Constitutional Law and the Regulatory State, 2012

Aspen Custom Publishing Series

Constitutional Law and the Regulatory State, 2012

Professor Noga Morag-Levine

Michigan State University College of Law

Wolters Kluwer

Law & Business

CONTENTS

United States v. Curtiss-Wright Export Corp. 386
Notes on Curtiss-Wright 388
2. Treaties and Executive Agreements 389
Dames & Moore v. Regan, Secretary of the Treasury 391
3. War Powers 393
Title 50. War and National Defense; Chapter 33 — War Powers Resolution 394

D. Presidential Power and the War on Terrorism 398
1. Detentions 398
Hamdi v. Rumsfeld 399
Boumediene v. Bush 411
2. Military Tribunals 425

E. Impeachment 433
The Appointment Power 438
Alexia Morrison, Independent Counsel v. Theodore B. Olson 438
The Removal Power 444
The Impeachment of Andrew Johnson 444
Free Enterprise Fund v. Public Company Accounting Oversight Board 452

8 AGENCIES IN THE STRUCTURE OF MODERN FEDERAL GOVERNMENT 459

A. What is an Agency? 459

B. Where do Agencies Fit in the Constitutional Structure? 462
The Constitution of the United States 464
Notes and Questions 465

9 CONTROL OF AGENCY ACTION 471

A. Presidential Control of Agency Action 471
1. Control of Agency Personnel 473

B. The Constitutional Problems of the Administrative State 474
1. The Non-Delegation Doctrine and Its Demise 475
A.L.A. Schechter Poultry Corp. v. United States 475
Panama Refining Co. v. Ryan 477
Whitman v. American Trucking Assn., Inc. 478
The Telephone Consumer Protection Act (1991) 481

C. Specificity and Delegation 482
1. The Constitutional Limits of Delegation 483
2. The Political Reasons for Delegation 485
David Epstein & Sharyn O'Halloran, The Nondelegation Doctrine and the Separation of Powers: A Political Science Approach 485
Notes and Questions 490
3. The Normative Implications of Delegation 491

CHAPTER 1

THE COMMON LAW AS A REGULATORY REGIME

Legend has it that a famous law professor, now a judge, began his first-year torts course each year with the following hypothetical:

> Extraterrestrials come to the United States and offer the American people a wonderful gift. The gift is the sort that will improve the efficiency of the society, the wealth of the society, and the happiness of the society. "Please accept our gift," implore the extraterrestrials. But here's the catch. "In exchange," the extraterrestrials continue, "your country must send us 45,000 people a year — men, women, and children — and they never will be seen or heard from again." What is the gift?

This hypothetical nicely presents the problem of auto safety. Motor vehicles are a wonderful gift. At the same time, they pose real risks to human life and health. The safety risks posed by the introduction of this technology provide a classic example of the social and economic issues that arise every day.

A familiar option for addressing the problem of auto safety is legislation and regulation, whether enacted at the federal or state level. It is within the constitutional power of Congress to enact a statute mandating that auto manufacturers install certain kinds of safety equipment, such as anti-lock brakes on new motor vehicles. Auto safety requirements, whether detailed in the statute or later developed by an agency through the issuance of regulations, might decrease the likelihood of auto accidents or mitigate their harmful effects.

Although such instances of government intervention are prevalent today, the law can respond in other ways to activities that generate risks to human safety and the like. Indeed, until the turn of the twentieth century, two other bodies of law — contract and tort — functioned as the primary mechanisms for addressing risks to human safety. Today, these bodies of law maintain an uneasy co-existence with statutes and regulations designed for that purpose.

Contract and tort law are part of the common law. The common law is a mode of government action — in other words, a regulatory regime. This may seem obvious, but law school courses tend to present the common law as the law itself, rather than as one source of law. In fact, the common law is nothing more than the particular set of legally binding rules that are made and implemented by judges in the course of resolving formal disputes between contesting parties.

How did the common law handle the problem of auto safety or the safety of any other products? We can start with contract law, which generally empowers individuals and entities to enter into legally binding agreements with one another. Prospective buyers of cars are always free to seek from sellers various safety features. Of course, the sellers may not be able to provide those safety features or may not offer them even if available. Likewise, consumers may not always have meaningful choices as to safety features if all the members of the auto industry basically offer the same features. Still, consumers usually have at least some degree of choice. For example, a person more concerned with auto safety than, say, fuel efficiency, can buy a larger car that is better able to withstand a crash than a smaller one. Similarly, consumers can choose to purchase special safety features such as side airbags or "crumple zones." These sorts of choices are legally enforceable in a particular way. If the safety feature fails to deliver a promised safety benefit, the buyer can sue the seller under contract law for breach of actual or implied warranty. A judge would determine whether the plaintiff was entitled to relief by considering whether a warranty was made, whether it was breached, and whether that breach caused the buyer to suffer a loss. In resolving contractual disputes, judges developed a set of rules that allocate the risk of harm between consumer and manufacturer.

For as long as there have been motorized vehicles (and, for that matter, horse-drawn wagons), Americans have also had the ability to bring a suit under tort law for harms caused by unsafe vehicles. Generally speaking, tort law, in contrast to contract law, imposes obligations independently of whether the person on whom the obligation is being imposed made any sort of promise or warranty to the person bringing the suit. For example, the buyer of a car whose steering mechanism fails while he is driving the car, resulting in an accident that injures him, could sue the manufacturer for the tort of negligence, regardless of whether the seller made any promise or warranty as to the soundness of the steering mechanism. If a judge or jury determined that the seller was at fault for the failure of the mechanism, then the court would order the seller to compensate the victim for his injuries. In this case-by-case manner, judges developed tort rules for what does and does not count as faulty conduct. In turn, these rules generated incentives for all auto manufacturers to design and build their vehicles in different ways to avoid future damages awards.

The current legal system still relies on contract and tort law but to a much lesser extent, in part because those bodies of law have been supplemented and, in some respects, superseded by statutes and regulations. *See* Barbara L. Atwell, *Products Liability and Preemption: A Judicial Framework*, 39 BUFF. L. REV. 181 (1991). This chapter examines the shift from the common law to statutes and regulations ("government regulation" for short). It begins by discussing the limitations of tort law for addressing safety risks, such as those from motor vehicles. It then discusses the limitations of markets and, indirectly, the limitations of contract law for addressing safety risks. The discussion of so-called "market failures" is part of a broader one about economic justifications for government regulation. The chapter then presents social justifications for government regulation. At times, society demands more for itself as a whole than any one individual would for herself. The chapter concludes by examining how these economic and social justifications apply to auto safety regulation.

A. The Limitations of Tort Law

In the early history of our legal system, tort law did not impose significant obligations on product manufacturers to take precautions against injury to the users of their products. From at least 1842 through 1916, the only individuals who could sue a manufacturer for injuries caused by a faulty product were those who had bought the product directly from that manufacturer. Consumers did not always buy products directly from the manufacturer, even though they were the intended users. As a result, they often could not bring suit. Many courts took the famous English decision of Winterbottom v. Wright, 152 Eng. Rep. 402 (1842), as authority for this regime.

In *Winterbottom v. Wright*, Wright had manufactured and maintained carriages and had a contract to provide the Postmaster-General with mail coaches. Under that contract, Wright agreed to keep these mail coaches in a safe condition for their use. The Postmaster-General, in turn, had a contract with another company to provide drivers for these coaches. One of these drivers, Winterbottom, suffered a severe injury to his leg when the wheel of one of Wright's coaches collapsed. Because Winterbottom was an employee of the company that had a contract to provide coaches to the Postmaster-General, he did not have a direct contractual relationship with either the Postmaster-General or with Wright.

Winterbottom sued Wright alleging that Wright had "improperly and negligently conducted himself" by failing to satisfy his duty to furnish mail coaches in a safe condition, free of "latent defects," and that as a result, Winterbottom suffered severe injury. The judges of the English Exchequer's court forcefully rejected Winterbottom's theory of liability. The chief judge, Lord Abinger, reasoned as follows:

> We ought not to permit a doubt to rest upon this subject, for our doing so might be the means of letting in upon us an infinity of actions. . . . There is no privity of contract between these parties; and if the plaintiff can sue, every passenger, or even any person passing along the road, who was injured by the upsetting of the coach, might bring a similar action. Unless we confine the operation of such contracts as this to the parties who entered into them, the most absurd and outrageous consequences, to which I can see no limit, would ensue. Where a party becomes responsible to the public, by undertaking a public duty, he is liable, though the injury may have arisen from the negligence of his servant or agent. . . . The plaintiff in this case could not have brought an action on the contract; if he could have done so, what would have been his situation, supposing the Postmaster-General had released the defendant? That would, at all events, have defeated his claim altogether. By permitting this

action, we should be working this injustice, that after the defendant had done everything to the satisfaction of his employer, and after all matters between them had
been adjusted, and all accounts settled on the footing of their contract, we should
subject them to be ripped open by this action of tort being brought against him.

Id. at 405-06.

Winterbottom stood for the proposition that manufacturers cannot be held
liable to consumers or other users of their products if those consumers or users are
not in contractual "privity" with the manufacturer. The idea of privity made sense
prior to the modern era. To buy a chair, you went to a carpenter, who built it for
you out of raw wood from the lumber mill; your fancy clothes were made to order
by a tailor or a dressmaker from cloth delivered to his shop in large rolls, or bolts;
bread came from the baker who made it from raw flour. In these circumstances,
the customer was generally in privity with the person most responsible for producing the purchased item. If there was something wrong with your purchase, it was
most likely the seller's fault, and if the raw material the seller used was defective,
well then, that was his or her responsibility. How could the owner of the lumber
mill or a flour mill know where the materials they produced were being used? It
was from the artisan who used the materials to produce a finished product that the
ultimate consumer bought.

These circumstances began to change in the nineteenth century when factories began producing finished products that bore the name of their manufacturer,
like Wedgwood china, Singer sewing machines, and Brewster carriages. (As late
as the 1930s, Cole Porter could still write, in his famous song *"You're the top!*

You're a Ritz hot toddy. You're the top! You're a Brewster body.") Items were completed by the manufacturer and sold to the public by retail stores that had no role in their manufacture. Department stores, carrying a variety of finished products, evolved in the U.S. during the mid to late nineteenth century. Many items continued to be sold in bulk; if you wanted to buy crackers, for example, you went to the general store, and the store keeper would scoop the desired quantity out of the proverbial cracker barrel. In 1898, the National Biscuit Company introduced Uneeda Biscuits, the first pre-packaged food product sold directly from a manufacturer to the public. The original purpose of marketing the product in this way was to protect it against moisture, and the product's symbol, a boy in a raincoat, was designed to advertise that virtue. The Morton Salt girl, a symbol that dates from the same era and is still in use, emphasized the same virtue for pre-packaged salt.

The fact that the crackers and salt had a symbol in the first place was groundbreaking because the symbol was specifically designed to market the product to the general public. Note also that the crackers did not bear the name of the manufacturer, but a made-up name generated by an advertising slogan ("Lest you forget, we say it yet, *you need a* biscuit"). In fact, advertising signs for Uneeda Biscuits appeared on the sides of buildings all across America. The surviving ones are often designated as landmarks.

As a result of these developments, the merchants with whom individuals regularly dealt were no longer the people who made the product, or even packaged it for sale. They were mere intermediaries, transferring a product that was produced, packaged, and labeled by remote manufacturers. These manufacturers, moreover, were now advertising their products directly to the public through newspaper and

magazine ads, signs on buildings, and, as the twentieth century progressed, radio and motion picture ads. Their ads necessarily contained various assertions and promises about the use, performance, and quality of the product being advertised.

In this new situation, what was the rationale for the doctrine of privity? Consider the famous decision printed below, which returns the discussion to auto safety:

MacPherson v. Buick Motor Co.

111 N.E. 1050 (N.Y. 1916)

CARDOZO, J.

The defendant is a manufacturer of automobiles. It sold an automobile to a retail dealer. The retail dealer resold to the plaintiff. While the plaintiff was in the car, it suddenly collapsed. He was thrown out and injured. One of the wheels was made of defective wood, and its spokes crumbled into fragments. The wheel was not made by the defendant; it was bought from another manufacturer. There is evidence, however, that its defects could have been discovered by reasonable inspection, and that inspection was omitted. There is no claim that the defendant knew of the defect and willfully concealed it. The charge is one, not of fraud, but of negligence. The question to be determined is whether the defendant owed a duty of care and vigilance to any one but the immediate purchaser.

The foundations of this branch of the law, at least in this state, were laid in *Thomas v. Winchester* (6 N.Y. 397). A poison was falsely labeled. The sale was made to a druggist, who in turn sold to a customer. The customer recovered damages from the seller who affixed the label. "The defendant's negligence," it was said, "put human life in imminent danger." A poison falsely labeled is likely to injure any one who gets it. Because the danger is to be foreseen, there is a duty to avoid the injury. Cases were cited by way of illustration in which manufacturers were not subject to any duty irrespective of contract. The distinction was said to be that their conduct, though negligent, was not likely to result in injury to any one except the purchaser. We are not required to say whether the chance of injury was always as remote as the distinction assumes. Some of the illustrations might be rejected to-day. The principle of the distinction is for present purposes the important thing.

Thomas v. Winchester became quickly a landmark of the law. In the application of its principle there may at times have been uncertainty or even error. There has never in this state been doubt or disavowal of the principle itself. The chief cases are well known, yet to recall some of them will be helpful. *Loop v. Litchfield* (42 N.Y. 351) is the earliest. It was the case of a defect in a small balance wheel used on a circular saw. The manufacturer pointed out the defect to the buyer, who wished a cheap article and was ready to assume the risk. The risk can hardly have been an imminent one, for the wheel lasted five years before it broke. In the meanwhile the buyer had made a lease of the machinery. It was held that the manufacturer was not answerable to the lessee. *Loop v. Litchfield* was followed in *Losee v. Clute* (51 N.Y. 494), the case of the explosion of a steam boiler. That decision has been criticized; but it must be confined to its special facts. It was put upon the ground that the risk of injury was too remote. The buyer in that case had not only accepted the boiler, but had tested it. The manufacturer knew that his own test was not the final one. The finality of the test has a bearing on the measure of diligence owing to persons other than the purchaser.

These early cases suggest a narrow construction of the rule. Later cases, however, evince a more liberal spirit. First in importance is *Devlin v. Smith* (89 N.Y. 470). The defendant, a contractor, built a scaffold for a painter. The painter's servants were injured. The contractor was held liable. He knew that the scaffold, if improperly constructed, was a most dangerous trap. He knew that it was to be used by the workmen. He was building it for that very purpose. Building it for their use, he owed them a duty, irrespective of his contract with their master, to build it with care.

From *Devlin v. Smith* we pass over intermediate cases and turn to the latest case in this court in which *Thomas v. Winchester* was followed. That case is *Statler v. Ray Mfg. Co.* (195 N.Y. 478, 480). The defendant manufactured a large coffee urn. It was installed in a restaurant. When heated, the urn exploded and injured the plaintiff. We held that the manufacturer was liable. We said that the urn "was of such a character inherently that, when applied to the purposes for which it was designed, it was liable to become a source of great danger to many people if not carefully and properly constructed."

It may be that *Devlin v. Smith* and *Statler v. Ray Mfg. Co.* have extended the rule of *Thomas v. Winchester*. If so, this court is committed to the extension. The defendant argues that things imminently dangerous to life are poisons, explosives, deadly weapons — things whose normal function it is to injure or destroy. But whatever the rule in *Thomas v. Winchester* may once have been, it has no longer that restricted meaning. A scaffold is not inherently a destructive instrument. It becomes destructive only if imperfectly constructed. A large coffee urn may have within itself, if negligently made, the potency of danger, yet no one thinks of it as an implement whose normal function is destruction. . . .

Devlin v. Smith was decided in 1882. A year later a very similar case came before the Court of Appeal in England (*Heaven v. Pender*, L. R. [11 Q. B. D.] 503). We find in the opinion of [Lord Esher], the same conception of a duty, irrespective of contract, imposed upon the manufacturer by the law itself: "Whenever one person supplies goods, or machinery, or the like, for the purpose of their being used by another person under such circumstances that every one of ordinary sense would, if he thought, recognize at once that unless he used ordinary care and skill with regard to the condition of the thing supplied or the mode of supplying it, there will be danger of injury to the person or property of him for whose use the thing is supplied, and who is to use it, a duty arises to use ordinary care and skill as to the condition or manner of supplying such thing." He then points out that for a neglect of such ordinary care or skill whereby injury happens, the appropriate remedy is an action for negligence. The right to enforce this liability is not to be confined to the immediate buyer. The right extends to the persons or class of persons for whose use the thing is supplied. It is enough that the goods "would in all probability be used at once . . . before a reasonable opportunity for discovering any defect which might exist," and that the thing supplied is of such a nature "that a neglect of ordinary care or skill as to its condition or the manner of supplying it would probably cause danger to the person or property of the person for whose use it was supplied, and who was about to use it." On the other hand, he would exclude a case "in which the goods are supplied under circumstances in which it would be a chance by whom they would be used or whether they would be used or not, or whether they would be used before there would probably be means of observing any defect," or where the goods are of such a nature that "a want of care or skill as to their condition or the manner of supplying them would not probably produce danger of injury to person or property." . . .

We hold, then, that the principle of *Thomas v. Winchester* is not limited to poisons, explosives, and things of like nature, to things which in their normal operation are implements of destruction. If the nature of a thing is such that it is reasonably certain to place life and limb in peril when negligently made, it is then a thing of danger. Its nature gives warning of the consequences to be expected. If to the element of danger there is added knowledge that the thing will be used by persons other than the purchaser, and used without new tests, then, irrespective of contract, the manufacturer of this thing of danger is under a duty to make it carefully. That is as far as we are required to go for the decision of this case. There must be knowledge of a danger, not merely possible, but probable. It is *possible* to use almost anything in a way that will make it dangerous if defective. That is not enough to charge the manufacturer with a duty independent of his contract. Whether a given thing is dangerous may be sometimes a question for the court and sometimes a question for the jury. There must also be knowledge that in the usual course of events the danger will be shared by others than the buyer. Such knowledge may often be inferred from the nature of the transaction. But it is possible that even knowledge of the danger and of the use will not always be enough. The proximity or remoteness of the relation is a factor to be considered. We are dealing now with the liability of the manufacturer of the finished product, who puts it on the market to be used without inspection by his customers. If he is negligent, where danger is to be foreseen, a liability will follow. We are not required at this time to say that it is legitimate to go back of the manufacturer of the finished product and hold the manufacturers of the component parts. To make their negligence a cause of imminent danger, an independent cause must often intervene; the manufacturer of the finished product must also fail in *his* duty of inspection. It may be that in those circumstances the negligence of the earlier members of the series is too remote to constitute, as to the ultimate user, an actionable wrong. We leave that question open . . . .

From this survey of the decisions, there thus emerges a definition of the duty of a manufacturer which enables us to measure this defendant's liability. Beyond all question, the nature of an automobile gives warning of probable danger if its construction is defective. This automobile was designed to go fifty miles an hour. Unless its wheels were sound and strong, injury was almost certain. It was as much a thing of danger as a defective engine for a railroad. The defendant knew the danger. It knew also that the car would be used by persons other than the buyer. This was apparent from its size; there were seats for three persons. It was apparent also from the fact that the buyer was a dealer in cars, who bought to resell. The maker of this car supplied it for the use of purchasers from the dealer just as plainly as the contractor in *Devlin v. Smith* supplied the scaffold for use by the servants of the owner. The dealer was indeed the one person of whom it might be said with some approach to certainty that by him the car would not be used. Yet the defendant would have us say that he was the one person whom it was under a legal duty to protect. The law does not lead us to so inconsequent a conclusion. Precedents drawn from the days of travel by stage coach do not fit the conditions of travel today. The principle that the danger must be imminent does not change, but the things subject to the principle do change. They are whatever the needs of life in a developing civilization require them to be. . . .

We think the defendant was not absolved from a duty of inspection because it bought the wheels from a reputable manufacturer. It was not merely a dealer in automobiles. It was a manufacturer of automobiles. It was responsible for the finished product. It was not at liberty to put the finished product on the market without subjecting the component parts to ordinary and simple tests. The obligation to inspect must vary with the nature of the thing to be inspected. The more probable the danger, the greater the need of caution. . . .

The judgment should be affirmed with costs.

NOTES AND QUESTIONS

1. Cardozo, who was subsequently appointed to the U.S. Supreme Court, is considered one of the greatest jurists in American history. Consider Cardozo's decision in light of the brief description we gave you above about changes in marketing practices at this time. Can you identify the sentences in the decision that take cognizance of these changes? What does Cardozo conclude from them? Why didn't he say so more explicitly?
2. How does Cardozo justify his decision? Are you convinced that the decision is simply an extension of prior cases? Why does Cardozo work so hard to show that it is?
3. Cardozo clearly changed the law. How do we justify judicial lawmaking? If we can't, how do we justify the common law, which, as described above, is a system of judge-made rules?

To the extent that *MacPherson* changed the law by jettisoning the privity rule, it also held the potential to change the future conduct of automakers. Under the privity rule, tort law had little effect on the future conduct of automakers because they faced no prospect of liability to buyers for negligently manufacturing an unsafe product. In response to *MacPherson*, do you suppose that Buick improved its inspection practices? Consider the following decision:

Rotche v. Buick Motor Co.

193 N.E. 529 (Ill. 1934)

PER CURIAM.

Nathan Rotche brought an action . . . against the Buick Motor Company and the Cicero Buick Sales Company, both corporations, to recover damages for personal injuries. The jury found the defendants guilty and assessed the plaintiff's damages at $20,000. . . . The Buick Motor Company applied to this court for a writ of certiorari, the writ was issued, and the record of the cause is submitted for a further review.

On August 13, 1929, Nathan Rotche, forty years of age, employed as a train guard on an elevated railway in the city of Chicago, bought a five-passenger Buick automobile from the Cicero Sales Company. Twenty-six days later, on September 8, 1929, accompanied by his son, he drove the automobile over a highway known as "Rand road." At a point about a mile northwest of the village of Des Plaines, the automobile, while running at a speed of thirty miles an hour, left the roadway, struck and damaged a concrete culvert, crossed a ditch adjoining the roadway, and came to a stop in a ploughed field at a point about twenty feet beyond the ditch. At rest, the automobile lay on its right side with the front of the car to the northwest. The right front tire and left front wheel were destroyed, the rear axle was bent, the top and sides of the body were damaged, and a clevis connecting a cable with the left front wheel-brake was missing. The automobile was first towed to a garage in the village of Des Plaines. About two weeks later the car was removed to another garage in Chicago. Rotche, the defendant in error, suffered injuries necessitating an operation upon his left leg and foot. As a result the leg is shortened and the foot turned outward. . . .

The garage owner who towed the automobile to Des Plaines made no particular examination of it at the time. Three or four weeks later, pursuant to a request made in behalf of the defendant in error, he examined the automobile in the garage in Chicago to which it had been removed. He then found that a clevis and two cotter pins were missing. Certain cotter pins on the left equalizer apparently had not been spread and could readily be removed.

The proprietor of the garage in Chicago made an examination of the car in Des Plaines on September 21, 1929, and found a loose cable. After the car had been taken to his garage, the left front wheel was removed. A clevis was missing. The cotter pins on the right side of the brake mechanism were properly clinched, while the free ends of some on the opposite side were not separated. Nothing in the mechanism underneath the left front fender was broken. . . .

Evidence was introduced showing the inspections to which Buick automobiles are subjected during the course of their construction. With respect to the brakes on these cars, two men at or near the end of a conveyor inspect all the parts as well as the adjustments. The brake inspectors examine every cotter key or pin to ascertain whether it is properly clinched to hold in place the clevis through which it extends. When any part of an automobile is found missing or defective, the car is tagged and excluded from the conveyor. No record is kept of the automobiles inspected except those found defective and therefore rejected. There was no record that the automobile in question was rejected for any defect in the construction or adjustment of the brakes or for any other defect.

The Buick Motor Company ships its automobiles to be sold to dealers in and about Chicago to its plant in the southwest part of that city. Two employees at this plant inspect the brakes of all automobiles received from the factory at Flint, Mich. They examine the pins and cotter keys in the brake connections and inspect the steering mechanism. Any defect found is reported to the superintendent. After inspection each automobile is tagged and kept for two weeks. The automobile concerning which the present controversy arises was sold and delivered to the Cicero Buick Sales Company on August 5, 1929.

The sales company also maintains a system of inspection. After a new automobile is sold, it is prepared for delivery to the purchaser and this process requires four and one-half or five hours. The inspection includes, among other things, the removal of the wheels, the greasing of the bearings, the oiling of brake connections, and the testing of the brakes by driving the car at a speed of thirty-five miles an hour. A mechanic employed by the sales company who inspected the car in question testified that the brake rods, cables, clevises, and cotter pins were in place and correctly adjusted and that the brakes were in perfect condition. The card which he filled out upon the completion of his inspection was introduced in evidence and showed that he had checked various items among which were the adjustments of the clutch, the pedals, and the brakes. He had an independent recollection of his inspection of the particular car because he permitted it to leave the possession of the sales company without a sufficient supply of gasoline.

Another employee of the sales company also inspected the car. He testified that he found all the cotter pins in place and properly spread or clinched; that the brakes were in the same condition when the car was sold to the defendant in error as when it was received from the manufacturer; that the cotter pin which witnesses called by the defendant in error testified was missing, he actually saw in its proper place; that it held the clevis; and that the ends of the cotter pin were spread or separated. . . .

The contentions of the plaintiff in error are that, even if, at the time the defendant in error bought the automobile from the sales company it was defective in the respect claimed by him, the defect charged was a patent one and would not subject the manufacturer of the automobile to liability to a third person for injuries suffered as the result of the defect; that, in any event, no competent evidence was adduced by the defendant in error to prove that the automobile was defective at the time it was delivered to the dealer or later when the accident occurred; and that, for either of the foregoing reasons, the motion to direct a verdict should have been granted.

The defendant in error seeks to trace the accident which gave rise to this case to an unspread cotter pin in the brake mechanism of his automobile. The plaintiff in error insists that such a defect or omission, if assumed, is a patent one, open and visible to every person and readily adjusted or corrected, and cannot, in the event personal injury or property damage ensues, charge the manufacturer with liability therefore. . . . Some cases hold that, since an automobile is not a dangerous instrumentality per se, a manufacturer owes no duty to third persons, irrespective of contractual relations, to use reasonable care in its manufacture and, consequently, is not liable to such persons for injuries caused by negligence in construction. On the other hand, courts have declared in later cases that a manufacturer who places in trade and commerce a manufactured article, such as an automobile, which is not inherently dangerous to life or limb, out which may become so, because of its negligence construction, is liable to one who sustains injury by reason of such negligent construction. *MacPherson v. Buick Motor Co.*, 217 N.Y. 382. . . .

Ordinary care in the building of an automobile requires that the free ends of a cotter pin used to hold a clevis in place be clinched or separated. It follows that a manufacturer will be liable to a purchaser from a dealer where the competent evidence shows that a cotter pin was not spread when the automobile left the factory and, in consequence, the pin fell from a clevis, the clevis worked out of place, and a cable was released so that, upon the application of sufficient pressure, the brake failed to operate and an accident and injuries to the purchaser resulted.

The plaintiff in error contends, however, that even if the cause of action alleged is maintainable, the defendant in error introduced no evidence to prove one of its essential elements, namely, that the automobile was negligently constructed, and, consequently, the motion to direct a verdict for the plaintiff in error should have been granted. . . .

The mere fact that an accident resulting in an injury to a person or in damage to property has occurred does not authorize a presumption or inference that the defendant was negligent. The burden was upon the defendant in error to prove by competent evidence, direct or circumstantial, that the plaintiff in error was guilty of negligence in the manufacture or assemblage of the automobile in question. Testimony concerning the condition of cotter pins in the brake mechanism several weeks after the accident occurred without proof that the condition of the pins remained unchanged was inadmissible and should have been excluded. Such testimony was not responsive to the allegations of the declaration and could not subject the plaintiff in error to liability. . . .

Defendant in error had driven the car about six hundred miles; he testified that, prior to the accident, the brakes had given him no trouble, and that, by their application, he could stop the car, when running at a speed of twenty-five miles an hour, within six or eight feet. The tire marks on the earth embankment made just before the automobile struck the concrete culvert showed that the brakes had been applied and apparently operated effectively. The uncontradicted evidence shows that the automobile was subjected to several inspections before it was delivered to the defendant in error. At the factory two men stationed at a conveyor inspected the parts and adjustments of the car. They examined every cotter pin to determine whether it was properly clinched. No car with a part missing or defective in any respect passed this inspection. At the manufacturer's plant in Chicago, two employees inspected the brakes, the cotter keys in the brake connections and the steering mechanism of all cars. The sales company caused further inspections to be made. One of its mechanics inspected the particular car and found the brake rods, cobles, clevises and cotter pins in place and correctly adjusted. Another employee of the same company found every cotter pin in place and clinched.

Whether there was negligence in the assembly of the parts of the automobile owned by the defendant in error, as a result of which the accident occurred, depends almost wholly upon the condition of the cotter pins previous to the sale of the car. With the incompetent testimony excluded, the competent evidence is not sufficiently definite to justify the conclusion that the automobile remained in the same condition from the time of the accident until it was examined by persons who testified that some of the cotter pins were unspread two weeks or more after the accident occurred.

The judgments of the Appellate and superior courts are reversed, and the cause is remanded to the superior court.

Reversed and remanded.

NOTES AND QUESTIONS

1. If *Rotche* is an indication, what changes did Buick make to its inspection practices by 1934? Automakers had begun inspecting all wheels using multiple tests by 1920, just four years after *MacPherson* was decided. By the time that *Rotche* was decided, isn't it clear that the common law worked to reduce the risk of auto accidents and corresponding harms?

2. The common law worked but to what extent? More specifically, to what extent did *MacPherson* prompt automakers to address the problem of auto safety beyond making changes to its inspection practices? If you were legal counsel to Buick or similar automakers, what other changes would you recommend that they make following *MacPherson*? Would they all involve safety improvements? Consider the following sorts of changes, drawn from CORNE-LIUS W. GILLAM, PRODUCTS LIABILITY IN THE AUTOMOBILE INDUSTRY: A Study in Strict Liability and Social Control (1960) and Sally H. Clarke, *Unmanageable Risks:* MacPherson v. Buick *and the Emergence of a Mass Consumer Market*, 23 LAW & HIST. REV. 1 (2005).

    a. *Advertising.* In the aftermath of *MacPherson*, automakers made their safety claims more realistic and cautious. For example, they changed their claims of "shatterproof glass" to claims of "safety glass."

    b. *Customer Service.* Automakers routinely began providing repair service not required by the terms of warranties to ensure customer satisfaction. But their generosity typically ended when drivers filed lawsuits. Indeed, automakers were quick to invoke disclaimers as bars against tort claims.

    c. *Business Organization.* Some automakers reorganized their businesses in complex ways to frustrate tort plaintiffs. McLean v. Goodyear Tire & Rubber Co., 85 F.2d 150 (5th Cir. 1936), provides a dramatic illustration. Goodyear manufactured tires in Ohio but transferred distribution to a Delaware corporation with the same name. A Texas plaintiff sued the Delaware distributor for injuries resulting from a blown tire. The Delaware distributor argued that it did not manufacture the tires and was therefore not liable. When the plaintiff moved to amend his complaint to include the Ohio manufacturer, the court held it had no jurisdiction over the Ohio corporation, which had no business in Texas. (Note that now the court would have jurisdiction over the Ohio corporation in Texas.)

d. *Disclaimers and Limited Warranties.* Automakers limited their liability as much as possible using limited warranties and disclaimers. Although a warranty is a promise of quality that, in principle, ought to work to the advantage of the buyer, warranties were often drafted with significant limitations that actually left consumers at a disadvantage. For example, an auto manufacturer might provide a warranty that lasted only for a few months. Or, it might limit recourse to replacement of the defective product or component part, rather than damages for the injuries suffered by the consumer in the accident.

e. *Products Liability Insurance.* Some automakers acquired greater products liability insurance throughout the early age of auto insurance, but many did not. Instead, these automakers chose to accept the risk of accidents. After all, they could extensively reduce their liability through warranties and disclaimers. They could also spread the costs of liability by increasing the price of new cars.

3. The common law worked in part to address the problem of auto safety, but how well did it work for MacPherson himself? MacPherson testified that he was driving carefully at only eight miles per hour when his left rear wheel collapsed and his car flipped over, breaking his wrist and gouging out his right eye. *See* Clarke, *supra*, at 2. For the injured party, does tort law provide too little too late?

4. Now focus on Buick. What advice do you suppose its lawyers provided before *MacPherson* was decided? Jeremy Bentham once disparagingly referred to the common law as "dog law" — i.e., akin to the practice of imposing a punishment on a pet who did not and could not have known that what he was doing was wrong until he was smacked on the nose for misbehaving. *MacPherson* put Buick in the doghouse in more ways than one, right?

5. In other contexts, tort law has additional limitations for regulating future conduct and preventing future harm. For example, how well does tort law work to prevent harm from airborne pollutants in the workplace when the health risk is obvious but the actual injury is latent — that is, the adverse effects may not materialize for years, or the full extent is unknown? How well does it work to prevent harms from airborne pollutants to the environment or the public at large? Did you ever read Dr. Seuss's *The Lorax* when you were a child, which is a parable about environmental degradation? Some might ask who speaks for the trees.

Note on the Limitations of Common Law Adjudication More Generally

Some of the limitations of tort law for addressing risks to society actually speak to the limitations of common law adjudication more generally. Courts are well suited to resolving concrete disputes between parties. How do they fare when attempting to craft general rules governing risk-generating conduct? Consider that question along the following lines:

Retrospective vs. Prospective: When a court announces a new rule, it applies that rule to prior conduct — which is to say, the conduct of the parties in the case. As a result, the parties may receive something of an unfair penalty or windfall. We were getting at this issue when asking what advice Buick's lawyers provided before *MacPherson* was decided, as compared to the advice they provided after the case was decided. Statutes typically apply to conduct that occurs after enactment, so they are typically not retroactive in the sense that common law judicial decisions can be.

Reactive vs. Proactive: A court can only address an issue when a party brings a case. A party can only bring a case if she suffers an injury. Thus, courts cannot reach out to prevent an injury, at least not all of them. We raised this issue when we asked whether tort law provided MacPherson himself too little too late. Legislatures and agencies can take action at any time. They need not await an injury.

Uncertainty: Courts often introduce uncertainty in the common law through a practice that Professor Melvin Eisenberg calls "transforming" prior precedent. MELVIN ARON EISENBERG, THE NATURE OF THE COMMON LAW 4-7, 58-60, 132-34 (1988). Courts do not forthrightly acknowledge that they are changing the law by overruling past decisions. Rather, courts recast those decisions in terms consistent with the present one. This practice leaves future parties and courts without a clear sense whether or to what extent the law has changed. As we asked above after *MacPherson*, did Judge Cardozo engage in transforming? Why would courts do this? Courts introduce other types of uncertainty in the common law. Even when courts acknowledge a change and other courts follow (courts are only bound by precedent in their own jurisdictions), they tend to approach broad legal questions from a narrow perspective. More specifically, they resolve such questions based on the facts of the case and only as necessary to decide the case. The resulting narrowness of judicial rules can decrease predictability for parties. Privity is no longer necessary for car purchasers to sue automakers, but exactly where else? Legislatures and agencies do not typically suffer from these sorts of uncertainty. First, federal statutes apply in all jurisdictions across the nation. Second, legislatures and agencies typically create rules of general application and future effect.

Institutional Competence: Courts are suited to resolve concrete disputes among parties. They are not well suited to redesign cars or other defective products. More generally, they lack the technical or specialized skill to craft the rules that govern risk-generating conduct. And while courts are well suited to award damages or issue injunctions, they are not well suited to set phase-in schedules for new requirements, which are often necessary to give regulated entities adequate time to change their conduct. Courts also lack the information gathering and processing capability that is necessary to craft and implement rules. In our civil system, courts do not initiate their own fact gathering. They are dependent on the parties for information, which means that information relevant to risk-related rules may be presented in a certain light or not at all. Even when courts have access to information, they are limited in the capacity to process it. No matter how intelligent or sophisticated, judges are generalists. They ordinarily lack the time let alone the experience to become experts in any given area. (The U.S. Court of Appeals for the D.C. Circuit is often said to be an expert in administrative law because so many cases involve such law, but the judges are still not experts in auto safety.) Legislatures and agencies have their own fact gathering apparatuses. Legislatures often hold hearings regarding bills that are being considered for enactment; in the context of these hearings, they can call witnesses and obtain documents. They can also talk to just about anyone they choose. Agencies are even better off in this respect. They have research staffs and continuous contacts with industry leaders, interest groups, and others with relevant information. They also house many specialists — lawyers, scientists, economists, and policymakers — and these specialists make agencies superior even to Congress for processing information.

Political Accountability: Judges, at least in the federal courts, are insulated from democratic politics. A judge cannot be voted off the bench no matter how much the people dislike her decisions. As a result, judges are less responsive to public preferences than elected officials. This political insulation is a deliberate constitutional choice, beneficial especially when judges are resolving disputes over unpopular rights. But when setting risk-related rules, it can be seen as somewhat less so. Such rules often involve complex political tradeoffs that elected officials or their agents are better suited to make. *See* Albert C. Lin, *Beyond Tort: Compensating Victims of Environmental Toxic Injury*, 78 S. CAL. L. REV. 1439, 1465-66 (2005).

Parties vs. Interested Participants: Adjudication before a court (as opposed to courts or judges themselves) is less pluralist in a different sense. It is restricted to the parties in the case, with some limited participation by others with a specific interest in the outcome. By contrast, the legislative process is open to anyone who can garner legislative attention. The administrative process is even more accessible; as you will see in Chapter 10, agencies have an obligation to solicit and consider the views of all interested parties.

Collective Action Problems: Adjudication before a court is dependent on private initiative, which not only requires an injury (see above) and a legal cause of action but the wherewithal to bring a lawsuit. Pursuing a lawsuit is notoriously expensive. Individuals have little incentive to bring lawsuits where the cost of litigation is likely to exceed the value of their recovery. Even when the value of recovery is likely to be greater than the cost of litigation, the inconvenience, not to mention the stress, may discourage individuals from bringing the suit. Note that certain litigation devices have helped by "collectivizing" similarly situated individuals and effectively spreading the costs among them. For example, the class action lawsuit provides a way of making litigation of many small-value claims practicable by effectively joining them together. But these and other devices do not completely eliminate the obstacles to addressing risk-generating conduct through adjudication. *See* Caroline Vaile Wright & Louise F. Fitzgerald, *Correlates of Joining a Sexual Harassment Class Action*, 33 LAW & HUM. BEHAV. 265 (2009).

B. Justifications for Regulation

Compensating for Spillovers (Externalities)

What Are Spillovers?

A considerable amount of regulation is justified on the ground that the unregulated price of a good does not reflect the true cost to society of producing that good. The differences between true social costs and unregulated price are "spillover" costs (or benefits) — usually referred to by economists as "externalities." If a train emits sparks that occasionally burn the crops of nearby farmers, the cost of destroyed crops is a spillover cost imposed upon the farmers by those who ship by train — so long as the shipper need not pay the farmer for the crop lost. Similarly, if honeybees fertilize nearby apple orchards, the beekeepers provide a spillover benefit to the orchard owners — so long as the latter do not pay the former for their service. Spillover benefits have sometimes been thought to justify government subsidy, as when free public education is argued to have societal benefits far exceeding the amount which students would willingly pay for its provision. Yet when one considers regulatory systems, spillover costs — not benefits — are ordinarily encountered.

The Classical Rationale for Regulation

Like the regulation of natural monopoly, the regulation of spillover costs is justified by the desirability of avoiding economic waste. Suppose a factory can produce sugar either through production method A or production method B. Method A costs 9 cents per unit of production but sends black smoke billowing throughout the neighborhood to the annoyance of neighbors for miles around. Method B costs 10 cents per unit of production and produces no smoke at all. The profit maximizing factory owner adopts A although, if those injured by the smoke would willingly pay more than 1 cent (per pound of sugar) to be rid of it, method A is socially more expensive. Then B, not A, should be chosen, because its total social costs — including costs of harm inflicted — are lower. As long as the affected public prefers reduced pollution to its noisome effect, it should bribe the producer to choose method B. Where the public prefers reduced pollution yet finds no practical way to bribe the producer, too many of society's resources are attracted (by lower prices not reflecting the cost of pollution) into polluting processes and products, and too few are attracted into pollution-free products and processes. Government intervention arguably is required to help eliminate this waste.

Objections to the Classical Rationale

It can be argued that spillover costs do not call for government intervention but, rather, for a rearrangement of private property rights.

First, as Ronald Coase has pointed out, if bargaining were costless, spillovers would not exist. Those suffering the pollution in the example above would simply band together and offer to pay the factory to use process B rather than A. The factory owner would switch only where the coalition was willing to pay more than 1 cent per pound. Precisely the same result would occur if the factory were required to compensate residents for pollution damage (both physical and psychological) it created, or if the government intervened and stopped pollution precisely and only in each instance where the public would rather pay abatement costs than suffer the effects of pollution. Thus, one might argue, why not let people bargain privately to abate pollution rather than introduce government regulation?

The answer to this question is that bargaining is not costless. Thus, the residents may suffer the pollution despite a willingness to pay more than 1 cent per pound to avoid it, simply because it is too difficult for them to band together. As the number of affected people increases, communication becomes more expensive, bargaining becomes more complicated, and a clear consensus is harder to obtain. Furthermore, there is the added problem that some participants may systematically underestimate the true value of abatement to them in the hope of minimizing their contribution to the cost of abatement. Thus, transaction costs may permit the continuance of spillover costs even though society would be better off without them. . . .

Of course, intervention itself is not costless. Moreover, intervention — or rearrangement of rights and liabilities — changes the distribution of wealth and income. Those who buy sugar (and the owners of sugar factories) are made poorer and those who suffer pollution are made richer by intervention or liability adjustments leading to reduced pollution. Insofar as intervention is designed to produce the result that would be paid for were bargaining feasible, those suffering pollution will gain more than the others lost. Whether this is a sufficient basis for intervening or altering liabilities may be debated. Traditionally it has been argued that changes should be made when the beneficiaries can compensate the losers out of their gains and have some gain left over; others have claimed that since the compensating is only hypothetical and not actually carried out, there is no clear justification for making the change. Regardless of the merits of these arguments, it is sufficient to note here that this rationale is one of "economic efficiency." To satisfy it is to move closer to a world in which all resources are used in a manner that maximizes the welfare of the world's individuals as measured by their preferences revealed in the marketplace. And it is the same rationale of allocative efficiency that underlies many governmental economic decisions and actions, including regulation of natural monopolies.

In sum, a spillover rationale must be phrased in terms of a particular product; it must assume that obstacles to bargaining lead to significantly greater use of a product (or production process) than would be the case if costless bargaining were possible; and it must assume that the result of intervention (taking into account the costs of intervention) will better approximate the bargained-for solution. If these assumptions are correct, then intervention will reduce allocative inefficiency. . . .

Inadequate Information

For a competitive market to function well, buyers must have sufficient information to evaluate competing products. They must identify the range of buying alternatives and understand the characteristics of the buying choices they confront. At the same time, information is a commodity that society must spend resources to produce. The buyer, looking for alternative suppliers, spends time, effort, and money in his search. The seller spends money on research, labeling, and advertising to make his identity and his product's qualities known. In well-functioning markets, one would expect to find as much information available as consumers are willing to pay for in order to lower the cost or to improve the quality of their choices.

The Classical Rationale for Regulation

Markets for information may on occasion not function well for several reasons. First, the incentives to produce and to disseminate information may be skewed. Some information (particularly that requiring detailed research) is expensive to produce initially but very cheap to make available once produced. Since it can be repeated by word of mouth, televised, or printed and reprinted at low cost, it may easily benefit many recipients who never pay its original producer. Thus, those in the best position to produce the information may not do so, or they may hesitate to disseminate it, for fear that the benefits will go not to themselves but only to others.

The importance of this problem varies considerably depending upon the type of information and its use. A firm that manufactures breakfast foods, for example, would have every incentive to produce information showing that its cereal was more nutritious than that of its competitors and to disseminate that information widely. Moreover, the production, use, and dissemination of much information is protected by copyright and patent laws. Further, the inadequate incentive to produce information typically leads to a demand not for regulation but for governmental support of production and dissemination.

Nonetheless, occasionally the problem may lead to a demand for regulation. Drug manufacturers, for example, are required to print the generic (general scientific) name of their product, as well as the brand name, on the label. Thus, the buyer sees that a host of competitors in fact offer to sell the same product. This labeling requirement can be seen as lowering the cost to buyers of searching for competing sellers, by quickly making them aware of the competitors' existence. And it does so by requiring those with the information most readily at hand to make it available.

Second, one of the parties to a transaction may seek deliberately to mislead the other, by conveying false information or by omitting key facts. A seller of securities may lie about the assets of the company; a seller of a used car may turn back the mileage indicator. Of course, false statements or active misrepresentations may be grounds for rescinding a contract or suing for damages. Yet the cost of court action is often high enough to weaken it or give it minimal effect as a deterrent. Nor can one necessarily rely upon fear of declining reputation to act as a deterrent. The importance of reputation in securing sales depends upon the particular product, the particular seller, and a host of other circumstances. The rationale for governmental action to prevent false or misleading information rests upon the assumption that court remedies and competitive pressures are not adequate to provide the consumer with the true information he would willingly pay for. Thus, the Securities and Exchange Commission (SEC) regulates the issuances of securities, while the buyer of used cars is typically left to his basic judicial remedies.

Third, even after locating potentially competing sellers, the buyer may not be able to evaluate the characteristics of the products or services they offer. The layman cannot readily evaluate the competence of a doctor or lawyer. Nor can he, unaided, evaluate the potential effectiveness or dangers of a drug. And he is unlikely at the time of purchase to know if a car is a lemon. Formal or informal understandings among those on the supply side — whether doctors, lawyers, or drug producers — may make difficult or impossible the creation of objectively applied labels that aid evaluation. Governmental intervention may be desired to prescribe the type of information that must be provided as well as to help buyers evaluate the information that is being supplied.

Fourth, the market may, on the supply side, be insufficiently competitive to provide all the information consumers would willingly pay for. Until the government required disclosure, accurate information was unavailable to most buyers concerning the durability of light bulbs, nicotine content of cigarettes, fuel economy for cars, or care requirements for textiles. In the 1930s automobile manufacturers advertised the comparative safety of their product. Subsequently this advertising disappeared, since auto makers felt that calling attention to safety problems hurt the industry more than it benefited individual firms. For similar reasons one does not find individual airlines advertising safety records. Since the airline industry is highly competitive in many respects, this fact suggests that tacit understandings not to supply certain varieties of information may be easier to reach (the industry need not be highly concentrated) than are tacit agreements not to compete in price or in service quality. . . .

Other Justifications

The reader should be aware of several other possible justifications for regulatory systems. While important, they have been used less often in the United States than elsewhere to justify governmental regulation of individual firms.

Unequal bargaining power. The assumption that the "best" or most efficient allocation of resources is achieved by free-market forces rests in part upon an assumption that there is a "proper" allocation of bargaining power among the parties affected. Where the existing division of such bargaining power is "unequal," it may be thought that regulation is justified in order to achieve a better balance. It is sometimes argued, for instance, that the "unequal bargaining power" of small sellers requires special legislative protection. While in principle one might regulate the "monopoly buyer" in order to protect these sellers, the more usual congressional response is to grant an exemption from the antitrust laws, thus allowing the sellers to organize in order to deal more effectively with the buyer. This rationale underlies the exemption granted not only to labor, but also to agricultural and fishing cooperatives.

Rationalization.   Occasionally governmental intervention is justified on the ground that, without it, firms in an industry would remain too small or would lack sufficient organization to produce their product efficiently. One would ordinarily expect such firms to grow or to cooperate through agreement, and to lower unit costs. But social or political factors may counteract this tendency. In such circumstances, agencies have sought to engage in industrywide "planning." In the 1960s, for example, the Federal Power Commission argued that increased coordination in the planning and operation of electric power generation and transmission facilities would significantly lower unit costs. The commission felt that environmental, political, regulatory, and managerial problems make it difficult for firms to plan jointly. The result was a relatively unsuccessful federal agency effort to encourage industrywide rationalization.

Moral hazard.   The term "moral hazard" is used to describe a situation in which someone other than a buyer pays for the buyer's purchase. The buyer feels no pocketbook constraint, and will purchase a good oblivious to the resource costs he imposes upon the economy. When ethical or other institutional constraints or direct supervision by the payer fail to control purchases, government regulation may be demanded.

The most obvious current example is escalating medical costs. As medical care is purchased to an ever greater extent by the government or by large private insurers (with virtually no constraint on the amount demanded by the individual users), medical costs have accounted for an ever greater proportion of the national product. The fact that purchases are paid for by others frees the individual from the need to consider that using more medical care means less production of other goods; thus, he may "unnecessarily" or "excessively" use medical resources. If one believed that too much of the gross national product is accounted for by medical treatment, and also believed that the problem of moral hazard prevents higher prices from acting as a check on individual demand for those resources (which in turn reduces incentive to hold down prices), one might advocate regulation to keep prices down, improve efficiency, or limit the supply of medical treatment.

Paternalism.   Although in some cases full and adequate information is available to decision makers in the marketplace, some argue that they nevertheless make irrational decisions and that therefore governmental regulation is needed. This justification is pure paternalism: the government supposedly knows better than individuals what they want or what is good for them. Such distrust of the ability of the purchaser to choose may be based on the alleged inability of the lay person to evaluate the information, as in the case of purchasing professional services, or the belief that, although the information could be accurately evaluated by the lay person, irrational human tendencies prevent this. The latter may be the case where small probabilities are involved, such as small risks of injury, or where matters of life and death are implicated, such as when those suffering from cancer will purchase a drug even though all reasonably reliable information indicates that it is worthless or even harmful. Whether the brand of paternalism based on mistrust of consumer rationality is consistent with the notions of freedom of choice that underlie the free market is questionable. However, it plays an important role in many governmental decisions.

Scarcity.   Regulation is sometimes justified in terms of scarcity. Regulation on the basis of this justification reflects a deliberate decision to abandon the market, because shortages or scarcity normally can be alleviated without regulation by allowing prices to rise. Nonetheless, one might decide to abandon price as an allocator in favor of using regulatory allocation to achieve a set of (often unspecified) "public interest" objectives, such as in the case of licensing television stations. Sometimes regulatory allocation is undertaken because of sudden supply failures: to rely on price might work too serious a hardship on many users who could not afford to pay the resulting dramatic price increases, as in the case of the Arab oil boycott. "Scarcity" or "shortage" calling for regulation may also be the result of the workings of an ongoing regulatory program, as when natural gas must be allocated because of rent control or when an agency awards licenses to enter an industry.

NOTES AND QUESTIONS

1. The concept of market failures helps to explain why citizens cannot always protect themselves through the forces of supply and demand, backed by the common law. Arguments over whether government intervention is a proper response typically center on whether the market will "clear" the failure and how soon. For example:

    a. *Monopoly.* If a monopolist is making exceptional profits, other entrepreneurs will be motivated to enter the market. The question then turns on whether there are "barriers to entry" and how high these barriers may be. In this era of globalization, foreign firms as well as domestic firms can serve as potential competitors (think of the U.S. auto industry).

    b. *Externalities.* Perhaps externalities can be overcome by affected individuals or groups getting together and bargaining for a solution in which the externalities they experience are "internalized" by the entity producing those spillover costs. If people near a factory are bothered by pollution, can't they convince the factory owner to install a pollution control system — or even contribute to the costs of paying for one? As Justice

Breyer writes, this solution is rarely simple because it requires collective action: "the residents may suffer the pollution despite a willingness to pay more than 1 cent per pound to avoid it, simply because it is too difficult for them to band together." Thus, collective action almost always imposes transaction costs: "As the number of affected people increases, communication becomes more expensive, bargaining becomes more complicated, and a clear consensus is harder to obtain." A legal default rule often is necessary to overcome these transaction costs by allocating responsibility for the harm to one party (i.e., the factory) rather than the other (i.e., the residents). Is the common law a candidate for solving the problem? Would that undermine the justification for regulation? For example, an expansion of nuisance law might grant people near a factory the right to sue the factory in tort; the factory owner would then need to compensate them for their damages or bargain with them to accept some contractual payment. Now we are back to the limitations of tort law.

c. *Rents.* Recognize that rents are not regarded by all as market failures. As Justice Breyer stated, "unlike a monopoly profit, the existence of a rent does not mean that there is 'inefficiency' or 'allocative waste.'" Thus, he comments that "[i]n many instances it seems perfectly fair that rents should accrue to producers who, through talents or skill, produced them." Even for those troubled by rents, the problem will eventually resolve itself. Sooner or later, by definition, the rent will disappear. Rents occur when a firm can supply goods for less than others because it has a more efficient production process. Over time, that firm will lose its advantage as others discover less expensive sources of supply. But will people agree on whether the wait time is acceptable?

d. *Information Asymmetries.* Competitors have an incentive to provide information in areas where their product has a market advantage. They want consumers to know why their product is the best. Will this incentive solve the problem and how soon?

2. Related, economists sometimes distinguish between market-displacing and market-correcting responses to market failure. For example, responding to a monopoly situation by setting prices displaces the operation of the market; responding to it by breaking up the monopolist into separate companies which will then compete with each other corrects the market. Can you identify market-displacing and market-correcting responses for rents, public goods, externalities, or information asymmetries? We offer an example of a market-correcting response to information asymmetries below.

3. Think about the "additional bases for regulation" that Justice Breyer lists: income transfer, fairness, and power. How general are these? Do they arise in the context of monopoly alone, as Justice Breyer seems to imply, or are they problems that pervade our entire economic system? Is comprehensive reliance on the market a foregone conclusion?

4. Not included in Justice Breyer's discussion is a type of market failure that economists often identify: the problem of public goods. Here is a description

of the problem from Robert Cooter & Thomas Ulen, LAW & ECONOMICS 45-46 (5th ed. 2008):

> A public good is a commodity with two very closely related characteristics:
>
> a. *nonrivalrous consumption*: consumption of a public good by one person does not leave less for any other consumer, and
>
> b. *nonexcludability*: the costs of excluding nonpaying beneficiaries who consume the good are so high that no private profit-maximizing firm is willing to supply the good.

Consider national defense. Suppose, for the purposes of illustration, that national defense was provided by competing private companies. For an annual fee a company would sell protection to its customers against loss from foreign invasion by air, land, or sea. Only those customers who purchase some company's services would be protected against foreign invasion. Perhaps these customers could be identified by special garments, and their property denoted by a large white X painted on the roof of their homes.

Who will purchase the services of these private national defense companies? Some will, but many will not. Many of the nonpurchasers will reason that if their neighbor will purchase a protection policy from a private national defense company, then they, too, will be protected: it will prove virtually impossible for the private company to protect the property and person of the neighbor without also providing security to the nearby nonpurchaser. Thus, the consumption of national defense is nonrivalrous: consumption by one person does not leave less for any other consumer. For that reason, there is a strong inducement for consumers of the privately provided public good to try to be *free riders*: they hope to benefit at no cost to themselves from the payment of others. How can public policy correct the market failure in the provision of public goods? There are two general correctives. First, the government may undertake to *subsidize* the private provision of the public good, either directly or indirectly through the tax system. An example might be research on basic science. Second, the government may undertake to provide the public good itself and to pay the costs of providing the service through the revenues raised by compulsory taxation. This is, in fact, how national defense is supplied.

One conventional regulatory response to information asymmetries, such as those between a purchaser of a car and the manufacturer, is to require the disclosure of more information. The idea is that with more information, private individuals or groups will be able to make choices on their own, reducing the need for government to compel particular conduct. The Securities Acts of 1933 and 1934 follow this model, requiring public corporations to disclose certain information through annual filings with the SEC.

A difficulty with this regulatory strategy is that people not only need access to information but the ability to make sense of it. The more technical the information, the harder it is to process. The less sophisticated the consumer of the information (contrast the typical car buyer to a car engineer), the greater it is still. To put this particular problem in a concrete context, read the following article, which contains a considerable amount of information, and see if you feel ready to make a decision on the subject.

1. Social Justifications for Regulation

Much government regulation stems from the recognition that, as a society, we may aspire to certain norms of conduct for their own sake. The 1960s and 1970s produced many statutes that fit this mold. Legislation exploded on the scene in diverse areas such as employment discrimination, environmental quality, consumer protection, and occupational safety. The 1966 auto safety statute is part of this wave of legislation. This statute may have addressed market failures, but that was not its only or sometimes even primary aim. So large was the wave of legislation that one scholar termed this period the Public Interest Era, *see* Robert L. Rabin, *Legitimacy, Discretion, and the Concept of Rights*, 92 YALE L.J. 1174 (1983), and another (see below) called it the Rights Revolution. As you read the excerpt from Professor Sunstein below, consider the ways in which the social justifications for government regulation that he discusses interact with the economic justifications for such regulation.

Cass Sunstein, After the Rights Revolution: Reconceiving the Regulatory State

57-69 (1990)

Collective Desires and Aspirations

Some statutes should be understood as an embodiment not of privately held preferences, but of what might be described as collective desires, including aspirations, "preferences about preferences," or considered judgments on the part of significant segments of society. Laws of this sort are a product of deliberative processes on the part of citizens and representatives. They cannot be understood as an attempt to aggregate or trade off private preferences. This understanding of politics recalls Madison's belief in deliberative democracy.

Frequently, political choices cannot easily be understood as a process of aggregating prepolitical desires. Some people may, for example, want nonentertainment broadcasting on television, even though their own consumption patterns favor situation comedies; they may seek stringent environmental laws even though they do not use the public parks; they may approve of laws calling for social security and welfare even though they do not save or give to the poor; they may support antidiscrimination laws even though their own behavior is hardly race- or gender-neutral. The choices people make as political participants are different from those they make as consumers. Democracy thus calls for an intrusion on markets. The widespread disjunction between political and consumption choices presents something of a puzzle. Indeed, it sometimes leads to the view that market ordering is undemocratic and that choices made through the political process are a preferable basis for social ordering.

A generalization of this sort would be far too broad in light of the multiple breakdowns of the political process and the advantages of market ordering in many arenas. But it would also be a mistake to suggest, as some do, that markets always reflect individual choice more reliably than politics, or that political choices differ from consumption outcomes only because of confusion, as voters fail to realize that they must ultimately bear the costs of the programs they favor. Undoubtedly consumer behavior is sometimes a better or more realistic reflection of actual preferences than is political behavior. But since preferences depend on context, the very notion of a "better reflection" of "actual" preferences is a confused one. Moreover, the difference might be explained by the fact that political behavior reflects a variety of influences that are distinctive to the context of politics.

These include four closely related phenomena. First, citizens may seek to fulfill individual and collective aspirations in political behavior, not in private consumption. As citizens, people may seek the aid of the law to bring about a social state in some sense higher than what emerges from market ordering. Second, people may, in their capacity as political actors, attempt to satisfy altruistic or other-regarding desires, which diverge from the self-interested preferences characteristic of markets. Third, political decisions might vindicate what might be called meta-preferences or second-order preferences. A law protecting environmental diversity and opposing consumption behaviors is an example. People have wishes about their wishes; and sometimes they try to vindicate those second-order wishes, or considered judgments about what is best, through law. Fourth, people may precommit themselves, with regulation, to a course of action that they consider to be in the general interest; the story of Ulysses and the Sirens is the model here. The adoption of a Constitution is itself an example of a precommitment strategy.

For all these reasons people seem to favor regulation designed to secure high-quality broadcasting even though their consumption patterns favor situation comedies — a phenomenon that helps justify certain controversial regulatory decisions by the Federal Communications Commission requiring nonentertainment broadcasting and presentations on issues of public importance. The same category of aspirations or public spiritedness includes measures designed to protect endangered species and natural preserves in the face of individual behavior that reflects little solicitude for them.

The collective character of politics, permitting a response to collective action problems, helps to explain these phenomena. People may not want to satisfy their meta-preferences, or to be altruistic, unless they are sure that others will be bound as well. More simply, people may prefer not to contribute to a collective benefit if donations are made individually, but their most favored system might be one in which they contribute if (but only if) there is assurance that others will do so. The collective character of politics might also overcome the problem, discussed below, of preferences and beliefs that have adapted to an unjust status quo or to limits in available opportunities. Without the possibility of collective action, the status quo may seem intractable, and private behavior will adapt accordingly. But if people can act in concert, preferences might take a quite different form; consider social movements involving the environment, labor, and race and sex discrimination.

In addition, social and cultural norms might incline people to express aspirational or altruistic goals in political behavior but not in markets. Such norms may press people, in their capacity as citizens, distinctly in the direction of a concern for others or for the public interest. The deliberative aspects of politics, bringing additional information and perspectives to bear, may also bring out or affect preferences as expressed through governmental processes.

Government action is a necessary response here. Possible examples include recycling programs, energy conservation programs, and contributions to the arts, to the poor, and to environmental protection. The collective action problem interacts with aspirations, altruistic desires, second-order preferences, and precommitment strategies; all of these are most likely to be enacted into law in the face of a question of collective action. Moreover, consumption decisions are a product of the criterion of private willingness to pay, which contains distortions of its own. Willingness to pay is a function of ability to pay, and it is an extremely crude proxy for utility. Political behavior removes this distortion (which is not to say that it does not introduce distortions of its own).

These general considerations suggest that statutes are sometimes a response to a considered judgment on the part of the electorate that the choices reflected in consumption patterns ought to be overcome. A related but more narrow justification is that statutes safeguard noncommodity values that an unregulated market protects inadequately. Social ordering through markets may have long-term, world-transforming effects that reflect a kind of collective myopia in the form of an emphasis on short-term considerations at the expense of the future. Here regulation is a natural response. Examples include promoting high-quality programming in broadcasting, supporting the arts, and ensuring diversity through protection of the environment and of endangered species. In all of these respects, political choices are not made by consulting given or private desires, but instead reflect a deliberative process designed to shape and reflect values. . . .

Social Subordination

Some regulatory statutes attempt not simply to redistribute resources, but to eliminate or reduce the social subordination of various social groups. Much of antidiscrimination law is designed as an attack on practices and beliefs that have adverse consequences for members of disadvantaged groups. Discriminatory attitudes and practices result in the social subordination of blacks, women, the handicapped, and gays and lesbians. Statutes designed to eliminate discrimination attempt to change both practices and attitudes. The motivating idea here is that differences that are irrelevant from the moral point of view ought not to be turned into social disadvantages, and they certainly should not be permitted to do so if the disadvantage is systemic. In all of these cases, social practices turn differences into systemic harms for the relevant group. Such measures as the Equal Pay Act, the Civil Rights Act of 1964, and the Developmentally Disabled Assistance and Bill of Rights Act attempt to supply correctives. As we will see, measures of this sort might be seen as a fulfillment of constitutional duties imposed by the fifth amendment on the Congress; and this is so even if those duties are not enforced by constitutional courts.

It is sometimes suggested that market pressures are sufficient to counteract social subordination, and that statutory intervention is therefore unnecessary. Businesses that discriminate will ultimately face economic pressure from those that do not. The refusal to hire qualified blacks and women will result in competitive injury to discriminators, who will therefore face higher costs and ultimately be driven from the marketplace. This process is said to make markets a good check on discrimination and on caste systems. Although such a process does occur in some settings, market pressures constitute, for several reasons, an inadequate constraint.

First, third parties might impose serious costs on those who agree to deal with members of disadvantaged groups; customers and others sometimes withdraw patronage or services. Consider, for example, the risks sometimes faced by firms that employ blacks, women, the disabled, and gays and lesbians. By their ability to impose costs, customers and others are well situated to prevent elimination of discriminatory practices. In these circumstances market pressures do not check discrimination, but instead guarantee that it will continue. A caste system of some sort is the predictable result. Undoubtedly such pressures have contributed to the perpetuation of discrimination in many settings.

Second, discriminatory behavior is sometimes a response to generalizations or stereotypes that, although quite overbroad and even invidious, provide an economically rational basis for market decisions. Because the behavior is economically rational, not based on a competitively harmful racial animus, it will persist as long as markets do. For example, an employer might act discriminatorily not because he hates or devalues blacks or women, or has a general desire not to associate with them, or is "prejudiced" in the ordinary sense, but because he has found that the stereotypes have sufficient truth to be a basis for employment decisions. Of course it will be exceptionally difficult to disentangle these various attitudes, and they will frequently overlap; but in light of the history of discrimination against both blacks and women, it would hardly be shocking if stereotyping was sometimes economically rational.

This form of discrimination is objectionable not because it is a reflection of ordinary bigotry or even irrationality, but because it works to perpetuate the second-class citizenship of members of disadvantaged groups. Markets will do nothing about such discrimination; civil rights legislation reduces it. The example suggests that the line between antidiscrimination laws and affirmative action is far thinner than is generally believed.

Third, private preferences of both beneficiaries and victims of discrimination tend to adapt to existing injustice, and to do so in such a way as to make significant change hard to undertake. People often have a "taste" for discrimination, and one of the purposes of antidiscrimination law is to alter that taste. The beneficiaries of the status quo take advantage of strategies that reduce cognitive dissonance, such as blaming the victim. The victims also reduce dissonance by adapting their preferences to the available opportunities or by adapting their aspirations to fit their persistent belief that the world is just. Psychological mechanisms of this sort furnish a formidable barrier to social change.

In a closely related phenomenon, members of disadvantaged groups faced with widespread discrimination on the part of employers may well respond to the relevant signals by deciding to invest less than other people in the acquisition of the skills valued by the market. Individual and group productivity is a function of demand; it is not independent of it. Members of a group that is the object of discrimination may therefore end up less productive, not only because their skin color or gender is devalued, but also because the market sends signals that it is less worthwhile for them to develop the skills necessary to compete.

Fourth, and most fundamentally, markets incorporate the practices and norms of the advantaged group. Conspicuous examples include the multiple ways in which employment settings, requirements, and expectations are structured for the able-bodied and for traditional male career patterns. In such cases, markets are the problem, not the solution. One goal of the advocates of antisubordination is to restructure market arrangements so as to put disadvantaged groups on a plane of equality — not by helping them to be "like" members of advantaged groups, but by changing the criteria themselves. A law cannot make it up to someone for being deaf or requiring a wheelchair; but it can aggravate or diminish the social consequences of deafness and lameness. Regulation requiring sign language and wheelchair ramps ensures that a difference is not turned into a systemic disadvantage. Here the conventional test of discrimination law — is the member of the disadvantaged group "similarly situated" to the member of the advantaged group? — itself reflects inequality, since it takes the norms and practices of the advantaged group as the baseline against which to measure inequality.

Statutes protecting the handicapped are the best example here. To say this is not to suggest the nature or degree of appropriate restructuring of the market — a difficult question in light of the sometimes enormous costs of adaptation to the norms and practices of disadvantaged groups. But it is to say that markets are far from a sufficient protection against social subordination. . . .

Irreversibility, Future Generations, Animals, and Nature

Some statutes are a response to the problem of irreversibility — the fact that a certain course of conduct, if continued, will lead to an outcome from which current and future generations will be able to recover not at all, or only at very high cost. Since markets reflect the preferences of current consumers, they do not take account of the effect of transactions on future generations. The consequences of reliance on market ordering will sometimes be an irretrievable loss. The protection of endangered species stems in part from this fear. Much of the impetus behind laws protecting natural areas is that environmental degradation is sometimes final or extraordinarily expensive to repair. Protection of cultural relics stems from a similar rationale.

To a large degree, social and economic regulation of this sort is produced by a belief in obligations owed by the present to future generations. Current practices may produce losses that might be acceptable if no one else were affected, but that are intolerable in light of their consequences for those who will follow. Effects on future generations thus amount to a kind of externality. Such externalities might include limitations in the available range of experiences or the elimination of potential sources of medicines and pesticides; consider the Endangered Species Act.

In more complex forms, arguments of this sort emphasize the multiple values of protecting species, animals, and nature. Some of these arguments are "anthrocentric," in the sense that they focus on the ultimate value of such protection to human beings. For example, many people enjoy seeing diversity in nature; and plants and animals furnish most of the raw materials for medicines, pesticides, and other substances with considerable instrumental worth to humanity. On this view, the loss or reduction of a species is a serious one for human beings. It is hard to monetize these values because of the difficulty of ascertaining, at any particular time, the many uses to which different species might be put.

A related but somewhat different argument emphasizes the value of natural diversity for the transformation of human values and for deliberation about the good. On this view, the preservation of diverse species and of natural beauty serves to alter existing preferences and provides an occasion for critical scrutiny of current desires and beliefs. Aesthetic experiences play an important role in shaping ideas and desires, and regulation may be necessary to ensure the necessary diversity.

On a different account, the elimination of a species, particular animals, and perhaps of waters and streams is objectionable quite apart from its effects on human beings, and indeed for its own sake. This account itself takes various forms. Sometimes the argument is a democratic one: most people believe that obligations are owed to nonhuman objects, and the majority deserves to rule. Sometimes the invocation of the rights of nonhuman creatures and objects can best be understood as a rhetorical device designed to inculcate social norms that will overcome collective action problems in preserving the environment — problems that are ultimately harmful to human beings. In many hands, however, the argument, sounding in what is sometimes called "deep ecology," does not even refer to human desires. The idea here is that animals, species as such, and perhaps even natural objects warrant respect for their own sake, and quite apart from their interactions with human beings. Sometimes such arguments posit general rights held by living creatures (and natural objects) against human depredations. In especially powerful forms, these arguments are utilitarian in character, stressing the often extreme and unnecessary suffering of animals who are hurt or killed. The Animal Welfare Act reflects these concerns.

NOTES AND QUESTIONS

1. As Sunstein explains, sometimes our "preferences about preferences" are entitled to more weight than the preferences that we act upon in our daily lives. If the government gives effect to our aspirations, how is this different from paternalism? In name only? Paternalism is often viewed as a poor justification for intervention. Is it always?

2. One way to view government intervention on the basis of public aspirations is leadership — i.e., the government is acting on our behalf with the expectation that we will catch up. When is the government entitled to lead? Is the government on firmer footing when a significant minority is already "with the program"? If so, where might we see such leadership today?

3. Consider anti-discrimination norms. Sunstein offers fours reasons why market pressures are insufficient to counter social subordination. Where might we see the reasons persist or materialize today?

4. In other parts of his book, Sunstein emphasizes a more general concern about the market as a natural, fixed baseline: "[M]arket outcomes — including prices and wages pursuant to a system of freedom of contract — are affected by a wide range of factors that are morally arbitrary. They include, for example, supply and demand at any particular place and time, unequally distributed opportunities before people become traders at all, existing tastes, the sheer number of purchasers and sellers, and even the unequal distribution of skills. There is no good reason for government to take these factors as natural or fixed, or to allow them to be turned into social and legal advantages, when it is deciding on the proper scope of regulation." SUNSTEIN, AFTER THE RIGHTS REVOLUTION 39. Thus, Sunstein argues that the market is a human creation and subject to evaluation on the same grounds as any other human creation, such as regulation. It need not only "fail" to be replaced, but can be rejected if another system is preferable. In a similar vein, Professor Neil Komesar proposes that we regard the market as just another means of regulation, which we can use or not depending on the results we want to achieve. *See* IMPERFECT ALTERNATIVES: CHOOSING INSTITUTIONS IN LAW, ECONOMICS, AND PUBLIC POLICY (1997). Do you see why arguments such as these are important?

5. We mentioned that auto safety legislation came on the scene in 1966 during the Rights Revolution. To what extent do social justifications support such legislation? Auto safety might be viewed as a societal right, along with other "rights" like workplace safety or environmental quality or employment equality: Every citizen is entitled to protection in their own vehicles, and the government can play a role in guaranteeing it. We were entering an age when technology could put a man on the moon; why not take the small steps necessary to make new cars safer for all?

From Justification to Legislation: A Note on the Role of Politics

Economic and social justifications for government regulation may play a role in the shift from the common law to the regulatory state, in general and in the auto safety context. They are also central to the public discourse about legislation. Specifically, they help courts, agencies, lawyers, and citizens understand what regulatory statutes mean and how they apply. But do these justifications explain why Congress enacts regulatory statutes?

Leading political scientists argue that they do not. Instead, they contend that Congress is motivated to enact a statute whenever that statute serves the self-interest of a majority of legislators. This claim is based on public choice theory, which holds that legislators, no different than any other rational actors, take actions that serve their self interest. *See, e.g.*, DENNIS C. MUELLER, PUBLIC CHOICE III (2003); DANIEL A. FARBER & PHILIP P. FRICKEY, LAW AND PUBLIC CHOICE: A CRITICAL INTRODUCTION (1991). For many legislators, this self-interest is reelection. Above all else, they want to keep their jobs for their own sakes. But even legislators who intend to pursue other, more public-minded goals must hold office to accomplish those goals. The consequence, by and large, is that legislators will cater to the preferences of wealthy and organized constituent groups because these groups fund reelection campaigns. Sometimes legislators are motivated by a different sort of self-interest, such as creating their own legacy, however long in office. They will take actions consistent with this goal. Note that political scientists are not making a normative claim; they are not contending that Congress *should* act this way or that statutes are justified on the basis of such legislative behavior. They are making a positive or descriptive claim: Congress *does* act in conformance with the self-interest of its members.

As we will see in the chapters that follow, there is a complex relationship between the justifications for government regulation and the political explanations for it. Consider, for instance, the question of statutory interpretation. When a court interprets a statute, is it the political explanation or the justification for the statute that matters? Theories of statutory interpretation diverge on that point. Some theories are based on the assumption that statutes reflect nothing more than legislative self-interest: the words are what it took to obtain legislative consensus and "do the deal" on behalf of powerful constituents, and, therefore, the words of the statute are all that should be subject to interpretation. Others posit that it is the justification for the statute — its purpose — that should guide statutory interpretation. The same questions arise as to how an agency should implement a statute. For now, the important point is seeing that both explanations and justifications for government regulation matter. What this also tells you is that there is more to the story of auto safety legislation than we have told you so far. In the next chapter, we turn to how auto safety legislation was enacted.

CHAPTER 2

LEGISLATION

The rise of the regulatory state is in part a story of the rise of legislation. Legislation is the legal basis of much modern social and economic policy. As a result, lawyers who operate in the regulatory state (which is to say nearly all lawyers) need to have an understanding of legislation. This chapter describes the basic aspects of the legislative process, the standard features of statutory design, and the main components of legislative drafting. Of course, every statute has its own particular history; we aim to capture the principal commonalities among them. By providing a view of the forces that shape statutes and the elements that they contain, we hope to provide a baseline for understanding the body of law that Congress enacts.

A. The Legislative Process

We begin our discussion of legislation with a snapshot of the process that generates it. Thus, we trace the path from bill to law, in a bit more detail than *Schoolhouse Rocks!* (pictured above). We then provide some theories of how the legislative process actually works and a specific example in the context of auto safety.

1. A General Description

When describing the legislative process, the place to start is with the Constitution. For a bill to become a law, the Constitution requires a majority vote of both houses of Congress (bicameralism) and a presidential signature (presentment), or a two-third majority vote of both houses of Congress to override a presidential veto. U.S. CONST., Art. 1, §7. Note how onerous these requirements are; few bills will survive them to become laws. The Framers of the Constitution seemed to have this very result in mind, as a formal check against the tyranny of the majority. *See* THE FEDERALIST No. 73 (Hamilton, viewing the requirements of bicameralism and presentment as an "an additional security against [the production] of improper laws"); THE FEDERALIST No. 63 (Madison, viewing the legislative process

as "suspend[ing] the blow mediated by the people themselves, until reason, justice, and truth can regain their authority over the public mind").

As onerous as the constitutional requirements are, most bills never make it to that stage. The modern legislative process is considerably more complicated. Both the House and the Senate maintain rules of procedure that allow smaller groups to derail a bill along the way. Thus, most bills actually "die in committee." Consider the following account:

Steven S. Smith, The American Congress

31-46 (1995)

The Standard Legislative Process

The modern legislative process gives a member who is interested in enacting a new law three basic procedural options. First, she could introduce her own bill and work to gain passage in both houses. Second, she could seek to have her ideas incorporated in legislation drafted by a committee or other members. And third, she could offer her proposal as an amendment to someone else's legislation. She might even pursue all three options simultaneously.

The standard legislative process in the modern Congress is outlined in Figure 2.1. I call it the standard process because it conforms to the standing rules and normal practices of the House and Senate. The houses are free to alter it for certain legislation, and they do so with some frequency. Even the standard process

Figure 2.1   The Standard Legislative Process for a Major Bill

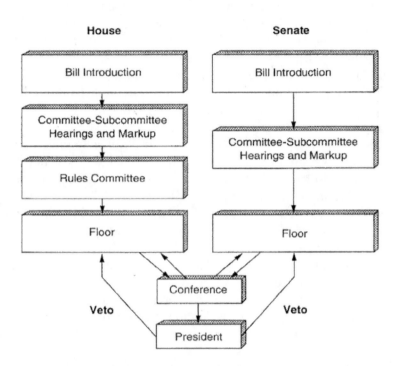

involves many options that are used regularly. The standard process involves multiple stages in each house, followed by steps for resolving House-Senate differences. . . . [A]fter the House and Senate agree on legislation, the Constitution provides for presidential approval or veto and veto override attempts. The standard process is like an obstacle course in which majorities must be created at several stages among different groups of legislators.

Introduction of Legislation

Legislation may be drafted by anyone — a member and his or her staff, a committee, lobbyists, executive branch officials, or any combination of insiders and outsiders — but it must be introduced by a member while Congress is in session. . . . In both houses, the chief sponsor of a measure may seek cosponsors. Legislation is designated as a bill, a joint resolution, a concurrent resolution, or a resolution and numbered as it is introduced. . . .

Committee Action

After introduction, the House Speaker or Senate's presiding officer refers legislation to the appropriate committees. In practice, the House and Senate parliamentarians inspect the content of legislation and recommend referral to the committee or committees with the appropriate jurisdiction. Careful drafting of legislation may influence the referral decision.

Legislation may be referred to more than one committee, an action called multiple referral, because committees sometimes share jurisdiction of certain kinds of legislation. Multiple referral has become quite common in the House. Since 1974, the Speaker of the House has been authorized to send legislation to committees jointly, sequentially, or by splitting it into parts. In the case of joint and sequential referral, the Speaker may set time limits on committee action. In recent Congresses, about one in ten House measures has been multiply referred; a higher proportion of important measures, closer to one in five has been multiply referred.

Senate committees may send legislation to a subcommittee, while most House committees must do so unless they vote to retain the legislation at the full committee. Committees and subcommittees may hold hearings to receive testimony on legislation from members, administration officials, interest-group representatives, outside experts, and others. They may commission studies from the Congressional Research Service or other congressional staff agencies. Committees and subcommittees may conduct "markups" on legislation — detailed consideration and amendment of the legislation. Committees may write their own legislation and have it introduced by their chairs. A measure may be reported by a committee with or without amendments or a recommendation that it pass, although most important reported legislation is amended and recommended to pass. A majority of a committee's members must be present to report a measure back to the House or Senate.

A bill reported from a committee must be accompanied by a committee report that provides the committee's justification for the bill. Committee reports are usually routinely drafted by staff and may include a statement of minority views on the legislation. On occasion, committee reports are controversial because they provide further interpretations of the bill that might guide later actions on the part of executive agencies or the courts. And committee reports sometimes help noncommittee members and their aides explain complicated legislation to constituents. In the House, the Ramsayer rule (named after the member who proposed it) requires that committee reports specify all of the changes in existing law that are made by the legislation.

Unless they are otherwise instructed by their parent chambers, committees are free to take no action on most legislation referred to them. Inaction at the committee stage dooms most legislation. In fact, most legislation dies in committee. In the 102d Congress (1991-1992), 4,245 bills and resolutions were introduced in the Senate and 7,184 were introduced in the House. But only 719 and 918 measures were reported by committees of the House and Senate, respectively — 17 and 13 percent.*

---

* [In the 110th Congress (Jan. 2008-Jan. 2009), 1,590 bills and resolutions were introduced in the Senate and 3,225 were introduced in the House; 452 and 404 measures were reported by committees of the House and Senate (29% and 13%). In the 111th Congress (Jan. 2009-Jan. 2010), 3,380 bills and resolutions were introduced in the Senate and 5,691 were introduced in the House; 199 and 367 measures were reported by committees of the House and Senate (less than 1% each). 2009-2010 was a presidential transition year. — EDS.]

Floor Scheduling

Legislation is listed in the order it is reported from committee on one of four calendars in the House and one of two calendars in the Senate. If each house did not have an alternative mechanism for scheduling legislation for floor consideration, priority legislation, which often is more complex and requires lengthy committee consideration, would get backlogged behind less important legislation. The exception is certain types of "privileged" legislation — such as budget and appropriations legislation — that the House allows committee leaders to call up directly on the floor. In both houses, the majority party leaders have assumed primary responsibility for scheduling, but the two houses have developed very different methods for setting the floor agenda.

The House. Minor legislation and major legislation are treated differently in the House. In recent years, minor bills have been called up most frequently by a unanimous consent request or a motion to suspend the rules. When legislation is called up by unanimous consent there typically is no discussion. Under a motion to suspend the rules, debate is limited to no more than forty minutes and no amendments are allowed, but a two-thirds majority is required for approval. The Speaker must recognize a member who seeks to bring up a minor measure by one of these means, so his cooperation is essential. A small number of measures are placed on the Consent Calendar, which is limited to measures involving spending of less than $1 million, supervised by a group of members from both parties, and considered twice each month. With very few exceptions, such measures are approved by unanimous consent — that is, without a formal vote.

Major, controversial legislation is more troublesome. Sponsors usually cannot obtain unanimous or even two-thirds majority support as is needed for minor legislation. Instead, the sponsors of a major or controversial bill go to the Committee on Rules to request a resolution, known as a special rule or, more briefly, a "rule." . . . The rule provides for priority consideration of the measure by allowing the Speaker to move the House into the Committee of the Whole, where the bill may be amended. . . . The rule limits general debate on the bill to one hour and allows only those amendments to the committee version that are listed in an accompanying report from the Rules Committee. This rule also sets aside objections (waives points of order) that may be made to the provisions of the bill or amendments that violate House rules.

Special rules are highly flexible tools for tailoring floor action to individual bills. Amendments may be limited or prohibited. The order of voting on amendments may be structured. For example, the House frequently adopts a special rule that is called king-of-the-hill. First used in 1982, such a rule provides for a sequence of votes on alternative amendments, usually full substitutes for the bill. The last amendment to receive a majority wins, even if it receives fewer votes than some other amendment. A king-of-the-hill rule allows members to vote for more than one version of the legislation, which gives them the freedom to support a version that is easy to defend at home and also vote for the version preferred by their party's leaders. Even more important, the procedure advantages the version voted on last, which usually is the proposal favored by the majority party leadership. If the Committee on Rules grants the rule and a majority of the House supports it, the way is paved for floor debate on the bill. Less than 10 percent of legislation reaching the House floor is important or controversial enough to warrant a special rule. . . .

The Senate. This is the first, but not the last, opportunity to note how different (some would say bizarre) the Senate is. In some respects, floor scheduling is simple in the Senate. Bringing up a bill is a matter of making a motion to proceed to its consideration. This is done by the majority leader and, while the motion technically requires a majority vote, it usually is approved by unanimous consent. The Senate has no Rules Committee empowered to report special rules.

What appears bizarre to many newcomers to Senate politics is that the motion to proceed is debatable and may be subject to a filibuster. . . . That is, senators may refuse to allow the majority leader's motion to come to a vote by conducting extended debate. In fact, they may not even have to conduct the filibuster because just the threat of doing so usually is enough to keep legislation of only moderate importance off the floor. The reason is that the majority leader usually cannot afford to create a logjam of legislation awaiting floor consideration by subjecting one measure to extended debate. Under Senate Rule 22, breaking a filibuster is a time-consuming process that requires a three-fifths constitutional majority — sixty senators — willing to invoke cloture. . . .

The ever-present threat of a filibuster requires that scheduling be a matter of consultation and negotiation among the majority leader, minority leader, bill sponsors, and other interested senators. These discussions, conducted in private, often yield bargains about how to proceed and may include compromises about substantive policy matters. The agreement, which may include limitations on debate and amendments, is then presented to the Senate. It requires unanimous approval to take effect. The process contrasts sharply with the formal Rules Committee hearings and majority approval of special rules in the House.

Floor Consideration

For most minor legislation that reaches the House or Senate floor, floor consideration is brief, no amendments are offered, and the legislation is approved by voice vote or by unanimous consent. On major legislation, many members usually want to speak and offer amendments, creating a need for procedures that will maintain order and expedite action. The two houses have quite different floor procedures for major legislation.

The House. Committee chairs write the Rules Committee requesting a hearing and a special rule for major legislation reported from their committees. Once the special rule for a measure is adopted, the House may resolve into the Committee of the Whole House on the State of the Union to conduct general debate and consider amendments. The Committee of the Whole, as it is usually abbreviated, consists of the full House meeting in the House chamber and operating under a special set of rules. For example, the quorum required to conduct business in the Committee of the Whole is smaller than for the House (100 versus 218), making it easier to conduct business while members are busy at other activities. A chair appointed by the Speaker presides over the Committee of the Whole. The Committee of the Whole first conducts general debate on the bill, and then moves to debate and votes on amendments. Legislation is considered section by section. An amendment must be relevant — germane — to the section under consideration, a requirement that is interpreted very restrictively. For example, an amendment to limit abortions cannot be considered when a bill on water treatment plants is being debated. Amendments sponsored by the committee originating the legislation are considered first for each section. Amendments in the Committee of the Whole are considered under the five-minute rule. That is, members are allowed to speak for five minutes on an amendment. The special rule providing for the consideration of a measure may — and often does — alter these standard procedures.

Voting on amendments in the Committee of the Whole can take one of three forms: voice vote, standing division vote, or recorded vote. On a voice vote, members yell out "yea" or "nay" and the presiding officer determines whether there were more yeas or nays. On a standing division vote, members voting "yea" stand and are counted, followed by those voting "nay." Since 1971, it has been possible to get a recorded vote on which each individual member's position is officially and publicly recorded. Under the current rule, a recorded vote in the Committee of the whole must be demanded by twenty-five members. Beginning in 1973, recorded voting has been done by electronic device, a computerized system in which members insert a credit-card sized identification card into a small voting box and push a yea, nay, or present button. This system is used for recording voting in the House as well. . . .

Legislation cannot be passed in the Committee of the Whole, so once debate and amending action are complete the measure, along with any approved amendments, is reported back to the House. Special rules usually provide that the "previous question" is ordered, preventing additional debate by the House. The amendments approved in the Committee of the Whole then may be subject to separate votes, but if no one demands a separate vote the amendments are approved en bloc. Next, a motion to recommit the legislation to committee, which by custom is made by a minority party member, is in order. If the motion to recommit is defeated, as it nearly always is, or simply not offered, the House moves to a vote on final passage.

The Senate. The Senate lacks detailed rules or a well-structured process for debating and amending legislation on the floor. What happens after the motion to proceed is adopted depends on whether unanimous consent has been obtained to limit or structure debate and amendments. In the absence of a unanimous consent agreement providing otherwise, Senate rules do not limit debate or amendments for most legislation. Debate and amending activity may go on for days — the Senate has no five-minute rule or general germaneness rule for amendments. The floor schedule becomes very unpredictable. Normally, the Senate muddles through controversial legislation with one or more unanimous consent agreements that limit debate, organize the consideration of amendments, and lend some predictability to its proceedings.

One reason consent for a time limitation agreement may be not acquired is that some senators may be filibustering the bill or some amendment. A filibuster, or sometimes just the threat of a filibuster, will force a compromise. But if a compromise is not possible, cloture must be invoked or the majority leader will be compelled to withdraw the measure from the floor. If cloture is invoked, thirty hours of debate are permitted under the current rule and germane amendments submitted before cloture can be considered. In fact, cloture sometimes is invoked to avoid nongermane amendments that may require embarrassing votes, complicate negotiations with the House, or stimulate a presidential veto.

The modern Senate does not use a committee of the whole. Floor voting can take one of three forms: voice vote, division vote, and roll-call votes. Voice and division votes are similar to those in the House; although the Senate very seldom uses division votes. The Senate does not have an electronic voting system, so its recorded votes which can be demanded by eleven senators, are conducted by a name-by-name call of the roll. A vote on final passage occurs as specified in a unanimous consent agreement or, in the absence of an agreement, whenever senators stop talking and offering amendments.

Resolving Differences Between the Houses

The two houses must approve identical legislation before it can be sent to the president. . . . . This can be accomplished in several ways. One house can accept a measure passed by the other house. The houses may exchange amendments until they agree on them. Or they may agree to hold a conference at which a resolution to the matters in dispute can be devised, sent back to the two houses, and approved. For legislation of much controversy and complexity, a conference is the only practical approach. No more than one in five measures goes to conference, although nearly one in two of measures receiving a House special rule goes to conference.

Members of conference committees, known as conferees, are appointed by the presiding officers of the two houses. Committee leaders' recommendations for conference delegation appointments usually are followed. Committee leaders take into account seniority, interest in the legislation, and other factors, and some committees have established traditions that the leaders observe. Conference delegations may be of any size. If a few of the large conferences for budget measures are excluded, the average conference has been twelve representatives and ten senators. Agreements between House and Senate conferees are written up as conference reports, which ports must be approved by majority votes in the House and Senate.

In the 102d Congress (1991-1992), eighty-seven conference reports were filed by conference committees. That represented only about 14 percent of the bills and joint resolutions enacted into law during the Congress. Plainly, most legislation is routine and noncontroversial and therefore does not require conference action. By the end of the 102d Congress, only about 6 percent of all bills introduced were enacted into law. . . .

Variations in the Legislative Process

From time to time the House and Senate have tailored their procedures to particular kinds of legislation or issues. In the last two decades, for example, Congress has created "fast-track" procedures for considering trade agreements negotiated by the executive branch with foreign governments. These procedures limit debate and bar amendments to speed congressional approval and limit congressional second-guessing of executive branch decisions.

An even more important class of legislation with special procedures concerns fiscal policy: decisions about federal spending, taxing, and budget deficits and surpluses. The Congressional Budget and Impoundment Control Act of 1974, often known simply as the Budget Act, established a process intended to coordinate congressional decisions that affect fiscal policy. In the 1980s and early 1990s, skyrocketing federal deficits motivated Congress to set tight rules constraining fiscal choices and adopt unique procedures for enforcing the new constraints. . . .

NOTES AND QUESTIONS

1. You can now appreciate the steps of the legislative process, many of which can also be described as hurdles or obstacles. Indeed, political scientists have used the concept of "vetogates" to describe the junctures in the legislative process where a proposed bill can be derailed by a relatively small number of individuals. *See* Mathew McCubbins, Roger Noll & Barry Weingast, *Legislative Intent, The Use of Positive Political Theory in Statutory Interpretation*, 57 LAW & CONTEMP. PROBS. 3 (1994). How many vetogates can you identify from the foregoing description of the process? Are they worrisome?
2. How can vetogates work in practice to the advantage of your client? Suppose your law firm represents companies that produce artificial honey through a chemical process. These companies think that their business will be destroyed by a bill that is about to be introduced into Congress, which will require them to list a series of disclosures on their product describing the way it was produced. They have hired you to go to Washington, D.C., and prevent the bill from being enacted into law. At which point in the legislative process do you think intervention would be most effective? Who would you contact? What would you say?
3. Can you identify the key moments in the legislative process when documents or statements other than the text of the bill are produced? These documents or statements form a part of the legislative history of the statute to which they relate. Whose views do these documents and statements reflect? Are there any that reflect the views of the majority of Congress? Which are most likely to be read by a majority of Congress? Which pieces are likely to capture the views of the minority or a dissenting legislator? We discuss the issue of legislative history later in this chapter as well as in Chapters 11 and 10.

Note on Theories of the Legislative Process

Over time, different theories have arisen to describe how the legislative process actually works. Although a full discussion of theories is best left to a course on legislation, we provide you with a brief introduction to some of the more important and influential ones:

Public Choice Theory and the Role of Interest Groups. What is the role of interest groups in the legislative process? In *The Logic of Collective Action* (1965), economist Mancur Olson asserted that it is more difficult to organize large groups with diffuse interests than small groups with common interests. Extending this logic, it is possible to see that small groups will have a disproportionate share of influence in the legislative process. The result is that "actual political choices [will be] determined by the efforts of individuals and groups to further their own interests." Gary Becker, A *Theory of Competition Among Pressure Groups for Political Influence*, 98 Q.J. ECON. 371, 372 (1983). Consistent with this theory, if you think that statutes reflect "the will of the people," think again. Statutes reflect the self-interest of the well-organized groups that prevail upon Congress to enact them. Why would Congress respond to interest groups in this fashion? The answer comes from public choice theory. Members of Congress are inclined to pursue their own self-interest, which is generally taken to be an interest in reelection. And well-organized, small interest groups can often promise members of Congress what they seek, while the diffuse public cannot. As Professors Daniel Farber and Philip Frickey have written:

> The core of the economic models is a jaundiced view of legislative motivation. In place of their prior assumption that legislators voted to promote their view of the public interest, economists now postulate that legislators are motivated solely by self-interest. In particular, legislators must maximize their likelihood of reelection. A legislator who is not reelected loses all the other possible benefits flowing from office.
>
> The question, then, is what do legislators have to do to get reelected? In other words, what determines the outcomes of elections? Economic models can be classified into two groups, depending on how they answer this question.
>
> Models in the first group assume that legislators attempt to maximize their appeal to their constituents. These constituents, in turn, vote according to their own economic self-interest. Thus, those models suggest that legislative votes can be easily predicted from the economic interests of constituents.
>
> Models in the second group give a greater role to special interest groups. Because voters don't know much about a legislator's conduct, elections may turn on financial backing, publicity, and endorsements. These forms of support, as well as other possible benefits including outright bribes, are likely to be provided by organized interest groups, which thereby acquire the ability to affect legislative action.
>
> The economic theory of interest groups can be traced to Mancur Olson's theory of collective action. Olson pointed out that political action generally benefits large groups. For example, everyone presumably benefits from improved national security. But any single person's efforts to protect national security normally can have only an infinitesimal effect. Hence, a rational person will try to "free ride" on the

efforts of others, contributing nothing to the national defense while benefiting from other people's actions.

This "free rider" problem suggests that it should be nearly impossible to organize large groups of individuals to seek broadly dispersed public goods. Instead, political activity should be dominated by small groups of individuals seeking to benefit themselves, usually at the public expense. The easiest groups to organize would presumably consist of a few individuals or firms seeking government benefits for themselves, which will be financed by the general public. Thus, if Olson is correct, politics should be dominated by "rent-seeking" special interest groups.

DANIEL A. FARBER & PHILIP P. FRICKEY, LAW AND PUBLIC CHOICE: A CRITICAL INTRODUCTION 22-23 (1991). On this theory, would Congress ever respond to the interests of the general public? It might if it believed that the public could be energized enough by a particular issue to vote on that basis. *See* R. DOUGLAS ARNOLD, THE LOGIC OF CONGRESSIONAL ACTION (1990).

Social Choice Theory and the Problem of Cycling. How does a multi-member body such as Congress ever agree on the details of legislation when confronted with multiple options? In *Social Choice and Individual Values* (2d ed. 1963), Kenneth Arrow demonstrated that a multi-member body with three or more options will engage in "cycling" if the options are voted on in pairs. (Social choice theory is similar to public choice theory; both rely on the economic, "rational actor" model of legislative behavior, which sees members of Congress as pursuing their own self-interest.) To see the point about cycling, assume a committee of three individuals (Alan, Betty, and Carol) is asked to award a contract to one of three states (Florida, Illinois, and Texas). The individuals on the committee each rank their preferences among the three states as follows, with the most preferred state at the top and the least preferred state at the bottom of each list:

Alan	*Betty*	*Carol*
Texas	Illinois	Florida
Illinois	Florida	Texas
Florida	Texas	Illinois

As between Texas and Illinois, which has majority support (two out of three votes)? The answer is Texas because both Alan and Carol prefer Texas to Illinois. But there's still another option: Florida. Maybe Florida has stronger support than Texas. As between Florida and Texas, which has majority support? The answer is Florida because both Betty and Carol prefer Florida to Texas. But neither Alan nor Betty prefer Florida over Illinois, so let's continue the contest for a third round. As between Illinois (which Alan and Betty prefer to Florida) and Texas, Texas wins. But we're back to the beginning again. According to Arrow's theorem, the only way to arrive at a choice is to end the cycling. In the legislative process, that result can be accomplished if one person, such as the chair of the committee, is given power to end the cycling by limiting the number of rounds. For discussion along these lines, *see* Kenenth Shepsle, *Congress Is a "They," Not an "It": Legislative Intent as Oxymoron*, 12 INT'L REV. L. & ECON. 239 (1992); Richard Pildes &

Elizabeth Anderson, *Slinging Arrow at Democracy: Public Choice Theory, Value Pluralism, and Democratic Politics*, 90 COLUM. L. REV. 2121 (1990). How is the result different if Betty discovers information about the preferences of her cohorts and changes her vote strategically to avoid her least favorite option?

Positive Political Theory and the Role of Institutions. Positive political theory provides a different window on the legislative process. Also growing out of economics, it turns the focus toward game theory. Individual legislators seek to ensure that legislation reflects their preferences, knowing that they are not the only players in the game. *See* William N. Eskridge, Jr. & John Ferejohn, *The Article I, Section 7 Game*, 80 Geo. L.J. 523 (1992); on positive political theory more generally, *see* Daniel Rodriguez & Barry Weingast, *The Positive Political Theory of Legislative History: New Perspective on the 1964 Civil Rights Act and its Interpretation*, 151 U. PA. L. REV. 1417 (2003); Mathew McCubbins, Roger Noll & Barry Weingast, *Legislative Intent: The Use of Positive Political Theory in Statutory Interpretation*, 57 LAW & CONTEMP. PROBS. 3 (1994). As a result, individual legislators develop statutes not only taking account of their own preferences but the reaction of others who participate in the process — for example, the median legislator and the President. The term "median legislator" refers to the legislator in the middle necessary to secure majority support for legislation. The political players must even anticipate the likely reaction of the Supreme Court, which may review the statute if subjected to judicial challenge. The situation is more complicated still if Congress selects an agency to implement the statute; then the players must anticipate the likely preferences of the agency. See Jonathan R. Macey, *Separated Powers and Positive Political Theory: The Tug of War Over Administrative Agencies*, 80 GEO. L.J. 671 (1992).

What do you think of the legislative process now? These theories of the legislative process begin to give you an idea of how the sausage is made, or, the metaphor that we prefer, what goes on underneath the hood. Such information is important not only in its own right but when considering how statutes are interpreted and applied. Keep it in mind as we go along.

2. A Specific Example: The Story of Auto Safety Legislation

With this description of the legislative process as background, it should be clear that every statute has a history, from introduction and floor debate to ultimate signature by the President. Not every statute follows the same "orthodox" path: some are fast-tracked, escape committee assignment, go forward without debate, and so on. But each statute has a story.

In a moment, we will introduce the National Traffic and Motor Vehicle Safety Act of 1966 to continue our study of legislation. This statute was the first piece of comprehensive federal auto safety legislation. What was its story? Who were the important players in Congress? Which committees were responsible for its passage? What were the key factors in avoiding a vetogate? We draw the following account from several leading sources, including RALPH NADER, UNSAFE AT ANY SPEED (1965), AND JERRY L. MASHAW & DAVID L. HARFST, THE STRUGGLE FOR AUTO SAFETY (1990).

Early efforts begin. With the enormous growth of the American auto industry in the 1950s and 1960s, the number of casualties from motor vehicle accidents kept rising. By the mid-1960s, Detroit expected to sell 8 million cars in an average year and 10 million in a good year. Although the rates of death and injury per passenger mile remained relatively flat, the dramatic increase in miles driven led to an increased toll on the roads. The number of deaths by the mid-1960s exceeded 50,000 per year. Government officials began to look with a more critical eye at the existing system of hands-off motor vehicle safety regulation.

The first efforts occurred at the state level. As Governor of Connecticut between 1955 and 1961, Abraham Ribicoff earned himself the nickname "Mr. Safety" for his dedication to and public focus on traffic safety issues. The New York State Legislature, under the leadership of State Senator Edward Speno, compelled auto manufacturers to install anchorage units for front seat belts in all cars sold in New York. State authorities did not reserve all their regulatory muscle for the auto manufacturers. Sen. Speno's committee, for example, took aim at the tire industry for its lack of safety performance standards. But this and other state initiatives were spotty and uncoordinated. Moreover, the auto industry often blocked state regulatory efforts by citing the difficulty of complying with a patchwork of different rules and implying that one state's stringent regulations might threaten the availability of cars in that state. By the mid-1960s, several states enacted laws mandating installation of manual seat belts in all cars sold within their borders; the auto industry had succeeded in delaying and limiting these efforts for years. All evidence indicated that the industry could continue to stall and convince legislatures in nearly every state to defer implementing any meaningful regulatory scheme.

Congress gets involved. Congress held its first auto safety hearings in 1956. A proposal to set and enforce brake fluid performance standards went nowhere, leading Congressman Kenneth Roberts of Alabama, who chaired the hearings, to exclaim, "I am getting tired of introducing bills and holding hearings on safety matters. This is certainly not a far-reaching bill. But it is a bill that can save a lot of lives." The other stakeholders seemed content to leave the old order in place.

Neither Congress generally nor the Eisenhower administration shared Rep. Roberts' interest in making motor vehicle designs safer. But Rep. Roberts did compile an impressive investigative record that lay the groundwork for future legislation. More importantly, he managed to get the executive branch into the business of setting auto safety standards, albeit through the back door. Using a new authority that Rep. Roberts pushed through the House, the federal General Services Administration (GSA), the executive branch's procurement department, began to set minimum safety parameters for the cars it purchased for the government's fleet. Because the federal fleet represented a substantial part of Detroit's sales in any given year, the GSA's standards induced manufacturers to comply so that they could keep their government contracts. However, the fundamental regulatory scheme did not change; the federal government merely exercised its power in the marketplace. Despite some effort to mandate federal regulation, the common law remained the primary source of legal rules regarding motor vehicle safety.

Senator Ribicoff takes the lead. In mid-1965, Abraham Ribicoff, now Senator from Connecticut and chair of the Senate Government Operations Committee's Subcommittee on Executive Reorganization, convened a new, comprehensive set of auto safety hearings. The Subcommittee heard impassioned testimony from Daniel Patrick Moynihan, then a Labor Department official, championing the citizen's right to safer cars, and citing the dramatic promise of the new science of accident prevention and mitigation. Waxing futuristic, he even envisioned a day when people would drive a vehicle that would automatically obey traffic laws and prevent accidents. But a parade of other administration officials testified approvingly of auto manufacturers' safety efforts and of the existing balance between federal and state regulation. Sen. Ribicoff adjourned his committee in the summer without producing any new legislative proposals.

Ralph Nader takes the spotlight. Late that fall, a new actor burst on the scene and changed the terms of the debate. Ralph Nader, a lawyer and among the first of what we now call consumer advocates, published *Unsafe at Any Speed*. Here is an excerpt from that book:

> The American automobile is produced exclusively to the standards which the manufacturer decides to establish. It comes into the marketplace unchecked. When a car becomes involved in an accident, the entire investigatory, enforcement and claims apparatus that makes up the post-accident response looks almost invariably to driver failure as the cause. The need to clear the highways rapidly after collisions contributes to further burying the vehicle's role. Should vehicle failure be obvious in some accidents, responsibility is seen in terms of inadequate maintenance by the motorist. Accommodated by superficial standards of accident investigation, the car manufacturers exude presumptions of engineering excellence and reliability, and this reputation is acceptable by unknowing motorists. . . .
>
> Today almost every [traffic safety] program is aimed at the driver — at educating him, exhorting him, watching him, judging him, punishing him, compiling records about his driving violations, and organizing him in citizen support activities. Resources and energy are directed into programs of enforcement, traffic laws, driver education, driver licensing, traffic courts, and vehicle inspection. The reasoning behind this philosophy of safety can be summarized in this way: Most accidents are in the class of driver fault; driver fault is in the class of violated traffic laws; therefore, observance of traffic laws by drivers would eliminate most accidents.
>
> The prevailing view of traffic safety is much more a political strategy to defend special interests than it is an empirical program to save lives and prevent injuries. For "traffic safety" is not just an abstract value to which lip service is paid. In the automobile industry, safety could represent an investment in research, a priority in production design and manufacturing, and a theme of marketing policy. But under existing business values potential safety advances are subordinated to other investments, priorities, preferences, and themes designed to maximize profit. Industry insists on maintaining the freedom to rank safety anywhere it pleases on its list of commercial considerations. In the protection of these considerations the industry supports and fosters the traffic safety policy focused on driver behavior; through lobbying and other close relations with state and municipal administrators the efforts of the automobile manufacturers have resulted not only in the perpetuation of that

policy but also in some side effects which help the industry preserve its exclusive control over vehicle design.

RALPH NADER, UNSAFE AT ANY SPEED 42-43, 235-36 (1965). Meanwhile, most of the book exposed in detail the deadly designs that auto manufacturers knowingly set on the roads. By pitting the underdog consumer against the biggest symbol of American corporate power, Nader could not have set up a morality play with greater clarity.

Rearmed by Nader, Sen. Ribicoff reopened his hearings when Congress reconvened for the 1966 session. This time, the Subcommittee had much greater visibility and a new tide of public opinion. Even a noted proponent of state, as opposed to federal, regulation testified in front of the committee that the problem required strong action.

Other political actors take an interest. With the new visibility also came new political actors looking for a share of the national spotlight and a hand in setting policy. President Johnson embraced the issue of auto safety as part of his wider call for centralized transportation policy under the umbrella of a new Department of Transportation. He said that a great transportation system was the mark of a great nation and that the United States was the only major nation in the world lacking such a system. On March 2, 1966, he delivered a Message on Transportation to Congress, proposing a far-reaching bill. *See* The American Presidency Project, *Lyndon B. Johnson: Special Message to the Congress on Transportation, http:// www.presidency.ucsb.edu/ws/index.php?pid=28114.*

After that, different groups competed to be the first to take significant action on auto safety. The Senate Commerce Committee, chaired by Warren Magnuson of Washington, proceeded to hold hearings on the administration's bill. Sen. Magnuson was eager to take public responsibility for the issue and claim credit with his constituents. Meanwhile, many, including members of Congress and Nader, complained in hearings that the administration's bill was too weak. The race was on in Congress to propose a stronger alternative.

But Sen. Ribicoff was the one who arguably tipped the balance in favor of regulation. Sen. Ribicoff called Nader to testify before his committee about General Motors. The substance of the hearings did not concern the design choices of the automaker, but its actions to discredit Nader himself in response to the momentum that his book had produced. The hearing revealed that GM had hired private detectives to dig up dirt about Nader's past and hired prostitutes to create new dirt about Nader's character. The man who had conducted the investigation on GM's behalf described his mission as: "They [GM] want to get something, somewhere, on this guy to get him out of their hair and to shut him up."

A statute is enacted. This revelation confirmed Nader's portrayal of auto manufacturers as callous peddlers of a dangerous product, and from that point, new auto safety legislation was all but inevitable. *Time* magazine, in those days a barometer of the nation's political center of gravity, soon ran a piece titled *Why Cars Must — And Can — Be Made Safer.* Congress faced continuous pressure to add new provisions to the bill that was pending before the Commerce Committee: new authority to federally supervise and publicize recalls, tougher compliance provisions, and independent research capacity quickly found their way into the legislation. The Senate soon passed its version of the auto safety bill virtually without opposition. Its ultimate report on the legislation concluded that "[t]he promotion of motor vehicle safety through voluntary standards has largely failed. The unconditional imposition of mandatory standards at the earliest practicable date is the only course commensurate with the highway death and injury toll."

The House, which many had expected to offer resistance, or at least some substantive changes, fell into line. Before the House Commerce Committee, even the auto manufacturers dropped their resistance to the legislation. After a perfunctory conference process that quickly reconciled the minor differences between the two bills, both houses passed the legislation by overwhelming margins. In early September, President Johnson signed it into law and officially created the federal auto safety regulatory scheme. When signing the legislation, he stated:

> For years, we have spent millions of dollars to understand polio and fight other childhood diseases. Yet until now we have tolerated a raging epidemic of highway death which has killed more of our youth than all other diseases combined. Through the Highway Safety Act, we are going to find out more about highway disease — and we aim to cure it.
>
> In this age of space, we are getting plenty of information about how to send men into space and how to bring them home. Yet we don't know for certain whether more auto accidents are caused by faulty brakes, or by soft shoulders, or by drunk drivers, or by deer crossing the highway.... [Auto safety] is no luxury item, no optional extra: it must be a normal cost of doing business.

NOTES AND QUESTIONS

1. According to the story above, how did auto safety first get the attention of Congress? What role, if any, did the following play: (a) individual members of Congress; (b) political entrepreneurs outside of Congress; (c) the President; (d) interest groups; and (e) public attitudes, perhaps in response to a crisis or series of events?

2. Once auto safety became a priority for Congress, was the path through the legislative process a fairly typical or "orthodox" one? Can you map parts of the story onto the general description of the legislative process provided above? As you compare the two, is there anything unusual or missing?

3. From the story above, we might gather a sense for the political motivations of certain actors, like Senator Ribicoff. What was in it for him? Does public choice theory help? As we mentioned above, public choice theory suggests that members of Congress enact statutes when doing so is in their own self-interest, which is mainly taken to be an interest in reelection. But, consistent with public choice theory, legislators can also have an interest in their own status or legacy. *See* RICHARD FENNO, CONGRESSMEN IN COMMITTEES (1973). If this is too cynical a view, what else might have motivated Senator Ribicoff?

4. Considering the role of interest groups from a social choice perspective, the 1966 Motor Vehicle Safety Act was not a strong candidate for enactment. On the one hand, a small and economically powerful group of manufacturers were to be burdened by the Act. At the time, the Big Three automakers — General Motors, Ford, and Chrysler — were the first, second, and fifth largest companies in the nation. MASHAW & HARFST, *supra*, at 49-50. Congress often seeks to please such groups because they can promise the most campaign funding and support. On the other hand, the potential beneficiaries of the Act were as numerous as automobile purchasers themselves. Diffuse groups such as these often face difficultly organizing to make their voice heard, and so Congress might fail to listen. What do you suppose happened in 1966 to belie this prediction? Professors Jerry Mashaw and David Harfst, who wrote the leading account of the politics surrounding the legislation, report that, by 1966, the auto industry lobby was "nearing collapse." MASHAW & HARFST, *supra*, at 57. Because motor vehicle production had never been federally regulated, the lobby had never developed strong connections to the corporate officials in Detroit and failed to keep them apprised as political momentum built. Moreover, the corporate officials themselves were "not in touch with large areas if social and political reality." *Id.* The corporate culture kept senior managers focused on their own business activities and professional circles rather than the world around them. Badly stung by this experience, where do you suppose the auto industry lobby focused its attention after Congress enacted the Act?

5. Can any theory of legislative behavior fully account for auto safety legislation? Mashaw and Harfst think not: "If the Nader-General Motors morality play was the spark that ignited the tinder, and congressman and reporters had personal and institutional interests in fanning the flame," the tinder itself was the ideological context of the moment. MASHAW & HARFST, *supra*, at 59. Consider that this legislation came about at the same time as the Civil Rights Act, the Clean Air Act, and many other right-based statutes. It also came about during a time of intense love for science and space, as President Johnson's statement makes clear. As Mashaw and Harfst describe the explanation for the legislation, it was "somewhere at the intersection of the civil rights movement and the space program — a wedding in the mid-1960's of egalitarian ethical judgment, scientific enthusiasm, and activist national politics." *Id.* Note how, in the Mashaw-Harfst description, the justifications for government regulation coincide with political explanations and even work with them.

6. A short postscript: After testifying about GM's behavior to Congress, Nader sued the automaker on a variety of legal claims. The case reached the New York Court of Appeals, which decided in his favor. *See* Nader v. General Motors Corp., 255 N.E. 2d 765 (N.Y. 1970). The court's decision articulated a new legal rule by creating the tort of "overzealous surveillance." (The common law lives!) Nader ultimately received $284,000 from GM, which he used to fund further regulatory efforts.

B. The National Traffic and Motor Vehicle Safety Act of 1966

We now present the actual statute that will facilitate our study of legislation. Below is the National Traffic and Motor Vehicle Safety Act of 1966 (which we will often refer to as the "1966 Motor Vehicle Safety Act"). It is reprinted in full, without any editing whatsoever.

The National Traffic and Motor Vehicle Safety Act of 1966

Pub. L. No. 89-563, 80 Stat. 718 (Sept. 9, 1966)

An Act

To provide for a coordinated national safety program and establishment of safety standards for motor vehicles in interstate commerce to reduce accidents involving motor vehicles and to reduce the deaths and injuries occurring in such accidents.

Be it enacted by the Senate and House of Representatives of the United States of America in Congress assembled, That Congress hereby declares that the purpose of this Act is to reduce traffic accidents and deaths and injuries to persons resulting from traffic accidents. Therefore, Congress determines that it is necessary to establish motor vehicle safety standards for motor vehicles and equipment in interstate commerce; to undertake and support necessary safety research and development; and to expand the national driver register.

Title I — Motor Vehicle Safety Standards

SEC. 101. This Act may be cited as the "National Traffic and Motor Vehicle Safety Act of 1966."

SEC. 102. As used in this title —

(1) "Motor vehicle safety" means the performance of motor vehicles or motor vehicle equipment in such a manner that the public is protected against unreasonable risk of accidents occurring as a result of the design, construction or performance of motor vehicles and is also protected against unreasonable risk of death or injury to persons in the event accidents do occur, and includes nonoperational safety of such vehicles.

(2) "Motor vehicle safety standards" means a minimum standard for motor vehicle performance, or motor vehicle equipment performance, which is practicable, which meets the need for motor vehicle safety and which provides objective criteria.

(3) "Motor vehicle" means any vehicle driven or drawn by mechanical power manufactured primarily for use on the public street, roads, and highways, except any vehicle operated exclusively on a rail or rails.

(4) "Motor vehicle equipment" means any system, part, or component of a motor vehicle as originally manufactured or any similar part or component

manufactured or sold for replacement or improvement of such system, part, or component or as an accessory, or addition to the motor vehicle.

(5) "Manufacturer" means any person engaged in the manufacturing or assembling of motor vehicles or motor vehicle equipment, including any person importing motor vehicles or motor vehicle equipment for resale.

(6) "Distributor" means any person primarily engaged in the sale and distribution of motor vehicles or motor vehicle equipment for resale.

(7) "Dealer" means any person who is engaged in the sale and distribution of new motor vehicles or motor vehicle equipment primarily to purchasers who in good faith purchase any such vehicle or equipment for purposes other than resale.

(8) "State" includes each of the several States, the District of Columbia, the Commonwealth of Puerto Rico, Guam, the Virgin Islands, the Canal Zone, and American Samoa.

(9) "Interstate commerce" means commerce between any place in a State and any place in another State, or between places in the same State through another State.

(10) "Secretary" means Secretary of Commerce.

(11) "Defect" includes any defect in performance, construction, components, or materials in motor vehicles or motor vehicle equipment.

(12) "United States district courts" means the Federal district courts of the United States and the United States courts of the Commonwealth of Puerto Rico, Guam, the Virgin Islands, the Canal Zone, and American Samoa.

(13) "Vehicle Equipment Safety Commission" means the Commission established pursuant to the joint resolution of the Congress relating to highway traffic safety, approved August 20, 1958 (72 Stat. 635), or as it may be hereafter reconstituted by law.

SEC. 103. (a) The Secretary shall establish by order appropriate Federal motor vehicle safety standards. Each such Federal motor vehicle safety standard shall be practicable, shall meet the need for motor vehicle safety, and shall be stated in objective terms.

(b) The Administrative Procedure Act shall apply to all orders establishing, amending, or revoking a Federal motor vehicle safety standard under this title.

(c) Each order establishing a Federal motor vehicle safety standard shall specify the date such standard is to take effect which shall not be sooner than one hundred and eighty days or later than one year from the date such order is issued, unless the Secretary finds, for good cause shown, that an earlier or later effective date is in the public interest, and publishes his reasons for such finding.

(d) Whenever a Federal motor vehicle safety standard established under this title is in effect, no State or political subdivision of a State shall have any authority either to establish, or to continue in effect, with respect to any motor vehicle or item of motor vehicle equipment any safety standard applicable to the same aspect of performance of such vehicle or item of equipment which is not identical to the Federal standard. Nothing in this section shall be construed to prevent the Federal Government or the government of any State or political subdivision thereof from establishing a safety requirement applicable to motor vehicles or motor vehicle equipment procured for its own use if such requirement imposes a higher standard of performance than that required to comply with the otherwise applicable Federal standard.

(e) The Secretary may by order amend or revoke any Federal motor vehicle safety standard established under this section. Such order shall specify the date on which such amendment or revocation is to take effect which shall not be sooner than one hundred and eighty days or later than one year from the date the order is issued, unless the Secretary finds, for good cause shown, that an earlier or later effective date is in the public interest, and publishes his reasons for such finding.

(f) In prescribing standards under this section, the Secretary shall —

(1) consider relevant available motor vehicle safety data, including the results of research, development, testing and evaluation activities conducted pursuant to this Act;

(2) consult with the Vehicle Equipment Safety Commission, and such other State or interstate agencies (including legislative committees) as he deems appropriate;

(3) consider whether any such proposed standard is reasonable, practicable and appropriate for the particular type of motor vehicle or item of motor vehicle equipment for which it is prescribed; and

(4) consider the extent to which such standards will contribute to carrying out the purposes of this Act.

(g) In prescribing safety regulations covering motor vehicles subject to part II of the Interstate Commerce Act, as amended (49 U.S.C. 301 et seq.), or the Transportation of Explosives Act, as amended (18 U.S.C. 831-835), the Interstate Commerce Commission shall not adopt or continue in effect any safety regulation which differs from a motor vehicle safety standard issued by the Secretary under this title, except that nothing in this subsection shall be deemed to prohibit the Interstate Commerce Commission from prescribing for any motor vehicle operated by a carrier subject to regulation under either or both of such Acts, a safety regulation which imposes a higher standard of performance subsequent to its manufacture than that required to comply with the applicable Federal standard at the time of manufacture.

(h) The Secretary shall issue initial Federal motor vehicle safety standards based upon existing safety standards on or before January 31, 1967. On or before January 31, 1968, the Secretary shall issue new and revised Federal motor vehicle safety standards under this title.

SEC. 104. (a) The Secretary shall establish a National Motor Vehicle Safety Advisory Council, a majority of which shall be representatives of the general public, including representatives of State and local governments, and the remainder shall include representatives of motor vehicle manufacturers, motor vehicle equipment manufacturers, and motor vehicle dealers.

(b) The Secretary shall consult with the Advisory Council on motor vehicle safety standards under this Act.

(c) Members of the National Motor Vehicle Safety Advisory Council may be compensated at a rate not to exceed $100 per diem (including travel time) when engaged in the actual duties of the Advisory Council. Such members, while away from their homes or regular places of business, may be allowed travel expenses, including per diem in lieu of subsistence as authorized by section 5 of the Administrative Expenses Act of 1946 (5 U.S.C 73b-2), for persons in the Government service employed intermittently. Payments under this section shall not render members of the Advisory Council employees or officials of the United States for any purpose.

Sec. 105. (a) (1) In a case of actual controversy as to the validity of any order under section 103, any person who will be adversely affected by such order when it is effective may at any time prior to the sixtieth day after such order is issued file a petition with the United States court of appeals for the circuit wherein such person resides or has his principal place of business, for a judicial review of such order. A copy of the petition shall be forthwith transmitted by the clerk of the court to the Secretary or other officer designated by him for that purpose. The Secretary thereupon shall file in the court the record of the proceedings on which the Secretary based his order, as provided in section 2112 of title 28 of the United States Code.

(2) If the petitioner applies to the court for leave to adduce additional evidence, and shows to the satisfaction of the court that such additional evidence is material and that there were reasonable grounds for the failure to adduce such evidence in the proceeding before the Secretary, the court may order such additional evidence (and evidence in rebuttal thereof) to be taken before the Secretary, and to be adduced upon the hearing, in such manner and upon such terms and conditions as to the court may seem proper. The Secretary may modify his findings as to the facts, or make new findings, by reason of the additional evidence so taken, and he shall file such modified or new findings, and his recommendation, if any, for the modification or setting aside of his original order, with the return of such additional evidence.

(3) Upon the filing of the petition referred to in paragraph (1) of this subsection, the court shall have jurisdiction to review the order in accordance with section 10 of the Administrative Procedure Act (5 U.S.C. 1009) and to grant appropriate relief as provided in such section.

(4) The judgment of the court affirming or setting aside, in whole or in part, any such order of the Secretary shall be final, subject to review by the Supreme Court of the United States upon certiorari or certification as provided in section 1254 of title 28 of the United States Code.

(5) Any action instituted under this subsection shall survive, notwithstanding any change in the person occupying the office of Secretary of any vacancy in such office.

(6) The remedies provided for in this subsection shall be in addition to and not in substitution for any other remedies provided by law.

(b) A certified copy of the transcript of the record and proceedings under this section shall be furnished by the Secretary to any interested party at his request, and payment of the costs thereof, and shall be admissible in any criminal, exclusion of imports, or other proceeding arising under or in respect of this title, irrespective of whether proceedings with respect to the order have previously been initiated or become final under subsection (a).

SEC. 106. (a) The Secretary shall conduct research, testing, development, and training necessary to carry out the purposes of this title, including, but not limited to —

(1) collecting data from any source for the purpose of determining the relationship between motor vehicle or motor vehicle equipment performance characteristics and (A) accidents involving motor vehicles, and (B) the occurrence of death, or personal injury resulting from such accidents;

(2) procuring (by negotiation or otherwise) experimental and other motor vehicles or motor vehicle equipment for research and testing purposes;

(3) selling or otherwise disposing of test motor vehicles and motor vehicle equipment and reimbursing the proceeds of such sale or disposal into the current appropriation available for the purpose of carrying out this title.

(b) The Secretary is authorized to conduct research, testing, development, and training as authorized to be carried out by subsection (a) of this section by making grants for the conduct of such research, testing, development, and training to States, interstate agencies, and nonprofit institutions.

(c) Whenever the Federal contribution for any research or development activity authorized by this Act encouraging motor vehicle safety is more than minimal, the Secretary shall include in any contract, grant, or other arrangement for such research or development activity, provisions effective to insure that all information, uses, processes, patents, and other developments resulting from that activity will be made freely and fully available to the general public. Nothing herein shall be construed to deprive the owner of any background patent or any right which he may have thereunder.

SEC. 107. The Secretary is authorized to advise, assist, and cooperate with, other Federal departments and agencies, and State and other interested public and private agencies, in the planning and development of —

(1) motor vehicle safety standards;

(2) methods for inspecting and testing to determine compliance with motor vehicle safety standards.

SEC. 108. (a) No person shall —

(1) manufacture for sale, sell, offer for sale, or introduce or deliver for introduction in interstate commerce, or import into the United States, any motor vehicle or item of motor vehicle equipment manufactured on or after the date any applicable Federal motor vehicle safety standard takes effect under this title unless it is in conformity with such standard except as provided in subsection (b) of this section;

(2) fail or refuse access to or copying of records, or fail to make reports or provide information, or fail or refuse to permit entry or inspection, as required under section 112;

(3) fail to issue a certificate required by section 114, or issue a certificate to the effect that a motor vehicle or item of motor vehicle equipment conforms to all applicable Federal motor vehicle safety standards, if such person in the exercise of due care has reason to know that such certificate is false or misleading in a material respect;

(4) fail to furnish notification of any defect as required by section 113.

(b) (1) Paragraph (1) of subsection (a) shall not apply to the sale, the offer for sale, or the introduction or delivery for introduction in interstate commerce of any motor vehicle or motor vehicle equipment after the first purchase of it in good faith for purposes other than resale. In order to assure a continuing and effective national traffic safety program, it is the policy of Congress to encourage and strengthen the enforcement of State inspection of used motor vehicles. Therefore to that end the Secretary shall conduct a thorough study and investigation to determine the adequacy of motor vehicle safety standards and motor vehicle inspection requirements and procedures applicable to used motor vehicles in each State, and the effect of programs authorized by this title upon such standards, requirements, and procedures for used motor vehicles, and as soon as practicable but not later than one year after the date of enactment of this title, the results of such study, and recommendations for such additional legislation as he deems necessary to carry out the purposes of this Act. As soon as practicable after the submission of such report, but no later than one year from the date of submission of such report, the Secretary, after consultation with the Council and such interested public and private agencies and groups as he deems advisable, shall establish uniform Federal motor vehicle safety standards applicable to all used motor vehicles. Such standards shall be expressed in terms of motor vehicle safety performance. The Secretary is authorized to amend or revoke such standards pursuant to this Act.

(2) Paragraph (1) of subsection (a) shall not apply to any person who establishes that he did not have reason to know in the exercise of due care that such vehicle or item of motor vehicle equipment is not in conformity with applicable Federal motor vehicle safety standards, or to any person who, prior to such first purchase, holds a certificate issued by the manufacturer or importer of such motor vehicle or motor vehicle equipment, to the effect that such vehicle or equipment conforms to all applicable Federal motor vehicle safety standards, unless such person knows that such vehicle or equipment does not so conform.

(3) A motor vehicle or item of motor vehicle equipment offered for importation in violation of paragraph (1) of subsection (a) shall be refused admission into the United States under joint regulations issued by the Secretary of the Treasury and the Secretary; except that the Secretary of the Treasury and the Secretary may, by such regulations, provide for authorizing the importation of such motor vehicle or item of motor vehicle equipment into the United States upon such terms and conditions (including the furnishing of a bond) as may appear to them appropriate to insure that any such motor vehicle or item of motor vehicle equipment will be brought into conformity with any applicable Federal motor vehicle safety standard prescribed under this title, or will be exported or abandoned to the United States.

(4) The Secretary of the Treasury and the Secretary may, by joint regulations, permit the temporary importation of any motor vehicle or item of motor vehicle equipment after the first purchase of it in good faith for purposes other than resale.

(5) Paragraph (1) of subsection (a) shall not apply in the case of a motor vehicle or item of motor vehicle equipment intended solely for export, and so

labeled or tagged on the vehicle or item itself and on the outside of the container, if any, which is exported.

(c) Compliance with any Federal motor vehicle safety standard issued under this title does not exempt any person from any liability under common law.

SEC. 109. (a) Whoever violates any provision of section 108, or any regulation issued thereunder, shall be subject to a civil penalty of not to exceed $1,000 for each such violation. Such violation of a provision of section 108, or regulations issued thereunder, shall constitute a separate violation with respect to each motor vehicle or item of motor vehicle equipment or with respect to each failure or refusal to allow or perform an act required thereby, except that the maximum civil penalty shall not exceed $400,000 for any related series of violations.

(b) Any such civil penalty may be compromised by the Secretary. In determining the amount of such penalty, or the amount agreed upon in compromise, the appropriateness of such penalty to the size of the business of the person charged and the gravity of the violation shall be considered. The amount of such penalty, when finally determined, or the amount agreed upon in compromise, may be deducted from any sums owing by the United States to the person charged.

SEC. 110. (a) The United States district courts shall have jurisdiction, for cause shown and subject to the provisions of rule 65(a) and (b) of the Federal Rules of Civil Procedure, to restrain violations of this title, or to restrain the sale, offer for sale, or the introduction or delivery for introduction, in interstate commerce, or the importation into the United States, of any motor vehicle or item of motor vehicle equipment which is determined, prior to the first purchase of such vehicle in good faith for purposes other than resale, not to conform to applicable Federal motor vehicle safety standards prescribed pursuant to this title, upon petition by the appropriate United States attorney or the Attorney General on behalf of the United States. Whenever practicable, the Secretary shall give notice to any person against whom an action for injunctive relief is contemplated and afford him an opportunity to present his views, and, except in the case of a knowing and willful violation, shall afford him reasonable opportunity to achieve compliance. The failure to give such notice and afford such opportunity shall not preclude the granting of appropriate relief.

(b) In any proceeding for criminal contempt for violation of an injunction or restraining order issued under this section, which violation also constitutes a violation of this title, trial shall be by the court or, upon demand of the accused, by a jury. Such trial shall be conducted in accordance with the practice and procedure applicable in the case of proceedings subject to the provisions of rule 42(b) of the Federal Rules of Criminal Procedure.

(c) Actions under subsection (a) of this section and section 109(a) of this title may be brought in the district wherein any act or transaction constituting the violation occurred, or in the district wherein the defendant is found or is an inhabitant or transacts business, and process in such cases may be served in any other district of which the defendant is an inhabitant or wherever the defendant may be found.

(d) In any actions brought under subsection (a) of this section and section 109(a) of this title, subpoenas for witnesses who are required to attend a United States district court may run into any other district.

(e) It shall be the duty of every manufacturer offering a motor vehicle or item of motor vehicle equipment for importation into the United States to designate in writing an agent upon whom service of all administrative and judicial processes, notices, orders, decisions and requirements may be made for and on behalf of said manufacturer, and to file such designation with the Secretary, which designation may from time to time be changed by like writing, similarly filed. Service of all administrative and judicial processes, notices, orders, decisions and requirements may be made upon said manufacturer by service upon such designated agent at his office or usual place of residence with like effect as if made personally upon said manufacturer, and in default of such designation of such agent, service of process, notice, order, requirement or decision in any proceeding before the Secretary or in any judicial proceeding for enforcement of this title or any standards prescribed pursuant to this title may be made by posting such process, notice, order, requirement or decision in the Office of the Secretary.

SEC. 111. (a) If any motor vehicle or item of motor vehicle equipment is determined not to conform to applicable Federal motor vehicle safety standards, or contains a defect which relates to motor vehicle safety, after the sale of such vehicle or item of equipment by a manufacturer or a distributor to a distributor or a dealer and prior to the sale of such vehicle or item of equipment by such distributor or dealer:

(1) The manufacturer or distributor, as the case may be, shall immediately repurchase such vehicle or item of motor vehicle equipment from such distributor or dealer at the price paid by such distributor or dealer, plus all transportation charges involved and a reasonable reimbursement of not less than 1 per centum per month of such price paid prorated from the date of notice of such nonconformance to the date of repurchase by the manufacturer or distributor; or

(2) In the case of motor vehicles, the manufacturer or distributor, as the case may be, at his own expense, shall immediately furnish the purchasing distributor or dealer the required conforming part or parts or equipment for installation by the distributor or dealer on or in such vehicle and for the installation involved the manufacturer shall reimburse such distributor or dealer for the reasonable value of such installation plus a reasonable reimbursement of not less than 1 per centum per month of the manufacturer's or distributor's selling price prorated from the date of notice of such nonconformance to the date such vehicle is brought into conformance, with applicable Federal standards: Provided, however, That the distributor or dealer proceeds with reasonable diligence with the installation after the required part, parts or equipment are received.

(b) In the event any manufacturer or distributor shall refuse to comply with the requirements of paragraphs (1) and (2) of subsection (a), then the distributor or dealer, as the case may be, to whom such nonconforming vehicle or equipment has been sold may bring suit against such manufacturer or distributor in any district court of the United States in the district in which said manufacturer or distributor resides, or is found, or has an agent, without respect to the amount in controversy, and shall recover the damage by him sustained, as well as all court costs plus reasonable attorneys' fees. Any action brought pursuant to this section shall be forever barred unless commenced within three years after the cause of action shall have accrued.

(c) The value of such installations and such reasonable reimbursements as specified in subsection (a) of this section shall be fixed by mutual agreement of the parties, or failing such agreement, by the court pursuant to the provisions of subsection (b) of this section.

SEC. 112. (a) The Secretary is authorized to conduct such inspection and investigation as may be necessary to enforce Federal vehicle safety standards established under this title. He shall furnish the Attorney General and, when appropriate, the Secretary of the Treasury any information obtained indicating noncompliance with such standards, for appropriate action.

(b) For purposes of enforcement of this title, officers or employees duly designated by the Secretary, upon presenting appropriate credentials and a written notice to the owner, operator, or agent in charge, are authorized (1) to enter, at reasonable times, any factory, warehouse, or establishment in which motor vehicles or items of motor vehicle equipment are manufactured, or held for introduction into interstate commerce or are held for sale after such introduction; and (2) to inspect, at reasonable times and within reasonable limits and in a reasonable manner, such factory, warehouse, or establishment. Each such inspection shall be commenced and completed with reasonable promptness.

(c) Every manufacturer of motor vehicles and motor vehicle equipment shall establish and maintain such records, make such reports, and provide such information as the Secretary may reasonably require to enable him to determine whether such manufacturer has acted or is acting in compliance with this title and motor vehicle safety standards prescribed pursuant to this title and shall, upon request of an officer or employee duly designated by the Secretary, permit such officer or employee to inspect appropriate books, papers, records, and documents relevant to determining whether such manufacturer has acted or is acting in compliance with this title and motor vehicle safety standards prescribed pursuant to this title.

(d) Every manufacturer of motor vehicles and motor vehicle equipment shall provide to the Secretary such performance data and other technical data related to performance and safety as may be required to carry out the purposes of this Act. The Secretary is authorized to require the manufacturer to give such notification of such performance and technical data at the time of original purchase to the first person who purchases a motor vehicle or item of equipment for purposes other than resale, as he determines necessary to carry out the purposes of this Act.

(e) All information reported to or otherwise obtained by the Secretary or his representative pursuant to subsection (b) or (c) which information contains or relates to a trade secret or other matter referred to in section 1905 of title 18 of the United States Code, shall be considered confidential for the purpose of that section, except that such information may be disclosed to other officers or employees concerned with carrying out this title or when relevant in any proceeding under this title. Nothing in this section shall authorize the withholding of information by the Secretary or any officer or employee under his control, from the duly authorized committees of the Congress.

SEC. 113. (a) Every manufacturer of motor vehicles shall furnish notification of any defect in any motor vehicle or motor vehicle equipment produced by such manufacturer which he determines, in good faith, relates to motor vehicle safety, to the purchaser (where known to the manufacturer) of such motor vehicle or motor vehicle equipment, within a reasonable time after such manufacturer has discovered such defect.

(b) The notification required by subsection (a) shall be accomplished —

(1) by certified mail to the first purchaser (not including any dealer of such manufacturer) of the motor vehicle or motor vehicle equipment containing such a defect, and to any subsequent purchaser to whom has been transferred any warranty on such motor vehicle or motor vehicle equipment; and

(2) by certified mail or other more expeditious means to the dealer or dealers of such manufacturer to whom such motor vehicle or equipment was delivered.

(c) The notification required by subsection (a) shall contain a clear description or such defect, an evaluation of the risk to traffic safety reasonably related to such defect, and a statement or the measures to be taken to repair such defect.

(d) Every manufacturer of motor vehicles shall furnish to the Secretary a true or representative copy of all notices, bulletins, and other communications to the dealers of such manufacturer or purchasers of motor vehicles or motor vehicle equipment of such manufacturer regarding any defect in such vehicle or equipment sold or serviced by such dealer. The Secretary shall disclose so much of the information contained in such notice or other information obtained under section 112(a) to the public as he deems will assist in carrying out the purposes of this Act, but he shall not disclose any information which contains or relates to a trade secret or other matter referred to in section 1905 of title 18 of the United States Code unless he determines that it is necessary to carry out the purposes of this Act.

(e) If through testing, inspection, investigation, or research carried out pursuant to this title, or examination of reports pursuant to subsection (d) of this section, or otherwise, the Secretary determines that any motor vehicle or item of motor vehicle equipment —

(1) does not comply with an applicable Federal motor vehicle safety standard prescribed pursuant to section 103; or

(2) contains a defect which relates to motor vehicle safety;

then he shall immediately notify the manufacturer of such motor vehicle or item of motor vehicle equipment of such defect or failure to comply. The notice shall contain the findings of the Secretary and shall include all information upon which the findings are based. The Secretary shall afford such manufacturer an opportunity to present his views and evidence in support thereof, to establish that there is no failure of compliance or that the alleged defect does not affect motor vehicle safety. If after such presentation by the manufacturer the Secretary determines that such vehicle or item of equipment does not comply with applicable Federal motor vehicle safety standards, or contains a defect which relates to motor vehicle safety, the Secretary shall direct the manufacturer to furnish the notification specified in subsection (c) of this section to the purchaser of such motor vehicle or item of motor vehicle equipment as provided in subsections (a) and (b) of this section.

SEC. 114. Every manufacturer or distributor of a motor vehicle or motor vehicle equipment shall furnish to the distributor or dealer at the time of delivery of such vehicle or equipment by such manufacturer or distributor the certification that each such vehicle or item of motor vehicle equipment conforms to all applicable Federal motor vehicle safety standards. In the case of an item of motor vehicle equipment such certification may be in the form of a label or tag on such item or on the outside of a container in which such item is delivered. In the case of an item of motor vehicle equipment such certification shall be in the form of a label or tag permanently affixed to such motor vehicle.

SEC. 115. The Secretary shall carry out the provisions of this Act through a National Traffic Safety Agency (hereinafter referred to as the "Agency"), which he shall establish in the Department of Commerce. The Agency shall be headed by a Traffic Safety Administrator who shall be appointed by the President, by and with the advice and consent of the Senate, and shall be compensated at the rate prescribed for level V of the Federal Executive Salary Schedule established by the Federal Executive Salary Act of 1964. The Administrator shall be a citizen of the United States, and shall be appointed with due regard for his fitness to discharge efficiently the powers and the duties delegated to him pursuant to this Act. The Administrator shall perform such duties as are delegated to him by the Secretary.

SEC. 116. Nothing contained herein shall be deemed to exempt from the antitrust laws of the United States any conduct that would otherwise be unlawful under such laws, or to prohibit under the antitrust laws of the United States any conduct that would be lawful under such laws.

SEC. 117. (a) The Act entitled "An Act to provide that hydraulic brake fluid sold or shipped in commerce for use in motor vehicles shall meet certain specifications prescribed by the Secretary of Commerce", approved September 5, 1962 (76 Stat. 437; Public Law 87-637), and the Act entitled "An Act to provide that seat belts sold or shipped in interstate commerce for use in motor vehicles shall meet certain safety standards", approved December 13, 1963 (77 Stat. 361; Public Law 88-201), are hereby repealed.

(b) Whoever, prior to the date of enactment of this section, knowingly and willfully violates any provision of law repealed by subsection (a) of this section, shall be punished in accordance with the provisions of such laws as in effect on the date such violation occurred.

(c) All standards issued under authority of the laws repealed by subsection (a) of this section which are in effect at the time this section takes effect, shall continue in effect as if they had been effectively issued under section 103 until amended or revoked by the Secretary, or a court of competent jurisdiction by operation of law.

(d) Any proceeding relating to any provision of law repealed by subsection (a) of this section which is pending at the time this section takes effect shall be continued by the Secretary as if this section had not been enacted, and orders issued in any such proceeding shall continue in effect as if they had been effectively issued under section 103 until amended or revoked by the Secretary in accordance with this title, or by operation of law.

(e) The repeals made by subsection (a) of this section shall not affect any suit, action, or other proceeding lawfully commenced prior to the date this section takes effect, and all such suits, actions, and proceedings, shall be continued, proceedings therein had, appeals therein taken, and judgments therein rendered, in the same manner and with the same effect as if this section had not been enacted. No suit, action, or other proceeding lawfully commenced by or against any agency or officer of the United States in relation to the discharge of official duties under any provision of law repealed by subsection (a) of this section shall abate by reason of such repeal, but the court, upon motion or supplemental petition filed at any time within 12 months after the date of enactment of this section showing the necessity for the survival of such suit, action, or other proceeding to obtain a settlement of the questions involved, may allow the same to be maintained.

SEC. 118. The Secretary, in exercising the authority under this title, shall utilize the services, research and testing facilities of public agencies to the maximum extent practicable in order to avoid duplication.

SEC. 119. The Secretary is authorized to issue, amend, and revoke such rules and regulations as he deems necessary to carry out this title.

SEC. 120. (a) The Secretary shall prepare and submit to the President for transmittal to the Congress on March 1 of each year a comprehensive report on the administration of this Act for the preceding calendar year. Such report shall include but not be restricted to (1) a thorough statistical compilation of the accidents and injuries occurring in such year; (2) a list of Federal motor vehicle safety standards prescribed or in effect in such year; (3) the degree of observance of applicable Federal motor vehicle standards; (4) a summary of all current research grants and contracts together with a description of the problems to be considered by such grants and contracts; (5) an analysis and evaluation, including relevant policy recommendations, of research activities completed and technological progress achieved during such year; and (6) the extent to which technical information was disseminated to the scientific community and consumer-oriented information was made available to the motoring public.

(b) The report required by subsection (a) of this section shall contain such recommendations for additional legislation as the Secretary deems necessary to promote cooperation among the several States in the improvement of traffic safety and to strengthen the national traffic safety program.

SEC. 121. (a) There is authorized to be appropriated for the purpose of carrying out the provisions of this title, other than those related to tire safety, not to exceed $11,000,000 for fiscal year 1967, $17,000,000 for fiscal year 1968, and $23,000,000 for the fiscal year 1969.

(b) There is authorized to be appropriated for the purpose of carrying out the provisions of this title related to tire safety and title II, not to exceed $2,900,000 for fiscal year 1967, and $1,450,000 per fiscal year for the fiscal years 1968 and 1969.

Sec. 122. The provisions of this title for certification of motor vehicles and items of motor vehicle equipment shall take effect on the effective date of the first standard actually issued under section 103 of this title.

Title: II — Tire Safety

Sec. 201. In all standards for pneumatic tires established under title I of this Act, the Secretary shall require that tires subject thereto be permanently and conspicuously labeled with such safety information as he determines to be necessary to carry out the purposes of this Act. Such labeling shall include —

(1) suitable identification of the manufacturer, or in the case of a retreaded tire suitable identification of the retreader, unless the tire contains a brand name other than the name of the manufacturer in which case it shall also contain a code mark which would permit the seller of such tire to identify the manufacturer thereof to the purchaser upon his request.

(2) the composition of the material used in the ply of the tire.

(3) the actual number of plies in the tire.

(4) the maximum permissible load for the tire.

(5) a recital that the tire conforms to Federal minimum safe performance standards, except that in lieu of such recital the Secretary may prescribe an appropriate mark or symbol for use by those manufacturers or retreaders who comply with such standards. The Secretary may require that additional safety related information be disclosed to the purchaser of a tire at the time of sale of the tire.

Sec. 202. In standards established under title I of this Act the Secretary shall require that each motor vehicle be equipped by the manufacturer or by the purchaser thereof at the time of the first purchase thereof in good faith for purposes other than resale with tires which meet the maximum permissible load standards when such vehicle is fully loaded with the maximum number of passengers it is designed to carry and a reasonable amount of luggage.

Sec. 203. In order to assist the consumer to make an informed choice in the purchase of motor vehicle tires, within two years after the enactment of this title, the Secretary shall, through standards established under title I of this Act, prescribe by order, and publish in the Federal Register, a uniform quality grading system for motor vehicle tires. Such order shall specify the date such system is to take effect which shall not be sooner than one hundred and eighty days or later than one year from the date such order is issued, unless the Secretary finds, for good cause shown, that an earlier or later effective date is in the public interest, and publishes his reasons for such finding. The Secretary shall also cooperate with industry and the Federal Trade Commission to the maximum extent practicable in efforts to eliminate deceptive and confusing tire nomenclature and marketing practices.

Sec. 204. (a) No person shall sell, offer for sale, or introduce for sale or deliver for introduction in interstate commerce, any tire or motor vehicle equipped with any tire which has been regrooved, except that the Secretary may by order permit the sale of regrooved tires and motor vehicles equipped with regrooved tires which he finds are designed and constructed in a manner consistent with the purposes of this Act.

(b) Violations of this section shall be subject to civil penalties and injunction in accordance with sections 109 and 110 of this Act.

(c) For the purposes of this section the term "regrooved tire" means a tire on which a new tread has been produced by cutting into the tread of a worn tire.

SEC. 205. In the event of any conflict between the requirements of orders or regulations issued by the Secretary under this title and title I of this Act applicable to motor vehicle tires and orders or administrative interpretations issued by the Federal Trade Commission, the provisions of orders or regulations issued by the Secretary shall prevail.

Title III — Accident and Injury Research and Test Facility

SEC. 301. The Secretary of Commerce is hereby authorized to make a complete investigation and study of the need for a facility or facilities to conduct research, development, and testing in traffic safety (including but not limited to motor vehicle and highway safety) authorized by law, and research, development, and testing relating to the safety of machinery used on highways or in connection with the maintenance of highways (with particular emphasis on tractor safety) as he deems appropriate and necessary.

SEC. 302. The Secretary shall report the results of his investigation and study to Congress not later than December 31, 1967. Such report shall include but not be limited to (1) an inventory of existing capabilities, equipment, and facilities, either publicly or privately owned or operated, which could be made available for use by the Secretary in carrying out the safety research, development, and testing referred to in section 301, (2) recommendations as to the site or sites for any recommended facility or facilities, (3) preliminary plans, specifications, and drawings for such recommended facility or facilities (including major research, development, and testing equipment), and (4) the estimated cost of the recommended sites, facilities, and equipment.

SEC. 303. There is hereby authorized to be appropriated not to exceed $3,000,000 for the investigation, study, and report authorized by this title. Any funds so appropriated shall remain available until expended.

Title IV — National Driver Register

SEC. 401. The Act entitled "An Act to provide for a register in the Department of Commerce in which shall be listed the names of certain persons who have had their motor vehicle operator's licenses revoked," approved July 14, 1960, as amended (74 Stat. 526; 23 U.S.C. 313 note), is hereby amended to read as follows: "That the Secretary of Commerce shall establish and maintain a register identifying each individual reported to him by a State, or political subdivision thereof, as an individual with respect to whom such State or political subdivision has denied, terminated, or temporarily withdrawn (except a withdrawal for less than six months based on a series of nonmoving violations) an individual's license or privilege to operate a motor vehicle.

"SEC. 2. Only at the request of a State, a political subdivision thereof, or a Federal department or agency, shall the Secretary furnish information contained in the register established under the first section of this Act, and such information shall be furnished only to the requesting party and only with respect to an individual applicant for a motor vehicle operator's license or permit.

"SEC. 3. As used in this Act, the term 'State' includes each of the several States, the Commonwealth of Puerto Rico, the District of Columbia, Guam, the Virgin Islands, the Canal Zone, and American Samoa."

Approved September 9, 1966, 1:10 P.M.

C. The Structure of a Modern Statute

The 1966 Motor Vehicle Safety Act might seem like a unique creature, and in some ways it is. No statute is constructed exactly like it or accomplishes exactly what it does. But the Act actually contains the same basic structure as many other statutes. Here is the list of standard statutory provisions from a leading treatise on statutory drafting, F. Reed Dickerson's *Legislative Drafting* (1954), which we have elaborated:

- **Title** ("*An Act to. . . .* "): The formal title states the basic purpose or function of the statute.
- **Enacting clause**: The enacting clause is meant to proclaim the fact that the statute has become law, but it often repeats the basic purpose and function of the statute.
- **Short title**: Statutes often have long titles and therefore need a shorter designation for the sake of reference. Often, the long title reduces to a clever acronym. Consider the statute entitled "Uniting and Strengthening America by Providing Appropriate Tools Required to Intercept and Obstruct Terrorism" Act. The fourteen words of this long title are thirteen more than were needed to name an anti-terrorism act, but they abbreviate to USA PATRIOT. We like VISTA for the Volunteers in Service to America statute because it sounds natural.

    The short title of a statute is also its Popular Name. In the old days, the Popular Name of a statute was typically the name of its primary sponsor or sponsors — the Sherman Act, the Mann Act, the Glass-Steagall Act — or the name of the agency it created — the Federal Trade Commission Act, the Federal Reserve Act. The first snazzy nickname was the Truth in Lending Act, which was originally called the Consumer Credit Labeling Act. The Popular Name can be an acronym.

    Popular Names are important because they are easy to find. The United States Code Annotated, which is the standard compilation of federal statutes, includes a Popular Name Index. The Popular Name is often the best way to find the text of a statute on the Internet.

- **Statement of purpose, preamble, and findings**: A statute may include a more elaborate statement of purpose than the ones in the formal title or enacting clause. In addition, it may have a preamble, which contains introductory information about the statute. Some statutes also add findings, which may simply restate the purpose of the law ("Congress finds that occupational retraining programs in the food industry are unsatisfactory"), but may include factual material that served as background for the statute ("Congress has found that the unemployment rate among food service workers who are dismissed from their position is 2.4 times the national average").

- **Definitions**: Typically but not always, definitions appear at the beginning of the statute. Although definitions are an optional component, they constitute operative language when they do appear. When defined terms are capitalized in the definitions section, they are usually capitalized each time they are used in the body of the statute. Very roughly, statutory definitions can serve three purposes:

  a. *Shorthand references to organizations.* These may be acronyms, short forms, or substituted terms. It would be awkward to refer to the National Oceanographic and Atmospheric Administration over and over again, so a statute might begin by defining the term "NOAA" and then use that designation thereafter. The statute might define the Department for Air and Water Quality Control and Industrial Employment Protection as "the Department," or the Committee on Scientific Integrity in Environmental Policymaking as "the Committee."

  b. *Shorthand references to repeated provisions.* Suppose a statute establishes a bidding process for awarding government contracts in a variety of different fields, and the process in each field is to issue a request for bids, consult with potential bidders in specified ways, receive bids on a special form, open them in a specified way, and then announce the awards at a given time after the bids are opened. It would clearly be awkward to repeat the entire description for each field, so the description can be provided once, in the definitions section, and then be referred to as "the Bidding Process" each time it appears in the subsequent statutory provisions.

  c. *Increased precision.* Statutes often use words in a particular sense, and that specialized meaning can be established in the definitions section. For example, the Endangered Species Act defines "plant" as "any member of the plant kingdom, including seeds, roots and other parts thereof." 16 U.S.C. §1532(14). Thus, it includes seeds, which we may not consider a plant, and excludes a factory or a spy, both of which are sometimes called "plants" in ordinary language. Some statutes also define terms more expansively than ordinary language would suggest. The Endangered Species Act prohibits people from "taking" certain animals, 16 U.S.C. §1538(a)(1), and states in its definitions section that "take" "means to harass, harm, pursue, hunt, shoot, wound, kill, trap, capture, or collect, or to attempt to engage in any such conduct." 16 U.S.C. §1532(19). By doing so, the drafters made sure that their prohibition applied to wounding an endangered animal as well as killing or capturing it, something that may not seem apparent from ordinary language.

Do not assume that a definition in a statute will eliminate all ambiguity about the meaning of a word. Drafters often reintroduce ambiguity, whether intentionally or unintentionally. In the government contracting example above, it seems perfectly reasonable to define the entire process as the "Bidding Process," but how can the drafter then refer to that element of the process when the actual bid is submitted without creating ambiguity? And if an ordinary word such as "take" is defined, what happens if the drafter uses that term in its ordinary sense? Having defined "take" in ways that the Endangered Species Act does, the drafters would be ill-advised to say: "Visitors to wildlife areas where endangered species are present will have part of their entrance fees remitted if they take their children."

- **Principal operative provisions**: Such provisions are the heart and soul of the statute. They contain the result that the statute is trying to achieve or the state of the world that it is designed to create. Some operative provisions impose prohibitions on private conduct — for example, prohibiting private contracts "in restraint of trade," as does the Sherman Antitrust Act, which is reprinted below. Others impose requirements on private conduct — for example, requiring auto manufacturers to comply with auto safety standards for new vehicles. Operative provisions can also seek to encourage or discourage certain conduct rather than requiring or prohibiting it outright — for example, they can provide industrial sources with "offsets" or credits for carbon emissions that can be sold if not used. Operative provisions can also transfer resources — for example, by imposing taxes or providing benefits. Note that some operative provisions are directed to government conduct rather than private conduct. And some are directed to both, as when a statute authorizes an agency to determine the prohibitions or set the requirements to which private actors are subject. We will have more to say about this sort of provision in a moment.

- **Subordinate operative provisions and exceptions**: A statute may contain other operative provisions that are separate from the principal operative provision. These provisions have an effect on the world but they are supportive of or secondary to the main objective. A statute may also contain exceptions to its principal operative provision in a separate section (e.g., "Nothing in this section shall be construed to prevent the importation or migration of foreigners and aliens under contract or agreement to perform as professional actors, artists, lecturers, or singers"). But a statute may also include exceptions, if any, in the principal operative provision.

- **Implementation provisions**: If the principal operative provisions are the heart and soul of a regulatory statute, the implementation provisions are its legs and arms. They enable the statute to do what it purports to do. All statutes require implementation, unless they are merely symbolic, but they do so in different ways. Criminal statutes impose criminal sanctions (for example, imprisonment) to enforce their operative provisions. Civil statutes impose other penalties (for example, monetary fines). Regulatory statutes do many things other than impose penalties, whether criminal or civil, to achieve their goals. They tend to contain rather distinctive implementation provisions, involving an agency in taking action to make a statute work. Implementation provisions are not always separate from operative provisions. As we noted above, an operative provision might direct an agency to establish requirements or prohibitions for private conduct. We discuss the relationship between operative and implementation provisions in more detail below.

- **Specific repeals and related amendments**: If a statute either repeals or amends a preexisting statute, it may contain a statement to that effect. Thus, a federal statute that repeals or amends another federal statute will generally contain a provision to that effect. Statutes can also repeal or amend prior statutes without expressly so stating, although repeals *by implication* are disfavored.

- **Preemption provision**: A preemption provision in a federal statute bars the application of state law. The Supremacy Clause of the U.S Constitution establishes the Constitution, federal statutes, and U.S. treaties as "the supreme law of the land," U.S. Const., Art. VI, §2, and therefore gives Congress the power to preempt any state law. But the scope of the preemption is not always clear. Does the federal statute preempt all state law, including state common law, state regulations, and state statutes, or only particular sources? Does it preempt any state law that is not identical to federal law or only those that are inconsistent with or less stringent than federal law? You must read these provisions carefully. Note that a statute can preempt state law *implicitly*, which means in the absence of an express preemption provision. We discuss this issue below.

- **Savings clause**: A savings clause preserves the application of state law in some respect. It may save a particular type of law, notwithstanding preemption of other types of law. It may provide information concerning the relationship between federal law and state law — for example, it may state that compliance with federal law is not a defense to liability in a state tort suit. Such a provision preserves state tort despite its overlap with the federal statute. As with preemption, you must read these provisions carefully. We also address this issue below.

- **Temporary provisions** (if any): Sometimes a statute will contain a provision that has only a limited duration, while the rest of the statute remains in effect until repealed or amended.

- **Expiration date**: A statute may contain a provision indicating that it will expire or "sunset" on a date specified. This is the exception, not the rule. Typically, statutes are conceived as continuing in perpetuity unless, of course, they are repealed or amended by a subsequent legislature.

- **Effective date** (if different from date of enactment): A statute may contain a provision indicating that it becomes effective on a specific date, generally later than the date of enactment. Statutes that apply to conduct that occurred before the date of enactment are said to apply "retroactively," and they are relatively uncommon.[1]

Note on the Relationship Between Operative and Implementation Provisions

Statutes do not always contain separate operative and implementation provisions. Thus, a statute might read, in part, as follows: "Sec. 3. No vehicle may be taken into the park." "Sec. 5. The Parks Department shall have the authority to enforce the prohibition in Section 3 by confiscating any vehicle in the park." But a statute may also read: "Sec. 4. The Parks Department may confiscate any vehicle that is taken into the park." Are these two provisions exactly the same? It is worth noting that, for some legal thinkers, they are not. This seemingly arcane point has been one of the central controversies of modern jurisprudence. *Compare* HANS KELSEN, GENERAL THEORY OF LAW AND THE STATE (1945) (defending the view that laws are of the second sort, stating a negative consequence the state would impose for a particular action), with H.L.A. HART, THE CONCEPT OF LAW (1961) (taking the view that the two are distinct and arguing that laws are general provisions that establish a norm of behavior government wants people to follow and impose sanctions in the case of disobedience). Similarly, there is a debate about whether a particular implementation provision is simply a price ("you can do x, but we will charge you y for doing so") or a sanction ("we don't want you to do x, and we will impose a penalty of y to deter you from doing so"). *See* Robert Cooter, *Prices and Sanctions*, 84 COLUM. L. REV. 1523 (1984). For our purposes, it is enough to note that statutes sometimes combine implementation and operative provisions and sometimes separate them.

Note on Preemption Provisions, Savings Clauses, and Federalism Issues

Congress often enacts regulatory statutes in areas where the states also have regulatory statutes and agencies. The interaction between federal and state regulatory efforts ranges from cooperative to competitive and every possible combination in between. On the cooperative end of the spectrum, federal statutes often enlist, or authorize the federal agency to enlist, state agencies to implement the statute or its regulations. Examples can be found in diverse areas such as environmental protection, consumer protection, and occupational safety. The Clean Air Act, reprinted below, is one. On the competitive side, federal statutes preclude state agencies from exercising any control over an area. Examples can be found in areas such as broadcasting, commercial aviation, and pharmaceutical licensing. There are many situations that fall somewhere in the middle. For example, the

---

[1] The Constitution actually forbids Congress from enacting retroactive criminal statutes, which are called ex post facto laws. See U.S. CONST., Art. I, §9. Thus, Congress cannot criminalize conduct that was legal when committed. While we are on the subject of constitutional limitations on criminal statutes, Congress also cannot enact bills of attainder, which impose criminal penalties on a specific person or group without a trial. See U.S. CONST., Art. I, §9. Congress can enact a private bill, which also singles out a specific person or group but not for criminal punishment.

Occupational Safety and Health Administration (OSHA) will defer to equivalent state agencies, but only if the "state OSHA" meets federal requirements. 29 U.S.C. §667. The Food and Drug Administration asserts comprehensive control over drug licensing, 21 U.S.C. §355, but state tort law may provide remedies against a drug company that mislabels its product, even if that product has been approved by the FDA. *See* Riegel v. Medtronics, Inc., 552 U.S. 312 (2008).

The legal basis for displacing or preempting state law is the Constitution's Supremacy Clause, which makes any federal enactment the "supreme Law of the Land." U.S. Const., Art. VI, §9, cl. 2. Although preemption is a constitutionally grounded doctrine, judicial determinations of preemption rarely turn on interpretation of the Constitution's language, because the typical question is not whether Congress can preempt state law (it can), but whether Congress intended to exercise this power in the particular statute under consideration. As we mentioned above, statutes may contain express preemption provisions, as well as express savings clauses. These typically require interpretation as to what sorts of state laws — state constitutional provisions, statutes, regulations, common law claims — they preempt or save. Note that, even in the absence of an express preemption provision, courts consider the issue of implied preemption, which occurs when compliance with both state law and federal law is impossible, or a state statute or regulation frustrates the operation of a federal one. *See* Freightliner Corp. v. Myrick, 514 U.S. 280 (1995); Florida Lime & Avocado Growers, Inc. v. Paul, 373 U.S. 132, 142-43 (1963). Courts are generally reluctant to find implied preemption because of the important federalism values at stake. For example, in Wyeth v. Levine, 129 S. Ct. 1187 (2009), the Supreme Court held that the Food, Drug, and Cosmetic Act did not preempt a state law failure-to-warn claim against a drug manufacturer that failed to adequately warn of dangers from administering an antihistamine through an IV-push rather than an IV-drip method. Preemption cases often pose some of the most challenging statutory interpretation issues that the courts confront. We have a bit more to say on this subject in Chapter 11.

CHAPTER 3

THE CONSTITUTION OF THE UNITED STATES

We the People of the United States, in Order to form a more perfect Union, establish justice, insure domestic Tranquility, provide for the common defence, promote the general Welfare, and secure the Blessings of Liberty to ourselves and our Posterity, do ordain and establish this Constitution for the United States of America.

A. Article I

Section 1. All legislative Powers herein granted shall be vested in a Congress of the United States which shall consist of a Senate and House of Representatives.

Section 2. [1] The House of Representatives shall be composed of Members chosen every second Year by the People of the several States, and the Electors in each State shall have the Qualifications requisite for Electors of the most numerous Branch of the State Legislature.

[2] No Person shall be a Representative who shall not have attained to the Age of twenty five Years, and been seven Years a Citizen of the United States, and who shall not, when elected, be an Inhabitant of that State in which he shall be chosen.

[3] Representatives and direct Taxes shall be apportioned among the several States which may be included within this Union, according to their respective Numbers, which shall be determined by adding to the whole Number of free Persons, including those bound to Service for a Term of Years, and excluding Indians not taxed, three fifths of all other Persons. The actual Enumeration shall be made within three Years after the first meeting of the Congress of the United States, and within every subsequent Term of ten Years, in such Manner as they shall by Law direct. The Number of Representatives shall not exceed one for every thirty Thousand, but each State shall have at Least One Representative; and until such enumeration shall be made, the State of New Hampshire shall be entitled to chuse three, Massachusetts eight, Rhode Island and Providence Plantations one,

Connecticut five, New York six, New Jersey four, Pennsylvania eight, Delaware one, Maryland six, Virginia ten, North Carolina five, South Carolina five, and Georgia three.

[4] When vacancies happen in the Representation from any State, the Executive Authority thereof shall issue Writs of Election to fill such Vacancies.

[5] The House of Representatives shall chuse their Speaker and other Officers; and shall have the sole Power of Impeachment.

Section 3. [1] The Senate of the United States shall be composed of two Senators from each State, chosen by the Legislature thereof, for six Years; and each Senator shall have one Vote.

[2] Immediately after they shall be assembled in Consequence of the first Election, they shall be divided as equally as may be into three Classes. The Seats of the Senators of the first Class shall be vacated at the Expiration of the second Year, of the second Class at the Expiration of the fourth Year, and of the third Class at the Expiration of the sixth Year, so that one third may be chosen every second Year; and if Vacancies happen by Resignation, or otherwise, during the Recess of the Legislature of any State, the Executive thereof may make temporary Appointments until the next Meeting of the Legislature, which shall then fill such Vacancies.

[3] No Person shall be a Senator who shall not have attained to the Age of thirty Years, and been nine Years a Citizen of the United States, and who shall not, when elected, be an Inhabitant of that State for which he shall be chosen.

[4] The Vice President of the United States shall be President of the Senate, but shall have no Vote, unless they be equally divided.

[5] The Senate shall chuse their other Officers, and also a President pro tempore, in the absence of the Vice President, or when he shall exercise the Office of President of the United States.

[6] The Senate shall have the sole Power to try all Impeachments. When sitting for that Purpose, they shall be on Oath or Affirmation. When the President of the United States is tried, the Chief Justice shall preside: And no Person shall be convicted without the Concurrence of two thirds of the Members present.

[7] Judgment in Cases of Impeachment shall not extend further than to removal from Office, and disqualification to hold and enjoy any Office of honor, Trust or Profit under the United States: but the Party convicted shall nevertheless be liable and subject to Indictment, Trial, judgment and Punishment, according to Law.

Section 4. [1] The Times, Places and Manner of holding Elections for Senators and Representatives, shall be prescribed in each State by the Legislature thereof; but the Congress may at any time by law make or alter such Regulations, except as to the Places of chusing Senators.

[2] The Congress shall assemble at least once in every Year, and such Meeting shall be on the first Monday in December, unless they shall by Law appoint a different Day.

Section 5. [1] Each house shall be the Judge of the Elections, Returns and Qualifications of its own members, and a Majority of each shall constitute a Quorum to do Business; but a smaller Number may adjourn from day to day, and may be authorized to compel the Attendance of absent members, in such Manner, and under such Penalties as each House may provide.

[2] Each House may determine the Rules of its Proceedings, punish its Members for disorderly Behavior, and, with the Concurrence of two thirds, expel a Member.

[3] Each House shall keep a Journal of its Proceedings, and from time to time publish the same, excepting such Parts as may in their Judgment require Secrecy; and the Yeas and Nays of the Members of either House on any question shall, at the Desire of one fifth of those Present, be entered on the Journal.

[4] Neither House, during the Session of Congress, shall, without the Consent of the other, adjourn for more than three days, nor to any other Place than that in which the two Houses shall be sitting.

Section 6. [1] The Senators and Representatives shall receive a Compensation for their Services, to be ascertained by Law, and paid out of the Treasury of the United States. They shall in all Cases, except Treason, Felony and Breach of the Peace, be privileged from Arrest during their Attendance at the Session of their respective Houses, and in going to and returning from the same; and for any Speech or Debate in either House, they shall not be questioned in any other Place.

[2] No Senator or Representative shall, during the time for which he was elected, be appointed to any civil Office under the Authority of the United States, which shall have been created, or the Emoluments whereof shall have been encreased during such time; and no Person holding any office under the United States, shall be a Member of either House during his Continuance in Office.

Section 7. [1] All Bills for raising Revenue shall originate in the House of Representatives; but the Senate may propose or concur with Amendments as on other Bills.

[2] Every Bill which shall have passed the House of Representatives and the Senate, shall, before it becomes a Law, be presented to the President of the United States; If he approve he shall sign it, but if not he shall return it, with his Objections to the House in which it shall have originated, who shall enter the Objections at large on their Journal, and proceed to reconsider it. If after such Reconsideration two thirds of that House shall agree to pass the Bill, it shall be sent, together with the Objections, to the other House, by which it shall likewise be reconsidered, and if approved by two thirds of that House, it shall become a Law. But in all such Cases the Votes of both Houses shall be determined by Yeas and Nays, and the Names of the Persons voting for and against the Bill shall be entered on the Journal of each House respectively. If any Bill shall not be returned by the President within ten Days (Sundays excepted) after it shall have been presented to him, the Same shall be a Law, in like Manner as if he had signed it, unless the Congress by their Adjournment prevents its Return, in which Case it shall not be a Law.

[3] Every Order, Resolution, or Vote to Which the Concurrence of the Senate and House of Representatives may be necessary (except on a question of Adjournment) shall be presented to the President of the United States; and before the Same shall take Effect, shall be approved by him, or being disapproved by him,

shall be repassed by two thirds of the Senate and House of Representatives, according to the Rules and Limitations prescribed in the Case of a Bill.

Section 8. [1] The Congress shall have Power To lay and collect Taxes, Duties, Imposts and Excises, to pay the Debts and provide for the common Defence and general Welfare of the United States; but all Duties, Imposts and Excises shall be uniform throughout the United States;

[2] To borrow money on the credit of the United States;

[3] To regulate Commerce with foreign Nations, and among the several States, and with the Indian Tribes;

[4] To establish an uniform Rule of Naturalization, and uniform Laws on the subject of Bankruptcies throughout the United States;

[5] To coin Money, regulate the Value thereof, and of foreign Coin, and fix the Standard of Weights and Measures;

[6] To provide the Punishment of counterfeiting the Securities and current Coin of the United States;

[7] To establish Post Offices and post Roads;

[8] To promote the Progress of Science and useful Arts, by securing for limited Times to Authors and Inventors the exclusive Right to their respective Writings and Discoveries;

[9] To constitute Tribunals inferior to the supreme Court;

[10] To define and punish Piracies and Felonies committed on the high Seas, and Offenses against the Law of Nations;

[11] To declare War, grant Letters of Marque and Reprisal, and make Rules concerning Captures on Land and Water;

[12] To raise and support Armies, but no Appropriation of Money to that Use shall be a longer Term than two Years;

[13] To provide and maintain a Navy;

[14] To make Rules for the Government and Regulation of the land and naval Forces;

[15] To provide for calling forth the Militia to execute the Laws of the Union, suppress Insurrections and repel Invasions;

[16] To provide for organizing, arming, and disciplining, the Militia, and for governing such Part of them as may be employed in the Service of the United States, reserving to the States respectively, the Appointment of the Officers, and the Authority of training the Militia according to the discipline prescribed by Congress;

[17] To exercise exclusive Legislation in all Cases whatsoever, over such District (not exceeding ten Miles square) as may, by Cession of particular States, and the Acceptance of Congress, become the Seat of the Government of the United States, and to exercise like Authority over all Places purchased by the Consent of the Legislature of the State in which the Same shall be, for the Erection of Forts, Magazines, Arsenals, dock-Yards, and other needful Buildings; — And

[18] To make all Laws which shall be necessary and proper for carrying into Execution the foregoing Powers, and all other Powers vested by this Constitution in the Government of the United States, or in any Department or Officer thereof.

Section 9. [1] The Migration or Importation of such Persons as any of the States now existing shall think proper to admit, shall not be prohibited by the Congress prior to the Year one thousand eight hundred and eight, but a Tax or duty may be imposed on such Importation, not exceeding ten dollars for each Person.

[2] The privilege of the Writ of Habeas Corpus shall not be suspended, unless when in Cases of Rebellion or Invasion the public Safety may require it.

[3] No Bill of Attainder or ex post facto Law shall be passed.

[4] No Capitation, or other direct, Tax shall be laid, unless in Proportion to the Census or Enumeration herein before directed to be taken.

[5] No Tax or Duty shall be laid on articles exported from any State.

[6] No Preference shall be given by any Regulation of Commerce or Revenue to the Ports of one State over those of another: nor shall Vessels bound to, or from, one State, be obliged to enter, clear, or pay Duties in another.

[7] No Money shall be drawn from the Treasury, but in Consequence of Appropriations made by Law; and a regular Statement and Account of the Receipts and Expenditures of all public Money shall be published from time to time.

[8] No title of Nobility shall be granted by the United States: And no Person holding any Office of Profit or Trust under them, shall, without the Consent of the Congress, accept of any present, Emolument, Office, or Title, of any kind whatever, from any King, Prince, or foreign State.

Section 10. [1] No State shall enter into any Treaty, Alliance, or Confederation; grant Letters of Marque and Reprisal; coin Money; emit Bills of Credit; make any Thing but gold and silver Coin a Tender in Payment of Debts; pass any Bill of Attainder, ex post facto Law, or Law impairing the Obligation of Contracts, or grant any title of Nobility.

[2] No State shall, without the Consent of the Congress, lay any Imposts or Duties on Imports or Exports, except what may be absolutely necessary for executing its inspection Laws: and the net Produce of all Duties and Imposts, laid by any State on Imports or Exports, shall be for the Use of the Treasury of the United States; and all such Laws be subject to the Revision and Controul of the Congress.

[3] No State shall, without the Consent of Congress, lay any Duty of Tonnage, keep Troops, or Ships of War in time of Peace, enter into any Agreement or Compact with another State, or with a foreign Power, or engage in War, unless actually invaded, or in such imminent Danger as will not admit of delay.

B. Article II

Section 1. [1] The executive Power shall be vested in a President of the United States of America. He shall hold his Office during the Term of four Years, and, together with the Vice President, chosen for the same Term, be elected, as follows:

[2] Each State shall appoint, in such Manner as the Legislature thereof may direct, a Number of Electors, equal to the whole Number of Senators and Representatives to which the State may be entitled in the Congress: but no Senator or Representative, or Person holding an Office of Trust or Profit under the United States, shall be appointed an Elector.

[3] The Electors shall meet in their respective States, and vote by Ballot for two Persons, of whom one at least shall not be an Inhabitant of the same State with themselves. And they shall make a List of all the Persons voted for, and of the Number of Votes for each; which List they shall sign and certify, and transmit sealed to the Seat of the Government of the United States, directed to the President of the Senate. The President of the Senate shall, in the Presence of the Senate and House of Representatives, open all the Certificates, and the Votes shall then be counted. The Person having the greatest Number of Votes shall be the President, if such Number be a Majority of the whole Number of Electors appointed; and if there be more than one who have such Majority, and have an equal Number of Votes, then the House of Representatives shall immediately chuse by Ballot one of them for President; and if no Person have a Majority, then from the five highest on the List the said House shall in like Manner chuse the President. But in chusing the President, the Votes shall be taken by States, the Representation from each State having one vote; a quorum for this Purpose shall consist of a Member or Members from two thirds of the States, and a Majority of all the States shall be necessary to a Choice. In every Case, after the Choice of the President, the Person having the Greatest Number of Votes of the Electors shall be the Vice President. But if there should remain two or more who have equal Votes, the Senate shall chuse from them by Ballot the Vice President.

[4] The Congress may determine the Time of chusing the Electors, and the Day on which they shall give their Votes; which Day shall be the same throughout the United States.

[5] No person except a natural born Citizen, or a Citizen of the United States, at the time of the Adoption of this Constitution, shall be eligible to the Office of President; neither shall any Person be eligible to that Office who shall not have attained to the Age of thirty five Years, and been fourteen Years a Resident within the United States.

[6] In case of the removal of the President from Office, or of his Death, Resignation, or Inability to discharge the Powers and Duties of the said Office, the Same shall devolve on the Vice President, and the Congress may by Law provide for the Case of Removal, Death, Resignation or Inability, both of the President and Vice President, declaring what Officer shall then act as President, and such Officer shall act accordingly, until the Disability be removed, or a President shall be elected.

[7] The President shall, at stated Times, receive for his Services, a Compensation, which shall neither be increased nor diminished during the Period for which he shall have been elected, and he shall not receive within that Period any other Emolument from the United States, or any of them.

[8] Before he enter on the Execution of his Office, he shall take the following Oath or Affirmation: "I do solemnly swear (or affirm) that I will faithfully execute

the Office of President of the United States, and will to the best of my Ability, preserve, protect and defend the Constitution of the United States."

Section 2. [1] The President shall be Commander in Chief of the Army and Navy of the United States, and of the Militia of the several States, when called into the actual Service of the United States; he may require the Opinion, in writing, of the principal Officer in each of the executive Departments, upon any subject relating to the Duties of their respective Offices, and he shall have Power to grant Reprieves and Pardons for Offenses against the United States, except in Cases of Impeachment.

[2] He shall have Power, by and with the Advice and Consent of the Senate, to make Treaties, provided two thirds of the Senators present concur; and he shall nominate, and by and with the Advice and Consent of the Senate, shall appoint Ambassadors, other public Ministers and Consuls, Judges of the supreme Court, and all other Officers of the United States, whose Appointments are not herein otherwise provided for, and which shall be established by Law: but the Congress may by Law vest the Appointment of such inferior Officers, as they think proper, in the President alone, to the Courts of Law, or in the Heads of Departments.

[3] The President shall have Power to fill up all Vacancies that may happen during the Recess of the Senate by granting Commissions which shall expire at the End of their next Session.

Section 3. He shall from time to time give to the Congress Information of the State of the Union, and recommend to their Consideration such Measures as he shall judge necessary and expedient; he may, on extraordinary Occasions, convene both Houses, or either of them, and in Case of Disagreement between them, with Respect to the time of Adjournment, he may adjourn them to such Time as he shall think proper; he shall receive Ambassadors and other public Ministers; he shall take Care that the Laws be faithfully executed, and shall Commission all the Officers of the United States.

Section 4. The President, Vice President and all civil Officers of the United States, shall be removed from Office on Impeachment for, and Conviction of, Treason, Bribery, or other high Crimes and Misdemeanors.

C. Article III

Section 1. The judicial Power of the United States, shall be vested in one supreme Court, and in such inferior Courts as the Congress may from time to time ordain and establish. The Judges, both of the supreme and inferior Courts, shall hold their Offices during good Behaviour, and shall, at stated Times, receive for their Services a Compensation, which shall not be diminished during their Continuance in Office.

Section 2. [1] The Judicial Power shall extend to all Cases, in Law and Equity, arising under this Constitution, the Laws of the United States, and Treaties made, or which shall be made, under their Authority; — to all Cases affecting Ambassadors, other public Ministers and Consuls; — to all Cases of admiralty and maritime Jurisdiction; — to Controversies to which the United States shall be a

Party; — to Controversies between two or more States; between a State and Citizens of another State; — between Citizens of different States; — between Citizens of the same State claiming Lands under Grants of different States, and between a State, or the Citizens thereof, and foreign States, Citizens or Subjects.

[2] In all cases affecting Ambassadors, other public Ministers and Consuls, and those in which a State shall be Party, the supreme Court shall have original Jurisdiction. In all the other Cases before mentioned, the supreme Court shall have appellate Jurisdiction, both as to Law and Fact, with such Exceptions, and under such Regulations as the Congress shall make.

[3] The trial of all Crimes, except in Cases of Impeachment, shall be by Jury; and such Trial shall be held in the State where the said Crimes shall have been committed; but when not committed within any State, the Trial shall be at such Place or Places as the Congress may by Law have directed.

Section 3. [1] Treason against the United States, shall consist only in levying War against them, or in adhering to their Enemies, giving them Aid and Comfort. No person shall be convicted of Treason unless on the Testimony of two Witnesses to the same over Act, or on Confession in open Court.

[2] The Congress shall have Power to declare the Punishment of Treason, but no Attainder of Treason shall work Corruption of Blood, or Forfeiture except during the Life of the Person attainted.

D. Article IV

Section 1. Full Faith and Credit shall be given in each State to the public Acts, Records, and judicial Proceedings of every other State. And the Congress may by general Laws prescribe the Manner in which such Acts, Records and Proceedings shall be proved, and the Effect thereof.

Section 2. [1] The Citizens of each State shall be entitled to all Privileges and Immunities of Citizens in the several States.

[2] A Person charged in any State with Treason, Felony, or other Crime, who shall flee from Justice, and be found in another State, shall on demand of the executive Authority of the State from which he fled, be delivered up, to be removed to the State having Jurisdiction of the Crime.

[3] No Person held to Service or Labour in one State, under the Laws thereof, escaping into another, shall, in Consequence of any Law or Regulation therein, be discharged from such Service or Labour, but shall be delivered up on Claim of the Party to whom such Service or Labour may be due.

Section 3. [1] New States may be admitted by the Congress into this Union; but no new State shall be formed or erected within the Jurisdiction of any other State; nor any State be formed by the Junction of two or more States, or Parts of States, without the Consent of the Legislatures of the States concerned as well as of the Congress.

[2] The Congress shall have Power to dispose of and make all needful Rules and Regulations respecting the Territory or other Property belonging to the

United States; and nothing in this Constitution shall be so construed as to Prejudice any Claims of the United States, or of any particular State.

Section 4. The United States shall guarantee to every State in this Union a Republican Form of Government, and shall protect each of them against Invasion; and on Application of the Legislature, or of the Executive (when the Legislature cannot be convened) against domestic Violence.

E. Article V

The Congress, whenever two thirds of both Houses shall deem it necessary, shall propose Amendments to this Constitution, or, on the Application of the Legislatures of two thirds of the several States, shall call a Convention for proposing Amendments, which, in either Case, shall be valid to all Intents and Purposes, as part of this Constitution, when ratified by the Legislatures of three fourths of the several States, or by Conventions in three fourths thereof, as the one or the other Mode of Ratification may be proposed by the Congress; Provided that no Amendment which may be made prior to the Year One thousand eight hundred and eight shall in any Manner affect the first and fourth Clauses in the Ninth Section of the first Article; and that no State, without its Consent, shall be deprived of its equal Suffrage in the Senate.

F. Article VI

[1] All Debts contracted and Engagements entered into, before the Adoption of this Constitution, shall be as valid against the United States under this Constitution, as under the Confederation.

[2] This Constitution, and the Laws of the United States which shall be made in Pursuance thereof; and all Treaties made, or which shall be made, under the Authority of the United States, shall be the supreme Law of the Land; and the Judges in every State shall be bound thereby, any Thing in the Constitution or Laws of any State to the Contrary notwithstanding.

[3] The Senators and Representatives before mentioned, and the Members of the several State Legislatures, and all executive and judicial Officers, both of the United States and of the several States, shall be bound by Oath or Affirmation, to support this Constitution; but no religious Test shall ever be required as a Qualification to any Office or public Trust under the United States.

G. Article VII

The Ratification of the Conventions of nine States shall be sufficient for the Establishment of this Constitution between the States so ratifying the Same.

Done in Convention by the Unanimous Consent of the States present the Seventeenth Day of September in the Year of our Lord one thousand seven hundred and Eighty seven and of the Independence of the United States of America the Twelfth.

ARTICLES IN ADDITION TO, AND AMENDMENT OF, THE CONSTITUTION OF THE UNITED STATES OF AMERICA, PROPOSED BY CONGRESS, AND RATIFIED BY THE LEGISLATURES OF THE SEVERAL STATES, PURSUANT TO THE FIFTH ARTICLE OF THE ORIGINAL CONSTITUTION.

H. Amendment I [1791]

Congress shall make no law respecting an establishment of religion, or prohibiting the free exercise thereof; or abridging the freedom of speech, or of the press; or the right of the people peaceably to assemble, and to petition the Government for a redress of grievances.

I. Amendment II [1791]

A well regulated Militia, being necessary to the security of a free State, the right of the people to keep and bear Arms, shall not be infringed.

J. Amendment III [1791]

No Soldier shall, in time of peace be quartered in any house, without the consent of the Owner, nor in time of war, but in a manner to be prescribed by law.

K. Amendment IV [1791]

The right of the people to be secure in their persons, houses, papers, and effects, against unreasonable searches and seizures, shall not be violated, and no Warrants shall issue, but upon probable cause, supported by Oath or affirmation, and particularly describing the place to be searched, and the persons or things to be seized.

L. Amendment V [1791]

No person shall be held to answer for a capital, or otherwise infamous crime, unless on a presentment or indictment of a Grand Jury, except in cases arising in the land or naval forces, or in the Militia, when in actual service in time of War or public danger; nor shall any person be subject for the same offence to be twice put in jeopardy of life or limb; nor shall be compelled in any criminal case to be a witness against himself, nor be deprived of life, liberty, or property, without due process of law; nor shall private property be taken for public use, without just compensation.

M. Amendment VI [1791]

In all criminal prosecutions, the accused shall enjoy the right to a speedy and public trial, by an impartial jury of the State and district wherein the crime shall have been committed, which district shall have been previously ascertained by law, and to be informed of the nature and cause of the accusation; to be confronted with the witnesses against him; to have compulsory process for obtaining witnesses in his favor, and to have the Assistance of Counsel for his defence.

N. Amendment VII [1791]

In Suits at common law, where the value in controversy shall exceed twenty dollars, the right of trial by jury shall be preserved, and no fact tried by a jury, shall be otherwise reexamined in any Court of the United States, than according to the rules of the common law.

O. Amendment VIII [1791]

Excessive bail shall not be required, nor excessive fines imposed, nor cruel and unusual punishments inflicted.

P. Amendment IX [1791]

The enumeration in the Constitution, of certain rights, shall not be construed to deny or disparage others retained by the people.

Q. Amendment X [1791]

The powers not delegated to the United States by the Constitution, nor prohibited by it to the States, are reserved to the States respectively, or to the people.

R. Amendment XI [1798]

The Judicial power of the United States shall not be construed to extend to any suit in law or equity, commenced or prosecuted against one of the United States by Citizens of another State, or by Citizens or Subjects of any Foreign State.

S. Amendment XII [1804]

The Electors shall meet in their respective states and vote by ballot for President and Vice-President, one of whom, at least, shall not be an inhabitant of the same state with themselves; they shall name in their ballots the person voted for as President, and in distinct ballots the person voted for as Vice-President, and they shall make distinct lists of all persons voted for as President, and of all persons voted for as Vice-President, and of the number of votes for each, which lists they shall sign and certify, and transmit sealed to the seat of the government of the United States, directed to the President of the Senate; — The President of the Senate shall, in the presence of the Senate and House of Representatives, open all the certificates and the votes shall then be counted; — The person having the greatest number of votes for President, shall be the President, if such number be a majority of the whole number of Electors appointed; and if no person have such majority, then from the persons having the highest numbers not exceeding three on the list of those voted for as President, the House of Representatives shall choose immediately, by ballot, the President. But in choosing the President, the votes shall be taken by states, the representation from each state having one vote; a quorum for this purpose shall consist of a member or members from two-thirds of the states, and a majority of all the states shall be necessary to a choice. And if the House of Representatives shall not choose a President whenever the right of choice shall devolve upon them, before the fourth day of March next following, then the Vice-President shall act as President, as in the case of the death or other constitutional disability of the President. — The person having the greatest number of votes as Vice-President, shall be the Vice-President, if such number be a majority of the whole number of Electors appointed, and if no person have a majority, then from the two highest numbers on the list, the Senate shall choose the Vice-President; a quorum for the purpose shall consist of two-thirds of the whole number of Senators, and a majority of the whole number shall be necessary to a choice. But no person constitutionally ineligible to the office of President shall be eligible to that of Vice-President of the United States.

T. Amendment XIII [1865]

Section 1. Neither slavery nor involuntary servitude, except as a punishment for crime whereof the party shall have been duly convicted, shall exist within the United States, or any place subject to their jurisdiction.

Section 2. Congress shall have power to enforce this article by appropriate legislation.

U. Amendment XIV [1868]

Section 1. All persons born or naturalized in the United States, and subject to the jurisdiction thereof, are citizens of the United States and of the State wherein they reside. No State shall make or enforce any law which shall abridge the privileges or immunities of citizens of the United States; nor shall any State deprive any person of life, liberty, or property, without due process of law; nor deny to any person within its jurisdiction the equal protection of the laws.

Section 2. Representatives shall be apportioned among the several States according to their respective numbers, counting the whole number of persons in each State, excluding Indians not taxed. But when the right to vote at any election for the choice of electors for President and Vice-President of the United States, Representatives in Congress, the Executive and Judicial officers of a State, or the members of the Legislature thereof, is denied to any of the male inhabitants of such State, being twenty-one years of age, and citizens of the United States, or in any way abridged, except for participation in rebellion, or other crime, the basis of representation therein shall be reduced in the proportion which the number of such male citizens shall bear to the whole number of male citizens twenty-one years of age in such State.

Section 3. No person shall be a Senator or Representative in Congress, or elector of President and Vice-President, or hold any office, civil or military, under the United States, or under any State, who, having previously taken an oath, as a member of Congress, or as an officer of the United States, or as a member of any State legislature, or as an executive or judicial officer of any State, to support the Constitution of the United States, shall have engaged in insurrection or rebellion against the same, or given aid or comfort to the enemies thereof. But Congress may by a vote of two-thirds of each House, remove such disability.

Section 4. The validity of the public debt of the United States, authorized by law, including debts incurred for payment of pensions and bounties for services in suppressing insurrection or rebellion, shall not be questioned. But neither the United States nor any State shall assume or pay any debt or obligation incurred in aid of insurrection or rebellion against the United States, or any claim for the loss of emancipation of any slave; but all such debts, obligations and claims shall be held illegal and void.

Section 5. The Congress shall have power to enforce, by appropriate legislation, the provisions of this article.

V. Amendment XV [1870]

Section 1. The right of citizens of the United States to vote shall not be denied or abridged by the United States or by any State on account of race, color, or previous condition of servitude.

Section 2. The Congress shall have power to enforce this article by appropriate legislation.

W. Amendment XVI [1913]

The Congress shall have power to lay and collect taxes on incomes, from whatever source derived, without apportionment among the several States, and without regard to any census or enumeration.

X. Amendment XVII [1913]

[1] The Senate of the United States shall be composed of two Senators from each State, elected by the people thereof, for six years, and each Senator shall have one vote. The electors in each State shall have the qualifications requisite for electors of the most numerous branch of the State legislatures.

[2] When vacancies happen in the representation of any State in the Senate, the executive authority of such State shall issue writs of election to fill such vacancies: *Provided*, That the legislature of any State may empower the executive thereof to make temporary appointments until the people fill the vacancies by election as the legislature may direct.

[3] This amendment shall not be so construed as to affect the election or term of any Senator chosen before it becomes valid as part of the Constitution.

Y. Amendment XVIII [1919]

Section 1. After one year from the ratification of this article the manufacture, sale, or transportation of intoxicating liquors within, the importation thereof into, or the exportation thereof from the United States and all territory subject to the jurisdiction thereof for beverage purposes is hereby prohibited.

Section 2. The Congress and the several States shall have concurrent power to enforce this article by appropriate legislation.

Section 3. This article shall be inoperative unless it shall have been ratified as an amendment to the Constitution by the legislatures of the several States, as provided in the Constitution, within seven years from the date of the submission hereof to the States by the Congress.

Z. Amendment XIX [1920]

[1] The right of citizens of the United States to vote shall not be denied or abridged by the United States or by any State on account of sex.

[2] Congress shall have power to enforce this article by appropriate legislation.

AA. Amendment XX [1933]

Section 1. The terms of the President and Vice President shall end at noon on the 20th day of January, and the terms of Senators and Representatives at noon on the 3d day of January, of the years in which such terms would have ended if this article had not been ratified; and the terms of their successor shall then begin.

Section 2. The Congress shall assemble at least once in every year, and such meeting shall begin at noon on the 3d day of January, unless they shall by law appoint a different day.

Section 3. If, at the time fixed for the beginning of the term of the President, the President elect shall have died, the Vice President elect shall become President. If a President shall not have been chosen before the time fixed for the beginning of his term, or if the President elect shall have failed to qualify, then the Vice President elect shall act as President until a President shall have qualified; and the Congress may by law provide for the case wherein neither a President elect nor a Vice President elect shall have qualified, declaring who shall then act as President, or the manner in which one who is to act shall be selected, and such person shall act accordingly until a President or Vice President shall have qualified.

Section 4. The Congress may by law provide for the case of the death of any of the persons from whom the House of Representatives may choose a President whenever the right of choice shall have devolved upon them, and for the case of the death of any of the persons from whom the Senate may choose a Vice President whenever the right of choice shall have devolved upon them.

Section 5. Sections 1 and 2 shall take effect on the 15th day of October following the ratification of this article.

Section 6. This article shall be inoperative unless it shall have been ratified as an amendment to the Constitution by the legislatures of three-fourths of the several States within seven years from the date of its submission.

AB. Amendment XXI [1933]

Section 1. The eighteenth article of amendment to the Constitution of the United States is hereby repealed.

Section 2. The transportation or importation into any State, Territory, or possession of the United States for delivery or use therein of intoxicating liquors, in violation of the laws thereof, is hereby prohibited.

Section 3. This article shall be inoperative unless it shall have been ratified as an amendment to the Constitution by conventions in the several States, as provided in the Constitution, within seven years from the date of the submissions hereof to the States by the Congress.

AC. Amendment XXII [1951]

Section 1. No person shall be elected to the office of the President more than twice, and no person who has held the office of President, or acted as President, for more than two years of a term to which some other person was elected President shall be elected to the office of the President more than once. But this Article shall not apply to any person holding the office of President when this Article was proposed by the Congress, and shall not prevent any person who may be holding the office of President, or acting as President, during the term within which the Article becomes operative from holding the office of President or acting as President during the remainder of such term.

Section 2. This article shall be inoperative unless it shall have been ratified as an amendment to the Constitution by the legislatures of three-fourths of the several States within seven years from the date of its submission to the States by the Congress.

AD. Amendment XXIII [1961]

Section 1. The District constituting the seat of Government of the United States shall appoint in such manner as the Congress may direct:

A number of electors of President and Vice President equal to the whole number of Senators and Representatives in Congress to which the District would be entitled if it were a State, but in no event more than the least populous State; they shall be in addition to those appointed by the States, but they shall be considered, for the purposes of the election of President and Vice President, to be electors appointed by a State; and they shall meet in the District and perform such duties as provided by the twelfth article of amendment.

Section 2. The Congress shall have power to enforce this article by appropriate legislation.

AE. Amendment XXIV [1964]

Section 1. The right of citizens of the United States to vote in any primary or other election for President or Vice President for electors for President or Vice President, or for Senator or Representative in Congress, shall not be denied or abridged by the United States or any State by reason of failure to pay any poll tax or other tax.

Section 2. The Congress shall have power to enforce this article by appropriate legislation.

AF. Amendment XXV [1967]

Section 1. In case of the removal of the President from office or of his death or resignation, the Vice President shall become President.

Section 2. Whenever there is a vacancy in the office of the Vice President, the President shall nominate a Vice President who shall take office upon confirmation by a majority vote of both Houses of Congress.

Section 3. Whenever the President transmits to the President pro tempore of the Senate and the Speaker of the House of Representatives his written declaration that he is unable to discharge the powers and duties of his office, and until he transmits to them a written declaration to the contrary, such powers and duties shall be discharged by the Vice President as Acting President.

Section 4. Whenever the Vice President and a Majority of either the principal officers of the executive departments or of such other body as Congress may by law provide, transmit to the President pro tempore of the Senate and the Speaker of the House of Representatives their written declaration that the President is unable to discharge the powers and duties of his office, the Vice President shall immediately assume the powers and duties of the office as Acting President.

Thereafter, when the President transmits to the President pro tempore of the Senate and the Speaker of the House of Representatives his written declaration that no inability exists, he shall resume the powers and duties of his office unless the Vice President and a majority of either the principal officers of the executive department or of such other body as Congress may by law provide, transmit within four days to the President pro tempore of the Senate and the Speaker of the House of Representatives their written declaration that the President is unable to discharge the powers and duties of his office. Thereupon Congress shall decide the issue, assembling within forty-eight hours for that purpose if not in session. If the Congress, within twenty-one days after receipt of the latter written declaration, or, if Congress is not in session, within twenty-one days after Congress is required to assemble, determined by two-thirds vote of both Houses that the President is unable to discharge the powers and duties of his office, the Vice President shall continue to discharge the same as Acting President; otherwise, the President shall resume the powers and duties of his office.

AG. Amendment XXVI [1971]

Section 1. The right of citizens of the United States, who are eighteen years of age or older, to vote shall not be denied or abridged by the United States or by any State on account of age.

Section 2. The Congress shall have power to enforce this article by appropriate legislation.

AH. Amendment XXVII [1992]

Section 1. No law, varying the Compensation for the services of the Senators and Representatives, shall take effect, unless an election of Representatives shall have intervened.

CHAPTER 4

HISTORICAL BACKGROUND AND CONTEMPORARY THEMES

A. The Constitution's Functions

Creates National Government and Separates Power

The Constitution creates a national government and divides power among the three branches. Article I creates the legislative power and vests it in Congress. Article II places the executive power in the president of the United States. Article III provides that the judicial power of the United States shall be in the Supreme Court and such inferior courts as Congress creates.

The division of powers among the branches was designed to create a system of checks and balances and lessen the possibility of tyrannical rule. In general, in order for the government to act, at least two branches must agree. Adopting a law requires passage by Congress and the signature of the president (unless it is adopted over his or her veto). Enforcing a law generally requires that the executive initiate a prosecution and that the judiciary convict. Chapters 2, 3, and 4 [Erwin Chemerinsky, Constitutional Law: Principles and Policies, 4th ed., (2011)] examine the powers of the judiciary, the legislature, and the executive, respectively. The conflicts and tensions among the branches is a constant theme throughout these chapters.

The Constitution specifies the term of each office among the three branches, the qualifications necessary to hold office, and the manner by which the office is to be filled. Article I, for example, provides for popular election of members of the House of Representatives to two-year terms and for selection of senators by state legislators for six-year terms. The Seventeenth Amendment changed this and provided for popular election of senators. Article I also provides that each member of the House shall be at least 25 years old, a citizen of the United States for at least seven years, and an inhabitant of the state from which he or she is elected.

A senator must be 30 years old, a citizen for at least nine years, and an inhabitant of the state from which he or she is elected.[1]

Article II outlines the method of choosing the president and vice president to a four-year term through the electoral college, a process that was modified by the Twelfth Amendment. The Twelfth Amendment eliminated the practice of making the runner-up in the presidential election the vice president, and established the procedure for the House of Representatives to choose the president when no candidate receives a majority in the electoral college.[2] Also, the Twenty-second Amendment provides that no person can be elected president more than twice. Article II also specifies that the president be at least 35 years old, a natural born citizen, and a resident of the United States for at least 14 years.

Article III provides that federal judges shall have life tenure, and Article II specifies that they will be selected by the president with the "advice and consent of the Senate." Interestingly, the Constitution specifies no other qualifications for being a federal judge.[3]

The length of office terms and the manner of selecting officeholders are crucial in defining the character of American government. The framers intentionally chose a scheme whereby one body of Congress, the House of Representatives, was popularly elected and all citizens were represented equally; the other body, the Senate, was selected by state legislatures, and every state had two senators. The Seventeenth Amendment, adopted in 1913, provided that senators would be directly elected by the voters. The president is chosen by the electoral college, not by majority vote, and the result has been that four times in history a president has been selected who received fewer popular votes than an opponent, most recently in November 2000.[4] Federal judges have life tenure so as to enhance the

---

[1] The Supreme Court held that states may not set additional qualifications for membership in Congress. Specifically, in *United States Term Limits v. Thornton*, 514 U.S. 779 (1995), the Court declared unconstitutional a state law that prevented individuals from being listed on the ballot after serving three terms in the House or two in the Senate. The Court ruled that states may not set term limits for members of Congress because the Constitution specifies the only qualifications for election to the House or Senate. In *Cook v. Gralike*, 531 U.S. 510 (2001), the Court reaffirmed this and declared unconstitutional a Missouri law that required that candidates' support or opposition to term limits be indicated on the ballot.

[2] If no candidate receives a majority in the electoral college, the Twelfth Amendment provides that the House of Representatives shall choose the president, with each state casting one vote. The Amendment does not specify how the state is to decide how to vote.

[3] In recent years, there have been many congressional battles over the confirmation of Supreme Court Justices. In 1969, the Senate rejected President Nixon's nominations of Harold Carswell and Clement Haynsworth, and in 1987 it rejected the nomination of Robert Bork. In 1991, there was a highly publicized battle over the confirmation of Clarence Thomas, who was confirmed by a vote of 52 to 48, the smallest margin in history for any justice confirmed by the Senate. In 2006, Samuel Alito was confirmed by a vote of 58 to 42.

[4] In the election of 1824, Andrew Jackson received the most popular votes with 152,933. John Quincy Adams received 115,696 votes. However, Jackson did not have a majority of the votes cast because William H. Crawford and Henry Clay each drew over 45,000 votes. Similarly, although Jackson received the most votes in the electoral college (99 compared to Adams's 84), Jackson did not receive a majority of the votes in the electoral college because Crawford and Clay received a total of 78 votes. In the subsequent election in the House of Representatives, Adams was elected president with 13 votes from the 24 states. Neal R. Peirce & Lawrence D. Longley, The People's President: The Electoral College in American History and the Direct Vote Alternative 50-51 (1981).

likelihood that their decisions will be based on the merits of the case and not on political pressure.

Divides Power Between the Federal and State Governments

The Constitution divides power vertically between the federal and state governments. "Federalism" is the term often used to refer to this vertical division of authority. The federalist structure of the government is much less apparent from the text of the Constitution than is the separation of powers. Article I begins by saying that "[a]ll legislative Powers herein granted shall be vested in a Congress." The implication is that Congress can act only if there is clear authority, with all other governance left to the states. But this is not made explicit in the text of the seven articles of the Constitution. Indeed, it was probably this lack of clarity that inspired the Tenth Amendment, which states: "The powers not delegated to the United States by the Constitution, nor prohibited by it to the States, are reserved to the States respectively, or to the people."

As discussed in detail in Chapter 3 [Erwin Chemerinsky, Constitutional Law: Principles and Policies, 4th ed., (2011)], there has been great debate throughout American history as to whether the Tenth Amendment reserves a zone of authority exclusively to the states and whether the judiciary should invalidate laws that infringe that zone.[5] Early in this century, the Court aggressively used the Tenth Amendment as a limit on Congress's power. After 1937, the Court rejected this view and did not see the Tenth Amendment as a basis for declaring federal laws unconstitutional. In the 1990s, however, the Tenth Amendment was once more used by the Supreme Court to invalidate federal statutes.[6]

One other provision that expressly relates to federalism is the supremacy clause found in Article VI of the Constitution. It declares that the "Constitution, and the Laws of the United States which shall be made in Pursuance thereof, and all Treaties made, or which shall be made, under the Authority of the United States, shall be the supreme Law of the Land." This provision sets up a clearly hierarchical relationship between the federal government and the states. Practically, the effect of the supremacy clause is that state and local laws are deemed preempted if they conflict with federal law. The issue of preemption is discussed in Chapter 5 [Erwin Chemerinsky, Constitutional Law: Principles and Policies, 4th ed., (2011)].

In the election of 1876, the Democrat Samuel J. Tilden received more popular votes than the Republican Rutherford B. Hayes. However, Hayes won 185 electoral college votes to Tilden's 184 and thereby gained the presidency. *Id.* at 53. In the election of 1888, Grover Cleveland received 95,096 more votes than Benjamin Harrison, but Harrison won the presidency with 233 votes in the electoral college compared to Cleveland's 168. *Id.* at 57-58. In the election of 2000, the Democrat Al Gore received more popular votes (50,992,335 votes) than the Republican George W. Bush (50,455,156 votes). Nevertheless, George W. Bush won the presidency by receiving 271 electoral college votes to Gore's 266.

[5] *See* §3.8 [Erwin Chemerinsky, Constitutional Law: Principles and Policies, 4th ed., (2011)].

[6] This history is discussed in detail in §3.8 [Erwin Chemerinsky, Constitutional Law: Principles and Policies, 4th ed., (2011)].

Finally, federalism limits the ability of states to impose burdens on each other. For example, since the country's earliest days, the Supreme Court has held that the grant of power to Congress to regulate commerce among the states limits the ability of states to regulate or tax commerce in a manner that places an undue burden on interstate commerce. This topic, sometimes called the dormant commerce clause, and the related issue of state taxation of interstate commerce, are discussed in Chapter 5 [Erwin Chemerinsky, Constitutional Law: Principles and Policies, 4th ed., (2011)].

Protects Individual Liberties

A third major function of the Constitution is to protect individual liberties. Although this is popularly regarded as the Constitution's most significant goal, there are few parts of the Constitution, apart from the Bill of Rights, that pertain to individual rights. Article I, §§9 and 10, respectively, say that neither the federal nor state governments can enact an ex post facto law or a bill of attainder.[7] An ex post facto law is one that criminally punishes conduct that was lawful when it was done or that increases the punishment for a crime after it was committed. A bill of attainder is a law that orders the punishment of a person without a trial. Article I, §10, also provides that no state shall impair the obligations of contracts.[8]

Article III, §2, ensures trial by jury of all crimes, except in cases of impeachment, in the state where the crime occurred. Article III, §3, limits the scope of treason to "levying War against [the United States], or in adhering to their Enemies, giving them Aid and Comfort." It also requires that a conviction be based on the testimony of two witnesses to an overt act or on a confession in open court. The punishment for treason is limited in that it cannot "work Corruption of Blood, or Forfeiture except during the Life of the Person attainted."

Article IV provides that the "Citizens of each State shall be entitled to all Privileges and Immunities of Citizens in the several States." This provision, which is discussed in detail in Chapter 5 [Erwin Chemerinsky, Constitutional Law: Principles and Policies, 4th ed., (2011)], limits the ability of a state to discriminate against out-of-state residents with regard to what are called "privileges and immunities." As described in Chapter 5 [Erwin Chemerinsky, Constitutional Law: Principles and Policies, 4th ed., (2011)], the Court has interpreted this phrase as referring to constitutional rights and the right of individuals to earn their livelihood.

The only other provisions of the Constitution, apart from the Bill of Rights, that deal with individual liberties focus on protecting the rights of slave owners. Article I, §9, prohibited Congress from banning the importation of slaves until 1808, and Article V, which concerns constitutional amendments, provides that this provision cannot be amended. Article IV, §2, contains the fugitive slave clause which required that a slave escaping from one state, even to a non–slave state, be returned to his or her owner. Slavery was very much a part of the fabric of

---

[7] These clauses are discussed in Chapter 6, §§6.2.2 and 6.2.3 [Erwin Chemerinsky, Constitutional Law: Principles and Policies, 4th ed., (2011)], respectively.

[8] This provision is discussed in §8.2 [Erwin Chemerinsky, Constitutional Law: Principles and Policies, 4th ed., (2011)].

the Constitution and it was not abolished until the Thirteenth Amendment was adopted in 1865 after the conclusion of the Civil War.

There are many explanations for the absence of a more elaborate statement of individual rights in the Constitution. Some believe that the framers thought it unnecessary because rights were adequately protected by the limitations on power of the national government. Also, the framers might have been fearful that enumerating some rights could be taken as implicitly denying the existence of other liberties. Thus, the Ninth Amendment to the Constitution declares: "The enumeration in the Constitution, of certain rights, shall not be construed to deny or disparage others retained by the people."

As described below, several states ratified the Constitution, but with the insistence that a Bill of Rights be added.[9] Almost immediately after Congress began its first session, James Madison started drafting amendments to the Constitution. Seventeen amendments passed the House of Representatives and were sent to the Senate. The Senate approved 12 of them. Interestingly, one that the Senate did not approve would have prohibited state infringement of freedom of conscience, speech, press, and jury trial; Madison referred to this as "the most valuable amendment in the whole lot."[10]

Of the 12 amendments that passed the House and the Senate, the states ratified ten. One that was not ratified would have provided a formula for the apportionment of the House of Representatives. The other amendment that was not ratified by the states provided: "No law, varying the compensation for the services of the Senators and Representatives shall take effect, until an election of Representatives shall have intervened." Only five states ratified this amendment between 1789 and 1791, when the first ten amendments were approved by the states. Between 1973 and 1992, 33 more states ratified it and it became a part of the Constitution in 1992, even though the ratification process extended over a 200-year period.[11]

Two characteristics about the protection of individual rights in the Constitution should be noted. First, the Constitution's protections of individual liberties apply only to the government; private conduct generally does not have to comply with the Constitution. Only the Thirteenth Amendment, which prohibits slavery and involuntary servitude, directly protects individuals from private conduct. The principle that the Constitution restricts only the government is sometimes called the "state action doctrine"; it is discussed in Chapter 6 [Erwin Chemerinsky, Constitutional Law: Principles and Policies, 4th ed., (2011)].

Second, the Bill of Rights provisions protecting individual liberties initially were deemed to apply only to the federal government and not to state or local governments.[12] Not until the twentieth century did the Supreme Court decide that most of the Bill of Rights apply to state and local governments through the due process clause of the Fourteenth Amendment.[13] This topic also is discussed in

---

[9] *See* John P. Kaminski, Restoring the Grand Security: The Debate over a Federal Bill of Rights, 1787-1792, 33 Santa Clara L. Rev. 887 (1993).

[10] Quoted in *id.* at 919.

[11] The Twenty-seventh Amendment is discussed in more detail below in Section 4.C.

[12] *See* Barron v. Mayor & City Council of Baltimore, 32 U.S. (7 Pet.) 243 (1833).

Chapter 6 [Erwin Chemerinsky, Constitutional Law: Principles and Policies, 4th ed., (2011)].

B. Why a Constitution?

As described above, the Constitution both empowers and limits government; it creates a framework for American government, but also limits the exercise of governing authority by protecting individual rights. The underlying question is why accomplish this through a Constitution?[14] Great Britain, for example, has no written constitution.

If no constitution existed in the United States, there likely would have been some initial informal agreement creating the institutions of government, and those institutions would have determined both the procedures of government and its substantive enactments. For example, the framers at the Constitutional Convention in Philadelphia in 1787 could have served as the initial legislature and, in that capacity, devised a structure of government embodied in a statute that could have been altered by subsequent legislatures.

A Constitution Is Unique Because It Is Difficult to Change

The key difference between this approach and the Constitution is that the latter is far more difficult to change. Whereas legislative enactments can be modified by another statute, the Constitution can be amended only by a much more elaborate and difficult procedure. Article V of the Constitution prescribes two alternative ways of amending the Constitution. One is for both houses of Congress, by two-thirds vote, to propose an amendment that becomes effective when ratified by three-fourths of the states. All 27 amendments to the Constitution were adopted through this procedure. The other mechanism outlined in Article V, though never used, is for two-thirds of the states to call for Congress to convene a constitutional convention which would propose amendments for the states to consider. These amendments, too, would require approval of three-fourths of the states in order to be ratified.[15]

Therefore, a defining characteristic of the American Constitution is that it is very difficult to alter. In focusing on the question, why have a Constitution, then,

---

[13] As discussed in §6.3.3 [Erwin Chemerinsky, Constitutional Law: Principles and Policies, 4th ed., (2011)], the Court has followed the approach of "selective incorporation," concluding that the Fourteenth Amendment does not incorporate all of the Bill of Rights, but only those parts that are deemed fundamental. All of the Bill of Rights, however, have been incorporated except the Third Amendment's right to not have soldiers quartered in a person's home, the Fifth Amendment's right to grand jury indictment in criminal cases, the Seventh Amendment's right to jury trial in civil cases, and the Eighth Amendment's right against excessive fines.

[14] A systematic examination of this question is undertaken in Michael J. Klarman, What's So Great About Constitutionalism? 93 Nw. U. L. Rev. 145 (1998).

[15] Thirty-two states have passed resolutions calling for a constitutional convention to draft a balanced budget amendment. See Stewart Dalzell & Eric J. Beste, Is the Twenty-Seventh Amendment 200 Years Too Late?, 62 Geo. Wash. L. Rev. 501, 506 (1994).

the real issue is: Why should a society generally committed to majority rule choose to be governed by a document that is very difficult to change? Professor Laurence Tribe puts the question succinctly: "[W]hy would a nation that rests legality on the consent of the governed choose to constitute its political life in terms of commitments to an original agreement — made by the people, binding on their children, and deliberately structured so as to be difficult to change?"[16]

It is hardly original or profound to answer this question by observing that the framers chose to create their government in a Constitution deliberately made difficult to change as a way of preventing tyranny of the majority, of protecting the rights of the minority from oppression by social majorities. If the structure of government was placed in a statute, there might be an overwhelming tendency to create dictatorial powers in times of crisis. If protections of individual liberties were placed in statutes only, a tyrannical government could overrule them. If terms of office were specified in a statute rather than in the Constitution, those in power could alter the rules to remain in power.

Thus, a constitution represents an attempt by society to limit itself to protect the values it most cherishes. A powerful analogy can be drawn to the famous story from mythology of Ulysses and the Sirens.[17] Ulysses, fearing the Sirens' song, which seduced sailors to their death, had himself bound to the ship's mast to protect himself from temptation. Ulysses's sailors plugged their ears with wax to be immune from the Sirens' call, whereas Ulysses, tied to the mast, heard the Sirens' song but was not harmed by it. Despite Ulysses's pleas for release, his sailors followed his earlier instructions and kept him bound and unable to heed the Sirens' song. His life was saved because he recognized his weakness and protected himself from it.

A constitution is society's attempt to tie its own hands, to limit its ability to fall prey to weaknesses that might harm or undermine cherished values. History teaches that the passions of the moment can cause people to sacrifice even the most basic principles of liberty and justice. The Constitution is society's attempt to protect itself from itself. The Constitution enumerates basic values — regular elections, separation of powers, individual rights, equality — and makes change or departure very difficult.

Although the analogy between the Constitution and Ulysses is appealing, there is a problem: Ulysses tied his own hands; a Constitution binds future generations. The survival of the Constitution likely is a reflection of the widespread belief, throughout American history, that it is desirable to be governed under it. Indeed, one enormous benefit of the Constitution is that it is written in terms sufficiently general and abstract that almost everyone in society can agree to them. For example, although people disagree about what speech should be protected and under what circumstances, there is almost universal agreement that there should be freedom of speech.[18] The Constitution thus serves as a unifying device, increasing the legitimacy of government and government actions.

---

[16] Laurence Tribe, American Constitutional Law 10 (3d ed. 2000).

[17] The analogy to Ulysses is developed in Jon Elster, Ulysses and the Sirens: Studies in Rationality and Irrationality (1979). The story of Ulysses is from Homer's Odyssey, Book XII (Harper Colophon ed. 1985).

Professor Thomas Grey observed that the Constitution "has been, virtually from the moment of its ratification, a sacred symbol, the potent emblem . . . of the nation itself."[19]

Implications

Viewing the Constitution in this manner has important implications that underlie the discussion throughout this book. First, the Constitution needs to be understood as an intentionally anti-majoritarian document. Simple claims that American democracy is based on majority rule — such as in criticizing the judiciary for being anti-majoritarian — should be viewed suspiciously.[20]

Second, the Constitution should be appraised from the perspective of whether it has succeeded in restraining the majority, especially in times of crisis, and successfully protecting minorities' rights.[21] Obviously, while there have been successes, there also have been significant failures, such as in the internment of Japanese Americans during World War II,[22] the long history of discrimination against racial minorities and women, and the persecution of alleged communists during the McCarthy era.[23]

Third, viewing the Constitution as a way of protecting long-term values from short-term passions poses a basic problem in constitutional interpretation. Interpretation is crucial to allow a document written for an eighteenth-century agrarian slave society to govern in the technological world of the late-twentieth and twenty-first centuries. Yet if each generation has broad license to interpret the Constitution, can it still serve as a constraint? The debate over how the Constitution should be interpreted is discussed specifically in Section 11.B and, of course, throughout this book.

---

[18] See Herbert McClosky & Alida Brill, Dimensions of Tolerance: What Americans Believe About Civil Liberties 39 (1983) (in opinion polls 97 percent of Americans say that they believe in freedom of speech, but only 18 percent would permit the Nazi party to use a public building for a meeting and only 23 percent would allow a group denouncing the government to use a public facility).

[19] Thomas Grey, The Constitution as Scripture 1, 3 (1984); see also Sanford Levinson, Constitutional Faith (1988); Max Lerner, Constitution and Court as Symbols, 46 Yale L.J. 1290, 1296 (1937).

[20] For an excellent development of this point, see Edward L. Rubin, Getting Past Democracy, 149 U. Pa. L. Rev. 711 (2001).

[21] The relationship between the Supreme Court and popular opinion is a complex one. See Barry Friedman, The Will of the People: How Pubic Opinion Has Influenced the Supreme Court and Shaped the Meaning of the Constitution (2009).

[22] See Korematsu v. United States, 323 U.S. 214 (1944), discussed in §9.3.2 [Erwin Chemerinsky, Constitutional Law: Principles and Policies, 4th ed., (2011)].

[23] See, e.g., Dennis v. United States, 341 U.S. 494 (1951), discussed in §11.3.2.4 [Erwin Chemerinsky, Constitutional Law: Principles and Policies, 4th ed., (2011)].

C. A Brief History of the Creation and Ratification of the Constitution and Its Amendments

The Constitution of the United States must be understood as a reaction to the events that preceded it. Many of its provisions — such as the Third Amendment, which prohibits quartering of soldiers in people's homes — only make sense in the context of history. Much of what is in the Constitution is the product of compromises made at the Constitutional Convention.

The Declaration of Independence, authored by Thomas Jefferson, was signed in 1776.[24] Although it has no binding legal authority, its ringing rhetoric often is invoked by courts and its complaints about British rule foreshadowed the protections that were placed in the Constitution and its Bill of Rights. After the Revolutionary War ended in 1781 (although the formal peace treaty was not signed until 1783), the 13 colonies ratified the Articles of Confederation.

Articles of Confederation

The Articles of Confederation were the first constitution of the United States. The Articles of Confederation created a very weak national government and embodied a strong commitment that state governments retained sovereignty. Indeed, the Articles of Confederation declared that "each state retains its sovereignty, freedom, and independence, and every Power, Jurisdiction, and right, which is not by this confederation expressly delegated to the United States, in Congress assembled." Under the Articles of Confederation there was no federal judiciary and no executive. There was a Confederation Congress, but its powers were greatly circumscribed. For example, under the Articles of Confederation, Congress had the authority to wage war, coin money, establish post offices, and deal with Indian tribes. However, the Congress had no power to tax and no authority to regulate commerce among the states. As Robert Clinton remarked, "Basically, the powers granted to Congress under the Articles represented the noncontroversial powers theretofore exercised by the Parliament and the Crown under the colonial system."[25]

Not surprisingly, serious problems developed under the Articles of Confederation. Most notably, states adopted laws that discriminated against goods and services from other states. For instance, New York, as a state with a port, imposed duties on goods destined for other states. To retaliate, these states then enacted taxes on commerce with New York. Many states tried to erect trade barriers to help their own economic interests. Congress, under the Articles of Confederation, was powerless to stop this.

Also, problems developed because of the lack of national executive or judicial authority. For instance, there was no way to ensure that states would comply with laws adopted by Congress.

---

[24] For a fascinating account of the events leading up to the Declaration of Independence and how Thomas Jefferson came to write it, *see* David McCullough, John Adams (2001).

[25] Robert N. Clinton, A Brief History of the Adoption of the United States Constitution, 75 Iowa L. Rev. 891, 893 (1990).

Constitutional Convention

The Constitutional Convention met in Philadelphia from May 25 until September 17, 1787.[26] An interesting question is whether the Convention acted unlawfully in proposing a new constitution, rather than in amending the Articles of Confederation.[27] The Constitutional Convention's mandate was to propose changes to the Articles of Confederation. Moreover, the Articles of Confederation required unanimous consent for revisions, but Article VII of the Constitution specified that "[t]he Ratification of the Conventions of nine States shall be sufficient for the Establishment of this Constitution between the States."

The first vote at the Convention, on May 30, was the adoption of a resolution "that a national government ought to be established consisting of a supreme legislative, judiciary and executive."[28] Thus, the Convention immediately agreed on abandoning, rather than amending, the Articles of Confederation, and on creating a new constitution.

Two competing plans were introduced for the new government. One, termed the "Virginia plan," emphasized creating a national government with relatively strong powers and the ability to regulate the conduct of individuals. The other, called the "New Jersey plan," would have created a unicameral legislature in which all states had equal representation and would have established the Supreme Court as the only federal court. Compromises were reached. One compromise was to create two houses in Congress: one with proportional representation based on population and one in which each state would have equal representation. Another compromise was to create a Supreme Court and to leave it up to Congress to decide whether to create lower federal courts.

After passing resolutions concerning the major aspects of the new government, the Convention formed a Committee on Detail to place the resolutions into a coherent document. The Committee on Detail, for example, drafted the list of the specific powers of Congress that are found in Article I of the Constitution. Then a Committee on Style was formed to reorder and renumber the provisions and revise the language where appropriate. After the Committee on Style presented its revised draft, there was a week of relatively hurried debate.[29] On September 17, 1787, the members of the Convention approved the document, signed it, and returned home to fight for its ratification.

---

[26] The authoritative record of the Convention is Max Farrand, ed., The Records of the Federal Convention of 1787 (1966); *see* Leonard W. Levy, Making the Constitution, in Judgments: Essays on American Constitutional History 5 (L. Levy ed. 1972).

[27] *See* Bruce Ackerman & Neal Katyal, Our Unconventional Founding, 62 U. Chi. L. Rev. 475, 481-482 (1995).

[28] The Records of the Federal Convention of 1787 30 (Max Farrand ed. 1966).

[29] *See, e.g.*, Clinton, *supra* note 25, at 910 (describing this as a "week of hurried and obviously impatient debate."). A key issue debated was whether there should be a right to a jury trial in civil cases, a proposal that was rejected. *Id.*

The Ratification Process

There were heated debates in many states over whether to ratify the Constitution. Antifederalists, who opposed the ratification, emphasized the powers of the new national government and its ability to relegate state governments to a secondary and relatively unimportant role.[30] The antifederalists also stressed the absence of an enumeration of individual rights in the Constitution.

The opposition was strong in several states. For example, North Carolina refused to ratify the Constitution in 1788 and did not change its position until 1789.[31] Rhode Island did not ratify until 1790 after it was threatened with exclusion from the new nation. It is estimated that a majority of the delegates initially opposed ratification in Massachusetts, New Hampshire, New York, and Virginia.[32]

As part of the ratification debates, the Constitution was thoroughly analyzed and discussed. The most detailed and famous defense of the Constitution was a series of 85 essays written by Alexander Hamilton, James Madison, and John Jay to help persuade the New York Convention to ratify the Constitution. These are known as the Federalist Papers and are regularly cited by the Supreme Court as evidencing the framers' intent.

Pennsylvania was the first state to hold a ratifying convention, which initially met on November 20, 1787, and on December 12 voted to ratify the Constitution by a vote of 46 to 23.[33] Meanwhile, Delaware unanimously ratified the Constitution on December 7 after only three hours of debate. New Jersey and Georgia also ratified quickly, on December 18 and January 2, respectively.[34]

The decision of Massachusetts, the second largest state, was pivotal. Initially, it was clear that a majority of the delegates were antifederalists and that the Constitution was likely to be defeated. Therefore the Federalists made a deal with antifederalist Governor John Hancock, who was also the president of the Massachusetts convention. The Federalists agreed not to oppose Hancock in the upcoming gubernatorial race and to propose him for vice president.[35] With Hancock's support, Massachusetts ratified the Constitution by the slim margin of 187 to 168.[36]

Maryland was the seventh state to ratify in April 1788, and South Carolina was the eighth state in May.[37] In Virginia, the antifederalists, led by Patrick Henry, mounted a strong opposition, but ultimately Virginia approved the Constitution by a margin of 89 to 79.[38] Likewise, there were heated battles in New York

---

[30] *See* Wilson Carey McWilliams, The Anti-Federalists, Representations and Party, 84 Nw. U. L. Rev. 12 (1989); *see generally* The Complete Anti-federalist (H. Storing ed. 1981).

[31] Forrest McDonald, A Constitutional History of the United States 31 (1982).

[32] *Id.*

[33] John P. Kaminski, Restoring the Grand Security: The Debate over a Federal Bill of Rights, 1787-1792, 33 Santa Clara L. Rev. 887, 897-899 (1993).

[34] *Id.* at 900.

[35] *Id.*

[36] *Id.* at 901.

[37] *Id.* at 902.

[38] *Id.* at 908.

and New Hampshire. These states also eventually approved the Constitution; by June 1788, ten states had ratified the Constitution, one more than the nine that Article VII requires.

The Addition of the Bill of Rights

As described above, the antifederalists opposed the Constitution, in part, because it failed to enumerate individual rights. In fact, several states approved the Constitution, but with a request that the new government immediately create a bill of rights. The New York and Virginia legislatures passed resolutions calling for a constitutional convention to create a bill of rights.[39]

To prevent another constitutional convention from occurring, James Madison, then in the House of Representatives, undertook to coalesce the various amendment proposals. In proposing a Bill of Rights, Madison declared: "If [guarantees of individual rights] are incorporated in the Constitution, independent tribunals of justice will consider themselves in a peculiar manner the guardians of these rights; they will be an impenetrable bulwark against every assumption of power in the Legislature or Executive; they will be naturally led to resist every encroachment upon rights expressly stipulated for in the Constitution by the declaration of rights."[40] As mentioned above, 17 were passed by the House, 12 by the Senate, and 10 by the states.[41] These came to be known as the Bill of Rights.

New Jersey was the first state to approve the Bill of Rights on November 20, 1789, and Virginia was the last state on December 15, 1791.

Amendments

Since 1791, 17 more amendments have been added to the Constitution.[42] They fit into three major categories. One type of amendment overrules specific Supreme Court decisions. Four amendments have been adopted to overrule the Court's interpretation of the Constitution. The Eleventh Amendment overturned *Chisholm v. Georgia*[43] and provided that states could not be sued in federal court by citizens of other states or citizens of foreign countries. Section 1 of the Fourteenth Amendment overturned the Court's decision in *Dred Scott v. Sandford*[44] and made it clear that slaves are persons and that all persons born or naturalized in the United States are citizens. The Sixteenth Amendment overturned the holding in *Pollock v. Farmers' Loan & Trust Co.*,[45] and permitted Congress to enact a

---

[39] *Id.* at 908, 912.

[40] James Madison's Speech to the House of Representatives Presenting the Proposed Bill of Rights, June 8, 1789, reprinted in Daniel Farber & Suzanna Sherry, A History of the American Constitution (1990).

[41] The Senate approved an eleventh of these initial 12 amendments in 1992 when Congress passed the Twenty-seventh Amendment.

[42] For an excellent history of the use of the amendment process, *see* David E. Kyvig, Explicit and Authentic Acts: Amending the U.S. Constitution, 1776-1995 (1996).

[43] 2 U.S. (2 Dall.) 419 (1793) (holding that states could be sued in federal court by citizens of other states).

[44] 60 U.S. (19 How.) 393 (1856).

personal income tax. Most recently, the Twenty-sixth Amendment overturned *Oregon v. Mitchell*[46] and provided anyone aged 18 or over the right to vote.

Second, some amendments were adopted to correct problems in the original Constitution. For example, the Twelfth Amendment, ratified in 1804, changed the procedure whereby the runner-up in a presidential election would become vice president. For obvious reasons, it was realized that it would be preferable that the vice president be of the same party as the president, rather than the president's opponent. The Twelfth Amendment also delineates the procedure that the House of Representatives shall use to choose a president if no candidate receives a majority of the votes in the electoral college.

Also, the Twenty-fifth Amendment, adopted in 1967, creates a procedure to choose a new vice president when there is a vacancy in that office. The procedure was used in 1973, when Gerald Ford was made vice president after Spiro Agnew resigned from the vice presidency. Less than a year later, the procedure was used for a second time when Richard Nixon resigned as president, Ford ascended to that office, and Nelson Rockefeller was made vice president. The Twenty-fifth Amendment also deals with the problem of a disabled president, a topic not addressed in the Constitution. The Twentieth Amendment, ratified in 1933, deals with the potential problem of the death of a president-elect, and specifies that terms of members of Congress begin on January 3 and the president and vice president are inaugurated on January 20.

Third, and most commonly, amendments have been added to the Constitution to reflect changes in social attitudes. The Thirteenth Amendment, adopted in 1865 after the Civil War, prohibits slavery and involuntary servitude. The Fourteenth Amendment was enacted in 1868 largely to protect the rights of the newly freed slaves and in its most important provisions says that no state can deny any person of equal protection of the laws or of life, liberty, or property without due process of law. The Fifteenth Amendment, ratified in 1870, provides that the right to vote shall not be denied on account of race or previous condition of servitude.

Several other amendments also seek to change and expand the electoral process. The Seventeenth Amendment, adopted in 1913, provides for popular election of senators.[47] The Nineteenth Amendment, approved in 1920, provides that "[t]he right of citizens of the United States to vote shall not be denied or abridged by the United States or by any State on account of sex." The Twenty-third Amendment, adopted in 1961, allows the District of Columbia to cast votes in the electoral college as if it were a state, but never more than the least populous state in the country. The Twenty-fourth Amendment, ratified in 1964, states that the right to vote in federal elections cannot be "denied or abridged by the United States or any State by reason of failure to pay any poll tax or other tax."

The Twenty-second Amendment, adopted in 1951, specifies that no person shall be elected more than twice to the office of president and "no person who has held the office of President, or acted as president, for more than two years of a

---

[45] 157 U.S. 429 (1895).

[46] 400 U.S. 112 (1970).

[47] *See* Vikram Amar, Indirect Effects of a Direct Election: A Structural Examination of the Seventeenth Amendment, 49 Vand. L. Rev. 1347 (1996).

term to which some other person was elected President shall be elected to the office of the President more than once." The amendment obviously was a reaction to President Franklin Roosevelt's being elected four times to the presidency; he was the only person in history to be elected more than twice.

The Eighteenth Amendment imposed prohibition and outlawed the "manufacture, sale, or transportation of intoxicating liquors." It was repealed in 1933, 14 years after it had been enacted, by the Twenty-first Amendment.

There is a story behind each amendment and each of the countless failed amendments.[48] Perhaps the most remarkable stories surround the adoption of the Fourteenth Amendment and the most recent amendment, the Twenty-seventh Amendment.

Of all the amendments since the Bill of Rights, the Fourteenth Amendment is the most important. It bestowed citizenship on the former slaves; prohibited states from denying any person equal protection; ensured that no person could be deprived of life, liberty, or property without due process of law; and empowered Congress to adopt legislation to implement it. It is through the Fourteenth Amendment that the Bill of Rights has been applied to the states.[49] Yet of all the amendments, the Fourteenth Amendment is the most questionable in terms of the procedures followed in its ratification.

Soon after the Fourteenth Amendment was proposed, the legislatures of Georgia, North Carolina, and South Carolina rejected it.[50] Congress was furious and saw this as an attempt by Southern states to undermine the North's victory in the Civil War. Therefore, in §5 of the Reconstruction Act, Congress specified that no rebel state would be readmitted to the Union and entitled to representation in Congress until it ratified the Fourteenth Amendment.[51]

New governments were created in these states, and the three states that had rejected it, along with most of the other Southern states, then ratified the Fourteenth Amendment. However, Ohio and New Jersey, which had ratified the amendment, subsequently passed resolutions withdrawing their ratification.

Nonetheless, on July 20, 1868, the Secretary of State issued a proclamation that the required three-fourths of the states (28 of the then-existing 37 states) had ratified the amendment. His list included the Southern states that had initially rejected the amendment but had later approved it because of coercion from Congress, *and* Ohio and New Jersey, which had rescinded their ratification. The following day, Congress passed a concurrent resolution declaring that the Fourteenth Amendment was a part of the Constitution because it had been ratified by

[48] *See* David E. Kyvig, Explicit and Authentic Acts: Amending the U.S. Constitution, 1776-1995 (1996).
[49] *See* §6.3.3 [Erwin Chemerinsky, Constitutional Law: Principles and Policies, 4th ed., (2011)].
[50] *See* Coleman v. Miller, 307 U.S. 433, 448 (1939) (describing the history of the ratification of the Fourteenth Amendment).
[51] 14 Stat. 429 (1867) ("[W]hen said State, by a vote of its legislature elected under said constitution, shall have adopted the amendment to the Constitution of the United States, proposed by the Thirty-ninth Congress, and known as article fourteen, and when said article shall have become a part of the Constitution of the United States, said State shall be declared entitled to representation in Congress.")

three-fourths of the states. The list of ratifying states included Ohio and New Jersey. Many years later, the Supreme Court recited this history and said that the "decision by the political departments of the Government as to the validity of the Fourteenth Amendment has been accepted."[52]

The Twenty-seventh Amendment also has an unusual, albeit less controversial, history. The Twenty-seventh Amendment states: "No law varying the compensation for the services of the Senators and Representatives shall take effect, until an election of Representatives shall have intervened."

The Twenty-seventh Amendment was drafted by James Madison when he was a member of the House of Representatives in 1789 and was one of 12 amendments passed by the Senate and sent to the states for ratification. Ten of the amendments were ratified and became the Bill of Rights, but only five states ratified this amendment. The amendment, however, contains no "expiration clause," that is, no requirement that it be ratified by a specified date in order to be effective. Therefore, in 1873, one additional state ratified the amendment.

The amendment never was the focus of much attention, but from time to time legislators in various states were successful in having it approved. From 1873 until 1992, 32 additional states approved the amendment. In 1992, Michigan was the thirty-eighth state to ratify it, providing the requisite approval of three-fourths of the states. The amendment is now a part of the Constitution, even though it took over 200 years for it to be ratified.[53]

D. Who Should be the Authoritative Interpreter of the Constitution?

The Issue

Regardless of the method of interpretation, who should interpret the Constitution? The correct answer is that all government officials and institutions are required to engage in constitutional interpretation. All elected officeholders take an oath to uphold the Constitution. Therefore, legislators — federal, state, and local — are obliged to consider the constitutionality of bills before ratifying them. The executive must consider constitutionality in deciding what laws to propose, which bills passed by the legislature to veto, and what executive policies to implement. Ever since *Marbury v. Madison*, the judiciary has had the authority to review the constitutionality of laws and of executive acts.[54] So the real question is not who should interpret the Constitution but, more specifically, who should be

---

[52] Coleman v. Miller, 307 U.S. at 450.

[53] *See* Sanford Levinson, Authorizing Constitutional Text: On the Purported Twenty-Seventh Amendment, 11 Const. Commentary 101, 102-107 (1994); William Van Alstyne, What Do You Think About the Twenty-Seventh Amendment, 10 Const. Commentary 9 (1993); Michael Stokes Paulsen, A General Theory of Article V: The Constitutional Lessons of the Twenty-Seventh Amendment, 103 Yale L.J. 677 (1993).

[54] U.S. (1 Cranch) 137 (1803). *Marbury* is discussed in detail in §2.2.1 [Erwin Chemerinsky, Constitutional Law: Principles and Policies, 4th ed., (2011)].

the authoritative interpreter of the Constitution? When there is a disagreement over how the Constitution should be interpreted, who resolves the conflict? This is an issue that arises in many ways throughout the book.

Approach 1: No Authoritative Interpreter

There are three possible answers to the question of who should be the authoritative interpreter of the Constitution. One approach is for no branch to be regarded as authoritative in constitutional interpretation. Each branch of the government would have equal authority to determine the meaning of constitutional provisions, and conflicts would be resolved through political power and compromise. If Congress and the president believe that a law is constitutional, they could disregard a judicial ruling of unconstitutionality. If the president believes a law to be unconstitutional, he or she could refuse to enforce it, notwithstanding declarations of its constitutionality from the legislature and judiciary.

This approach to constitutional interpretation finds support early in United States history from presidents such as Thomas Jefferson and Andrew Jackson. Jefferson wrote:

> [N]othing in the Constitution has given . . . [the judges] a right to decide for the Executive, more than the Executive to decide for them. Both magistrates are equally independent in the sphere of action assigned to them. The judges, believing the law constitutional, had a right to pass a sentence of fine and imprisonment; because that power was placed in their hands by the Constitution. But the Executive, believing the law to be unconstitutional, was bound to remit the execution of it, because that power has been confided to him by the constitution. That instrument meant that its coordinate branches should be checks on each other. But the opinion which gives to the judges the right to decide what laws are constitutional, and what not, not only for themselves in their own sphere of action, but for the legislature and executive also in their spheres, would make the judiciary a despotic branch.[55]

Similarly, in vetoing a bill to recharter the Bank of the United States, President Andrew Jackson declared:

> The Congress, the Executive, and the Court must each for itself be guided by its own opinion of the Constitution. Each public officer who takes an oath to support the Constitution swears that he will support it as he understands it, and not as it is understood by others. It is as much the duty of the House of Representatives, of the Senate, and of the President to decide upon the constitutionality of any bill or resolution which may be presented to them for passage or approval as it is of the supreme judges when it may be brought before them for judicial decision. The opinion of the judges has no more authority over Congress than the opinion of Congress has over the judges, and on that point, the President is independent of both.[56]

---

[55] Thomas Jefferson, letter to Abigail Adams, September 11, 1804, 8 The Writings of Thomas Jefferson 310 (Ford ed. 1897).

[56] Andrew Jackson, Veto Message, 2 Messages and Papers of the President 576, 581-583 (Richardson ed. 1896).

In the 1980s, Attorney General Edwin Meese took exactly this position. Meese challenged the view that the judiciary is the ultimate arbiter of constitutional questions and argued that each branch has equal authority to decide for itself the meaning of constitutional provisions.[57] Meese remarked: "The Supreme Court, then, is not the only interpreter of the Constitution. Each of the three coordinate branches of government created and empowered by the Constitution — the executive and legislative no less than the judicial — has a duty to interpret the Constitution in the performance of its official functions."[58] More recently, advocates of "popular constitutionalism" have criticized what they regard as "judicial supremacy."[59] Although these terms are not defined with precision, a core aspect is to challenge the Court as ultimate arbiter of the meaning of the Constitution.[60]

Approach 2: Each Branch Is Authoritative in Certain Areas

A second approach to the question of who is the authoritative interpreter of the Constitution is that for each part of the Constitution one branch of government is assigned the role of being the final arbiter of disputes, but it is not the same branch for all parts of the Constitution. Thus, each branch would be the authoritative interpreter for some constitutional provisions. Because the Constitution does not specify who should interpret the document, some institution would need to allocate interpretive authority among the branches of government.

Arguably, the second approach is the one that best describes the current system of constitutional interpretation. The judiciary has declared that certain parts of the Constitution pose political questions and are matters to be decided by branches of government other than the courts.[61] For example, the courts frequently have held that challenges to the president's conduct of foreign policy — such as whether the Vietnam War was constitutional — pose a political question not to be resolved by the judiciary.[62] By declaring a matter to be a political question, the Court states that it is for the other branches of government to interpret the constitutional provisions in question and determine whether the Constitution is violated. The effect of the political question doctrine is that for each part of the Constitution there is a final arbiter, but it is not the same branch for all constitutional provisions.

---

[57] Edwin Meese III, The Law of the Constitution, 61 Tul. L. Rev. 979 (1987). *See also* Edwin Meese III, Putting the Federal Judiciary Back on the Constitutional Track, 14 Ga. St. U. L. Rev. 781 (1998).

[58] *Id.* at 985-986. *See also* Edward J. Hartnett, A Matter of Judgment, Not a Matter of Opinion, 74 N.Y.U. L. Rev. 123 (1999).

[59] *See, e.g.*, Larry D. Kramer, The People Themselves: Popular Constitutionalism and Judicial Review (2004). For a critique of popular constitutionalism, *see* Erwin Chemerinsky, In Defense of Judicial Review: The Perils of Popular Constitutionalism, 2004 U. Ill. L. Rev. 673.

[60] In a recent book, James MacGregor Burns wrote "that the Constitution never granted the judiciary a supremacy over the government, nor had the Framers ever conceived it." James MacGregor Burns, Packing the Court: The Rise of Judicial Power and the Coming Crisis of the Supreme Court 253 (2009).

[61] The political question doctrine is discussed in detail in Section 10.F.

[62] *See* Section 10.F.4.

Approach 3: The Judiciary Is the Authoritative Interpreter

A third and final approach is to assign to one branch of government final authority for all constitutional interpretation. Although every governmental institution interprets the Constitution, one branch is assigned the role of umpire; its views resolve disputes and are final until reversed by constitutional amendment.[63] Arguably, *Marbury v. Madison* endorses this approach in Chief Justice John Marshall's famous declaration: "It is emphatically the province and duty of the judicial department to say what the law is."[64] Similarly, in *United States v. Nixon*, the Supreme Court held that it was the judiciary's duty to determine the meaning of the Constitution.[65] In rejecting the president's claim that it was for the executive to determine the scope of executive privilege, Chief Justice Warren Burger, writing for the Court, stated: "The President's counsel . . . reads the Constitution as providing an absolute privilege of confidentiality for all Presidential communications. Many decisions of this Court, however, have unequivocally reaffirmed the holding *of Marbury v. Madison* that '[i]t is emphatically the province and duty of the judicial department to say what the law is.'"[66]

But *Marbury* and *Nixon* also can be read as ambiguous and as not resolving the question of which of these three approaches is preferable. *Marbury* could be read narrowly as holding only that the Court is the final arbiter of the meaning of Article III of the Constitution, which defines the judicial power. The specific issue in *Marbury*, which is discussed in §2.2 [Erwin Chemerinsky, Constitutional Law: Principles and Policies, 4th ed., (2011)], is whether a section of the Judiciary Act of 1789 is consistent with Article III of the Constitution. Accordingly, *Marbury* could be interpreted, consistent with the second approach described above, as assigning to the judiciary only the responsibility for interpreting Article III.

In fact, *Marbury* even could be seen as consistent with the first approach, that there is no final arbiter of the meaning of the Constitution. By this view, *Marbury* simply holds that the judiciary may interpret the Constitution in deciding cases — it is one voice — and that it is not required to defer to legislative or executive interpretations. *Marbury*, according to this argument, says nothing about whether other branches of government are bound to follow the Court's interpretation. Chief Justice Marshall's declaration could be understood as emphatically declaring that courts do have a voice.

Likewise, *United States v. Nixon* could be viewed as a limited ruling that the judiciary has the final word in cases raising the question of access to evidence necessary for criminal trials. The Court in *Nixon* emphasized the judiciary's special role in ensuring fair trials.[67] Thus, the case could be seen as holding only that the

---

[63] For an excellent scholarly exposition and development of this view, *see* Larry Alexander & Frederick Schauer, On Extrajudicial Constitutional Interpretation, 110 Harv. L. Rev. 1359 (1997).

[64] 5 U.S. at 177, *Marbury* is discussed in §2.2.1 [Erwin Chemerinsky, Constitutional Law: Principles and Policies, 4th ed., (2011)].

[65] 418 U.S. 683 (1974), discussed in §4.3 [Erwin Chemerinsky, Constitutional Law: Principles and Policies, 4th ed., (2011)].

[66] *Id.* at 703.

[67] *Id.* at 709.

Court is the final arbiter in matters relating to the judiciary's powers under Article III.

Like the debate over the method of constitutional interpretation, there is no definitive answer to the question of who should be the authoritative interpreter of the Constitution. There is an obvious benefit to having a single institution — the judiciary — resolve disputes. The federal judiciary, with its greater insulation from majoritarian politics, is arguably best suited to interpret and enforce the anti-majoritarian American Constitution. But there is also value in allowing each institution to decide for itself the meaning of the Constitution, or in allowing each branch a realm where it is the final arbiter of the Constitution's meaning. The anti-majoritarian nature of the federal judiciary is seen by some as a reason to restrict its role.

Although this issue does not often arise explicitly, it underlies many constitutional issues. For example, should there be a political question doctrine where the interpretation of particular constitutional provisions is left to the political branches of government, or should the judiciary decide these questions?[68] Can Congress use its power to create "exceptions and regulations" to the Supreme Court's appellate jurisdiction to attempt to change the law, such as by keeping the Court from hearing challenges to state abortion laws?[69] Can Congress use its powers under §5 of the Fourteenth Amendment to enact laws that interpret the amendment differently from the Supreme Court and thus effectively overrule Supreme Court decisions?[70] All of these issues require consideration of who is the authoritative interpreter of the Constitution.

---

[68] *See* Section 10.F.

[69] This topic is discussed in §2.9 [Erwin Chemerinsky, Constitutional Law: Principles and Policies, 4th ed., (2011)].

[70] Discussed in §3.6.2 [Erwin Chemerinsky, Constitutional Law: Principles and Policies, 4th ed., (2011)].

CHAPTER 5

THE FEDERAL JUDICIAL POWER

A. The Authority for Judicial Review

In studying constitutional law, you will be reading countless Supreme Court cases deciding the constitutionality of federal, state, and local laws and executive actions. Surprisingly, the Constitution is silent as to whether the Supreme Court and other federal courts have the authority to engage in such judicial review. In England, for example, both in 1787 and today, no court has the authority to invalidate an act of Parliament. In 1787, the framers of the United States Constitution, in Philadelphia, did not discuss whether the federal judiciary should have the power of judicial review.

The authority for judicial review was first announced by the Supreme Court in Marbury v. Madison in 1803.[1] *Marbury* establishes the authority for judicial review of both federal executive and legislative acts. The historical background of the case is important in understanding the decision that follows. In November 1800, the incumbent President, John Adams, lost in a hotly contested election. Thomas Jefferson received a majority of the popular vote but tied in the electoral college vote with Aaron Burr. Jefferson ultimately prevailed, based on a vote in the House of Representatives.

Adams was a Federalist, and the Federalists were determined to exercise their influence before the Republican, Jefferson, took office. In January 1801, Adams's Secretary of State, John Marshall, was named to serve as the third Chief Justice of the United States Supreme Court. Throughout the remainder of Adams's presidency, Marshall served as both Secretary of State and Chief Justice.

On February 13, 1801, Congress enacted the Circuit Judge Act, which reduced the number of Supreme Court Justices from six to five, decreasing the opportunity for Republican control of the Court. The Act also eliminated the Supreme Court Justices' duty to serve as circuit judges and created 16 new

---

[1] For excellent, in-depth analysis of Marbury v. Madison, *see* James A. O'Fallon, *Marbury*, 44 Stan. L. Rev. 219 (1992); William W. Van Alstyne, *A Critical Guide to Marbury v. Madison*, 1969 Duke L.J. 1.

judgeships on the circuit courts. However, this change was short-lived; in 1802, Congress repealed this statute, restoring the practice of circuit riding by Supreme Court Justices and eliminating the newly created circuit court judgeships. The constitutionality of congressional abolition of judgeships was not tested in the courts.

On February 27, 1801, less than a week before the end of Adams's term, Congress adopted the Organic Act of the District of Columbia, which authorized the President to appoint 42 justices of the peace. Adams announced his nominations on March 2, and on March 3, the day before Jefferson's inauguration, the Senate confirmed the nominees. Immediately, Secretary of State (and Chief Justice) John Marshall signed the commissions for these individuals and dispatched his brother, James Marshall, to deliver them. A few commissions, including one for William Marbury, were not delivered before Jefferson's inauguration. President Jefferson instructed his Secretary of State, James Madison, to withhold the undelivered commissions.

William Marbury filed suit in the United States Supreme Court seeking a writ of mandamus to compel Madison, as Secretary of State, to deliver the commission. A writ of mandamus is a petition to a court asking it to order a government officer to perform a duty. Marbury claimed that the Judiciary Act of 1789 authorized the Supreme Court to grant mandamus in a proceeding filed initially in the Supreme Court. Although Marbury's petition was filed in December 1801, the Supreme Court did not hear the case until 1803 because Congress, by statute, abolished the June and December 1802 Terms of the Supreme Court.

In reading Marbury v. Madison, it will be useful to focus on the following questions: (1) How does the Court justify judicial review of executive actions and, according to the Court, when is such judicial review available and when is it unavailable? (2) Why does the Court find the Judiciary Act of 1789 unconstitutional? and (3) How does the Court justify judicial review of legislative acts?

Marbury v. Madison

5 U.S. (1 Cranch) 137 (1803)

Mr. Chief Justice MARSHALL delivered the opinion of the court.

The following questions have been considered and decided.

1. Has the applicant a right to the commission he demands?

2. If he has a right, and that right has been violated, do the laws of his country afford him a remedy?

3. If they do afford him a remedy, is it a mandamus issuing from this court?

The first object of inquiry is,

1. Has the applicant a right to the commission he demands?

This is an appointment made by the president, by and with the advice and consent of the senate, and is evidenced by no act but the commission itself. In such a case therefore the commission and the appointment seem inseparable; it being almost impossible to show an appointment otherwise than by proving the existence of a commission: still the commission is not necessarily the appointment; though conclusive evidence of it.

In considering this question, it has been conjectured that the commission may have been assimilated to a deed, to the validity of which, delivery is essential.

It has also occurred as possible, and barely possible, that the transmission of the commission, and the acceptance thereof, might be deemed necessary to complete the right of the plaintiff. The transmission of the commission is a practice directed by convenience, but not by law.

It is therefore decidedly the opinion of the court, that when a commission has been signed by the president, the appointment is made; and that the commission is complete when the seal of the United States has been affixed to it by the secretary of state.

To withhold the commission, therefore, is an act deemed by the court not warranted by law, but violative of a vested legal right.

2. If he has a right, and that right has been violated, do the laws of his country afford him a remedy?

The very essence of civil liberty certainly consists in the right of every individual to claim the protection of the laws, whenever he receives an injury. One of the first duties of government is to afford that protection.

The government of the United States has been emphatically termed a government of laws, and not of men. It will certainly cease to deserve this high appellation, if the laws furnish no remedy for the violation of a vested legal right. It behooves us then to inquire whether there be in its composition any ingredient which shall exempt from legal investigation, or exclude the injured party from legal redress.

Is it in the nature of the transaction? Is the act of delivering or withholding a commission to be considered as a mere political act belonging to the executive department alone, for the performance of which entire confidence is placed by our constitution in the supreme executive; and for any misconduct respecting which, the injured individual has no remedy?

It follows then that the question, whether the legality of an act of the head of a department be examinable in a court of justice or not, must always depend on the nature of that act. If some acts be examinable, and others not, there must be some rule of law to guide the court in the exercise of its jurisdiction.

By the constitution of the United States, the president is invested with certain important political powers, in the exercise of which he is to use his own discretion, and is accountable only to his country in his political character, and to his own conscience. To aid him in the performance of these duties, he is authorized to appoint certain officers, who act by his authority and in conformity with his orders.

In such cases, their acts are his acts; and whatever opinion may be entertained of the manner in which executive discretion may be used, still there exists, and can exist, no power to control that discretion. The subjects are political. They respect the nation, not individual rights, and being entrusted to the executive, the decision of the executive is conclusive. The application of this remark will be perceived by adverting to the act of congress for establishing the department of foreign affairs. This officer, as his duties were prescribed by that act, is to conform precisely to the will of the president. He is the mere organ by whom that will is communicated. The acts of such an officer, as an officer, can never be examinable by the courts.

But when the legislature proceeds to impose on that officer other duties; when he is directed peremptorily to perform certain acts; when the rights of individuals are dependent on the performance of those acts; he is so far the officer of the law; is amenable to the laws for his conduct; and cannot at his discretion sport away the vested rights of others.

The conclusion from this reasoning is, that where the heads of departments are the political or confidential agents of the executive, merely to execute the will of the president, or rather to act in cases in which the executive possesses a constitutional or legal discretion, nothing can be more perfectly clear than that their acts are only politically examinable. But where a specific duty is assigned by law, and individual rights depend upon the performance of that duty, it seems equally clear that the individual who considers himself injured has a right to resort to the laws of his country for a remedy.

The question whether a right has vested or not, is, in its nature, judicial, and must be tried by the judicial authority. If, for example, Mr. Marbury had taken the oaths of a magistrate, and proceeded to act as one; in consequence of which a suit had been instituted against him, in which his defence had depended on his being a magistrate; the validity of his appointment must have been determined by judicial authority.

So, if he conceives that by virtue of his appointment he has a legal right either to the commission which has been made out for him or to a copy of that commission, it is equally a question examinable in a court, and the decision of the court upon it must depend on the opinion entertained of his appointment.

It remains to be inquired whether,

3. He is entitled to the remedy for which he applies. This depends on,

1. The nature of the writ applied for. And,
2. The power of this court.

1. The Nature of the Writ

This writ, if awarded, would be directed to an officer of government, and its mandate to him would be, to use the words of Blackstone, "to do a particular thing therein specified, which appertains to his office and duty, and which the court has previously determined or at least supposes to be consonant to right and justice." These circumstances certainly concur in this case.

Still, to render the mandamus a proper remedy, the officer to whom it is to be directed, must be one to whom, on legal principles, such writ may be directed; and the person applying for it must be without any other specific and legal remedy.

The province of the court is, solely, to decide on the rights of individuals, not to inquire how the executive, or executive officers, perform duties in which they have a discretion. Questions, in their nature political, or which are, by the constitution and laws, submitted to the executive, can never be made in this court.

If one of the heads of departments commits any illegal act, under colour of his office, by which an individual sustains an injury, it cannot be pretended that his office alone exempts him from being sued in the ordinary mode of proceeding, and being compelled to obey the judgment of the law. How then can his office exempt him from this particular mode of deciding on the legality of his conduct, if the case be such a case as would, were any other individual the party complained of, authorize the process?

It is not by the office of the person to whom the writ is directed, but the nature of the thing to be done, that the propriety or impropriety of issuing a mandamus is to be determined. Where he is directed by law to do a certain act affecting the absolute rights of individuals, in the performance of which he is not placed under the particular direction of the president, [mandamus is appropriate].

This, then, is a plain case of a mandamus, either to deliver the commission, or a copy of it from the record; and it only remains to be inquired.

Whether it can issue from this court.

The act to establish the judicial courts of the United States authorizes the supreme court "to issue writs of mandamus, in cases warranted by the principles and usages of law, to any courts appointed, or persons holding office, under the authority of the United States."

The secretary of state, being a person, holding an office under the authority of the United States, is precisely within the letter of the description; and if this court is not authorized to issue a writ of mandamus to such an officer, it must be because the law is unconstitutional, and therefore absolutely incapable of conferring the authority, and assigning the duties which its words purport to confer and assign.

In the distribution of this power it is declared that "the supreme court shall have original jurisdiction in all cases affecting ambassadors, other public ministers and consuls, and those in which a state shall be a party. In all other cases, the supreme court shall have appellate jurisdiction."

It has been insisted at the bar, that as the original grant of jurisdiction to the supreme and inferior courts is general, and the clause, assigning original jurisdiction to the supreme court, contains no negative or restrictive words; the power remains to the legislature to assign original jurisdiction to that court in other cases than those specified in the article which has been recited; provided those cases belong to the judicial power of the United States.

If it had been intended to leave it in the discretion of the legislature to apportion the judicial power between the supreme and inferior courts according to the will of that body, it would certainly have been useless to have proceeded further than to have defined the judicial power, and the tribunals in which it should be vested. The subsequent part of the section is mere surplusage, is entirely without meaning, if such is to be the construction. If congress remains at liberty to give this court appellate jurisdiction, where the constitution has declared their jurisdiction shall be original; and original jurisdiction where the constitution has declared it shall be appellate; the distribution of jurisdiction made in the constitution, is form without substance.

It cannot be presumed that any clause in the constitution is intended to be without effect; and therefore such construction is inadmissible, unless the words require it.

When an instrument organizing fundamentally a judicial system, divides it into one supreme, and so many inferior courts as the legislature may ordain and establish; then enumerates its powers, and proceeds so far to distribute them, as to define the jurisdiction of the supreme court by declaring the cases in which it shall take original jurisdiction, and that in others it shall take appellate jurisdiction, the plain import of the words seems to be, that in one class of cases its jurisdiction is original, and not appellate; in the other it is appellate, and not original. If any other construction would render the clause inoperative, that is an additional reason for rejecting such other construction, and for adhering to the obvious meaning.

It is the essential criterion of appellate jurisdiction, that it revises and corrects the proceedings in a cause already instituted, and does not create that case. Although, therefore, a mandamus may be directed to courts, yet to issue such a writ to an officer for the delivery of a paper, is in effect the same as to sustain an original action for that paper, and therefore seems not to belong to appellate, but to original jurisdiction. Neither is it necessary in such a case as this, to enable the court to exercise its appellate jurisdiction.

The authority, therefore, given to the supreme court, by the act establishing the judicial courts of the United States, to issue writs of mandamus to public officers, appears not to be warranted by the constitution; and it becomes necessary to inquire whether a jurisdiction, so conferred, can be exercised.

The question, whether an act, repugnant to the constitution, can become the law of the land, is a question deeply interesting to the United States; but, happily, not of an intricacy proportioned to its interest. It seems only necessary to recognise certain principles, supposed to have been long and well established, to decide it.

This original and supreme will organizes the government, and assigns to different departments their respective powers. It may either stop here; or establish certain limits not to be transcended by those departments.

The government of the United States is of the latter description. The powers of the legislature are defined and limited; and that those limits may not be mistaken or forgotten, the constitution is written. To what purpose are powers limited, and to what purpose is that limitation committed to writing; if these limits may, at any time, be passed by those intended to be restrained? The distinction between a government with limited and unlimited powers is abolished, if those limits do not confine the persons on whom they are imposed, and if acts prohibited and acts allowed are of equal obligation. It is a proposition too plain to be contested, that the constitution controls any legislative act repugnant to it; or, that the legislature may alter the constitution by an ordinary act.

Between these alternatives there is no middle ground. The constitution is either a superior, paramount law, unchangeable by ordinary means, or it is on a level with ordinary legislative acts, and like other acts, is alterable when the legislature shall please to alter it.

If the former part of the alternative be true, then a legislative act contrary to the constitution is not law: if the latter part be true, then written constitutions are absurd attempts, on the part of the people, to limit a power in its own nature illimitable.

Certainly all those who have framed written constitutions contemplate them as forming the fundamental and paramount law of the nation, and consequently the theory of every such government must be, that an act of the legislature repugnant to the constitution is void.

This theory is essentially attached to a written constitution, and is consequently to be considered by this court as one of the fundamental principles of our society. It is not therefore to be lost sight of in the further consideration of this subject.

If an act of the legislature, repugnant to the constitution, is void, does it, notwithstanding its invalidity, bind the courts and oblige them to give it effect? Or, in other words, though it be not law, does it constitute a rule as operative as if it was a law? This would be to overthrow in fact what was established in theory; and would seem, at first view, an absurdity too gross to be insisted on. It shall, however, receive a more attentive consideration.

It is emphatically the province and duty of the judicial department to say what the law is. Those who apply the rule to particular cases, must of necessity expound and interpret that rule. If two laws conflict with each other, the courts must decide on the operation of each.

So if a law be in opposition to the constitution: if both the law and the constitution apply to a particular case, so that the court must either decide that case conformably to the law, disregarding the constitution; or conformably to the constitution, disregarding the law: the court must determine which of these conflicting rules governs the case. This is of the very essence of judicial duty.

If then the courts are to regard the constitution; and the constitution is superior to any ordinary act of the legislature; the constitution, and not such ordinary act, must govern the case to which they both apply.

Those then who controvert the principle that the constitution is to be considered, in court, as a paramount law, are reduced to the necessity of maintaining that courts must close their eyes on the constitution, and see only the law.

This doctrine would subvert the very foundation of all written constitutions. It would declare that an act, which, according to the principles and theory of our government, is entirely void, is yet, in practice, completely obligatory. It would declare, that if the legislature shall do what is expressly forbidden, such act, notwithstanding the express prohibition, is in reality effectual. It would be giving to the legislature a practical and real omnipotence with the same breath which professes to restrict their powers within narrow limits. It is prescribing limits, and declaring that those limits may be passed at pleasure.

That it thus reduces to nothing what we have deemed the greatest improvement on political institutions — a written constitution, would of itself be sufficient, in America where written constitutions have been viewed with so much reverence, for rejecting the construction. But the peculiar expressions of the constitution of the United States furnish additional arguments in favour of its rejection.

The judicial power of the United States is extended to all cases arising under the constitution.

Could it be the intention of those who gave this power, to say that, in using it, the constitution should not be looked into? That a case arising under the constitution should be decided without examining the instrument under which it arises? This is too extravagant to be maintained.

In some cases then, the constitution must be looked into by the judges. And if they can open it at all, what part of it are they forbidden to read, or to obey?

There are many other parts of the constitution which serve to illustrate this subject.

The constitution declares that "no bill of attainder or ex post facto law shall be passed." If, however, such a bill should be passed and a person should be prosecuted under it, must the court condemn to death those victims whom the constitution endeavours to preserve?

"No person," says the constitution, "shall be convicted of treason unless on the testimony of two witnesses to the same overt act, or on confession in open court." Here the language of the constitution is addressed especially to the courts. It prescribes, directly for them, a rule of evidence not to be departed from. If the legislature should change that rule, and declare one witness, or a confession out of court, sufficient for conviction, must the constitutional principle yield to the legislative act?

From these and many other selections which might be made, it is apparent, that the framers of the constitution contemplated that instrument as a rule for the government of courts, as well as of the legislature.

Why otherwise does it direct the judges to take an oath to support it? This oath certainly applies, in an especial manner, to their conduct in their official character. How immoral to impose it on them, if they were to be used as the instruments, and the knowing instruments, for violating what they swear to support!

Why does a judge swear to discharge his duties agreeably to the constitution of the United States, if that constitution forms no rule for his government? if it is closed upon him and cannot be inspected by him.

It is also not entirely unworthy of observation, that in declaring what shall be the supreme law of the land, the constitution itself is first mentioned; and not the laws of the United States generally, but those only which shall be made in pursuance of the constitution, have that rank.

Thus, the particular phraseology of the constitution of the United States confirms and strengthens the principle, supposed to be essential to all written constitutions, that a law repugnant to the constitution is void, and that courts, as well as other departments, are bound by that instrument.

NOTES ON MARBURY v. MADISON

Marbury v. Madison establishes a number of key propositions that continue to this day. First, it creates the authority for judicial review of executive actions.

The Court draws a distinction between areas in which there are individual rights, and therefore government duties, and those in which the executive has discretion as to how to act. In the latter, the Court says that only the political process is the check on the executive branch.

Second, *Marbury* establishes that Article III is the ceiling of federal court jurisdiction. The precise holding is that Congress cannot expand the original jurisdiction of the Supreme Court. More generally, *Marbury* stands for the proposition that Article III authorizes the maximum jurisdiction of the federal courts. As a result, Congress cannot authorize federal courts to hear cases beyond what is specified in Article III, and federal courts cannot gain jurisdiction by consent.

Third, *Marbury* establishes the authority for judicial review of legislative acts. This, of course, is what Marbury v. Madison is most renowned for establishing. *Marbury* does this by declaring unconstitutional a provision of a federal law, the Judiciary Act of 1789, which the Court interprets as authorizing the Supreme Court to exercise mandamus on original jurisdiction. Yet, a careful reading of that provision makes it questionable whether the provision authorizes this. The relevant portion of section 13 of the Judiciary Act stated:

> The Supreme Court shall also have appellate jurisdiction from the circuit courts and courts of the several states, in the cases hereinafter specially provided for; . . . and shall have power to issue writs of prohibition . . . to the district courts, when proceeding as courts of admiralty and maritime jurisdiction, and writs of mandamus, in cases warranted by the principles and usages of law, to any court appointed, or persons holding office, under the authority of the United States.

The statute seems to be about appellate jurisdiction and not original jurisdiction. If the Court had interpreted the law this way, *Marbury* would have lost on jurisdictional grounds and the Court never would have had occasion to reach the issue of whether the Supreme Court can review the constitutionality of federal laws.

That, of course, is part of the brilliance of Marbury v. Madison: Chief Justice John Marshall established judicial review while declaring unconstitutional a statute that he read as expanding the Court's powers. Politically, Marshall had no choice but to deny Marbury relief; the Jefferson administration surely would have refused to comply with a court order to deliver the commission. In addition, there was a real possibility that Jefferson might seek the impeachment of the Federalist justices in an attempt to gain Republican control of the judiciary. One judge, albeit a clearly incompetent jurist, already had been impeached, and not long after his removal, the House of Representatives impeached Justice Samuel Chase on the grounds that he had made electioneering statements from the bench and had criticized the repeal of the 1801 Circuit Court Act. Yet John Marshall did more than simply rule in favor of the Jefferson administration; he used the occasion of deciding Marbury v. Madison to establish the power of the judiciary and to articulate a role for the federal courts that survives to this day.

The Supreme Court did not declare another federal statute unconstitutional until 1857 in the infamous case of Dred Scott v. Sandford, 60 U.S. (19 How.) 393 (1857), which invalidated the Missouri Compromise and helped to precipitate the Civil War.[2] By then, the power of the Court to consider the constitutionality of federal laws was an accepted part of American government.

Marbury v. Madison has been invoked by the Supreme Court in some of the most important cases in American history. For example, in Cooper v. Aaron, 358 U.S. 1 (1958), the Supreme Court responded to Arkansas's refusal to obey a federal court order desegregating the Little Rock public schools by relying on the authority of Marbury v. Madison. In an unusual opinion, signed individually by each Justice, the Court rejected Arkansas's position and emphatically declared: "Article VI of the Constitution makes the Constitution 'the supreme Law of the Land.' . . . Marbury v. Madison . . . declared the basic principle that the federal judiciary is supreme in the exposition of the law of the Constitution, and that principle has ever since been respected by this Court and the Country as a permanent and indispensable feature of our constitutional system. . . . Every state legislator and executive and judicial officer is solemnly committed by oath . . . 'to support this Constitution.'"

Similarly, in United States v. Nixon, 418 U.S. 683 (1974), the Supreme Court ordered President Richard Nixon to produce tapes of White House conversations in connection with the Watergate investigation. In response to the President's claims that he alone should determine the scope of executive privilege, Chief Justice Warren Burger, writing for the Court, stated: "The President's counsel . . . reads the Constitution as providing an absolute privilege of confidentiality for all Presidential communications. Many decisions of this Court, however, have unequivocally reaffirmed the holding of Marbury v. Madison that '[i]t is emphatically the province and duty of the judicial department to say what the law is.'"

Marbury v. Madison thus provides the foundation for American constitutional law by establishing the authority for judicial review of executive and legislative acts.

AUTHORITY FOR JUDICIAL REVIEW OF STATE JUDGMENTS

Marbury v. Madison establishes only the authority for judicial review of federal executive and legislative actions. The authority for judicial review of state court decisions was established in two decisions early in the nineteenth century: Martin v. Hunter's Lessee and Cohens v. Virginia.

---

[2] *Dred Scott* is discussed in Chapter 7 [Erwin Chemerinsky, Constitutional Law, 3rd ed., (2009)], which focuses on equal protection.

MARTIN v. HUNTER'S LESSEE, 14 U.S. (1 Wheat.) 304 (1816):   There were two competing claims to certain land within the state of Virginia. Martin claimed title to the land based on inheritance from Lord Fairfax, a British citizen who owned the property. The United States and England had entered into two treaties protecting the rights of British citizens to own land in the United States. However, Hunter claimed that Virginia had taken the land before the treaties came into effect and, hence, Martin did not have a valid claim to the property.

The Virginia Court of Appeals ruled in favor of Hunter and, in essence, in favor of the state's authority to have taken and disposed of the land. The United States Supreme Court issued a writ of error and reversed the Virginia decision. The Supreme Court held that the federal treaty was controlling and that it established Lord Fairfax's ownership and thus the validity of inheritance pursuant to his will. The Virginia Court of Appeals, however, declared that the Supreme Court lacked the authority to review state court decisions. The Virginia court stated that the "Courts of the United States, therefore, belonging to one sovereignty, cannot be appellate Courts in relation to the State Courts, which belong to a different sovereignty — and, of course, their commands or instructions impose no obligation."

The United States Supreme Court again granted review and declared the authority to review state court judgments. Justice Joseph Story wrote the opinion for the Court. Chief Justice John Marshall did not participate because he and his brother had contracted to purchase a large part of the Fairfax estate that was at issue in the litigation.

Justice Story argued that the structure of the Constitution presumes that the Supreme Court may review state court decisions. Story argued that the Constitution creates a Supreme Court and gives Congress discretion whether to create lower federal courts. But if Congress chose not to establish such tribunals, then the Supreme Court would be powerless to hear any cases, except for the few fitting within its original jurisdiction, unless it could review state court rulings.

Additionally, Justice Story explained the importance of Supreme Court review of state courts. Justice Story said that although he assumed that "judges of the state courts are, and always will be, of as much learning, integrity, and wisdom as those of courts of the United States," the Constitution is based on a recognition that "state attachments, state prejudices, state jealousies, and state interests might sometimes obstruct, or control, or be supposed to obstruct or control, the regular administration of justice." Furthermore, Justice Story observed that Supreme Court review is essential to ensure uniformity in the interpretation of federal law. Justice Story concluded that the very nature of the Constitution, the contemporaneous understanding of it, and many years of experience all established the Supreme Court's authority to review state court decisions.

COHENS v. VIRGINIA, 19 U.S. (6 Wheat.) 264 (1821):   Two brothers were convicted in Virginia state court of selling District of Columbia lottery tickets in violation of Virginia law. The defendants sought review in the United States Supreme Court because they claimed the Constitution prevented their prosecution for selling tickets authorized by Congress. Virginia argued: (1) in general, the Supreme Court had no authority to review state court decisions; and (2) in particular, review was not allowed in criminal cases and in cases where a state government was a party.

The Supreme Court, in an opinion by Chief Justice John Marshall, reaffirmed the constitutionality of §25 of the Judiciary Act and the authority of the Supreme Court to review state court judgments. The Court emphasized that state courts often could not be trusted to adequately protect federal rights because "[i]n many States the judges are dependent for office and for salary on the will of the legislature." The Court thus declared that criminal defendants could seek Supreme Court review when they claimed that their conviction violated the Constitution.

B. Limits on the Federal Judicial Power

The judicial power to say what the law is gives to unelected federal judges great authority. There thus has been an ongoing, unresolved debate over how this power is constrained and whether the limits on judicial authority are sufficient. Three primary limits exist: interpretive limits; congressional limits; and justiciability limits. Interpretive limits raise the question of how the Constitution should be interpreted; some approaches seek to greatly narrow the judicial power, while others accord judges broad latitude in deciding the meaning of the Constitution. Congressional limits refer to the ability of Congress to restrict federal court jurisdiction. Justiciability limits refer to a series of judicially created doctrines that limit the types of matters that federal courts can decide.

1. *Interpretive Limits*

Much of the Constitution is written in broad, open-textured language. How should the Court, or anyone seeking to interpret the Constitution, give meaning to these words? What weight should be given to the text, to the framers' intent, to the practices at the time the constitutional provision was adopted, to tradition, to social policy needs? There is no agreement among Justices or scholars as to the appropriate method of constitutional interpretation. Yet the resolution of every issue of constitutional law turns on this question.

The issue of how courts should interpret the Constitution is particularly controversial and, of course, at the core of the issues discussed throughout this book. On the one hand, some believe that it is essential that the Court's discretion in interpreting the Constitution be narrowly circumscribed to limit the judicial power. They argue that democracy means rule by electorally accountable officials and that judicial review by unelected federal judges is inconsistent with this. The late Yale Law Professor Alexander Bickel said that judicial review is a "deviant institution in American democracy" because it permits unelected judges to overturn the decisions of popularly accountable officials.[3] Robert Bork similarly

---

[3] Alexander Bickel, *The Least Dangerous Branch* 18 (1962).

remarked that a "Court that makes rather than implements value choices cannot be squared with the presuppositions of a democratic society."[4]

Those adopting this approach seek to constrain courts interpreting the Constitution. Some argue, for example, that the Court is justified in protecting constitutional rights only if they are clearly stated in the text or intended by the framers. Those who adopt this theory, often called originalism, defend it as a desirable way to limit unelected judges in a democratic society.[5] Originalism is the view that "judges deciding constitutional issues should confine themselves to enforcing norms that are stated or clearly implicit in the written Constitution."[6]

Others disagree with these theories and argue that it is desirable for the Court to have substantial discretion in determining the meaning of the Constitution. Often called "non-originalists," they argue that it is important that the Constitution evolve by interpretation and not only by amendment. Non-originalism is the "view that courts should go beyond that set of references and enforce norms that cannot be discovered within the four corners of the document."[7] The claim is that non-originalist review is essential so that the Constitution does not remain virtually static, so that it can evolve to meet the needs of a society that is advancing technologically and morally.

Non-originalists argue, for example, that equal protection in the last half of the twentieth century must mean that government-mandated racial segregation is unacceptable; yet there is strong evidence that the framers of the Fourteenth Amendment approved this practice. The drafters of the Equal Protection Clause did not intend to protect women from discrimination, but it is widely accepted that the Clause should apply to gender discrimination. Indeed, the argument is made that under originalism it would be unconstitutional to elect a woman as President or Vice President because the Constitution refers to these office-holders with the word, "he," and the framers clearly intended that they be male.

Originalists believe that the Court should find a right to exist in the Constitution only if it is expressly stated in the text or was clearly intended by its framers. If the Constitution is silent, originalists say it is for the legislature, unconstrained by the courts, to decide the law. Non-originalists think that it is permissible for the Court to interpret the Constitution to protect rights that are not expressly stated or clearly intended. Originalists believe that the Constitution should evolve solely by amendment; non-originalists believe that the Constitution's meaning can evolve by amendment and by interpretation.

But within these theories there are a wide range of different approaches. Some originalists argue that the framers' specific intent must be followed, while others maintain that only the framers' abstract intent is controlling. Justice Scalia has argued that the focus should not be on the framers' intentions, but on the meaning of the Constitution as evidenced by the text and the practices at the time the Constitution was ratified. Similarly, among non-originalists there are those who emphasize tradition, those who stress natural law principles, those who say

---

[4] Robert Bork, *Neutral Principles and Some First Amendment Problems*, 47 Ind. L.J. 1, 6 (1971).
[5] *See, e.g.*, Raoul Berger, *Ely's Theory of Judicial Review*, 42 Ohio St. L.J. 87, 87 (1981).
[6] John Hart Ely, *Democracy and Distrust* 1 (1980).
[7] *Id.*

constitutional law should be about improving the processes of government, those who emphasize contemporary values, and other variants too. Often, the Supreme Court has looked to tradition in deciding whether a right is protected by the Constitution.[8]

The debate over how the Constitution should be interpreted — and the extent to which the method of interpretation should limit the judiciary — arises in all areas of constitutional law.

2. Congressional Limits

Article III of the Constitution provides that the "Supreme Court shall have appellate jurisdiction, both as to Law and Fact, with such Exceptions, and under such Regulations as the Congress shall make." May Congress use this authority to restrict Supreme Court jurisdiction to hear particular types of cases so as to effectively overrule Supreme Court decisions? There is no definitive answer to this question, although many proposals have been introduced into Congress in an attempt to restrict jurisdiction to change the substantive law.

For example, during the 1950s, the Supreme Court invalidated some loyalty oaths for government workers and attorneys.[9] In response, the Jennings-Butler Bill was introduced in the United States Senate to prevent review of State Board of Bar Examiners' decisions concerning who could practice law in a state.[10] Altogether, since the 1940s, over 100 proposals were introduced in Congress to restrict federal court jurisdiction over particular topics.[11] During the 1980s, there were proposals in Congress to prevent federal courts from hearing cases involving challenges to state laws permitting school prayers or state laws restricting access to abortions.[12] Most recently, in June 2004, the House of Representatives passed a bill to prevent the Supreme Court or lower federal courts from interpreting or hearing challenges to the Defense of Marriage Act.[13] And in September 2004, the House passed a bill to preclude judicial review of the constitutionality of the Pledge of Allegiance.[14]

In large part, the debate centers on two major constitutional issues: What does the language of Article III mean when it says that Supreme Court jurisdiction

---

[8] Compare Bowers v. Hardwick, 478 U.S. 186 (1986) (refusing to find constitutional protection for a right to engage in private consensual homosexual activity, in part, because of the lack of a tradition of providing such protection), with Moore v. City of East Cleveland, Ohio, 431 U.S. 494 (1977) (finding constitutional protection for the right of an extended family to live together because of the tradition of protecting such families). Both cases are presented in Chapter 8 [Erwin Chemerinsky, Constitutional Law, 3rd ed., (2009)].

[9] See, e.g., Schware v. Board of Bar Examiners, 353 U.S. 232 (1957); Konigsberg v. State Bar, 353 U.S. 252 (1957).

[10] S. 3386, 85th Cong., 2d Sess. (1958).

[11] Paul Bator, Daniel Meltzer, Paul Mishkin, & David Shapiro, Hart & Wechsler's The Federal Courts and the Federal System 377 (3d ed. 1988).

[12] See, e.g., S. 158, 97th Cong., 1st Sess. (1981); H.R. 3225, 97th Cong., 1st Sess. (1981) (bills restricting federal court jurisdiction in abortion cases); S. 481, 97th Cong., 1st Sess. (1981); H.R. 4756, 97th Cong., 1st Sess. (1981) (bills restricting federal court jurisdiction over cases that involve voluntary school prayers).

[13] H.R. 3313, 108th Cong., 2d Sess. (2004).

[14] H.R. 2023, 108th Cong., 2d Sess. (2004).

exists subject to such "exceptions and regulations" as Congress shall make? Does separation of powers limit the ability of Congress to restrict Supreme Court jurisdiction?

THE EXCEPTIONS AND REGULATIONS CLAUSE

Even after more than 200 years of American history, there is no consensus as to what the Constitution means when it provides that the Supreme Court possesses appellate jurisdiction "both as to Law and Fact, with such Exceptions, and under such Regulations as the Congress shall make." On one side of the debate are those who believe that this provides Congress with broad powers to remove matters from the Supreme Court's purview. The argument, in part, is that the framers of the Constitution intended such congressional control as a check on the judiciary's power.[15] Evidence of this intent, it is argued, is found in the fact that the first Congress did not vest the Supreme Court with appellate jurisdiction over all of the types of cases and controversies enumerated in Article III. For example, under the Judiciary Act of 1789, the Supreme Court had authority only to review decisions of a state's highest court that ruled against a federal constitutional claim.[16] It was not until the twentieth century that the Supreme Court was accorded power to review decisions of a state court that ruled in favor of a constitutional right.[17]

On the other side of the debate are those who believe that Congress is limited in its ability to control Supreme Court jurisdiction. Some argue that the term "Exceptions" in Article III was intended to modify the word "Fact."[18] The contention is that the framers were concerned about the Supreme Court's ability to overturn fact-finding by lower courts, especially when done by juries. Under this view, Congress could create an exception to the Supreme Court's jurisdiction for review of matters of fact, but Congress could not eliminate the Court's appellate jurisdiction for issues of law.

Alternatively, it is argued that even though Congress is given authority to limit Supreme Court jurisdiction under the text of Article III, this power — like all congressional powers — cannot be used in a manner that violates the Constitution. Opponents of jurisdiction restriction contend that congressional preclusion of Supreme Court review of particular topics would violate other parts of the Constitution.[19]

---

[15] *See, e.g.,* Herbert Wechsler, *The Courts and the Constitution*, 65 Colum. L. Rev. 1001, 1005-1006 (1965).

[16] Act of Sept. 24, 1789, 1 Stat. 73; *see* Peter W. Low & John Jeffries, Jr., *Federal Courts and the Law of Federal-State Relations* 171 (3d ed. 1994).

[17] Act of Dec. 23, 1914, 38 Stat. 790.

[18] *See* Raoul Berger, *Congress v. The Supreme Court* 285-296 (1969).

[19] *See, e.g.,* Leonard G. Ratner, *Congressional Power over the Appellate Jurisdiction of the Supreme Court*, 109 U. Pa. L. Rev. 157 (1960); Lawrence Gene Sager, *Foreword: Constitutional Limitations on Congress' Authority to Regulate the Jurisdiction of the Federal Courts*, 95 Harv. L. Rev. 17 (1981); Laurence A. Tribe, *Jurisdictional Gerrymandering: Zoning Disfavored Rights out of the Federal Courts*, 16 Harv. C.R.-C.L. L. Rev. 129 (1981).

The primary Supreme Court case interpreting the Exceptions and Regulations Clause is Ex parte McCardle. In reading *McCardle*, consider whether it is precedent for a federal law precluding Supreme Court review of particular types of cases or whether it is distinguishable.

Ex Parte McCardle

74 U.S. 506 (1868)

[McCardle was a newspaper editor in Vicksburg, Mississippi, who was arrested by federal officials for writing a series of newspaper articles that were highly critical of Reconstruction and especially of the military rule of the South following the Civil War. McCardle filed a petition for a writ of habeas corpus pursuant to a statute adopted in 1867 that permitted federal courts to grant habeas corpus relief to anyone held in custody in violation of the Constitution or laws of the United States by either a state government or the federal government. Before 1867, under the Judiciary Act of 1789, which was supplemented but not replaced by the 1867 law, federal courts could hear habeas petitions only of those who were held in federal custody.

McCardle contended that the Military Reconstruction Act was unconstitutional in that it provided for military trials for civilians. He also claimed that his prosecution violated specific Bill of Rights' provisions, including the First, Fifth, and Sixth Amendments. The United States government argued that the federal courts lacked jurisdiction to grant habeas corpus to McCardle under the 1867 Act. The federal government read the 1867 statute, despite its language to the contrary, as providing federal court relief only for state prisoners. The Supreme Court rejected this contention and set the case for argument on the merits of McCardle's claim that the Military Reconstruction Act and his prosecution were unconstitutional.

On March 9, 1868, the Supreme Court held oral arguments on McCardle's constitutional claims. Three days later, on March 12, 1868, Congress adopted a rider to an inconsequential tax bill that repealed that part of the 1867 statute that authorized Supreme Court appellate review of writs of habeas corpus. Members of Congress stated that their purpose was to remove the *McCardle* case from the Supreme Court's docket and thus prevent the Court from potentially invalidating Reconstruction. Representative Wilson declared that the "amendment [repealing Supreme Court authority under the 1867 Act is] aimed at striking at a branch of the jurisdiction of the Supreme Court . . . thereby sweeping the [*McCardle*] case from the docket by taking away the jurisdiction of the Court."

On March 25, 1868, President Andrew Johnson vetoed the attempted repeal of Supreme Court jurisdiction. This was five days before the Senate was scheduled to begin its impeachment trial of President Johnson and the grounds for impeachment focused solely on his alleged obstruction of Reconstruction. Congress immediately overrode President Johnson's veto on March 27, 1868.

The Supreme Court then considered whether it had jurisdiction to hear McCardle's constitutional claims in light of the recently adopted statute denying it authority to hear appeals under the 1867 Act that was the basis for jurisdiction in McCardle's petition.]

Chief Justice CHASE delivered the opinion of the court.

The first question necessarily is that of jurisdiction; for, if the act of March, 1868, takes away the jurisdiction defined by the act of February, 1867, it is useless, if not improper, to enter into any discussion of other questions.

It is quite true, as was argued by the counsel for the petitioner, that the appellate jurisdiction of this court is not derived from acts of Congress. It is, strictly speaking, conferred by the Constitution. But it is conferred "with such exceptions and under such regulations as Congress shall make."

It is unnecessary to consider whether, if Congress had made no exceptions and no regulations, this court might not have exercised general appellate jurisdiction under rules prescribed by itself. The exception to appellate jurisdiction in the case before us, however, is not an inference from the affirmation of other appellate jurisdiction. It is made in terms. The provision of the act of 1867, affirming the appellate jurisdiction of this court in cases of habeas corpus is expressly repealed. It is hardly possible to imagine a plainer instance of positive exception.

We are not at liberty to inquire into the motives of the legislature. We can only examine into its power under the Constitution; and the power to make exceptions to the appellate jurisdiction of this court is given by express words.

What, then, is the effect of the repealing act upon the case before us? We cannot doubt as to this. Without jurisdiction the court cannot proceed at all in any cause. Jurisdiction is power to declare the law, and when it ceases to exist, the only function remaining to the court is that of announcing the fact and dismissing the cause. And this is not less clear upon authority than upon principle.

It is quite clear, therefore, that this court cannot proceed to pronounce judgment in this case, for it has no longer jurisdiction of the appeal; and judicial duty is not less fitly performed by declining ungranted jurisdiction than in exercising firmly that which the Constitution and the laws confer.

Counsel seem to have supposed, if effect be given to the repealing act in question, that the whole appellate power of the court, in cases of habeas corpus, is denied. But this is an error. The act of 1868 does not except from that jurisdiction any cases but appeals from Circuit Courts under the act of 1867. It does not affect the jurisdiction which was previously exercised.

NOTES ON EX PARTE MCCARDLE

Less than a year after its decision in *McCardle*, the Supreme Court in Ex parte Yerger, 75 U.S. (8 Wall.) 85 (1868), held that it had authority to review habeas corpus decisions of lower federal courts under the Judiciary Act of 1789. Like *McCardle, Yerger* involved a newspaper editor's challenge to the constitutionality of the Military Reconstruction Act. After the Supreme Court upheld its jurisdiction to decide Yerger's constitutional claims, the federal military authorities dismissed all charges against him, thereby again preventing Supreme Court review of the constitutionality of Reconstruction.

SEPARATION OF POWERS AS A LIMIT ON CONGRESS'S AUTHORITY

To what extent does separation of powers limit the ability of Congress to exercise control over Supreme Court decision making? The primary Supreme Court decision finding a federal law unconstitutional on the grounds that it violates separation of powers is United States v. Klein. In reading *Klein*, consider what limits it imposes on Congress's ability to control or restrict Supreme Court jurisdiction.

United States v. Klein

80 U.S. 128 (1871)

Chief Justice CHASE delivered the opinion of the court.

[In 1863, Congress adopted a statute providing that individuals whose property was seized during the Civil War could recover the property, or compensation for it, upon proof that they had not offered aid or comfort to the enemy during the war. The Supreme Court subsequently held that a presidential pardon fulfilled the statutory requirement of demonstrating that an individual was not a supporter of the rebellion.

In response to this decision and frequent pardons issued by the president, Congress quickly adopted a statute providing that a pardon was inadmissible as evidence in a claim for return of seized property. Moreover, the statute provided that a pardon, without an express disclaimer of guilt, was proof that the person aided the rebellion and would deny the federal courts jurisdiction over the claims. The statute declared that upon "proof of such pardon . . . the jurisdiction of the court in the case shall cease, and the court shall forthwith dismiss the suit of such claimant."]

The substance of this enactment is that an acceptance of a pardon, without disclaimer, shall be conclusive evidence of the acts pardoned, but shall be null and void as evidence of the rights conferred by it, both in the Court of Claims and in this court on appeal.

It was urged in argument that the right to sue the government in the Court of Claims is a matter of favor; but this seems not entirely accurate. It is as much the duty of the government as of individuals to fulfil its obligations. Before the establishment of the Court of Claims claimants could only be heard by Congress. That court was established in 1855 for the triple purpose of relieving Congress, and of protecting the government by regular investigation, and of benefiting the claimants by affording them a certain mode of examining and adjudicating upon their claims. It was required to hear and determine upon claims founded upon any law of Congress, or upon any regulation of an executive department, or upon any contract, express or implied, with the government of the United States.

Undoubtedly the legislature has complete control over the organization and existence of that court and may confer or withhold the right of appeal from its decisions. And if this act did nothing more, it would be our duty to give it effect. If it simply denied the right of appeal in a particular class of cases, there could be no doubt that it must be regarded as an exercise of the power of Congress to make "such exceptions from the appellate jurisdiction" as should seem to it expedient.

But the language of the proviso shows plainly that it does not intend to withhold appellate jurisdiction except as a means to an end. Its great and controlling purpose is to deny to pardons granted by the President the effect which this court had adjudged them to have. The proviso declares that pardons shall not be considered by this court on appeal. We had already decided that it was our duty to consider them and give them effect, in cases like the present, as equivalent to proof of loyalty. It provides that whenever it shall appear that any judgment of the Court of Claims shall have been founded on such pardons, without other proof of loyalty, the Supreme Court shall have no further jurisdiction of the case and shall dismiss the same for want of jurisdiction. The proviso further declares that every pardon granted to any suitor . . . if accepted in writing without disclaimer of the fact recited, be taken as conclusive evidence in that court and on appeal, of the act recited; and on proof of pardon or acceptance, summarily made on motion or otherwise, the jurisdiction of the court shall cease and the suit shall be forthwith dismissed.

It is evident from this statement that the denial of jurisdiction to this court, as well as to the Court of Claims, is founded solely on the application of a rule of decision, in causes pending, prescribed by Congress. The court has jurisdiction of the cause to a given point; but when it ascertains that a certain state of things exists, its jurisdiction is to cease and it is required to dismiss the cause for want of jurisdiction.

It seems to us that this is not an exercise of the acknowledged power of Congress to make exceptions and prescribe regulations to the appellate power.

The court is required to ascertain the existence of certain facts and thereupon to declare that its jurisdiction on appeal has ceased, by dismissing the bill. What is this but to prescribe a rule for the decision of a cause in a particular way? In the case before us, the Court of Claims has rendered judgment for the claimant and an appeal has been taken to this court. We are directed to dismiss the appeal, if we find that the judgment must be affirmed, because of a pardon granted to the intestate of the claimants. Can we do so without allowing one party to the controversy to decide it in its own favor? Can we do so without allowing that the legislature may prescribe rules of decision to the Judicial Department of the government in cases pending before it?

We must think that Congress has inadvertently passed the limit which separates the legislative from the judicial power. It is of vital importance that these powers be kept distinct. The Constitution provides that the judicial power of the United States shall be vested in one Supreme Court and such inferior courts as the Congress shall from time to time ordain and establish. The same instrument, in the last clause of the same article, provides that in all cases other than those of original jurisdiction, "the Supreme Court shall have appellate jurisdiction both as to law and fact, with such exceptions and under such regulations as the Congress shall make."

Congress has already provided that the Supreme Court shall have jurisdiction of the judgments of the Court of Claims on appeal. Can it prescribe a rule in conformity with which the court must deny to itself the jurisdiction thus conferred, because and only because its decision, in accordance with settled law, must be adverse to the government and favorable to the suitor? This question seems to us to answer itself.

The rule prescribed is also liable to just exception as impairing the effect of a pardon, and thus infringing the constitutional power of the Executive. It is the intention of the Constitution that each of the great co-ordinate departments of the government — the Legislative, the Executive, and the Judicial — shall be, in its sphere, independent of the others. To the executive alone is intrusted the power of pardon; and it is granted without limit. Pardon includes amnesty. It blots out the offence pardoned and removes all its penal consequences. It may be granted on conditions. In these particular pardons, that no doubt might exist as to their character, restoration of property was expressly pledged, and the pardon was granted on condition that the person who availed himself of it should take and keep a prescribed oath.

NOTES ON UNITED STATES v. KLEIN

There have been many occasions in which Congress has reacted to a Supreme Court decision interpreting a statute by adopting a law effectively overruling the Court's ruling. In essence, Congress is directing the results in future cases. The key question is whether this is distinguishable from *Klein*. The Supreme Court distinguished *Klein* in the following more recent case:

ROBERTSON v. SEATTLE AUDUBON SOCIETY, 503 U.S. 429 (1992): The Department of Interior and Related Agencies Appropriations Act of 1990 required the Bureau of Land Management to offer specified land for sale and also imposed restrictions on harvesting from other land. Additionally, the Act expressly noted two pending cases and said that "Congress hereby determines and directs that management of areas according to subsections (b)(3) and (b)(5) of this section on [the specified lands] is adequate consideration for the purpose of meeting the statutory requirements that are the basis for [the two lawsuits]."

The Supreme Court rejected the argument that Congress was directing the outcome of the pending litigation. The Supreme Court held that Congress had changed the law itself and did not direct findings or results under the old law. The Court said that *Klein* applies in a situation where Congress directs the judiciary as to decision making under an existing law and does not apply when Congress adopts a new law. The Court found that as a new law the statute was constitutional.

These cases establish no clear principles as to what the phrase "exceptions and regulations" means or when separation of powers prevents Congress from changing the law in response to a Supreme Court decision interpreting a statute. Ultimately, the arguments about Congress's ability to check the federal judiciary, like so many areas of constitutional law, turn on disputes about the meaning of the Constitution's language, the intent of its framers, and the competing policy considerations.

CHAPTER 6

THE FEDERAL LEGISLATIVE POWER

A. Introduction: Congress and the States

When may Congress act? What laws may Congress adopt? A basic principle of American government is that Congress may act only if there is express or implied authority in the Constitution, whereas states may act unless the Constitution prohibits the action. Article I of the Constitution, which creates the federal legislative power, begins by stating: "All legislative powers herein granted shall be vested in a Congress of the United States which shall consist of a Senate and House of Representatives." Additionally, the Tenth Amendment declares: "The powers not delegated to the United States by the Constitution, nor prohibited by it to the States, are reserved to the States respectively, or to the people."

In evaluating the constitutionality of any act of Congress, there are always two questions. First, does Congress have the authority under the Constitution to legislate? This requires defining the scope of the powers granted to Congress, particularly in Article I, §8 of the Constitution. Second, if so, does the law violate another constitutional provision or doctrine, such as by infringing separation of powers or interfering with individual liberties?

In answering both of these questions the issue has arisen throughout American history as to the extent to which concern for state governments and their prerogatives should matter. During some eras of constitutional history, such as between the late nineteenth century and 1937 and again in the past decade, concern for state governments has profoundly answered how the Court has dealt with both of these questions. The Court during these times limited Congressional power to leave areas of governance to state governments. During these times, the Court also directly protected state sovereignty, concluding that even valid exercises of legislative power are unconstitutional when they infringe state sovereignty. The Court has used the Tenth Amendment as the basis for this protection of state governments from federal encroachment.

During other times of American history, however, the Court has refused to use concern over state governments either as a basis for narrowly interpreting the scope of Congress's powers or as a limit through the Tenth Amendment on the reach of federal legislation. From the 1930s until the 1990s, the Court broadly defined the scope of Congress's authority under Article I of the Constitution and refused to use the Tenth Amendment as a limit on federal power.

In other words, throughout American history, Congress's powers have been defined relative to the states. Some of the most important political battles in American history — abolition of slavery, Reconstruction, progressive labor legislation, the New Deal, the Civil Rights movement — have been fought over how power should be allocated between the federal and state governments.

The division of power between Congress and the states is the focus of this chapter. The chapter considers how Congress's powers enumerated in the Constitution should be defined. It also considers whether and when the Tenth Amendment, and its protection of state governments, is and should be a limit on Congressional power.

The chapter begins with McCulloch v. Maryland, an enormously important case concerning the relationship between federal and state governments. Following *McCulloch*, the issue is raised as to the values to be gained and lost by safeguarding state government entities. Subsequent sections of this chapter examine particular federal powers, especially Congress's Commerce Clause authority (section 6.B), its taxing and spending power (section C [Erwin Chemerinsky, Constitutional Law, 3rd ed., (2009)]), its authority under §5 of the Fourteenth Amendment (section 6.D), and its power to authorize suits against state governments (section E [Erwin Chemerinsky, Constitutional Law, 3rd ed., (2009)]).

THE FRAMEWORK FOR ANALYSIS: MCCULLOCH v. MARYLAND

McCulloch v. Maryland is the most important Supreme Court decision in American history defining the scope of Congress's powers and delineating the relationship between the federal government and the states. The issue in *McCulloch* is whether it is constitutional for the State of Maryland to tax the Bank of the United States.

Some historical background is likely to be useful in understanding the decision. The controversy over the Bank of the United States began early in George Washington's presidency, in 1790, with a major dispute in both Congress and the executive branch as to whether Congress had the authority to create such a bank.[1] Secretary of the Treasury Alexander Hamilton strongly favored creating a Bank of the United States, but he was opposed by Secretary of State Thomas Jefferson and Attorney General Edmund Randolph. Both Jefferson and Randolph argued that Congress lacked the authority under the Constitution to create such a bank and that doing so would usurp state government prerogatives. Ultimately, Hamilton

---

[1] A thorough discussion of the history of the Bank of the United States can be found in 1 Charles Warren, *The Supreme Court in United States History* 499-540 (1st ed. 1922).

persuaded President George Washington to support creating the bank, but the debate continued in Congress. James Madison, then in the House of Representatives, echoed the views of Jefferson and Randolph, and opposed the bank. Despite this opposition, Congress created the first Bank of the United States.

The bank existed for 21 years until its charter expired in 1811. However, after the War of 1812, the country experienced serious economic problems, and the Bank of the United States was re-created in 1816. In fact, although he had opposed such a bank a quarter of a century earlier, President James Madison endorsed its re-creation. The U.S. government actually owned only 20 percent of the new bank.

The Bank of the United States did not solve the country's economic problems and, indeed, many blamed the bank's monetary policies for aggravating a serious depression. State governments were particularly angry at the bank because the bank called in loans owed by the states. Several states adopted laws designed to limit the operation of the bank. Some states adopted laws prohibiting its operation within their borders. Others, such as Maryland, taxed it. The Maryland law required that any bank not chartered by the State pay either an annual tax of $15,000 or a tax of 2 percent on all of its notes that needed to be on special stamped paper.

The bank refused to pay the Maryland tax, and John James sued for himself and the State of Maryland in the County Court of Baltimore to recover the money owed under the tax. The defendant, McCulloch, was the cashier of that branch of the Bank of the United States. The trial court rendered judgment in favor of the plaintiffs, James and the State of Maryland, and the Maryland Court of Appeals affirmed.

McCulloch v. Maryland

17 U.S. (4 Wheat.) 316 (1819)

MARSHALL, Ch. J., delivered the opinion of the court.

In the case now to be determined, the defendant, a sovereign state, denies the obligation of a law enacted by the legislature of the Union, and the plaintiff, on his part, contests the validity of an act which has been passed by the legislature of that state. The constitution of our country, in its most interesting and vital parts, is to be considered; the conflicting powers of the government of the Union and of its members, as marked in that constitution, are to be discussed; and an opinion given, which may essentially influence the great operations of the government. No tribunal can approach such a question without a deep sense of its importance, and of the awful responsibility involved in its decision. But it must be decided peacefully, or remain a source of hostile legislation, perhaps, of hostility of a still more serious nature; and if it is to be so decided, by this tribunal alone can the decision be made. On the supreme court of the United States has the constitution of our country devolved this important duty.

[I]

The first question made in the cause is — has congress power to incorporate a bank? It has been truly said, that this can scarcely be considered as an open question, entirely unprejudiced by the former proceedings of the nation respecting it. The principle now contested was introduced at a very early period of our history, has been recognised by many successive legislatures, and has been acted upon by the judicial department, in cases of peculiar delicacy, as a law of undoubted obligation.

It will not be denied, that a bold and daring usurpation might be resisted, after an acquiescence still longer and more complete than this. But it is conceived, that a doubtful question, one on which human reason may pause, and the human judgment be suspended, in the decision of which the great principles of liberty are not concerned, but the respective powers of those who are equally the representatives of the people, are to be adjusted; if not put at rest by the practice of the government, ought to receive a considerable impression from that practice. An exposition of the constitution, deliberately established by legislative acts, on the faith of which an immense property has been advanced, ought not to be lightly disregarded.

The power now contested was exercised by the first congress elected under the present constitution. The bill for incorporating the Bank of the United States did not steal upon an unsuspecting legislature, and pass unobserved. Its principle was completely understood, and was opposed with equal zeal and ability. After being resisted, first, in the fair and open field of debate, and afterwards, in the executive cabinet, with as much persevering talent as any measure has ever experienced, and being supported by arguments which convinced minds as pure and as intelligent as this country can boast, it became a law. The original act was permitted to expire; but a short experience of the embarrassments to which the refusal to revive it exposed the government, convinced those who were most prejudiced against the measure of its necessity, and induced the passage of the present law. It would require no ordinary share of intrepidity, to assert that a measure adopted under these circumstances, was a bold and plain usurpation, to which the constitution gave no countenance.

In discussing this question, the counsel for the state of Maryland have deemed it of some importance, in the construction of the constitution, to consider that instrument, not as emanating from the people, but as the act of sovereign and independent states. The powers of the general government, it has been said, are delegated by the states, who alone are truly sovereign; and must be exercised in subordination to the states, who alone possess supreme dominion. It would be difficult to sustain this proposition. The convention which framed the constitution was indeed elected by the state legislatures. But the instrument, when it came from their hands, was a mere proposal, without obligation, or pretensions to it. It was reported to the then existing congress of the United States, with a request that it might "be submitted to a convention of delegates, chosen in each state by the people thereof, under the recommendation of its legislature, for their assent and ratification."

This mode of proceeding was adopted; and by the convention, by congress, and by the state legislatures, the instrument was submitted to the people. They acted upon it in the only manner in which they can act safely, effectively and wisely, on such a subject, by assembling in convention. It is true, they assembled in their several states — and where else should they have assembled? No political dreamer was ever wild enough to think of breaking down the lines which separate the states, and of compounding the American people into one common mass. Of consequence, when they act, they act in their states. But the measures they adopt do not, on that account, cease to be the measures of the people themselves, or become the measures of the state governments.

From these conventions, the constitution derives its whole authority. The government proceeds directly from the people; is "ordained and established," in the name of the people; and is declared to be ordained, "in order to form a more perfect union, establish justice, insure domestic tranquillity, and secure the blessings of liberty to themselves and to their posterity." The assent of the states, in their sovereign capacity, is implied, in calling a convention, and thus submitting that instrument to the people. But the people were at perfect liberty to accept or reject it; and their act was final. It required not the affirmance, and could not be negatived, by the state governments. The constitution, when thus adopted, was of complete obligation, and bound the state sovereignties.

It has been said, that the people had already surrendered all their powers to the state sovereignties, and had nothing more to give. But, surely, the question whether they may resume and modify the powers granted to government, does not remain to be settled in this country. Much more might the legitimacy of the general government be doubted, had it been created by the states. The powers delegated to the state sovereignties were to be exercised by themselves, not by a distinct and independent sovereignty, created by themselves. To the formation of a league, such as was the confederation, the state sovereignties were certainly competent. But when, "in order to form a more perfect union," it was deemed necessary to change this alliance into an effective government, possessing great and sovereign powers, and acting directly on the people, the necessity of referring it to the people, and of deriving its powers directly from them, was felt and acknowledged by all. The government of the Union, then (whatever may be the influence of this fact on the case), is, emphatically and truly, a government of the people. In form, and in substance, it emanates from them. Its powers are granted by them, and are to be exercised directly on them, and for their benefit.

This government is acknowledged by all, to be one of enumerated powers. The principle, that it can exercise only the powers granted to it, would seem too apparent, to have required to be enforced by all those arguments, which its enlightened friends, while it was depending before the people, found it necessary to urge; that principle is now universally admitted. But the question respecting the extent of the powers actually granted, is perpetually arising, and will probably continue to arise, so long as our system shall exist. In discussing these questions, the conflicting powers of the general and state governments must be brought into view, and the supremacy of their respective laws, when they are in opposition, must be settled.

If any one proposition could command the universal assent of mankind, we might expect it would be this — that the government of the Union, though limited in its powers, is supreme within its sphere of action. This would seem to result, necessarily, from its nature. It is the government of all; its powers are delegated by all; it represents all, and acts for all. Though any one state may be willing to control its operations, no state is willing to allow others to control them. The nation, on those subjects on which it can act, must necessarily bind its component parts. But this question is not left to mere reason: the people have, in express terms, decided it, by saying, "this constitution, and the laws of the United States, which shall be made in pursuance thereof," "shall be the supreme law of the land," and by requiring that the members of the state legislatures, and the officers of the executive and judicial departments of the states, shall take the oath of fidelity to it. The government of the United States, then, though limited in its powers, is supreme; and its laws, when made in pursuance of the constitution, form the supreme law of the land, "anything in the constitution or laws of any state to the contrary notwithstanding."

Among the enumerated powers, we do not find that of establishing a bank or creating a corporation. But there is no phrase in the instrument which, like the articles of confederation, excludes incidental or implied powers; and which requires that everything granted shall be expressly and minutely described. Even the 10th amendment, which was framed for the purpose of quieting the excessive jealousies which had been excited, omits the word "expressly," and declares only, that the powers "not delegated to the United States, nor prohibited to the states, are reserved to the states or to the people;" thus leaving the question, whether the particular power which may become the subject of contest, has been delegated to the one government, or prohibited to the other, to depend on a fair construction of the whole instrument. The men who drew and adopted this amendment had experienced the embarrassments resulting from the insertion of this word in the articles of confederation, and probably omitted it, to avoid those embarrassments. A constitution, to contain an accurate detail of all the subdivisions of which its great powers will admit, and of all the means by which they may be carried into execution, would partake of the prolixity of a legal code, and could scarcely be embraced by the human mind. It would, probably, never be understood by the public. Its nature, therefore, requires, that only its great outlines should be marked, its important objects designated, and the minor ingredients which compose those objects, be deduced from the nature of the objects themselves. That this idea was entertained by the framers of the American constitution, is not only to be inferred from the nature of the instrument, but from the language. Why else were some of the limitations, found in the 9th section of the 1st article, introduced? It is also, in some degree, warranted, by their having omitted to use any restrictive term which might prevent its receiving a fair and just interpretation. In considering this question, then, we must never forget that it is a constitution we are expounding.

Although, among the enumerated powers of government, we do not find the word "bank" or "incorporation," we find the great powers, to lay and collect taxes; to borrow money; to regulate commerce; to declare and conduct a war; and to raise and support armies and navies. The sword and the purse, all the external relations, and no inconsiderable portion of the industry of the nation, are intrusted to its government. It can never be pretended, that these vast powers draw after them others of inferior importance, merely because they are inferior. Such an idea can never be advanced. But it may with great reason be contended, that a government, intrusted with such ample powers, on the due execution of which the happiness and prosperity of the nation so vitally depends, must also be intrusted with ample means for their execution. The power being given, it is the interest of the nation to facilitate its execution. It can never be their interest, and cannot be presumed to have been their intention, to clog and embarrass its execution, by withholding the most appropriate means. Can we adopt that construction (unless the words imperiously require it), which would impute to the framers of that instrument, when granting these powers for the public good, the intention of impeding their exercise, by withholding a choice of means? If, indeed, such be the mandate of the constitution, we have only to obey; but that instrument does not profess to enumerate the means by which the powers it confers may be executed; nor does it prohibit the creation of a corporation, if the existence of such a being be essential, to the beneficial exercise of those powers. It is, then, the subject of fair inquiry, how far such means may be employed.

It is not denied, that the powers given to the government imply the ordinary means of execution. That, for example, of raising revenue, and applying it to national purposes, is admitted to imply the power of conveying money from place to place, as the exigencies of the nation may require, and of employing the usual means of conveyance. The government which has a right to do an act, and has imposed on it, the duty of performing that act, must, according to the dictates of reason, be allowed to select the means; and those who contend that it may not select any appropriate means, that one particular mode of effecting the object is excepted, take upon themselves the burden of establishing that exception.

But the constitution of the United States has not left the right of congress to employ the necessary means, for the execution of the powers conferred on the government, to general reasoning. To its enumeration of powers is added, that of making "all laws which shall be necessary and proper, for carrying into execution the foregoing powers, and all other powers vested by this constitution, in the government of the United States, or in any department thereof." The counsel for the state of Maryland have urged various arguments, to prove that this clause, though, in terms, a grant of power, is not so, in effect; but is really restrictive of the general right, which might otherwise be implied, of selecting means for executing the enumerated powers. In support of this proposition, they have found it necessary to contend, that this clause was inserted for the purpose of conferring on congress the power of making laws. That, without it, doubts might be entertained, whether congress could exercise its powers in the form of legislation.

But the argument on which most reliance is placed, is drawn from that peculiar language of this clause. Congress is not empowered by it to make all laws, which may have relation to the powers confered on the government, but such only as may be "necessary and proper" for carrying them into execution. The word "necessary" is considered as controlling the whole sentence, and as limiting the right to pass laws for the execution of the granted powers, to such as are indispensable, and without which the power would be nugatory. That it excludes the choice of means, and leaves to congress, in each case, that only which is most direct and simple.

Is it true, that this is the sense in which the word "necessary" is always used? Does it always import an absolute physical necessity, so strong, that one thing to which another may be termed necessary, cannot exist without that other? We think it does not. If reference be had to its use, in the common affairs of the world, or in approved authors, we find that it frequently imports no more than that one thing is convenient, or useful, or essential to another. To employ the means necessary to an end, is generally understood as employing any means calculated to produce the end, and not as being confined to those single means, without which the end would be entirely unattainable. Such is the character of human language, that no word conveys to the mind, in all situations, one single definite idea; and nothing is more common than to use words in a figurative sense. Almost all compositions contain words, which, taken in a their rigorous sense, would convey a meaning different from that which is obviously intended. It is essential to just construction, that many words which import something excessive, should be understood in a more mitigated sense — in that sense which common usage justifies. The word "necessary" is of this description. It has not a fixed character, peculiar to itself. It admits of all degrees of comparison; and is often connected with other words, which increase or diminish the impression the mind receives of the urgency it imports. A thing may be necessary, very necessary, absolutely or indispensably necessary. To no mind would the same idea be conveyed by these several phrases. This word, then, like others, is used in various senses; and, in its construction, the subject, the context, the intention of the person using them, are all to be taken into view.

Let this be done in the case under consideration. The subject is the execution of those great powers on which the welfare of a nation essentially depends. It must have been the intention of those who gave these powers, to insure, so far as human prudence could insure, their beneficial execution. This could not be done, by confiding the choice of means to such narrow limits as not to leave it in the power of congress to adopt any which might be appropriate, and which were conducive to the end. This provision is made in a constitution, intended to endure for ages to come, and consequently, to be adapted to the various crises of human affairs. To have prescribed the means by which government should, in all future time, execute its powers, would have been to change, entirely, the character of the instrument, and give it the properties of a legal code. It would have been an unwise attempt to provide, by immutable rules, for exigencies which, if foreseen at all, must have been seen dimly, and which can be best provided for as they occur. To have declared, that the best means shall not be used, but those alone, without which the power given would be nugatory, would have been to deprive the legislature of the capacity to avail itself of experience, to exercise its reason, and to accommodate its legislation to circumstances.

So, with respect to the whole penal code of the United States: whence arises the power to punish, in cases not prescribed by the constitution? All admit, that the government may, legitimately, punish any violation of its laws; and yet, this is not among the enumerated powers of congress. The right to enforce the observance of law, by punishing its infraction, might be denied, with the more plausibility, because it is expressly given in some cases.

Take, for example, the power "to establish post-offices and post-roads." This power is executed, by the single act of making the establishment. But, from this has been inferred the power and duty of carrying the mail along the post-road, from one post-office to another. And from this implied power, has again been inferred the right to punish those who steal letters from the post-office, or rob the mail. It may be said, with some plausibility, that the right to carry the mail, and to punish those who rob it, is not indispensably necessary to the establishment of a post-office and post-road. This right is indeed essential to the beneficial exercise of the power, but not indispensably necessary to its existence. So, of the punishment of the crimes of stealing or falsifying a record or process of a court of the United States, or of perjury in such court. To punish these offences, is certainly conducive to the due administration of justice. But courts may exist, and may decide the causes brought before them, though such crimes escape punishment.

In ascertaining the sense in which the word "necessary" is used in this clause of the constitution, we may derive some aid from that with which it it is associated. Congress shall have power "to make all laws which shall be necessary and proper to carry into execution" the powers of the government. If the word "necessary" was used in that strict and rigorous sense for which the counsel for the state of Maryland contend, it would be an extraordinary departure from the usual course of the human mind, as exhibited in composition, to add a word, the only possible effect of which is, to qualify that strict and rigorous meaning; to present to the mind the idea of some choice of means of legislation, not strained and compressed within the narrow limits for which gentlemen contend.

We think so for the following reasons: 1st. The clause is placed among the powers of congress, not among the limitations on those powers. 2d. Its terms purport to enlarge, not to diminish the powers vested in the government. It purports to be an additional power, not a restriction on those already granted. No reason has been, or can be assigned, for thus concealing an intention to narrow the discretion of the national legislature, under words which purport to enlarge it. The framers of the constitution wished its adoption, and well knew that it would be endangered by its strength, not by its weakness. Had they been capable of using language which would convey to the eye one idea, and, after deep reflection, impress on the mind, another, they would rather have disguised the grant of power, than its limitation. If, then, their intention had been, by this clause, to restrain the free use of means which might otherwise have been implied, that intention would have been inserted in another place, and would have been expressed in terms resembling these. "In carrying into execution the foregoing powers, and all others," &c., "no laws shall be passed but such as are necessary and proper." Had the intention been to make this clause restrictive, it would unquestionably have been so in form as well as in effect.

We admit, as all must admit, that the powers of the government are limited, and that its limits are not to be transcended. But we think the sound construction of the constitution must allow to the national legislature that discretion, with respect to the means by which the powers it confers are to be carried into execution, which will enable that body to perform the high duties assigned to it, in the manner most beneficial to the people. Let the end be legitimate, let it be within the scope of the constitution, and all means which are appropriate, which are plainly adapted to that end, which are not prohibited, but consist with the letter and spirit of the constitution, are constitutional.

Should congress, in the execution of its powers, adopt measures which are prohibited by the constitution; or should congress, under the pretext of executing its powers, pass laws for the accomplishment of objects not intrusted to the government; it would become the painful duty of this tribunal, should a case requiring such a decision come before it, to say, that such an act was not the law of the land. But where the law is not prohibited, and is really calculated to effect any of the objects intrusted to the government, to undertake here to inquire into the decree of its necessity, would be to pass the line which circumscribes the judicial department, and to tread on legislative ground. This court disclaims all pretensions to such a power.

[II]

Whether the state of Maryland may, without violating the constitution, tax that branch? That the power of taxation is one of vital importance; that it is retained by the states; that it is not abridged by the grant of a similar power to the government of the Union; that it is to be concurrently exercised by the two governments — are truths which have never been denied. But such is the paramount character of the constitution, that its capacity to withdraw any subject from the action of even this power, is admitted. The states are expressly forbidden to lay any duties on imports or exports, except what may be absolutely necessary for executing their inspection laws. If the obligation of this prohibition must be conceded — if it may restrain a state from the exercise of its taxing power on imports and exports — the same paramount character would seem to restrain, as it certainly may restrain, a state from such other exercise of this power, as is in its nature incompatible with, and repugnant to, the constitutional laws of the Union. A law, absolutely repugnant to another, as entirely repeals that other as if express terms of repeal were used.

On this ground, the counsel for the bank place its claim to be exempted from the power of a state to tax its operations. There is no express provision for the case, but the claim has been sustained on a principle which so entirely pervades the constitution, is so intermixed with the materials which compose it, so interwoven with its web, so blended with its texture, as to be incapable of being separated from it, without rending it into shreds. This great principle is, that the constitution and the laws made in pursuance thereof are supreme; that they control the constitution and laws of the respective states, and cannot be controlled by them. From this, which may be almost termed an axiom, other propositions are deduced as corollaries, on the truth or error of which, and on their application to this case, the cause has been supposed to depend. These are, 1st. That a power to create implies a power to preserve: 2d. That a power to destroy, if wielded by a different hand, is hostile to, and incompatible with these powers to create and to preserve: 3d. That where this repugnancy exists, that authority which is supreme must control, not yield to that over which it is supreme.

The power of congress to create, and of course, to continue, the bank, was the subject of the preceding part of this opinion; and is no longer to be considered as questionable. That the power of taxing it by the states may be exercised so as to destroy it, is too obvious to be denied. But taxation is said to be an absolute power, which acknowledges no other limits than those expressly prescribed in the constitution, and like sovereign power of every other description, is intrusted to the discretion of those who use it. But the very terms of this argument admit, that the sovereignty of the state, in the article of taxation itself, is subordinate to, and may be controlled by the constitution of the United States. How far it has been controlled by that instrument, must be a question of construction. In making this construction, no principle, not declared, can be admissible, which would defeat the legitimate operations of a supreme government. It is of the very essence of supremacy, to remove all obstacles to its action within its own sphere, and so to modify every power vested in subordinate governments, as to exempt its own operations from their own influence. This effect need not be stated in terms. It is so involved in the declaration of supremacy, so necessarily implied in it, that the expression of it could not make it more certain. We must, therefore, keep it in view, while construing the constitution. The argument on the part of the state of Maryland, is, not that the states may directly resist a law of congress, but that they may exercise their acknowledged powers upon it, and that the constitution leaves them this right, in the confidence that they will not abuse it. Before we proceed to examine this argument, and to subject it to test of the constitution, we must be permitted to bestow a few considerations on the nature and extent of this original right of taxation, which is acknowledged to remain with the states. It is admitted, that the power of taxing the people and their property, is essential to the very existence of government, and may be legitimately exercised on the objects to which it is applicable, to the utmost extent to which the government may choose to carry it. The only security against the abuse of this power, is found in the structure of the government itself. In imposing a tax, the legislature acts upon its constituents. This is, in general, a sufficient security against erroneous and oppressive taxation.

The people of a state, therefore, give to their government a right of taxing themselves and their property, and as the exigencies of government cannot be limited, they prescribe no limits to the exercise of this right, resting confidently on the interest of the legislator, and on the influence of the constituent over their representative, to guard them against its abuse. But the means employed by the government of the Union have no such security, nor is the right of a state to tax them sustained by the same theory. Those means are not given by the people of a particular state, not given by the constituents of the legislature, which claim the right to tax them, but by the people of all the states. They are given by all, for the benefit of all — and upon theory, should be subjected to that government only which belongs to all.

It may be objected to this definition, that the power of taxation is not confined to the people and property of a state. It may be exercised upon every object brought within its jurisdiction. The sovereignty of a state extends to everything which exists by its own authority, or is introduced by its permission; but does it extend to those means which are employed by congress to carry into execution powers conferred on that body by the people of the United States? We think it demonstrable, that it does not. Those powers are not given by the people of a single state. They are given by the people of the United States, to a government whose laws, made in pursuance of the constitution, are declared to be supreme. Consequently, the people of a single state cannot confer a sovereignty which will extend over them.

That the power to tax involves the power to destroy; that the power to destroy may defeat and render useless the power to create; that there is a plain repugnance in conferring on one government a power to control the constitutional measures of another, which other, with respect to those very measures, is declared to be supreme over that which exerts the control, are propositions not to be denied. But all inconsistencies are to be reconciled by the magic of the word confidence. Taxation, it is said, does not necessarily and unavoidably destroy. To carry it to the excess of destruction, would be an abuse, to presume which, would banish that confidence which is essential to all government. But is this a case of confidence? Would the people of any one state trust those of another with a power to control the most insignificant operations of their state government? We know they would not. Why, then, should we suppose, that the people of any one state should be willing to trust those of another with a power to control the operations of a government to which they have confided their most important and most valuable interests? In the legislature of the Union alone, are all represented. The legislature of the Union alone, therefore, can be trusted by the people with the power of controlling measures which concern all, in the confidence that it will not be abused. This, then, is not a case of confidence, and we must consider it is as it really is.

If we apply the principle for which the state of Maryland contends, to the constitution, generally, we shall find it capable of changing totally the character of that instrument. We shall find it capable of arresting all the measures of the government, and of prostrating it at the foot of the states. The American people have declared their constitution and the laws made in pursuance thereof, to be supreme; but this principle would transfer the supremacy, in fact, to the states. If the states may tax one instrument, employed by the government in the execution of its powers, they may tax any and every other instrument. They may tax the mail; they may tax the mint; they may tax patent-rights; they may tax the papers of the custom-house; they may tax judicial process; they may tax all the means employed by the government, to an excess which would defeat all the ends of government. This was not intended by the American people. They did not design to make their government dependent on the states.

The court has bestowed on this subject its most deliberate consideration. The result is a conviction that the states have no power, by taxation or otherwise, to retard, impede, burden, or in any manner control, the operations of the constitutional laws enacted by congress to carry into execution the powers vested in the general government. This is, we think, the unavoidable consequence of that supremacy which the constitution has declared. We are unanimously of opinion, that the law passed by the legislature of Maryland, imposing a tax on the Bank of the United Sates, is unconstitutional and void.

B. The Commerce Power

Article I, §8 states: "The Congress shall have the power . . . [t]o regulate Commerce with foreign Nations, and among the several States, and with the Indian Tribes. . . ." Practically speaking, this provision has been the authority for a broad array of federal legislation, ranging from criminal statutes to securities laws to civil rights laws to environmental laws. From the perspective of constitutional law, the Commerce Clause has been the focus of the vast majority of Supreme Court decisions that have considered the scope of congressional power and federalism.

There have been roughly four eras of Commerce Clause jurisprudence. During the initial era, from early in American history until the 1890s, the commerce power was broadly defined but minimally used. In a period from the 1890s until 1937, the Court narrowly defined the scope of Congress's commerce power and used the Tenth Amendment as a limit. The era from 1937 until the 1990s was a time when the Court expansively defined the scope of the commerce power and refused to apply the Tenth Amendment as a limit. Since the 1990s, the Court has again narrowed the scope of the commerce power and revived the Tenth Amendment as an independent, judicially enforceable limit on federal actions.

Throughout these eras, the Court is considering three questions. First: What is "commerce"? Is it one stage of business, or does it include all aspects of business — even life in the United States? Second: What does "among the several states" mean? Is it limited to instances where there is a direct effect on interstate commerce, or does any effect on interstate activities suffice? And third: Does the Tenth Amendment limit Congress? If Congress is acting within the scope of its commerce power, can a law be declared unconstitutional as violating the Tenth Amendment?

1. *The Initial Era: Gibbons v. Ogden Defines the Commerce Power*

The New York legislature granted a monopoly to Robert Fulton and Robert Livingston for operating steamboats in New York waters. Fulton and Livingston licensed Aaron Ogden to operate a ferry boat between New York City and Elizabethtown Port in New Jersey. Thomas Gibbons operated a competing ferry service and thus violated the exclusive rights given to Fulton and Livingston, and their licensee Ogden, under the monopoly. Gibbons maintained that he had the right to operate his ferry because it was licensed under a federal law as "vessels in the coasting trade." Nonetheless, Ogden successfully sued for an injunction in the New York state courts.

The Supreme Court considered the scope of Congress's powers and then whether the New York grant of a monopoly was constitutional. The latter aspect of the case, the permissibility of the state law, is discussed in Chapter 4 [Erwin Chemerinsky, Constitutional Law, 3rd ed., (2009)]. Below is the Court's discussion of the scope of Congress's commerce power.

Gibbons v. Ogden

22 U.S. (9 Wheat.) 1 (1824)

Chief Justice MARSHALL delivered the opinion of the Court.

As preliminary to the very able discussions of the constitution, which we have heard from the bar, and as having some influence on its construction, reference has been made to the political situation of these States, anterior to its formation. It has been said, that they were sovereign, were completely independent, and were connected with each other only by a league. This is true. But, when these allied sovereigns converted their league into a government, when they converted their Congress of Ambassadors, deputed to deliberate on their common concerns, and to recommend measures of general utility, into a Legislature, empowered to enact laws on the most interesting subjects, the whole character in which the States appear, underwent a change, the extent of which must be determined by a fair consideration of the instrument by which that change was effected.

This instrument contains an enumeration of powers expressly granted by the people to their government. It has been said, that these powers ought to be construed strictly. But why ought they to be so construed? Is there one sentence in the constitution which gives countenance to this rule? In the last of the enumerated powers, that which grants, expressly, the means for carrying all others into execution, Congress is authorized "to make all laws which shall be necessary and proper" for the purpose.

The words are, "Congress shall have power to regulate commerce with foreign nations, and among the several States, and with the Indian tribes." The subject to be regulated is commerce; and our constitution being one of enumeration, and not of definition, to ascertain the extent of the power, it becomes necessary to settle the meaning of the word. The counsel for the appellee would limit it to traffic, to buying and selling, or the interchange of commodities, and do not admit that it comprehends navigation. This would restrict a general term, applicable to many objects, to one of its significations. Commerce, undoubtedly, is traffic, but it is something more: it is intercourse. It describes the commercial intercourse between nations, and parts of nations, in all its branches, and is regulated by prescribing rules for carrying on that intercourse. The mind can scarcely conceive a system for regulating commerce between nations, which shall exclude all laws concerning navigation, which shall be silent on the admission of the vessels of the one nation into the ports of the other, and be confined to prescribing rules for the conduct of individuals, in the actual employment of buying and selling, or of barter.

If commerce does not include navigation, the government of the Union has no direct power over that subject, and can make no law prescribing what shall constitute American vessels, or requiring that they shall be navigated by American seamen. Yet this power has been exercised from the commencement of the government, has been exercised with the consent of all, and has been understood by all to be a commercial regulation. All America understands, and has uniformly understood, the word "commerce," to comprehend navigation. It was so understood, and must have been so understood, when the constitution was framed.

The power over commerce, including navigation, was one of the primary objects for which the people of America adopted their government, and must have been contemplated in forming it. The convention must have used the word in that sense, because all have understood it in that sense; and the attempt to restrict it comes too late.

The word used in the constitution, then, comprehends, and has been always understood to comprehend, navigation within its meaning; and a power to regulate navigation, is as expressly granted, as if that term had been added to the word "commerce."

To what commerce does this power extend? The constitution informs us, to commerce "with foreign nations, and among the several States, and with the Indian tribes."

It has, we believe, been universally admitted, that these words comprehend every species of commercial intercourse between the United States and foreign nations. No sort of trade can be carried on between this country and any other, to which this power does not extend. It has been truly said, that commerce, as the word is used in the constitution, is a unit, every part of which is indicated by the term.

The subject to which the power is next applied, is to commerce "among the several States." The word "among" means intermingled with. A thing which is among others, is intermingled with them. Commerce among the States, cannot stop at the external boundary line of each State, but may be introduced into the interior.

It is not intended to say that these words comprehend that commerce, which is completely internal, which is carried on between man and man in a State, or between different parts of the same State, and which does not extend to or affect other States. Such a power would be inconvenient, and is certainly unnecessary.

Comprehensive as the word "among" is, it may very properly be restricted to that commerce which concerns more States than one. The phrase is not one which would probably have been selected to indicate the completely interior traffic of a State, because it is not an apt phrase for that purpose; and the enumeration of the particular classes of commerce, to which the power was to be extended, would not have been made, had the intention been to extend the power to every description. The enumeration presupposes something not enumerated; and that something, if we regard the language or the subject of the sentence, must be the exclusively internal commerce of a State. The genius and character of the whole government seem to be, that its action is to be applied to all the external concerns of the nation, and to those internal concerns which affect the States generally; but not to those which are completely within a particular State, which do not affect other States, and with which it is not necessary to interfere, for the purpose of executing some of the general powers of the government. The completely internal commerce of a State, then, may be considered as reserved for the State itself.

But, in regulating commerce with foreign nations, the power of Congress does not stop at the jurisdictional lines of the several States. It would be a very useless power, if it could not pass those lines. The commerce of the United States with foreign nations, is that of the whole United States. Every district has a right to participate in it. The deep streams which penetrate our country in every direction, pass through the interior of almost every State in the Union, and furnish the means of exercising this right. If Congress has the power to regulate it, that power must be exercised whenever the subject exists. If it exists within the States, if a foreign voyage may commence or terminate at a port within a State, then the power of Congress may be exercised within a State.

We are now arrived at the inquiry — What is this power?

It is the power to regulate; that is, to prescribe the rule by which commerce is to be governed. This power, like all others vested in Congress, is complete in itself, may be exercised to its utmost extent, and acknowledges no limitations, other than are prescribed in the constitution. If, as has always been understood, the sovereignty of Congress, though limited to specified objects, is plenary as to those objects, the power over commerce with foreign nations, and among the several States, is vested in Congress as absolutely as it would be in a single government, having in its constitution the same restrictions on the exercise of the power as are found in the constitution of the United States. The wisdom and the discretion of Congress, their identity with the people, and the influence which their constituents possess at elections, are, in this, as in many other instances, as that, for example, of declaring war, the sole restraints on which they have relied, to secure them from its abuse. They are the restraints on which the people must often rely, in all representative governments.

During the remainder of the nineteenth century, until the 1890s, there were relatively few cases considering the scope of Congress's Commerce Clause power. In the years after *Gibbons* and before the Civil War, the Supreme Court rarely considered challenges to federal legislation adopted under Congress's Commerce Clause authority. After the Civil War, there were a few cases concerning the scope of the commerce power. Some of the cases continued *Gibbons*'s expansive definition of commerce. For example, in *The Daniel Ball*, 77 U.S. (1 Wall.) 557 (1871), the Court accorded Congress broad authority to license ships, even those operating entirely intrastate, so long as the boats were carrying goods that had come from another state or that ultimately would go to another state. The Court explained that unsafe ships in intrastate commerce could affect and harm ships in interstate commerce.

Yet, there also were a few cases that departed from *Gibbons* and invalidated federal legislation as exceeding the scope of the commerce power. The first case to overturn a federal law in this way was United States v. Dewitt, 76 U.S. (9 Wall.) 41 (1869), in 1870. A federal law outlawed the sale of naphtha and other illuminating oils that could ignite at less than 110 degrees Fahrenheit. The Court held that the law was "a police regulation, relating exclusively to the internal trade of the States." In a precursor to decisions that followed after the 1890s, the Court declared the law unconstitutional because it was "a virtual denial of any power to interfere with the internal trade and business of the separate States."

In *The Trademark Cases*, 100 U.S. (10 Otto) 82 (1878), the Court invalidated the federal law that established a federal system for registering trademarks. The Court concluded that the law was unconstitutional because it applied to wholly intrastate businesses and business transactions and therefore "is obviously the exercise of a power not confided to Congress."

U.S. v. Comstock

130 S.Ct. 1949 (2010)

Justice BREYER delivered the opinion of the Court.

A federal civil-commitment statute authorizes the Department of Justice to detain a mentally ill, sexually dangerous federal prisoner beyond the date the prisoner would otherwise be released. We have previously examined similar statutes enacted under state law to determine whether they violate the Due Process Clause. See *Kansas v. Hendricks*, (1997); *Kansas v. Crane* (2002). But this case presents a different question. Here we ask whether the Federal Government has the authority under Article I of the Constitution to enact this federal civil-commitment program or whether its doing so falls beyond the reach of a government "of enumerated powers." *McCulloch v. Maryland* (1819). We conclude that the Constitution grants Congress the authority to enact §4248 as "necessary and proper for carrying into Execution" the powers "vested by" the "Constitution in the Government of the United States.

I

The federal statute before us allows a district court to order the civil commitment of an individual who is currently "in the custody of the [Federal] Bureau of Prisons," if that individual (1) has previously "engaged or attempted to engage in sexually violent conduct or child molestation," (2) currently "suffers from a serious mental illness, abnormality, or disorder," and (3) "as a result of" that mental illness, abnormality, or disorder is "sexually dangerous to others," in that "he would have serious difficulty in refraining from sexually violent conduct or child molestation if released."

In order to detain such a person, the Government (acting through the Department of Justice) must certify to a federal district judge that the prisoner meets the conditions just described, *i.e.*, that he has engaged in sexually violent activity or child molestation in the past and that he suffers from a mental illness that makes him correspondingly dangerous to others. When such a certification is filed, the statute automatically stays the individual's release from prison, thereby giving the Government an opportunity to prove its claims at a hearing through psychiatric (or other) evidence. The statute provides that the prisoner "shall be represented by counsel" and shall have "an opportunity" at the hearing "to testify, to present evidence, to subpoena witnesses on his behalf, and to confront and cross-examine" the Government's witnesses.

If the Government proves its claims by "clear and convincing evidence," the court will order the prisoner's continued commitment in "the custody of the

Attorney General," who must "make all reasonable efforts to cause" the State where that person was tried, or the State where he is domiciled, to "assume responsibility for his custody, care, and treatment." If either State is willing to assume that responsibility, the Attorney General "shall release" the individual "to the appropriate official" of that State. But if, "notwithstanding such efforts, neither such State will assume such responsibility," then "the Attorney General shall place the person for treatment in a suitable [federal] facility."

Confinement in the federal facility will last until either (1) the person's mental condition improves to the point where he is no longer dangerous (with or without appropriate ongoing treatment), in which case he will be released; or (2) a State assumes responsibility for his custody, care, and treatment, in which case he will be transferred to the custody of that State. The statute establishes a system for ongoing psychiatric and judicial review of the individual's case, including judicial hearings at the request of the confined person at six-month intervals.

In November and December 2006, the Government instituted proceedings in the Federal District Court for the Eastern District of North Carolina against the five respondents in this case. Three of the five had previously pleaded guilty in federal court to possession of child pornography, and the fourth had pleaded guilty to sexual abuse of a minor. With respect to each of them, the Government claimed that the respondent was about to be released from federal prison, that he had engaged in sexually violent conduct or child molestation in the past, and that he suffered from a mental illness that made him sexually dangerous to others. During that same time period, the Government instituted similar proceedings against the fifth respondent, who had been charged in federal court with aggravated sexual abuse of a minor, but was found mentally incompetent to stand trial. Each of the five respondents moved to dismiss the civil-commitment proceeding on constitutional grounds.

II

The question presented is whether the Necessary and Proper Clause, Art. I, §8, cl. 18, grants Congress authority sufficient to enact the statute before us. In resolving that question, we assume, but we do not decide, that other provisions of the Constitution-such as the Due Process Clause-do not prohibit civil commitment in these circumstances. In other words, we assume for argument's sake that the Federal Constitution would permit a State to enact this statute, and we ask solely whether the Federal Government, exercising its enumerated powers, may enact such a statute as well. On that assumption, we conclude that the Constitution grants Congress legislative power sufficient to enact §4248. We base this conclusion on five considerations, taken together.

First, the Necessary and Proper Clause grants Congress broad authority to enact federal legislation. Nearly 200 years ago, this Court stated that the Federal "[G]overnment is acknowledged by all to be one of enumerated powers," *McCulloch*, which means that "[e]very law enacted by Congress must be based on one or more of" those powers. But, at the same time, "a government, entrusted with such" powers "must also be entrusted with ample means for their execution."

Accordingly, the Necessary and Proper Clause makes clear that the Constitution's grants of specific federal legislative authority are accompanied by broad power to enact laws that are "convenient, or useful" or "conducive" to the authority's "beneficial exercise." "Let the end be legitimate, let it be within the scope of the constitution, and all means which are appropriate, which are plainly adapted to that end, which are not prohibited, but consist with the letter and spirit of the constitution, are constitutional."

We have since made clear that, in determining whether the Necessary and Proper Clause grants Congress the legislative authority to enact a particular federal statute, we look to see whether the statute constitutes a means that is rationally related to the implementation of a constitutionally enumerated power.

We have also recognized that the Constitution "addresse[s]" the "choice of means" "primarily . . . to the judgment of Congress. If it can be seen that the means adopted are really calculated to attain the end, the degree of their necessity, the extent to which they conduce to the end, the closeness of the relationship between the means adopted and the end to be attained, are matters for congressional determination alone."

Thus, the Constitution, which nowhere speaks explicitly about the creation of federal crimes beyond those related to "counterfeiting," "treason," or "Piracies and Felonies committed on the high Seas" or "against the Law of Nations," nonetheless grants Congress broad authority to create such crimes. And Congress routinely exercises its authority to enact criminal laws in furtherance of, for example, its enumerated powers to regulate interstate and foreign commerce, to enforce civil rights, to spend funds for the general welfare, to establish federal courts, to establish post offices, to regulate bankruptcy, to regulate naturalization, and so forth.

Similarly, Congress, in order to help ensure the enforcement of federal criminal laws enacted in furtherance of its enumerated powers, "can cause a prison to be erected at any place within the jurisdiction of the United States, and direct that all persons sentenced to imprisonment under the laws of the United States shall be confined there." Moreover, Congress, having established a prison system, can enact laws that seek to ensure that system's safe and responsible administration by, for example, requiring prisoners to receive medical care and educational training, and can also ensure the safety of the prisoners, prison workers and visitors, and those in surrounding communities by, for example, creating further criminal laws governing entry, exit, and smuggling, and by employing prison guards to ensure discipline and security.

Neither Congress' power to criminalize conduct, nor its power to imprison individuals who engage in that conduct, nor its power to enact laws governing prisons and prisoners, is explicitly mentioned in the Constitution. But Congress nonetheless possesses broad authority to do each of those things in the course of "carrying into Execution" the enumerated powers "vested by" the "Constitution in the Government of the United States."

Second, the civil-commitment statute before us constitutes a modest addition to a set of federal prison-related mental-health statutes that have existed for many decades. We recognize that even a longstanding history of related federal action does not demonstrate a statute's constitutionality. A history of involvement, however, can nonetheless be "helpful in reviewing the substance of a congressional statutory scheme," and, in particular, the reasonableness of the relation between the new statute and pre-existing federal interests.

Here, Congress has long been involved in the delivery of mental health care to federal prisoners, and has long provided for their civil commitment. In 1855 it established Saint Elizabeth's Hospital in the District of Columbia to provide treatment to "the insane of the army and navy . . . and of the District of Columbia." In 1857 it provided for confinement at Saint Elizabeth's of any person within the District of Columbia who had been "charged with [a] crime" and who was "insane" or later became "insane during the continuance of his or her sentence in the United States penitentiary." In 1874, expanding the geographic scope of its statutes, Congress provided for civil commitment in federal facilities (or in state facilities if a State so agreed) of "*all* persons who have been or shall be convicted of any offense in *any* court of the United States" and who are or "shall become" insane "during the term of their imprisonment." And in 1882 Congress provided for similar commitment of those "*charged*" with federal offenses who become "insane" while in the "custody" of the United States. Thus, over the span of three decades, Congress created a national, federal civil-commitment program under which any person who was either charged with or convicted of any federal offense in any federal court could be confined in a federal mental institution.

In 2006, Congress enacted the particular statute before us. It differs from earlier statutes in that it focuses directly upon persons who, due to a mental illness, are sexually dangerous. Notably, many of these individuals were likely already subject to civil commitment under §4246, which, since 1949, has authorized the postsentence detention of federal prisoners who suffer from a mental illness and who are thereby dangerous (whether sexually or otherwise). Aside from its specific focus on sexually dangerous persons, §4248 is similar to the provisions first enacted in 1949. In that respect, it is a modest addition to a longstanding federal statutory framework, which has been in place since 1855.

Third, Congress reasonably extended its longstanding civil-commitment system to cover mentally ill and sexually dangerous persons who are already in federal custody, even if doing so detains them beyond the termination of their criminal sentence. For one thing, the Federal Government is the custodian of its prisoners. As federal custodian, it has the constitutional power to act in order to protect nearby (and other) communities from the danger federal prisoners may pose. If a federal prisoner is infected with a communicable disease that threatens others, surely it would be "necessary and proper" for the Federal Government to take action, pursuant to its role as federal custodian, to refuse (at least until the threat diminishes) to release that individual among the general public, where he might infect others. And if confinement of such an individual is a "necessary and proper" thing to do, then how could it not be similarly "necessary and proper" to confine an individual whose mental illness threatens others to the same degree?

Moreover, §4248 is "reasonably adapted," to Congress' power to act as a responsible federal custodian. Congress could have reasonably concluded that federal inmates who suffer from a mental illness that causes them to "have serious difficulty in refraining from sexually violent conduct," would pose an especially high danger to the public if released. And Congress could also have reasonably concluded (as detailed in the Judicial Conference's report) that a reasonable number of such individuals would likely *not* be detained by the States if released from federal custody, in part because the Federal Government itself severed their claim to "legal residence in any State" by incarcerating them in remote federal prisons.

Fourth, the statute properly accounts for state interests. Respondents and the dissent contend that §4248 violates the Tenth Amendment because it "invades the province of state sovereignty" in an area typically left to state control. But the Tenth Amendment's text is clear: "The powers *not delegated to the United States* by the Constitution, nor prohibited by it to the States, are reserved to the States respectively, or to the people." The powers "delegated to the United States by the Constitution" include those specifically enumerated powers listed in Article I along with the implementation authority granted by the Necessary and Proper Clause. Virtually by definition, these powers are not powers that the Constitution "reserved to the States."

Nor does this statute invade state sovereignty or otherwise improperly limit the scope of "powers that remain with the States." To the contrary, it requires *accommodation* of state interests.

Fifth, the links between §4248 and an enumerated Article I power are not too attenuated. Neither is the statutory provision too sweeping in its scope. Invoking the cautionary instruction that we may not "pile inference upon inference" in order to sustain congressional action under Article I, respondents argue that, when legislating pursuant to the Necessary and Proper Clause, Congress' authority can be no more than one step removed from a specifically enumerated power. But this argument is irreconcilable with our precedents. And, as we have explained, from the implied power to punish we have *further* inferred both the power to imprison, and, in *Greenwood*, the federal civil-commitment power.

Indeed even the dissent acknowledges that Congress has the implied power to criminalize any conduct that might interfere with the exercise of an enumerated power, and also the additional power to imprison people who violate those (inferentially authorized) laws, and the additional power to provide for the safe and reasonable management of those prisons, and the additional power to regulate the prisoners' behavior even after their release. And the same enumerated power that justifies the creation of a federal criminal statute, and that justifies the additional implied federal powers that the dissent considers legitimate, justifies civil commitment under §4248 as well. Thus, we must reject respondents' argument that the Necessary and Proper Clause permits no more than a single step between an enumerated power and an Act of Congress.

Nor need we fear that our holding today confers on Congress a general "police power, which the Founders denied the National Government and reposed in the States." As the Solicitor General repeatedly confirmed at oral argument, §4248 is narrow in scope. It has been applied to only a small fraction of federal prisoners. Thus, far from a "general police power," §4248 is a reasonably adapted and narrowly tailored means of pursuing the Government's legitimate interest as a federal custodian in the responsible administration of its prison system.

2. *The 1890s-1937: A Limited Federal Commerce Power*

In the late nineteenth century, concurrent with the Industrial Revolution and the growth of the national economy, Congress began using the Commerce Clause much more extensively to regulate businesses. The Interstate Commerce Act in 1887 was largely meant to provide for federal regulation of railroads, and the Sherman Antitrust Act in 1890 was intended to combat monopolies and restraints of trade.

Beginning in the 1890s, the Supreme Court took a very different approach to the Commerce Clause than that expressed in Gibbons v. Ogden. The Court narrowly interpreted the scope of Congress's commerce power based on an expressed concern for leaving regulatory matters to the state governments. Additionally, the Court applied the Tenth Amendment to reserve a zone of activities for exclusive state control and invalidated federal laws that were within Congress's commerce power that usurped state prerogatives. The Court applied three doctrines: First, it narrowly defined "commerce"; second, it applied a restrictive conception of what is "among the states"; and third, it held that Congress violates the Tenth Amendment when it regulates matters left to state governments. Each of these three doctrinal developments is discussed in turn below.

To understand these cases, it is important to recognize that the Supreme Court's majority during this era was deeply committed to a laissez-faire, unregulated economy. The hostility to government economic regulation reflected in the federalism cases to follow was paralleled by the Court's also invalidating state laws regulating the economy. As discussed in detail in Chapter 6 [Erwin Chemerinsky, Constitutional Law, 3rd ed., (2009)], from the late nineteenth century until 1937, the Court often declared unconstitutional state laws regulating employment and commercial transactions as violating freedom of contract protected under the Due Process Clause.

Although the constitutional doctrines were different and thus are presented in two different chapters, they both stemmed from the Court's hostility to government regulations. If Congress, for example, enacted a minimum wage law, it would be invalidated based on the federalism cases discussed below. If a state government adopted the same law, it would be invalidated based on freedom of contract under the Due Process Clause, discussed in Chapter 6 [Erwin Chemerinsky, Constitutional Law, 3rd ed., (2009)]. Together, these doctrines reflected a view about the proper role of government and also about the appropriate role of the Court. This era was the first time in American history in which the Court on a fairly regular basis invalidated important and popular federal and state laws.

a. What Is "Commerce"?
United States v. E.C. Knight Co.
156 U.S. 1 (1895)

Chief Justice FULLER delivered the opinion of the court.

By the purchase of the stock of the four Philadelphia refineries with shares of its own stock the American Sugar Refining Company acquired nearly complete control of the manufacture of refined sugar within the United States. The bill charged that the contracts under which these purchases were made constituted combinations in restraint of trade, and that in entering into them the defendants combined and conspired to restrain the trade and commerce in refined sugar among the several states and with foreign nations, contrary to the act of congress of July 2, 1890.

The fundamental question is whether, conceding that the existence of a monopoly in manufacture is established by the evidence, that monopoly can be directly suppressed under the act of congress in the mode attempted by this bill.

It cannot be denied that the power of a state to protect the lives, health, and property of its citizens, and to preserve good order and the public morals, "the power to govern men and things within the limits of its dominion," is a power originally and always belonging to the states, not surrendered by them to the general government, nor directly restrained by the constitution of the United States, and essentially exclusive.

The argument is that the power to control the manufacture of refined sugar is a monopoly over a necessary of life, to the enjoyment of which by a large part of the population of the United States interstate commerce is indispensable, and that, therefore, the general government, in the exercise of the power to regulate commerce, may repress such monopoly directly, and set aside the instruments which have created it. But this argument cannot be confined to necessaries of life merely, and must include all articles of general consumption. Doubtless the power to control the manufacture of a given thing involves, in a certain sense, the control of its disposition, but this is a secondary, and not the primary, sense; and, although the exercise of that power may result in bringing the operation of commerce into play, it does not control it, and affects it only incidentally and indirectly. Commerce succeeds to manufacture, and is not a part of it. The power to regulate commerce is the power to prescribe the rule by which commerce shall be governed, and is a power independent of the power to suppress monopoly. But it may operate in repression of monopoly whenever that comes within the rules by which commerce is governed, or whenever the transaction is itself a monopoly of commerce.

It is vital that the independence of the commercial power and of the police power, and the delimitation between them, however sometimes perplexing, should always be recognized and observed, for, while the one furnishes the strongest bond of union, the other is essential to the preservation of the autonomy of the states as required by our dual form of government; and acknowledged evils, however grave and urgent they may appear to be, had better be borne, than the risk be run, in the effort to suppress them, of more serious consequences by resort to expedients of even doubtful constitutionality.

Justice HARLAN, dissenting.

The court holds it to be vital in our system of government to recognize and give effect to both the commercial power of the nation and the police powers of the states, to the end that the Union be strengthened, and the autonomy of the states preserved. In this view I entirely concur. Undoubtedly, the preservation of the just authority of the states is an object of deep concern to every lover of his country. No greater calamity could befall our free institutions than the destruction of that authority, by whatever means such a result might be accomplished. But it is equally true that the preservation of the just authority of the general government is essential as well to the safety of the states as to the attainment of the important ends for which that government was ordained by the people of the United States; and the destruction of that authority would be fatal to the peace and well-being of the American people. The constitution, which enumerates the powers committed to the nation for objects of interest to the people of all the states, should not, therefore, be subjected to an interpretation so rigid, technical, and narrow that those objects cannot be accomplished.

Under the power with which it is invested, congress may remove unlawful obstructions, of whatever kind, to the free course of trade among the states. In so doing it would not interfere with the "autonomy of the states," because the power thus to protect interstate commerce is expressly given by the people of all the states. It is the constitution, the supreme law of the land, which invests congress with power to protect commerce among the states against burdens and exactions arising from un-lawful restraints by whatever authority imposed. Surely, a right secured or granted by that instrument is under the protection of the government which that instrument creates. Any combination, therefore, that disturbs or unreasonably obstructs freedom in buying and selling articles manufactured to be sold to persons in other states, or to be carried to other states, — a freedom that cannot exist if the right to buy and sell is fettered by unlawful restraints that crush out competition, — affects, not incidentally, but directly, the people of all the states; and the remedy for such an evil is found only in the exercise of powers confided to a government which, this court has said, was the government of all, exercising powers delegated by all, representing all, acting for all.

The Court's narrow definition of "commerce" continued throughout the era, from the 1890s until 1937. The following case from 1936 invalidated an important piece of New Deal legislation.

Carter v. Carter Coal Co.

298 U.S. 238 (1936)

Justice SUTHERLAND delivered the opinion of the Court.

The purposes of the "Bituminous Coal Conservation Act of 1935," involved in these suits, as declared by the title, are to stabilize the bituminous coal-mining industry and promote its interstate commerce; to provide for co-operative marketing of bituminous coal; to levy a tax on such coal and provide for a drawback under certain conditions; to declare the production, distribution, and use of such coal to be affected with a national public interest; to conserve the national resources of such coal; to provide for the general welfare, and for other purposes. The constitutional validity of the act is challenged in each of the suits.

Without repeating the long and involved provisions with regard to the fixing of minimum prices, it is enough to say that the act confers the power to fix the minimum price of coal at each and every coal mine in the United States, with such price variations as the board may deem necessary and proper. There is also a provision authorizing the commission, when deemed necessary in the public interest, to establish maximum prices in order to protect the consumer against unreasonably high prices. All sales and contracts for the sale of coal are subject to the code prices provided for and in effect when such sales and contracts are made. Various unfair methods of competition are defined and forbidden.

The labor provisions of the code, found in part 3 of the same section, require that to effectuate the purposes of the act employees to be given the right to organize and bargain collectively, through representatives of their own choosing, free from interference, restraint, or coercion of employers or their agents in respect of their concerted activities.

Every journey to a forbidden end begins with the first step; and the danger of such a step by the federal government in the direction of taking over the powers of the states is that the end of the journey may find the states so despoiled of their powers, or — what may amount to the same thing — so relieved of the responsibilities which possession of the powers necessarily enjoins, as to reduce them to little more than geographical subdivisions of the national domain.

In exercising the authority conferred by this clause of the Constitution, Congress is powerless to regulate anything which is not commerce, as it is powerless to do anything about commerce which is not regulation. We first inquire, then — What is commerce? No all embracing definition has ever been formulated.

As used in the Constitution, the word "commerce" is the equivalent of the phrase "intercourse for the purposes of trade," and includes transportation, purchase, sale, and exchange of commodities between the citizens of the different states. And the power to regulate commerce embraces the instruments by which commerce is carried on. A pretension as far reaching as this, would extend to contracts between citizen and citizen of the same State, would control the pursuits of the planter, the grazier, the manufacturer, the mechanic, the immense operations of the collieries and mines and furnaces of the country.

That commodities produced or manufactured within a state are intended to be sold or transported outside the state does not render their production or manufacture subject to federal regulation under the commerce clause.

We have seen that the word "commerce" is the equivalent of the phrase "intercourse for the purposes of trade." Plainly, the incidents leading up to and culminating in the mining of coal do not constitute such intercourse. The employment of men, the fixing of their wages, hours of labor, and working conditions, the bargaining in respect of these things — whether carried on separately or collectively — each and all constitute intercourse for the purposes of production, not of trade. The latter is a thing apart from the relation of employer and employee, which in all producing occupations is purely local in character. Extraction of coal from the mine is the aim and the completed result of local activities. Commerce in the coal mined is not brought into being by force of these activities, but by negotiations, agreements and circumstances entirely apart from production. Mining brings the subject-matter of commerce into existence. Commerce disposes of it.

A consideration of the foregoing, and of many cases which might be added to those already cited, renders inescapable the conclusion that the effect of the labor provisions of the act, including those in respect of minimum wages, wage agreements, collective bargaining, and the Labor Board and its powers, primarily falls upon production and not upon commerce; and confirms the further resulting conclusion that production is a purely local activity. It follows that none of these essential antecedents of production constitutes a transaction in or forms any part of interstate commerce. Everything which moves in interstate commerce has had a local origin. Without local production somewhere, interstate commerce, as now carried on, would practically disappear. Nevertheless, the local character of mining, of manufacturing, and of crop growing is a fact, and remains a fact, whatever may be done with the products.

Much stress is put upon the evils which come from the struggle between employers and employees over the matter of wages, working conditions, the right of collective bargaining, etc., and the resulting strikes, curtailment, and irregularity of production and effect on prices; and it is insisted that interstate commerce is greatly affected thereby. But, in addition to what has just been said, the conclusive answer is that the evils are all local evils over which the federal government has no legislative control. The relation of employer and employee is a local relation. Such effect as they may have upon commerce, however extensive it may be, is secondary and indirect. An increase in the greatness of the effect adds to its importance. It does not alter its character.

A.L.A. Schechter Poultry Corp. v. United States

295 U.S. 495 (1935)

Chief Justice HUGHES delivered the opinion of the Court.

Petitioners were convicted in the District Court of the United States for the Eastern District of New York on eighteen counts of an indictment charging violations of what is known as the "Live Poultry Code," and on an additional count for conspiracy to commit such violations.[2] [The Code required sellers to sell only entire coops or half-coops of chickens, and made it illegal for buyers to reject individual chickens. The Code also regulated employment by requiring collective bargaining, prohibiting child labor, and by establishing a 40-hour work week and a minimum wage.]

New York City is the largest live poultry market in the United States. Ninety-six per cent of the live poultry there marketed comes from other states. Three-fourths of this amount arrives by rail and is consigned to commission men or receivers. Most of these freight shipments (about 75 per cent) come in at the Manhattan Terminal of the New York Central Railroad, and the remainder at one of the four terminals in New Jersey serving New York City. The commission men transact by far the greater part of the business on a commission basis, representing the shippers as agents, and remitting to them the proceeds of sale, less commissions, freight, and handling charges. Otherwise, they buy for their own account. They sell to slaughterhouse operators who are also called marketmen.

The defendants are slaughterhouse operators of the latter class. A.L.A. Schechter Poultry Corporation and Schechter Live Poultry Market are corporations conducting wholesale poultry slaughterhouse markets in Brooklyn, New York City. Defendants ordinarily purchase their live poultry from commission men at the West Washington Market in New York City or at the railroad terminals serving the city, but occasionally they purchase from commission men in Philadelphia. They buy the poultry for slaughter and resale. After the poultry is trucked to their slaughterhouse markets in Brooklyn, it is there sold, usually within twenty-four hours, to retail poultry dealers and butchers who sell directly to consumers. The poultry purchased from defendants is immediately slaughtered, prior to delivery, by shochtim in defendants' employ. Defendants do not sell poultry in interstate commerce.

[P]rovisions relate to the hours and wages of those employed by defendants in their slaughterhouses in Brooklyn and to the sales there made to retail dealers and butchers. Were these transactions "in" interstate commerce? Much is made of the fact that almost all the poultry coming to New York is sent there from other states. But the code provisions, as here applied, do not concern the transportation of the poultry from other states to New York, or the transactions of the commission men or others to whom it is consigned, or the sales made by such consignees to defendants. When defendants had made their purchases, whether at the West Washington Market in New York City or at the railroad terminals serving the city, or elsewhere, the poultry was trucked to their slaughterhouses in Brooklyn for local disposition. The interstate transactions in relation to that poultry then ended. Defendants held the poultry at their slaughterhouse markets for slaughter and local sale to retail dealers and butchers who in turn sold directly to consumers.

---

[2] In addition to finding that the law exceeded the scope of Congress's Commerce Clause authority, the Court also found there was an excessive delegation of legislative power. The delegation issue is considered in Chapter 7. [Footnote by casebook author.]

Neither the slaughtering nor the sales by defendants were transactions in interstate commerce.

The undisputed facts thus afford no warrant for the argument that the poultry handled by defendants at their slaughterhouse markets was in a "current" or "flow" of interstate commerce, and was thus subject to congressional regulation. The mere fact that there may be a constant flow of commodities into a state does not mean that the flow continues after the property has arrived and has become commingled with the mass of property within the state and is there held solely for local disposition and use. So far as the poultry here in question is concerned, the flow in interstate commerce had ceased. The poultry had come to a permanent rest within the state. It was not held, used, or sold by defendants in relation to any further transactions in interstate commerce and was not destined for transportation to other states. Hence decisions which deal with a stream of interstate commerce — where goods come to rest within a state temporarily and are later to go forward in interstate commerce — and with the regulations of transactions involved in that practical continuity of movement, are not applicable here.

In determining how far the federal government may go in controlling intrastate transactions upon the ground that they "affect" interstate commerce, there is a necessary and well-established distinction between direct and indirect effects. The precise line can be drawn only as individual cases arise, but the distinction is clear in principle. Direct effects are illustrated by the railroad cases. But where the effect of intrastate transactions upon interstate commerce is merely indirect, such transactions remain within the domain of state power. If the commerce clause were construed to reach all enterprises and transactions which could be said to have an indirect effect upon interstate commerce, the federal authority would embrace practically all the activities of the people, and the authority of the state over its domestic concerns would exist only by sufferance of the federal government. Indeed, on such a theory, even the development of the state's commercial facilities would be subject to federal control.

While these decisions related to the application of the Federal statute, and not to its constitutional validity, the distinction between direct and indirect effects of intrastate transactions upon interstate commerce must be recognized as a fundamental one, essential to the maintenance of our constitutional system. Otherwise, as we have said, there would be virtually no limit to the federal power, and for all practical purposes we should have a completely centralized government. We must consider the provisions here in question in the light of this distinction.

In *Schechter*, the Court, in part, concludes that the federal regulation of the poultry business could not be justified on the ground that it is part of the stream of commerce. The "stream of commerce" approach to defining "among the states" was used in many cases during this time period. For example, in Swift & Co. v. United States 196 U.S. 375 (1905), the Court upheld the application of the Sherman Antitrust Act to an agreement among meat dealers to fix the price at which they would purchase meat from stockyards. Although the stockyard was intrastate, the Court stressed that it was only a temporary stop for the cattle. Justice Holmes, writing for the Court, explained that the stockyards were in "a current of commerce among the States, and the purchase of the cattle is a part and incident of such commerce."

Similarly, in Stafford v. Wallace, 258 U.S. 495 (1922), the Court upheld the Packers and Stockyards Act of 1921 which authorized the Secretary of Commerce to regulate rates and prescribe standards for the operation of stockyards where livestock was kept. The law was designed to protect consumers by lessening collusion between stockyard managers and packers and also by decreasing the ability of packers to set prices for livestock. The Supreme Court upheld the federal law emphasizing that the stockyards are in the stream of commerce. Chief Justice Taft, writing for the Court, explained that the "stockyards are but a throat through which the current flows, and the transactions which occur therein are only incident to this current from the West to the East, and from one State to another. Such transactions can not be separated from the movement to which they contribute and necessarily take on its character."

The Court relied on this stream of commerce approach to allow Congress to prohibit the sale of impure or adulterated food or drugs,[3] to require retail labeling for items traveling in interstate commerce,[4] and to restrict the sale of intoxicating beverages to Indians.[5]

The Court, however, did not consistently apply its stream of commerce approach. For example, in Railroad Retirement Board v. Alton R.R. Co., 295 U.S. 330 (1935), the Court declared unconstitutional the Railroad Retirement Act of 1934, which provided a pension system for railroad workers. Railroads obviously were part of the stream of interstate commerce, and the Court had upheld other federal regulations of railroads.[6] But in the *Alton R.R. Co.* case the Court struck down the requirement for a pension for railroad workers and distinguished the other cases as concerning the safety or efficiency of the railroads. The Court said that Congress could not use its commerce power to require a pension program for railroad employees because the law was only to help "the social welfare of the worker, and therefore [was] remote from any regulation of commerce."

Thus, during the era from the 1890s until 1937, the Court, at times, more broadly defined "among the states," such as in the *Shreveport Rate Cases* and in the stream of commerce decisions. At other times, the Court more narrowly defined "among the states," such as in requiring a direct effect on commerce in *Schechter* and in rejecting the stream of commerce argument in that case and in *Alton*.

---

[3] Hipolite Egg. Co. v. United States, 220 U.S. 451 (1911).
[4] McDermott v. Wisconsin, 228 U.S. 115 (1913).
[5] United States v. Nice, 241 U.S. 591 (1916).
[6] *See, e.g.,* Southern Railway v. United States, 222 U.S. 20 (1911) (upholding the Federal Safety Appliance Acts, which regulated couplers on railroad cars): Baltimore & Ohio Railroad Co. v. Interstate Commerce Commission, 221 U.S. 612 (1911) (upholding a federal law that set maximum hours for railroad workers).

3. *1937-1990s: Broad Federal Commerce Power*

By the mid-1930s, there were enormous pressures for a change in the Supreme Court's narrow approach to defining the scope of Congress's power. It must be remembered that during this time the Court also was narrowly interpreting the scope of other congressional powers, such as the spending power (discussed below), and greatly restricting the ability of state governments to regulate the economy by protecting freedom of contract under substantive due process (discussed in Chapter 6 [Erwin Chemerinsky, Constitutional Law, 3rd ed., (2009)]).

The economic crisis caused by the Depression made the Supreme Court's hostility to economic regulation and its commitment to a laissez-faire economy seem anachronistic and harmful. Unemployment was widespread, and the wages of those with jobs were low. Business failure was endemic, and production was substantially lessened. Foreclosures of home and farm mortgages were common.

Strong political pressure developed for change. President Franklin Roosevelt won a landslide reelection victory in 1936 and saw this as a strong endorsement for the New Deal programs that the Court was invalidating, such as in Carter v. Carter Coal and Schechter Poultry v. United States. In March 1937, Roosevelt proposed that Congress adopt legislation to increase the size of the Supreme Court.[7] Under the proposal, one Justice would be added to the Court for each Justice over age 70, up to a maximum of 15 Justices. In light of the ages of the Justices then on the Court, Roosevelt would have been able to add six new Justices and thus secure a majority on the Court to uphold the New Deal programs.

Roosevelt's Court packing plan drew intense opposition, even from some supporters of New Deal programs, on the ground that it was a threat to the independence of the federal judiciary. It is worth noting, however, that nothing in the Constitution mandated or even suggested a number of Justices for the Court. The first Judiciary Act prescribed a Court of six. This was temporarily reduced to five in 1801 and increased back to six in 1802. The number of Justices was increased to seven in 1807, to nine in 1837, and to ten in 1864. Generally, the increase in the size of the Court was a result of the addition of a new federal circuit court of appeals. Supreme Court Justices were responsible for "riding circuit" and sitting as federal appeals court judges; an additional Justice was created each time the country expanded and a new circuit was added.

In 1866, with unpopular President Andrew Johnson in the White House, Congress reduced the size of the Supreme Court to seven. This kept Johnson from filling an existing vacancy on the Court and meant that the next two vacancies also would go unfilled in order to bring the Court's size down from ten to seven. In 1869, after Ulysses Grant became President, the number on the Court was increased to nine, where it has been ever since.

Although the number of Justices was not specified in the Constitution, Roosevelt's Court packing plan was intensely opposed as a threat to judicial independence. In 1937, Justice Owen Roberts changed his position and was the fifth to

---

[7] The "Court packing" proposal is discussed in detail in Robert Jackson, *The Struggle for Judicial Supremacy* (1941).

uphold two laws of the type that previously had been invalidated: a state minimum wage law for women and a federal law regulating labor relations.[8] There is a debate over whether Roberts was influenced by the political pressure of the Court packing plan or whether he planned to change his vote prior to Roosevelt's proposal. Whatever the cause, Roberts's change in sentiment will forever be known as "the switch in time that saved nine."

KEY DECISIONS CHANGING THE COMMERCE CLAUSE DOCTRINE

Three decisions — NLRB v. Jones & Laughlin Steel Corp. in 1937, United States v. Darby in 1941, and Wickard v. Filburn in 1942 — overruled the earlier era of decisions and expansively defined the scope of Congress's commerce power. Indeed, because of these three decisions, from 1937 until 1995, not one federal law was declared unconstitutional as exceeding the scope of Congress's commerce power. These three key rulings are presented and then followed by consideration of how the Court defined "commerce among the states" after these decisions and how the Court treated the Tenth Amendment prior to the 1990s.

NLRB v. Jones & Laughlin Steel Corp.

301 U.S. 1 (1937)

Chief Justice HUGHES delivered the opinion of the Court.

In a proceeding under the National Labor Relations Act of 1935 the National Labor Relations Board found that the respondent, Jones & Laughlin Steel Corporation, had violated the act by engaging in unfair labor practices affecting commerce. The unfair labor practices charged were that the corporation was discriminating against members of the union with regard to hire and tenure of employment, and was coercing and intimidating its employees in order to interfere with their self-organization. The discriminatory and coercive action alleged was the discharge of certain employees.

The facts as to the nature and scope of the business of the Jones & Laughlin Steel Corporation have been found by the Labor Board, and, so far as they are essential to the determination of this controversy, they are not in dispute. The corporation is organized under the laws of Pennsylvania and has its principal office at Pittsburgh. It is engaged in the business of manufacturing iron and steel in plants

---

[8] West Coast Hotel v. Parish, 300 U.S. 379 (1937) (upholding a state minimum wage law for women), discussed in Chapter 6 [Erwin Chemerinsky, Constitutional Law, 3rd ed., (2009)]; NLRB v. Jones & Laughlin Steel Corp., 301 U.S. 1 (1937) (upholding federal regulation of the steel industry), discussed below.

situated in Pittsburgh and nearby Aliquippa, Pa. It manufactures and distributes a widely diversified line of steel and pig iron, being the fourth largest producer of steel in the United States. With its subsidiaries — nineteen in number — it is a completely integrated enterprise, owning and operating ore, coal and limestone properties, lake and river transportation facilities and terminal railroads located at its manufacturing plants. It owns or controls mines in Michigan and Minnesota. It operates four ore steamships on the Great Lakes, used in the transportation of ore to its factories. It owns coal mines in Pennsylvania. It operates towboats and steam barges used in carrying coal to its factories. It owns limestone properties in various places in Pennsylvania and West Virginia. It owns the Monongahela connecting railroad which connects the plants of the Pittsburgh works and forms an interconnection with the Pennsylvania, New York Central and Baltimore & Ohio Railroad systems. It owns the Aliquippa & Southern Railroad Company, which connects the Aliquippa works with the Pittsburgh & Lake Erie, part of the New York Central system. Much of its product is shipped to its warehouses in Chicago, Detroit, Cincinnati and Memphis, — to the last two places by means of its own barges and transportation equipment. In Long Island City, New York, and in New Orleans it operates structural steel fabricating shops in connection with the warehousing of semifinished materials sent from its works. Through one of its wholly-owned subsidiaries it owns, leases, and operates stores, warehouses, and yards for the distribution of equipment and supplies for drilling and operating oil and gas wells and for pipe lines, refineries and pumping stations. It has sales offices in twenty cities in the United States and a wholly-owned subsidiary which is devoted exclusively to distributing its product in Canada. Approximately 75 percent of its product is shipped out of Pennsylvania.

Summarizing these operations, the Labor Board concluded that the works in Pittsburgh and Aliquippa "might be likened to the heart of a self-contained, highly integrated body. They draw in the raw materials from Michigan, Minnesota, West Virginia, Pennsylvania in part through arteries and by means controlled by the respondent; they transform the materials and then pump them out to all parts of the nation through the vast mechanism which the respondent has elaborated."

To carry on the activities of the entire steel industry, 33,000 men mine ore, 44,000 men mine coal, 4,000 men quarry limestone, 16,000 men manufacture coke, 343,000 men manufacture steel, and 83,000 men transport its product. Respondent has about 10,000 employees in its Aliquippa plant, which is located in a community of about 30,000 persons.

The act is challenged in its entirety as an attempt to regulate all industry, thus invading the reserved powers of the States over their local concerns. It is asserted that the references in the act to interstate and foreign commerce are colorable at best; that the act is not a true regulation of such commerce or of matters which directly affect it, but on the contrary has the fundamental object of placing under the compulsory supervision of the federal government all industrial labor relations within the nation.

If this conception of terms, intent and consequent inseparability were sound, the act would necessarily fall by reason of the limitation upon the federal power which inheres in the constitutional grant, as well as because of the explicit reservation of the Tenth Amendment. The authority of the federal government may not be pushed to such an extreme as to destroy the distinction, which the commerce clause itself establishes, between commerce "among the several States" and the internal concerns of a state. That distinction between what is national and what is local in the activities of commerce is vital to the maintenance of our federal system.

We think it clear that the National Labor Relations Act may be construed so as to operate within the sphere of constitutional authority. There can be no question that the commerce thus contemplated by the act (aside from that within a Territory or the District of Columbia) is interstate and foreign commerce in the constitutional sense. The act also defines the term "affecting commerce": "The term 'affecting commerce' means in commerce, or burdening or obstructing commerce or the free flow of commerce, or having led or tending to lead to a labor dispute burdening or obstructing commerce or the free flow of commerce."

This definition is one of exclusion as well as inclusion. The grant of authority to the Board does not purport to extend to the relationship between all industrial employees and employers. Its terms do not impose collective bargaining upon all industry regardless of effects upon interstate or foreign commerce. It purports to reach only what may be deemed to burden or obstruct that commerce and, thus qualified, it must be construed as contemplating the exercise of control within constitutional bounds. It is a familiar principle that acts which directly burden or obstruct interstate or foreign commerce, or its free flow, are within the reach of the congressional power. Acts having that effect are not rendered immune because they grow out of labor disputes. It is the effect upon commerce, not the source of the injury, which is the criterion.

Respondent says that, whatever may be said of employees engaged in interstate commerce, the industrial relations and activities in the manufacturing department of respondent's enterprise are not subject to federal regulation. The argument rests upon the proposition that manufacturing in itself is not commerce.

The congressional authority to protect interstate commerce from burdens and obstructions is not limited to transactions which can be deemed to be an essential part of a "flow" of interstate or foreign commerce. Burdens and obstructions may be due to injurious action springing from other sources. The fundamental principle is that the power to regulate commerce is the power to enact "all appropriate legislation" for its "protection or advancement"; to adopt measures "to promote its growth and insure its safety"; "to foster, protect, control, and restrain." That power is plenary and may be exerted to protect interstate commerce "no matter what the source of the dangers which threaten it." Although activities may be intrastate in character when separately considered, if they have such a close and substantial relation to interstate commerce that their control is essential or appropriate to protect that commerce from burdens and obstructions, Congress cannot be denied the power to exercise that control.

The close and intimate effect which brings the subject within the reach of federal power may be due to activities in relation to productive industry although the industry when separately viewed is local. It is thus apparent that the fact that the employees here concerned were engaged in production is not determinative. The question remains as to the effect upon interstate commerce of the labor practice involved.

Giving full weight to respondent's contention with respect to a break in the complete continuity of the "stream of commerce" by reason of respondent's manufacturing operations, the fact remains that the stoppage of those operations by industrial strife would have a most serious effect upon interstate commerce. In view of respondent's far-flung activities, it is idle to say that the effect would be indirect or remote. It is obvious that it would be immediate and might be catastrophic. We are asked to shut our eyes to the plainest facts of our national life and to deal with the question of direct and indirect effects in an intellectual vacuum. Because there may be but indirect and remote effects upon interstate commerce in connection with a host of local enterprises throughout the country, it does not follow that other industrial activities do not have such a close and intimate relation to interstate commerce as to make the presence of industrial strife a matter of the most urgent national concern. When industries organize themselves on a national scale, making their relation to interstate commerce the dominant factor in their activities, how can it be maintained that their industrial labor relations constitute a forbidden field into which Congress may not enter when it is necessary to protect interstate commerce from the paralyzing consequences of industrial war?

Experience has abundantly demonstrated that the recognition of the right of employees to self-organization and to have representatives of their own choosing for the purpose of collective bargaining is often an essential condition of industrial peace. Refusal to confer and negotiate has been one of the most prolific causes of strife.

Justice McREYNOLDS delivered the following dissenting opinion.

Justice VAN DEVANTER, Justice SUTHERLAND, Justice BUTLER and I are unable to agree with the decisions just announced. The Court as we think departs from well-established principles followed in Schechter Poultry Corporation v. United States, and Carter v. Carter Coal Co. In each cause the Labor Board formulated and then sustained a charge of unfair labor practices towards persons employed only in production. It ordered restoration of discharged employees to former positions with payment for losses sustained. These orders were declared invalid below upon the ground that respondents while carrying on production operations were not thereby engaging in interstate commerce; that labor practices in the course of such operations did not directly affect interstate commerce; consequently respondents' actions did not come within congressional power.

The wide sweep of the statute will more readily appear if consideration be given to the Board's proceedings against the smallest and relatively least important — the Clothing Company. If the act applies to the relations of that Company to employees in production, of course it applies to the larger respondents with like business elements although the affairs of the latter may present other characteristics. Though differing in some respects, all respondents procure raw materials outside the state where they manufacture, fabricate within and then ship beyond the state. Manifestly that view of congressional power would extend it into almost every field of human industry.

Wickard v. Filburn

317 U.S. 111 (1942)

Justice JACKSON delivered the opinion of the Court.

The appellee for many years past has owned and operated a small farm in Montgomery County, Ohio, maintaining a herd of dairy cattle, selling milk, raising poultry, and selling poultry and eggs. It has been his practice to raise a small acreage of winter wheat, sown in the Fall and harvested in the following July; to sell a portion of the crop; to feed part to poultry and livestock on the farm, some of which is sold; to use some in making flour for home consumption; and to keep the rest for the following seeding. The intended disposition of the crop here involved has not been expressly stated.

In July of 1940, pursuant to the Agricultural Adjustment Act of 1938, as then amended, there were established for the appellee's 1941 crop a wheat acreage allotment of 11.1 acres and a normal yield of 20.1 bushels of wheat an acre. He was given notice of such allotment in July of 1940 before the Fall planting of his 1941 crop of wheat, and again in July of 1941, before it was harvested. He sowed, however, 23 acres, and harvested from his 11.9 acres of excess acreage 239 bushels, which under the terms of the Act as amended on May 26,1941, constituted farm marketing excess, subject to a penalty of 49 cents a bushel, or $117.11 in all.

The general scheme of the Agricultural Adjustment Act of 1938 as related to wheat is to control the volume moving in interstate and foreign commerce in order to avoid surpluses and shortages and the consequent abnormally low or high wheat prices and obstructions to commerce. Within prescribed limits and by prescribed standards the Secretary of Agriculture is directed to ascertain and proclaim each year a national acreage allotment for the next crop of wheat, which is then apportioned to the states and their counties, and is eventually broken up into allotments for individual farms.

It is urged that under the Commerce Clause of the Constitution, Article I, §8, clause 3, Congress does not possess the power it has in this instance sought to exercise. The question would merit little consideration since our decision in United States v. Darby, sustaining the federal power to regulate production of goods for commerce except for the fact that this Act extends federal regulation to production not intended in any part for commerce but wholly for consumption on the farm. Appellee says that this is a regulation of production and consumption of wheat. Such activities are, he urges, beyond the reach of Congressional power under the Commerce Clause, since they are local in character, and their effects upon interstate commerce are at most "indirect."

We believe that a review of the course of decision under the Commerce Clause will make plain, however, that questions of the power of Congress are not to be decided by reference to any formula which would give controlling force to nomenclature such as "production" and "indirect" and foreclose consideration of the actual effects of the activity in question upon interstate commerce.

Once an economic measure of the reach of the power granted to Congress in the Commerce Clause is accepted, questions of federal power cannot be decided simply by finding the activity in question to be "production" nor can consideration of its economic effects be foreclosed by calling them "indirect." Whether the subject of the regulation in question was "production," "consumption," or "marketing" is, therefore, not material for purposes of deciding the question of federal power before us. But even if appellee's activity be local and though it may not be regarded as commerce, it may still, whatever its nature, be reached by Congress if it exerts a substantial economic effect on interstate commerce and this irrespective of whether such effect is what might at some earlier time have been defined as "direct" or "indirect."

The parties have stipulated a summary of the economics of the wheat industry. Commerce among the states in wheat is large and important. The effect of consumption of homegrown wheat on interstate commerce is due to the fact that it constitutes the most variable factor in the disappearance of the wheat crop. Consumption on the farm where grown appears to vary in an amount greater than 20 percent of average production. The total amount of wheat consumed as food varies but relatively little, and use as seed is relatively constant.

The maintenance by government regulation of a price for wheat undoubtedly can be accomplished as effectively by sustaining or increasing the demand as by limiting the supply. The effect of the statute before us is to restrict the amount which may be produced for market and the extent as well to which one may forestall resort to the market by producing to meet his own needs. That appellee's own contribution to the demand for wheat may be trivial by itself is not enough to remove him from the scope of federal regulation where, as here, his contribution, taken together with that of many others similarly situated, is far from trivial.

It is well established by decisions of this Court that the power to regulate commerce includes the power to regulate the prices at which commodities in that commerce are dealt in and practices affecting such prices. One of the primary purposes of the Act in question was to increase the market price of wheat and to that end to limit the volume thereof that could affect the market. It can hardly be denied that a factor of such volume and variability as home-consumed wheat would have a substantial influence on price and market conditions. This may arise because being in marketable condition such wheat overhangs the market and if induced by rising prices tends to flow into the market and check price increases. But if we assume that it is never marketed, it supplies a need of the man who grew it which would otherwise be reflected by purchases in the open market. Home-grown wheat in this sense competes with wheat in commerce. The stimulation of commerce is a use of the regulatory function quite as definitely as prohibitions or restrictions thereon. This record leaves us in no doubt that Congress may properly have considered that wheat consumed on the farm where grown if wholly outside the scheme of regulation would have a substantial effect in defeating and obstructing its purpose to stimulate trade therein at increased prices.

These three cases adopt broad definitions of "commerce" and "among the states" and reject the Tenth Amendment as a limit on Congress's Commerce Clause power. Commerce includes all stages of business; no longer is a distinction drawn between commerce and other stages of business such as mining, manufacture, and production. Congress can regulate any activity, intrastate or interstate, that has a substantial effect on interstate commerce. Indeed, Congress can regulate activities that themselves have little effect on interstate commerce if the activity, looked at cumulatively throughout the country has a substantial effect on commerce. The Tenth Amendment, *as Darby* states, is simply a reminder that for Congress to legislate it must point to express or implied power. The Tenth Amendment is no longer seen as reserving a zone of activities for exclusive state control.

This expansive definition of Congress's commerce power continued from 1937 until the 1990s. From 1937 until 1992, not one federal law was invalidated as exceeding the scope of Congress's Commerce Clause authority and only once was a federal law found to violate the Tenth Amendment, and that case was expressly overruled less than a decade later. In describing the law after *Jones Laughlin*, *Darby*, and *Wickard*, initially the cases concerning the meaning of "commerce among the states" are described, followed by an examination of cases concerning the Tenth Amendment during this time period.

The Test for the Commerce Clause After 1937

Taken together, *NLRB v. Jones & Laughlin Steel Corp.*, *United States v. Darby*, and *Wickard v. Filburn* expansively defined the scope of Congress's commerce clause power.[9] No longer did the Court distinguish between commerce and other stages of business such as mining, manufacturing, and production; instead, Congress could exercise control over all phases of business. No longer did the Court distinguish between direct and indirect effects on interstate commerce; rather, Congress could regulate any activity that taken cumulatively had an effect on interstate commerce. No longer was the Tenth Amendment a limit on congressional power; instead, a federal law would be upheld so long as it was within the scope of Congress's power, and the commerce clause was interpreted so broadly that seemingly any law would meet this requirement.

Thus, after 1937 until 1995, not one federal law was declared unconstitutional as exceeding the scope of Congress's commerce power. The law of the commerce clause during this era could be simply stated: Congress could regulate any activity if there was a substantial effect on interstate commerce. Of course, after *Wickard v. Filburn*, it was not necessary that the particular person or entity being regulated have a substantial effect on commerce; the requirement was only that the activity, looked at cumulatively across the country, have a substantial effect on commerce.

---

[9] These were not the only decisions in this period that broadly defined the scope of Congress's commerce power. *See also* Kentucky Whip & Collar Co. v. Illinois Central R.R., 299 U.S. 334 (1937) (upholding a ban on shipments in interstate commerce of convict-made goods into states forbidding their use); United States v. Rock Royal Co-operative, 307 U.S. 533 (1939) (upholding a federal regulation of the handling of milk in the New York metropolitan area); United States v. Wrightwood Dairy Co., 315 U.S. 110 (1942) (upholding the power of Congress to regulate milk that was produced and sold intrastate, but was in competition with interstate dairy products).

In fact, in some cases, the Court even deleted the word "substantial" and declared that Congress could regulate anything under the commerce clause so long as there was a rational basis for believing that there was an effect on commerce. In *Hodel v. Indiana*, in 1981, the Court stated: "A court may invalidate legislation enacted under the Commerce Clause only if it is clear that there is no rational basis for a congressional finding that the regulated activity affects interstate commerce, or that there is no reasonable connection between the regulatory means selected and the asserted ends."[10]

Under this test, it is difficult to imagine anything that Congress could not regulate under the commerce clause so long as it was not violating another constitutional provision. As such, since 1937, a wide array of federal legislation has been adopted under the aegis of the commerce clause. To illustrate the breadth of the Supreme Court's interpretation of the commerce clause, consider three types of federal laws adopted under it: regulatory laws, civil rights laws, and criminal laws.

Regulatory Laws

A key aspect of American government since 1937 has been the dramatic increase in the number of federal administrative and regulatory agencies and in the scope of authority they possess.[11] The Court's broad definition of the commerce clause power facilitated this expansion. The Court held that Congress can set the terms for items shipped in interstate commerce. This includes virtually anything that potentially can travel across state lines. For instance, the Court has held that Congress can regulate intangible items such as insurance policies or stock under its commerce power.[12]

Congress can regulate purely intrastate activities, including all aspects of business, if there is a rational basis for believing that there is an interstate effect. For example, the Court held that Congress could regulate strip mining on land even though the land was not a part of interstate commerce and even though regulating land use has been a traditional state government function.[13] The Court deferred to congressional findings that "many surface mining operations result in

---

[10] 452 U.S. 314, 323-324 (1981). It is worth noting that not all of the Justices agreed with this broad definition of the commerce power, though Justice Rehnquist wrote separately to stress that there must be a "substantial effect" in order for Congress to act: "It would be a mistake to conclude that Congress' power to regulate . . . is unlimited. Some activities may be so private or local in nature that they may not be in commerce. . . . [The] Court asserts that regulation will be upheld if Congress had a rational basis for finding that the regulated activity affects interstate commerce. . . . [But] it has long been established that . . . [t]here must instead be a showing that the regulated activity has a *substantial effect* on that commerce." Hodel v. Virginia Surface Mining & Reclamation Assn., Inc., 452 U.S. 264, 310-312 (1981) (Rehnquist, J., concurring in the judgment). As discussed below, in *United States v. Lopez*, 514 U.S. 549 (1995), the Court, in an opinion by Chief Justice Rehnquist, held that the test is that there must be a "substantial effect" on interstate commerce.

[11] The constitutional problems posed by these agencies are discussed in more detail in §3.9 [Erwin Chemerinsky, Constitutional Law: Principles and Policies, 4th ed., (2011)].

[12] *See* United States v. South-Eastern Underwriters Assn., 322 U.S. 533 (1944) (Congress's authority to regulate interstate insurance transactions); American Power & Light Co. v. SEC, 329 U.S. 90 (1946) (Congress's authority to regulate stock in public utilities).

[13] *See* Hodel v. Virginia Surface Mining & Reclamation Assn., Inc., 452 U.S. 264 (1981); Hodel v. Indiana, 452 U.S. 314 (1981)

disturbances of surface areas that burden and adversely affect commerce and the public welfare by destroying or diminishing the utility of land . . . by causing erosion and landslides, by contributing to floods, by polluting the water, by destroying fish and wildlife habitat, by impairing natural beauty, by damaging the property of citizens, by creating hazards dangerous to life and property . . . , and by counteracting government programs and efforts to conserve soil, water, and other natural resources."[14]

Also, Congress can regulate intrastate activities if necessary to protect its regulation of interstate activities. In fact, the Court has held that Congress's regulatory power extends even after an item has been shipped in interstate commerce. For example, the Court upheld the authority of the Food and Drug Administration to impose labeling requirements for items that have been a part of interstate commerce.[15]

Civil Rights Laws

Among the most important laws ever adopted in American history is the 1964 Civil Rights Act, which, in part, prohibits private employment discrimination based on race, gender, or religion, and which forbids discrimination by places of public accommodation such as hotels and restaurants. Congress enacted this legislation under its commerce clause power, and the Supreme Court upheld it on that basis.

Logically it might seem that the civil rights law would be most easily justified under Congress's authority pursuant to §5 of the Fourteenth Amendment. However, the Supreme Court, in 1883, had held that Congress only could regulate government conduct and could not regulate private behavior under the Fourteenth Amendments.[16] Therefore, in 1964, it was uncertain whether Congress could use its Fourteenth Amendment power to outlaw private discrimination in employment and public accommodations. Congress thus chose the commerce clause as the authority for this landmark legislation.[17]

In *Heart of Atlanta Motel Inc. v. United States*, the Court upheld the constitutionality of Title II of the Civil Rights Act, which prohibited discrimination by places of public accommodation.[18] The Heart of Atlanta Motel was located in downtown Atlanta and had 216 rooms and about 75 percent of its registered guests

---

[14] *Id.* at 277. In *Hodel v. Virginia Surface Mining and Reclamation Association*, the Court upheld the general constitutionality of the Surface Mining Control and Reclamation Act of 1977. In the companion case of *Hodel v. Indiana* the Court upheld the prime farmland provisions of the Act that required a demonstration of the ability to restore cropland before it was subjected to strip mining operations.

[15] United States v. Sullivan, 332 U.S. 689 (1948) (affirming the conviction of a retail druggist for "misbranding" two pill boxes).

[16] The Civil Rights Cases, 109 U.S. 3 (1883). This decision is discussed in detail in §3.6.1 and §6.4 [Erwin Chemerinsky, Constitutional Law: Principles and Policies, 4th ed., (2011)].

[17] Earlier cases had upheld the ability of Congress to prohibit discrimination in the channels of interstate commerce. See, e.g., Morgan v. Virginia, 328 U.S. 373 (1946); Boynton v. Virginia, 364 U.S. 454 (1960).

[18] 379 U.S. 241 (1964).

from out of state.[19] The Court upheld the application of the Act to the motel, which had a policy of refusing to provide accommodations to blacks.

The Court said that in evaluating the law and its application "[t]he only questions are: (1) whether Congress had a rational basis for finding that racial discrimination by motels affected commerce, and (2) if it had such a basis, whether the means it selected to eliminate that evil are reasonable and appropriate."[20] The Court concluded that the "voluminous testimony [before Congress] presents overwhelming evidence that discrimination by hotels and motels impedes interstate travel."[21] The Court noted that it did not matter that Congress's motive, in part, was moral; many federal laws, stretching back to the *Lottery Case*, had been adopted under the commerce power to remedy moral wrongs. Also, the Court said that it did not matter if the motel was "of a purely local character;" the Court said "[i]f it is interstate commerce that feels the pinch, it does not matter how local the operation which applies the squeeze."[22]

In a companion case, *Katzenbach v. McClung*, the Court upheld the application of the Act to a small business: Ollie's Barbecue, a family-owned restaurant in Birmingham, Alabama.[23] The Court's recitation of the facts emphasized the interstate connections of the restaurant. For example, 46 percent of the meat that it purchased annually came from out of state.[24] The Court's decision, however, was not based on the interstate impact of this particular restaurant. Rather, the Court found that Congress rationally had concluded that discrimination by restaurants cumulatively had an impact on interstate commerce. The Court found that the testimony before Congress "afforded ample basis for the conclusion that established restaurants in such areas sold less interstate goods because of the discrimination, that interstate travel was obstructed directly by it, that business in general suffered and that many new businesses refrained from establishing there as a result of it."[25] The Court upheld the Civil Rights Act and its application to Ollie's Barbecue because "[t]he power of Congress [under the commerce clause] is broad and sweeping."[26]

Although both *Heart of Atlanta Motel* and *Katzenbach v. McClung* were unanimous decisions, Justices Douglas and Goldberg concurred in each and said that they would have preferred to have the law upheld as constitutional under §5 of the Fourteenth Amendment.[27] The scope of Congress's power under this constitutional provision is discussed in §3.6 [Erwin Chemerinsky, Constitutional Law: Principles and Policies, 4th ed., (2011)] below.

---

[19] *Id.* at 243.
[20] *Id.* at 258-259.
[21] *Id.* at 253.
[22] *Id.* at 258 (citation omitted).
[23] 379 U.S. 294 (1964).
[24] *Id.* at 297.
[25] *Id.* at 300.
[26] *Id.* at 305.
[27] 379 U.S. at 280 (Douglas, J., concurring) ("I would prefer to rest the assertion of legislative power [on] §5 of the Fourteenth Amendment"); *id.* at 293 (Goldberg, J., concurring) (Congress had the authority under both the commerce clause and under §5 of the Fourteenth Amendment).

These decisions reflect the breadth of Congress's commerce power, but they are not surprising under the doctrines developed since 1937. Under *Wickard*, racial discrimination by hotels and restaurants, looked at cumulatively across the country, surely has an effect on interstate commerce. Nor is there any reason why it should matter that Congress's primary purpose was based more on a moral judgment to eliminate discrimination than on concern for enhancing the economy. The Court has been consistently unwilling to limit Congress to acting under the commerce clause only to advance economic efficiency.

Criminal Laws

Not surprisingly, Congress has used its broad commerce clause power to enact many federal criminal laws. Some of these laws were adopted before 1937, such as the Mann Act, which makes it a crime to take a woman across state lines for immoral purposes,[28] and the Lindbergh Act, which prohibits kidnapping.[29]

Perez v. United States illustrates the Court's willingness to uphold federal criminal laws adopted under the commerce power.[30] Title II of the Consumer Credit Protection Act prohibited loan sharking activities such as charges of excess interest, violence, and threats of violence to collect debts. The defendant had been convicted of violating the law, but argued to the Supreme Court that the law could not be constitutionally applied to him because his business wholly operated in New York and there was no proof that he had engaged in organized crime.

The Court rejected these arguments and upheld the federal law. The Court concluded that it was rational for Congress to believe that even intrastate loan sharking activities had a sufficient effect on interstate commerce. The Court said that particularized findings were not required in order for a law to be upheld; it was sufficient that Congress had a rational belief that even "purely intrastate [loan sharking] . . . nevertheless directly affect[s] interstate and foreign commerce."[31]

After *Perez*, Congress used this authority to adopt one of the broadest and most important contemporary statutes: the federal RICO law. Title IX of the Organized Crime Control Act of 1970 contains the Racketeer Influenced and Corrupt Organizations (RICO) Act, which makes it a federal crime for "any person employed by or associated with any enterprise engaged, or the activities of which affect, interstate or foreign commerce, to conduct or participate, directly or indirectly, in a pattern of racketeering activity."[32] Racketeering is broadly defined to include everything from prostitution, obscenity, and gambling to arson, extortion, and bribery.[33]

---

[28] *See* Hoke v. United States, 227 U.S. 308 (1913); Caminetti v. United States, 242 U.S. 470 (1917).
[29] Gooch v. United States, 297 U.S. 124 (1936).
[30] 402 U.S. 146 (1971).
[31] *Id.* at 155-156.
[32] 18 U.S.C. §1962 (c).
[33] 19 U.S.C. §1961(1).

Is the Broad Definition of the Commerce Power Desirable?

These decisions illustrate the breadth of the commerce power between 1937 and 1995. The key question is whether this is a desirable recognition of the need for federal legislation or whether it is an undesirable abandonment of basic constitutional principles. On the one hand, the complex problems facing American society in the twentieth century necessitate that Congress have authority to act beyond the narrow confines created by the Court in the pre-1937 area.

On the other hand, a core principle of American constitutional law is that the federal government has limited powers with most governance left to the states. The Court's expansive approach to the commerce clause puts virtually nothing beyond the reach of Congress, so long as it does not violate another constitutional provision.

Closely related to this issue is the question whether the judiciary should protect the states or whether the only check on Congress is through the political process. This is discussed more fully in §3.8 [Erwin Chemerinsky, Constitutional Law: Principles and Policies, 4th ed., (2011)], below. These basic normative questions are key in evaluating the desirability of the shift in the law since 1995 as the Court has narrowed the scope of the commerce power.

4. The Commerce Clause After United States v. Lopez

Between 1936 and April 26, 1995, the Supreme Court did not find one federal law unconstitutional as exceeding the scope of Congress's commerce power. Then in *United States v. Lopez*[34] by a 5-to-4 margin, the Supreme Court declared unconstitutional the Gun-Free School Zones Act of 1990, which made it a federal crime to have a gun within 1,000 feet of a school.[35] Splitting along ideological lines, the Court ruled that the relationship to interstate commerce was too tangential and uncertain to uphold the law as a valid exercise of Congress's commerce power. Chief Justice Rehnquist wrote the opinion of the Court and was joined by Justices O'Connor, Kennedy, Scalia, and Thomas. Justices Stevens, Souter, Ginsburg, and Breyer dissented.

The Court followed its decision in *Lopez* with *United States v. Morrison*,[36] in 2000, in which it declared unconstitutional the civil damages provision of the Violence Against Women Act, which created a federal cause of action for victims of gender-motivated violence.[37] *Morrison* had the identical split among the Justices as *Lopez*. As discussed below, *Morrison* goes significantly further than *Lopez* in limiting the scope of Congress's commerce power by holding that Congress cannot regulate a noneconomic activity by finding that, looked at cumulatively, it has a substantial effect on interstate commerce.

---

[34] 514 U.S. 549 (1995).
[35] 18 U.S.C. §922(q)(2)(a); §921(a)(25).
[36] 529 U.S. 598 (2000).
[37] 42 U.S.C. §13981.

Additionally, in two subsequent cases, *United States v. Jones*[38] and *Solid Waste Agency of Northern Cook County v. United States Army Corps of Engineers*[39] the Court interpreted federal laws narrowly to avoid "constitutional doubts" that would be raised by a broader interpretation. In each instance, the Court said that applying the federal law would raise serious questions as to whether Congress had exceeded its commerce power. To avoid these constitutional doubts the Court narrowly interpreted the federal laws.

However, in its two most recent cases concerning the scope of Congress's commerce power — *Pierce County, Washington v. Guillen*[40] and *Gonzales v. Raich*[41] — the Court rejected challenges and upheld federal statutes.

These cases are discussed in turn below. There is no doubt that these cases, especially when considered together with the Court's narrowing in the scope of Congress's powers under §5 of the Fourteenth Amendment and its revival of the Tenth Amendment,[42] are one of the most important developments in constitutional law in recent years.[43] It is uncertain whether the Roberts Court will continue down this path and further limit the scope of Congress's commerce power. In its first five years, the Roberts Court decided no cases concerning the scope of Congress's powers under the commerce clause. Its only decision about the scope of congressional authority was *United States v. Comstock*,[44] which upheld as a valid exercise of Congress's authority under the necessary and proper clause a law providing for the indefinite commitment of "sexually dangerous" individuals in the custody of the Federal Bureau of Prisons.

United States v. Lopez

Alfonso Lopez was a twelfth grade student at Edison High School in San Antonio, Texas, in 1992 when he was arrested for carrying a concealed .38 caliber handgun and five bullets. He was charged with violating the Gun-Free School Zones Act of 1990, which made it a federal offense "for any individual knowingly to possess a firearm at a place that the individual knows, or has reasonable cause to believe, is a school zone."[45] The law defines a school zone as "in, or on the grounds of, a public, parochial, or private school"[46] or "within a distance of 1,000

---

[38] 529 U.S. 848 (2000).
[39] 531 U.S. 159 (2001).
[40] 537 U.S. 129 (2003).
[41] 125 S. Ct. 2195 (2005).
[42] The narrowing of Congress's power under §5 of the Fourteenth Amendment is discussed below in §3.6.1 [Erwin Chemerinsky, Constitutional Law: Principles and Policies, 4th ed., (2011)], and the revival of the Tenth Amendment as a limit on federal power is considered in §3.9 [Erwin Chemerinsky, Constitutional Law: Principles and Policies, 4th ed., (2011)].
[43] Understandably, a great deal of academic attention has been devoted to these decisions. *See, e.g.*, Isabelle Katz Pinzler, Toward a More Perfect Union: Understanding and Countering the Federalism Revolution (2002); Richard H. Fallon, Jr., The Conservative Paths of the Rehnquist Court's Federalism Decisions, 69 U. Chi. L. Rev. 429 (2002); Robert A. Schapiro & William W. Buzbee, Unidimensional Federalism: Power and Perspective in Commerce Clause Adjudication, 88 Cornell L. Rev. 1199 (2003).
[44] 130 S. Ct. 1949 (2010), discussed above in §3.2 [Erwin Chemerinsky, Constitutional Law: Principles and Policies, 4th ed., (2011)].
[45] 18 U.S.C. §922(q)(2)(A).
[46] 18 U.S.C. §921(a)(25)(A).

feet from the grounds of a public, parochial, or private school."[47] Lopez was convicted of violating this law and sentenced to six months of imprisonment and two
years of supervised release.

Lopez appealed on the ground that the Gun-Free School Zones Act of 1990
was an unconstitutional exercise of Congress's commerce power. The United
States Court of Appeals for the Fifth Circuit found that the law was unconstitutional because there were inadequate findings by Congress as to a sufficient relationship to interstate commerce.

The United States Supreme Court affirmed, but on different grounds. The
Court's decision was not based on the absence of adequate findings by Congress;
rather, the Court concluded that the law was unconstitutional because it was not
substantially related to interstate commerce.

Chief Justice Rehnquist's opinion for the Court began by emphasizing that
the Constitution creates a national government of enumerated powers.[48] In other
words, the Court returned to the notion that Article I limits Congress's legislative
powers to those that are express or implied in the Constitution.

After reviewing the history of decisions under the commerce clause, the Court
identified three types of activities that Congress can regulate under this power.
First, Congress can "regulate the use of the channels of interstate commerce."[49]
The Court cited *Heart of Atlanta Motel, Inc. v. United States*, which upheld the
federal law prohibiting discrimination by hotels and restaurants as an example of
protecting the channels of interstate commerce.[50]

Second, the Court said that Congress may legislate "to regulate and protect
the instrumentalities of interstate commerce."[51] The Court said that this includes
the power to regulate persons and things in interstate commerce. The Court here
cited several cases which upheld congressional power to regulate the railroads
under its commerce power.[52]

Finally, the Court said that Congress may "regulate those activities having a
substantial relation to interstate commerce."[53] Chief Justice Rehnquist said that
the prior case law was uncertain as to whether an activity must "affect" or "substantially affect" interstate commerce to be regulated under this approach. Chief
Justice Rehnquist concluded that the more restrictive interpretation of congressional power is preferable and that "the proper test requires an analysis of whether
the regulated activity 'substantially affects' interstate commerce."[54]

The Court concluded that the presence of a gun near a school did not substantially affect interstate commerce and that therefore the federal law was unconstitutional. Chief Justice Rehnquist noted that nothing in the Act limited its

[47] 18 U.S.C. §921(a)(25)(B).
[48] 514 U.S. 549, 552.
[49] *Id.* at 558.
[50] 379 U.S. 241 (1964), discussed above in §3.3.4 [Erwin Chemerinsky, Constitutional Law: Principles and Policies, 4th ed., (2011)].
[51] *Id.* at 558-559, citing Jones & Laughlin Steel Corp. v. United States, 301 U.S. at 37.
[52] *See, e.g.,* Shreveport Rate Cases, 234 U.S. 342 (1914), discussed above in §3.3.3 [Erwin Chemerinsky, Constitutional Law: Principles and Policies, 4th ed., (2011)], (1937).
[53] 514 U.S. at 558.
[54] *Id.* at 559.

application to instances where there was proof that the gun had been part of inter-state commerce. The Court specifically rejected the federal government's claim that regulation was justified under the commerce clause because possession of a gun near a school may result in violent crime that can adversely affect the economy.

Concurring opinions were written by Justice Thomas and also by Justice Kennedy, whose opinion was joined by Justice O'Connor. Justice Thomas's opinion was notable because it urged a much narrower view of congressional power than adopted by the majority. Thomas's approach would have returned the Court to the limits on the commerce authority that the Court followed between 1887 and 1937. Justices Kennedy and O'Connor stressed federalism and the relationship between limiting Congress's authority and protecting state prerogatives. They also emphasized the lack of necessity for the federal law because the vast majority of states already had laws prohibiting guns near schools.

Justices Stevens, Souter, and Breyer wrote dissenting opinions. Justice Breyer's dissent was the most thorough and was joined by the other dissenting Justices: Stevens, Souter, and Ginsburg. The dissent criticized the majority for engaging in undue judicial activism; for abandoning almost 60 years of precedent; and for invalidating an important federal statute. Justice Breyer argued that the judiciary should uphold a federal law as a valid exercise of the commerce power so long as there is a "rational basis" that an activity affects interstate commerce.[55] Justice Breyer then explained why guns inherently are a part of interstate commerce and why guns near schools have an economic impact that justifies federal regulation under the commerce power.

United States v. Morrison

United States v. Morrison presented the question as to whether the civil damages provision of the federal Violence Against Women Act is constitutional.[56] The provision authorizes victims of gender-motivated violence to sue for money damages. Congress enacted the Violence Against Women Act based on detailed findings of the inadequacy of state laws in protecting women who are victims of domestic violence and sexual assaults. For example, Congress found that gender-motivated violence costs the American economy billions of dollars a year and is a substantial constraint on freedom of travel by women throughout the country.

The case was brought by Christy Brzonkala, who allegedly was raped by football players while a freshman at Virginia Polytechnic Institute. The players were not criminally prosecuted and ultimately avoided even sanctions by the university. Brzonkala filed suit against her assailants and the university under the civil damages provision of the Violence Against Women Act.

The issue before the Supreme Court was whether the civil damages provision of the Act could be upheld, either as an exercise of Congress's commerce clause authority or as permissible under Congress's power pursuant to §5 of the Fourteenth Amendment. In a 5-to-4 decision, the Court held that Congress lacked the

---

[55] *Id.* at 618 (Breyer, J., dissenting).
[56] 42 U.S.C. §13981.

authority to adopt the provision under either of these powers.[57] The split was the same as in all of the recent federalism rulings: Chief Justice Rehnquist wrote the opinion for the Court, joined by Justices O'Connor, Scalia, Kennedy, and Thomas. Justices Stevens, Souter, Ginsburg, and Breyer dissented.

In *Morrison,* the Court reaffirmed the three-part test for Congress's commerce clause authority that was articulated in *United States v. Lopez.* Congress may regulate (a) the channels of interstate commerce, (b) the instrumentalities of interstate commerce and persons or things in interstate commerce, and (c) activities that have a substantial effect on interstate commerce. The United States government and the plaintiff, Christy Brzonkala, defended the law based on the third part of the test, on the ground that violence against women has a substantial effect on the national economy. There was a lengthy legislative history of the Violence Against Women Act in which Congress found that assaults against women, when looked at cumulatively across the country, have a substantial effect on interstate commerce. The Supreme Court expressly rejected this argument as insufficient to sustain the law. Chief Justice Rehnquist emphasized that Congress was regulating noneconomic activity that has traditionally been dealt with by state laws. He wrote: "Gender-motivated crimes of violence are not, in any sense of the phrase, economic activity. While we need not adopt a categorical rule against aggregating the effects of any noneconomic activity in order to decide these cases, thus far in our Nation's history our cases have upheld Commerce Clause regulation of intrastate activity only where that activity is economic in nature."[58] The Supreme Court found Congress's findings of impact on the economy to be inadequate to sustain the law under the commerce clause. Chief Justice Rehnquist declared: "But the existence of congressional findings is not sufficient, by itself, to sustain the constitutionality of Commerce Clause legislation. As we stated in Lopez, '[S]imply because Congress may conclude that a particular activity substantially affects interstate commerce does not necessarily make it so.'"[59] The Court said that Congress was relying on a "but-for" causal chain "from the initial occurrence of violent crime . . . to every attenuated effect upon interstate commerce."[60] The Court said that "[i]f accepted, petitioners' reasoning would allow Congress to regulate any crime as long as the nationwide, aggregated impact of that crime has substantial effects on employment, production, transit or consumption."[61] By this reasoning, the Court explained, Congress could regulate all violent crimes in the United States. The Court thus concluded: "We accordingly reject the argument that Congress may regulate noneconomic, violent criminal conduct based solely on that conduct's aggregated effect on interstate commerce. The Constitution requires a distinction between what is truly national and what is truly local."[62]

---

[57] The Court's discussion of Congress's power to enact the law pursuant to §5 of the Fourteenth Amendment is considered below in §3.6.1 [Erwin Chemerinsky, Constitutional Law: Principles and Policies, 4th ed., (2011)].

[58] 529 U.S. 598, 613 (2000).

[59] *Id.* at 614 (citation omitted).

[60] *Id.* at 615.

[61] *Id.*

[62] *Id.* at 617-618.

Justice Clarence Thomas wrote a concurring opinion in which he again objected, as in *Lopez*, to the "substantial effects" test as a way of justifying congressional action under the commerce power. He wrote: "[T]he very notion of a 'substantial effects' test under the Commerce Clause is inconsistent with the original understanding of Congress' powers and with this Court's early Commerce Clause cases. By continuing to apply this rootless and malleable standard, however circumscribed, the Court has encouraged the Federal Government to persist in its view that the Commerce Clause has virtually no limits. Until this Court replaces its existing Commerce Clause jurisprudence with a standard more consistent with the original understanding, we will continue to see Congress appropriating state police powers under the guise of regulating commerce."[63] In other words, Justice Thomas would go significantly further than the majority in limiting the scope of Congress's commerce power; the majority in *Morrison* would allow Congress to regulate economic activities based on their cumulative impact on the economy, but not Justice Thomas.

Justice Souter wrote a dissenting opinion, joined by Justices Stevens, Ginsburg, and Souter. Justice Souter stressed the need for judicial deference to congressional fact-finding: "Congress has the power to legislate with regard to activity that, in the aggregate, has a substantial effect on interstate commerce. The fact of such a substantial effect is not an issue for the courts in the first instance, but for the Congress, whose institutional capacity for gathering evidence and taking testimony far exceeds ours. By passing legislation, Congress indicates its conclusion, whether explicitly or not, that facts support its exercise of the commerce power. The business of the courts is to review the congressional assessment, not for soundness but simply for the rationality of concluding that a jurisdictional basis exists in fact."[64]

Justice Souter stressed that Congress had conducted voluminous hearings and found that violence against women has an enormous effect on the American economy. He wrote: "But the sufficiency of the evidence before Congress to provide a rational basis for the finding cannot seriously be questioned. Indeed, the legislative record here is far more voluminous than the record compiled by Congress and found sufficient in two prior cases upholding Title II of the Civil Rights Act of 1964 against Commerce Clause challenges."[65]

Thus, *Morrison* goes further than *Lopez* in limiting the scope of Congress's commerce power by narrowing the ability of Congress to regulate based on findings of "substantial effect" on interstate commerce. At least in areas that the Court regards as traditionally regulated by the states, Congress cannot regulate noneconomic activity based on a cumulative substantial effect on interstate commerce.

---

[63] *Id.* at 627 (Thomas, J., concurring).
[64] *Id.* at 628 (Souter, J., dissenting).
[65] *Id.* at 634.

Narrowly Interpreting Laws to Avoid "Constitutional Doubts"

In two subsequent cases, *United States v. Jones*[66] and *Solid Waste Agency of Northern Cook County v. United States Army Corps of Engineers*,[67] the Supreme Court has narrowly interpreted federal laws to avoid "constitutional doubts" as to whether Congress exceeded its commerce power. In each instance, the Court did not declare the federal statute unconstitutional, but instead used the recent restrictive interpretations of the commerce power as a reason for limiting the scope of the federal laws.

In *Jones*, the Court considered whether arson of a dwelling violates the federal law that makes arson of property in interstate commerce a federal crime.[68] The United States government argued that the residence was part of interstate commerce in that it had insurance policies and it received utility service. But the Supreme Court, in a unanimous decision, interpreted the arson act to not apply to arson of a dwelling. Justice Ginsburg wrote the opinion for the Court and said that allowing the law to be applied to arson of a residence would raise "constitutional doubts" as to whether Congress had exceeded the scope of its commerce clause power.[69] To avoid the constitutional issue, the Court interpreted the federal statute narrowly to not include arson of dwellings.

In *Solid Waste Agency of Northern Cook County v. United States Army Corps of Engineers*,[70] the Supreme Court held that the Army Corps of Engineers could not apply the federal Water Pollution Control Act to intrastate waters based on the presence of migratory birds. A consortium of suburbs of Chicago sought to buy an abandoned gravel pit to dispose of nonhazardous solid wastes. Water within the gravel pit was used by migratory birds. The Army Corps of Engineers had promulgated rules concerning when the Water Pollution Control Act applied, and one of these, the "migratory bird rule," was used to require compliance in the use of the abandoned gravel pit.

The Supreme Court, in a 5-to-4 decision, interpreted the federal Act narrowly to avoid "constitutional doubts" and thus held that the presence of migratory birds is not sufficient to bring intrastate waters within the scope of the Water Pollution Control Act. The government argued that the migratory bird rule was constitutional because "protection of migratory birds is a 'national interest of very nearly the first magnitude,' . . . and that, as the Court of Appeals found, millions of people spend over a billion dollars annually on recreational pursuits relating to migratory birds."[71] Chief Justice Rehnquist, writing for the Court, said that whether these justifications are sufficient under the commerce clause, especially in light of *Lopez* and *Morrison*, is a "significant constitutional question."[72]

---

[66] 529 U.S. 848 (2000).
[67] 531 U.S. 159 (2001).
[68] 18 U.S.C. §844.
[69] 529 U.S. at 858.
[70] 531 U.S. 159 (2001).
[71] *Id.* at 173.
[72] *Id.*

To avoid the constitutional issue, the Court said that it would interpret the statute to not apply. Chief Justice Rehnquist explained: "These are significant constitutional questions raised by respondents' application of their regulations, and yet we find nothing approaching a clear statement from Congress that it intended §404(a) to reach an abandoned sand and gravel pit such as we have here. Permitting respondents to claim federal jurisdiction over ponds and mudflats falling within the 'Migratory Bird Rule' would result in a significant impingement of the States' traditional and primary power over land and water use. We thus read the statute as written to avoid the significant constitutional and federalism questions raised by respondents' interpretation, and therefore reject the request for administrative deference."[73]

Although interpreting laws narrowly to avoid constitutional doubts is not new, its application to the commerce clause gives a powerful tool to lawyers challenging the application of federal civil and criminal laws. They need not persuade the Court that a federal statute is unconstitutional on its face or as applied. Instead, they only need to show that the application of the law would raise "constitutional doubts." The Supreme Court never has explained how serious the constitutional doubts must be; nor has it indicated how plausible the narrowing construction has to be. Together, *Jones* and *Solid Waste Agency* indicate another way in which the Rehnquist Court's recent narrow interpretation of the commerce power is manifesting itself.

Upholding Federal Laws and Rejecting Commerce Clause Challenges

The two most recent commerce clause cases, as of this writing, both refused to extend limits on Congress's powers and upheld the federal statutes. In *Pierce County, Washington v. Guillen*,[74] the Court unanimously reaffirmed broad authority for Congress to legislate concerning road safety as part of its power to regulate the channels of interstate commerce. A federal statute provides that if a local government does a traffic study as part of applying for federal funds, that study is not discoverable. Congress's concern was that local governments would refrain from conducting such investigations if they could be used as evidence against them in suits arising from automobile accidents.

Guillen involved two separate accidents at intersections in the State of Washington and the local governments had recently conducted studies of traffic conditions at both locations. The plaintiffs sued the local governments and sought access to the traffic studies. The Washington Supreme Court declared unconstitutional the federal law that exempted these studies from discovery. The United States Supreme Court, in an opinion by Justice Clarence Thomas, unanimously reversed and upheld the federal law. Justice Thomas explained that "[i]t is well established that the Commerce Clause gives Congress authority to regulate the use of the channels of interstate commerce. . . . [The statutes] can be viewed as

---

[73] *Id.* at 174.
[74] 537 U.S. 129 (2003). For a discussion of this decision and its implications, *see* Mitchell N. Berman, *Guillen* and Gullability: Piercing the Surface of Commerce Clause Doctrine, 89 Iowa L. Rev. 1487 (2004).

legislation aimed at improving safety in the channels of interstate commerce and increasing protection for the instrumentalities of interstate commerce. As such, they fall within Congress' Commerce Clause power."[75]

More dramatically, in *Gonzales v. Raich*,[76] the Court held that Congress constitutionally may use its power to regulate commerce among the states to prohibit the cultivation and possession of small amounts of marijuana for medicinal purposes. Although California has created an exemption to its state marijuana laws for medical uses, no such exemption exists to the federal law. In a 6-to-3 decision, with the majority opinion written by Justice Stevens, the Court upheld the federal law. Justices Kennedy, Souter, Ginsburg, and Breyer joined the majority opinion, and Justice Scalia concurred in the judgment. Justice Stevens explained that for almost 70 years Congress has had the authority to regulate activities that have a substantial effect on interstate commerce. The Court concluded that marijuana, looked at cumulatively, including that grown for medical purposes, has a substantial effect on interstate commerce. Justice Stevens's opinion relied on a precedent from over 60 years ago: *Wickard v. Filburn*, discussed above, which held that Congress may regulate the amount of wheat that farmers grow for their own home consumption.

How does *Gonzales v. Raich* fit into the Court's recent commerce clause jurisprudence? The Court did not change the test for the commerce clause that it has followed since *Lopez* in 1995: Congress, under the commerce clause, may regulate the channels of interstate commerce, the instrumentalities of interstate commerce and persons or things in interstate commerce, and activities which have a substantial effect on interstate commerce. Nor did the Court revisit its holding in *Morrison* that in regulating noneconomic activities, substantial effect cannot be based on cumulative impact. Instead, *Gonzales v. Raich* stands for the proposition that intrastate production of a commodity sold in interstate commerce is economic activity and thus substantial effect can be based on cumulative impact. Justice Scalia concurred in the judgment, and emphasized that Congress, pursuant to the necessary and proper clause, has the authority to control intrastate production of goods that are of a type that end up in interstate commerce.

Implications

Lopez was dramatic simply because it was the first time in almost 60 years that a federal law has been declared unconstitutional as exceeding the scope of Congress's commerce power. *Morrison, Jones*, and *Solid Waste Agency* show that *Lopez* is not an aberration, but the beginning of a major change in the Court's approach to the commerce clause. Interestingly, except for *Jones*, these were all 5-to-4 decisions, with the five most conservative Justices — one who was appointed by President Nixon, three who were appointed by President Reagan, and one who was appointed by President Bush — in the majority.[77] Although these Justices are

---

[75] *Id.* at 146-147.

[76] 545 U.S. 1 (2005).

[77] Some have described these cases as conservative "judicial activism." *See, e.g.,* Herbert Hovencamp, Judicial Restraint and Constitutional Federalism: The Supreme Court's *Lopez* and *Seminole Tribe* Decisions, 96 Colum. L. Rev. 2213, 2213 (1996).

most commonly associated with advocating judicial restraint, in these cases they abandoned almost 60 years of deference to the legislature under the commerce clause. On the other hand, it is not surprising that it would be conservative Justices who are most concerned with limiting the scope of congressional powers and protecting the prerogatives of state governments.

These decisions leave many questions unanswered and therefore invite challenges to countless federal laws. How far can Congress go to protect the channels of interstate commerce? What is Congress's authority to regulate the instrumentalities of interstate commerce and persons and things in interstate commerce? Perhaps most important, what is a "substantial effect" on interstate commerce? How is the line between economic and noneconomic activities, drawn in *Morrison* and dealt with in *Raich*, to be defined? Do *Pierce County* and *Raich* reflect a shift away from a Court seeking to limit the commerce power or are they merely a pause in what will turn out to be major restrictions on federal power?

A great deal depends on the answers to these questions. Innumerable federal laws — from drug laws to RICO,[78] from environmental laws[79] to civil rights laws — might now be vulnerable. So far, the vast majority of these challenges have failed in the lower courts.[80]

A major issue concerning the scope of Congress's commerce power that seems destined to reach the Supreme Court is the constitutionality of the "individual mandate" — the requirement that individuals purchase health insurance or pay a penalty — in the Patient Protection and Affordable Care Act.[81] At issue is §1501 of the Act, commonly known as the Minimum Essential Coverage Provision. The Minimum Essential Coverage Provision requires that every United States citizen, other than those falling within specified exceptions, maintain a minimum level of health insurance coverage for each month beginning in 2014. As of the end of 2010, there is a split among the federal district courts, with two upholding the constitutionality of the law as a valid exercise of Congress's commerce power,[82] and one striking it down.[83] On the one hand, the challengers argue that Congress forcing people to purchase is unprecedented and those who do not want to buy health insurance are, by definition, not engaged in commerce. On the other hand, if we accept that Congress may regulate economic activity that

---

[78] In *United States v. Robertson*, 514 U.S. 669 (1995), the Court upheld a federal RICO conviction by finding a sufficient connection to interstate commerce. *Robertson* involved a fraud concerning a gold mine in Alaska, and the Court emphasized that Robertson was from Arizona, that he had hired out-of-staters to work in the gold mine, and that he had taken profits out of Alaska. The Court thus avoided any need to consider limits on the scope of RICO in light of *Lopez*.

[79] For a discussion of the constitutionality of environmental laws, such as the Endangered Species Act, after *Lopez*, see John Copeland Nagle, The Commerce Clause Meets the Delhi Sands Flower-Loving Fly, 97 Mich. L. Rev. 174 (1998).

[80] *See* Glenn H. Reynolds & Brannon P. Denning, Lower Court Readings of *Lopez*, Or What If the Supreme Court Held a Constitutional Revolution and Nobody Came?, 2000 Wis. L. Rev. 369 (describing the pattern of lower courts rejecting constitutional challenges to federal laws based on *Lopez*).

[81] Pub.L. No. 111-148, 124 Stat. 119 (2010).

[82] Baldwin v. Sebelius, 2010 WL 3418436 (Aug. 27, 2010); Thomas More Law Center v. Obama, 720 F. Supp. 2d 882 (E.D. Mich. 2010).

[83] Commonwealth ex rel. Cuccinella, 2010 WL 5059718 (E.D. Va. Dec. 13, 2010).

has a substantial effect on commerce, supporters maintain that buying, or not buying, health insurance is an economic choice and point out that, taken cumulatively, the health insurance industry has a trillion-dollar effect on the economy. The argument is that if Congress can regulate Angela Raich growing marijuana for her own personal use, it surely can regulate health care, including by requiring individuals to purchase care or pay a tax. This well could provide the next major commerce clause decision from the United States Supreme Court.

5. 1990s-???: Narrowing of the Commerce Power and Revival of the Tenth Amendment as a Constraint on Congress

In the 1990s, the Supreme Court once more changed course with regard to the scope of Congress's powers under the Commerce Clause and whether the Tenth Amendment is a limit on federal power. In 1995, in United States v. Lopez, the Supreme Court for the first time in almost 60 years found that a federal law exceeded Congress's Commerce Clause authority. *Lopez* led to challenges to literally dozens of federal laws. In 2000, the Court reaffirmed *Lopez* in United States v. Morrison. Additionally, in 1992, in New York v. United States and in 1997, in Printz v. United States, the Court again used the Tenth Amendment to protect state governments from federal encroachments. All of these cases are presented below.

Obviously, it is too soon to know how far the Court will go in limiting Congress's powers or using the Tenth Amendment as a constraint on federal authority. All of these decisions limiting the scope of Congress's Commerce Clause power were 5-4 rulings, with the majority comprising Chief Justice Rehnquist and Justices O'Connor, Scalia, Kennedy, and Thomas. There have not been decisions on the scope of the Commerce Clause or the meaning of the Tenth Amendment since Chief Justice Roberts and Justice Alito replaced Justices Rehnquist and O'Connor.

In reading these recent decisions concerning the Commerce Clause and the Tenth Amendment, it will be helpful to focus on two questions, one descriptive and one normative. Descriptively, what principles does the Court articulate as to when Congress exceeds the scope of its Commerce Clause authority and when Congress violates the Tenth Amendment? Normatively, does the Court persuasively justify the desirability of these limits on federal powers?

a. What Is Congress's Authority to Regulate "Commerce Among the States"?

United States v. Lopez

514 U.S. 549 (1995)

Chief Justice REHNQUIST delivered the opinion of the Court.

In the Gun-Free School Zones Act of 1990, Congress made it a federal offense "for any individual knowingly to possess a firearm at a place that the individual knows, or has reasonable cause to believe, is a school zone." 18 U.S.C. §922(q)(1)(A). The Act neither regulates a commercial activity nor contains a requirement that the possession be connected in any way to interstate commerce. We hold that the Act exceeds the authority of Congress "[t]o regulate Commerce . . . among the several States. . . ."

On March 10, 1992, respondent, who was then a 12th-grade student, arrived at Edison High School in San Antonio, Texas, carrying a concealed .38-caliber handgun and five bullets. Acting upon an anonymous tip, school authorities confronted respondent, who admitted that he was carrying the weapon. He was arrested and charged under Texas law with firearm possession on school premises. The next day, the state charges were dismissed after federal agents charged respondent by complaint with violating the Gun-Free School Zones Act of 1990. The term "school zone" is defined as "in, or on the grounds of, a public, parochial or private school" or "within a distance of 1,000 feet from the grounds of a public, parochial or private school."

Respondent waived his right to a jury trial. The District Court conducted a bench trial, found him guilty, and sentenced him to six months' imprisonment and two years' supervised release.

We start with first principles. The Constitution creates a Federal Government of enumerated powers. As James Madison wrote: "The powers delegated by the proposed Constitution to the federal government are few and defined. Those which are to remain in the State governments are numerous and indefinite." The Federalist No. 45. This constitutionally mandated division of authority "was adopted by the framers to ensure protection of our fundamental liberties." "Just as the separation and independence of the coordinate branches of the Federal Government serve to prevent the accumulation of excessive power in any one branch, a healthy balance of power between the States and the Federal Government will reduce the risk of tyranny and abuse from either front."

[The Court then reviewed the history of Commerce Clause decisions from Gibbons v. Ogden through the early 1940s.] *Jones & Laughlin Steel*, *Darby*, and *Wickard* ushered in an era of Commerce Clause jurisprudence that greatly expanded the previously defined authority of Congress under that Clause. In part, this was a recognition of the great changes that had occurred in the way business was carried on in this country. Enterprises that had once been local or at most regional in nature had become national in scope. But the doctrinal change also reflected a view that earlier Commerce Clause cases artificially had constrained the authority of Congress to regulate interstate commerce.

But even these modern-era precedents which have expanded congressional power under the Commerce Clause confirm that this power is subject to outer limits. In *Jones & Laughlin Steel*, the Court warned that the scope of the interstate commerce power "must be considered in the light of our dual system of government and may not be extended so as to embrace effects upon interstate commerce so indirect and remote that to embrace them, in view of our complex society, would effectually obliterate the distinction between what is national and what is local and create a completely centralized government." Since that time, the Court has heeded that warning and undertaken to decide whether a rational basis existed for concluding that a regulated activity sufficiently affected interstate commerce. See, e.g., Hodel v. Virginia Surface Mining & Reclamation Assn., Inc.

(1981); Perez v. United States (1971); Katzenbach v. McClung (1964); Heart of Atlanta Motel, Inc. v. United States (1964).

Consistent with this structure, we have identified three broad categories of activity that Congress may regulate under its commerce power. First, Congress may regulate the use of the channels of interstate commerce. See, e.g., *Darby*; *Heart of Atlanta Motel*. Second, Congress is empowered to regulate and protect the instrumentalities of interstate commerce, or persons or things in interstate commerce, even though the threat may come only from intrastate activities. See, e.g., *Shreveport Rate Cases* (1914); *Southern R. Co. v. United States* (1911) (upholding amendments to Safety Appliance Act as applied to vehicles used in intrastate commerce). Finally, Congress's commerce authority includes the power to regulate those activities having a substantial relation to interstate commerce, *Jones & Laughlin Steel*, i.e., those activities that substantially affect interstate commerce.

Within this final category, admittedly, our case law has not been clear whether an activity must "affect" or "substantially affect" interstate commerce in order to be within Congress's power to regulate it under the Commerce Clause. We conclude, consistent with the great weight of our case law, that the proper test requires an analysis of whether the regulated activity "substantially affects" interstate commerce.

We now turn to consider the power of Congress, in the light of this framework, to enact §922(q). The first two categories of authority may be quickly disposed of: §922(q) is not a regulation of the use of the channels of interstate commerce, nor is it an attempt to prohibit the interstate transportation of a commodity through the channels of commerce; nor can §922(q) be justified as a regulation by which Congress has sought to protect an instrumentality of interstate commerce or a thing in interstate commerce. Thus, if §922(q) is to be sustained, it must be under the third category as a regulation of an activity that substantially affects interstate commerce.

First, we have upheld a wide variety of congressional Acts regulating intrastate economic activity where we have concluded that the activity substantially affected interstate commerce. Examples include the regulation of intrastate coal mining; *Hodel*, supra, intrastate extortionate credit transactions, *Perez*, restaurants utilizing substantial interstate supplies, *McClung*, inns and hotels catering to interstate guests, *Heart of Atlanta Motel*, and production and consumption of homegrown wheat, Wickard v. Filburn. These examples are by no means exhaustive, but the pattern is clear. Where economic activity substantially affects interstate commerce, legislation regulating that activity will be sustained. Even *Wickard*, which is perhaps the most far reaching example of Commerce Clause authority over intrastate activity, involved economic activity in a way that the possession of a gun in a school zone does not.

Section 922(q) is a criminal statute that by its terms has nothing to do with "commerce" or any sort of economic enterprise, however broadly one might define those terms. Section 922(q) is not an essential part of a larger regulation of economic activity, in which the regulatory scheme could be undercut unless the intrastate activity were regulated. It cannot, therefore, be sustained under our cases upholding regulations of activities that arise out of or are connected with a commercial transaction, which viewed in the aggregate, substantially affects interstate commerce.[84]

Second, §922(q) contains no jurisdictional element which would ensure, through case-by-case inquiry, that the firearm possession in question affects interstate commerce. For example, in United States v. Bass (1971), the Court interpreted former 18 U.S.C. §1202(a), which made it a crime for a felon to "receiv[e], posses[s], or transpor[t] in commerce or affecting commerce . . . any firearm." The Court interpreted the possession component of §1202(a) to require an additional nexus to interstate commerce both because the statute was ambiguous and because "unless Congress conveys its purpose clearly, it will not be deemed to have significantly changed the federal-state balance." Unlike the statute in *Bass*, §922(q) has no express jurisdictional element which might limit its reach to a discrete set of firearm possessions that additionally have an explicit connection with or effect on interstate commerce.

Although as part of our independent evaluation of constitutionality under the Commerce Clause we of course consider legislative findings, and indeed even congressional committee findings, regarding effect on interstate commerce, the Government concedes that "[n]either the statute nor its legislative history contain[s] express congressional findings regarding the effects upon interstate commerce of gun possession in a school zone." We agree with the Government that Congress normally is not required to make formal findings as to the substantial burdens that an activity has on interstate commerce. But to the extent that congressional findings would enable us to evaluate the legislative judgment that the activity in question substantially affected interstate commerce, even though no such substantial effect was visible to the naked eye, they are lacking here.

The Government's essential contention, is that we may determine here that §922(q) is valid because possession of a firearm in a local school zone does indeed substantially affect interstate commerce. The Government argues that possession of a firearm in a school zone may result in violent crime and that violent crime can be expected to affect the functioning of the national economy in two ways. First, the costs of violent crime are substantial, and, through the mechanism of insurance, those costs are spread throughout the population. Second, violent crime reduces the willingness of individuals to travel to areas within the country that are perceived to be unsafe. The Government also argues that the presence of guns in schools poses a substantial threat to the educational process by threatening the learning environment. A handicapped educational process, in turn, will result in a less productive citizenry. That, in turn, would have an adverse effect on the

---

[84] Under our federal system, the "'States possess primary authority for defining and enforcing the criminal law.'" Brecht v. Abrahamson (1982). Under our federal system the administration of criminal justice rests with the States except as Congress, acting within the scope of those delegated powers, has created offenses against the United States. When Congress criminalizes conduct already denounced as criminal by the States, it effects a "'change in the sensitive relation between federal and state criminal jurisdiction.'" United States v. Enmons (1973). The Government acknowledges that §922(q) "displace[s] state policy choices in . . . that its prohibitions apply even in States that have chosen not to outlaw the conduct in question." [Footnote by the Court.]

Nation's economic well-being. As a result, the Government argues that Congress could rationally have concluded that §922(q) substantially affects interstate commerce.

We pause to consider the implications of the Government's arguments. The Government admits, under its "costs of crime" reasoning, that Congress could regulate not only all violent crime, but all activities that might lead to violent crime, regardless of how tenuously they relate to interstate commerce. Similarly, under the Government's "national productivity" reasoning, Congress could regulate any activity that it found was related to the economic productivity of individual citizens: family law (including marriage, divorce, and child custody), for example. Under the theories that the Government presents in support of §922(q), it is difficult to perceive any limitation on federal power, even in areas such as criminal law enforcement or education where States historically have been sovereign. Thus, if we were to accept the Government's arguments, we are hard pressed to posit any activity by an individual that Congress is without power to regulate.

Although Justice BREYER argues that acceptance of the Government's rationales would not authorize a general federal police power, he is unable to identify any activity that the States may regulate but Congress may not. Justice BREYER posits that there might be some limitations on Congress's commerce power, such as family law or certain aspects of education. These suggested limitations, when viewed in light of the dissent's expansive analysis, are devoid of substance.

For instance, if Congress can, pursuant to its Commerce Clause power, regulate activities that adversely affect the learning environment, then, a fortiori, it also can regulate the educational process directly. Congress could determine that a school's curriculum has a "significant" effect on the extent of classroom learning. As a result, Congress could mandate a federal curriculum for local elementary and secondary schools because what is taught in local schools has a significant "effect on classroom learning," and that, in turn, has a substantial effect on interstate commerce.

Admittedly, a determination whether an intrastate activity is commercial or noncommercial may in some cases result in legal uncertainty. But, so long as Congress's authority is limited to those powers enumerated in the Constitution, and so long as those enumerated powers are interpreted as having judicially enforceable outer limits, congressional legislation under the Commerce Clause always will engender "legal uncertainty." The Constitution mandates this uncertainty by withholding from Congress a plenary police power that would authorize enactment of every type of legislation.

These are not precise formulations, and in the nature of things they cannot be. But we think they point the way to a correct decision of this case. The possession of a gun in a local school zone is in no sense an economic activity that might, through repetition elsewhere, substantially affect any sort of interstate commerce. Respondent was a local student at a local school; there is no indication that he had recently moved in interstate commerce, and there is no requirement that his possession of the firearm have any concrete tie to interstate commerce.

To uphold the Government's contentions here, we would have to pile inference upon inference in a manner that would bid fair to convert congressional authority under the Commerce Clause to a general police power of the sort retained by the States. Admittedly, some of our prior cases have taken long steps down that road, giving great deference to congressional action. The broad language in these opinions has suggested the possibility of additional expansion, but we decline here to proceed any further. To do so would require us to conclude that the Constitution's enumeration of powers does not presuppose something not enumerated, and that there never will be a distinction between what is truly national and what is truly local. This we are unwilling to do.

Justice KENNEDY, with whom Justice O'CONNOR joins, concurring.

The history of the judicial struggle to interpret the Commerce Clause during the transition from the economic system the Founders knew to the single, national market still emergent in our own era counsels great restraint before the Court determines that the Clause is insufficient to support an exercise of the national power. That history gives me some pause about today's decision, but I join the Court's opinion with these observations on what I conceive to be its necessary though limited holding.

The history of our Commerce Clause decisions contains at least two lessons of relevance to this case. The first, as stated at the outset, is the imprecision of content-based boundaries used without more to define the limits of the Commerce Clause. The second, related to the first but of even greater consequence, is that the Court as an institution and the legal system as a whole have an immense stake in the stability of our Commerce Clause jurisprudence as it has evolved to this point. Stare decisis operates with great force in counseling us not to call in question the essential principles now in place respecting the congressional power to regulate transactions of a commercial nature. That fundamental restraint on our power forecloses us from reverting to an understanding of commerce that would serve only an 18th-century economy, dependent then upon production and trading practices that had changed but little over the preceding centuries; it also mandates against returning to the time when congressional authority to regulate undoubted commercial activities was limited by a judicial determination that those matters had an insufficient connection to an interstate system. Congress can regulate in the commercial sphere on the assumption that we have a single market and a unified purpose to build a stable national economy.

It would be mistaken and mischievous for the political branches to forget that the sworn obligation to preserve and protect the Constitution in maintaining the federal balance is their own in the first and primary instance. At the same time, the absence of structural mechanisms to require those officials to undertake this principled task, and the momentary political convenience often attendant upon their failure to do so, argue against a complete renunciation of the judicial role. Although it is the obligation of all officers of the Government to respect the constitutional design, the federal balance is too essential a part of our constitutional structure and plays too vital a role in securing freedom for us to admit inability to intervene when one or the other level of Government has tipped the scales too far.

The statute before us upsets the federal balance to a degree that renders it an unconstitutional assertion of the commerce power, and our intervention is required. As the Chief Justice explains, unlike the earlier cases to come before the Court here neither the actors nor their conduct has a commercial character, and neither the purposes nor the design of the statute has an evident commercial nexus. The statute makes the simple possession of a gun within 1,000 feet of the grounds of the school a criminal offense. In a sense any conduct in this interdependent world of ours has an ultimate commercial origin or consequence, but we have not yet said the commerce power may reach so far. If Congress attempts that extension, then at the least we must inquire whether the exercise of national power seeks to intrude upon an area of traditional state concern.

An interference of these dimensions occurs here, for it is well established that education is a traditional concern of the States. Milliken v. Bradley (1974); Epperson v. Arkansas (1968). The proximity to schools, including of course schools owned and operated by the States or their subdivisions, is the very premise for making the conduct criminal. In these circumstances, we have a particular duty to ensure that the federal-state balance is not destroyed.

While it is doubtful that any State, or indeed any reasonable person, would argue that it is wise policy to allow students to carry guns on school premises, considerable disagreement exists about how best to accomplish that goal. In this circumstance, the theory and utility of our federalism are revealed, for the States may perform their role as laboratories for experimentation to devise various solutions where the best solution is far from clear.

If a State or municipality determines that harsh criminal sanctions are necessary and wise to deter students from carrying guns on school premises, the reserved powers of the States are sufficient to enact those measures. Indeed, over 40 States already have criminal laws outlawing the possession of firearms on or near school grounds.

Other, more practicable means to rid the schools of guns may be thought by the citizens of some States to be preferable for the safety and welfare of the schools those States are charged with maintaining. These might include inducements to inform on violators where the information leads to arrests or confiscation of the guns; programs to encourage the voluntary surrender of guns with some provision for amnesty; penalties imposed on parents or guardians for failure to supervise the child; laws providing for suspension or expulsion of gun-toting students.

The statute now before us forecloses the States from experimenting and exercising their own judgment in an area to which States lay claim by right of history and expertise, and it does so by regulating an activity beyond the realm of commerce in the ordinary and usual sense of that term. The tendency of this statute to displace state regulation in areas of traditional state concern is evident from its territorial operation. There are over 100,000 elementary and secondary schools in the United States. Each of these now has an invisible federal zone extending 1,000 feet beyond the (often irregular) boundaries of the school property. Yet throughout these areas, school officials would find their own programs for the prohibition of guns in danger of displacement by the federal authority unless the State chooses to enact a parallel rule.

Absent a stronger connection or identification with commercial concerns that are central to the Commerce Clause, that interference contradicts the federal balance the framers designed and that this Court is obliged to enforce.

For these reasons, I join in the opinion and judgment of the Court.

Justice THOMAS, concurring.

The Court today properly concludes that the Commerce Clause does not grant Congress the authority to prohibit gun possession within 1,000 feet of a school, as it attempted to do in the Gun-Free School Zones Act of 1990. Although I join the majority, I write separately to observe that our case law has drifted far from the original understanding of the Commerce Clause. In a future case, we ought to temper our Commerce Clause jurisprudence in a manner that both makes sense of our more recent case law and is more faithful to the original understanding of that Clause.

While the principal dissent concedes that there are limits to federal power, the sweeping nature of our current test enables the dissent to argue that Congress can regulate gun possession. But it seems to me that the power to regulate "commerce" can by no means encompass authority over mere gun possession, any more than it empowers the Federal Government to regulate marriage, littering, or cruelty to animals, throughout the 50 States. Our Constitution quite properly leaves such matters to the individual States, notwithstanding these activities' effects on interstate commerce. Any interpretation of the Commerce Clause that even suggests that Congress could regulate such matters is in need of reexamination.

In an appropriate case, I believe that we must further reconsider our "substantial effects" test with an eye toward constructing a standard that reflects the text and history of the Commerce Clause without totally rejecting our more recent Commerce Clause jurisprudence.

Today, however, I merely support the Court's conclusion with a discussion of the text, structure, and history of the Commerce Clause and an analysis of our early case law. My goal is simply to show how far we have departed from the original understanding and to demonstrate that the result we reach today is by no means "radical." I also want to point out the necessity of refashioning a coherent test that does not tend to "obliterate the distinction between what is national and what is local and create a completely centralized government."

At the time the original Constitution was ratified, "commerce" consisted of selling, buying, and bartering, as well as transporting for these purposes. See 1 S. Johnson, A Dictionary of the English Language 361 (4th ed. 1773) (defining commerce as "Intercour[s]e; exchange of one thing for another; interchange of any thing; trade; traffick"); N. Bailey, An Universal Etymological English Dictionary (26th ed. 1789) ("trade or traffic"); T. Sheridan, A Complete Dictionary of the English Language (6th ed. 1796) ("Exchange of one thing for another; trade, traffick"). As one would expect, the term "commerce" was used in contradistinction to productive activities such as manufacturing and agriculture.

Moreover, interjecting a modern sense of commerce into the Constitution generates significant textual and structural problems. For example, one cannot replace "commerce" with a different type of enterprise, such as manufacturing. When a manufacturer produces a car, assembly cannot take place "with a foreign nation" or "with the Indian Tribes." Parts may come from different States or other nations and hence may have been in the flow of commerce at one time, but manufacturing takes place at a discrete site. Agriculture and manufacturing involve the production of goods; commerce encompasses traffic in such articles.

The Constitution not only uses the word "commerce" in a narrower sense than our case law might suggest, it also does not support the proposition that Congress has authority over all activities that "substantially affect" interstate commerce. The Commerce Clause does not state that Congress may "regulate matters that substantially affect commerce with foreign Nations, and among the several States, and with the Indian Tribes."

Put simply, much if not all of Art. I, §8 (including portions of the Commerce Clause itself), would be surplusage if Congress had been given authority over matters that substantially affect interstate commerce. An interpretation of cl. 3 that makes the rest of §8 superfluous simply cannot be correct. Yet this Court's Commerce Clause jurisprudence has endorsed just such an interpretation: The power we have accorded Congress has swallowed Art. I, §8.

Indeed, if a "substantial effects" test can be appended to the Commerce Clause, why not to every other power of the Federal Government? There is no reason for singling out the Commerce Clause for special treatment. Accordingly, Congress could regulate all matters that "substantially affect" the Army and Navy, bankruptcies, tax collection, expenditures, and so on. In that case, the Clauses of §8 all mutually overlap, something we can assume the Founding Fathers never intended.

I am aware of no cases prior to the New Deal that characterized the power flowing from the Commerce Clause as sweepingly as does our substantial effects test. My review of the case law indicates that the substantial effects test is but an innovation of the 20th century.

As recently as 1936, the Court continued to insist that the Commerce Clause did not reach the wholly internal business of the States. See Carter v. Carter Coal Co. (1936); see also A.L.A. Schechter Poultry Corp. v. United States (1935). The Federal Government simply could not reach such subjects regardless of their effects on interstate commerce.

These cases all establish a simple point: From the time of the ratification of the Constitution to the mid-1930's, it was widely understood that the Constitution granted Congress only limited powers, notwithstanding the Commerce Clause. Moreover, there was no question that activities wholly separated from business, such as gun possession, were beyond the reach of the commerce power. If anything, the "wrong turn" was the Court's dramatic departure in the 1930's from a century and a half of precedent.

Apart from its recent vintage and its corresponding lack of any grounding in the original understanding of the Constitution, the substantial effects test suffers from the further flaw that it appears to grant Congress a police power over the Nation. The substantial effects test suffers from this flaw, in part, because of its "aggregation principle." Under so-called "class of activities" statutes, Congress can regulate whole categories of activities that are not themselves either "interstate" or "commerce." In applying the effects test, we ask whether the class of activities as a whole substantially affects interstate commerce, not whether any specific activity within the class has such effects when considered in isolation.

The aggregation principle is clever, but has no stopping point. Suppose all would agree that gun possession within 1,000 feet of a school does not substantially affect commerce, but that possession of weapons generally (knives, brass knuckles, nunchakus, etc.) does. Under our substantial effects doctrine, even though Congress cannot single out gun possession, it can prohibit weapon possession generally. But one always can draw the circle broadly enough to cover an activity that, when taken in isolation, would not have substantial effects on commerce. Under our jurisprudence, if Congress passed an omnibus "substantially affects interstate commerce" statute, purporting to regulate every aspect of human existence, the Act apparently would be constitutional. Even though particular sections may govern only trivial activities, the statute in the aggregate regulates matters that substantially affect commerce.

Unless the dissenting Justices are willing to repudiate our long-held understanding of the limited nature of federal power, I would think that they, too, must be willing to reconsider the substantial effects test in a future case. If we wish to be true to a Constitution that does not cede a police power to the Federal Government, our Commerce Clause's boundaries simply cannot be "defined" as being "'commensurate with the national needs'" or self-consciously intended to let the Federal Government "'defend itself against economic forces that Congress decrees inimical or destructive of the national economy.'" Such a formulation of federal power is no test at all: It is a blank check.

At an appropriate juncture, I think we must modify our Commerce Clause jurisprudence. Today, it is easy enough to say that the Clause certainly does not empower Congress to ban gun possession within 1,000 feet of a school.

Justice STEVENS, dissenting.

The welfare of our future "Commerce with foreign Nations, and among the several States," U.S. Const., Art. I, §8, cl. 3, is vitally dependent on the character of the education of our children. I therefore agree entirely with Justice BREYER's explanation of why Congress has ample power to prohibit the possession of firearms in or near schools — just as it may protect the school environment from harms posed by controlled substances such as asbestos or alcohol. I also agree with Justice SOUTER's exposition of the radical character of the Court's holding and its kinship with the discredited, pre-Depression version of substantive due process.

Guns are both articles of commerce and articles that can be used to restrain commerce. Their possession is the consequence, either directly or indirectly, of commercial activity. In my judgment, Congress's power to regulate commerce in firearms includes the power to prohibit possession of guns at any location because of their potentially harmful use; it necessarily follows that Congress may also prohibit their possession in particular markets. The market for the possession of handguns by school-age children is, distressingly, substantial. Whether or not the

national interest in eliminating that market would have justified federal legislation in 1789, it surely does today.

Justice SOUTER, dissenting.

In reviewing congressional legislation under the Commerce Clause, we defer
to what is often a merely implicit congressional judgment that its regulation
addresses a subject substantially affecting interstate commerce "if there is any
rational basis for such a finding." Hodel v. Virginia Surface Mining & Reclamation Assn., Inc. (1981). If that congressional determination is within the realm of
reason, "the only remaining question for judicial inquiry is whether 'the means
chosen by Congress [are] reasonably adapted to the end permitted by the
Constitution.'"

The practice of deferring to rationally based legislative judgments "is a paradigm of judicial restraint." In judicial review under the Commerce Clause, it
reflects our respect for the institutional competence of the Congress on a subject
expressly assigned to it by the Constitution and our appreciation of the legitimacy
that comes from Congress's political accountability in dealing with matters open
to a wide range of possible choices.

It was not ever thus, however, as even a brief overview of Commerce Clause
history during the past century reminds us. The modern respect for the competence and primacy of Congress in matters affecting commerce developed only
after one of this Court's most chastening experiences, when it perforce repudiated
an earlier and untenably expansive conception of judicial review in derogation of
congressional commerce power. A look at history's sequence will serve to show
how today's decision tugs the Court off course, leading it to suggest opportunities
for further developments that would be at odds with the rule of restraint to which
the Court still wisely states adherence.

There is today, however, a backward glance at both the old pitfalls, as the
Court treats deference under the rationality rule as subject to gradation according
to the commercial or noncommercial nature of the immediate subject of the challenged regulation. The distinction between what is patently commercial and what
is not looks much like the old distinction between what directly affects commerce
and what touches it only indirectly. And the act of calibrating the level of deference by drawing a line between what is patently commercial and what is less
purely so will probably resemble the process of deciding how much interference
with contractual freedom was fatal. Thus, it seems fair to ask whether the step
taken by the Court today does anything but portend a return to the untenable
jurisprudence from which the Court extricated itself almost 60 years ago. The
answer is not reassuring. To be sure, the occasion for today's decision reflects the
century's end, not its beginning. But if it seems anomalous that the Congress of
the United States has taken to regulating school yards, the Act in question is still
probably no more remarkable than state regulation of bake shops 90 years ago. In
any event, there is no reason to hope that the Court's qualification of rational basis
review will be any more successful than the efforts at substantive economic review
made by our predecessors as the century began. Taking the Court's opinion on its
own terms, Justice BREYER has explained both the hopeless porosity of

"commercial" character as a ground of Commerce Clause distinction in America's highly connected economy, and the inconsistency of this categorization with our rational basis precedents from the last 50 years.

Justice BREYER, with whom Justice STEVENS, Justice SOUTER, and Justice GINSBURG join, dissenting.

The issue in this case is whether the Commerce Clause authorizes Congress to enact a statute that makes it a crime to possess a gun in, or near, a school. In my view, the statute falls well within the scope of the commerce power as this Court has understood that power over the last half century.

In reaching this conclusion, I apply three basic principles of Commerce Clause interpretation. First, the power to "regulate Commerce . . . among the several States," U.S. Const., Art. I, §8, cl. 3, encompasses the power to regulate local activities insofar as they significantly affect interstate commerce. See, e.g., Gibbons v. Ogden (1824); Wickard v. Filburn. As the majority points out, the Court, in describing how much of an effect the Clause requires, sometimes has used the word "substantial" and sometimes has not.

Second, in determining whether a local activity will likely have a significant effect upon interstate commerce, a court must consider, not the effect of an individual act (a single instance of gun possession), but rather the cumulative effect of all similar instances (i.e., the effect of all guns possessed in or near schools). See, e.g., Wickard.

Third, the Constitution requires us to judge the connection between a regulated activity and interstate commerce, not directly, but at one remove. Courts must give Congress a degree of leeway in determining the existence of a significant factual connection between the regulated activity and interstate commerce — both because the Constitution delegates the commerce power directly to Congress and because the determination requires an empirical judgment of a kind that a legislature is more likely than a court to make with accuracy. The traditional words "rational basis" capture this leeway. Thus, the specific question before us, as the Court recognizes, is not whether the "regulated activity sufficiently affected interstate commerce," but, rather, whether Congress could have had "a rational basis" for so concluding.

Applying these principles to the case at hand, we must ask whether Congress could have had a rational basis for finding a significant (or substantial) connection between gun-related school violence and interstate commerce. Or, to put the question in the language of the explicit finding that Congress made when it amended this law in 1994: Could Congress rationally have found that "violent crime in school zones," through its effect on the "quality of education," significantly (or substantially) affects "interstate" or "foreign commerce"? As long as one views the commerce connection, not as a "technical legal conception," but as "a practical one," the answer to this question must be yes. Numerous reports and studies — generated both inside and outside government — make clear that Congress could reasonably have found the empirical connection that its law, implicitly or explicitly, asserts.

For one thing, reports, hearings, and other readily available literature make clear that the problem of guns in and around schools is widespread and extremely serious. These materials report, for example, that four percent of American high school students (and six percent of inner-city high school students) carry a gun to school at least occasionally, Centers for Disease Control 2342; Sheley, McGee, & Wright 679; that 12 percent of urban high school students have had guns fired at them, *ibid.*; that 20 percent of those students have been threatened with guns, *ibid.*; and that, in any 6-month period, several hundred thousand schoolchildren are victims of violent crimes in or near their schools, U.S. Dept. of Justice 1 (1989); House Select Committee Hearing 15 (1989). And, they report that this widespread violence in schools throughout the Nation significantly interferes with the quality of education in those schools. See, e.g., House Judiciary Committee Hearing 44 (1990) (linking school violence to dropout rate); U.S. Dept. of Health 118-119 (1978) (school-violence victims suffer academically). Based on reports such as these, Congress obviously could have thought that guns and learning are mutually exclusive. Congress could therefore have found a substantial educational problem — teachers unable to teach, students unable to learn — and concluded that guns near schools contribute substantially to the size and scope of that problem.

Having found that guns in schools significantly undermine the quality of education in our Nation's classrooms, Congress could also have found, given the effect of education upon interstate and foreign commerce, that gun-related violence in and around schools is a commercial, as well as a human, problem. Education, although far more than a matter of economics, has long been inextricably intertwined with the Nation's economy.

In recent years the link between secondary education and business has strengthened, becoming both more direct and more important. [T]here is evidence that, today more than ever, many firms base their location decisions upon the presence, or absence, of a work force with a basic education.

Specifically, Congress could have found that gun-related violence near the classroom poses a serious economic threat (1) to consequently inadequately educated workers who must endure low paying jobs, and (2) to communities and businesses that might (in today's "information society") otherwise gain, from a well-educated work force, an important commercial advantage, of a kind that location near a railhead or harbor provided in the past. Congress might also have found these threats to be no different in kind from other threats that this Court has found within the commerce power, such as the threat that loan sharking poses to the "funds" of "numerous localities," Perez v. United States, and that unfair labor practices pose to instrumentalities of commerce. As I have pointed out, Congress has written that "the occurrence of violent crime in school zones" has brought about a "decline in the quality of education" that "has an adverse impact on interstate commerce and the foreign commerce of the United States." The violence-related facts, the educational facts, and the economic facts, taken together, make this conclusion rational. And, because under our case law, the sufficiency of the constitutionally necessary Commerce Clause link between a crime of violence and interstate commerce turns simply upon size or degree, those same facts make the statute constitutional.

To hold this statute constitutional is not to "obliterate" the "distinction between what is national and what is local," . . . ; nor is it to hold that the Commerce Clause permits the Federal Government to "regulate any activity that it found was related to the economic productivity of individual citizens," to regulate "marriage, divorce, and child custody," or to regulate any and all aspects of education. First, this statute is aimed at curbing a particularly acute threat to the educational process — the possession (and use) of life-threatening firearms in, or near, the classroom. The empirical evidence that I have discussed above unmistakably documents the special way in which guns and education are incompatible. Second, the immediacy of the connection between education and the national economic well-being is documented by scholars and accepted by society at large in a way and to a degree that may not hold true for other social institutions. It must surely be the rare case, then, that a statute strikes at conduct that (when considered in the abstract) seems so removed from commerce, but which (practically speaking) has so significant an impact upon commerce.

The majority's holding — that §922 falls outside the scope of the Commerce Clause — creates three serious legal problems. First, the majority's holding runs contrary to modern Supreme Court cases that have upheld congressional actions despite connections to interstate or foreign commerce that are less significant than the effect of school violence.

The second legal problem the Court creates comes from its apparent belief that it can reconcile its holding with earlier cases by making a critical distinction between "commercial" and noncommercial "transaction[s]." That is to say, the Court believes the Constitution would distinguish between two local activities, each of which has an identical effect upon interstate commerce, if one, but not the other, is "commercial" in nature. As a general matter, this approach fails to heed this Court's earlier warning not to turn "questions of the power of Congress" upon "formula[s]" that would give "controlling force to nomenclature such as 'production' and 'indirect' and foreclose consideration of the actual effects of the activity in question upon interstate commerce."

The third legal problem created by the Court's holding is that it threatens legal uncertainty in an area of law that, until this case, seemed reasonably well settled. Congress has enacted many statutes (more than 100 sections of the United States Code), including criminal statutes (at least 25 sections), that use the words "affecting commerce" to define their scope, see, e.g., 18 U.S.C. §844(i) (destruction of buildings used in activity affecting interstate commerce), and other statutes that contain no jurisdictional language at all, see, e.g., 18 U.S.C. §922(o)(1) (possession of machineguns). Do these, or similar, statutes regulate noncommercial activities? If so, would that alter the meaning of "affecting commerce" in a jurisdictional element?

Upholding this legislation would do no more than simply recognize that Congress had a "rational basis" for finding a significant connection between guns in or near schools and (through their effect on education) the interstate and foreign commerce they threaten. For these reasons, I would reverse the judgment of the Court of Appeals. Respectfully, I dissent.

United States v. Morrison

529 U.S. 598 (2000)

Chief Justice REHNQUIST delivered the opinion of the Court.

In these cases we consider the constitutionality of 42 U.S.C. §13981, which provides a federal civil remedy for the victims of gender-motivated violence. The United States Court of Appeals for the Fourth Circuit, sitting en banc, struck down §13981 because it concluded that Congress lacked constitutional authority to enact the section's civil remedy. [W]e affirm.

I

Petitioner Christy Brzonkala enrolled at Virginia Polytechnic Institute (Virginia Tech) in the fall of 1994. In September of that year, Brzonkala met respondents Antonio Morrison and James Crawford, who were both students at Virginia Tech and members of its varsity football team. Brzonkala alleges that, within 30 minutes of meeting Morrison and Crawford, they assaulted and repeatedly raped her. After the attack, Morrison allegedly told Brzonkala, "You better not have any . . . diseases." In the months following the rape, Morrison also allegedly announced in the dormitory's dining room that he "like[d] to get girls drunk and. . . ." The omitted portions, quoted verbatim in the briefs on file with this Court, consist of boasting, debased remarks about what Morrison would do to women, vulgar remarks that cannot fail to shock and offend.

Brzonkala alleges that this attack caused her to become severely emotionally disturbed and depressed. She sought assistance from a university psychiatrist, who prescribed antidepressant medication. Shortly after the rape Brzonkala stopped attending classes and withdrew from the university.

In early 1995, Brzonkala filed a complaint against respondents under Virginia Tech's Sexual Assault Policy. During the school-conducted hearing on her complaint, Morrison admitted having sexual contact with her despite the fact that she had twice told him "no." After the hearing, Virginia Tech's Judicial Committee found insufficient evidence to punish Crawford, but found Morrison guilty of sexual assault and sentenced him to immediate suspension for two semesters.

Virginia Tech's dean of students upheld the judicial committee's sentence. However, in July 1995, Virginia Tech informed Brzonkala that Morrison intended to initiate a court challenge to his conviction under the Sexual Assault Policy. University officials told her that a second hearing would be necessary to remedy the school's error in prosecuting her complaint under that policy, which had not been widely circulated to students. Following this second hearing the Judicial Committee again found Morrison guilty and sentenced him to an identical 2-semester suspension. This time, however, the description of Morrison's offense was, without explanation, changed from "sexual assault" to "using abusive language."

Morrison appealed his second conviction through the university's administrative system. On August 21, 1995, Virginia Tech's senior vice president and provost set aside Morrison's punishment. After learning from a newspaper that Morrison would be returning to Virginia Tech for the fall 1995 semester, she dropped out of the university.

In December 1995, Brzonkala sued Morrison, Crawford, and Virginia Tech in the United States District Court for the Western District of Virginia. Section 13981 was part of the Violence Against Women Act of 1994. It states that "[a]ll persons within the United States shall have the right to be free from crimes of violence motivated by gender." To enforce that right, subsection (c) declares: "A person (including a person who acts under color of any statute, ordinance, regulation, custom, or usage of any State) who commits a crime of violence motivated by gender and thus deprives another of the right declared in subsection (b) of this section shall be liable to the party injured, in an action for the recovery of compensatory and punitive damages, injunctive and declaratory relief, and such other relief as a court may deem appropriate." Section 13981 defines a "crim[e] of violence motivated by gender" as "a crime of violence committed because of gender or on the basis of gender, and due, at least in part, to an animus based on the victim's gender."

[II]

Due respect for the decisions of a coordinate branch of Government demands that we invalidate a congressional enactment only upon a plain showing that Congress has exceeded its constitutional bounds. With this presumption of constitutionality in mind, we turn to the question whether §13981 falls within Congress's power under Article I, §8, of the Constitution. Brzonkala and the United States rely upon the third clause of the Article, which gives Congress power "[t]o regulate Commerce with foreign Nations, and among the several States, and with the Indian Tribes."[85]

As we discussed at length in, *Lopez,* our interpretation of the Commerce Clause has changed as our Nation has developed. We need not repeat that detailed review of the Commerce Clause's history here; it suffices to say that, in the years since NLRB v. Jones & Laughlin Steel Corp. (1937), Congress has had considerably greater latitude in regulating conduct and transactions under the Commerce Clause than our previous case law permitted. *Lopez* emphasized, however, that even under our modern, expansive interpretation of the Commerce Clause, Congress's regulatory authority is not without effective bounds.

As we observed in *Lopez,* modern Commerce Clause jurisprudence has "identified three broad categories of activity that Congress may regulate under its commerce power." "First, Congress may regulate the use of the channels of interstate commerce." "Second, Congress is empowered to regulate and protect the instrumentalities of interstate commerce, or persons or things in interstate commerce, even though the threat may come only from intrastate activities." "Finally, Congress's commerce authority includes the power to regulate those activities

---

[85] The Court also considered the constitutionality of the Violence Against Women Act as an exercise of Congress's power under §5 of the Fourteenth Amendment. This aspect of *Morrison* is presented below. [Footnote by casebook author.]

having a substantial relation to interstate commerce, . . . i.e., those activities that substantially affect interstate commerce."

Petitioners do not contend that these cases fall within either of the first two of these categories of Commerce Clause regulation. They seek to sustain §13981 as a regulation of activity that substantially affects interstate commerce. Given §13981's focus on gender-motivated violence wherever it occurs (rather than violence directed at the instrumentalities of interstate commerce, interstate markets, or things or persons in interstate commerce), we agree that this is the proper inquiry.

[In *Lopez*] we observed that [the Gun-Free School Zones Act] was "a criminal statute that by its terms has nothing to do with 'commerce' or any sort of economic enterprise, however broadly one might define those terms." Reviewing our case law, we noted that "we have upheld a wide variety of congressional Acts regulating intrastate economic activity where we have concluded that the activity substantially affected interstate commerce."

Both petitioners and Justice SOUTER's dissent downplay the role that the economic nature of the regulated activity plays in our Commerce Clause analysis. But a fair reading of *Lopez* shows that the noneconomic, criminal nature of the conduct at issue was central to our decision in that case.

The second consideration that we found important in [*Lopez*] was that the statute contained "no express jurisdictional element which might limit its reach to a discrete set of firearm possessions that additionally have an explicit connection with or effect on interstate commerce." Such a jurisdictional element may establish that the enactment is in pursuance of Congress's regulation of interstate commerce.

Third, we noted that neither §922(q) " 'nor its legislative history contain[s] express congressional findings regarding the effects upon interstate commerce of gun possession in a school zone.' " Finally, our decision in *Lopez* rested in part on the fact that the link between gun possession and a substantial effect on interstate commerce was attenuated.

With these principles underlying our Commerce Clause jurisprudence as reference points, the proper resolution of the present cases is clear. Gender-motivated crimes of violence are not, in any sense of the phrase, economic activity. While we need not adopt a categorical rule against aggregating the effects of any noneconomic activity in order to decide these cases, thus far in our Nation's history our cases have upheld Commerce Clause regulation of intrastate activity only where that activity is economic in nature.

Like the Gun-Free School Zones Act at issue in *Lopez*, §13981 contains no jurisdictional element establishing that the federal cause of action is in pursuance of Congress's power to regulate interstate commerce. In contrast with the lack of congressional findings that we faced in *Lopez*, §13981 is supported by numerous findings regarding the serious impact that gender-motivated violence has on victims and their families. But the existence of congressional findings is not sufficient, by itself, to sustain the constitutionality of Commerce Clause legislation. As we stated in *Lopez*, " '[S]imply because Congress may conclude that a particular activity substantially affects interstate commerce does not necessarily make it so.' "

In these cases, Congress's findings are substantially weakened by the fact that they rely so heavily on a method of reasoning that we have already rejected as unworkable if we are to maintain the Constitution's enumeration of powers. Congress found that gender-motivated violence affects interstate commerce "by deterring potential victims from traveling interstate, from engaging in employment in interstate business, and from transacting with business, and in places involved in interstate commerce; . . . by diminishing national productivity, increasing medical and other costs, and decreasing the supply of and the demand for interstate products." H.R. Conf. Rep. No. 103-711.

The reasoning that petitioners advance seeks to follow the but-for causal chain from the initial occurrence of violent crime (the suppression of which has always been the prime object of the States' police power) to every attenuated effect upon interstate commerce. If accepted, petitioners' reasoning would allow Congress to regulate any crime as long as the nationwide, aggregated impact of that crime has substantial effects on employment, production, transit, or consumption. Indeed, if Congress may regulate gender-motivated violence, it would be able to regulate murder or any other type of violence since gender-motivated violence, as a subset of all violent crime, is certain to have lesser economic impacts than the larger class of which it is a part. Petitioners' reasoning, moreover, will not limit Congress to regulating violence but may, as we suggested in *Lopez*, be applied equally as well to family law and other areas of traditional state regulation since the aggregate effect of marriage, divorce, and childrearing on the national economy is undoubtedly significant. Given these findings and petitioners' arguments, the concern that we expressed in *Lopez* that Congress might use the Commerce Clause to completely obliterate the Constitution's distinction between national and local authority seems well founded.

We accordingly reject the argument that Congress may regulate noneconomic, violent criminal conduct based solely on that conduct's aggregate effect on interstate commerce. The Constitution requires a distinction between what is truly national and what is truly local. In recognizing this fact we preserve one of the few principles that has been consistent since the Clause was adopted.

Justice THOMAS, concurring.

The majority opinion correctly applies our decision in United States v. Lopez (1995), and I join it in full. I write separately only to express my view that the very notion of a "substantial effects" test under the Commerce Clause is inconsistent with the original understanding of Congress's powers and with this Court's early Commerce Clause cases. By continuing to apply this rootless and malleable standard, however circumscribed, the Court has encouraged the Federal Government to persist in its view that the Commerce Clause has virtually no limits. Until this Court replaces its existing Commerce Clause jurisprudence with a standard more consistent with the original understanding, we will continue to see Congress appropriating state police powers under the guise of regulating commerce.

Justice SOUTER, with whom Justice STEVENS, Justice GINSBURG, and Justice BREYER join, dissenting.

Our cases, which remain at least nominally undisturbed, stand for the following propositions. Congress has the power to legislate with regard to activity that, in the aggregate, has a substantial effect on interstate commerce. The fact of such a substantial effect is not an issue for the courts in the first instance, but for the Congress, whose institutional capacity for gathering evidence and taking testimony far exceeds ours. By passing legislation, Congress indicates its conclusion, whether explicitly or not, that facts support its exercise of the commerce power. The business of the courts is to review the congressional assessment, not for soundness but simply for the rationality of concluding that a jurisdictional basis exists in fact. Any explicit findings that Congress chooses to make, though not dispositive of the question of rationality, may advance judicial review by identifying factual authority on which Congress relied.

Applying those propositions in these cases can lead to only one conclusion. One obvious difference from United States v. Lopez, is the mountain of data assembled by Congress, here showing the effects of violence against women on interstate commerce. Passage of the Act in 1994 was preceded by four years of hearings. Congress thereby explicitly stated the predicate for the exercise of its Commerce Clause power. Is its conclusion irrational in view of the data amassed? True, the methodology of particular studies may be challenged, and some of the figures arrived at may be disputed. But the sufficiency of the evidence before Congress to provide a rational basis for the finding cannot seriously be questioned. Indeed, the legislative record here is far more voluminous than the record compiled by Congress and found sufficient in two prior cases upholding Title II of the Civil Rights Act of 1964 against Commerce Clause challenges.

While Congress did not, to my knowledge, calculate aggregate dollar values for the nationwide effects of racial discrimination in 1964, in 1994 it did rely on evidence of the harms caused by domestic violence and sexual assault, citing annual costs of $3 billion in 1990. Equally important, though, gender-based violence in the 1990's was shown to operate in a manner similar to racial discrimination in the 1960's in reducing the mobility of employees and their production and consumption of goods shipped in interstate commerce. Like racial discrimination, "[g]ender-based violence bars its most likely targets — women — from full partic[ipation] in the national economy."

Why is the majority tempted to reject the lesson so painfully learned in 1937? If we now ask why the formalistic economic/noneconomic distinction might matter today, after its rejection in Wickard, the answer is not that the majority fails to see causal connections in an integrated economic world. The answer is that in the minds of the majority there is a new animating theory that makes categorical formalism seem useful again. Just as the old formalism had value in the service of an economic conception, the new one is useful in serving a conception of federalism.

It is the instrument by which assertions of national power are to be limited in favor of preserving a supposedly discernible, proper sphere of state autonomy to legislate or refrain from legislating as the individual States see fit. The legitimacy of the Court's current emphasis on the noncommercial nature of regulated activity, then, does not turn on any logic serving the text of the Commerce Clause or on the realism of the majority's view of the national economy.

The Court finds it relevant that the statute addresses conduct traditionally subject to state prohibition under domestic criminal law, a fact said to have some heightened significance when the violent conduct in question is not itself aimed directly at interstate commerce or its instrumentalities. Again, history seems to be recycling, for the theory of traditional state concern as grounding a limiting principle has been rejected previously, and more than once.

All of this convinces me that today's ebb of the commerce power rests on error, and at the same time leads me to doubt that the majority's view will prove to be enduring law. There is yet one more reason for doubt. Although we sense the presence of *Carter Coal, Schechter,* and *Usery* once again, the majority embraces them only at arm's-length. Where such decisions once stood for rules, today's opinion points to considerations by which substantial effects are discounted. Cases standing for the sufficiency of substantial effects are not overruled; cases overruled since 1937 are not quite revived. As our predecessors learned then, the practice of such ad hoc review cannot preserve the distinction between the judicial and the legislative, and this Court, in any event, lacks the institutional capacity to maintain such a regime for very long. This one will end when the majority realizes that the conception of the commerce power for which it entertains hopes would inevitably fail the test expressed in Justice Holmes's statement that "[t]he first call of a theory of law is that it should fit the facts." O. Holmes, The Common Law 167 (Howe ed. 1963). The facts that cannot be ignored today are the facts of integrated national commerce and a political relationship between States and Nation much affected by their respective treasuries and constitutional modifications adopted by the people. The federalism of some earlier time is no more adequate to account for those facts today than the theory of laissez-faire was able to govern the national economy 70 years ago.

In two cases, the Court has narrowly construed some federal laws to avoid the question of whether they exceed the scope of Congress's commerce power. In United States v. Jones, 529 U.S. 848 (2000), the Supreme Court unanimously held that the federal Arson Act does not apply to arson of a dwelling. The Court, in an opinion by Justice Ginsburg, said that applying the Arson Act to arson of a private residence would raise serious constitutional issues concerning Congress's power under the Commerce Clause. As a result, the Court said to avoid "constitutional doubts" it would interpret the law to not apply to such acts.

The Court took the same approach, although in a much more closely divided decision, in Solid Waste Agency of Northern Cook County v. United States Army Corps of Engineers, 531 U.S. 159 (2001). The issue was whether the Clean Water Act, which applies to "navigable waters," could be applied to intrastate waters because of the presence of migratory birds. The Court, 5-4, said no, holding that it would interpret the statute this way so as to avoid constitutional doubts.

Chief Justice Rehnquist, working for the Court Stated:

Where an administrative interpretation of a statute invokes the outer limits of Congress' power, we expect a clear indication that Congress intended that result. This requirement stems from our prudential desire not to needlessly reach constitutional issues and our assumption that Congress does not casually authorize administrative agencies to interpret a statute to push the limit of congressional authority. This concern is heightened where the administrative interpretation alters the federal-state framework by permitting federal encroachment upon a traditional state power. Thus, "where an otherwise acceptable construction of a statute would raise serious constitutional problems, the Court will construe the statute to avoid such problems unless such construction is plainly contrary to the intent of Congress."

Twice in the past six years we have reaffirmed the proposition that the grant of authority to Congress under the Commerce Clause, though broad, is not unlimited. See United States v. Morrison (2000); United States v. Lopez (1995). Respondents argue that the "Migratory Bird Rule" falls within Congress' power to regulate intrastate activities that "substantially affect" interstate commerce. They note that the protection of migratory birds is a "national interest of very nearly the first magnitude," Missouri v. Holland (1920), and that, as the Court of Appeals found, millions of people spend over a billion dollars annually on recreational pursuits relating to migratory birds. These arguments raise significant constitutional questions. For example, we would have to evaluate the precise object or activity that, in the aggregate, substantially affects interstate commerce. This is not clear, for although the Corps has claimed jurisdiction over petitioner's land because it contains water areas used as habitat by migratory birds, respondents now focus upon the fact that the regulated activity is petitioner's municipal landfill, which is "plainly of a commercial nature." But this is a far cry, indeed, from the "navigable waters" and "waters of the United States" to which the statute by its terms extends.

These are significant constitutional questions raised by respondents' application of their regulations, and yet we find nothing approaching a clear statement from Congress that it intended §404(a) to reach an abandoned sand and gravel pit such as we have here. Permitting respondents to claim federal jurisdiction over ponds and mudflats falling within the "Migratory Bird Rule" would result in a significant impingement of the States' traditional and primary power over land and water use. We thus read the statute as written to avoid the significant constitutional and federalism questions raised by respondents' interpretation, and therefore reject the request for administrative deference.

Justice Stevens, writing for the four dissenting Justices, argued that the Army Corps of Engineers had the authority to apply the Clean Water Act to intrastate waters because of the presence of migratory birds. He wrote:

Contrary to the Court's suggestion, the Corps' interpretation of the statute does not "encroac[h]" upon "traditional state power" over land use. "Land use planning in essence chooses particular uses for the land; environmental regulation, at its core, does not mandate particular uses of the land but requires only that, however the land is used, damage to the environment is kept within prescribed limits." California Coastal Comm'n v. Granite Rock Co. (1987). The CWA is not a land-use code; it is a paradigm of environmental regulation. Such regulation is an accepted exercise of federal power. Hodel v. Virginia Surface Mining & Reclamation Assn., Inc. (1981).

The Corps' exercise of its §404 permitting power over "isolated" waters that serve as habitat for migratory birds falls well within the boundaries set by this Court's Commerce Clause jurisprudence. In United States v. Lopez (1995), this Court identified "three broad categories of activity that Congress may regulate under its commerce power": (1) channels of interstate commerce; (2) instrumentalities of interstate commerce, or persons and things in interstate commerce; and (3) activities that "substantially affect" interstate commerce. The migratory bird rule at issue here is properly analyzed under the third category. In order to constitute a proper exercise of Congress' power over intrastate activities that "substantially affect" interstate commerce, it is not necessary that each individual instance of the activity substantially affect commerce; it is enough that, taken in the aggregate, the class of activities in question has such an effect.

The activity being regulated in this case (and by the Corps' §404 regulations in general) is the discharge of fill material into water. The Corps did not assert jurisdiction over petitioner's land simply because the waters were "used as habitat by migratory birds." It asserted jurisdiction because petitioner planned to discharge fill into waters "used as habitat by migratory birds." Had petitioner intended to engage in some other activity besides discharging fill (i.e., had there been no activity to regulate), or, conversely, had the waters not been habitat for migratory birds (i.e., had there been no basis for federal jurisdiction), the Corps would never have become involved in petitioner's use of its land. There can be no doubt that, unlike the class of activities Congress was attempting to regulate in United States v. Morrison (2000) ("[g]ender-motivated crimes"), and *Lopez* (possession of guns near school property), the discharge of fill material into the Nation's waters is almost always undertaken for economic reasons.

Moreover, no one disputes that the discharge of fill into "isolated" waters that serve as migratory bird habitat will, in the aggregate, adversely affect migratory bird populations. Nor does petitioner dispute that the particular waters it seeks to fill are home to many important species of migratory birds, including the second-largest breeding colony of Great Blue Herons in northeastern Illinois, and several species of waterfowl protected by international treaty and Illinois endangered species laws.

The power to regulate commerce among the several States necessarily and properly includes the power to preserve the natural resources that generate such commerce. Moreover, the protection of migratory birds is a well-established federal responsibility. As Justice Holmes noted in Missouri v. Holland, the federal interest in protecting these birds is of "the first magnitude." Because of their transitory nature, they "can be protected only by national action."

During the last few years of the Rehnquist Court, two challenges to federal laws as exceeding the scope of the commerce power were rejected. One, Pierce County, Washington v. Guillen, was unanimous and did not engender controversy. The other, Gonzales v. Raich, was enormously controversial and led some commentators to argue that the Court was shifting away from significant limits on Congress's commerce power.

Pierce County, Washington v. Guillen

537 U.S. 129 (2003)

Justice THOMAS delivered the opinion of the Court.

We address in this case whether 23 U.S.C. §409, which protects information "compiled or collected" in connection with certain federal highway safety programs from being discovered or admitted in certain federal or state trials, is a valid exercise of Congress's authority under the Constitution.

Beginning with the Highway Safety Act of 1966, Congress has endeavored to improve the safety of our Nation's highways by encouraging closer federal and state cooperation with respect to road improvement projects. To that end, Congress has adopted several programs to assist the States in identifying highways in need of improvements and in funding those improvements. Of relevance to this case is the Hazard Elimination Program (Program) which provides state and local governments with funding to improve the most dangerous sections of their roads. To be eligible for funds under the Program, a state or local government must undertake a thorough evaluation of its public roads. Specifically, §152(a)(1) requires them to "conduct and systematically maintain an engineering survey of all public roads to identify hazardous locations, sections, and elements, including roadside obstacles and unmarked or poorly marked roads, which may constitute a danger to motorists, bicyclists, and pedestrians, assign priorities for the correction of such locations, sections, and elements, and establish and implement a schedule of projects for their improvement."

Not long after the adoption of the Hazard Elimination Program, the Secretary of Transportation reported to Congress that the States objected to the absence of any confidentiality with respect to their compliance measures under §152. According to the Secretary's report, the States feared that diligent efforts to identify roads eligible for aid under the Program would increase the risk of liability for accidents that took place at hazardous locations before improvements could be made. In 1983, concerned that the States' reluctance to be forthcoming and thorough in their data collection efforts undermined the Program's effectiveness, the United States Department of Transportation (DOT) recommended the adoption of legislation prohibiting the disclosure of information compiled in connection with the Hazard Elimination Program.

To address the concerns expressed by the States and the DOT, in 1987, Congress adopted 23 U.S.C. §409, which now reads:

"Notwithstanding any other provision of law, reports, surveys, schedules, lists, or data compiled or collected for the purpose of identifying, evaluating, or planning the safety enhancement of potential accident sites, hazardous roadway conditions, or railway-highway crossings, pursuant to sections 130, 144, and 152 of this title or for the purpose of developing any highway safety construction improvement project which may be implemented utilizing Federal-aid highway funds shall not be subject to discovery or admitted into evidence in a Federal or State court proceeding or considered for other purposes in any action for damages arising from any occurrence at a location mentioned or addressed in such reports, surveys, schedules, lists, or data."

Ignacio Guillen's wife, Clementina Guillen-Alejandre, died on July 5, 1996, in an automobile accident at the intersection of 168th Street East and B Street East (168/B intersection), in Pierce County, Washington. Several months before the accident, petitioner had requested §152 funding for this intersection, but the request had been denied. Petitioner renewed its application for funding on April 3, 1996, and the second request was approved on July 26, 1996, only three weeks after the accident occurred.

Beginning on August 16, 1996, counsel for respondents sought to obtain from petitioner information about accidents that had occurred at the 168/B intersection. Petitioner declined to provide any responsive information, asserting that any relevant documents were protected by §409. After informal efforts failed to resolve this discovery dispute, respondents turned to the Washington courts.

While the appeal in the PDA action was pending, respondents filed a separate action, asserting that petitioner had been negligent in failing to install proper traffic controls at the 168/B intersection. In connection with the tort action, respondents served petitioner with interrogatories seeking information regarding accidents that had occurred at the 168/B intersection. Petitioner refused to comply with the discovery request, once again relying on §409. Respondents successfully sought an order to compel, and petitioner moved for discretionary appellate review of the trial judge's interlocutory order.

We now consider whether §409 is a proper exercise of Congress's authority under the Constitution. We conclude that it is. It is well established that the Commerce Clause gives Congress authority to "regulate the use of the channels of interstate commerce." United States v. Lopez (1995). In addition, under the Commerce Clause, Congress "is empowered to regulate and protect the instrumentalities of interstate commerce, or persons or things in interstate commerce, even though the threat may come only from intrastate activities." Congress adopted §152 to assist state and local governments in reducing hazardous conditions in the Nation's channels of commerce. That effort was impeded, however, by the States' reluctance to comply fully with the requirements of §152, as such compliance would make state and local governments easier targets for negligence actions by providing would-be plaintiffs a centralized location from which they could obtain much of the evidence necessary for such actions. In view of these circumstances, Congress could reasonably believe that adopting a measure eliminating an unforeseen side effect of the information-gathering requirement of §152 would result in more diligent efforts to collect the relevant information, more candid discussions of hazardous locations, better informed decisionmaking, and, ultimately, greater safety on our Nation's roads.

Consequently, both the original §409 and the 1995 amendment can be viewed as legislation aimed at improving safety in the channels of commerce and increasing protection for the instrumentalities of interstate commerce. As such, they fall within Congress's Commerce Clause power.

Gonzales v. Raich

545 U.S. 1 (2005)

Justice STEVENS delivered the opinion of the Court.

California is one of at least nine States that authorize the use of marijuana for medicinal purposes. The question presented in this case is whether the power vested in Congress by Article I, §8, of the Constitution "[t]o make all Laws which shall be necessary and proper for carrying into Execution" its authority to "regulate Commerce with foreign Nations, and among the several States" includes the power to prohibit the local cultivation and use of marijuana in compliance with California law.

I

California has been a pioneer in the regulation of marijuana. In 1913, California was one of the first States to prohibit the sale and possession of marijuana, and at the end of the century, California became the first State to authorize limited use of the drug for medicinal purposes. In 1996, California voters passed Proposition 215, now codified as the Compassionate Use Act of 1996. The proposition was designed to ensure that "seriously ill" residents of the State have access to marijuana for medical purposes, and to encourage Federal and State Governments to take steps towards ensuring the safe and affordable distribution of the drug to patients in need. The Act creates an exemption from criminal prosecution for physicians, as well as for patients and primary caregivers who possess or cultivate marijuana for medicinal purposes with the recommendation or approval of a physician.

Respondents Angel Raich and Diane Monson are California residents who suffer from a variety of serious medical conditions and have sought to avail themselves of medical marijuana pursuant to the terms of the Compassionate Use Act. They are being treated by licensed, board-certified family practitioners, who have concluded, after prescribing a host of conventional medicines to treat respondents' conditions and to alleviate their associated symptoms, that marijuana is the only drug available that provides effective treatment. Both women have been using marijuana as a medication for several years pursuant to their doctors' recommendation, and both rely heavily on cannabis to function on a daily basis. Indeed, Raich's physician believes that forgoing cannabis treatments would certainly cause Raich excruciating pain and could very well prove fatal.

On August 15, 2002, county deputy sheriffs and agents from the federal Drug Enforcement Administration (DEA) came to Monson's home. After a thorough investigation, the county officials concluded that her use of marijuana was entirely lawful as a matter of California law. Nevertheless, after a 3-hour standoff, the federal agents seized and destroyed all six of her cannabis plants. Respondents thereafter brought this action against the Attorney General of the United States and the head of the DEA seeking injunctive and declaratory relief prohibiting the enforcement of the federal Controlled Substances Act (CSA) to the extent it prevents them from possessing, obtaining, or manufacturing cannabis for their personal medical use.

The case is made difficult by respondents' strong arguments that they will suffer irreparable harm because, despite a congressional finding to the contrary, marijuana does have valid therapeutic purposes. The question before us, however, is not whether it is wise to enforce the statute in these circumstances; rather, it is whether Congress' power to regulate interstate markets for medicinal substances encompasses the portions of those markets that are supplied with drugs produced and consumed locally. Well-settled law controls our answer. The CSA is a valid exercise of federal power, even as applied to the troubling facts of this case. We accordingly vacate the judgment of the Court of Appeals.

II

Shortly after taking office in 1969, President Nixon declared a national "war on drugs." As the first campaign of that war, Congress set out to enact legislation that would consolidate various drug laws on the books into a comprehensive statute, provide meaningful regulation over legitimate sources of drugs to prevent diversion into illegal channels, and strengthen law enforcement tools against the traffic in illicit drugs. That effort culminated in the passage of the Comprehensive Drug Abuse Prevention and Control Act of 1970.

[Subsequently, Congress enacted the CSA and] Congress devised a closed regulatory system making it unlawful to manufacture, distribute, dispense, or possess any controlled substance except in a manner authorized by the CSA. The CSA categorizes all controlled substances into five schedules. The drugs are grouped together based on their accepted medical uses, the potential for abuse, and their psychological and physical effects on the body. Each schedule is associated with a distinct set of controls regarding the manufacture, distribution, and use of the substances listed therein. The CSA and its implementing regulations set forth strict requirements regarding registration, labeling and packaging, production quotas, drug security, and recordkeeping.

In enacting the CSA, Congress classified marijuana as a Schedule I drug. Schedule I drugs are categorized as such because of their high potential for abuse, lack of any accepted medical use, and absence of any accepted safety for use in medically supervised treatment.

III

Respondents in this case do not dispute that passage of the CSA, as part of the Comprehensive Drug Abuse Prevention and Control Act, was well within Congress' commerce power. Nor do they contend that any provision or section of the CSA amounts to an unconstitutional exercise of congressional authority. Rather, respondents' challenge is actually quite limited; they argue that the CSA's categorical prohibition of the manufacture and possession of marijuana as applied to the intrastate manufacture and possession of marijuana for medical purposes pursuant to California law exceeds Congress' authority under the Commerce Clause.

In assessing the validity of congressional regulation, none of our Commerce Clause cases can be viewed in isolation. As charted in considerable detail in

United States v. Lopez, our understanding of the reach of the Commerce Clause, as well as Congress' assertion of authority thereunder, has evolved over time. Cases decided during that "new era," which now spans more than a century, have identified three general categories of regulation in which Congress is authorized to engage under its commerce power. First, Congress can regulate the channels of interstate commerce. Second, Congress has authority to regulate and protect the instrumentalities of interstate commerce, and persons or things in interstate commerce. Third, Congress has the power to regulate activities that substantially affect interstate commerce. Only the third category is implicated in the case at hand.

Our case law firmly establishes Congress' power to regulate purely local activities that are part of an economic "class of activities" that have a substantial effect on interstate commerce. See, e.g., *Wickard v. Filburn* (1942). As we stated in *Wickard*, "even if appellee's activity be local and though it may not be regarded as commerce, it may still, whatever its nature, be reached by Congress if it exerts a substantial economic effect on interstate commerce." We have never required Congress to legislate with scientific exactitude. When Congress decides that the "'total incidence'" of a practice poses a threat to a national market, it may regulate the entire class. In this vein, we have reiterated that when "'a general regulatory statute bears a substantial relation to commerce, the de minimis character of individual instances arising under that statute is of no consequence.'"

Our decision in *Wickard* is of particular relevance. In *Wickard*, we upheld the application of regulations promulgated under the Agricultural Adjustment Act of 1938, which were designed to control the volume of wheat moving in interstate and foreign commerce in order to avoid surpluses and consequent abnormally low prices. *Wickard* thus establishes that Congress can regulate purely intrastate activity that is not itself "commercial," in that it is not produced for sale, if it concludes that failure to regulate that class of activity would undercut the regulation of the interstate market in that commodity.

The similarities between this case and *Wickard* are striking. Like the farmer in *Wickard*, respondents are cultivating, for home consumption, a fungible commodity for which there is an established, albeit illegal, interstate market. Just as the Agricultural Adjustment Act was designed "to control the volume [of wheat] moving in interstate and foreign commerce in order to avoid surpluses . . ." and consequently control the market price, a primary purpose of the CSA is to control the supply and demand of controlled substances in both lawful and unlawful drug markets. In *Wickard*, we had no difficulty concluding that Congress had a rational basis for believing that, when viewed in the aggregate, leaving home-consumed wheat outside the regulatory scheme would have a substantial influence on price and market conditions. Here too, Congress had a rational basis for concluding that leaving home-consumed marijuana outside federal control would similarly affect price and market conditions.

More concretely, one concern prompting inclusion of wheat grown for home consumption in the 1938 Act was that rising market prices could draw such wheat into the interstate market, resulting in lower market prices. The parallel concern making it appropriate to include marijuana grown for home consumption in the

CSA is the likelihood that the high demand in the interstate market will draw such marijuana into that market. While the diversion of homegrown wheat tended to frustrate the federal interest in stabilizing prices by regulating the volume of commercial transactions in the interstate market, the diversion of home-grown marijuana tends to frustrate the federal interest in eliminating commercial transactions in the interstate market in their entirety. In both cases, the regulation is squarely within Congress' commerce power because production of the commodity meant for home consumption, be it wheat or marijuana, has a substantial effect on supply and demand in the national market for that commodity.[86]

In assessing the scope of Congress' authority under the Commerce Clause, we stress that the task before us is a modest one. We need not determine whether respondents' activities, taken in the aggregate, substantially affect interstate commerce in fact, but only whether a "rational basis" exists for so concluding. Given the enforcement difficulties that attend distinguishing between marijuana cultivated locally and marijuana grown elsewhere, 21 U.S.C. §801(5), and concerns about diversion into illicit channels, we have no difficulty concluding that Congress had a rational basis for believing that failure to regulate the intrastate manufacture and possession of marijuana would leave a gaping hole in the CSA. Thus, as in *Wickard*, when it enacted comprehensive legislation to regulate the interstate market in a fungible commodity, Congress was acting well within its authority to "make all Laws which shall be necessary and proper" to "regulate Commerce . . . among the several States." U.S. Const., Art. I, §8. That the regulation ensnares some purely intrastate activity is of no moment. As we have done many times before, we refuse to excise individual components of that larger scheme.

IV

To support their contrary submission, respondents rely heavily on two of our more recent Commerce Clause cases. In their myopic focus, they overlook the larger context of modern-era Commerce Clause jurisprudence preserved by those cases. Moreover, even in the narrow prism of respondents' creation, they read those cases far too broadly. Those two cases, of course, are *United States v. Lopez* (1995) and *United States v. Morrison* (2000). As an initial matter, the statutory challenges at issue in those cases were markedly different from the challenge respondents pursue in the case at hand. Here, respondents ask us to excise individual applications of a concededly valid statutory scheme. In contrast, in both *Lopez* and *Morrison*, the parties asserted that a particular statute or provision fell outside Congress' commerce power in its entirety. This distinction is pivotal for we have often reiterated that "[w]here the class of activities is regulated and that class is within the

---

[86] To be sure, the wheat market is a lawful market that Congress sought to protect and stabilize, whereas the marijuana market is an unlawful market that Congress sought to eradicate. This difference, however, is of no constitutional import. It has long been settled that Congress' power to regulate commerce includes the power to prohibit commerce in a particular commodity. [Footnote by the Court.]

reach of federal power, the courts have no power 'to excise, as trivial, individual instances' of the class."

Unlike those at issue in *Lopez* and *Morrison*, the activities regulated by the CSA are quintessentially economic. "Economics" refers to "the production, distribution, and consumption of commodities." Webster's Third New International Dictionary (1966). The CSA is a statute that regulates the production, distribution, and consumption of commodities for which there is an established, and lucrative, interstate market. Prohibiting the intrastate possession or manufacture of an article of commerce is a rational (and commonly utilized) means of regulating commerce in that product. Such prohibitions include specific decisions requiring that a drug be withdrawn from the market as a result of the failure to comply with regulatory requirements as well as decisions excluding Schedule I drugs entirely from the market. Because the CSA is a statute that directly regulates economic, commercial activity, our opinion in *Morrison* casts no doubt on its constitutionality.

V

Respondents also raise a substantive due process claim and seek to avail themselves of the medical necessity defense. These theories of relief were set forth in their complaint but were not reached by the Court of Appeals. We therefore do not address the question whether judicial relief is available to respondents on these alternative bases. We do note, however, the presence of another avenue of relief. As the Solicitor General confirmed during oral argument, the statute authorizes procedures for the reclassification of Schedule I drugs. But perhaps even more important than these legal avenues is the democratic process, in which the voices of voters allied with these respondents may one day be heard in the halls of Congress.

Justice SCALIA, concurring in the judgment.

I agree with the Court's holding that the Controlled Substances Act (CSA) may validly be applied to respondents' cultivation, distribution, and possession of marijuana for personal, medicinal use. I write separately because my understanding of the doctrinal foundation on which that holding rests is, if not inconsistent with that of the Court, at least more nuanced.

Since *Perez v. United States* (1971), our cases have mechanically recited that the Commerce Clause permits congressional regulation of three categories: (1) the channels of interstate commerce; (2) the instrumentalities of interstate commerce, and persons or things in interstate commerce; and (3) activities that "substantially affect" interstate commerce. The first two categories are self-evident, since they are the ingredients of interstate commerce itself. The third category, however, is different in kind, and its recitation without explanation is misleading and incomplete.

It is misleading because, unlike the channels, instrumentalities, and agents of interstate commerce, activities that substantially affect interstate commerce are not themselves part of interstate commerce, and thus the power to regulate them cannot come from the Commerce Clause alone. Rather, Congress's regulatory authority over intrastate activities that are not themselves part of interstate commerce (including activities that have a substantial effect on interstate commerce) derives from the Necessary and Proper Clause. And the category of "activities that substantially affect interstate commerce" is incomplete because the authority to enact laws necessary and proper for the regulation of interstate commerce is not limited to laws governing intrastate activities that substantially affect interstate commerce. Where necessary to make a regulation of interstate commerce effective, Congress may regulate even those intrastate activities that do not themselves substantially affect interstate commerce.

Today's principal dissent objects that, by permitting Congress to regulate activities necessary to effective interstate regulation, the Court reduces *Lopez* and *Morrison* to "little more than a drafting guide." I think that criticism unjustified. Unlike the power to regulate activities that have a substantial effect on interstate commerce, the power to enact laws enabling effective regulation of interstate commerce can only be exercised in conjunction with congressional regulation of an interstate market, and it extends only to those measures necessary to make the interstate regulation effective. As *Lopez* itself states, and the Court affirms today, Congress may regulate noneconomic intrastate activities only where the failure to do so "could . . . undercut" its regulation of interstate commerce. This is not a power that threatens to obliterate the line between "what is truly national and what is truly local."

Lopez and *Morrison* affirm that Congress may not regulate certain "purely local" activity within the States based solely on the attenuated effect that such activity may have in the interstate market. But those decisions do not declare noneconomic intrastate activities to be categorically beyond the reach of the Federal Government. Neither case involved the power of Congress to exert control over intrastate activities in connection with a more comprehensive scheme of regulation. To dismiss this distinction as "superficial and formalistic," . . . (O'Connor, J., dissenting), is to misunderstand the nature of the Necessary and Proper Clause, which empowers Congress to enact laws in effectuation of its enumerated powers that are not within its authority to enact in isolation. See *McCulloch v. Maryland* (1819).

And there are other restraints upon the Necessary and Proper Clause authority. As Chief Justice Marshall wrote in *McCulloch v. Maryland*, even when the end is constitutional and legitimate, the means must be "appropriate" and "plainly adapted" to that end. Moreover, they may not be otherwise "prohibited" and must be "consistent with the letter and spirit of the constitution." These phrases are not merely hortatory.

The application of these principles to the case before us is straightforward. In the CSA, Congress has undertaken to extinguish the interstate market in Schedule I controlled substances, including marijuana. The Commerce Clause unquestionably permits this. The power to regulate interstate commerce "extends not only to those regulations which aid, foster and protect the commerce, but embraces those which prohibit it." To effectuate its objective, Congress has prohibited almost all intrastate activities related to Schedule I substances — both economic activities (manufacture, distribution, possession with the intent to distribute) and noneconomic activities (simple possession). That simple possession is a noneconomic activity is immaterial to whether it can be prohibited as a necessary part of a larger regulation. Rather, Congress's authority to enact all of these prohibitions of intrastate controlled-substance activities depends only upon whether they are appropriate means of achieving the legitimate end of eradicating Schedule I substances from interstate commerce.

By this measure, I think the regulation must be sustained. Not only is it impossible to distinguish "controlled substances manufactured and distributed intrastate" from "controlled substances manufactured and distributed interstate," but it hardly makes sense to speak in such terms. Drugs like marijuana are fungible commodities. As the Court explains, marijuana that is grown at home and possessed for personal use is never more than an instant from the interstate market — and this is so whether or not the possession is for medicinal use or lawful use under the laws of a particular State. Congress need not accept on faith that state law will be effective in maintaining a strict division between a lawful market for "medical" marijuana and the more general marijuana market.

I thus agree with the Court that, however the class of regulated activities is subdivided, Congress could reasonably conclude that its objective of prohibiting marijuana from the interstate market "could be undercut" if those activities were excepted from its general scheme of regulation. That is sufficient to authorize the application of the CSA to respondents.

Justice O'CONNOR, with whom the Chief Justice and Justice THOMAS join as to all but Part III, dissenting.

We enforce the "outer limits" of Congress' Commerce Clause authority not for their own sake, but to protect historic spheres of state sovereignty from excessive federal encroachment and thereby to maintain the distribution of power fundamental to our federalist system of government. *United States v. Lopez* (1995). One of federalism's chief virtues, of course, is that it promotes innovation by allowing for the possibility that "a single courageous State may, if its citizens choose, serve as a laboratory; and try novel social and economic experiments without risk to the rest of the country." *New State Ice Co. v. Liebmann* (1932) (Brandeis, J., dissenting).

This case exemplifies the role of States as laboratories. The States' core police powers have always included authority to define criminal law and to protect the health, safety, and welfare of their citizens. Exercising those powers, California (by ballot initiative and then by legislative codification) has come to its own conclusion about the difficult and sensitive question of whether marijuana should be available to relieve severe pain and suffering. Today the Court sanctions an application of the federal Controlled Substances Act that extinguishes that experiment, without any proof that the personal cultivation, possession, and use of marijuana for medicinal purposes, if economic activity in the first place, has a substantial effect on interstate commerce and is therefore an appropriate subject of federal regulation. In so doing, the Court announces a rule that gives Congress a perverse incentive to legislate broadly pursuant to the Commerce Clause — nestling questionable assertions of its authority into comprehensive regulatory schemes — rather than with precision. That rule and the result it produces in this case are irreconcilable with our decisions in *Lopez* and *Morrison*. Accordingly I dissent.

The Court's principal means of distinguishing *Lopez* from this case is to observe that the Gun-Free School Zones Act of 1990 was a "brief, single-subject statute," whereas the CSA is "a lengthy and detailed statute creating a comprehensive framework for regulating the production, distribution, and possession of five classes of 'controlled substances.'" Thus, according to the Court, it was possible in *Lopez* to evaluate in isolation the constitutionality of criminalizing local activity (there gun possession in school zones), whereas the local activity that the CSA targets (in this case cultivation and possession of marijuana for personal medicinal use) cannot be separated from the general drug control scheme of which it is a part.

Today's decision allows Congress to regulate intrastate activity without check, so long as there is some implication by legislative design that regulating intrastate activity is essential (and the Court appears to equate "essential" with "necessary") to the interstate regulatory scheme. Seizing upon our language in *Lopez* that the statute prohibiting gun possession in school zones was "not an essential part of a larger regulation of economic activity, in which the regulatory scheme could be undercut unless the intrastate activity were regulated," the Court appears to reason that the placement of local activity in a comprehensive scheme confirms that it is essential to that scheme. If the Court is right, then *Lopez* stands for nothing more than a drafting guide: Congress should have described the relevant crime as "transfer or possession of a firearm anywhere in the nation" — thus including commercial and noncommercial activity, and clearly encompassing some activity with assuredly substantial effect on interstate commerce. Had it done so, the majority hints, we would have sustained its authority to regulate possession of firearms in school zones. Furthermore, today's decision suggests we would readily sustain a congressional decision to attach the regulation of intrastate activity to a pre-existing comprehensive (or even not-so-comprehensive) scheme. If so, the Court invites increased federal regulation of local activity even if, as it suggests, Congress would not enact a new interstate scheme exclusively for the sake of reaching intrastate activity. I cannot agree that our decision in *Lopez* contemplated such evasive or overbroad legislative strategies with approval. Until today, such arguments have been made only in dissent.

Lopez and *Morrison* did not indicate that the constitutionality of federal regulation depends on superficial and formalistic distinctions. Likewise I did not understand our discussion of the role of courts in enforcing outer limits of the Commerce Clause for the sake of maintaining the federalist balance our Constitution requires as a signal to Congress to enact legislation that is more extensive and more intrusive into the domain of state power. If the Court always defers to Congress as it does today, little may be left to the notion of enumerated powers.

The hard work for courts, then, is to identify objective markers for confining the analysis in Commerce Clause cases. Here, respondents challenge the constitutionality of the CSA as applied to them and those similarly situated. I agree with the Court that we must look beyond respondents' own activities. Otherwise, individual litigants could always exempt themselves from Commerce Clause regulation merely by pointing to the obvious — that their personal activities do not have a substantial effect on interstate commerce. The task is to identify a mode of analysis that allows Congress to regulate more than nothing (by declining to reduce each case to its litigants) and less than everything (by declining to let Congress set the terms of analysis). The analysis may not be the same in every case, for it depends on the regulatory scheme at issue and the federalism concerns implicated.

A number of objective markers are available to confine the scope of constitutional review here. Both federal and state legislation — including the CSA itself, the California Compassionate Use Act, and other state medical marijuana legislation — recognize that medical and nonmedical (i.e., recreational) uses of drugs are realistically distinct and can be segregated, and regulate them differently. Respondents challenge only the application of the CSA to medicinal use of marijuana. Moreover, because fundamental structural concerns about dual sovereignty animate our Commerce Clause cases, it is relevant that this case involves the interplay of federal and state regulation in areas of criminal law and social policy, where "States lay claim by right of history and expertise." Under our precedents, the conduct is economic and, in the aggregate, substantially affects interstate commerce. Even if intrastate cultivation and possession of marijuana for one's own medicinal use can properly be characterized as economic, and I question whether it can, it has not been shown that such activity substantially affects interstate commerce. Similarly, it is neither self-evident nor demonstrated that regulating such activity is necessary to the interstate drug control scheme.

The Court's definition of economic activity is breathtaking. It defines as economic any activity involving the production, distribution, and consumption of commodities. And it appears to reason that when an interstate market for a commodity exists, regulating the intrastate manufacture or possession of that commodity is constitutional either because that intrastate activity is itself economic, or because regulating it is a rational part of regulating its market. Putting to one side the problem endemic to the Court's opinion — the shift in focus from the activity at issue in this case to the entirety of what the CSA regulates — the Court's definition of economic activity for purposes of Commerce Clause jurisprudence threatens to sweep all of productive human activity into federal regulatory reach.

Even assuming that economic activity is at issue in this case, the Government has made no showing in fact that the possession and use of homegrown marijuana for medical purposes, in California or elsewhere, has a substantial effect on interstate commerce. Similarly, the Government has not shown that regulating such activity is necessary to an interstate regulatory scheme. Whatever the specific theory of "substantial effects" at issue (i.e., whether the activity substantially affects interstate commerce, whether its regulation is necessary to an interstate regulatory scheme, or both), a concern for dual sovereignty requires that Congress' excursion into the traditional domain of States be justified.

That is why characterizing this as a case about the Necessary and Proper Clause does not change the analysis significantly. Congress must exercise its authority under the Necessary and Proper Clause in a manner consistent with basic constitutional principles. Likewise, that authority must be used in a manner consistent with the notion of enumerated powers — a structural principle that is as much part of the Constitution as the Tenth Amendment's explicit textual command. Accordingly, something more than mere assertion is required when Congress purports to have power over local activity whose connection to an intrastate market is not self-evident. Otherwise, the Necessary and Proper Clause will always be a back door for unconstitutional federal regulation. Indeed, if it were enough in "substantial effects" cases for the Court to supply conceivable justifications for intrastate regulation related to an interstate market, then we could have surmised in *Lopez* that guns in school zones are "never more than an instant from the interstate market" in guns already subject to extensive federal regulation, recast *Lopez* as a Necessary and Proper Clause case, and thereby upheld the Gun-Free School Zones Act of 1990.

There is simply no evidence that homegrown medicinal marijuana users constitute, in the aggregate, a sizable enough class to have a discernable, let alone substantial, impact on the national illicit drug market — or otherwise to threaten the CSA regime.

The Government has not overcome empirical doubt that the number of Californians engaged in personal cultivation, possession, and use of medical marijuana, or the amount of marijuana they produce, is enough to threaten the federal regime. Nor has it shown that Compassionate Use Act marijuana users have been or are realistically likely to be responsible for the drug's seeping into the market in a significant way. The Government does cite one estimate that there were over 100,000 Compassionate Use Act users in California in 2004, but does not explain, in terms of proportions, what their presence means for the national illicit drug market.

Relying on Congress' abstract assertions, the Court has endorsed making it a federal crime to grow small amounts of marijuana in one's own home for one's own medicinal use. This overreaching stifles an express choice by some States, concerned for the lives and liberties of their people, to regulate medical marijuana differently. If I were a California citizen, I would not have voted for the medical marijuana ballot initiative; if I were a California legislator I would not have supported the Compassionate Use Act. But whatever the wisdom of California's experiment with medical marijuana, the federalism principles that have driven our Commerce Clause cases require that room for experiment be protected in this case. For these reasons I dissent.

Justice THOMAS, dissenting.

Respondents Diane Monson and Angel Raich use marijuana that has never been bought or sold, that has never crossed state lines, and that has had no demonstrable effect on the national market for marijuana. If Congress can regulate this under the Commerce Clause, then it can regulate virtually anything — and the Federal Government is no longer one of limited and enumerated powers.

Respondents' local cultivation and consumption of marijuana is not "Commerce . . . among the several States." By holding that Congress may regulate activity that is neither interstate nor commerce under the Interstate Commerce

Clause, the Court abandons any attempt to enforce the Constitution's limits on federal power. The majority supports this conclusion by invoking, without explanation, the Necessary and Proper Clause. Regulating respondents' conduct, however, is not "necessary and proper for carrying into Execution" Congress' restrictions on the interstate drug trade. Thus, neither the Commerce Clause nor the Necessary and Proper Clause grants Congress the power to regulate respondents' conduct.

As I explained at length in *United States v. Lopez* (1995), the Commerce Clause empowers Congress to regulate the buying and selling of goods and services trafficked across state lines. The Clause's text, structure, and history all indicate that, at the time of the founding, the term "'commerce' consisted of selling, buying, and bartering, as well as transporting for these purposes." Commerce, or trade, stood in contrast to productive activities like manufacturing and agriculture.

Even the majority does not argue that respondents' conduct is itself "Commerce among the several States." Monson and Raich neither buy nor sell the marijuana that they consume. They cultivate their cannabis entirely in the State of California — it never crosses state lines, much less as part of a commercial transaction. Certainly no evidence from the founding suggests that "commerce" included the mere possession of a good or some purely personal activity that did not involve trade or exchange for value. In the early days of the Republic, it would have been unthinkable that Congress could prohibit the local cultivation, possession, and consumption of marijuana.

More difficult, however, is whether the CSA is a valid exercise of Congress' power to enact laws that are "necessary and proper for carrying into Execution" its power to regulate interstate commerce. The Necessary and Proper Clause is not a warrant to Congress to enact any law that bears some conceivable connection to the exercise of an enumerated power. Nor is it, however, a command to Congress to enact only laws that are absolutely indispensable to the exercise of an enumerated power.

On its face, a ban on the intrastate cultivation, possession and distribution of marijuana may be plainly adapted to stopping the interstate flow of marijuana. Unregulated local growers and users could swell both the supply and the demand sides of the interstate marijuana market, making the market more difficult to regulate. But respondents do not challenge the CSA on its face. Instead, they challenge it as applied to their conduct. The question is thus whether the intrastate ban is "necessary and proper" as applied to medical marijuana users like respondents.

Respondents are not regulable simply because they belong to a large class (local growers and users of marijuana) that Congress might need to reach, if they also belong to a distinct and separable subclass (local growers and users of state-authorized, medical marijuana) that does not undermine the CSA's interstate ban. California's Compassionate Use Act sets respondents' conduct apart from other intrastate producers and users of marijuana.

In sum, neither in enacting the CSA nor in defending its application to respondents has the Government offered any obvious reason why banning medical marijuana use is necessary to stem the tide of interstate drug trafficking. Congress' goal of curtailing the interstate drug trade would not plainly be thwarted if it could not apply the CSA to patients like Monson and Raich. That is, unless Congress' aim is really to exercise police power of the sort reserved to the States in order to eliminate even the intrastate possession and use of marijuana.

The majority prevents States like California from devising drug policies that they have concluded provide much-needed respite to the seriously ill. It does so without any serious inquiry into the necessity for federal regulation or the propriety of "displac[ing] state regulation in areas of traditional state concern." The majority's rush to embrace federal power "is especially unfortunate given the importance of showing respect for the sovereign States that comprise our Federal Union." Our federalist system, properly understood, allows California and a growing number of other States to decide for themselves how to safeguard the health and welfare of their citizens. I would affirm the judgment of the Court of Appeals.

C. The Taxing and Spending Power

1. *The Scope of the Taxing and Spending Power*

Article I, §8 of the Constitution states that "Congress shall have Power To lay and collect Taxes, Duties, Imposts and Excises, to pay the Debts and provide for the common Defence and general Welfare of the United States; but all Duties, Imposts and Excises shall be uniform throughout the United States." Under the Articles of Confederation, the limited federal government had no taxing power and therefore no revenue to spend. Obviously, in the twentieth century, the power to tax and spend is one of the most important of all congressional powers.

For What Purposes May Congress Tax and Spend?

Is Congress limited to taxing and spending only to carry out other powers specifically enumerated in Article I, or does Congress have broad authority to tax and spend for the general welfare? The Court adopted the latter, much more expansive, view in *United States v. Butler*.[87] *Butler* concerned the constitutionality of the Agricultural Adjustment Act of 1933, which sought to stabilize production in agriculture by offering subsidies to farmers to limit their crops. By restricting the supply of agricultural products, Congress sought to ensure a fair price and thus to encourage agricultural production.

Butler declared the Agricultural Adjustment Act unconstitutional on the ground that it violated the Tenth Amendment because it regulated production;

---

[87] 297 U.S. 1 (1936).

the regulation of production, according to the Court, was left to the states.[88] This aspect of *Butler* has never been followed and is discussed in more detail in §3.8 [Erwin Chemerinsky, Constitutional Law: Principles and Policies, 4th ed., (2011)], which considers the Tenth Amendment. However, the *Butler* Court's holding concerning the scope of the taxing and spending powers remains good law.

The Court began by noting that the debate over the scope of the taxing and spending power goes back to a dispute between James Madison and Alexander Hamilton. Madison took the view that Congress was limited to taxing and spending to carry out the other powers specifically granted in Article I of the Constitution. The Court explained that "Madison asserted it amounted to no more than a reference to the other powers enumerated in the subsequent clauses of the same section; that, as the United States is a government of limited and enumerated powers, the grant of power to tax and spend for the general national welfare must be confined to the enumerated legislative fields committed to the Congress."[89]

In contrast, Hamilton took the position that Congress could tax and spend for any purpose that it believed served the general welfare, so long as Congress did not violate another constitutional provision. The Court noted that "Hamilton . . . maintained that the clause confers a power separate and distinct from those later enumerated, is not restricted in meaning by the grant of them, and Congress consequently has a substantive power to tax and to appropriate, limited only by the requirement that it shall be exercised to provide for the general welfare of the United States."[90]

The Court expressly endorsed Hamilton's position as "the correct one."[91] Thus, Congress has broad power to tax and spend for the general welfare so long as it does not violate other constitutional provisions. For example, a tax that was calculated or administered in a racially discriminatory fashion would be unconstitutional, not as exceeding the scope of Congress's Article I powers, but as violating the equal protection guarantee of the Fifth Amendment.[92]

Subsequent cases affirmed Congress's expansive authority under the taxing and spending clauses. In *Steward Machine Co. v. Davis*, the Court upheld the constitutionality of the federal unemployment compensation system created by the Social Security Act.[93] In *Helvering v. Davis*, the Court upheld the constitutionality of the Social Security Act's old age pension program, which was supported exclusively by federal taxes.[94] Justice Benjamin Cardozo, writing for the Court, stated: "The discretion [to decide whether taxing and spending advances

---

[88] The Court adopted a similar limit on Congress's commerce power between 1887 and 1937, holding that regulating production was left to the states. *See* §3.3.3 [Erwin Chemerinsky, Constitutional Law: Principles and Policies, 4th ed., (2011)].

[89] 297 U.S. at 65.

[90] *Id.* at 65.

[91] *Id.* at 66.

[92] As discussed in §9.1.1 [Erwin Chemerinsky, Constitutional Law: Principles and Policies, 4th ed., (2011)], equal protection applies to state and local governments through the Fourteenth Amendment and to the federal government through the Fifth Amendment.

[93] 301 U.S. 548 (1937).

[94] 301 U.S. 619 (1937).

the general welfare] belongs to Congress, unless the choice is clearly wrong, a display of arbitrary power, not an exercise of judgment. . . . Nor is the concept of the general welfare static. Needs that were narrow or parochial a century ago may be interwoven in our day with the well-being of the Nation."[95]

In light of the narrowing of Congress's commerce power, some have urged similar restrictions on Congress's spending power and even an overruling of *United States v. Butler*'s expansive interpretation of this authority.[96] Thus far, though, the Court has not indicated any such change in the law.

2. *The Taxing Power*

Historically, the Court drew distinctions between direct and indirect taxes, and between revenue raising and regulatory taxes, in considering the constitutionality of taxes. Neither of these distinctions has any significance today.[97]

Direct and Indirect Taxes

Article I, §2, of the Constitution states that "direct Taxes shall be apportioned among the several States which may be included within this Union, according to their respective Numbers." Article I, §9, provides that "[n]o Capitation, or other direct, Tax shall be laid, unless in Proportion to the Census." In its initial cases considering these provisions, the Court narrowly defined a *direct* tax and thus accorded Congress broad authority to impose various kinds of taxes. Under the earlier cases, direct taxes seemed limited to taxes on real property; therefore, all other taxes could be imposed by Congress without concern about apportionment among the states. For example, in *Hylton v. United States*, in 1796, the Court held that a federal tax on carriages was indirect and therefore did not need to be apportioned among the states.[98]

In *Veazie Bank v. Fenno*, in 1869, the Court upheld the constitutionality of a federal tax on state bank notes.[99] The Court concluded that this was an indirect tax and declared that "direct taxes have been limited to taxes on land and appurtenances, and taxes on polls, or capitation taxes."[100] The Court repeated this view in *Springer v. United States*, where the Court upheld the constitutionality of the Civil War Income Tax.[101]

---

[95] *Id.* at 640-641.
[96] John C. Eastman, Restoring the "General" to the General Welfare Clause, 4 Chapman L. Rev. 63 (2001).
[97] Another limit on Congress's taxing power, which remains important, is the Export Clause found in Article I, §9: "No Tax or Duty shall be laid on Articles exported from any State." The Supreme Court held that this provision prohibits Congress from assessing nondiscriminatory federal taxes on goods in export transit. United States v. International Business Machines Corporation, 517 U.S. 843 (1996). The Court also ruled that a tax on policies insuring exports is functionally the same as a tax on exports.
[98] 3 U.S. (3 Dall.) 171 (1796).
[99] 75 U.S. (8 Wall.) 533 (1869).
[100] *Id.* at 544.
[101] 102 U.S. (12 Otto.) 586, 602 (1880).

However, in *Pollock v. Farmer's Loan & Trust Co.*, the Court, by a 5-to-4 margin, declared unconstitutional the federal income tax.[102] The Court explained that because the income tax collected revenue gained from property, among other sources, it was a direct tax and had to be apportioned among the states. In 1913, 18 years after *Pollock*, the Sixteenth Amendment was ratified to overturn that decision and to allow a federal income tax. The Sixteenth Amendment provides: "The Congress shall have power to lay and collect taxes on incomes, from whatever source derived, without apportionment among the several States, and without regard to any census or enumeration."

The Court eventually abandoned the distinction between direct and indirect taxes.[103] In *Flint v. Stone Tracy Co.*, the Court upheld the Corporation Excise Tax of 1909, which imposed a tax on corporations doing business in states or territories.[104] Similarly, the Court upheld taxes such as those on estates[105] and gifts.[106] The constitutional provisions quoted above, requiring apportionment of direct taxes, seem limited, at most, to taxes on real property. In other words, unless Congress were to create a national property tax, all other taxes are very likely to be deemed indirect and therefore are constitutional even without apportionment among the states.

Regulatory and Revenue Raising Taxes

Unlike the distinction between direct and indirect taxes, which is drawn in the text of the Constitution, the distinction between *regulatory* and *revenue raising taxes* was judicially created. However, like the distinction between direct and indirect taxes, the distinction between regulatory and revenue raising taxes no longer has any practical significance.

In the *Child Labor Tax Case, Bailey v. Drexel Furniture Co.*, the Court declared unconstitutional a federal tax on companies that shipped in interstate commerce goods made by child labor.[107] As discussed above, the Supreme Court earlier had declared unconstitutional a federal law that prohibited the shipment in interstate commerce of goods made by child labor.[108] The Court found that the law violated the Tenth Amendment and usurped prerogatives reserved to the states. Not surprisingly, the Court declared unconstitutional the federal tax that attempted to accomplish the same thing as the earlier federal law that had been invalidated.

The Court based its decision on a distinction between a true tax and a penalty for a violation of a commercial regulation. The Court explained that although taxes could have an "incidental" regulatory effect, a tax is unconstitutional when

---

[102] 157 U.S. 429 (1895).

[103] *But see* Eisner v. Macomber, 252 U.S. 189 (1920) (stock dividends are not income prior to their sale or conversion and therefore are not taxable without apportionment).

[104] 220 U.S. 107 (1911).

[105] Bank & Trust Co. of New York v. Eisner, 256 U.S. 345 (1921).

[106] Bromley v. McCaughn, 280 U.S. 124 (1929).

[107] 259 U.S. 20 (1922).

[108] Hammer v. Dagenhart, 247 U.S. 251 (1918), discussed in §3.3.3 [Erwin Chemerinsky, Constitutional Law: Principles and Policies, 4th ed., (2011)].

"in the extension of the penalizing features of the so-called tax . . . it loses its character as such and becomes a mere penalty with the characteristics of regulation and punishment."[109]

At the same time, in *Hill v. Wallace*, the Court declared unconstitutional a federal tax on grain future contracts.[110] The law imposed a tax on grain contracts unless the contracts had been approved by a board of trade that was sanctioned by the United States Department of Agriculture. As in the *Child Labor Tax Case*, the Court found that the regulation was unconstitutional because it was a penalty and not a true tax.

In *United States v. Constantine*, in 1935, the Court declared unconstitutional a federal tax on liquor dealers who had violated state liquor laws.[111] The Court again based its decision on a distinction between regulatory taxes and taxes that are designed to raise revenue. The Court stated: "[The tax] exhibits . . . an intent to prohibit and to punish violations of state law [and therefore] remove all semblance of a revenue act, and stamp the sum it exacts as a penalty."[112]

The problem with these cases is that they draw a false distinction between taxes that generate revenue and taxes that are penalties. Obviously, a tax can be both at the same time. Congress can use a tax law simultaneously to regulate and to generate funds. Therefore, deciding whether a tax should be characterized as regulatory or revenue generating is inherently arbitrary. Additionally, it is questionable why Congress cannot use taxes for a regulatory purpose; it is unclear what constitutional principle allows taxes for one purpose and not the other.

In fact, prior to the *Child Labor Tax Case* and *Hill v. Wallace*, the Court repeatedly had rejected such a distinction between regulatory taxes and revenue raising taxes. In *Veazie Bank v. Fenno*, the Court upheld a federal tax on state bank notes, even though the primary purpose of the tax was to eliminate such state notes.[113] In *United States v. Doremus*, the Court upheld the Narcotics Drug Act of 1914, which both taxed narcotics and imposed extensive regulations on their sale.[114] The Court rejected any distinction between regulatory taxes and those designed to raise revenues. The Court stated: "If the legislation enacted has some reasonable relation to the exercise of the taxing authority conferred by the Constitution, it cannot be invalidated because of the supposed [regulatory] motives which induced it."[115]

Similarly, in *McCray v. United States*, the Court upheld a federal tax on colored oleomargarine.[116] The Court expressly rejected the argument that the tax was unconstitutional because it was a penalty and intended primarily for regulatory purposes. The Court declared: "Since . . . the taxing power conferred by the Constitution knows no limits except those expressly stated in that instrument, it

---

[109] 259 U.S. at 38.
[110] 259 U.S. 44 (1922).
[111] 296 U.S. 287 (1935).
[112] *Id.* at 295.
[113] 75 U.S. (8 Wall.) 27 (1869).
[114] 249 U.S. 86 (1919).
[115] *Id.* at 93.
[116] 195 U.S. 27 (1904).

must follow, if a tax be within the lawful power, the exertion of that power may not be judicially restrained because of the results to arise from its exercise."[117]

Therefore, it is not surprising that the distinction between regulatory taxes and revenue raising taxes was relatively short-lived. In 1937, the Court upheld a federal tax on firearm dealers.[118] The Court explained that "[e]very tax is in some measure regulatory. . . . But [it] is not any less a tax because it has a regulatory effect. . . . Inquiry into the hidden motives which may move Congress to exercise a power constitutionally conferred upon it is beyond the competency of the courts."[119] Subsequently, the Court upheld a federal tax on bookmakers and said that regulatory taxes are constitutional because "[u]nless there are provisions extraneous to any tax need, courts are without authority to limit the exercise of the taxing power."[120]

3. The Spending Power

Broad Scope of the Spending Power

As described above, the Court has held that Congress has broad power to spend funds to advance the "general welfare."[121] In *United States v. Butler*, the Court held that Congress is not limited to spending only to achieve the specific powers granted in Article I of the Constitution.[122] Rather, Congress may spend in any way it believes would serve the general welfare, so long as it does not violate another constitutional provision. Thus, in *Steward Machine Co. v. Davis*,[123] the Court upheld provisions of the Social Security Act that provided unemployment compensation, and in *Helvering v. Davis*,[124] the Court upheld the provisions of the Social Security Act that provided for an old age pension program. In both cases, the Court emphasized the broad scope of Congress's spending power.

The Court recently reaffirmed the broad scope of Congress's spending power. In *Sabri v. United States*,[125] the Court unanimously upheld the constitutionality of a federal law that prohibits bribery of state, local, and tribal officials of entities that receive at least $10,000 in federal funds.[126] An individual convicted under this law argued that his activities had nothing to do with the area of local government that received federal funds and that Congress exceeded the scope of its spending power. The claim was that Congress only could prohibit bribery as to those state, local, and tribal activities that actually got federal money.

The Supreme Court expressly rejected this argument. In an opinion by Justice David Souter, the Court explained: "Money is fungible, bribed officials are

---

[117] *Id.* at 59.
[118] Sonzinsky v. United States, 300 U.S. 506 (1937).
[119] *Id.* at 513 (citations omitted).
[120] United States v. Kahriger, 345 U.S. 22, 31 (1953).
[121] *See* Section 6.C.1.
[122] 297 U.S. 1 (1936), discussed above in Section 6.C.1.
[123] 301 U.S. 548 (1937).
[124] 301 U.S. 619 (1937).
[125] 541 U.S. 600 (2004).
[126] 18 U.S.C. §666(a)(2).

untrustworthy stewards of federal funds, and corrupt contractors do not deliver dollar-for-dollar value."[127] The Court expressly rejected the federalism challenge to the law and concluded that the criminal law was constitutional because Congress has the "power to bring federal power to bear directly on individuals who convert public spending into unearned private gain, not a means for bringing federal economic might to bear on a State's own choices of public policy."[128]

Conditions on Grants to State Governments

One important issue involving the spending power concerns the ability of Congress to place conditions on grants to state and local governments. The Court has held that Congress may place conditions on such grants, so long as the conditions are expressly stated and have some relationship to the purpose of the spending program.

In *Oklahoma v. Civil Service Commission*, the Court upheld a provision of the federal Hatch Act that granted federal funds to state governments on the condition that the states adopt civil service systems and limit the political activities of many categories of government workers.[129] The Court explained that Congress has broad power to set conditions for the receipt of federal funds even as to areas that Congress might otherwise not be able to regulate. The Court stated: "While the United States is not concerned with, and has no power to regulate, local political activities as such of state officials, it does have power to fix the terms upon which its money allotments to states shall be disbursed."[130]

The Court affirmed this decision in *South Dakota v. Dole*.[131] A federal law sought to create a 21-year-old drinking age by withholding a portion of federal highway funds from any state government that failed to impose such a drinking age. Specifically, 5 percent of federal highway funds would be denied to any state that did not create a 21-year-old drinking age.

The Court, in an opinion by Chief Justice Rehnquist, approved this condition on federal money. The Court emphasized that the condition imposed by Congress was directly related to one of the main purposes behind federal highway money: creating safe interstate travel. The Court recognized that at some point "the financial inducement offered by Congress might be so coercive as to pass the point at which pressure turns into compulsion."[132] But the Court said that in this case, the condition of federal highway money was a "relatively mild encouragement" and was constitutional "[e]ven if Congress might lack the power to impose a national minimum drinking age directly, we conclude that encouragement to state action . . . is a valid use of the spending power."[133]

---

[127] 541 U.S. at 606.
[128] *Id.* at 608.
[129] 330 U.S. 127 (1947).
[130] *Id.* at 143.
[131] 483 U.S. 203 (1987).
[132] *Id.* at 211 (citation omitted).
[133] *Id.* at 212.

In *Pennhurst State School and Hospital v. Halderman*, the Supreme Court held that Congress may place strings on grants to state and local governments so long as the conditions are expressly stated.[134] The Developmentally Disabled Assistance and Bill of Rights Act of 1975 created a federal grant program for state governments to provide for better care for the developmentally disabled. The Act included a "bill of rights" for the developmentally disabled. The Pennhurst State School and Hospital, a facility run by the State of Pennsylvania, was sued for violating the bill of rights contained in the Act.

The Court ruled in favor of the state, holding that "if Congress intends to impose a condition on the grant of federal moneys it must do so unambiguously."[135] The Court explained that conditions must be clearly stated so that states will know the consequences of their choosing to take federal funds. The Court concluded that the Act failed to require that states meet the bill of rights as a condition for accepting federal money.

It is possible that as the Supreme Court narrows the scope of other congressional powers and revives the Tenth Amendment as a limit on Congress's powers, the Court might impose greater restrictions on conditional spending. However, in *New York v. United States*, the Supreme Court held that although Congress cannot directly compel state legislative or regulatory action, it can induce behavior by putting conditions on grants.[136] The Tenth Amendment, including *New York v. United States*, is discussed in more detail in §3.8 [Erwin Chemerinsky, Constitutional Law: Principles and Policies, 4th ed., (2011)].

In sum, Congress possesses expansive power to spend for the general welfare so long as it does not violate another constitutional provision. Congress may impose conditions on grants to state and local governments so long as the conditions relate to the purpose of the spending and are clearly stated.[137]

D. Congress's Powers Under the Post-Civil War Amendments

After the Civil War, three extremely important amendments were added to the Constitution. The Thirteenth Amendment, adopted in 1865, prohibits slavery and involuntary servitude, except as a punishment for a crime, and also provides in §2, "Congress shall have power to enforce this article by appropriate legislation." The Fourteenth Amendment, adopted in 1868, provides that all persons born or naturalized in the United States are citizens and that no state can abridge the privileges or immunities of such citizens; nor may states deprive any person of life, liberty, or property without due process of law or deny any person of equal protection of the laws. Section 5 of the Fourteenth Amendment states: "the

---

[134] 451 U.S. 1, 17 (1981).

[135] *Id.* at 20.

[136] 505 U.S. 144, 166-167 (1992).

[137] For a strong criticism of this doctrine, urging limits on Congress's ability to set conditions on federal money received by state governments, *see* Lynn A. Baker & Mitchell N. Berman, Getting off the *Dole:* Why the Court Should Abandon Its Spending Doctrine, and How a Too-Clever Congress Could Provoke It to Do So, 78 Ind. L.J. 459 (2003).

Congress shall have power to enforce, by appropriate legislation, the provisions of this article."

The Fifteenth Amendment declares that "[t]he right of citizens of the United States to vote shall not be denied or abridged by the United States or by any State on account of race, color, or previous condition of servitude." Section 2 again provides that Congress has the power to enforce it by appropriate legislation.

The three Reconstruction era amendments thus contain provisions that empower Congress to enact civil rights legislation. Two major questions arise concerning the scope of this power. First, may Congress regulate private conduct under this authority, or is Congress limited to regulating only government actions? Second, what is the scope of Congress's power under these amendments?

1. Whom May Congress Regulate Under the Post-Civil War Amendments?

In the *Civil Rights Cases*, 109 U.S. 3 (1883), the Court held that Congress, pursuant to §2 of the Thirteenth Amendment and §5 of the Fourteenth Amendment, may regulate only state and local government actions, not private conduct.[138] The Civil Rights Act of 1875 provided that all persons were "entitled to the full and equal enjoyment of the accommodations, advantages, facilities and privileges of inns, public conveyances, on land or water, theatres, and other places of public amusement; subject only to the conditions and limitations established by law, and applicable to citizens of every race and color, regardless of any previous condition of servitude." In other words, the law broadly prohibited private racial discrimination by hotels, restaurants, transportation, and other public accommodations.

By an 8-1 decision, the Court held that the Act was unconstitutional and adopted a restrictive view as to the power of Congress to use these provisions to regulate private behavior. As to the Thirteenth Amendment, the Court recognized that it applies to private conduct; it prohibits people from being or owning slaves. The Court, however, said that Congress's power was limited to ensuring an end to slavery; Congress could not use this power to eliminate discrimination. The Court explained that "[i]t would be running the slavery argument into the ground to make it apply to every act of discrimination which a person may see fit to make as to the guests he will entertain, or as to the people he will take into his coach or cab or car, or admit to his concert or theatre, or deal with in other matters of intercourse or business." Indeed, the Court stated that Congress could abolish "all badges and incidents of slavery," but it could not use its power under the Thirteenth Amendment to "adjust what may be called the social rights of men and races in the community."

The Court, writing less than 20 years after the Civil War, said that slavery was a thing of the past and that there was little need for civil rights legislation to protect blacks. Justice Bradley, writing for the Court, stated: "When a man has

---

[138] The *Civil Rights Cases* are presented in Chapter 5 [Erwin Chemerinsky, Constitutional Law, 3rd ed., (2009)].

emerged from slavery, and by the aid of beneficent legislation has shaken off the inseparable concomitants of that state, there must be some stage in the progress of his elevation when he takes the rank of a mere citizen and ceases to be the special favorite of the laws, and when his rights as a citizen, or a man, are to be protected in the ordinary modes by which other men's rights are protected."

The Court also held that Congress lacked the authority to enact the law under the Fourteenth Amendment. In fact, the Court broadly declared that the Fourteenth Amendment only applies to government action and that therefore it cannot be used by Congress to regulate private behavior. The Court stated that "the fourteenth amendment is prohibitory . . . upon the states. [Individual] invasion of individual rights is not the subject matter of the amendment." The Court made it clear that Congress's authority was only over state and local governments and their officials, not over private conduct: "It does not authorize Congress to create a code of municipal law for the regulation of private rights; but to provide modes of redress against the operation of State laws, and the actions of State officers."

Now, however, it is well established that Congress, pursuant to §2 of the Thirteenth Amendment, may prohibit private racial discrimination. In Jones v. Alfred H. Mayer Co., 392 U.S. 409 (1968), the Court held that Congress could prohibit private discrimination in selling and leasing property. The case involved a private real estate developer who refused to sell housing or land to African Americans. An African-American couple sued under 42 U.S.C. §1982, which provides that all citizens have "the same right, in every State and Territory, as is enjoyed by white citizens thereof to inherit, purchase, lease, sell, hold and convey real and personal property."

The Court held that §1982 applies to prohibit private discrimination and that Congress had the authority under the Thirteenth Amendment to adopt the law. The Court said that Congress has broad legislative power under the Thirteenth Amendment: "Congress has the power under the Thirteenth Amendment rationally to determine what are the badges and incidents of slavery, and the authority to translate that determination into effective legislation."

Similarly, in Runyon v. McCrary, 427 U.S. 160 (1976), the Court held that 42 U.S.C. §1981 applies to prohibit discrimination in private contracting and that this is within the scope of Congress's power under §2 of the Thirteenth Amendment. Section 1981 provides that "[a]ll persons within the jurisdiction of the United States shall have the same right in every State and Territory to make and enforce contracts, to sue, be parties, give evidence, and to the full and equal benefit of all laws and proceedings for the security of persons and property as is enjoyed by white citizens." Runyon raised the question of whether §1981 prohibits private schools from excluding qualified African-American children solely because of their race.

The Supreme Court saw no basis for distinguishing Jones v. Alfred H. Mayer Co and concluded "that §1981, like §1982, reaches private conduct." The Court unanimously reaffirmed this conclusion in 1989 in Patterson v. McLean Credit Union, 491 U.S. 164 (1989).

However, the Supreme Court recently reaffirmed that Congress cannot regulate private behavior under the Fourteenth Amendment. In United States v.

Guest, 383 U.S. 745 (1966), five Justices, although not in a single opinion, concluded that Congress may outlaw private discrimination pursuant to §5 of the Fourteenth Amendment. *Guest* involved the federal law which makes it a crime for two or more persons to go "in disguise on the highway, or on the premises of another, with intent to prevent or hinder his free exercise or enjoyment of any right or privilege." 18 U.S.C. §241. The Court held that interference with the use of facilities in interstate commerce violated the law, whether or not motivated by a racial animus.

The majority opinion did not reach the question of whether Congress could regulate private conduct under §5 of the Fourteenth Amendment. However, six of the Justices — three in a concurring opinion and three in a dissenting opinion — expressed the view that Congress could prohibit private discrimination under its §5 powers. Justice Tom Clark, in a concurring opinion joined by Justices Hugo Black and Abe Fortas, said that "the specific language of §5 empowers the Congress to enact laws punishing all conspiracies — with or without state action — that interfere with Fourteenth Amendment rights." Likewise, Justice William Brennan in an opinion that concurred in part and dissented in part, and that was joined by Chief Justice Earl Warren and Justice William Douglas, concluded that Congress may prohibit private discrimination pursuant to §5. However, the Supreme Court recently overruled *Guest* and held that Congress cannot regulate private behavior under §5.

United States v. Morrison

529 U.S. 598 (2000)

[The case is presented above in connection with the Commerce Clause. The issue is the constitutionality of the civil damages provision of the Violence Against Women Act. The case involves a woman, who while a freshman at Virginia Tech University was allegedly raped by football players. She sued under the civil remedies provision of the Act. In the first part of the majority opinion, the Court held that it exceeded the scope of Congress's Commerce Clause authority.[139] In the alternative, the government argued that the law was constitutional as an exercise of Congress's power under §5 of the Fourteenth Amendment.]

Chief Justice REHNQUIST delivered the opinion of the Court:

Because we conclude that the Commerce Clause does not provide Congress with authority to enact §13981, we address petitioners' alternative argument that the section's civil remedy should be upheld as an exercise of Congress's remedial power under §5 of the Fourteenth Amendment. As noted above, Congress expressly invoked the Fourteenth Amendment as a source of authority to enact §13981.

---

[139] The portion of the opinion concerning the Commerce Clause is presented above in Section 6.B of this chapter. [Footnote by casebook author.]

Petitioners' §5 argument is founded on an assertion that there is pervasive bias in various state justice systems against victims of gender-motivated violence. This assertion is supported by a voluminous congressional record.

The principles governing an analysis of congressional legislation under §5 are well settled. [T]he language and purpose of the Fourteenth Amendment place certain limitations on the manner in which Congress may attack discriminatory conduct. These limitations are necessary to prevent the Fourteenth Amendment from obliterating the framers' carefully crafted balance of power between the States and the National Government.

Foremost among these limitations is the time-honored principle that the Fourteenth Amendment, by its very terms, prohibits only state action. "[T]he principle has become firmly embedded in our constitutional law that the action inhibited by the first section of the Fourteenth Amendment is only such action as may fairly be said to be that of the States. That Amendment erects no shield against merely private conduct, however discriminatory or wrongful." Shelley v. Kraemer (1948).

Shortly after the Fourteenth Amendment was adopted, we decided two cases interpreting the Amendment's provisions, United States v. Harris (1883), and the *Civil Rights Cases* (1883). We concluded that th[e] law[s] exceeded Congress's §5 power because the law was "directed exclusively against the action of private persons, without reference to the laws of the State, or their administration by her officers." The force of the doctrine of stare decisis behind these decisions stems not only from the length of time they have been on the books, but also from the insight attributable to the Members of the Court at that time. Every Member had been appointed by President Lincoln, Grant, Hayes, Garfield, or Arthur — and each of their judicial appointees obviously had intimate knowledge and familiarity with the events surrounding the adoption of the Fourteenth Amendment.

Petitioners rely on United States v. Guest (1966), for the proposition that the rule laid down in the *Civil Rights Cases* is no longer good law. In *Guest*, the Court reversed the construction of an indictment under 18 U.S.C. §241, saying in the course of its opinion that "we deal here with issues of statutory construction, not with issues of constitutional power." Three Members of the Court, in a separate opinion by Justice Brennan, expressed the view that the *Civil Rights Cases* were wrongly decided, and that Congress could under §5 prohibit actions by private individuals. Three other Members of the Court, who joined the opinion of the Court, joined a separate opinion by Justice Clark which in two or three sentences stated the conclusion that Congress could "punis[h] all conspiracies — with or without state action — that interfere with Fourteenth Amendment rights."

Though these three Justices saw fit to opine on matters not before the Court in *Guest*, the Court had no occasion to revisit the *Civil Rights Cases* and *Harris*, having determined "the indictment [charging private individuals with conspiring to deprive blacks of equal access to state facilities] in fact contain[ed] an express allegation of state involvement."

Section 13981 is not aimed at proscribing discrimination by officials which the Fourteenth Amendment might not itself proscribe; it is directed not at any State or state actor, but at individuals who have committed criminal acts motivated by gender bias. In the present cases, for example, §13981 visits no consequence whatever on any Virginia public official involved in investigating or prosecuting Brzonkala's assault. The section is, therefore, unlike any of the §5 remedies that we have previously upheld.

Petitioner Brzonkala's complaint alleges that she was the victim of a brutal assault. But Congress's effort in §13981 to provide a federal civil remedy can be sustained neither under the Commerce Clause nor under §5 of the Fourteenth Amendment. If the allegations here are true, no civilized system of justice could fail to provide her a remedy for the conduct of respondent Morrison. But under our federal system that remedy must be provided by the Commonwealth of Virginia, and not by the United States.

Justice BREYER dissenting.

Given my conclusion on the Commerce Clause question, I need not consider Congress's authority under §5 of the Fourteenth Amendment. Nonetheless, I doubt the Court's reasoning rejecting that source of authority. The Court points out that in United States v. Harris (1883), and the *Civil Rights Cases* (1883), the Court held that §5 does not authorize Congress to use the Fourteenth Amendment as a source of power to remedy the conduct of private persons. That is certainly so. The Federal Government's argument, however, is that Congress used §5 to remedy the actions of state actors, namely, those States which, through discriminatory design or the discriminatory conduct of their officials, failed to provide adequate (or any) state remedies for women injured by gender-motivated violence — a failure that the States, and Congress, documented in depth.

But why can Congress not provide a remedy against private actors? Those private actors, of course, did not themselves violate the Constitution. But this Court has held that Congress at least sometimes can enact remedial "[l]egislation . . . [that] prohibits conduct which is not itself unconstitutional." It intrudes little upon either States or private parties. It may lead state actors to improve their own remedial systems, primarily through example. It restricts private actors only by imposing liability for private conduct that is, in the main, already forbidden by state law. Why is the remedy "disproportionate"? And given the relation between remedy and violation — the creation of a federal remedy to substitute for constitutionally inadequate state remedies — where is the lack of "congruence"?

Despite my doubts about the majority's §5 reasoning, I need not, and do not, answer the §5 question, which I would leave for more thorough analysis if necessary on another occasion. Rather, in my view, the Commerce Clause provides an adequate basis for the statute before us. And I would uphold its constitutionality as the "necessary and proper" exercise of legislative power granted to Congress by that Clause.

2. *What Is the Scope of Congress's Power?*

There are two different views as to the scope of Congress's power under the post-Civil War Amendments and particularly under §5 of the Fourteenth Amendment. One approach is narrow and accords Congress only authority to prevent or provide remedies for violations of rights recognized by the Supreme Court; under this view, Congress cannot expand the scope of rights or provide additional rights. An alternative approach also accords Congress authority to interpret the Fourteenth Amendment to expand the scope of rights or even to create new rights. Under this view, Congress may create rights by statute where the Court has not found them in the Constitution, but Congress cannot dilute or diminish constitutional rights.

The choice between these two views is in part about a textual argument concerning what §5 means when it empowers Congress "to enforce" the Amendment by appropriate legislation. Those who take the narrower view contend that Congress is not "enforcing" if it is creating new rights. But those who take the broader view argue that Congress is enforcing the Amendment by creating greater protections than those found by the Court.

The dispute over these two views also is about the appropriate roles of the Court and Congress in deciding the substantive content of rights. Those who take the narrow position see it as solely the Court's role to decide the rights protected under the Constitution; Congress's role is limited to enacting laws to prevent and remedy violations. But those who adopt the broader view of Congress's §5 power see both Congress and the Court as having authority to recognize and protect rights under the Constitution.

As with all of the material in this chapter, there also is an important underlying issue concerning the allocation of power between the federal and state governments. Advocates of the narrow view see it as limiting federal power, reserving more governance for the states, and lessening the instances in which the federal government can regulate state and local actions. In contrast, supporters of the broader approach defend it as creating needed national power to protect civil rights and civil liberties.

In Katzenbach v. Morgan, the first case presented, the Court seemed to adopt the broader approach and accord Congress expansive authority under §5 of the Fourteenth Amendment. In three recent cases, City of Boerne v. Flores, Florida Prepaid v. College Savings Bank, and Kimel v. Florida Board of Regents, the Court clearly chose the narrow view and limited Congress's power under §5.

Katzenbach v. Morgan & Morgan

384 U.S. 641 (1966)

Justice BRENNAN delivered the opinion of the Court.

These cases concern the constitutionality of §4(e) of the Voting Rights Act of 1965. That law, in the respects pertinent in these cases, provides that no person who has successfully completed the sixth primary grade in a public school in, or a private school accredited by, the Commonwealth of Puerto Rico in which the language of instruction was other than English shall be denied the right to vote in any election because of his inability to read or write English. Appellees, registered voters in New York City, brought this suit to challenge the constitutionality of §4(e) insofar as it pro tanto prohibits the enforcement of the election laws of New York requiring an ability to read and write English as a condition of voting.

The Attorney General of the State of New York argues that an exercise of congressional power under §5 of the Fourteenth Amendment that prohibits the enforcement of a state law can only be sustained if the judicial branch determines that the state law is prohibited by the provisions of the Amendment that Congress sought to enforce. More specifically, he urges that §4(e) cannot be sustained as appropriate legislation to enforce the Equal Protection Clause unless the judiciary decides — even with the guidance of a congressional judgment — that the application of the English literacy requirement prohibited by §4(e) is forbidden by the Equal Protection Clause itself. We disagree. Neither the language nor history of §5 supports such a construction. A construction of §5 that would require a judicial determination that the enforcement of the state law precluded by Congress violated the Amendment, as a condition of sustaining the congressional enactment, would depreciate both congressional resourcefulness and congressional responsibility for implementing the Amendment. It would confine the legislative power in this context to the insignificant role of abrogating only those state laws that the judicial branch was prepared to adjudge unconstitutional, or of merely informing the judgment of the judiciary by particularizing the "majestic generalities" of §1 of the Amendment.

Thus our task in this case is not to determine whether the New York English literacy requirement as applied to deny the right to vote to a person who successfully completed the sixth grade in a Puerto Rican school violates the Equal Protection Clause. Accordingly, our decision in Lassiter v. Northampton County Bd. of Election, sustaining the North Carolina English literacy requirement as not in all circumstances prohibited by the first sections of the Fourteenth and Fifteenth Amendments, is inapposite. *Lassiter* did not present the question before us here: Without regard to whether the judiciary would find that the Equal Protection Clause itself nullifies New York's English literacy requirement as so applied, could Congress prohibit the enforcement of the state law by legislating under §5 of the Fourteenth Amendment? In answering this question, our task is limited to determining whether such legislation is, as required by §5, appropriate legislation to enforce the Equal Protection Clause.

By including §5 the draftsmen sought to grant to Congress, by a specific provision applicable to the Fourteenth Amendment, the same broad powers expressed in the Necessary and Proper Clause, Art. I, §8, cl. 18. We therefore proceed to the consideration whether §4(e) is "appropriate legislation" to enforce the Equal Protection Clause, that is, under the McCulloch v. Maryland standard, whether §4(e) may be regarded as an enactment to enforce the Equal Protection Clause, whether it is "plainly adapted to that end" and whether it is not prohibited by but is consistent with "the letter and spirit of the [C]onstitution."[140]

---

[140] Contrary to the suggestion of the dissent, infra, §5 does not grant Congress power to exercise discretion in the other direction and to enact "statutes so as in effect to dilute equal protection and due process decisions of this Court." We emphasize that Congress's power under §5 is limited to adopting measures to enforce the guarantees of the Amendment; §5 grants Congress no power to restrict, abrogate, or dilute these guarantees. Thus, for example, an enactment authorizing the States to establish racially segregated systems of educaion would not be — as required by §5 — a measure "to enforce" the Equal Protection Clause since that clause of its own force prohibits such state laws. [Footnote in original opinion.]

There can be no doubt that §4(e) may be regarded as an enactment to enforce the Equal Protection Clause. Congress explicitly declared that it enacted §4(e) "to secure the rights under the [F]ourteenth [A]mendment of persons educated in American-flag schools in which the predominant classroom language was other than English." The persons referred to include those who have migrated from the Commonwealth of Puerto Rico to New York and who have been denied the right to vote because of their inability to read and write English, and the Fourteenth Amendment rights referred to include those emanating from the Equal Protection Clause. More specifically, §4(e) may be viewed as a measure to secure for the Puerto Rican community residing in New York nondiscriminatory treatment by government — both in the imposition of voting qualifications and the provision or administration of governmental services, such as public schools, public housing and law enforcement.

Section 4(e) may be readily seen as "plainly adapted" to furthering these aims of the Equal Protection Clause. The practical effect of §4(e) is to prohibit New York from denying the right to vote to large segments of its Puerto Rican community. Congress has thus prohibited the State from denying to that community the right that is "preservative of all rights." This enhanced political power will be helpful in gaining nondiscriminatory treatment in public services for the entire Puerto Rican community. Section 4(e) thereby enables the Puerto Rican minority better to obtain "perfect equality of civil rights and the equal protection of the laws." It was well within congressional authority to say that this need of the Puerto Rican minority for the vote warranted federal intrusion upon any state interests served by the English literacy requirement. It was for Congress, as the branch that made this judgment, to assess and weigh the various conflicting considerations. It is not for us to review the congressional resolution of these factors. It is enough that we be able to perceive a basis upon which the Congress might resolve the conflict as it did. There plainly was such a basis to support §4(e) in the application in question in this case. Any contrary conclusion would require us to be blind to the realities familiar to the legislators.

Since Congress undertook to legislate so as to preclude the enforcement of the state law, and did so in the context of a general appraisal of literacy requirements for voting, to which it brought a specially informed legislative competence, it was Congress's prerogative to weigh these competing considerations. Here again, it is enough that we perceive a basis upon which Congress might predicate a judgment that the application of New York's English literacy requirement to deny the right to vote to a person with a sixth grade education in Puerto Rican schools in which the language of instruction was other than English constituted an invidious discrimination in violation of the Equal Protection Clause.

We therefore conclude that §4(e), in the application challenged in this case, is appropriate legislation to enforce the Equal Protection Clause and that the judgment of the District Court must be and hereby is reversed.

Justice HARLAN, whom Justice STEWART joins, dissenting.

Worthy as its purposes may be thought by many, I do not see how §4(e) of the Voting Rights Act of 1965, can be sustained except at the sacrifice of fundamentals in the American constitutional system — the separation between the legislative and judicial function and the boundaries between federal and state political authority. By the same token I think that the validity of New York's literacy test, a question which the Court considers only in the context of the federal statute, must be upheld. It will conduce to analytical clarity if I discuss the second issue first.

Any analysis of this problem must begin with the established rule of law that the franchise is essentially a matter of state concern, subject only to the overriding requirements of various federal constitutional provisions dealing with the franchise, e.g., the Fifteenth, Seventeenth, Nineteenth, and Twenty-fourth Amendments, and, as more recently decided, to the general principles of the Fourteenth Amendment.

In 1959, in Lassiter v. Northampton Election Bd., this Court dealt with substantially the same question and resolved it unanimously in favor of the legitimacy of a state literacy qualification. There a North Carolina English literacy test was challenged. We held that there was "wide scope" for State qualifications of this sort. I believe the same interests recounted in *Lassiter* indubitably point toward upholding the rationality of the New York voting test.

The pivotal question in this instance is what effect the added factor of a congressional enactment has on the straight equal protection argument dealt with above. The Court declares that since §5 of the Fourteenth Amendment gives to the Congress power to "enforce" the prohibitions of the Amendment by "appropriate" legislation, the test for judicial review of any congressional determination in this area is simply one of rationality; that is, in effect, was Congress acting rationally in declaring that the New York statute is irrational? Although §5 most certainly does give to the Congress wide powers in the field of devising remedial legislation to effectuate the Amendment's prohibition on arbitrary state action, I believe the Court has confused the issue of how much enforcement power Congress possesses under §5 with the distinct issue of what questions are appropriate for congressional determination and what questions are essentially judicial in nature.

When recognized state violations of federal constitutional standards have occurred, Congress is of course empowered by §5 to take appropriate remedial measures to redress and prevent the wrongs. But it is a judicial question whether the condition with which Congress has thus sought to deal is in truth an infringement of the Constitution, something that is the necessary prerequisite to bringing the §5 power into play at all.

Section 4(e), however, presents a significantly different type of congressional enactment. The question here is not whether the statute is appropriate remedial legislation to cure an established violation of a constitutional command, but whether there has in fact been an infringement of that constitutional command, that is, whether a particular state practice or, as here, a statute is so arbitrary or irrational as to offend the command of the Equal Protection Clause of the Fourteenth Amendment. That question is one for the judicial branch ultimately to determine. Were the rule otherwise, Congress would be able to qualify this Court's constitutional decisions under the Fourteenth and Fifteenth

Amendments let alone those under other provisions of the Constitution, by resorting to congressional power under the Necessary and Proper Clause. In view of this Court's holding in *Lassiter*, that an English literacy test is a permissible exercise of state supervision over its franchise, I do not think it is open to Congress to limit the effect of that decision as it has undertaken to do by §4(e). In effect the Court reads §5 of the Fourteenth Amendment as giving Congress the power to define the substantive scope of the Amendment. If that indeed be the true reach of §5, then I do not see why Congress should not be able as well to exercise its §5 "discretion" by enacting statutes so as in effect to dilute equal protection and due process decisions of this Court. In all such cases there is room for reasonable men to differ as to whether or not a denial of equal protection or due process has occurred, and the final decision is one of judgment. Until today this judgment has always been one for the judiciary to resolve.

To deny the effectiveness of this congressional enactment is not of course to disparage Congress's exertion of authority in the field of civil rights; it is simply to recognize that the Legislative Branch like the other branches of federal authority is subject to the governmental boundaries set by the Constitution. To hold, on this record, that §4(e) overrides the New York literacy requirement seems to me tantamount to allowing the Fourteenth Amendment to swallow the State's constitutionally ordained primary authority in this field. For if Congress by what, as here, amounts to mere ipse dixit can set that otherwise permissible requirement partially at naught I see no reason why it could not also substitute its judgment for that of the States in other fields of their exclusive primary competence as well.

In City of Boerne v. Flores, the Court appeared to adopt a very different view of the scope of Congress's authority under §5 of the Fourteenth Amendment than that taken by a majority in *Katzenbach*. To understand *City of Boerne*, which follows, a bit of background is necessary. In Employment Div., Dept. of Human Resources of Oregon v. Smith, 494 U.S. 872 (1990), the Supreme Court significantly narrowed the scope of the Free Exercise Clause.[141] Oregon law prohibited the consumption of peyote, a hallucinogenic substance. Native Americans challenged this law claiming that it infringed free exercise of religion because their religious rituals required the use of peyote. Under prior Supreme Court precedents, government actions burdening religion are upheld only if they are necessary to achieve a compelling government purpose. The Supreme Court, in *Smith*, changed the law and held that the Free Exercise Clause cannot be used to challenge neutral laws of general applicability. The Oregon law prohibiting consumption of peyote was deemed neutral because it was not motivated by a desire to interfere with religion and it was a law of general applicability.

In response to this decision, in 1993, Congress overwhelmingly adopted the Religious Freedom Restoration Act, which was signed into law by President

---

[141] Employment Division v. Smith is presented in Chapter 10 [Erwin Chemerinsky, Constitutional Law, 3rd ed., (2009)] in the discussion of free exercise of religion.

Clinton. The Religious Freedom Restoration Act was express in stating that its goal was to overturn *Smith* and restore the test that was followed before that decision. The Act requires courts considering free exercise challenges, including to neutral laws of general applicability, to uphold the government's actions only if they are necessary to achieve a compelling purpose. In City of Boerne v. Flores, the Court declared the Religious Freedom Restoration Act unconstitutional.

City of Boerne v. Flores

521 U.S. 507 (1997)

Justice KENNEDY delivered the opinion of the Court.

A decision by local zoning authorities to deny a church a building permit was challenged under the Religious Freedom Restoration Act of 1993 (RFRA). The case calls into question the authority of Congress to enact RFRA. We conclude the statute exceeds Congress's power.

I

Situated on a hill in the city of Boerne, Texas, some 28 miles northwest of San Antonio, is St. Peter Catholic Church. Built in 1923, the church's structure replicates the mission style of the region's earlier history. The church seats about 230 worshippers, a number too small for its growing parish. Some 40 to 60 parishioners cannot be accommodated at some Sunday masses. In order to meet the needs of the congregation the Archbishop of San Antonio gave permission to the parish to plan alterations to enlarge the building.

A few months later, the Boerne City Council passed an ordinance authorizing the city's Historic Landmark Commission to prepare a preservation plan with proposed historic landmarks and districts. Under the ordinance, the Commission must preapprove construction affecting historic landmarks or buildings in a historic district.

Soon afterwards, the Archbishop applied for a building permit so construction to enlarge the church could proceed. City authorities, relying on the ordinance and the designation of a historic district (which, they argued, included the church), denied the application. The Archbishop brought this suit challenging the permit denial in the United States District Court for the Western District of Texas. The complaint contained various claims, but to this point the litigation has centered on RFRA and the question of its constitutionality. The Archbishop relied upon RFRA as one basis for relief from the refusal to issue the permit.

II

Congress enacted RFRA in direct response to the Court's decision in Employment Div., Dept. of Human Resources of Oregon v. Smith (1990). RFRA prohibits "[g]overnment" from "substantially burden[ing]" a person's exercise of religion even if the burden results from a rule of general applicability unless the government can demonstrate the burden "(1) is in furtherance of a compelling governmental interest; and (2) is the least restrictive means of furthering that compelling governmental interest."

III

A

The parties disagree over whether RFRA is a proper exercise of Congress's §5 power "to enforce" by "appropriate legislation" the constitutional guarantee that no State shall deprive any person of "life, liberty, or property, without due process of law" nor deny any person "equal protection of the laws."

All must acknowledge that §5 is "a positive grant of legislative power" to Congress, Katzenbach v. Morgan (1966). Legislation which deters or remedies constitutional violations can fall within the sweep of Congress's enforcement power even if in the process it prohibits conduct which is not itself unconstitutional and intrudes into "legislative spheres of autonomy previously reserved to the States." We have also concluded that other measures protecting voting rights are within Congress's power to enforce the Fourteenth and Fifteenth Amendments, despite the burdens those measures placed on the States.

It is also true, however, that "[a]s broad as the congressional enforcement power is, it is not unlimited." In assessing the breadth of §5's enforcement power, we begin with its text. Congress has been given the power "to enforce" the "provisions of this article." We agree with respondent, of course, that Congress can enact legislation under §5 enforcing the constitutional right to the free exercise of religion. The "provisions of this article," to which §5 refers, include the Due Process Clause of the Fourteenth Amendment.

Congress's power under §5, however, extends only to "enforc[ing]" the provisions of the Fourteenth Amendment. The Court has described this power as "remedial." The design of the Amendment and the text of §5 are inconsistent with the suggestion that Congress has the power to decree the substance of the Fourteenth Amendment's restrictions on the States. Legislation which alters the meaning of the Free Exercise Clause cannot be said to be enforcing the Clause. Congress does not enforce a constitutional right by changing what the right is. It has been given the power "to enforce," not the power to determine what constitutes a constitutional violation. Were it not so, what Congress would be enforcing would no longer be, in any meaningful sense, the "provisions of [the Fourteenth Amendment]."

While the line between measures that remedy or prevent unconstitutional actions and measures that make a substantive change in the governing law is not easy to discern, and Congress must have wide latitude in determining where it lies, the distinction exists and must be observed. There must be a congruence and proportionality between the injury to be prevented or remedied and the means adopted to that end. Lacking such a connection, legislation may become substantive in operation and effect. History and our case law support drawing the distinction, one apparent from the text of the Amendment.

1

The Fourteenth Amendment's history confirms the remedial, rather than substantive, nature of the Enforcement Clause. The Joint Committee on Reconstruction of the 39th Congress began drafting what would become the Fourteenth Amendment in January 1866. The objections to the Committee's first draft of the Amendment, and the rejection of the draft, have a direct bearing on the central issue of defining Congress's enforcement power. In February, Republican Representative John Bingham of Ohio reported the following draft amendment to the House of Representatives on behalf of the Joint Committee: "The Congress shall have power to make all laws which shall be necessary and proper to secure to the citizens of each State all privileges and immunities of citizens in the several States, and to all persons in the several States equal protection in the rights of life, liberty, and property."

The proposal encountered immediate opposition, which continued through three days of debate. Members of Congress from across the political spectrum criticized the Amendment, and the criticisms had a common theme: The proposed Amendment gave Congress too much legislative power at the expense of the existing constitutional structure. Democrats and conservative Republicans argued that the proposed Amendment would give Congress a power to intrude into traditional areas of state responsibility, a power inconsistent with the federal design central to the Constitution.

Section 1 of the new draft Amendment imposed self-executing limits on the States. Section 5 prescribed that "[t]he Congress shall have power to enforce, by appropriate legislation, the provisions of this article." Under the revised Amendment, Congress's power was no longer plenary but remedial. Congress was granted the power to make the substantive constitutional prohibitions against the States effective. Representative Bingham said the new draft would give Congress "the power . . . to protect by national law the privileges and immunities of all the citizens of the Republic . . . whenever the same shall be abridged or denied by the unconstitutional acts of any State." Representative Stevens described the new draft Amendment as "allow[ing] Congress to correct the unjust legislation of the States."

The design of the Fourteenth Amendment has proved significant also in maintaining the traditional separation of powers between Congress and the Judiciary. The first eight Amendments to the Constitution set forth self-executing prohibitions on governmental action, and this Court has had primary authority to interpret those prohibitions. The Bingham draft, some thought, departed from that tradition by vesting in Congress primary power to interpret and elaborate on the meaning of the new Amendment through legislation. Under it, "Congress, and not the courts, was to judge whether or not any of the privileges or immunities were not secured to citizens in the several States." The power to interpret the Constitution in a case or controversy remains in the Judiciary.

2

The remedial and preventive nature of Congress's enforcement power, and the limitation inherent in the power, were confirmed in our earliest cases on the

Fourteenth Amendment. In the Civil Rights Cases (1883), the Court invalidated sections of the Civil Rights Act of 1875 which prescribed criminal penalties for denying to any person "the full enjoyment of" public accommodations and conveyances, on the grounds that it exceeded Congress's power by seeking to regulate private conduct. The Enforcement Clause, the Court said, did not authorize Congress to pass "general legislation upon the rights of the citizen, but corrective legislation; that is, such as may be necessary and proper for counteracting such laws as the States may adopt or enforce, and which, by the amendment, they are prohibited from making or enforcing. . . ." Although the specific holdings of these early cases might have been superseded or modified, *see, e.g.*, Heart of Atlanta Motel, Inc. v. United States (1964); United States v. Guest (1966), their treatment of Congress's §5 power as corrective or preventive, not definitional, has not been questioned.

3

Any suggestion that Congress has a substantive, non-remedial power under the Fourteenth Amendment is not supported by our case law. If Congress could define its own powers by altering the Fourteenth Amendment's meaning, no longer would the Constitution be "superior paramount law, unchangeable by ordinary means." It would be "on a level with ordinary legislative acts, and, like other acts, . . . alterable when the legislature shall please to alter it." Marbury v. Madison. Under this approach, it is difficult to conceive of a principle that would limit congressional power. Shifting legislative majorities could change the Constitution and effectively circumvent the difficult and detailed amendment process contained in Article V.

We now turn to consider whether RFRA can be considered enforcement legislation under §5 of the Fourteenth Amendment.

B

Respondent contends that RFRA is a proper exercise of Congress's remedial or preventive power. The Act, it is said, is a reasonable means of protecting the free exercise of religion as defined by *Smith*. It prevents and remedies laws which are enacted with the unconstitutional object of targeting religious beliefs and practices. If Congress can prohibit laws with discriminatory effects in order to prevent racial discrimination in violation of the Equal Protection Clause, then it can do the same, respondent argues, to promote religious liberty.

While preventive rules are sometimes appropriate remedial measures, there must be a congruence between the means used and the ends to be achieved. The appropriateness of remedial measures must be considered in light of the evil presented. Strong measures appropriate to address one harm may be an unwarranted response to another, lesser one.

A comparison between RFRA and the Voting Rights Act is instructive. In contrast to the record which confronted Congress and the judiciary in the voting rights cases, RFRA's legislative record lacks examples of modern instances of generally applicable laws passed because of religious bigotry. The history of persecution in this country detailed in the hearings mentions no episodes occurring in the past 40 years. Regardless of the state of the legislative record, RFRA cannot be considered remedial, preventive legislation, if those terms are to have any meaning. RFRA is so out of proportion to a supposed remedial or preventive object that it cannot be understood as responsive to, or designed to prevent, unconstitutional behavior. It appears, instead, to attempt a substantive change in constitutional protections. Preventive measures prohibiting certain types of laws may be appropriate when there is reason to believe that many of the laws affected by the congressional enactment have a significant likelihood of being unconstitutional.

RFRA is not so confined. Sweeping coverage ensures its intrusion at every level of government, displacing laws and prohibiting official actions of almost every description and regardless of subject matter. RFRA's restrictions apply to every agency and official of the Federal, State, and local Governments. RFRA applies to all federal and state law, statutory or otherwise, whether adopted before or after its enactment. RFRA has no termination date or termination mechanism. Any law is subject to challenge at any time by any individual who alleges a substantial burden on his or her free exercise of religion. The reach and scope of RFRA distinguish it from other measures passed under Congress's enforcement power, even in the area of voting rights.

The stringent test RFRA demands of state laws reflects a lack of proportionality or congruence between the means adopted and the legitimate end to be achieved. If an objector can show a substantial burden on his free exercise, the State must demonstrate a compelling governmental interest and show that the law is the least restrictive means of furthering its interest. Claims that a law substantially burdens someone's exercise of religion will often be difficult to contest. Requiring a State to demonstrate a compelling interest and show that it has adopted the least restrictive means of achieving that interest is the most demanding test known to constitutional law. Laws valid under *Smith* would fall under RFRA without regard to whether they had the object of stifling or punishing free exercise. We make these observations not to reargue the position of the majority in *Smith* but to illustrate the substantive alteration of its holding attempted by RFRA. Even assuming RFRA would be interpreted in effect to mandate some lesser test, say one equivalent to intermediate scrutiny, the statute nevertheless would require searching judicial scrutiny of state law with the attendant likelihood of invalidation. This is a considerable congressional intrusion into the States' traditional prerogatives and general authority to regulate for the health and welfare of their citizens.

The substantial costs RFRA exacts, both in practical terms of imposing a heavy litigation burden on the States and in terms of curtailing their traditional general regulatory power, far exceed any pattern or practice of unconstitutional conduct under the Free Exercise Clause as interpreted in *Smith*. Simply put, RFRA is not designed to identify and counteract state laws likely to be unconstitutional because of their treatment of religion. In most cases, the state laws to which RFRA applies are not ones which will have been motivated by religious bigotry. If a state law disproportionately burdened a particular class of religious observers, this circumstance might be evidence of an impermissible legislative motive.

Our national experience teaches that the Constitution is preserved best when each part of the government respects both the Constitution and the proper actions and determinations of the other branches. When the Court has interpreted the Constitution, it has acted within the province of the Judicial Branch, which embraces the duty to say what the law is. Marbury v. Madison. When the political branches of the Government act against the background of a judicial interpretation of the Constitution already issued, it must be understood that in later cases and controversies the Court will treat its precedents with the respect due them under settled principles, including stare decisis, and contrary expectations must be disappointed. RFRA was designed to control cases and controversies, such as the one before us; but as the provisions of the federal statute here invoked are beyond congressional authority, it is this Court's precedent, not RFRA, which must control.

Broad as the power of Congress is under the Enforcement Clause of the Fourteenth Amendment, RFRA contradicts vital principles necessary to maintain separation of powers and the federal balance. The judgment of the Court of Appeals sustaining the Act's constitutionality is reversed.

Justice O'CONNOR, with whom Justice BREYER joins except as to a portion of Part I, dissenting.

I dissent from the Court's disposition of this case. I agree with the Court that the issue before us is whether the Religious Freedom Restoration Act (RFRA) is a proper exercise of Congress's power to enforce §5 of the Fourteenth Amendment. But as a yardstick for measuring the constitutionality of RFRA, the Court uses its holding in Employment Div., Dept. of Human Resources of Oregon v. Smith (1990), the decision that prompted Congress to enact RFRA, as a means of more rigorously enforcing the Free Exercise Clause. I remain of the view that Smith was wrongly decided, and I would use this case to reexamine the Court's holding there. Therefore, I would direct the parties to brief the question whether Smith represents the correct understanding of the Free Exercise Clause and set the case for reargument. If the Court were to correct the misinterpretation of the Free Exercise Clause set forth in Smith, it would simultaneously put our First Amendment jurisprudence back on course and allay the legitimate concerns of a majority in Congress who believed that Smith improperly restricted religious liberty. We would then be in a position to review RFRA in light of a proper interpretation of the Free Exercise Clause.

Justice SOUTER, dissenting.

To decide whether the Fourteenth Amendment gives Congress sufficient power to enact the Religious Freedom Restoration Act, the Court measures the legislation against the free-exercise standard of Employment Div., Dept. of Human Resources of Oregon v. Smith (1990). I have serious doubts about the precedential value of the Smith rule and its entitlement to adherence. These doubts are intensified today by the historical arguments going to the original understanding of the Free Exercise Clause presented in Justice O'CONNOR'S opinion, which raises very substantial issues about the soundness of the Smith rule. In order to provide full adversarial consideration, this case should be set down for reargument permitting plenary reexamination of the issue. Since the Court declines to follow that course, our free-exercise law remains marked by an "intolerable tension," and the constitutionality of the Act of Congress to enforce the free-exercise right cannot now be soundly decided. I would therefore dismiss the writ of certiorari as improvidently granted, and I accordingly dissent from the Court's disposition of this case.

_____

Since *Boerne*, the Supreme Court has had occasion to consider the scope of Congress's §5 power in several cases that involve the authority of Congress to authorize suits against state governments. Each of these decisions is presented below in the final section of the chapter, which examines the authority of Congress to authorize suits against state governments.

As discussed below, the Supreme Court has held that Congress can authorize suits against state governments pursuant to §5 of the Fourteenth Amendment, but not under any other congressional power. The Court thus has had to consider whether federal laws authorizing suits against state governments for patent infringement are within the scope of Congress's §5 power. These cases apply City of Boerne v. Flores and provide further elaboration of its restrictive view of Congress's §5 authority. They are presented below because they arise in the context of Congress's power to authorize suits against state governments.

DOES THE TENTH AMENDMENT LIMIT CONGRESSIONAL POWERS?

The Tenth Amendment states: "The powers not delegated to the United States by the Constitution, nor prohibited by it to the States, are reserved to the States respectively, or to the people." The key question about the Tenth Amendment is whether it is a judicially enforceable limit on Congress's powers; can federal laws, otherwise within the scope of Congress's authority, be declared unconstitutional as violating this constitutional provision?

There are two different ways of answering this question. One is that the Tenth Amendment is not a separate constraint on Congress, but rather is simply a reminder that Congress only may legislate if it has authority under the Constitution. Under this approach, a federal law never would be found unconstitutional as violating the Tenth Amendment, but it could be invalidated as exceeding the scope of Congress's powers under Article I of the Constitution or for violating another constitutional provision.

The alternate approach is that the Tenth Amendment protects state sovereignty from federal intrusion. Under this approach, the Tenth Amendment is a key protection of states' rights and federalism. The Tenth Amendment reserves a zone of activity to the states for their exclusive control, and federal laws intruding into this zone should be declared unconstitutional by the courts.

In Gibbons v. Ogden, the Court took the former position and held that a federal law was constitutional so long as Congress was acting within the scope of its authority. In the first third of this century, until 1937, the Court adopted the latter view and found that the Tenth Amendment reserved to the states control over production, and federal laws attempting to regulate production were unconstitutional. The key case in this regard was Hammer v. Dagenhart.

Hammer v. Dagenhart

247 U.S. 251 (1918)

Justice DAY delivered the opinion of the Court.

A bill was filed in the United States District Court for the Western District of North Carolina by a father in his own behalf and as next friend of his two minor sons, one under the age of fourteen years and the other between the ages of fourteen and sixteen years, employees in a cotton mill at Charlotte, North Carolina, to enjoin the enforcement of the act of Congress intended to prevent interstate commerce in the products of child labor.

The controlling question for decision is: Is it within the authority of Congress in regulating commerce among the states to prohibit the transportation in interstate commerce of manufactured goods, the product of a factory in which, within thirty days prior to their removal therefrom, children under the age of fourteen have been employed or permitted to work, or children between the ages of fourteen and sixteen years have been employed or permitted to work more than eight hours in any day, or more than six days in any week, or after the hour of 7 o'clock P.M., or before the hour of 6 o'clock A.M.?

The power essential to the passage of this act, the government contends, is found in the commerce clause of the Constitution which authorizes Congress to regulate commerce with foreign nations and among the states.

[It] is insisted that adjudged cases in this court establish the doctrine that the power to regulate given to Congress incidentally includes the authority to prohibit the movement of ordinary commodities and therefore that the subject is not open for discussion.

The thing intended to be accomplished by this statute is the denial of the facilities of interstate commerce to those manufacturers in the states who employ children within the prohibited ages. The act in its effect does not regulate transportation among the states, but aims to standardize the ages at which children may be employed in mining and manufacturing within the states. The goods shipped are of themselves harmless. When offered for shipment, and before transportation begins, the labor of their production is over, and the mere fact that they were intended for interstate commerce transportation does not make their production subject to federal control under the commerce power.

Over interstate transportation, or its incidents, the regulatory power of Congress is ample, but the production of articles, intended for interstate commerce, is a matter of local regulation. "When the commerce begins is determined, not by the character of the commodity, nor by the intention of the owner to transfer it to another state for sale, nor by his preparation of it for transportation, but by its actual delivery to a common carrier for transportation, or the actual commencement of its transfer to another state." If it were otherwise, all manufacture intended for interstate shipment would be brought under federal control to the practical exclusion of the authority of the states, a result certainly not contemplated by the framers of the Constitution when they vested in Congress the authority to regulate commerce among the states.

It is further contended that the authority of Congress may be exerted to control interstate commerce in the shipment of childmade goods because of the effect of the circulation of such goods in other states where the evil of this class of labor has been recognized by local legislation, and the right to thus employ child labor has been more rigorously restrained than in the state of production. In other words, that the unfair competition, thus engendered, may be controlled by closing the channels of interstate commerce to manufacturers in those states where the local laws do not meet what Congress deems to be the more just standard of other states.

There is no power vested in Congress to require the states to exercise their police power so as to prevent possible unfair competition. Many causes may cooperate to give one state, by reason of local laws or conditions, an economic advantage over others. The commerce clause was not intended to give to Congress a general authority to equalize such conditions. In some of the states laws have been passed fixing minimum wages for women, in others the local law regulates the hours of labor of women in various employments. Business done in such states may be at an economic disadvantage when compared with states which have no such regulations; surely, this fact does not give Congress the power to deny transportation in interstate commerce to those who carry on business where the hours of labor and the rate of compensation for women have not been fixed by a standard in use in other states and approved by Congress.

The grant of power of Congress over the subject of interstate commerce was to enable it to regulate such commerce, and not to give it authority to control the states in their exercise of the police power over local trade and manufacture.

The grant of authority over a purely federal matter was not intended to destroy the local power always existing and carefully reserved to the states in the Tenth Amendment to the Constitution.

Police regulations relating to the internal trade and affairs of the states have been uniformly recognized as within such control. That there should be limitations upon the right to employ children in mines and factories in the interest of their own and the public welfare, all will admit. That such employment is generally deemed to require regulation is shown by the fact that the brief of counsel states that every state in the Union has a law upon the subject, limiting the right to thus employ children. In North Carolina, the state wherein is located the factory in which the employment was had in the present case, no child under twelve years of age is permitted to work.

To sustain this statute would not be in our judgment a recognition of the lawful exertion of congressional authority over interstate commerce, but would sanction an invasion by the federal power of the control of a matter purely local in its character, and over which no authority has been delegated to Congress in conferring the power to regulate commerce among the states.

In our view the necessary effect of this act is, by means of a prohibition against the movement in interstate commerce of ordinary commercial commodities to regulate the hours of labor of children in factories and mines within the states, a purely state authority. Thus the act in a two-fold sense is repugnant to the Constitution. It not only transcends the authority delegated to Congress over commerce but also exerts a power as to a purely local matter to which the federal authority does not extend. The far reaching result of upholding the act cannot be more plainly indicated than by pointing out that if Congress can thus regulate matters entrusted to local authority by prohibition of the movement of commodities in interstate commerce, all freedom of commerce will be at an end, and the power of the states over local matters may be eliminated, and thus our system of government be practically destroyed.

Justice HOLMES, dissenting.

The single question in this case is whether Congress has power to prohibit the shipment in interstate or foreign commerce of any product of a cotton mill situated in the United States, in which within thirty days before the removal of the product children under fourteen have been employed, or children between fourteen and sixteen have been employed more than eight hours in a day, or more than six days in any week, or between seven in the evening and six in the morning. The objection urged against the power is that the States have exclusive control over their methods of production and that Congress cannot meddle with them. But if an act is within the powers specifically conferred upon Congress, it seems to me that it is not made any less constitutional because of the indirect effects that it may have, however obvious it may be that it will have those effects, and that we are not at liberty upon such grounds to hold it void.

The first step in my argument is to make plain what no one is likely to dispute — that the statute in question is within the power expressly given to Congress if considered only as to its immediate effects and that if invalid it is so only upon some collateral ground. The statute confines itself to prohibiting the carriage of certain goods in interstate or foreign commerce. Congress is given power to regulate such commerce in unqualified terms. It would not be argued today that the power to regulate does not include the power to prohibit.

The question then is narrowed to whether the exercise of its otherwise constitutional power by Congress can be pronounced unconstitutional because of its possible reaction upon the conduct of the States in a matter upon which I have admitted that they are free from direct control. I should have thought that matter had been disposed of so fully as to leave no room for doubt. I should have thought that the most conspicuous decisions of this Court had made it clear that the power to regulate commerce and other constitutional powers could not be cut down or qualified by the fact that it might interfere with the carrying out of the domestic policy of any State.

But I had thought that the propriety of the exercise of a power admitted to exist in some cases was for the consideration of Congress alone and that this Court always had disavowed the right to intrude its judgment upon questions of policy or morals. It is not for this Court to pronounce when prohibition is necessary to regulation if it ever may be necessary — to say that it is permissible as against strong drink but not as against the product of ruined lives.

The Act does not meddle with anything belonging to the States. They may regulate their internal affairs and their domestic commerce as they like. But when they seek to send their products across the State line they are no longer within their rights. If there were no Constitution and no Congress their power to cross the line would depend upon their neighbors. Under the Constitution such commerce belongs not to the States but to Congress to regulate. It may carry out its views of public policy whatever indirect effect they may have upon the activities of the States.

THE TENTH AMENDMENT BETWEEN 1937 AND THE 1990S

In United States v. Darby, above, the Court declared that the Tenth Amendment is "but a truism," simply a reminder that for Congress to act it must have authority under the Constitution. This approach to the Tenth Amendment was followed without exception until 1976, when the Court invalidated a federal law for violating the Tenth Amendment. The case was National League of Cities v. Usery and it attracted enormous attention from scholars and litigants who began bringing Tenth Amendment challenges to other federal laws.

National League of Cities v. Usery
426 U.S. 833 (1976)

Justice REHNQUIST delivered the opinion of the Court.

Nearly 40 years ago Congress enacted the Fair Labor Standards Act, and required employers covered by the Act to pay their employees a minimum hourly wage and to pay them at one and one-half times their regular rate of pay for hours worked in excess of 40 during a work week. This Court unanimously upheld the Act as a valid exercise of congressional authority under the commerce power in United States v. Darby. [The Court then reviewed the federal laws, including one adopted in 1974, that applied the law to public employees.]

Appellants in no way challenge these decisions establishing the breadth of authority granted Congress under the commerce power. Their contention, on the contrary, is that when Congress seeks to regulate directly the activities of States as public employers, it transgresses an affirmative limitation on the exercise of its power akin to other commerce power affirmative limitations contained in the Constitution. Appellants' essential contention is that the 1974 amendments to the Act, while undoubtedly within the scope of the Commerce Clause, encounter a similar constitutional barrier because they are to be applied directly to the States and subdivisions of States as employers.

This Court has never doubted that there are limits upon the power of Congress to override state sovereignty, even when exercising its otherwise plenary powers to tax or to regulate commerce which are conferred by Art. I of the Constitution. While the Tenth Amendment has been characterized as a "truism," it is not without significance. The Amendment expressly declares that Congress may not exercise power in a fashion that impairs the states' integrity or their ability to function effectively in a federal system.

One undoubted attribute of state sovereignty is the States' power to determine the wages which shall be paid to those whom they employ in order to carry out their governmental functions, what hours those persons will work, and what compensation will be provided where these employees may be called upon to work overtime. The question we must resolve here, then, is whether these determinations are " 'functions essential to separate and independent existence,' " so that Congress may not abrogate the States' otherwise plenary authority to make them.

In their complaint appellants advanced estimates of substantial costs which will be imposed upon them by the 1974 amendments. Judged solely in terms of increased costs in dollars, these allegations show a significant impact on the functioning of the governmental bodies involved. The Metropolitan Government of Nashville and Davidson County, Tenn., for example, asserted that the Act will increase its costs of providing essential police and fire protection, without any increase in service or in current salary levels, by $938,000 per year. Cape Girardeau, Mo., estimated that its annual budget for fire protection may have to be increased by anywhere from $250,000 to $400,000 over the current figure of $350,000. The State of Arizona alleged that the annual additional expenditures which will be required if it is to continue to provide essential state services may total $2.5 million. The State of California, which must devote significant portions of its budget to fire-suppression endeavors, estimated that application of the Act to its employment practices will necessitate an increase in its budget of between $8 million and $16 million.

Increased costs are not, of course, the only adverse effects which compliance with the Act will visit upon state and local governments, and in turn upon the citizens who depend upon those governments. In its complaint in intervention, for example, California asserted that it could not comply with the overtime costs (approximately $750,000 per year) which the Act required to be paid to California Highway Patrol cadets during their academy training program. California reported that it had thus been forced to reduce its academy training program from 2,080 hours to only 960 hours, a compromise undoubtedly of substantial importance to those whose safety and welfare may depend upon the preparedness of the California Highway Patrol.

Quite apart from the substantial costs imposed upon the States and their political subdivisions, the Act displaces state policies regarding the manner in which they will structure delivery of those governmental services which their citizens require. The Act, speaking directly to the States qua States, requires that they shall pay all but an extremely limited minority of their employees the minimum wage rates currently chosen by Congress. It may well be that as a matter of economic policy it would be desirable that States, just as private employers, comply with these minimum wage requirements. But it cannot be gainsaid that the federal requirement directly supplants the considered policy choices of the States' elected officials and administrators as to how they wish to structure pay scales in state employment. The State might wish to employ persons with little or no training, or those who wish to work on a casual basis, or those who for some other reason do not possess minimum employment requirements, and pay them less than the federally prescribed minimum wage. It may wish to offer part-time or summer employment to teenagers at a figure less than the minimum wage, and if unable to do so may decline to offer such employment at all. But the Act would forbid such choices by the States. The only "discretion" left to them under the Act is either to attempt to increase their revenue to meet the additional financial burden imposed upon them by paying congressionally prescribed wages to their existing complement of employees, or to reduce that complement to a number which can be paid the federal minimum wage without increasing revenue.

This congressionally imposed displacement of state decisions may substantially restructure traditional ways in which the local governments have arranged their affairs. Our examination of the effect of the 1974 amendments, as sought to be extended to the States and their political subdivisions, satisfies us that both the minimum wage and the maximum hour provisions will impermissibly interfere with the integral governmental functions of these bodies. Even if we accept appellee's assessments concerning the impact of the amendments, their application will nonetheless significantly alter or displace the States' abilities to structure employer-employee relationships in such areas as fire prevention, police protection, sanitation, public health, and parks and recreation. These activities are typical of those performed by state and local governments in discharging their dual functions of administering the public law and furnishing public services. Indeed, it is functions such as these which governments are created to provide, services such as these which the States have traditionally afforded their citizens. If Congress may withdraw from the States the authority to make those fundamental employment decisions upon which their systems for performance of these functions must rest, we think there would be little left of the States' "separate and independent existence." This exercise of congressional authority does not comport with the federal system of government embodied in the Constitution. We hold that insofar as the challenged amendments operate to directly displace the States' freedom to structure integral operations in areas of traditional governmental functions, they are not within the authority granted Congress by Art. I, §8, cl. 3.

Justice BLACKMUN, concurring.

The Court's opinion and the dissents indicate the importance and significance of this litigation as it bears upon the relationship between the Federal Government and our States. Although I am not untroubled by certain possible implications of the Court's opinion some of them suggested by the dissents I do not read the opinion so despairingly as does my Brother BRENNAN. In my view, the result with respect to the statute under challenge here is necessarily correct. I may misinterpret the Court's opinion, but it seems to me that it adopts a balancing approach, and does not outlaw federal power in areas such as environmental protection, where the federal interest is demonstrably greater and where state facility compliance with imposed federal standards would be essential. With this understanding on my part of the Court's opinion, I join it.

Justice BRENNAN, with whom Justice WHITE and Justice MARSHALL join, dissenting.

The Court concedes, as of course it must, that Congress enacted the 1974 amendments pursuant to its exclusive power under Art. I, §8, cl. 3, of the Constitution "[t]o regulate Commerce . . . among the several States." It must therefore be surprising that my Brethren should choose this bicentennial year of our independence to repudiate principles governing judicial interpretation of our Constitution settled since the time of Chief Justice John Marshall, discarding his postulate that the Constitution contemplates that restraints upon exercise by Congress of its plenary commerce power lie in the political process and not in the judicial process.

My Brethren do not successfully obscure today's patent usurpation of the role reserved for the political process by their purported discovery in the Constitution of a restraint derived from sovereignty of the States on Congress's exercise of the commerce power.

My Brethren thus have today manufactured an abstraction without substance, founded neither in the words of the Constitution nor on precedent. An abstraction having such profoundly pernicious consequences is not made less so by characterizing the 1974 amendments as legislation directed against the "States qua States." Today's repudiation of this unbroken line of precedents that firmly reject my Brethren's ill-conceived abstraction can only be regarded as a transparent cover for invalidating a congressional judgment with which they disagree. The only analysis even remotely resembling that adopted today is found in a line of opinions dealing with the Commerce Clause and the Tenth Amendment that ultimately provoked a constitutional crisis for the Court in the 1930s. E.g., Carter v. Carter Coal Co.; United States v. Butler; Hammer v. Dagenhart.

Justice STEVENS, dissenting.

The Court holds that the Federal Government may not interfere with a sovereign State's inherent right to pay a substandard wage to the janitor at the state capitol. The principle on which the holding rests is difficult to perceive.

The Federal Government may, I believe, require the State to act impartially when it hires or fires the janitor, to withhold taxes from his paycheck, to observe safety regulations when he is performing his job, to forbid him from burning too much soft coal in the capitol furnace, from dumping untreated refuse in an adjacent waterway, from overloading a state-owned garbage truck, or from driving either the truck or the Governor's limousine over 55 miles an hour. Even though these and many other activities of the capitol janitor are activities of the State qua State, I have no doubt that they are subject to federal regulation.

———

In the decade after *National League of Cities*, the Supreme Court rejected Tenth Amendment challenges to several other federal laws and continually narrowed the Tenth Amendment protection provided in that decision. In each case, Justice Blackmun voted with the majority, often as the crucial fifth vote refusing to extend or apply National League of Cities v. Usery.

In Hodel v. Virginia Surface Mining & Reclamation Association, 452 U.S. 264 (1981), the Court made it clear that *Usery* only applied when Congress was regulating state governments, not when Congress was regulating private conduct. In *Hodel*, the Court upheld a federal law that regulated strip mining and required reclamation of strip-mined land. The Court clarified its test for the Tenth Amendment in light of *Usery*. The Court said that for a federal law to violate the Tenth Amendment, it needed to regulate "the States as States"; it must "address matters that are indisputably attribute[s] of state sovereignty"; it must directly impair the States' ability to "structure integral operations in areas of traditional governmental functions"; and it must not be such that "the nature of the federal interest . . . justifies state submission." The Court in *Hodel* found that the law, the Surface Mining Control and Reclamation Act of 1977, was constitutional because it did not regulate the states as states. In several other cases, the Court also rejected Tenth Amendment challenges to federal laws.[142]

In 1985, the Court expressly overruled *National League of Cities*.

Garcia v. San Antonio Metropolitan Transit Authority

469 U.S. 528 (1985)

Justice Blackmun delivered the opinion of the Court.

We revisit in these cases an issue raised in National League of Cities v. Usery. In that litigation, this Court, by a sharply divided vote, ruled that the Commerce Clause does not empower Congress to enforce the minimum-wage and overtime provisions of the Fair Labor Standards Act (FLSA) against the States "in areas of

———

[142] United Transportation Union v. Long Island R.R. Co., 455 U.S. 678 (1982) (application of the Railway Labor Act to a state-owned railroad did not violate the Tenth Amendment); Federal Energy Regulatory Commission (FERC) v. Mississippi, 456 U.S. 742 (1982) (rejecting a challenge to the Public Utilities Regulatory Policies Act of 1978, which required that state utility commissions consider FERC proposals); Equal Employment Opportunity Commission v. Wyoming, 460 U.S. 226 (1983) (upholding a federal law forcing states to comply with the Age Discrimination in Employment Act violated the Tenth Amendment).

traditional governmental functions." Although *National League of Cities* supplied some examples of "traditional governmental functions," it did not offer a general explanation of how a "traditional" function is to be distinguished from a "nontraditional" one. Since then, federal and state courts have struggled with the task, thus imposed, of identifying a traditional function for purposes of state immunity under the Commerce Clause.

Our examination of this "function" standard applied in these and other cases over the last eight years now persuades us that the attempt to draw the boundaries of state regulatory immunity in terms of "traditional governmental function" is not only unworkable but is also inconsistent with established principles of federalism and, indeed, with those very federalism principles on which *National League of Cities* purported to rest. That case, accordingly, is overruled.

Thus far, this Court itself has made little headway in defining the scope of the governmental functions deemed protected under *National League of Cities*. Many constitutional standards involve "undoubte[d] . . . gray areas," and, despite the difficulties that this Court and other courts have encountered so far, it normally might be fair to venture the assumption that case-by-case development would lead to a workable standard for determining whether a particular governmental function should be immune from federal regulation under the Commerce Clause.

We believe, however, that there is a more fundamental problem at work here, a problem that explains why an attempt to draw distinctions with respect to federal regulatory authority under *National League of Cities* is unlikely to succeed regardless of how the distinctions are phrased. The problem is that neither the governmental/proprietary distinction nor any other that purports to separate out important governmental functions can be faithful to the role of federalism in a democratic society. The essence of our federal system is that within the realm of authority left open to them under the Constitution, the States must be equally free to engage in any activity that their citizens choose for the common weal, no matter how unorthodox or unnecessary anyone else — including the judiciary — deems state involvement to be. Any rule of state immunity that looks to the "traditional," "integral," or "necessary" nature of governmental functions inevitably invites an unelected federal judiciary to make decisions about which state policies it favors and which ones it dislikes.

We therefore now reject, as unsound in principle and unworkable in practice, a rule of state immunity from federal regulation that turns on a judicial appraisal of whether a particular governmental function is "integral" or "traditional." Any such rule leads to inconsistent results at the same time that it disserves principles of democratic self-governance, and it breeds inconsistency precisely because it is divorced from those principles. If there are to be limits on the Federal Government's power to interfere with state functions — as undoubtedly there are — we must look elsewhere to find them.

The central theme of *National League of Cities* was that the States occupy a special position in our constitutional system and that the scope of Congress's authority under the Commerce Clause must reflect that position. Of course, the Commerce Clause by its specific language does not provide any special limitation on Congress's actions with respect to the States.

What has proved problematic is not the perception that the Constitution's federal structure imposes limitations on the Commerce Clause, but rather the nature and content of those limitations. We doubt that courts ultimately can identify principled constitutional limitations on the scope of Congress's Commerce Clause powers over the States merely by relying on a priori definitions of state sovereignty. In part, this is because of the elusiveness of objective criteria for "fundamental" elements of state sovereignty, a problem we have witnessed in the search for "traditional governmental functions."

Apart from the limitation on federal authority inherent in the delegated nature of Congress's Article I powers, the principal means chosen by the framers to ensure the role of the States in the federal system lies in the structure of the Federal Government itself.[143] It is no novelty to observe that the composition of the Federal Government was designed in large part to protect the States from overreaching by Congress. The framers thus gave the States a role in the selection both of the Executive and the Legislative Branches of the Federal Government. The States were vested with indirect influence over the House of Representatives and the Presidency by their control of electoral qualifications and their role in Presidential elections. U.S. Const., Art. I, §2, and Art. II, §1. They were given more direct influence in the Senate, where each State received equal representation and each Senator was to be selected by the legislature of his State. Art. I, §3. The significance attached to the States' equal representation in the Senate is underscored by the prohibition of any constitutional amendment divesting a State of equal representation without the State's consent. Art. V.

The extent to which the structure of the Federal Government itself was relied on to insulate the interests of the States is evident in the views of the framers. James Madison explained that the Federal Government "will partake sufficiently of the spirit [of the States], to be disinclined to invade the rights of the individual States, or the prerogatives of their governments." The Federalist No. 46.

The effectiveness of the federal political process in preserving the States' interests is apparent even today in the course of federal legislation. On the one hand, the States have been able to direct a substantial proportion of federal revenues into their own treasuries in the form of general and program-specific grants in aid. The federal role in assisting state and local governments is a longstanding one; Congress provided federal land grants to finance state governments from the beginning of the Republic, and direct cash grants were awarded as early as 1887 under the Hatch Act. In the past quarter-century alone, federal grants to States and localities have grown from $7 billion to $96 billion. As a result, federal grants now account for about one-fifth of state and local government expenditures. The States have obtained federal funding for such services as police and fire protection, education, public health and hospitals, parks and recreation, and sanitation. Moreover, at the same time that the States have exercised their influence to obtain

---

[143] *See, e.g.,* J. Choper, Judicial Review and the National Political Process 175-184 (1980); Wechsler, The Political Safeguards of Federalism: The Role of the States in the Composition and Selection of the National Government, 54 Colum. L. Rev. 543 (1954); La Pierre, the Political Safeguards of Federalism Redux: Intergovernmental Immunity and the States as Agents of the Nation, 60 Wash. U. L.Q. 779 (1982). [Footnote by the Court.]

federal support, they have been able to exempt themselves from a wide variety of obligations imposed by Congress under the Commerce Clause.

We realize that changes in the structure of the Federal Government have taken place since 1789, not the least of which has been the substitution of popular election of Senators by the adoption of the Seventeenth Amendment in 1913, and that these changes may work to alter the influence of the States in the federal political process. Nonetheless, against this background, we are convinced that the fundamental limitation that the constitutional scheme imposes on the Commerce Clause to protect the "States as States" is one of process rather than one of result. Any substantive restraint on the exercise of Commerce Clause powers must find its justification in the procedural nature of this basic limitation, and it must be tailored to compensate for possible failings in the national political process rather than to dictate a "sacred province of state autonomy."

Insofar as the present cases are concerned, then, we need go no further than to state that we perceive nothing in the overtime and minimum-wage requirements of the FLSA, as applied to SAMTA, that is destructive of state sovereignty or violative of any constitutional provision. SAMTA faces nothing more than the same minimum-wage and overtime obligations that hundreds of thousands of other employers, public as well as private, have to meet.

Of course, we continue to recognize that the States occupy a special and specific position in our constitutional system and that the scope of Congress's authority under the Commerce Clause must reflect that position. But the principal and basic limit on the federal commerce power is that inherent in all congressional action — the built-in restraints that our system provides through state participation in federal governmental action. The political process ensures that laws that unduly burden the States will not be promulgated. In the factual setting of these cases the internal safeguards of the political process have performed as intended.

National League of Cities v. Usery is overruled.

Justice POWELL, with whom the Chief Justice, Justice REHNQUIST, and Justice O'CONNOR join, dissenting.

The Court today, in its 5-4 decision, overrules National League of Cities v. Usery, a case in which we held that Congress lacked authority to impose the requirements of the Fair Labor Standards Act on state and local governments. Because I believe this decision substantially alters the federal system embodied in the Constitution, I dissent.

There are, of course, numerous examples over the history of this Court in which prior decisions have been reconsidered and overruled. There have been few cases, however, in which the principle of stare decisis and the rationale of recent decisions were ignored as abruptly as we now witness. The reasoning of the Court in National League of Cities, and the principle applied there, have been reiterated consistently over the past eight years.

Whatever effect the Court's decision may have in weakening the application of stare decisis, it is likely to be less important than what the Court has done to the Constitution itself. A unique feature of the United States is the federal system of government guaranteed by the Constitution and implicit in the very name of our

country. Despite some genuflecting in the Court's opinion to the concept of federalism, today's decision effectively reduces the Tenth Amendment to meaningless
rhetoric when Congress acts pursuant to the Commerce Clause.

To leave no doubt about its intention, the Court renounces its decision in
National League of Cities because it "inevitably invites an unelected federal judiciary to make decisions about which state policies it favors and which ones it dislikes." In other words, the extent to which the States may exercise their authority,
when Congress purports to act under the Commerce Clause, henceforth is to be
determined from time to time by political decisions made by members of the Federal Government, decisions the Court says will not be subject to judicial review. I
note that it does not seem to have occurred to the Court that it — an unelected
majority of five Justices — today rejects almost 200 years of the understanding of
the constitutional status of federalism. In doing so, there is only a single passing
reference to the Tenth Amendment. Nor is so much as a dictum of any court cited
in support of the view that the role of the States in the federal system may depend
upon the grace of elected federal officials, rather than on the Constitution as interpreted by this Court.

The Court finds that the test of state immunity approved in *National League
of Cities* and its progeny is unworkable and unsound in principle. In finding the
test to be unworkable, the Court begins by mischaracterizing *National League of
Cities* and subsequent cases. In concluding that efforts to define state immunity
are unsound in principle, the Court radically departs from long-settled constitutional values and ignores the role of judicial review in our system of government.

Today's opinion does not explain how the States' role in the electoral process
guarantees that particular exercises of the Commerce Clause power will not
infringe on residual state sovereignty. Members of Congress are elected from the
various States, but once in office they are Members of the Federal Government.
Although the States participate in the Electoral College, this is hardly a reason to
view the President as a representative of the States' interest against federal
encroachment. We noted recently "[t]he hydraulic pressure inherent within each
of the separate Branches to exceed the outer limits of its power...." INS v.
Chadha (1983). The Court offers no reason to think that this pressure will not
operate when Congress seeks to invoke its powers under the Commerce Clause,
notwithstanding the electoral role of the States.

The Court apparently thinks that the State's success at obtaining federal funds
for various projects and exemptions from the obligations of some federal statutes
is indicative of the "effectiveness of the federal political process in preserving the
States' interests...." But such political success is not relevant to the question
whether the political processes are the proper means of enforcing constitutional
limitations. The fact that Congress generally does not transgress constitutional
limits on its power to reach state activities does not make judicial review any less
necessary to rectify the cases in which it does do so. The States' role in our system
of government is a matter of constitutional law, not of legislative grace. "The
powers not delegated to the United States by the Constitution, nor prohibited by
it to the States, are reserved to the States, respectively, or to the people." U.S.
Const., Amdt. 10.

More troubling than the logical infirmities in the Court's reasoning is the result of its holding, i.e., that federal political officials, invoking the Commerce Clause, are the sole judges of the limits of their own power. This result is inconsistent with the fundamental principles of our constitutional system. See, e.g., The Federalist No. 78 (Hamilton). At least since Marbury v. Madison (1803), it has been the settled province of the federal judiciary "to say what the law is" with respect to the constitutionality of Acts of Congress. In rejecting the role of the judiciary in protecting the States from federal overreaching, the Court's opinion offers no explanation for ignoring the teaching of the most famous case in our history.

[T]he Court today propounds a view of federalism that pays only lipservice to the role of the States. Although it says that the States "unquestionably do 'retai[n] a significant measure of sovereign authority,'" it fails to recognize the broad, yet specific areas of sovereignty that the framers intended the States to retain. Indeed, the Court barely acknowledges that the Tenth Amendment exists. Indeed, the Court's view of federalism appears to relegate the States to precisely the trivial role that opponents of the Constitution feared they would occupy.

Justice REHNQUIST, dissenting.

I join both Justice POWELL's and Justice O'CONNOR's thoughtful dissents. [U]nder any one of these approaches the judgment in these cases should be affirmed, and I do not think it incumbent on those of us in dissent to spell out further the fine points of a principle that will, I am confident, in time again command the support of a majority of this Court.

E. Does the Tenth Amendment Limit Congress's Authority?

The first indication of the revival of the Tenth Amendment occurred in Gregory v. Ashcroft, 501 U.S. 452 (1991). State court judges in Missouri challenged a provision of the Missouri Constitution that set a mandatory retirement age as violating the federal Age Discrimination in Employment Act. The Supreme Court held that a federal law will be applied to important state government activities only if there is a clear statement from Congress that the law was meant to apply. The Court did not use the Tenth Amendment to invalidate the federal law on its face or as applied. Instead, the Court used the Tenth Amendment and federalism considerations as a rule of construction. The Court ruled that a federal law that imposes a substantial burden on a state government will be applied only if Congress clearly indicated that it wanted the law to apply. The Age Discrimination in Employment Act lacks such a clear statement, and hence the Court refused to apply it to preempt the Missouri mandatory retirement age. Justice O'Connor, writing for the Court, discussed the importance of autonomous state governments as a check on possible federal tyranny and stressed the significance of the Tenth Amendment as a constitutional protector of state sovereignty.

There have been two decisions following Gregory v. Ashcroft that used the Tenth Amendment to invalidate federal laws: New York v. United States and Printz v. United States.

New York v. United States

505 U.S. 144 (1992)

Justice O'CONNOR delivered the opinion of the Court.

These cases implicate one of our Nation's newest problems of public policy and perhaps our oldest question of constitutional law. The public policy issue involves the disposal of radioactive waste: In these cases, we address the constitutionality of three provisions of the Low-Level Radioactive Waste Policy Amendments Act of 1985. The constitutional question is as old as the Constitution: It consists of discerning the proper division of authority between the Federal Government and the States. We conclude that while Congress has substantial power under the Constitution to encourage the States to provide for the disposal of the radioactive waste generated within their borders, the Constitution does not confer upon Congress the ability simply to compel the States to do so.

I

We live in a world full of low level radioactive waste. Radioactive material is present in luminous watch dials, smoke alarms, measurement devices, medical fluids, research materials, and the protective gear and construction materials used by workers at nuclear power plants. Low level radioactive waste is generated by the Government, by hospitals, by research institutions, and by various industries. The waste must be isolated from humans for long periods of time, often for hundreds of years. Millions of cubic feet of low level radioactive waste must be disposed of each year.

The 1985 Act was based largely on a proposal submitted by the National Governors' Association. The Act provides three types of incentives to encourage the States to comply with their statutory obligation to provide for the disposal of waste generated within their borders. [The Court described the first two as monetary incentives to encourage opening waste sites and access incentives, allowing states without sites to be denied access to other states' sites. The focus of the case is on the third type of incentive.]

The take title provision. The third type of incentive is the most severe. The Act provides:

> If a State (or, where applicable, a compact region) in which low-level radioactive waste is generated is unable to provide for the disposal of all such waste generated within such State or compact region by January 1, 1996, each State in which such waste is generated, upon the request of the generator or owner of the waste, shall take title to the waste, be obligated to take possession of the waste, and shall be liable for all damages directly or indirectly incurred by such generator or owner as a

consequence of the failure of the State to take possession of the waste as soon after January 1, 1996, as the generator or owner notifies the State that the waste is available for shipment.

II

A

The task of ascertaining the constitutional line between federal and state power has given rise to many of the Court's most difficult and celebrated cases.

These questions can be viewed in either of two ways. In some cases the Court has inquired whether an Act of Congress is authorized by one of the powers delegated to Congress in Article I of the Constitution. See, e.g., Perez v. United States (1971); McCulloch v. Maryland (1819). In other cases the Court has sought to determine whether an Act of Congress invades the province of state sovereignty reserved by the Tenth Amendment. See, e.g., Garcia v. San Antonio Metropolitan Transit Authority (1985). In a case like these, involving the division of authority between federal and state governments, the two inquiries are mirror images of each other. If a power is delegated to Congress in the Constitution, the Tenth Amendment expressly disclaims any reservation of that power to the States; if a power is an attribute of state sovereignty reserved by the Tenth Amendment, it is necessarily a power the Constitution has not conferred on Congress.

Congress exercises its conferred powers subject to the limitations contained in the Constitution. Thus, for example, under the Commerce Clause Congress may regulate publishers engaged in interstate commerce, but Congress is constrained in the exercise of that power by the First Amendment. The Tenth Amendment likewise restrains the power of Congress, but this limit is not derived from the text of the Tenth Amendment itself, which, as we have discussed, is essentially a tautology. Instead, the Tenth Amendment confirms that the power of the Federal Government is subject to limits that may, in a given instance, reserve power to the States. The Tenth Amendment thus directs us to determine, as in this case, whether an incident of state sovereignty is protected by a limitation on an Article I power.

The benefits of this federal structure have been extensively cataloged elsewhere, but they need not concern us here. Our task would be the same even if one could prove that federalism secured no advantages to anyone. It consists not of devising our preferred system of government, but of understanding and applying the framework set forth in the Constitution. "The question is not what power the Federal Government ought to have but what powers in fact have been given by the people." United States v. Butler (1936).

B

Petitioners do not contend that Congress lacks the power to regulate the disposal of low level radioactive waste. Space in radioactive waste disposal sites is frequently sold by residents of one State to residents of another. Regulation of the resulting interstate market in waste disposal is therefore well within Congress's authority under the Commerce Clause. Petitioners likewise do not dispute that under the Supremacy Clause Congress could, if it wished, pre-empt state radioactive waste regulation. Petitioners contend only that the Tenth Amendment limits the power of Congress to regulate in the way it has chosen. Rather than addressing the problem of waste disposal by directly regulating the generators and disposers of waste, petitioners argue, Congress has impermissibly directed the States to regulate in this field.

Most of our recent cases interpreting the Tenth Amendment have concerned the authority of Congress to subject state governments to generally applicable laws. This litigation presents no occasion to apply or revisit the holdings of any of these cases, as this is not a case in which Congress has subjected a State to the same legislation applicable to private parties.

This litigation instead concerns the circumstances under which Congress may use the States as implements of regulation; that is, whether Congress may direct or otherwise motivate the States to regulate in a particular field or a particular way. Our cases have established a few principles that guide our resolution of the issue.

1

As an initial matter, Congress may not simply "commandee[r] the legislative processes of the States by directly compelling them to enact and enforce a federal regulatory program." While Congress has substantial powers to govern the Nation directly, including in areas of intimate concern to the States, the Constitution has never been understood to confer upon Congress the ability to require the States to govern according to Congress's instructions.

Indeed, the question whether the Constitution should permit Congress to employ state governments as regulatory agencies was a topic of lively debate among the framers. In providing for a stronger central government, therefore, the framers explicitly chose a Constitution that confers upon Congress the power to regulate individuals, not States. As we have seen, the Court has consistently respected this choice. We have always understood that even where Congress has the authority under the Constitution to pass laws requiring or prohibiting certain acts, it lacks the power directly to compel the States to require or prohibit those acts. The allocation of power contained in the Commerce Clause, for example, authorizes Congress to regulate interstate commerce directly; it does not authorize Congress to regulate state governments' regulation of interstate commerce.

2

This is not to say that Congress lacks the ability to encourage a State to regulate in a particular way, or that Congress may not hold out incentives to the States as a method of influencing a State's policy choices. Our cases have identified a variety of methods, short of outright coercion, by which Congress may urge a State to adopt a legislative program consistent with federal interests. Two of these methods are of particular relevance here.

First, under Congress's spending power, "Congress may attach conditions on the receipt of federal funds." South Dakota v. Dole (1986). Such conditions must (among other requirements) bear some relationship to the purpose of the federal spending; otherwise, of course, the spending power could render academic the Constitution's other grants and limits of federal authority. Where the recipient of federal funds is a State, as is not unusual today, the conditions attached to the funds by Congress may influence a State's legislative choices.

Second, where Congress has the authority to regulate private activity under the Commerce Clause, we have recognized Congress's power to offer States the choice of regulating that activity according to federal standards or having state law pre-empted by federal regulation. This arrangement, which has been termed "a program of cooperative federalism," is replicated in numerous federal statutory schemes. These include the Clean Water Act; the Occupational Safety and Health Act of 1970; the Resource Conservation and Recovery Act of 1976, and the Alaska National Interest Lands Conservation Act.

By either of these methods, as by any other permissible method of encouraging a State to conform to federal policy choices, the residents of the State retain the ultimate decision as to whether or not the State will comply. If a State's citizens view federal policy as sufficiently contrary to local interests, they may elect to decline a federal grant. If state residents would prefer their government to devote its attention and resources to problems other than those deemed important by Congress, they may choose to have the Federal Government rather than the State bear the expense of a federally mandated regulatory program, and they may continue to supplement that program to the extent state law is not pre-empted. Where Congress encourages state regulation rather than compelling it, state governments remain responsive to the local electorate's preferences; state officials remain accountable to the people.

By contrast, where the Federal Government compels States to regulate, the accountability of both state and federal officials is diminished. If the citizens of New York, for example, do not consider that making provision for the disposal of radioactive waste is in their best interest, they may elect state officials who share their view. That view can always be pre-empted under the Supremacy Clause if it is contrary to the national view, but in such a case it is the Federal Government that makes the decision in full view of the public, and it will be federal officials that suffer the consequences if the decision turns out to be detrimental or unpopular. But where the Federal Government directs the States to regulate, it may be state officials who will bear the brunt of public disapproval, while the federal officials who devised the regulatory program may remain insulated from the electoral ramifications of their decision. Accountability is thus diminished when, due to federal coercion, elected state officials cannot regulate in accordance with the views of the local electorate in matters not pre-empted by federal regulation.

With these principles in mind, we turn to the three challenged provisions of the Low-Level Radioactive Waste Policy Amendments Act of 1985.

III

[The Court upheld the monetary and access incentives created by Congress for states to open waste sites. The Court found that the former was permissible as an exercise of the spending power. The Court found the second was permissible under Congress's authority to encourage compacts among the states.]

C

The take title provision is of a different character. In this provision, Congress has crossed the line distinguishing encouragement from coercion.

The take title provision offers state governments a "choice" of either accepting ownership of waste or regulating according to the instructions of Congress. Respondents do not claim that the Constitution would authorize Congress to impose either option as a freestanding requirement. On one hand, the Constitution would not permit Congress simply to transfer radioactive waste from generators to state governments. Such a forced transfer, standing alone, would in principle be no different than a congressionally compelled subsidy from state governments to radioactive waste producers. The same is true of the provision requiring the States to become liable for the generators' damages. Standing alone, this provision would be indistinguishable from an Act of Congress directing the States to assume the liabilities of certain state residents. Either type of federal action would "commandeer" state governments into the service of federal regulatory purposes, and would for this reason be inconsistent with the Constitution's division of authority between federal and state governments. On the other hand, the second alternative held out to state governments — regulating pursuant to Congress's direction — would, standing alone, present a simple command to state governments to implement legislation enacted by Congress. As we have seen, the Constitution does not empower Congress to subject state governments to this type of instruction.

Because an instruction to state governments to take title to waste, standing alone, would be beyond the authority of Congress, and because a direct order to regulate, standing alone, would also be beyond the authority of Congress, it follows that Congress lacks the power to offer the States a choice between the two. A choice between two unconstitutionally coercive regulatory techniques is no choice at all. Either way, "the Act commandeers the legislative processes of the States by directly compelling them to enact and enforce a federal regulatory program," Hodel v. Virginia Surface Mining & Reclamation Assn., Inc., an outcome that has never been understood to lie within the authority conferred upon Congress by the Constitution.

Respondents emphasize the latitude given to the States to implement Congress's plan. The Act enables the States to regulate pursuant to Congress's instructions in any number of different ways. States may avoid taking title by contracting with sited regional compacts, by building a disposal site alone or as part of a compact, or by permitting private parties to build a disposal site. States that host sites may employ a wide range of designs and disposal methods, subject only to broad federal regulatory limits. This line of reasoning, however, only underscores the critical alternative a State lacks: A State may not decline to administer the federal program. No matter which path the State chooses, it must follow the direction of Congress.

The take title provision appears to be unique. No other federal statute has been cited which offers a state government no option other than that of implementing legislation enacted by Congress. Whether one views the take title provision as lying outside Congress's enumerated powers, or as infringing upon the core of state sovereignty reserved by the Tenth Amendment, the provision is inconsistent with the federal structure of our Government established by the Constitution.

The United States argues that the Constitution's prohibition of congressional directives to state governments can be overcome where the federal interest is sufficiently important to justify state submission. But whether or not a particularly strong federal interest enables Congress to bring state governments within the orbit of generally applicable federal regulation, no Member of the Court has ever suggested that such a federal interest would enable Congress to command a state government to enact state regulation. No matter how powerful the federal interest involved, the Constitution simply does not give Congress the authority to require the States to regulate. The Constitution instead gives Congress the authority to regulate matters directly and to pre-empt contrary state regulation. Where a federal interest is sufficiently strong to cause Congress to legislate, it must do so directly; it may not conscript state governments as its agents. The sited state respondents focus their attention on the process by which the Act was formulated. They correctly observe that public officials representing the State of New York lent their support to the Act's enactment. Respondents note that the Act embodies a bargain among the sited and unsited States, a compromise to which New York was a willing participant and from which New York has reaped much benefit. Respondents then pose what appears at first to be a troubling question: How can a federal statute be found an unconstitutional infringement of state sovereignty when state officials consented to the statute's enactment?

The answer follows from an understanding of the fundamental purpose served by our Government's federal structure. The Constitution does not protect the sovereignty of States for the benefit of the States or state governments as abstract political entities, or even for the benefit of the public officials governing the States. To the contrary, the Constitution divides authority between federal and state governments for the protection of individuals. State sovereignty is not just an end in itself: "Rather, federalism secures to citizens the liberties that derive from the diffusion of sovereign power. Just as the separation and independence of the coordinate branches of the Federal Government serves to prevent the accumulation of excessive power in any one branch, a healthy balance of power between the States and the Federal Government will reduce the risk of tyranny and abuse from either front." Gregory v. Ashcroft (1991).

Where Congress exceeds its authority relative to the States, therefore, the departure from the constitutional plan cannot be ratified by the "consent" of state officials. An analogy to the separation of powers among the branches of the

Federal Government clarifies this point. The Constitution's division of power among the three branches is violated where one branch invades the territory of another, whether or not the encroached-upon branch approves the encroachment. State officials thus cannot consent to the enlargement of the powers of Congress beyond those enumerated in the Constitution.

States are not mere political subdivisions of the United States. State governments are neither regional offices nor administrative agencies of the Federal Government. The positions occupied by state officials appear nowhere on the Federal Government's most detailed organizational chart. The Constitution instead "leaves to the several States a residuary and inviolable sovereignty," The Federalist No. 39, reserved explicitly to the States by the Tenth Amendment. Whatever the outer limits of that sovereignty may be, one thing is clear: The Federal Government may not compel the States to enact or administer a federal regulatory program. The Constitution permits both the Federal Government and the States to enact legislation regarding the disposal of low level radioactive waste. The Constitution enables the Federal Government to pre-empt state regulation contrary to federal interests, and it permits the Federal Government to hold out incentives to the States as a means of encouraging them to adopt suggested regulatory schemes. It does not, however, authorize Congress simply to direct the States to provide for the disposal of the radioactive waste generated within their borders. While there may be many constitutional methods of achieving regional self-sufficiency in radioactive waste disposal, the method Congress has chosen is not one of them.

Justice WHITE, with whom Justice BLACKMUN and Justice STEVENS join, concurring in part and dissenting in part.

The Court today affirms the constitutionality of two facets of the Low-Level Radioactive Waste Policy Amendments Act of 1985 (1985 Act). These provisions include the monetary incentives from surcharges collected by States with low-level radioactive waste storage sites, and the "access incentives," which deny access to disposal sites for States that fail to meet certain deadlines for low-level radioactive waste disposal management. The Court strikes down and severs a third component of the 1985 Act, the "take title" provision, which requires a noncomplying State to take title to or to assume liability for its low-level radioactive waste if it fails to provide for the disposal of such waste by January 1, 1996. The Court deems this last provision unconstitutional under principles of federalism. Because I believe the Court has mischaracterized the essential inquiry, misanalyzed the inquiry it has chosen to undertake, and undervalued the effect the seriousness of this public policy problem should have on the constitutionality of the take title provision, I respectfully dissent from [this aspect] of its opinion.

I

My disagreement with the Court's analysis begins at the basic descriptive level of how the legislation at issue in these cases came to be enacted. The Court goes some way toward setting out the bare facts, but its omissions cast the statutory context of the take title provision in the wrong light. To read the Court's version of events, one would think that Congress was the sole proponent of a solution to the Nation's low-level radioactive waste problem. Not so. The Low-Level Radioactive Waste Policy Act of 1980 (1980 Act), and its amendatory 1985 Act, resulted from the efforts of state leaders to achieve a state-based set of remedies to the waste problem. They sought not federal pre-emption or intervention, but rather congressional sanction of interstate compromises they had reached.

The two signal events in 1979 that precipitated movement toward legislation were the temporary closing of the Nevada disposal site in July 1979, after several serious transportation-related incidents, and the temporary shutting of the Washington disposal site because of similar transportation and packaging problems in October 1979. At that time the facility in Barnwell, South Carolina, received approximately three-quarters of the Nation's low-level radioactive waste, and the Governor ordered a 50 percent reduction in the amount his State's plant would accept for disposal. The Governor of Washington threatened to shut down the Hanford, Washington, facility entirely by 1982 unless "some meaningful progress occurs toward" development of regional solutions to the waste disposal problem. Only three sites existed in the country for the disposal of low-level radioactive waste, and the "sited" States confronted the undesirable alternatives either of continuing to be the dumping grounds for the entire Nation's low-level waste or of eliminating or reducing in a constitutional manner the amount of waste accepted for disposal.

The imminence of a crisis in low-level radioactive waste management cannot be overstated. Accordingly, the National Governors' Association Task Force urged that "each state should accept primary responsibility for the safe disposal of low-level radioactive waste generated within its borders" and that "the states should pursue a regional approach to the low-level waste disposal problem."

A movement thus arose to achieve a compromise between the sited and the unsited States, in which the sited States agreed to continue accepting waste in exchange for the imposition of stronger measures to guarantee compliance with the unsited States' assurances that they would develop alternative disposal facilities. The bill that in large measure became the 1985 Act "represent[ed] the diligent negotiating undertaken by" the National Governors' Association and "embodied" the "fundamentals of their settlement."

Unlike legislation that directs action from the Federal Government to the States, the 1980 and 1985 Acts reflected hard-fought agreements among States as refereed by Congress. The distinction is key, and the Court's failure properly to characterize this legislation ultimately affects its analysis of the take title provision's constitutionality.

II

Even were New York not to be estopped from challenging the take title provision's constitutionality, I am convinced that, seen as a term of an agreement entered into between the several States, this measure proves to be less constitutionally odious than the Court opines. First, the practical effect of New York's position is that because it is unwilling to honor its obligations to provide in-state storage facilities for its low-level radioactive waste, other States with such plants must accept New York's waste, whether they wish to or not. Otherwise, the many economically and socially beneficial producers of such waste in the State would have to cease their operations. The Court's refusal to force New York to accept responsibility for its own problem inevitably means that some other State's sovereignty will be impinged by it being forced, for public health reasons, to accept New York's low-level radioactive waste. I do not understand the principle of federalism to impede the National Government from acting as referee among the States to prohibit one from bullying another.

Moreover, it is utterly reasonable that, in crafting a delicate compromise between the three overburdened States that provided low-level radioactive waste disposal facilities and the rest of the States, Congress would have to ratify some punitive measure as the ultimate sanction for noncompliance. The take title provision, though surely onerous, does not take effect if the generator of the waste does not request such action, or if the State lives up to its bargain of providing a waste disposal facility either within the State or in another State pursuant to a regional compact arrangement or a separate contract.

III

The Court announces that it has no occasion to revisit such decisions as Gregory v. Ashcroft (1991); South Carolina v. Baker (1988); Garcia v. San Antonio Metropolitan Transit Authority (1985); EEOC v. Wyoming (1983); and National League of Cities v. Usery (1976). Although this statement sends the welcome signal that the Court does not intend to cut a wide swath through our recent Tenth Amendment precedents, it nevertheless is unpersuasive. I have several difficulties with the Court's analysis in this respect: It builds its rule around an insupportable and illogical distinction in the types of alleged incursions on state sovereignty; it derives its rule from cases that do not support its analysis; it fails to apply the appropriate tests from the cases on which it purports to base its rule; and it omits any discussion of the most recent and pertinent test for determining the take title provision's constitutionality.

The Court's distinction between a federal statute's regulation of States and private parties for general purposes, as opposed to a regulation solely on the activities of States, is unsupported by our recent Tenth Amendment cases. In no case has the Court rested its holding on such a distinction. Moreover, the Court makes no effort to explain why this purported distinction should affect the analysis of Congress's power under general principles of federalism and the Tenth Amendment. The distinction, facilely thrown out, is not based on any defensible theory. An incursion on state sovereignty hardly seems more constitutionally acceptable if the federal statute that "commands" specific action also applies to private parties. The alleged diminution in state authority over its own affairs is not any less because the federal mandate restricts the activities of private parties.

Given the scanty textual support for the majority's position, it would be far more sensible to defer to a coordinate branch of government in its decision to devise a solution to a national problem of this kind. Certainly in other contexts, principles of federalism have not insulated States from mandates by the National Government. The Court has upheld congressional statutes that impose clear directives on state officials, including those enacted pursuant to the Extradition Clause, see, e.g., Puerto Rico v. Branstad (1987), the post-Civil War Amendments, see, e.g., South Carolina v. Katzenbach (1966), as well as congressional statutes that require state courts to hear certain actions, see, e.g., Testa v. Katt (1947).

IV

Though I disagree with the Court's conclusion that the take title provision is unconstitutional, I do not read its opinion to preclude Congress from adopting a similar measure through its powers under the Spending or Commerce Clauses. The Court makes clear that its objection is to the alleged "commandeer[ing]" quality of the take title provision. The spending power offers a means of enacting a take title provision under the Court's standards. Congress could, in other words, condition the payment of funds on the State's willingness to take title if it has not already provided a waste disposal facility.

Similarly, should a State fail to establish a waste disposal facility by the appointed deadline (under the statute as presently drafted, January 1, 1996) Congress has the power pursuant to the Commerce Clause to regulate directly the producers of the waste. Thus, as I read it, Congress could amend the statute to say that if a State fails to meet the January 1, 1996, deadline for achieving a means of waste disposal, and has not taken title to the waste, no low-level radioactive waste may be shipped out of the State of New York. This background suggests that the threat of federal pre-emption may suffice to induce States to accept responsibility for failing to meet critical time deadlines for solving their low-level radioactive waste disposal problems, especially if that federal intervention also would strip state and local authorities of any input in locating sites for low-level radioactive waste disposal facilities. And should Congress amend the statute to meet the Court's objection and a State refuse to act, the National Legislature will have ensured at least a federal solution to the waste management problem.

Finally, our precedents leave open the possibility that Congress may create federal rights of action in the generators of low-level radioactive waste against persons acting under color of state law for their failure to meet certain functions designated in federal-state programs.

V

The ultimate irony of the decision today is that in its formalistically rigid obeisance to "federalism," the Court gives Congress fewer incentives to defer to the wishes of state officials in achieving local solutions to local problems. By invalidating the measure designed to ensure compliance for recalcitrant States, such as New York, the Court upsets the delicate compromise achieved among the States and forces Congress to erect several additional formalistic hurdles to clear before achieving exactly the same objective. Because the Court's justifications for undertaking this step are unpersuasive to me, I respectfully dissent.

Justice STEVENS, concurring in part and dissenting in part.

Under the Articles of Confederation, the Federal Government had the power to issue commands to the States. Because that indirect exercise of federal power proved ineffective, the framers of the Constitution empowered the Federal Government to exercise legislative authority directly over individuals within the States, even though that direct authority constituted a greater intrusion on state sovereignty. Nothing in that history suggests that the Federal Government may not also impose its will upon the several States as it did under the Articles. The Constitution enhanced, rather than diminished, the power of the Federal Government.

The notion that Congress does not have the power to issue "a simple command to state governments to implement legislation enacted by Congress," is incorrect and unsound. There is no such limitation in the Constitution. The Tenth Amendment surely does not impose any limit on Congress's exercise of the powers delegated to it by Article I. Nor does the structure of the constitutional order or the values of federalism mandate such a formal rule. To the contrary, the Federal Government directs state governments in many realms. The Government regulates state-operated railroads, state school systems, state prisons, state elections, and a host of other state functions. Similarly, there can be no doubt that, in time of war, Congress could either draft soldiers itself or command the States to supply their quotas of troops. I see no reason why Congress may not also command the States to enforce federal water and air quality standards or federal standards for the disposition of low-level radioactive wastes.

Printz v. United States

521 U.S. 898 (1997)

Justice SCALIA delivered the opinion of the Court.

The question presented in these cases is whether certain interim provisions of the Brady Handgun Violence Prevention Act, commanding state and local law enforcement officers to conduct background checks on prospective handgun purchasers and to perform certain related tasks, violate the Constitution.

I

The Gun Control Act of 1968 (GCA), establishes a detailed federal scheme governing the distribution of firearms. In 1993, Congress amended the GCA by enacting the Brady Act. The Act requires the Attorney General to establish a national instant background check system by November 30, 1998, and immediately puts in place certain interim provisions until that system becomes operative. Under the interim provisions, [state and local law enforcement personnel must do background checks before issuing permit for firearms].

Petitioners Jay Printz and Richard Mack, the chief law enforcement officers [CLEOs] for Ravalli County, Montana, and Graham County, Arizona, respectively, filed separate actions challenging the constitutionality of the Brady Act's interim provisions.

II

From the description set forth above, it is apparent that the Brady Act purports to direct state law enforcement officers to participate, albeit only temporarily, in the administration of a federally enacted regulatory scheme. Regulated firearms dealers are required to forward Brady Forms not to a federal officer or employee, but to the CLEOs, whose obligation to accept those forms is implicit in the duty imposed upon them to make "reasonable efforts" within five days to determine whether the sales reflected in the forms are lawful. While the CLEOs are subjected to no federal requirement that they prevent the sales determined to be unlawful (it is perhaps assumed that their state-law duties will require prevention or apprehension), they are empowered to grant, in effect, waivers of the federally prescribed 5-day waiting period for handgun purchases by notifying the gun dealers that they have no reason to believe the transactions would be illegal.

The petitioners here object to being pressed into federal service, and contend that congressional action compelling state officers to execute federal laws is unconstitutional. Because there is no constitutional text speaking to this precise question, the answer to the CLEOs' challenge must be sought in historical understanding and practice, in the structure of the Constitution, and in the jurisprudence of this Court. We treat those three sources, in that order, in this and the next two sections of this opinion.

Petitioners contend that compelled enlistment of state executive officers for the administration of federal programs is, until very recent years at least, unprecedented. The Government contends, to the contrary, that "the earliest Congresses enacted statutes that required the participation of state officials in the implementation of federal laws," Brief for United States 28. The Government's contention demands our careful consideration, since early congressional enactments "provid[e] 'contemporaneous and weighty evidence' of the Constitution's meaning," Bowsher v. Synar (1986). Indeed, such "contemporaneous legislative exposition of the Constitution . . . , acquiesced in for a long term of years, fixes the construction to be given its provisions." Myers v. United States (1926) (citing numerous cases). Conversely if, as petitioners contend, earlier Congresses avoided use of this highly attractive power, we would have reason to believe that the power was thought not to exist.

The Government observes that statutes enacted by the first Congresses required state courts to record applications for citizenship, to transmit abstracts of citizenship applications and other naturalization records to the Secretary of State, and to register aliens seeking naturalization and issue certificates of registry. It may well be, however, that these requirements applied only in States that authorized their courts to conduct naturalization proceedings.

These early laws establish, at most, that the Constitution was originally understood to permit imposition of an obligation on state judges to enforce federal prescriptions, insofar as those prescriptions related to matters appropriate for the judicial power. [W]e do not think the early statutes imposing obligations on state courts imply a power of Congress to impress the state executive into its service. Indeed, it can be argued that the numerousness of these statutes, contrasted with the utter lack of statutes imposing obligations on the States' executive (notwith-standing the attractiveness of that course to Congress), suggests an assumed absence of such power.

Not only do the enactments of the early Congresses, as far as we are aware, contain no evidence of an assumption that the Federal Government may command the States' executive power in the absence of a particularized constitutional authorization, they contain some indication of precisely the opposite assumption. On September 23, 1789 — the day before its proposal of the Bill of Rights, see 1 Annals of Congress 912-913 — the First Congress enacted a law aimed at obtaining state assistance of the most rudimentary and necessary sort for the enforcement of the new Government's laws: the holding of federal prisoners in state jails at federal expense. Significantly, the law issued not a command to the States' executive, but a recommendation to their legislatures. Moreover, when Georgia refused to comply with the request, Congress's only reaction was a law authorizing the marshal in any State that failed to comply with the Recommendation of September 23, 1789, to rent a temporary jail until provision for a permanent one could be made.

To complete the historical record, we must note that there is not only an absence of executive-commandeering statutes in the early Congresses, but there is an absence of them in our later history as well, at least until very recent years. The Government points to a number of federal statutes enacted within the past few decades that require the participation of state or local officials in implementing federal regulatory schemes. Some of these are connected to federal funding measures, and can perhaps be more accurately described as conditions upon the grant of federal funding than as mandates to the States; others, which require only the provision of information to the Federal Government, do not involve the precise issue before us here, which is the forced participation of the States' executive in the actual administration of a federal program. For deciding the issue before us here, they are of little relevance. Even assuming they represent assertion of the very same congressional power challenged here, they are of such recent vintage that they are no more probative than the statute before us of a constitutional tradition that lends meaning to the text.

III

The constitutional practice we have examined above tends to negate the existence of the congressional power asserted here, but is not conclusive. We turn next to consideration of the structure of the Constitution, to see if we can discern among its "essential postulate[s]," a principle that controls the present cases.

A

It is incontestible that the Constitution established a system of "dual sovereignty." Gregory v. Ashcroft (1991). Although the States surrendered many of their powers to the new Federal Government, they retained "a residuary and inviolable sovereignty," The Federalist No. 39 (J. Madison). This is reflected throughout the

Constitution's text, including (to mention only a few examples) the prohibition on any involuntary reduction or combination of a State's territory, Art. IV, §3; the Judicial Power Clause, Art III, §2, and the Privileges and Immunities Clause, Art. IV, §2, which speak of the "Citizens" of the States; the amendment provision, Article V, which requires the votes of three-fourths of the States to amend the Constitution; and the Guarantee Clause, Art. IV, §4, which "presupposes the continued existence of the states and . . . those means and instrumentalities which are the creation of their sovereign and reserved rights." Residual state sovereignty was also implicit, of course, in the Constitution's conferral upon Congress of not all governmental powers, but only discrete, enumerated ones, Art. I, §8, which implication was rendered express by the Tenth Amendment's assertion that "[t]he powers not delegated to the United States by the Constitution, nor prohibited by it to the States, are reserved to the States respectively, or to the people."

The framers' experience under the Articles of Confederation had persuaded them that using the States as the instruments of federal governance was both ineffectual and provocative of federal-state conflict. See The Federalist No. 15. Preservation of the States as independent political entities being the price of union, and "[t]he practicality of making laws, with coercive sanctions, for the States as political bodies" having been, in Madison's words, "exploded on all hands," 2 Records of the Federal Convention of 1787, p. 9 (M. Farrand ed. 1911), the framers rejected the concept of a central government that would act upon and through the States, and instead designed a system in which the state and federal governments would exercise concurrent authority over the people — who were, in Hamilton's words, "the only proper objects of government," The Federalist No. 15, at 109.

This separation of the two spheres is one of the Constitution's structural protections of liberty. "Just as the separation and independence of the coordinate branches of the Federal Government serve to prevent the accumulation of excessive power in any one branch, a healthy balance of power between the States and the Federal Government will reduce the risk of tyranny and abuse from either front."

B

We have thus far discussed the effect that federal control of state officers would have upon the first element of the "double security" alluded to by Madison: the division of power between State and Federal Governments. It would also have an effect upon the second element: the separation and equilibration of powers between the three branches of the Federal Government itself. The Constitution does not leave to speculation who is to administer the laws enacted by Congress; the President, it says, "shall take Care that the Laws be faithfully executed," Art. II, §3, personally and through officers whom he appoints (save for such inferior officers as Congress may authorize to be appointed by the "Courts of Law" or by "the Heads of Departments" who are themselves presidential appointees), Art. II, §2. The Brady Act effectively transfers this responsibility to thousands of CLEOs in the 50 States, who are left to implement the program without meaningful

Presidential control (if indeed meaningful Presidential control is possible without the power to appoint and remove). The insistence of the framers upon unity in the Federal Executive — to insure both vigor and accountability — is well known. That unity would be shattered, and the power of the President would be subject to reduction, if Congress could act as effectively without the President as with him, by simply requiring state officers to execute its laws.

IV

Finally, and most conclusively in the present litigation, we turn to the prior juris-prudence of this Court. When we were at last confronted squarely with a federal statute that unambiguously required the States to enact or administer a federal regulatory program, our decision should have come as no surprise. At issue in New York v. United States (1992) were the so-called "take title" provisions of the Low-Level Radioactive Waste Policy Amendments Act of 1985, which required States either to enact legislation providing for the disposal of radioactive waste generated within their borders, or to take title to, and possession of the waste. We concluded that Congress could constitutionally require the States to do neither. "The Federal Government," we held, "may not compel the States to enact or administer a federal regulatory program."

The Government contends that New York is distinguishable on the following ground: unlike the "take title" provisions invalidated there, the background-check provision of the Brady Act does not require state legislative or executive officials to make policy, but instead issues a final directive to state CLEOs.

The Government's distinction between "making" law and merely "enforcing" it, between "policymaking" and mere "implementation," is an interesting one. Executive action that has utterly no policymaking component is rare, particularly at an executive level as high as a jurisdiction's chief law-enforcement officer. Is it really true that there is no policymaking involved in deciding, for example, what "reasonable efforts" shall be expended to conduct a background check?

Even assuming, moreover, that the Brady Act leaves no "policymaking" dis-cretion with the States, we fail to see how that improves rather than worsens the intrusion upon state sovereignty. Preservation of the States as independent and autonomous political entities is arguably less undermined by requiring them to make policy in certain fields than by "reduc[ing] [them] to puppets of a ventrilo-quist Congress." It is an essential attribute of the States' retained sovereignty that they remain independent and autonomous within their proper sphere of author-ity. It is no more compatible with this independence and autonomy that their offi-cers be "dragooned" into administering federal law, than it would be compatible with the independence and autonomy of the United States that its officers be impressed into service for the execution of state laws.

Finally, the Government puts forward a cluster of arguments that can be grouped under the heading: "The Brady Act serves very important purposes, is most efficiently administered by CLEOs during the interim period, and places a minimal and only temporary burden upon state officers." Assuming all the men-tioned factors were true, they might be relevant if we were evaluating whether the incidental application to the States of a federal law of general applicability excessively interfered with the functioning of state governments. But where, as here, it is the whole object of the law to direct the functioning of the state executive, and hence to compromise the structural framework of dual sovereignty, such a "balancing" analysis is inappropriate. It is the very principle of separate state sovereignty that such a law offends, and no comparative assessment of the various interests can overcome that fundamental defect.

We adhere to that principle today, and conclude categorically, as we concluded categorically in *New York*: "The Federal Government may not compel the States to enact or administer a federal regulatory program." The mandatory obligation imposed on CLEOs to perform background checks on prospective handgun purchasers plainly runs afoul of that rule.

We held in *New York* that Congress cannot compel the States to enact or enforce a federal regulatory program. Today we hold that Congress cannot circumvent that prohibition by conscripting the State's officers directly. The Federal Government may neither issue directives requiring the States to address particular problems, nor command the States' officers, or those of their political subdivisions, to administer or enforce a federal regulatory program. It matters not whether policymaking is involved, and no case-by-case weighing of the burdens or benefits is necessary; such commands are fundamentally incompatible with our constitutional system of dual sovereignty.

Justice THOMAS, concurring.

The Court today properly holds that the Brady Act violates the Tenth Amendment in that it compels state law enforcement officers to "administer or enforce a federal regulatory program." Although I join the Court's opinion in full, I write separately to emphasize . . . [i]n my "revisionist" view, the Federal Government's authority under the Commerce Clause, which merely allocates to Congress the power "to regulate Commerce . . . among the several states," does not extend to the regulation of wholly intra state, point-of-sale transactions. See United States v. Lopez (1995) (concurring opinion). Absent the underlying authority to regulate the intrastate transfer of firearms, Congress surely lacks the corollary power to impress state law enforcement officers into administering and enforcing such regulations.

Although this Court has long interpreted the Constitution as ceding Congress extensive authority to regulate commerce (interstate or otherwise), I continue to believe that we must "temper our Commerce Clause jurisprudence" and return to an interpretation better rooted in the Clause's original understanding.

Even if we construe Congress's authority to regulate interstate commerce to encompass those intrastate transactions that "substantially affect" interstate commerce, I question whether Congress can regulate the particular transactions at issue here. The Constitution, in addition to delegating certain enumerated powers to Congress, places whole areas outside the reach of Congress's regulatory authority. The First Amendment, for example, is fittingly celebrated for preventing Congress from "prohibiting the free exercise" of religion or "abridging the freedom of speech." The Second Amendment similarly appears to contain an express limitation on the government's authority. That Amendment provides: "[a] well regulated Militia, being necessary to the security of a free State, the right of the people to keep and bear arms, shall not be infringed." This Court has not had recent occasion to consider the nature of the substantive right safeguarded by the Second Amendment. If, however, the Second Amendment is read to confer a personal right to "keep and bear arms," a colorable argument exists that the Federal Government's regulatory scheme, at least as it pertains to the purely intrastate sale or possession of firearms, runs afoul of that Amendment's protections. As the parties did not raise this argument, however, we need not consider it here. Perhaps, at some future date, this Court will have the opportunity to determine whether Justice Story was correct when he wrote that the right to bear arms "has justly been considered, as the palladium of the liberties of a republic." 3 J. Story, Commentaries (1833). In the meantime, I join the Court's opinion striking down the challenged provisions of the Brady Act as inconsistent with the Tenth Amendment.

Justice STEVENS, with whom Justice SOUTER, Justice GINSBURG, and Justice BREYER join, dissenting.

When Congress exercises the powers delegated to it by the Constitution, it may impose affirmative obligations on executive and judicial officers of state and local governments as well as ordinary citizens. This conclusion is firmly supported by the text of the Constitution, the early history of the Nation, decisions of this Court, and a correct understanding of the basic structure of the Federal Government.

These cases do not implicate the more difficult questions associated with congressional coercion of state legislatures addressed in New York v. United States (1992). Nor need we consider the wisdom of relying on local officials rather than federal agents to carry out aspects of a federal program, or even the question whether such officials may be required to perform a federal function on a permanent basis. The question is whether Congress, acting on behalf of the people of the entire Nation, may require local law enforcement officers to perform certain duties during the interim needed for the development of a federal gun control program. It is remarkably similar to the question, heavily debated by the framers of the Constitution, whether the Congress could require state agents to collect federal taxes. Or the question whether Congress could impress state judges into federal service to entertain and decide cases that they would prefer to ignore.

Indeed, since the ultimate issue is one of power, we must consider its implications in times of national emergency. Matters such as the enlistment of air raid wardens, the administration of a military draft, the mass inoculation of children to forestall an epidemic, or perhaps the threat of an international terrorist, may require a national response before federal personnel can be made available to respond. If the Constitution empowers Congress and the President to make an appropriate response, is there anything in the Tenth Amendment, "in historical understanding and practice, in the structure of the Constitution, [or] in the jurisprudence of this Court," that forbids the enlistment of state officers to make that response effective? More narrowly, what basis is there in any of those sources for concluding that it is the Members of this Court, rather than the elected representatives of the people, who should determine whether the Constitution contains the unwritten rule that the Court announces today?

Perhaps today's majority would suggest that no such emergency is presented by the facts of these cases. But such a suggestion is itself an expression of a policy judgment. And Congress's view of the matter is quite different from that implied by the Court today.

The Brady Act was passed in response to what Congress described as an "epidemic of gun violence." H. Rep. No. 103-344, 103rd Cong. 1st Sess. 1985. The Act's legislative history notes that 15,377 Americans were murdered with firearms in 1992, and that 12,489 of these deaths were caused by handguns. Congress expressed special concern that "[t]he level of firearm violence in this country is, by far, the highest among developed nations." The partial solution contained in the Brady Act, a mandatory background check before a handgun may be purchased, has met with remarkable success. Between 1994 and 1996, approximately 6,600 firearm sales each month to potentially dangerous persons were prevented by Brady Act checks; over 70% of the rejected purchasers were convicted or indicted felons. Whether or not the evaluation reflected in the enactment of the Brady Act is correct as to the extent of the danger and the efficacy of the legislation, the congressional decision surely warrants more respect than it is accorded in today's unprecedented decision.

I

The text of the Constitution provides a sufficient basis for a correct disposition of this case. Article I, §8, grants the Congress the power to regulate commerce among the States. Putting to one side the revisionist views expressed by Justice THOMAS, there can be no question that provision adequately supports the regulation of commerce in handguns effected by the Brady Act. Moreover, the additional grant of authority in that section of the Constitution "[t]o make all Laws which shall be necessary and proper for carrying into Execution the foregoing Powers" is surely adequate to support the temporary enlistment of local police officers in the process of identifying persons who should not be entrusted with the possession of handguns. In short, the affirmative delegation of power in Article I provides ample authority for the congressional enactment.

Unlike the First Amendment, which prohibits the enactment of a category of laws that would otherwise be authorized by Article I, the Tenth Amendment imposes no restriction on the exercise of delegated powers. Using language that plainly refers only to powers that are "not" delegated to Congress, it provides: "The powers not delegated to the United States by the Constitution, nor prohibited by it to the States, are reserved to the States respectively, or to the people." The Amendment confirms the principle that the powers of the Federal Government are limited to those affirmatively granted by the Constitution, but it does not purport to limit the scope or the effectiveness of the exercise of powers that are delegated to Congress.

There is not a clause, sentence, or paragraph in the entire text of the Constitution of the United States that supports the proposition that a local police officer can ignore a command contained in a statute enacted by Congress pursuant to an express delegation of power enumerated in Article I.

II

Under the Articles of Confederation the National Government had the power to issue commands to the several sovereign states, but it had no authority to govern individuals directly. Thus, it raised an army and financed its operations by issuing requisitions to the constituent members of the Confederacy, rather than by creating federal agencies to draft soldiers or to impose taxes.

That method of governing proved to be unacceptable, not because it demeaned the sovereign character of the several States, but rather because it was cumbersome and inefficient. The basic change in the character of the government that the framers conceived was designed to enhance the power of the national government, not to provide some new, unmentioned immunity for state officers.

Indeed, the historical materials strongly suggest that the Founders intended to enhance the capacity of the federal government by empowering it — as a part of the new authority to make demands directly on individual citizens — to act through local officials. Hamilton made clear that the new Constitution, "by extending the authority of the federal head to the individual citizens of the several States, will enable the government to employ the ordinary magistracy of each, in the execution of its laws." The Federalist No. 27, at 180. Hamilton's meaning was unambiguous; the federal government was to have the power to demand that local officials implement national policy programs.

More specifically, during the debates concerning the ratification of the Constitution, it was assumed that state agents would act as tax collectors for the federal government. The Court's response to this powerful historical evidence is weak. The majority suggests that "none of these statements necessarily implies... Congress could impose these responsibilities without the consent of the States." No fair reading of these materials can justify such an interpretation. As Hamilton explained, the power of the government to act on "individual citizens" — including "employ[ing] the ordinary magistracy" of the States — was an answer to the problems faced by a central government that could act only directly "upon the States in their political or collective capacities." The Federalist, No. 27.

More importantly, the fact that Congress did elect to rely on state judges and the clerks of state courts to perform a variety of executive functions, is surely evidence of a contemporary understanding that their status as state officials did not immunize them from federal service. The majority's description of these early statutes is both incomplete and at times misleading.

III

The Court's "structural" arguments are not sufficient to rebut that presumption. The fact that the framers intended to preserve the sovereignty of the several States simply does not speak to the question whether individual state employees may be required to perform federal obligations, such as registering young adults for the draft, creating state emergency response commissions designed to manage the release of hazardous substances, collecting and reporting data on underground storage tanks that may pose an environmental hazard, and reporting traffic fatalities, and missing children, to a federal agency.

As we explained in Garcia v. San Antonio Metropolitan Transit Authority (1985): "[T]he principal means chosen by the framers to ensure the role of the States in the federal system lies in the structure of the Federal Government itself. It is no novelty to observe that the composition of the Federal Government was designed in large part to protect the States from overreaching by Congress." Given the fact that the Members of Congress are elected by the people of the several States, with each State receiving an equivalent number of Senators in order to ensure that even the smallest States have a powerful voice in the legislature, it is quite unrealistic to assume that they will ignore the sovereignty concerns of their constituents. It is far more reasonable to presume that their decisions to impose modest burdens on state officials from time to time reflect a considered judgment that the people in each of the States will benefit therefrom.

Recent developments demonstrate that the political safeguards protecting Our Federalism are effective. The majority expresses special concern that were its rule not adopted the Federal Government would be able to avail itself of the services of state government officials "at no cost to itself." But this specific problem of federal actions that have the effect of imposing so-called "unfunded mandates" on the States has been identified and meaningfully addressed by Congress in recent legislation. See Unfunded Mandates Reform Act of 1995, Pub.L. 104-4, 109 Stat. 48.

Nor is there force to the assumption undergirding the Court's entire opinion that if this trivial burden on state sovereignty is permissible, the entire structure of federalism will soon collapse. These cases do not involve any mandate to state legislatures to enact new rules. When legislative action, or even administrative rulemaking, is at issue, it may be appropriate for Congress either to pre-empt the State's lawmaking power and fashion the federal rule itself, or to respect the State's power to fashion its own rules. But this case, unlike any precedent in which the Court has held that Congress exceeded its powers, merely involves the imposition of modest duties on individual officers. The Court seems to accept the fact that Congress could require private persons, such as hospital executives or school administrators, to provide arms merchants with relevant information about a prospective purchaser's fitness to own a weapon; indeed, the Court does not disturb the conclusion that flows directly from our prior holdings that the burden on police officers would be permissible if a similar burden were also imposed on private parties with access to relevant data. A structural problem that vanishes when the statute affects private individuals as well as public officials is not much of a structural problem.

IV

Finally, the Court advises us that the "prior jurisprudence of this Court" is the most conclusive support for its position. That "prior jurisprudence" is New York v. United States. Our statements, taken in context, clearly did not decide the question presented here, whether state executive officials — as opposed to state legislators — may in appropriate circumstances be enlisted to implement federal policy. The "take title" provision at issue in New York was beyond Congress's authority to enact because it was "in principle . . . no different than a congressionally compelled subsidy from state governments to radioactive waste producers," almost certainly a legislative act.

The provision of the Brady Act that crosses the Court's newly defined constitutional threshold is more comparable to a statute requiring local police officers to report the identity of missing children to the Crime Control Center of the Department of Justice than to an offensive federal command to a sovereign state. If Congress believes that such a statute will benefit the people of the Nation, and serve the interests of cooperative federalism better than an enlarged federal bureaucracy, we should respect both its policy judgment and its appraisal of its constitutional power.

Accordingly, I respectfully dissent.

There has been one other Tenth Amendment decision in the current era: Reno v. Condon in January 2000. In Reno v. Condon, the Supreme Court rejected a Tenth Amendment challenge to the federal Driver's Privacy Protection Act that prohibits state departments of motor vehicles from releasing personal information such as home addresses and Social Security numbers. Strikingly, Reno v. Condon was a unanimous decision by the Supreme Court. As you read the decision, it is important to focus on how the Court distinguishes New York v. United States and Printz v. United States and what principles thus emerge for when Congress can and cannot regulate state governments.

Reno v. Condon

528 U.S. 141 (2000)

Chief Justice REHNQUIST delivered the opinion of the Court.

The Driver's Privacy Protection Act of 1994 (DPPA or Act) regulates the disclosure of personal information contained in the records of state motor vehicle departments (DMVs). We hold that in enacting this statute Congress did not run afoul of the federalism principles enunciated in New York v. United States (1992) and Printz v. United States (1997).

The DPPA regulates the disclosure and resale of personal information contained in the records of state DMVs. State DMVs require drivers and automobile owners to provide personal information, which may include a person's name, address, telephone number, vehicle description, Social Security number, medical information, and photograph, as a condition of obtaining a driver's license or registering an automobile. Congress found that many States, in turn, sell this personal information to individuals and businesses. These sales generate significant revenues for the States.

The DPPA establishes a regulatory scheme that restricts the States' ability to disclose a driver's personal information without the driver's consent. The DPPA generally prohibits any state DMV, or officer, employee, or contractor thereof, from "knowingly disclos[ing] or otherwise mak[ing] available to any person or entity personal information about any individual obtained by the department in connection with a motor vehicle record." The DPPA defines "personal information" as any information "that identifies an individual, including an individual's photograph, Social Security number, driver identification number, name, address (but not the 5-digit zip code), telephone number, and medical or disability information," but not including "information on vehicular accidents, driving violations, and driver's status."

The DPPA's provisions do not apply solely to States. The Act also regulates the resale and redisclosure of drivers' personal information by private persons who have obtained that information from a state DMV. The DPPA establishes several penalties to be imposed on States and private actors that fail to comply with its requirements.

South Carolina law conflicts with the DPPA's provisions. Under that law, the information contained in the State's DMV records is available to any person or entity that fills out a form listing the requester's name and address and stating that the information will not be used for telephone solicitation.

Following the DPPA's enactment, South Carolina and its Attorney General, respondent Condon, filed suit in the United States District Court for the District of South Carolina, alleging that the DPPA violates the Tenth and Eleventh Amendments to the United States Constitution.

We of course begin with the time-honored presumption that the DPPA is a "constitutional exercise of legislative power." The United States asserts that the DPPA is a proper exercise of Congress's authority to regulate interstate commerce under the Commerce Clause. The United States bases its Commerce Clause argument on the fact that the personal, identifying information that the DPPA regulates is a "thin[g] in interstate commerce," and that the sale or release of that information in interstate commerce is therefore a proper subject of congressional regulation. United States v. Lopez (1995). We agree with the United States' contention. The motor vehicle information which the States have historically sold is used by insurers, manufacturers, direct marketers, and others engaged in interstate commerce to contact drivers with customized solicitations. The information is also used in the stream of interstate commerce by various public and private entities for matters related to interstate motoring. Because drivers' information is, in this context, an article of commerce, its sale or release into the interstate stream of business is sufficient to support congressional regulation.

But the fact that drivers' personal information is, in the context of this case, an article in interstate commerce does not conclusively resolve the constitutionality of the DPPA. In New York and Printz, we held federal statutes invalid, not because Congress lacked legislative authority over the subject matter, but because those statutes violated the principles of federalism contained in the Tenth Amendment.

South Carolina contends that the DPPA violates the Tenth Amendment because it "thrusts upon the States all of the day-to-day responsibility for administering its complex provisions," and thereby makes "state officials the unwilling implementors of federal policy." South Carolina emphasizes that the DPPA requires the State's employees to learn and apply the Act's substantive restrictions, which are summarized above, and notes that these activities will consume the employees' time and thus the State's resources. South Carolina further notes that the DPPA's penalty provisions hang over the States as a potential punishment should they fail to comply with the Act.

We agree with South Carolina's assertion that the DPPA's provisions will require time and effort on the part of state employees, but reject the State's argument that the DPPA violates the principles laid down in either *New York* or *Printz*. We think, instead, that this case is governed by our decision in South Carolina v. Baker (1988). In *Baker*, we upheld a statute that prohibited States from issuing unregistered bonds because the law "regulate[d] state activities," rather than "seek[ing] to control or influence the manner in which States regulate private parties." We further noted:

> The NGA [National Governor's Association] nonetheless contends that §310 has commandeered the state legislative and administrative process because many state legislatures had to amend a substantial number of statutes in order to issue bonds in registered form and because state officials had to devote substantial effort to determine how best to implement a registered bond system. Such "commandeering" is, however, an inevitable consequence of regulating a state activity. Any federal regulation demands compliance. That a State wishing to engage in certain activity must take administrative and sometimes legislative action to comply with federal standards regulating that activity is a commonplace that presents no constitutional defect.

Like the statute at issue in *Baker*, the DPPA does not require the States in their sovereign capacity to regulate their own citizens. The DPPA regulates the States as the owners of databases. It does not require the South Carolina Legislature to enact any laws or regulations, and it does not require state officials to assist in the enforcement of federal statutes regulating private individuals. We accordingly conclude that the DPPA is consistent with the constitutional principles enunciated in *New York* and *Printz*.

As a final matter, we turn to South Carolina's argument that the DPPA is unconstitutional because it regulates the States exclusively. The essence of South Carolina's argument is that Congress may only regulate the States by means of "generally applicable" laws, or laws that apply to individuals as well as States. But we need not address the question whether general applicability is a constitutional requirement for federal regulation of the States, because the DPPA is generally applicable. The DPPA regulates the universe of entities that participate as suppliers to the market for motor vehicle information — the States as initial suppliers of the information in interstate commerce and private resellers or redisclosers of that information in commerce.

F. Preemption of State and Local Laws

As described above, Article VI of the Constitution contains the Supremacy Clause, which provides that the Constitution, and laws and treaties made pursuant to it, are the supreme law of the land. If there is a conflict between federal and state law, the federal law controls and the state law is invalidated because federal law is supreme. In Gibbons v. Ogden, 22 U.S. (9 Wheat.) 1, 211 (1824), Chief Justice John Marshall said: "[A]cts of the State Legislatures . . . [that] interfere with, or are contrary to the laws of Congress [are to be invalidated because] [i]n every such case, the act of Congress . . . is supreme; and the law of State, though enacted in the exercise of powers not controverted, must yield to it." Much more recently the Supreme Court declared: "[U]nder the Supremacy Clause, from which our pre-emption doctrine is derived, 'any state law, however clearly within a State's acknowledged power, which interferes with or is contrary to federal law, must yield.' " Gade v. National Solid Wastes Management Association (1992).

The difficulty, of course, is in deciding whether a particular state or local law is preempted by a specific federal statute or regulation. As in so many other areas of constitutional law, there is no clear rule for deciding whether a state or local law should be invalidated on preemption grounds. The Supreme Court once remarked that there is not "an infallible constitutional test or an exclusive constitutional yardstick. In the final analysis, there can be no one crystal clear distinctly marked formula."[144]

Traditionally, the Supreme Court has identified two major situations where preemption occurs. One is where a federal law expressly preempts state or local law. The other situation is where preemption is implied by a clear congressional intent to preempt state or local law.

In one of its most recent preemption cases, Gade v. National Solid Wastes Management, the Court summarized the tests for preemption:

> Pre-emption may be either express or implied, and is compelled whether Congress' command is explicitly stated in the statute's language or implicitly contained in its structure and purpose. Absent explicit pre-emptive language, we have recognized at least two types of implied pre-emption: field pre-emption, where the scheme of federal regulation is so pervasive as to make reasonable the inference that Congress left no room for the States to supplement it, and conflict pre-emption, where compliance with both federal and state regulations is a physical impossibility, or where state law stands as an obstacle to the accomplishment and execution of the full purposes and objectives of Congress.

Although these categories, or minor variations, are frequently used, they are not distinct. For example, even if there is statutory language expressly preempting state law, Congress rarely is clear about the scope of what is preempted or how particular situations should be handled. Courts must decide what is preempted, and this inevitably leads to an inquiry into congressional intent.[145] Conversely, implied preemption is often a function of both perceived congressional intent and the language used in the statute or regulation.

---

[144] Hines v. Davidowitz, 312 U.S. 52, 67 (1941).

[145] See Catherine Fisk, *The Last Article About the Language of ERISA Preemption? A Case Study of the Failure of Textualism*, 33 Harv. J. Legis. 37 (1996) (arguing that the distinction between express and implied preemption is one without much difference).

The Supreme Court has recognized that in both express and implied preemption the issue is discerning congressional intent. The Court has said that "[t]he question whether a certain state action is pre-empted by federal law is one of congressional intent."[146] It has remarked that "'[t]he purpose of Congress is the ultimate touchstone' in every preemption case."[147] The problem, of course, is that Congress's intent, especially as to the scope of preemption, is rarely expressed or clear. Therefore, although the Court purports to be finding congressional intent, it often is left to make guesses about purpose based on fragments of statutory language, random statements in the legislative history, and the degree of detail of the federal regulation.

For the sake of clarity, this section is organized parallel to the test for preemption articulated by the Supreme Court in Gade v. National Solid Wastes Management that is quoted above and that has been frequently repeated by the Court.[148] There are two major situations where preemption is found. First, express preemption occurs where there is explicit preemptive language. Second, there is implied preemption. The Court has identified three types of implied preemption. One is termed "field preemption" — where the scheme of federal law and regulation is "so pervasive as to make reasonable the inference that Congress left no room for the States to supplement it."[149] Another type of implied preemption is where there is a conflict between federal and state law. Even if federal law does not expressly preempt state law, preemption will be found where "compliance with both federal and state regulations is a physical impossibility."[150]

Implied preemption also will be found if state law impedes the achievement of a federal objective. Even if federal and state law are not mutually exclusive and even if there is no congressional expression of a desire to preempt state law, preemption will be found if state law "stands as an obstacle to the accomplishment and execution of the full purposes and objectives of Congress."[151]

Ultimately, preemption doctrines are about allocating governing authority between the federal and state governments. A broad view of preemption leaves less room for governance by state and local governments. It is for this reason that, at times, the Court has declared that the preemption analysis "start[s] with the assumption that the historic powers of the States [are] not to be superseded by . . . Federal Act unless that [is] the clear and manifest purpose of Congress."[152] But a very narrow preemption doctrine minimizes the reach of federal law and risks undermining the federal objectives.

The basic question is how willing courts should be to find preemption. Should there be a strong presumption against a court concluding that there is preemption? If so, what should be sufficient to overcome this presumption?

[146] Gade v. National Soild Wastes Management, 505 U.S. 88, 96 (1992) (citations omitted).
[147] See Medtronic Inc. v. Lohr, 518 U.S. 470, 485 (1996), quoting Retail Clerks v. Schermerhorn, 375 U.S. 96, 103 (1963).
[148] 505 U.S. at 96. See, e.g., Freightliner Corp. v. Myrick, 514 U.S. 208, 287 (1995); Wisconsin Public Intervenor v. Mortier, 501 U.S. 597, 604-605 (1991).
[149] Rice v. Santa Fe Elevator Corp., 331 U.S. 218, 230 (1947).
[150] Florida Lime & Avocado Growers, Inc v. Paul, 373 U.S. 132, 142-143 (1963).
[151] Hines v. Davidowitz, 312 U.S. 52, 67 (1941).
[152] Rice v. Santa Fe Elevator Corp., 331 U.S. 218, 230 (1947).

Or should courts be willing to find preemption whenever doing so would effectuate the purposes of federal law?

1. *Express Preemption*

Whenever Congress has the authority to legislate, Congress can make federal law exclusive in a field. The clearest way for Congress to do this is to expressly preclude state or local regulation in an area. Thus, some federal laws contain clauses that expressly preempt state and local laws. For example, the federal Employee Retirement Income Security Act of 1974 (ERISA) states that it "supersede[s] any and all State laws insofar as they may now or hereafter relate to any employee benefit plan."[153] The following case is illustrative of the issues that arise when courts deal with issues of express preemption.

Lorillard Tobacco Co. v. Reilly

533 U.S. 525 (2001)

O'CONNOR, J., delivered the opinion of the Court, Parts I, II-C, and II-D of which were unanimous; Parts II-A, II-B of which were joined by REHNQUIST, C.J., and SCALIA, KENNEDY, and THOMAS, JJ.

In January 1999, the Attorney General of Massachusetts promulgated comprehensive regulations governing the advertising and sale of cigarettes, smokeless tobacco, and cigars. The first question presented for our review is whether certain cigarette advertising regulations are pre-empted by the Federal Cigarette Labeling and Advertising Act (FCLAA).

I

In January 1999, pursuant to his authority to prevent unfair or deceptive practices in trade, the Massachusetts Attorney General (Attorney General) promulgated regulations governing the sale and advertisement of cigarettes, smokeless tobacco, and cigars. The purpose of the regulations is "to eliminate deception and unfairness in the way tobacco products are marketed, sold and distributed in Massachusetts in order to address the incidence of tobacco use by children under legal age . . . [and] in order to prevent access to such products by underage consumers."

The cigarette and smokeless tobacco regulations being challenged before this Court provide:

(2) Retail Outlet Sales Practices. Except as otherwise provided, it shall be an unfair or deceptive act or practice for any person who sells or distributes cigarettes or smokeless tobacco products through a retail outlet located within Massachusetts to engage in any of the following retail outlet sales practices:

(c) Using self-service displays of cigarettes or smokeless tobacco products;

---

[153] 29 U.S.C. §1144(a).

(d) Failing to place cigarettes and smokeless tobacco products out of the reach of all consumers, and in a location accessible only to outlet personnel.

(5) Advertising Restrictions. Except as provided, it shall be an unfair or deceptive act or practice for any manufacturer, distributor or retailer to engage in any of the following practices:

(a) Outdoor advertising, including advertising in enclosed stadiums and advertising from within a retail establishment that is directed toward or visible from the outside of the establishment, in any location that is within a 1,000 foot radius of any public playground, playground area in a public park, elementary school or secondary school;

(b) Point-of-sale advertising of cigarettes or smokeless tobacco products any portion of which is placed lower than five feet from the floor of any retail establishment which is located within a one thousand foot radius of any public playground, playground area in a public park, elementary school or secondary school, and which is not an adult-only retail establishment.

II

Before reaching the First Amendment issues, we must decide to what extent federal law pre-empts the Attorney General's regulations. The cigarette petitioners contend that the FCLAA pre-empts the Attorney General's cigarette advertising regulations.

A

In the FCLAA, Congress has crafted a comprehensive federal scheme governing the advertising and promotion of cigarettes. The FCLAA's pre-emption provision provides:

(a) Additional statements

No statement relating to smoking and health, other than the statement required by section 1333 of this title, shall be required on any cigarette package.

(b) State regulations

No requirement or prohibition based on smoking and health shall be imposed under State law with respect to the advertising or promotion of any cigarettes the packages of which are labeled in conformity with the provisions of this chapter.

The FCLAA's pre-emption provision does not cover smokeless tobacco or cigars.

In this case, our task is to identify the domain expressly pre-empted, because "an express definition of the pre-emptive reach of a statute . . . supports a reasonable inference . . . that Congress did not intend to pre-empt other matters." Congressional purpose is the "ultimate touchstone" of our inquiry. Because "federal law is said to bar state action in [a] fiel[d] of traditional state regulation," namely, advertising, we "wor[k] on the assumption that the historic police powers of the States [a]re not to be superseded by the Federal Act unless that [is] the clear and manifest purpose of Congress." In the pre-emption provision, Congress unequivocally precludes the requirement of any additional statements on "cigarette packages beyond those provided in [the statute]." Congress further precludes States or localities from imposing any requirement or prohibition based on smoking and health with respect to the advertising and promotion of cigarettes. Without question, the second clause is more expansive than the first; it employs far more sweeping language to describe the state action that is pre-empted. We must give meaning to each element of the pre-emption provision. We are aided in our interpretation by considering the predecessor pre-emption provision and the circumstances in which the current language was adopted.

In 1964, the groundbreaking Report of the Surgeon General's Advisory Committee on Smoking and Health concluded that "[c]igarette smoking is a health hazard of sufficient importance in the United States to warrant appropriate remedial action." In 1965, Congress enacted the FCLAA as a proactive measure in the face of impending regulation by federal agencies and the States. The purpose of the FCLAA was twofold: to inform the public adequately about the hazards of cigarette smoking, and to protect the national economy from interference due to diverse, nonuniform, and confusing cigarette labeling and advertising regulations with respect to the relationship between smoking and health. The FCLAA prescribed a label for cigarette packages. Section 5 of the FCLAA included a pre-emption provision in which "Congress spoke precisely and narrowly." Subsection 5(a) prohibited any requirement of additional statements on cigarette packaging. Subsection 5(b) provided that "[n]o statement relating to smoking and health shall be required in the advertising of any cigarettes the packages of which are labeled in conformity with the provisions of this Act."

In 1969, House and Senate committees held hearings about the health effects of cigarette smoking and advertising by the cigarette industry. The bill that emerged from the House of Representatives strengthened the warning and maintained the pre-emption provision. The Senate amended that bill, adding the ban on radio and television advertising, and changing the pre-emption language to its present form.

The final result was the Public Health Cigarette Smoking Act of 1969, in which Congress, following the Senate's amendments, made three significant changes to the FCLAA. First, Congress drafted a new label that read: "Warning: The Surgeon General Has Determined That Cigarette Smoking Is Dangerous to Your Health." Second, Congress declared it unlawful to advertise cigarettes on any medium of electronic communication subject to the jurisdiction of the FCC. Finally, Congress enacted the current pre-emption provision, which proscribes any "requirement or prohibition based on smoking and health . . . imposed under State law with respect to the advertising or promotion" of cigarettes. The new subsection 5(b) did not pre-empt regulation by federal agencies, freeing the FTC to impose warning requirements in cigarette advertising. The new pre-emption provision, like its predecessor, only applied to cigarettes, and not other tobacco products.

In 1984, Congress again amended the FCLAA in the Comprehensive Smoking Education Act. The purpose of the Act was to "provide a new strategy for making Americans more aware of any adverse health effects of smoking, to assure the

timely and widespread dissemination of research findings and to enable individuals to make informed decisions about smoking." The Act established a series of
warnings to appear on a rotating basis on cigarette packages and in cigarette advertising, and directed the Health and Human Services Secretary to create and
implement an educational program about the health effects of cigarette smoking.

The FTC has continued to report on trade practices in the cigarette industry.
In 1999, the first year since the master settlement agreement, the FTC reported
that the cigarette industry expended $8.24 billion on advertising and promotions,
the largest expenditure ever. Substantial increases were found in point-of-sale promotions, payments made to retailers to facilitate sales, and retail offers such as buy
one, get one free, or product giveaways. Substantial decreases, however, were
reported for outdoor advertising and transit advertising.

The scope and meaning of the current pre-emption provision become
clearer once we consider the original pre-emption language and the amendments to the FCLAA. Without question, "the plain language of the pre-emption
provision in the 1969 Act is much broader." Rather than preventing only "statements," the amended provision reaches all "requirement[s] or prohibition[s] . . .
imposed under State law." And, although the former statute reached only statements "in the advertising," the current provision governs "with respect to the
advertising or promotion" of cigarettes. Congress expanded the pre-emption provision with respect to the States, and at the same time, it allowed the FTC to regulate cigarette advertising. Congress also prohibited cigarette advertising in
electronic media altogether. Viewed in light of the context in which the current
pre-emption provision was adopted, we must determine whether the FCLAA
pre-empts Massachusetts' regulations governing outdoor and point-of-sale advertising of cigarettes.

B

Turning first to the language in the pre-emption provision relied upon by the
Court of Appeals, we reject the notion that the Attorney General's cigarette advertising regulations are not "with respect to" advertising and promotion. The Attorney General argues that the cigarette advertising regulations are not "based on
smoking and health," because they do not involve health-related content in cigarette advertising but instead target youth exposure to cigarette advertising. To be
sure, Members of this Court have debated the precise meaning of "based on
smoking and health," but we cannot agree with the Attorney General's narrow
construction of the phrase.

As Congress enacted the current pre-emption provision, Congress did not
concern itself solely with health warnings for cigarettes. In the 1969 amendments,
Congress not only enhanced its scheme to warn the public about the hazards of
cigarette smoking, but also sought to protect the public, including youth, from
being inundated with images of cigarette smoking in advertising. In pursuit of the
latter goal, Congress banned electronic media advertising of cigarettes. And to the
extent that Congress's contemplated additional targeted regulation of cigarette
advertising, it vested that authority in the FTC.

The context in which Congress crafted the current pre-emption provision leads us to conclude that Congress prohibited state cigarette advertising regulations motivated by concerns about smoking and health. Massachusetts has attempted to address the incidence of underage cigarette smoking by regulating advertising, much like Congress's ban on cigarette advertising in electronic media. At bottom, the concern about youth exposure to cigarette advertising is intertwined with the concern about cigarette smoking and health. Thus the Attorney General's attempt to distinguish one concern from the other must be rejected.

The Attorney General next claims that the State's outdoor and point-of-sale advertising regulations for cigarettes are not pre-empted because they govern the location, and not the content, of advertising. This is also Justice Stevens' main point with respect to pre-emption.

The content versus location distinction has some surface appeal. The pre-emption provision immediately follows the section of the FCLAA that prescribes warnings. The pre-emption provision itself refers to cigarettes "labeled in conformity with" the statute. But the content/location distinction cannot be squared with the language of the pre-emption provision, which reaches all "requirements" and "prohibitions" "imposed under State law." A distinction between the content of advertising and the location of advertising in the FCLAA also cannot be reconciled with Congress' own location-based restriction, which bans advertising in electronic media, but not elsewhere. We are not at liberty to pick and choose which provisions in the legislative scheme we will consider, but must examine the FCLAA as a whole.

Justice Stevens maintains that Congress did not intend to displace state regulation of the location of cigarette advertising. There is a critical distinction, however, between generally applicable zoning regulations, and regulations targeting cigarette advertising. The latter type of regulation, which is inevitably motivated by concerns about smoking and health, squarely contradicts the FCLAA. The FCLAA's comprehensive warnings, advertising restrictions, and pre-emption provision would make little sense if a State or locality could simply target and ban all cigarette advertising.

In sum, we fail to see how the FCLAA and its pre-emption provision permit a distinction between the specific concern about minors and cigarette advertising and the more general concern about smoking and health in cigarette advertising, especially in light of the fact that Congress crafted a legislative solution for those very concerns. We also conclude that a distinction between state regulation of the location as opposed to the content of cigarette advertising has no foundation in the text of the pre-emption provision. Congress pre-empted state cigarette advertising regulations like the Attorney General's because they would upset federal legislative choices to require specific warnings and to impose the ban on cigarette advertising in electronic media in order to address concerns about smoking and health. Accordingly, we hold that the Attorney General's outdoor and point-of-sale advertising regulations targeting cigarettes are pre-empted by the FCLAA.

Justice STEVENS, with whom Justices SOUTER, GINSBURG, and BREYER join, dissenting [on the preemption issue].

As the majority acknowledges, under prevailing principles, any examination of the scope of a preemption provision must "'start with the assumption that the historic police powers of the States [are] not to be superseded by . . . Federal Act unless that [is] the clear and manifest purpose of Congress.'" Cipollone v. Liggett Group, Inc. (1992). As the regulations at issue in this suit implicate two powers that lie at the heart of the States' traditional police power — the power to regulate land usage and the power to protect the health and safety of minors — our precedents require that the Court construe the preemption provision "narrow[ly]." If Congress's intent to preempt a particular category of regulation is ambiguous, such regulations are not preempted.

The text of the preemption provision must be viewed in context, with proper attention paid to the history, structure, and purpose of the regulatory scheme in which it appears. An assessment of the scope of a preemption provision must give effect to a "reasoned understanding of the way in which Congress intended the statute and its surrounding regulatory scheme to affect business, consumers, and the law."

This task, properly performed, leads inexorably to the conclusion that Congress did not intend to preempt state and local regulations of the location of cigarette advertising when it adopted the provision at issue in this suit. In both 1965 and 1969, Congress made clear the purposes of its regulatory endeavor, explaining with precision the federal policies motivating its actions. According to the acts, Congress adopted a "comprehensive Federal program to deal with cigarette labeling and advertising with respect to any relationship between smoking and health," for two reasons: (1) to inform the public that smoking may be hazardous to health and (2) to ensure that commerce and the interstate economy not be "impeded by diverse, nonuniform, and confusing cigarette labeling and advertising regulations with respect to any relationship between smoking and health."

In order to serve the second purpose it was necessary to preempt state regulation of the content of both cigarette labels and cigarette advertising. If one State required the inclusion of a particular warning on the package of cigarettes while another State demanded a different formulation, cigarette manufacturers would have been forced into the difficult and costly practice of producing different packaging for use in different States. To foreclose the waste of resources that would be entailed by such a patchwork regulatory system, Congress expressly precluded other regulators from requiring the placement on cigarette packaging of any "statement relating to smoking and health." Similar concerns applied to cigarette advertising. If different regulatory bodies required that different warnings or statements be used when cigarette manufacturers advertised their products, the text and layout of a company's ads would have had to differ from locale to locale. The resulting costs would have come with little or no health benefit. Moreover, given the nature of publishing, it might well have been the case that cigarette companies would not have been able to advertise in national publications without violating the laws of some jurisdictions. In response to these concerns, Congress adopted a parallel provision preempting state and local regulations requiring inclusion in cigarette advertising of any "statement relating to smoking and health."

There was, however, no need to interfere with state or local zoning laws or other regulations prescribing limitations on the location of signs or billboards. Laws prohibiting a cigarette company from hanging a billboard near a school in Boston in no way conflict with laws permitting the hanging of such a billboard in other jurisdictions. Nor would such laws even impose a significant administrative burden on would-be advertisers, as the great majority of localities impose general restrictions on signage, thus requiring advertisers to examine local law before posting signs whether or not cigarette-specific laws are preempted.

The legislative history of the provision also supports such a reading. The record does not contain any evidence that Congress intended to expand the scope of preemption beyond content restrictions. To the contrary, the Senate Report makes it clear that the changes merely "clarified" the scope of the original provision. Even as amended, Congress perceived the provision as "narrowly phrased" and emphasized that its purpose is to "avoid the chaos created by a multiplicity of conflicting regulations." According to the Senate Report, the changes "in no way affect the power of any state or political subdivision of any state with respect to . . . the sale of cigarettes to minors . . . or similar police regulations."

I am firmly convinced that, when Congress amended the preemption provision in 1969, it did not intend to expand the application of the provision beyond content regulations. I, therefore, find the conclusion inescapable that the zoning regulation at issue in this suit is not a "requirement or prohibition . . . with respect to . . . advertising" within the meaning of the 1969 Act. Even if I were not so convinced, however, I would still dissent from the Court's conclusion with regard to preemption, because the provision is, at the very least, ambiguous. The historical record simply does not reflect that it was Congress's " 'clear and manifest purpose,' " to preempt attempts by States to utilize their traditional zoning authority to protect the health and welfare of minors. Absent such a manifest purpose, Massachusetts and its sister States retain their traditional police powers.

Another more recent case concerning the scope of an express preemption provision was Riegel v. Medtronic, 128 S. Ct. 999 (2008). The Medical Devices Amendments of 1976, 21 U.S.C. §360k, preempt states from imposing "requirements" different from federal law after the Food and Drug Administration approves a medical device. The Court held, 8-1, that this preempts state tort liability against manufacturers for devices approved by the FDA. The Court reasoned that tort liability, like regulation, changes behavior and essentially creates requirements. Justice Ginsburg was alone in dissent and stressed that there should be a presumption against preemption. She said that if Congress wanted to preempt tort liability, it could do so, but that this law only preempted states from imposing "requirements."

2. Implied Preemption

a. Conflicts Preemption

If a federal and a state law are mutually exclusive, so that a person cannot comply with both, the state law is deemed preempted. This is called "conflicts preemption." The difficulty often lies in determining whether the laws actually conflict. For example, if the federal government sets a standard for air pollution control, but a state sets a stricter standard, is there conflicts preemption? It depends entirely on the intent of the federal government. If the federal government made the express decision to allow pollution above that level, then a stricter state regulation is in conflict with the federal law. But if the federal government was just setting the minimum standard, the floor of regulation, then a stricter state law is not in conflict with the federal law and would not be preempted. The following case raises exactly this issue.

Florida Lime & Avocado Growers, Inc. v. Paul, Director, Dept. of Agriculture of California

373 U.S. 132 (1963)

Justice BRENNAN delivered the opinion of the Court.

Section 792 of California's Agricultural Code, which gauges the maturity of avocados by oil content, prohibits the transportation or sale in California of avocados which contain "less than 8 per cent of oil, by weight excluding the skin and seed." In contrast, federal marketing orders approved by the Secretary of Agriculture gauge the maturity of avocados grown in Florida by standards which attribute no significance to oil content. This case presents the question of the constitutionality of the California statute insofar as it may be applied to exclude from California markets certain Florida avocados which, although certified to be mature under the federal regulations, do not uniformly meet the California requirement of 8% of oil.

We consider first appellants' challenge under the Supremacy Clause. That the California statute and the federal marketing orders embody different maturity tests is clear. However, this difference poses, rather than disposes of the problem before us.

A holding of federal exclusion of state law is inescapable and requires no inquiry into congressional design where compliance with both federal and state regulations is a physical impossibility for one engaged in interstate commerce. That would be the situation here if, for example, the federal orders forbade the picking and marketing of any avocado testing more than 7% oil, while the California test excluded from the State any avocado measuring less than 8% oil content. No such impossibility of dual compliance is presented on this record, however. As to those Florida avocados of the hybrid and Guatemalan varieties which were actually rejected by the California test, the District Court indicated that the Florida growers might have avoided such rejections by leaving the fruit on the trees beyond the earliest picking date permitted by the federal regulations, and nothing in the record contradicts that suggestion. Nor is there a lack of evidentiary support for the District Court's finding that the Florida varieties marketed in California "attain or exceed 8% oil content while in a prime commercial marketing condition," even though they may be "mature enough to be acceptable prior to the time that they reach that content." Thus the present record demonstrates no inevitable collision between the two schemes of regulation, despite the dissimilarity of the standards.

b. Preemption Because State Law Impedes the Achievement of a Federal Objective

Preemption also can be found if a state or local law is deemed to impede the achievement of a federal objective. In other words, even if the federal and state laws are not mutually exclusive, preemption will be found if the state or local law interferes with attaining a federal legislative goal. In applying this type of preemption, the courts must determine the federal objective and must decide the point at which state regulation unduly interferes with achieving the goal. The following cases illustrate this inquiry.

Pacific Gas & Electric Co. v. State Energy Resources Conservation & Development Commn.
461 U.S. 190 (1983)

Justice WHITE delivered the opinion of the Court.

The turning of swords into plowshares has symbolized the transformation of atomic power into a source of energy in American society. To facilitate this development the federal government relaxed its monopoly over fissionable materials and nuclear technology, and in its place, erected a complex scheme to promote the civilian development of nuclear energy, while seeking to safeguard the public and the environment from the unpredictable risks of a new technology. Early on, it was decided that the states would continue their traditional role in the regulation of electricity production. The interrelationship of federal and state authority in the nuclear energy field has not been simple; the federal regulatory structure has been frequently amended to optimize the partnership.

This case emerges from the intersection of the federal government's efforts to ensure that nuclear power is safe with the exercise of the historic state authority over the generation and sale of electricity. At issue is whether provisions in the 1976 amendments to California's Warren-Alquist Act, which condition the construction of nuclear plants on findings by the State Energy Resources Conservation and Development Commission that adequate storage facilities and means of disposal are available for nuclear waste, are preempted by the Atomic Energy Act of 1954.

I

A nuclear reactor must be periodically refueled and the "spent fuel" removed. This spent fuel is intensely radioactive and must be carefully stored. The general practice is to store the fuel in a water-filled pool at the reactor site. For many years, it was assumed that this fuel would be reprocessed; accordingly, the storage pools were designed as short-term holding facilities with limited storage capacities. As expectations for reprocessing remained unfulfilled, the spent fuel accumulated in the storage pools, creating the risk that nuclear reactors would have to be shut down. This could occur if there were insufficient room in the pool to store spent fuel and also if there were not enough space to hold the entire fuel core when certain inspections or emergencies required unloading of the reactor. In recent years, the problem has taken on special urgency. Some 8,000 metric tons of spent nuclear fuel have already accumulated, and it is projected that by the year 2000 there will be some 72,000 metric tons of spent fuel. Government studies indicate that a number of reactors could be forced to shut down in the near future due to the inability to store spent fuel.

There is a second dimension to the problem. Even with water-pools adequate to store safely all the spent fuel produced during the working lifetime of the reactor, permanent disposal is needed because the wastes will remain radioactive for thousands of years. A number of long-term nuclear waste management strategies have been extensively examined. These range from sinking the wastes in stable deep seabeds, to placing the wastes beneath ice sheets in Greenland and Antarctica, to ejecting the wastes into space by rocket. The greatest attention has been focused on disposing of the wastes in subsurface geologic repositories such as salt deposits. Problems of how and where to store nuclear wastes has engendered considerable scientific, political, and public debate. There are both safety and economic aspects to the nuclear waste issue: first, if not properly stored, nuclear wastes might leak and endanger both the environment and human health; second, the lack of a long-term disposal option increases the risk that the insufficiency of interim storage space for spent fuel will lead to reactor-shutdowns, rendering nuclear energy an unpredictable and uneconomical adventure.

The California laws at issue here are responses to these concerns. Two [provisions] are before us. Section 25524.1(b) provides that before additional nuclear plants may be built, the Energy Commission must determine on a case-by-case basis that there will be "adequate capacity" for storage of a plant's spent fuel rods "at the time such nuclear facility requires such . . . storage." The law also requires that each utility provide continuous, on-site, "full core reserve storage capacity" in order to permit storage of the entire reactor core if it must be removed to permit repairs of the reactor.

Section 25524.2 deals with the long-term solution to nuclear wastes. This section imposes a moratorium on the certification of new nuclear plants until the Energy Commission "finds that there has been developed and that the United States through its authorized agency has approved and there exists a demonstrated technology or means for the disposal of high-level nuclear waste." "Disposal" is defined as a "method for the permanent and terminal disposition of high-level nuclear waste. . . ." Such a finding must be reported to the state legislature, which may nullify it.

[II]

Petitioners, the United States, and supporting amici, present three major lines of argument as to why §25524.2 is preempted. First, they submit that the statute — because it regulates construction of nuclear plants and because it is allegedly predicated on safety concerns — ignores the division between federal and state authority created by the Atomic Energy Act, and falls within the field that the federal government has preserved for its own exclusive control. Second, the statute, and the judgments that underlie it, conflict with decisions concerning the nuclear waste disposal issue made by Congress and the Nuclear Regulatory Commission. Third, the California statute frustrates the federal goal of developing nuclear technology as a source of energy. We consider each of these contentions in turn.

A

Even a brief perusal of the Atomic Energy Act reveals that, despite its comprehensiveness, it does not at any point expressly require the States to construct or authorize nuclear power plants or prohibit the States from deciding, as an absolute or conditional matter, not to permit the construction of any further reactors. Instead, petitioners argue that the Act is intended to preserve the federal government as the sole regulator of all matters nuclear, and that §25524.2 falls within the scope of this impliedly preempted field. But as we view the issue, Congress, in passing the 1954 Act and in subsequently amending it, intended that the federal government should regulate the radiological safety aspects involved in the construction and operation of a nuclear plant, but that the States retain their traditional responsibility in the field of regulating electrical utilities for determining questions of need, reliability, cost, and other related state concerns.

Need for new power facilities, their economic feasibility, and rates and services, are areas that have been characteristically governed by the States. [This] is not particularly controversial. But deciding how §25524.2 is to be construed and classified is a more difficult proposition. At the outset, we emphasize that the statute does not seek to regulate the construction or operation of a nuclear powerplant. It would clearly be impermissible for California to attempt to do so, for such regulation, even if enacted out of non-safety concerns, would nevertheless directly conflict with the NRC's exclusive authority over plant construction and operation. Respondents appear to concede as much. Respondents do broadly argue, however, that although safety regulation of nuclear plants by states is forbidden, a state may completely prohibit new construction until its safety concerns are satisfied by the federal government. We reject this line of reasoning. State safety regulation is not preempted only when it conflicts with federal law. Rather, the federal government has occupied the entire field of nuclear safety concerns, except the limited powers expressly ceded to the states. A state moratorium on nuclear construction grounded in safety concerns falls squarely within the prohibited field. Moreover, a state judgment that nuclear power is not safe enough to be further developed would conflict directly with the countervailing judgment of the NRC, that nuclear construction may proceed notwithstanding extant uncertainties as to waste disposal. A state prohibition on nuclear construction for safety reasons would also be in the teeth of the Atomic Energy Act's objective to insure that nuclear technology be safe enough for widespread development and use — and would be preempted for that reason.

That being the case, it is necessary to determine whether there is a non-safety rationale for §25524.2. California has maintained, and the Court of Appeals agreed, that §25524.2 was aimed at economic problems, not radiation hazards. The California Assembly Committee on Resources, Land Use, and Energy, which proposed a package of bills including §25524.2, reported that the waste disposal problem was "largely economic or the result of poor planning, not safety related." Without a permanent means of disposal, the nuclear waste problem could become critical leading to unpredictably high costs to contain the problem or, worse, shutdowns in reactors.

B

Petitioners' second major argument concerns federal regulation aimed at the nuclear waste disposal problem itself. It is contended that §25524.2 conflicts with federal regulation of nuclear waste disposal, with the NRC's decision that it is permissible to continue to license reactors, notwithstanding uncertainty surrounding the waste disposal problem, and with Congress' recent passage of legislation directed at that problem.

Pursuant to its authority under the Act, the AEC, and later the NRC, promulgated extensive and detailed regulations concerning the operation of nuclear facilities and the handling of nuclear materials. The NRC's imprimatur, however, indicates only that it is safe to proceed with such plants, not that it is economically wise to do so. Because the NRC order does not and could not compel a utility to develop a nuclear plant, compliance with both it and §25524.2 are possible. Moreover, because the NRC's regulations are aimed at insuring that plants are safe, not necessarily that they are economical, §25524.2 does not interfere with the objective of the federal regulation.

C

Finally, it is strongly contended that §25524.2 frustrates the Atomic Energy Act's purpose to develop the commercial use of nuclear power. It is well established that state law is preempted if it "stands as an obstacle to the accomplishment of the full purposes and objectives of Congress." Hines v. Davidowitz (1941).

There is little doubt that a primary purpose of the Atomic Energy Act was, and continues to be, the promotion of nuclear power. The Act itself states that it is a program "to encourage widespread participation in the development and utilization of atomic energy for peaceful purposes to the maximum extent consistent with the common defense and security and with the health and safety of the public."

The Court of Appeals is right, however, that the promotion of nuclear power is not to be accomplished "at all costs." The elaborate licensing and safety provisions and the continued preservation of state regulation in traditional areas belie that. Moreover, Congress has allowed the States to determine — as a matter of economics — whether a nuclear plant vis-à-vis a fossil fuel plant should be built. The decision of California to exercise that authority does not, in itself, constitute a basis for preemption. Therefore, while the argument of petitioners and the United States has considerable force, the legal reality remains that Congress has left sufficient authority in the states to allow the development of nuclear power to be slowed or even stopped for economic reasons. Given this statutory scheme, it is for Congress to rethink the division of regulatory authority in light of its possible exercise by the states to undercut a federal objective. The courts should not assume the role which our system assigns to Congress.

c. Preemption Because Federal Law Occupies the Field

A final form of implied preemption is where federal law wholly occupies a field. Even though federal law does not expressly preempt state law, preemption will be found if there is a clear congressional intent to have federal law occupy a particular area of law. The most important example of this is immigration law. As the following case indicates, the Supreme Court long has held that federal law is exclusive in regulating immigration.

Hines, Secretary of Labor & Industry of Pennsylvania v. Davidowitz

312 U.S. 52 (1941)

Justice BLACK delivered the opinion of the Court.

This case involves the validity of an Alien Registration Act adopted by the Commonwealth of Pennsylvania. The Act, passed in 1939, requires every alien 18 years or over, with certain exceptions, to register once each year; provide such information as is required by the statute, plus any "other information and details" that the Department of Labor and Industry may direct; pay $1 as an annual registration fee; receive an alien identification card and carry it at all times; show the card whenever it may be demanded by any police officer or any agent of the Department of Labor and Industry; and exhibit the card as a condition precedent to registering a motor vehicle in his name or obtaining a license to operate one. The Department of Labor and Industry is charged with the duties of classifying the registrations for "the purpose of ready reference," and furnishing a copy of the classification to the Pennsylvania Motor Police. Nonexempt aliens who fail to register are subject to a fine of not more than $100 or imprisonment for not more than 60 days, or both. For failure to carry an identification card or for failure to show it upon proper demand, the punishment is a fine of not more than $10, or imprisonment for not more than 10 days, or both.

But in 1940, Congress enacted a federal Alien Registration Act. We must therefore pass upon the state Act in the light of the Congressional Act. The federal Act provides for a single registration of aliens 14 years of age and over; detailed information specified by the Act, plus "such additional matters as may be prescribed by the Commissioner, with the approval of the Attorney General"; finger-printing of all registrants; and secrecy of the federal files, which can be "made available only to such persons or agencies as may be designated by the Commissioner, with the approval of the Attorney General." No requirement that aliens carry a registration card to be exhibited to police or others is embodied in the law, and only the wilful failure to register is made a criminal offense; punishment is fixed at a fine of not more than $1000, imprisonment for not more than 6 months, or both.

The basic subject of the state and federal laws is identical — registration of aliens as a distinct group. That the supremacy of the national power in the general field of foreign affairs, including power over immigration, naturalization and deportation, is made clear by the Constitution was pointed out by authors of The Federalist in 1787, and has since been given continuous recognition by this Court. When the national government by treaty or statute has established rules and regulations touching the rights, privileges, obligations or burdens of aliens as such, the treaty or statute is the supreme law of the land. No state can add to or take from the force and effect of such treaty or statute for Article VI of the Constitution provides that "This Constitution, and the Laws of the United States which shall be made in Pursuance thereof; and all Treaties made, or which shall be made, under the Authority of the United States, shall be the supreme Law of the Land; and the Judges in every State shall be bound thereby, any Thing in the Constitution or Laws of any State to the Contrary notwithstanding." The Federal Government, representing as it does the collective interests of the forty-eight states, is entrusted with full and exclusive responsibility for the conduct of affairs with foreign sovereignties.

One of the most important and delicate of all international relationships, recognized immemorially as a responsibility of government, has to do with the protection of the just rights of a country's own nationals when those nationals are in another country. Experience has shown that international controversies of the gravest moment, sometimes even leading to war, may arise from real or imagined wrongs to another's subjects inflicted, or permitted, by a government. This country, like other nations, has entered into numerous treaties of amity and commerce since its inception — treaties entered into under express constitutional authority, and binding upon the states as well as the nation. Among those treaties have been many which not only promised and guaranteed broad rights and privileges to aliens sojourning in our own territory, but secured reciprocal promises and guarantees for our own citizens while in other lands. And apart from treaty obligations, there has grown up in the field of international relations a body of customs defining with more or less certainty the duties owing by all nations to alien residents — duties which our State Department has often successfully insisted foreign nations must recognize as to our nationals abroad. In general, both treaties and international practices have been aimed at preventing injurious discriminations against aliens.

It cannot be doubted that both the state and the federal registration laws belong "to that class of laws which concern the exterior relation of this whole nation with other nations and governments." Consequently the regulation of aliens is so intimately blended and intertwined with responsibilities of the national government that where it acts, and the state also acts on the same subject, "the act of congress, or the treaty, is supreme; and the law of the state, though enacted in the exercise of powers not controverted, must yield to it." And where the federal government, in the exercise of its superior authority in this field, has enacted a complete scheme of regulation and has therein provided a standard for the registration of aliens, states cannot, inconsistently with the purpose of Congress, conflict or interfere with, curtail or complement, the federal law, or enforce additional or auxiliary regulations.

Having the constitutional authority so to do, Congress has provided a standard for alien registration in a single integrated and all-embracing system in order to obtain the information deemed to be desirable in connection with aliens, When it made this addition to its uniform naturalization and immigration laws, it plainly manifested a purpose to do so in such a way as to protect the personal liberties of law-abiding aliens through one uniform national registration system, and to leave them free from the possibility of inquisitorial practices and police surveillance that might not only affect our international relations but might also generate the very disloyalty which the law has intended guarding against.

Justice STONE, dissenting.

Undoubtedly Congress, in the exercise of its power to legislate in aid of powers granted by the Constitution to the national government may greatly enlarge the exercise of federal authority and to an extent which need not now be defined, it may, if such is its will, thus subtract from the powers which might otherwise be exercised by the states. Assuming, as the Court holds, that Congress could constitutionally set up an exclusive registration system for aliens, I think it has not done so and that it is not the province of the courts to do that which Congress has failed to do.

At a time when the exercise of the federal power is being rapidly expanded through Congressional action, it is difficult to overstate the importance of safeguarding against such diminution of state power by vague inferences as to what Congress might have intended if it had considered the matter or by reference to our own conceptions of a policy which Congress has not expressed and which is not plainly to be inferred from the legislation which it has enacted. The Judiciary of the United States should not assume to strike down a state law which is immediately concerned with the social order and safety of its people unless the statute plainly and palpably violates some right granted or secured to the national government by the Constitution or similarly encroaches upon the exercise of some authority delegated to the United States for the attainment of objects of national concern.

G. The Dormant Commerce Clause

The "dormant Commerce Clause" is the principle that state and local laws are unconstitutional if they place an undue burden on interstate commerce. There is no constitutional provision that expressly declares that states may not burden interstate commerce. Rather, the Supreme Court has inferred this from the grant of power to Congress in Article I, §8, to regulate commerce among the states.

If Congress has legislated, the issue is whether the federal law preempts the state or local law — the issue discussed above. But even if Congress has not acted or no preemption is found, the state or local law can be challenged on the ground that it excessively burdens commerce among the states. In other words, even if Congress has not acted — even if its commerce power lies dormant, state and local laws still can be challenged as unduly impeding interstate commerce. As Felix Frankfurter explained: "[T]he doctrine [is] that the Commerce Clause, by its own force and without national legislation, puts it into the power of the Court to place limits on state authority."[154]

The Commerce Clause thus has two distinct functions. One is an authorization for congressional actions. The scope of Congress's power to legislate under the Commerce Clause is discussed in Chapter 6. The other function of the Commerce Clause is in limiting state and local regulation. This is the dormant or "negative" Commerce Clause.[155]

The dormant Commerce Clause is not the only way of challenging state laws that burden interstate commerce, especially if the state or local law discriminates against out-of-staters. For example, if the state or local government discriminates against out-of-staters with regard to a fundamental right or important economic activities, a challenge can be brought under the Privileges and Immunities Clause of Article IV, §2. The Privileges and Immunities Clause is discussed in the next subsection. Also, laws that discriminate against out-of-staters can be challenged under the Equal Protection Clause of the Fourteenth Amendment.

The discussion of the dormant Commerce Clause begins in part 1 of this section by examining whether there should be a dormant Commerce Clause. Understanding the policies underlying the dormant Commerce Clause is important in considering the cases that follow. Also, there is a debate among Justices and scholars as to whether there should be a dormant Commerce Clause and under what circumstances courts should use it.

Part 2 then describes the Court's nineteenth-century dormant Commerce Clause cases. These older precedents often are invoked in modern decisions, even though the tests used in contemporary cases are quite different from those used in the nineteenth century.

Part 3 presents the key cases concerning the contemporary dormant Commerce Clause. The central question in dormant Commerce Clause analysis is whether the state or local law discriminates against out-of-staters or whether it treats in-staters and out-of-staters alike. If a law is found to discriminate, it is very likely to be declared unconstitutional. If a law is deemed non-discriminatory, the law is likely to be upheld. Therefore, part 3 proceeds in three steps: First, how is it

---

[154] Felix Frankfurter, *The Commerce Clause under Marshall, Taney and Waits*, 18 (1937).

[155] There is a vast literature on the dormant Commerce Clause. Some of the most important and best articles include Donald H. Regan, *The Supreme Court and State. Protectionism: Making Sense of the Dormant Commerce Clause*, 84 Mich. L. Rev. 1091 (1986); Julian M. Eule, *Laying the Dormant Commerce Clause to Rest*, 91 Yale L.J. 425 (1982).

determined whether a law is discriminatory? Second, what is the analysis for laws that are discriminatory? And finally, what is the analysis for laws that are not discriminatory?

Part 4 then considers exceptions to the dormant Commerce Clause, that is, situations where laws that otherwise would violate the dormant Commerce Clause will be allowed. One exception is if Congress approves the state or local action. Congress has plenary power to regulate commerce among the states and may authorize laws that otherwise would violate the dormant Commerce Clause. The other major exception is termed "the market participant exception." Under the market participant exception, a state or local government may favor its own citizens in receiving benefits from state or local governments or in dealing with government-owned businesses.

1. Why a Dormant Commerce Clause?

Congress always has the authority under its commerce power to preempt state or local regulation of commerce. Therefore, Congress could invalidate any state or local law that it deems to place an undue burden on interstate commerce. The crucial issue with regard to the dormant Commerce Clause is whether the judiciary, in the absence of congressional action, should invalidate state and local laws because they place an undue burden on interstate commerce.

The Supreme Court explains the justifications for the dormant Commerce Clause in the following case.

H.P. Hood & Sons, Inc. v. Du Mond, Commissioner of Agriculture & Markets of New York

336 U.S. 525 (1949)

Justice JACKSON delivered the opinion of the Court.

This case concerns the power of the State of New York to deny additional facilities to acquire and ship milk in interstate commerce where the grounds of denial are that such limitation upon interstate business will protect and advance local economic interests.

H.P. Hood & Sons, Inc., a Massachusetts corporation, has long distributed milk and its products to inhabitants of Boston. That city obtains about 90% of its fluid milk from states other than Massachusetts. Dairies located in New York State since about 1900 have been among the sources of Boston's supply, their contribution having varied but during the last ten years approximately 8%.

The controversy concerns a proposed additional plant for the same kind of operation at Greenwich, New York [which the state seeks to deny to the Massachusetts company].

Our decision in a milk litigation most relevant to the present controversy deals with the converse of the present situation. Baldwin v. G. A. F. Seelig, Inc. In that case, New York placed conditions and limitations on the local sale of milk imported from Vermont designed in practical effect to exclude it, while here its order proposes to limit the local facilities for purchase of additional milk so as to withhold milk from export. The State agreed then, as now, that the Commerce Clause prohibits it from directly curtailing movement of milk into or out of the State. This Court unanimously rejected the State's contention in the *Seelig* case and held that the Commerce Clause, even in the absence of congressional action, prohibits such regulations for such ends. The opinion was by Mr. Justice Cardozo, experienced in the milk problems of New York and favorably disposed toward the efforts of the State to control the industry. It recognized, as do we, broad power in the State to protect its inhabitants against perils to health or safety, fraudulent traders and highway hazards even by use of measures which bear adversely upon interstate commerce. But it laid repeated emphasis upon the principle that the State may not promote its own economic advantages by curtailment or burdening of interstate commerce.

The Constitution, said Mr. Justice Cardozo for the unanimous Court, "was framed upon the theory that the peoples of the several states must sink or swim together, and that in the long run prosperity and salvation are in union and not division." He reiterated that the economic objective, as distinguished from any health, safety and fair-dealing purpose of the regulation, was the root of its invalidity. The action of the State would "neutralize the economic consequences of free trade among the states." "Such a power, if exerted, will set a barrier to traffic between one state and another as effective as if customs duties, equal to the price differential, had been laid upon the thing transported." "If New York, in order to promote the economic welfare of her farmers, may guard them against competition, with the cheaper prices of Vermont, the door has been opened to rivalries and reprisals that were meant to be averted by subjecting commerce between the states to the power of the nation." And again, "Neither the power to tax nor the police power may be used by the state of destination with the aim and effect of establishing an economic barrier against competition with the products of another state or the labor of its residents. Restrictions so contrived are an unreasonable clog upon the mobility of commerce. They set up what is equivalent to a rampart of customs duties designed to neutralize advantages belonging to the place of origin. They are thus hostile in conception as well as burdensome in result."

This distinction between the power of the State to shelter its people from menaces to their health or safety and from fraud, even when those dangers emanate from interstate commerce, and its lack of power to retard, burden or constrict the flow of such commerce for their economic advantage, is one deeply rooted in both our history and our law.

When victory relieved the Colonies from the pressure for solidarity that war had exerted, a drift toward anarchy and commercial warfare between states began. "[E]ach state would legislate according to its estimate of its own interests, the importance of its own products, and the local advantages or disadvantages of its position in a political or commercial view." This came "to threaten at once the peace and safety of the Union." Story, The Constitution. The sole purpose for which Virginia initiated the movement which ultimately produced the Constitution was "to take into consideration the trade of the United States; to examine the relative situations and trade of the said states; to consider how far a uniform system in their commercial regulation may be necessary to their common interest and their permanent harmony" and for that purpose the General Assembly of Virginia in January of 1786 named commissioners and proposed their meeting with those from other states. The desire of the Forefathers to federalize regulation of foreign and interstate commerce stands in sharp contrast to their jealous preservation of power over their internal affairs. No other federal power was so universally assumed to be necessary, no other state power was so readily relinquished.

The necessity of centralized regulation of commerce among the states was so obvious and so fully recognized that the few words of the Commerce Clause were little illuminated by debate. But the significance of the clause was not lost and its effect was immediate and salutary.

The material success that has come to inhabitants of the states which make up this federal free trade unit has been the most impressive in the history of commerce, but the established interdependence of the states only emphasizes the necessity of protecting interstate movement of goods against local burdens and repressions. We need only consider the consequences if each of the few states that produce copper, lead, high-grade iron ore, timber, cotton, oil or gas should decree that industries located in that state shall have priority. What fantastic rivalries and dislocations and reprisals would ensue if such practices were begun! Or suppose that the field of discrimination and retaliation be industry. May Michigan provide that automobiles cannot be taken out of that State until local dealers' demands are fully met? Would she not have every argument in the favor of such a statute that can be offered in support of New York's limiting sales of milk for out-of-state shipment to protect the economic interests of her competing dealers and local consumers? Could Ohio then pounce upon the rubber-tire industry, on which she has a substantial grip, to retaliate for Michigan's auto monopoly?

Our system, fostered by the Commerce Clause, is that every farmer and every craftsman shall be encouraged to produce by the certainty that he will have free access to every market in the Nation, that no home embargoes will withhold his export, and no foreign state will by customs duties or regulations exclude them. Likewise, every consumer may look to the free competition from every producing area in the Nation to protect him from exploitation by any. Such was the vision of the Founders; such has been the doctrine of this Court which has given it reality.

The State, however, insists that denial of the license for a new plant does not restrict or obstruct interstate commerce, because petitioner has been licensed at its other plants without condition or limitation as to the quantities it may purchase. Hence, it is said, all that has been denied petitioner is a local convenience — that of being able to buy and receive at Greenwich, quantities of milk it is free to buy at Eagle Bridge and Salem. It suggests that, by increased efficiency or enlarged capacity at its other plants, petitioner might sufficiently increase its supply through those facilities.

The weakness of this contention is that a buyer has to buy where there is a willing seller, and the peculiarities of the milk business necessitate location of a receiving and cooling station for nearby producers. The Commissioner has not made and there is nothing to persuade us that he could have made findings that petitioner can obtain such additional supplies through its existing facilities;

indeed he found that "applicant has experienced some difficulty during the flush season because of the inability of the plant facilities to handle the milk by 9 A.M.," the time its receipt is required by Boston health authorities unless it is cooled by the farmer before delivery, and a substantial part of it is not.

The Court in Hood & Sons v. Du Mond presents the traditional arguments for having a dormant Commerce Clause. First, there is a historical argument for the dormant Commerce Clause: The framers intended to prevent state laws that interfered with interstate commerce. Second, there is an economic justification for the dormant Commerce Cause: The economy is better off if state and local laws impeding interstate commerce are invalidated. As Professor Regan notes, "protectionism is inefficient because it diverts business away from presumptively low-cost producers without any colorable justification in terms of a benefit that deserves approval from the point of view of the nation as a whole."[156]

Third, there is a political justification for the dormant Commerce Clause: States and their citizens should not be harmed by laws in other states where they lack political representation. In McCulloch v. Maryland, the Supreme Court invalidated Maryland's tax on the Bank of the United States, in part, because it was a tax that ultimately would be borne by those in other states that obviously did not have representation in the Maryland political process.[157] Similarly, the political process cannot be trusted when a state is helping itself at the expense of out-of-staters who have no representation. Justice Stone explained: "Underlying the stated rule has been the thought, often expressed in judicial opinion, that when the regulation is of such a character that its burden falls principally upon those without the state, legislative action is not likely to be subjected to those political restraints which are normally exerted on legislation where it affects adversely some interests within the state."[158]

But others argue against the existence of a dormant Commerce Clause. The strongest recent criticism of the existence of the dormant Commerce Clause was by Justice Clarence Thomas in a dissenting opinion in Camps Newfound/ Owatonna, Inc. v. Town of Harrison, 520 U.S. 564 (1997). The majority of the Supreme Court declared unconstitutional on dormant Commerce Clause grounds a state property tax because its exemption for property owned by charitable institutions excluded organizations operated principally for the benefit of nonresidents.

Justice Thomas dissented and strongly criticized the dormant Commerce Clause, especially in instances where the state does not discriminate against out-of-staters. Thomas wrote:

---

[156] Regan, *supra* note 155, at 1118.
[157] 17 U.S. (4 Wheat.) 316, 429-430 (1819), presented in Chapter 6.
[158] South Carolina State Highway Department v. Barnwell Brothers, Inc., 303 U.S. 177, 185 (1938).

The negative Commerce Clause has no basis in the text of the Constitution, makes little sense, and has proved virtually unworkable in application. In one fashion or another, every Member of the current Court and a goodly number of our predecessors have at least recognized these problems, if not been troubled by them.

To cover its exercise of judicial power in an area for which there is no textual basis, the Court has historically offered two different theories in support of its negative Commerce Clause jurisprudence. The first theory posited was that the Commerce Clause itself constituted an exclusive grant of power to Congress. See, e.g., Passenger Cases (1849). The "exclusivity" rationale was likely wrong from the outset, however. And, in any event, the Court has long since "repudiated" the notion that the Commerce Clause operates as an exclusive grant of power to Congress, and thereby forecloses state action respecting interstate commerce. Freeman v. Hewit (1946) (Rutledge, J., concurring). Indeed, the Court's early view that the Commerce Clause, on its own, prohibited state impediments to interstate commerce such that "Congress cannot re-grant, or in any manner reconvey to the states that power," Cooley v. Board of Wardens of Port of Philadelphia ex rel. Soc. for Relief of Distressed Pilots (1852), quickly proved untenable. And, as this Court's definition of the scope of congressional authority under the positive Commerce Clause has expanded, the exclusivity rationale has moved from untenable to absurd.

The second theory offered to justify creation of a negative Commerce Clause is that Congress, by its silence, pre-empts state legislation. See Robbins v. Shelby County Taxing Dist. (1887) (asserting that congressional silence evidences congressional intent that there be no state regulation of commerce). In other words, we presumed that congressional "inaction" was "equivalent to a declaration that inter-State commerce shall be free and untrammelled." Welton v. Missouri (1876). To the extent that the "pre-emption-by-silence" rationale ever made sense, it, too, has long since been rejected by this Court in virtually every analogous area of the law.

Even were we wrongly to assume that congressional silence evidenced a desire to pre-empt some undefined category of state laws, and an intent to delegate such policy-laden categorization to the courts, treating unenacted congressional intent as if it were law would be constitutionally dubious.

In sum, neither of the Court's proffered theoretical justifications — exclusivity or pre-emption-by-silence — currently supports our negative Commerce Clause jurisprudence, if either ever did. Despite the collapse of its theoretical foundation, I suspect we have nonetheless adhered to the negative Commerce Clause because we believed it necessary to check state measures contrary to the perceived spirit, if not the actual letter, of the Constitution.

Moreover, our negative Commerce Clause jurisprudence has taken us well beyond the invalidation of obviously discriminatory taxes on interstate commerce. We have used the Clause to make policy-laden judgments that we are ill equipped and arguably unauthorized to make. Any test that requires us to assess (1) whether a particular statute serves a "legitimate" local public interest; (2) whether the effects of the statute on interstate commerce are merely "incidental" or "clearly excessive in relation to the putative benefits"; (3) the "nature" of the local interest; and (4) whether there are alternative means of furthering the local interest that have a "lesser impact" on interstate commerce, and even then makes the question "one of degree," surely invites us, if not compels us, to function more as legislators than as judges. Moreover, our open-ended balancing tests in this area have allowed us to reach different results based merely "on differing assessments of the force of competing analogies."

In my view, none of this policy-laden decisionmaking is proper. Rather, the Court should confine itself to interpreting the text of the Constitution, which itself seems to prohibit in plain terms certain of the more egregious state taxes on interstate commerce described above, and leaves to Congress the policy choices necessary for any further regulation of interstate commerce.

The argument against the dormant Commerce Clause is, in part, textual. The drafters of the Constitution could have included a provision prohibiting states from interfering with interstate commerce. Also, opponents of the dormant Commerce Clause argue that the Constitution gives Congress the power to regulate commerce and Congress can act to invalidate state laws that unduly burden interstate commerce. The argument is that this should not be a task for an unelected federal judiciary. Thus, this is an argument based partially on separation of powers — the task of reviewing state laws should be done by Congress and not by the courts — and partially on federalism — minimizing the instances where state and local laws are invalidated.

In reading the cases that follow, consider these competing policy considerations, whether there should be a dormant Commerce Clause, and especially when it should apply.

2. *The Dormant Commerce Clause Before 1938*

The dormant Commerce Clause can be traced back to Gibbons v. Ogden, 22 U.S. (9 Wheat.) 1 (1824). The issue in *Gibbons* was whether the state of New York could grant an exclusive monopoly for operating steamboats in New York waters and thereby prevent a person with a federal license from operating in New York. As presented in Chapter 6, Chief Justice John Marshall, writing for the Court, used *Gibbons* as the occasion for broadly defining the scope of Congress's power under the Commerce Clause. Marshall said that "commerce" refers to all stages of business and that "among the states" includes matters that affect more than one state and are not purely internal. Chief Justice John Marshall also used *Gibbons* for considering the Commerce Clause as an independent limit on state power, even where Congress has not acted. Marshall explained that "when a State proceeds to regulate commerce with foreign nations, or among the several states, it is exercising the very power that is granted to Congress, and is doing the very thing which Congress is authorized to do." This argument would seem to imply that Congress's commerce power is exclusive; that any state regulation of commerce is inconsistent with federal power. The idea appears to be that the power to regulate commerce is the authority to decide that commerce should not be regulated and that states therefore should not be able to act with regard to commerce unless specifically authorized by Congress.

Chief Justice Marshall, however, did not go nearly this far in limiting state authority. Rather, Marshall drew a distinction between a state's exercise of its police power and a state exercising the federal power over commerce. Marshall said, for example, that state inspection laws are constitutional even though they may have a "considerable influence on commerce" because they are a "portion of that great immense of legislation, which embraces every thing within the territory of a State, not surrendered to the general government; all which can be most advantageously exercised by the States themselves. Inspection laws, quarantine laws, health laws of every description, as well as laws for regulating the internal commerce of a State, and those which respect turnpike roads, ferries, etc., are component parts of this mass."

In several cases following *Gibbons*, the Court applied this approach in evaluating state laws under the Commerce Clause. For example, in Willson v. The Black Bird Creek Marsh Co., 27 U.S. (2 Pet.) 245 (1829), the Court considered whether a state could construct a dam that obstructed an interstate waterway. The Court rejected a challenge by the owner of a federally licensed ship, because construction of the dam was a permissible exercise of the state's police power. Similarly, in Mayor, Aldermen and Commonalty of New York v. Miln, 36 U.S. (11 Pet.) 102 (1837), the Court upheld a state law requiring passenger identification lists for all ships arriving from other states or countries. The Court said that the law was "not a regulation of commerce but of police," apparently because it was based on a desire to protect public safety by guarding against the arrival of undesirables.

The Court has struggled ever since *Gibbons* with attempting to articulate criteria for when state laws burdening commerce should be upheld as valid exercises of the police power and when they should be invalidated as violating the dormant Commerce Clause.[159] Cooley v. Board of Wardens is a particularly important case in which the Court drew a distinction between subject matter that is national, in which case state laws are invalidated under the dormant Commerce Clause, and subject matter that is local, in which case state laws are allowed.

Aaron B. Cooley v. The Board of Wardens of the Port of Philadelphia

53 U.S. (12 How.) 299 (1851)

[A Pennsylvania law required all ships entering or leaving the Port of Philadelphia to use a local pilot or to pay a fine that went to support retired pilots.]

We think this particular regulation concerning half-pilotage fees, is an appropriate part of a general system of regulations of this subject. Testing it by the practice of commercial states and countries legislating on this subject, we find it has usually been deemed necessary to make similar provisions.

---

[159] *See, e.g.,* The Passenger Cases, 48 U.S. (7 How.) 283 (1849), where the Court split 5-4, with every Justice writing a separate opinion, and invalidated a state law requiring every incoming passenger to pay for the costs of health inspections and treatment; *see also The License Cases,* 46 U.S. (5 How.) 504 (1847).

[We] cannot pronounce a law which does this, to be so far removed from the usual and fit scope of laws for the regulation of pilots and pilotage, as to be deemed, for this cause, a covert attempt to legislate upon another subject under the appearance of legislating on this one. It is urged that the second section of the act of the Legislature of Pennsylvania, of the 11th of June, 1832, proves that the state had other objects in view than the regulation of pilotage.

It must be remembered, that the fair objects of a law imposing half-pilotage when a pilot is not received, may be secured, and at the same time some classes of vessels exempted from such charge. Thus the very section of the act of 1803, now under consideration, does not apply to coasting vessels of less burden than seventy-five tons, not to those bound to, or sailing from, a port in the river Delaware. The purpose of the law being to cause masters of such vessels as generally need a pilot, to employ one, and to secure to the pilots a fair remuneration for cruising in search of vessels, or waiting for employment in port, there is an obvious propriety in having reference to the number, size, and nature of employment of vessels frequenting the port; and it will be found, by an examination of the different systems of these regulations, which have from time to time been made in this and other countries, that the legislative discretion has been constantly exercised in making discriminations, founded on differences both in the character of the trade, and the tonnage of vessels engaged therein.

We do not perceive anything in the nature or extent of this particular discrimination in favor of vessels engaged in the coal trade, which would enable us to declare it to be other than a fair exercise of legislative discretion, acting upon the subject of the regulation of the pilotage of this port of Philadelphia, with a view to operate upon the masters of those vessels, who, as a general rule, ought to take a pilot, and with the further view of relieving from the charge of half-pilotage, such vessels as from their size, or the nature of their employment, should be exempted from contributing to the support of pilots, except so far as they actually receive their services.

The Act of 1789 contains a clear and authoritative declaration by the first Congress that the nature of this subject is such that it should be left to the legislation of the states; that it is local and not national; that it is likely to be the best provided for, not by one system or plan for regulations, but by as many as the legislative discretion of the several states should deem applicable to the local peculiarities of the parts within their limits.

Many cases applied the *Cooley* test throughout the nineteenth century and into the twentieth century. In Welton v. Missouri, 91 U.S. (1 Otto) 275 (1875), the Court used the *Cooley* approach to invalidate a law that required peddlers of out-of-state merchandise to pay a tax and obtain a license, whereas no similar requirements existed for in-state merchants. The Court said that "transportation and exchange of commodities is of national importance, and admits and requires uniformity of regulation." Similarly, in Wabash, St. Louis & Pacific Ry. Co. v. Illinois, 118 U.S. 557 (1886), the Court used the *Cooley* approach to invalidate a state law that regulated railway rates for goods brought to or from other states. The Court emphasized that there would be enormous burdens on interstate commerce if all states adopted such laws and thus concluded that it was an area that required national uniformity and not local regulation.

But during this same time the Court upheld other state laws on the ground that they were in areas where diverse regulation was desirable. For instance, in Smith v. Alabama, 124 U.S. 465 (1888), the Court upheld a state law requiring that all locomotive engineers operating in the state be licensed by a state board of examiners. Likewise, in Erb v. Morasch, 177 U.S. 584 (1900), the Court upheld a city's ordinance that restricted train speed within the city. In Atchinson Topeka & Santa Fe Ry. Co. v. Railroad Commn., 283 U.S. 380 (1931), the Court upheld a state law that required electric headlights of prescribed brightness on all trains operating within the state.

3. The Contemporary Test for the Dormant Commerce Clause

a. The Shift to a Balancing Approach

The nineteenth century's approaches summarized above — the police power/commerce power test of *Gibbons* and the local/national subject matter test of *Cooley* — attempted to draw rigid categories of areas where federal law was exclusive and those where states could regulate. The modern approach is based not on rigid categories, but rather on courts balancing the benefits of a law against the burdens that it imposes on interstate commerce. It should be noted, however, that the Court never has expressly overruled any of the earlier tests and sometimes invokes them in explaining a particular result.

The Court's shift to a balancing approach for the dormant Commerce Clause is evident from comparing two cases, South Carolina State Highway Dept. v. Barnwell Bros. and Southern Pacific Co. v. Arizona.

South Carolina State Highway Dept. v. Barnwell Bros., Inc.

303 U.S. 177 (1938)

Justice STONE delivered the opinion of the Court.

Act No. 259 of the General Assembly of South Carolina, of April 28, 1933, prohibits use on the state highways of motor trucks and "semitrailer motortrucks" whose width exceeds 90 inches, and whose weight including load exceeds 20,000 pounds. For purposes of the weight limitation, section 2 of the statute provides that a semitrailer motortruck, which is a motor propelled truck with a trailer whose front end is designed to be attached to and supported by the truck, shall be considered a single unit. The principal question for decision is whether these prohibitions impose an unconstitutional burden upon interstate commerce.

South Carolina has built its highways and owns and maintains them. It has received from the federal government, in aid of its highway improvements, money grants which have been expended upon the highways to which the injunction applies. But appellees do not challenge here the ruling of the District Court that Congress has not undertaken to regulate the weight and size of motor vehicles in interstate motor traffic and has left undisturbed whatever authority in that regard the states have retained under the Constitution.

The Commerce Clause by its own force, prohibits discrimination against interstate commerce, whatever its form or method, and the decisions of this Court have recognized that there is scope for its like operation when state legislation nominally of local concern is in point of fact aimed at interstate commerce, or by its necessary operation is a means of gaining a local benefit by throwing the attendant burdens on those without the state. It was to end these practices that the Commerce Clause was adopted. The Commerce Clause has also been thought to set its own limitation upon state control of interstate rail carriers so as to preclude the subordination of the efficiency and convenience of interstate traffic to local service requirements.

Few subjects of state regulation are so peculiarly of local concern as is the use of state highways. There are few, local regulation of which is so inseparable from a substantial effect on interstate commerce. Unlike the railroads, local highways are built, owned, and maintained by the state or its municipal subdivisions. The state has a primary and immediate concern in their safe and economical administration. The present regulations, or any others of like purpose, if they are to accomplish their end, must be applied alike to interstate and intrastate traffic both moving in large volume over the highways. The fact that they affect alike shippers in interstate and intrastate commerce in large number within as well as without the state is a safeguard against their abuse.

[O]ur decisions [have held] that a state may impose nondiscriminatory restrictions with respect to the character of motor vehicles moving in interstate commerce as a safety measure and as a means of securing the economical use of its highways. [C]ourts do not sit as Legislatures, either state or national. They cannot act as Congress does when, after weighing all the conflicting interests, state and national, it determines when and how much the state regulatory power shall yield to the larger interests of a national commerce. And in reviewing a state highway regulation where Congress has not acted, a court is not called upon, as are state Legislatures, to determine what, in its judgment, is the most suitable restriction to be applied of those that are possible, or to choose that one which in its opinion is best adapted to all the diverse interests affected.

Since the adoption of one weight or width regulation, rather than another, is a legislative, not a judicial, choice, its constitutionality is not to be determined by weighing in the judicial scales the merits of the legislative choice and rejecting it if the weight of evidence presented in court appears to favor a different standard. The choice of a weight limitation based on convenience of application and consequent lack of need for rigid supervisory enforcement is for the Legislature, and we cannot say that its preference for the one over the other is in any sense arbitrary or unreasonable. The choice is not to be condemned because the Legislature prefers a workable standard, less likely to be violated than another under which the violations will probably be increased but more easily detected. It is for the Legislature to say whether the one test or the other will in practical operation better protect the highways from the risk of excessive loads. The regulatory measures taken by South Carolina are within its legislative power. They do not infringe the Fourteenth Amendment, and the resulting burden on interstate commerce is not forbidden.

Southern Pacific Co. v. Arizona ex rel. Sullivan, Attorney General

325 U.S. 761 (1945)

Chief Justice STONE delivered the opinion of the Court.

The Arizona Train Limit Law of May 16, 1912 makes it unlawful for any person or corporation to operate within the state a railroad train of more than fourteen passenger or seventy freight cars, and authorizes the state to recover a money penalty for each violation of the Act.

Although the Commerce Clause conferred on the national government power to regulate commerce, its possession of the power does not exclude all state power of regulation. Ever since Willson v. Black-Bird Creek Marsh Co., and Cooley v. Board of Wardens, it has been recognized that, in the absence of conflicting legislation by Congress, there is a residuum of power in the state to make laws governing matters of local concern which nevertheless in some measure affect interstate commerce or even, to some extent, regulate it. When the regulation of matters of local concern is local in character and effect, and its impact on the national commerce does not seriously interfere with its operation, and the consequent incentive to deal with them nationally is slight, such regulation has been generally held to be within state authority.

In the application of these principles some enactments may be found to be plainly within and others plainly without state power. But between these extremes lies the infinite variety of cases in which regulation of local matters may also operate as a regulation of commerce, in which reconciliation of the conflicting claims of state and national power is to be attained only by some appraisal and accommodation of the competing demands of the state and national interests involved. Hence the matters for ultimate determination here are the nature and extent of the burden which the state regulation of interstate trains, adopted as a safety measure, imposes on interstate commerce, and whether the relative weights of the state and national interests involved are such as to make inapplicable the rule, generally observed, that the free flow of interstate commerce and its freedom from local restraints in matters requiring uniformity of regulation are interests safeguarded by the Commerce Clause from state interference.

The findings show that the operation of long trains, that is trains of more than fourteen passenger and more than seventy freight cars, is standard practice over the main lines of the railroads of the United States, and that, if the length of trains is to be regulated at all, national uniformity in the regulation adopted, such as only Congress can prescribe, is practically indispensable to the operation of an efficient and economical national railway system. On many railroads passenger trains of more than fourteen cars and freight trains of more than seventy cars are operated, and on some systems freight trains are run ranging from one hundred and twenty-five to one hundred and sixty cars in length. Outside of Arizona, where the length of trains is not restricted, appellant runs a substantial proportion of long trains. In 1939 on its comparable route for through traffic through Utah and Nevada from 66 to 85% of its freight trains were over 70 cars in length and over 43% of its passenger trains included more than fourteen passenger cars. In Arizona, approximately 93% of the freight traffic and 95% of the passenger traffic is interstate. Because of the Train Limit Law appellant is required to haul over 30% more trains in Arizona than would otherwise have been necessary.

The record shows a definite relationship between operating costs and the length of trains, the increase in length resulting in a reduction of operating costs per car. The additional cost of operation of trains complying with the Train Limit Law in Arizona amounts for the two railroads traversing that state to about $1,000,000 a year. The reduction in train lengths also impedes efficient operation. More locomotives and more manpower are required; the necessary conversion and reconversion of train lengths at terminals and the delay caused by breaking up and remaking long trains upon entering and leaving the state in order to comply with the law, delays the traffic and diminishes its volume moved in a given time, especially when traffic is heavy.

The unchallenged findings leave no doubt that the Arizona Train Limit Law imposes a serious burden on the interstate commerce conducted by appellant. It materially impedes the movement of appellant's interstate trains through that state and interposes a substantial obstruction to the national policy proclaimed by Congress, to promote adequate, economical and efficient railway transportation service. Enforcement of the law in Arizona, while train lengths remain unregulated or are regulated by varying standards in other states, must inevitably result in an impairment of uniformity of efficient railroad operation because the railroads are subjected to regulation which is not uniform in its application. Compliance with a state statute limiting train lengths requires interstate trains of a length lawful in other states to be broken up and reconstituted as they enter each state according as it may impose varying limitations upon train lengths. The alternative is for the carrier to conform to the lowest train limit restriction of any of the states through which its trains pass, whose laws thus control the carriers' operations both within and without the regulating state.

If one state may regulate train lengths, so may all the others, and they need not prescribe the same maximum limitation. The practical effect of such regulation is to control train operations beyond the boundaries of the state exacting it because of the necessity of breaking up and reassembling long trains at the nearest terminal points before entering and after leaving the regulating state. The serious impediment to the free flow of commerce by the local regulation of train lengths and the practical necessity that such regulation, if any, must be prescribed by a single body having a nation-wide authority are apparent.

The trial court found that the Arizona law had no reasonable relation to safety, and made train operation more dangerous. Examination of the evidence and the detailed findings makes it clear that this conclusion was rested on facts found which indicate that such increased danger of accident and personal injury as may result from the greater length of trains is more than offset by the increase in the number of accidents resulting from the larger number of trains when train lengths are reduced.

We think, as the trial court found, that the Arizona Train Limit Law, viewed as a safety measure, affords at most slight and dubious advantage, if any, over unregulated train lengths, because it results in an increase in the number of trains and train operations and the consequent increase in train accidents of a character generally more severe than those due to slack action. Its undoubted effect on the commerce is the regulation, without securing uniformity, of the length of trains operated in interstate commerce, which lack is itself a primary cause of preventing the free flow of commerce by delaying it and by substantially increasing its cost and impairing its efficiency.

In recent years, some Justices, most notably Rehnquist, Scalia, and Thomas, have objected to this balancing test and have argued in favor of upholding all state laws that are deemed non-discriminatory. Justice Scalia contended: "This process is ordinarily called 'balancing,' but the scale analogy is not really appropriate, since the interests on both sides are incommensurate. It is more like judging whether a particular line is longer than a particular rock is heavy. . . . Weighing the governmental interests of a State against the needs of interstate commerce is, by contrast, a task squarely within the responsibility of Congress, and ill suited to the judicial function."[160] As quoted above, Justice Thomas also has been very critical of the balancing test in dormant Commerce Clause cases.[161]

The question, of course, is what should replace the balancing test. The categorical approaches that preceded it were not useful in deciding whether a particular law violated the dormant Commerce Clause. Justice Scalia's answer is to eliminate dormant Commerce Clause review where the state is not discriminating against out-of-staters. Scalia wrote: "I would therefore abandon the balancing approach to these negative Commerce Clause cases . . . and leave essentially legislative judgments to the Congress. . . . In my view, a state statute is invalid under the Commerce Clause if, and only if, it accords discriminatory treatment to interstate commerce in a respect not required to achieve a lawful state purpose."[162]

The question that Justices Scalia and Thomas raise is whether there should be any dormant Commerce Clause review when a state law is deemed non-discriminatory.

On the one hand, assuring a free flow of commerce among the states is best achieved by eliminating burdens on interstate commerce. On the other hand, there is no reason to distrust the political process when it is treating in-staters and

---

[160] Bendix Autolite Corp. v. Midwesco Enterprises, Inc., 486 U.S. 888 (1988) (Scalia, J., dissenting).
[161] Camps Newfound/Owatonna, Inc. v. Town of Harrison, 520 U.S. 564 (1997) (Thomas, J., dissenting), quoted above.
[162] Bendix Autolite Corp. v. Midwesco Enterprises, Inc., 486 U.S. 888 (1988) (Scalia, J., dissenting).

out-of-staters alike. Limiting the scope of the dormant Commerce Clause has the benefits of minimizing the judicial role and maximizing the deference paid to state and local governments.

b. Determining Whether a Law Is Discriminatory

The balancing prescribed by the Supreme Court is not the same in all dormant Commerce Clause cases, but instead varies depending upon whether the state or local law discriminates against out-of-staters or treats in-staters and out-of-staters alike. As discussed below, if the Court concludes that a state is discriminating against out-of-staters, then there is a strong presumption against the law and it will be upheld only if it is necessary to achieve an important purpose. In contrast, if the Court concludes that the law is non-discriminatory, then the presumption is in favor of upholding the law, and it will be invalidated only if it is shown that the law's burdens on interstate commerce outweigh its benefits.

Thus, the threshold question is determining whether the state law is discriminatory against out-of-staters. This makes sense in light of the purposes of the dormant Commerce Clause. The framers were most concerned about stopping protectionist state legislation, where a state would discriminate against out-of-staters to benefit its citizens at the expense of out-of-staters. Also, it is thought that protectionist laws are most likely to interfere with the economy. Besides, if a law applies to in-staters and out-of-staters equally, then at least some of those affected by the law are represented in the political process.

Sometimes laws are facially discriminatory against out-of-staters; that is, the laws in their very terms draw a distinction between in-staters and out-of-staters. Other times, laws are facially neutral, but might be motivated by a desire to help in-staters at the expense of out-of-staters or might have a discriminatory impact against those from other states. The first set of cases presented below involves facial discrimination; then presented are cases involving claims of facially neutral laws with discriminatory purpose or impact. After these cases, the next subsection looks at the analysis used when a law is deemed discriminatory; following this is a subsection examining the analysis for when a law is deemed not discriminatory.

FACIALLY DISCRIMINATORY LAWS

Sometimes, a law clearly favors in-staters over out-of-staters. For example, in Granholm v. Heald, 544 U.S. 460 (2005), the Court struck down state laws that allowed in-state wineries, but not out-of-state wineries, to sell wine directly to consumers through the mail. In recent years, many of the cases before the Supreme Court involving the dormant Commerce Clause have involved challenges to state and local environmental regulations. Below are three important Supreme Court decisions considering local laws designed to deal with solid-waste disposal problems.

City of Philadelphia v. New Jersey

437 U.S. 617 (1978)

Justice STEWART delivered the opinion of the Court.

A New Jersey law prohibits the importation of most "solid or liquid waste which originated or was collected outside the territorial limits of the State. . . ." In this case we are required to decide whether this statutory prohibition violates the Commerce Clause of the United States Constitution.

I

The statutory provision in question is ch. 363 of 1973 N.J. Laws, which took effect in early 1974. In pertinent part it provides: "No person shall bring into this State any solid or liquid waste which originated or was collected outside the territorial limits of the State, except garbage to be fed to swine in the State of New Jersey, until the commissioner [of the State Department of Environmental Protection] shall determine that such action can be permitted without endangering the public health, safety and welfare and has promulgated regulations permitting and regulating the treatment and disposal of such waste in this State."

Immediately affected by these developments were the operators of private landfills in New Jersey, and several cities in other States that had agreements with these operators for waste disposal. They brought suit against New Jersey and its Department of Environmental Protection in state court, attacking the statute and regulations on a number of state and federal grounds.

All objects of interstate trade merit Commerce Clause protection; none is excluded by definition at the outset. Hence, we reject the state court's suggestion that the banning of "valueless" out-of-state wastes by ch. 363 implicates no constitutional protection. Just as Congress has power to regulate the interstate movement of these wastes, States are not free from constitutional scrutiny when they restrict that movement.

[II]

Although the Constitution gives Congress the power to regulate commerce among the States, many subjects of potential federal regulation under that power inevitably escape congressional attention "because of their local character and their number and diversity." South Carolina State Highway Dept. v. Barnwell Bros., Inc. (1939). In the absence of federal legislation, these subjects are open to control by the States so long as they act within the restraints imposed by the Commerce Clause itself.

The opinions of the Court through the years have reflected an alertness to the evils of "economic isolation" and protectionism, while at the same time recognizing that incidental burdens on interstate commerce may be unavoidable when a State legislates to safeguard the health and safety of its people. Thus, where simple economic protectionism is effected by state legislation, a virtually per se rule of invalidity has been erected. The clearest example of such legislation is a law that overtly blocks the flow of interstate commerce at a State's borders.

The crucial inquiry, therefore, must be directed to determining whether ch. 363 is basically a protectionist measure, or whether it can fairly be viewed as a law directed to legitimate local concerns, with effects upon interstate commerce that are only incidental.

The purpose of ch. 363 is set out in the statute itself as follows: "The Legislature finds and determines that . . . the volume of solid and liquid waste continues to rapidly increase, that the treatment and disposal of these wastes continues to pose an even greater threat to the quality of the environment of New Jersey, that the available and appropriate land fill sites within the State are being diminished, that the environment continues to be threatened by the treatment and disposal of waste which originated or was collected outside the State, and that the public health, safety and welfare require that the treatment and disposal within this State of all wastes generated outside of the State be prohibited."

[I]t does not matter whether the ultimate aim of ch. 363 is to reduce the waste disposal costs of New Jersey residents or to save remaining open lands from pollution, for we assume New Jersey has every right to protect its residents' pocketbooks as well as their environment. And it may be assumed as well that New Jersey may pursue those ends by slowing the flow of all waste into the State's remaining landfills, even though interstate commerce may incidentally be affected. But whatever New Jersey's ultimate purpose, it may not be accomplished by discriminating against articles of commerce coming from outside the State unless there is some reason, apart from their origin, to treat them differently. Both on its face and in its plain effect, ch. 363 violates this principle of nondiscrimination.

The Court has consistently found parochial legislation of this kind to be constitutionally invalid, whether the ultimate aim of the legislation was to assure a steady supply of milk by erecting barriers to allegedly ruinous outside competition, or to create jobs by keeping industry within the State, or to preserve the State's financial resources from depletion by fencing out indigent immigrants. In each of these cases, a presumably legitimate goal was sought to be achieved by the illegitimate means of isolating the State from the national economy.

The New Jersey law at issue in this case falls squarely within the area that the Commerce Clause puts off limits to state regulation. On its face, it imposes on out-of-state commercial interests the full burden of conserving the State's remaining landfill space. The New Jersey law blocks the importation of waste in an obvious effort to saddle those outside the State with the entire burden of slowing the flow of refuse into New Jersey's remaining landfill sites. That legislative effort is clearly impermissible under the Commerce Clause of the Constitution. Today, cities in Pennsylvania and New York find it expedient or necessary to send their waste into New Jersey for disposal, and New Jersey claims the right to close its borders to such traffic. Tomorrow, cities in New Jersey may find it expedient or necessary to send their waste into Pennsylvania or New York for disposal, and those States might then claim the right to close their borders. The Commerce Clause will protect New Jersey in the future, just as it protects her neighbors now, from efforts by one State to isolate itself in the stream of interstate commerce from a problem shared by all.

Justice REHNQUIST, with whom the Chief Justice joins, dissenting.

A growing problem in our Nation is the sanitary treatment and disposal of solid waste. For many years, solid waste was incinerated. Because of the significant environmental problems attendant on incineration, however, this method of solid waste disposal has declined in use in many localities, including New Jersey. "Sanitary" landfills have replaced incineration as the principal method of disposing of solid waste. In ch. 363 of the 1973 N.J. Laws, the State of New Jersey legislatively recognized the unfortunate fact that landfills also present extremely serious health and safety problems. First, in New Jersey, "virtually all sanitary landfills can be expected to produce leachate, a noxious and highly polluted liquid which is seldom visible and frequently pollutes . . . ground and surface waters." The natural decomposition process which occurs in landfills also produces large quantities of methane and thereby presents a significant explosion hazard. Landfills can also generate "health hazards caused by rodents, fires and scavenger birds" and, "needless to say, do not help New Jersey's aesthetic appearance nor New Jersey's noise or water or air pollution problems."

The health and safety hazards associated with landfills present appellees with a currently unsolvable dilemma. Other, hopefully safer, methods of disposing of solid wastes are still in the development stage and cannot presently be used. But appellees obviously cannot completely stop the tide of solid waste that its citizens will produce in the interim. For the moment, therefore, appellees must continue to use sanitary landfills to dispose of New Jersey's own solid waste despite the critical environmental problems thereby created.

The question presented in this case is whether New Jersey must also continue to receive and dispose of solid waste from neighboring States, even though these will inexorably increase the health problems discussed above. The Court answers this question in the affirmative. New Jersey must either prohibit all landfill operations, leaving itself to cast about for a presently nonexistent solution to the serious problem of disposing of the waste generated within its own borders, or it must accept waste from every portion of the United States, thereby multiplying the health and safety problems which would result if it dealt only with such wastes generated within the State. Because past precedents establish that the Commerce Clause does not present appellees with such a Hobson's choice, I dissent.

C & A Carbone, Inc. v. Town of Clarkstown, New York

511 U.S. 383 (1994)

Justice KENNEDY delivered the opinion of the Court.

As solid waste output continues apace and landfill capacity becomes more costly and scarce, state and local governments are expending significant resources to develop trash control systems that are efficient, lawful, and protective of the environment. The difficulty of their task is evident from the number of recent cases that we have heard involving waste transfer and treatment. The case decided today, while perhaps a small new chapter in that course of decisions, rests nevertheless upon well-settled principles of our Commerce Clause jurisprudence.

We consider a so-called flow control ordinance, which requires all solid waste to be processed at a designated transfer station before leaving the municipality. The avowed purpose of the ordinance is to retain the processing fees charged at the transfer station to amortize the cost of the facility. Because it attains this goal by depriving competitors, including out-of-state firms, of access to a local market, we hold that the flow control ordinance violates the Commerce Clause.

The town of Clarkstown, New York, lies in the lower Hudson River Valley. In August 1989, Clarkstown entered into a consent decree with the New York State Department of Environmental Conservation. The town agreed to close its landfill located on Route 303 in West Nyack and build a new solid waste transfer station on the same site. The station would receive bulk solid waste and separate recyclable from nonrecyclable items. Recyclable waste would be baled for shipment to a recycling facility; nonrecyclable waste, to a suitable landfill or incinerator.

The cost of building the transfer station was estimated at $1.4 million. A local private contractor agreed to construct the facility and operate it for five years, after which the town would buy it for $1. During those five years, the town guaranteed a minimum waste flow of 120,000 tons per year, for which the contractor could charge the hauler a so-called tipping fee of $81 per ton. If the station received less than 120,000 tons in a year, the town promised to make up the tipping fee deficit. The object of this arrangement was to amortize the cost of the transfer station: The town would finance its new facility with the income generated by the tipping fees.

The problem, of course, was how to meet the yearly guarantee. This difficulty was compounded by the fact that the tipping fee of $81 per ton exceeded the disposal cost of unsorted solid waste on the private market. The solution the town adopted was the flow control ordinance here in question. The ordinance requires all non-hazardous solid waste within the town to be deposited at the Route 303 transfer station. Noncompliance is punishable by as much as a $1,000 fine and up to 15 days in jail.

The petitioners in this case are C & A Carbone, Inc., a company engaged in the processing of solid waste, and various related companies or persons, all of whom we designate Carbone. Carbone operates a recycling center in Clarkstown, where it receives bulk solid waste, sorts and bales it, and then ships it to other processing facilities — much as occurs at the town's new transfer station. While the flow control ordinance permits recyclers like Carbone to continue receiving solid waste, it requires them to bring the nonrecyclable residue from that waste to the Route 303 station. It thus forbids Carbone to ship the nonrecyclable waste itself, and it requires Carbone to pay a tipping fee on trash that Carbone has already sorted.

In March 1991, a tractor-trailer containing 23 bales of solid waste struck an overpass on the Palisades Interstate Parkway. When the police investigated the accident, they discovered the truck was carrying household waste from Carbone's Clarkstown plant to an Indiana landfill. The Clarkstown police put Carbone's plant under surveillance and in the next few days seized six more tractor-trailers leaving the facility. The trucks also contained nonrecyclable waste, originating both within and without the town, and destined for disposal sites in Illinois, Indiana, West Virginia, and Florida.

The real question is whether the flow control ordinance is valid despite its undoubted effect on interstate commerce. For this inquiry, our case law yields two lines of analysis: first, whether the ordinance discriminates against interstate commerce, Philadelphia v. New Jersey (1978); and second, whether the ordinance imposes a burden on interstate commerce that is "clearly excessive in relation to the putative local benefits," Pike v. Bruce Church, Inc. (1970). As we find that the ordinance discriminates against interstate commerce, we need not resort to the *Pike* test.

The central rationale for the rule against discrimination is to prohibit state or municipal laws whose object is local economic protectionism, laws that would excite those jealousies and retaliatory measures the Constitution was designed to prevent. We have interpreted the Commerce Clause to invalidate local laws that impose commercial barriers or discriminate against an article of commerce by reason of its origin or destination out of State.

Clarkstown protests that its ordinance does not discriminate because it does not differentiate solid waste on the basis of its geographic origin. All solid waste, regardless of origin, must be processed at the designated transfer station before it leaves the town. Unlike the statute in Philadelphia, says the town, the ordinance erects no barrier to the import or export of any solid waste but requires only that the waste be channeled through the designated facility.

Our initial discussion of the effects of the ordinance on interstate commerce goes far toward refuting the town's contention that there is no discrimination in its regulatory scheme. The town's own arguments go the rest of the way. As the town itself points out, what makes garbage a profitable business is not its own worth but the fact that its possessor must pay to get rid of it. In other words, the article of commerce is not so much the solid waste itself, but rather the service of processing and disposing of it. With respect to this stream of commerce, the flow control ordinance discriminates, for it allows only the favored operator to process waste that is within the limits of the town. The ordinance is no less discriminatory because in-state or in-town processors are also covered by the prohibition.

In this light, the flow control ordinance is just one more instance of local processing requirements that we long have held invalid. The essential vice in laws of this sort is that they bar the import of the processing service. Out-of-state meat inspectors, or shrimp hullers, or milk pasteurizers, are deprived of access to local demand for their services. Put another way, the offending local laws hoard a local resource for the benefit of local businesses that treat it. The flow control ordinance has the same design and effect. It hoards solid waste, and the demand to get rid of it, for the benefit of the preferred processing facility. The only conceivable distinction from the cases cited above is that the flow control ordinance favors a single local proprietor. But this difference just makes the protectionist effect of the ordinance more acute. The flow control ordinance at issue here squelches competition in the waste-processing service altogether, leaving no room for investment from outside.

Discrimination against interstate commerce in favor of local business or investment is per se invalid, save in a narrow class of cases in which the municipality can demonstrate, under rigorous scrutiny, that it has no other means to advance a legitimate local interest. Maine v. Taylor (1986) (upholding Maine's ban on the import of baitfish because Maine had no other way to prevent the spread of parasites and the adulteration of its native fish species). A number of amici contend that the flow control ordinance fits into this narrow class. They suggest that as landfill space diminishes and environmental cleanup costs escalate, measures like flow control become necessary to ensure the safe handling and proper treatment of solid waste.

The teaching of our cases is that these arguments must be rejected absent the clearest showing that the unobstructed flow of interstate commerce itself is unable to solve the local problem. The Commerce Clause presumes a national market free from local legislation that discriminates in favor of local interests. Here Clarkstown has any number of nondiscriminatory alternatives for addressing the health and environmental problems alleged to justify the ordinance in question. The most obvious would be uniform safety regulations enacted without the object to discriminate. These regulations would ensure that competitors like Carbone do not underprice the market by cutting corners on environmental safety.

Nor may Clarkstown justify the flow control ordinance as a way to steer solid waste away from out-of-town disposal sites that it might deem harmful to the environment. To do so would extend the town's police power beyond its jurisdictional bounds. States and localities may not attach restrictions to exports or imports in order to control commerce in other States.

The flow control ordinance does serve a central purpose that a nonprotectionist regulation would not: It ensures that the town-sponsored facility will be profitable, so that the local contractor can build it and Clarkstown can buy it back at nominal cost in five years. In other words, as the most candid of amici and even Clarkstown admit, the flow control ordinance is a financing measure. By itself, of course, revenue generation is not a local interest that can justify discrimination against interstate commerce. Otherwise States could impose discriminatory taxes against solid waste originating outside the State.

State and local governments may not use their regulatory power to favor local enterprise by prohibiting patronage of out-of-state competitors or their facilities.

Justice SOUTER, with whom the Chief Justice and Justice BLACKMUN join, dissenting.

The majority may invoke "well-settled principles of our Commerce Clause jurisprudence," but it does so to strike down an ordinance unlike anything this Court has ever invalidated. Previous cases have held that the "negative" or "dormant" aspect of the Commerce Clause renders state or local legislation unconstitutional when it discriminates against out-of-state or out-of-town businesses such as those that pasteurize milk, hull shrimp, or mill lumber, and the majority relies on these cases because of what they have in common with this one: out-of-state processors are excluded from the local market (here, from the market for trash processing services). What the majority ignores, however, are the differences between our local processing cases and this one: the exclusion worked by Clarkstown's Local Law 9 bestows no benefit on a class of local private actors, but instead directly aids the government in satisfying a traditional governmental responsibility. The law does not differentiate between all local and all out-of-town providers of a service, but instead between the one entity responsible for ensuring that the job gets done and all other enterprises, regardless of their location. The ordinance thus falls outside that class of tariff or protectionist measures that the Commerce Clause has traditionally been thought to bar States from enacting against each other, and when the majority subsumes the ordinance within the class of laws this Court has struck down as facially discriminatory (and so avails itself of our "virtually per se rule" against such statutes, see Philadelphia v. New Jersey (1978)), the majority is in fact greatly extending the Clause's dormant reach.

There are, however, good and sufficient reasons against expanding the Commerce Clause's inherent capacity to trump exercises of state authority such as the ordinance at issue here. There is no indication in the record that any out-of-state trash processor has been harmed, or that the interstate movement or disposition of trash will be affected one whit. To the degree Local Law 9 affects the market for trash processing services, it does so only by subjecting Clarkstown residents and businesses to burdens far different from the burdens of local favoritism that dormant Commerce Clause jurisprudence seeks to root out. The town has found a way to finance a public improvement, not by transferring its cost to out-of-state economic interests, but by spreading it among the local generators of trash, an equitable result with tendencies that should not disturb the Commerce Clause and should not be disturbed by us.

In United Haulers Assn., Inc. v. Oneida-Herkimer Solid Waste Management Authority, the Court distinguished Carbone and upheld the law. The key question in reading this case is whether there is a meaningful distinction between the decisions.

United Haulers Assn., Inc. v. Oneida-Herkimer Solid Waste Management Authority

127 S. Ct. 1786 (2007)

Chief Justice ROBERTS delivered the opinion of the Court, except as to Part II-D.

"Flow control" ordinances require trash haulers to deliver solid waste to a particular waste processing facility. In *C & A Carbone, Inc. v. Clarkstown* (1994), this Court struck down under the Commerce Clause a flow control ordinance that forced haulers to deliver waste to a particular private processing facility. In this case, we face flow control ordinances quite similar to the one invalidated in *Carbone*. The only salient difference is that the laws at issue here require haulers to bring waste to facilities owned and operated by a state-created public benefit corporation. We find this difference constitutionally significant. Disposing of trash has been a traditional government activity for years, and laws that favor the government in such areas — but treat every private business, whether in-state or out-of-state, exactly the same — do not discriminate against interstate commerce for purposes of the Commerce Clause. Applying the Commerce Clause test reserved for regulations that do not discriminate against interstate commerce, we uphold these ordinances because any incidental burden they may have on interstate commerce does not outweigh the benefits they confer on the citizens of Oneida and Herkimer Counties.

I

Located in central New York, Oneida and Herkimer Counties span over 2,600 square miles and are home to about 306,000 residents. Traditionally, each city, town, or village within the Counties has been responsible for disposing of its own waste. Many had relied on local landfills, some in a more environmentally responsible fashion than others.

By the 1980's, the Counties confronted what they could credibly call a solid waste "crisis." Many local landfills were operating without permits and in violation of state regulations. Sixteen were ordered to close and remediate the surrounding environment, costing the public tens of millions of dollars. These environmental problems culminated in a federal clean-up action against a land-fill in Oneida County; the defendants in that case named over 600 local businesses and several municipalities and school districts as third-party defendants.

The "crisis" extended beyond health and safety concerns. The Counties had an uneasy relationship with local waste management companies, enduring price fixing, pervasive overcharging, and the influence of organized crime. Dramatic price hikes were not uncommon: In 1986, for example, a county contractor doubled its waste disposal rate on six weeks' notice.

Responding to these problems, the Counties requested and New York's Legislature and Governor created the Oneida-Herkimer Solid Waste Management Authority (Authority), a public benefit corporation. The Authority is empowered to collect, process, and dispose of solid waste generated in the Counties. To further the Authority's governmental and public purposes, the Counties may impose "appropriate and reasonable limitations on competition" by, for instance, adopting "local laws requiring that all solid waste . . . be delivered to a specified solid waste management-resource recovery facility"

In 1989, the Authority and the Counties entered into a Solid Waste Management Agreement, under which the Authority agreed to manage all solid waste within the Counties. Private haulers would remain free to pick up citizens' trash from the curb, but the Authority would take over the job of processing the trash, sorting it, and sending it off for disposal. To fulfill its part of the bargain, the

Authority agreed to purchase and develop facilities for the processing and disposal of solid waste and recyclables generated in the Counties.

The Authority collected "tipping fees" to cover its operating and maintenance costs for these facilities.[163] The tipping fees significantly exceeded those charged for waste removal on the open market, but they allowed the Authority to do more than the average private waste disposer. In addition to landfill transportation and solid waste disposal, the fees enabled the Authority to provide recycling of 33 kinds of materials, as well as composting, household hazardous waste disposal, and a number of other services. If the Authority's operating costs and debt service were not recouped through tipping fees and other charges, the agreement provided that the Counties would make up the difference.

As described, the agreement had a flaw: Citizens might opt to have their waste hauled to facilities with lower tipping fees. To avoid being stuck with the bill for facilities that citizens voted for but then chose not to use, the Counties enacted "flow control" ordinances requiring that all solid waste generated within the Counties be delivered to the Authority's processing sites. Private haulers must obtain a permit from the Authority to collect waste in the Counties. Penalties for noncompliance with the ordinances include permit revocation, fines, and imprisonment.

Petitioners are United Haulers Association, Inc., a trade association made up of solid waste management companies, and six haulers that operated in Oneida and Herkimer Counties when this action was filed. In 1995, they sued the Counties and the Authority alleging that the flow control laws violate the Commerce Clause by discriminating against interstate commerce. They submitted evidence that without the flow control laws and the associated $86-per-ton tipping fees, they could dispose of solid waste at out-of-state facilities for between $37 and $55 per ton, including transportation.

II

A

The Commerce Clause provides that "Congress shall have Power . . . [t]o regulate Commerce with foreign Nations, and among the several States." Although the Constitution does not in terms limit the power of States to regulate commerce, we have long interpreted the Commerce Clause as an implicit restraint on state authority, even in the absence of a conflicting federal statute.

To determine whether a law violates this so-called "dormant" aspect of the Commerce Clause, we first ask whether it discriminates on its face against interstate commerce. In this context, " 'discrimination' simply means differential treatment of in-state and out-of-state economic interests that benefits the former and

---

[163] Tipping fees are disposal charges levied against collectors who drop off waste at a processing facility. They are called "tipping" fees because garbage trucks literally tip their back end to dump out the carried waste. As of 1995, haulers in the Counties had to pay tipping fees of at least $86 per ton, a price that ballooned to as much as $172 per ton if a particular load contained more than 25% recyclables. [Footnote by Chief Justice Roberts.]

burdens the latter." Discriminatory laws motivated by "simple economic protectionism" are subject to a "virtually per se rule of invalidity," which can only be overcome by a showing that the State has no other means to advance a legitimate local purpose, *Maine v. Taylor* (1986).

B

[T]he haulers argue vigorously that the Counties' ordinances discriminate against interstate commerce under *Carbone*. In *Carbone*, the town of Clarkstown, New York, hired a private contractor to build a waste transfer station. According to the terms of the deal, the contractor would operate the facility for five years, charging an above-market tipping fee of $81 per ton; after five years, the town would buy the facility for one dollar. The town guaranteed that the facility would receive a certain volume of trash per year. To make good on its promise, Clarkstown passed a flow control ordinance requiring that all nonhazardous solid waste within the town be deposited at the transfer facility. This Court struck down the ordinance, holding that it discriminated against interstate commerce by "hoard[ing] solid waste, and the demand to get rid of it, for the benefit of the preferred processing facility." The dissent pointed out that all of this Court's local processing cases involved laws that discriminated in favor of private entities, not public ones. According to the dissent, Clarkstown's ostensibly private transfer station was "essentially a municipal facility," and this distinction should have saved Clarkstown's ordinance because favoring local government is by its nature different from favoring a particular private company. The majority did not comment on the dissent's public-private distinction.

The parties in this case draw opposite inferences from the majority's silence. The haulers say it proves that the majority agreed with the dissent's characterization of the facility, but thought there was no difference under the dormant Commerce Clause between laws favoring private entities and those favoring public ones. The Counties disagree, arguing that the majority studiously avoided the issue because the facility in *Carbone* was private, and therefore the question whether public facilities may be favored was not properly before the Court.

We believe the latter interpretation of *Carbone* is correct. If the Court thought Clarkstown's processing facility was public, that additional distinction was not merely "conceivable" — it was conceived, and discussed at length, by three Justices in dissent. *Carbone* cannot be regarded as having decided the public-private question.

C

The flow control ordinances in this case benefit a clearly public facility, while treating all private companies exactly the same. Because the question is now squarely presented on the facts of the case before us, we decide that such flow control ordinances do not discriminate against interstate commerce for purposes of the dormant Commerce Clause.

Compelling reasons justify treating these laws differently from laws favoring particular private businesses over their competitors. States and municipalities are not private businesses — far from it. Unlike private enterprise, government is vested with the responsibility of protecting the health, safety, and welfare of its citizens. These important responsibilities set state and local government apart from a typical private business.

Given these differences, it does not make sense to regard laws favoring local government and laws favoring private industry with equal skepticism. As our local processing cases demonstrate, when a law favors in-state business over out-of-state competition, rigorous scrutiny is appropriate because the law is often the product of "simple economic protectionism." Laws favoring local government, by contrast, may be directed toward any number of legitimate goals unrelated to protectionism. Here the flow control ordinances enable the Counties to pursue particular policies with respect to the handling and treatment of waste generated in the Counties, while allocating the costs of those policies on citizens and businesses according to the volume of waste they generate.

The contrary approach of treating public and private entities the same under the dormant Commerce Clause would lead to unprecedented and unbounded interference by the courts with state and local government. The dormant Commerce Clause is not a roving license for federal courts to decide what activities are appropriate for state and local government to undertake, and what activities must be the province of private market competition. In this case, the citizens of Oneida and Herkimer Counties have chosen the government to provide waste management services, with a limited role for the private sector in arranging for transport of waste from the curb to the public facilities. The citizens could have left the entire matter for the private sector, in which case any regulation they undertook could not discriminate against interstate commerce. But it was also open to them to vest responsibility for the matter with their government, and to adopt flow control ordinances to support the government effort. It is not the office of the Commerce Clause to control the decision of the voters on whether government or the private sector should provide waste management services.

We should be particularly hesitant to interfere with the Counties' efforts under the guise of the Commerce Clause because "[w]aste disposal is both typically and traditionally a local government function." Finally, it bears mentioning that the most palpable harm imposed by the ordinances — more expensive trash removal — is likely to fall upon the very people who voted for the laws. Our dormant Commerce Clause cases often find discrimination when a State shifts the costs of regulation to other States, because when "the burden of state regulation falls on interests outside the state, it is unlikely to be alleviated by the operation of those political restraints normally exerted when interests within the state are affected." Here, the citizens and businesses of the Counties bear the costs of the ordinances. There is no reason to step in and hand local businesses a victory they could not obtain through the political process.

We hold that the Counties' flow control ordinances, which treat in-state private business interests exactly the same as out-of-state ones, do not "discriminate against interstate commerce" for purposes of the dormant Commerce Clause.[164]

D

The Counties' flow control ordinances are properly analyzed under the test set forth in *Pike v. Bruce Church, Inc.* (1970), which is reserved for laws "directed to legitimate local concerns, with effects upon interstate commerce that are only incidental." Under the *Pike* test, we will uphold a nondiscriminatory statute like this one "unless the burden imposed on [interstate] commerce is clearly excessive in relation to the putative local benefits."

After years of discovery, both the Magistrate Judge and the District Court could not detect any disparate impact on out-of-state as opposed to in-state businesses. We find it unnecessary to decide whether the ordinances impose any incidental burden on interstate commerce because any arguable burden does not exceed the public benefits of the ordinances.

The ordinances give the Counties a convenient and effective way to finance their integrated package of waste-disposal services. While "revenue generation is not a local interest that can justify discrimination against interstate commerce," we think it is a cognizable benefit for purposes of the *Pike* test.

At the same time, the ordinances are more than financing tools. They increase recycling in at least two ways, conferring significant health and environmental benefits upon the citizens of the Counties. First, they create enhanced incentives for recycling and proper disposal of other kinds of waste. Solid waste disposal is expensive in Oneida-Herkimer, but the Counties accept recyclables and many forms of hazardous waste for free, effectively encouraging their citizens to sort their own trash. Second, by requiring all waste to be deposited at Authority facilities, the Counties have markedly increased their ability to enforce recycling laws. If the haulers could take waste to any disposal site, achieving an equal level of enforcement would be much more costly, if not impossible. For these reasons, any arguable burden the ordinances impose on interstate commerce does not exceed their public benefits.

Justice SCALIA, concurring in part.

I join Part I and Parts II-A through II-C of the Court's opinion. I write separately to reaffirm my view that "the so-called 'negative' Commerce Clause is an

---

[164] The Counties and their amicus were asked at oral argument if affirmance would lead to the "Oneida-Herkimer Hamburger Stand," accompanied by a "flow control" law requiring citizens to purchase their burgers only from the state-owned producer. We doubt it. "The existence of major in-state interests adversely affected by [a law] is a powerful safeguard against legislative abuse." Recognizing that local government may facilitate a customary and traditional government function such as waste disposal, without running afoul of the Commerce Clause, is hardly a prescription for state control of the economy. In any event, Congress retains authority under the Commerce Clause as written to regulate interstate commerce, whether engaged in by private or public entities. It can use this power, as it has in the past, to limit state use of exclusive franchises. [Footnote by the Court.]

unjustified judicial invention, not to be expanded beyond its existing domain." "The historical record provides no grounds for reading the Commerce Clause to be other than what it says — an authorization for Congress to regulate commerce."

I have been willing to enforce on stare decisis grounds a "negative" self- executing Commerce Clause in two situations: "(1) against a state law that facially discriminates against interstate commerce, and (2) against a state law that is indistinguishable from a type of law previously held unconstitutional by the Court." As today's opinion makes clear, the flow-control law at issue in this case meets neither condition. It benefits a public entity performing a traditional local-government function and treats all private entities precisely the same way. "Disparate treatment constitutes discrimination only if the objects of the disparate treatment are, for the relevant purposes, similarly situated." None of this Court's cases concludes that public entities and private entities are similarly situated for Commerce Clause purposes. To hold that they are "would broaden the negative Commerce Clause beyond its existing scope, and intrude on a regulatory sphere traditionally occupied by . . . the States."

I am unable to join Part II-D of the principal opinion, in which the plurality performs so-called "*Pike* balancing." Generally speaking, the balancing of various values is left to Congress — which is precisely what the Commerce Clause (the real Commerce Clause) envisions.

Justice THOMAS, concurring in the judgment.

I concur in the judgment. Although I joined C & A Carbone, Inc. v. Clarkstown (1994), I no longer believe it was correctly decided. The negative Commerce Clause has no basis in the Constitution and has proved unworkable in practice. As the debate between the majority and dissent shows, application of the negative Commerce Clause turns solely on policy considerations, not on the Constitution. Because this Court has no policy role in regulating interstate commerce, I would discard the Court's negative Commerce Clause jurisprudence.

Because I believe that the power to regulate interstate commerce is a power given to Congress and not the Court, I concur in the judgment of the Court.

Justice ALITO, with whom Justice STEVENS and Justice KENNEDY join, dissenting.

In C & A Carbone, Inc. v. Clarkstown (1994), we held that "a so-called flow control ordinance, which require[d] all solid waste to be processed at a designated transfer station before leaving the municipality," discriminated against interstate commerce and was invalid under the Commerce Clause because it "depriv[ed] competitors, including out-of-state firms, of access to a local market." Because the provisions challenged in this case are essentially identical to the ordinance invalidated in *Carbone*, I respectfully dissent.

This case cannot be meaningfully distinguished from *Carbone*. As the Court itself acknowledges, "[t]he only salient difference" between the cases is that the ordinance invalidated in *Carbone* discriminated in favor of a privately owned facility, whereas the laws at issue here discriminate in favor of "facilities owned and operated by a state-created public benefit corporation." The Court relies on the distinction between public and private ownership to uphold the flow-control laws, even though a straightforward application of *Carbone* would lead to the opposite result. The public-private distinction drawn by the Court is both illusory and without precedent.

The fact that the flow control laws at issue discriminate in favor of a government-owned enterprise does not meaningfully distinguish this case from *Carbone*. The only real difference between the facility at issue in *Carbone* and its counterpart in this case is that title to the former had not yet formally passed to the municipality. The Court exalts form over substance in adopting a test that turns on this technical distinction, particularly since, barring any obstacle presented by state law, the transaction in *Carbone* could have been restructured to provide for the passage of title at the beginning, rather than the end, of the 5-year period.

For this very reason, it is not surprising that in *Carbone* the Court did not dispute the dissent's observation that the preferred facility was for all practical purposes owned by the municipality. To the contrary, the Court repeatedly referred to the transfer station in terms suggesting that the transfer station did in fact belong to the town.

Today the Court dismisses those statements as "at best inconclusive." The Court, however, fails to offer any explanation as to what other meaning could possibly attach to *Carbone*'s repeated references to Clarkstown's transfer station as a municipal facility. It also ignores the fact that the ordinance itself, which was included in its entirety in an appendix to the Court's opinion, repeatedly referred to the station as "the Town of Clarkstown solid waste facility." The Court likewise fails to acknowledge that the parties in *Carbone* openly acknowledged the municipal character of the transfer station.

I see no ambiguities in those statements, much less any reason to dismiss them as "at best inconclusive"; they reflect a clear understanding that the station was, for all purposes relevant to the dormant Commerce Clause, a municipal facility.

In any event, we have never treated discriminatory legislation with greater deference simply because the entity favored by that legislation was a government-owned enterprise. The Court has long subjected discriminatory legislation to strict scrutiny, and has never, until today, recognized an exception for discrimination in favor of a state-owned entity.

Nor has this Court ever suggested that discriminatory legislation favoring a state-owned enterprise is entitled to favorable treatment. To be sure, state-owned entities are accorded special status under the market-participant doctrine. But that doctrine is not applicable here.

Under the market-participant doctrine, a State is permitted to exercise " 'independent discretion as to parties with whom [it] will deal.' " The doctrine thus allows States to engage in certain otherwise-discriminatory practices (e.g., selling exclusively to, or buying exclusively from, the State's own residents), so long as the State is "acting as a market participant, rather than as a market regulator."

Respondents are doing exactly what the market-participant doctrine says they cannot: While acting as market participants by operating a fee-for-service business enterprise in an area in which there is an established interstate market, respondents are also regulating that market in a discriminatory manner and claiming that their special governmental status somehow insulates them from a dormant Commerce Clause challenge.

The fallacy in the Court's approach can be illustrated by comparing a law that discriminates in favor of an in-state facility, owned by a corporation whose shares are publicly held, and a law discriminating in favor of an otherwise identical facility that is owned by the State or municipality. Those who are favored and disfavored by these two laws are essentially the same with one major exception: The law favoring the corporate facility presumably benefits the corporation's shareholders, most of whom are probably not local residents, whereas the law favoring the government-owned facility presumably benefits the people of the enacting State or municipality. I cannot understand why only the former law, and not the latter, should be regarded as a tool of economic protectionism. Nor do I think it is realistic or consistent with our precedents to condemn some discriminatory laws as protectionist while upholding other, equally discriminatory laws as lawful measures designed to serve legitimate local interests unrelated to protectionism.

For these reasons, I cannot accept the proposition that laws discriminating in favor of state-owned enterprises are so unlikely to be the product of economic protectionism that they should be exempt from the usual dormant Commerce Clause standards.

Thus, if the legislative means are themselves discriminatory, then regardless of how legitimate and nonprotectionist the underlying legislative goals may be, the legislation is subject to strict scrutiny. Similarly, the fact that a discriminatory law "may [in some sense] be directed toward any number of legitimate goals unrelated to protectionism" does not make the law nondiscriminatory. The existence of such goals is relevant, not to whether the law is discriminatory, but to whether the law can be allowed to stand even though it discriminates against interstate commerce. And even then, the existence of legitimate goals is not enough; discriminatory legislation can be upheld only where such goals cannot adequately be achieved through nondiscriminatory means.

Equally unpersuasive is the Court's suggestion that the flow-control laws do not discriminate against interstate commerce because they "treat in-state private business interests exactly the same as out-of-state ones." Again, the critical issue is whether the challenged legislation discriminates against interstate commerce. If it does, then regardless of whether those harmed by it reside entirely outside the State in question, the law is subject to strict scrutiny. Indeed, this Court has long recognized that "'a burden imposed by a State upon interstate commerce is not to be sustained simply because the statute imposing it applies alike to the people of all the States, including the people of the State enacting such statute.'"

The dormant Commerce Clause has long been understood to prohibit the kind of discriminatory legislation upheld by the Court in this case.

———————

Many cases involving facially discriminatory laws have dealt with attempts by state and local governments to conserve their natural resources for use by their own residents. The following case is illustrative of such a state law that facially discriminates in this way.

Hughes v. Oklahoma

441 U.S. 322 (1979)

Justice BRENNAN delivered the opinion of the Court.

The question presented for decision is whether [an] Oklahoma Statute violates the Commerce Clause, of the United States Constitution, insofar as it provides that "[n]o person may transport or ship minnows for sale outside the state which were seined or procured within the waters of this state. . . ."

The burden to show discrimination rests on the party challenging the validity of the statute, but "[w]hen discrimination against commerce . . . is demonstrated, the burden falls on the State to justify it both in terms of the local benefits flowing from the statute and the unavailability of non-discriminatory alternatives adequate to preserve the local interests at stake." Furthermore, when considering the purpose of a challenged statute, this Court is not bound by the name, description or characterization given it by the legislature or the courts of the State, but will determine for itself the practical impact of the law.

Section 4-115(B) on its face discriminates against interstate commerce. It forbids the transportation of natural minnows out of the State for purposes of sale, and thus "overtly blocks the flow of interstate commerce at [the] State's borders." Such facial discrimination by itself may be a fatal defect, regardless of the State's purpose, because "the evil of protectionism can reside in legislative means as well as legislative ends." At a minimum such facial discrimination invokes the strictest scrutiny of any purported legitimate local purpose and of the absence of nondiscriminatory alternatives.

Oklahoma argues that §4-115(B) serves a legitimate local purpose in that it is "readily apparent as a conservation measure." The State's interest in maintaining the ecological balance in state waters by avoiding the removal of inordinate numbers of minnows may well qualify as a legitimate local purpose. We consider the States' interests in conservation and protection of wild animals as legitimate local purposes similar to the States' interests in protecting the health and safety of their citizens. But the fiction of state ownership may no longer be used to force those outside the State to bear the full costs of "conserving" the wild animals within its borders when equally effective nondiscriminatory conservation measures are available. Far from choosing the least discriminatory alternative, Oklahoma has chosen to "conserve" its minnows in the way that most overtly discriminate against interstate commerce. The State places no limits on the numbers of minnows that can be taken by licensed minnow dealers; nor does it limit in any way how these minnows may be disposed of within the State. Yet it forbids the transportation of any commercially significant number of natural minnows out of the State for sale. Section 4-115(B) is certainly not a "last ditch" attempt at conservation after nondiscriminatory alternatives have proved unfeasible. It is rather a choice of the most discriminatory means even though nondiscriminatory alternatives would seem likely to fulfill the State's purported legitimate local purpose more effectively.

———————

The Court has held that reciprocity requirements — a state allows out-of-staters to have access to markets or resources only when the out-of-staters are from states that grant similar benefits — are facially discriminatory. For instance, in Great A. & P. Tea Co. v. Cottrell, 424 U.S. 366 (1976), the Court unanimously invalidated a Mississippi law that provided that milk could be shipped into Mississippi from another state only if it had a public health certificate and only if the other state would accept milk from Mississippi on a reciprocal basis. Likewise, in Sporhase v. Nebraska, 458 U.S. 941 (1982), the Court found that a state law was discriminatory when it denied a permit to draw and use water for use in another state unless that state granted reciprocal rights to draw water for use in Nebraska.

FACIALLY NEUTRAL LAWS

The Supreme Court has held that facially neutral laws can be found to be discriminatory if they either have the purpose or the effect of discriminating against out-of-staters. The Court has declared: "A court may find that a state law constitutes 'economic protectionism' on proof either of discriminatory effect or of discriminatory purpose." Minnesota v. Clover Leaf Creamery Co., 450 U.S. 1027 (1981). This is very different from analysis under the Equal Protection Clause, discussed in Chapter 7 [Erwin Chemerinsky, Constitutional Law, 3rd ed., (2009)], where a facially neutral law is deemed discriminatory only if there is both a discriminatory purpose and a discriminatory effect.

The difficulty for courts is in deciding whether a particular law has a discriminatory purpose or a legitimate non-discriminatory objective and whether a law should be deemed to have a discriminatory impact. This difficulty is illustrated by comparing the following cases. In the first case presented, Hunt v. Washington State Apple Advertising Commn., the Court found that discriminatory impact is sufficient for a law to be deemed discriminatory and concluded that the state's statute was impermissibly discriminatory in its effects. In the second case, Exxon Corp. v. Governor of Maryland, the Court found that the law was not discriminatory and upheld its constitutionality. As you read these cases, compare their discriminatory effects and consider whether there is a meaningful difference in this regard between the decisions.

Hunt, Governor of the State of North Carolina v. Washington State Apple Advertising Commn.

432 U.S. 333 (1977)

Chief Justice BURGER delivered the opinion of the Court.

Washington State is the Nation's largest producer of apples, its crops accounting for approximately 30% of all apples grown domestically and nearly half of all apples shipped in closed containers in interstate commerce. As might be expected, the production and sale of apples on this scale is a multimillion dollar enterprise which plays a significant role in Washington's economy. Because of the importance of the apple industry to the State, its legislature has undertaken to protect and enhance the reputation of Washington apples by establishing a stringent, mandatory inspection program, administered by the State's Department of Agriculture, which requires all apples shipped in interstate commerce to be tested under strict quality standards and graded accordingly. In all cases, the Washington State grades, which have gained substantial acceptance in the trade, are the equivalent of, or superior to, the comparable grades and standards adopted by the United States Department of Agriculture (USDA). Compliance with the Washington inspection scheme costs the State's growers approximately $1 million each year.

In 1973, North Carolina enacted a statute which required all closed containers of apples sold, offered for sale, or shipped into the State to bear "no grade other than the applicable U.S. grade or standard." State grades were expressly prohibited. In addition to its obvious consequence prohibiting the display of Washington State apple grades on containers of apples shipped into North Carolina, the regulation presented the Washington apple industry with a marketing problem of potentially nationwide significance. Washington apple growers annually ship in commerce approximately 40 million closed containers of apples, nearly 500,000 of which eventually find their way into North Carolina, stamped with the applicable Washington State variety and grade. It is the industry's practice to purchase these containers preprinted with the various apple varieties and grades, prior to harvest. After these containers are filled with apples of the appropriate type and grade, a substantial portion of them are placed in cold-storage warehouses where the grade labels identify the product and facilitate its handling. These apples are then shipped as needed throughout the year; after February 1 of each year, they constitute approximately two-thirds of all apples sold in fresh markets in this country. Since the ultimate destination of these apples is unknown at the time they are placed in storage, compliance with North Carolina's unique regulation would have required Washington growers to obliterate the printed labels on containers shipped to North Carolina, thus giving their product a damaged appearance. Alternatively, they could have changed their marketing practices to accommodate the needs of the North Carolina market, i.e., repack apples to be shipped to North Carolina in containers bearing only the USDA grade, and/or store the estimated portion of the harvest destined for that market in such special containers. As a last resort, they could discontinue the use of the preprinted containers entirely. None of these costly and less efficient options was very attractive to the industry.

Moreover, in the event a number of other States followed North Carolina's lead, the resultant inability to display the Washington grades could force the Washington growers to abandon the State's expensive inspection and grading system which their customers had come to know and rely on over the 60-odd years of its existence.

As the District Court correctly found, the challenged statute has the practical effect of not only burdening interstate sales of Washington apples, but also discriminating against them. This discrimination takes various forms. The first, and most obvious, is the statute's consequence of raising the costs of doing business in the North Carolina market for Washington apple growers and dealers, while leaving those of their North Carolina counterparts unaffected. As previously noted, this disparate effect results from the fact that North Carolina apple producers, unlike their Washington competitors, were not forced to alter their marketing practices in order to comply with the statute. They were still free to market their wares under the USDA grade or none at all as they had done prior to the statute's enactment. Obviously, the increased costs imposed by the statute would tend to shield the local apple industry from the competition of Washington apple growers and dealers who are already at a competitive disadvantage because of their great distance from the North Carolina market.

Second, the statute has the effect of stripping away from the Washington apple industry the competitive and economic advantages it has earned for itself through its expensive inspection and grading system. The record demonstrates that the Washington apple-grading system has gained nationwide acceptance in the apple trade.

Third, by prohibiting Washington growers and dealers from marketing apples under their State's grades, the statute has a leveling effect which insidiously operates to the advantage of local apple producers. As noted earlier, the Washington State grades are equal or superior to the USDA grades in all corresponding categories. Hence, with free market forces at work, Washington sellers would normally enjoy a distinct market advantage vis-à-vis local producers in those categories where the Washington grade is superior. However, because of the statute's operation, Washington apples which would otherwise qualify for and be sold under the superior Washington grades will now have to be marketed under their inferior USDA counterparts. Such "downgrading" offers the North Carolina apple industry the very sort of protection against competing out-of-state products that the Commerce Clause was designed to prohibit. At worst, it will have the effect of an embargo against those Washington apples in the superior grades as Washington dealers withhold them from the North Carolina market. At best, it will deprive Washington sellers of the market premium that such apples would otherwise command.

When discrimination against commerce of the type we have found is demonstrated, the burden falls on the State to justify it both in terms of the local benefits flowing from the statute and the unavailability of nondiscriminatory alternatives adequate to preserve the local interests at stake. Dean Milk Co. v. Madison (1951). North Carolina has failed to sustain that burden on both scores. The several States unquestionably possess a substantial interest in protecting their citizens from confusion and deception in the marketing of foodstuffs, but the challenged statute does remarkably little to further that laudable goal at least with respect to Washington apples and grades. The statute, as already noted, permits the marketing of closed containers of apples under no grades at all. Such a result can hardly be thought to eliminate the problems of deception and confusion created by the multiplicity of differing state grades; indeed, it magnifies them by depriving purchasers of all information concerning the quality of the contents of closed apple containers. Moreover, although the statute is ostensibly a consumer protection measure, it directs its primary efforts, not at the consuming public at large, but at apple wholesalers and brokers who are the principal purchasers of closed containers of apples. And those individuals are presumably the most knowledgeable individuals in this area. Since the statute does nothing at all to purify the flow of information at the retail level, it does little to protect consumers against the problems it was designed to eliminate.

In addition, it appears that nondiscriminatory alternatives to the outright ban of Washington State grades are readily available. For example, North Carolina could effectuate its goal by permitting out-of-state growers to utilize state grades only if they also marked their shipments with the applicable USDA label. In that case, the USDA grade would serve as a benchmark against which the consumer could evaluate the quality of the various state grades.

Exxon Corp. v. Governor of Maryland

437 U.S. 117 (1978)

Justice STEVENS delivered the opinion of the Court.

A Maryland statute provides that a producer or refiner of petroleum products (1) may not operate any retail service station within the State, and (2) must extend all "voluntary allowances" uniformly to all service stations it supplies.

The Maryland statute is an outgrowth of the 1973 shortage of petroleum. In response to complaints about inequitable distribution of gasoline among retail stations, the Governor of Maryland directed the State Comptroller to conduct a market survey. The results of that survey indicated that gasoline stations operated by producers or refiners had received preferential treatment during the period of short supply. The Comptroller therefore proposed legislation which was "designed to correct the inequities in the distribution and pricing of gasoline reflected by the survey."

The essential facts alleged in the complaint are not in dispute. All of the gasoline sold by Exxon in Maryland is transported into the State from refineries located elsewhere. Although Exxon sells the bulk of this gas to wholesalers and independent retailers, it also sells directly to the consuming public through 36 company-operated stations. Exxon uses these stations to test innovative marketing concepts or products. Focusing primarily on the Act's requirement that it discontinue its operation of these 36 retail stations, Exxon's complaint challenged the validity of the statute.

Plainly, the Maryland statute does not discriminate against interstate goods, nor does it favor local producers and refiners. Since Maryland's entire gasoline supply flows in interstate commerce and since there are no local producers or refiners, such claims of disparate treatment between interstate and local commerce would be meritless. Appellants, however, focus on the retail market arguing that the effect of the statute is to protect in-state independent dealers from out-of-state competition. They contend that the divestiture provisions "create a protected enclave for Maryland independent dealers. . . ." As support for this proposition, they rely on the fact that the burden of the divestiture requirements falls solely on interstate companies. But this fact does not lead, either logically or as a practical matter, to a conclusion that the State is discriminating against interstate commerce at the retail level.

As the record shows, there are several major interstate marketers of petroleum that own and operate their own retail gasoline stations. These interstate dealers, who compete directly with the Maryland independent dealers, are not affected by the Act because they do not refine or produce gasoline. In fact, the Act creates no barriers whatsoever against interstate independent dealers; it does not prohibit the flow of interstate goods, place added costs upon them, or distinguish between in-state and out-of-state companies in the retail market. The absence of any of these factors fully distinguishes this case from those in which a State has been found to have discriminated against interstate commerce. See, e.g., Hunt v. Washington Apple Advertising Commn. For instance, the Court in *Hunt* noted that the challenged state statute raised the cost of doing business for out-of-state dealers, and, in various other ways, favored the in-state dealer in the local market. No comparable claim can be made here. While the refiners will no longer enjoy their same status in the Maryland market, in-state independent dealers will have no competitive advantage over out-of-state dealers. The fact that the burden of a state regulation falls on some interstate companies does not, by itself, establish a claim of discrimination against interstate commerce.

Appellants argue, however, that this fact does show that the Maryland statute impermissibly burdens interstate commerce. They point to evidence in the record which indicates that, because of the divestiture requirements, at least three refiners will stop selling in Maryland, and which also supports their claim that the elimination of company-operated stations will deprive the consumer of certain special services. Even if we assume the truth of both assertions, neither warrants a finding that the statute impermissibly burdens interstate commerce. Some refiners may choose to withdraw entirely from the Maryland market, but there is no reason to assume that their share of the entire supply will not be promptly replaced by other interstate refiners. The source of the consumers' supply may switch from company-operated stations to independent dealers, but interstate commerce is not subjected to an impermissible burden simply because an otherwise valid regulation causes some business to shift from one interstate supplier to another.

Appellants claim that the statute "will surely change the market structure by weakening the independent refiners. . . ." We cannot, however, accept appellants' underlying notion that the Commerce Clause protects the particular structure or methods of operation in a retail market. [T]he Clause protects the interstate market, not particular interstate firms, from prohibitive or burdensome regulations. It may be true that the consuming public will be injured by the loss of the high-volume, low-priced stations operated by the independent refiners, but again that argument relates to the wisdom of the statute, not to its burden *on* commerce.

Justice BLACKMUN, dissenting.

I dissent from the Court's opinion because it fails to condemn impermissible discrimination against interstate commerce in *retail* gasoline marketing. The divestiture provisions preclude out-of-state competitors from retailing gasoline within Maryland. The effect is to protect in-state retail service station dealers from the competition of the out-of-state businesses. This protectionist discrimination is not justified by any legitimate state interest that cannot be vindicated by more even-handed regulation. [The law,] therefore, violate[s] the Commerce Clause.

In Maryland the retail marketing of gasoline is interstate commerce, for all petroleum products come from outside the State. Retailers serve interstate travelers. To the extent that particular retailers succeed or fail in their businesses, the interstate wholesale market for petroleum products is affected.

The Commerce Clause forbids discrimination against interstate commerce, which repeatedly has been held to mean that States and localities may not discriminate against the transactions of out-of-state actors in interstate markets. The discrimination need not appear on the face of the state or local regulation. "The Commerce Clause forbids discrimination, whether forthright or ingenious. In each case it is our duty to determine whether the statute under attack, whatever its name may be, will in its practical operation work discrimination against interstate commerce." The state or local authority need not intend to discriminate in order to offend the policy of maintaining a free-flowing national economy. As demonstrated in *Hunt*, a statute that on its face restricts both intrastate and interstate transactions may violate the Clause by having the "practical effect" of discriminating in its operation. If discrimination results from a statute, the burden falls upon the state or local government to demonstrate legitimate local benefits justifying the inequality and to show that less discriminatory alternatives cannot protect the local interests.

With this background, the unconstitutional discrimination in the Maryland statute becomes apparent. No facial inequality exists; §§(b) and (c) preclude all refiners and producers from marketing gasoline at the retail level. But given the structure of the retail gasoline market in Maryland, the effect of §§(b) and (c) is to exclude a class of predominantly out-of-state gasoline retailers while providing protection from competition to a class of nonintegrated retailers that is overwhelmingly composed of local businessmen.

In 1974, of the 3,780 gasoline service stations in the State, 3,547 were operated by nonintegrated local retail dealers. Of the 233 company-operated stations, 197 belonged to out-of-state integrated producers or refiners. Thirty-four were operated by nonintegrated companies that would not have been affected immediately by the Maryland statute. The only in-state integrated petroleum firm, Crown Central Petroleum, Inc., operated just two service stations. Of the class of stations statutorily insulated from the competition of the out-of-state integrated firms, then, more than 99% were operated by local business interests. Of the class of enterprises excluded entirely from participation in the retail gasoline market, 95% were out-of-state firms, operating 98% of the stations in the class.

The discrimination suffered by the out-of-state integrated producers and refiners is significant. Five of the excluded enterprises, Ashland Oil, Inc., BP Oil, Inc., Kayo Oil Co., Petroleum Marketing Corp., and Southern States Cooperative, Inc., market nonbranded gasoline through price competition rather than through brand recognition. Of the 98 stations marketing gasoline in this manner, all but 6 are company operated. The record also contains testimony that the discrimination will burden the operations of major branded companies, such as appellants Exxon, Phillips, Shell, and Gulf, all of which are out-of-state firms. Most importantly, §§(b) and (c) will preclude these companies, as well as those mentioned in the previous paragraph, from competing directly for the profits of retail marketing.

[T]he State appears to be concerned about unfair competitive behavior such as predatory pricing or inequitable allocation of petroleum products by the integrated firms. These are the only examples of specific misconduct asserted in the State's answers. But none of the concerns support the discrimination in §§(b) and (c). There is no proof in the record that any significant portion of the class of out-of-state firms burdened by the divestiture sections has engaged in such misconduct. Furthermore, predatory pricing and unfair allocation already have been prohibited by both state and federal law. Less discriminatory legislation, which would regulate the leasing of all service stations, not just those owned by the out-of-state integrated producers and refiners, could prevent whatever evils arise from short-term leases.

Facially neutral laws also can be found to be discriminatory if they were enacted for a protectionist purpose: helping in-staters at the expense of out-of-staters. Although the following two cases involve discussion of both purpose and effect, in the former, West Lynn Creamery, Inc. v. Healy, the Court invalidated a state law largely because of its discriminatory purpose; but in the latter case, Minnesota v. Clover Leaf Creamery Co., the Court upheld the law by finding that the law did not have a discriminatory objective.

West Lynn Creamery, Inc. v. Healy, Commissioner of Massachusetts Dept. of Food & Agriculture

512 U.S. 186 (1994)

Justice STEVENS delivered the opinion of the Court.

A Massachusetts pricing order imposes an assessment on all fluid milk sold by dealers to Massachusetts retailers. About two-thirds of that milk is produced out of State. The entire assessment, however, is distributed to Massachusetts dairy farmers. The question presented is whether the pricing order unconstitutionally discriminates against interstate commerce. We hold that it does.

Petitioner West Lynn Creamery, Inc., is a milk dealer licensed to do business in Massachusetts. It purchases raw milk, which it processes, packages, and sells to wholesalers, retailers, and other milk dealers. About 97% of the raw milk it purchases is produced by out-of-state farmers. Petitioner LeComte's Dairy, Inc., is also a licensed Massachusetts milk dealer. It purchases all of its milk from West Lynn and distributes it to retail outlets in Massachusetts.

In the 1980s and early 1990s, Massachusetts dairy farmers began to lose market share to lower cost producers in neighboring States. In response, the Governor of Massachusetts appointed a Special Commission to study the dairy industry. The commission found that many producers had sold their dairy farms during the past decade and that if prices paid to farmers for their milk were not significantly increased, a majority of the remaining farmers in Massachusetts would be "forced out of business within the year."

On January 28, 1992, relying on the commission's report, the Commissioner of the Massachusetts Department of Food and Agriculture (respondent) declared a State of Emergency. [T]he Massachusetts order requires dealers to make payments into a fund that is disbursed to farmers on a monthly basis. The assessments, however, are only on Class I sales and the distributions are only to Massachusetts farmers.

The Commerce Clause also limits the power of the Commonwealth of Massachusetts to adopt regulations that discriminate against interstate commerce. "This 'negative' aspect of the Commerce Clause prohibits economic protectionism — that is, regulatory measures designed to benefit in-state economic interests by burdening out-of-state competitors. . . . Thus, state statutes that clearly discriminate against interstate commerce are routinely struck down . . . unless the discrimination is demonstrably justified by a valid factor unrelated to economic protectionism. . . ." New Energy Co. of Ind. v. Limbach (1988).

Respondent's principal argument is that, because "the milk order achieves its goals through lawful means," the order as a whole is constitutional. He argues that the payments to Massachusetts dairy farmers from the Dairy Equalization Fund are valid, because subsidies are constitutional exercises of state power, and that the order premium which provides money for the fund is valid, because it is a nondiscriminatory tax. Therefore the pricing order is constitutional, because it is merely the combination of two independently lawful regulations. In effect, respondent argues, if the State may impose a valid tax on dealers, it is free to use the proceeds of the tax as it chooses; and if it may independently subsidize its farmers, it is free to finance the subsidy by means of any legitimate tax.

Even granting respondent's assertion that both components of the pricing order would be constitutional standing alone, the pricing order nevertheless must fall. A pure subsidy funded out of general revenue ordinarily imposes no burden on interstate commerce, but merely assists local business. The pricing order in this case, however, is funded principally from taxes on the sale of milk produced in other States. By so funding the subsidy, respondent not only assists local farmers, but burdens interstate commerce. The pricing order thus violates the cardinal principle that a State may not "benefit in-state economic interests by burdening out-of-state competitors."

More fundamentally, respondent errs in assuming that the constitutionality of the pricing order follows logically from the constitutionality of its component parts. By conjoining a tax and a subsidy, Massachusetts has created a program more dangerous to interstate commerce than either part alone. Nondiscriminatory measures, like the evenhanded tax at issue here, are generally upheld, in spite of any adverse effects on interstate commerce, in part because "[t]he existence of major in-state interests adversely affected . . . is a powerful safeguard against legislative abuse." Minnesota v. Clover Leaf Creamery Co. (1981). However, when a nondiscriminatory tax is coupled with a subsidy to one of the groups hurt by the tax, a State's political processes can no longer be relied upon to prevent legislative abuse, because one of the in-state interests which would otherwise lobby against the tax has been mollified by the subsidy. So, in this case, one would ordinarily have expected at least three groups to lobby against the order premium, which, as a tax, raises the price (and hence lowers demand) for milk: dairy farmers, milk dealers, and consumers. But because the tax was coupled with a subsidy, one of the most powerful of these groups, Massachusetts dairy farmers, instead of exerting their influence against the tax, were in fact its primary supporters.

More fundamentally, respondent ignores the fact that Massachusetts dairy farmers are part of an integrated interstate market. [T]he purpose and effect of the pricing order are to divert market share to Massachusetts dairy farmers. This diversion necessarily injures the dairy farmers in neighboring States. Preservation of local industry by protecting it from the rigors of interstate competition is the hallmark of the economic protectionism that the Commerce Clause prohibits.

State of Minnesota v. Clover Leaf Creamery Co.

449 U.S. 456 (1981)

Justice BRENNAN delivered the opinion of the Court.

In 1977, the Minnesota Legislature enacted a statute banning the retail sale of milk in plastic nonreturnable, nonrefillable containers, but permitting such sale in other nonreturnable, nonrefillable containers, such as paperboard milk cartons. The purpose of the Minnesota statute is set out as §1: "The legislature finds that the use of nonreturnable, nonrefillable containers for the packaging of milk and other milk products presents a solid waste management problem for the state, promotes energy waste, and depletes natural resources. The legislature therefore determines that the use of nonreturnable, nonrefillable containers for packaging milk and other milk products should be discouraged and that the use of returnable and reusable packaging for these products is preferred and should be encouraged." Proponents of the legislation argued that it would promote resource conservation, ease solid waste disposal problems, and conserve energy. Relying on the results of studies and other information, they stressed the need to stop introduction of the plastic nonreturnable container before it became entrenched in the market.

After the Act was passed, respondents filed suit in Minnesota District Court, seeking to enjoin its enforcement. The court further found that, contrary to the statement of purpose in §1, the "actual basis" for the Act "was to promote the economic interests of certain segments of the local dairy and pulpwood industries at the expense of the economic interests of other segments of the dairy industry and the plastics industry." The court therefore declared the Act "null, void, and unenforceable."

When legislating in areas of legitimate local concern, such as environmental protection and resource conservation, States are nonetheless limited by the Commerce Clause. If a state law purporting to promote environmental purposes is in reality "simple economic protectionism," we have applied a "virtually per se rule of invalidity." Philadelphia v. New Jersey (1978). Even if a statute regulates "even-handedly," and imposes only "incidental" burdens on interstate commerce, the courts must nevertheless strike it down if "the burden imposed on such commerce is clearly excessive in relation to the putative local benefits." Pike v. Bruce Church, Inc. (1970). Moreover, "the extent of the burden that will be tolerated will of course depend on the nature of the local interest involved, and on whether it could be promoted as well with a lesser impact on interstate activities."

A court may find that a state law constitutes "economic protectionism" on proof either of discriminatory effect or of discriminatory purpose. Respondents advance a "discriminatory purpose" argument, relying on a finding by the District Court that the Act's "actual basis was to promote the economic interests of certain segments of the local dairy and pulpwood industries at the expense of the economic interests of other segments of the dairy industry and the plastics industry."

Minnesota's statute does not effect "simple protectionism," but "regulates even-handedly" by prohibiting all milk retailers from selling their products in plastic, nonreturnable milk containers, without regard to whether the milk, the containers, or the sellers are from outside the State. This statute is therefore unlike statutes discriminating against interstate commerce, which we have consistently struck down. E.g., Hughes v. Oklahoma (1979); Philadelphia v. New Jersey [(1978)]; Hunt v. Washington Apple Advertising Comm'n [(1977)]. Since the statute does not discriminate between interstate and intrastate commerce, the controlling question is whether the incidental burden imposed on interstate commerce by the Minnesota Act is "clearly excessive in relation to the putative local benefits." We conclude that it is not.

The burden imposed on interstate commerce by the statute is relatively minor. Milk products may continue to move freely across the Minnesota border, and since most dairies package their products in more than one type of container, the inconvenience of having to conform to different packaging requirements in Minnesota and the surrounding States should be slight. Within Minnesota, business will presumably shift from manufacturers of plastic nonreturnable containers to producers of paperboard cartons, refillable bottles, and plastic pouches, but there is no reason to suspect that the gainers will be Minnesota firms, or the losers out-of-state firms. Indeed, two of the three dairies, the sole milk retailer, and the sole milk container producer challenging the statute in this litigation are Minnesota firms.

Pulpwood producers are the only Minnesota industry likely to benefit significantly from the Act at the expense of out-of-state firms. Respondents point out that plastic resin, the raw material used for making plastic nonreturnable milk jugs, is produced entirely by non-Minnesota firms, while pulpwood, used for making paperboard, is a major Minnesota product. Nevertheless, it is clear that respondents exaggerate the degree of burden on out-of-state interests, both because plastics will continue to be used in the production of plastic pouches, plastic returnable bottles, and paperboard itself, and because out-of-state pulpwood producers will presumably absorb some of the business generated by the Act. Even granting that the out-of-state plastics industry is burdened relatively more heavily than the Minnesota pulpwood industry, we find that this burden is not "clearly excessive" in light of the substantial state interest in promoting conservation of energy and other natural resources and easing solid waste disposal problems, which we have already reviewed in the context of equal protection analysis. We find these local benefits ample to support Minnesota's decision under the Commerce Clause. Moreover, we find no approach with "a lesser impact on interstate activities."

c. Analysis If a Law Is Deemed Discriminatory

The cases presented above demonstrate that the crucial initial inquiry in dormant Commerce Clause cases is whether the law is discriminatory against out-of-staters. In City of Philadelphia v. New Jersey, the Court said "where simple economic protectionism is effected by state legislation, a virtually per se rule of invalidity has been erected." In C & A Carbone, Inc. v. Town of Clarkstown, the Court declared: "Discrimination against interstate commerce in favor of local business or investment is per se invalid, save in a narrow class of cases in which the municipality can demonstrate, under rigorous scrutiny, that it has no other means to advance a legitimate local interest." In Hunt v. Washington State Apple Advertising Commission, the Court stated: "When discrimination against commerce of the type we have found is demonstrated, the burden falls on the State to justify it both in terms of the local benefits flowing from the statute and the unavailability of nondiscriminatory alternatives adequate to preserve the local interests at stake."

The initial case, Dean Milk Co. v. City of Madison, illustrates the rigorous scrutiny used when laws are deemed discriminatory. Following it is Maine v. Taylor, the only case thus far in which the Supreme Court has upheld a discriminatory state law challenged under the dormant Commerce Clause.

Dean Milk Co. v. City of Madison, Wisconsin

340 U.S. 349 (1951)

This appeal challenges the constitutional validity of [a] section of an ordinance of the City of Madison, Wisconsin, regulating the sale of milk and milk products within the municipality's jurisdiction. [The] section in issue makes it unlawful to sell any milk as pasteurized unless it has been processed and bottled at an approved pasteurization plant within a radius of five miles from the central square of Madison. Appellant is an Illinois corporation engaged in distributing milk and milk products in Illinois and Wisconsin. It contended below, as it does here, that both the five-mile limit on pasteurization plants and the twenty-five-mile limit on sources of milk violate the Commerce Clause and the Fourteenth Amendment to the Federal Constitution.

The City of Madison is the county seat of Dane County. Within the county are some 5,600 dairy farms with total raw milk production in excess of 600,000,000 pounds annually and more than ten times the requirements of Madison. Aside from the milk supplied to Madison, fluid milk produced in the county moves in large quantities to Chicago and more distant consuming areas, and the remainder is used in making cheese, butter and other products.

Appellant purchases and gathers milk from approximately 950 farms in northern Illinois and southern Wisconsin, none being within twenty-five miles of Madison. Its pasteurization plants are located at Chemung and Huntley, Illinois, about 65 and 85 miles respectively from Madison. Appellant was denied a license to sell its products within Madison solely because its pasteurization plants were more than five miles away. It is conceded that the milk which appellant seeks to sell in Madison is supplied from farms and processed in plants licensed and inspected by public health authorities of Chicago, and is labeled "Grade A" under the Chicago ordinance which adopts the rating standards recommended by the United States Public Health Service.

Upon these facts we find it necessary to determine only the issue raised under the Commerce Clause, for we agree with appellant that the ordinance imposes an undue burden on interstate commerce. [T]his regulation in practical effect excludes from distribution in Madison wholesome milk produced and pasteurized in Illinois. In thus erecting an economic barrier protecting a major local industry against competition from without the State, Madison plainly discriminates against interstate commerce. This it cannot do, even in the exercise of its unquestioned power to protect the health and safety of its people, if reasonable nondiscriminatory alternatives, adequate to conserve legitimate local interests, are available. It is immaterial that Wisconsin milk from outside the Madison area is subjected to the same proscription as that moving in interstate commerce.

It appears that reasonable and adequate alternatives are available. If the City of Madison prefers to rely upon its own officials for inspection of distant milk sources, such inspection is readily open to it without hardship for it could charge the actual and reasonable cost of such inspection to the importing producers and processors. Moreover, appellee Health Commissioner of Madison testified that as proponent of the local milk ordinance he had submitted the provisions here in controversy and an alternative proposal based on the Model Milk Ordinance recommended by the United States Public Health Service. The model provision imposes no geographical limitation on location of milk sources and processing plants but excludes from the municipality milk not produced and pasteurized conformably to standards as high as those enforced by the receiving city. In implementing such an ordinance, the importing city obtains milk ratings based on uniform standards and established by health authorities in the jurisdiction where production and processing occur. The receiving city may determine the extent of enforcement of sanitary standards in the exporting area by verifying the accuracy of safety ratings of specific plants or of the milkshed in the distant jurisdiction through the United States Public Health Service, which routinely and on request spot checks the local ratings.

To permit Madison to adopt a regulation not essential for the protection of local health interests and placing a discriminatory burden on interstate commerce would invite a multiplication of preferential trade areas destructive of the very purpose of the Commerce Clause. Under the circumstances here presented, the regulation must yield to the principle that "one state in its dealings with another may not place itself in a position of economic isolation."

Maine v. Taylor & United States

477 U.S. 131 (1986)

Justice BLACKMUN delivered the opinion of the Court.

Once again, a little fish has caused a commotion. See Hughes v. Oklahoma (1979); TVA v. Hill (1978). The fish in this case is the golden shiner, a species of minnow commonly used as live bait in sport fishing. Appellee Robert J. Taylor operates a bait business in Maine. Despite a Maine statute prohibiting the importation of live baitfish, he arranged to have 158,000 live golden shiners delivered to him from outside the State. The shipment was intercepted, and a federal grand jury in the District of Maine indicted Taylor for violating and conspiring to violate the Lacey Act Amendments of 1981. Section 3(a)(2)(A) of those Amendments makes it a federal crime "to import, export, transport, sell, receive, acquire, or purchase in interstate or foreign commerce . . . any fish or wildlife taken, possessed, transported, or sold in violation of any law or regulation of any State or in violation of any foreign law."

Taylor moved to dismiss the indictment on the ground that Maine's import ban unconstitutionally burdens interstate commerce and therefore may not form the basis for a federal prosecution under the Lacey Act. Maine intervened to defend the validity of its statute, arguing that the ban legitimately protects the State's fisheries from parasites and nonnative species that might be included in shipments of live baitfish.

Maine's statute restricts interstate trade in the most direct manner possible, blocking all inward shipments of live baitfish at the State's border. Still, this fact alone does not render the law unconstitutional. The limitation imposed by the Commerce Clause on state regulatory power "is by no means absolute," and "the States retain authority under their general police powers to regulate matters of 'legitimate local concern,' even though interstate commerce may be affected." In determining whether a State has overstepped its role in regulating interstate commerce, this Court has distinguished between state statutes that burden interstate transactions only incidentally, and those that affirmatively discriminate against such transactions. While statutes in the first group violate the Commerce Clause only if the burdens they impose on interstate trade are "clearly excessive in relation to the putative local benefits," Pike v. Bruce Church, Inc. (1970), statutes in the second group are subject to more demanding scrutiny. The Court explained in Hughes v. Oklahoma, that once a state law is shown to discriminate against interstate commerce "either on its face or in practical effect," the burden falls on the State to demonstrate both that the statute "serves a legitimate local purpose," and that this purpose could not be served as well by available nondiscriminatory means.

[At] the evidentiary hearing [in] the District Court, [t]hree scientific experts testified for the prosecution and one for the defense. The prosecution experts testified that live baitfish imported into the State posed two significant threats to Maine's unique and fragile fisheries. First, Maine's population of wild fish — including its own indigenous golden shiners — would be placed at risk by three types of parasites prevalent in out-of-state baitfish, but not common to wild fish in Maine. Second, nonnative species inadvertently included in shipments of live baitfish could disturb Maine's aquatic ecology to an unpredictable extent by competing with native fish for food or habitat, by preying on native species, or by disrupting the environment in more subtle ways. The prosecution experts further testified that there was no satisfactory way to inspect shipments of live baitfish for parasites or commingled species. According to their testimony, the small size of baitfish and the large quantities in which they are shipped made inspection for commingled species "a physical impossibility." Parasite inspection posed a separate set of difficulties because the examination procedure required destruction of the fish.

Although the proffered justification for any local discrimination against interstate commerce must be subjected to "the strictest scrutiny," Hughes v. Oklahoma, the empirical component of that scrutiny, like any other form of factfinding, is the basic responsibility of district courts, rather than appellate courts. After reviewing the expert testimony presented to the Magistrate, however, we cannot say that the District Court clearly erred in finding that substantial scientific uncertainty surrounds the effect that baitfish parasites and nonnative species could have on Maine's fisheries. Moreover, we agree with the District Court that Maine has a legitimate interest in guarding against imperfectly understood environmental risks, despite the possibility that they may ultimately prove to be negligible. The constitutional principles underlying the Commerce Clause cannot be read as requiring the State of Maine to sit idly by and wait until potentially irreversible environmental damage has occurred or until the scientific community agrees on what disease organisms are or are not dangerous before it acts to avoid such consequences.

Justice STEVENS, dissenting.

There is something fishy about this case. Maine is the only State in the Union that blatantly discriminates against out-of-state baitfish by flatly prohibiting their importation. Although golden shiners are already present and thriving in Maine (and, perhaps not coincidentally, the subject of a flourishing domestic industry), Maine excludes golden shiners grown and harvested (and, perhaps not coincidentally sold) in other States. This kind of stark discrimination against out-of-state articles of commerce requires rigorous justification by the discriminating State. "When discrimination against commerce of the type we have found is demonstrated, the burden falls on the State to justify it both in terms of the local benefits flowing from the statute and the unavailability of nondiscriminatory alternatives adequate to preserve the local interests at stake." Hunt v. Washington State Apple Advertising Comm'n (1977).

Like the District Court, the Court concludes that uncertainty about possible ecological effects from the possible presence of parasites and nonnative species in shipments of out-of-state shiners suffices to carry the State's burden of proving a legitimate public purpose. The Court similarly concludes that the State has no obligation to develop feasible inspection procedures that would make a total ban unnecessary. It seems clear, however, that the presumption should run the other way. Since the State engages in obvious discrimination against out-of-state commerce, it should be put to its proof. Ambiguity about dangers and alternatives should actually defeat, rather than sustain, the discriminatory measure.

This is not to derogate the State's interest in ecological purity. But the invocation of environmental protection or public health has never been thought to confer some kind of special dispensation from the general principle of nondiscrimination in interstate commerce. If Maine wishes to rely on its interest in ecological preservation, it must show that interest, and the infeasibility of other alternatives, with far greater specificity. Otherwise, it must further that asserted interest in a manner far less offensive to the notions of comity and cooperation that underlie the Commerce Clause. Maine's unquestionable natural splendor notwithstanding, the State has not carried its substantial burden of proving why it cannot meet its environmental concerns in the same manner as other States with the same interest in the health of their fish and ecology. I respectfully dissent.

d. Analysis If a Law Is Deemed Non-Discriminatory

If the court concludes that a state's law is not discriminatory — that is, it treats in-staters and out-of-staters alike — then it is subjected to a much less demanding test. Non-discriminatory laws are upheld so long as the benefits to the government outweigh the burdens on interstate commerce. As presented earlier, it should be remembered that some Justices — most notably Chief Justice Rehnquist and Justices Scalia and Thomas — object to the subjectivity of this balancing test and even question whether the dormant Commerce Clause should apply in the absence of state discrimination against out-of-staters. Their arguments should be considered during the reading of the following cases.

The initial case presented below, Pike v. Bruce Church, is the decision most frequently cited as establishing the test used in analyzing laws that are not discriminatory.

Loren J. Pike v. Bruce Church, Inc.

397 U.S. 137 (1970)

Justice STEWART delivered the opinion of the Court.

The appellee is a company engaged in extensive commercial farming operations in Arizona and California. The appellant is the official charged with enforcing the Arizona Fruit and Vegetable Standardization Act. A provision of the Act requires that, with certain exceptions, all cantaloupes grown in Arizona and offered for sale must "be packed in regular compact arrangement in closed standard containers approved by the supervisor. . . ." Invoking his authority under that provision, the appellant issued an order prohibiting the appellee company from transporting uncrated cantaloupes from its Parker, Arizona, ranch to nearby Blythe, California, for packing and processing. The company then brought this action in a federal court to enjoin the order as unconstitutional.

The facts are not in dispute, having been stipulated by the parties. The appellee company has for many years been engaged in the business of growing, harvesting, processing, and packing fruits and vegetables at numerous locations in Arizona and California for interstate shipment to markets throughout the Nation. One of the company's newest operations is at Parker, Arizona, where, pursuant to a 1964 lease with the Secretary of the Interior, the Colorado River Indian Agency, and the Colorado River Indian Tribes, it undertook to develop approximately 6,400 acres of uncultivated, arid land for agricultural use. The company has spent more than $3,000,000 in clearing, leveling, irrigating, and otherwise developing this land. The company began growing cantaloupes on part of the land in 1966, and has harvested a large cantaloupe crop there in each subsequent year. The cantaloupes are considered to be of higher quality than those grown in other areas of the State. Because they are highly perishable, cantaloupes must upon maturity be immediately harvested, processed, packed, and shipped in order to prevent spoilage. The processing and packing operations can be performed only in packing sheds. Because the company had no such facilities at Parker, it transported its 1966 Parker cantaloupe harvest in bulk loads to Blythe, California, 31 miles away, where it operated centralized and efficient packing shed facilities. There the melons were sorted, inspected, packed, and shipped. In 1967 the company again sent its Parker cantaloupe crop to Blythe for sorting, packing, and shipping. In 1968, however, the appellant entered the order here in issue, prohibiting the company from shipping its cantaloupes out of the State unless they were packed in containers in a manner and of a kind approved by the appellant. Because cantaloupes in the quantity involved can be so packed only in packing sheds, and because no such facilities were available to the company at Parker or anywhere else nearby in Arizona, the company faced imminent loss of its anticipated 1968 cantaloupe crop in the gross amount of $700,000.

Although the criteria for determining the validity of state statutes affecting interstate commerce have been variously stated, the general rule that emerges can be phrased as follows: Where the statute regulates even-handedly to effectuate a legitimate local public interest, and its effects on interstate commerce are only incidental, it will be upheld unless the burden imposed on such commerce is clearly excessive in relation to the putative local benefits. If a legitimate local purpose is found, then the question becomes one of degree. And the extent of the burden that will be tolerated will of course depend on the nature of the local interest involved, and on whether it could be promoted as well with a lesser impact on interstate activities.

We are not dealing here with "state legislation in the field of safety where the propriety of local regulation has long been recognized," or with an Act designed to protect consumers in Arizona from contaminated or unfit goods. Its purpose and design are simply to protect and enhance the reputation of growers within the State. These are surely legitimate state interests.

But the State's tenuous interest in having the company's cantaloupes identified as originating in Arizona cannot constitutionally justify the requirement that the company build and operate an unneeded $200,000 packing plant in the State. The nature of that burden is, constitutionally, more significant than its extent. For the Court has viewed with particular suspicion state statutes requiring business operations to be performed in the home State that could more efficiently be performed elsewhere. Even where the State is pursuing a clearly legitimate local interest, this particular burden on commerce has been declared to be virtually per se illegal.

While the order issued under the Arizona statute does not impose such rigidity on an entire industry, it does impose just such a straitjacket on the appellee company with respect to the allocation of its interstate resources. Such an incidental consequence of a regulatory scheme could perhaps be tolerated if a more compelling state interest were involved. But here the State's interest is minimal at best — certainly less substantial than a State's interest in securing employment for its people. If the Commerce Clause forbids a State to require work to be done within its jurisdiction to promote local employment, then surely it cannot permit a State to require a person to go into a local packing business solely for the sake of enhancing the reputation of other producers within its borders.

The following two cases, Bibb v. Navajo Freight Lines and Consolidated Freightways Corp. v. Kassell, are examples of where the Court has used the balancing test to find non-discriminatory laws unconstitutional.

Bibb, Director, Dept. of Public Safety of Illinois v. Navajo Freight Lines, Inc.

359 U.S. 520 (1959)

Justice DOUGLAS delivered the opinion of the Court.

We are asked in this case to hold that an Illinois statute requiring the use of a certain type of rear fender mudguard on trucks and trailers operated on the highways of that State conflicts with the Commerce Clause of the Constitution. The statutory specification for this type of mudguard provides that the guard shall contour the rear wheel, with the inside surface being relatively parallel to the top 90 degrees of the rear 180 degrees of the whole surface. The surface of the guard must extend downward to within 10 inches from the ground when the truck is loaded to its maximum legal capacity. The guards must be wide enough to cover the width of the protected tire, must be installed not more than 6 inches from the tire surface when the vehicle is loaded to maximum capacity, and must have a lip or flange on its outer edge of not less than 2 inches.

Appellees, interstate motor carriers holding certificates from the Interstate Commerce Commission, challenged the constitutionality of the Illinois Act. A specially constituted three-judge District Court concluded that it unduly and unreasonably burdened and obstructed interstate commerce, because it made the conventional or straight mudflap, which is legal in at least 45 States, illegal in Illinois, and because the statute, taken together with a Rule of the Arkansas Commerce Commission requiring straight mudflaps, rendered the use of the same motor vehicle equipment in both States impossible. The statute was declared to be violative of the Commerce Clause and appellants were enjoined from enforcing it.

The power of the State to regulate the use of its highways is broad and pervasive. We have recognized the peculiarly local nature of this subject of safety, and have upheld state statutes applicable alike to interstate and intrastate commerce, despite the fact that they may have an impact on interstate commerce. South Carolina State Highway Dept. v. Barnwell Bros. (1939).

These safety measures carry a strong presumption of validity when challenged in court. If there are alternative ways of solving a problem, we do not sit to determine which of them is best suited to achieve a valid state objective. Policy decisions are for the state legislature, absent federal entry into the field. Unless we can conclude on the whole record that "the total effect of the law as a safety measure in reducing accidents and casualties is so slight or problematical as not to outweigh the national interest in keeping interstate commerce free from interferences which seriously impede it," we must uphold the statute.

The District Court found that "since it is impossible for a carrier operating in interstate commerce to determine which of its equipment will be used in a particular area, or on a particular day, or days, carriers operating into or through Illinois . . . will be required to equip all their trailers in accordance with the requirements of the Illinois Splash Guard statute." With two possible exceptions the mudflaps required in those States which have mudguard regulations would not meet the standards required by the Illinois statute. The cost of installing the contour mudguards is $30 or more per vehicle. The District Court found that the initial cost of installing those mudguards on all the trucks owned by the appellees ranged from $4,500 to $45,840. There was also evidence in the record to indicate that the cost of maintenance and replacement of these guards is substantial.

Illinois introduced evidence seeking to establish that contour mudguards had a decided safety factor in that they prevented the throwing of debris into the faces of drivers of passing cars and into the windshields of a following vehicle. But the District Court in its opinion stated that it was "conclusively shown that the contour mud flap possesses no advantages over the conventional or straight mud flap previously required in Illinois and presently required in most of the states," and that "there is rather convincing testimony that use of the contour flap creates hazards previously unknown to those using the highways." These hazards were found to be occasioned by the fact that this new type of mudguard tended to cause an accumulation of heat in the brake drum, thus decreasing the effectiveness of brakes, and by the fact that they were susceptible of being hit and bumped when the trucks were backed up and of falling off on the highway.

An order of the Arkansas Commerce Commission requires that trailers operating in that State be equipped with straight or conventional mudflaps. Vehicles equipped to meet the standards of the Illinois statute would not comply with Arkansas standards, and vice versa. Thus if a trailer is to be operated in both States, mudguards would have to be interchanged, causing a significant delay in an operation where prompt movement may be of the essence. It was found that from two to four hours of labor are required to install or remove a contour mudguard. Moreover, the contour guard is attached to the trailer by welding and if the trailer is conveying a cargo of explosives (e.g., for the United States Government) it would be exceedingly dangerous to attempt to weld on a contour mudguard without unloading the trailer.

It was also found that the Illinois statute seriously interferes with the "interline" operations of motor carriers — that is to say, with the interchanging of trailers between an originating carrier and another carrier when the latter serves an area not served by the former. These "interline" operations provide a speedy through-service for the shipper. Interlining contemplates the physical transfer of the entire trailer; there is no unloading and reloading of the cargo. The interlining process is particularly vital in connection with shipment of perishables, which would spoil if unloaded before reaching their destination, or with the movement of explosives carried under seal. Of course, if the originating carrier never operated in Illinois, it would not be expected to equip its trailers with contour mudguards. Yet if an interchanged trailer of that carrier were hauled to or through Illinois, the statute would require that it contain contour guards. Since carriers which operate in and through Illinois cannot compel the originating carriers to equip their trailers with contour guards, they may be forced to cease interlining with those who do not meet the Illinois requirements. Over 60 percent of the business of 5 of the 6 plaintiffs is interline traffic. For the other it constitutes 30 percent. All of the plaintiffs operate extensively in interstate commerce, and the annual mileage in Illinois of none of them exceeds 7 percent of total mileage.

We deal not with absolutes but with questions of degree. The state legislatures plainly have great leeway in providing safety regulations for all vehicles — interstate as well as local. Our decisions so hold. Yet the heavy burden which the Illinois mudguard law places on the interstate movement of trucks and trailers seems to us to pass the permissible limits even for safety regulations.

Consolidated Freightways Corp. of Delaware v. Raymond Kassel

455 U.S. 329 (1981)

Justice POWELL announced the judgment of the Court and delivered an opinion, in which Justice WHITE, Justice BLACKMUN, and Justice STEVENS joined.

The question is whether an Iowa statute that prohibits the use of certain large trucks within the State unconstitutionally burdens interstate commerce.

I

Appellee Consolidated Freightways Corporation of Delaware (Consolidated) is one of the largest common carriers in the country. It offers service in 48 States under a certificate of public convenience and necessity issued by the Interstate Commerce Commission. Among other routes, Consolidated carries commodities through Iowa on Interstate 80, the principal east-west route linking New York, Chicago, and the west coast, and on Interstate 35, a major north-south route.

Consolidated mainly uses two kinds of trucks. One consists of a three-axle tractor pulling a 40-foot two-axle trailer. This unit, commonly called a single, or "semi," is 55 feet in length overall. Such trucks have long been used on the Nation's highways. Consolidated also uses a two-axle tractor pulling a single-axle trailer which, in turn, pulls a single-axle dolly and a second single-axle trailer. This combination, known as a double, or twin, is 65 feet long overall. Many trucking companies, including Consolidated, increasingly prefer to use doubles to ship certain kinds of commodities. Doubles have larger capacities, and the trailers can be detached and routed separately if necessary. Consolidated would like to use 65-foot doubles on many of its trips through Iowa.

The State of Iowa, however, by statute restricts the length of vehicles that may use its highways. Unlike all other States in the West and Midwest, Iowa generally prohibits the use of 65-foot doubles within its borders. Instead, most truck combinations are restricted to 55 feet in length. Doubles, mobile homes, trucks carrying vehicles such as tractors and other farm equipment, and singles hauling livestock, are permitted to be as long as 60 feet. Notwithstanding these restrictions, Iowa's statute permits cities abutting the state line by local ordinance to adopt the length limitations of the adjoining State. Where a city has exercised this option, otherwise oversized trucks are permitted within the city limits and in nearby commercial zones.

Because of Iowa's statutory scheme, Consolidated cannot use its 65-foot doubles to move commodities through the State. Instead, the company must do one of four things: (i) use 55-foot singles; (ii) use 60-foot doubles; (iii) detach the trailers of a 65-foot double and shuttle each through the State separately; or (iv) divert 65-foot doubles around Iowa. Dissatisfied with these options, Consolidated filed this suit in the District Court averring that Iowa's statutory scheme unconstitutionally burdens interstate commerce. Iowa defended the law as a reasonable safety measure enacted pursuant to its police power. The State asserted that 65-foot doubles are more dangerous than 55-foot singles and, in any event, that the law promotes safety and reduces road wear within the State by diverting much truck traffic to other States.

In a 14-day trial, both sides adduced evidence on safety, and on the burden on interstate commerce imposed by Iowa's law. On the question of safety, the District Court found that the "evidence clearly establishes that the twin is as safe as the semi." For that reason, "there is no valid safety reason for barring twins from Iowa's highways because of their configuration. The evidence convincingly, if not overwhelmingly, establishes that the 65-foot twin is as safe as, if not safer than, the 60-foot twin and the 55-foot semi. . . . Twins and semis have different characteristics. Twins are more maneuverable, are less sensitive to wind, and create less splash and spray. However, they are more likely than semis to jackknife or upset. They can be backed only for a short distance. The negative characteristics are not such that they render the twin less safe than semis overall. Semis are more stable but are more likely to 'rear end' another vehicle."

In light of these findings, the District Court applied the standard we enunciated in Raymond Motor Transportation, Inc. v. Rice (1978), and concluded that the state law impermissibly burdened interstate commerce.

We conclude that the Iowa truck-length limitations unconstitutionally burden interstate commerce. In Raymond Motor Transportation, Inc. v. Rice, the Court held that a Wisconsin statute that precluded the use of 65-foot doubles violated the Commerce Clause. This case is *Raymond* revisited. Here, as in *Raymond*, the State failed to present any persuasive evidence that 65-foot doubles are less safe than 55-foot singles. Moreover, Iowa's law is now out of step with the laws of all other Midwestern and Western States. Iowa thus substantially burdens the interstate flow of goods by truck. In the absence of congressional action to set uniform standards, some burdens associated with state safety regulations must be tolerated. But where, as here, the State's safety interest has been found to be illusory, and its regulations impair significantly the federal interest in efficient and safe interstate transportation, the state law cannot be harmonized with the Commerce Clause.

Iowa made a more serious effort to support the safety rationale of its law than did Wisconsin in *Raymond*, but its effort was no more persuasive. As noted above, the District Court found that the "evidence clearly establishes that the twin is as safe as the semi." The record supports this finding.

The trial focused on a comparison of the performance of the two kinds of trucks in various safety categories. The evidence showed, and the District Court found, that the 65-foot double was at least the equal of the 55-foot single in the ability to brake, turn, and maneuver. The double, because of its axle placement, produces less splash and spray in wet weather. And, because of its articulation in the middle, the double is less susceptible to dangerous "off-tracking," and to wind.

Consolidated, meanwhile, demonstrated that Iowa's law substantially burdens interstate commerce. Trucking companies that wish to continue to use 65-foot doubles must route them around Iowa or detach the trailers of the doubles and ship them through separately. Alternatively, trucking companies must use the smaller 55-foot singles or 60-foot doubles permitted under Iowa law. Each of these options engenders inefficiency and added expense. The record shows that Iowa's law added about $12.6 million each year to the costs of trucking companies. Consolidated alone incurred about $2 million per year in increased costs.

In addition to increasing the costs of the trucking companies (and, indirectly, of the service to consumers), Iowa's law may aggravate, rather than ameliorate, the problem of highway accidents. Fifty-five foot singles carry less freight than 65-foot doubles. Either more small trucks must be used to carry the same quantity of goods through Iowa, or the same number of larger trucks must drive longer distances to bypass Iowa. In either case, as the District Court noted, the restriction requires more highway miles to be driven to transport the same quantity of goods.

Other things being equal, accidents are proportional to distance traveled. Thus, if 65-foot doubles are as safe as 55-foot singles, Iowa's law tends to increase the number of accidents, and to shift the incidence of them from Iowa to other States. Because Iowa has imposed this burden without any significant countervailing safety interest, its statute violates the Commerce Clause.

Justice REHNQUIST, with whom Chief Justice BURGER and Justice STEWART join, dissenting.

The result in this case suggests, to paraphrase Justice Jackson, that the only state truck-length limit "that is valid is one which this Court has not been able to get its hands on." Although the plurality opinion and the opinion concurring in the judgment strike down Iowa's law by different routes, I believe the analysis in both opinions oversteps our limited authority to review state legislation under the Commerce Clause and seriously intrudes upon the fundamental right of the States to pass laws to secure the safety of their citizens. Accordingly, I dissent.

It is necessary to elaborate somewhat on the facts as presented in the plurality opinion to appreciate fully what the Court does today. Iowa's action in limiting the length of trucks which may travel on its highways is in no sense unusual. Every State in the Union regulates the length of vehicles permitted to use the public roads. Nor is Iowa a renegade in having length limits which operate to exclude the 65-foot doubles favored by Consolidated. These trucks are prohibited in other areas of the country as well, some 17 States and the District of Columbia, including all of New England and most of the Southeast. While pointing out that Consolidated carries commodities through Iowa on Interstate 80, "the principal east-west route linking New York, Chicago, and the west coast," the plurality neglects to note that both Pennsylvania and New Jersey, through which Interstate 80 runs before reaching New York, also ban 65-foot doubles. In short, the persistent effort in the plurality opinion to paint Iowa as an oddity standing alone to block commerce carried in 65-foot doubles is simply not supported by the facts.

A determination that a state law is a rational safety measure does not end the Commerce Clause inquiry. A "sensitive consideration" of the safety purpose in relation to the burden on commerce is required. When engaging in such a consideration the Court does not directly compare safety benefits to commerce costs and strike down the legislation if the latter can be said in some vague sense to "outweigh" the former. Such an approach would make an empty gesture of the strong presumption of validity accorded state safety measures, particularly those governing highways. It would also arrogate to this Court functions of forming public policy, functions which, in the absence of congressional action, were left by the framers of the Constitution to state legislatures. These admonitions are peculiarly apt when, as here, the question involves the difficult comparison of financial losses and "the loss of lives and limbs of workers and people using the highways."

The purpose of the "sensitive consideration" referred to above is rather to determine if the asserted safety justification, although rational, is merely a pretext for discrimination against interstate commerce. We will conclude that it is if the safety benefits from the regulation are demonstrably trivial while the burden on commerce is great. Iowa defends its statute as a highway safety regulation. There can be no doubt that the challenged statute is a valid highway safety regulation and thus entitled to the strongest presumption of validity against Commerce Clause challenges.

———

One particular type of non-discriminatory law is worth noting: The Court has consistently declared unconstitutional state laws that regulate the out-of-state conduct of businesses. In Edgar v. MITE Corp., 457 U.S. 624 (1982), the Court declared unconstitutional an Illinois law that required the Secretary of State to adjudicate the fairness of tender offers for the purchase of corporate stock and to reject the transaction if the offer was inequitable or would work a fraud on the sellers. The Court said that the law was a "direct restraint on interstate commerce" because the state was controlling "conduct beyond the boundaries of the state." The state law regulated sales of stock that occurred outside of Illinois. The Court applied the balancing test and found that the law was unconstitutional because it substantially burdened interstate commerce by "hindering the reallocation of economic resources to their highest-valued use," but there was "nothing to be weighed in the balance to sustain the law."

Similarly, Brown-Forman Distillers Corp. v. New York State Liquor Authority, 476 U.S. 573 (1986), involved a New York law that required liquor distillers selling wholesale in the state to file a monthly price schedule, to sell at those prices in New York, and to sell at the lowest prices the distiller charged wholesale in any other state for the same month. The Court found the latter provision to violate the dormant Commerce Clause because it had the "practical effect of . . . control[ling] liquor prices in other states." The Court explained: "While New York may regulate the sale of liquor within its borders, and may seek low prices for its residents, it may not project its legislation into other States by regulating the price to be paid for liquor in those states."

In Healy v. The Beer Institute, 491 U.S. 324 (1989), the Court declared unconstitutional a Connecticut law that required beer companies to post their prices each month and to attest that the prices were not higher than their prices in the four states bordering Connecticut. The Court noted that "the Commerce Clause . . . precludes the application of a state statute to commerce that takes place wholly outside the State's borders, whether or not the commerce has effects within the State." The Court said therefore that "[t]he critical inquiry is whether the practical effect of the regulation is to control conduct beyond the boundaries of the State." The Connecticut law was declared unconstitutional because it affected the prices charged out of the state.

SUMMARY

State laws that discriminate against out-of-staters are almost always declared unconstitutional. Such a law will be allowed only if it is proven that the law is necessary — the least restrictive means — to achieve a non-protectionist purpose. If a law does not discriminate against out-of-staters, the Court balances its burdens on interstate commerce against its benefits. The inquiry is fact dependent and the outcome obviously turns on how the Court appraises the burdens and the benefits.

e. Exceptions to the Dormant Commerce Clause

There are two exceptions where laws that otherwise would violate the dormant Commerce Clause will be allowed. One exception is if Congress approves the state law. Even a clearly unconstitutional, discriminatory state law will be allowed if approved by Congress because Congress has plenary power to regulate commerce among the states. The second exception is termed the "market participant exception": A state may favor its own citizens in receiving benefits from government programs or in dealing with government-owned businesses. Each exception is presented in turn.

4. Background on the Eleventh Amendment and State Sovereign Immunity

The Eleventh Amendment states, "The Judicial power of the United States shall not be construed to extend to any suit in law or equity, commenced or prosecuted against one of the United States by Citizens of another State, or by Citizens or Subjects of any foreign state." The Eleventh Amendment was intended to strike from the Constitution clauses of Article III, §2, of the Constitution which states that the judicial power of the United States extends to suits "between a State and Citizens of another State" and "between a State, or the Citizens thereof, and foreign States, Citizens or subjects."

More specifically, the Eleventh Amendment was adopted to overrule the Supreme Court's decision in Chisholm v. Georgia, 2 U.S. (2 Dall.) 419 (1793). *Chisholm* involved an attempt by a South Carolina citizen to recover money owed by the state of Georgia. He sued in federal court pursuant to the language of Article III that expressly allows federal courts to hear suits against state governments by citizens of other states. The State of Georgia claimed that it had sovereign immunity and could not be sued without its consent. The Supreme Court, in a four-to-one decision, ruled in Chisholm's favor. They concluded that the clear language of Article III authorized suits against a state by citizens of another state.

State legislators and governors were outraged by the Supreme Court's decision in Chisholm v. Georgia. Georgia adopted a statute declaring that anyone attempting to enforce the Supreme Court's decision is "hereby declared to be guilty of a felony, and shall suffer death, without the benefit of clergy by being hanged."[165] The intense reaction to *Chisholm* is reflected in the speed with which

---

[165] Peter W. Low & John C. Jeffries, Jr., *Federal Courts and the Law of Federal-State Relations* 810 (4th ed. 1998).

a constitutional amendment to overturn the decision was adopted. The Supreme Court decided *Chisholm* on February 14, 1794. By March 4, 1794, less than three weeks later, both houses of Congress had approved the Eleventh Amendment. Within a year, the requisite number of states ratified it, although it was three more years until the President issued a proclamation declaring the Eleventh Amendment to have been properly ratified.

In 1890, in Hans v. Louisiana, 134 U.S. 1 (1890), the Court held that the Eleventh Amendment also bars suits against a state by its own citizens. Although the terms of the amendment only prohibit suits against a state by citizens of other states and foreign countries, Hans v. Louisiana held that it would be "anomalous" to allow states to be sued by their own citizens. Thus, since *Hans*, states have been immune to suits both by their own citizens and by citizens of other states.

There is great disagreement among scholars and Justices as to the proper interpretation of the Eleventh Amendment. Some, including a majority of the current Court, believe that sovereign immunity creates a constitutional restriction on federal court subject matter jurisdiction for all suits against state governments. By this view, the Eleventh Amendment is part of a broader constitutional limitation on federal court jurisdiction created by sovereign immunity.[166]

A second view of the Eleventh Amendment treats it as restricting only the diversity jurisdiction of federal courts.[167] The language of the Eleventh Amendment clearly is directed at modifying this latter provision. In fact, the Amendment simply states: "The Judicial Power of the United States shall not be construed to extend to any suit . . . against one of the United States by Citizens of another state." Because *Chisholm* only involved this latter part of Article III, it makes sense to view the Eleventh Amendment as restricting only diversity suits against state governments. Therefore, according to this view, the Eleventh Amendment does not bar suits against states based on other parts of Article III. Most notably, the Amendment does not preclude suits based on federal question jurisdiction. Thus, all claims of state violations of the United States Constitution or federal laws could be heard in federal courts. Four Justices on the current Court accept this view.

The Eleventh Amendment, under the former view adopted by a majority of the current Court, creates a major hurdle for those seeking to enforce federal laws against state governments.[168] States cannot be sued in federal court, even for egregious violations of federal rights. There are three ways around the Eleventh Amendment to hold state governments accountable in federal court.

One is that state officers may be sued in federal court, even when state governments cannot be sued. The Eleventh Amendment does not preclude suits against

---

[166] *See, e.g.,* Alden v. Maine, 527 U.S. 706 (1999), presented below.

[167] *See* John J. Gibbons, *The Eleventh Amendment and State Sovereign Immunity: A Reinterpretation,* 83 Colum. L. Rev. 1889 (1983); William A. Fletcher, *A Historical Interpretation of the Eleventh Amendment: A Narrow Construction of an Affirmative Grant of Jurisdiction Rather than a Prohibition Against Jurisdiction,* 35 Stan. L. Rev. 1033 (1983).

[168] The Supreme Court has held that the Eleventh Amendment does not bar suits against local governments. Mt. Healthy City School Dist. Bd. of Educ. v. Doyle, 429 U.S. 274 (1977); Lincoln County v. Luning, 133 U.S. 529 (1890).

state officers for injunctive relief, even when the remedy will enjoin the implementation of an official state policy. Ex parte Young, 209 U.S. 123 (1908), is widely credited with establishing this principle. Simply stated, state officers may be sued for injunctive relief or for damages to be paid by them, but state officers cannot be sued where it is the state treasury that will be paying damages to compensate for past wrongs.[169]

Second, states may waive their Eleventh Amendment immunity and may consent to be sued in federal court. Although allowing such waivers seems inconsistent with viewing the Eleventh Amendment as a restriction on the federal courts' subject matter jurisdiction, it is firmly established that "if a State waives its immunity and consents to suit in federal court, the Eleventh Amendment does not bar the action."[170] If a state waives its Eleventh Amendment immunity, then it may be sued directly in federal court, even for retroactive relief to be paid out of the state treasury. However, the Court has stated clearly that the "test for determining whether a state has waived its [Eleventh Amendment] immunity from federal-court jurisdiction is a stringent one."[171] The Court has held that waivers must be explicit; there is no doctrine of implied or constructive waiver of the Eleventh Amendment.[172]

Third, the Supreme Court has held that Congress, acting pursuant to §5 of the Fourteenth Amendment may authorize suits against state governments. This authority is established in the cases in the next section. Following the cases creating this authority, the three recent Supreme Court decisions construing the scope of Congress's §5 power are presented. Finally, the section concludes by presenting the Supreme Court's recent decision in Alden v. Maine, holding that Congress cannot authorize suits against state governments in state courts. *Alden* held that state governments have sovereign immunity and cannot be sued in state courts without their consent even for violations of federal laws.

5. Congress's Power to Authorize Suits Against State Governments

a. The Basic Rule: Congress May Authorize Suits Against States Pursuant Only to §5 of the Fourteenth Amendment

The Supreme Court has considered the ability of Congress to override sovereign immunity and authorize suits against state governments. Fitzpatrick v. Bitzer was a key, initial case.

---

[169] There is a large body of law as to when suits against state officers are allowed and when they are not permitted. For a discussion of this law, *see* Erwin Chemerinsky, *Federal Jurisdiction* (4th ed. 2003), Chapter 7 [Erwin Chemerinsky, Constitutional Law, 3rd ed., (2009)].

[170] Atascadero State Hosp. v. Scanlon, 473 U.S. 234, 238 (1985).

[171] Atascadero State Hosp. v. Scanlon, 473 U.S. at 241.

[172] College Savings Bank v. Florida Prepaid Postsecondary Educ. Expense Bd., 527 U.S. 666 (1999).

Fitzpatrick v. Bitzer

427 U.S. 445 (1976)

Justice REHNQUIST delivered the opinion of the Court.

In the 1972 Amendments to Title VII of the Civil Rights Act of 1964, Congress, acting under section 5 of the Fourteenth Amendment, authorized federal courts to award money damages in favor of a private individual against a state government found to have subjected that person to employment discrimination on the basis of "race, color, religion, sex, or national origin." The principal question presented by these cases is whether, as against the shield of sovereign immunity afforded the State by the Eleventh Amendment, Congress has the power to authorize Federal courts to enter such an award against the State as a means of enforcing the substantive guarantees of the Fourteenth Amendment.

The impact of the Fourteenth Amendment upon the relationship between the Federal Government and the States, and the reach of congressional power under §5, were examined at length by this Court in Ex parte State of Virginia (1880). A state judge had been arrested and indicted under a federal criminal statute prohibiting the exclusion on the basis of race of any citizen from service as a juror in a state court. The judge claimed that the statute was beyond Congress's power to enact under either the Thirteenth or the Fourteenth Amendment. The Court first observed that these Amendments "were intended to be, what they really are, limitations of the power of the States and enlargements of the power of Congress." It then addressed the relationship between the language of §5 and the substantive provisions of the Fourteenth Amendment:

> The prohibitions of the Fourteenth Amendment are directed to the States, and they are to a degree restrictions of State power. It is these which Congress is empowered to enforce, and to enforce against State action, however put forth, whether that action be executive, legislative, or judicial. Such enforcement is no invasion of State sovereignty. No law can be, which the people of the States have, by the Constitution of the United States, empowered Congress to enact.

It is true that none of these previous cases presented the question of the relationship between the Eleventh Amendment and the enforcement power granted to Congress under §5 of the Fourteenth Amendment. But we think that the Eleventh Amendment, and the principle of state sovereignty which it embodies, see Hans v. Louisiana (1890), are necessarily limited by the enforcement provisions of §5 of the Fourteenth Amendment. In that section Congress is expressly granted authority to enforce "by appropriate legislation" the substantive provisions of the Fourteenth Amendment, which themselves embody significant limitations on state authority. When Congress acts pursuant to §5, not only is it exercising legislative authority that is plenary within the terms of the constitutional grant, it is exercising that authority under one section of a constitutional Amendment whose other sections by their own terms embody limitations on state authority. We think that Congress may, in determining what is "appropriate legislation" for the purpose of enforcing the provisions of the Fourteenth Amendment, provide for private suits against States or state officials which are constitutionally impermissible in other contexts.

In Pennsylvania v. Union Gas Co., 491 U.S. 1 (1989), the Supreme Court held five to four that Congress may override the Eleventh Amendment and authorize suits against state governments pursuant to any of its constitutional powers, so long as the law in its text expressly authorizes such suits. In the case, the Supreme Court confronted two questions: (1) Does the Comprehensive Environmental Response, Compensation, and Liability Act of 1980 (CERCLA), as amended by the Superfund Amendments and Reauthorization Act of 1986 (SARA), authorize suits against state governments in federal court? (2) If so, does Congress, when legislating pursuant to the Commerce Clause, have the authority to create such state government liability?

The Court answered both questions affirmatively. However, the Court did so without a majority opinion and was very splintered. There were five votes that CERCLA permits states to be sued for monetary liability in federal court: Justices Brennan, Marshall, Blackmun, Stevens, and Scalia. There also were five votes that Congress, acting pursuant to its Commerce Clause authority, can create such federal court jurisdiction: Justices Brennan, Marshall, Blackmun, Stevens, and White.

Between 1989, when Pennsylvania v. Union Gas was decided, and 1996, when Seminole Tribe v. Florida was decided, there was a significant change in the composition of the Supreme Court. Four of the Justices in majority in Pennsylvania v. Union Gas had left the Court — Justices Brennan, Marshall, Blackmun, and White. All four of the dissenters in Pennsylvania v. Union Gas remained on the Court. They were joined by Justice Clarence Thomas and overruled Pennsylvania v. Union Gas by a five to four margin.

Seminole Tribe of Florida v. Florida

517 U.S. 44 (1996)

Chief Justice REHNQUIST delivered the opinion of the Court.

The Indian Gaming Regulatory Act provides that an Indian tribe may conduct certain gaming activities only in conformance with a valid compact between the tribe and the State in which the gaming activities are located. The Act, passed by Congress under the Indian Commerce Clause, U.S. Const., Art. I, §8, cl. 3, imposes upon the States a duty to negotiate in good faith with an Indian tribe toward the formation of a compact and authorizes a tribe to bring suit in federal court against a State in order to compel performance of that duty. We hold that notwithstanding Congress's clear intent to abrogate the States' sovereign immunity, the Indian Commerce Clause does not grant Congress that power, and therefore §2710(d)(7) cannot grant jurisdiction over a State that does not consent to be sued.

I

Congress passed the Indian Gaming Regulatory Act in 1988 in order to provide a statutory basis for the operation and regulation of gaming by Indian tribes. [The Act requires that states negotiate in "good faith" with Indian Tribes to permit gambling on Native American reservations and authorizes suits against state governments to enforce the law.]

In September 1991, the Seminole Tribe of Florida, petitioner, sued the State of Florida and its Governor, Lawton Chiles, respondents. Invoking jurisdiction under 25 U.S.C. §2710(d)(7)(A), as well as 28 U.S.C. §§1331 and 1362, petitioner alleged that respondents had "refused to enter into any negotiation for inclusion of [certain gaming activities] in a tribal-state compact," thereby violating the "requirement of good faith negotiation" contained in §2710(d)(3). Respondents moved to dismiss the complaint, arguing that the suit violated the State's sovereign immunity from suit in federal court.

II

Petitioner argues that Congress through the Act abrogated the States' immunity from suit. In order to determine whether Congress has abrogated the States' sovereign immunity, we ask two questions: first, whether Congress has "unequivocally expresse[d] its intent to abrogate the immunity," Green v. Mansour (1985); and second, whether Congress has acted "pursuant to a valid exercise of powers."

A

Congress's intent to abrogate the States' immunity from suit must be obvious from "a clear legislative statement." This rule arises from a recognition of the important role played by the Eleventh Amendment and the broader principles that it reflects. Here, we agree with the parties, with the Eleventh Circuit in the decision below, and with virtually every other court that has confronted the question that Congress has in §2710(d)(7) provided an "unmistakably clear" statement of its intent to abrogate. Section 2710(d)(7)(A)(i) vests jurisdiction in "[t]he United States district courts . . . over any cause of action . . . arising from the failure of a State to enter into negotiations . . . or to conduct such negotiations in good faith."

B

Having concluded that Congress clearly intended to abrogate the States' sovereign immunity through §2710(d)(7), we turn now to consider whether the Act was passed "pursuant to a valid exercise of power." [O]ur inquiry into whether Congress has the power to abrogate unilaterally the States' immunity from suit is narrowly focused on one question: Was the Act in question passed pursuant to a constitutional provision granting Congress the power to abrogate? See, e.g., Fitzpatrick v. Bitzer (1976). Previously, in conducting that inquiry, we have found authority to abrogate under only two provisions of the Constitution. In *Fitzpatrick*, we recognized that the Fourteenth Amendment, by expanding federal power at the expense of state autonomy, had fundamentally altered the balance of state and federal power struck by the Constitution. We noted that §1 of the Fourteenth Amendment contained prohibitions expressly directed at the States and that §5 of the Amendment expressly provided that "The Congress shall have power to enforce, by appropriate legislation, the provisions of this article." We held that through the Fourteenth Amendment, federal power extended to intrude upon the province of the Eleventh Amendment and therefore that §5 of the Fourteenth Amendment allowed Congress to abrogate the immunity from suit guaranteed by that Amendment.

In only one other case has congressional abrogation of the States' Eleventh Amendment immunity been upheld. In Pennsylvania v. Union Gas Co. (1989), a plurality of the Court found that the Interstate Commerce Clause, Art. I, §8, cl. 3, granted Congress the power to abrogate state sovereign immunity, stating that the power to regulate interstate commerce would be "incomplete without the authority to render States liable in damages." Justice White added the fifth vote necessary to the result in that case, but wrote separately in order to express that he "[did] not agree with much of [the plurality's] reasoning."

The Court in *Union Gas* reached a result without an expressed rationale agreed upon by a majority of the Court. We have already seen that Justice Brennan's opinion received the support of only three other Justices. Of the other five, Justice White, who provided the fifth vote for the result, wrote separately in order to indicate his disagreement with the plurality's rationale, and four Justices joined together in a dissent that rejected the plurality's rationale. Since it was issued, *Union Gas* has created confusion among the lower courts that have sought to understand and apply the deeply fractured decision.

The plurality's rationale also deviated sharply from our established federalism jurisprudence and essentially eviscerated our decision in Hans v. Lousiana (1890). Never before the decision in *Union Gas* had we suggested that the bounds of Article III could be expanded by Congress operating pursuant to any constitutional provision other than the Fourteenth Amendment. Indeed, it had seemed fundamental that Congress could not expand the jurisdiction of the federal courts beyond the bounds of Article III. Marbury v. Madison (1803).

In the five years since it was decided, *Union Gas* has proved to be a solitary departure from established law. Reconsidering the decision in *Union Gas*, we conclude that none of the policies underlying stare decisis require our continuing adherence to its holding. The decision has, since its issuance, been of questionable precedential value, largely because a majority of the Court expressly disagreed with the rationale of the plurality. The case involved the interpretation of the Constitution and therefore may be altered only by constitutional amendment or revision by this Court. Finally, both the result in *Union Gas* and the plurality's rationale depart from our established understanding of the Eleventh Amendment and undermine the accepted function of Article III. We feel bound to conclude that *Union Gas* was wrongly decided and that it should be, and now is, overruled.

In overruling *Union Gas* today, we reconfirm that the background principle of state sovereign immunity embodied in the Eleventh Amendment is not so ephemeral as to dissipate when the subject of the suit is an area, like the regulation of Indian commerce, that is under the exclusive control of the Federal Government. Even when the Constitution vests in Congress complete law-making authority over a particular area, the Eleventh Amendment prevents congressional authorization of suits by private parties against unconsenting States. The Eleventh Amendment restricts the judicial power under Article III, and Article I cannot be used to circumvent the constitutional limitations placed upon federal jurisdiction. Petitioner's suit against the State of Florida must be dismissed for a lack of jurisdiction.

Justice STEVENS, dissenting.

This case is about power — the power of the Congress of the United States to create a private federal cause of action against a State, or its Governor, for the violation of a federal right. [I]n a sharp break with the past, today the Court holds that with the narrow and illogical exception of statutes enacted pursuant to the Enforcement Clause of the Fourteenth Amendment, Congress has no such power.

The importance of the majority's decision to overrule the Court's holding in Pennsylvania v. Union Gas Co. cannot be overstated. The majority's opinion does not simply preclude Congress from establishing the rather curious statutory scheme under which Indian tribes may seek the aid of a federal court to secure a State's good-faith negotiations over gaming regulations. Rather, it prevents Congress from providing a federal forum for a broad range of actions against States, from those sounding in copyright and patent law, to those concerning bankruptcy, environmental law, and the regulation of our vast national economy.

There may be room for debate over whether, in light of the Eleventh Amendment, Congress has the power to ensure that such a cause of action may be enforced in federal court by a citizen of another State or a foreign citizen. There can be no serious debate, however, over whether Congress has the power to ensure that such a cause of action may be brought by a citizen of the State being sued. Congress's authority in that regard is clear.

The fundamental error that continues to lead the Court astray is its failure to acknowledge that its modern embodiment of the ancient doctrine of sovereign immunity "has absolutely nothing to do with the limit on judicial power contained in the Eleventh Amendment." It rests rather on concerns of federalism and comity that merit respect but are nevertheless, in cases such as the one before us, subordinate to the plenary power of Congress.

Justice SOUTER, with whom Justice GINSBURG and Justice BREYER join, dissenting.

In holding the State of Florida immune to suit under the Indian Gaming Regulatory Act, the Court today holds for the first time since the founding of the Republic that Congress has no authority to subject a State to the jurisdiction of a federal court at the behest of an individual asserting a federal right.

The fault I find with the majority today is not in its decision to reexamine *Union Gas*, for the Court in that case produced no majority for a single rationale supporting congressional authority. Instead, I part company from the Court because I am convinced that its decision is fundamentally mistaken, and for that reason I respectfully dissent.

It is useful to separate three questions: (1) whether the States enjoyed sovereign immunity if sued in their own courts in the period prior to ratification of the National Constitution; (2) if so, whether after ratification the States were entitled to claim some such immunity when sued in a federal court exercising jurisdiction either because the suit was between a State and a nonstate litigant who was not its citizen, or because the issue in the case raised a federal question; and (3) whether any state sovereign immunity recognized in federal court may be abrogated by Congress.

The answer to the first question is not clear, although some of the framers assumed that States did enjoy immunity in their own courts. The second question was not debated at the time of ratification, except as to citizen-state diversity jurisdiction; there was no unanimity, but in due course the Court in Chisholm v. Georgia (1793), answered that a state defendant enjoyed no such immunity. As to federal-question jurisdiction, state sovereign immunity seems not to have been debated prior to ratification, the silence probably showing a general understanding at the time that the States would have no immunity in such cases.

The adoption of the Eleventh Amendment soon changed the result in *Chisholm*, not by mentioning sovereign immunity, but by eliminating citizen-state diversity jurisdiction over cases with state defendants. I will explain why the Eleventh Amendment did not affect federal-question jurisdiction, a notion that needs to be understood for the light it casts on the soundness of *Hans*'s holding that States did enjoy sovereign immunity in federal-question suits. The *Hans* Court erroneously assumed that a State could plead sovereign immunity against a noncitizen suing under federal-question jurisdiction, and for that reason held that a State must enjoy the same protection in a suit by one of its citizens. The error of *Hans*'s reasoning is underscored by its clear inconsistency with the Founders' hostility to the implicit reception of common-law doctrine as federal law, and with the Founders' conception of sovereign power as divided between the States and the National Government for the sake of very practical objectives.

The Court's answer today to the third question is likewise at odds with the Founders' view that common law, when it was received into the new American legal system, was always subject to legislative amendment. In ignoring the reasons for this pervasive understanding at the time of the ratification, and in holding that a non-textual common-law rule limits a clear grant of congressional power under Article I, the Court follows a course that has brought it to grief before in our history, and promises to do so again.

The doctrine of sovereign immunity comprises two distinct rules, which are not always separately recognized. The one rule holds that the King or the Crown, as the font of law, is not bound by the law's provisions; the other provides that the King or Crown, as the font of justice, is not subject to suit in its own courts. The one rule limits the reach of substantive law; the other, the jurisdiction of the courts. We are concerned here only with the latter rule, which took its common-law form in the high Middle Ages.

The significance of this doctrine in the nascent American law is less clear, however, than its early development and steady endurance in England might suggest. While some colonial governments may have enjoyed some such immunity, the scope (and even the existence) of this governmental immunity in pre-Revolutionary America remains disputed.

Whatever the scope of sovereign immunity might have been in the Colonies, however, or during the period of Confederation, the proposal to establish a National Government under the Constitution drafted in 1787 presented a prospect unknown to the common law prior to the American experience: [T]he States would become parts of a system in which sovereignty over even domestic matters would be divided or parcelled out between the States and the Nation, the latter to be invested with its own judicial power and the right to prevail against the States whenever their respective substantive laws might be in conflict.

The history and structure of the Eleventh Amendment convincingly show that it reaches only to suits subject to federal jurisdiction exclusively under the Citizen-State Diversity Clauses. In precisely tracking the language in Article III providing for citizen-state diversity jurisdiction, the text of the Amendment does, after all, suggest to common sense that only the Diversity Clauses are being addressed. If the framers had meant the Amendment to bar federal-question suits as well, they could not only have made their intentions clearer very easily, but could simply have adopted the first post-*Chisholm* proposal, introduced in the House of Representatives by Theodore Sedgwick of Massachusetts on instructions from the Legislature of that Commonwealth. Its provisions would have had exactly that expansive effect:

> [N]o state shall be liable to be made a party defendant, in any of the judicial courts, established, or which shall be established under the authority of the United States, at the suit of any person or persons, whether a citizen or citizens, or a foreigner or foreigners, or of any body politic or corporate, whether within or without the United States.

Three critical errors in Hans v. Louisiana weigh against constitutionalizing its holding as the majority does today. The first we have already seen: the *Hans* Court misread the Eleventh Amendment. It also misunderstood the conditions under which common-law doctrines were received or rejected at the time of the founding, and it fundamentally mistook the very nature of sovereignty in the young Republic that was supposed to entail a State's immunity to federal-question jurisdiction in a federal court. While I would not, as a matter of stare decisis, overrule *Hans* today, an understanding of its failings on these points will show how the Court today simply compounds already serious error in taking *Hans* the further step of investing its rule with constitutional inviolability against the considered judgment of Congress to abrogate it.

Because neither text, precedent, nor history supports the majority's abdication of our responsibility to exercise the jurisdiction entrusted to us in Article III, I would reverse the judgment of the Court of Appeals.

The Eleventh Amendment and Congress's Power to Override It

The Eleventh Amendment states, "The Judicial power of the United States shall not be construed to extend to any suit in law or equity, commenced or prosecuted against one of the United States by Citizens of another State, or by Citizens or Subjects of any foreign state." The Supreme Court long has interpreted this provision as barring suits against state governments without their consent both by their own citizens and by citizens of other states.[173]

In *Fitzpatrick v. Bitzer,* the Court ruled that Congress could authorize suits against state governments if it acts pursuant to §5 of the Fourteenth Amendment.[174] In *Fitzpatrick,* the Court held that state governments may be sued for violating Title VII of the 1964 Civil Rights Act, which prevents employment discrimination based on race, gender, and religion.[175] The Court, in an opinion by then-Justice Rehnquist, explained that the Fourteenth Amendment followed the Eleventh Amendment and thus can modify it. More importantly, the Court said that the Fourteenth Amendment was intended as a limit on state power. Justice Rehnquist explained: "When Congress acts pursuant to §5, not only is it exercising legislative authority that is plenary within the terms of the constitutional grant, it is exercising that authority under one section of a constitutional Amendment whose other sections by their own terms embody limitations on state authority. We think that Congress may, in determining what is 'appropriate legislation' for the purpose of enforcing the provisions of the Fourteenth Amendment, provide for private suits against States or state officials which are constitutionally impermissible in other contexts."[176]

In *Pennsylvania v. Union Gas Co.,* in 1989, the Supreme Court held, 5 to 4, that Congress may override the Eleventh Amendment and authorize suits against state governments pursuant to any of its constitutional powers, so long as the law in its text expressly authorizes such suits.[177] In this case, the Court ruled that state governments could be sued pursuant to a federal environmental law, CERCLA, because Congress was clear in acting under the commerce clause in authorizing suits against state governments.

Seven years later, in *Seminole Tribe v. Florida,*[178] the Supreme Court expressly overturned *Pennsylvania v. Union Gas.* The simple reality is that between 1989, when *Union Gas* was decided, and 1996, when *Seminole Tribe* was decided, there was a significant change in the composition of the Supreme Court. Four of the Justices in majority in *Pennsylvania v. Union Gas* had left the Court: Justices Brennan, Marshall, Blackmun, and White. All four of the dissenters in *Pennsylvania v. Union Gas* remained on the Court. They were joined by Justice Clarence Thomas and overruled *Pennsylvania v. Union Gas* by a 5-to-4 margin.

---

[173] Hans v. Louisiana, 134 U.S. 1 (1890). The Eleventh Amendment and sovereign immunity are discussed in detail in §2.10 [Erwin Chemerinsky, Constitutional Law: Principles and Policies, 4th ed., (2011)].
[174] 427 U.S. 445 (1976).
[175] 42 U.S.C. §2000e.
[176] 427 U.S. at 456.
[177] 491 U.S. 1 (1989).
[178] 517 U.S. 44 (1996).

Chief Justice Rehnquist wrote for the Court and stressed that *Pennsylvania v. Union Gas* is an unprecedented expansion in Congress's power to authorize suits against state governments. He explained:

> Even when the Constitution vests in Congress complete law-making authority over a particular area, the Eleventh Amendment prevents congressional authorization of suits by private parties against unconsenting States. The Eleventh Amendment restricts the judicial power under Article III, and Article I cannot be used to circumvent the constitutional limitations placed upon federal jurisdiction.[179]

The Court held that Congress only can authorize suits against state governments, and override the Eleventh Amendment, when it acts pursuant to §5 of the Fourteenth Amendment.[180]

A year after *Seminole Tribe*, the Court decided *City of Boerne v. Flores* and narrowed the scope of Congress's §5 powers. There is an obvious and crucial interrelationship of these two cases: In deciding whether a state can be sued under a federal statute, the court must decide whether the law is a valid exercise of Congress's §5 powers. If the Court upholds the law as permissible under §5, the state may be sued, otherwise the litigation cannot go forward against the state government. Five times so far the Court has considered whether a law is a valid exercise of power under Congress's §5 authority and whether the law can be used to sue a state government. In the first three cases — *Florida Prepaid Postsecondary Education Expense Board v. College Savings Bank*,[181] *Kimel v. Florida Board of Regents*,[182] and *University of Alabama v. Garrett*,[183] the Court applied *City of Boerne v. Flores* and found the law invalid as an exercise of Congress's §5 powers and precluded the suit against the state government. But in the two most recent cases — *Nevada Department of Human Resources v. Hibbs*[184] and *Tennessee v. Lane*[185] the Court found statutes to fit within Congress's §5 authority and allowed suits against the states. In *United States v. Georgia*, the Court held that Congress may authorize suits to remedy constitutional violations.[186] These cases are described below and followed by a consideration of the principle that emerges from them.

---

[179] *Id.* at 72-73.

[180] For an excellent criticism of *Seminole Tribe*, see Laura S. Fitzgerald, Beyond *Marbury*: Jurisdictional Self-Dealing in *Seminole Tribe*, 52 Vand. L. Rev. 407 (1999); Vicki C. Jackson, *Seminole Tribe*, The Eleventh Amendment, and the Potential Evisceration of *Ex parte Young*, 72 N.Y.U. L. Rev. 495 (1997); Herbert Hovencamp, Judicial Restraint and Constitutional Federalism: The Supreme Court's *Lopez* and *Seminole Tribe* Decisions, 96 Colum. L. Rev. 2213 (1996).

[181] 527 U.S. 627 (1999).

[182] 528 U.S. 62 (2000).

[183] 531 U.S. 356 (2001).

[184] 538 U.S. 721 (2003).

[185] 541 U.S. 509 (2004).

[186] 546 U.S. 151 (2006).

Florida Prepaid Postsecondary Expense Education Board v. College Savings Bank

College Savings Bank, a New Jersey company, devised a system, which it patented, for students to use to save money to later pay for their college education. Florida Prepaid, an agency of the Florida government, copied this system for use by Florida residents to save money to attend Florida schools. College Savings Bank sued Florida Prepaid for, among other things,[187] patent infringement.

In 1992, Congress expressly amended the patent laws to authorize suits against state governments for patent infringement.[188] The Supreme Court, however, held that the law was not a valid exercise of power under §5 of the Fourteenth Amendment and thus could not be used to sue the state government. Although patents unquestionably are property and the Fourteenth Amendment protects property from being denied by state governments without due process, the Court found that the authorization of suits was impermissible because it was not "proportionate" or "congruent" to remedy constitutional violations.

Chief Justice Rehnquist, writing for the Court, stated: "In enacting the Patent Remedy Act, however, Congress identified no pattern of patent infringement by the States, let alone a pattern of constitutional violations. Unlike the undisputed record of racial discrimination confronting Congress in the voting rights cases, Congress came up with little evidence of infringing conduct on the part of the States."[189] The Court held that the law was not valid under §5 because "[t]he legislative record thus suggests that the Patent Remedy Act does not respond to a history of 'widespread and persisting deprivation of constitutional rights' of the sort Congress has faced in enacting proper prophylactic §5 legislation."[190]

Florida Prepaid follows from *Seminole Tribe* and *City of Boerne*: The Court reaffirmed that Congress can authorize suits against states only pursuant to §5, and it concluded, based on *City of Boerne*, that the law authorizing suits for patent infringement did not fit within this power. However, what is striking about *Florida Prepaid* is that it involved patent law, an area in which federal courts have exclusive jurisdiction. Barring patent infringement suits against state governments in federal court means that a state government can infringe patents without ever facing a lawsuit.[191]

Kimel v. Florida Board of Regents

Several cases were consolidated in *Kimel v. Florida Board of Regents*[192] The named case involved a suit by current and former faculty and librarians at Florida State University, including Daniel Kimel, Jr. They alleged that the university's

---

[187] College Savings Bank also sued for a violation of the Lanham Act, but the Supreme Court, in a separate opinion, also found that this was barred by sovereign immunity. College Sav. Bank v. Florida Prepaid Postsecondary Expense Educ. Bd., 527 U.S. 666 (1999).

[188] 35 U.S.C. §271.

[189] 527 U.S. at 640.

[190] *Id.*

[191] Although the state government cannot be sued, the state official may be sued. Ex parte Young, 209 U.S. 123 (1908). Thus, the state official may be sued for an injunction to stop future infringements, but the state government may not be sued for damages.

[192] 528 U.S. 62 (2000).

failure to provide promised pay adjustments discriminated against older workers and thus violated the ADEA. A companion case was brought by Wellington Dickson, an employee of the Florida Department of Corrections, who claimed that he was denied promotions because of his age. Another of the consolidated cases involved faculty members at a state university in Alabama who claimed age discrimination.

The Supreme Court held that all of these claims against state agencies are barred by the Eleventh Amendment. By a 7-to-2 margin with only Kennedy and Thomas dissenting, the Court concluded that the ADEA is an express authorization of suit against the states. The Court then ruled 5 to 4 that the ADEA is not a valid exercise of Congress's power under §5 and that therefore it cannot be used to sue state governments.

Justice O'Connor wrote the majority opinion and was joined by Chief Justice Rehnquist and Justices Scalia, Kennedy, and Thomas. The Court concluded that the burdens the ADEA imposes on state and local governments are disproportionate to any unconstitutional behavior that might exist. The Court emphasized that under prior decisions, only rational basis review is used for age discrimination.[193] The Court explained that there is not a "history of purposeful discrimination" based on age and that "age also does not define a discrete and insular minority because all persons, if they live out their normal life spans," will experience it.[194] Indeed, the Court said that states "may discriminate based on age without offending the Fourteenth Amendment if the age classification is rationally related to a legitimate state interest."[195] The Court said that age often is a relevant criteria for employers.

Therefore, the Court concluded that the broad prohibition of age discrimination in the ADEA was deemed to exceed the scope of Congress's power. The Court declared: "Judged against the backdrop of our equal protection jurisprudence, it is clear that the ADEA is so out of proportion to a supposed remedial core preventive object that it cannot be understood as responsive to, or designed to prevent, unconstitutional behavior."[196]

The Court stressed that the ADEA prohibits a great deal of conduct that is otherwise constitutional. The Court also emphasized that there were not "findings" by Congress of substantial age discrimination by state governments. Therefore, the Court stated that because of "the lack of evidence of widespread and unconstitutional age discrimination by the States, we hold that the ADEA is not a valid exercise of power under section 5 of the Fourteenth Amendment."

Where does this leave state employees who are victims of age discrimination? Justice O'Connor concludes the majority opinion by saying that their recourse is under state law in state courts. She states: "Our decision does not signal the end of the line for employees who find themselves subject to age discrimination at the hands of state employers. . . . State employees are protected by state age

---

[193] *See, e.g.,* Vance v. Bradley, 440 U.S. 93 (1979); Massachusetts Bd. of Retirement v. Murgia, 427 U.S. 307 (1976).

[194] 528 U.S. at 83.

[195] *Id.*

[196] *Id.* at 86.

discrimination statutes, and may recover money damages from their state employers, in almost every State of the Union. Those avenues of relief remain available today, just as they were before the decision."[197] State courts and state law are the only recourse for an attorney seeking redress for a state employee who has suffered age discrimination.

University of Alabama v. Garrett

In *University of Alabama v. Garrett*,[198] the Court considered whether state governments may be sued for violating Title I of the Americans with Disabilities Act, which prohibits employment discrimination against the disabled and requires reasonable accommodation for disabilities by employers. The plaintiffs' key argument to the Court was that the elaborate legislative history documenting government discrimination against the disabled made the Americans with Disabilities Act different from other laws the Court had considered in the last few years. The Supreme Court, in a 5-to-4 decision, rejected this argument and held that state governments may not be sued for violating Title I of the ADA.

Patricia Garrett was the director of nursing at the University of Alabama, Birmingham hospital. She was diagnosed with breast cancer and took time off work to have surgery, chemotherapy, and radiation. When she returned to work, she was informed that her position as director of nursing was no longer available. She sued under Title I of the ADA.

Chief Justice Rehnquist's majority opinion began by stating that the ADA was a substantial expansion of rights compared to the Constitution. He explained that under equal protection, discrimination based on disability only need meet a rational basis test, being rationally related to a legitimate government purpose.[199] The ADA prohibits much more than would fail a rational basis test, and its requirement for reasonable accommodation of disabilities is significantly greater than the Constitution requires.

The Court then concluded that Title I of the ADA is not "proportionate" or "congruent" to preventing and remedying constitutional violations. Chief Justice Rehnquist declared: "The legislative record of the ADA, however, simply fails to show that Congress did in fact identify a pattern of irrational state discrimination in employment against the disabled."[200] Justice Breyer attached a 39-page appendix to his dissenting opinion in which he listed the numerous references in the legislative history to government discrimination against the disabled.[201] Chief Justice Rehnquist's majority opinion found these insufficient. He said that some were just anecdotes.[202] He said that most involved local governments, not state governments, and local governments are not protected by state sovereign immunity.[203] He said that some of the evidence concerns government discrimination against

[197] *Id.* at 17.
[198] 531 U.S. 356 (2001).
[199] 531 U.S. at 366, citing City of Cleburne v. Cleburne Living Center, 473 U.S. 432.
[200] *Id.* at 965.
[201] *Id.* at 389-390. (Breyer, J., dissenting).
[202] *Id.* at 370-371.
[203] *Id.*

the disabled in providing services, and that is Title II, not Title I, of the ADA. He observed that: "In 1990, the States alone employed more than 4.5 million people. It is telling, we think, that given these large numbers, Congress assembled only such minimal evidence of unconstitutional state discrimination in employment against the disabled."[204]

Chief Justice Rehnquist contrasted the legislative record for the Voting Rights Act of 1965, which he said was in "stark" contrast to the ADA. He noted the statistical findings by Congress in enacting the Voting Rights Act, such as "an otherwise inexplicable 50-percentage-point gap in the registration of white and African-American voters in some States."[205] He concluded that the congressional findings for the ADA were insufficient in comparison. He wrote: "[I]n order to authorize private individuals to recover money damages against the States, there must be a pattern of discrimination by the States which violates the Fourteenth Amendment, and the remedy imposed by Congress must be congruent and proportional to the targeted violation. Those requirements are not met here, and to uphold the Act's application to the States would allow Congress to rewrite the Fourteenth Amendment law laid down by this Court in Cleburne. Section 5 does not so broadly enlarge congressional authority."[206]

Chief Justice Rehnquist, however, added a footnote to make clear that the Court was not declaring the ADA unconstitutional as applied to state governments, but rather only holding that state governments could not be sued by individuals for violations.[207] He explained that the federal government still could sue the states to enforce the law and that suits against individual government officers for injunctive relief were also permissible.[208] But damages actions against state governments are barred.

Nevada Department of Human Resources v. Hibbs

In contrast, in *Nevada Department of Human Resources v. Hibbs*,[209] the Supreme Court held that the family leave provision of the Family and Medical Leave Act (FMLA) fits within the scope of Congress's §5 powers and can be used to sue state governments. The FMLA requires that employers, including government employers, provide their employees with unpaid leave time for family and medical care. The Supreme Court in *Hibbs*, by a 6-to-3 margin, held that the family leave provision is a valid congressional abrogation of state sovereign immunity.[210] Chief Justice Rehnquist, writing for the Court, stressed that the "FMLA aims to protect the right to be free from gender-based discrimination in the workplace."[211] The Court said that Congress, recognizing social realities, found that

---

[204] *Id.* at 370.
[205] *Id.* at 373.
[206] *Id.* at 374
[207] *Id.* at 374 n.9.
[208] *Id.*
[209] 538 U.S. 721 (2003).
[210] For an excellent discussion of the issue presented in *Hibbs, see* Robert C. Post & Reva B. Siegel, Legislative Constitutionalism and Section Five Power: Policentric Interpretation of the Family and Medical Leave Act, 112 Yale L.J. 1943 (2003).
[211] 538 U.S. at 728.

the absence of family leave policies disadvantaged women in the workplace. Although the FMLA is gender neutral in that it requires leaves be granted to both men and women, and Hibbs was male, the Court said that Congress clearly intended the law to prevent gender discrimination in employment.

Chief Justice Rehnquist distinguished *Kimel* and *Garrett* on the grounds that they involved types of discrimination which receive only rational basis review, whereas gender discrimination triggers intermediate scrutiny under equal protection. The Court explained: "Here, however, Congress directed its attention to state gender discrimination, which triggers a heightened level of scrutiny. Because the standard for demonstrating the constitutionality of a gender-based classification is more difficult to meet than our rational basis test, . . . it was easier for Congress to show a pattern of constitutional violations."[212]

Tennessee v. Lane

The Court followed and extended *Hibbs* in *Tennessee v. Lane*.[213] The case involved a criminal defendant who literally climbed on his hands and knees to get to a second-floor courtroom because it was not accessible to those with disabilities. He sued the state government pursuant to Title II of the Americans with Disabilities Act,[214] which prohibits state and local governments from discriminating against people with disabilities in government programs, services, and activities.

The Court, in a 5-to-4 decision, held that Lane's suit against the state was not barred by sovereign immunity. The Court, in an opinion by Justice Stevens, emphasized that there is a well-established fundamental right of access to the courts. The Court recognized that Congress has greater latitude to legislate under §5 when dealing with a claim that receives heightened judicial scrutiny, whether because it is a fundamental right or a type of discrimination that receives heightened scrutiny. *Tennessee v. Lane* does not address whether states can be sued under Title II when there is not a fundamental right that is implicated.

United States v. Georgia

United States v. Georgia also involved Title II of the Americans with Disabilities Act, specifically a suit by a paraplegic prisoner.[215] The Court, in a unanimous opinion written by Justice Scalia, held that sovereign immunity did not bar the suit because the prisoner alleged violations of his constitutional rights under the Eighth Amendment. The Court explained: "Thus, insofar as Title II creates a private cause of action for damages against the States for conduct that *actually* violates the Fourteenth Amendment, Title II validly abrogates state sovereign immunity."[216]

United States v. Georgia thus holds that Congress may authorize suits against states pursuant to §5 of the Fourteenth Amendment for actions that actually violate the Fourteenth Amendment. *Hibbs* and *Lane* hold that for rights or types of

---

[212] *Id.* at 736.
[213] 541 U.S. 509 (2004).
[214] 42 U.S.C. §12131.
[215] 546 U.S. 151 (2006).
[216] *Id.* at 159.

discrimination that receive heightened scrutiny, Congress has much greater authority to permit suits against state governments than for claims that receive only rational basis review.

Future Implications

There are two key questions in appraising these recent decisions: Descriptively what are they likely to mean in terms of the ability to sue state governments to enforce other federal civil rights laws; and normatively are they desirable in their protection of state sovereign immunity and in the distinctions drawn as to when state governments may be sued?

Descriptively, the law seems to be that if it is a claim that receives heightened scrutiny, based on the type of discrimination or the presence of a fundamental right, Congress has broad authority to legislate. Indeed, based on *Hibbs*, there is no need for a congressional finding of pervasive constitutional violations when Congress is dealing with areas that receive heightened judicial scrutiny. In *Hibbs*, Congress never found any *unconstitutional* gender discrimination. On the other hand, if it is a claim that receives only rational basis review, then even an elaborate legislative record, as in *Garrett*, is unlikely to be enough to allow suits against state governments. Unless Congress finds pervasive unconstitutional state conduct, it cannot authorize suits against the states.

Normatively, there are questions as to whether the distinctions drawn in these cases are desirable and more generally whether Congress should be able to authorize suits against state governments. The Court offered little explanation as to why the level of scrutiny matters in determining the scope of Congress's powers under §5. Perhaps it is that in areas receiving heightened scrutiny there already are sufficient findings of historical violations such that there is no need for congressional documentation. But critics, including the dissenting Justices, argue that Congress's power under §5 is not altered by the level of scrutiny used by the courts.

Defenders of the Court's recent decisions in *Florida Prepaid*, *Kimel*, and *Garrett* contend that the rulings are an appropriate protection of state sovereign immunity and a proper limit on Congress's §5 powers.[217] They argue that sovereign immunity is an important aspect of the Constitution's protection of state governments and that Congress's power to authorize suits against state governments must be limited. As explained above in the discussion of *City of Boerne v. Flores*, its defenders argue that the decision properly interpreted §5 based on the text of the provision, its framers' intent, and the need to preserve the Supreme Court's role in determining the meaning of the Constitution.

But critics of these decisions disagree with their premise that sovereign immunity is an inherent part of the Constitution's design. Indeed, those objecting

---

[217] *See, e.g.*, James Eugene Fitzgerald, State Sovereign Immunity: Searching for Stability, 48 UCLA L. Rev. 1203 (2001); Alfred Hill, In Defense of Our Law of Sovereign Immunity, 42 B.C. L. Rev. 485 (2001); William J; Rich, Privileges or Immunities: The Missing Link in Establishing Congressional Power to Abrogate State Eleventh Amendment Immunity, 28 Hastings Const. L.Q. 235 (2001).

to the decisions contend that sovereign immunity is not authorized by the text of the Constitution,[218] and that such immunity undermines the basic constitutional principle of government accountability.[219] Critics also argue, as discussed above, that *City of Boerne* was wrongly decided and that Congress should have the authority under §5 to expand the scope of rights. The critics contend that all of these recent decisions are undue conservative judicial activism: The five most conservative Justices are striking down important federal laws based on principles nowhere found in the Constitution.

This debate is likely to continue for the foreseeable future as the federal courts continue to apply *City of Boerne* and *Seminole Tribe*. Ultimately, the disagreement is over basic constitutional principles concerning separation of powers, federalism, and the protection of individual rights under the Constitution. There also is the prospect of change in the near future because of the presence of two new Justices. *Hibbs* was a 6-to-3 decision, with Chief Justice Rehnquist and Justice O'Connor in the majority. *Lane* was a 5-to-4 ruling, with Justice O'Connor in the majority. The presence of four new Justices — Roberts, Alito, Sotomayor, and Kagan — may steer the Court in a different direction and call into question the distinctions drawn in the recent cases.

---

[218] The Eleventh Amendment's text only bars suits against state governments by citizens of other states or citizens of foreign countries. There is strong historical evidence that this was meant to preclude only suits based on diversity of citizenship against state governments. *See* William A. Fletcher, A Historical Interpretation of the Eleventh Amendment: A Narrow Construction of an Affirmative Grant of Jurisdiction Rather Than a Prohibition Against Jurisdiction, 35 Stan. L. Rev. 1033 (1983); John J. Gibbons, The Eleventh Amendment and State Sovereign Immunity: A Reinterpretation, 83 Colum. L. Rev. 1889 (1983).

[219] *See, e.g.,* Erwin Chemerinsky, Against Sovereign Immunity, 53 Stan. L. Rev. 1201 (2001).

CHAPTER 7

THE FEDERAL EXECUTIVE POWER

This chapter examines the powers of the presidency and the executive branch. It particularly focuses on the tensions between the executive and legislative powers. The prior chapter examined the federal legislative power in relationship to state governments. This chapter, in contrast, centers on the relationship between two branches of the federal government.

Six topics are examined. First, Section 7.A focuses on the issue of inherent presidential power and the question of when, if at all, the President may act without constitutional or statutory authority. The issue of executive privilege is considered as an example of this controversy. Second, Section 7.B looks at the ability of Congress to expand presidential powers beyond those enumerated in the Constitution, specifically examining the Supreme Court's recent decision in the line-item veto case.

Third, Section 9.B considers the constitutional problems posed by administrative agencies. The section begins by considering the non-delegation doctrine and its demise and then examines the legislative veto as a possible alternative check on administrative agencies. In light of the demise of the legislative veto, the chapter then considers other alternative checks on agencies, including the use of the removal power.

Fourth, Section 7.C looks at the allocation of decision-making authority in the area of foreign policy. In particular, responsibilities with regard to treaties and war powers are considered. Fifth, Section 7.D examines executive power and the war on terrorism.

Finally, Section F [Erwin Chemerinsky, Constitutional Law, 3rd ed., (2009)] concludes by examining checks on the executive, including civil suits for money damages and impeachment.

A. Inherent Presidential Power

INTRODUCTION

When, if ever may the President act without express constitutional or statutory authorization? If the President has explicit constitutional authority for particular conduct, then the issues are solely whether the President is acting within the scope of the granted power and whether the President is violating some other constitutional provision. If there is a statute authorizing the President's conduct, then the question is whether that law is constitutional. But what if there is neither constitutional nor statutory authority?

The debate over this question began in the earliest days of the nation and had impeccable authorities on each side of the dispute. Early in the presidency of George Washington, Alexander Hamilton and James Madison clashed over this issue and whether the President could issue a neutrality proclamation as to a war occurring between England and France. Alexander Hamilton argued that the difference in the wording of Articles I and II reveals the framers' intention to create inherent presidential powers.[1] Article I initially states, "All legislative Powers herein granted shall be vested in a Congress of the United States." Article II of the Constitution begins, "The executive Power shall be vested in a President of the United States of America." Because Article II does not limit the President to powers "herein granted," Hamilton argued that the President has authority not specifically delineated in the Constitution.

Others, beginning with James Madison,[2] have disputed this interpretation of Article II, contending that the opening language of Article II was "simply to settle the question whether the executive branch should be plural or single and to give the executive a title."[3] According to this position, the President has no powers that are not enumerated in Article II and, indeed, such unenumerated authority would be inconsistent with a Constitution creating a government of limited authority.

The leading Supreme Court decision concerning this issue is Youngstown Sheet & Tube Co. v. Sawyer. In reading this decision, focus on how each of the opinions would answer the question of when the President may act without express constitutional or statutory authority. Following this case, a specific, important example is presented: When, if at all, may the President claim executive privilege?

---

[1] Alexander Hamilton, First Letter of *Pacificus* (June 29, 1793), reprinted in William M. Goldsmith, *The Growth of Presidential Power: A Documented History* 398, 401 (1974).

[2] James Madison, The First letter of *Helvidius*, reprinted in W. Goldsmith, *supra* note 1, at 405.

[3] Edward S. Corwin, *The Steel Seizure Case: A Judicial Brick Without Straw*, 53 Colum. L. Rev. 53, 53 (1953).

Youngstown Sheet & Tube Co. v. Sawyer

343 U.S. 579 (1952)

Justice BLACK delivered the opinion of the Court.

We are asked to decide whether the President was acting within his constitutional power when he issued an order directing the Secretary of Commerce to take possession of and operate most of the Nation's steel mills. The mill owners argue that the President's order amounts to lawmaking, a legislative function which the Constitution has expressly confided to the Congress and not to the President. The Government's position is that the order was made on findings of the President that his action was necessary to avert a national catastrophe which would inevitably result from a stoppage of steel production, and that in meeting this grave emergency the President was acting within the aggregate of his constitutional powers as the Nation's Chief Executive and the Commander in Chief of the Armed Forces of the United States. The issue emerges here from the following series of events:

In the latter part of 1951, a dispute arose between the steel companies and their employees over terms and conditions that should be included in new collective bargaining agreements. Long-continued conferences failed to resolve the dispute. On December 18, 1951, the employees' representative, United Steelworkers of America, C.I.O., gave notice of an intention to strike when the existing bargaining agreements expired on December 31. The Federal Mediation and Conciliation Service then intervened in an effort to get labor and management to agree. This failing, the President on December 22, 1951, referred the dispute to the Federal Wage Stabilization Board to investigate and make recommendations for fair and equitable terms of settlement. This Board's report resulted in no settlement. On April 4, 1952, the Union gave notice of a nationwide strike called to begin at 12:01 A.M. April 9. The indispensability of steel as a component of substantially all weapons and other war materials led the President to believe that the proposed work stoppage would immediately jeopardize our national defense and that governmental seizure of the steel mills was necessary in order to assure the continued availability of steel. Reciting these considerations for his action, the President, a few hours before the strike was to begin, issued Executive Order 10340. The order directed the Secretary of Commerce to take possession of most of the steel mills and keep them running. The Secretary immediately issued his own possessory orders, calling upon the presidents of the various seized companies to serve as operating managers for the United States. They were directed to carry on their activities in accordance with regulations and directions of the Secretary. The next morning the President sent a message to Congress reporting his action. Twelve days later he sent a second message. Congress has taken no action.

Obeying the Secretary's orders under protest, the companies brought proceedings against him in the District Court. Their complaints charged that the seizure was not authorized by an act of Congress or by any constitutional provisions.

The President's power, if any, to issue the order must stem either from an act of Congress or from the Constitution itself. There is no statute that expressly authorizes the President to take possession of property as he did here. Nor is there any act of Congress to which our attention has been directed from which such a power can fairly be implied. Indeed, we do not understand the Government to rely on statutory authorization for this seizure. There are two statutes which do authorize the President to take both personal and real property under certain conditions. However, the Government admits that these conditions were not met and that the President's order was not rooted in either of the statutes.

Moreover, the use of the seizure technique to solve labor disputes in order to prevent work stoppages was not only unauthorized by any congressional enactment; prior to this controversy, Congress had refused to adopt that method of settling labor disputes. When the Taft-Hartley Act was under consideration in 1947, Congress rejected an amendment which would have authorized such governmental seizures in cases of emergency. Apparently it was thought that the technique of seizure, like that of compulsory arbitration, would interfere with the process of collective bargaining. Consequently, the plan Congress adopted in that Act did not provide for seizure under any circumstances. Instead, the plan sought to bring about settlements by use of the customary devices of mediation, conciliation, investigation by boards of inquiry, and public reports. In some instances temporary injunctions were authorized to provide cooling-off periods. All this failing, unions were left free to strike after a secret vote by employees as to whether they wished to accept their employers' final settlement offer.

It is clear that if the President had authority to issue the order he did, it must be found in some provisions of the Constitution. And it is not claimed that express constitutional language grants this power to the President. The contention is that presidential power should be implied from the aggregate of his powers under the Constitution. Particular reliance is placed on provisions in Article II which say that "the executive Power shall be vested in a President . . ."; that "he shall take Care that the Laws be faithfully executed"; and that he "shall be Commander in Chief of the Army and Navy of the United States."

The order cannot properly be sustained as an exercise of the President's military power as Commander in Chief of the Armed Forces. The Government attempts to do so by citing a number of cases upholding broad powers in military commanders engaged in day-to-day fighting in a theater of war. Such cases need not concern us here. Even though "theater of war" be an expanding concept, we cannot with faithfulness to our constitutional system hold that the Commander in Chief of the Armed Forces has the ultimate power as such to take possession of private property in order to keep labor disputes from stopping production. This is a job for the Nation's lawmakers, not for its military authorities.

Nor can the seizure order be sustained because of the several constitutional provisions that grant executive power to the President. In the framework of our Constitution, the President's power to see that the laws are faithfully executed refutes the idea that he is to be a lawmaker. The Constitution limits his functions in the lawmaking process to the recommending of laws he thinks wise and the vetoing of laws he thinks bad. And the Constitution is neither silent nor equivocal about who shall make laws which the President is to execute.

The Founders of this Nation entrusted the lawmaking power to the Congress alone in both good and bad times. It would do no good to recall the historical events, the fears of power and the hopes for freedom that lay behind their choice. Such a review would but confirm our holding that this seizure order cannot stand.

Mr. Justice JACKSON, concurring in the judgment and opinion of the Court.

That comprehensive and undefined presidential powers hold both practical advantages and grave dangers for the country will impress anyone who has served as legal adviser to a President in time of transition and public anxiety. A judge, like an executive adviser, may be surprised at the poverty of really useful and unambiguous authority applicable to concrete problems of executive power as they actually present themselves. Just what our forefathers did envision, or would have envisioned had they foreseen modern conditions, must be divined from materials almost as enigmatic as the dreams Joseph was called upon to interpret for Pharaoh. A century and a half of partisan debate and scholarly speculation yields no net result but only supplies more or less apt quotations from respected sources on each side of any question. They largely cancel each other. And court decisions are indecisive because of the judicial practice of dealing with the largest questions in the most narrow way.

We may well begin by a somewhat over-simplified grouping of practical situations in which a President may doubt, or others may challenge, his powers, and by distinguishing roughly the legal consequences of this factor of relativity.

1. When the President acts pursuant to an express or implied authorization of Congress, his authority is at its maximum, for it includes all that he possesses in his own right plus all that Congress can delegate. In these circumstances, and in these only, may he be said (for what it may be worth), to personify the federal sovereignty. If his act is held unconstitutional under these circumstances, it usually means that the Federal Government as an undivided whole lacks power. A seizure executed by the President pursuant to an Act of Congress would be supported by the strongest of presumptions and the widest latitude of judicial interpretation, and the burden of persuasion would rest heavily upon any who might attack it.

2. When the President acts in absence of either a congressional grant or denial of authority, he can only rely upon his own independent powers, but there is a zone of twilight in which he and Congress may have concurrent authority, or in which its distribution is uncertain. Therefore, congressional inertia, indifference or quiescence may sometimes, at least as a practical matters, enable, if not invite, measures of independent presidential responsibility. In this area, any actual test of power is likely to depend on the imperatives of events and contemporary imponderables rather than on abstract theories of law.

3. When the President takes measures incompatible with the expressed or implied will of Congress, his power is at its lowest ebb, for then he can rely only upon his own constitutional powers minus any constitutional powers of Congress over the matter. Courts can sustain exclusive Presidential control in such a case only by disabling the Congress from acting upon the subject. Presidential claim to a power at once so conclusive and preclusive must be scrutinized with caution, for what is at stake is the equilibrium established by our constitutional system.

Into which of these classifications does this executive seizure of the steel industry fit? It is eliminated from the first by admission, for it is conceded that no congressional authorization exists for this seizure. That takes away also the support of the many precedents and declarations which were made in relation, and must be confined, to this category.

Can it then be defended under flexible tests available to the second category? It seems clearly eliminated from that class because Congress has not left seizure of private property an open field but has covered it by three statutory policies inconsistent with this seizure.

This leaves the current seizure to be justified only by the severe tests under the third grouping, where it can be supported only by any remainder of executive power after subtraction of such powers as Congress may have over the subject. In short, we can sustain the President only by holding that seizure of such strike-bound industries is within his domain and beyond control by Congress. Thus, this Court's first review of such seizures occurs under circumstances which leave Presidential power most vulnerable to attack and in the least favorable of possible constitutional postures.

The clause on which the Government relies is that "The President shall be Commander in Chief of the Army and Navy of the United States. . . ." These cryptic words have given rise to some of the most persistent controversies in our constitutional history. Assuming that we are in a war de facto, whether it is or is not a war de jure, does that empower the Commander-in-Chief to seize industries he thinks necessary to supply our army? The Constitution expressly places in Congress power "to raise and support Armies" and "to provide and maintain a Navy." This certainly lays upon Congress primary responsibility for supplying the armed forces. Congress alone controls the raising of revenues and their appropriation and may determine in what manner and by what means they shall be spent for military and naval procurement. I suppose no one would doubt that Congress can take over war supply as a Government enterprise. On the other hand, if Congress sees fit to rely on free private enterprise collectively bargaining with free labor for support and maintenance of our armed forces, can the Executive because of lawful disagreements incidental to that process, seize the facility for operation upon Government-imposed terms?

There are indications that the Constitution did not contemplate that the title Commander-in-Chief of the Army and Navy will constitute him also Commander-in-Chief of the country, its industries and its inhabitants. He has no monopoly of "war powers," whatever they are. While Congress cannot deprive the President of the command of the army and navy, only Congress can provide him an army or navy to command. That military powers of the Commander-in-Chief were not to supersede representative government of internal affairs seems obvious from the Constitution and from elementary American history.

The executive action we have here originates in the individual will of the President and represents an exercise of authority without law. No one, perhaps not even the President, knows the limits of the power he may seek to exert in this instance and the parties affected cannot learn the limit of their rights. We do not know today what powers over labor or property would be claimed to flow from

Government possession if we should legalize it, what rights to compensation would be claimed or recognized, or on what contingency it would end. With all its defects, delays and inconveniences, men have discovered no technique for long preserving free government except that the Executive be under the law, and that the law be made by parliamentary deliberations. Such institutions may be destined to pass away. But it is the duty of the Court to be last, not first, to give them up.

Justice DOUGLAS, concurring.

There can be no doubt that the emergency which caused the President to seize these steel plants was one that bore heavily on the country. But the emergency did not create power; it merely marked an occasion when power should be exercised. And the fact that it was necessary that measures be taken to keep steel in production does not mean that the President, rather than the Congress, had the constitutional authority to act. The Congress, as well as the President, is trustee of the national welfare. The President can act more quickly than the Congress. The President with the armed services at his disposal can move with force as well as with speed. All executive power — from the reign of ancient kings to the rule of modern dictators — has the outward appearance of efficiency.

Legislative power, by contrast, is slower to exercise. There must be delay while the ponderous machinery of committees, hearings, and debates is put into motion. That takes time; and while the Congress slowly moves into action, the emergency may take its toll in wages, consumer goods, war production, the standard of living of the people, and perhaps even lives. Legislative action may indeed often be cumbersome, time-consuming, and apparently inefficient. But as Mr. Justice Brandeis stated in his dissent in Myers v. United States:

> The doctrine of the separation of powers was adopted by the Convention of 1787 not to promote efficiency but to preclude the exercise of arbitrary power. The purpose was not to avoid friction, but, by means of the inevitable friction incident to the distribution of the governmental powers among three departments, to save the people from autocracy.

We therefore cannot decide this case by determining which branch of government can deal most expeditiously with the present crisis. The answer must depend on the allocation of powers under the Constitution. That in turn requires an analysis of the conditions giving rise to the seizure and of the seizure itself.

The legislative nature of the action taken by the President seems to me to be clear. When the United States takes over an industrial plant to settle a labor controversy, it is condemning property. The seizure of the plant is a taking in the constitutional sense. A permanent taking would amount to the nationalization of the industry. A temporary taking falls short of that goal. But though the seizure is only for a week or a month, the condemnation is complete and the United States must pay compensation for the temporary possession.

The President has no power to raise revenues. That power is in the Congress by Article I, Section 8 of the Constitution. The President might seize and the

Congress by subsequent action might ratify the seizure. But until and unless Congress acted, no condemnation would be lawful. The branch of government that has the power to pay compensation for a seizure is the only one able to authorize a seizure or make lawful one that the President had effected. That seems to me to be the necessary result of the condemnation provision in the Fifth Amendment. It squares with the theory of checks and balances expounded by Mr. Justice BLACK in the opinion of the Court in which I join.

Justice FRANKFURTER, concurring.

We must therefore put to one side consideration of what powers the President would have had if there had been no legislation whatever bearing on the authority asserted by the seizure, or if the seizure had been only for a short, explicitly temporary period, to be terminated automatically unless Congressional approval were given. These and other questions, like or unlike, are not now here. I would exceed my authority were I to say anything about them.

The question before the Court comes in this setting. Congress has frequently — at least 16 times since 1916 — specifically provided for executive seizure of production, transportation, communications, or storage facilities. In every case it has qualified this grant of power with limitations and safeguards. The power to seize has uniformly been given only for a limited period or for a defined emergency, or has been repealed after a short period. Its exercise has been restricted to particular circumstances such as "time of war or when war is imminent," the needs of "public safety" or of "national security or defense," or "urgent and impending need." The period of governmental operation has been limited, as, for instance, to "sixty days after the restoration of productive efficiency." Congress also has not left to implication that just compensation be paid: it has usually legislated in detail regarding enforcement of this litigation-breeding general requirement.

Congress in 1947 was again called upon to consider whether governmental seizure should be used to avoid serious industrial shutdowns. Congress decided against conferring such power generally and in advance, without special congressional enactment to meet each particular need. Under the urgency of telephone and coal strikes in the winter of 1946, Congress addressed itself to the problems raised by "national emergency" strikes and lockouts. The termination of wartime seizure powers on December 31, 1946, brought these matters to the attention of Congress with vivid impact. A proposal that the President be given powers to seize plants to avert a shutdown where the "health or safety" of the nation was endangered, was thoroughly canvassed by Congress and rejected. No room for doubt remains that the proponents as well as the opponents of the bill which became the Labor Management Relations Act of 1947 clearly understood that as a result of that legislation the only recourse for preventing a shutdown in any basic industry, after failure of mediation, was Congress. Authorization for seizure as an available remedy for potential dangers was unequivocally put aside. An amendment presented in the House providing that where necessary "to preserve and protect the public health and security" the President might seize any industry in which there is an impending curtailment of production, was voted down after debate, by a vote of more than three to one.

[N]othing can be plainer than that Congress made a conscious choice of policy in a field full of perplexity and peculiarly within legislative responsibility for choice. In formulating legislation for dealing with industrial conflicts, Congress could not more clearly and emphatically have withheld authority than it did in 1947. Perhaps as much so as is true of any piece of modern legislation, Congress acted with full consciousness of what it was doing and in the light of much recent history. Previous seizure legislation had subjected the powers granted to the President to restrictions of varying degrees of stringency. Instead of giving him even limited powers, Congress in 1947 deemed it wise to require the President, upon failure of attempts to reach a voluntary settlement, to report to Congress if he deemed the power of seizure a needed shot for his locker. The President could not ignore the specific limitations of prior seizure statutes. No more could he act in disregard of the limitation put upon seizure by the 1947 Act.

It cannot be contended that the President would have had power to issue this order had Congress explicitly negated such authority in formal legislation. Congress has expressed its will to withhold this power from the President as though it had said so in so many words.

Deeply embedded traditional ways of conducting government cannot supplant the Constitution or legislation, but they give meaning to the words of a text or supply them. It is an inadmissibly narrow conception of American constitutional law to confine it to the words of the Constitution and to disregard the gloss which life has written upon them. In short, a systematic, unbroken, executive practice, long pursued to the knowledge of the Congress and never before questioned, engaged in by Presidents who have also sworn to uphold the Constitution, making as it were such exercise of power part of the structure of our government, may be treated as a gloss on "executive Power" vested in the President by §1 of Art. II. Down to the World War II period, then, the record is barren of instances comparable to the one before us.

A scheme of government like ours no doubt at times feels the lack of power to act with complete, all-embracing, swiftly moving authority. No doubt a government with distributed authority, subject to be challenged in the courts of law, at least long enough to consider and adjudicate the challenge, labors under restrictions from which other governments are free. It has not been our tradition to envy such governments. In any event our government was designed to have such restrictions. The price was deemed not too high in view of the safeguards which these restrictions afford.

Chief Justice VINSON, with whom Justice REED and Justice MINTON join, dissenting.

The President of the United States directed the Secretary of Commerce to take temporary possession of the Nation's steel mills during the existing emergency because "a work stoppage would immediately jeopardize and imperil our national defense and the defense of those joined with us in resisting aggression, and would add to the continuing danger of our soldiers, sailors and airmen engaged in combat in the field."

In passing upon the question of Presidential powers in this case, we must first consider the context in which those powers were exercised. Those who suggest that this is a case involving extraordinary powers should be mindful that these are extraordinary times. A world not yet recovered from the devastation of World War II has been forced to face the threat of another and more terrifying global conflict.

In 1950, when the United Nations called upon member nations "to render every assistance" to repel aggression in Korea, the United States furnished its vigorous support. For almost two full years, our armed forces have been fighting in Korea, suffering casualties of over 108,000 men. Hostilities have not abated. The "determination of the United Nations to continue its action in Korea to meet the aggression" has been reaffirmed. Congressional support of the action in Korea has been manifested by provisions for increased military manpower and equipment and for economic stabilization, as hereinafter described. Alert to our responsibilities, which coincide with our own self preservation through mutual security, Congress has enacted a large body of implementing legislation. As an illustration of the magnitude of the over-all program, Congress has appropriated $130 billion for our own defense and for military assistance to our allies since the June, 1950, attack in Korea.

The President has the duty to execute the foregoing legislative programs. Their successful execution depends upon continued production of steel and stabilized prices for steel. Accordingly, when the collective bargaining agreements between the Nation's steel producers and their employees, represented by the United Steel Workers, were due to expire on December 31, 1951, and a strike shutting down the entire basic steel industry was threatened, the President acted to avert a complete shutdown of steel production.

One is not here called upon even to consider the possibility of executive seizure of a farm, a corner grocery store or even a single industrial plant. Such considerations arise only when one ignores the central fact of this case — that the Nation's entire basic steel production would have shut down completely if there had been no Government seizure. Even ignoring for the moment whatever confidential information the President may possess as "the Nation's organ for foreign affairs," the uncontroverted affidavits in this record amply support the finding that "a work stoppage would immediately jeopardize and imperil our national defense."

Plaintiffs do not remotely suggest any basis for rejecting the President's finding that any stoppage of steel production would immediately place the Nation in peril. At the time of seizure there was not, and there is not now, the slightest evidence to justify the belief that any strike will be of short duration. The Union and the steel companies may well engage in a lengthy struggle. Plaintiff's counsel tells us that "sooner or later" the mills will operate again. That may satisfy the steel companies and, perhaps, the Union. But our soldiers and our allies will hardly be cheered with the assurance that the ammunition upon which their lives depend will be forthcoming — "sooner or later," or, in other words, "too little and too late."

Accordingly, if the President has any power under the Constitution to meet a critical situation in the absence of express statutory authorization, there is no basis whatever for criticizing the exercise of such power in this case.

A review of executive action demonstrates that our Presidents have on many occasions exhibited the leadership contemplated by the framers when they made the President Commander in Chief, and imposed upon him the trust to "take Care that the Laws be faithfully executed." With or without explicit statutory authorization, Presidents have at such times dealt with national emergencies by acting promptly and resolutely to enforce legislative programs, at least to save those programs until Congress could act. Congress and the courts have responded to such executive initiative with consistent approval.

Focusing now on the situation confronting the President on the night of April 8, 1952, we cannot but conclude that the President was performing his duty under the Constitution to "take Care that the Laws be faithfully executed" — a duty described by President Benjamin Harrison as "the central idea of the office." The President reported to Congress the morning after the seizure that he acted because a work stoppage in steel production would immediately imperil the safety of the Nation by preventing execution of the legislative programs for procurement of military equipment. And, while a shutdown could be averted by granting the price concessions requested by plaintiffs, granting such concessions would disrupt the price stabilization program also enacted by Congress. Rather than fail to execute either legislative program, the President acted to execute both

Much of the argument in this case has been directed at straw men. We do not now have before us the case of a President acting solely on the basis of his own notions of the public welfare. Nor is there any question of unlimited executive power in this case. The President himself closed the door to any such claim when he sent his Message to Congress stating his purpose to abide by any action of Congress, whether approving or disapproving his seizure action. Here, the President immediately made sure that Congress was fully informed of the temporary action he had taken only to preserve the legislative programs from destruction until Congress could act.

Faced with the duty of executing the defense programs which Congress had enacted and the disastrous effects that any stoppage in steel production would have on those programs, the President acted to preserve those programs by seizing the steel mills. There is no question that the possession was other than temporary in character and subject to congressional direction — either approving, disapproving or regulating the manner in which the mills were to be administered and returned to the owners. The President immediately informed Congress of his action and clearly stated his intention to abide by the legislative will. No basis for claims of arbitrary action, unlimited powers or dictatorial usurpation of congressional power appears from the facts of this case. On the contrary, judicial, legislative and executive precedents throughout our history demonstrate that in this case the President acted in full conformity with his duties under the Constitution.

B. The Authority of Congress to Increase Executive Power

The prior section focused on the power of the President to act without express constitutional or statutory authority. This section focuses on the power of

Congress to enhance the powers of the President by conferring authority not contained in the Constitution. Underlying this issue are two different views of separation of powers. One approach sees separation of powers as appropriately resolved, whenever possible, between the President and Congress; if the two branches agree, the courts only rarely should invalidate their actions. The other view sees separation of powers as constitutionally mandated and therefore envisions a crucial judicial role in enforcing its requirements.

The issue of Congress's authority to increase executive power arises again, importantly, in the next section, which focuses on the ability of Congress to delegate legislative power to administrative agencies. Here the focus is on a recent Supreme Court decision, Clinton v. City of New York, which involved the constitutionality of a federal statute that created the line-item veto. The statute empowered the President to veto (or more precisely to "cancel") particular parts of appropriation bills while allowing the rest to go into effect.

William J. Clinton, President of the United States v. City of New York

524 U.S. 417 (1998)

Justice STEVENS delivered the opinion of the Court.

The Line Item Veto Act (Act), was enacted in April 1996 and became effective on January 1, 1997.

I

We begin by reviewing the canceled items that are at issue in these cases. Title XIX of the Social Security Act, as amended, authorizes the Federal Government to transfer huge sums of money to the States to help finance medical care for the indigent. In 1991, Congress directed that those federal subsidies be reduced by the amount of certain taxes levied by the States on health care providers. In 1994, the Department of Health and Human Services (HHS) notified the State of New York that 15 of its taxes were covered by the 1991 Act, and that as of June 30, 1994, the statute therefore required New York to return $955 million to the United States. New York turned to Congress for relief. On August 5, 1997, Congress enacted a law that resolved the issue in New York's favor. Section 4722(c) of the Balanced Budget Act of 1997 identifies the disputed taxes and provides that they "are deemed to be permissible health care related taxes and in compliance with the requirements" of the relevant provisions of the 1991 statute.

On August 11, 1997, the President sent identical notices to the Senate and to the House of Representatives canceling "one item of new direct spending," specifying §4722(c) as that item, and stating that he had determined that "this cancellation will reduce the Federal budget deficit." He explained that §4722(c) would have permitted New York "to continue relying upon impermissible provider taxes to finance its Medicaid program" and that "[t]his preferential treatment would have increased Medicaid costs, would have treated New York differently from all other States, and would have established a costly precedent for other States to request comparable treatment."

A person who realizes a profit from the sale of securities is generally subject to a capital gains tax. In §968 of the Taxpayer Relief Act of 1997, Congress amended §1042 of the Internal Revenue Code to permit owners of certain food refiners and processors to defer the recognition of gain if they sell their stock to eligible farmers' cooperatives. The purpose of the amendment, as repeatedly explained by its sponsors, was "to facilitate the transfer of refiners and processors to farmers' cooperatives." The amendment to §1042 was one of the 79 "limited tax benefits" authorized by the Taxpayer Relief Act of 1997 and specifically identified in Title XVII of that Act as "subject to [the] line item veto."

On the same date that he canceled the "item of new direct spending" involving New York's health care programs, the President also canceled this limited tax benefit. In his explanation of that action, the President endorsed the objective of encouraging "value-added farming through the purchase by farmers' cooperatives of refiners or processors of agricultural goods," but concluded that the provision lacked safeguards and also "failed to target its benefits to small- and medium-size cooperatives."

II

Appellees filed two separate actions against the President and other federal officials challenging these two cancellations. The plaintiffs in the first case are the City of New York, two hospital associations, one hospital, and two unions representing health care employees. The plaintiffs in the second are a farmers' cooperative consisting of about 30 potato growers in Idaho and an individual farmer who is a member and officer of the cooperative.

The Line Item Veto Act gives the President the power to "cancel in whole" three types of provisions that have been signed into law: "(1) any dollar amount of discretionary budget authority; (2) any item of new direct spending; or (3) any limited tax benefit." It is undisputed that the New York case involves an "item of new direct spending" and that the Snake River case involves a "limited tax benefit" as those terms are defined in the Act. It is also undisputed that each of those provisions had been signed into law pursuant to Article I, §7, of the Constitution before it was canceled.

The Act requires the President to adhere to precise procedures whenever he exercises his cancellation authority. In identifying items for cancellation he must consider the legislative history, the purposes, and other relevant information about the items. He must determine, with respect to each cancellation, that it will "(i) reduce the Federal budget deficit; (ii) not impair any essential Government functions; and (iii) not harm the national interest." Moreover, he must transmit a special message to Congress notifying it of each cancellation within five calendar days (excluding Sundays) after the enactment of the canceled provision. It is undisputed that the President meticulously followed these procedures in these cases.

A cancellation takes effect upon receipt by Congress of the special message from the President. If, however, a "disapproval bill" pertaining to a special message is enacted into law, the cancellations set forth in that message become "null and void." The Act sets forth a detailed expedited procedure for the consideration of a "disapproval bill," but no such bill was passed for either of the cancellations involved in these cases. A majority vote of both Houses is sufficient to enact a disapproval bill. The Act does not grant the President the authority to cancel a disapproval bill, but he does, of course, retain his constitutional authority to veto such a bill.

In both legal and practical effect, the President has amended two Acts of Congress by repealing a portion of each. "[R]epeal of statutes, no less than enactment, must conform with Art. I." INS v. Chadha (1983). There is no provision in the Constitution that authorizes the President to enact, to amend, or to repeal statutes.

Both Article I and Article II assign responsibilities to the President that directly relate to the lawmaking process, but neither addresses the issue presented by these cases. The President "shall from time to time give to the Congress Information on the State of the Union, and recommend to their Consideration such Measures as he shall judge necessary and expedient. . . ." Art. II, §3. Thus, he may initiate and influence legislative proposals. Moreover, after a bill has passed both Houses of Congress, but "before it become[s] a Law," it must be presented to the President. If he approves it, "he shall sign it, but if not he shall return it, with his Objections to that House in which it shall have originated, who shall enter the Objections at large on their Journal, and proceed to reconsider it." Art. I, §7, cl. 2. His "return" of a bill, which is usually described as a "veto," is subject to being overridden by a two-thirds vote in each House.

There are important differences between the President's "return" of a bill pursuant to Article I, §7, and the exercise of the President's cancellation authority pursuant to the Line Item Veto Act. The constitutional return takes place before the bill becomes law; the statutory cancellation occurs after the bill becomes law. The constitutional return is of the entire bill; the statutory cancellation is of only a part. Although the Constitution expressly authorizes the President to play a role in the process of enacting statutes, it is silent on the subject of unilateral Presidential action that either repeals or amends parts of duly enacted statutes.

There are powerful reasons for construing constitutional silence on this profoundly important issue as equivalent to an express prohibition. The procedures governing the enactment of statutes set forth in the text of Article I were the product of the great debates and compromises that produced the Constitution itself. Familiar historical materials provide abundant support for the conclusion that the power to enact statutes may only "be exercised in accord with a single, finely wrought and exhaustively considered, procedure." Our first President understood the text of the Presentment Clause as requiring that he either "approve all the parts of a Bill, or reject it in toto."

What has emerged in these cases from the President's exercise of his statutory cancellation powers, however, are truncated versions of two bills that passed both Houses of Congress. They are not the product of the "finely wrought" procedure that the framers designed.

[III]

[W]e express no opinion about the wisdom of the procedures authorized by the Line Item Veto Act. Many members of both major political parties who have served in the Legislative and the Executive Branches have long advocated the enactment of such procedures for the purpose of "ensur[ing] greater fiscal accountability in Washington." H.R. Conf. Rep. 104-491, p. 15 (1996). The text of the Act was itself the product of much debate and deliberation in both Houses of Congress and that precise text was signed into law by the President. We do not lightly conclude that their action was unauthorized by the Constitution.

If there is to be a new procedure in which the President will play a different role in determining the final text of what may "become a law," such change must come not by legislation but through the amendment procedures set forth in Article V of the Constitution.

Justice KENNEDY, concurring.

A nation cannot plunder its own treasury without putting its Constitution and its survival in peril. The statute before us, then, is of first importance, for it seems undeniable the Act will tend to restrain persistent excessive spending. Nevertheless, for the reasons given by Justice Stevens in the opinion for the Court, the statute must be found invalid. Failure of political will does not justify unconstitutional remedies.

I write to respond to my colleague Justice Breyer, who observes that the statute does not threaten the liberties of individual citizens, a point on which I disagree. The argument is related to his earlier suggestion that our role is lessened here because the two political branches are adjusting their own powers between themselves. To say the political branches have a somewhat free hand to reallocate their own authority would seem to require acceptance of two premises: first, that the public good demands it, and second, that liberty is not at risk. The former premise is inadmissible. The Constitution's structure requires a stability which transcends the convenience of the moment. The latter premise, too, is flawed. Liberty is always at stake when one or more of the branches seek to transgress the separation of powers. Separation of powers was designed to implement a fundamental insight: concentration of power in the hands of a single branch is a threat to liberty.

Justice BREYER, with whom Justice O'CONNOR and Justice SCALIA join, dissenting.

[I]

I approach the constitutional question before us with three general considerations in mind. First, the Act represents a legislative effort to provide the President with the power to give effect to some, but not to all, of the expenditure and revenue-diminishing provisions contained in a single massive appropriations bill. And this objective is constitutionally proper.

When our Nation was founded, Congress could easily have provided the President with this kind of power. In that time period, our population was less than four million, federal employees numbered fewer than 5,000, annual federal budget outlays totaled approximately $4 million, and the entire operative text of Congress's first general appropriations law [was two sentences long]. At that time, a Congress, wishing to give a President the power to select among appropriations, could simply have embodied each appropriation in a separate bill, each bill subject to a separate Presidential veto.

Today, however, our population is about 250 million, the Federal Government employs more than four million people, the annual federal budget is $1.5 trillion, and a typical budget appropriations bill may have a dozen titles, hundreds of sections, and spread across more than 500 pages of the Statutes at Large. Congress cannot divide such a bill into thousands, or tens of thousands, of separate appropriations bills, each one of which the President would have to sign, or to veto, separately. Thus, the question is whether the Constitution permits Congress to choose a particular novel means to achieve this same, constitutionally legitimate, end.

Second, the case in part requires us to focus upon the Constitution's generally phrased structural provisions, provisions that delegate all "legislative" power to Congress and vest all "executive" power in the President. The Court, when applying these provisions, has interpreted them generously in terms of the institutional arrangements that they permit.

Third, we need not here referee a dispute among the other two branches. And, as the majority points out, " 'When this Court is asked to invalidate a statutory provision that has been approved by both Houses of the Congress and signed by the President, particularly an Act of Congress that confronts a deeply vexing national problem, it should only do so for the most compelling constitutional reasons.' " (quoting Bowsher v. Synar (1986) (STEVENS, J., concurring in judgment)).

These three background circumstances mean that, when one measures the literal words of the Act against the Constitution's literal commands, the fact that the Act may closely resemble a different, literally unconstitutional, arrangement is beside the point. To drive exactly 65 miles per hour on an interstate highway closely resembles an act that violates the speed limit. But it does not violate that limit, for small differences matter when the question is one of literal violation of law. No more does this Act literally violate the Constitution's words.

[II]

The Court believes that the Act violates the literal text of the Constitution. A simple syllogism captures its basic reasoning:

Major Premise: The Constitution sets forth an exclusive method for enacting, repealing, or amending laws.

Minor Premise: The Act authorizes the President to "repea[l] or amen[d]" laws in a different way, namely by announcing a cancellation of a portion of a previously enacted law.

Conclusion: The Act is inconsistent with the Constitution.

I find this syllogism unconvincing, however, because its Minor Premise is faulty. When the President "canceled" the two appropriation measures now before us, he did not repeal any law nor did he amend any law. He simply followed the law, leaving the statutes, as they are literally written, intact.

To take a simple example, a legal document, say a will or a trust instrument, might grant a beneficiary the power (a) to appoint property "to Jones for his life, remainder to Smith for 10 years so long as Smith . . . etc., and then to Brown," or (b) to appoint the same property "to Black and the heirs of his body," or (c) not to exercise the power of appointment at all. To choose the second or third of these alternatives prevents from taking effect the legal consequences that flow from the first alternative, which the legal instrument describes in detail. Any such choice, made in the exercise of a delegated power, renders that first alternative language without "legal force or effect." But such a choice does not "repeal" or "amend" either that language or the document itself. The will or trust instrument, in delegating the power of appointment, has not delegated a power to amend or to repeal the instrument; to the contrary, it requires the delegated power to be exercised in accordance with the instrument's terms.

These features of the law do not mean that the delegated power is, or is just like, a power to appoint property. But they do mean that it is not, and it is not just like, the repeal or amendment of a law, or, for that matter, a true line item veto (despite the Act's title). Because one cannot say that the President's exercise of the power the Act grants is, literally speaking, a "repeal" or "amendment," the fact that the Act's procedures differ from the Constitution's exclusive procedures for enacting (or repealing) legislation is beside the point. The Act itself was enacted in accordance with these procedures, and its failure to require the President to satisfy those procedures does not make the Act unconstitutional.

C. Separation of Powers and Foreign Policy

The Constitution says very little about foreign policy decision making. Article I, §8 grants Congress the power to regulate commerce with foreign nations, "To declare War, grant letters of Marque and Reprisal, and make Rules concerning Captures on Land and Water," to raise and support armies, and to "define and punish Piracies and Felonies committed on the high Seas, and Offenses against the Law of Nations." Article II says that the "President shall be Commander in Chief of the Army and Navy of the United States, and of the Militia of the several States, when called into the actual Service of the United States." Article II also provides that the President "shall have Power, by and with Advice and Consent of the Senate, to make Treaties, provided two thirds of the Senators present concur."

These relatively few provisions raise many difficult and important issues. For example, what is the relationship between Congress's power to declare war and the President's authority as Commander in Chief? When may the President use troops, including in war situations, without a congressional declaration of war? Another illustration of the Constitution's ambiguity is whether the President can use executive agreements instead of treaties in dealing with foreign countries. Is this an appropriate exercise of the power of the Chief Executive or is it an unconstitutional usurpation of the Senate's power?

This is an area of constitutional law where reliance on the framers' intent is particularly difficult. A world of instantaneous communications, missiles that can be sent across the world in minutes, and troops that can be sent anywhere within hours is vastly different from that which existed in 1787.

This area of constitutional law is different in another way as well: the relative absence of judicial decisions. As described in Chapter 5, the Supreme Court frequently has declared that issues concerning foreign policy are non-justiciable political questions; matters for the executive and legislature to resolve without judicial review. *See, e.g.*, Goldwater v. Carter, 444 U.S. 996 (1979) (holding nonjusticiable a challenge to the President's rescission of the United States treaty with Taiwan) (included in Chapter 5).

This section considers three issues. First, are foreign policy and domestic affairs different under the Constitution? Does the President have more inherent authority regarding foreign policy than as to domestic affairs? Second, what are the constitutional limits on agreements with foreign nations? In particular, may the President use executive agreements rather than treaties? Finally, how is decision-making authority over war powers allocated?

1. Are Foreign Policy and Domestic Affairs Different?

Do the same principles of separation of powers apply in foreign policy as in domestic affairs? Should the Constitution be interpreted as according the President more inherent powers as to foreign policy? The leading case supporting this view is United States v. Curtiss-Wright Export Corp. The issue in the case is the constitutionality of a congressional delegation of power to the President in the area of foreign policy. As you read the decision, it is important to remember that the Supreme Court was aggressively enforcing the non-delegation doctrine — the principle that Congress cannot delegate legislative power to executive agencies — at the time the case was decided.

United States v. Curtiss-Wright Export Corp.

299 U.S. 304 (1936)

Justice SUTHERLAND delivered the opinion of the Court.

Congress passed a resolution authorizing the President to stop sales of arms to countries involved in the Chaco border dispute. President Roosevelt immediately issued an order prohibiting munitions sales to the warring nations in the Chaco border dispute.

On January 27, 1936, an indictment was returned in the court below, the first count of which charges that appellees, beginning with the 29th day of May, 1934, conspired to sell in the United States certain arms of war, namely, fifteen machine guns, to Bolivia, a country then engaged in armed conflict in the Chaco, in violation of the Joint Resolution of Congress approved May 28, 1934, and the provisions of a proclamation issued on the same day by the President of the United States pursuant to authority conferred by section 1 of the resolution.

Whether, if the Joint Resolution had related solely to internal affairs, it would be open to the challenge that it constituted an unlawful delegation of legislative power to the Executive, we find it unnecessary to determine. The whole aim of the resolution is to affect a situation entirely external to the United States, and falling within the category of foreign affairs. The determination which we are called to make, therefore, is whether the Joint Resolution, as applied to that situation, is vulnerable to attack under the rule that forbids a delegation of the lawmaking power. In other words, assuming (but not deciding) that the challenged delegation, if it were confined to internal affairs, would be invalid, may it nevertheless be sustained on the ground that its exclusive aim is to afford a remedy for a hurtful condition within foreign territory?

It will contribute to the elucidation of the question if we first consider the differences between the powers of the federal government in respect of foreign or external affairs and those in respect of domestic or internal affairs. That there are differences between them, and that these differences are fundamental, may not be doubted.

The two classes of powers are different, both in respect of their origin and their nature. The broad statement that the federal government can exercise no powers except those specifically enumerated in the Constitution, and such implied powers as are necessary and proper to carry into effect the enumerated powers, is categorically true only in respect of our internal affairs. In that field, the primary purpose of the Constitution was to carve from the general mass of legislative powers then possessed by the states such portions as it was thought desirable to vest in the federal government, leaving those not included in the enumeration still in the states. That this doctrine applies only to powers which the states had is self-evident. And since the states severally never possessed international powers, such powers could not have been carved from the mass of state powers but obviously were transmitted to the United States from some other source. During the Colonial period, those powers were possessed exclusively by and were entirely under the control of the Crown.

It results that the investment of the federal government with the powers of external sovereignty did not depend upon the affirmative grants of the Constitution. The powers to declare and wage war, to conclude peace, to make treaties, to maintain diplomatic relations with other sovereignties, if they had never been mentioned in the Constitution, would have vested in the federal government as necessary concomitants of nationality.

Not only, as we have shown, is the federal power over external affairs in origin and essential character different from that over internal affairs, but participation in the exercise of the power is significantly limited. In this vast external realm, with its important, complicated, delicate and manifold problems, the President alone has the power to speak or listen as a representative of the nation. He makes treaties with the advice and consent of the Senate; but he alone negotiates. Into the field of negotiation the Senate cannot intrude; and Congress itself is powerless to invade it. As Marshall said in his great argument of March 7, 1800, in the House of Representatives, "The President is the sole organ of the nation in its external relations, and its sole representative with foreign nations."

It is important to bear in mind that we are here dealing not alone with an authority vested in the President by an exertion of legislative power, but with such an authority plus the very delicate, plenary and exclusive power of the President as the sole organ of the federal government in the field of international relations — a power which does not require as a basis for its exercise an act of Congress, but which, of course, like every other governmental power, must be exercised in subordination to the applicable provisions of the Constitution. It is quite apparent that if, in the maintenance of our international relations, embarrassment — perhaps serious embarrassment — is to be avoided and success for our aims achieved, congressional legislation which is to be made effective through negotiation and inquiry within the international field must often accord to the President a degree of discretion and freedom from statutory restriction which would not be admissible were domestic affairs alone involved. Moreover, he, not Congress, has the better opportunity of knowing the conditions which prevail in foreign countries, and especially is this true in time of war. He has his confidential sources of information. He has his agents in the form of diplomatic, consular and other officials. Secrecy in respect of information gathered by them may be highly necessary, and the premature disclosure of it productive of harmful results.

NOTES ON CURTISS-WRIGHT

Justice Sutherland's broad interpretation of presidential power in foreign affairs has been challenged by constitutional scholars. First, some contend that his view is inconsistent with a written Constitution that contains provisions concerning foreign policy. If Sutherland's view were correct, there would have been no reason for the Constitution to enumerate any powers in the area of foreign affairs; all powers would exist automatically as part of national sovereignty. The detailing of authority for conducting foreign policy rebuts the assumption that the President has complete control over foreign affairs simply by virtue of being Chief Executive.[4]

Second, many have criticized the historical account that is the foundation for Justice Sutherland's opinion. Professor Charles Lofgren notes that the "history on

---

[4] See David M. Levitan, *The Foreign Relations Power: An Analysis of Mr. Justice Sutherland's Theory*, 55 Yale L.J. 467, 493-494 (1946).

which [*Curtiss-Wright*] rest[s] is 'shockingly inaccurate' " and not based on either the text of the Constitution or the framers' intent.[5] In his view, the framers intended that the President, like all branches of the federal government, have limited powers, not the expansive inherent authority described in *Curtiss-Wright*.

If the President has broad inherent power in foreign policy as indicated in *Curtiss-Wright*, does this mean that congressional actions to limit the President in this realm are unconstitutional? The issue arose during the 1980s in connection with an attempt by the Reagan Administration to circumvent a federal law prohibiting aid to the contras in Nicaragua. The Boland Amendment to the appropriation bills barred any "agency or entity of the United States involved in intelligence activities" from spending funds "to support military or paramilitary operations in Nicaragua."[6]

Some high-level members of the Reagan Administration intentionally violated the Boland Amendment by raising funds from third parties to fund the contras and by selling arms to Iran to fund the contras.[7] Some have defended these actions on the ground that the Boland Amendment was an impermissible restriction on the President's power to conduct foreign policy. For example, a Republican minority report to a House Committee report declared: "[The] Constitution gives the President some power to act on his own in foreign affairs. . . . Congress may not use its control over appropriations, including salaries, to prevent the executive or judiciary from fulfilling Constitutionally mandated obligations."[8]

Others, including the Democratic majority on the House Committee, argued that Congress controls the power of the purse and therefore should be able to control government spending. The Boland Amendment was a restriction on expenditures. Moreover, Article I gives Congress the power to regulate foreign commerce. Thus, supporters of the Boland Amendment contended that it was constitutional and the President has no authority to disobey a constitutional statute in the conduct of foreign or domestic affairs.

The Boland Amendment thus poses a relatively recent example concerning the scope of the President's powers in foreign policy and the ability of Congress to impose limits.

2. Treaties and Executive Agreements

Article II, §2 states that the President "shall have Power, by and with the Advice and Consent of the Senate, to make Treaties, provided two thirds of the

---

[5] Charles A. Lofgren, *United States v. Curtiss-Wright Export Corp.: A Historical Reassessment*, 83 Yale L.J. 1, 32 (1973).

[6] 101 Stat. 1011 (1987).

[7] *See* Lawrence E. Walsh, *Final Report of the Independent Counsel for Iran/Contra Matters* (1993); Michael Arthur Ledeen, *Perilous Statecraft: An Insider's Account of the Iran-Contra Affair* (1988).

[8] Report of the Congressional Committees Investigating the Iran-Contra Affair, S. Rep. No. 100-216, H. Rep. No. 100-433 (1987) at 473 (minority report).

Senators present concur." The major constitutional issue that has arisen concerns the authority of the President to use executive agreements rather than treaties for foreign policy commitments. A treaty is an agreement between the United States and a foreign country that is negotiated by the President and is effective when ratified by the Senate.[9] An executive agreement, in contrast, is an agreement between the United States and a foreign country that is effective when signed by the President and the head of the other government. In other words, if the document is labeled "treaty," Senate approval is required. If the document is titled "executive agreement," no Senate ratification is necessary.

Although the Constitution does not mention executive agreements, it is well established that such agreements are constitutional. Indeed, based on past experience, it appears that executive agreements can be used for any purpose; that is, anything that can be done by treaty can be done by executive agreement. Never in American history has the Supreme Court declared an executive agreement unconstitutional as usurping the Senate's treaty-approving function. Even major foreign policy commitments have been implemented through executive agreements. For example, in 1940, the "Destroyer-Bases Agreement" substantially expanded American involvement in World War II when President Roosevelt agreed to loan Great Britain 50 naval destroyers in exchange for the United States receiving free 99-year leases to develop military bases on several sites in the Caribbean and Newfoundland.[10]

The Court has sided with the President each time there has been a challenge to an executive agreement. In United States v. Pink[11] and United States v. Belmont,[12] the Supreme Court upheld an executive agreement, the Litvinov Agreement, whereby the United States recognized the Soviet Union in exchange for the Soviet Union assigning to the United States its interests in a Russian insurance company in New York. The Soviet Union had nationalized the interest in this insurance company in 1918 and 1919. The United States would use these assets to pay claims that it and others had against the Soviet Union.[13]

The Court upheld the executive agreement and explained that because it was not a treaty, Senate approval was not required. New York courts had refused to enforce the Litvinov Agreement, but the Court ruled that states must comply with executive agreements. Executive agreements, like treaties, prevail over state law and policy. Justice Douglas, writing for the Court in *Pink*, explained: "A treaty is a 'Law of the Land' under the supremacy clause [of Article VI] of the Constitution.

---

[9] For an argument that there is a new form of presidential-congressional international agreement, approved by both houses of Congress but not requiring approval of two-thirds of the Senate, *see* Bruce Ackerman & David Golove, *Is NAFTA Constitutional?* 108 Harv. L. Rev. 799 (1995); *but see* Laurence H. Tribe, *Taking Text and Structure Seriously: Reflections on Free-Form Method in Constitutional Interpretation*, 108 Harv. L. Rev. 1221 (1995) (strongly objecting to such an approach).

[10] Richard W. Leopold, *The Growth of American Foreign Policy*, 565-566 (1962).

[11] 315 U.S. 203 (1942).

[12] 301 U.S. 324 (1937).

[13] In *Pink*, the Court also rejected a claim that the agreement was an impermissible taking of property without just compensation in violation of the Fifth Amendment. The Court noted that the Litvinov Agreement did not bar compensation for claims, although it did give the United States priority as a creditor.

Such international compacts and agreements as the Litvinov Assignment have a similar dignity."[14] Similarly, in United States v. Belmont, the Court stated that "in the case of all international compacts and agreements ... complete power over international affairs is in the national government and is not and cannot be subject to any curtailment or interference on the part of the several states."[15]

A more recent example of the Supreme Court upholding an executive agreement was Dames & Moore v. Regan in 1981.

Dames & Moore v. Regan, Secretary of the Treasury
453 U.S. 654 (1981)

Justice REHNQUIST delivered the opinion of the Court.

The questions presented by this case touch fundamentally upon the manner in which our Republic is to be governed. Throughout the nearly two centuries of our Nation's existence under the Constitution, this subject has generated considerable debate. We have had the benefit of commentators such as John Jay, Alexander Hamilton, and James Madison writing in The Federalist Papers at the Nation's very inception, the benefit of astute foreign observers of our system such as Alexis deTocqueville and James Bryce writing during the first century of the Nation's existence, and the benefit of many other treatises as well as more than 400 volumes of reports of decisions of this Court. As these writings reveal it is doubtless both futile and perhaps dangerous to find any epigrammatical explanation of how this country has been governed. Indeed, as Justice Jackson noted, "[a] judge ... may be surprised at the poverty of really useful and unambiguous authority applicable to concrete problems of executive power as they actually present themselves."

I

On November 4, 1979, the American Embassy in Tehran was seized and our diplomatic personnel were captured and held hostage. In response to that crisis, President Carter, acting pursuant to the International Emergency Economic Powers Act (hereinafter IEEPA) declared a national emergency on November 14, 1979, and blocked the removal or transfer of "all property and interests in property of the Government of Iran, its instrumentalities and controlled entities and the Central Bank of Iran which are or become subject to the jurisdiction of the United States. ..." Exec. Order No. 12170.

On January 20, 1981, the Americans held hostage were released by Iran pursuant to an Agreement entered into the day before and embodied in two Declarations of the Democratic and Popular Republic of Algeria. The Agreement stated that "[i]t is the purpose of [the United States and Iran] ... to terminate all litigation as between the Government of each party and the nationals of the other, and

[14] 315 U.S. at 230.
[15] 301 U.S. at 331.

to bring about the settlement and termination of all such claims through binding arbitration." In furtherance of this goal, the Agreement called for the establishment of an Iran-United States Claims Tribunal which would arbitrate any claims not settled within six months. Awards of the Claims Tribunal are to be "final and binding" and "enforceable . . . in the courts of any nation in accordance with its laws." Under the Agreement, the United States is obligated "to terminate all legal proceedings in United States courts involving claims of United States persons and institutions against Iran and its state enterprises, to nullify all attachments and judgments obtained therein, to prohibit all further litigation based on such claims, and to bring about the termination of such claims through binding arbitration."

On April 28, 1981, petitioner filed this action in the District Court for declaratory and injunctive relief against the United States and the Secretary of the Treasury, seeking to prevent enforcement of the Executive Orders and Treasury Department regulations implementing the Agreement with Iran. In its complaint, petitioner alleged that the actions of the President and the Secretary of the Treasury implementing the Agreement with Iran were beyond their statutory and constitutional powers and, in any event, were unconstitutional to the extent they adversely affect petitioner's final judgment against the Government of Iran and the Atomic Energy Organization, its execution of that judgment in the State of Washington, its prejudgment attachments, and its ability to continue to litigate against the Iranian banks.

Not infrequently in affairs between nations, outstanding claims by nationals of one country against the government of another country are "sources of friction" between the two sovereigns. United States v. Pink (1942). To resolve these difficulties, nations have often entered into agreements settling the claims of their respective nationals. As one treatise writer puts it, international agreements settling claims by nationals of one state against the government of another "are established international practice reflecting traditional international theory." L. Henkin, Foreign Affairs and the Constitution 262 (1972). Consistent with that principle, the United States has repeatedly exercised its sovereign authority to settle the claims of its nationals against foreign countries. Though those settlements have sometimes been made by treaty, there has also been a longstanding practice of settling such claims by executive agreement without the advice and consent of the Senate. Under such agreements, the President has agreed to renounce or extinguish claims of United States nationals against foreign governments in return for lump-sum payments or the establishment of arbitration procedures. It is clear that the practice of settling claims continues today. Since 1952, the President has entered into at least 10 binding settlements with foreign nations, including an $80 million settlement with the People's Republic of China.

Crucial to our decision today is the conclusion that Congress has implicitly approved the practice of claim settlement by executive agreement. This is best demonstrated by Congress' enactment of the International Claims Settlement Act of 1949. The Act had two purposes: (1) to allocate to United States nationals funds received in the course of an executive claims settlement with Yugoslavia, and (2) to provide a procedure whereby funds resulting from future settlements could be distributed. To achieve these ends Congress created the International Claims Commission, now the Foreign Claims Settlement Commission, and gave it jurisdiction to make final and binding decisions with respect to claims by United States nationals against settlement funds. By creating a procedure to implement future settlement agreements, Congress placed its stamp of approval on such agreements. Indeed, the legislative history of the Act observed that the United States was seeking settlements with countries other than Yugoslavia and that the bill contemplated settlements of a similar nature in the future.

Over the years Congress has frequently amended the International Claims Settlement Act to provide for particular problems arising out of settlement agreements, thus demonstrating Congress' continuing acceptance of the President's claim settlement authority. In addition to congressional acquiescence in the President's power to settle claims, prior cases of this Court have also recognized that the President does have some measure of power to enter into executive agreements without obtaining the advice and consent of the Senate. In United States v. Pink (1942), for example, the Court upheld the validity of the Litvinov Assignment, which was part of an Executive Agreement whereby the Soviet Union assigned to the United States amounts owed to it by American nationals so that outstanding claims of other American nationals could be paid.

Finally, we re-emphasize the narrowness of our decision. We do not decide that the President possesses plenary power to settle claims, even as against foreign governmental entities. But where, as here, the settlement of claims has been determined to be a necessary incident to the resolution of a major foreign policy dispute between our country and another, and where, as here, we can conclude that Congress acquiesced in the President's action, we are not prepared to say that the President lacks the power to settle such claims.

During the 1940s and 1950s, Senator Bricker proposed a constitutional amendment, known as the Bricker Amendment, that would have prevented the use of executive agreements. The Amendment never was passed by Congress, but it reflects deep concern over the President's ability to circumvent the treaty ratification process by using executive agreements instead.

3. *War Powers*

The Constitution is an invitation for a struggle between the President and Congress over control of the war power. The Constitution, in Article I, grants Congress the power to declare war and the authority to raise and support the army and the navy. Article II makes the President the Commander in Chief.

Basic, unresolved questions exist concerning these powers. First, what constitutes a declaration of war? Must it be a formal declaration of war, such as was adopted by Congress after the bombing of Pearl Harbor to authorize America's entry into World War II? Or may it be less explicit? For example, was the Gulf of Tonkin Resolution, which authorized the use of military force in Southeast Asia, sufficient to constitute a declaration of war for the Vietnam War? Might even repeated congressional approval of funding for a war be regarded as sufficient even without passage of a resolution explicitly approving the war?

Second, when may the President use American troops in hostilities without congressional approval? To what extent does the President's power as Commander in Chief authorize the use of troops in foreign countries without a formal declaration of war? Neither of these questions ever has been clearly answered by the Supreme Court. In fact, given the Court's view that such foreign policy disputes constitute a political question, answers are unlikely to come from the judiciary.

Thus, the Supreme Court rarely has spoken as to the constitutionality of the President using troops in a war or war-like circumstances without congressional approval. In fact, the only Supreme Court case to address the issue was in the unique context of the Civil War and the actions of the President to deal with the rebellion. In the *Prize Cases*, the Court ruled that the President had the power to impose a blockade on Southern states without a congressional declaration of war.[16] No other Supreme Court case has addressed the constitutionality of presidential war-making without a congressional declaration of war. Therefore, little exists in the way of law regarding the circumstances in which the President may use troops without congressional approval or as to what Congress may do to suspend American involvement in a war.

In 1973, Congress adopted the War Powers Resolution to address these two questions.[17] The War Powers Resolution was a response to the Vietnam War in which two Presidents, Lyndon Johnson and Richard Nixon, fought a highly unpopular war with great cost in lives and dollars without a formal declaration of war from Congress.

Title 50. War and National Defense; Chapter 33 — War Powers Resolution

§1541.   PURPOSE AND POLICY

(a)   CONGRESSIONAL DECLARATION

It is the purpose of this chapter to fulfill the intent of the framers of the Constitution of the United States and insure that the collective judgment of both the Congress and the President will apply to the introduction of United States Armed Forces into hostilities, or into situations where imminent involvement in hostilities is clearly indicated by the circumstances, and to the continued use of such forces in hostilities or in such situations.

---

[16] 67 U.S. (2 Black) 635 (1862).

[17] 50 U.S.C. §1541. Although it is called "The War Powers Resolution," it is a properly adopted federal statute.

(b)   CONGRESSIONAL LEGISLATIVE POWER UNDER NECESSARY AND PROPER CLAUSE

Under article I, section 8, of the Constitution, it is specifically provided that the Congress shall have the power to make all laws necessary and proper for carrying into execution, not only its own powers but also all other powers vested by the Constitution in the Government of the United States, or in any department or officer thereof.

(c)   PRESIDENTIAL EXECUTIVE POWER AS COMMANDER-IN-CHIEF; LIMITATION

The constitutional powers of the President as Commander-in-Chief to introduce United States Armed Forces into hostilities, or into situations where imminent involvement in hostilities is clearly indicated by the circumstances, are exercised only pursuant to (1) a declaration of war, (2) specific statutory authorization, or (3) a national emergency created by attack upon the United States, its territories or possessions, or its armed forces.

§1542.   CONSULTATION; INITIAL AND REGULAR CONSULTATIONS

The President in every possible instance shall consult with Congress before introducing United States Armed Forces into hostilities or into situations where imminent involvement in hostilities is clearly indicated by the circumstances, and after every such introduction shall consult regularly with the Congress until United States Armed Forces are no longer engaged in hostilities or have been removed from such situations.

§1543.   REPORTING REQUIREMENT

(a)   WRITTEN REPORT; TIME OF SUBMISSION; CIRCUMSTANCES NECESSITATING SUB-MISSION; INFORMATION REPORTED

In the absence of a declaration of war, in any case in which United States Armed Forces are introduced —

(1) into hostilities or into situations where imminent involvement in hostilities is clearly indicated by the circumstances;

(2) into the territory, airspace or waters of a foreign nation, while equipped for combat, except for deployments which relate solely to supply, replacement, repair, or training of such forces; or

(3) in numbers which substantially enlarge United States Armed Forces equipped for combat already located in a foreign nation

the President shall submit within 48 hours to the Speaker of the House of Representatives and to the President pro tempore of the Senate a report, in writing, setting forth —

(A) the circumstances necessitating the introduction of United States Armed Forces;

(B) the constitutional and legislative authority under which such introduction took place; and

(C) the estimated scope and duration of the hostilities or involvement.

(b)   OTHER INFORMATION REPORTED

The President shall provide such other information as the Congress may request in the fulfillment of its constitutional responsibilities with respect to committing the Nation to war and to the use of United States Armed Forces abroad.

(c)   PERIODIC REPORTS; SEMIANNUAL REQUIREMENT

Whenever United States Armed Forces are introduced into hostilities or into any situation described in subsection (a) of this section, the President shall, so long as such armed forces continue to be engaged in such hostilities or situation, report to the Congress periodically on the status of such hostilities or situation as well as on the scope and duration of such hostilities or situation, but in no event shall he report to the Congress less often than once every six months.

§1544.   CONGRESSIONAL ACTION

(a)   TRANSMITTAL OF REPORT AND REFERRAL TO CONGRESSIONAL COMMITTEES; JOINT REQUEST FOR CONVENING CONGRESS

Each report submitted pursuant to section 1543(a)(1) of this title shall be transmitted to the Speaker of the House of Representatives and to the President pro tempore of the Senate on the same calendar day.

(b)   TERMINATION OF USE OF UNITED STATES ARMED FORCES; EXCEPTIONS; EXTENSION PERIOD

Within sixty calendar days after a report is submitted or is required to be submitted pursuant to section 1543(a)(1) of this title, whichever is earlier, the President shall terminate any use of United States Armed Forces with respect to which such report was submitted (or required to be submitted), unless the Congress (1) has declared war or has enacted a specific authorization for such use of United States Armed Forces, (2) has extended by law such sixty-day period, or (3) is physically unable to meet as a result of an armed attack upon the United States. Such sixty-day period shall be extended for not more than an additional thirty days if the President determines and certifies to the Congress in writing that unavoidable military necessity respecting the safety of United States Armed Forces requires the continued use of such armed forces in the course of bringing about a prompt removal of such forces.

(c)   CONCURRENT RESOLUTION FOR REMOVAL BY PRESIDENT OF UNITED STATES ARMED FORCES

Notwithstanding subsection (b) of this section, at any time that United States Armed Forces are engaged in hostilities outside the territory of the United States, its possessions and territories without a declaration of war or specific statutory authorization, such forces shall be removed by the President if the Congress so directs by concurrent resolution.

§1547.   INTERPRETATION OF JOINT RESOLUTION

(a)   INFERENCES FROM ANY LAW OR TREATY

Authority to introduce United States Armed Forces into hostilities or into situations wherein involvement in hostilities is clearly indicated by the circumstances shall not be inferred —

(1) from any provision of law (whether or not in effect before November 7, 1973), including any provision contained in any appropriation Act, unless such provision specifically authorizes the introduction of United States Armed Forces into hostilities or into such situations and states that it is intended to constitute specific statutory authorization within the meaning of this chapter; or

(2) from any treaty heretofore or hereafter ratified unless such treaty is implemented by legislation specifically authorizing the introduction of United States Armed Forces into hostilities or into such situations and stating that it is intended to constitute specific statutory authorization within the meaning of this chapter.

(b)   JOINT HEADQUARTERS OPERATIONS OF HIGH-LEVEL MILITARY COMMANDS

Nothing in this chapter shall be construed to require any further specific statutory authorization to permit members of United States Armed Forces to participate jointly with members of the armed forces of one or more foreign countries in the headquarters operations of high-level military commands which were established prior to November 7, 1973, and pursuant to the United Nations Charter or any treaty ratified by the United States prior to such date.

(c)   INTRODUCTION OF UNITED STATES ARMED FORCES

For purposes of this chapter, the term "introduction of United States Armed Forces" includes the assignment of members of such armed forces to command, coordinate, participate in the movement of, or accompany the regular or irregular military forces of any foreign country or government when such military forces are engaged, or there exists an imminent threat that such forces will become engaged, in hostilities.

(d)   CONSTITUTIONAL AUTHORITIES OR EXISTING TREATIES UNAFFECTED; CONSTRUCTION AGAINST GRANT OF PRESIDENTIAL AUTHORITY RESPECTING USE OF UNITED STATES ARMED FORCES

Nothing in this chapter —

(1) is intended to alter the constitutional authority of the Congress or of the President, or the provisions of existing treaties; or

(2) shall be construed as granting any authority to the President with respect to the introduction of United States Armed Forces into hostilities or into situations wherein involvement in hostilities is clearly indicated by the circumstances which authority he would not have had in the absence of this chapter.

§1548.   SEPARABILITY OF PROVISIONS

If any provision of this chapter or the application thereof to any person or circumstance is held invalid, the remainder of the chapter and the application of such provision to any other person or circumstance shall not be affected thereby.

The constitutionality of the War Powers Resolution has not been tested. In 1999, Representative Tom Campbell brought a lawsuit arguing that the bombing of Yugoslavia was in violation of the War Powers Resolution. The United States District Court for the District of Columbia dismissed the case for lack of standing and the United States Court of Appeals for the District of Columbia Circuit affirmed. Campbell v. Clinton, 52 F. Supp. 2d 34 (D.D.C. 1999), aff'd 203 F.3d 19 (D.C. Cir. 2000). In 2003, a lawsuit was brought to have the impending war in Iraq declared unconstitutional. It, too, was dismissed as non-justiciable. Doe v. Bush, 323 F.3d 133 (1st Cir. 2003). It is quite possible that every challenge to a President's actions as violating the War Powers Resolution will be dismissed on justiciability grounds, either for lack of standing or as a political question.

Nonetheless, the underlying constitutional issue remains: Is the War Powers Resolution an unconstitutional intrusion on the President's powers as Commander in Chief? Or is the War Powers Resolution a permissible effort by Congress to interpret the Constitution and ensure checks and balances?

D. Presidential Power and the War on Terrorism

The tragic events of September 11, 2001, have led to many government actions that will raise important difficult constitutional questions: Is the indefinite detention of "unlawful combatants" constitutional? Are secret deportation proceedings constitutional? Is it permissible for the government to hold individuals indefinitely as "material witnesses"? Are provisions of the USA Patriot Act, which include expanded authorization for electronic eavesdropping by the government, constitutional?

The materials below consider two issues: When may the Executive detain American enemy combatants; and when, if at all, are military tribunals constitutional?

1. Detentions

In June 2004, the Supreme Court decided three major cases concerning civil liberties and the war on terrorism. Two were resolved largely on non-constitutional grounds. In Rasul v. Bush, 542 U.S. 466 (2004), the Supreme Court held that detainees being held at Guantanamo Bay, Cuba, had a right to have their habeas corpus petition heard in a federal court. In Padilla v. Rumsfeld, 542 U.S. 426 (2004), the Court held that an American citizen, apprehended in the United States and held as an enemy combatant in a military prison in South Carolina could not present a habeas corpus petition in federal court in New York, where he was earlier held. Rather, the habeas petition needed to be refiled in South Carolina.

But in Hamdi v. Rumsfeld, below, the Court considered whether an American citizen apprehended in a foreign country could be indefinitely detained as an enemy combatant without any form of due process. By a 5-4 margin, though without a majority opinion, the Court ruled that there was sufficient legal authority to detain Hamdi as an enemy combatant. But the Court, by an 8-1 margin, concluded that Hamdi must be accorded due process, including a meaningful factual hearing. In October 2004, Hamdi was released from custody after agreeing to renounce his United States citizenship, not take up arms against the United States, and not to return to this country.

Hamdi v. Rumsfeld

542 U.S. 507 (2004)

Justice O'CONNOR announced the judgment of the Court and delivered an opinion, in which the Chief Justice, Justice KENNEDY, and Justice BREYER join.

At this difficult time in our Nation's history, we are called upon to consider the legality of the Government's detention of a United States citizen on United States soil as an "enemy combatant" and to address the process that is constitutionally owed to one who seeks to challenge his classification as such. The United States Court of Appeals for the Fourth Circuit held that petitioner's detention was legally authorized and that he was entitled to no further opportunity to challenge his enemy-combatant label. We now vacate and remand. We hold that although Congress authorized the detention of combatants in the narrow circumstances alleged here, due process demands that a citizen held in the United States as an enemy combatant be given a meaningful opportunity to contest the factual basis for that detention before a neutral decisionmaker.

I

On September 11, 2001, the al Qaeda terrorist network used hijacked commercial airliners to attack prominent targets in the United States. Approximately 3,000 people were killed in those attacks. One week later, in response to these "acts of treacherous violence," Congress passed a resolution authorizing the President to "use all necessary and appropriate force against those nations, organizations, or persons he determines planned, authorized, committed, or aided the terrorist attacks" or "harbored such organizations or persons, in order to prevent any future acts of international terrorism against the United States by such nations, organizations or persons." Soon thereafter, the President ordered United States Armed Forces to Afghanistan, with a mission to subdue al Qaeda and quell the Taliban regime that was known to support it.

This case arises out of the detention of a man whom the Government alleges took up arms with the Taliban during this conflict. His name is Yaser Esam Hamdi. Born an American citizen in Louisiana in 1980, Hamdi moved with his family to Saudi Arabia as a child. By 2001, the parties agree, he resided in Afghanistan. At some point that year, he was seized by members of the Northern Alliance, a coalition of military groups opposed to the Taliban government, and eventually was turned over to the United States military. The Government asserts that it initially detained and interrogated Hamdi in Afghanistan before transferring him to the United States Naval Base in Guantanamo Bay in January 2002. In

April 2002, upon learning that Hamdi is an American citizen, authorities transferred him to a naval brig in Norfolk, Virginia, where he remained until a recent transfer to a brig in Charleston, South Carolina. The Government contends that Hamdi is an "enemy combatant," and that this status justifies holding him in the United States indefinitely — without formal charges or proceedings — unless and until it makes the determination that access to counsel or further process is warranted.

II

The threshold question before us is whether the Executive has the authority to detain citizens who qualify as "enemy combatants." There is some debate as to the proper scope of this term, and the Government has never provided any court with the full criteria that it uses in classifying individuals as such. It has made clear, however, that, for purposes of this case, the "enemy combatant" that it is seeking to detain is an individual who, it alleges, was " 'part of or supporting forces hostile to the United States or coalition partners' " in Afghanistan and who " 'engaged in an armed conflict against the United States' " there. We therefore answer only the narrow question before us: whether the detention of citizens falling within that definition is authorized.

The Government maintains that no explicit congressional authorization is required, because the Executive possesses plenary authority to detain pursuant to Article II of the Constitution. We do not reach the question whether Article II provides such authority, however, because we agree with the Government's alternative position, that Congress has in fact authorized Hamdi's detention.

Our analysis on that point, set forth below, substantially overlaps with our analysis of Hamdi's principal argument for the illegality of his detention. He posits that his detention is forbidden by 18 U.S.C. §4001(a). Section 4001(a) states that "[n]o citizen shall be imprisoned or otherwise detained by the United States except pursuant to an Act of Congress." Congress passed §4001(a) in 1971 as part of a bill to repeal the Emergency Detention Act of 1950, which provided procedures for executive detention, during times of emergency, of individuals deemed likely to engage in espionage or sabotage. Congress was particularly concerned about the possibility that the Act could be used to reprise the Japanese internment camps of World War II.

The Government again presses two alternative positions. First, it argues that §4001(a) applies only to "the control of civilian prisons and related detentions," not to military detentions. Second, it maintains that §4001(a) is satisfied, because Hamdi is being detained "pursuant to an Act of Congress" — the [Authorization for Use of Military Force]. Again, because we conclude that the Government's second assertion is correct, we do not address the first. In other words, for the reasons that follow, we conclude that the AUMF is explicit congressional authorization for the detention of individuals in the narrow category we describe (assuming, without deciding, that such authorization is required), and that the AUMF satisfied §4001(a)'s requirement that a detention be "pursuant to an Act of Congress" (assuming, without deciding, that §4001(a) applies to military detentions).

The AUMF authorizes the President to use "all necessary and appropriate force" against "nations, organizations, or persons" associated with the September 11, 2001, terrorist attacks. There can be no doubt that individuals who fought against the United States in Afghanistan as part of the Taliban, an organization known to have supported the al Qaeda terrorist network responsible for those attacks, are individuals Congress sought to target in passing the AUMF. We conclude that detention of individuals falling into the limited category we are considering, for the duration of the particular conflict in which they were captured, is so fundamental and accepted an incident to war as to be an exercise of the "necessary and appropriate force" Congress has authorized the President to use.

The capture and detention of lawful combatants and the capture, detention, and trial of unlawful combatants, by "universal agreement and practice," are "important incident[s] of war." *Ex parte Quirin.* The purpose of detention is to prevent captured individuals from returning to the field of battle and taking up arms once again. [I]t is of no moment that the AUMF does not use specific language of detention. Because detention to prevent a combatant's return to the battlefield is a fundamental incident of waging war, in permitting the use of "necessary and appropriate force," Congress has clearly and unmistakably authorized detention in the narrow circumstances considered here.

Hamdi contends that the AUMF does not authorize indefinite or perpetual detention. Certainly, we agree that indefinite detention for the purpose of interrogation is not authorized. Further, we understand Congress's grant of authority for the use of "necessary and appropriate force" to include the authority to detain for the duration of the relevant conflict, and our understanding is based on long-standing law-of-war principles. If the practical circumstances of a given conflict are entirely unlike those of the conflicts that informed the development of the law of war, that understanding may unravel. But that is not the situation we face as of this date. Active combat operations against Taliban fighters apparently are ongoing in Afghanistan. The United States may detain, for the duration of these hostilities, individuals legitimately determined to be Taliban combatants who "engaged in an armed conflict against the United States." If the record establishes that United States troops are still involved in active combat in Afghanistan, those detentions are part of the exercise of "necessary and appropriate force," and therefore are authorized by the AUMF.

Ex parte Milligan (1866) does not undermine our holding about the Government's authority to seize enemy combatants, as we define that term today. In that case, the Court made repeated reference to the fact that its inquiry into whether the military tribunal had jurisdiction to try and punish Milligan turned in large part on the fact that Milligan was not a prisoner of war, but a resident of Indiana arrested while at home there. That fact was central to its conclusion. Had Milligan been captured while he was assisting Confederate soldiers by carrying a rifle against Union troops on a Confederate battlefield, the holding of the Court might well have been different. The Court's repeated explanations that Milligan was not a prisoner of war suggest that had these different circumstances been present he could have been detained under military authority for the duration of the conflict, whether or not he was a citizen.[18]

III

Even in cases in which the detention of enemy combatants is legally authorized, there remains the question of what process is constitutionally due to a citizen who disputes his enemy-combatant status. Hamdi argues that he is owed a meaningful and timely hearing and that "extra-judicial detention [that] begins and ends with the submission of an affidavit based on third-hand hearsay" does not comport with the Fifth and Fourteenth Amendments. The Government counters that any more process than was provided below would be both unworkable and "constitutionally intolerable." Our resolution of this dispute requires a careful examination both of the writ of habeas corpus, which Hamdi now seeks to employ as a mechanism of judicial review, and of the Due Process Clause, which informs the procedural contours of that mechanism in this instance.

A

Though they reach radically different conclusions on the process that ought to attend the present proceeding, the parties begin on common ground. All agree that, absent suspension, the writ of habeas corpus remains available to every individual detained within the United States. Only in the rarest of circumstances has Congress seen fit to suspend the writ. All agree suspension of the writ has not occurred here. Thus, it is undisputed that Hamdi was properly before an Article III court to challenge his detention.

First, the Government urges the adoption of the Fourth Circuit's holding below — that because it is "undisputed" that Hamdi's seizure took place in a combat zone, the habeas determination can be made purely as a matter of law, with no further hearing or factfinding necessary. This argument is easily rejected. As the dissenters from the denial of rehearing en banc noted, the circumstances surrounding Hamdi's seizure cannot in any way be characterized as "undisputed," as "those circumstances are neither conceded in fact, nor susceptible to concession in law, because Hamdi has not been permitted to speak for himself or even through counsel as to those circumstances." Further, the "facts" that constitute the alleged concession are insufficient to support Hamdi's detention. Under the definition of enemy combatant that we accept today as falling within the scope of Congress's authorization, Hamdi would need to be "part of or supporting forces hostile to the United States or coalition partners" and "engaged in an armed conflict against the United States" to justify his detention in the United States for the duration of the relevant conflict. The habeas petition states only that "[w]hen

---

[18] Here the basis asserted for detention by the military is that Hamdi was carrying a weapon against American troops on a foreign battlefield; that is, that he was an enemy combatant. The legal category of enemy combatant has not been elaborated upon in great detail. The permissible bounds of the category will be defined by the lower courts as subsequent cases are presented to them. [Footnote by Justice O'Connor.]

seized by the United States Government, Mr. Hamdi resided in Afghanistan." An assertion that one *resided* in a country in which combat operations are taking place is not a concession that one was "*captured* in a zone of active combat operations in a foreign theater of war," and certainly is not a concession that one was "part of or supporting forces hostile to the United States or coalition partners" and "engaged in an armed conflict against the United States." Accordingly, we reject any argument that Hamdi has made concessions that eliminate any right to further process.

The Government's second argument requires closer consideration. This is the argument that further factual exploration is unwarranted and inappropriate in light of the extraordinary constitutional interests at stake. Under the Government's most extreme rendition of this argument, "[r]espect for separation of powers and the limited institutional capabilities of courts in matters of military decision-making in connection with an ongoing conflict" ought to eliminate entirely any individual process, restricting the courts to investigating only whether legal authorization exists for the broader detention scheme. At most, the Government argues, courts should review its determination that a citizen is an enemy combatant under a very deferential "some evidence" standard. Under this review, a court would assume the accuracy of the Government's articulated basis for Hamdi's detention, as set forth in the Mobbs Declaration, and assess only whether that articulated basis was a legitimate one.

In response, Hamdi emphasizes that this Court consistently has recognized that an individual challenging his detention may not be held at the will of the Executive without recourse to some proceeding before a neutral tribunal to determine whether the Executive's asserted justifications for that detention have basis in fact and warrant in law.

Both of these positions highlight legitimate concerns. And both emphasize the tension that often exists between the autonomy that the Government asserts is necessary in order to pursue effectively a particular goal and the process that a citizen contends he is due before he is deprived of a constitutional right. The ordinary mechanism that we use for balancing such serious competing interests, and for determining the procedures that are necessary to ensure that a citizen is not "deprived of life, liberty, or property, without due process of law," is the test that we articulated in Mathews v. Eldridge (1976). *Mathews* dictates that the process due in any given instance is determined by weighing "the private interest that will be affected by the official action" against the Government's asserted interest, "including the function involved" and the burdens the Government would face in providing greater process. The *Mathews* calculus then contemplates a judicious balancing of these concerns, through an analysis of "the risk of an erroneous deprivation" of the private interest if the process were reduced and the "probable value, if any, of additional or substitute safeguards." We take each of these steps in turn.

1

It is beyond question that substantial interests lie on both sides of the scale in this case. Hamdi's "private interest . . . affected by the official action," is the most elemental of liberty interests — the interest in being free from physical detention by one's own government. Nor is the weight on this side of the *Mathews* scale off-set by the circumstances of war or the accusation of treasonous behavior, for "[i]t is clear that commitment for *any* purpose constitutes a significant deprivation of liberty that requires due process protection," and at this stage in the *Mathews* calculus, we consider the interest of the *erroneously* detained individual. Indeed, as *amicus* briefs from media and relief organizations emphasize, the risk of erroneous deprivation of a citizen's liberty in the absence of sufficient process here is very real. Moreover, as critical as the Government's interest may be in detaining those who actually pose an immediate threat to the national security of the United States during ongoing international conflict, history and common sense teach us that an unchecked system of detention carries the potential to become a means for oppression and abuse of others who do not present that sort of threat. We reaffirm today the fundamental nature of a citizen's right to be free from involuntary confinement by his own government without due process of law, and we weigh the opposing governmental interests against the curtailment of liberty that such confinement entails.

2

On the other side of the scale are the weighty and sensitive governmental interests in ensuring that those who have in fact fought with the enemy during a war do not return to battle against the United States. As discussed above, the law of war and the realities of combat may render such detentions both necessary and appropriate, and our due process analysis need not blink at those realities. Without doubt, our Constitution recognizes that core strategic matters of warmaking belong in the hands of those who are best positioned and most politically accountable for making them.

The Government also argues at some length that its interests in reducing the process available to alleged enemy combatants are heightened by the practical difficulties that would accompany a system of trial-like process. In its view, military officers who are engaged in the serious work of waging battle would be unnecessarily and dangerously distracted by litigation half a world away, and discovery into military operations would both intrude on the sensitive secrets of national defense and result in a futile search for evidence buried under the rubble of war. To the extent that these burdens are triggered by heightened procedures, they are properly taken into account in our due process analysis.

3

Striking the proper constitutional balance here is of great importance to the Nation during this period of ongoing combat. But it is equally vital that our calculus not give short shrift to the values that this country holds dear or to the privilege that is American citizenship. It is during our most challenging and uncertain moments that our Nation's commitment to due process is most severely tested; and it is in those times that we must preserve our commitment at home to the principles for which we fight abroad.

We therefore hold that a citizen-detainee seeking to challenge his classification as an enemy combatant must receive notice of the factual basis for his classification, and a fair opportunity to rebut the Government's factual assertions before a neutral decision maker. These essential constitutional promises may not be eroded.

At the same time, the exigencies of the circumstances may demand that, aside from these core elements, enemy-combatant proceedings may be tailored to alleviate their uncommon potential to burden the Executive at a time of ongoing military conflict. Hearsay, for example, may need to be accepted as the most reliable available evidence from the Government in such a proceeding. Likewise, the Constitution would not be offended by a presumption in favor of the Government's evidence, so long as that presumption remained a rebuttable one and fair opportunity for rebuttal were provided. Thus, once the Government puts forth credible evidence that the habeas petitioner meets the enemy-combatant criteria, the onus could shift to the petitioner to rebut that evidence with more persuasive evidence that he falls outside the criteria. A burden-shifting scheme of this sort would meet the goal of ensuring that the errant tourist, embedded journalist, or local aid worker has a chance to prove military error while giving due regard to the Executive once it has put forth meaningful support for its conclusion that the detainee is in fact an enemy combatant. In the words of *Mathews*, process of this sort would sufficiently address the "risk of erroneous deprivation" of a detainee's liberty interest while eliminating certain procedures that have questionable additional value in light of the burden on the Government.

We think it unlikely that this basic process will have the dire impact on the central functions of warmaking that the Government forecasts. The parties agree that initial captures on the battlefield need not receive the process we have discussed here; that process is due only when the determination is made to *continue* to hold those who have been seized.

D

In so holding, we necessarily reject the Government's assertion that separation of powers principles mandate a heavily circumscribed role for the courts in such circumstances. Indeed, the position that the courts must forgo any examination of the individual case and focus exclusively on the legality of the broader detention scheme cannot be mandated by any reasonable view of separation of powers, as this approach serves only to *condense* power into a single branch of government. We have long since made clear that a state of war is not a blank check for the President when it comes to the rights of the Nation's citizens. Whatever power the United States Constitution envisions for the Executive in its exchanges with other nations or with enemy organizations in times of conflict, it most assuredly envisions a role for all three branches when individual liberties are at stake. Thus, while we do not question that our due process assessment must pay keen attention to the particular burdens faced by the Executive in the context of military action, it would turn our system of checks and balances on its head to suggest that a citizen could not make his way to court with a challenge to the factual basis for his detention by his government, simply because the Executive opposes making available such a challenge. Absent suspension of the writ by Congress, a citizen detained as an enemy combatant is entitled to this process.

Because we conclude that due process demands some system for a citizen detainee to refute his classification, the proposed "some evidence" standard is inadequate. Any process in which the Executive's factual assertions go wholly unchallenged or are simply presumed correct without any opportunity for the alleged combatant to demonstrate otherwise falls constitutionally short.

Justice SOUTER, with whom Justice GINSBURG joins, concurring in part, dissenting in part, and concurring in the judgment.

The plurality accept[s] the Government's position that if Hamdi's designation as an enemy combatant is correct, his detention (at least as to some period) is authorized by an Act of Congress as required by §4001(a), that is, by the Authorization for Use of Military Force. Here, I disagree and respectfully dissent. The Government has failed to demonstrate that the Force Resolution authorizes the detention complained of here even on the facts the Government claims. If the Government raises nothing further than the record now shows, the Non-Detention Act entitles Hamdi to be released.

[I]

The threshold issue is how broadly or narrowly to read the Non-Detention Act, the tone of which is severe: "No citizen shall be imprisoned or otherwise detained by the United States except pursuant to an Act of Congress." Should the severity of the Act be relieved when the Government's stated factual justification for incommunicado detention is a war on terrorism, so that the Government may be said to act "pursuant" to congressional terms that fall short of explicit authority to imprison individuals? With one possible though important qualification, the answer has to be no. For a number of reasons, the prohibition within §4001(a) has to be read broadly to accord the statute a long reach and to impose a burden of justification on the Government.

First, the circumstances in which the Act was adopted point the way to this interpretation. The provision superseded a cold-war statute, the Emergency Detention Act of 1950, which had authorized the Attorney General, in time of emergency, to detain anyone reasonably thought likely to engage in espionage or sabotage. That statute was repealed in 1971 out of fear that it could authorize a repetition of the World War II internment of citizens of Japanese ancestry; Congress meant to preclude another episode like the one described in Korematsu v. United States (1944). The fact that Congress intended to guard against a repetition of the World War II internments when it repealed the 1950 statute and gave us §4001(a) provides a powerful reason to think that §4001(a) was meant to require clear congressional authorization before any citizen can be placed in a cell. Congress's understanding of the need for clear authority before citizens are kept detained is itself therefore clear, and §4001(a) must be read to have teeth in its demand for congressional authorization.

Finally, even if history had spared us the cautionary example of the internments in World War II, there would be a compelling reason to read §4001(a) to demand manifest authority to detain before detention is authorized. The defining character of American constitutional government is its constant tension between security and liberty, serving both by partial helpings of each. In a government of separated powers, deciding finally on what is a reasonable degree of guaranteed liberty whether in peace or war (or some condition in between) is not well entrusted to the Executive Branch of Government, whose particular responsibility is to maintain security. For reasons of inescapable human nature, the branch of the Government asked to counter a serious threat is not the branch on which to rest the Nation's entire reliance in striking the balance between the will to win and the cost in liberty on the way to victory; the responsibility for security will naturally amplify the claim that security legitimately raises. A reasonable balance is more likely to be reached on the judgment of a different branch, just as Madison said in remarking that "the constant aim is to divide and arrange the several offices in such a manner as that each may be a check on the other — that the private interest of every individual may be a sentinel over the public rights." The Federalist No. 51. Hence the need for an assessment by Congress before citizens are subject to lockup, and likewise the need for a clearly expressed congressional resolution of the competing claims.

Since the Government has given no reason either to deflect the application of §4001(a) or to hold it to be satisfied, I need to go no further; the Government hints of a constitutional challenge to the statute, but it presents none here. I will, however, stray across the line between statutory and constitutional territory just far enough to note the weakness of the Government's mixed claim of inherent, extrastatutory authority under a combination of Article II of the Constitution and the usages of war. It is in fact in this connection that the Government developed its argument that the exercise of war powers justifies the detention, and what I have just said about its inadequacy applies here as well. Beyond that, it is instructive to recall Justice Jackson's observation that the President is not Commander in Chief of the country, only of the military. Youngstown Sheet & Tube Co. v. Sawyer (1952) (concurring opinion) (presidential authority is "at its lowest ebb" where the President acts contrary to congressional will).

There may be room for one qualification to Justice Jackson's statement, however: in a moment of genuine emergency, when the Government must act with no time for deliberation, the Executive may be able to detain a citizen if there is reason to fear he is an imminent threat to the safety of the Nation and its people (though I doubt there is any want of statutory authority). This case, however, does not present that question, because an emergency power of necessity must at least be limited by the emergency; Hamdi has been locked up for over two years.

Whether insisting on the careful scrutiny of emergency claims or on a vigorous reading of §4001(a), we are heirs to a tradition given voice 800 years ago by Magna Carta, which, on the barons' insistence, confined executive power by "the law of the land."

[II]

Because I find Hamdi's detention forbidden by §4001(a) and unauthorized by the Force Resolution, I would not reach any questions of what process he may be due in litigating disputed issues in a proceeding under the habeas statute or prior to the habeas enquiry itself. For me, it suffices that the Government has failed to justify holding him in the absence of a further Act of Congress, criminal charges, a showing that the detention conforms to the laws of war, or a demonstration that §4001(a) is unconstitutional.

Since this disposition does not command a majority of the Court, however, the need to give practical effect to the conclusions of eight members of the Court rejecting the Government's position calls for me to join with the plurality in ordering remand on terms closest to those I would impose. Although I think litigation of Hamdi's status as an enemy combatant is unnecessary, the terms of the plurality's remand will allow Hamdi to offer evidence that he is not an enemy combatant, and he should at the least have the benefit of that opportunity.

Justice SCALIA, with whom Justice STEVENS joins, dissenting.

Petitioner, a presumed American citizen, has been imprisoned without charge or hearing in the Norfolk and Charleston Naval Brigs for more than two years, on the allegation that he is an enemy combatant who bore arms against his country for the Taliban. His father claims to the contrary, that he is an inexperienced aid worker caught in the wrong place at the wrong time. This case brings into conflict the competing demands of national security and our citizens' constitutional right to personal liberty. Although I share the Court's evident unease as it seeks to reconcile the two, I do not agree with its resolution.

Where the Government accuses a citizen of waging war against it, our constitutional tradition has been to prosecute him in federal court for treason or some other crime. Where the exigencies of war prevent that, the Constitution's Suspension Clause, Art. I, §9, cl. 2, allows Congress to relax the usual protections temporarily. Absent suspension, however, the Executive's assertion of military exigency has not been thought sufficient to permit detention without charge. No one contends that the congressional Authorization for Use of Military Force, on which the Government relies to justify its actions here, is an implementation of the Suspension Clause. Accordingly, I would reverse the decision below.

The very core of liberty secured by our Anglo-Saxon system of separated powers has been freedom from indefinite imprisonment at the will of the Executive. The allegations here, of course, are no ordinary accusations of criminal activity. Yaser Esam Hamdi has been imprisoned because the Government believes he participated in the waging of war against the United States. The relevant question, then, is whether there is a different, special procedure for imprisonment of a citizen accused of wrongdoing *by aiding the enemy in wartime*.

Justice O'CONNOR, writing for a plurality of this Court, asserts that captured enemy combatants (other than those suspected of war crimes) have traditionally been detained until the cessation of hostilities and then released. That is probably an accurate description of wartime practice with respect to enemy *aliens*. The tradition with respect to American citizens, however, has been quite different. Citizens aiding the enemy have been treated as traitors subject to the criminal process.

There are times when military exigency renders resort to the traditional criminal process impracticable. English law accommodated such exigencies by allowing legislative suspension of the writ of habeas corpus for brief periods. Our Federal Constitution contains a provision explicitly permitting suspension, but limiting the situations in which it may be invoked: "The privilege of the Writ of Habeas Corpus shall not be suspended, unless when in Cases of Rebellion or Invasion the public Safety may require it." The Suspension Clause was by design a safety valve, the Constitution's only "express provision for exercise of extraordinary authority because of a crisis."

Several limitations give my views in this matter a relatively narrow compass. They apply only to citizens, accused of being enemy combatants, who are detained within the territorial jurisdiction of a federal court. This is not likely to be a numerous group; currently we know of only two, Hamdi and Jose Padilla. Where the citizen is captured outside and held outside the United States, the constitutional requirements may be different. Moreover, even within the United States, the accused citizen-enemy combatant may lawfully be detained once prosecution is in progress or in contemplation. The Government has been notably successful in securing conviction, and hence long-term custody or execution, of those who have waged war against the state.

I frankly do not know whether these tools are sufficient to meet the Government's security needs, including the need to obtain intelligence through interrogation. It is far beyond my competence, or the Court's competence, to determine that. But it is not beyond Congress's. If the situation demands it, the Executive can ask Congress to authorize suspension of the writ — which can be made subject to whatever conditions Congress deems appropriate, including even the procedural novelties invented by the plurality today. To be sure, suspension is limited by the Constitution to cases of rebellion or invasion. But whether the attacks of September 11, 2001, constitute an "invasion," and whether those attacks still justify suspension several years later, are questions for Congress rather than this Court. If civil rights are to be curtailed during wartime, it must be done openly and democratically, as the Constitution requires, rather than by silent erosion through an opinion of this Court.

Justice THOMAS, dissenting.

The Executive Branch, acting pursuant to the powers vested in the President by the Constitution and with explicit congressional approval, has determined that Yaser Hamdi is an enemy combatant and should be detained. This detention falls squarely within the Federal Government's war powers, and we lack the expertise and capacity to second-guess that decision. As such, petitioner's habeas challenge should fail, and there is no reason to remand the case. The plurality reaches a contrary conclusion by failing adequately to consider basic principles of the constitutional structure as it relates to national security and foreign affairs and by using the balancing scheme of Mathews v. Eldridge (1976). I do not think that the Federal Government's war powers can be balanced away by this Court. Arguably, Congress could provide for additional procedural protections, but until it does, we have no right to insist upon them. But even if I were to agree with the general approach the plurality takes, I could not accept the particulars. The plurality utterly fails to account for the Government's compelling interests and for our own institutional inability to weigh competing concerns correctly. I respectfully dissent.

Although the President very well may have inherent authority to detain those arrayed against our troops, I agree with the plurality that we need not decide that question because Congress has authorized the President to do so. The Authorization for Use of Military Force (AUMF) authorizes the President to "use all necessary and appropriate force against those nations, organizations, or persons he determines planned, authorized, committed, or aided the terrorist attacks" of September 11, 2001. But I do not think that the plurality has adequately explained the breadth of the President's authority to detain enemy combatants, an authority that includes making virtually conclusive factual findings. In my view, the structural considerations discussed above, as recognized in our precedent, demonstrate that we lack the capacity and responsibility to second-guess this determination.

The Government's asserted authority to detain an individual that the President has determined to be an enemy combatant, at least while hostilities continue, comports with the Due Process Clause. As these cases also show, the Executive's decision that a detention is necessary to protect the public need not and should not be subjected to judicial second-guessing. Indeed, at least in the context of enemy-combatant determinations, this would defeat the unity, secrecy, and dispatch that the Founders believed to be so important to the warmaking function.

Accordingly, I conclude that the Government's detention of Hamdi as an enemy combatant does not violate the Constitution. By detaining Hamdi, the President, in the prosecution of a war and authorized by Congress, has acted well within his authority. Hamdi thereby received all the process to which he was due under the circumstances. I therefore believe that this is no occasion to balance the competing interests, as the plurality unconvincingly attempts to do.

Undeniably, Hamdi has been deprived of a serious interest, one actually protected by the Due Process Clause. Against this, however, is the Government's overriding interest in protecting the Nation. If a deprivation of liberty can be justified by the need to protect a town, the protection of the Nation, *a fortiori*, justifies it.

In October 2006, Congress passed and President Bush signed the Military Commission Act of 2006, Pub. L. No. 109-366, 120 Stat. 2600 (2006). Among other things, the Act provides that non-citizens held as enemy combatants shall not have access to federal court via a writ of habeas corpus. Instead, they must go through military proceedings and then seek review in the United States Court of

Appeals for the District of Columbia Circuit. The D.C. Circuit is limited to hearing claims under the Constitution and federal statutes; it cannot hear claims under treaties such as the Geneva Accords. The Military Commission Act creates express statutory authority for military commissions and defines their procedures.

In February 2007, the United States Court of Appeals for the District of Columbia Circuit upheld the constitutionality of the Military Commission Act, rejecting a challenge that it was an unconstitutional suspension of the writ of habeas corpus. Boumediene v. Bush, 476 F.3d 981 (D.C. Cir. 2007).

In June 2008, the Supreme Court reversed the D.C. Circuit. The decision focuses on what the Constitution requires in terms of the availability of habeas corpus; specifically, what is an unconstitutional suspension of the writ? Underlying the majority and the dissenting opinions are very different views about the appropriate role of the judiciary in the war on terror.

Boumediene v. Bush

128 S. Ct. 2229 (2008)

Justice KENNEDY delivered the opinion of the Court.

Petitioners are aliens designated as enemy combatants and detained at the United States Naval Station at Guantanamo Bay, Cuba. There are others detained there, also aliens, who are not parties to this suit.

Petitioners present a question not resolved by our earlier cases relating to the detention of aliens at Guantanamo: whether they have the constitutional privilege of habeas corpus, a privilege not to be withdrawn except in conformance with the Suspension Clause, Art. I, §9, cl. 2. We hold these petitioners do have the habeas corpus privilege. Congress has enacted a statute, the Detainee Treatment Act of 2005 (DTA), that provides certain procedures for review of the detainees' status. We hold that those procedures are not an adequate and effective substitute for habeas corpus. Therefore §7 of the Military Commissions Act of 2006 (MCA) operates as an unconstitutional suspension of the writ. We do not address whether the President has authority to detain these petitioners nor do we hold that the writ must issue. These and other questions regarding the legality of the detention are to be resolved in the first instance by the District Court.

I

Under the Authorization for Use of Military Force (AUMF), the President is authorized "to use all necessary and appropriate force against those nations, organizations, or persons he determines planned, authorized, committed, or aided the terrorist attacks that occurred on September 11, 2001, or harbored such organizations or persons, in order to prevent any future acts of international terrorism against the United States by such nations, organizations or persons."

In Hamdi v. Rumsfeld (2004), five Members of the Court recognized that detention of individuals who fought against the United States in Afghanistan "for the duration of the particular conflict in which they were captured, is so funda-mental and accepted an incident to war as to be an exercise of the 'necessary and appropriate force' Congress has authorized the President to use." After *Hamdi*, the Deputy Secretary of Defense established Combatant Status Review Tribunals (CSRTs) to determine whether individuals detained at Guantanamo were "enemy combatants," as the Department defines that term. A later memorandum established procedures to implement the CSRTs. The Government maintains these procedures were designed to comply with the due process requirements identified by the plurality in *Hamdi*.

Interpreting the AUMF, the Department of Defense ordered the detention of these petitioners, and they were transferred to Guantanamo. Some of these indi-viduals were apprehended on the battlefield in Afghanistan, others in places as far away from there as Bosnia and Gambia. All are foreign nationals, but none is a citizen of a nation now at war with the United States. Each denies he is a member of the al Qaeda terrorist network that carried out the September 11 attacks or of the Taliban regime that provided sanctuary for al Qaeda. Each petitioner appeared before a separate CSRT; was determined to be an enemy combatant; and has sought a writ of habeas corpus in the United States District Court for the District of Columbia.

The first actions commenced in February 2002. We granted certiorari and reversed, holding that 28 U.S.C. §2241 extended statutory habeas corpus jurisdic-tion to Guantanamo. See Rasul v. Bush (2004). After *Rasul*, petitioners' cases were consolidated and entertained in two separate proceedings. In the first set of cases, Judge Richard J. Leon granted the Government's motion to dismiss, hold-ing that the detainees had no rights that could be vindicated in a habeas corpus action. In the second set of cases Judge Joyce Hens Green reached the opposite conclusion, holding the detainees had rights under the Due Process Clause of the Fifth Amendment.

While appeals were pending from the District Court decisions, Congress passed the DTA. Subsection (e) of §1005 of the DTA amended 28 U.S.C. §2241 to provide that "no court, justice, or judge shall have jurisdiction to hear or consider . . . an application for a writ of habeas corpus filed by or on behalf of an alien detained by the Department of Defense at Guantanamo Bay, Cuba." Sec-tion 1005 further provides that the Court of Appeals for the District of Columbia Circuit shall have "exclusive" jurisdiction to review decisions of the CSRTs. Ibid.

In Hamdan v. Rumsfeld (2006), the Court held this provision did not apply to cases (like petitioners') pending when the DTA was enacted. Congress responded by passing the MCA.

II

As a threshold matter, we must decide whether MCA §7 denies the federal courts jurisdiction to hear habeas corpus actions pending at the time of its enactment. We hold the statute does deny that jurisdiction, so that, if the statute is valid, peti-tioners' cases must be dismissed.

As amended by the terms of the MCA, 28 U.S.C.A. §2241(e) now provides:

"(1) No court, justice, or judge shall have jurisdiction to hear or consider an application for a writ of habeas corpus filed by or on behalf of an alien detained by the United States who has been determined by the United States to have been properly detained as an enemy combatant or is awaiting such determination.

"(2) Except as provided in [§§1005(e)(2) and (e)(3) of the DTA] no court, justice, or judge shall have jurisdiction to hear or consider any other action against the United States or its agents relating to any aspect of the detention, transfer, treatment, trial, or conditions of confinement of an alien who is or was detained by the United States and has been determined by the United States to have been properly detained as an enemy combatant or is awaiting such determination."

Section 7(b) of the MCA provides the effective date for the amendment of §2241(e). It states: "The amendment made by [MCA §7(a)] shall take effect on the date of the enactment of this Act, and shall apply to all cases, without exception, pending on or after the date of the enactment of this Act which relate to any aspect of the detention, transfer, treatment, trial, or conditions of detention of an alien detained by the United States since September 11, 2001."

If this ongoing dialogue between and among the branches of Government is to be respected, we cannot ignore that the MCA was a direct response to *Hamdan*'s holding that the DTA's jurisdiction-stripping provision had no application to pending cases. The Court of Appeals was correct to take note of the legislative history when construing the statute, and we agree with its conclusion that the MCA deprives the federal courts of jurisdiction to entertain the habeas corpus actions now before us.

V

In light of this holding the question becomes whether the statute stripping jurisdiction to issue the writ avoids the Suspension Clause mandate because Congress has provided adequate substitute procedures for habeas corpus.

The gravity of the separation-of-powers issues raised by these cases and the fact that these detainees have been denied meaningful access to a judicial forum for a period of years render these cases exceptional.

Our case law does not contain extensive discussion of standards defining suspension of the writ or of circumstances under which suspension has occurred. This simply confirms the care Congress has taken throughout our Nation's history to preserve the writ and its function. Indeed, most of the major legislative enactments pertaining to habeas corpus have acted not to contract the writ's protection but to expand it or to hasten resolution of prisoners' claims.

We do not endeavor to offer a comprehensive summary of the requisites for an adequate substitute for habeas corpus. We do consider it uncontroversial, however, that the privilege of habeas corpus entitles the prisoner to a meaningful opportunity to demonstrate that he is being held pursuant to "the erroneous application or interpretation" of relevant law. And the habeas court must have the power to order the conditional release of an individual unlawfully detained — though release need not be the exclusive remedy and is not the appropriate one in every case in which the writ is granted.

Where a person is detained by executive order, rather than, say, after being tried and convicted in a court, the need for collateral review is most pressing. A criminal conviction in the usual course occurs after a judicial hearing before a tribunal disinterested in the outcome and committed to procedures designed to ensure its own independence. These dynamics are not inherent in executive detention orders or executive review procedures. In this context the need for habeas corpus is more urgent. The intended duration of the detention and the reasons for it bear upon the precise scope of the inquiry. Habeas corpus proceedings need not resemble a criminal trial, even when the detention is by executive order. But the writ must be effective. The habeas court must have sufficient authority to conduct a meaningful review of both the cause for detention and the Executive's power to detain.

To determine the necessary scope of habeas corpus review, therefore, we must assess the CSRT process, the mechanism through which petitioners' designation as enemy combatants became final. Whether one characterizes the CSRT process as direct review of the Executive's battlefield determination that the detainee is an enemy combatant — as the parties have and as we do — or as the first step in the collateral review of a battlefield determination makes no difference in a proper analysis of whether the procedures Congress put in place are an adequate substitute for habeas corpus. What matters is the sum total of procedural protections afforded to the detainee at all stages, direct and collateral.

Petitioners identify what they see as myriad deficiencies in the CSRTs. The most relevant for our purposes are the constraints upon the detainee's ability to rebut the factual basis for the Government's assertion that he is an enemy combatant. As already noted, at the CSRT stage the detainee has limited means to find or present evidence to challenge the Government's case against him. He does not have the assistance of counsel and may not be aware of the most critical allegations that the Government relied upon to order his detention. The detainee can confront witnesses that testify during the CSRT proceedings. But given that there are in effect no limits on the admission of hearsay evidence — the only requirement is that the tribunal deem the evidence "relevant and helpful," — the detainee's opportunity to question witnesses is likely to be more theoretical than real.

Even if we were to assume that the CSRTs satisfy due process standards, it would not end our inquiry. Habeas corpus is a collateral process that exists, in Justice Holmes' words, to "cu[t] through all forms and g[o] to the very tissue of the structure. It comes in from the outside, not in subordination to the proceedings, and although every form may have been preserved opens the inquiry whether they have been more than an empty shell." Even when the procedures authorizing detention are structurally sound, the Suspension Clause remains applicable and the writ relevant.

Although we make no judgment as to whether the CSRTs, as currently constituted, satisfy due process standards, we agree with petitioners that, even when all the parties involved in this process act with diligence and in good faith, there is considerable risk of error in the tribunal's findings of fact. And given that the consequence of error may be detention of persons for the duration of hostilities that may last a generation or more, this is a risk too significant to ignore.

For the writ of habeas corpus, or its substitute, to function as an effective and proper remedy in this context, the court that conducts the habeas proceeding must have the means to correct errors that occurred during the CSRT proceedings. This includes some authority to assess the sufficiency of the Government's evidence against the detainee. It also must have the authority to admit and consider relevant exculpatory evidence that was not introduced during the earlier proceeding. Federal habeas petitioners long have had the means to supplement the record on review, even in the postconviction habeas setting. Here that opportunity is constitutionally required.

The extent of the showing required of the Government in these cases is a matter to be determined. We need not explore it further at this stage. We do hold that when the judicial power to issue habeas corpus properly is invoked the judicial officer must have adequate authority to make a determination in light of the relevant law and facts and to formulate and issue appropriate orders for relief, including, if necessary, an order directing the prisoner's release.

C

We now consider whether the DTA allows the Court of Appeals to conduct a proceeding meeting these standards. The DTA does not explicitly empower the Court of Appeals to order the applicant in a DTA review proceeding released should the court find that the standards and procedures used at his CSRT hearing were insufficient to justify detention. This is troubling. Yet, for present purposes, we can assume congressional silence permits a constitutionally required remedy. The absence of a release remedy and specific language allowing AUMF challenges are not the only constitutional infirmities from which the statute potentially suffers, however. The more difficult question is whether the DTA permits the Court of Appeals to make requisite findings of fact. Assuming the DTA can be construed to allow the Court of Appeals to review or correct the CSRT's factual determinations, as opposed to merely certifying that the tribunal applied the correct standard of proof, we see no way to construe the statute to allow what is also constitutionally required in this context: an opportunity for the detainee to present relevant exculpatory evidence that was not made part of the record in the earlier proceedings.

On its face the statute allows the Court of Appeals to consider no evidence outside the CSRT record.

Under the DTA the Court of Appeals has the power to review CSRT determinations by assessing the legality of standards and procedures. This implies the power to inquire into what happened at the CSRT hearing and, perhaps, to remedy certain deficiencies in that proceeding. But should the Court of Appeals determine that the CSRT followed appropriate and lawful standards and procedures, it will have reached the limits of its jurisdiction. There is no language in the DTA that can be construed to allow the Court of Appeals to admit and consider newly discovered evidence that could not have been made part of the CSRT record because it was unavailable to either the Government or the detainee when the CSRT made its findings. This evidence, however, may be critical to the detainee's argument that he is not an enemy combatant and there is no cause to detain him.

By foreclosing consideration of evidence not presented or reasonably available to the detainee at the CSRT proceedings, the DTA disadvantages the detainee by limiting the scope of collateral review to a record that may not be accurate or complete.

Although we do not hold that an adequate substitute must duplicate §2241 in all respects, it suffices that the Government has not established that the detainees' access to the statutory review provisions at issue is an adequate substitute for the writ of habeas corpus. MCA §7 thus effects an unconstitutional suspension of the writ. In view of our holding we need not discuss the reach of the writ with respect to claims of unlawful conditions of treatment or confinement.

VI

The real risks, the real threats, of terrorist attacks are constant and not likely soon to abate. The ways to disrupt our life and laws are so many and unforeseen that the Court should not attempt even some general catalogue of crises that might occur. Certain principles are apparent, however. Practical considerations and exigent circumstances inform the definition and reach of the law's writs, including habeas corpus. The cases and our tradition reflect this precept.

In cases involving foreign citizens detained abroad by the Executive, it likely would be both an impractical and unprecedented extension of judicial power to assume that habeas corpus would be available at the moment the prisoner is taken into custody. If and when habeas corpus jurisdiction applies, as it does in these cases, then proper deference can be accorded to reasonable procedures for screening and initial detention under lawful and proper conditions of confinement and treatment for a reasonable period of time. Domestic exigencies, furthermore, might also impose such onerous burdens on the Government that here, too, the Judicial Branch would be required to devise sensible rules for staying habeas corpus proceedings until the Government can comply with its requirements in a responsible way. Here, as is true with detainees apprehended abroad, a relevant consideration in determining the courts' role is whether there are suitable alternative processes in place to protect against the arbitrary exercise of governmental power.

The cases before us, however, do not involve detainees who have been held for a short period of time while awaiting their CSRT determinations. Were that the case, or were it probable that the Court of Appeals could complete a prompt review of their applications, the case for requiring temporary abstention or exhaustion of alternative remedies would be much stronger. These qualifications no longer pertain here. In some of these cases six years have elapsed without the judicial oversight that habeas corpus or an adequate substitute demands. And there has been no showing that the Executive faces such onerous burdens that it cannot respond to habeas corpus actions. To require these detainees to complete DTA review before proceeding with their habeas corpus actions would be to require additional months, if not years, of delay. The detainees in these cases are entitled to a prompt habeas corpus hearing.

Our decision today holds only that the petitioners before us are entitled to seek the writ; that the DTA review procedures are an inadequate substitute for habeas corpus; and that the petitioners in these cases need not exhaust the review procedures in the Court of Appeals before proceeding with their habeas actions in the District Court. The only law we identify as unconstitutional is MCA §7. Accordingly, both the DTA and the CSRT process remain intact. Our holding with regard to exhaustion should not be read to imply that a habeas court should intervene the moment an enemy combatant steps foot in a territory where the writ runs. The Executive is entitled to a reasonable period of time to determine a detainee's status before a court entertains that detainee's habeas corpus petition.

In considering both the procedural and substantive standards used to impose detention to prevent acts of terrorism, proper deference must be accorded to the political branches. There are further considerations, however. Security subsists, too, in fidelity to freedom's first principles. Chief among these are freedom from arbitrary and unlawful restraint and the personal liberty that is secured by adherence to the separation of powers. It is from these principles that the judicial authority to consider petitions for habeas corpus relief derives.

Our opinion does not undermine the Executive's powers as Commander in Chief. On the contrary, the exercise of those powers is vindicated, not eroded, when confirmed by the Judicial Branch. Within the Constitution's separation-of-powers structure, few exercises of judicial power are as legitimate or as necessary as the responsibility to hear challenges to the authority of the Executive to imprison a person. Some of these petitioners have been in custody for six years with no definitive judicial determination as to the legality of their detention. Their access to the writ is a necessity to determine the lawfulness of their status, even if, in the end, they do not obtain the relief they seek.

Because our Nation's past military conflicts have been of limited duration, it has been possible to leave the outer boundaries of war powers undefined. If, as some fear, terrorism continues to pose dangerous threats to us for years to come, the Court might not have this luxury. This result is not inevitable, however. The political branches, consistent with their independent obligations to interpret and uphold the Constitution, can engage in a genuine debate about how best to preserve constitutional values while protecting the Nation from terrorism.

It bears repeating that our opinion does not address the content of the law that governs petitioners' detention. That is a matter yet to be determined. We hold that petitioners may invoke the fundamental procedural protections of habeas corpus. The laws and Constitution are designed to survive, and remain in force, in extraordinary times. Liberty and security can be reconciled; and in our system they are reconciled within the framework of the law. The Framers decided that habeas corpus, a right of first importance, must be a part of that framework, a part of that law.

Justice SOUTER, with whom Justice GINSBURG and Justice BREYER join, concurring.

I join the Court's opinion in its entirety and add this afterword only to emphasize two things one might overlook after reading the dissents.

Four years ago, this Court in Rasul v. Bush (2004) held that statutory habeas jurisdiction extended to claims of foreign nationals imprisoned by the United States at Guantanamo Bay, "to determine the legality of the Executive's potentially indefinite detention" of them. Subsequent legislation eliminated the statutory habeas jurisdiction over these claims, so that now there must be constitutionally based jurisdiction or none at all. But no one who reads the Court's opinion in *Rasul* could seriously doubt that the jurisdictional question must be answered the same way in purely constitutional cases, given the Court's reliance on the historical background of habeas generally in answering the statutory question.

A second fact insufficiently appreciated by the dissents is the length of the disputed imprisonments, some of the prisoners represented here today having been locked up for six years. Hence the hollow ring when the dissenters suggest that the Court is somehow precipitating the judiciary into reviewing claims that the military (subject to appeal to the Court of Appeals for the District of Columbia Circuit) could handle within some reasonable period of time. These suggestions of judicial haste are all the more out of place given the Court's realistic acknowledgment that in periods of exigency the tempo of any habeas review must reflect the immediate peril facing the country. After six years of sustained executive detentions in Guantanamo, subject to habeas jurisdiction but without any actual habeas scrutiny, today's decision is no judicial victory, but an act of perseverance in trying to make habeas review, and the obligation of the courts to provide it, mean something of value both to prisoners and to the Nation.

Chief Justice ROBERTS, with whom Justice SCALIA, Justice THOMAS, and Justice ALITO join, dissenting.

Today the Court strikes down as inadequate the most generous set of procedural protections ever afforded aliens detained by this country as enemy combatants. The political branches crafted these procedures amidst an ongoing military conflict, after much careful investigation and thorough debate. The Court rejects them today out of hand, without bothering to say what due process rights the detainees possess, without explaining how the statute fails to vindicate those rights, and before a single petitioner has even attempted to avail himself of the law's operation. And to what effect? The majority merely replaces a review system designed by the people's representatives with a set of shapeless procedures to be defined by federal courts at some future date. One cannot help but think, after surveying the modest practical results of the majority's ambitious opinion, that this decision is not really about the detainees at all, but about control of federal policy regarding enemy combatants.

The majority is adamant that the Guantanamo detainees are entitled to the protections of habeas corpus — its opinion begins by deciding that question. I regard the issue as a difficult one, primarily because of the unique and unusual jurisdictional status of Guantanamo Bay. I nonetheless agree with Justice Scalia's analysis of our precedents and the pertinent history of the writ, and accordingly join his dissent. The important point for me, however, is that the Court should have resolved these cases on other grounds. Habeas is most fundamentally a procedural right, a mechanism for contesting the legality of executive detention. The critical threshold question in these cases, prior to any inquiry about the writ's scope, is whether the system the political branches designed protects whatever rights the detainees may possess. If so, there is no need for any additional process, whether called "habeas" or something else.

Congress entrusted that threshold question in the first instance to the Court of Appeals for the District of Columbia Circuit, as the Constitution surely allows Congress to do. But before the D.C. Circuit has addressed the issue, the Court cashiers the statute, and without answering this critical threshold question itself. The Court does eventually get around to asking whether review under the DTA is, as the Court frames it, an "adequate substitute" for habeas, but even then its opinion fails to determine what rights the detainees possess and whether the DTA system satisfies them. The majority instead compares the undefined DTA process to an equally undefined habeas right — one that is to be given shape only in the future by district courts on a case-by-case basis. This whole approach is misguided.

It is also fruitless. How the detainees' claims will be decided now that the DTA is gone is anybody's guess. But the habeas process the Court mandates will most likely end up looking a lot like the DTA system it replaces, as the district court judges shaping it will have to reconcile review of the prisoners' detention with the undoubted need to protect the American people from the terrorist threat — precisely the challenge Congress undertook in drafting the DTA. All that today's opinion has done is shift responsibility for those sensitive foreign policy and national security decisions from the elected branches to the Federal Judiciary.

I believe the system the political branches constructed adequately protects any constitutional rights aliens captured abroad and detained as enemy combatants may enjoy. I therefore would dismiss these cases on that ground. With all respect for the contrary views of the majority, I must dissent.

The majority's overreaching is particularly egregious given the weakness of its objections to the DTA. Simply put, the Court's opinion fails on its own terms. The majority strikes down the statute because it is not an "adequate substitute" for habeas review, but fails to show what rights the detainees have that cannot be vindicated by the DTA system.

The majority is equally wrong to characterize the CSRTs as part of that initial determination process. They are instead a means for detainees to challenge the Government's determination. The Executive designed the CSRTs to mirror Army Regulation 190-8, the very procedural model the plurality in *Hamdi* said provided the type of process an enemy combatant could expect from a habeas court. The CSRTs operate much as habeas courts would if hearing the detainee's collateral challenge for the first time: They gather evidence, call witnesses, take testimony, and render a decision on the legality of the Government's detention. If the CSRT finds a particular detainee has been improperly held, it can order release.

The majority insists that even if "the CSRTs satisf[ied] due process standards," full habeas review would still be necessary, because habeas is a collateral remedy available even to prisoners "detained pursuant to the most rigorous proceedings imaginable." This comment makes sense only if the CSRTs are incorrectly viewed as a method used by the Executive for determining the prisoners' status, and not as themselves part of the collateral review to test the validity of that determination. The majority can deprecate the importance of the CSRTs only by treating them as something they are not.

In short, the *Hamdi* plurality concluded that this type of review would be enough to satisfy due process, even for citizens. Congress followed the Court's lead, only to find itself the victim of a constitutional bait and switch.

Given the statutory scheme the political branches adopted, and given *Hamdi*, it simply will not do for the majority to dismiss the CSRT procedures as "far more limited" than those used in military trials, and therefore beneath the level of process "that would eliminate the need for habeas corpus review." The question is not how much process the CSRTs provide in comparison to other modes of adjudication. The question is whether the CSRT procedures — coupled with the judicial review specified by the DTA — provide the "basic process" *Hamdi* said the Constitution affords American citizens detained as enemy combatants.

To what basic process are these detainees due as habeas petitioners? We have said that "at the absolute minimum," the Suspension Clause protects the writ "'as it existed in 1789.'" The majority admits that a number of historical authorities suggest that at the time of the Constitution's ratification, "common-law courts abstained altogether from matters involving prisoners of war." If this is accurate, the process provided prisoners under the DTA is plainly more than sufficient — it allows alleged combatants to challenge both the factual and legal bases of their detentions.

Assuming the constitutional baseline is more robust, the DTA still provides adequate process, and by the majority's own standards. The DTA system — CSRT review of the Executive's determination followed by D.C. Circuit review for sufficiency of the evidence and the constitutionality of the CSRT process — meets these criteria.

All told, the DTA provides the prisoners held at Guantanamo Bay adequate opportunity to contest the bases of their detentions, which is all habeas corpus need allow. The DTA provides more opportunity and more process, in fact, than that afforded prisoners of war or any other alleged enemy combatants in history.

Despite these guarantees, the Court finds the DTA system an inadequate habeas substitute, for one central reason: Detainees are unable to introduce at the appeal stage exculpatory evidence discovered after the conclusion of their CSRT proceedings. The Court hints darkly that the DTA may suffer from other infirmities, but it does not bother to name them, making a response a bit difficult. As it stands, I can only assume the Court regards the supposed defect it did identify as the gravest of the lot.

If this is the most the Court can muster, the ice beneath its feet is thin indeed. As noted, the CSRT procedures provide ample opportunity for detainees to introduce exculpatory evidence — whether documentary in nature or from live witnesses — before the military tribunals. And if their ability to introduce such evidence is denied contrary to the Constitution or laws of the United States, the D.C. Circuit has the authority to say so on review.

For all its eloquence about the detainees' right to the writ, the Court makes no effort to elaborate how exactly the remedy it prescribes will differ from the procedural protections detainees enjoy under the DTA. The Court objects to the detainees' limited access to witnesses and classified material, but proposes no alternatives of its own. Indeed, it simply ignores the many difficult questions its holding presents. What, for example, will become of the CSRT process? The majority says federal courts should generally refrain from entertaining detainee challenges until after the petitioner's CSRT proceeding has finished. But to what deference, if any, is that CSRT determination entitled?

There are other problems. Take witness availability. What makes the majority think witnesses will become magically available when the review procedure is labeled "habeas"? Will the location of most of these witnesses change — will they suddenly become easily susceptible to service of process? Or will subpoenas issued by American habeas courts run to Basra? And if they did, how would they be enforced? Speaking of witnesses, will detainees be able to call active-duty military officers as witnesses? If not, why not?

The majority has no answers for these difficulties. What it does say leaves open the distinct possibility that its "habeas" remedy will, when all is said and done, end up looking a great deal like the DTA review it rejects.

The majority rests its decision on abstract and hypothetical concerns. Step back and consider what, in the real world, Congress and the Executive have actually granted aliens captured by our Armed Forces overseas and found to be enemy combatants:

- The right to hear the bases of the charges against them, including a summary of any classified evidence.
- The ability to challenge the bases of their detention before military tribunals modeled after Geneva Convention procedures. Some 38 detainees have been released as a result of this process.
- The right, before the CSRT, to testify, introduce evidence, call witnesses, question those the Government calls, and secure release, if and when appropriate.
- The right to the aid of a personal representative in arranging and presenting their cases before a CSRT.
- Before the D.C. Circuit, the right to employ counsel, challenge the factual record, contest the lower tribunal's legal determinations, ensure compliance with the Constitution and laws, and secure release, if any errors below establish their entitlement to such relief.

In sum, the DTA satisfies the majority's own criteria for assessing adequacy. This statutory scheme provides the combatants held at Guantanamo greater procedural protections than have ever been afforded alleged enemy detainees — whether citizens or aliens — in our national history.

So who has won? Not the detainees. The Court's analysis leaves them with only the prospect of further litigation to determine the content of their new habeas right, followed by further litigation to resolve their particular cases, followed by further litigation before the D.C. Circuit — where they could have started had they invoked the DTA procedure. Not Congress, whose attempt to "determine — through democratic means — how best" to balance the security of the American people with the detainees' liberty interests, has been unceremoniously brushed aside. Not the Great Writ, whose majesty is hardly enhanced by its extension to a jurisdictionally quirky outpost, with no tangible benefit to anyone. Not the rule of law, unless by that is meant the rule of lawyers, who will now arguably have a greater role than military and intelligence officials in shaping policy for alien enemy combatants. And certainly not the American people, who today lose a bit more control over the conduct of this Nation's foreign policy to unelected, politically unaccountable judges.

Justice SCALIA, with whom the Chief Justice, Justice THOMAS, and Justice ALITO join, dissenting.

Today, for the first time in our Nation's history, the Court confers a constitutional right to habeas corpus on alien enemies detained abroad by our military forces in the course of an ongoing war. The Chief Justice's dissent, which I join, shows that the procedures prescribed by Congress in the Detainee Treatment Act provide the essential protections that habeas corpus guarantees; there has thus been no suspension of the writ, and no basis exists for judicial intervention beyond what the Act allows. My problem with today's opinion is more fundamental still: The writ of habeas corpus does not, and never has, run in favor of aliens abroad; the Suspension Clause thus has no application, and the Court's intervention in this military matter is entirely ultra vires.

I shall devote most of what will be a lengthy opinion to the legal errors contained in the opinion of the Court. Contrary to my usual practice, however, I think it appropriate to begin with a description of the disastrous consequences of what the Court has done today.

America is at war with radical Islamists. The enemy began by killing Americans and American allies abroad: 241 at the Marine barracks in Lebanon, 19 at the Khobar Towers in Dhahran, 224 at our embassies in Dar es Salaam and Nairobi, and 17 on the USS Cole in Yemen. On September 11, 2001, the enemy brought the battle to American soil, killing 2,749 at the Twin Towers in New York City, 184 at the Pentagon in Washington, D.C., and 40 in Pennsylvania. It has threatened further attacks against our homeland; one need only walk about buttressed and barricaded Washington, or board a plane anywhere in the country, to know that the threat is a serious one. Our Armed Forces are now in the field against the enemy, in Afghanistan and Iraq. Last week, 13 of our countrymen in arms were killed.

The game of bait-and-switch that today's opinion plays upon the Nation's Commander in Chief will make the war harder on us. It will almost certainly cause more Americans to be killed. That consequence would be tolerable if necessary to preserve a time-honored legal principle vital to our constitutional

Republic. But it is this Court's blatant abandonment of such a principle that produces the decision today. The President relied on our settled precedent in Johnson v. Eisentrager (1950), when he established the prison at Guantanamo Bay for enemy aliens. Citing that case, the President's Office of Legal Counsel advised him "that the great weight of legal authority indicates that a federal district court could not properly exercise habeas jurisdiction over an alien detained at [Guantanamo Bay]." Memorandum from Patrick F. Philbin and John C. Yoo, Deputy Assistant Attorneys General, Office of Legal Counsel, to William J. Haynes II, General Counsel, Dept. of Defense (Dec. 28, 2001). Had the law been otherwise, the military surely would not have transported prisoners there, but would have kept them in Afghanistan, transferred them to another of our foreign military bases, or turned them over to allies for detention. Those other facilities might well have been worse for the detainees themselves.

In the long term, then, the Court's decision today accomplishes little, except perhaps to reduce the well-being of enemy combatants that the Court ostensibly seeks to protect. In the short term, however, the decision is devastating. At least 30 of those prisoners hitherto released from Guantanamo Bay have returned to the battlefield. See S.Rep. No. 110-90, pt. 7, p. 13 (2007) (Minority Views of Sens. Kyl, Sessions, Graham, Cornyn, and Coburn) (hereinafter Minority Report). Some have been captured or killed. See also Mintz, Released Detainees Rejoining the Fight, Washington Post, Oct. 22, 2004, pp. A1, A12. But others have succeeded in carrying on their atrocities against innocent civilians. In one case, a detainee released from Guantanamo Bay masterminded the kidnapping of two Chinese dam workers, one of whom was later shot to death when used as a human shield against Pakistani commandoes. Another former detainee promptly resumed his post as a senior Taliban commander and murdered a United Nations engineer and three Afghan soldiers. Mintz, supra. Still another murdered an Afghan judge. It was reported only last month that a released detainee carried out a suicide bombing against Iraqi soldiers in Mosul, Iraq. See White, Ex-Guantanamo Detainee Joined Iraq Suicide Attack, Washington Post, May 8, 2008, p. A18.

These, mind you, were detainees whom the military had concluded were not enemy combatants. Their return to the kill illustrates the incredible difficulty of assessing who is and who is not an enemy combatant in a foreign theater of operations where the environment does not lend itself to rigorous evidence collection. Astoundingly, the Court today raises the bar, requiring military officials to appear before civilian courts and defend their decisions under procedural and evidentiary rules that go beyond what Congress has specified. As The Chief Justice's dissent makes clear, we have no idea what those procedural and evidentiary rules are, but they will be determined by civil courts and (in the Court's contemplation at least) will be more detainee-friendly than those now applied, since otherwise there would no reason to hold the congressionally prescribed procedures unconstitutional. If they impose a higher standard of proof (from foreign battlefields) than the current procedures require, the number of the enemy returned to combat will obviously increase.

But even when the military has evidence that it can bring forward, it is often foolhardy to release that evidence to the attorneys representing our enemies. And one escalation of procedures that the Court is clear about is affording the detainees increased access to witnesses (perhaps troops serving in Afghanistan?) and to classified information. During the 1995 prosecution of Omar Abdel Rahman, federal prosecutors gave the names of 200 unindicted co-conspirators to the "Blind Sheik's" defense lawyers; that information was in the hands of Osama Bin Laden within two weeks. In another case, trial testimony revealed to the enemy that the United States had been monitoring their cellular network, whereupon they promptly stopped using it, enabling more of them to evade capture and continue their atrocities.

And today it is not just the military that the Court elbows aside. A mere two Terms ago in Hamdan v. Rumsfeld (2006), when the Court held (quite amazingly) that the Detainee Treatment Act of 2005 had not stripped habeas jurisdiction over Guantanamo petitioners' claims, four Members of today's five-Justice majority joined an opinion saying the following: "Nothing prevents the President from returning to Congress to seek the authority [for trial by military commission] he believes necessary."

Turns out they were just kidding. For in response, Congress, at the President's request, quickly enacted the Military Commissions Act, emphatically reasserting that it did not want these prisoners filing habeas petitions. It is therefore clear that Congress and the Executive — both political branches — have determined that limiting the role of civilian courts in adjudicating whether prisoners captured abroad are properly detained is important to success in the war that some 190,000 of our men and women are now fighting. As the Solicitor General argued, "the Military Commissions Act and the Detainee Treatment Act . . . represent an effort by the political branches to strike an appropriate balance between the need to preserve liberty and the need to accommodate the weighty and sensitive governmental interests in ensuring that those who have in fact fought with the enemy during a war do not return to battle against the United States."

But it does not matter. The Court today decrees that no good reason to accept the judgment of the other two branches is "apparent." "The Government," it declares, "presents no credible arguments that the military mission at Guantanamo would be compromised if habeas corpus courts had jurisdiction to hear the detainees' claims." What competence does the Court have to second-guess the judgment of Congress and the President on such a point? None whatever. But the Court blunders in nonetheless. Henceforth, as today's opinion makes unnervingly clear, how to handle enemy prisoners in this war will ultimately lie with the branch that knows least about the national security concerns that the subject entails.

Today the Court warps our Constitution in a way that goes beyond the narrow issue of the reach of the Suspension Clause, invoking judicially brainstormed separation-of-powers principles to establish a manipulable "functional" test for the extraterritorial reach of habeas corpus (and, no doubt, for the extraterritorial reach of other constitutional protections as well). It blatantly misdescribes important precedents, most conspicuously Justice Jackson's opinion for the Court in Johnson v. Eisentrager. It breaks a chain of precedent as old as the common law that prohibits judicial inquiry into detentions of aliens abroad absent statutory authorization. And, most tragically, it sets our military commanders the impossible task of proving to a civilian court, under whatever standards this Court devises in the future, that evidence supports the confinement of each and every enemy prisoner.

The Nation will live to regret what the Court has done today. I dissent.

---

2. Military Tribunals

In November 2001, President Bush issued an order for military tribunals. The order for military tribunals raises many basic questions: Does the President, as Commander in Chief, have the authority to create military tribunals or is creating courts entirely a congressional power under the Constitution? Can the government suspend provisions of the Bill of Rights in trying non-citizens accused of terrorism or supporting terrorism? More generally, how should the Constitution be interpreted during war time?

There is one major Supreme Court decision concerning military tribunals prior to the current era: *Ex parte Quirin*, from World War II:

EX PARTE QUIRIN, 317 U.S. 1 (1942):   Chief Justice STONE delivered the opinion of the Court.

The question for decision is whether the detention of petitioners by respondent for trial by Military Commission, appointed by Order of the President of July 2, 1942, on charges preferred against them purporting to set out their violations of the law of war and of the Articles of War, is in conformity to the laws and Constitution of the United States.

After denial of their applications by the District Court, petitioners asked leave to file petitions for habeas corpus in this Court. In view of the public importance of the questions raised by their petitions and of the duty which rests on the courts, in time of war as well as in time of peace, to preserve unimpaired the constitutional safeguards of civil liberty, and because in our opinion the public interest required that we consider and decide those questions without any avoidable delay, we directed that petitioners' applications be set down for full oral argument at a special term of this Court, convened on July 29, 1942.

The following facts appear from the petitions or are stipulated. Except as noted they are undisputed. All the petitioners were born in Germany; all have lived in the United States. All returned to Germany between 1933 and 1941. All except petitioner Haupt are admittedly citizens of the German Reich, with which the United States is at war. Haupt came to this country with his parents when he was five years old; it is contended that he became a citizen of the United States by virtue of the naturalization of his parents during his minority and that he has not since lost his citizenship. The Government, however, takes the position that on attaining his majority he elected to maintain German allegiance and citizenship or in any case that he has by his conduct renounced or abandoned his United

States citizenship. For reasons presently to be stated we do not find it necessary to resolve these contentions.

After the declaration of war between the United States and the German Reich, petitioners received training at a sabotage school near Berlin, Germany, where they were instructed in the use of explosives and in methods of secret writing. Thereafter petitioners, with a German citizen, Dasch, proceeded from Germany to a seaport in Occupied France, where petitioners Burger, Heinck and Quirin, together with Dasch, boarded a German submarine which proceeded across the Atlantic to Amagansett Beach on Long Island, New York. The four were there landed from the submarine in the hours of darkness, on or about June 13, 1942, carrying with them a supply of explosives, fuses and incendiary and timing devices. While landing they wore German Marine Infantry uniforms or parts of uniforms. Immediately after landing they buried their uniforms and the other articles mentioned and proceeded in civilian dress to New York City.

The remaining four petitioners at the same French port boarded another German submarine, which carried them across the Atlantic to Ponte Vedra Beach, Florida. On or about June 17, 1942, they came ashore during the hours of darkness wearing caps of the German Marine Infantry and carrying with them a supply of explosives, fuses, and incendiary and timing devices. They immediately buried their caps and the other articles mentioned and proceeded in civilian dress to Jacksonville, Florida, and thence to various points in the United States. All were taken into custody in New York or Chicago by agents of the Federal Bureau of Investigation. All had received instructions in Germany from an officer of the German High Command to destroy war industries and war facilities in the United States, for which they or their relatives in Germany were to receive salary payments from the German Government. They also had been paid by the German Government during their course of training at the sabotage school and had received substantial sums in United States currency, which were in their possession when arrested. The currency had been handed to them by an officer of the German High Command, who had instructed them to wear their German uniforms while landing in the United States.

The President, as President and Commander in Chief of the Army and Navy, by Order of July 2, 1942, appointed a Military Commission and directed it to try petitioners for offenses against the law of war and the Articles of War, and prescribed regulations for the procedure on the trial and for review of the record of the trial and of any judgment or sentence of the Commission. On the same day, by Proclamation, the President declared that "all persons who are subjects, citizens or residents of any nation at war with the United States or who give obedience to or act under the direction of any such nation, and who during time of war enter or attempt to enter the United States . . . through coastal or boundary defenses, and are charged with committing or attempting or preparing to commit sabotage, espionage, hostile or warlike acts, or violations of the law of war, shall be subject to the law of war and to the jurisdiction of military tribunals."

The Proclamation also stated in terms that all such persons were denied access to the courts. Pursuant to direction of the Attorney General, the Federal Bureau of Investigation surrendered custody of petitioners to respondent, Provost

Marshal of the Military District of Washington, who was directed by the Secretary of War to receive and keep them in custody, and who thereafter held petitioners for trial before the Commission.

On July 3, 1942, the Judge Advocate General's Department of the Army prepared and lodged with the Commission the following charges against petitioners, supported by specifications:

1. Violation of the law of war.
2. Violation of Article 81 of the Articles of War, defining the offense of relieving or attempting to relieve, or corresponding with or giving intelligence to, the enemy.
3. Violation of Article 82, defining the offense of spying.
4. Conspiracy to commit the offenses alleged in charges 1, 2 and 3.

The Commission met on July 8, 1942, and proceeded with the trial, which continued in progress while the causes were pending in this Court. On July 27th, before petitioners' applications to the District Court, all the evidence for the prosecution and the defense had been taken by the Commission and the case had been closed except for arguments of counsel. It is conceded that ever since petitioners' arrest the state and federal courts in Florida, New York, and the District of Columbia, and in the states in which each of the petitioners was arrested or detained, have been open and functioning normally.

Petitioners' main contention is that the President is without any statutory or constitutional authority to order the petitioners to be tried by military tribunal for offenses with which they are charged; that in consequence they are entitled to be tried in the civil courts with the safeguards, including trial by jury, which the Fifth and Sixth Amendments guarantee to all persons charged in such courts with criminal offenses. In any case it is urged that the President's Order, in prescribing the procedure of the Commission and the method for review of its findings and sentence, and the proceedings of the Commission under the Order, conflict with Articles of War adopted by Congress and are illegal and void.

The Government challenges each of these propositions. But regardless of their merits, it also insists that petitioners must be denied access to the courts, both because they are enemy aliens or have entered our territory as enemy belligerents, and because the President's Proclamation undertakes in terms to deny such access to the class of persons defined by the Proclamation, which aptly describes the character and conduct of petitioners. It is urged that if they are enemy aliens or if the Proclamation has force no court may afford the petitioners a hearing. But there is certainly nothing in the Proclamation to preclude access to the courts for determining its applicability to the particular case. And neither the Proclamation nor the fact that they are enemy aliens forecloses consideration by the courts of petitioners' contentions that the Constitution and laws of the United States constitutionally enacted forbid their trial by military commission. [W]e have resolved those questions by our conclusion that the Commission has jurisdiction to try the charge preferred against petitioners. There is therefore no occasion to decide contentions of the parties unrelated to this issue. We pass at once to the consideration of the basis of the Commission's authority.

We are not here concerned with any question of the guilt or innocence of petitioners. Constitutional safeguards for the protection of all who are charged with offenses are not to be disregarded in order to inflict merited punishment on some who are guilty. But the detention and trial of petitioners — ordered by the President in the declared exercise of his powers as Commander in Chief of the Army in time of war and of grave public danger — are not to be set aside by the courts without the clear conviction that they are in conflict with the Constitution or laws of Congress constitutionally enacted.

Congress and the President, like the courts, possess no power not derived from the Constitution. But one of the objects of the Constitution, as declared by its preamble, is to "provide for the common defence." As a means to that end the Constitution gives to Congress the power to "provide for the common Defence," Art. I, §8, cl. 1; "To raise and support Armies," "To provide and maintain a Navy," Art. I, §8, cls. 12, 13; and "To make Rules for the Government and Regulation of the land and naval Forces," Art. I, §8, cl. 14. Congress is given authority "To declare War, grant Letters of Marque and Reprisal, and make Rules concerning Captures on Land and Water," Art. I, §8, cl. 11; and "To define and punish Piracies and Felonies committed on the high Seas, and Offenses against the Law of Nations," Art. I, §8, cl. 10. And finally the Constitution authorizes Congress "To make all Laws which shall be necessary and proper for carrying into Execution the foregoing Powers, and all other Powers vested by this Constitution in the Government of the United States, or in any Department or Officer thereof." Art. I, §8, cl. 18.

The Constitution confers on the President the "executive Power," Art II, §1, cl. 1, and imposes on him the duty to "take Care that the Laws be faithfully executed." Art. II, §3. It makes him the Commander in Chief of the Army and Navy, Art. II, §2, cl. 1, and empowers him to appoint and commission officers of the United States. Art. H, §3, cl. 1.

By the Articles of War, Congress has provided rules for the government of the Army. It has provided for the trial and punishment, by courts martial, of violations of the Articles by members of the armed forces and by specified classes of persons associated or serving with the Army. Arts. 1, 2. But the Articles also recognize the "military commission" appointed by military command as an appropriate tribunal for the trial and punishment of offenses against the law of war not ordinarily tried by court martial. *See* Arts. 12, 15. Articles 38 and 46 authorize the President, with certain limitations, to prescribe the procedure for military commissions. Articles 81 and 82 authorize trial, either by court martial or military commission, of those charged with relieving, harboring or corresponding with the enemy and those charged with spying. And Article 15 declares that "the provisions of these articles conferring jurisdiction upon courts-martial shall not be construed as depriving military commission . . . or other military tribunals of concurrent jurisdiction in respect of offenders or offenses that by statute or by the law of war may be triable by such military commissions . . . or other military tribunals." Article 2 includes among those persons subject to military law the personnel of our own military establishment. But this, as Article 12 provides, does not exclude from that class "any other person who by the law of war is subject to trial by military tribunals" and who under Article 12 may be tried by court martial or under Article 15 by military commission.

From the very beginning of its history this Court has recognized and applied the law of war as including that part of the law of nations which prescribes, for the conduct of war, the status, rights and duties of enemy nations as well as of enemy individuals. By the Articles of War, and especially Article 15, Congress has explicitly provided, so far as it may constitutionally do so, that military tribunals shall have jurisdiction to try offenders or offenses against the law of war in appropriate cases. Congress, in addition to making rules for the government of our Armed Forces, has thus exercised its authority to define and punish offenses against the law of nations by sanctioning, within constitutional limitations, the jurisdiction of military commissions to try persons for offenses which, according to the rules and precepts of the law of nations, and more particularly the law of war, are cognizable by such tribunals. And the President, as Commander in Chief, by his Proclamation in time of war has invoked that law. By his Order creating the present Commission he has undertaken to exercise the authority conferred upon him by Congress, and also such authority as the Constitution itself gives the Commander in Chief, to direct the performance of those functions which may constitutionally be performed by the military arm of the nation in time of war.

An important incident to the conduct of war is the adoption of measures by the military command not only to repel and defeat the enemy, but to seize and subject to disciplinary measures those enemies who in their attempt to thwart or impede our military effort have violated the law of war. It is unnecessary for present purposes to determine to what extent the President as Commander in Chief has constitutional power to create military commissions without the support of Congressional legislation. For here Congress has authorized trial of offenses against the law of war before such commissions. We are concerned only with the question whether it is within the constitutional power of the national government to place petitioners upon trial before a military commission for the offenses with which they are charged. We must therefore first inquire whether any of the acts charged is an offense against the law of war cognizable before a military tribunal, and if so whether the Constitution prohibits the trial. We may assume that there are acts regarded in other countries, or by some writers on international law, as offenses against the law of war which would not be triable by military tribunal here, either because they are not recognized by our courts as violations of the law of war or because they are of that class of offenses constitutionally triable only by a jury. It was upon such grounds that the Court denied the right to proceed by military tribunal in *Ex parte Milligan*, supra. But as we shall show, these petitioners were charged with an offense against the law of war which the Constitution does not require to be tried by jury.

It is no objection that Congress in providing for the trial of such offenses has not itself undertaken to codify that branch of international law or to mark its precise boundaries, or to enumerate or define by statute all the acts which that law condemns. An Act of Congress punishing "the crime of piracy as defined by the law of nations" is an appropriate exercise of its constitutional authority, Art. I, §8, cl. 10, "to define and punish" the offense since it has adopted by reference the sufficiently precise definition of international law. Similarly by the reference in the 15th Article of War to "offenders or offenses that . . . by the law of war may be triable by such military commissions," Congress has incorporated by reference, as within the jurisdiction of military commissions, all offenses which are defined as such by the law of war and which may constitutionally be included within that jurisdiction. Congress had the choice of crystallizing in permanent form and in minute detail every offense against the law of war, or of adopting the system of common law applied by military tribunals so far as it should be recognized and deemed applicable by the courts. It chose the latter course.

By universal agreement and practice the law of war draws a distinction between the armed forces and the peaceful populations of belligerent nations and also between those who are lawful and unlawful combatants. Lawful combatants are subject to capture and detention as prisoners of war by opposing military forces. Unlawful combatants are likewise subject to capture and detention, but in addition they are subject to trial and punishment by military tribunals for acts which render their belligerency unlawful. The spy who secretly and without uniform passes the military lines of a belligerent in time of war, seeking to gather military information and communicate it to the enemy, or an enemy combatant who without uniform comes secretly through the lines for the purpose of waging war by destruction of life or property, are familiar examples of belligerents who are generally deemed not to be entitled to the status of prisoners of war, but to be offenders against the law of war subject to trial and punishment by military tribunals.

Such was the practice of our own military authorities before the adoption of the Constitution, and during the Mexican and Civil Wars. During the Civil War the military commission was extensively used for the trial of offenses against the law of war. By a long course of practical administrative construction by its military authorities, our Government has likewise recognized that those who during time of war pass surreptitiously from enemy territory into our own, discarding their uniforms upon entry, for the commission of hostile acts involving destruction of life or property, have the status of unlawful combatants punishable as such by military commission. This precept of the law of war has been so recognized in practice both here and abroad, and has so generally been accepted as valid by authorities on international law that we think it must be regarded as a rule or principle of the law of war recognized by this Government by its enactment of the Fifteenth Article of War.

Specification 1 of the First charge is sufficient to charge all the petitioners with the offense of unlawful belligerency, trial of which is within the jurisdiction of the Commission, and the admitted facts affirmatively show that the charge is not merely colorable or without foundation. Specification 1 states that petitioners "being enemies of the United States and acting for . . . the German Reich, a belligerent enemy nation, secretly and covertly passed, in civilian dress, contrary to the law of war, through the military and naval lines and defenses of the United States . . . and went behind such lines, contrary to the law of war, in civilian dress . . . for the purpose of committing . . . hostile acts, and, in particular, to destroy certain war industries, war utilities and war materials within the United States."

This specification so plainly alleges violation of the law of war as to require but brief discussion of petitioners' contentions. As we have seen, entry upon our territory in time of war by enemy belligerents, including those acting under the direction of the armed forces of the enemy, for the purpose of destroying property used or useful in prosecuting the war, is a hostile and war-like act. It subjects those who participate in it without uniform to the punishment prescribed by the law of war for unlawful belligerents. It is without significance that petitioners were not alleged to have borne conventional weapons or that their proposed hostile acts did not necessarily contemplate collision with the Armed Forces of the United States. Paragraphs 351 and 352 of the Rules of Land Warfare, already referred to, plainly contemplate that the hostile acts and purposes for which unlawful belligerents may be punished are not limited to assaults on the Armed Forces of the United States. Modern warfare is directed at the destruction of enemy war supplies and the implements of their production and transportation quite as much as at the armed forces. Every consideration which makes the unlawful belligerent punishable is equally applicable whether his objective is the one or the other. The law of war cannot rightly treat those agents of enemy armies who enter our territory, armed with explosives intended for the destruction of war industries and supplies, as any the less belligerent enemies than are agents similarly entering for the purpose of destroying fortified places or our Armed Forces. By passing our boundaries for such purposes without uniform or other emblem signifying their belligerent status, or by discarding that means of identification after entry, such enemies become unlawful belligerents subject to trial and punishment.

Citizenship in the United States of an enemy belligerent does not relieve him from the consequences of a belligerency which is unlawful because in violation of the law of war. Citizens who associate themselves with the military arm of the enemy government, and with its aid, guidance and direction enter this country bent on hostile acts are enemy belligerents within the meaning of the Hague Convention and the law of war. It is as an enemy belligerent that petitioner Haupt is charged with entering the United States, and unlawful belligerency is the gravamen of the offense of which he is accused.

Nor are petitioners any the less belligerents if, as they argue, they have not actually committed or attempted to commit any act of depredation or entered the theatre or zone of active military operations. The argument leaves out of account the nature of the offense which the Government charges and which the Act of Congress, by incorporating the law of war, punishes. It is that each petitioner, in circumstances which gave him the status of an enemy belligerent, passed our military and naval lines and defenses or went behind those lines, in civilian dress and with hostile purpose. The offense was complete when with that purpose they entered — or, having so entered, they remained upon — our territory in time of war without uniform or other appropriate means of identification. For that reason, even when committed by a citizen, the offense is distinct from the crime of treason defined in Article III, §3 of the Constitution, since the absence of uniform essential to one is irrelevant to the other.

But petitioners insist that even if the offenses with which they are charged are offenses against the law of war, their trial is subject to the requirement of the Fifth

Amendment that no person shall be held to answer for a capital or otherwise infamous crime unless on a presentment or indictment of a grand jury, and that such trials by Article III, §2, and the Sixth Amendment must be by jury in a civil court. Before the Amendments, §2 of Article III, the Judiciary Article, had provided: "The Trial of all Crimes, except in Cases of Impeachment, shall be by Jury," and had directed that "such Trial shall be held in the State where the said Crimes shall have been committed."

Presentment by a grand jury and trial by a jury of the vicinage where the crime was committed were at the time of the adoption of the Constitution familiar parts of the machinery for criminal trials in the civil courts. But they were procedures unknown to military tribunals, which are not courts in the sense of the Judiciary Article, and which in the natural course of events are usually called upon to function under conditions precluding resort to such procedures. As this Court has often recognized, it was not the purpose or effect of §2 of Article III, read in the light of the common law, to enlarge the then existing right to a jury trial. The object was to preserve unimpaired trial by jury in all those cases in which it had been recognized by the common law and in all cases of a like nature as they might arise in the future, but not to bring within the sweep of the guaranty those cases in which it was then well understood that a jury trial could not be demanded as of right. The Fifth and Sixth Amendments, while guaranteeing the continuance of certain incidents of trial by jury which Article III, §2 had left unmentioned, did not enlarge the right to jury trial as it had been established by that Article.

All these are instances of offenses committed against the United States, for which a penalty is imposed, but they are not deemed to be within the provisions of the Fifth and Sixth Amendments relating to "crimes" and "criminal prosecutions." In the light of this long-continued and consistent interpretation we must conclude that §2 of Article III and the Fifth and Sixth Amendments cannot be taken to have extended the right to demand a jury to trials by military commission, or to have required that offenses against the law of war not triable by jury at common law be tried only in the civil courts. It has not hitherto been challenged, and so far as we are advised it has never been suggested in the very extensive literature of the subject that an alien spy, in time of war, could not be tried by military tribunal without a jury.

The exception from the Amendments of "cases arising in the land or naval forces" was not aimed at trials by military tribunals, without a jury, of such offenses against the law of war. Its objective was quite different — to authorize the trial by court martial of the members of our Armed Forces for all that class of crimes which under the Fifth and Sixth Amendments might otherwise have been deemed triable in the civil courts. The cases mentioned in the exception are not restricted to those involving offenses against the law of war alone, but extend to trial of all offenses, including crimes which were of the class traditionally triable by jury at common law.

We cannot say that Congress in preparing the Fifth and Sixth Amendments intended to extend trial by jury to the cases of alien or citizen offenders against the law of war otherwise triable by military commission, while withholding it from members of our own armed forces charged with infractions of the Articles of War punishable by death. It is equally inadmissible to construe the Amendments — whose primary purpose was to continue unimpaired present-ment by grand jury and trial by petit jury in all those cases in which they had been customary — as either abolishing all trials by military tribunals, save those of the personnel of our own armed forces, or what in effect comes to the same thing, as imposing on all such tribunals the necessity of proceeding against unlawful enemy belligerents only on presentment and trial by jury. We con-clude that the Fifth and Sixth Amendments did not restrict whatever authority was conferred by the Constitution to try offenses against the law of war by mili-tary commission, and that petitioners, charged with such an offense not required to be tried by jury at common law, were lawfully placed on trial by the Commis-sion without a jury.

Accordingly, we conclude that Charge I, on which petitioners were detained for trial by the Military Commission, alleged an offense which the President is authorized to order tried by military commission; that his Order convening the Commission was a lawful order and that the Commission was lawfully consti-tuted; that the petitioners were held in lawful custody and did not show cause for their discharge.

In June 2006, in Hamdan v. Rumsfeld, 548 U.S. 557 (2006), the Court ruled, by a 5-3 margin, that the military tribunals provided pursuant to an Executive Order by President Bush were invalid. The Court found that the procedures vio-lated the Uniform Code of Military Justice and the Geneva Accords. The Court did not consider the constitutional issues raised. Congress responded by enacting the Military Commission Act of 2006. The procedures ordered under it have not yet been ruled upon by the Supreme Court, though the Court invalidated the restrictions on habeas corpus in the Act in Boumediene v. Bush, above.

E. Impeachment

The ultimate check on presidential power is impeachment and removal. Article II, §4 of the Constitution provides: "The President, Vice President and all civil Officers of the United States, shall be removed from Office on Impeachment for, and Conviction of, Treason, Bribery, or other high Crimes and Misdemeanors." Article I, §2 provides that the House of Representatives has the sole power to impeach. If there is an impeachment by the House, then a trial is held in the Sen-ate. Article I, §3 gives the Senate the sole power to try impeachments and pre-scribes that "no Person shall be convicted without the Concurrence of two thirds of the Members present."

Two major issues remain unresolved concerning these provisions. First, what are "high Crimes and Misdemeanors"? At one end of the spectrum is the view that these are limited to acts that violate the criminal law and that can be deemed a serious threat to society.[19] At the opposite pole is the statement of Gerald Ford, who was a Congressman from Michigan when he proposed the impeachment of Supreme Court Justice William Douglas largely because of Douglas's liberal views: "[A]n impeachable offense is whatever a majority of the House of Representatives considers [it] to be."[20]

Second, what procedures must be followed when there is an impeachment and removal proceeding? For example, is it permissible for the Senate to have a committee hear the evidence and make a recommendation to the entire body, or must the Senate sit as a tribunal to hear the case?

There is no definitive answer to either of these questions.[21] There is no Supreme Court case addressing either. In fact, none is likely in the future because the Supreme Court has held that challenges to the impeachment and removal process pose non-justiciable political questions.[22]

Although there are not judicial precedents to guide Congress, there is historical experience. Three times there have been serious efforts to impeach the President, and two Presidents have been impeached.

Andrew Johnson was the first President to be impeached. He was impeached in 1867 for firing Secretary of War Edwin Stanton in violation of the Tenure in Office Act.[23] After the end of the Civil War, Congress became increasingly frustrated with Johnson, a Southerner from Tennessee, presiding over Reconstruction. Congress adopted the Tenure in Office Act of 1867 to keep Johnson from firing Lincoln's cabinet. The Act declared that such a firing would be deemed a "high misdemeanor," indicating that Congress was considering the possibility of impeachment from the outset. The Supreme Court subsequently held that the Tenure in Office Act violated separation of powers.[24] Nonetheless, the House impeached and Johnson avoided removal by just one vote in the Senate.

The second serious attempt to impeach a President occurred in 1974 and was directed against Richard Nixon. The House Judiciary Committee voted three Articles of Impeachment. One was for obstruction of justice in connection with the Watergate cover-up; one was for using government agencies, such as the FBI and the IRS, for political advantages; and the final article was for failing to comply with subpoenas. Before the matter could be considered by the entire House, Nixon resigned.

---

[19] See Charles L. Black, Jr., Impeachment: A Handbook 39-40 (1974) (a violation of the criminal law is not essential, but a good indicator of a high crime or misdemeanor).

[20] 116 Cong. Rec. 11913 (1970).

[21] For an excellent scholarly treatment of these and other issues surrounding impeachment, see Michael J. Gerhardt, The Federal Impeachment Process (2d ed. 2000).

[22] See Nixon v. United States, 506 U.S. 224 (1993) (dismissing as a political question a suit brought by federal district court Judge Walter Nixon objecting to the Senate assigning a committee the responsibility of hearing the evidence against him following impeachment by the House of Representatives).

[23] See, e.g., Michael Les Benedict, The Impeachment and Trial of Andrew Johnson (1973); Milton Lomask, Andrew Johnson: President on Trial (1973); Gene Smith, High Crimes and Misdemeanors: The Impeachment and Trial of Andrew Johnson (1977); Gerhardt, supra note 21, at 10 n.30.

[24] Myers v. United States, 272 U.S. 52 (1926) (included earlier in this chapter).

Most recently, of course, President Bill Clinton was impeached by the House of Representatives in 1998, but the Senate did not convict him. A short version of a long story begins after the Supreme Court decided Clinton v. Jones, above, and allowed Paula Jones's civil suit against Bill Clinton to proceed. The United States District Court then allowed Jones's attorney to depose President Clinton and permitted questions to be asked about Clinton's other sexual relationships.

Monica Lewinsky, a former White House aide, had described to her friend Linda Tripp a sexual relationship that Lewinsky had with the President that included many phone calls, private meetings, phone sex, and oral sex. Tripp informed Jones's lawyers of this, and on the eve of Mr. Clinton's deposition in the *Jones* case, Mrs. Tripp secretly met for hours with lawyers for Ms. Jones and briefed them about Ms. Lewinsky.

On January 17, 1998, Clinton's deposition was taken and he was asked about Ms. Lewinsky. Below is the key part of Clinton's statement during the deposition:

Q.   Did you have an extramarital sexual affair with Monica Lewinsky?
Clinton: No.
Q.   If she told someone that she had a sexual affair with you beginning in November of   1995, would that be a lie?
Clinton: It's certainly not the truth. It would not be the truth.
Q.   I think I used the term "sexual affair." And so the record is completely clear, have you ever had sexual relations with Monica Lewinsky, as that term is defined in   Deposition Exhibit 1, as modified by the Court?
Bennett: I object because I don't know that he can remember —
J. Wright: Well, it's real short. He can — I will permit the question and you may show the witness definition number one.
Clinton: I have never had sexual relations with Monica Lewinsky. I've never had an affair with her.

The possibility that the President had committed perjury was brought to the attention of Attorney General Janet Reno. She authorized Independent Counsel Kenneth Starr, who was investigating the Whitewater land scandal for possible presidential involvement, to broaden his investigation to consider whether the President had committed perjury or obstructed justice. Starr conducted a lengthy investigation, including having the President testify before a grand jury.

On August 17, 1998, Clinton testified before the grand jury. His testimony later became the basis for a separate accusation of perjury. In his grand jury testimony, President Clinton refused to answer any specific questions of a sexual nature about his relationship with Monica Lewinsky; instead, he read and referred to the following prepared statement:

When I was alone with Ms. Lewinsky on certain occasions in early 1996 and once in early 1997, I engaged in conduct that was wrong. These encounters did not consist of sexual intercourse; they did not constitute "sexual relations" as I understood that term to be defined at my January 17, 1998, deposition; but they did involve inappropriate intimate contact. These inappropriate encounters ended, at my insistence, in early 1997. . . .

While I will provide the grand jury whatever other information I can, because of privacy considerations affecting my family, myself, and others, and in an effort to preserve the dignity of the Office I hold, this is all I will say about the specifics of these particular matters.

President Clinton did engage in extended hypothetical and definitional discussions as to what would or would not constitute sexual relations or fall within his definition of the term "sexual relations." The following was the most important exchange, with Clinton answering the questions:

A.   You are free to infer that my testimony is that I did not have sexual relations, as I understood this term to be defined.
Q.   Including touching her breast, kissing her breast, or touching her genitalia?
A.   That's correct.

In the fall of 1998, Independent Counsel Kenneth Starr released a very detailed report documenting the relationship between Monica Lewinsky and Bill Clinton. The report described the progress of their relationship, many phone calls over a long period of time, sexual touchings, and oral sex. The House Judiciary Committee then conducted impeachment hearings and voted four Articles of Impeachment against the President. The vote in the House Judiciary Committee was entirely along partisan lines, with all of the Republican members voting for impeachment and the Democrats voting against.

The first article of the Articles of Impeachment stated:

In his conduct while President of the United States, William Jefferson Clinton, in violation of his constitutional oath faithfully to execute the office of President of the United States and, to the best of his ability, preserve, protect, and defend the Constitution of the United States . . . has willfully corrupted and manipulated the judicial process of the United States for his personal gain and exoneration, impeding the administration of justice [through his perjury before the grand jury concerning this prior relationship with an intern and his prior sworn testimony]. . . .

In doing this, William Jefferson Clinton has undermined the integrity of his office, has brought disrepute on the Presidency, has betrayed his trust as President, and has acted in a manner subversive of the rule of law and justice, to the manifest injury of the people of the United States.[25]

Article Two stated:

In his conduct while President of the United States, William Jefferson Clinton, in violation of his constitutional oath faithfully to execute the office of President of the United States and, to the best of his ability, preserve, protect, and defend the Constitution of the United States, and in violation of his constitutional duty to take care that the laws be faithfully executed, has willfully corrupted and manipulated the

---

[25] H.R. Res. 611, 105th Cong. (1998) (enacted), reprinted in 144 Cong. Rec. H11, 11774 (daily ed. Dec. 18, 1998). The second paragraph was repeated in each of the four Articles of Impeachment.

judicial process of the United States for his personal gain and exoneration, impeding the administration of justice [through acts of deception and perjury]. . . . [26]

Article Three stated:

In his conduct while President of the United States, William Jefferson Clinton, in violation of his constitutional oath faithfully to execute the office of President of the United States and, to the best of his ability, preserve, protect, and defend the Constitution of the United States, and in violation of his constitutional duty to take care that the laws be faithfully executed, has prevented, obstructed, and impeded the administration of justice, and has to that end engaged personally, and through his subordinates and agents, in a course of conduct or scheme designed to delay, impede, cover up, and conceal the existence of evidence and testimony related to a Federal civil rights action brought against him in a duly instituted judicial proceeding. . . . [27]

Article Four stated:

Using the powers and influence of the office of President of the United States, William Jefferson Clinton, in violation of his constitutional oath faithfully to execute the office of President of the United States and, to the best of his ability, preserve, protect, and defend the Constitution of the United States, and in disregard of his constitutional duty to take care that the laws be faithfully executed, has engaged in conduct that resulted in misuse and abuse of his high office, impaired the due and proper administration of justice and the conduct of lawful inquiries, and contravened the authority of the legislative branch and the truth seeking purpose of a coordinate investigative proceeding, in that, as President, William Jefferson Clinton refused and failed to respond to certain written requests for admission and willfully made perjurious, false and misleading sworn statements in response to certain written requests for admission propounded to him as part of the impeachment inquiry. . . . [28]

On December 19, 1998, the House of Representatives passed two Articles of Impeachment. The first article passed by a vote of 228-206, with five Democrats defecting to vote for impeachment and five Republicans defecting to vote against impeachment. Article Three passed by a vote of 221-212, with five Democrats defecting to vote for impeachment and five Republicans defecting to vote against impeachment. On Article Two, alleging perjury in the civil deposition, 28 Republicans crossed party lines to vote against the article, defeating the article 205-229. On Article Four, alleging perjury in the President's answer to Congress, 81 Republicans crossed party lines in favor of the President, while one Democrat crossed party lines in favor of Article Four, for a final vote of 148-285.

[26] Id., reprinted in 144 Cong. Rec. H11, 11774 (daily ed. Dec. 18, 1998).
[27] Id., reprinted in 144 Cong. Rec. H11, 11774-11775 (daily ed. Dec. 18, 1998).
[28] Id., reprinted in 144 Cong. Rec. H11, 11774-11775 (daily ed. Dec. 18, 1998).

The U.S. Senate then conducted a trial of President Clinton on the two Articles of Impeachment. The Chief Justice of the United States, as prescribed by the Constitution, presided. In accord with Senate rules, the Senators' deliberations were entirely in closed session. Neither Article of Impeachment received the two-thirds vote needed to remove the President.

———

It is unclear what lesson is to be learned from any of these experiences concerning what constitutes "high crimes and misdemeanors." All of these instances were highly partisan and all raise the fundamental question of what should be regarded as an impeachable offense.

THE APPOINTMENT POWER

Article II, §2 provides that the President "shall nominate, and by and with the Advice and Consent of the Senate, shall appoint Ambassadors, other public Ministers and Consuls, Judges of the Supreme Court, and all other Officers of the United States, whose Appointments are not herein otherwise provided for, and which shall be established by Law: but the Congress may by Law vest the Appointment of such inferior Officers, as they think proper, in the President alone, to the Courts of Law, or in the Heads of Departments."

The key constitutional issue here concerns who may possess the appointment power. Morrison v. Olson is the leading case dealing with this issue.

Alexia Morrison, Independent Counsel v. Theodore B. Olson

487 U.S. 654 (1988)

Chief Justice REHNQUIST delivered the opinion of the Court.

This case presents us with a challenge to the independent counsel provisions of the Ethics in Government Act of 1978. We hold today that these provisions of the Act do not violate the Appointments Clause of the Constitution, the limitations of Article III, nor do they impermissibly interfere with the President's authority under Article II in violation of the constitutional principle of separation of powers.

I

Briefly stated, Title VI of the Ethics in Government Act allows for the appointment of an "independent counsel" to investigate and, if appropriate, prosecute certain high-ranking Government officials for violations of federal criminal laws. The Act requires the Attorney General, upon receipt of information that he determines is "sufficient to constitute grounds to investigate whether any person [covered by the Act] may have violated any Federal criminal law," to conduct a preliminary investigation of the matter. When the Attorney General has completed this investigation, or 90 days has elapsed, he is required to report to a special court (the Special Division) created by the Act "for the purpose of appointing independent counsels." If the Attorney General determines that "there are no reasonable grounds to believe that further investigation is warranted," then he must notify the Special Division of this result. In such a case, "the division of the court shall have no power to appoint an independent counsel."

If, however, the Attorney General has determined that there are "reasonable grounds to believe that further investigation or prosecution is warranted," then he "shall apply to the division of the court for the appointment of an independent counsel." Upon receiving this application, the Special Division "shall appoint an appropriate independent counsel and shall define that independent counsel's prosecutorial jurisdiction."

With respect to all matters within the independent counsel's jurisdiction, the Act grants the counsel "full power and independent authority to exercise all investigative and prosecutorial functions and powers of the Department of Justice, the Attorney General, and any other officer or employee of the Department of Justice." Under §594(a)(9), the counsel's powers include "initiating and conducting prosecutions in any court of competent jurisdiction, framing and signing indictments, filing informations, and handling all aspects of any case, in the name of the United States."

Two statutory provisions govern the length of an independent counsel's tenure in office. The first defines the procedure for removing an independent counsel. Section 596(a)(1) provides: "An independent counsel appointed under this chapter may be removed from office, other than by impeachment and conviction, only by the personal action of the Attorney General and only for good cause, physical disability, mental incapacity, or any other condition that substantially impairs the performance of such independent counsel's duties."

If an independent counsel is removed pursuant to this section, the Attorney General is required to submit a report to both the Special Division and the Judiciary Committees of the Senate and the House "specifying the facts found and the ultimate grounds for such removal." Under the current version of the Act, an independent counsel can obtain judicial review of the Attorney General's action by filing a civil action in the United States District Court for the District of Columbia. The reviewing court is authorized to grant reinstatement or "other appropriate relief."

The other provision governing the tenure of the independent counsel defines the procedures for "terminating" the counsel's office. Under §596(b)(1), the office of an independent counsel terminates when he or she notifies the Attorney General that he or she has completed or substantially completed any investigations or prosecutions undertaken pursuant to the Act. In addition, the Special Division, acting either on its own or on the suggestion of the Attorney General, may terminate the office of an independent counsel at any time if it finds that "the investigation of all matters within the prosecutorial jurisdiction of such independent counsel . . . have been completed or so substantially completed that it would be appropriate for the Department of Justice to complete such investigations and prosecutions."

Finally, the Act provides for congressional oversight of the activities of independent counsel. An independent counsel may from time to time send Congress statements or reports on his or her activities.

[II]

The Appointments Clause of Article II reads as follows:

> "[The President] shall nominate, and by and with the Advice and Consent of the Senate, shall appoint Ambassadors, other public Ministers and Consuls, Judges of the Supreme Court, and all other Officers of the United States, whose Appointments are not herein otherwise provided for, and which shall be established by Law: but the Congress may by Law vest the Appointment of such inferior Officers, as they think proper, in the President alone, in the Courts of Law, or in the Heads of Departments." U.S. Const., Art. II, §2, cl. 2.

The parties do not dispute that "[t]he Constitution for purposes of appointment . . . divides all its officers into two classes." As we stated in Buckley v. Valeo (1976): "[P]rincipal officers are selected by the President with the advice and consent of the Senate. Inferior officers Congress may allow to be appointed by the President alone, by the heads of departments, or by the Judiciary." The initial question is, accordingly, whether appellant is an "inferior" or a "principal" officer. If she is the latter, as the Court of Appeals concluded, then the Act is in violation of the Appointments Clause.

The line between "inferior" and "principal" officers is one that is far from clear, and the framers provided little guidance into where it should be drawn. We need not attempt here to decide exactly where the line falls between the two types of officers, because in our view appellant clearly falls on the "inferior officer" side of that line. Several factors lead to this conclusion.

First, appellant is subject to removal by a higher Executive Branch official. Although appellant may not be "subordinate" to the Attorney General (and the President) insofar as she possesses a degree of independent discretion to exercise the powers delegated to her under the Act, the fact that she can be removed by the Attorney General indicates that she is to some degree "inferior" in rank and authority. Second, appellant is empowered by the Act to perform only certain, limited duties. An independent counsel's role is restricted primarily to investigation and, if appropriate, prosecution for certain federal crimes. Admittedly, the Act delegates to appellant "full power and independent authority to exercise all investigative and prosecutorial functions and powers of the Department of Justice," but this grant of authority does not include any authority to formulate policy for the Government or the Executive Branch, nor does it give appellant any administrative duties outside of those necessary to operate her office. The Act specifically provides that in policy matters appellant is to comply to the extent possible with the policies of the Department.

Third, appellant's office is limited in jurisdiction. Not only is the Act itself restricted in applicability to certain federal officials suspected of certain serious federal crimes, but an independent counsel can only act within the scope of the jurisdiction that has been granted by the Special Division pursuant to a request by the Attorney General. Finally, appellant's office is limited in tenure. There is concededly no time limit on the appointment of a particular counsel. Nonetheless, the office of independent counsel is "temporary" in the sense that an independent counsel is appointed essentially to accomplish a single task, and when that task is over the office is terminated, either by the counsel herself or by action of the Special Division. Unlike other prosecutors, appellant has no ongoing responsibilities that extend beyond the accomplishment of the mission that she was appointed for and authorized by the Special Division to undertake. In our view, these factors relating to the "ideas of tenure, duration . . . and duties" of the independent counsel are sufficient to establish that appellant is an "inferior" officer in the constitutional sense.

Justice SCALIA, dissenting.

That is what this suit is about. Power. The allocation of power among Congress, the President, and the courts in such fashion as to preserve the equilibrium the Constitution sought to establish — so that "a gradual concentration of the several powers in the same department," Federalist No. 51 (J. Madison), can effectively be resisted. Frequently an issue of this sort will come before the Court clad, so to speak, in sheep's clothing: the potential of the asserted principle to effect important change in the equilibrium of power is not immediately evident, and must be discerned by a careful and perceptive analysis. But this wolf comes as a wolf.

To repeat, Article II, §1, cl. 1, of the Constitution provides: "The executive Power shall be vested in a President of the United States."

This does not mean some of the executive power, but all of the executive power. It seems to me, therefore, that the decision of the Court of Appeals invalidating the present statute must be upheld on fundamental separation-of-powers principles if the following two questions are answered affirmatively: (1) Is the conduct of a criminal prosecution (and of an investigation to decide whether to prosecute) the exercise of purely executive power? (2) Does the statute deprive the President of the United States of exclusive control over the exercise of that power? Surprising to say, the Court appears to concede an affirmative answer to both questions, but seeks to avoid the inevitable conclusion that since the statute vests some purely executive power in a person who is not the President of the United States it is void.

The Court concedes that "[t]here is no real dispute that the functions performed by the independent counsel are 'executive,'" though it qualifies that concession by adding "in the sense that they are law enforcement functions that typically have been undertaken by officials within the Executive Branch."

The qualifier adds nothing but atmosphere. In what other sense can one identify "the executive Power" that is supposed to be vested in the President (unless it includes everything the Executive Branch is given to do) except by reference to what has always and everywhere — if conducted by government at all — been conducted never by the legislature, never by the courts, and always by the executive. There is no possible doubt that the independent counsel's functions fit this description. She is vested with the "full power and independent authority to exercise all investigative and prosecutorial functions and powers of the Department of Justice [and] the Attorney General." Governmental investigation and prosecution of crimes is a quintessentially executive function.

As for the second question, whether the statute before us deprives the President of exclusive control over that quintessentially executive activity: The Court does not, and could not possibly, assert that it does not. That is indeed the whole object of the statute. Instead, the Court points out that the President, through his Attorney General, has at least some control. That concession is alone enough to invalidate the statute, but I cannot refrain from pointing out that the Court greatly exaggerates the extent of that "some" Presidential control. "Most importan[t]" among these controls, the Court asserts, is the Attorney General's "power to remove the counsel for 'good cause.'" This is somewhat like referring to shackles as an effective means of locomotion.

The utter incompatibility of the Court's approach with our constitutional traditions can be made more clear, perhaps, by applying it to the powers of the other two branches. Is it conceivable that if Congress passed a statute depriving itself of less than full and entire control over some insignificant area of legislation, we would inquire whether the matter was "so central to the functioning of the Legislative Branch" as really to require complete control, or whether the statute gives Congress "sufficient control over the surrogate legislator to ensure that Congress is able to perform its constitutionally assigned duties"? Of course we would have none of that. Once we determined that a purely legislative power was at issue we would require it to be exercised, wholly and entirely, by Congress. Or to bring the point closer to home, consider a statute giving to non-Article III judges just a tiny bit of purely judicial power in a relatively insignificant field, with substantial control, though not total control, in the courts — perhaps "clear error" review, which would be a fair judicial equivalent of the Attorney General's "for cause" removal power here. Is there any doubt that we would not pause to inquire whether the matter was "so central to the functioning of the Judicial Branch" as really to require complete control, or whether we retained "sufficient control over the matters to be decided that we are able to perform our constitutionally assigned duties"? We would say that our "constitutionally assigned duties" include complete control over all exercises of the judicial power. We should say here that the President's constitutionally assigned duties include complete control over investigation and prosecution of violations of the law, and that the inexorable command of Article II is clear and definite: the executive power must be vested in the President of the United States.

Is it unthinkable that the President should have such exclusive power, even when alleged crimes by him or his close associates are at issue? No more so than that Congress should have the exclusive power of legislation, even when what is at issue is its own exemption from the burdens of certain laws. No more so than that this Court should have the exclusive power to pronounce the final decision on justiciable cases and controversies, even those pertaining to the constitutionality of a statute reducing the salaries of the Justices. A system of separate and coordinate powers necessarily involves an acceptance of exclusive power that can theoretically be abused. As we reiterate this very day, "[i]t is a truism that constitutional protections have costs." While the separation of powers may prevent us from righting every wrong, it does so in order to ensure that we do not lose liberty.

In sum, this statute does deprive the President of substantial control over the prosecutory functions performed by the independent counsel, and it does substantially affect the balance of powers. That the Court could possibly conclude otherwise demonstrates both the wisdom of our former constitutional system, in which the degree of reduced control and political impairment were irrelevant, since all purely executive power had to be in the President; and the folly of the new system of standardless judicial allocation of powers we adopt today.

The authority for creating an Independent Counsel, the Ethics in Government Act, expired in 1999. After the investigation of President Bill Clinton by Independent Counsel Kenneth Starr, described more fully in the last section of this chapter, Congress simply let the Act expire and did not renew the authority for the creation of an Independent Counsel. Some believe that this is a vindication for the views expressed by Justice Scalia in his dissent in Morrison v. Olson, while others contend that the expiration of the authority for an Independent Counsel is a serious mistake that will be regretted when there are future scandals involving the President or high-level executive officials.

The Court has imposed one important limit on who may possess the appointment power: The Court has held that Congress cannot give the appointment power to itself or to its officers. Article II specifies several possibilities as to who may possess the appointment power; Congress is not among them. In Buckley v. Valeo, 424 U.S. 1 (1976), the Court held unconstitutional a federal law that empowered the Speaker of the House of Representatives and the President Pro Tempore of the Senate to appoint four of the six members of the Federal Election Commission.

The Court emphasized the text of Article II, which specifies who may possess the appointment power. The Court said that under Article II, Congress could vest the appointment power for inferior offices in the President, the heads of departments, or the lower federal courts. The Speaker of the House and the President Pro Tem of the Senate are obviously none of these and therefore the Court found that they could not possess the appointment power.

THE REMOVAL POWER

There is no provision of the Constitution concerning the President's authority to remove executive branch officials. The principle that has emerged from the cases is that, in general, the President may remove executive officials unless removal is limited by statute. Congress, by statute, may limit removal both if it is an office where independence from the President is desirable, and if the law does not prohibit removal but, rather, limits removal to instances where good cause is shown.

No single case has clearly articulated this principle. Rather it comes from the experience of Andrew Johnson's impeachment and from five Supreme Court decisions that have considered the removal power, all reviewed below. The section then concludes by describing the law concerning the removal power that emerges from this authority.

THE IMPEACHMENT OF ANDREW JOHNSON

Consideration of the removal power must begin with an incident that was never directly reviewed in the courts: the impeachment of President Andrew Johnson for firing the Secretary of War in violation of a federal law that prohibited the removal.[29] After the assassination of President Abraham Lincoln, there was great consternation that a Southerner, Andrew Johnson from Tennessee, was the President at the end of the Civil War. The perception was that Johnson's sympathies were with the South and that he was obstructing reconstruction and the North's claiming the benefits of its victory. Congress passed the Tenure in Office Act of 1867 to prevent him from removing key members of the cabinet.

Secretary of War Edwin Stanton openly challenged the President's authority and Johnson fired Stanton, even though that violated the Tenure in Office Act. The House of Representatives voted Articles of Impeachment based almost entirely on this removal. The vote in the Senate, however, was one short of the two-thirds necessary for removal and thus Johnson completed his term as President.

MYERS v. UNITED STATES, 272 U.S. 52 (1926):   Chief Justice TAFT delivered the opinion of the Court.

---

[29] For a detailed description of the facts of this impeachment, *see* Raoul Berger, *Impeachment: The Constitutional Problem* (1973).

This case presents the question whether under the Constitution the President has the exclusive power of removing executive officers of the United States whom he has appointed by and with the advice and consent of the Senate.

Myers, appellant's intestate, was on July 21,1917, appointed by the President, by and with the advice and consent of the Senate, to be a postmaster of the first class at Portland, Or., for a term of four years. On January 20, 1920, Myers' resignation was demanded. He refused the demand. On February 2, 1920, he was removed from office by order of the Postmaster General, acting by direction of the President. He protested to the department against his removal, and continued to do so until the end of his term. He pursued no other occupation and drew compensation for no other service during the interval. On April 21, 1921, he brought this suit in the Court of Claims for his salary from the date of his removal, which, as claimed by supplemental petition filed after July 21, 1921, the end of his term, amounted to $8,838.71.

The question where the power of removal of executive officers appointed by the President by and with the advice and consent of the Senate was vested, was presented early in the first session of the First Congress. There is no express provision respecting removals in the Constitution, except as section 4 of article 2, above quoted, provides for removal from office by impeachment. The subject was not discussed in the Constitutional Convention.

The power to prevent the removal of an officer who has served under the President is different from the authority to consent to or reject his appointment. When a nomination is made, it may be presumed that the Senate is, or may become, as well advised as to the fitness of the nominee as the President, but in the nature of things the defects in ability or intelligence or loyalty in the administration of the laws of one who has served as an officer under the President are facts as to which the President, or his trusted subordinates, must be better informed than the Senate, and the power to remove him may therefore be regarded as confined for very sound and practical reasons, to the governmental authority which has administrative control. The power of removal is incident to the power of appointment, not to the power of advising and consenting to appointment, and when the grant of the executive power is enforced by the express mandate to take care that the laws be faithfully executed, it emphasizes the necessity for including within the executive power as conferred the exclusive power of removal.

It is reasonable to suppose also that had it been intended to give to Congress power to regulate or control removals in the manner suggested, it would have been included among the specifically enumerated legislative powers in Article 1, or in the specified limitations on the executive power in Article 2. The difference between the grant of legislative power under Article 1 to Congress which is limited to powers therein enumerated, and the more general grant of the executive power to the President under Article 2 is significant. The fact that the executive power is given in general terms strengthened by specific terms where emphasis is appropriate, and limited by direct expressions where limitation is needed, and that no express limit is placed on the power of removal by the executive is a convincing indication that none was intended.

HUMPHREY'S EXECUTOR v. UNITED STATES, 295 U.S. 602 (1935):   Justice SUTHERLAND delivered the opinion of the Court.

Plaintiff brought suit in the Court of Claims against the United States to recover a sum of money alleged to be due the deceased for salary as a Federal Trade Commissioner from October 8, 1933, when the President undertook to remove him from office, to the time of his death on February 14, 1934. William E. Humphrey, the decedent, on December 10, 1931, was nominated by President Hoover to succeed himself as a member of the Federal Trade Commission, and was confirmed by the United States Senate. He was duly commissioned for a term of seven years, expiring September 25, 1938; and, after taking the required oath of office, entered upon his duties. On July 25, 1933, President Roosevelt addressed a letter to the commissioner asking for his resignation, on the ground "that the aims and purposes of the Administration with respect to the work of the Commission can be carried out most effectively with personnel of my own selection," but disclaiming any reflection upon the commissioner personally or upon his services. The commissioner replied, asking time to consult his friends. The commissioner declined to resign; and on October 7, 1933, the President wrote him: "Effective as of this date you are hereby removed from the office of Commissioner of the Federal Trade Commission."

The provisions of section 1 of the Federal Trade Commission Act, stat[e] that "any commissioner may be removed by the President for inefficiency, neglect of duty, or malfeasance in office." The question first to be considered is whether, by the provisions of section 1 of the Federal Trade Commission Act already quoted, the President's power is limited to removal for the specific causes enumerated therein.

The commission is to be nonpartisan; and it must, from the very nature of its duties, act with entire impartiality. It is charged with the enforcement of no policy except the policy of the law. Its duties are neither political nor executive, but predominantly quasi judicial and quasi legislative. Like the Interstate Commerce Commission, its members are called upon to exercise the trained judgment of a body of experts "appointed by law and informed by experience."

The legislative reports in both houses of Congress clearly reflect the view that a fixed term was necessary to the effective and fair administration of the law. The debates in both houses demonstrate that the prevailing view was that the Commission was not to be "subject to anybody in the government but . . . only to the people of the United States"; free from "political domination or control" or the "probability or possibility of such a thing"; to be "separate and apart from any existing department of the government — not subject to the orders of the President."

Thus, the language of the act, the legislative reports, and the general purposes of the legislation as reflected by the debates, all combine to demonstrate the congressional intent to create a body of experts who shall gain experience by length of service; a body which shall be independent of executive authority, except in its selection, and free to exercise its judgment without the leave or hindrance of any other official or any department of the government. To the accomplishment of these purposes, it is clear that Congress was of opinion that length and certainty of tenure would vitally contribute. And to hold that, nevertheless, the members of the commission continue in office at the mere will of the President, might be to thwart, in large measure, the very ends which Congress sought to realize by definitely fixing the term of office.

To support its contention that the removal provision of section 1, as we have just construed it, is an unconstitutional interference with the executive power of the President, the government's chief reliance is Myers v. United States.

The office of a postmaster is so essentially unlike the office now involved that the decision in the Myers Case cannot be accepted as controlling our decision here. A postmaster is an executive officer restricted to the performance of executive functions. He is charged with no duty at all related to either the legislative or judicial power. The actual decision in the Myers Case finds support in the theory that such an officer is merely one of the units in the executive department and, hence, inherently subject to the exclusive and illimitable power of removal by the Chief Executive, whose subordinate and aid he is. It goes no farther; much less does it include an officer who occupies no place in the executive department and who exercises no part of the executive power vested by the Constitution in the President.

The Federal Trade Commission is an administrative body created by Congress to carry into effect legislative policies embodied in the statute in accordance with the legislative standard therein prescribed, and to perform other specified duties as a legislative or as a judicial aid. Such a body cannot in any proper sense be characterized as an arm or an eye of the executive. Its duties are performed without executive leave and, in the contemplation of the statute, must be free from executive control. In administering the provisions of the statute in respect of "unfair methods of competition," that is to say, in filling in and administering the details embodied by that general standard, the commission acts in part quasi legislatively and in part quasi judicially. In making investigations and reports thereon for the information of Congress under section 6, in aid of the legislative power, it acts as a legislative agency. Under section 7, which authorizes the commission to act as a master in chancery under rules prescribed by the court, it acts as an agency of the judiciary. To the extent that it exercises any executive function, as distinguished from executive power in the constitutional sense, it does so in the discharge and effectuation of its quasi legislative or quasi judicial powers, or as an agency of the legislative or judicial departments of the government.

We think it plain under the Constitution that illimitable power of removal is not possessed by the President in respect of officers of the character of those just named. The authority of Congress, in creating quasi legislative or quasi judicial agencies, to require them to act in discharge of their duties independently of executive control cannot well be doubted; and that authority includes, as an appropriate incident, power to fix the period during which they shall continue, and to forbid their removal except for cause in the meantime. For it is quite evident that one who holds his office only during the pleasure of another cannot be depended upon to maintain an attitude of independence against the latter's will.

WIENER v. UNITED STATES, 357 U.S. 349 (1958):   Justice FRANK-
FURTER delivered the opinion of the Court.

This is a suit for back pay, based on petitioner's alleged illegal removal as a
member of the War Claims Commission. The facts are not in dispute. By the
War Claims Act of 1948, Congress established that Commission with "jurisdiction to receive and adjudicate according to law," claims for compensating intern-
ees, prisoners of war, and religious organizations, who suffered personal injury or
property damage at the hands of the enemy in connection with World War II.
The Commission was to be composed of three persons, at least two of whom were
to be members of the bar, to be appointed by the President, by and with the advice
and consent of the Senate. The Commission was to wind up its affairs not later
than three years after the expiration of the time for filing claims. This limit on the
Commission's life was the mode by which the tenure of the Commissioners was
defined, and Congress made no provision for removal of a Commissioner.

Having been duly nominated by President Truman, the petitioner was confirmed on June 2, 1950, and took office on June 8, following. On his refusal to
heed a request for his resignation, he was, on December 10, 1953, removed by
President Eisenhower.

[T]he most reliable factor for drawing an inference regarding the President's
power of removal in our case is the nature of the function that Congress vested in
the War Claims Commission. What were the duties that Congress confided to
this Commission? And can the inference fairly be drawn from the failure of Congress to provide for removal that these Commissioners were to remain in office at
the will of the President? For such is the assertion of power on which petitioner's
removal must rest. The ground of President Eisenhower's removal of petitioner
was precisely the same as President Roosevelt's removal of Humphrey. Both Presidents desired to have Commissioners, one on the Federal Trade Commission, the
other on the War Claims Commission, "of my own selection." They wanted these
Commissioners to be their men. The terms of removal in the two cases are identical and express the assumption that the agencies of which the two Commissioners
were members were subject in the discharge of their duties to the control of the
Executive. An analysis of the Federal Trade Commission Act left this Court in no
doubt that such was not the conception of Congress in creating the Federal Trade
Commission. The terms of the War Claims Act of 1948 leave no doubt that such
was not the conception of Congress regarding the War Claims Commission.

The history of this legislation emphatically underlines this fact. The Commission was established as an adjudicating body with all the paraphernalia by which
legal claims are put to the test of proof, with finality of determination "not subject
to review by any other official of the United States or by any court by mandamus
or otherwise." The claims were to be "adjudicated according to law," that is, on
the merits of each claim, supported by evidence and governing legal considerations, by a body that was "entirely free from the control or coercive influence,
direct or indirect," Humphrey's Executor v. United States, either the Executive or
the Congress. If, as one must take for granted, the War Claims Act precluded the
President from influencing the Commission in passing on a particular claim, a
fortiori must it be inferred that Congress did not wish to have hang over the

Commission the Damocles' sword of removal by the President for no reason other than that he preferred to have on that Commission men of his own choosing.

For such is this case. We have not a removal for cause involving the rectitude of a member of an adjudicatory body, nor even a suspensory removal until the Senate could act upon it by confirming the appointment of a new Commissioner or otherwise dealing with the matter. Judging the matter in all the nakedness in which it is presented, namely, the claim that the President could remove a member of an adjudicatory body like the War Claims Commission merely because he wanted his own appointees on such a Commission, we are compelled to conclude that no such power is given to the President directly by the Constitution, and none is impliedly conferred upon him by statute simply because Congress said nothing about it. The philosophy of *Humphrey's Executor*, in its explicit language as well as its implications, precludes such a claim.

BOWSHER v. SYNAR, 478 U.S 714 (1986):   Chief Justice BURGER delivered the opinion of the Court.

The question presented by these appeals is whether the assignment by Congress to the Comptroller General of the United States of certain functions under the Balanced Budget and Emergency Deficit Control Act of 1985 violates the doctrine of separation of powers.

On December 12, 1985, the President signed into law the Balanced Budget and Emergency Deficit Control Act of 1985, popularly known as the "Gramm-Rudman-Hollings Act." The purpose of the Act is to eliminate the federal budget deficit. To that end, the Act sets a "maximum deficit amount" for federal spending for each of fiscal years 1986 through 1991. The size of that maximum deficit amount progressively reduces to zero in fiscal year 1991. If in any fiscal year the federal budget deficit exceeds the maximum deficit amount by more than a specified sum, the Act requires across-the-board cuts in federal spending to reach the targeted deficit level, with half of the cuts made to defense programs and the other half made to nondefense programs. The Act exempts certain priority programs from these cuts.

The Constitution does not contemplate an active role for Congress in the supervision of officers charged with the execution of the laws it enacts. We conclude that Congress cannot reserve for itself the power of removal of an officer charged with the execution of the laws except by impeachment. To permit the execution of the laws to be vested in an officer answerable only to Congress would, in practical terms, reserve in Congress control over the execution of the laws.

To permit an officer controlled by Congress to execute the laws would be, in essence, to permit a congressional veto. Congress could simply remove, or threaten to remove, an officer for executing the laws in any fashion found to be unsatisfactory to Congress. This kind of congressional control over the execution of the laws, *Chadha* makes clear, is constitutionally impermissible.

The dangers of congressional usurpation of Executive Branch functions have long been recognized. "[T]he debates of the Constitutional Convention, and the Federalist Papers, are replete with expressions of fear that the Legislative Branch of the National Government will aggrandize itself at the expense of the other two branches." Buckley v. Valeo (1976). Indeed, we also have observed only recently that "[t]he hydraulic pressure inherent within each of the separate Branches to exceed the outer limits of its power, even to accomplish desirable objectives, must be resisted." With these principles in mind, we turn to consideration of whether the Comptroller General is controlled by Congress.

The critical factor lies in the provisions of the statute defining the Comptroller General's office relating to removability. Although the Comptroller General is nominated by the President from a list of three individuals recommended by the Speaker of the House of Representatives and the President pro tempore of the Senate, and confirmed by the Senate, he is removable only at the initiative of Congress. He may be removed not only by impeachment but also by joint resolution of Congress "at any time" resting on any one of the following bases: "(i) permanent disability; (ii) inefficiency; (iii) neglect of duty; (iv) malfeasance; or (v) a felony or conduct involving moral turpitude."

It is clear that Congress has consistently viewed the Comptroller General as an officer of the Legislative Branch. Over the years, the Comptrollers General have also viewed themselves as part of the Legislative Branch. By placing the responsibility for execution of the Balanced Budget and Emergency Deficit Control Act in the hands of an officer who is subject to removal only by itself, Congress in effect has retained control over the execution of the Act and has intruded into the executive function. The Constitution does not permit such intrusion.

MORRISON v. OLSON, 487 U.S. 654 (1988): Chief Justice REHNQUIST delivered the opinion of the Court.

[The case involved the constitutionality of the provisions of the Ethics in Government Act, which provide for the appointment of an independent counsel to investigate alleged wrong-doing by the President and other high-level executive officials. The portion of the opinion concerning the constitutionality of the Act's having appointment of the independent counsel done by federal court judges is presented above. This is the part of the opinion concerning the removal power.]

We now turn to consider whether the Act is invalid under the constitutional principle of separation of powers. The first is whether the provision of the Act restricting the Attorney General's power to remove the independent counsel to only those instances in which he can show "good cause," taken by itself, impermissibly interferes with the President's exercise of his constitutionally appointed functions.

Unlike both *Bowsher* and *Myers*, this case does not involve an attempt by Congress itself to gain a role in the removal of executive officials other than its established powers of impeachment and conviction. The Act instead puts the removal power squarely in the hands of the Executive Branch; an independent counsel may be removed from office, "only by the personal action of the Attorney General, and only for good cause." There is no requirement of congressional approval of the Attorney General's removal decision, though the decision is subject to judicial review. In our view, the removal provisions of the Act make this case more analogous to Humphrey's Executor v. United States (1935), and Wiener v. United States (1958), than to *Myers* or *Bowsher*.

Appellees contend that *Humphrey's Executor* and *Wiener* are distinguishable from this case because they did not involve officials who performed a "core executive function." They argue that our decision in *Humphrey's Executor* rests on a distinction between "purely executive" officials and officials who exercise "quasi-legislative" and "quasi-judicial" powers. In their view, when a "purely executive" official is involved, the governing precedent is *Myers*, not *Humphrey's Executor*. And, under *Myers*, the President must have absolute discretion to discharge "purely" executive officials at will.

We undoubtedly did rely on the terms "quasi-legislative" and "quasi-judicial" to distinguish the officials involved in *Humphrey's Executor* and *Wiener* from those in *Myers*, but our present considered view is that the determination of whether the Constitution allows Congress to impose a "good cause"-type restriction on the President's power to remove an official cannot be made to turn on whether or not that official is classified as "purely executive." The analysis contained in our removal cases is designed not to define rigid categories of those officials who may or may not be removed at will by the President, but to ensure that Congress does not interfere with the President's exercise of the "executive power" and his constitutionally appointed duty to "take care that the laws be faithfully executed" under Article II. *Myers* was undoubtedly correct in its holding, and in its broader suggestion that there are some "purely executive" officials who must be removable by the President at will if he is to be able to accomplish his constitutional role.

At the other end of the spectrum from *Myers*, the characterization of the agencies in *Humphrey's Executor* and *Wiener* as "quasi-legislative" or "quasi-judicial" in large part reflected our judgment that it was not essential to the President's proper execution of his Article II powers that these agencies be headed up by individuals who were removable at will. We do not mean to suggest that an analysis of the functions served by the officials at issue is irrelevant. But the real question is whether the removal restrictions are of such a nature that they impede the President's ability to perform his constitutional duty, and the functions of the officials in question must be analyzed in that light.

Considering for the moment the "good cause" removal provision in isolation from the other parts of the Act at issue in this case, we cannot say that the imposition of a "good cause" standard for removal by itself unduly trammels on executive authority. Although the counsel exercises no small amount of discretion and judgment in deciding how to carry out his or her duties under the Act, we simply do not see how the President's need to control the exercise of that discretion is so central to the functioning of the Executive Branch as to require as a matter of constitutional law that the counsel be terminable at will by the President.

Nor do we think that the "good cause" removal provision at issue here impermissibly burdens the President's power to control or supervise the independent counsel, as an executive official, in the execution of his or her duties under the Act. This is not a case in which the power to remove an executive official has been completely stripped from the President, thus providing no means for the President to ensure the "faithful execution" of the laws. Rather, because the independent counsel may be terminated for "good cause," the Executive, through the Attorney General, retains ample authority to assure that the counsel is competently performing his or her statutory responsibilities in a manner that comports with the provisions of the Act. Although we need not decide in this case exactly what is encompassed within the term "good cause" under the Act, the legislative history of the removal provision also makes clear that the Attorney General may remove an independent counsel for "misconduct." We do not think that this limitation as it presently stands sufficiently deprives the President of control over the independent counsel to interfere impermissibly with his constitutional obligation to ensure the faithful execution of the laws.

Together, these cases seem to establish that the President may fire any executive official. Congress, however, can limit removal by statute if both it is an office where independence from the President is desirable and the statute does not prohibit removal, but limits it to where there is good cause.

Ultimately the question is whether these mechanisms for controlling administrative agencies — statutes, budget, informal committee controls, appointment, and removal — are sufficient. Some Justices have suggested that it would be desirable to revive the non-delegation doctrine. Justice Scalia seemed to be arguing for this in his dissent in Morrison v. Olson, above. Additionally, in the early 1980s, Justice Rehnquist took a similar position. In Industrial Union Dept., AFL-CIO v. American Petroleum Institute, 448 U.S. 607 (1980), the Court upheld provisions of the Occupational Safety and Health Act that authorized the Secretary of Labor to adopt standards that are "reasonably necessary or appropriate to provide safe or healthful employment" and to "set the standard which most adequately assures, to the extent feasible, on the basis of the best available evidence, that no employee will suffer material impairment of health." Justice Rehnquist, in a dissenting opinion, argued that these provisions should have been invalidated as an excessive delegation of legislative power. He wrote: "When fundamental policy decisions underlying important legislation about to be enacted are to be made, the buck stops with Congress and the President insofar as he exercises his constitutional role in the legislative process." If the Court were to follow the views of Rehnquist and Scalia, the issue then would become how to distinguish permissible from impermissible delegations of power.

Free Enterprise Fund v. Public Company Accounting Oversight Board

130 S.Ct. 3138 (2010)

Chief Justice ROBERTS delivered the opinion of the Court.

Our Constitution divided the "powers of the new Federal Government into three defined categories, Legislative, Executive, and Judicial." Article II vests "[t]he executive Power . . . in a President of the United States of America," who must "take Care that the Laws be faithfully executed." In light of "[t]he impossibility that one man should be able to perform all the great business of the State," the Constitution provides for executive officers to "assist the supreme Magistrate in discharging the duties of his trust."

Since 1789, the Constitution has been understood to empower the President to keep these officers accountable-by removing them from office, if necessary. This Court has determined, however, that this authority is not without limit. In *Humphrey's Executor v. United States* (1935), we held that Congress can, under certain circumstances, create independent agencies run by principal officers appointed by the President, whom the President may not remove at will but only for good cause. Likewise, in *United States v. Perkins* (1886), and *Morrison v. Olson* (1988), the Court sustained similar restrictions on the power of principal executive officers-themselves responsible to the President-to remove their own inferiors. The parties do not ask us to reexamine any of these precedents, and we do not do so.

We are asked, however, to consider a new situation not yet encountered by the Court. The question is whether these separate layers of protection may be combined. May the President be restricted in his ability to remove a principal officer, who is in turn restricted in his ability to remove an inferior officer, even though that inferior officer determines the policy and enforces the laws of the United States?

We hold that such multilevel protection from removal is contrary to Article II's vesting of the executive power in the President. The President cannot "take Care that the Laws be faithfully executed" if he cannot oversee the faithfulness of the officers who execute them. Here the President cannot remove an officer who enjoys more than one level of good-cause protection, even if the President determines that the officer is neglecting his duties or discharging them improperly. That judgment is instead committed to another officer, who may or may not agree with the President's determination, and whom the President cannot remove simply because that officer disagrees with him. This contravenes the President's "constitutional obligation to ensure the faithful execution of the laws."

I

After a series of celebrated accounting debacles, Congress enacted the Sarbanes-Oxley Act of 2002 (or Act). Among other measures, the Act introduced tighter regulation of the accounting industry under a new Public Company Accounting Oversight Board. The Board is composed of five members, appointed to staggered 5-year terms by the Securities and Exchange Commission. It was modeled on private self-regulatory organizations in the securities industry — such as the New York Stock Exchange — that investigate and discipline their own members subject to Commission oversight. Congress created the Board as a private "nonprofit corporation," and Board members and employees are not considered Government "officer[s] or employee[s]" for statutory purposes. The Board can thus recruit its members and employees from the private sector by paying salaries far above the standard Government pay scale.[30]

---

[30] The current salary for the Chairman is $673,000. Other Board members receive $547,000. [Footnote by the Court.]

Unlike the self-regulatory organizations, however, the Board is a Government-created, Government-appointed entity, with expansive powers to govern an entire industry. Every accounting firm — both foreign and domestic — that participates in auditing public companies under the securities laws must register with the Board, pay it an annual fee, and comply with its rules and oversight. The Board is charged with enforcing the Sarbanes-Oxley Act, the securities laws, the Commission's rules, its own rules, and professional accounting standards. To this end, the Board may regulate every detail of an accounting firm's practice, including hiring and professional development, promotion, supervision of audit work, the acceptance of new business and the continuation of old, internal inspection procedures, professional ethics rules, and "such other requirements as the Board may prescribe."

The Board promulgates auditing and ethics standards, performs routine inspections of all accounting firms, demands documents and testimony, and initiates formal investigations and disciplinary proceedings. The willful violation of any Board rule is treated as a willful violation of the Securities Exchange Act of 1934, a federal crime punishable by up to 20 years' imprisonment or $25 million in fines ($5 million for a natural person). And the Board itself can issue severe sanctions in its disciplinary proceedings, up to and including the permanent revocation of a firm's registration, a permanent ban on a person's associating with any registered firm, and money penalties of $15 million ($750,000 for a natural person). Despite the provisions specifying that Board members are not Government officials for statutory purposes, the parties agree that the Board is "part of the Government" for constitutional purposes, and that its members are "'Officers of the United States'" who "exercis[e] significant authority pursuant to the laws of the United States."

The Act places the Board under the SEC's oversight, particularly with respect to the issuance of rules or the imposition of sanctions (both of which are subject to Commission approval and alteration). But the individual members of the Board — like the officers and directors of the self-regulatory organizations — are substantially insulated from the Commission's control. The Commission cannot remove Board members at will, but only "for good cause shown," "in accordance with" certain procedures.

Those procedures require a Commission finding, "on the record" and "after notice and opportunity for a hearing," that the Board member "(A) has willfully violated any provision of th[e] Act, the rules of the Board, or the securities laws; (B) has willfully abused the authority of that member; or (C) without reasonable justification or excuse, has failed to enforce compliance with any such provision or rule, or any professional standard by any registered public accounting firm or any associated person thereof." Removal of a Board member requires a formal Commission order and is subject to judicial review. The parties agree that the Commissioners cannot themselves be removed by the President except under the *Humphrey's Executor* standard of "inefficiency, neglect of duty, or malfeasance in office."

[II]

We hold that the dual for-cause limitations on the removal of Board members contravene the Constitution's separation of powers.

The Constitution provides that "[t]he executive Power shall be vested in a President of the United States of America." As Madison stated on the floor of the First Congress, "if any power whatsoever is in its nature Executive, it is the power of appointing, overseeing, and controlling those who execute the laws."

The landmark case of *Myers v. United States* reaffirmed the principle that Article II confers on the President "the general administrative control of those executing the laws." It is *his* responsibility to take care that the laws be faithfully executed. The buck stops with the President, in Harry Truman's famous phrase. As we explained in *Myers*, the President therefore must have some "power of removing those for whom he can not continue to be responsible."

Nearly a decade later in *Humphrey's Executor*, this Court held that *Myers* did not prevent Congress from conferring good-cause tenure on the principal officers of certain independent agencies. That case concerned the members of the Federal Trade Commission, who held 7-year terms and could not be removed by the President except for "'inefficiency, neglect of duty, or malfeasance in office.'" The Court distinguished *Myers* on the ground that *Myers* concerned "an officer [who] is merely one of the units in the executive department and, hence, inherently subject to the exclusive and illimitable power of removal by the Chief Executive, whose subordinate and aid he is." By contrast, the Court characterized the FTC as "quasi-legislative and quasi-judicial" rather than "purely executive," and held that Congress could require it "to act . . . independently of executive control." Because "one who holds his office only during the pleasure of another, cannot be depended upon to maintain an attitude of independence against the latter's will," the Court held that Congress had power to "fix the period during which [the Commissioners] shall continue in office, and to forbid their removal except for cause in the meantime."

Humphrey's Executor did not address the removal of inferior officers, whose appointment Congress may vest in heads of departments. If Congress does so, it is ordinarily the department head, rather than the President, who enjoys the power of removal. This Court has upheld for-cause limitations on that power as well.

As explained, we have previously upheld limited restrictions on the President's removal power. In those cases, however, only one level of protected tenure separated the President from an officer exercising executive power. It was the President — or a subordinate he could remove at will — who decided whether the officer's conduct merited removal under the good-cause standard.

The Act before us does something quite different. It not only protects Board members from removal except for good cause, but withdraws from the President any decision on whether that good cause exists. That decision is vested instead in other tenured officers — the Commissioners — none of whom is subject to the President's direct control. The result is a Board that is not accountable to the President, and a President who is not responsible for the Board.

The added layer of tenure protection makes a difference. Without a layer of insulation between the Commission and the Board, the Commission could remove a Board member at any time, and therefore would be fully responsible for what the Board does. The President could then hold the Commission to account for its supervision of the Board, to the same extent that he may hold the Commission to account for everything else it does.

A second level of tenure protection changes the nature of the President's review. Now the Commission cannot remove a Board member at will. The President therefore cannot hold the Commission fully accountable for the Board's conduct, to the same extent that he may hold the Commission accountable for everything else that it does. The Commissioners are not responsible for the Board's actions. They are only responsible for their own determination of whether the Act's rigorous good-cause standard is met. And even if the President disagrees with their determination, he is powerless to intervene-unless that determination is so unreasonable as to constitute "inefficiency, neglect of duty, or malfeasance in office."

This novel structure does not merely add to the Board's independence, but transforms it. Neither the President, nor anyone directly responsible to him, nor even an officer whose conduct he may review only for good cause, has full control over the Board. The President is stripped of the power our precedents have preserved, and his ability to execute the laws — by holding his subordinates accountable for their conduct — is impaired.

That arrangement is contrary to Article II's vesting of the executive power in the President. Without the ability to oversee the Board, or to attribute the Board's failings to those whom he *can* oversee, the President is no longer the judge of the Board's conduct. He is not the one who decides whether Board members are abusing their offices or neglecting their duties. He can neither ensure that the laws are faithfully executed, nor be held responsible for a Board member's breach of faith. This violates the basic principle that the President "cannot delegate ultimate responsibility or the active obligation to supervise that goes with it," because Article II "makes a single President responsible for the actions of the Executive Branch."

Indeed, if allowed to stand, this dispersion of responsibility could be multiplied. If Congress can shelter the bureaucracy behind two layers of good-cause tenure, why not a third? At oral argument, the Government was unwilling to concede that even *five* layers between the President and the Board would be too many. The officers of such an agency — safely encased within a Matryoshka doll of tenure protections — would be immune from Presidential oversight, even as they exercised power in the people's name.

The diffusion of power carries with it a diffusion of accountability. The people do not vote for the "Officers of the United States." They instead look to the President to guide the "assistants or deputies . . . subject to his superintendence." Without a clear and effective chain of command, the public cannot "determine on whom the blame or the punishment of a pernicious measure, or series of pernicious measures ought really to fall." That is why the Framers sought to ensure that "those who are employed in the execution of the law will be in their proper situation, and the chain of dependence be preserved; the lowest officers, the middle grade, and the highest, will depend, as they ought, on the President, and the President on the community."

By granting the Board executive power without the Executive's oversight, this Act subverts the President's ability to ensure that the laws are faithfully executed — as well as the public's ability to pass judgment on his efforts. The Act's restrictions are incompatible with the Constitution's separation of powers.

Respondents and the dissent resist this conclusion, portraying the Board as "the kind of practical accommodation between the Legislature and the Executive that should be permitted in a 'workable government.'" No one doubts Congress's power to create a vast and varied federal bureaucracy. But where, in all this, is the role for oversight by an elected President? The Constitution requires that a President chosen by the entire Nation oversee the execution of the laws. And the "'fact that a given law or procedure is efficient, convenient, and useful in facilitating functions of government, standing alone, will not save it if it is contrary to the Constitution,'" for "'[c]onvenience and efficiency are not the primary objectives-or the hallmarks-of democratic government.'"

One can have a government that functions without being ruled by functionaries, and a government that benefits from expertise without being ruled by experts. Our Constitution was adopted to enable the people to govern themselves, through their elected leaders. The growth of the Executive Branch, which now wields vast power and touches almost every aspect of daily life, heightens the concern that it may slip from the Executive's control, and thus from that of the people. This concern is largely absent from the dissent's paean to the administrative state.

Calls to abandon those protections in light of "the era's perceived necessity," are not unusual. Nor is the argument from bureaucratic expertise limited only to the field of accounting. The failures of accounting regulation may be a "pressing national problem," but "a judiciary that licensed extraconstitutional government with each issue of comparable gravity would, in the long run, be far worse." Neither respondents nor the dissent explains why the Board's task, unlike so many others, requires *more* than one layer of insulation from the President — or, for that matter, why only two. The point is not to take issue with for-cause limitations in general; we do not do that. The question here is far more modest. We deal with the unusual situation, never before addressed by the Court, of two layers of for-cause tenure. And though it may be criticized as "elementary arithmetical logic," two layers are not the same as one.

[III]

[P]etitioners argue that Board members are principal officers requiring Presidential appointment with the Senate's advice and consent. We held in *Edmond v. United States*, (1997), that "[w]hether one is an 'inferior' officer depends on whether he has a superior," and that "'inferior officers' are officers whose work is directed and supervised at some level" by other officers appointed by the President with the Senate's consent. In particular, we noted that "[t]he power to remove officers" at will and without cause "is a powerful tool for control" of an inferior. As explained above, the statutory restrictions on the Commission's power to remove Board members are unconstitutional and void. Given that the Commission is properly viewed, under the Constitution, as possessing the power to remove Board members at will, and given the Commission's other oversight authority, we have no hesitation in concluding that the Board members are inferior officers whose appointment Congress may permissibly vest in a "Hea[d] of Departmen[t]."

In light of the foregoing, petitioners are not entitled to broad injunctive relief against the Board's continued operations. But they are entitled to declaratory relief sufficient to ensure that the reporting requirements and auditing standards to which they are subject will be enforced only by a constitutional agency accountable to the Executive.

CHAPTER 8

AGENCIES IN THE STRUCTURE OF MODERN FEDERAL GOVERNMENT

The regulatory state is the collection of federal government institutions and laws that determine many aspects of social and economic policy. Administrative agencies are chief among those institutions. The purpose of this chapter is to describe how agencies fit in the structure of modern federal government. We describe what an agency is, examine its constitutional foundations, explain its principal forms, and discuss who within them makes decisions. With this introduction, we can go on in subsequent chapters to show you how agencies function — and in particular, how agencies make the decisions of law and policy that are at the heart of the regulatory state.

In this chapter, we describe only the basics of how agencies fit in the structure of modern federal government. For this reason, we do not explore in detail the Supreme Court's decisions on the structure of modern federal government. We leave that inquiry to courses in constitutional law. Nor do we consider in depth the variations among agencies. We leave that to courses in administrative law, environmental law, food and drug law, labor law, telecommunications law, and the like. Our aim is exceedingly practical: to provide just enough information for you to understand the place of agencies within our federal system. For example, you cannot understand how agencies implement regulatory statutes without an understanding of *who* within agencies makes decisions. This understanding also furnishes a standpoint from which to evaluate whether agencies operate in a normatively acceptable or legitimate fashion.

A. What is an Agency?

An agency is a unit of government created by statute. It owes its existence, form, and power to legislation. In this book, we are primarily concerned with *federal* agencies, which are established through *federal* legislation. Although the President occasionally will establish an agency by executive order, Congress usually follows by enacting a statute establishing the agency and delegating authority to it.

The Environmental Protection Agency and the Department of Homeland Security are the most well-known examples of agencies that were first established by executive order and then delegated authority by statute. By and large, statutes create and specify the powers of agencies.

Agencies play a prominent role in public law for the simple reason that they possess considerable power. Many agencies possess the power to act with the force of law, just as Congress or a court does. They do so by issuing rules (sometimes called regulations), which are analogous to statutes, and by issuing orders, after conducting an adjudication that is similar to a judicial, trial-type hearing. Agencies have power to do many other things short of issuing legally binding statements — conduct research, provide public information, produce guidance documents, issue opinion letters, write internal office manuals, inspect premises, and more. Indeed, people in regulated industries often find themselves immersed in fairly continuous interactions with the relevant regulator.

Even focusing only on rules or regulations, it becomes immediately clear why agencies are paramount. As a matter of sheer volume, the number of regulations issued by agencies far exceeds the number of statutes issued by Congress. For instance, in 2008, there were considerably fewer statutes than regulations:

- 284 statutes[1]
- 3,955 regulations[2]

But these numbers only tell a small part of the story. As we will examine in depth, statutes frequently delegate to agencies many of the most significant decisions of social and economic policy. The startling contrast between the number of regulations and statutes likely understates how much authority agencies have in establishing rules that govern society. Agencies also adjudicate more cases than the entire federal judiciary.

Another window on agency authority concerns the costs of compliance with regulations. Although the estimates vary, the federal government itself estimates that the cost of compliance with regulations is one-tenth of the gross domestic product. *See* COUNCIL OF ECONOMIC ADVISORS, ECONOMIC REPORT OF THE PRESIDENT 296 (Feb. 2004), available at *www.gpoaccess.gov/eop/index.html*. With such great social and economic implications, it is no wonder that regulations play so large a role in public and corporate life — not to mention lawyer workload.

A final consideration is the sheer size of the federal bureaucracy. It is difficult for private parties to engage in any commercial or professional endeavor without encountering an agency. When you apply for a school loan or pick up your snail mail, you are encountering an agency. The regulatory state is comprised of 15 cabinet departments and their sub-cabinet agencies, along with a large number of other "alphabet soup" agencies. Here is a list of the cabinet departments and other agencies:

---

[1] Pub. L. No. 110-176 (signed January 4, 2008) through Pub. L. No. 110-460 (signed December 23, 2008).

[2] This data comes from the Office of the Federal Register (last contacted Feb. 18, 2010).

Cabinet Departments

Department of Agriculture (USDA)	Department of Commerce	Department of Defense (DOD)
Department of Education (ED)	Department of Energy (DOE)	Department of Health and Human Services (HHS)
Department of Homeland Security	Department of Housing and Urban Development (HUD)	Department of the Interior
Department of Justice (DOJ)	Department of Labor (DOL)	Department of State
Department of Transportation (DOT)	Department of the Treasury	Department of Veterans Affairs

Other Agencies

Central Intelligence Agency (CIA)	Commodity Futures Trading Commission (CFTC)	Consumer Product Safety Commission (CPSC)
Defense Nuclear Facilities Safety Board (DNFSB)	Environmental Protection Agency (EPA)	Equal Employment Opportunity Commission (EEOC)
Export-Import Bank of the United States	Farm Credit Administration	Federal Communications Commission (FCC)
Federal Deposit Insurance Corporation (FDIC)	Federal Election Commission (FEC)	Federal Housing Finance Board
Federal Labor Relations Authority	Federal Maritime Commission	Federal Mine Safety and Health Review Commission
Federal Reserve System (FRS)	Federal Trade Commission (FTC)	General Services Administration (GSA)
Merit Systems Protection Board (MSPB)	National Aeronautics and Space Administration (NASA)	National Archives and Records Administration (NARA)

National Capital Planning Commission	National Credit Union Administration (NCUA)	National Foundation on the Arts and the Humanities
National Labor Relations Board (NLRB)	National Mediation Board	National Railroad Passenger Corporation (Amtrak)
National Science Foundation (NSF)	National Transportation Safety Board	Nuclear Regulatory Commission (NRC)
Occupational Safety and Health Review Commission (OSHRC)	Office of Government Ethics	Office of Personnel Management (OPM)
Office of Special Counsel (OSC)	Peace Corps	Pension Benefit Guaranty Corporation
Postal Rate Commission	Railroad Retirement Board	Securities and Exchange Commission (SEC)
Selective Service System	Social Security Administration (SSA)	Small Business Administration (SBA)
Tennessee Valley Authority	United States Agency for International Development (USAID)	United States Trade and Development Agency
United States Commission on Civil Rights	United States International Trade Commission (USITC)	United States Postal Service

The federal government employs over 2.5 million workers, more than 1,100 full- and part-time Senate-confirmed political appointees, as well as other presidential appointees, career civil servants, and other non-political government workers. Anne Joseph O'Connell, *Vacant Offices: Delays in Staffing Top Agency Positions*, 82 S. Cal. L. Rev. 913 (2009); *see also* David E. Lewis, The Politics of Presidential Appointments 20-30 (2008) (describing the types of employees and officers that make up federal government). Given the place that agencies occupy in our federal system, there is a continual quest for control of their decisions by the President, Congress, regulated parties, public interest groups, and even the courts. We focus on these issues later in the book.

B. Where do Agencies Fit in the Constitutional Structure?

Considering the prevalence of agencies in our federal system, it is logical to ask how the United States Constitution provides for them. The Constitution is the principal source of information concerning the institutions of the federal government. What does it say about agencies? The answer: it is virtually silent on these institutions.

Without intending to convert this course into one on constitutional law, some discussion of constitutional basics is helpful. The first three Articles of the Constitution create the three branches of government, the legislative, the executive, and the judicial:

- Article I provides that "[a]ll legislative Powers herein granted shall be vested in a Congress of the United States, which shall consist of a Senate and a House of Representatives." U.S. CONST., Art. I, §1. Article I authorizes Congress to enact statutes and specifies the scope of Congress's power to do so.
- Article II provides that "[t]he executive Power shall be vested in a President." U.S. CONST., Art. II, §1. Article II authorizes the President to ensure that the law is faithfully executed or enforced. U.S. CONST., Art.II, §3.
- Article III provides that "[t]he judicial power of the United States, shall be vested in one supreme Court," and establishes limits on the judicial power to be exercised by federal courts that Congress chooses to create. It authorizes the courts to adjudicate "[c]ases" or "[c]ontroversies" that arise between or among parties. U.S. CONST., Art. III, §2.

In a nutshell, these Articles vest, enumerate, limit, separate, and balance federal power. By bestowing power in the branches (vesting), the Articles create or constitute our federal government. By granting the branches only certain powers and no more (enumerating and limiting), the Articles delineate and cabin the scope of federal power, thereby reserving power to the states. At the same time, the Articles collectively ensure that each federal power rests with the institution best qualified to exercise it. Legislation is committed to Congress, elected by the people and therefore able to represent them in the formulation of national policy. The execution or enforcement of the law is committed to the President, who is not only elected but, as a single actor, is uniquely situated to act with the dispatch and decisiveness that law enforcement requires. Adjudication of the law is committed to the courts, which are positioned to exercise impartial judgment when deciding cases under the law precisely because they are not elected and have the protection of life tenure in office. By dividing power among the branches (separation), the Articles ensure that no branch has the power to simultaneously make, enforce, and interpret the law. By creating co-equal branches (balancing), the Articles aim to allow each branch tools to protect its own powers and check the other branches. In these Articles, then, it is possible to see the explicit vesting, enumerating, and limiting of power as well as the implicit principles of federalism, separation of powers, and checks and balances. The vesting constitutes the government but the rest, including all three implicit principles, divide the government to prevent tyranny; they thus rest on a fundamental mistrust of consolidated power.

Where are agencies in the Constitution? Agencies are not described. The Constitution does provide for officers other than elected officials or appointed judges and offices apart from the President, Congress, and judiciary. But the references do not specify the powers or procedures of agencies with anywhere near the detail necessary to understand their operation.

It is worthwhile to take a first-hand look. Here is what the Constitution has to say about the structure of government, in the first three Articles (the full text of these Articles appears in the Appendix):

The Constitution of the United States

Article I

Section 1.

All legislative Powers herein granted shall be vested in a Congress of the United States, which shall consist of a Senate and House of Representatives.

Section 8.

1: The Congress shall have Power To lay and collect Taxes, Duties, Imposts and Excises, to pay the Debts and provide for the common Defense and general Welfare of the United States; but all Duties, Imposts and Excises shall be uniform throughout the United States; . . .

3: To regulate Commerce with foreign Nations, and among the several States, and with the Indian Tribes; . . .

9: To constitute Tribunals inferior to the supreme Court; . . .

18: To make all Laws which shall be necessary and proper for carrying into Execution the foregoing Powers, and all other Powers vested by this Constitution in the Government of the United States, or in any Department or Officer thereof . . . .

Article II

Section 1.

1: The executive Power shall be vested in a President of the United States of America . . . .

Section 2.

1: The President shall be Commander in Chief of the Army and Navy of the United States, and of the Militia of the several States, when called into the actual Service of the United States; he may require the Opinion, in writing, of the principal Officer in each of the executive Departments, upon any Subject relating to the Duties of their respective Offices, and he shall have Power to grant Reprieves and Pardons for Offences against the United States, except in Cases of Impeachment.

2: He shall have Power, by and with the Advice and Consent of the Senate, to make Treaties, provided two thirds of the Senators present concur; and he shall nominate, and by and with the Advice and Consent of the Senate, shall appoint Ambassadors, other public Ministers and Consuls, Judges of the supreme Court, and all other Officers of the United States, whose Appointments are not herein otherwise provided for, and which shall be established by Law: but the Congress may by Law vest the Appointment of such inferior Officers, as they think proper, in the President alone, in the Courts of Law, or in the Heads of Departments . . . .

Article III

Section 1.

The judicial Power of the United States, shall be vested in one supreme Court, and in such inferior Courts as the Congress may from time to time ordain and establish.

Section 2.

1: The judicial Power shall extend to all Cases, in Law and Equity, arising under this Constitution, the Laws of the United States, and Treaties made, or which shall be made, under their Authority; — to all Cases affecting Ambassadors, other public Ministers and Consuls; — to all Cases of admiralty and maritime Jurisdiction; — to Controversies to which the United States shall be a Party; — to Controversies between two or more States; — *between a State and Citizens of another State [this phrase was changed by Amendment XI]]* — between Citizens of different States, — between Citizens of the same State claiming Lands under Grants of different States, and between a State, or the Citizens thereof, and foreign States, Citizens or Subjects . . . .

NOTES AND QUESTIONS

1. Why doesn't the Constitution, which establishes the basic structure of our government, tell us what agencies are, how they are organized, and who controls them? Perhaps the Framers were not thinking about agencies at all. But isn't this answer foreclosed by the text? Although the Framers certainly did not anticipate the size and extent of the modern regulatory state, they knew that a national government would need agencies of some sort. At the same time, the text is confusing. Note the reference to "the principal officer in each of the Executive Departments" in Art. II, §2, cl. 1. The only thing this reference tells us is that the President may demand a written opinion from the heads of the departments. But what are these departments, how are they organized, and who controls them? If the President controls them, then his ability to obtain a written opinion from the head of the department would

seem to go without saying. Does this secondary form of control suggest that someone else is exercising the primary control, and if so, who? In contrast, consider that the departments are mentioned only in Article II, and they are described as "Executive Departments," which suggests that they are under the President's control because Article II says that the "executive Power shall be vested in a President." Which is it?

2. The historical record of the Constitutional Convention provides a partial explanation for this confusing text. From the records of the Constitutional Convention, it appears that the somewhat elusive clause in Art. II, §2, cl. 1, is the remnant of a longer provision that the Framers deleted because they decided that their own ideas about the executive departments should not be enshrined in the constitutional document. Was this decision wise or did it leave too much up for grabs? This book might affect your view.

3. However wise, the bottom line is that the Constitution imposes few requirements on the creation and operation of agencies. What powers may an agency possess? What process must an agency adhere to? Which branch of government can lay claim to controlling agencies, for example, by reversing their actions or removing their top managers? By and large, the entire subject of the regulatory state will come from elsewhere — it is *extra-constitutional*. Understanding the extra-constitutional requirements and constraints is the purpose of this book.

4. For clarity's sake, understand that agencies are not *unconstitutional* simply because the rules concerning them are *extra-constitutional*. The Supreme Court has long held that Congress has authority to create agencies, subject to fairly minimal constraints. *See, e.g.*, United States v. Rock Royal Co-op, Inc., 307 U.S. 533, 574 (1939) (from the earliest days Congress has granted authority to executive offers, and its power to do so is well established); J.W. Hampton, Jr. & Co. v. United States, 276 U.S. 394, 409 (1928) (Congress possesses the authority to create an agency to exercise federal functions as long as it includes in the statute some instruction or "intelligible principle" to guide the agency). We address the issue of delegation to agencies in Chapter 2, pp. 483.

Just because the Constitution does not say much about the structure and powers of agencies does not mean that it is irrelevant to agencies. To the contrary, agencies must comport with general constitutional principles, just as institutions expressly created by the Constitution must comply with these principles. Indeed, the fact that the Constitution says little about the structure and powers of agencies actually may make the question of how agencies comply with general constitutional principles all the more pressing; how is it that institutions run by unelected officials can be responsible for decisions of such social and economic significance? These questions also are urgent given the unique blend of powers agencies wield; how is it that a single agency can be responsible for making, enforcing, and interpreting the law, as many are? In this respect, the "legitimacy" of agencies has been an on-going subject of discussion. Agencies are defended (and criticized) in different terms, some clearly traceable to the Constitution, and others less so. By way of introduction, consider the following:

a. *Expertise.* Agencies are often seen as possessing institutional competence — or expertise — for solving the complex problems that confront modern society. Agencies have broad access to information, specialized knowledge, and trained staff. They also have time to devote to a particular set of problems. Moreover, agencies can develop a systemic perspective on regulatory issues, helping to integrate diverse policies and balance multiple goals. The legitimacy of agencies may depend in part on their expertise, thought superior to Congress's, for making generally applicable, forward-looking rules.

b. *Fairness and Rationality.* The Constitution provides specific procedures for certain actions, such as bicameralism and presentment for legislation and trials for adjudication. The legislative process famously slows the production of improvident or hasty law by requiring a significant degree of political support for the enactment of any statute. The judicial process secures individual rights by providing for an impartial decision maker and an opportunity to be heard. The Due Process Clause and other provisions also provide guarantees of fairness. Might agencies be subject to procedures that could have similar effects on their decisions? If so, agencies might gain legitimacy based in part on those procedures.

Where might those procedures come from? In addition to certain constraints imposed by the Due Process Clause, agencies are subject to procedural requirements imposed by statute. Most significantly, the Administrative Procedure Act (APA), 5 U.S.C. §§551 *et seq.*, provides default procedures for agencies to use for making law and policy, as well as the standards that courts apply when reviewing such action. At a general level, the APA helps to ensure that agency decisions comport with the rule of law — that they are fair and deliberative. (The APA is reproduced in Appendix B.)

Here is a bit more background on the APA that will be useful throughout the book. The APA divides agency action into two basic categories: formal and informal. Formal action requires an agency to conduct a trial-type hearing, much like a judicial hearing, and it can result in an order resolving a dispute between two parties, which is called formal adjudication, or a rule with future effect and general application, called formal rulemaking. *See* APA, 5 U.S.C. §§554-55. As a practical matter, agencies rarely engage in formal rulemaking, so the category of action requiring a trial-type hearing basically includes formal adjudication. Informal action does not require agencies to hold trial-type hearings. For so-called notice-and-comment rulemaking, agencies rely on written submissions from interested parties, *see* APA, 5 U.S.C. §553, and for other action, unhelpfully called informal adjudication, agencies rely on even less formal procedures. In fact, the APA prescribes virtually no procedures for informal adjudication. It is really a catch-all category that may include such diverse activities as planning decisions, strategic decisions, advice, guidance, or resource allocation. Agencies may elect to follow formalized procedures for informal adjudication (or notice-and-comment rulemaking), but the APA does not so require. We have more to say about administrative procedures in Chapter 10.

The APA also provides standards for judicial review of agency action, which help to ensure the rationality of agency action. For instance, the APA authorizes courts to strike down agency action that is "arbitrary" or "capricious." 5 U.S.C. §706(2)(A). Even based on this basic description of the APA, can you see why it might be included as part of the "constitutional law" of the regulatory state?

Does the APA require even more fairness and rationality for regulation than the Constitution guarantees for legislation? Why might we expect even more from agencies than from Congress when they are the ones making law?

c. *Interest Representation.* When agencies act through processes that are open and accessible to a wide range of interests, they can provide a form of interest representation that might also enhance their legitimacy. For example, agencies that issue regulations through the notice-and-comment rulemaking process can do as the name of that process suggests: they can afford interested parties notice and an opportunity to comment on proposed policies. Moreover, agencies have incentives to consider and accommodate different views to minimize the issues that parties later seek to challenge in the courts. Why exactly is representation and participation important? Do parties get more consideration here than at the legislative level?

d. *Political Accountability.* Although agencies are run by unelected bureaucrats, they can be seen as accountable to the people, not directly, but indirectly, because the President supervises their decisions. The President can be held responsible at the polls for unpopular agency decisions, affording electoral accountability. In addition, the President can engraft his preferences on agency decisions, affording a form of democratic accountability that some say is superior even to Congress's. The President is the one official elected by and therefore representative of a national constituency. Is this argument stronger for some agencies as opposed to others?

Are there other values that contribute to agency legitimacy, whether or not directly traceable to constitutional principles? Consider the following:

a. *Efficacy and Flexibility.* Agencies might be able to implement policies that are preferred or needed when gridlock grips Congress. Many agencies have the capacity to respond quickly to changing circumstances, whether the result of technological advances, market conditions, consumer preferences, demographic shifts, emergencies, and so on. This attribute might also enhance their legitimacy.

b. *Coordination.* Agencies might be at their best when not pursuing their missions in isolation but coordinating their policies with other agencies across government. The coordination of agency policies can allow for consistent and uniform regulatory regimes to develop. Thus, agencies are often judged in terms of their coordination (or lack thereof). In this regard, note that the President can help agencies coordinate their policies by requiring them to report their planned and proposed regulations to the Office of Management and Budget and giving that office an opportunity to respond.

c. *Efficiency*. Finally, agencies might do well to issue efficient regulations. They have the resources to consider the expected costs and benefits of regulations. Indeed, under executive orders that recent Presidents have issued, agencies must perform cost-benefit analyses for all proposed major regulations (basically those with costs of $100 million or more). Many (though not all) believe that agencies are more legitimate when adhering to cost-benefit analysis.

Again, the point of thinking in these terms is to address a persistent normative question about agencies: are they "legitimate" given their place in the structure of modern government? The answer will depend on the extent to which agencies actually exhibit these and other values, and how legal structures promote (or impede) them. We will need the rest of the book to see. For now, understand that agencies have a curious constitutional pedigree, which only amplifies questions about their legitimacy.

CHAPTER 9

CONTROL OF AGENCY ACTION

When agencies implement their statutes, they understand that each branch of government will have an interest in how they do so. Roughly speaking, political officials, such as the President or members of Congress, will seek to ensure that agency action tracks their preferences. Courts will seek to ensure that agency action comports with legal standards. But this is only the beginning. In this chapter, we examine the various tools that each branch uses in asserting control of agency action. We discuss the efficacy of these tools as well as the normative implications of their use, such as promoting (or undermining) accountability and expertise.

Lawyers have ample reason to study control of agency action. Not only is that subject important for a complete understanding of how agencies implement their statutes, but lawyers are involved in how political officials and courts assert control over agencies. For agency decisionmaking that is underway, gaining the attention of the White House or a member of Congress can help prompt intervention in the agency action. Once agency action is final, lawyers are the ones who seek to invoke judicial control in the context of litigation challenging such action.

Although we introduce control on a branch-by-branch and tool-by-tool basis, all of the branches may assert control over the same agency action and may use more than one tool. In this sense, control is dynamic. We illustrate this interaction through a case study involving the very passive restraints rescission that you have been studying in this book.

A. Presidential Control of Agency Action

In looking at the regulatory state, one fact is certain: the President seeks to assert control of agency action. The President does so in a number of ways that differ in terms of their formality, transparency, and effectiveness. At one end of the spectrum, the President can request that an agency voluntarily take a particular action, and can make such a request in a meeting or other informal, non-public manner.

At the other end, the President can take the formal, visible, and effective step of replacing recalcitrant agency officials with individuals more amenable to administration views or withhold funding until agency officials change course. Perhaps in the middle, the President can set up an entire process for requiring agencies to submit their proposed regulations to the White House for review under specified principles. In this section, we introduce you to these tools and more. We will not focus on the informal means per se, but rather on the more formal and transparent means by which presidential administrations assert control over agencies. We also examine the different officials who exert influence.

At the outset, you might ask why the President seeks to assert control of agency action. As we noted in the introduction to this chapter, many believe that the President asserts control to ensure that agency action roughly tracks administration preferences. In this way, the President can better implement his agenda and enhance the prospects of reelection. Or the President can build a lasting legacy. "Because voters and history judge presidents for the performance of the entire federal government during their tenure," Presidents have incentives "to ensure that policy outcomes, both legislative and administrative, are under their control." David E. Lewis, The Politics of Presidential Appointments 55 (2008).

The President also has a responsibility to supervise agency action. In this respect, note that the Constitution provides that the President "shall take Care that the laws be faithfully executed." U.S. Const. Art. II, §3, cl. 3. Some believe that the Take Care Clause, together with the Vesting Clause, mean that the President has an obligation to supervise all law execution. *See, e.g.,* Steven G. Calabresi & Saikrishna B. Prakash, *The President's Power to Execute the Laws,* 104 Yale L.J. 541, 570-99 (1994). Some read these clauses more pragmatically, as granting the President the authority but not the formal obligation to supervise agency action. *See, e.g.,* Elena Kagan, *Presidential Administration,* 114 Harv. L. Rev. 2245, 2331-32 (2001); Jerry L. Mashaw, *Prodelegation: Why Administrators Should Make Political Decisions,* 1 J.L. Econ. & Org. 81, 95 (1985). On this account, the President asserts control of agency action as necessary to ensure that such action is consistent with overall government priorities and popular preferences.

What are the normative implications of presidential control? First and foremost, it is often said that presidential control can enhance the accountability of agency action. The President is the one official elected by a national constituency and can confer his unique brand of representation on unelected agency officials by asserting control of their actions. In addition, voters can hold the President responsible for agency actions that they dislike. Second, it is frequently said that presidential control can improve the efficacy of agency action. The President can coordinate the actions of agencies across the government, avoiding redundant or conflicting regulations. The President can spur a sluggish agency into action. The President can require agencies to consider factors that they may have neglected or misapplied, including the costs and benefits of their proposed regulations. In this last respect, it is said that presidential control can improve the efficiency of agency action. Note, however, that presidential control is not without potential downsides. What if the President seeks to influence agency action in a way that contravenes scientific findings or statutory considerations? In such instances, presidential control can be said to decrease the expertise and even the legality of agency action.

As you encounter the tools below, consider how each works for the President. Evaluate the differing degrees of formality, transparency, and effectiveness. Think about the various normative implications.

1. Control of Agency Personnel

Chief among the President's powers for asserting control of agency action is the power to appoint and to fire the heads of agencies.[1] Through appointment of Senate-confirmed officers, the President is able to select individuals who will follow administration priorities either because they share those priorities or are loyal on party or personal grounds. If the President makes the right appointments, he will rarely need means for later exerting control over an agency; the political appointee will know what needs to be done.

In the event of disagreement over general priorities or specific policies, the President has the authority to fire the heads of executive-branch agencies. The President can replace those officials with individuals more amenable to administration views. But the actual removal of such leaders is politically costly for the President. It draws considerable publicity and creates the need for a replacement acceptable to the Senate. How can the President avoid some of the spectacle and still control an official? The threat of removal often creates strong incentives for agency leaders to comply with the President's wishes or to resign "voluntarily" from their positions. To get a sense for how the threat of removal might operate in practice, go back to Chapter 8 and reread the materials regarding former EPA Administrator Whitman. *See* pp. 787.

Control of agency officials plays out differently for independent agencies. The President cannot fire the commissioners or board members of independent agencies for policy disagreements, even if inclined to take the heat and find a replacement. Those officials, for the most part, are protected by statute from presidential removal except for specified cause. As discussed in Chapter 8, Congress can create independent agencies as long as they do not interfere with the President's constitutional duty to take care that the laws are faithfully executed. But the President still has the ability to assert some control over those agencies and their political officials. A good cause restriction is not complete insulation from presidential removal. Nor is it complete insulation from presidential control. Furthermore, the President possesses other means to assert control of independent agencies. As with executive-branch agencies, the President has the power to appoint their leaders (with Senate confirmation) and may also have the power to select the chair of the agency from among its members. The President assists independent agencies in their budget negotiations with Congress and can use this

---

[1] The President also influences agency policy by appointing other officials, including members of the Senior Executive Service and individuals with so called "Schedule C" appointments whose responsibilities are of a confidential or policy-making nature. *See* LEWIS, THE POLITICS OF PRESIDENTIAL APPOINTMENTS at 23-25.

power to influence independent agencies, as described in the next section. The President also controls executive-branch agency officials who work with independent agency officials and thereby shape their policy decisions. For example, the Secretary of the Treasury works closely with the Federal Reserve Board Chair and the commissioners of the SEC on matters of financial policy.

Is it possible for Congress to provide too much distance between independent agency officials and the President? For example, what if such officials could be removed only by *other* independent agency officials rather than by the President or even an executive-branch official, such as the Attorney General? Congress could certainly expand the range of possibilities for regulatory governance to include many innovative forms.[2] How far can it go? *See* Free Enterprise Fund v. Public Company Accounting Oversight Bd., 537 F.3d 667 (D.C. Cir. 2008), *cert. granted*, 129 S. Ct. 2378 (2009) (concerning the constitutionality of the Public Company Accounting Oversight Board, the members of which are removable for cause by the Securities and Exchange Commission).

B. The Constitutional Problems of the Administrative State

One of the most dramatic changes in American government since the Constitution was written in 1787 has been the growth of administrative agencies. Although federal agencies and departments have existed in some form since the beginning of American history, it is only in the last century that Congress has routinely delegated its legislative power to executive agencies. The creation of the Interstate Commerce Commission in 1887 ushered in a new era for the federal government: the creation of federal administrative agencies with broad powers. Over the course of the next century, a vast array of federal agencies were created, such as the Federal Communications Commission, the Securities and Exchange Commission, the Food and Drug Administration, the Environmental Protection Agency, the Nuclear Regulatory Commission, and countless more.

These agencies exercise all of the powers of government: legislative, executive, and judicial. Administrative agencies generally have legislative power, as they possess the authority to promulgate rules that have the force of law. Administrative agencies also have executive power, because they are responsible for bringing enforcement actions against those who violate the relevant federal laws and regulations. Finally, administrative agencies frequently have judicial power in that

---

[2] An important movement in modern legal scholarship, sometimes called New Public Governance, gives a prominent role to collaborative arrangements between quasi-private entities and public agencies. *See, e.g.*, IAN AYRES & JOHN BRAITHWAITE, RESPONSIVE REGULATION: TRANSCENDING THE DEREGULATION DEBATE (1992); NEIL GUNNINGHAM & PETER GRABOSKY, SMART REGULATION: DESIGNING ENVIRONMENTAL POLICY (1998); Jody Freeman, *Collaborative Governance in the Administrative State*, 45 UCLAL. REV. 1 (1997); Orly Lobel, *The Renew Deal: The Fall of Regulation and the Rise of Governance in Contemporary Legal Thought*, 89 MINN. L. REV. 342 (2004); Victoria Nourse & Gregory Shaffer, *Varieties of New Legal Realism: Can New World Order Prompt a New Legal Theory*, 95 CORNELL L. REV. 61 (2009).

they employ administrative law judges who hear cases brought by agency officials against those accused of violating the agency's regulations.

The combination of legislative, executive, and judicial power in the same hands is troubling. James Madison wrote: "The accumulation of all powers, legislative, executive, and judiciary, in the same hands . . . may justly be pronounced the very definition of tyranny." The Federalist No. 47, p. 301 (Clinton Rossiter ed., 1961). More generally, controlling and checking administrative agencies poses an important constitutional problem, unaddressed by the text or the framers' intent.

Subsection 1 considers the non-delegation doctrine, the principle that Congress cannot delegate legislative power, and its demise. The existence of broad delegations of legislative authority to administrative agencies is part of the constitutional problem posed by administrative agencies. One possible check on administrative agencies is the "legislative veto": Congress, acting pursuant to statutory authorization, invalidates an agency's action by a resolution that is not presented to the President for a possible veto. However, as presented in Subsection 2, the Supreme Court declared this tool unconstitutional. Subsection 3 then examines other checks on administrative agencies, including the appointment and removal power, judicial review, and Congress delegating authority to itself.

The tension explored throughout this section is on how to reconcile the practical need for administrative agencies in the complex, modern world with basic principles of separation of powers and checks and balances.

1. The Non-Delegation Doctrine and Its Demise

One solution to the constitutional problems posed by administrative agencies is the non-delegation doctrine: the principle that Congress may not delegate its legislative power to administrative agencies. The non-delegation doctrine forces a politically accountable Congress to make the policy choices, rather than leaving this to unelected administrative officials.

The height of the Court's enforcement of the non-delegation doctrine was in the mid-1930s in two decisions that invalidated New Deal legislation. The National Industrial Recovery Act, a key piece of New Deal legislation, authorized the President to approve "codes of fair competition" developed by boards of various industries.

A.L.A. Schechter Poultry Corp. v. United States

295 U.S. 495 (1935)

[The A.L.A. Schechter Poultry Corporation was indicted for an alleged conspiracy and for violations of the Code of Fair Competition for the Live Poultry Industry of the metropolitan area in and about the city of New York. The Code of Fair Competition prescribed labor standards for poultry businesses and many aspects of how such businesses could operate. The Code was created by a business group delegated this authority by a federal law, the National Industrial Recovery Act.]

Chief Justice HUGHES delivered the opinion of the Court.[3]

The question, then, turns upon the authority which section 3 of the Recovery Act vests in the President to approve or prescribe. If the codes have standing as penal statutes, this must be due to the effect of the executive action. But Congress cannot delegate legislative power to the President to exercise an unfettered discretion to make whatever laws he thinks may be needed or advisable for the rehabilitation and expansion of trade or industry.

Accordingly we turn to the Recovery Act to ascertain what limits have been set to the exercise of the President's discretion: First, the President, as a condition of approval, is required to find that the trade or industrial associations or groups which propose a code "impose no inequitable restrictions on admission to membership" and are "truly representative." That condition, however, relates only to the status of the initiators of the new laws and not to the permissible scope of such laws. Second, the President is required to find that the code is not "designed to promote monopolies or to eliminate or oppress small enterprises and will not operate to discriminate against them." And to this is added a proviso that the code "shall not permit monopolies or monopolistic practices." But these restrictions leave virtually untouched the field of policy envisaged by section 1, and, in that wide field of legislative possibilities, the proponents of a code, refraining from monopolistic designs, may roam at will, and the President may approve or disapprove their proposals as he may see fit. That is the precise effect of the further finding that the President is to make — that the code "will tend to effectuate the policy of this title."

Section 3 of the Recovery Act is without precedent. It supplies no standards for any trade, industry, or activity. It does not undertake to prescribe rules of conduct to be applied to particular states of fact determined by appropriate administrative procedure. Instead of prescribing rules of conduct, it authorizes the making of codes to prescribe them. For that legislative undertaking, section 3 sets up no standards, aside from the statement of the general aims of rehabilitation, correction, and expansion described in section 1. In view of the scope of that broad declaration and of the nature of the few restrictions that are imposed, the discretion of the President in approving or prescribing codes, and thus enacting laws for the government of trade and industry throughout the country, is virtually unfettered. We think that the code-making authority thus conferred is an unconstitutional delegation of legislative power.

---

[3] The Court also found the law unconstitutional as exceeding the scope of Congress's Commerce Clause authority. This aspect of the decision is discussed in Chapter 6.

Panama Refining Co. v. Ryan

293 U.S. 388 (1935)

[A provision of the National Industrial Recovery Act authorized the President to prohibit transportation in interstate and foreign commerce of petroleum produced in excess of the amount permitted by state.]

Chief Justice HUGHES delivered the opinion of the Court.

On July 11, 1933, the President, by Executive Order No. 6199 prohibited "the transportation in interstate and foreign commerce of petroleum and the products thereof produced or withdrawn from storage in excess of the amount permitted to be produced or withdrawn from storage by any State law or valid regulation or order prescribed thereunder, by any board, commission, officer, or other duly authorized agency of a State." This action was based on section 9(c) of title 1 of the National Industrial Recovery Act of June 16, 1933.

[The federal law] contains nothing as to the circumstances or conditions in which transportation of petroleum or petroleum products should be prohibited — nothing as to the policy of prohibiting or not prohibiting the transportation of production exceeding what the states allow.

It is no answer to insist that deleterious consequences follow the transportation of "hot oil" — oil exceeding state allowances. The Congress did not prohibit that transportation. The Congress did not undertake to say that transportation of "hot oil" was injurious. The Congress did not say that transportation of that oil was "unfair competition." The Congress did not declare in what circumstances that transportation should be forbidden, or require the President to make any determination as to any facts or circumstances. Among the numerous and diverse objectives broadly stated, the President was not required to choose. The President was not required to ascertain and proclaim the conditions prevailing in the industry which made the prohibition necessary. The Congress left the matter to the President without standard or rule, to be dealt with as he pleased.

The Constitution provides that "All legislative Powers herein granted shall be vested in a Congress of the United States, which shall consist of a Senate and House of Representatives." And the Congress is empowered "To make all Laws which shall be necessary and proper for carrying into Execution" its general powers. The Congress manifestly is not permitted to abdicate or to transfer to others the essential legislative functions with which it is thus vested. Undoubtedly legislation must often be adapted to complex conditions involving a host of details with which the national Legislature cannot deal directly. The Constitution has never been regarded as denying to the Congress the necessary resources of flexibility and practicality, which will enable it to perform its function in laying down policies and establishing standards, while leaving to selected instrumentalities the making of subordinate rules within prescribed limits and the determination of facts to which the policy as declared by the Legislature is to apply. Without capacity to give authorizations of that sort we should have the anomaly of a legislative power which in many circumstances calling for its exertion would be but a futility. But the constant recognition of the necessity and validity of such provisions and the wide range of administrative authority which has been developed by means of them cannot be allowed to obscure the limitations of the authority to delegate, if our constitutional system is to be maintained.

If section 9(c) were held valid, it would be idle to pretend that anything would be left of limitations upon the power of the Congress to delegate its lawmaking function. The reasoning of the many decisions we have reviewed would be made vacuous and their distinctions nugatory. Instead of performing its lawmaking function, the Congress could at will and as to such subjects as it chooses transfer that function to the President or other officer or to an administrative body. The question is not of the intrinsic importance of the particular statute before us, but of the constitutional processes of legislation which are an essential part of our system of government.

———————

In the almost 70 years since *Panama Oil* and *Schechter*, not a single federal law has been declared an impermissible delegation of legislative power by the Supreme Court. Although these decisions have not been expressly overruled, they never have been followed either. All delegations, no matter how broad, have been upheld. Although the Court says that when Congress delegates its legislative power it must provide criteria to guide the agency's exercise of discretion,[4] all delegations, even without any criteria, have been upheld. Undoubtedly, this reflects a judicial judgment that broad delegations were necessary in the complex world of the late twentieth century and that the judiciary is ill equipped to draw meaningful lines. For example, in Mistretta v. United States, 488 U.S. 361 (1989), the Supreme Court upheld the Federal Sentencing Reform Act, which created the United States Sentencing Commission, an agency located in the judicial branch with broad discretion to promulgate sentencing guidelines to determine the punishments for those convicted of federal crimes.

Many have predicted a revival of the non-delegation doctrine, but it has not happened, as illustrated by the Supreme Court's most recent case on the topic: Whitman v. American Trucking Association, Inc.

Whitman v. American Trucking Assn., Inc.

531 U.S. 457 (2001)

Justice SCALIA delivered the opinion of the Court.

These cases present the question [w]hether §109(b)(1) of the Clean Air Act (CAA) delegates legislative power to the Administrator of the Environmental Protection Agency (EPA).[5]

———————

[4] *See, e.g.*, National Cable Television Assn. v. United States, 415 U.S 336 (1974).

[5] There also were statutory questions presented in this case, including "[w]hether the Administrator may consider the costs of implementation in setting national ambient air quality standards (NAAQS) under §109(b)(1); [w]hether the Court of Appeals had jurisdiction to review the EPA's interpretation of Part D of Title I of the CAA, with respect to implementing the revised ozone NAAQS; [i]f so, whether the EPA's interpretation of that part was permissible." The Court's discussion of these issues is not included because these are statutory and not constitutional questions. [Footnote by casebook author.]

Section 109(a) of the CAA requires the Administrator of the EPA to promulgate [National Ambient Air Quality Standards] NAAQS for each air pollutant for which "air quality criteria" have been issued. Once a NAAQS has been promulgated, the Administrator must review the standard (and the criteria on which it is based) "at five-year intervals" and make "such revisions . . . as may be appropriate." These cases arose when, on July 18, 1997, the Administrator revised the NAAQS for particulate matter (PM) and ozone.

The District of Columbia Circuit agreed with the respondents that §109(b)(1) delegated legislative power to the Administrator in contravention of the United States Constitution, Art. I, §1, because it found that the EPA had interpreted the statute to provide no "intelligible principle" to guide the agency's exercise of authority. The court thought, however, that the EPA could perhaps avoid the unconstitutional delegation by adopting a restrictive construction of §109(b)(1), so instead of declaring the section unconstitutional the court remanded the NAAQS to the agency.

[I]

In Lead Industries Assn., Inc. v. EPA, the District of Columbia Circuit held that "economic considerations [may] play no part in the promulgation of ambient air quality standards under Section 109" of the CAA. In the present cases, the court adhered to that holding, as it had done on many other occasions. Respondents argue that these decisions are incorrect. We disagree; and since the first step in assessing whether a statute delegates legislative power is to determine what authority the statute confers, we address that issue of interpretation first and reach respondents' constitutional arguments in Part [II].

Section 109(b)(1) instructs the EPA to set primary ambient air quality standards "the attainment and maintenance of which . . . are requisite to protect the public health" with "an adequate margin of safety." Here were it not for the hundreds of pages of briefing respondents have submitted on the issue, one would have thought it fairly clear that this text does not permit the EPA to consider costs in setting the standards. The language, as one scholar has noted, "is absolute." D. Currie, Air Pollution: Federal Law and Analysis 4-15 (1981). The EPA, "based on" the information about health effects contained in the technical "criteria" documents compiled under §108(a)(2), is to identify the maximum airborne concentration of a pollutant that the public health can tolerate, decrease the concentration to provide an "adequate" margin of safety, and set the standard at that level. Nowhere are the costs of achieving such a standard made part of that initial calculation. The text of §109(b), interpreted in its statutory and historical context and with appreciation for its importance to the CAA as a whole, unambiguously bars cost considerations from the NAAQS-setting process, and thus ends the matter for us as well as the EPA.

[II]

Section 109(b)(1) of the CAA instructs the EPA to set "ambient air quality standards the attainment and maintenance of which in the judgment of the

Administrator, based on [the] criteria [documents of §108] and allowing an adequate margin of safety, are requisite to protect the public health." The Court of Appeals held that this section as interpreted by the Administrator did not provide an "intelligible principle" to guide the EPA's exercise of authority in setting NAAQS. "[The] EPA," it said, "lack[ed] any determinate criteria for drawing lines. It has failed to state intelligibly how much is too much." The court hence found that the EPA's interpretation (but not the statute itself) violated the nondelegation doctrine. We disagree.

In a delegation challenge, the constitutional question is whether the statute has delegated legislative power to the agency. Article I, §1, of the Constitution vests "[a]ll legislative Powers herein granted . . . in a Congress of the United States." This text permits no delegation of those powers, and so we repeatedly have said that when Congress confers decision-making authority upon agencies Congress must "lay down by legislative act an intelligible principle to which the person or body authorized to [act] is directed to conform." We have never suggested that an agency can cure an unlawful delegation of legislative power by adopting in its discretion a limiting construction of the statute. The idea that an agency can cure an unconstitutionally standardless delegation of power by declining to exercise some of that power seems to us internally contradictory. The very choice of which portion of the power to exercise — that is to say, the prescription of the standard that Congress had omitted — would itself be an exercise of the forbidden legislative authority. Whether the statute delegates legislative power is a question for the courts, and an agency's voluntary self-denial has no bearing upon the answer.

We agree with the Solicitor General that the text of §109(b)(1) of the CAA at a minimum requires that "[f]or a discrete set of pollutants and based on published air quality criteria that reflect the latest scientific knowledge, [the] EPA must establish uniform national standards at a level that is requisite to protect public health from the adverse effects of the pollutant in the ambient air." Requisite, in turn, "mean[s] sufficient, but not more than necessary." These limits on the EPA's discretion are strikingly similar to the ones we approved in Touby v. United States (1991), which permitted the Attorney General to designate a drug as a controlled substance for purposes of criminal drug enforcement if doing so was "necessary to avoid an imminent hazard to the public safety." They also resemble the Occupational Safety and Health Act provision requiring the agency to "set the standard which most adequately assures, to the extent feasible, on the basis of the best available evidence, that no employee will suffer any impairment of health" — which the Court upheld in Industrial Union Dept., AFL-CIO v. American Petroleum Institute (1980), and which even then-Justice Rehnquist, who alone in that case thought the statute violated the nondelegation doctrine, would have upheld if, like the statute here, it did not permit economic costs to be considered.

The scope of discretion §109(b)(1) allows is in fact well within the outer limits of our non-delegation precedents. In the history of the Court we have found the requisite "intelligible principle" lacking in only two statutes, one of which provided literally no guidance for the exercise of discretion, and the other of which conferred authority to regulate the entire economy on the basis of no more precise a standard than stimulating the economy by assuring "fair competition." *See* Panama Refining Co. v. Ryan (1935); A.L.A. Schechter Poultry Corp. v. United States (1935). We have, on the other hand, upheld the validity of §11(b)(2) of the Public Utility Holding Company Act of 1935, which gave the Securities and Exchange Commission authority to modify the structure of holding company systems so as to ensure that they are not "unduly or unnecessarily complicate[d]" and do not "unfairly or inequitably distribute voting power among security holders." American Power & Light Co. v. SEC (1946). We have approved the wartime conferral of agency power to fix the prices of commodities at a level that "will be generally fair and equitable and will effectuate the [in some respects conflicting] purposes of th[e] Act." Yakus v. United States (1944). And we have found an "intelligible principle" in various statutes authorizing regulation in the "public interest." *See, e.g.,* National Broadcasting Co. v. United States (1943) (FCC's power to regulate airwaves); New York Central Securities Corp. v. United States (1932) (ICC's power to approve railroad consolidations). In short, we have "almost never felt qualified to second-guess Congress regarding the permissible degree of policy judgment that can be left to those executing or applying the law."

[E]ven in sweeping regulatory schemes we have never demanded, as the Court of Appeals did here, that statutes provide a "determinate criterion" for saying "how much [of the regulated harm] is too much." It is therefore not conclusive for delegation purposes that, as respondents argue, ozone and particulate matter are "nonthreshold" pollutants that inflict a continuum of adverse health effects at any airborne concentration greater than zero, and hence require the EPA to make judgments of degree. "[A] certain degree of discretion, and thus of lawmaking, inheres in most executive or judicial action." Mistretta v. United States (Scalia, J., dissenting). Section 109(b)(1) of the CAA, which to repeat we interpret as requiring the EPA to set air quality standards at the level that is "requisite" — that is, not lower or higher than is necessary — to protect the public health with an adequate margin of safety, fits comfortably within the scope of discretion permitted by our precedent. We therefore reverse the judgment of the Court of Appeals.

The Telephone Consumer Protection Act (1991)

Pub. L. No. 102-243, §3, 105 Stat. 2394, 2397 (provision below codified as amended at 47 U.S.C. §227)

(c) Protection of subscriber privacy rights

    (1) Rulemaking proceeding required

    Within 120 days after December 20, 1991, the Commission shall initiate a rulemaking proceeding concerning the need to protect residential telephone subscribers' privacy rights to avoid receiving telephone solicitations to which they object. The proceeding shall —

        (A) compare and evaluate alternative methods and procedures (including the use of electronic databases, telephone network technologies, special directory markings, industry-based or company-specific "do not call" systems, and any other alternatives, individually or in combination) for their effectiveness in protecting such privacy rights, and in terms of their cost and other advantages and disadvantages;

(B) evaluate the categories of public and private entities that would have the capacity to establish and administer such methods and procedures;

(C) consider whether different methods and procedures may apply for local telephone solicitations, such as local telephone solicitations of small businesses or holders of second class mail permits;

(D) consider whether there is a need for additional Commission authority to further restrict telephone solicitations, including those calls exempted under subsection (a)(3) of this section, and, if such a finding is made and supported by the record, propose specific restrictions to the Congress; and

(E) develop proposed regulations to implement the methods and procedures that the Commission determines are most effective and efficient to accomplish the purposes of this section.

(2) Regulations

Not later than 9 months after December 20, 1991, the Commission shall conclude the rulemaking proceeding initiated under paragraph (1) and shall prescribe regulations to implement methods and procedures for protecting the privacy rights described in such paragraph in an efficient, effective, and economic manner and without the imposition of any additional charge to telephone subscribers.

C. Specificity and Delegation

When Congress writes a statute, it must decide whether to resolve the problems that the statute addresses with a greater or lesser degree of specificity. This decision is crucial for the regulatory state because it determines how much authority Congress delegates to the implementing institution. For example, Congress can write a statute that seeks to promote auto safety by specifically requiring that automakers install airbags in new vehicles. NHTSA would merely ensure that automakers comply with the requirement. Or Congress can write a statute that seeks to promote motor vehicle safety by "reducing the occurrence of accidents by x% of vehicles sold per year, and the occurrence of injuries or deaths by y% percent of vehicles sold per year." NHTSA would determine the means for accomplishing this goal, as well as ensuring automaker compliance with those means. The 1966 Motor Vehicle Safety Act actually requires NHTSA to issue auto safety standards that are "practicable" and meet "the need for motor vehicle safety," §103, and defines "motor vehicle safety" as preventing an "unreasonable risk of accidents occurring . . . and an unreasonable risk of death or injury to persons in the event accidents do occur."§102(1). This is the broadest formulation of the three, granting NHTSA the greatest degree of authority to set auto safety standards. Note that a statute may be relatively specific or general whether it is implemented by an agency or a court. For example, the Sherman Antitrust Act, reprinted above, prohibits certain private contracts, combinations, and conspiracies "in restraint of trade." This language is relatively general, and courts determine how it applies in particular cases.

When Congress foregoes specificity, the result is a delegation of authority, but not every delegation is explicit in the statute. Look at the Sherman Antitrust Act: the provision does not expressly grant courts authority to determine which contracts, etc., are "in restraint of trade." The delegation is implicit, as are all delegations to courts. In fact, we may not even acknowledge that courts possess delegations. *See* Margaret H. Lemos, *The Consequences of Congress's Choice of Delegate: Judicial and Agency Interpretations of Title VII*, 63 VAND. L. REV. 363, 365 (2010). This may reflect the view that courts find law rather than make it. Regardless, vague language leaves courts, like agencies, substantial discretion. *See id.* As one of us has noted, a statue that applies directly to citizens and that a court implements can be called "transitive," which is distinct from those that do not and which can be called "intransitive."*See* Edward L. Rubin, *Law and Legislation in the Administrative State*, 89 COLUM. L. REV. 369, 381-85 (1989).

With regard to agencies, the delegation of authority from Congress is often explicit in the statute. The 1966 Motor Vehicle Safety Act contains a good example. The Act directs NHTSA to issue regulations determining the actual safety requirements that auto manufacturers have to meet, providing only broad guidance on the content. Congress also makes implicit delegations to agencies by the very act of writing ambiguous language — or at least the Supreme Court has so stated in a famous case that we study in Chapters 10 and 9 called *Chevron U.S.A., Inc., v. Natural Resources Defense Council*. When Congress leaves a term or phrase imprecise, it typically intends for agencies to determine the meaning.

For the most part, Congress does not write very specific statutes but shifts crucial policy choices to courts or agencies. Thus, as between specificity and delegation, Congress frequently chooses delegation. Many might describe delegation as the defining characteristic of modern government. Because delegation is central to the issues that we consider in this book, we pause to examine several aspects of it.

1. The Constitutional Limits of Delegation

One persistent question about the delegation of authority from Congress to agencies is whether it is constitutionally permissible. The constitutional argument against such delegation is that Congress is vested with legislative power and cannot delegate that power to other institutions. The Supreme Court has considered this argument on many occasions, but it has only enforced the so-called "nondelegation doctrine" in two 1935 decisions. Those decisions involved different provisions of the same usually sweeping statute, the National Industrial Recovery Act ("NIRA"). *See* Panama Refining Co. v. Ryan, 293 U.S. 388 (1935); A.L.A. Schechter Poultry Corp. v. United States, 295 U.S. 495 (1935). The NIRA was intended to stem the economic effects of the Great Depression. It granted the President authority to approve codes that ensured "fair competition" across virtually every aspect of the economy — from employment wages and hours to the price and quality of livestock. Thus, the statute was broad along two dimensions: it contained a general license to improve economic conditions, rather than a specific directive, and it reached almost every aspect of the economy, not a particular problem or industry. Furthermore, individual codes were actually set by members of the industry to which they applied; the President merely rubber stamped them. The Court had little hesitation in striking down the delegation of authority, which was not only "unconfined and vagrant" but effectively placed government power in private hands. *Schechter Poultry*, 295 U.S. at 537, 551 (Cardozo, J., concurring).

With the exception of these two early decisions, the Court has gone out of its way to uphold broad delegating statutes as long as they contain an "intelligible principle" to constrain the agency.[6] An "intelligible principle" is language in an operative provision (sometimes together with language in the definition section) of a statute that provides the agency some guidance on its mission. Few intelligible principles provide any more guidance than the vague instruction to the Secretary in the 1966 Motor Vehicle Safety Act to issue regulations that are "practicable" and "meet the need for auto safety" (§103(a)) or that avoid an "unreasonable risk" of injury or death (§102(1)). Nevertheless, the Court has been clear that language such as this satisfies the intelligible principle requirement. *See, e.g.*, Whitman v. Am. Trucking Ass'ns, 531 U.S. 457 (2001) (upholding the Clean Air Act as containing an intelligible principle in the words "requisite to protect the public health" and noting other equally vague examples).[7] Thus, the Court has suggested that no delegation is likely to fail muster on constitutional nondelegation grounds.

The Court has justified this permissive approach in pragmatic terms: Some delegation is unavoidable given the demands on modern government, and once the Court allows some delegation, it has no basis for distinguishing constitutional from unconstitutional ones. In Justice Scalia's words, "the debate over unconstitutional delegation becomes a debate not over a point of principle but over a question of degree." *Mistretta*, 488 U.S. at 415 (Scalia, J., dissenting). Because this determination requires consideration of facts "both multifarious and (in the nonpartisan sense) highly political," he continued, the Court has "almost never felt qualified to second-guess Congress regarding the permissible degree of policy judgment that be left to those executing or applying the law."*Id.* at 416 (Scalia, J., dissenting).

Although the Court has shown an unwillingness to invalidate broad delegations on constitutional nondelegation grounds, it has continued to raise nondelegation concerns and address them through a non-constitutional route: statutory

---

[6] The "intelligible principle" formulation actually came from a pre-1935 case. *See* J.W. Hampton, Jr. & Co. v. United States, 276 U.S. 394, 409 (1928).

[7] For other decisions upholding broad delegations, see Yakus v. United States, 321 U.S. 414 (1944) (upholding the Emergency Price Control Act, which enabled the administrator to set "fair and equitable prices"); Mistretta v. United States, 488 U.S. 361 (1989) (upholding a delegation to the Federal Sentencing Commission to "promulgate sentencing guidelines for every criminal offense"); Touby v. United States, 500 U.S. 160 (1991) (upholding a delegation to the Attorney General to add certain drugs to those listed in the statute, the possession or sale of which would constitute a crime, on the basis of standards that require the Attorney General to consider the levels of use of a particular drug and the impact on public health); Loving v. United States, 517 U.S. 748, 768-69 (1996) (upholding a delegation to the President to define "aggravating factors" that permit the imposition of the death penalty in a court martial).

interpretation. Thus, the Court has interpreted statutes narrowly in some instances to deprive an agency of what it plainly considers to be overbroad authority. *See, e.g.*, Industrial Union Dep't, AFL-CIO v. American Petroleum Inst., 448 U.S. 607 (1980). We discuss this approach in Chapters 11 and 9.

2. *The Political Reasons for Delegation*

Assuming that Congress has the constitutional ability to delegate, a practical political question is why Congress delegates so much authority to agencies. If it has the choice, why does it forego resolving an issue itself in favor of delegating that issue to an agency? Political scientists working in public choice and positive political theory have attempted to identify the circumstances that are conducive to delegation. Consider the following:

David Epstein & Sharyn O'Halloran, The Nondelegation Doctrine and the Separation of Powers: A Political Science Approach

20 Cardozo L. Rev. 947, 960-67 (1999)

II. Theory: The Political Logic of Delegation

We now juxtapose the legislative organization literature with the delegation literature to address our central questions of how much authority Congress delegates to the executive branch, and why Congress delegates more authority in some policy areas than in others. The starting point for our analysis, as with all political analyses, is the equation that preferences are filtered through institutions to produce policy. That is, individuals and their preferences are the fundamental building blocks for political outcomes, but they do not, in and of themselves, predict a particular policy; one must also know the institutions that aggregate these preferences, as well as how they operate in a given circumstance. When predicting the outcome of a legislative election, for instance, one must not only know the partisan preferences of the electorate, but also the electoral system being used, e.g., proportional representation or plurality-winner elections, district-based or at-large, primaries or no primaries, and so on.

Here, we wish to explain delegation from the legislative to the executive branch and the impact of this delegation on public policy. The key actors in this situation are legislators, the President, and executive agencies. We assume the preferences of legislators and the President to be, first and foremost, reelection. They may have other concerns as well, such as the desire for power, rewarding friends, and good government, but to satisfy any of the above they must first retain public office. The preferences of bureaucrats are more difficult to specify, as they lack any direct electoral motivation. The bureaucracy literature suggests that they may be controlled by their political superiors, driven by the desire to expand their budgets, seek to protect their professional reputation, or angle for lucrative post-agency positions. We will concentrate here on the former motivation — control by other political actors — as it is the most sensitive to variation in external political conditions.

We further assume that political actors who seek reelection will, on any given policy, attempt to bring final outcomes as close as possible to the median voter in their politically relevant constituency. Note that legislators will not necessarily take into account the preferences of all voters in their district if only a subset are mobilize on a particular issue, hence the possibility for special interest politics. On some issues, though, such as Social Security, minimum wage, and health care, a large proportion of the electorate will be mobilized, in which case the legislator will try to satisfy this broader constituency. Furthermore, we assume that actors' preferences over policy outcomes differ because they respond to different constituents. For instance, the fact that presidents have a national constituency usually means that they will be less susceptible to the demands of any one special interest, as opposed to House members who represent more narrowly defined geographical bases.

A. Choosing How to Decide

Our institutional analysis begins with the observation that there are two alternative modes for specifying the details of public policy. Policy can be made through the typical legislative process, in which a committee considers a bill and reports it to the floor of the chamber, and then a majority of the floor members must agree on a policy to enact. Alternatively, Congress can pass a law that delegates authority to regulatory agencies, allowing them to fill in some or all of the details of policy. The key is that, given a fixed amount of policy details to be specified, these two modes of policymaking are substitutes for each other. To the degree that one is used more, the other will perforce be used less.

Note also that it is Congress who chooses where policy is made. Legislators can either write detailed, exacting laws, in which case the executive branch will have little or no substantive input into policy, they can delegate the details to agencies, thereby giving the executive branch a substantial role in the policymaking process, or they can pick any point in between. Since legislators' primary goal is reelection, it follows that policy will be made so as to maximize legislators' reelection chances. Thus, delegation will follow the natural fault lines of legislators' political advantage.

In making this institutional choice, legislators face costs either way. Making explicit laws requires legislative time and energy that might be profitably spent on more electorally productive activities. After all, one of the reasons bureaucracies are created is for agencies to implement policies in areas where Congress has neither the time nor expertise to micromanage policy decisions, and by restricting flexibility, Congress would be limiting agencies' ability to adjust to changing circumstances. This tradeoff is captured well by Terry Moe in his discussion of regulatory structure:

> The most direct way [to control agencies] is for today's authorities to specify, in excruciating detail, precisely what the agency is to do and how it is to do it, leaving

as little as possible to the discretionary judgment of bureaucrats-and thus as little as possible for future authorities to exercise control over, short of passing new legislation. . . . Obviously, this is not a formula for creating effective organizations. In the interests of public protection, agencies are knowingly burdened with cumbersome, complicated, technically inappropriate structures that undermine their capacity to perform their jobs well.

Where oversight and monitoring problems do not exist, legislators would readily delegate authority to the executive branch, taking advantage of agency expertise, conserving scarce resources of time, staff, and energy, and avoiding the logrolls, delays, and informational inefficiencies associated with the committee system.

Consider, for example, the issue of airline safety, which is characterized on the one hand by the need for technical expertise, and on the other hand by an almost complete absence of potential political benefits. That is, policymakers will receive little credit if airlines run well and no disasters occur, but they will have to withstand intense scrutiny if something goes wrong. Furthermore, legislative and executive preferences on this issue would tend to be almost perfectly aligned — have fewer accidents as long as the costs to airlines are not prohibitive. The set of individuals receiving benefits, the public who use the airlines, is diffused and ill organized, while those paying the costs of regulation, the airline companies, are well-organized and politically active. Furthermore, keeping in mind that deficiencies in the system are easily detectable, delegated power is relatively simple to monitor. For all these reasons, even if legislators had unlimited time and resources of their own (which they do not), delegation to the executive branch would be the preferred mode of policymaking.

However, delegation implies surrendering at least some control over policy, and legislators will be loathe to relinquish authority in politically sensitive policy areas where they cannot be assured that the executive branch will carry out their intent. To the extent that legislators delegate to the executive branch, they face principal-agent problems of oversight and control since agencies will be influenced by the President, by interest groups, by the courts, and by the bureaucrats themselves. If agencies are so influenced, they may abuse their discretionary authority and enact policies with which Congress is likely to disagree.

Take, by way of illustration, the issue of tax policy, where Congress uses considerable resources to write detailed legislation that leaves the executive branch with little or no leeway in interpretation. The political advantages of controlling tax policy do not come from the duty of setting overall rates, which taxpayers tend to resent, but from the possibility of granting corporations and other well-organized lobby groups special tax breaks, so-called corporate welfare. If designed correctly, these benefits can target a specific industry or group and are paid for by the general public, either through taxes paid into general revenues or by the decrease in revenue stemming from the tax break. Such political benefits are not lightly foregone, and they would be difficult to replicate through a delegation scheme with open-ended mandates. Thus, Congress continues to make tax policy itself, despite the demands of time and expertise that this entails.

So, when deciding where policy will be made, legislators will trade off the internal costs of policymaking in committees against the external costs of delegating authority to regulatory agencies. We can think of Congress's decision of where to make policy as equivalent to a firm's make-or-buy decision-legislators can either produce policy internally, or they can subcontract it out (delegate) to the Executive. In making this decision, legislators face a continuum of possibilities: Congress can do everything itself by writing specific legislation and leave nothing to the Executive; it can give everything to the Executive by writing very general laws and do nothing itself; or it can choose any alternative in between. So, Congress will choose the point along this continuum — how much discretionary authority to delegate — that balances these two types of costs at the margin.

As a result, Congress delegates to the Executive in those areas which it handles least efficiently, where the committee system is most prone to over-logrolling and/or the under-provision of expertise. Conversely, it retains control over those areas where the political disadvantages of delegation — loss of control due to the principal-agent problem — outweigh the advantages. Just as companies subcontract out the jobs that they perform less efficiently than the market, legislators subcontract out the details of policy that they produce at a greater political cost than executive agencies.

B. The Pyramid of Power

To illustrate our argument, Figure 9.1 summarizes legislators' alternatives over the structure of policymaking. Each node of the tree represents a policy decision to be made in a given law, ranging from the most elemental decisions at the top (e.g., who will receive Social Security, and on what basis benefits will be paid) to the fine-grained details of implementation on the bottom (e.g., when and how to mail the benefit checks). The shaded area represents those details spelled out in the enacting legislation, so the boundaries between the shaded and unshaded regions are the boundaries of the administrative state in that policy area.

Note that the uppermost nodes fall within the sphere of legislative policymaking. This is where the nondelegation doctrine comes into play. Congress must make the basic policy decisions in any law; it cannot delegate without also specifying an "intelligible principle" for agencies to follow.But, this standard imposes only a minimal constraint on Congress, which in practice is easily satisfied by reference to some reasonableness standard for bureaucrats. At the bottom of the diagram, Congress will usually not find it useful or even possible to specify the most intricate details of policy implementation. Consequently, the scope of detail in a given piece of legislation will be limited, making explicit some policy choices and leaving others to executive actors. And the boundaries between legislative and executive action will be adjusted over time as one mode of policy production or the other better fulfills legislators' reelection needs.

Figure 9.1   Boundaries of the Administrative State

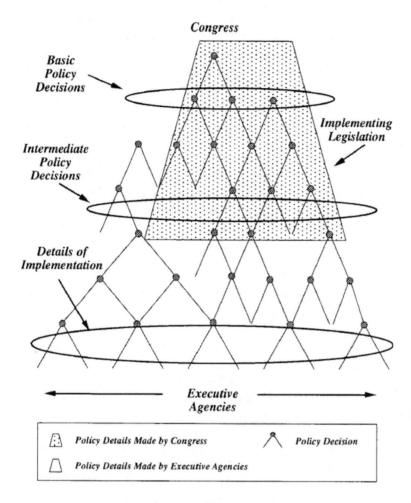

C. Empirical Predictions

If this theory aptly describes legislators' preferences over delegation, then what patterns should we expect to see in executive discretion from law to law? To begin with, legislators should be more willing to delegate authority to executive branch actors who share their preferences than to those who do not, as such actors are less likely to use their discretion in the pursuit of policy goals contrary to legislators' desires. To the extent that partisan affiliation can serve as a proxy for preferences, and to the extent that the President can control agency actions through appointment powers, we should expect to see Congress delegate more authority to Presidents of their own party than to Presidents of the opposite party.

In a similar vein, legislators should be more apt to rely on committees whose membership mirrors that of the floor, and to distrust outlying committees. The legislative organization literature reviewed above emphasizes that committees whose preferences differ from those of the floor will not receive procedural benefits such as closed rules and deference in the policymaking process. If our theory is correct, then these should also be the committees that lose authority to their executive branch counterparts.

A third prediction arising from our approach concerns the informational as opposed to distributive nature of policymaking. As policy becomes more complex, Congress will rationally rely more on the executive branch to fill in policy details. This occurs for two reasons. The first and most obvious reason is that the executive branch is filled (or can be filled) with policy experts who can run tests and experiments, gather data, and otherwise determine the wisest course of policy, much more so than can 535 members of Congress and their staff. The second, less obvious reason has to do with the fact that expertise garnered in legislative committees cannot be transformed directly into policy outcomes. Rather, it must first pass through the floor, which may decide to make some alterations to the committee's proposals. The existence of the floor as a policy middle-man gives committees less incentive to gather information in the first place. Executive agencies, on the other hand, are not hampered by the need to obtain congressional approval; their rulings become law directly. Therefore, even purely policy-motivated executive agencies will be more informationally efficient than will be congressional committees.

Bringing together these statements, we predict that Congress would delegate more authority to the Executive:

1. The closer are the preferences of the Executive to the median floor voter, so that divided government leads to less discretion;
2. The higher the level of conflict between the committee and the median floor voter, so that committee outliers lead Congress to delegate less authority; and
3. The more complex is a policy area.

Note that our theory, if correct, contradicts the key predictions of the nondelegation forces. Rather than portraying Congress as delegating ever-increasing authority to executive actors, we assert that levels of delegation will rise and fall over time in response to changing external factors. Instead of assuming that legislators have no interest in monitoring delegated authority, we assert that they will empower interest groups, the courts, and other actors to challenge agency actions through administrative procedures as well as direct oversight. Finally, a revitalized nondelegation doctrine would have the effect of shifting back to Congress precisely those policy areas, such as the reduction of pork barrel benefits, that it handles poorly relative to the Executive, so limits on delegation would only tend to diminish the efficacy of the political process.

NOTES AND QUESTIONS

1. The first section of the Epstein and O'Halloran article states the behavioral assumptions of public choice theory. Recall that public choice theory begins from the premise that people, as rational actors, try to maximize their material

self-interest. In the case of legislators, this is generally taken to be an interest in reelection. Take a moment to consider whether this explanation is satisfying. Is it too cynical? Note that even those legislators who are motivated to serve the public must hold and maintain their jobs to do so.

2. Epstein and O'Halloran assert that Congress must balance the benefits and costs of delegation. What are the benefits and costs that they identify? In which circumstances is Congress more likely to delegate? In which circumstances is it less likely to delegate?

3. What if an issue is complex — militating toward delegation — but the opposite political party holds the White House — increasing monitoring costs and militating against delegation? Can you think of strategies for Congress to maintain the benefits without incurring the costs of delegation? Here are Epstein and O'Halloran again:

> One method by which delegated authority is circumscribed lies in the administrative procedures that constrain executive branch actions. . . . But structural choices also include the particular actors to whom authority is delegated: cabinet departments, independent agencies, or state-level actors. Legislators must first decide whether to give authority to the executive or to the states — this is the *federalism* question. And if the authority will be located in the executive branch, Congress must choose the type of executive actor to receive the delegated authority — this is the *locational* question.

DAVID EPSTEIN & SHARYN O'HALLORAN, DELEGATING POWERS: A TRANSACTION COST APPROACH TO POLICY MAKING UNDER SEPARATE POWERS 153 (1999).

3. The Normative Implications of Delegation

Although Congress may choose to delegate for strategic reasons, that choice has normative implications. What exactly are the normative advantages and disadvantages of delegation? This question has divided legal scholars for some time. Consider the following positions, which are somewhat representative but by no means exhaustive.

David Schoenbrod, Power Without Responsibility: How Congress Abuses the People Through Delegation

10-12 (1993)

Congress and the president delegate for much the same reason that they continue to run budget deficits. With deficit spending, they can claim credit for the benefits of their expenditures yet escape blame for the costs. The public must pay ultimately of course, but through taxes levied at some future time by some other officials. The point is not that deficits always have bad economic consequences, but that they have the political consequence of allowing officials to duck responsibility for costs.

Likewise, delegation allows legislators to claim credit for the benefits which a regulatory statute promises yet escape the blame for the burdens it will impose, because they do not issue the laws needed to achieve those benefits. The public inevitably must suffer regulatory burdens to realize regulatory benefits, but the laws will come from an agency that legislators can then criticize for imposing excessive burdens on their constituents. Just as deficit spending allows legislators to appear to deliver money to some people without taking it from others, delegation allows them to appear to deliver regulatory benefits without imposing regulatory costs. It provides "a handy set of mirrors — so useful in Washington — by which a politician can appear to kiss both sides of the apple."

Politicians understand that delegation helps them to avoid blame. For example, in 1988 legislators used delegation to try to give themselves a 50-percent pay raise without losing votes in the next election. They enacted a statute that delegated to a commission the power to set pay for themselves and other top officials whose pay they linked to their own. Under the statute, if the commission grants a pay increase, another statute passed before (but not after) the increase goes into effect could cancel it. When the commission recommended the 50-percent increase, some legislators introduced bills to cancel it. But that action was part of a plan in which the congressional leadership would prevent a vote on the bills until it was too late to stop the increase. Legislators could then tell their constituents that they would have voted against the increase if given a chance. Thus they could get the pay raise and also credit for opposing it. However, the size of the increase, in an atmosphere of antipathy to Congress, provoked such a storm of protest and publicity that the public came to see through the charade. Embarrassed, the House leadership conducted a secret ballot among members to determine whether to hold a roll-call vote on the pay increase. Fifty-seven percent of the members who responded opposed a roll call, although 95 percent of the House members surveyed by the Public Citizen group claimed that they had supported it. After public opposition to the pay increase rose to an extraordinary 88 percent, Congress passed a bill to cancel it.

The pay raise controversy illustrates the willingness of Congress to use delegation to manipulate voters' perceptions of its activities. In this instance the manipulation failed — indeed backfired — because the public came to see it for what it was. Yet such manipulation is usually successful because routine government action is neither so readily understood nor so pregnant with symbolic value as the pay raise was, and so eludes the sustained attention of the press and the public.

So far, I have suggested that delegation as well as budget deficits help lawmakers escape blame for the direct costs of federal regulation, such as the higher grocery prices caused by marketing orders. Both budget deficits and delegation also impose important indirect costs on the public. Budget deficits require interest payments on the new debt, increase inflation, and raise interest rates. Delegation has indirect costs of even greater consequence, as illustrated by the environmental statutes that I tried to make work in my own career.

In those statutes, Congress and the president generally did not resolve the key conflicts between business and environmental groups but instead promised to satisfy each side and instructed the Environmental Protection Agency (EPA) to make the laws accordingly. Subsequently, when EPA attempted to issue a law that industry did not like, legislators — sometimes even those who took the strongest environmental positions on the floor of Congress — would tell EPA to back off. And, on the other hand, should EPA fail to satisfy environmentalists, legislators-sometimes even those with close ties to industry would strike environmentalist poses. To camouflage the statute's lack of substance, our elected lawmakers had included all the decisions on procedures that any constituent might want — for example, the agency shall issue a law to protect the public from pollutant x by deadline y, but not before preparing an analysis of the impact on industry z although they knew that the agency could never come close to discharging these duties with the time, resources, and political power given to it.

This experience . . . illustrates the profound indirect costs of delegation:

- It undercuts the government's capacity to resolve disputes through compromise by allowing the only officials with authoritative power to impose compromises to instead claim to be all things to all interests.
- It allows disputes to be prolonged and keeps standards of conduct murky, because pressure from legislators and the complicated procedures imposed upon agencies turn lawmaking into an excruciatingly slow process. Agencies typically report that they have issued only a small fraction of the laws that their longstanding statutory mandates require. Competing interests devote large sums of money and many of their best minds to this seemingly interminable process. Meanwhile, those potentially subject to regulation have no reliable way to plan their activities, as they do not know what the law eventually will be. The public is unprotected during these struggles: a statute that delegates provides no law until an agency makes one.

In the very act of allowing our elected lawmakers to shape laws that make themselves look like heroes, delegation renders them less responsible to the people and less responsive to their interests.

Jerry L. Mashaw, Greed, Chaos & Governance: Using Public Choice to Improve Public Law

146-47, 152-55 (1997)

. . . I do not believe that failure to reach consensus on detail should disable legislators from legislating because I see no reason to believe that it has negative consequences either for public welfare or for political accountability. A decision to go forward notwithstanding continuing ambiguity or disagreement about the details of implementation is a decision that the polity is better off legislating generally than maintaining the status quo. Citizens may disagree, but they can also hold legislators accountable for their choice. If citizens want more specific statutes, or fear that legislating without serious agreement on implementing details is danger-ous, they can, after all, throw the bums out.

To be sure, it may be argued that this requires a significant level of sophistica-tion on the part of voters. But that is precisely the problem with the suggestion that broad delegations of authority in legislation enhance the ability of representatives either to dissemble or to be inconsistent, by comparison with more specific legisla-tive action. The sad truth is that legislators can as easily convey information selec-tively or take up inconsistent positions in specific statutes as in more general ones.

The Clean Air Act that Schoenbrod uses as an example for his view as easily supports mine. There are indeed some critical gaps in this statute and its many amendments that leave substantial policy discretion to administrators. On the other hand, the statute goes on for hundreds of pages, many of them containing hyper technical provisions that few citizens could possibly understand. Moreover, to the extent that the Clean Air Act and its amendments do things that dramati-cally depart from citizens' expectation, I would suggest that they are largely in the detailed provisions, not in the broad aspirational sections. Voters do not read bills and would have little chance of understanding most of them if they did. Hence, legislators can selectively convey information about legislation whether they legis-late specifically or generally.

Nor does specificity help voters police for inconsistency in legislators' ideolog-ical positions. Indeed, it would seem to me much easier for a voter to detect the inconsistency in a legislator's statement that he or she intended "to protect the public health through strict air quality regulation while avoiding any serious eco-nomic dislocation" than by attempting to figure out that the specific provisions of a bill were indeed trading off these values and in precisely what ways.

Consider a different, but now well-known, example: The most specific legisla-tion that comes out of the Congress these days is perhaps the gargantuan and mind-numbingly detailed legislation drafted by the Budget, Appropriations, and Finance Committees. But an Omnibus Budget Reconciliation Act can hardly be carried, much less read. And perhaps nowhere in American politics do legislators make better use of selective information and creative incoherence than in explain-ing to the American people what has been done in constructing the federal budget. . . .

Edward L. Rubin, Law and Legislation in the Administrative State

89 Columbia L. Rev. 369, 388-92 (1984)

In doctrinal terms, delegation has very little relevance to modern legislation. A proper use of the term in our contemporary context shows that Congress has virtu-ally never delegated any of its power. The entire concept was born from a misun-derstanding of the administrative state and from an image of modern legislation restricted to transitive rules.

When the legislature directs an agency to implement a program of some sort, the legislature is exercising its power, not giving that power away. The "legislative power" does not consist of a monopoly on the enactment of a certain set of preexisting rules. Rather, it is the power to issue directives that allocate resources among citizens and government agencies, form public and private organizations, and authorize regulatory action by administrative agencies. When the legislature takes such actions, when it creates an agency, allocates resources to it, or authorizes it to act, the legislature is simply carrying out its basic task: it is exercising the legislative power it possesses.

A legislature could conceivably delegate its power, that is, give away the legislative power itself. It could do so by authorizing some other body to enact and repeal a broad range, or perhaps all, of the statutes that lie within the legislature's jurisdiction. But the enactment of a particular statute hardly represents such a delegation. Rather, it represents the mode of legislative action demanded by the separation of powers doctrine, the very doctrine from which delegation itself is derived. A central feature of this doctrine is that the legislature may not enforce its legislation or engage in similar operational activities. Such activities are reserved to implementation mechanisms — agencies and courts — belonging to the executive and judicial branches. Thus, the separation of powers doctrine obligates the legislature to act by granting power. Whether a particular statute is broadly or narrowly worded, it represents an exercise of the legislative power, not a delegation of it.

The reason why modern legislation is often regarded as a delegation of the legislative power is that it grants to an implementation mechanism the power to make rules. According to this view, while the power to adjudicate is separate from the legislative process, the power to make rules is the power of the legislature itself, and a grant of this power represents at least a partial surrender of the legislature's own prerogatives. But rule-making power cannot be equated with legislation in a modern administrative state. Such power must be exercised by other governmental units, and the legislature must act in ways that do not involve rule making. As has frequently been pointed out, rule making is an intrinsic and unavoidable part of the process by which administrative agencies implement statutes. An agency that exercises any degree of planning or any prosecutorial or inspection function, that operates an institution, or that makes any positive effort to secure compliance, must engage in rule making of some sort. At the same time, a modern legislature must engage in many activities that cannot be described as rule making, such as creating administrative agencies and allocating resources to them.

Lisa Schultz Bressman, *Schechter Poultry* at the Millennium: A Delegation Doctrine for the Administrative State

109 Yale L.J. 1399, 1415-16, 1422-26 (2000)

[Consider a new] delegation doctrine [that] requires administrative agencies to issue rules containing reasonable limits on their discretion in exchange for broad grants of regulatory authority. Thus, the new delegation doctrine upholds the congressional transfer of lawmaking authority to administrative agencies, but imposes restraints on the exercise of that authority. Instead of demanding intelligible principles from Congress, it permits agencies to select their own standards, consistent with the broad purposes of the statutory scheme. (Administrative limiting standards are distinct from congressional intelligible principles because the former are not discernible from the statute itself, but rather are chosen by the agency in accordance with the broad purposes of the statute. Both serve, however, to define the parameters of permissible administrative action.) These administrative limiting standards, once promulgated, function no differently than if Congress had written them into the original statute — that is, they bind agencies in implementing the statutory provision to which they apply. In this way, the standards serve to limit administrative discretion and prevent arbitrary administrative decisionmaking....

The current scholarly debate might have difficulty making sense of the new delegation doctrine in terms of democracy. Schoenbrod's side of the debate might find that the administrative-standards requirement perpetuates the general abdication of democratic values in this area because it fails to ensure that Congress makes the hard choices. On the other side, Mashaw . . . might conclude that the administrative-standards requirement arbitrarily intrudes on democratic values because it interferes with the legitimate exercise of administrative lawmaking authority. Put simply, one side might claim that the administrative-standards requirement does too little, and the other side might contend that it does too much.

Whatever the merits of each side's argument, the entire debate falls short of addressing the particular conception of democracy reinforced by the new delegation doctrine and its administrative-standards requirement. The new delegation doctrine does not focus on the proper locus of lawmaking authority, which is the issue that has seemed to dominate at least one side of the current scholarly debate. Rather, it accepts Congress's assignment of power and consequent relinquishment of policy control. But it does not thereby abdicate responsibility for promoting and protecting democracy. Nor does it arbitrarily interfere with legitimate delegations. Instead, it restrains the exercise of delegated authority by invoking a principle — an obligation to provide limiting standards — that reflects classic democratic values in precisely those cases that raise familiar concerns about democracy.

This principle can be understood to advance democracy in several ways. For example, it may increase congressional accountability by improving congressional oversight of agency action. Administrative limiting standards may enhance congressional oversight by providing an additional piece of information for Congress to consider in evaluating a controversial agency proposal. Moreover, that piece of information is particularly useful to Congress in formulating a legislative response because it provides insight not only into the agency's rationale but also into its overarching regulatory theory.

Administrative limiting standards also may spur calls for oversight hearings. Traditionally, Congress has used such hearings sparingly and for matters of some prominence. Interest groups may increase the pressure for congressional review of agency standards they dislike, either before or after those standards are promulgated. Or interest groups, fearing unfavorable administrative standards, may push for more precise and protective standards in the initial statute. To the extent that this occurs, the new delegation doctrine may force Congress to make more basic choices up front — the result that Schoenbrod seeks to achieve through use of the original nondelegation doctrine. . . .

Perhaps more significantly and intuitively, the new delegation doctrine promotes the rule of law. As Jerry Mashaw succinctly explains,

> A consistent strain of our constitutional politics asserts that legitimacy flows from "the rule of law." By that is meant a system of objective and accessible commands, law which can be seen to flow from collective agreement rather than from the exercise of discretion or preference by those persons who happen to be in positions of authority. By reducing discretion, and thereby the possibility for the exercise of the individual preferences of officials, specific rules reinforce the rule of law.

The rule-of-law rationale for delegation review is hardly new. It has always been present in the Court's intelligible-principle requirement. Although the Court has primarily understood this requirement to preserve separation of powers, it has made it clear that the requirement also serves an important role in controlling administrative discretion. Thus, the rule of law has always supplied a partial doctrinal basis for the nondelegation principle.

Moreover, the rule of law has furnished a major theoretical underpinning of delegation review for some time. In his 1978 treatise, Kenneth Culp Davis stated:

> The purpose [of a nondelegation doctrine] should be to do what can be done through such a doctrine to protect private parties against injustice on account of unnecessary and uncontrolled discretionary power.
>
> Instead of saying that delegations are unlawful or that delegations are unlawful unless accompanied by meaningful standards, the courts should affirmatively assert that delegations are lawful and desirable, as long as the broad legislative purpose is discernible and as long as protections against arbitrary power are provided. . . .
>
> The change in the basic purpose is essential because the underlying problem is broader than control of delegation; the problem is to provide effective protection against administrative arbitrariness. . . .
>
> . . . The courts should continue their requirement of meaningful standards, except that when the legislative body fails to prescribe the required standards for discretionary action in particular cases, the administrators should be allowed to satisfy the requirement by prescribing them within a reasonable time.

Thus, Davis understood the purpose of delegation review as advancing rule-of-law values and further recognized that administrative, as well as congressional, standards could serve those values. Davis certainly was not alone on this point. As Judge Leventhal recognized in the important case of *Amalgamated Meat Cutters v. Connally*, an administrative-standards requirement "means that however broad the discretion of the Executive at the outset, the standards once developed limit the latitude of subsequent executive action."

NOTES AND QUESTIONS

1. How does the Schoenbrod argument against delegation fit in with the Epstein and O'Halloran account of delegation? Is the desire to escape blame a reelection strategy that favors delegation?
2. Schoenbrod assumes that the Supreme Court, by reinvigorating the nondelegation doctrine, can help to reform the legislative process. Is this a proper role for the Court? What would Rubin say? Is delegation a legislative failure, or the essence of modern legislation?
3. Will reinvigorating the nondelegation doctrine work to reform the legislative process? Or will it, as Mashaw suggests, simply shut down modern government? Is the risk worth running if Congress can escape blame anyway through specific legislation?
4. Does your answer change if Congress truly cannot provide detailed rules in some area that it nonetheless wants to regulate? For example, some rules may require information that can only be obtained through the regulatory process itself; this was arguably the case with the 1966 Motor Vehicle Safety Act. Take a look at the Act again and see if you can identify some areas where Congress expected the regulatory process to generate relevant information.
5. Does accountability argue for locating policy decisions in a single elected legislature rather than in administrative agencies headed by political appointees and supervised by the President? This is one point of disagreement between Schoenbrod and Mashaw.
6. If given the choice, Schoenbrod would have courts invalidate broad delegations and Mashaw would have courts uphold them. Is there a middle ground? As we briefly mentioned above, in certain circumstances, a court can interpret a statute narrowly rather than invalidate or approve it wholesale. *See, e.g.,* Cass R. Sunstein, *Nondelegation Canons*, 67 U. Chi. L. Rev. 315 (2000). This approach is widely used, though not without limits. Bressman suggests another possibility: courts can prod agencies to issue "limiting standards," which would function no differently than standards that Congress itself might supply in the statute. A different approach is for courts to interpret regulatory statutes as requiring the agency to state reasons for its actions. *See* SEC v. Chenery Corp., 318 U.S. 80, 87 (1943) (a court may uphold an agency's action only for reasons stated by the agency at the time it acted). *See* Kevin M. Stack, *The Constitutional Foundations of* Chenery, 116 Yale L.J. 952, 958 (2007). What is gained and lost through approaches such as these?

D. What do Agencies Look Like?

If you were looking at agencies from a distance, you would see many similarities among them. The only clearly distinguishing feature would be their varied subject areas. Closer up, other notable distinctions would emerge. In this section, we provide a mid-range snapshot of agencies, discussing some features that unite and divide them.

1. Executive-Branch and Independent Agencies

When Congress creates an agency, one design decision stands out above the rest: whether to create an executive-branch agency or a so-called "independent" agency. Executive-branch agencies appear under the President in the government organizational chart and are run by officials who can be fired at will by the President. The most familiar executive-branch agencies include:

- Each "Department" headed by a "Secretary" (or in the case of the Department of Justice, the Attorney General)
- Subdivisions of Departments, such as the National Highway Safety Transportation Administration (NHTSA) within the Department of Transportation or the Food and Drug Administration (FDA) within the Department of Health and Human Services
- Environmental Protection Agency (EPA)

Independent agencies are different. Their heads serve fixed terms that expire in staggered years and are removable by the President only "for cause" or "good cause." Thus, these agencies are independent in the sense that their heads are not subject to plenary presidential removal. In addition, there is a difference in their form. Independent agencies generally are run by multi-member commissions or boards rather than a single administrator. The most well-known independent agencies are the Federal Communications Commission (FCC), the Federal Reserve Board (the Fed), and the Securities and Exchange Commission (SEC). The Paperwork Reduction Act defines "independent regulatory agencies" to include:

Board of Governors of the Federal Reserve System
Commodity Futures Trading Commission
Consumer Product Safety Commission
Federal Communications Commission
Federal Deposit Insurance Corporation
Federal Energy Regulatory Commission
Federal Housing Finance Agency
Federal Maritime Commission
Federal Trade Commission
Interstate Commerce Commission
Mine Enforcement Safety and Health Review Commission

National Labor Relations Board
Nuclear Regulatory Commission
Occupational Safety and Health Review Commission
Postal Regulatory Commission
Securities and Exchange Commission

44 U.S.C. §3502(5).

Independent agencies are different in structure from executive-branch agencies, but they also have some variations in structure from one another. For example:

The five members of the Federal Trade Commission serve seven-year terms and are removable by the President for "inefficiency, neglect of duty, or malfeasance in office." 15 U.S.C. §41. In addition, not more than three of the Commissioners can "be members of the same political party." *Id.* This is known as a bipartisan requirement, and it serves as an additional check on political imbalance. The President selects the chairperson, who customarily steps down to allow a new President to select his or her own chairperson. Because the chairperson has the power to influence the agency's agenda, the ability to select the chairperson is significant from the President's perspective.

By contrast, the five commissioners of the Securities and Exchange Commission are appointed for five-year terms, and no more than three of the five members may belong to the same political party. 15 U.S.C. §78d. The SEC is not governed by a statutory removal restriction, but the removal power belongs to the President and is "commonly understood" as limited to "inefficiency, neglect of duty, or malfeasance in office." *See* MFS Securities Corp. v. SEC, 380 F.3d 611, 619-20 (2d Cir. 2004) (quoting SEC v. Blinder, Robinson & Co., 855 F.2d 677, 681 (10th Cir. 1988)). The chairperson, selected by the President, customarily steps down to allow a new President to appoint his or her own chairperson. The commissioners also have limitations on their employment activities and business interests. 15 U.S.C. §78d ("No commissioner shall engage in any other business, vocation, or employment than that of serving as commissioner, nor shall any commissioner participate, directly or indirectly, in any stock-market operations or transactions of a character subject to regulation by the Commission pursuant to this chapter.").

The seven members of the Federal Reserve Board serve 14-year terms and are removable by the President only "for cause." 12 U.S.C. §§241-42. Not more than one Board member "may be selected from any one Federal Reserve district." Additionally, the President, in selecting members, "shall have due regard to a fair representation of the financial, agricultural, industrial, and commercial interests, and geographical divisions of the country." The Chair is selected by the President and serves for a four-year term. But the Chair does not step down upon the election of a new President, making the Federal Reserve Board more insulated from this sort of presidential control than other independent agencies. 12 U.S.C. §242.

Here are two other examples drawn directly from the statutes so that you may see their features in context. The National Labor Relations Board, like the FTC, contains a specific statutory removal restriction, as well as other qualifications.

29 U.S.C. §153. National Labor Relations Board

(a) Creation, composition, appointment, and tenure; Chairman; removal of members

The National Labor Relations Board (hereinafter called the "Board") created by this subchapter prior to its amendment by the Labor Management Relations Act, 1947 [29 U.S.C.A. §§141 *et seq.*], is hereby continued as an agency of the United States, except that the Board shall consist of five instead of three members, appointed by the President by and with the advice and consent of the Senate. Of the two additional members so provided for, one shall be appointed for a term of five years and the other for a term of two years. Their successors, and the successors of the other members, shall be appointed for terms of five years each, excepting that any individual chosen to fill a vacancy shall be appointed only for the unexpired term of the member whom he shall succeed. The President shall designate one member to serve as Chairman of the Board. Any member of the Board may be removed by the President, upon notice and hearing, for neglect of duty or malfeasance in office, but for no other cause.

The FCC, like the SEC, lacks a specific statutory limitation on removal, but it nevertheless is understood to have one. It also has limitations on the financial interests of its members:

47 U.S.C. §154. Federal Communications Commission

(a) Number of commissioners; appointment

The Federal Communications Commission (in this chapter referred to as the "Commission") shall be composed of five commissioners appointed by the President, by and with the advice and consent of the Senate, one of whom the President shall designate as chairman.

(b) Qualifications

(1) Each member of the Commission shall be a citizen of the United States.

(2)(A) No member of the Commission or person employed by the Commission shall —

(i) be financially interested in any company or other entity engaged in the manufacture or sale of telecommunications equipment which is subject to regulation by the Commission;

(ii) be financially interested in any company or other entity engaged in the business of communication by wire or radio or in the use of the electromagnetic spectrum;

(iii) be financially interested in any company or other entity which controls any company or other entity specified in clause (i) or clause (ii), or which derives a significant portion of its total income from ownership of stocks, bonds, or other securities of any such company or other entity; or

(iv) be employed by, hold any official relation to, or own any stocks, bonds, or other securities of, any person significantly regulated by the Commission under this chapter;

except that the prohibitions established in this subparagraph shall apply only to financial interests in any company or other entity which has a

significant interest in communications, manufacturing, or sales activities
which are subject to regulation by the Commission . . . .

(5) The maximum number of commissioners who may be members of the
same political party shall be a number equal to the least number of commissioners which constitutes a majority of the full membership of the
Commission . . . .

(c) Terms of office; vacancies

Commissioners shall be appointed for terms of five years and until their successors are appointed and have been confirmed and taken the oath of office, except
that they shall not continue to serve beyond the expiration of the next session of
Congress subsequent to the expiration of said fixed term of office; except that any
person chosen to fill a vacancy shall be appointed only for the unexpired term of
the Commissioner whom he succeeds. No vacancy in the Commission shall
impair the right of the remaining commissioners to exercise all the powers of the
Commission.

Note on the Constitutionality of Independent Agencies

Independent agencies have been subject to constitutional challenge. The
issue is not whether independent agencies are unconstitutional by virtue of the
broad authority that they possess; executive-branch agencies also possess broad
powers, and an assault on such powers raises constitutional issues that we briefly
address in connection with our discussion of legislative delegation in Chapter 2,
see pp. 483. Rather, independent agencies are subject to particular challenge
because, unlike executive-branch agencies, their leaders are not removable by the
President at will. If the members of independent agencies are not subject to the
plenary control of the President, does the President posses sufficient control of
such agencies to ensure, as the Constitution requires, that the laws are faithfully
executed?

At first, the answer seemed to be no. In a famous early decision authored by
(former President) Chief Justice Taft, Myers v. United States, 272 U.S. 52 (1926),
the Supreme Court articulated a very broad view of the President's removal
power, suggesting that the President's power of removal be unrestricted as to all
officers the President appoints. "The imperative reasons requiring an unrestricted
power to remove the most important of his subordinates in their most important
duties must, therefore, control the interpretation of the Constitution as to all
appointed by him." Id. at 134.

But, in a New Deal decision, the Court limited Myers and upheld a removal
restriction on members of the FTC over the objection of President Franklin Roosevelt, who sought to remove a commissioner for policy disagreement rather than
"inefficiency, neglect of duty, or malfeasance in office." Humphrey's Executor v.
United States, 295 U.S. 602 (1935). In Humphrey's Executor, the Court emphasized
the functions of the officials: Congress could restrict the ability of the President to
remove FTC members without violating the principle of separations of powers
because those members exercised "quasi-legislative" and "quasi-judicial" functions
rather than executive ones. See id. at 628-29; see also Wiener v. United States, 357

U.S. 349 (1958) (construing statute to create removal restrictions on the members of the War Claims Commission and upholding its constitutionality).

Since then, the Court has gone out of its way to preserve the constitutionality of independent agencies when called into question. When asked to consider a removal restriction on an inferior officer with "purely executive" functions, it validated that restriction using a more forgiving functional analysis. *See* Morrison v. Olson, 487 U.S. 654 (1988) (upholding the constitutionality of the independent counsel statute). It stated that Congress may impose removal restrictions on agency officials as long as the restriction does not unduly "interfere with the President's exercise of the 'executive power' and his constitutionally appointed duty to 'take care that the laws be faithfully executed' under Article II." *Id.* at 690, 693. So, unless things change, independent agencies have a secure constitutional status.

Interestingly, the question of how much protection a "good cause" removal provision provides has not been tested. Most assume that "good cause" must amount to something more than a mere disagreement about policy or priorities, but it is not clear how much more. Indeed, one of the basic points of the Court's decision in *Morrison v. Olson* was that the removal provision still provided the President, through the Attorney General, "ample" authority to supervise the conduct of the independent counsel. See *Morrison*, 487 U.S. at 692; *see also* Kevin M. Stack, *The Story of* Morrison v. Olson: *The Independent Counsel and Independent Agencies in Watergate's Wake, in* PRESIDENTIAL POWER STORIES 401, 435-37 (Christopher H. Schroeder & Curtis A. Bradley eds., 2009).

2. *The Practical Significance of Agency Independence*

Even if the special provisions that create independent agencies do not render such agencies unconstitutional, an important question remains about the effect of these provisions in practice. On that question, consider the following excerpt from Professor Peter Strauss's foundational treatment of agencies in the structure of modern government:

Peter L. Strauss, The Place of Agencies in Government: Separation of Powers and the Fourth Branch

84 Colum. L. Rev. 573, 584 (1984)

The allocation of law-administration among these forms does not follow simple functional lines. Although administrative law students and others sometimes talk uncritically as if the performance of regulation were a lodestone — as if all regulatory agencies were "independent regulatory commissions" — regulatory and policymaking responsibilities are scattered among independent and executive-branch agencies in ways that belie explanation in terms of the work agencies do. Take, for example, workplace safety: the Mine Safety Act is wholly administered by an executive department, at first the Department of the Interior and more recently the Department of Labor; the Occupational Safety and Health Act is administered in part by an executive agency, the Occupational Safety and Health Administration, and in part by an independent commission, the Occupational Safety and Health Review Commission, both placed in the Department of Labor; nuclear safety is in the charge of a fully independent agency, the Nuclear Regulatory Commission. Similar dispersions could be noted respecting antitrust policy, economic policy, consumer protection from fraudulent advertising, and even rate regulation. The diversity is characteristic of our pragmatic ways with government, reflecting the circumstances of the particular regulatory regime, the temper of presidential/congressional relations at the time, or the perceived success or failure of an existing agency performing like functions, more than any grand scheme of government.

The diversity of form, however, ought not to conceal the substantial commonalities of internal structure, function, and procedure. Despite the attention often given asserted differences between single, politically responsible administrators and multimember independent commissions, these organizations are more similar than different below the highest levels. In its regulatory work each is subdivided in accordance with the same principles of bureaucratic organization, relies upon staff protected by the same civil service laws, performs the same functions, employs the same public procedures, and settles disputes using the same types of decisional personnel.

Imagine, for example, a single corporation operating a coal mine, a manufacturing plant, and a nuclear power station. The safety of its workplaces would be regulated by the three agencies noted above — the Department of Labor, OSHA/OSHRC (also within the Department), and the NRC. From its perspective, the placement of these regulatory agencies in the structure of government is essentially irrelevant. Each "legislates" in adopting the rules the corporation is compelled to obey; each engages in executive activity in conducting investigations, adopting policies within the "legislative" framework, or deciding to initiate formal proceedings; each "adjudicates" the ensuing complaints. The Administrative Procedure Act [APA] applies equally to all agency types. Case law involving agency procedure, judicial review, or presidential and congressional oversight gives no hint that an agency's "independence" vel non could be a significant factor in any decision about appropriate or fair procedures.

Beyond the identity of public procedures and the frequently mixed character of agency function lies the essential similarity of the human resources of all agencies. All are predominantly staffed by civil servants protected from political reprisal in the performance of their jobs. In consequence, even agency work outside the public procedures of the APA is substantially independent of political influence, whatever the apparent place of the agency in the governmental structure. As Presidents and political scientists are fond of remarking, the White House does not control policymaking in the executive departments. The President and a few hundred political appointees are at the apex of an enormous bureaucracy whose members enjoy tenure in their jobs, are subject to the constraints of statutes whose history and provisions they know in detail, and often have strong views of the public good in the field in which they work. The ability to contribute to what he regards as beneficial change is often what has motivated the bureaucrat to choose public employment. Presidents come and go while the governing statutes, the bureaucrat's values, and the interactions he enjoys with fellow workers, remain more or less constant. To be sure, he can be influenced by outside pressures; obedience to authority, avoidance of the pain of antagonistic committee hearings or budget reductions, and a general desire for the good will of the political leadership are undoubted factors in his behavior. Winning budget support in Congress, or office space, or effective representation in judicial proceedings, are not trivial goods — even absent the political loyalties that may derive from appointment or the sharing of general aspirations about government policy. Nonetheless the bureaucracy constitutes an independent force — indeed, that fact is in some respects the dominating problem of the current administrative law literature — and its cooperation must be won to achieve any desired outcome . . . .

The independent agencies are often free, at least in a formal sense, of other relationships with the White House that characterize the executive-branch agencies. The President's influence reaches somewhat more deeply into the top layers of bureaucracy at an executive agency than at an independent commission. Where subsidiary officers in the executive agencies may be subject to presidential appointment and certainly require White House clearance, in the independent agencies only commissioners are appointed with required executive participation; staff appointments, even at the highest level, are made by the commission. The requirement that commission membership be at least nominally bipartisan does not prevent the appointment of political friends but doubtless lowers the political temperature. Typically, the independents have more authority to conduct their own litigation than executive-branch agencies do, although not exclusive authority. Executive-branch agencies have an obligation to clear legislative matters — draft statutes, budget submission, even testimony — with the Office of Management and Budget, an obligation from which some of the independents are excused. One recent statute, the Paperwork Reduction Act of 1980, specifically empowers the independents to overrule by majority the Presidential directives respecting the collection of information to which executive branch agencies are bound. As a political matter, recent Presidents have not required the independent commissions to participate in the centralized oversight of rulemaking associated with presidentially required cost-benefit analyses of major proposals for rulemaking.

Yet these differences are at best matters of degree, overstated if taken to imply rigorous control within the executive branch. Even in executive agencies, the layer over which the President enjoys direct control of personnel is very thin and political factors may make it difficult for him to exercise even those controls to the fullest. An administrator with a public constituency and mandate, such as William Ruckelshaus, cannot be discharged — and understands that he cannot be discharged — without substantial political cost. Also for political reasons, one may be certain that independent commission consultation with the White House about appointments often occurs, even if subdued — as in so many other matters — by the lack of obligation so to consult.

Presidential influence over the independent agencies is heightened by the special ties existing between the President and the chairmen of almost all of the independent regulatory commissions. Although all commissioners, including the chairmen, are appointed to fixed terms as commissioners, the chairman generally holds that special post at the President's pleasure. His position, moreover, gives him special influence over the agency's course, making it particularly likely that his views will find acceptance. Professor David Welborn's interesting and thorough study of regulatory commission chairmen reveals that they almost completely dominate the administrative side of commission business, selecting most staff, setting budgetary policy, and as a consequence commanding staff loyalties. These administrative responsibilities, corresponding to presidential responsibilities for the government as a whole, doubtless underlie Congress's general recognition of the President's special claim to have his own choice as chairman. Perhaps more surprisingly, the chairmen also dominate commission policymaking: commanding the staff, they are far less often in dissent from commission policy decisions than their colleagues. Here the White House connection is often less direct and generally more subtle, but consultation and coordination on general policy issues of national interest naturally occurs.

NOTES AND QUESTIONS

1. As Professor Strauss notes, executive-branch and independent agencies have a lot in common when viewed from mid-range. Both are subject to the APA and its provisions on administrative process and judicial review. They have a similar range of functions and powers. They also employ similar staff. Are the differences overstated?

2. According to Strauss, which practical political means does the President possess to control independent agencies?

3. To what extent does diminished presidential control of independent agencies mean increased congressional control of such agencies? Is increased congressional control a positive or a negative? We will return to the topic of political control at the end of the book. For now, understand that independent and executive-branch agencies are differently situated in terms of political control.

4. Why does Congress create independent agencies? Political scientists might answer "because it can." *See* David Epstein & Sharyn O'Halloran, Delegating Powers 154-55 (1999). Congress has created independent agencies during times when the President is from the opposite political party and relatively weak. Perhaps less cynically, Congress also has created independent agencies to keep certain decisions at a distance from politics. Consider two classic cases. The first is when an agency is adjudicating cases involving individual rights. No decision maker should find someone guilty of a crime, or judge her liable in a civil case for political reasons, right? The other classic case for independence is when an agency is setting monetary policy. Political officials might be tempted to adjust interest rates for short-term political gains at public expense. Might Congress have a self-regarding, electoral interest in preventing these results?

Figure 9.2   DOT

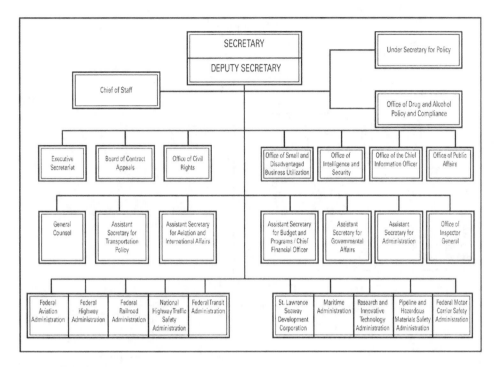

Source: http://www.dot.gov/dotorgchart.pdf.

3. *Organizational Charts*

As Professor Strauss observes, executive-branch and independent agencies follow similar organizational principles. We think illustrations are useful to demonstrate the similarities. On the executive-branch side, we provide the organizational chart of the Department of Transportation, as well as the organizational chart of its auto safety subunit, the National Highway and Traffic Safety Administration. On the independent side, we provide the organizational chart of the Federal Communications Commission. These examples will not only allow you to see similarities between the two broad types of agencies but to better appreciate what agencies generally look like.

NOTES AND QUESTIONS

---

1. The structure that is depicted on an organizational chart is called the formal structure by organization theorists. Note how complex the formal structure of a federal agency is. NHTSA is just one of 28 boxes in the general organizational chart of the Department of Transportation. Yet that one box can be depicted as an organizational chart of its own, with 22 separate boxes. Nearly

Figure 9.3   NHTSA

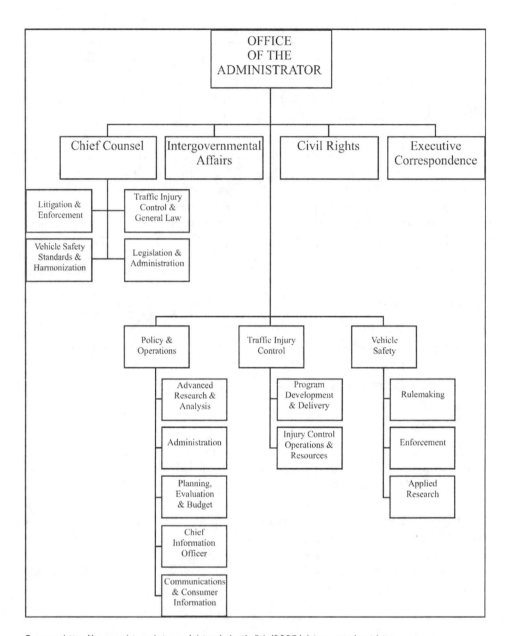

Source: http://www.nhtsa.dot.gov/nhtsa/whatis/bb/2005/nhtsa-orgchart.htm.

all the boxes on the NHTSA chart could be expanded as well. Think how massive and complex the DOT chart would be if it included all these subsidiary boxes.

2. Agency organizational structures often reflect an effort to separate policymaking, enforcement, and adjudicatory functions. Literally, different officials within different offices or divisions perform different tasks. This internal division of

Figure 9.4   FCC

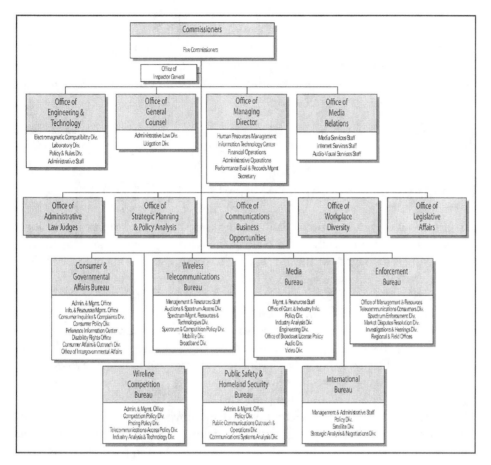

Source: http://www.fcc.gov/fccorgchart.html.

functions allows a single agency to address all aspects of an overarching problem — such as auto safety or environmental protection — without sacrificing fairness and impartiality in particular cases. This is important; the Constitution itself separates powers so as to prevent government officials from making law with particular prosecutions or dispositions in mind. What prevents agency officials from meeting in the hallways to discuss issues with one another? If separate offices are insufficient, how about separate buildings? Could Congress solve the problem more effectively or efficiently by devising rules of conduct for agency officials to follow? What might those rules look like?

3. Many agencies, such as the DOT, are sub-divided according to the specific problems that they address — for example, aviation, highway, railroad, etc. What implications might this organizational structure have for the way in which agency employees conceive of their overall mission?

4. Agencies also have specialized offices or divisions, such as general counsel offices, technology offices, or media relations offices. These offices provide

legal advice or other services to the sub-divisions. Look for a moment at NHTSA's organizational chart. The General Counsel has a Vehicle Safety Standards and Harmonization division (NHTSA rules are called "standards"). Meanwhile, the Vehicle Safety Division has a rulemaking office. How might you imagine that these offices would work together on a proposed standard requiring auto manufacturers to install airbags in new cars? Where would the proposal originate? When would the other office get involved? Is this information clear from the organizational chart?

E. Who Shapes Policy in an Agency?

To describe agencies, we must do more than sketch a picture from an institutional perspective. The reason is that agencies possess no decisional capacity apart from the individuals who work within them. Furthermore, the identity of these individuals affects the substance of the policy that agencies produce. If placed in NHTSA, who would you expect to issue more stringent rules concerning auto safety: an official selected from a consumer welfare group or from the auto industry? Who would have more expertise in determining the crashworthiness of a vehicle equipped with certain safety features: an agency scientist or a political official? Who would have a better sense of the resources available to devote to auto safety issues in view of overall governmental priorities? These are extreme examples. The more general point is that people matter.

Agencies are run by two different types of employees, political appointees and civil service members. Political appointees are those selected by the President and confirmed by the Senate for their positions as well as many appointed by the President alone or by agency heads. There are about 3,000 of them (roughly 40 percent requiring Senate confirmation). Civil service members are hired through a non-political process. There are more than 2 million of them. Not only do they greatly outnumber political appointees, they also greatly outlast them.

In this section, we describe the people who exercise power and responsibility within agencies. We not only describe the appointment and removal processes for these two groups, but we describe how the two groups interact with one another. All of these dynamics affect the people who hold the jobs and the policy that they generate.

1. Political Appointees

Note that the Constitution requires some high-level officials to be appointed by the President and confirmed by the Senate. Political appointees include these officials as well as the relatively greater number of non-Senate confirmed presidential appointees. When a new President is elected, these positions are up for grabs. Turnover among political appointees is widespread, particularly when the new President is from the opposite political party of the outgoing President. The newly elected President begins to identify nominees for political appointments even before taking office. There is continual turnover throughout an administration because political appointees serve in a position an average of two years before departing for other opportunities.

a. Getting the Job

Because political appointees occupy the top rung of leadership and management within an agency, they can dramatically shape the direction of that agency. How do political appointees get these influential positions? Most would say it is a combination of who you know and what you know. The President seeks out those in whom he has confidence — for without trustworthy individuals, the President cannot discharge his own constitutional responsibilities. It is only natural for the President to have confidence in those whom he knows, either personally or professionally. The President also seeks to reward those who, during the campaign, were close advisors and supporters. In this respect, note that some departments and agencies receive a large share of presidential "friends," such as the Commerce Department or the Small Business Administration. *See* David E. Rosenbaum & Steven Labaton, *Amid Many Fights Over Qualifications, a Bush Nomination Stalls in the Senate*, N.Y. TIMES (Sept. 24, 2005). For most jobs, qualifications clearly matter. A President does himself, let alone the country, no good by selecting individuals who lack the requisite skills to perform the tasks at hand.

Convincing the President that you deserve the job is not enough for the most influential positions. The Senate retains a formal role in the confirmation process of some political appointees. *See* U.S. CONST., Art. II, §2, cl. 2. How does that formal role play out in actual practice? The next two excerpts offer different visions of the confirmation process.

GAO Report to the Chairman, Subcommittee on Oversight of Government Management, Restructuring, and the District of Columbia, Committee on Governmental Affairs

U.S. Senate, GAO/GGD-00-174, August 11, 2000

B-284958
August 11, 2000
The Honorable George V. Voinovich
Chairman, Subcommittee on Oversight of Government Management, Restructuring, and the District of Columbia
Committee on Governmental Affairs
United States Senate

Dear Mr. Chairman:

On February 17, 2000, you wrote to us regarding your concern that some political appointees in the executive branch lack the requisite leadership and management skills and background to successfully address the challenges facing federal agencies. You asked that we suggest questions to assist the Senate in its constitutional role of confirming nominees, to help ensure that future political appointees have the requisite skills to be results-oriented leaders and managers. Appendix I of this letter transmits those questions.

The questions cover the following four categories:

- results-oriented decisionmaking,
- financial management,
- information and technology management, and
- human capital management.

During the 1990s, Congress responded to long-standing shortcomings in the way federal agencies were managed by creating a framework for more results-oriented management; the three major areas addressed by the reforms were results-oriented decisionmaking, financial management, and information technology management. No consensus has yet emerged to address what some see as the major remaining gap in that framework — strategic human capital management. The Senate can facilitate progress in these key management areas by confirming nominees who have the skills and abilities to help make these key reforms a reality.

Recognizing that the positions nominees may fill can range from the heads of major departments and agencies to program managers, we have attempted to order the questions in the first three categories from the general (more appropriate for agency heads) to the specific (more appropriate for program managers). The final category — human capital management — is organized based on a five-part strategy discussed in our September 1999 report.

Realistically, there may be too many questions to expect each nominee to answer them all, and some questions may not be appropriate for all nominees. This does not detract from their usefulness because each Senate committee planning a confirmation hearing can decide which questions to include on the pre-hearing questionnaire, depending on the position to be confirmed and the amount of other information the committee may require the nominee to provide.

We believe that asking questions on selected leadership and management issues will send a strong message that the Senate considers such issues to be a priority for all nominees for senior agency positions. The questions can also help ensure that nominees have the requisite skills to deal effectively with the broad array of complex management challenges facing the federal government in the 21st century. In addition, if the Senate asks these questions as part of the confirmation process, then future Presidents may place added importance on ensuring that nominees have the requisite leadership and management experience for their positions before submitting their names to the Senate for confirmation.

As agreed with your office, unless you announce the contents of this report earlier, we plan no further distribution until 30 days after its issue date. At that time, we will send copies of the report to Senator Richard J. Durbin, Ranking Minority Member, Subcommittee on Oversight of Government Management,

Restructuring, and the District of Columbia, and to Senator Fred Thompson, Chairman, and Senator Joseph Lieberman, Ranking Minority Member, Senate Committee on Governmental Affairs. We will also send copies to Jacob J. Lew, Director, Office of Management and Budget. In addition, we will make copies available to others upon request.

Key contributors to these questions were Nancy Kingsbury, J. Christopher Mihm, Al Stapleton, Stephen Altman, David Plocher, George Stalcup, Kevin Tansey, and Dennise Stickley of GAO. We would also like to acknowledge the important role of Pat McGinrus and principals and staff from the Council for Excellence in Government. The Council organized an extremely valuable and informative focus group involving over 20 of its principals to help us develop questions to ask nominees. We solicited further suggestions from a broad range of individuals with expertise in public management issues. The following experts and organizations responded and offered insights and suggestions that we used in crafting the questions: Don Kettle from the University of Wisconsin, Susan Shaw and her colleagues from the National Treasury Employees Union, Mark Huddleston from the University of Delaware, Anne Lillis and her colleagues from the American Society for Public Administration, and Virginia Thomas from the Heritage Foundation.

We recognize that the nomination and confirmation of agency leaders with appropriate management skills is only one step in transforming the cultures of federal agencies so that they become high performance organizations. We look forward to working with you and other Members of Congress and executive branch officials in this important work.

If you have any questions, please call Christopher Mihm or Al Stapleton on (202) 512-8676.

Sincerely yours,

David M. Walker
Comptroller General
of the United States

2. Career Civil Servants

Political appointees are not the only people who shape policy in agencies. It takes a staff to run an institution, particularly one as large as an agency. To entice workers to join an agency, some general employment protections are essential. As a lawyer, you might hesitate to commit your professional talents to an agency if you knew that your tenure and terms were only as secure as the current presidential administration, which may serve four, or at most eight, years. Enter the statutorily based civil service system. The civil service is a merit system, where positions in government agencies are awarded on the basis of competitive examination. Pay is determined by position and seniority, with fixed salary steps set by statute and regulation. Employees do not serve "at will," which would mean that they could be removed from office for any reason. Rather, they can only be dismissed "for cause" — absenteeism, proven incompetence, dishonesty, and the like.

What are the implications of civil service protections for regulatory policy? There are advantages and disadvantages. An advantage is that civil service protections ensure a stable workforce in the face of political turnover. They also reduce political "cronyism." Career staffers also tend to possess more specialized training and skill than their political bosses. Among them are the scientists, the economists, and the lawyers. The flip side is that civil service protections create inefficiencies, guaranteeing job security to workers despite suboptimal performance. Another concern is that civil service protections create a bureaucracy cut off from the control of elected officials.

How the advantages and disadvantages sort out depends in part on the interplay between political appointees and career staffers. In theory, each agency is structured so that a small number of political appointees direct policy in accordance with the wishes of the popularly elected President, and a large number of credentialed staff members carry out that policy in a competent, professional manner. In reality, there is considerable push and pull between the two groups. At best, the dynamic helps to improve policy. Each group effectively supplies what the other is missing. At worst, the dynamic produces conflict rather than cooperation. The following excerpt highlights the issues.

Francis E. Rourke, Bureaucracy, Politics, and Public Policy

127-32 (3d ed. 1984)

A relationship that is fundamental to determining policy in any governmental bureaucracy is the interaction between political executives at the top of the administrative pyramid and career officials subordinate to them. In a democratic state political executives usually represent the political party that has been victorious at the polls . . . .

In American bureaucracy, . . . [a]lthough the career official has advantages in . . . [the relationship with the political executive], including continuity in office and greater familiarity with the work of the agency, the political executive is far from powerless. For one thing political executives preside over a hierarchic system in which their office is a primary source of legitimate authority. Whether elected or appointed, the political executive is in a way a symbol of public control over the governmental process. In a society highly impregnated with democratic ideology, as the United States certainly is, this is a formidable source of authority.

Consequently, the tendency is strong for career bureaucrats to tailor their recommendations to fit what they believe are the policy views of the political executive. And once the executive has made up his or her mind on a policy question, these career officials will ordinarily support the decision, even if they disagree with it. To be sure, mavericks in some agencies may publicly challenge their superior's decisions. But though these cases often receive great publicity, they are exceptions to the bureaucrat's general willingness to go along with policies decided upon at a higher level . . . .

Usually bureaucratic opposition to official policy is covert rather than open — guerrilla warfare rather than a frontal assault. Career officials will confide their doubts about the wisdom of the policies being followed by their political superiors to friendly legislators or reporters, or they may alert pressure groups with which they have an intimate relationship that policy changes being contemplated by the administration in power are adverse to their interests. They thus convert disputes with political executives into conflicts between their superiors and outside organizations. In this way, they can pursue their objectives without jeopardy to the forms of bureaucratic life or the safety of their own position. Moreover, by avoiding an open break with their superior, they can continue to pass ammunition to the political executive's critics from the security of their intimate participation in the affairs and deliberations of the agency. In this surreptitious way, career officials can incite political conflict in the outside world without risking their own safety by directly participating in the combat. Many of these tactics were used by career employees at the EPA in their struggles with political appointees during the early years of the Reagan administration.

Such warfare is not a frequent occurrence. More commonly, the relationship between political executives and career officials can be described, in Charles E. Lindblom's terms, as one of "mutual accommodation." Career subordinates have good reason for deferring to their political superior, who is invested with the authority of office in a bureaucratic environment in which rank is an impressive symbol of power. Members of Congress may be prepared to treat departmental executives with familiarity if not contempt. Ordinary bureaucrats are not.

Moreover, while representing the authority of the community in the agency, the political executive also represents the agency in the community. Bureaucrats cannot publicly undermine the executive without risking injury to the organization with which their personal fortunes are linked. They have a stake in his or her success. The political executive is the best salesperson they have for achieving the agency's goals and continuously replenishing its resources. Any executive who is truly effective in speaking for the agency will be highly regarded by career officials, whether or not they agree with the executive on policy issues. As secretary of labor during the Nixon administration, George Shultz was greatly respected by departmental officials, even when they were not enthusiastic about the administration's labor policies. Though he remained friendly with the department's trade union constituency, Shultz had extremely good access to the president, and was thus in a strong position to advance and protect the department's interests at the White House.

Of course, political executives cannot run roughshod over the views of their career subordinates. Even if they have the legal power to coerce these subordinates into obedience, they cannot force them to perform their duties enthusiastically, which is essential if the agency is to attain substantial effectiveness. Moreover, career subordinates have a formidable capacity to make trouble for executives in the outside community, as we have seen, and this threat requires political executives to exercise diplomacy in their dealings with these officials. Such diplomacy may sometimes lead a chief executive to call for improved salary and fringe benefits for an agency's staff as a means of purchasing their support for policy goals.

In the formal theory of public administration, the role of the career staff is regarded as primarily that of ensuring competence in the design of policy — they are expected to see to it that the techniques used to achieve goals are the most effective available. In practice, however, the career staff also tends to develop a fine sensitivity to the political pressures to which an agency is subject. A political executive's best advice on how to operate politically may well come from career subordinates. They know their way around the political thickets that surround the agency; political executives may not. Moreover, legislators tend to seek advice on policy questions from career officials, because they often regard these officials as more knowledgeable and trustworthy in answering questions dealing with policy issues than political executives, who may try to defend or protect the party in power. The phrase Herbert Storing uses to describe the role of senior bureaucrats in the governmental process is that of "closet statesmen."

On the other hand, the politically appointed head of an executive agency often has at least as much competence in the agency area of expertise as the career staff. This happens especially often in agencies like the National Science Foundation, where outside professional groups insist that a top executive with first-rate scientific credentials be appointed. In situations of this sort, a political appointee is expected to take the lead in policy development, while the career officials help avoid political pitfalls in the agency's dealings with the community, Congress, and other executive agencies.

NOTES AND QUESTIONS

1. Political appointees and careers staffers bring different talents and limitations to the table. In many ways, the two groups are better together than either alone. Career staffers handle technical details and daily operations, and political appointees handle policy decisions and overall priorities. By dividing power in this way, each side can discipline the other and prevent an excessive concentration of power *within* the agency. *See* Neal Kumar Katyal, *Internal Separation of Powers*, 115 YALE L.J. 2314 (2006). Does this view ease concerns about the "legitimacy" of agencies? If so, how?

2. Is an internal separation of powers model realistic? That model suggests that each group should stick to their designated roles. What happens if one side crosses the line, either inadvertently or intentionally? For example, career staffers may let their view of whether a particular health or safety risk is worth running (a policy judgment) influence their judgment concerning the extent to which that risk exists (a scientific judgment). Or political appointees may recast the science to suit their policy preferences. *See* Karen Tumulty & Mark Thompson, *The Political Science Test*, TIME (Feb. 5, 2006); Daniel Smith, *Political Science*, N.Y. TIMES MAGAZINE (Sept. 4, 2005). We will return to these issues in Chapter 10 when we discuss agency regulation.

3. While the dynamic between the two groups can be a positive force, it can also be a deleterious one. Having a new boss every four or eight years can damage

the morale of those in it for the long haul. And having stalwarts from the prior administration (or even the administration before that) can impede the progress of those implementing a new vision. Can you think of what career staffers might do to protect their turf in general or while waiting out the current administration?

4. Conversely, what might the President do to change the career staff? Are political considerations ever permissible? According to a report from the Justice Department's inspector general, ideological considerations played a role in hiring decisions for Honors Program and summer intern positions (which go to recent law school graduates and law school students!) at the Justice Department's civil rights division between 2001 and 2007. Carrie Johnson, *Study Finds Ideology Fueled Justice Dept. Hirings*, WASH. POST (Jan. 13, 2009). Specifically, political appointees eliminated candidates with connections to liberal organizations or causes. During the same period, the report states, career staffers were transferred out of the civil rights division because of their political views or race. Carrie Johnson, *Report Cites Political and Racial Bias at Justice*, WASH. POST (Jan. 14, 2009). Hiring into career spots on the basis of ideological, political, or race-based considerations violates Justice Department policy and civil service laws.

5. Who gets better grades for managing agency operations — political appointees or career staffers? Professor David E. Lewis published a study of 614 federal programs managed by 245 different agencies. *See* David E. Lewis, *Testing Pendleton's Premise: Do Political Appointees Make Worse Bureaucrats?*, 69 J. POL. 1073 (2007). Using a scale developed by the Office of Management and Budget in the White House to measure how well a program functions, Lewis found that programs get systematically lower management grades when run by political appointees rather than civil service officers. What might explain this finding? What does this analysis suggest about who should do the work within agencies? Should political appointees still manage agencies because only they promote accountability, even if efficiency suffers?

You now have a sense for the place of agencies in the structure of modern federal government. You understand that agencies are the central actors, although the Constitution has little to say about them. Information about the form and power of agencies comes from other sources. You understand that agencies fall into two basic categories: executive-branch and independent. This distinction has given rise to constitutional challenges, but the Supreme Court for the most part has not prevented Congress from creating independent agencies. Furthermore, you understand that the differences between executive-branch and independent agencies, though real in terms of agency form and presidential control, can be overstated and do not detract from the similarities among agencies. Agencies have similar functions. They have similar internal organizational divisions. They have similar personnel, managed by political officials and operated by career civil servants. On this subject, you understand that who actually runs agencies is noteworthy not simply in its own right but because ultimately people not "institutions" exercise power.

With this background in mind, the next chapter discusses how we got to this place. Why have agencies come to dominate not only our federal government but our social and economic policy? There was a time when the federal government largely stayed out of financial, health, safety, and environmental issues. Instead, people protected *themselves* through the market and the common law — say, by demanding from automakers certain safety features when buying a car, or by suing automakers under state tort law when injured by a dangerous car. What were the limitations of this regulatory regime?

CHAPTER 10

STATUTORY IMPLEMENTATION BY AGENCIES

Agencies are the institutions primarily responsible for implementing regulatory statutes. This chapter examines how they perform that function. We examine the different tools or types of analyses that agencies use in implementing regulatory statutes. Furthermore, we focus on one particular process that agencies use for implementing regulatory statutes: the notice-and-comment rulemaking process. This process generates rules, also called regulations, which are legally binding on government officials and private parties, similar to statutes. At the end of the chapter, we discuss some other forms of statutory implementation, including formal adjudication and guidance. We also address some leading theories of agency behavior.

Before we begin, it is worth highlighting some of the features that make agencies distinctive as institutions for implementing statutes. First, and perhaps most fundamentally, agencies are designed to deploy technical expertise. As discussed in Chapter 2, a central reason why Congress creates agencies is to capitalize on their specialized skill. Agencies employ scientists, economists, and other professionals who are trained and knowledgeable about the important aspects of complex regulatory problems. Agencies also have the ability to obtain and process technical information as well as to develop long-term experience with implementing policy in particular regulatory areas. Courts, by contrast, are generalists. They have relatively limited access to technical staff, limited ability to obtain and process technical information, and limited familiarity with regulatory schemes.

Second, agencies have considerable control over their agenda. Although some statutes impose specific deadlines for when an agency must complete a specific task, most grant agencies discretion within a general area about what problems to tackle, when to tackle them, and through which means. Many agencies have the ability to refrain from taking any action at all; a statute grants them authority but imposes no obligation to use it. NHTSA is not such an agency; the 1966 Motor Vehicle Safety Act requires it to issue auto safety standards within a certain period. But even NHTSA has discretion concerning the content and timing of such standards. In this respect, agencies are like prosecutors or Congress. Prosecutors can pick their cases. Likewise, Congress has considerable control over its agenda. Congress is not required to pass any particular kind of legislation; it may be health care this year and financial reform next. In contrast, courts depend upon lawsuits to present issues for their resolution. While the Supreme Court has some ability to control the issues it decides and when, in general courts are reactive institutions. Agencies generally have the power set the agenda within their regulatory spheres.

Third, as discussed in Chapters 8 and 2, agencies are structured to be responsive, or accountable, to political officials. Agencies have an ongoing relationship with both of the political branches, and this relationship is most evident when agencies are making major policy decisions. Congress not only creates the statutes that grant agencies authority but continues to monitor how they exercise their authority. The President is also involved on an ongoing basis, particularly in the work of executive-branch agencies. If an agency does something unpopular, members of Congress and the President will hear about it. Federal courts, by contrast, are relatively insulated from politics, not only because federal judges have life tenure, but also because due process principles insulate adjudication from direct outside influences.

As you will see, these distinctive features affect how agencies implement their statutes. Even when agencies are interpreting statutes in the course of implementing them, they are not simply "mini" courts. They have different capabilities as well as different constraints. Take note of the ways in which these capabilities and constraints manifest themselves throughout the chapter.

A. The Notice-and-Comment Rulemaking Process

Just as Congress generally follows a relatively predictable process for enacting statutes, agencies generally follow a relatively predictable process for issuing regulations. That process is known as the "notice-and-comment" rulemaking process. The procedural requirements for this process are found in 5 U.S.C. §553 of the Administrative Procedure Act (APA). As we have mentioned, the APA provides procedural requirements for agencies to follow unless their organic statutes contain more specific ones. Below we provide an overview of the process; for a more detailed account, see A *Blackletter Statement of Federal Administrative Law*, 54 ADMIN. L. REV. 1 (2002).

Initiating the Process.   An agency initiates the notice-and-comment rulemaking process in response to a *Petition for Rulemaking* from private parties, at the prompting of other government officials, or on its own. Once an agency decides to go ahead, the first step usually is to issue a *Notice of Proposed Rulemaking* (NPRM), which contains one or more proposed rules and is published in the *Federal Register*. We reproduce a NPRM in the next section. *See* pp. 526. Sometimes an agency will issue a document in advance of the NPRM, called (not surprisingly) an *Advanced Notice of Proposed Rulemaking*. This step is useful to winnow proposals prior to issuing an NPRM. When an executive-branch agency is in the initiation phase, it must submit any proposed rule with anticipated costs of $100 million or more for review to the Office of Information and Regulatory Affairs (OIRA) in the White House. *See* Exec. Order No. 12866, 58 Fed. Reg. 51735 §6 (Sept. 30, 1993), as amended by Exec. Order No. 13497, 74 Fed Reg. 6113 (Jan. 30, 2009). Note that this review requirement comes from executive order, not the APA.

Under APA §553, an NPRM must contain a "reference to the legal authority under which the rule is promulgated," "either the terms or substance of the proposed rule or description of the subjects involved," and a statement of time and place of any public proceedings. *See* APA, 5 U.S.C. §553(b). Judicial interpretations of the APA have also required the agency to make available the data and studies that are the basis for its rule. *See* American Radio Relay League, Inc. v. FCC, 524 F.3d 227, 236-38 (D.C. Cir. 2008); United States v. Nova Scotia Food Products Corp., 568 F.2d 240, 252 (2d Cir. 1977). The disclosure of data is necessary for interested parties to effectively comment on the rule. As you will see, agencies end up producing very elaborate statements in the NPRM.

Conducting the Process.   After the agency publishes the NPRM in the *Federal Register*, it must provide a reasonable time for interested parties to submit written comments on the proposed rule. These comments are the means for interested parties to be "heard" on the proposed rule. One purpose of the notice-and-comment rulemaking process is to replace an oral, trial-type hearing with a written one. To make the paper process meaningful, the agency has an obligation to consider the comments that parties submit as part of the rulemaking docket; these written comments are now available for easy viewing on the internet. *See, e.g., www.regulations.gov.* Many comments, particularly those from industry groups such as automakers or insurance companies, include detailed analysis of the proposals and are frequently drafted by lawyers. But any person may submit a comment on any proposal, and the agency has the same obligation to consider it.

After receiving comments, an agency sometimes realizes that a new proposal is worth consideration alongside, or in lieu of, existing ones. If that proposal is not a "logical outgrowth" of the existing proposals, *see* CSX Transportation, Inc. v. Surface Transportation Bd., 584 F.3d 1076, 1079-80 (D.C. Cir. 2009) (NPRM is logical outgrowth if parties should have anticipated that change was possible and thus reasonably should have filed their comments during notice and comment), then the agency must conduct a new round of notice and comment. It typically does so by issuing a *Supplemental Notice of Proposed Rulemaking* (SNPRM). It is possible for an agency to conduct multiple rounds, although that is not the norm. Can you see why? An agency can gather a sense for the range of options before issuing an NPRM by seeking information through informal contacts with affected parties or by issuing an ANPRM.

Completing the Process.   The agency completes the notice-and-comment rulemaking process by issuing a final rule. The APA requires the agency to include with its final rule a statement of the basis for the rule: "After consideration of the relevant matter presented, the agency shall incorporate in the rules adopted a concise general statement of their basis and purpose." *See* APA, §553(c). The statement of "basis and purpose" must, at a minimum, set forth the rationale and legal authority for the rule. Although the "basis and purpose" language in the APA is rather sparse, the Supreme Court has required agencies to provide an extensive explanation for their final rules, mainly to facilitate judicial review of such rules under a different section of the APA, 5 U.S.C. §702. *See* Motor Vehicle Manufacturers Ass'n v. State Farm Insurance Co., 463 U.S. 29, 43-44 (1983); Citizens to Preserve Overton Park v. Volpe, 401 U.S. 402, 416 (1971). Sometimes an agency determines after completing the notice-and-comment rulemaking process that no final rule is warranted. The agency must provide an explanation for that decision as well. Note that a host of other statutes require agencies to evaluate the impact of their regulations on certain interests — for example, on small businesses and the environment. *See* pp. 547. Agencies often include a section called "impact analyses" in their final rules, which demonstrates their compliance with these statutes. This section also may contain any cost-benefit analysis that an agency performed to comply with the executive order on this issue.

If an agency wants to amend or rescind a final rule, it also must do so through the rulemaking process. Put differently, the agency must issue a new rule. This principle should be familiar by analogy to the legislative process: Congress can amend or repeal a statute only by enacting a new statute. For both Congress and agencies, this principle generally holds regardless of the magnitude of the change. Thus, even if an agency wants to change a relatively minor detail of a final rule, such as extending a phase-in schedule, it must issue a new rule.

NOTES AND QUESTIONS

1. We have said that the notice-and-comment rulemaking process is analogous to the legislative process in that it produces rules with effects similar to statutes. What are the most obvious differences from the legislative process?
2. Based on the description above, do you have any sense for who writes NPRMs or final rules? Agency rulemaking staff? Agency lawyers? Agency political officials? All of the above? The agency head must sign every rule. Do you suppose that she has familiarity with the content of the rules, even if she did not pen all the words? Or is she like Congress relative to the committees responsible for bills? We revisit questions like these as we go along in this chapter.
3. Does the notice-and-comment rulemaking process seem "burdensome" to you? Is it less burdensome than a trial-type hearing? What sort of alternative might the agency prefer?
4. Why does the notice-and-comment rulemaking process look the way that it does? Why would Congress have designed it this way? What values does it serve?

B. Standard 208

The cars that we drive today are equipped with airbags. We can trace that result in large part to the 1966 Motor Vehicle Safety Act. Yet the Act did not mandate airbags, or any other safety feature, per se. Rather, it delegated authority to an agency. NHTSA issued a final rule, so-called Standard 208, which is principally responsible for airbags. But the story was far more complicated than that. Beginning in 1973 and unfolding over a decade, NHTSA issued the rule, amended the rule, suspended the rule, rescinded the rule, and reintroduced the rule. Thus, NHTSA went through an extended period of intense regulatory activity, mainly through successive notice-and-comment rulemaking proceedings, where it addressed what are called "passive restraints" — that is, vehicle safety devices that protect occupants without requiring them to buckle up (hence the name "passive"). The most familiar are automatic seatbelts (belts that typically attach to the door of car and swing forward to meet the occupant when the door closes) and airbags (inflatable cushions that deploy on impact). NHTSA finally settled on airbags.

In this section, we provide the two documents from the middle of the story: the 1981 Notice of Proposed Rulemaking and Final Rule. In these documents, NHTSA *rescinded* the requirement that manufacturers install passive restraints. We have selected these documents because they reveal in a particularly interesting way the key tools of agency statutory implementation, not because they are the final word on passive restraints.

Before turning to these two agency documents, it is first helpful to recall the provisions of the 1966 Motor Vehicle Safety Act that required NHTSA to issue motor vehicle safety standards:

Sec. 103. (a) The Secretary shall establish by order appropriate Federal motor vehicle safety standards. Each such Federal motor vehicle safety standard shall be practicable, shall meet the need for motor vehicle safety, and shall be stated in objective terms.

(b) The Administrative Procedure Act shall apply to all orders establishing, amending, or revoking a Federal motor vehicle safety standard under this title.

(c) Each order establishing a Federal motor vehicle safety standard shall specify the date such standard is to take effect which shall not be sooner than one hundred and eighty days or later than one year from the date such order is issued, unless the Secretary finds, for good cause shown, that an earlier or later effective date is in the public interest, and publishes his reasons for such finding.

(d) Whenever a Federal motor vehicle safety standard established under this title is in effect, no State or political subdivision of a State shall have any authority either to establish, or to continue in effect, with respect to any motor vehicle or item of motor vehicle equipment any safety standard applicable to the same aspect of performance of such vehicle or item of equipment, which is not identical to the Federal standard. Nothing in this section shall be construed to prevent the Federal Government or the government of any State or political subdivision thereof from establishing a safety requirement applicable to motor vehicles or motor vehicle equipment procured for its own use if such requirement imposes a higher standard of performance than that required to comply with the otherwise applicable Federal standard.

(e) The Secretary may by order amend or revoke any Federal motor vehicle safety standard established under this section. Such order shall specify the date on which such amendment or revocation is to take effect, which shall not be sooner than one hundred and eighty days or later than one year from the date the order is issued, unless the Secretary finds, for good cause shown, that an earlier or later effective date is in the public interest, and publishes his reasons for such finding.

(f) In prescribing standards under this section, the Secretary shall —

(1) consider relevant available motor vehicle safety data, including the results of research, development, testing and evaluation activities conducted pursuant to this Act;

(2) consult with the Vehicle Equipment Safety Commission, and such other State or interstate agencies (including legislative committees) as he deems appropriate;

(3) consider whether any such proposed standard is reasonable practicable and appropriate for the particular type of motor vehicle or item of motor vehicle equipment for which it is prescribed; and

(4) consider the extent to which such standards will contribute to carrying out the purposes of this Act.

Pub. L. No. 89-563, 80 Stat. 718, 719-20 (1966).

It is also helpful to have a sense of the broader political and social context of Standard 208. The history of that regulation *is* complex, and providing some fore-grounding will assist you in reading the actual agency documents. For a more detailed account, see JERRY L. MASHAW & DAVID L. HARFST, THE STRUGGLE FOR AUTO SAFETY (1990).

In the Beginning: Manual Seatbelts. When the Department of Transportation initially promulgated Standard 208 in 1967, the agency did not require auto manufacturers to install passive restraints in new motor vehicles. Rather, it required only that auto manufacturers install manual seatbelts. Manual seatbelts, if used properly, have always been (and continue to be) an effective means to reduce the occurrence of secondary collisions or the incidence of injury or death from such collisions when they do occur. But manual seatbelt use was so low during this initial period that traffic injuries and fatalities were still very high. People simply refused to buckle up on their own. So the agency began to study the option of "passive" occupant restraint systems, which would not depend upon an affirmative action by the occupant to produce safety benefits. The Department began investigating two different types of passive restraints: the automatic seatbelt and the airbag.

Enter Passive Restraints. In 1969, the Department issued a proposal (again, called a Notice of Proposed Rulemaking or NPRM) to require auto manufacturers to install passive restraints in new vehicles. In 1970 and 1972, it issued a final rule revising Standard 208 to require auto manufacturers to install passive restraints, ultimately for all front seat occupants in vehicles manufactured after

1975. In the interim before 1975, the agency required auto manufacturers either to install passive restraints or couple a manual seatbelt with an "ignition interlock," a device that emitted an audible warning buzzer and prevented the vehicle from starting if the seatbelts were not fastened. In 1972, the Court of Appeals for the Sixth Circuit upheld the revised Standard 208 against a challenge by auto manufacturers. *See* Chrysler Corp. v. Department of Transportation, 472 F.2d 659 (6th Cir. 1972). Auto manufacturers then began to comply, by and large choosing to install ignition interlocks in the short run.

Drivers and Congress React; NHTSA responds. The American public had an extremely strong adverse reaction to ignition interlocks. Just as car owners resented the intrusion of manual seat belts, they opposed the annoying reminder to fasten them. Congress took note. In 1974, Congress amended the 1966 Motor Vehicle Safety Act to prohibit NHTSA from allowing an ignition interlock or an audible buzzer. *See* 49 U.S.C. §30124. In addition, Congress required the agency to submit any passive restraint regulation to Congress, which it could then veto by a concurrent resolution of the House and Senate. In 1975, William T. Coleman, the Secretary of Transportation under President Ford, postponed the installation of passive restraints and then suspended altogether the installation of passive restraints. Secretary Coleman instead established a demonstration project to facilitate public acceptance, allowing manufacturers to install passive restraints in up to 500,000 new cars.

A New Administration Weighs In. When President Carter took office in 1977, he replaced Secretary Coleman with Secretary Brock Adams. NHTSA also got a new leader: Joan Claybrook, a former congressional staffer who had worked on the 1966 Motor Vehicle Safety Act. Secretary Adams and Administrator Claybrook saw things differently from the prior administration. They believed that the demonstration project was unnecessary to facilitate public acceptance. Accordingly, NHTSA modified Standard 208 to require a phase-in of passive restraints by 1982 for large model cars, and by 1984 for small model cars. *See* 42 Fed. Reg. 34289 (1977). The Court of Appeals for the D.C. Circuit upheld this version of Standard 208. *See* Pacific Legal Foundation v. Department of Transportation, 593 F.2d 1338, 1339 (D.C. Cir. 1979).

Another New Administration Changes Course. In 1981, Standard 208 faced yet another reversal in the hands of yet another new presidential administration. President Reagan campaigned for office on a platform of deregulation. As part of that plan, he supported easing regulatory burdens on the ailing domestic auto industry. On April 6, 1981, NHTSA delayed compliance with the passive restraint requirement for large cars, moving it from September 1, 1981, to September 1, 1982. It also proposed a more dramatic overhaul of the passive restraint regulations. On October 29, 1981, the agency issued a final rule rescinding the passive restraints requirement.

What follows are the two basic documents for NHTSA's 1981 notice-and-comment rulemaking: the Notice of Proposed Rulemaking and the Final Rule, as first published in the *Federal Register*. These documents look like no other you have previously seen in this book. Read them as you would any written text, attending both to their formal features and their reasoning.

---

49 C.F.R. 571, Federal Motor Vehicle Safety Standards; Occupant Crash Protection

[Docket No. 74-14; Notice 22], April 6, 1981

[46 Fed. Reg. 21205 (1981)]

AGENCY: Department of Transportation

ACTION: Notice of proposed rulemaking

SUMMARY: The purpose of this notice is to seek comment on a series of alternative amendments to the automatic restraint requirements of Safety Standard No. 208, Occupant Crash Protection. As amended by a final rule published in today's Federal Register, those requirements are currently scheduled to become effective for large cars and mid-size cars on September 1, 1982, and for small cars on September 1, 1983.

Under the first alternative being considered, the sequence of compliance would be changed so that small cars would be required to comply on September 1, 1982, mid-size cars on September 1, 1983, and large cars on September 1, 1984.

The second alternative would require all cars sizes to begin compliance on March 1, 1983. In addition, the first and second alternatives would amend the automatic restraint requirements so that those restraints would not be required in the front center seating position.

The third alternative would rescind the automatic restraint requirements.

This action is being taken to ensure that Standard No. 208 reflects the changes in circumstances that have occurred since the automatic restraint requirements were issued in 1977, and to ensure that the standard meets the requirements of the National Traffic and Motor Vehicle Safety Act of 1966 and Executive Order 12291, "Federal Regulation," (February 17, 1981).

DATE: Comments on this proposal must be received by: May 26, 1981.

ADDRESS: Comments should refer to the docket number and to the number of this notice and be submitted to: Docket Section, Room 5109, Nassif Building, 400 Seventh Street, S.W., Washington, D.C. 20590. (Docket hours are 8:00 a.m. to 4:00 pm.)

FOR FURTHER INFORMATION CONTACT: Mr. Michael Finkelstein, Office of Rulemaking, National Highway Traffic Safety Administration, Washington, D.C. 20590 (202-426-1810).

SUPPLEMENTARY INFORMATION: On February 12, 1981, the Department of Transportation published a proposal for a one year delay in the application of the automatic restraint requirements of Safety Standard No. 208 to large cars (46 FR 12033). That action was proposed in light of circumstances which made it necessary and appropriate to extend the effective date, and to provide an opportunity to review the requirements and determine the need for further revisions in the standard. In today's issue of Federal Register, the Department has published a final rule adopting the one year delay.

The purpose of this notice is to gather public comment to aid the review process. The notice proposes a wide range of possible changes to the automatic restraint requirements in order to encourage broad and creative public participation. The Department, desires to ensure that it is taking the most effective and reasonable approach to addressing the serious safety problem posed by the low rate of safety belt use in all cars and by the steadily decreasing average size of new cars sold in this country. As discussed below, the Department is also undertaking an intensive campaign to inform and encourage the public on the need for increased manual belt usage.

Background

The automatic restraint requirements of Standard No. 208 were adopted by the Department in 1977 (42 FR 34289; July 5, 1977). That decision was based on a variety of factors. The Department was confronted with a substantial safety problem. Approximately 25,000 occupants in the front seats of passenger cars were being killed annually in crashes. Although the cars were equipped with manual safety belts under Safety Standard No. 208, relatively few people were being protected since most people did not use manual belts. Studies showed that usage was about 20 percent for all types of belt systems.

The Department anticipated that this safety problem would progressively worsen as people began to switch to smaller, more fuel efficient cars. Generally, the chance of death or serious injury in a crash increases as car size decreases.

The Department concluded that there was no available way of increasing manual belt use. Although mandatory belt use laws had been used in combination in other countries to achieve dramatic increases in the rate of belt use, similar opportunities do not exist in this country. Based on Congressional action indicating disfavor with these laws and lack of State interest, enactment of mandatory use laws was not deemed to be a viable alternative.

To provide a solution to the problems of a high death and injury toll and of a low manual belt use rate, the Department turned to requiring the use of automatic

restraints. Then, as now, the two systems that qualified as automatic restraints were air cushion restraints (air bags) and automatic seat belts (belts that automatically move into place when an occupants enters a vehicle and closes the door). Automatic restraints were found to be superior to manual belts because they were as effective as manual belts in preventing death and injury and would provide protection in a much higher percentage of crashes. (Persons wishing to learn additional details about that and earlier rulemaking relating to automatic restraints are urged to consult dockets 69-7, 73-8 and 74-14 and the rulemaking notices associated with those dockets.)

The Department anticipated substantial safety benefits from the automatic restraint requirements. According to NHTSA's analysis, 9,000 fatalities and 65,000 serious injuries would be prevented annually once all cars on the road had automated restraints, i.e., ten years after initial implementation.

As the Department indicated in its February 12, 1981 proposal, the 1977 decision was based on a variety of key assumptions which, in the light of subsequent events, are no longer valid. The Department assumed that consumers would freely be able to choose between air bags and automatic belts, with 60 percent of cars having the former and 40 percent having the latter. The air bag percentage was based on the expectation that all large cars and intermediates, and half of the compacts would be equipped with those systems. The Department also believed that some of the even smaller cars would be equipped with air bags. These factors, together with the greater design problems and absence of experience in installing air bags in smaller cars, led the Department to phase-in the automatic requirements beginning with large cars.

Current manufacturer plans contemplate almost no installation of air bags, only about 1 percent of the total fleet of new cars. As a result, the phasing-in of the requirements with large cars first and small cars last requires reexamination.

The phase-in sequence is further called into question by the accelerated switch from large cars to less safe, smaller ones. The Department recognized that a switch would occur as a result of the 1973-74 oil shock and the impending implementation of. fuel economy standards. It did not, however, anticipate that the switch would occur as rapidly as it had, due in large measure to the subsequent oil cut-off of 1979. In 1977, NHTSA estimated that size mix in the early 1980's would be 24 percent small cars, 53 percent mid-size cars, and 23 percent large cars. Now the expectation is that the new car fleet will consist of 1 percent large cars, 58 percent mid-size cars and 41 percent small cars. When the numbers of large and small cars in the early-mid 1980's was expected to be approximately the same, the sequence of implementation had no significance in terms of the cars equipped with automatic restraints. Given the currently expected fleet mix of large and small cars, the sequence has substantial significance, especially since smaller cars are less safe.

In 1977, NHTSA believed that automatic belts would cost only 34 dollars more than manual belts and that air bags would cost approximately 154 dollars more than manual belts. Today, NHTSA's comparable figures are 105 dollars for the incremental cost of automatic belts, and at least 400 dollars for air bags at high production volumes and as much as 1,100 dollars at low volumes.

The Department has now undertaken to review the automatic restraint requirements and their implementation schedule in view of changed circumstances which undermine the reasonableness of the existing implementation schedule, the substantial impact of automatic restraints on manufacturer and consumer costs and the accentuation of those manufacturer impacts by the economic difficulties of the automobile industry.

In the analysis which preceded the February 12 proposal, the Department determined that a number of additional factors were relevant. Among these factors is the unnecessary character of the costs which would be incurred by application of automatic restraint requirements to large cars scheduled to be phased out in the near future. These costs would arise largely from the loss of sales due to increased costs, and to the loss of the middle front seating position in large cars.

Another factor is the possibility that initial public acceptance of automatic restraints might have been adversely affected by the decision of large car manufacturers not to make air bags available in model year 1982. Still another factor was the effect of current automatic belt designs on public acceptance and usage.

Based on all of these factors, the Department decided to adopt the one year delay for installing those restraints in large cars.

In conjunction with this decision, the Department is preparing to undertake an intensive public education campaign to induce the public to use their safety belts: This campaign would affect not only the 1982 model year cars which now will be equipped almost exclusively with manual belts but also all other belt-equipped vehicles on the road today. The number of seat belt-equipped vehicles is over 150 million. Accordingly, it is expected that a properly conceived and sustained program, aided by manufacturers and other levels of government, would

make an important contribution to vehicle safety.

The same factors underlying the one year delay also led the Department to issue this notice and propose three principal alternatives.

Principal Proposals

1. Reversal of phase-in sequence. Under this proposal, the automatic restraint requirements would become effective for small cars (wheelbase of 100 inches or less) on September 1, 1982, for mid-size cars (wheelbase greater than 100 inches and less than 114 inches) on September 1, 1983, and for large cars (wheelbase of 114 inches or greater) on September 1, 1984. This proposal would have the advantage of ensuring that automatic restraints are first placed in the car size class which presents the greatest safety risk.

If adopted as proposed, it could produce greater net benefits than implementation of the automatic restraint requirements in accordance with the original phase-in schedule established in 1977. This gain would result from the greater safety risk posed by small cars than by large cars and the increasingly greater number of small cars over large ones.

The Department notes also that requiring small cars instead of large cars to comply first would require a much larger proportion of manufacturers to begin compliance simultaneously rather than under the original schedule. Thus, the new schedule would be more equitable and reasonable. Still another advantage of this proposal is that it would avoid, to a large extent, the necessity and extra cost of redesigning and equipping large cars with automatic restraints for the few years that these cars will continue to be produced. In view of the substantial experience of several manufacturers with designing and producing small cars with automatic

belts, it is believed that there is sufficient leadtime to implement this proposal.

2. Simultaneous compliance. Under this proposal, all size classes would be required to begin compliance at the same time, i.e., March 1, 1983. This proposal allows compliance to begin a half year later than under the first proposal, to offset switching from a phase-in compliance schedule to a simultaneous one. Like the first proposal, this proposal could yield benefits greater than the original phase-in schedule by accelerating the date on which all cars must be equipped with automatic restraints. This proposal could be construed as even more equitable than the first in that all manufacturers would have to bring all of their cars into compliance at the same time.

3. Rescission. The third principal proposal is to rescind the automatic restraint requirements. The principal considerations underlying this proposal are the unlikelihood of public acceptability of automatic restraints in the absence of any significant degree of choice between automatic belts and air bags, the public acceptability of the specific automatic belt designs currently planned by the automobile manufacturers, uncertainties about the general public's rate of future usage of both automatic and manual belt systems, and the substantial cost of air bags even if produced in large volumes.

Additional Proposals

In conjunction with the first and second principal proposals, the Department is also proposing to except the front center seating position of cars from automatic restraint requirements. With that exception, manufacturers could equip that seating position with either a manual belt or with an automatic restraint. This exception is intended to solve a dilemma presented manufacturers in bringing six seat passenger cars into compliance with the current automatic restraint requirements. Since the only known type of automatic restraint for the center seating position is the air bag, manufacturers are faced with a choice of either equipping all three front seating positions with the relatively expensive air bags, or removing the center position and equipping the remaining two with automatic belts.

The latter choice permits use of the less expensive type of automatic restraint, but has the offsetting disadvantage of reducing the utility of the car. The advantage of such an exception is that it would enable manufacturers to retain the center position and equip the two outer front positions with automatic belts. If the automatic belts were the detachable type, they would permit ready access to the center position. The Department recognizes that the usage rate of detachable automatic belts may be less than that for nondetachable types.

The Department also seeks comment on the desirability of and authority for adopting a suggestion made by Volvo in commenting on the February 12 proposal. Out of concern about the perceived marketing need for flexibility in the beginning of new model years and about the relative inflexibility of the normal agency practice of treating September 1 as the beginning of the model year, Volvo suggested that effective dates be specified as "September 1 or the date of production start of the new model year if this date falls between September 1 and December 31."

Impacts of Proposals

The Department has considered the impacts of these proposals and determined that each of the three principal proposals in the notice is a major rulemaking within the meaning of E.O. 12291. A preliminary regulatory impact analysis is being placed in the docket simultaneously with the publication of this notice. A copy of the analysis may be obtained by contacting the docket at the address given at the beginning of this notice.

As noted above, it is expected that both the reversal proposal and the simultaneous compliance proposal could produce benefits equal or greater than the benefits of the revised schedule. This would result primarily from the earlier compliance by small cars which pose greater safety risks than large or mid-size cars. Rescission of the automatic restraint requirements could, after ten years, cause a loss of 750-7,500 lives annually based on the benefits to be expected from all cars on the road having been equipped with automatic restraints by that time.

The precise safety impacts of these and the other proposals depend largely on the usage rate of automatic belts and the effectiveness of the planned public information campaign. As set forth in more detail in the regulatory impact analysis accompanying the Final Rule published elsewhere in this issue of the Federal Register, NHTSA now anticipates a usage rate in the range of 15-60 percent. The rate will ultimately depend on how the public reacts to the automatic belt designs, especially the detachable ones which now appear likely to become the predominant type.

The cost effects of the reversal and simultaneous compliance proposals would be mixed. For example, the reversal proposal would cause the manufacturing and consumer costs of model year 1983 small cars to increase and of model year 1983 mid-size and large cars to decrease. Some slight loss of sales or deferral of purchases of model year 1983 small cars and model year 1984 mid-size cars could occur, although such effects should be minimized by the market forces pushing consumers toward smaller, more fuel efficient cars.

The cost impacts of the simultaneous compliance proposal would depend on how near the manufacturers come to beginning compliance on March 1, 1983. If they begin precisely on that date, then the manufacturer and consumer costs would decrease for the mid-size and large cars produced during the first half of model year 1983 and would increase for the small cars produced during the latter half of that model year. The effect on individual company sales should be minimized by this proposal, since competitive effects among manufacturers and different car size classes would be eliminated.

The rescission proposal would produce substantial savings in manufacturer capital investments and variable costs and in consumer costs. The savings in capital investments alone would be at least several hundred million dollars. The annual savings in manufacturing and consumer costs would be much greater, based on the costs that would otherwise be incurred in installing automatic restraints in all new cars.

The effects of this notice on small entities have been considered under the Regulatory Flexibility Act. Interested persons should consult both the preliminary regulatory impact analysis prepared for this notice and also the final regulatory impact analysis for the one year delay notice published today.

Although almost none if the direct or indirect suppliers of air bags and automatic belts are considered to be "small businesses," the Department did examine the impact on those suppliers. It is believed that the impact of the reversal and simultaneous compliance proposals should be minimal, because those proposals accelerate the compliance of some cars while delaying the compliance of others and since, in the case of automatic belt manufacturers, these businesses produce both automatic and manual belts.

Rescission of the automatic restraint requirements would adversely affect both automatic belt manufacturers and air bag manufacturers. To the extent that the profit to these manufacturers from automatic belt sales exceeds that from manual belt sales, the revenue of these manufacturers will decrease. Given the decision of the car manufacturers to use automatic belts almost exclusively in complying with the automatic restraint requirements, the impact of a rescission on air bag manufacturers may actually be quite limited. Nevertheless, the Department notes that air bag suppliers responding to its February 12 proposal stated that any further delay or uncertainty regarding the automatic restraint effective dates would adversely affect their prospect.

The only proposal that would more than minimally affect small governments and other small fleet purchasers would appear to be rescission. Its adoption would give them a cost savings similar to the one created for purchasers of large 1982 model year cars by the one year delay.

In accordance with the National Environmental Policy Act of 1969, the Department has considered the environmental impacts of the proposals in this notice. A Draft Environmental Impact Statement will be placed in the docket for this rulemaking.

Interested persons are also urged to consult the Final Environmental Impact Statement for the 1977 rule

establishing the automatic restraint requirements.

Interested persons are invited to submit comments on the proposal. It is requested but not required that 10 copies be submitted.

All comments must be limited not to exceed 15 pages in length. Necessary attachments may be appended to these submissions without regard to the 15 page limit. This limitation is intended to encourage commenters to detail their primary arguments in a concise fashion.

If a commenter wishes to submit certain information under a claim of confidentiality, three copies of the complete submission, including purportedly confidential information, should be submitted to the Chief Counsel, NHTSA, at the street address given above, and seven copies from which the purportedly confidential information has been deleted should be submitted to the Docket Section. Any claim of confidentiality must be supported by a statement demonstrating that the information falls within 5 U.S.C. section 552(b)(4), and that disclosure of the information is likely to result in substantial competitive damage; specifying the period during which the information must be withheld to avoid that damage; and showing that earlier disclosure would result in that damage. In addition, the commenter or, in the case of a corporation, a responsible corporate official authorized to speak for the corporation must certify in writing that each item for which confidential treatment is requested is in fact confidential within the meaning of section 552(b)(4)

and that a diligent search has been conducted by the commenter or its employees to assure that none of the specified items has previously been disclosed or otherwise become available to the public.

All comments received before the close of business on the comment closing date indicated above will be considered, and will be available for examination in the docket at the above address both before and after that date. To the extent possible, comments filed after the closing date will also be considered. However, the rulemaking action may proceed at any time after that date, and comments received after the closing date and too late for consideration in regard to the action will be treated as suggestions for future rulemaking. NHTSA will continue to file relevant material as it becomes available in the docket after the closing date, and it is recommended that interested persons continue to examine the docket for new material.

Those persons desiring to be notified upon receipt of their comments in the rules docket should enclose, in the envelope with their comments, a self addressed stamped postcard. Upon receiving the comments, the docket supervisor will return the postcard by mail.

(Secs. 103, 119, Pub. L. 89-563, 80 Stat. 718 (15 U.S.C. 1392, 1407))

Issued on April 6, 1981.

Andrew L. Lewis, Jr.,
Secretary of Transportation
[FR Doc. 81-10709 Filed 4-6-81; 2:25 pm]
BILLING CODE 4910-59-M

NOTES AND QUESTIONS

1. Create an outline of the NPRM and describe the function or content of each section. Does the title of each indicate its purpose or seem to have a more specialized meaning? Why might the agency prepare the document in this form? Do you suppose that the form is typical for NHTSA? All agencies?

2. What reasons does the agency give for seeking a change to Standard 208? Was it incorrect about the safety benefits of the passive restraints requirement?
3. The NPRM contains three alternative proposals. Is each proposal equally supported by the information in the background section? If NHTSA favored one proposal, is there any indication of that? Can you think of any other proposal that NHTSA should have considered?
4. After NHTSA sets forth its proposals, it considers the "impacts" of those proposals. Which impacts does it assess? Why does it assess these particular impacts? E.O. 12,291 is an executive ordered issued by President Reagan that requires agencies to prepare a regulatory impact analysis, evaluating the costs and benefits of their proposals. We discuss this below and again in Chapter 9. The Regulatory Flexibility Act, 5 U.S.C. §§601 *et seq.*, is a federal statute that requires agencies to consider the effect of their proposals on small entities, including businesses and governments. The National Environmental Policy Act of 1969, 42 U.S.C. §§4321 *et seq.*, is a federal statute that requires agencies to prepare an environmental impact statement, evaluating the effect of their proposals on the environment. We also discuss these below.
5. As you might imagine, given the stakes for the domestic and foreign auto industries and the auto insurance industry, not to mention the public, NHTSA received a mountain of comments. If you were a lawyer for one of these organizations or for a consumer protection organization, what comments would you file with the agency?

Now read the final rule that NHTSA issued in 1981 rescinding the passive restraints requirement. As with the NPRM, you should pay careful attention to its formal features as well as the agency's reasoning. You should also seek to identify the ways in which it is similar to and different from the NPRM.

49 C.F.R. Part 571
National Highway Traffic Safety Administration

[Docket No. 74-14; Notice 25], Thursday, October 29, 1981

[46 Fed. Reg. 53419 (1981)]

Federal Motor Vehicle Safety Standards; Occupant Crash Protection

AGENCY: National Highway Traffic Safety Administration, Department of Transportation.

ACTION: Final rule.

SUMMARY: The purpose of this notice is to amend Federal Motor Vehicle Safety Standard No. 208, Occupant Crash Protection, to rescind the requirements for installation of automatic restraints in the front seating positions of passenger cars. Those requirements were scheduled to become effective for large and mid-size cars on September 1, 1982, and for small cars on September 1, 1983.

The automatic restraint requirements are being rescinded because of uncertainty about the public acceptability and probable usage rate of the type of automatic restraint which the car manufacturers planned to make available to most new car buyers. This uncertainty and the relatively substantial cost of automatic restraints preclude the agency from determining that the standard is at this time reasonable and practicable. The reasonableness of the automatic restraint requirements is further called into question by the fact that all new car buyers would be required to pay for automatic belt systems that may induce only a few additional people to take advantage of the benefits of occupant restraints.

The agency is also seriously concerned about the possibility that adverse public reaction to the cost and presence of automatic restraints could have a significant adverse effect on present and future public acceptance of highway safety efforts.

Under the amended standard, car manufacturers will continue to have the current option of providing either automatic or manual occupant restraints.

DATES: The rescission of the automatic restraint requirements of Standard No. 208 is effective December 8, 1981. Any petitions for reconsideration must be received by the agency not later than December 3, 1981.

ADDRESS: Any petitions for reconsideration should refer to the docket number and notice number of this notice and be submitted to: Administrator, National Highway Traffic Safety Administration, 400 Seventh Street, S.W., Washington, D.C. 20590.

FOR FURTHER INFORMATION CONTACT: Mr. Michael Finkelstein,

Associate Administrator for Rulemaking, National Highway Traffic Safety Administration, Washington, D.C. 20590 (202-426-1810).

SUPPLEMENTARY INFORMATION: On April 9, 1981, the Department of Transportation published a notice of proposed rulemaking (NPRM) setting forth alternative amendments to the automatic restraint requirements of Standard No. 208 (46 FR 21205). The purpose of proposing the alternatives was to ensure that Standard No. 208 reflects the changes in circumstances since the automatic restraint requirements were issued (42 FR 34289; July 5, 1977) and to ensure that the standard meets the requirements of the National Traffic and Motor Vehicle Safety Act of 1966 and Executive Order 12291, "Federal Regulations" (February 17, 1981).

Background and NPRM

The automatic restraint requirements were adopted in 1977 in response to the high number of passenger car occupants killed annually in crashes and to the persistent low usage rate of manual belts. The manual belt is the type of belt which is found in most cars today and which the occupant must place around himself or herself and buckle in order to gain its protection. Then, as now, there were two types of automatic restraints, i.e., restraints that require no action by vehicle occupants, such as buckling a belt, in order to be effective. One type is the air cushion restraint (air bag) and the other is the automatic belt (a belt which automatically envelops an occupant when the occupant enters a vehicle and closes the door).

In view of the greater experience with air bags in large cars and to spread out capital investments, the Department established a large-to-small car compliance schedule. Under that schedule, large cars were required to begin compliance

on September 1, 1981, mid-size cars on September 1, 1982, and small cars on September 1, 1983.

On April 6, 1981, after providing notice and opportunity for comment, the Department delayed the compliance date for large cars from September 1, 1981, to September 1, 1982. As explained in the April 6, final rule, that delay was adopted . . . because of the effects of implementation in model year 1982 on large car manufacturers, because of the added significance which those effects assume due to the change in economic circumstances since the schedule was adopted in 1977, and because of the undermining by subsequent events of the rationale underlying the original phase-in schedule.

Simultaneous with publishing the one-year delay in the effective date for large cars, the Department also issued a proposal for making further changes in the automatic restraint requirements. This action was taken in response to a variety of factors that raised questions whether the automatic restraint requirements represented the most reasonable and effective approach to the problem of the low usage of safety belts. Among these factors were the uncertainty about public acceptability of automatic restraints in view of the absence of any significant choice between automatic belts and air bags and the nature of the automatic belt designs planned by the car manufacturers, the consequent uncertainties about the rate of usage of automatic restraints, and the substantial costs of air bags even if produced in large volumes.

The three principal proposals were reversal of phase-in sequence, simultaneous compliance, and rescission. The reversal proposal would have changed the large-to-small car order of compliance to a requirement that small cars commence compliance on September 1, 1982, mid-size cars on September 1, 1983, and large cars on September 1, 1984. The proposal for simultaneous compliance would have required all size classes to begin compliance on the same date, March 1, 1983. The rescission proposal would have retained the manufacturers' current option of equipping their cars with either manual or automatic restraints.

In addition, the Department proposed that, under both the first and second alternatives, the automatic restraint requirements be amended so that such restraints would not be required in the front center seating position.

Following the close of the period for written comments on the April NPRM, NHTSA decided, in its discretion, to hold a public meeting on the alternatives. The purpose of the meeting was to permit interested parties to present their views and arguments orally before the Administrator and ensure that all available data were submitted to the agency. The notice announcing the meeting indicated that participants at the hearing would be permitted to supplement their previous comments. The notice also urged participants to consider the issues raised in former Secretary Coleman's June 14, 1976 proposal regarding occupant restraints and in former Secretary Adams' March 24, 1977 proposal regarding automatic restraints.

Rationale for Agency Decision

The decision to rescind the automatic restraint requirements was difficult for the agency to make. NHTSA has long pursued the goal of achieving substantial increases in the usage of safety belts and other types of occupant restraints. Former Secretary Adams clearly believed that he had ensured the achievement of that goal in July 1977 when he promulgated the automatic restraint requirements. Now that goal appears as elusive as ever. Instead of being equipped with automatic restraints that will protect substantially greater numbers of persons than current manual belts, most new cars would have had a type of automatic belt that might not have been any more acceptable to the public than manual belts. The usage of those automatic belts might, therefore, have been only slightly higher than that of manual belts. While most of the anticipated benefits have virtually disappeared, the costs have not. Vehicle price increases would have amounted to approximately $1 billion per year.

This turn of events may in part reflect the failure of the Department in the years following 1977 to conduct a long term effort to educate the public about the various types of restraints and the need to use them. The need for such an undertaking was seen by former Secretary Coleman in announcing his decision in 1976 to conduct an automatic restraint demonstration project prior to deciding whether to mandate automatic restraints. His instruction that NHTSA undertake significant new steps to promote safety belt usage was never effectively carried out. The result of such an effort could have been that a substantial portion of the public would have been receptive to a variety of automatic restraint designs. As a result of concern over public acceptance, manufacturers have designed their automatic restraints to avoid creating a significant adverse reaction. Unfortunately, the elements of design intended to minimize adverse reaction would also minimize the previously anticipated increases in belt usage and safety benefits of requiring new cars to have automatic restraints instead of manual belts.

The uncertainty regarding the usage of the predominant type of planned automatic restraint has profound implications for the determinations which NHTSA must make regarding a standard under the National Traffic and Motor Vehicle Safety Act. NHTSA has a duty under the Vehicle Safety Act and E.O. 12291 to review the automatic restraint requirements in light of changing events and to ensure that the requirements continue to meet the criteria which each Federal Motor Vehicle Safety Standard must satisfy. If the criteria cannot be satisfied, the agency must make whatever changes in the standard are warranted. The agency must also have the flexibility to modify its standards and programs in its efforts to find effective methods for accomplishing its safety mission.

The agency believes that the post-1977 events have rendered it incapable of finding now, as it was able to do in 1977, that the automatic restraint requirements would meet all of the applicable criteria in the Vehicle Safety Act. Section 103(a) of the Vehicle Safety Act requires that each Federal Motor Vehicle Safety Standard meet the need for safety and be practicable and objective. Each standard must also be reasonable, practicable and appropriate for each type of vehicle or equipment to which it applies (Section 103(f)(3). To meet the need for safety, a standard must be reasonably likely to reduce deaths and injuries. To be found practicable, the agency must conclude that the public will in fact avail themselves of the safety devices installed pursuant to the standard. (*Pacific Legal Foundation v. Department of Transportation*, 593 F.2d 1338, at 1345-6 (D.C. Cir. 1979). To be reasonable and practicable, a standard must be economically and technologically feasible, and the costs of implementation must be reasonable. (S. Rep.

No. 1301, 89th Cong., 2d Sess. 6 (1966).}

In reaching the decision announced by this notice, NHTSA has reviewed the enormous record compiled by this agency over the past decade on automatic restraints. Particular attention was paid to the information and issues relating to the notices which the Agency or Department has issued regarding automatic restraints since 1976. All comments submitted in response to the April 1981 proposal by proponents and opponents of the automatic restraint requirements have been thoroughly considered. A summary of the major comments is included as an appendix to this notice. The agency's analysis of those comments may be found in this notice and the final regulatory impact analysis. A copy of the analysis has been placed in the public docket.

Usage of automatic restraints and safety benefits. As in the case of the comments submitted concerning the one-year delay in automatic restraint requirements for large cars, the commenters on the April 1981 proposal expressed sharply divergent views and arguments and reached widely differing conclusions concerning the likely usage rates and benefits of the automatic restraints planned for installation in response to the automatic restraint requirements. The wide distance between the positions of the proponents and opponents of these requirements stems primarily from the lack of any directly relevant data on the most important issue, i.e., the public reaction to and usage rate of detachable automatic belts. These disagreements once again demonstrate the difficulty in reaching reliable conclusions due to the uncertainty created by the lack of adequate data.

In issuing the automatic restraint requirements in 1977, NHTSA assumed that the implementation of those requirements would produce substantial benefits. According to the analysis which NHTSA performed in that year, automatic restraints were expected to prevent 9,000 deaths and 65,000 serious injuries once all cars on the road were equipped with those devices. That prediction was premised on several critical assumptions. Most important among the assumptions were those concerning the safety benefits of automatic restraints — reductions in death and injury — which in turn are a function of the types of automatic restraints to be placed in each year's production of new cars.

The agency assumed that the combination of air bags and lap belts would be approximately 66 percent effective in preventing fatalities and that automatic belts would have a 50% level of effectiveness. The agency assumed also that air bags would be placed in more than 60 percent of new cars and that automatic belts would be placed in the remaining approximately 40 percent. The agency's analysis predicted that air bags would provide protection in virtually all crashes of sufficient severity to cause deployment of the air bags. It was further assumed that the automatic belts would be used by 60 to 70 percent of the occupants of those cars.

As to public reaction, the agency anticipated that the public would, as a whole, accept automatic restraints because it could choose between the two types of those restraints. Those not wanting automatic belts would select an air bag. Partly as a function of the expected large volume of air bag installation, the agency projected that the cost of air bags would be only slightly more than $100 (in 1977 dollars) more than manual belts.

As part of its efforts to monitor and facilitate implementation of the automatic restraint requirements, the agency continued its gathering of data about the use and effectiveness of air bags and of automatic belts with use-inducing features, the only type of automatic belt available to the public. With respect to automatic belts, this effort was carried out through a contract with Opinion Research Corporation. Under that contract, observations were made of seat belt usage during the two year period beginning November 1977. These observations provided data on usage of manual and automatic belts in model year 1975-79 VW Rabbits and of manual belts in model year 1978-79 GM Chevettes, As a result of voluntary decisions by VW and GM, a number of the Rabbits and Chevettes were equipped with automatic belts. The observation data showed usage rates of about 36 percent for manual belts and about 81 percent for automatic belts in the Rabbits. The observed rate of manual belt usage in Chevettes was 11 percent. There were insufficient numbers of model year 1978-79 Chevettes equipped with automatic belts to develop reliable usage figures.

Several telephone surveys were also made under contract with Opinion Research. The first survey involved owners of model year 1979 VW Rabbits and GM Chevettes equipped with automatic belts and was conducted during 1979. This survey showed that 89 percent of Rabbit owners and 72 percent of Chevette owners said that they used their automatic belts. A second survey was conducted in late 1979 and early 1980. It covered owners of model year 1980 Rabbits and Chevettes. The usage rates found by the second survey were almost identical to those in the first survey.

Now, however, the validity of the benefit predictions in 1977 and the relevancy of the extensive data gathered by NHTSA on air bags and on automatic belts with use-inducing features have been substantially if not wholly undermined by drastic changes in the types of automatic restraints that would have been installed under the automatic restraint requirements. Instead of installing air bags in approximately 60 percent of new cars, the manufacturers apparently planned to install them in less than 1 percent of new cars. Thus, automatic belts would have been the predominant means of compliance, and installed in approximately 99% of new cars. Thus, the assumed life-saving potential of air bags would not have been realized.

Manufacturers have stated that they chose belt systems for compliance because of the competitive disadvantage of offering the relatively expensive, inadequately understood air bag when other manufacturers would have been providing automatic belts. These explanations seem credible.

The other drastic change concerns the type of automatic belt to be installed. Although some aspects of the car manufacturers' automatic belt plans are still tentative, it now appears reasonably certain that if the automatic restraint requirements were implemented, the overwhelming majority of new cars would be equipped with automatic belts that are detachable, unlike the automatic belts in Rabbits and Chevettes. Most planned automatic belts would be like today's manual lap and shoulder belts in that they can be easily detached and left that way permanently.

Again, this design choice would appear to have arisen out of concern that without such features emergency exit could be inhibited, and, in part as a result of a perception of this fact, public refusal to accept new designs would be widespread. The agency shares this concern, and has since 1977 required that all such belts provide for emergency exit. Agency concerns on this point have been validated by recent related attitudinal research, discussed below.

In its final rule delaying the initial effective date of the automatic restraint requirements, the April 1981 proposal and the associated documents analyzing the impacts of those actions, NHTSA expressly confronted the lack of usage data directly relevant to the type of automatic belts now planned to be installed in most new cars. The agency stated that there were several reasons why the available data was of limited utility in attempting to make any reliable predictions about the usage of easily detachable automatic belts. The most important reason, which has already been noted, is that the predominant type of planned automatic belt would not have had features to ensure that these belts are not detached.

Second, all of the available data relate to only two subcompacts, the Rabbit and the Chevette. Due to a combination of owner demographics and a correlation between driver perception of risk and the size of the car being driven, belt usage rates are typically higher in small cars than in larger ones. Therefore, the usage rates for the two subcompacts cannot simply be adopted as the usage rates for automatic belts in all car size classes.

Third, most of the Rabbit and Chevette owners knew that their new car would come with an automatic belt and had it demonstrated for them, even if many state that they did not consciously choose that type of belt. Having voluntarily invested in automatic restraints, they are more likely to use those restraints than someone who is compelled to buy them.

The significance of the fundamental difference between the nondetachable and detachable automatic belt bears further discussion. The Rabbit automatic belts are, as a practical matter, not permanently detachable since they are equipped with an ignition interlock. If the belt is disconnected, the interlock prevents the starting of the car. Each successive use would therefore require re-connection before engine start. The Chevette automatic belts also were initially equipped with an ignition interlock. Beginning in model year 1980, the Chevette belts were made both practically and literally nondetachable. They consist of a continuous, nondetachable shoulder belt. Additional webbing can be played out to produce slack in the belt; however, the belt remains attached at both ends.

By contrast, the automatic belts now planned for most cars do not have any effect on the starting of the cars and are easily detachable. Some belt designs may be detached and permanently stowed as readily as the current manual lap and shoulder belts. Once a detachable automatic belt is detached, it becomes identical to a manual belt. Contrary to assertions of some supporters of the standard, its use thereafter requires the same type of affirmative action that is the stumbling block to obtaining high usage levels of manual belts. If the car owners perceive the belts as simply a different configuration of the current manual belts, this stumbling block is likely to remain. They may treat the belt as a manual one and thus never develop the habit of simply leaving the belt attached so that it can act as an automatic belt.

The agency recognizes the possibility that the exposure of some new car purchasers to attached automatic belts may convert some previously occasional users of manual belts to full time belt users. Present attitudinal survey data clearly establish the existence of a population of such occupants who could be influenced by some external factor to convert to relatively constant users. However, the agency believes that many purchasers of new cars having detachable automatic belts would not experience the potential use-inducing character of attached automatic belts unless they had taken the initiative themselves to attach the belts.

Thus, the change in car manufacturers' plans has left the agency without any factual basis for reliably predicting the likely usage increases due to detachable automatic belts, or for even predicting the likelihood of any increase at all. The only tentative conclusion that can be drawn from available data is that the installation of nondetachable automatic belts in other subcompacts could result in usage rates near those found in Rabbits and Chevettes. Even that use of the Rabbit and Chevette data may be questionable, however, given the element of voluntarism in the purchase of automatic belts by many of the Rabbit and Chevette owners. Thus, the data on automatic belt use in Rabbits and Chevettes may do little more than confirm the lesson of the model year 1974-75 cars equipped with manual belts and ignition interlocks, i.e., that the addition to a belt system of a feature that makes the belt nondetachable or necessitates its attachment before a car can be started can substantially increase the rate of belt usage.

In estimating automatic belt usage rates for the purposes of the April final rule and proposal, the agency recognized the substantial uncertainty regarding the effects of easily detachable automatic belts on belt usage. NHTSA attempted to compensate for the lack of directly relevant data by using two different techniques to predict a potential range of usage.

One technique was to assume a consistent multiplier effect, whereby belt usage in cars of all size classes would be assumed to be more than slightly double as it had in Rabbits. A doubling of the current 10-11 percent manual belt usage rate projected over the general car fleet would

mean a 22 percent rate could be achieved with the installation of automatic belts. The other technique was to assume that there would be a consistent additive effect, whereby the same absolute percentage point increase in belt usage would occur as there had been in the case with Rabbits. Use of this method would result in a predicted 50 percentage point increase in belt usage, over the entire fleet, from the current 10-11 percent to approximately 60 percent.

The agency used the results of these two techniques in an attempt to construct a range of possible increases in belt usage. Thus, a range of 15 to 60 percent was used in both the final regulatory impact analysis for the April rulemaking to defer the effective date for one year and the preliminary analysis for the current action. The figure of 15 percent was derived by doubling the observed 7 percent usage levels in the large type cars affected by the deferral. A figure of 22 percent would have been more appropriate as the low end of the range for the current action, since it would represent a doubling of the current usage rate of the car fleet as a whole. This latter figure has been used in addressing this question in the current final regulatory analysis.

Although the agency had no definitive way of resolving the uncertainty about the usage of detachable automatic belts, the agency estimated that belt usage with automatic belts would most likely fall near the lower end of either range. This estimate was based on a variety of factors. Most relate to the previously discussed limitations in the relevancy of the observations and surveys of Rabbit and Chevette owners. In addition, those data were on their face inconsistent with data regarding automatic belt usage in crashes involving Rabbits. Those crash data indicated a usage rate of 55-57 percent instead of the better than 80

percent rate indicated by the observation study and telephone surveys.

Thus, the agency made the preliminary judgment in its impact analyses that the switch from manual belts to detachable automatic belts could approximately double belt usage. However, the April 1981 final rule noted that the actual belt usage might be lower, even substantially so. With respect to cars with current low usage rates, that notice stated that the usage rate of detachable automatic belts might only approach levels similar to those currently achieved with manual belts.

The commenters on the April 1981 NPRM did not present any new factual data that could have reduced the substantial uncertainty confronting the agency. Instead, the commenters relied on the same data examined by the agency in its impact analyses.

The commenters were sharply divided on the question of usage rates. Proponents of the automatic restraint requirements did not in their analyses address the significance of the use-inducing nature of the nondetachable automatic belts in the Rabbits and Chevettes or the demographic factors relating to those car purchasers. Instead, they asserted that the usage rates achieved in Rabbits and Chevettes would, with slight adjustments, also be achieved in other car size classes. In reaching this conclusion, they asserted that the usage rate increases of automatic belts shown by Rabbit and Chevette owners were the same regardless of whether the automatic belts were purchased knowingly or unknowingly. There was an exception to this pattern of comment among the proponents. One public spokesperson for an interest group acknowledged that automatic belts could be designed in a way that they so closely resembled manual belts that their usage rates would be the same.

Opponents of the automatic restraint requirements, relying on the similarity of detachable automatic belts to manual belts, predicted that the automatic belts would not have any substantial effect on belt usage. The opponents of the requirements also dismissed the experience of the Rabbit and Chevette owners on the grounds that the automatic belts in those cars had been voluntarily purchased and were nondetachable.

While the public comments did not provide the agency with any different or more certain basis for estimating belt usage than it already had, they did induce the agency to reexamine its assumption about the possible automatic belt usage rates. Although it is nearly impossible to sort out with precision the individual contributions made by nondetachability, interlocks, car size, demographics and other factors, NHTSA believes that the usage of automatic belts in Rabbits and Chevettes would have been substantially lower if the automatic belts in those cars were not equipped with a use-inducing device inhibiting detachment.

In the agency's judgment, there is a reasonable basis for believing that most of the increase in automatic belt Rabbits and Chevettes is due to the nondetachability feature, whether an interlock or other design feature, of their belt systems. Necessitating the attachment of belts by the addition of interlocks to 1974-75 cars resulted in an increase in manual belt usage by as much as 40 percent in cars subject to that requirement. A similar effect in the case of the Rabbit would account for four-fifths of the increase observed in the automatic belt vehicles. A significant portion of the remaining increase could in fact be attributable to the fact many owners of automatic belt Rabbits and Chevettes knowingly and voluntarily bought the automatic belts. By

the principle of self-selection, these people would be more inclined to use their belts than the purchasers of 1974-75 Rabbits who did not have any choice regarding the purchase of a manual belt equipped with an interlock. This factor would not, of course, be present in the fleet subject to the standard.

The most appropriate way of accounting for the detachability problem and other limitations on the validity of that Rabbit and Chevette data would be to recognize that the levels of usage resulting from both the point estimates are based on uncertain conclusion and adjust each appropriately. The agency's estimate in the final regulatory impact analysis for the April 1981 final rule that usage would likely fall near the lower end of the range had the effect of substantially adjusting downward the usage rate (60 percent) produced by the technique relying on the absolute percentage point increase (50 percentage points) in belt usage in automatic belt Rabbits and Chevettes. A similar adjustment could also be made in the usage rate (15 percent) indicated by the multiplier technique.

Throughout these sequential analyses, the agency has examined the extremely sparse factual data, applied those factors which are known to externally affect usage rates, and defined for analytical purposes the magnitude of potential safety effects. Aside from the initial data points, all such analyses in all cases necessarily involve exercises of discretion and informed judgment. Resultant conclusions are indications of probable usage which always have been and always must be relied upon by the agency in the absence of additional objective data.

The agency believes that the results produced by both techniques must be adjusted to account for the effects of detachability and the other factors affecting usage rates. Therefore, as the April 1981

final rule recognized, the incremental usage attributable to the automatic aspect of the subject belts may be substantially less than 11 percent.

The agency's analysis of the public comments and other available information leads it to conclude that it cannot reliably predict even a 5 percentage point increase as the minimum level of expected usage increase. The adoption of a few percentage points increase as the minimum would, in the agency's judgment, be more consistent with the substantial uncertainty about the usage rate of detachable automatic belts. Based on the data available to it, NHTSA is unable to assess the probability that the actual incremental usage would fall nearer a 0 percentage point increase or nearer some higher value like a 5 or 10 percentage point increase.

Thus, the agency concludes that the data on automatic belt usage in Rabbits and Chevettes does not provide a sufficient basis for reliably extrapolating the likely range of usage of detachable automatic belts by the general motoring public in all car size classes. Those data are not even sufficient for demonstrating the likelihood that those belts would be used in perceptibly greater numbers than the current manual belts. If the percentage increase is zero or extremely small due to the substantial similarity of the design and methods of using detachable automatic belts and manual belts, then the data regarding manual belt usage would be as reliable a guide to the effects of detachable automatic belts on belt usage as data regarding usage of nondetachable automatic belts. Indeed, the manual belt data may even be a more reliable guide since the data are based on usage by the general motoring public in cars from all size and demographic classes.

In view of the uncertainty about the incremental safety

benefits of detachable automatic belts, it is difficult for the agency to determine that the automatic restraint requirements in their present form meet the need for safety.

In concluding that for this reason detachable automatic belts may contribute little to achieving higher belt usage rates, the question then arises whether the agency should amend the standard to require that automatic belts have a use-inducing feature like that of the Rabbit and Chevette automatic belts. NHTSA believes that such features would increase belt usage. The agency does not, however, believe that such devices should be mandated, for the reasons discussed in detail below.

Costs of automatic restraints

In view of the possibly minimal safety benefits and substantial costs of implementing the automatic restraint requirements, the agency is unable to conclude that the incremental costs of the requirements are reasonable. The requirements are, in that respect, impracticable. While the car manufacturers have already made some of the capital expenditures necessary to comply with the automatic restraint requirements, they still face substantial, recurring variable costs. The average price increase per car is estimated to be $89. The costs of air bags and some designs of automatic belts would be substantially higher. With a total annual production of more than 10 million cars for sale in this country, there would be a price effect of approximately $1 billion.

While the car manufacturers might be able to pass along some or all of their costs to consumers, the necessary price increases would reduce sales. There might not be any net revenue loss since the extra revenue from the higher prices could offset the revenue loss from the lower volume of sales. However, those sale losses would cause net employment losses. Additional sales losses might occur due to consumer uncertainty about or antipathy toward the detachable automatic belts which do not stow so unobtrusively as current manual lap and shoulder belts.

Consumers would probably not be able to recoup their loss of disposable income due to the higher car prices. There does not appear to be any certainty that owners of cars with detachable automatic belts would receive offsetting discounts in insurance costs. Testimony and written comments submitted to the agency indicate premium reductions generally are available only to owners of cars equipped with air bags, not automatic belts. Some large insurance companies do not now offer discounts to any automatic restraint-equipped cars, even those with air bags. If insurance cost discounts were to be given owners of cars having detachable automatic belts, such discounts would be given only after the automatic belts had produced significant increases in belt usage, and in turn significant decreases in deaths and serious injuries. The apparent improbability of any economic effect approaching the magnitude of the consumer cost means that the discounts would not likely materialize on a general basis.

Insurance company statements at the August 1981 public meeting reaffirmed this belief as they state that they could not now assure reductions in insurance premiums but would have to first collect a considerable amount of claim data.

Finally, the weight added to cars by the installation of automatic belts would cause either increased fuel costs for consumers or further new car price increases to cover the incorporation of offsetting fuel economy improvements.

The agency does not believe that it would be reasonable to require car manufacturers or consumers to bear such substantial costs without more adequate assurance that they will produce benefits. Given the plans of the car manufacturers to rely primarily on detachable automatic belts and the absence of relevant data to resolve the usage question, implementation of the automatic restraint requirements amounts to an expensive federal regulatory risk. The result if the detachable automatic belts fail to achieve significant increases in belt usage could be a substantial waste of resources.

The agency believes that the costs are particularly unreasonable in view of the likelihood that other alternatives available to the agency, the states and the private sector could accomplish the goal of the automatic restraint requirements at greatly reduced cost. Like those requirements, the agency's planned educational campaign is addressed primarily to the substantial portion of the motoring public who are currently occasional users of manual belts.

Effect on public attitude toward safety

Although the issue of public acceptance of automatic restraints has already been discussed as it relates to the usage rate of detachable automatic restraints, there remains the question of the effect of automatic restraints on the public attitude toward safety regulation in general. Whether or not there would be more than minimal safety benefits, implementation of the automatic restraint requirements might cause significant long run harm to the safety program.

No regulatory policy is of lasting value if it ultimately proves unacceptable to the public. Public acceptability is at issue in any vehicle safety rulemaking proceeding in which the required safety equipment would be obtrusive, relatively expensive and beneficial only to the extent that significant portions of the motoring public will cooperate and use it. Automatic belt requirements exhibit all of those characteristics. The agency has given the need for public acceptability of automatic restraints substantial weight since it will clearly determine not only the level of safety benefits but also the general public attitude toward related safety initiatives by the government or the private sector.

As noted above, detachable automatic belts may not be any more acceptable to the public than manual belts at any given point in time. If the detachable automatic belts do not produce more than negligible safety benefits, then regardless of the benefits attributable to the small number of other types of automatic restraints planned to be installed, the public may resent being required to pay substantially more for the automatic systems. Many if not most consumers could well conclude that the automatic belts would in fact provide them with no different freedom of choice about usage or levels of protection than manual belts currently offer. As a result, it is not unreasonable to conclude that the public may regard the automatic restraint requirements as an expensive example of ineffective regulation.

Thus, whether or not the detachable automatic belts might have been successful in achieving higher belt usage rates, mandates requiring such belts could well adversely affect public attitude toward the automatic restraint requirements in particular and safety measures in general. As noted in more detail in the 1976 Decision of Secretary Coleman.

Rejection by the public would lead to administrative or Congressional reversal of a passive restraint requirement that could result in hundreds of millions of dollars of wasted resources, severe damage to the nation's economy, and, equally important, a poisoning of popular sentiment toward efforts to improve occupant restraint systems in the future.

It can only be concluded that the public attitude described by the Secretary at that time is at least as prevalent today. The public might ultimately have sought the legislative rescission of the requirements. Action-forcing safety measures have twice before been overturned by Congress. In the mid-1970's, Congress rescinded the ignition interlock provision and provided that agency could not require the States to adopt and enforce motorcycle helmet use laws. Some people might also have cut the automatic belts out of their cars, thus depriving subsequent owners of the cars of the protection of any occupant restraint system. These are serious concerns for an agency charged by statute with taking steps appropriate for addressing safety problems that arise not only in the short term but also the long term. The agency must be able to react effectively to the expected increases in vehicle deaths and injuries during the 1980's.

Equity

Another relevant factor affecting the reasonableness of the automatic restraint requirements and of their costs is the equity of the distribution of such costs among the affected consumers. Responsible regulatory policy should generally strive to ensure that the beneficiaries of regulation bear the principal costs of that regulation. The higher the costs of a given regulation, the more serious the potential equity problem. The automatic restraint requirements of the standard would have required the current regular user of manual belts not only to pay himself for a system that affords him no additional safety protection, but in part to subsidize the current nonuser of belts who may or may not be induced by the automatic restraints to commence regular restraint usage.

Option of Adopting Use-Compelling Features

As noted above, some commenters have suggested that the only safety belts which are truly "passive" are those with use-compelling features. Such commenters have recommended that the agency amend the standard so as to require such features. For example, an ignition interlock which prohibits the car from starting unless the belt is secured is a use-compelling feature. Another example is a passive belt design which is simply not detachable, because no buckle and latch release mechanism is provided. While NHTSA agrees that such use-compelling features could significantly increase usage of passive belts, NHTSA cannot agree that use-compelling features could be required consistent with the interests of safety. In the case of the ignition interlock, NHTSA clearly has no authority to require such a use-compelling feature. The history of the Congressional action which removed this authority from NHTSA suggests that Congress would look with some disfavor upon any similar attempt to impose a use-compelling feature on a belt system.

But, even if NHTSA were to require that passive belts contain use-compelling features, the agency believes that the requirement could be counterproductive. Recent attitudinal research conducted by NHTSA confirms a widespread, latent and irrational fear in many members of the public that they could be trapped by the seat belt after a crash. Such apprehensions may well be contributing factors in decisions by many people not to wear a seat belt at all. This apprehension is clearly a question which can be addressed through education, but pending its substantial reduction, it would be highly inappropriate to impose a technology which by its very nature could heighten or trigger that concern.

In addition, the agency believes there are compelling safety reasons why it should not mandate use-compelling features on passive belts. In the event of accident, occupants wearing belts suffer significantly reduced risk of loss of consciousness, and are commonly able to extricate themselves with relative ease. However, the agency would be unable to find the cause of safety served by imposing any requirement which would further complicate the extrication of any occupant from his or her car, as some use-compelling features would. NHTSA's regulations properly recognize the need for all safety belts to have some kind of release mechanism, either a buckle and latch mechanism or a spool-out release which feeds a length of belt long enough to extricate a car occupant.

Alternative methods of increasing restraint usage

Finally, the agency believes that it is possible to induce increased belt usage, and enhance public understanding and awareness of belt mechanisms in general, by means that are at least as effective but much less costly than the installation of millions of detachable automatic belts.

In the decision noted above, Secretary Coleman noted the obligation of the Department of Transportation to undertake efforts to encourage the public to use occupant restraints, active or passive. Toward this point, Secretary Coleman directed the Administrator of NHTSA to undertake significant new steps to promote seat belt usage during the demonstration program. This instruction of the Secretary

was not effectively carried out and, unfortunately, we do not enjoy today the benefits of a prolonged Departmental campaign to encourage seat belt usage. Had such a program been successfully carried out, increased seat belt usage could have saved many lives each year, beginning in 1977.

Rather than allowing the Coleman demonstration program and its accompanying education effort to come to fruition, the Department reconsidered Secretary Coleman's 1976 decision during 1977. At the conclusion of the reconsideration period, the Department reversed that decision, and amended the standard to require the provision of automatic restraints in new passenger cars, in accordance with a phased-in schedule.

The benefits of any such belt use enhancement efforts could have already substantially exceeded those projected for the automatic restraint requirements of this standard. Over the next ten years, the requirements of the standard would have addressed primarily those occasional belt users amenable to change who buy new cars during the mid and late 1980's.

Prior to the initiation of rulemaking in February of this year, the Department had resolved to undertake a major educational effort to enhance voluntary belt usage levels. Such efforts will be closely coordinated with new and preexisting major initiatives at the State level and in the private sector, many of which were discussed at the public meeting on the present rulemaking. These efforts will address not only those users/purchasers amenable to change, but also those currently driving and riding in cars, multipurpose passenger vehicles and trucks on the road today. The potential for immediate impact is thus many times greater. Further, with the much greater number of

persons directly impacted, educational efforts would need to raise safety belt usage in the vehicles on the road during the 1980's by only a few percentage points to achieve far greater safety benefits than the automatic restraint requirements could have achieved during the same time period.

This is in no sense to argue or suggest that nonregulatory alternatives are or should be considered in all cases appropriate to limit Federal regulation. However, the existence of such efforts, and their relevance to calculations of benefits in the present case, must be and has been considered to the extent discussed herein.

Summary of Agency Conclusion

As originally conceived, the automatic restraint requirement was a far reaching technology forcing regulation that could have resulted in a substantial reduction in injuries and loss of life on our highways.

As it would be implemented in the mid-1980's, however, the requirement has turned into a billion dollar Federal effort whose main technological advance would be to require seat belts that are anchored to the vehicle door rather than the vehicle body, permitting these belts to be used either as conventional active belts or as automatic belts.

To gain this advantage, under the standard as drafted, consumers would see the end of the six passenger car and an average vehicle price increase on the order of $89 per car. The almost certain benefits that had been anticipated as a result of the use of air bag technology have been replaced by the gravely uncertain benefit estimates associated with belt systems that differ little from existing manual belts.

In fact, with the change in manufacturers' plans that in essence replaced air bags with automatic belts, the central issue in this proceeding has become whether automatic belts would induce higher belt usage rates than are occurring with manual belts.

Many of the comments in the course of this rulemaking were directed specifically at the question of belt use. Most addressed themselves to the information in the docket on the usage witnessed in the VW Rabbit and Chevette equipped with automatic belts.

The Agency's own analysis of the available information concludes that it is virtually impossible to develop an accurate and supportable estimate of future belt use increases based upon the Rabbit and Chevette automatic belt observations. The Agency further believes that it is impossible to disaggregate the roles that demographics, use inducing devices, and automatic aspects of the belt played in the observed increases.

Faced with this level of uncertainty, and the wide margins of possible error, the agency is simply unable to comply with its statutory mandate to consider and conclude that the automatic restraint requirements are at this time practicable or reasonable within the meaning of the Vehicle Safety Act. On the other hand, the agency is not able to agree with assertions that there will be absolutely no increase in belt use as a result of automatic belts. Certainly, while a large portion of the population appears to find safety belts uncomfortable or refuses to wear them for other reasons, there is a sizeable segment of the population that finds belts acceptable but still does not use them. It is plausible to assume that some people in this group who would not otherwise use manual belts would not disconnect automatic belts.

It is this same population that will generate all of the benefits that result directly and solely from this regulation. This is a population that can also be

reached in other ways. The Agency, state governments and the private sector are in the process of expanding and initiating major national belt use educational programs of unprecedented scale. While undertaken entirely apart from the pending proceeding, the fact remains that this effort will predominantly affect the same population that the automatic belts would be aimed at.

On the one hand, it could be argued that, the success of any belt use program would only be enhanced by the installation of automatic belts. Individuals who can be convinced of the utility of safety belts would presumably have an easier time accepting an automatic belt. On the other hand, there is little evidence that the standard itself will materially increase usage levels above those otherwise achievable.

However, the agency is not merely faced with uncertainty as to the actual benefits that would result from detachable automatic safety belts. When the uncertain nature of the benefits is considered together with the risk of adverse safety consequences that might result from the maintenance of this regulation, the agency must conclude that such retention would not be reasonable, and would not meet the need for motor vehicle safety.

It is useful to summarize precisely what the agency believes these risks might be. The principal risk is that adverse public reaction could undermine the effectiveness of both the standard itself and future or related efforts.

The agency also concludes, however, that retention would present serious risk of jeopardizing other separate efforts to increase manual belt usage by the Federal government, States and the private sector. A public that believes it is the victim of too much government regulation by virtue of the standard might well resist such parallel efforts to enhance voluntary belt usage. Further, to the

extent that States begin to consider belt use laws as an option, a Federal regulation addressing the same issue could undermine those attempts as well.

While one cannot be certain of the adverse effects on net belt usage increases, it would be irresponsible to fail to consider them. A decision to retain the regulation under any of the schedules now being considered would not get automatic belts on the road until 1983 and would not apply to the entire fleet of new cars until 1984. By the end of the 1984 model year, under most options, there would have been fewer than 20 million vehicles equipped with automatic belts on the road.

By the same time, however, there will be upward of 150 million vehicles equipped with only manual belts, drivers and occupants of which will have been exposed to interim belt usage encouragement efforts.

Agency analysis indicates that external efforts of whatever kind that increase usage by only 5 percent, will save more than 1300 lives per year beginning in 1983. Installation of automatic belts could save an equal number of lives in 1983 only with 95 percent belt usage.

Further, even if one is convinced that automatic belts can double belt usage and alternative efforts would only increase usage by 5 percent, it would not be until 1989 that total life savings attributable to automatic belts installed under the automatic restraint requirements would reach the total life savings achieved through such other efforts.

NHTSA fully recognizes that neither outcome is a certainty. Much closer to the truth is that both outcomes are uncertain. However, neither is significantly more likely than the other. That being the case, to impose the $1 billion cost on the public does not appear to be reasonable.

It is particularly unreasonable in light of the fact that the rescission does not foreclose the option to again reopen rulemaking if enhanced usage levels of both manual and automatic belts do not materialize. Long before there would have been any substantial number of vehicles on the road mandatorily equipped with automatic belts as a result of this standard, NHTSA will conclusively know whether other efforts to increase belt use have succeeded either in achieving acceptable usage levels or in increased public understanding and acceptance of the need for further use-inducing or automatic protection alternatives. If so obviously no further action would be needed. If such is not the case, rulemaking would again be a possibility. Any such rulemaking, following even partially successful efforts to increase belt use, would be much less likely to face public rejection.

It has been said that the Vehicle Safety Act is a "technology-forcing" statute. The agency concurs completely.

However, the issue of automatic restraints now before the agency is not a "technology-forcing" issue. The manual seat belt available in every car sold today offers the same, or more, protection than either the automatic seat belt or the air bag. Instead, the agency today faces a decision to force people to accept protection that they do not choose for themselves. It is difficult to conclude that the Vehicle Safety Act is, or in light of past experience could become, a "people-forcing" statute.

NHTSA cannot find that the automatic restraint requirements meet the need for motor vehicle safety by offering any greater protection than is already available.

After 12 years of rulemaking, NHTSA has not yet succeeded in its original intent, the widespread offering of automatic crash protection that will produce substantial benefits. The agency is still committed to this goal and intends immediately to initiate efforts with automobile manufacturers to ensure that the public will have such types of technology available. If this does not succeed, the agency will consider regulatory action to assure that the last decade's enormous advances in crash protection technology will not be lost.

Impact Analyses

NHTSA has considered the impacts of this final rule and determined that it is a major rulemaking within the meaning of E.O. 12291 and a significant rule within the meaning of the Department of Transportation regulatory policies and procedures. A final regulatory impact analysis is being placed in the public docket simultaneously with the publication of this notice. A copy of the analysis may be obtained by writing to: National Highway Traffic Safety Administration, Docket Section, Room 5109, 400 Seventh Street, S.W., Washington, D.C. 20590.

The agency's determination that the rule is major and significant is based primarily upon the substantial savings in variable manufacturing costs and in consumer costs that result from the rescission of the automatic restraint requirements. These costs would have amounted to approximately $1 billion once all new cars became subject to the requirements. The costs would have recurred annually as long as the requirements remained in effect. There is also a recurring savings in fuel costs of approximately $150 million annually. Implementation of the automatic restraint requirements would have increased the weight of cars and reduced their fuel economy. In addition, the car manufacturers will be able to reallocate $400 million in capital investment that they would have had to allocate for the purpose of completing their efforts to comply with the automatic restraint requirements.

The agency finds it difficult to provide a reliable estimate of any adverse safety effects of rescinding the automatic restraint requirements. There might have been significant safety loss if the installation of detachable automatic belts resulted in a doubling of belt usage and if the question were simply one of the implementation or rescission of the automatic restraint requirements. The April 1981 NPRM provided estimates of the additional deaths that might occur as a result of rescission. However, those estimates included carefully drafted caveats. The notice expressly stated that the impacts of rescission would depend upon the usage rate of automatic belts and of the effectiveness of the agency's educational campaign. The agency has now determined that there is no certainty that the detachable automatic belts would produce more than a several percentage point increase in usage. The small number of cars that would have been equipped with automatic belts having use-inducing features or with air bags would not have added more than several more percentage points to that amount. Further, any potential safety losses associated with the rescission must be balanced against the expected results of the agency's planned educational program about safety belts. That campaign will be addressed to the type of person who might be induced by the detachable automatic belts to begin regular safety belt usage, i.e., the occasional user of manual belts. Since that campaign will affect occasional users in all vehicles on the road today instead of only those in new cars, the campaign can yield substantially greater benefits than the detachable automatic belts even with a much lower effectiveness level.

The agency has also considered the impact of this action on automatic restraint suppliers, new car dealers and small organizations and governmental units. Since the agency certifies that the rescission would not have a significant effect on a substantial number of small entities, a final regulatory flexibility analysis has not been prepared. However, the impacts of the rescission on the suppliers, dealers and other entities are discussed in the final Regulatory Impact Analysis.

The impact on air bag manufacturers is likely to be minimal. Earlier this year, General Motors, Ford and most other manufacturers cancelled their air bag programs for economic reasons. These manufacturers planned instead to rely almost wholly on detachable automatic belts. Therefore, it is not accurate to say, as some commenters did, that rescission of the automatic restraint requirements will "kill" the air bag. Rescission will not affect the air bag manufacturers to any significant degree. Further, the agency plans to undertake new steps to promote the continued development and production of air bags.

The suppliers of automatic belts are generally the same firms that supply manual belts. Thus, the volume of sales of these firms is not expected to be affected by the rescission. However, there will be some loss of economic activity that would have been associated with developing and producing the more sophisticated automatic belts.

The effects of the rescission on new car dealers would be positive. Due to reduced new car purchase prices and more favorable reaction to manual belts than to automatic belts, sales increases of 395,000 cars were estimated by GM and 235,000 cars by Ford. While these figures appear to be overstated, the agency agrees that rescission will increase new car sales.

Small organizations and governmental units would be benefited by the reduced cost of purchasing and operating new cars. Given the indeterminacy of the usage rate that detachable automatic belts would have achieved, it is not possible to estimate the effects, if any, of the rescission on the safety of persons employed by these groups.

In accordance with the National Environmental Policy Act of 1969, NHTSA has considered the environmental impacts of the rescission and the alternatives proposed in the April 1981 NPRM. The option selected is disclosed by the analysis to result in the largest reductions in the consumption of plastics, steel, glass and fuel/energy. A Final Environmental Impact Statement is being placed in the public docket simultaneously with the publication of this notice.

This amendment is being made effective in less than 180 days because the date on which the car manufacturers would have to make expenditure commitments to meet the automatic restraint requirements for model year 1983 falls within that 180-day period.

Part 571 Federal Motor Vehicle Safety Standards 49 C.F.R. §571.208

In consideration of the foregoing, Federal Motor Vehicle Safety Standard No. 208, Occupant Crash Protection (49 CFR 571.208), is amended as set forth below.

49 C.F.R. §571.208 §571.208 [Amended]

1. §4.1.2 is amended by revising it to read:
§4.1.2 Passenger cars manufactured on or after September 1, 1973. Each passenger car manufactured on or after September 1, 1973, shall meet the requirements of §4.1.2.1, §4.1.2.2 or §4.1.2.3. A protection system that meets the requirements of §4.1.2.1 or §4.1.2.2 may be installed at one or more designated seating positions of a vehicle that otherwise meets the requirements of §4.1.2.3.
2. The heading of §4.1.2.1 is amended by revising it to read:
§4.1.2.1 First option — Frontal/Angular Automatic protection system.
. . .
§4.1.3 [Removed]
3. §4.1.3. is removed.
(Secs. 103, 119, Pub. L. 89-563, 80 Stat. 718 (15 Stat. 1392, 1407); delegation of authority at 49 CFR 1.50)

Issued on October 23, 1981. Raymond A. Peck, Jr., Administrator.

Appendix
Editorial

Note. — This appendix will not appear in the Code of Federal Regulations.

Following is a summary of the major comments submitted in response to the April 9, 1981 notice of proposed rulemaking. A more detailed summary of comments has been placed in NHTSA Docket No. 74-14: Notice 22. This summary is organized in broad terms according to the interest groups from which the comments were received.

Insurance Companies

All commenting insurance companies strongly favored retention of the automatic restraint requirements. Many favored maintaining the present implementation schedule (i.e., September 1, 1982, for large and medium-sized cars and September 1, 1983, for small cars), although several companies stated they would support a change to require that small cars are phased in first or a simultaneous implementation date. Several insurance companies stated that air bags offer the best technology for saving lives and reducing injuries. These companies pointed out that repeated surveys have indicated that consumers appear to favor air bags, even if higher costs are likely. Several insurers argued that a retreat from the standard represents a breach of the Secretary's statutory obligation to reduce traffic accidents and deaths and injuries which result from them. One company argued that a delay in the standard (i.e., the delay and reversal alternative) would produce no measurable economic benefit to car makers and might possibly result in an economic loss to them. Nearly all the companies argued that the standard is cost-beneficial and represents the optimum approach to resolving this country's most pressing public health problem. Many companies stated that reduced insurance premiums resulting from the lives saved and injuries prevented by automatic restraints would help offset the cost of those systems to consumers.

A majority of the insurance companies argued that seat belt use campaigns will not be effective in raising the current use rate of manual belts significantly. The companies pointed to the failures of all past campaigns to have any substantial impact on use rates. On the other hand, these companies believe that the use rate of automatic belts will be significant. The companies point to the current use data for automatic belts on VW Rabbits and Chevettes as evidence that automatic belt use will be significant. The companies believe that seat belt use campaigns should only be complimentary to automatic restraints, not a substitute.

Several insurance companies pointed to the huge economic losses resulting from traffic accidents. One company stated that these losses mount to over 1 billion dollars per year and result in recurring costs because of continuing medical problems such as epilepsy and quadriplegia. One company cited Professor William Nordhaus's analysis of the consequences of rescinding the standard as being equivalent to society's loss if the tuberculosis vaccine had not been developed, or if Congress repealed the Clean Air Act. In his submission on behalf of the insurance companies, Professor Nordhaus stated that fatalities will increase by 6,400 each year and injuries by 120,000 if the standard is rescinded. One company argued that the standard is cost-beneficial if automatic belt use rates increase usage only 5 percent. However, this company stated that use rates as high as 70 percent could be expected, and that the costs of rescinding the standard could reach as much as 2 billion dollars per year. This company also argued that the economic condition of the vehicle industry is no excuse for any delay in the standard and is not a statutorily justified reason for rescinding the standard.

Consumer Groups and Health Organizations

There were many consumer groups and health-related organizations which strongly urged that the automatic restraint requirements be maintained and that there be no further delays in the implementation schedule. Most of these groups argued that the cost of both air bags and automatic belts are greatly exaggerated by vehicle manufacturers. One group stated that the three alternative proposals are "naive and exhibit a callous disregard for human lives that flouts the agency's mandated safety mission." This group argued that a worst alternative is to rescind the standard and rely on education programs to increase the use of manual belts, since seat belt campaigns have failed repeatedly in this country. The group stated that the simultaneous implementation alternative in March 1983 ignores the industry's background of introducing safety changes only at the beginning of a new model year. Regarding a reversed phase-in schedule, the group stated that the requirement that small cars have automatic restraints by September 1, 1982, would not likely provide sufficient lead time for small car manufacturers. Additionally, with approximately 2 to 1 difference in seat belt use in small cars versus larger cars, it is not at all clear that the proposed reversal would make up for the delay in implementation in the larger cars in terms of lives saved. The group argued that the best alternative is to maintain the existing implementation schedule.

Several consumer groups argued that the center seating position should not be eliminated from the requirements for several reasons. First, they argued, this position is likely to be occupied by children. Second, the center seat requirement is one factor that will lead to the installation of air bags in some vehicles since current automatic belt designs cannot be applied to the center seat. Nearly all consumer groups argued that benefits of the automatic restraint standard far outweigh the costs.

One association stated that the air bag supplier industry could be forced out of business if substantial modifications and further delays are made to the standard. This would mean, the association argued, that the life-saving air bag technology could be lost forever. The association would support some modifications to the standard if there were some clear commitment by the Department that some car models would be required to offer the consumer the choice of air bags. The group noted that air bag suppliers have indicated that a sufficient production volume would result in air bag systems priced in the 200 to 300 dollar range.

Various health groups and medical experts argued that the pain and suffering resulting from epilepsy and paraplegia, as well as mental suffering and physical disfigurement, could be greatly reduced by the automatic restraint standard. These persons argued that the standard should be implemented as soon as possible.

One consumer oriented group did not support the automatic restraint standard. That foundation argued that the standard is not justified, particularly if it is complied with by means of air bags. The group stated that air bag effectiveness is overestimated since the agency does not include non-frontal crashes in its statistics. The organization argued that in many situations air bags are actually unsafe. This group also argued that the public acceptability of automatic seat belts is uncertain, and that a well-founded finding of additional safety benefits by the Department is required in order to justify retention of the standard.

Vehicle Manufacturers

The vehicle manufacturers, both foreign and domestic, were unanimously opposed to retention of the automatic restraint standard. Most manufacturers stated the predominate means of complying with the standard would be with automatic belts, and that such belts are not likely to increase usage substantially. This is because most automatic belts will be designed to be easily detachable because of emergency egress considerations and to avoid a potential backlash by consumers that would be counterproductive to the cause of motor vehicle safety. The domestic manufacturers argued that the public would not accept coercive automatic belts (i.e., automatic belts with interlocks or some other use-inducing feature). Eliminating any coercive element produces, in effect, a manual belt, which will be used no more than existing manual systems.

The domestic manufacturers also argued that air bags would not be economically practicable and

would, therefore, be unacceptable to the public. One manufacturer noted that current belt users will object strenuously to paying additional money for automatic belts that will not offer any more protection than their existing belts.

One manufacturer argued that the injury criteria specified in the standard is not representative of real injuries and should be replaced with only static test requirements for belt systems. The company argued that there are many problems with test repeatability under the 208 requirements.

All manufacturers of small cars stated that it would be impossible for them to comply with the standard by September 1, 1982, i.e., under the reversal proposal. These manufacturers stated that there is insufficient lead time to install automatic restraints in small cars by that date, and several foreign manufacturers stated they would not be able to sell their vehicles in that model year if the schedule is reversed. Most of the manufacturers, both domestic and foreign, stated that it is also too late to install automatic restraints in their small cars even six months earlier than the existing schedule, i.e., under the March 1983 simultaneous implementation proposal. Many manufacturers supported a simultaneous implementation if the standard is not rescinded, but requested that the effective date be September 1, 1983, or later. The manufacturers argued that an effective date for small cars prior to September 1, 1983, would not allow enough time to develop acceptable, reliable and high quality automatic belts.

Nearly all vehicle manufacturers believe that an intensive seat belt education campaign can be just as effective as automatic restraints and without the attendant high costs of automatic restraints. Additionally, most foreign manufacturers recommended

that mandatory seat belt use laws be enacted in lieu of automatic restraints.

One foreign manufacturer requested that any effective date for automatic restraints be "September 1 or the date of production start of the new model year if this date falls between September 1 and December 31." The company stated that this would allow manufacturers to continue production for several months of models that would then be phased out of production. However, a domestic vehicle manufacturer argued that this would give foreign manufacturers an unfair competitive advantage, and that current practice of September 1 effective dates should be retained.

Most manufacturers supported the proposal to exclude the center seating position from the automatic restraint requirements, in order to give manufacturers more design flexibility. However, the two domestic manufacturers which would be most affected by such an exception stated that it is too late for them to make use of such an exception for 1983 models. The two companies stated that such an exception would have benefits in the long run, however, and would allow them to continue production of six-seat passenger cars in the mid-1980's.

Suppliers and Trade Groups

Suppliers of air bag system components supported continuation of the automatic restraint requirements. One commenter stated that having to buckle-up is an act which requires a series of psychological and physical reactions which are responsible for the low rate of manual seat belts. Also, this company stated that educational campaigns to increase belt use will not work.

One motor vehicle trade group stated that a study by the Canadian government has established the superiority of manual seat belt systems. This group argued that the automatic restraint requirements cannot be justified because any expected benefits are speculative.

One trade group voiced its concern about sodium azide (an air bag propellant) as it pertains to possible hazards posed to the scrap processing industry.

A group representing seat belt manufacturers stated that the most effective way of guaranteeing belt use is through mandatory belt use laws. That group believes that belt usage can be increased through public education, and that simple, easy to use automatic belts such as are currently on the VW Rabbit will also increase belt usage. This group did not support a simultaneous implementation date for automatic restraints, stating that this could put a severe strain on the supplier industry. The group did support elimination of the automatic restraint requirements for center seating positions.

An automobile association recommended equipping small cars with automatic restraints first. The association stated that a reversed phase-in schedule would protect a significantly large segment of the public at an earlier date, would reduce a foreign competitive advantage (under the existing schedule), and would give needed economic relief to large car manufacturers. This organization also recommended that, as an alternative, automatic restraints be required only at the driver's position. This would achieve three-quarters of the reductions in deaths and serious injuries now projected for full-front seat systems, yet cost only half as much.

Congressional comments

Mr. Timothy E. Wirth, Chairman of the House Subcommittee on Telecommunications, Consumer Protection and Finance, made the following comments:

- The automatic restraint requirements would produce benefits to society far in excess of costs.
- The Committee findings strongly point to the necessity of requiring the installation of automatic crash protection systems, at a minimum, on a substantial portion of the new car fleet at the earliest possible date. Mr. Wirth suggested that the effective date for small cars be September 1, 1982, and for intermediate and large cars September 1, 1983.
- The economic conditions of the automobile industry should not be relevant to the NHTSA's decision on matters of safety. NHTSA's decision must be guided solely by safety-related concerns.
- The agency should not discount its own findings indicating high use of automatic belts (referring to the existing VW and Chevette automatic belt use data).

In a joint letter to the Secretary, eighteen Congressmen urged that the automatic restraint requirements be maintained. This letter noted that over 50,000 people are killed each year on the highways and stated: "While the tragedy of their deaths cannot be measured in economic terms, the tragedy of their serious injuries cost all of us billions of dollars each year in higher insurance costs, increased welfare payments, unemployment and social security payments and rehabilitation costs paid to support the injured and the families of those who have been killed." The letter stressed the Congressmen's belief that the automatic crash protection standard would produce benefits to society far in excess of its cost.

In a letter addressed to Administrator Peck, fifty-nine Congressmen urged that the automatic restraint standard be rescinded. That letter stated: "The 208 standard persists as one of the more controversial federal regulations to be forced on the automobile industry. . . . The industry continues to spend hundreds of thousands of dollars every day in order to meet this standard, despite considerable evidence that any safety benefits realized by enforcing the standard would be minimal."

Private Citizens

In addition to comments from the above groups and organizations, the agency also received general comments from numerous private citizens. These comments were almost equally divided in their support or opposition to the automatic restraint standard.

[FR Doc. 81-31189 Filed 10-23-81; 3:46 pm]
BILLING CODE 4910-59-M

NOTES AND QUESTIONS

1. What are the differences between the final rule and the NPRM? In terms of format, the final rule is similar to the NPRM. It contains similar headings (e.g., summary, supplementary information, etc.). In terms of effect, the final rule is not the same as the NPRM. It sets forth the agency's final action. Simply put, those subject to the rule — the so-called regulated entities, which are

automakers in this instance — face legal sanctions for noncompliance with the requirements or prohibitions in the final rule. Furthermore, the agency itself is obligated to follow the rule unless and until it changes the rule through another round of notice-and-comment rulemaking. Thus, NHTSA cannot reintroduce a passive restraint requirement in any other way. What substantive differences can you identify between the NPRM and the final rule? Read them side by side to see what the agency learned from the rule-making process.

2. In the NPRM, the agency set forth three principle proposals, and in the final rule, it adopted just one. How did it make that decision? In the remaining questions, let's try to break down the agency's rationale.

   a. What words of the statute were relevant? How does NHTSA decide what those words mean in relation to passive restraints?

   b. NHTSA includes a discussion of the Rabbit/Chevette study. What did that study show? Why did the agency discount it? Was doing so reasonable?

   c. What is the role of economic analysis in the decision? What was the cost of the rule? Who felt the effects — automakers, consumers, others? Why was $89 per car such an indefensible amount to pay for safety, given the overall cost of new cars?

   d. What is the role of public attitudes? How does the agency factor them in? What are the options for addressing public attitudes? Did NHTSA select a rational course?

   e. As we recounted above, President Reagan was committed to easing burdens on the ailing domestic auto industry. Passive restraints contributed significantly to such burdens. Where is that factor mentioned in the rationale for the final rule? Should it be mentioned?

C. The Standard form of Regulations

You have just read an NPRM and a final rule. To what extent do other NPRMs and final rules resemble these? Quite a bit, as it happens. Although every rulemaking document is suited to its own issues, such documents have distinctive and predictable features. To really appreciate those features, it is useful to compare them to the structural features of statutes.

Recall the features of statutes:

- Title ("*An Act to . . . .*")
- Enacting clause
- Short title
- Statement of purpose
- Definitions
- Principal operative provisions

- Subordinate operative provisions
- Implementation provisions
- Temporary provisions
- Specific repeals
- Preemption provision
- Savings clause
- Expiration date
- Effective date

Do the agency documents map these sections? The answer is not exactly. Consider the features of NHTSA's final rule described in general terms:

- **Caption:** The caption of a final rule serves a similar purpose as the title of a statute. It identifies the regulation, not by short name but by citation, subject, and agency. Agencies issue too many regulations, even on a single subject, to distinguish them by casual reference. That said, some of the more significant rules or repeat players are identified for purposes of discussion by number, such as Standard 208.
- **Summary:** In some sense, the summary of a rule is like the title or purpose of a statute ("*An Act to . . .* "). The summary indicates upfront, in brief, the purpose of the rule. It generally contains more elaboration than the purpose clause of a statute, but then again, the rule generally contains more elaboration than the statute.
- **Supplementary Information:** This section contains the explanation for the rule. First, it supplies the *background* for the rule, which is analogous, if you will, to the factual and procedural posture section of a judicial opinion. It also provides a *rationale* for the rule. As part of the rationale for the rule, the agency addresses the comments that parties submitted. Statutes rarely contain explicit rationales (or responses to citizen suggestions); as we have seen, rationales are often produced in the legislative history, if at all. Supplementary Information also contains *impact analyses*. When issuing regulations, agencies are obligated to consider the effect of their decisions on certain interests. By executive order, many must perform a regulatory impact analysis, including a cost-benefit analysis, for all major regulations (basically, those with costs of $100 million or more). *See, e.g.,* Exec. Order No. 12,866, 58 Fed. Reg. 51735 (Sept. 30, 1993), *as amended by* Exec. Order No. 13,497, 74 Fed. Reg. 6113 (Jan. 30, 2009). Under the Regulatory Flexibility Act, 5 U.S.C. §§601, 604, agencies must prepare a "regulatory flexibility analysis" (RFA) if the rulemaking could "have a significant impact on a substantial number of small entities," including businesses and governments. Under the National Environmental Policy Act, 42, U.S.C. §§4321 *et seq.*, and related statutes and executive orders, agencies must prepare an environmental impact statement for "major Federal actions significantly affecting the quality of the human environment." 42 U.S.C. §4332. Agencies face other legal obligations as well. For example, under the Unfunded Mandates Act, 2 U.S.C. §1532, an agency must prepare a

written statement about benefits and costs of their rules that may result in aggregate expenditure by State, local, and tribal governments, or by the private sector, of $100 million or more in any one year (adjusted annually for inflation). Under the Paperwork Reduction Act, 44 U.S.C. §§3501 *et seq.*, agencies must consider whether their rules (or other actions) will create any additional information collection, paperwork, or recordkeeping burdens. Agencies include a summary of their impact analyses in their final rules (as well as in their NPRMs). Statutes include no equivalent section because Congress faces no similar obligation to analyze the impacts of legislation.

- **Appendix:** The agency's final rule may contain an appendix that includes a summary of party comments or technical data — basically material that is necessary to support the explanation for the rule. The NPRM may also have an appendix section, particularly if technical data is necessary for parties to meaningfully comment on the proposals. The appendix of the final rule is a part of the record on which the agency's decision will be reviewed. Statutes rarely contain such backup material, although they do occasionally contain "findings" sections. In addition, the legislative history frequently contains testimony transcripts and written submissions.
- **Codification:** After the agency publishes its final rule in the *Federal Register*, the operative provisions of the rule will be codified in the *Code of Federal Regulations* (C.F.R.). These operative provisions are what alter the legal requirements imposed on private parties. Thus, these provisions are most closely analogous to actual text of a statute codified in the *United States Code*.

The most striking difference between an agency rule and a statute is the narrative style. In this respect, the agency rule seems more like the Senate Report that you have read, or perhaps a judicial opinion. But there is a very important difference. The narrative explanation is necessary to the validity of the rule. Recall that when an agency engages in notice-and-comment rulemaking, the APA requires the agency, "[a]fter consideration of the relevant matter presented [in the comment period]" to "incorporate in the rules adopted a concise statement of their basis and purpose." APA, §553(c). An agency that issued a rule without a concise statement of its basis and purpose would violate this requirement of the APA and face judicial reversal on that ground. Furthermore, the Supreme Court has required a more detailed explanation to facilitate judicial review of agency rules, as we discuss in the note below. No constitutional procedure or legislative rule requires Congress to provide an explanation, though it may provide more or less detail in the purpose section of a statute.

Note on the Formalization of the Agency Explanation

It is worth taking a minute to elaborate why an agency like NHTSA would provide an extensive explanation for its rule, given the relatively minimal requirements in §553 of the APA. The most likely reason is that the Supreme Court has required such explanations to facilitate judicial review. The APA directs courts to reverse agency action that is "arbitrary, capricious, [or] an abuse of discretion," APA, §706. In a famous decision, Motor Vehicle Manufacturers Ass'n v. State Farm Mutual Insurance Co. 463 U.S. 29 (1983), the Court required that agencies provide an explanation containing the reasons for their rules in order for those rules to survive review under the "arbitrary and capricious" standard. We will read this decision in Chapter 9; it actually involves judicial review of the very rule that you just read. For now, however, observe that the result of *State Farm* and other decisions is to require that agencies provide fairly extensive explanations for their decisions. Drawing on those decisions, it is fair to say that, at a minimum, an agency must demonstrate that it has:

- Based its decision on relevant factors and no irrelevant factors;
- Considered all important aspects of the problem;
- Considered alternatives within the ambit of existing regulation;
- Made a rational connection between the evidence and its conclusions;
- Offered a plausible policy, even if not the one that a court would adopt;
- Justified changes in course from prior policy;
- Disclosed scientific or other data upon which it relied;
- Considered comments submitted in response to the NPRM.

In addition, the Court has insisted that agencies furnish these extensive explanations at the time when they act; a reviewing court will not uphold an agency decision "unless the grounds upon which the agency acted in exercising its power were those upon which its action can be sustained." SEC v. Chenery Corp., 318 U.S. 80, 95 (1943). Thus, the agency cannot supply a "post hoc" rationale for a rule, say, in the course of defending such a rule in court. Nor will a court supply a rationale, as it might when reviewing a statute or a lower court decision. *See* Kevin M. Stack, *The Constitutional Foundation of* Chenery, 116 YALE L.J. 952, 955, 966-71 (2007).

The result of these judicial doctrines has been to "formalize" informal, notice-and-comment rulemaking. If agencies are interested in protecting their regulations from judicial reversal and remand — an order returning the regulation to the agency for further proceedings consistent with the opinion of the court — they must produce explanations that contain the basis for their decisions. Of course, agencies may have other reasons for providing explanations for their decisions. For example, they might think that this exercise not only protects their decisions from judicial reversal and remand but from political reprisal. In other words, offering an explanation reduces the chance of the President or Congress reacting adversely to their decisions. Agencies may also think that providing an explanation increases compliance by regulated entities and approval by citizens. If parties understand a regulation, they are more likely to follow and accept it. And agencies may think that providing an explanation reflects best practices from an internal management standpoint. If forced to explain their regulations in rational terms, agency officials will be encouraged to develop regulations in rational terms. Similarly, agency officials will be encouraged to follow a regularized process across diverse issues. The bottom line is that for some or all of these reasons, agencies have come to provide extensive explanations in the predictable form that you have seen.

D. The Tools of Statutory Implementation

In a certain sense, the explanation that an agency provides reveals the factors that it considered or analyses that it performed when making a decision. Consider what NHTSA stated in its explanation when amending Standard 208 in response to a 1998 airbags statute:

> Before we made decisions on which provisions should be included in this rule to improve air bag performance as required by TEA 21 [The Transportation Equity Act for the 21st Century, 49 U.S.C. §30127], we carefully considered the available information and the public comments, the underlying safety problems, the performance of air bag systems in current motor vehicles, the ability (including lead time needs) of vehicle manufacturers to achieve better performance in future motor vehicles, the air bag technology (including advanced air bag technology) currently available or being developed, the cost of compliance, and other factors. Because the comments on the SNPRM [Supplemental Notice of Proposed Rulemaking] focused on the alternatives for improving the protection provided by air bags, we were particularly careful in considering the comments concerning the costs, benefits and risks associated with each of those alternatives.
>
> The requirements in today's rule for improving protection and minimizing risk are challenging and will push the vehicle manufacturers to make needed safety improvements in air bag performance. Our decisions regarding the selection of those requirements [were] based on available test data and analysis, and our informed judgment about the best way of implementing the requirements of TEA 21.

See Department of Transportation, Federal Motor Vehicle Safety Standards; Occupant Crash Protection, Final Rule, 65 Fed. Reg. 30680 (May 12, 2001).

In this section, which comprises the bulk of this chapter, we consider the factors that agencies consider and the analyses that they perform in some detail. It is important for lawyers to understand these "tools" of statutory implementation. They often furnish the grounds for influencing, challenging, defending, or applying agency decisions. Here is a brief overview, explained in terms of the 1981 rule rescinding passive restraints, which you read above:

- **Statutory:** The agency considers the authority that the statute grants (e.g., "establish . . . appropriate Federal motor vehicle safety standards") and the instructions that it provides (e.g., establish standards that are "practicable" and "meet the need for auto safety") to determine what actions are required and permitted; it often interprets the language of its statute before applying that language, just as courts do.
- **Scientific:** It examines the scientific data that the problem requires (e.g., on the potential of passive restraints to prevent crashes or save lives and minimize injuries in the event of crashes, relying on existing studies or

producing new ones); it examines the existing and potential technology for responding to risks (e.g., advanced airbags).

- **Economic:** It assesses the costs (e.g., to automakers and consumers of passive restraints requirements) in relation to the benefits (e.g., to passengers and others of such requirements) of different alternatives.
- **Political:** It considers other important aspects of the problem, like public attitudes (e.g., public resistance to future auto safety regulation) and political preferences (e.g., presidential desire to minimize federal regulation, especially burdens on the domestic auto industry, though such consideration is not evident in the final rule rescinding passive restraints).

Note that agencies do not perform all of these analyses for every regulation. For example, an agency may issue a regulation without scientific or technical analysis if that regulation simply interprets a statutory term, such as "take" for purposes of the Endangered Species Act, as you may recall from the *Sweet Home* decision in the previous chapter. Or it may forego statutory analysis if the regulation is clearly authorized and purely technical. In addition, a particular statute may preclude or limit a certain analysis. The Clean Air Act, for example, precludes EPA from allowing the costs of regulating pollutants to control. A statute may restrict particular policy considerations, like the financial health of automakers (did the Motor Vehicle Safety Act of 1966 restrict this consideration?). A statute may require an agency to rely on the scientific conclusions of the National Academy of Sciences, as you will see later on in this chapter when we discuss the disposition of nuclear waste. Given these possibilities, an agency may have to determine as part of its *statutory* analysis whether its statute precludes or limits other analyses, such as economic or scientific analyses. Lawyers working with regulatory statutes are never relieved of the responsibility to read actual statutes to see what they specify.

Note also that agencies must find a way to integrate these tools when making a decision. Regulations reflect all-things-considered judgments, not a series of isolated considerations. Similarly, agencies must find a way to integrate the people who apply these tools, from political appointees to career staff, policymakers to lawyers to scientists to economists. These individuals within an agency possess expertise in different areas. Some internal structure is necessary to ensure that they work in a cooperative fashion rather than a counter-productive one. We address these issues after presenting the tools.

1. Statutory Analysis

An agency must ensure that its regulations are (a) within the scope of its statute and (b) consistent with the terms of its statute. Both are issues of statutory interpretation. The first issue is one of "jurisdiction": does this statute authorize this agency to reach a particular subject. A statute that authorizes an agency to regulate "vehicles" does not authorize them to regulate air conditioners no matter what "vehicles" means (interestingly, it might authorize an agency to regulate air pollutants, at least indirectly, as part of regulating vehicle fuel economy).

Even if an agency has jurisdiction over a particular subject, it may only regulate that subject in the manner that the statute permits. Thus, the second issue: an agency may not rely on prohibited or irrelevant statutory factors and it must consider mandatory or relevant statutory factors. For example, a statute might prohibit reliance on a particular policy factor, such as the health of the auto industry, notwithstanding the President's contrary wishes. Or a statute might make that factor irrelevant in light of the interests that it does prioritize, such as the safety of auto passengers. Furthermore, a statute might require an agency to consider certain factors, such as whether an auto safety standard is "practicable" or meets "the need for auto safety." The agency is not entitled to disregard statutorily mandated factors. Nor is it entitled to ignore a factor that the statute makes relevant among others, but not necessarily determinative in the overall judgment.

Logically, issues of statutory interpretation come before all other analyses, such as scientific, economic, and political. The agency has to resolve questions about its authority before it proceeds to exercise that authority. Indeed, such questions may determine how an agency conducts the other analyses. For example, the word "feasible" in a statute might require (or prohibit) a particular type of economic analysis. As a practical matter, agencies often engage in statutory analysis concurrently or even after other analyses. It is only once a viable policy alternative has surfaced based on other tools that the agency needs to seriously engage in statutory analysis; and of course, at that point, or if the agency has a strong policy preference, it may conduct statutory analysis in that light. You can consider this issue from the personnel perspective as well: often, agency lawyers are brought onto a matter at the same time as or even after agency policymakers, scientists, and economists have begun to work.

You have already seen some agency statutory analysis or interpretation in the chapter on judicial statutory interpretation. For example, consider *Sweet Home*, in which the Court addressed the meaning of "take" for purposes of the Endangered Species Act. It found that "take," which was further defined to include "harm," could include significant habitat modification or degradation. *See* pp. 202-11. The Department of Interior had issued that interpretation through notice-and-comment rulemaking before the Court ever got there. We did not focus on the role of the agency when discussing that case. Now we address it directly. In so doing, we are interested in how agency lawyers address questions of statutory interpretation and whether they do so differently from courts. Statutory analysis is the bread and butter for agency lawyers, and a central occupation for lawyers who seek to influence agency action.

a. NHTSA Illustration

In the document that we reprint below, NHTSA denied a petition by two automakers to retroactively reduce the fuel economy standards the agency had set for cars in a certain model year. The automakers filed the petition after they had failed to meet the fuel economy standards and were subject to significant penalties as a result. In denying the petition, NHTSA provided a detailed statutory analysis:

49 C.F.R. 531
Passenger Automobile Average Fuel Economy Standards; Denial of Petitions for Rulemaking

[Docket No. FE-87-02; Notice 1], April 28, 1988

[53 Fed. Reg. 39115 (1988)]

AGENCY: National Highway Traffic Safety Administration (NHTSA), DOT.

ACTION: Denial of petitions for rulemaking.

SUMMARY: This notice denies petitions for rulemaking submitted by Mercedes-Benz of North America and the General Motors Corporation. Mercedes asked the agency to retroactively reduce the model year 1984 and 1985 corporate average fuel economy (CAFE) standards for passenger automobiles to 26.0 miles per gallon or below. General Motors asked the agency to retroactively reduce the model year 1985 standard to 26.0 miles per gallon or below. The model year 1984 standard was set by the agency; the model year 1985 standard, by Congress in the CAFE statute. The agency is denying both petitions for the reasons set forth in this notice. . . .

SUPPLEMENTARY INFORMATION:

. . . Title V of the Motor Vehicle Information and Cost Savings Act (Cost Savings Act), which is codified at 15 U.S.C. 2001-2012, provides for an automotive fuel economy regulatory program under which standards are established for the corporate average fuel economy (CAFE) of the annual production fleets of passenger automobiles and of light trucks. Title V was added in 1975 to the Cost Savings Act by the Energy Policy and Conservation Act (EPCA). Responsibility for the automotive fuel economy program was delegated by the Secretary of Transportation to the Administrator of NHTSA. . . .

Section 502 [of Title V] specified CAFE standards for passenger automobiles of 18, 19 and 20 mpg for model years 1978, 1979, and 1980, respectively, and 27.5 mpg for model year 1985 and thereafter. The Secretary of Transportation was required to establish standards for model years 1981-84 by July 1, 1977. Section 502(a)(3) requires that the standards for each of those model years be set at a level which (1) is the maximum feasible average fuel economy level and (2) would result in steady progress toward meeting the standard for model year 1985. On June 30, 1977, NHTSA adopted CAFE standards for passenger automobiles for model years 1981-84 (42 FR 33534). These standards were 22 mpg for 1981, 24 mpg for 1982, 26 mpg for 1983, and 27 mpg for 1984.

Section 502(f)(1) provides that the model year 1981-84 standards may be amended, from time to time, as long as the amended standards are set at the maximum feasible level and at a level representing steady progress toward the model year 1985 standard. In 1979, General Motors and Ford did informally request that rulemaking be initiated to reduce the model year 1981-84 standards. NHTSA denied the request on the ground that there was no showing that the standards were infeasible, but invited petitions in the future if there were any inaccuracies in the agency's analysis of the requests or any new facts significant enough to warrant commencing rulemaking. (See "Report on Requests by General Motors and Ford to Reduce Fuel Economy Standards for MY 1981-84 Passenger Automobiles" June 1979, and the accompanying notice of availability, June 25, 1979; 44 FR 37104). General Motors and Ford did suggest in August 1986 in their comments on a supplemental NPRM on the reduction of the model year 1987-88 standards for passenger automobiles that the agency retroactively reduce the model year 1984-85 standards if it did not reduce the model year 1987-88 standards to 26.0 mpg. . . . [T]he standards for model year 1987-88 were reduced to 26.0 mpg. No petition for rulemaking to reduce the model year 1984-85 standards was submitted until August 1987.

Section 502(a)(4) authorizes (but does not require) the agency to amend the standard of 27.5 mpg for model year 1985 or any subsequent model year if it finds that the maximum feasible fuel economy level is higher or lower than 27.5 mpg in that year and sets the standard at that level. The agency has not previously amended the statutory standard of 27.5 for model year 1985, and did affirm the feasibility of that standard on several occasions. (For example, see the preamble to the June 1977 final rule adopting the model year 1981-1984 standards, and the June 1979 report on requests by General Motors and Ford to reduce the model year 1981-84 standards.) In response to timely petitions, the agency did reduce the passenger automobile standards for model years 1986-88 from 27.5 mpg to 26.0 mpg (50 FR 40528, October 4, 1985, for model year 1986 and 51 FR 35594, October 6, 1986, for model years 1987-88). Also, in response to a timely petition, the agency did reduce the 1985 light truck CAFE standard. (October 22, 1984; 49 FR 41250). . . .

Title V provides for civil penalties for violating a CAFE standard and credits for exceeding one, in the amount of $5 for each 0.1 mpg that a manufacturer's fleet is below (above, in the case of credits) the standard, multiplied by the number of automobiles in that fleet. The credits may be used to offset a shortfall that occurs when a manufacturer does not achieve in a model year the CAFE required by the standard for that year. Manufacturers may carry credits as far back as three model years before the year in which they are earned or as far forward as three model years after the year in which they are earned. (See sections 502(l), 507 and 508 of the Cost Savings Act.)

If information available to the agency indicates that a manufacturer's CAFE for a model year fell below the standard for that year, and the manufacturer does not have sufficient carry-forward credits to offset the shortfall, the agency is required by section 502(l)(1)(C)(iv) to notify the manufacturer of that fact and provide a reasonable period for the manufacturer to submit a plan for earning sufficient credits in the three following model years to offset that shortfall completely. If a carry-back plan is not submitted and approved, the agency is required by section 508 to commence a proceeding under that section to determine whether the manufacturer has violated section 507(a)(1), which makes it unlawful to fail to comply with a CAFE standard for passenger automobiles. If the agency makes that determination, on the record following opportunity for agency hearing, the agency assesses civil penalties according to the formula described above.

Finally, under section 508, penalties may be compromised, modified or remitted in only three circumstances: If necessary to prevent insolvency or bankruptcy of a manufacturer; if a manufacturer shows that the violation was the result of an act of God, strike, or fire; or if the Federal Trade Commission certifies (in response to a request by a manufacturer for relief) that a modification of the penalty is necessary to prevent a substantial lessening of competition. . . .

Petitions for rulemaking to reduce the model year 1984-85 standards were submitted after the agency notified several manufacturers of apparent noncompliance with one or both of those standards. . . .

The agency has concluded that such retroactive amendment [i.e., amending a CAFE standard for a past year, namely 1984-1985] is

inconsistent with several aspects of the statutory scheme. First, the agency believes that the statutory scheme of establishing annual standards, but permitting the attainment of compliance through the earning and applying of credits to handle shortfalls, is not consistent with retroactive amendment of a standard after the end of the applicable model year. Congress included a one year carry-back/carry-forward provision in Title V in 1975 to provide the manufacturers some flexibility in dealing with the problems created by falling short of a standard. When Congress amended Title V in 1980 to extend the availability of credits from one year to three, and provided for the submission of carry-back plans for the use of credits in advance of their actually being earned, the legislative history made it clear that Congress believed it was increasing the manufacturers flexibility regarding the problems associated with shortfalls. The Senate Report stated that the extension "to provide greater flexibility in the application of existing rules covering carry-forward/carry-back of civil penalties (sic; should have read "credits") will relieve some of the burden of present regulation on automobile manufacturers." Sen. Rpt. No 96-642, March 25, 1980, page 4. With respect to the requirement for submittal of a plan, the Report stated that:

[S]ubmittal of such a plan offers useful deterrent to a scenario (improbable though it may be) in which a manufacturer might fail over a successive period of as many as 3 years to meet each year's CAFE standard and then appeal for economic relief from a massive civil penalty accrued over that period. *Ibid*, page 7.

The flexibility of carry-forward and carry-back credits would not have been needed if the agency could (or must, as the petitions imply) retroactively amend standards to account for industrywide shortfalls. The fact that Congress did extend the availability of credits suggests that retroactive amendment was not thought to be an available option. It further suggests that Congress recognized that there would be some years in which shortfalls might occur for a variety of reasons. Instead of directing the agency to remedy such shortfalls through retroactive rulemaking, Congress chose to expand the availability of credits to offset these potential shortfalls.

Other aspects of the statutory scheme that would be disturbed by retroactive amendments are the precise and narrow provisions for commencing a proceeding to determine the existence of a noncompliance and to assess civil penalties and for mitigation of civil penalties in the event that a shortfall cannot be offset by credits. Congress chose to restrict this authority of the Secretary of Transportation quite specifically. With respect to mitigation of penalties, Congress provided for mitigation in three specific instances only, specifying express limitations on the exercise of discretion in two of the instances and requiring consultation with the Federal Trade Commission in the other instance. If retroactive rulemaking amounted to an indirect attempt by the agency to remit penalties, it would be contrary to the statutory scheme.

Finally, the statutory scheme for making refunds to manufacturers for civil penalties already paid would also be disturbed by retroactive amendment. Sections 507 and 508 together provide that a manufacturer which has violated a standard (i.e., has fallen short of a standard and has not obtained agency approval of a plan projecting its earning of sufficient credits in the three

following years to completely offset its shortfall) must pay the civil penalty for the shortfall, and later apply for a partial refund in the amount of any credits actually earned during those subsequent three years. The provision in section 508 regarding the refund of civil penalties is the only provision in Title V dealing with that subject. Yet, the retroactive amendment sought by these two petitioners would cause refunds to be made in excess of $3 million to two manufacturers that paid civil penalties for one or both of model years 1984-85. These refunds would be made, not because those manufacturers earned credits in subsequent years, as the statute contemplates, but because the standards would have been retroactively amended.

Further, reducing a standard for a model year after the year is over would raise questions about equity of such an amendment for manufacturers which absorbed the costs of compliance with the standard for a particular model year. While not directly disturbing the statutory scheme in the same manner as the examples above, these perceived inequities must be considered by the agency in the context of whether the manufacturers that did comply (with or without credits) might decline to make efforts in the future, counting instead on retroactive amendment. If this were to occur, the statutory scheme would indeed be disturbed. . . .

In its 1984 interpretation, the agency noted that while the statute does not contain explicit language concerning an amendment which lowers a CAFE standard, it does contain language that suggests that reductions are to be made prospectively, i.e., before the beginning of the model year in question. The agency cited arguments by Chrysler that amendments reducing the stringency of standards must be made at least 18 months before the beginning of the

model year and that, therefore, Ford's petition regarding model year 1984-5 light truck standards was too late with respect to both models years. Chrysler argued that section 502(b) calls for 18 months leadtime for any light truck standards being prescribed and that changes in standards come within that requirement. Chrysler argued also that the 18 month requirement of section 502(f)(2) was applicable since granting Ford's request would in effect make the standards more stringent for Chrysler. Section 502(f)(2) applies to amendments to passenger automobile standards as well as those to light truck standards.

On the other hand, there are other statutory provisions that some past commenters have interpreted to the opposite effect. Section 502(f)(1) provides that amendments to the 1981-84 car standards may be made "from time to time." Some manufacturers have interpreted that language to indicate that there is no temporal limitation on amendments reducing standards. They have also noted the absence of any express limitation in the statute on the time period in which an amendment reducing a standard may be adopted.

To aid in resolving this issue, the agency carefully examined the legislative history of section 502. The relevant legislative history of section 502 is found in the Conference Report on EPCA which contains the following discussion:

Average fuel economy standards prescribed by the ST (Secretary of Transportation) for passenger automobiles in model years after 1980, for non-passenger automobiles, and for passenger automobiles manufactured by manufacturers of fewer than 10,000 passenger automobiles may be amended from time to time as long as each such amendment satisfies the 18 month rule — i.e., any amendment which has the effect of making an average fuel economy standard more stringent must be promulgated at least 18 months prior to the beginning of the model year to which such amendment will apply. An amendment which has the effect of making an average fuel economy standard less stringent can be promulgated at any time prior to the beginning of the model year in question. *See* Sen. Rep. 94-516, 94th Cong., 1st Sess. (1975) at 157. (Emphasis added.)

The agency reaffirms its belief that the language in the legislative history is clear. Amendments increasing standards may be made at any time up to 18 months before the model year, while amendments reducing a standard may be made at any time up to the beginning of the model year. If no limit on the timing of amendments reducing the standards had been intended, the second-quoted sentence would have ended with the words "promulgated at any time."

As to the petitioners arguments about the absence of any express deadline in Title V for amendments reducing a standard, the agency notes that deadlines are generally specified in Title V, as in the agency's other vehicle regulatory statutes, to ensure that the agency completes its rulemaking establishing new requirements far enough in advance of the effective date to provide adequate leadtime for regulated parties to achieve compliance. Although Title V does not contain an express requirement that an amendment reducing a standard be issued before the beginning of the model year to which it applies, the agency does not interpret the fact of that absence to indicate that Congress permits retroactive amendment of the standards. In light of the legislative history, it is likely that Congress viewed a provision expressly specifying such a deadline as unnecessary.

General Motors made a related argument that the conference committee's choice of the House's 18-month deadline for amendments increasing standards over the Senate's 18 month deadline for all amendments to standards indicates that Congress desired that there be no deadline for amendments reducing standards. The legislative history of Title V provides no indication that Congress wanted to authorize retroactive rulemaking. The agency believes that the choice of the House version indicates only that Congress recognized that no leadtime was necessary to enable manufacturers to conform their conduct to a relaxing amendment and sought to allow the issuance of such amendments right up to the beginning of the model year. Cutting these amendments off 18 months before the beginning of the model year would have been inconsistent with the provision in the APA allowing a rule relieving a restriction to become effective immediately upon issuance.

NOTES AND QUESTIONS

1. Which provisions of the statute were relevant to NHTSA's decision?
2. What tools of statutory interpretation does NHTSA use? Specifically, see if you can identify the canons of construction on which it relies. Do you have a sense that NHTSA uses the tools differently than a court would? *See* General Motors Corp. v. National Highway Traffic & Safety Administration 898 F.2d 165 (D.C. Cir. 1990).
3. How does the agency use legislative history? On which sources does it rely? What inferences does it draw from them? Does NHTSA use legislative history any differently than a court would?
4. Later in 1988, GM again asked NHTSA to grant a retroactive amendment, and NHTSA again denied the petition. *See* 53 Fed. Reg. 39115 (Oct. 5, 1988). Two months after the agency denied GM's second petition, the Supreme Court issued a new decision on the issue of retroactive rulemaking. Bowen v. Georgetown University Hospital, 488 U.S. 204 (1988). In that decision, the Court held that a statute will not be understood "to encompass the power to promulgate retroactive rules unless that power is conveyed in express terms." *Id.* at 208. This rule is the agency analogue to the presumption against

retroactivity that we discussed in Chapter 11, pp. 274-75. If NHTSA applied this rule, how would it change its analysis?

---

2. Scientific Analysis

We now depart statutory analysis for scientific analysis, which often plays a significant part in how agencies implement their statutes. Scientific analysis helps agencies to evaluate the risk of a bad event occurring and to develop appropriate responses. It is important for lawyers both inside and outside the agency to understand the basics of scientific analysis. Even though lawyers are generally not scientists themselves, they may be asked to integrate or challenge the scientific data or methodologies. They may be asked to offer alternative interpretations of the data or responses in light of the data. They may be asked to evaluate or critique the state of technology. They may also be asked to determine whether what stands for scientific analysis is actually politics, and vice versa, affecting who is responsible for making decisions and whether those decisions are valid.

We provide a broad overview of how agencies use scientific analysis. An agency has to acquire relevant information from reliable sources. Which sources are reliable, given the limited ability to test human subjects? An agency has to draw appropriate conclusions based on the data that it obtains. Was NHTSA correct to discount the Rabbit/Chevette study, for example? Was that a purely "scientific" determination? Who should make such judgments within the agency — the career scientists who have expertise or the political appointees who have accountability? What about the career economists, who might also have relevant information on the costs and benefits of particular options? Consider also that science cannot always produce a factual basis for making a decision. Agencies must decide how to proceed in the face of scientific uncertainty. Should scientists or policymakers determine how?

a. NHTSA Illustration

The following NHTSA final rule shows the agency wrestling with many of these aspects of scientific analysis:

49 C.F.R. 552, 571, 585, 595

Federal Motor Vehicle Safety Standards; Occupant Crash Protection

[Docket No. NHTSA 00-7013; Notice 1], Friday, May 12, 2000

[65 Fed. Reg. 30680 (2000)]

AGENCY: National Highway Traffic Safety Administration (NHTSA). DOT.

ACTION: Final rule; interim final rule.

SUMMARY: This rule amends our occupant crash protection standard to require that future air bags be designed to create less risk of serious air bag-induced injuries than current air bags, particularly for small women and young children; and provide improved frontal crash protection for all occupants, by means that include advanced air bag technology. To achieve these goals, it adds a wide variety of new requirements, test procedures, and injury criteria, using an assortment of new dummies. It replaces the sled test with a rigid barrier crash test for assessing the protection of unbelted occupants.

The issuance of this rule completes the implementation of our 1996 comprehensive plan for reducing air bag risks. It is also required by the Transportation Equity Act for the 21st Century (TEA 21), which was enacted in 1998. . . .

The number of lives saved annually by air bags is continuing to increase as the percentage of air bag-equipped vehicles on the road increases. We estimate that air bags will save more than 3,200 lives annually in passenger cars and light trucks when all light vehicles on the road are equipped with driver and passenger air bags. This estimate is based on an anticipated fleet of vehicles meeting all of the requirements in this rule and on 1997 seat belt use rates (66.9 percent, according to State-reported surveys). However, if observed seat belt use rates were to reach 85 percent, the annual savings of lives due to air bags would be reduced to approximately 2,400. . . .

While air bags are saving an increasing number of people in moderate and high speed crashes, they have occasionally caused fatalities, especially to unrestrained, out-of-position children, in relatively low speed crashes. As of April 1, 2000, NHTSA's Special Crash Investigation (SCI) program had confirmed a total of 158 fatalities induced by the deployment of an air bag. Of that total, 92 were children, 60 were drivers, and 6 were adult passengers. An additional 38 fatalities were under investigation by SCI on that date, but they had not been confirmed as having been induced by air bags.

Changes have already occurred that are reducing the number of persons killed by air bags. Some changes are behavioral. As a result of public education programs, improved labeling and media coverage, the public is much more aware of the dangers air bags pose to children in the front seat and to drivers sitting too close to the air bag and is taking steps to reduce those dangers. For example, more children are being put in the back seat. More short-statured drivers are moving back from the steering wheel.

Other changes are technological. First, as NHTSA noted in its report, "Air Bag Technology in Light Passenger Vehicles" (December 1999), the air bag outputs (i.e., pressure rise rate and the peak pressure) were reduced significantly in many MY 1998 and later motor vehicles in comparison to the earlier vehicles. Hence, the sled test option successfully expedited the depowering of existing air bags. While there are many means by which air bag aggressiveness can be reduced, reducing air bag outputs is a quick means of accomplishing this goal. The agency's analyses also show that, between MY 1997 and MY 1998, 50 to 60 percent of the vehicles in the fleet covered by the 1997 IR lowered the output of the driver-side air bag, while about 40 to 50 percent of the vehicles in that fleet lowered the output for the passenger side. Comparison of the data for MY 1997 and MY 1998 vehicles shows that, on average, the pressure rise rate in MY 1998 vehicles decreased about 22 percent for the driver air bag and 14 percent for the passenger air bags. . . .

To address the problems that arose with the air bags installed in many motor vehicles, the agency announced a comprehensive plan in November 1996. The plan set forth an array of immediate, interim and long-term measures. The immediate and interim measures focused on behavioral changes and relatively modest technological changes. The long-term measures focused on more significant technological changes, i.e., advanced air bag technologies. The immediate steps included expanding efforts to persuade parents to place their children in the rear seat; requiring new labels with eye-catching graphics and colors and strong, clear warning messages; extending the period of time for permitting the installation of original equipment on-off switches in new vehicles which either lacked a rear seat or had a rear seat too small to permit the installation of a child restraint system; and permitting the installation of retrofit on-off switches in vehicles-in-use to protect people in at-risk groups. Because of the lead time needed to develop and install advanced air bag technologies, NHTSA announced plans to propose an interim measure to accelerate manufacturer efforts to redesign their air bags. In the long term, the agency said that it would conduct rulemaking to require the installation of advanced air bags. . . .

To implement the interim phase of the comprehensive plan and speed the redesigning and recertifying of air bags to reduce the risks to out-of-position occupants, we amended Standard No. 208, Occupant Crash Protection, 49 CFR 571.208, to establish a temporary option under which vehicle manufacturers could certify their vehicles based on a 48 km/h (30 mph) unbelted sled test using a 50th percentile adult male dummy, instead of the 48 km/h (30 mph) unbelted rigid barrier crash test using that dummy. 62 F.R. 12960; March 19, 1997.

Available data indicate that the redesigned air bags, together with behavioral changes, such as placing more children in the back seat, have reduced the risks from air bags for the at-risk populations. Although these real-world data reflect only about two years of field experience with redesigned air bags, they preliminarily indicate that the redesigned air bags in model year (MY) 1998 and 1999 vehicles provide the same level of frontal crash protection as that provided by earlier air bags.

While the redesigned air bags in current motor vehicles have contributed to the reduction in the risk of air bag-induced injuries, they can still cause death or serious injury to unrestrained occupants. We selected the provisions adopted in this rule to ensure that future air bags provide more frontal crash protection, and reduce risk further, than either the current redesigned air bags or air bags that would have been minimally compliant with the sled test. . . .

The rule will improve protection and minimize risk by requiring new tests and injury criteria and specifying the use of an entire family of test dummies: the existing dummy representing 50th percentile adult males, and new dummies representing 5th percentile adult females, six-year old children, three-year old children, and one-year old infants. With the addition of those dummies, our occupant crash protection standard will more fully reflect the range in sizes of vehicle occupants. As noted above, most aspects of this rule are supported by most commenters on this rulemaking, including vehicle manufacturers, air bag manufacturers, insurance companies, public interest groups, academia, and the NTSB [National Transportation Safety Board]. . . .

The provisions of this rule, particularly the maximum test speed for the unbelted rigid barrier test, reflect the uncertainty associated with simultaneously achieving the twin goals of TEA 21.* This uncertainty leads us to take an approach that best assures improved air bag protection for occupants of all sizes, without compromising efforts to reduce the risks of injury to vulnerable occupants, including children and short women seated very close to air bags and out-of-position occupants. Such an approach is one that involves the least uncertainty for the occupants who have been most at risk. As long as the manufacturers improve the already substantial overall level of real world protection provided by current redesigned air bags, the uncertainty associated with the challenge of simultaneously achieving the twin goals of TEA 21 is best resolved at this point in favor of minimizing risk. This is especially true in the early stages of the introduction of advanced air bag technologies.

In light of that uncertainty, we are selecting the lower of two proposed speeds as the maximum test speed for the unbelted rigid barrier crash test and issuing that part of this rule as an interim final rule. To resolve that uncertainty, we are planning a multi-year effort to obtain additional data. We will issue a final decision regarding the maximum test speed after giving notice and seeking public comment. If we were to increase the speed, we would provide leadtime commensurate with the extent of that increase. . . .

---

*[The Transportation Equity Act for the 21st Century (TEA 21), 49 U.S.C. §30127, enacted by Congress in June 1998, requires NHTSA to issue a rule amending Federal Motor Vehicle Safety Standard No. 208, Occupant Crash Protection: "to improve occupant protection for occupants of different sizes, belted and unbelted, under Federal Motor Vehicle Safety Standard No. 208, while minimizing the risk to infants, children, and other occupants from injuries and deaths caused by air bags, by means that include advanced air bags." — EDS.]

The agency drafted the risk minimization requirements to give vehicle manufacturers a broad choice among those advanced air bag technologies that can be used either to turn air bags off in appropriate circumstances or cause air bags to deploy in a low risk manner. Thus, the vehicle manufacturers will have the freedom to choose from a variety of available technological solutions or to innovate by developing new ones if they so desire.

We estimate that if advanced air bag technologies (suppression and low risk deployment) are 100 percent reliable, they could have eliminated 95 percent of the known air bag fatalities that have occurred to date in low speed crashes. For example, weight sensors can be installed in the passenger seat so that the passenger air bag is turned off when children, from infants up to the typical 6-year-old, are present. The use of weight sensors for that purpose should essentially eliminate the risk of air bag-induced fatal injuries for children in that size and age range. Based on available data, it does not appear that turning air bags off for those young children would result in the loss of any benefits. There is an element of uncertainty about the level of reliability and effectiveness of the suppression for children from 0 to 6 years old and low risk deployment designs that will be actually installed in vehicles. We also note that we do not currently have a dummy suitable for assessing the effectiveness of suppression and low risk deployment for children ages 7-12. (See the section below entitled, "Future Rulemaking Plans.") Our decision concerning the maximum test speed for the unbelted rigid barrier test reflects, in part, these uncertainties and limitations.

The availability of advanced air bag technologies for minimizing risks is not just a theoretical possibility. Vehicle manufacturers are very actively working on completing their development and testing of weight sensor systems so that they will be ready for installation for the passenger air bags in their motor vehicles. Installation could begin as early as the next model year. Means of reducing risk for drivers, including dual-stage air bags coupled with sensors for driver seat belt use and driver seat position, are already being installed in some vehicles. . . .

NOTES AND QUESTIONS

1. Airbags have significant health and safety benefits, but they are not an unmitigated good. In particular, they can cause significant injuries and fatalities to children and small-stature adults. How does NHTSA estimate the risks from airbags to children and small-stature adults?
2. How does NHTSA address these risks? Note the role of behavioral changes and technological changes. How do they affect the standards that NHTSA adopts?
3. NHTSA states that scientific "uncertainty" plays a role. What is the uncertainty? How does it affect the standards that NHTSA adopts?

b. Assessing Risk

As you have seen, many regulatory statutes grant agencies authority to address risks to human health and safety, to the environment, to animal populations, and more. But what exactly constitutes a risk? Professor Kip Viscusi defines risk as follows:

It is helpful to distinguish among risk, uncertainty, and ignorance. In the situation of risk, we know that states of the world that may prevail (a flipped coin will show one or two faces) and the precise probability of each state (heads and tails are equally likely). In the case of uncertainty, we may not even be able to define what states of the world are possible.

The real world is rife with uncertainty. Even if we can make direct environmental measurements (e.g., for atmospheric pollution), interpretation of our observations may be problematic. Does an unusually high temperature this year indicate an upward trend, or does it represent random variation around an unchanging mean?

As our technological capabilities grow and economic activity imposes further strains on the environment, we will increasingly find ourselves in situations of ignorance. As we enter apparently benign but uncharted territory, we cannot be confident that if there were threats, we would detect them. Many individual decisions, as well as scientific risk analyses, are afflicted by ignorance. California studies of transportation safety in the event of an earthquake, for example, failed to capture the full range of effects that may have led to the highway damage experienced in October 1989. Under ignorance, the potential for bad society decisions is particularly great. Conceivably, for example, environmental releases of genetically engineered organisms might alter the current ecological balance in ways we cannot anticipate.

KIP VISCUSI, FATAL TRADEOFFS 153-54 (1992).

Agencies charged with regulating risk follow a two-step process. They first acquire and process information about risk. This step is known as "risk assessment." Agencies then determine how to respond to such risk. This step is known as "risk management." Professors Celia Campbell-Mohn and John Applegate provide a succinct account of the difference between risk assessment and risk management in the toxic substances context:

Risk assessment is a process for calculating the probability and magnitude of identified adverse effects, most commonly excess deaths from cancer caused by exposure to a chemical or radiological agent. The process is used to identify activities that require regulatory attention, to select the nature and stringency of an appropriate regulatory response, and to choose among the many potential objects of regulators' efforts. Risk assessment aims to "organize and express what can be stated about risks that are not subject to direct observation and measurement" based on an analysis of data concerning toxicity and exposure.

A 1983 NAS [National Academy of Sciences] report, *Risk Assessment in the Federal Government: Managing the Process* (the "Red Book") set out the general methodology for human-health-related risk assessment . . . . [1]

The Red Book distinguished this process from *risk management*, the substantive decision to take or withhold regulatory action. The latter, unlike risk assessment, explicitly involves political, social, and economic policy questions, such as the acceptable level of risk and the appropriate regulatory response. As a rigid dichotomy, of course, this split is an unrealistic view of government action and of science. Political and judgmental factors pervade the entire assessment function. Operating in a world of uncertainty, incomplete data, and genuine differences between scientists in interpretation of and inferences from the available data, risk assessors must make many assumptions and estimates. The choice, for example, among

---

[1] Professors Cambell-Mohn and Applegate analogize a risk assessment requirement "to the Environmental Impact Statement ("EIS") process in the NEPA, which mandates no particular substantive result, because the EIS informs but is clearly distinct from the final agency decision."

conservative, risk-preferring, or middle-ground assumptions is clearly a policy question. Rather than paper over the role of policy in risk assessment, the relationship between risk assessment and risk management should be acknowledged.

Celia Campbell-Mohn & John S. Applegate, *Learning from NEPA: Guidelines for Responsible Risk Legislation*, 23 HARV. ENVTL. L. REV. 93, 95-98 (1999). [2]

Note that the distinction between scientific questions and policy questions separates risk assessment from risk management. There are some questions that science can answer and some questions that science cannot. A decision how or whether to regulate cannot turn solely on the scientific "facts." It involves "political, social, and economic policy questions, such as the acceptable level of risk and the appropriate regulatory response." But, as Professors Campbell-Mohn and Applegate acknowledge, judgment calls pervade the principal methodologies for performing risk assessment — that is, for obtaining the scientific "facts." The next excerpt outlines those methodologies and shows some of the junctures where the distinction between science and policy blurs.

David Ropeik & George Gray, Risk!

8-13 (2002)

As we try to judge what's risky and what's not, we look to science for answers. But even with all the facts that science can provide, much uncertainty remains, for a number of reasons. First, the sciences by which risk is investigated-toxicology, epidemiology, and statistical analysis are inherently imprecise. Second, there are a lot of risk questions science simply hasn't asked yet. New risks like using a cell phone while driving or eating genetically modified food haven't been studied nearly enough for us to have all the answers. And third, even for risks that have been studied, the facts as we know them are constantly changing as scientific answers to one set of questions reveal more questions. . . .

---

[2] OMB has offered guidelines to agency heads for performing risk assessment, with a fairly turgid history. In 1995, OMB and the Office of Science and Technology Policy in the Executive Office of the President first provided a set of principles. See U.S. Office of Mgmt. and Budget (OMB), Memo for Regulatory Working Group, Principles for Risk Analysis (1995). In 2006, OMB issued a Proposed Risk Assessment Bulletin for comment, and requested that the National Academy of Sciences conduct an expert peer review on the 2006 Bulletin. The National Academy found that the 2006 Bulletin was "fundamentally flawed," and it recommended that OMB withdraw it. See Scientific Review of the Proposed Risk Assessment Bulletin from the Office of Management and Budget 6 (National Research Council, 2007). In response, OMB declined to issue the 2006 Bulletin in final form, and instead issued a memorandum to heads of executive departments and agencies specifying its guidelines for risk assessment. See Memorandum to Heads of Exec. Departments and Agencies from Susan Dudley & Sharon Hays, Updated Principles of Risk Analysis (Sept. 17, 2007). These guidelines require the assumptions, both quantitative and qualitative, underlying risk assessments to be explicitly stated. These guidelines also direct agencies to make significant risk management decisions to create the greatest net improvements in social welfare.

Toxicology

Most simply described, toxicology is the study of poisons: But because of that very definition, you can understand why toxicologists usually can't test the agent they're investigating on human subjects. So animals are used as surrogates. But toxicologists admit that they can't say for sure what a compound will do in humans based on evidence of what it does in animals. As one toxicologist says, "With stuff that might kill people, animal testing, as imprecise as it is, is the best we can do. But despite what you might think of your boss or some people you don't like, humans aren't rats." Toxicologists don't know which lab animal species serve as the best indicators of what would happen in people, nor do they know which species are better indicators for which kinds of hazards. So extrapolating from lab animals to humans is imprecise. As one example, cyclamate, an artificial sweetener, causes one type of liver tumor in only one species of rat, and then only in males, and doesn't cause it in any other test animals. Yet test data from the experiments on those rats caused the food additive to be banned for human consumption.

Another imprecision from toxicology arises because testing of lab animals often involves subjecting the animals to massive doses of an agent. In testing for carcinogenicity, animals routinely get doses, each day, far greater than you would be exposed to in your entire lifetime. Toxicologists call this dose the MTD, for "maximum tolerated dose." They use this technique when testing for cancer in order to maximize the chance that they'll find any effect that might occur and that might not show up from a milder dose.

Using these [maximum tolerated doses], toxicologists presume that if the substance they're testing causes an effect at a high dose, it might cause the same effect at a lower dose. This approach seems like a rational way to deal with potentially dangerous chemicals and other agents; if high doses cause harm, assume that low doses might too. But sometimes the size of the dose is what's really causing the harm. Think of aspirin, for example. One or two aspirin are fine. Too many will kill you. The standard toxicological approach of subjecting lab animals to high doses of a test compound can reveal subtle effects, but it can also produce misleading results.

A further imprecision arises in toxicology because in vivo tests in living lab animals, or in vitro tests of cells in a lab dish or beaker, isolate and test just one compound at a time. That's a smart way to find out with precision whether that particular agent is hazardous. But in the real world we're exposed to a stew of agents, and the mix can lead to different outcomes than exposure to any individual component. (Radon and smoking, for instance, apparently work synergistically and increase the risk of lung cancer more than the sum of one risk plus the other risk.) In addition, while the environment in the lab is stable and uniform, the real world is full of variables such as our environment, our health, our food, our emotional states, and our genetic makeup from one generation to the next and from one person to the next. These factors and many others affect how we react to a compound or circumstance.

In short, while toxicology can tell us a lot about the biological hazard of a particular chemical or element or compound, it can't tell us with absolute accuracy just what the substance being tested — at high doses to another species in a controlled lab — will do at lower doses to humans in the complicated real world.

Epidemiology

When we can't test a substance or hazard on people but we want to know whether it might be a threat to public health, we look around for circumstances in which people might already have been exposed. Studying what has happened, or is currently happening, to real populations in the real world, and trying to make sense of which hazards and exposures might be associated with which consequences, is the essence of epidemiology.

Like toxicologists, epidemiologists readily acknowledge that their science is imprecise. Epidemiology can usually provide only associations, not absolute proof, that some particular exposure may be what's causing some particular consequence. For example, in one kind of study epidemiologists investigate a specific small group of people who get sick. The book and movie A Civil Action, for instance, made famous the polluted drinking water in Woburn, Massachusetts.

A higher-than-expected number of cases of childhood leukemia showed up in just a few years in a small neighborhood. Epidemiologists investigated to find out what sources of exposure to potential hazards the neighbors shared. They discovered that one thing the neighbors had in common was that those who drank from a certain water supply had a higher rate of illness. Therefore, something about the water was the likely cause of the leukemia. They tested the water for chemicals suspected to cause that illness and estimated how much of the water people drank, for how long, and how polluted it was when people drank it. In the end, a peer-reviewed epidemiological study showed an association between how much of the well water pregnant mothers drank and the frequency of childhood leukemia in their offspring. The more they drank, the more likely it was that their children developed leukemia.

But that's not proof. Perhaps a couple of the neighbors were exposed to something else the researchers didn't ask about. Maybe the researchers never detected something else in the well water. These other factors are known as "confounders," hidden clues that can muddy the epidemiological waters and lead to an inaccurate assumption that A caused B. Hidden confounders can never be completely ruled out.

This isn't to suggest that the findings of epidemiology are weak or of little use in judging risks. In good epidemiological studies, researchers give the research subjects in-depth questionnaires about their health, their lifestyle, their diet, their social and economic characteristics, even their residential history (where they have lived and when), trying to rule out all confounders. They compare a group of people suffering some kind of health problem, like those families in Woburn, with other "control" groups, populations of similar size and socioeconomic status somewhere else, who presumably were not exposed to the same things. For the bigger long-term population studies, epidemiologists carry out multiple research programs in different places at different times to see if their results agree. With such techniques, epidemiologists can rule out every other possibility they can think of. They can become more and more certain of the associations they find.

But, like toxicologists, they can rarely be completely sure.

Statistical Analysis

In addition to the findings of toxicology and epidemiology, risk analysts also look for their clues among large sets of statistics. Those data collections are compilations of real-world information, on either morbidity (nonfatal health problems) or mortality (deaths). These databases can offer rich details, like how many people were injured or killed in motor vehicle accidents, categorized by speed, vehicle size, whether the victim was male, female, old, young, wearing a seat belt or not, and so on. There are data sets on hundreds of risks that offer information on the age, gender, and race of the affected population and the circumstances that led to the death or illness, such as the number of food poisoning cases connected with restaurants, or the number of workers murdered on the job. Other data collections provide risk analysts with information about hazardous materials emissions, local water or air pollution levels, or the presence of harmful chemicals in our blood or the food we eat. These details all offer insights about the hazard, exposure, consequence, and probability of various risks.

But the numbers in these data collections usually suffer from some imprecision. Not everybody who suffers food poisoning after dining at a restaurant, for example, actually goes to a doctor to report his illness. Not every police officer fills out every last detail on every accident report. Not every factory keeps accurate, or honest, records of its emissions. And not every government information collection system gathers the information and enters it into its database accurately.

Numbers are also subject to interpretation. Here's an example. According to national motor vehicle crash statistics, drivers 75 years old or over are involved in four times as many fatal crashes as the average of all other age groups. But does that mean that elderly drivers are killing other people, or just that because of frail health they're more likely to die themselves whenever they're in a crash? You can't tell by that statistic. The numbers don't tell you everything you need to know. As Mark Twain said, "There are three kinds of lies — lies, damned lies, and statistics."

Finally, no matter how precise and narrow statistical categories are, they lump everybody in that category together. For example, federal motor vehicle crash statistics group data by age, gender, the day and time of crashes, and the kind of vehicle involved. So you can determine how many 15- to 24-year-old males were involved in crashes on Sundays at 5 P.M. in pickup trucks. As narrow as that seems, that's still a large group of people and not everyone in it is the same. Individuals within that group have all sorts of differences in health, lifestyle, education, genetics, body size and shape, and on and on.

Risk statistics are generalities, and by definition cannot specifically answer the question we all want answered: "What is the risk to *me*?"...As we've stated, because you are unique none of those numbers will accurately and precisely answer your question. Risk numbers can be only a general guide. They give you a sense of which risks are bigger and which ones are smaller, and sometimes they can tell you which risks are higher or lower for the demographic groups to which you belong. But even risk numbers that define the categories as narrowly as possible still can't calculate the risk for each unique individual.

In sum, the sciences that supply the facts about risk, while growing more and more powerful, are still imprecise. They can provide us with valuable insights. But their results are uncertain and open to interpretation. There are very few unequivocal answers when it comes to defining and quantifying the risks we face. That's why in this guide our approach is to offer information in ranges: the *range* of exposures, the *range* of consequences, and so forth. . . .

NOTES AND QUESTIONS

1. No methodology for evaluating risk answers every question. For example, any test that does not rely on human subjects to estimate risk about human populations is inherently imprecise. What are the sources of imprecision in the various methodologies?
2. Agencies rely on scientific analyses despite their imprecision. How does an agency determine whether a particular mouse study (or a Rabbit study) is reliable? The answer is: the agency makes a judgment call based on its estimation of the relevant similarities and differences of mice and men or owners of Rabbits and others cars with respect to the particular risk at issue. Mice may have biological systems that are sufficiently similar for one purpose, say the effect of a drug on the nervous system, but not for others, say the effect on the endocrine system.
3. Where do crash-test-dummy studies, like the ones that NHTSA uses, fit among the methodologies that Ropeik and Gray describe? What are the limits of such simulations? You might imagine that computers often perform simulations without the need to crash an actual car or airplane or other craft.
4. Assuming agencies can acquire information about risk, they must process such information when using it to make a decision. Let's say a mouse study predicted a small risk of non-fatal side effects in humans from a particular drug. Is this a significant risk or a trivial risk? Would more information help? Let's say that the drug is intended for children, so that the risk is to children. Let's also say that the drug may disrupt normal growth and have lasting reproductive effects. How are you responding now to the "small risk of non-fatal side effects"?
5. If policy judgment inheres in every aspect of risk assessment, perhaps the most important question is who within the agency should decide. Are scientists best able to evaluate whether the particular biological system of mice is similar enough to the comparable system of people? What about whether Rabbit owners are representative of the average car passenger? Aren't judgment calls supposed to be made by political officials within agencies because only those officials have the requisite accountability? We return to the question of "who should decide" below, and through the entire discussion of agency statutory implementation. The allocation of authority within an agency affects the ultimate decision as much as the allocation between agencies and others institutions.

NOTES AND QUESTIONS

1. Trans-scientific questions "arise from a variety of practical and theoretical limitations on scientific experimentation." As a result, agency decisions that are based on scientific data or conclusions (e.g., the decision to limit exposure of a toxin at a particular concentration, the decision to require the installation of passive restraints) reflect substantial numbers of policy judgments. The mixture is inevitable; both science and trans-science are necessary to a final agency regulation, but typically, neither is sufficient. Who should decide trans-scientific questions? Even if your answer is political officials, why must agency scientists nonetheless maintain some sort of a role?

2. Professors Campbell-Mohn and Applegate, who earlier gave us the distinction between risk assessment and risk management, caution against too rigid a separation at the EPA:

    > The call to keep these two functions distinct was originally articulated in response to a widespread perception that EPA was making judgments on the risk posed by a particular substance not on the basis of science, but rather on the basis of its willingness to regulate the substance. The purpose of separation, however, was not to prevent any exercise of policy judgment at all when evaluating science or to prevent risk managers from influencing the type of information that assessors would collect, analyze, or present. Indeed, the Red Book made it clear that judgment (also referred to as risk-assessment policy or science policy) would be required even during the phase of risk assessment. The present committee concludes further that the science-policy judgments that EPA makes in the course of risk assessment would be improved if they were more clearly informed by the agency's priorities and goals in risk management. Protecting the integrity of the risk assessment, while building more productive linkages to make risk assessment more accurate and relevant to risk management, will be essential as the agency proceeds to regulate the residual risks of hazardous air pollutants.

    Celia Campbell-Mohn & John S. Applegate, *Learning from NEPA: Guidelines for Responsible Risk Legislation*, 23 HARV. ENVTL. L. REV. 93, 97-98 (1999), citing National Research Council, Committee on Risk Assessment of Hazardous Air Pollutants, Science and Judgment in Risk Assessment 259-60 (1994). If separation is not the answer, then what is?

3. Think back to NHTSA's reason for discounting the Rabbit/Chevette study: the owners of those smaller cars were not representative of the average passenger, and the automatic belt systems in those cars were not representative of the one that the agency was considering. These determinations concerning the relevance of the study were not scientific conclusions but trans-scientific judgments. What were the scientific facts or conclusions that the Rabbit/Chevette study revealed?

c. Scientific Uncertainty

One important aspect of how agencies use science is how they respond to uncertainty. NHTSA helps to demonstrate the point in concrete, not overly technical, terms. In its rule rescinding passive restraints, NHTSA stated that "the changes in car manufacturers' plans has left the agency without any factual basis for reliably predicting the likely usage increases due to detachable automatic seat belts, or for even predicting the likelihood of any increase at all." 46 Fed. Reg. 53422. This is a claim of factual uncertainty, analogous to scientific uncertainty.

In general, how should an agency respond in the face of scientific uncertainty? This question is the subject of intense academic debate. Many agencies actually believe it supports precautionary action. Consider the following from Professor Viscusi:

> Government efforts aimed at developing risk information are not guided by the formal statistical properties of the risk but rather by administrative procedures incorporating various types of "conservatism." Although risk assessment biases may operate in both directions, most approved procedures tend to overstate the actual risk. In regulated toxic substances, for example, results from the most sensitive animal species are often used, and government agencies such as the EPA routinely focus on the upper end of the 95 confidence interval as the risk level rather than use the mean of the distribution. A series of such conservative assumptions (e.g., on exposure by focusing on the most sensitive humans) can overstate the mean probability of an unfavorable outcome by several orders of magnitude.

Viscusi, Fatal Tradeoffs, 156-57.

When lives are at stake, the impulse in the face of scientific uncertainty often is to follow a conservative approach (which tends to justify more regulation, not less). But where do we stop? Would you ban cell phones because of the risk that they cause brain tumors as a result of radiation emitted to the brain? There is scientific uncertainty on the causal link. If not, would you mandate potentially life-saving devices (e.g., an earpiece that puts distance between the phone and the brain) in excess of caution? In other contexts, would you withhold potentially life-saving precautions (e.g., drugs or vaccines) until the science can demonstrate their safety?

Agencies are inconsistent in their responses to scientific uncertainty. As a practical matter, agencies often respond to scientific uncertainty by offering ranges of risk reduction. This is how NHTSA dealt with factual uncertainty in its final rule rescinding passive restraints requirements. After determining that the Rabbit/Chevette study was not reliable because of the demographics of the subjects and type of automatic restraints in their cars, the agency considered two different methods for using that study to construct a range of possible increases in belt usage as a result of the installation of automatic seatbelts (15-60%). In the end, it concluded that usage would likely be at the low end of the range.

A particularly difficult issue arises when an agency has no reliable data on which to proceed but is nevertheless obligated to act. Here is a real example (greatly simplified) of regulation in the face of scientific uncertainty. It involves an issue of utmost importance: the disposal of the nation's nuclear waste. By the year 2035, the United States will have produced 105,000 metric tons of nuclear waste, which is roughly twice the amount that currently exists. Furthermore, nuclear waste has potentially devastating effects on human health over a time period far longer than recorded human history. EPA is required to address the disposal of nuclear waste under a highly complex regulatory scheme. But its resolution was further complicated by scientific uncertainty. Consider this description, drawn in large part from the D.C. Circuit decision remanding the regulation back to the agency, Nuclear Energy Institute, Inc. v. EPA, 373 F.3d 1251, 1258-68 (D.C. Cir. 2004):

After years of consideration, Congress designated Yucca Mountain, Nevada, as the country's nuclear waste disposal site. In 1982, it enacted the Nuclear Waste Policy Act, which required the EPA to establish standards health and safety for the site. 42 U.S.C. §§1010 et seq. (1982). Specifically, the statute required EPA "based upon and consistent with the findings and recommendations of the National Academy of Sciences, [to] promulgate, by rule, public health and safety standards for protection of the public from releases from radioactive materials stored or disposed of in the repository at the Yucca Mountain site."

The EPA issued a rule, 40 C.F.R. part 197, to protect both individuals living near the disposal site and local ground-water supplies from excessive exposure to radiation releases. That rule required the agency responsible for managing the Yucca Mountain site, the Department of Energy, to demonstrate a reasonable expectation that, for 10,000 years following disposal, the "reasonable minimally exposed individual" receives no more than an annual committed effective dose equivalent of 150 microsieverts (15 millirems) from releases from the undisturbed Yucca Mountain disposal system. This is the "individual-risk standard." In addition, EPA established a standard for individual risk in the event of "human intrusion" — drilling, whether intentional or unintentional — and one for ground-water protection. Both also involved a 10,000 year compliance period.

But the National Academy of Sciences arrived at a different number. NAS found "no scientific basis for limiting the time period of the individual-risk standard to 10,000 years or any other value." Rather, NAS found that "compliance assessment is feasible for most physical and geologic aspects of repository performance on the time scale of the long-term stability of the fundamental geologic regime — a time scale that is on the order of 10^6 [one million] years at Yucca Mountain." Furthermore, NAS stated that humans may not face peak radiation risks until tens to hundreds of thousands of years after disposal, "or even farther into the future." Given these findings, NAS "recommend[ed] that compliance assessment be conducted for the time when the greatest risk occurs, within the limits imposed by the long-term stability of the geologic environment." NAS stated, however, that "although the selection of a time period of applicability has scientific elements, it also has policy aspects that we have not addressed," including (in the D.C. Circuit's words) "the goal of establishing consistent policies for managing various kinds of long-lived, hazardous materials."

In its final rule, EPA explained the reasons for rejecting NAS's compliance assessment. It acknowledged NAS's finding that it is necessary to protect individuals at the time of peak radiation risks and that it is scientifically possible to predict repository performance for approximately one million years. Nevertheless, EPA concluded that "such an approach is not practical for regulatory decision-making." 66 Fed. Reg. at 32,097. As EPA stated,

> Despite NAS's recommendation, we conclude that there is still considerable uncertainty as to whether current modeling capability allows development of computer models that will provide sufficiently meaningful and reliable projections over a time frame up to tens-of-thousands to hundreds-of-thousands of years. Simply because such models can provide projections for those time periods does not mean those projections are meaningful and reliable enough to establish a rational basis for regulatory decisionmaking.

EPA also stated that its decision "involves both technical and policy considerations." As the D.C. Circuit summarized the EPA's decision, five considerations played a role: "(1) the agency uses 10,000 years for programs involving the disposal of other long-lived, hazardous materials, (2) the individual-protection requirements in 40 C.F.R. part 191, EPA's generally applicable nuclear waste disposal standards, use such a time frame, and "consistency [is] appropriate because both sets of standards apply to the same types of waste," (3) many international geologic disposal programs use 10,000 years, (4) setting the standard to peak dose times "could lead to a period of regulation that has never been implemented in a national or international radiation regulatory program," and focusing on 10,000 years forces more emphasis on features that humans can control such as repository design, and (5) projecting human exposure levels over long periods of time involves great uncertainty." *Nuclear Energy Institutes, Inc.*, 73 F.3d at 1268. As to scientific uncertainty, EPA stated that "we believe that NAS might not have fully addressed two aspects of uncertainty" — namely, "the impact of long-term natural changes in climate and its effect upon choosing an appropriate RMEI," and "the range of possible biosphere conditions and human behavior." 66 Fed. Reg. at 32,097.

3. *Economic Analysis*

When moving from risk assessment to risk management, an agency must decide whether to regulate, and if so, how stringently. One of the major tools for making such policy judgments is economic analysis. Agencies use economic analysis to assign a dollar amount to the benefits of a regulation and then to examine those benefits in relation to their costs.

Where does economic analysis come from? When agencies make decisions, common sense suggests that they ought to consider costs in some respect, even if they ultimately choose to prioritize another factor. We live in a world of finite resources; agencies should determine whether we are getting the most for our money. Furthermore, we run our lives generally in consideration of the costs and benefits of our actions. When deciding whether to cross a street against the light, you (at least implicitly) weigh the benefits of crossing against the costs of such action. If you wait to walk, it is because you are better off that way.

Common sense is not the only factor that prompts agencies to consider costs and benefits. Many statutes invite consideration of costs and benefits, and some require it. Only a very few prohibit it. In addition, as noted above, executive orders since President Reagan have required cost-benefit analysis (CBA) for all proposed major regulations (basically, those with costs of $100 million or more). Thus, there is a standing presidential requirement of CBA, backed by an executive order. We will not dwell here on the reasons why agencies choose to comply with the dictates of common sense or the terms of their organic statutes and executive orders. For now, suffice it to say that they do.

NHTSA is a good example. When NHTSA originally mandated the installation of passive restraints in 1977, it estimated that its rule would yield significant benefits:

> According to the analysis which NHTSA performed in that year, automatic restraints were expected to prevent 9,000 deaths and 65,000 serious injuries once all cars on the road were equipped with those devices. That prediction was premised on several critical assumptions. Most important among the assumptions were those concerning the safety benefits of automatic restraints — reductions in death and injury — which in turn are a function of the types of automatic restraints to be placed in each year's production of new cars.
>
> The agency assumed that the combination of airbags and lap belts would be approximately 66 percent effective in preventing fatalities and that automatic belts would have a 50 percent level of effectiveness. The agency also assumed also that airbags would be placed in more than 60 percent of new cars and that automatic belts would be placed in the remaining approximately 40 percent. The agency's analysis predicted that airbags would provide protection in virtually all crashes of sufficient severity to cause deployment of the airbags. It was further assumed that the automatic belts would be used by 60 to 70 percent of the occupants of those cars.

NHTSA, Federal Vehicle Safety Standards, Final Rule, 46, Fed. Reg. 53419, 53420 (Oct. 29, 1981).

NHTSA's assumptions about the benefits of its passive restraints requirements did not materialize because automakers overwhelmingly chose to install automatic seatbelts rather than airbags. Furthermore, the agency found that the benefits of automatic seatbelts were uncertain: no data existed showing that people would use such seatbelts any more often than they were using manual seatbelts. As a result, Standard 208 would cost $89 per vehicle (the cost to install automatic seatbelts) and eliminate the middle seat or sixth seat passenger position without any countervailing benefits. The quality of the CBA depends on the accuracy of the assumptions the agency makes when conducting it.

More generally, how do agencies perform CBA? What are the criticisms of that approach? What are the other variations of economic analysis that statutes prescribe or agencies perform? We consider these issues in some detail because, for good or bad, the regulatory state is at present a "cost-benefit state." *See* CASS R. SUNSTEIN, THE COST-BENEFIT STATE (2002). Economic considerations play a pivotal role in the work of agencies and therefore in the work of lawyers, both inside and outside of those agencies.

a. The Mechanics of Cost-Benefit Analysis

At a basic level, conducting CBA involves monetizing — or assigning a dollar value to — the benefits and costs of a regulation. That can be a difficult task. It involves putting a price tag on risk reductions, making economic assumptions, and discounting future values to present ones. We address these issues below.

1. Valuing Statistical Lives: In economic terms, what was the benefit of requiring the installation of passive restraints, as NHTSA first envisioned it? The agency assumed that its rule would prevent 9,000 deaths and 65,000 serious injuries. What is that benefit worth to society in dollars? It is necessary to monetize these benefits to evaluate them against the costs of the regulation.

In monetizing benefits for regulations that protect human health and safety, agencies confront the question of what a human life is worth in dollars. To set a dollar value, agencies use a statistical "value of human life" number. That number can vary wildly among agencies — from $50,000 per life to more than $8 million per life. What is the basis for these numbers? Consider the following:

W. Kip Viscusi, Fatal Tradeoffs

17-19 (1992)

2.1 Valuation Methodology

Traditionally, issues pertaining to the valuation of human life had been treated a strictly moral concepts, not matters to be degraded through economic analysis of choices and tradeoffs. However, as Schelling (1968) observed, substantial insight can be obtained by assessing the benefits of risk reduction in the same manner as we value other economic effects. In general, the appropriate benefit measure for risk reductions is the willingness to pay to produce the particular outcome. Similarly, the selling price for changes in risk establishes the value for risk increases. In the usual risk policy decision — for example, determining what safety characteristics to provide in automobiles — the policy result to be assessed is an incremental risk reduction rather than a shift involving the certainty of life or death. This need to think in terms of statistical lives as opposed to certain lives defines the main character of our choice problems. In particular, the matter of interest is individuals' valuation of lotteries involving life and death.

Addressing value-of-life issues by focusing on our attitudes toward lotteries involving small risks of death provides a methodology for formulating these issues in a sound economic manner. This approach also avoids the more difficult task of confronting the valuation of lives at risk of certain death, which understandably raises a different class of ethical issues. Nevertheless, even when only small risks are involved, the concerns involved remain inherently sensitive, and we should not be cavalier in making these judgments. Because of the central role of individual preferences, individual values of life may differ considerably, just as do other tastes. A central concern is who is valuing the life and for what reason. A particular life may have one value to the individual, another to his or her family, and still another to society at large.

As the willingness-to-pay methodology has become better understood, the controversy surrounding the entire line of research on the value of life has diminished. Much of the early opposition to the economic valuation of life stemmed from the reliance on value-of-life concepts that had been developed to inform decisions on compensating survivors rather than on reducing risks to life. Initial efforts consequently sought to value life using the human capital approach. In particular, [some early analyses] estimated values of life based on various measures of earnings. This technique, which continues to be used throughout the United States court system to assess damages for personal injury, addresses only the financial losses involved. The death of a family member, for example, would impose a financial loss on survivors, which would be measured as the present value of the income the deceased would have earned net of taxes and his or her consumption. Similarly, the present value of taxes the deceased would have paid represents the financial loss to the rest of society. . . .

2.2 The Value of Statistical Lives

The ultimate purpose of the value-of-life literature is to provide some basis for sensitive social decisions. Before investigating how society should make decisions involving the saving of lives, we will first assess whether we can establish an empirical reference point for making tradeoffs involving life and health. In the absence of such empirical information, there will be few operational contexts in which economic analysis of value-of-life decisions is instructive. Some sense of the order of magnitude of the value-of-life estimates will also assuage many of the concerns expressed about the morality of this line of work. If the appropriate economic value of life is over $1 million, resistance to this methodology will probably be much less than if the estimate is, say, $200,000.

The basic approach to establishing a value of risk reduction parallels the technique for benefit assessment for other contexts. If, for example, one were attempting to assign benefits to the building of a new public parking garage, the appropriate benefit measure would be the sum of the willingness to pay of all the residents for this new facility. In a similar manner, when assessing the benefits of risk reduction, the pertinent value is the willingness to pay for the risk reduction. What we are purchasing with our tax dollars is not the certainty of survival. Rather, it is the incremental reduction in the probability of an adverse outcome that might otherwise have affected some random member of our community. What is at stake is consequently statistical lives, not certain identified lives.

In the case of risks that we must bear, the concern shifts from our willingness to pay for added safety to the amount that we require to bear the risk, which is usually termed our willingness-to-accept amount. For sufficiently small changes in risk, the willingness-to-pay and willingness-to-accept amounts should be approximately equal, but in practice they are not. [T]here is often an alarmist reaction to increases in risk above the accustomed level so that willingness-to-accept amounts may dwarf the willingness-to-pay amounts if we respond irrationally to the risks.

In each case, the underlying concern is with a lottery involving a small probability of an adverse outcome. Our attitude toward this lottery defines the terms of trade that we believe are appropriate, where these terms of trade represent our risk dollar tradeoff.

1. The statistical value of a human life is different from tort measures of economic damages, such as lost earnings. Why is it more appropriate when monetizing the benefits of regulation to ask individuals what they would be willing to pay for a small reduction in the risk of harm?
2. What does "statistical" mean? When economists survey individuals concerning their willingness to pay for risk reduction, those individuals are not valuing their own lives or the lives of those they know. Rather, they are placing a price tag on "the incremental reduction in the probability of an adverse outcome that might otherwise have affected some random member of our community." Why is this important to accurately estimate the benefits of regulation?
3. What does "life" mean? Individuals are not being asked how much they would be willing to pay for "the certainty of survival." They are simply valuing a small reduction in risk. Why is that important to accurately estimate the benefits of regulation?

Further Note on Monetization: Professor Viscusi provides the basic framework for valuing statistical lives, but other issues arise in the process. Consider the following:

Heterogeneity of Life.   Are all lives worth the same? What if a regulation mainly benefits future generations? Suppose people tend to value their own lives more. What about a regulation that mainly benefits the elderly? Or the poor? Suppose people tend to value the lives of the elderly or the poor less. What are the pros and cons of allowing the heterogeneity of statistical life to enter into the calculation? For a critical analysis of these issues, *see* RICHARD L. REVESZ & MICHAEL LIVERMORE, RETAKING RATIONALITY: HOW COST-BENEFIT ANALYSIS CAN BETTER PROTECT THE ENVIRONMENT AND OUR HEALTH 77-84 (elderly), 107-118 (future generations) (2008).

Stated Preferences vs. Revealed Preferences.   How do economists measure "willingness to pay"? Is what we say different from how we behave — put simply, do we put our money where our mouths are? The answer is not always. To account for the divergence, economists measure both stated and revealed preferences. They measure stated preferences by surveying individuals about how much they are willing to pay to avoid increased risks. They measure revealed preferences by, for example, observing in job market data how much workers demand in hazard pay to accept risky jobs. Professor Viscusi terms this measure "willingness to accept" and says it is useful for risks that we must bear. He also notes that what individuals are willing to accept to incur exposure to a risk and willing to pay to avoid exposure are different; the former is higher. Think about your own behavior. Can you explain why?

Variations Among Agencies and Issues.   When economists perform studies and evaluate market data, they can particularize the analysis for differences among risks across agencies or even within a single agency. That is why different agencies maintain divergent valuations and why some agencies use different numbers for different problems. For an extended discussion, *see* VISCUSI, FATAL TRADE-OFFS 34-39; REVESZ & LIVERMORE, RETAKING RATIONALITY: HOW COST-BENEFIT ANALYSIS CAN BETTER PROTECT THE ENVIRONMENT AND OUR HEALTH 47-48.

Updating Valuations Over Time.   The value of a statistical life can be expected to change over time as people's preferences about risk change. Economists update the numbers periodically. And so do agencies. But not all updates are on the up and up. For example, in 2008, EPA set the value of a statistical life at $6.9 million, a drop of $1 million from 2005. *See* Seth Borenstein, *An American Life Worth Less Today*, Associated Press, July 10, 2008. The agency itself did not call attention to the change; rather, the Associated Press discovered it after reviewing the cost-benefit analyses in EPA regulations. *See id.* Professor Viscusi was quoted in the Associated Press article as saying that EPA's is change "doesn't make sense" because "[a]s people become more affluent, the value of statistical lives go up as well." *Id.* By contrast, the Department of Transportation increased its statistical life valuation twice over this same time. *See id.* Consider another example. In 2002, the EPA decided to reduce the value of statistical life by 38 percent for the elderly but then reversed itself when the change became public. *Id.* Do these experiences suggest that valuation is not only driven by economics? Under the circumstances, perhaps the question we ought to be asking is *who* should select the appropriate valuation? Agency career economists? Agency political appointees? OIRA officials who combine economics with politics when performing regulatory review on behalf of the White House? Elected officials themselves? As in the scientific context, "who decides" questions are crucial to the policy that results.

Cognitive Biases.   People suffer from predictable irrationalities or cognitive biases that cause them to misperceive risk. These biases then affect the statistical life valuation. What people are willing to pay for a small reduction in risk depends on how they view that risk. Here is Professor Viscusi:

MISTAKES IN ESTIMATION
    Whereas people generally overestimate the likelihood of low-probability events (death by tornado), they underestimate higher risk levels (heart disease or stroke). We are particularly likely to overestimate previously unrecognized risks in the aftermath of an unfavorable outcome. Such perceptional biases account for the emotional public response to such events as Three Mile Island, or occasional incidents of deliberate poisoning of foodstuffs or medicines.
    Risk perceptions may also be affected by the visibility of a risk, by fear associated with it, and by the extent to which individuals believe they can exercise control over

it. Consider the greenhouse effect. Although global warming is a prime concern of the Environmental Protection Agency, it ranks only twenty-third among the U.S. public's environmental concerns. The high risk of automobile fatality-car accidents kill one in 5,000 Americans each year might perhaps be reduced significantly if drivers informed with a more realistic sense of what they can and cannot do to control the risk drank less alcohol and wore seat belts more often.

Because experience tells us little about low-probability risks, we appropriately examine correlated indicators that pose less serious problems. For example, the record high temperatures of 1988 mayor may not have been signals of an impending greenhouse effect. Unfortunately, such signals are seldom as informative as canaries in the coal mine. Adverse events may occur without warning; witness the San Francisco earthquake in October 1989. Moreover, happenstance warnings may bear little relation to the magnitude, likelihood, or nature of a problem. Forest management efforts should not have to await the chance burning of national parks and forests.

DISTORTIONS IN MONETARY VALUATION

Economic valuations of risk also tend to be distorted by underlying misweighting of risks. For example, from an expected utility perspective, individuals generally place too high a value on preventing increases in a risk from its current level (the so-called status quo bias or reference risk effect). These tendencies are reflected in government policy. Products causing new forms of cancer tend to arouse greater public concern and new technologies are often regulated much more strictly than are old technologies and familiar risks. Man-made carcinogens are carefully scrutinized, while much higher levels of natural carcinogens may be tolerated. Because of this imbalance, we pay more dollars for our products and end up with greater risks to our lives.

Studies of consumers show that many individuals would be willing to pay a premium for the assured elimination of a risk. The Russian roulette problem illustrates. Consider two alternative scenarios for a forced round of play. In the first, you have the option to purchase and remove one bullet from a gun that has three bullets in its six chambers. How much would you pay for this reduction in risk? (Assume you are unmarried, with no children.) In the second situation, the gun has only a single bullet. How much would you pay to buy back this bullet? From an economic standpoint, you should always be willing to pay at least as much and typically more in the first situation since there is some chance you will be killed by one of the remaining bullets, in which case money is worthless (or worth less). However, experiments find respondents are typically willing to pay more when a single bullet is in the gun, because its removal will ensure survival. . . .

The valuation of a risk is likely to depend on how the risk is generated. We tolerate voluntarily assumed risks more than those, such as environmental hazards over which we have no control. We regard acts of commission as much more serious than acts of omission. In pharmaceutical screening, for example, the Food and Drug Administration (FDA) worries more about introducing harmful new drugs than about missing opportunities for risk reduction offered by new pharmaceutical products.

VISCUSI, FATAL TRADEOFFS 152-54.

II. Other Economic Assumptions: In monetizing the benefits of a regulation, agencies often make other assumptions. For example, in a 2008 regulation, NHTSA made the following assumption about the price of a gallon of gasoline to calculate the costs and benefits of improved fuel economy standards:

> The total costs for manufacturers just complying with the [fuel economy] standards for [model year or "MY"] 2011–2015 passenger cars would be approximately $16 billion, compared to the costs they would incur if the standards remained at the adjusted baseline. The resulting vehicle price increases to buyers of MY 2015 passenger cars would be recovered or paid back in additional fuel savings in an average of 56 months, assuming fuel prices ranging from $2.26 per gallon in 2016 to $2.51 per gallon in 2030. The total costs for manufacturers just complying with the standards for MY2011–2015 light trucks would be approximately $31 billion, compared to the costs they would incur if the standards remained at the adjusted baseline. The resulting vehicle price increases to buyers of MY 2015 light trucks would be paid back in additional fuel savings in an average of 50 months, assuming fuel prices ranging from $2.26 to $2.51 per gallon.

73 Fed. Reg. 24352, 24356 (May 2, 2008).

When NHTSA made this assumption about gas prices in May 2008, those prices were hovering around the $4.00/gallon mark. (What are gas prices as you read this material?) But models projecting future gas prices were this optimistic. What is the effect of the agency's low-ball assumption on the economic analysis that it is performing? What is the effect on the fuel economy standards that it is proposing?

III. Selecting a Discount Rate: It is useful to know how people today value a life and what they are willing to pay to avoid a risk. But many of the costs and benefits of regulation affect the future. What is a small reduction in the risk of cancer in 25 years worth to you in today's dollars? Similarly, what does a gallon of gas priced at $2.51 in the year 2030 cost in today's dollars? To deal with this aspect of regulation, agencies select a discount rate to convert future costs and benefits to present dollars. But the choice is often quite difficult to make.

The choice of discount rate is an issue that arises frequently. Agencies often propose different discount rates and seek comment on the proper choice. Even when agencies do not solicit input on the discount rate or propose more than one, commentators often challenge their selection. As you can gather, understanding and questioning the discount rate (as well as the other components of cost-benefit analysis) is the work of lawyers and not just economists. That is why we expose you to the issue here. To see the importance of discount rates from a lawyer's perspective, consider this example from another regulation setting fuel economy standards:

49 C.F.R. Parts 523, 533 and 537
Average Fuel Economy Standards for Light Trucks Model Years 2008-2011

[Docket No. NHTSA 2006-24306], Thursday, April 6, 2006

[71 Fed. Reg. 17566 (2006)]

AGENCY: National Highway Traffic Safety Administration (NHTSA), Department of Transportation.
ACTION: Final rule.

. . .

Discounting future fuel savings and other benefits is intended to measure the reduction in the value to society of these benefits when they are deferred until some future date rather than received immediately. The discount rate expresses the percent decline in the value of these benefits — as viewed from today's perspective — for each year they are deferred into the future. The agency used a discount rate of 7 percent per year to discount the value of future fuel savings and other benefits when it analyzed the CAFE standards proposed in the NPRM.

The Alliance, General Motors, the Mercatus Center, and Criterion Economics all argued that in assessing benefits and costs associated with the CAFE standards, the agency should rely on a discount rate greater than 7 percent. The Alliance stated that the Congressional Budget Office discounts consumers' fuel savings at a rate of 12 percent per year and that other recent studies of CAFE standards have also used that rate. According to the Alliance, that rate is slightly higher than the average interest rate that consumers reported paying to finance used car purchases in the most recent Consumer Expenditure Survey. The Alliance argued further that consumers can be expected to discount the value of future fuel savings at a rate at least as high as their cost for financing the purchase of a vehicle whose higher price was justified by its higher fuel economy.

The Alliance based its assertion for use of 12 percent because, as it stated, this value was used in the NAS [National Academy of Science] report and approximates the used car loan rate published in the Consumer Expenditure Survey. However, we note that the NAS report did not use a single discount rate. Instead, the NAS used both 12 percent and 0 percent discount rates due to the assumption that the proper discount rate was "subjective." Therefore, NAS did not advocate a discount rate. As explained below, the vehicle loan rate faced by consumers is an appropriate measure of the discount rate.

General Motors suggested a discount rate of 9 percent, based on its assertions that new vehicles are financed at 8 percent and used vehicles at 10 percent. Essentially, General Motors is recommending that the agency rely on the interest for a car loan as the discount rate. General Motors also argued that fuel economy is not the only thing which consumers value and that the agency should take efforts to separate private benefits from public externalities. While we are uncertain as to what General Motors is recommending, we assume that its comment suggests that a higher discount rate, based on car loan rates, is appropriate for discounting private benefits (those to buyers), while a lower rate is appropriate for social benefits (such as reductions in externalities). Criterion Economics also recommended use of a 9 percent discount rate in its comments, which it suggested is a conservative rate between the average real rates for new and used cars that adequately accounts for volatility in future energy prices.

As discussed further below, we agree in that loan rates for new and used cars should be considered when determining the appropriate discount rate. However, loan estimates made by both General Motors and Criterion Economics are considerably higher than data provided by the Federal Reserve Board, which estimates new loan rates (as of October 2005) of 6 percent for new cars and 9 percent for used cars.

The Mercatus Center stated that the 7 percent discount

rate selected by the agency is too low, and as a result, it results in the setting of standards that are inequitable, particularly to low-income households. According to published academic research referenced by the Mercatus Center, most households have discount rates higher than 7 percent, with low-income households having particularly high discount rate. Therefore, the Mercatus Center urged NHTSA to rely on discount rates of 12 percent for all households and as high as 20 percent for low-income households in evaluating proposed standards. However, the studies cited by Mercatus Center to justify these discount rates examine the implied discount rate for future energy savings that result when households purchase more energy-efficient appliances such as furnaces and air conditioners. These studies were generally conducted in the late 1970's and early 1980's and may not be representative of the discount rates for motor vehicles of the economic conditions 20-25 years later.

Environmental Defense, NRDC [Natural Resources Defense Council], and the Union of Concerned Scientists provided comments endorsing use of a lower discount rate. These organizations expressed their belief that a 7-percent discount rate is too high, proposing instead a rate of 3 percent. Environmental Defense and NRDC stated that OMB Circular A-4, Regulatory analysis (2003), recommends a discount rate of 3 percent when the regulation directly affects private consumption. These commenters asserted that the proposed CAFE regulation primarily and directly affects private consumption (i.e., by affecting the sales price of new vehicles and reducing the per-mile cost of driving). NRDC also argued that OMB Circular A-4 further indicates that lower rates may be appropriate for rules that produce benefits over multiple generations.

Thus, these commenters recommended that a discount rate reflecting the social rate of time preference (i.e., a 3 percent real rate) should be used.

In response to Environmental Defense, the Union of Concerned Scientists, and NRDC, the guidelines in OMB circular A-4, New Guidelines for the Conduct of Regulatory Analysis, state that the agency should analyze the costs and benefits of a regulation at 3 percent and 7 percent discount rates, as suggested by guidance issued by the federal OMB. The 3 percent and 7 percent rates reflect two potential evaluations of impacts: Foregone private consumption and foregone capital investment, respectively. In accordance with these guidelines, the agency analyzes the impacts of costs and benefits using both discount rates. However, this guidance does not state what discount rate should be used to determine the standards.

There are several reasons for the agency's choice of 7 percent as the appropriate discount rate to determine the standards. First, OMB Circular A-4 indicates that this rate reflects the economy-wide opportunity cost of capital. The agency believes that a substantial portion of the cost of this regulation may come at the expense of other investments the auto manufacturers might otherwise make. Several large manufacturers are resource-constrained with respect to their engineering and product-development capabilities. As a result, other uses of these resources will be foregone while they are required to be applied to technologies that improve fuel economy.

Second, 7 percent is also an appropriate rate to the extent that the costs of the regulation come at the expense of consumption as opposed to investment. As explained below, the agency believes a car loan rate is an appropriate discount rate because it reflects the opportunity cost faced by consumers when buying vehicles with greater fuel economy and a higher purchase price. The agency assumed that a majority of both new and used vehicles is financed and since the vast majority of the benefits of higher fuel economy standards accrue to vehicle purchasers in the form of fuel savings, the appropriate discount rate is the car loan interest rate paid by consumers.

According to the Federal Reserve, the interest rate on new car loans made through commercial banks has closely tracked the rate on 10-year treasury notes, but exceeded it by about 3 percent. The official Administration forecast is that real interest rates on 10-year treasury notes will average about 3 percent through 2016, implying that 6 percent is a reasonable forecast for the real interest rate on new car loans. During the last five years, the interest rate on used car loans made

through automobile financing companies has closely tracked the rate on new car loans made through commercial banks, but exceeded it by about 3 percent. Consideration is given to the loan rate of used cars because some of the fuel savings resulting from improved fuel economy accrue to used car buyers. Given the 6 percent estimate for new car loans, a reasonable forecast for used car loans is 9 percent. Since the benefits of fuel economy accrue to both new and used car owners, a discount rate between 6 and 9 percent is appropriate. Assuming that new car buyers discount fuel savings at 6 percent for 5 years (the average duration of a new car loan) and that used car buyers discount fuel savings at 9 percent for 5 years (the average duration of a used car loan), the single constant discount rate that yields equivalent present value fuel savings is very close to 7 percent.

Further, reliance on the consumer borrowing rate is consistent with that of the Department of Energy (DOE) program for energy efficient appliances. For more than a decade, the Department of Energy has used consumer borrowing interest rates or "finance cost" to discount the value of future energy savings in establishing minimum energy efficiency standards for household appliances. This includes (1) the financial cost of any debt incurred to purchase appliances, principally interest charges on debt, or (2) the opportunity cost of any equity used to purchase appliances, principally interest earnings on household equity. For example, for appliances purchased in conjunction with a new home, DOE uses real mortgage interest rates to discount future energy savings. This approach is analogous to NHTSA's use of real auto loan rates to discount future gasoline savings in establishing CAFE standards.

b. The Controversy Over Cost-Benefit Analysis

Although the centrality of CBA is unarguable, the wisdom of relying on it as a critical tool for determining regulatory policy is controversial. Compare the following:

Cass R. Sunstein, Cost-Benefit Default Principles

99 Mich. L. Rev. 1651, 1656-63 (2001)

The rise of interest in cost-benefit balancing signals a dramatic shift from the initial stages of national risk regulation. Those stages were undergirded by what might be called "1970s environmentalism," which placed a high premium on immediate responses to long-neglected problems, which emphasized the existence of problems rather than their magnitude, and which was often rooted in moral indignation directed at the behavior of those who created pollution and other risks to safety and health. Defining aspects of 1970s environmentalism can be found in the apparently cost-blind national ambient air quality provisions of the Clean Air Act and in statutory provisions requiring that standards be set on the basis of "standards of performance" for which costs are a secondary consideration.

No one should deny that 1970s environmentalism has done an enormous amount of good, helping to produce dramatic improvements in many domains, above all in the context of air pollution, where ambient air quality has improved for all major pollutants. Indeed, 1970s environmentalism appears, by most accounts, to survive cost-benefit balancing, producing aggregate benefits in the trillions of dollars, well in excess of the aggregate costs. The EPA's own estimates suggest that, as a result of the Clean Air Act, there were 184,000 fewer premature deaths among people thirty years of age or older in 1990 — and also that there were 39,000 fewer cases of congestive heart failure, 89,000 fewer cases of hospital admissions for respiratory problems, 674,000 fewer cases of chronic bronchitis, and 850,000 fewer asthma attacks. The EPA finds annual costs of air pollution control at $37 billion, hardly a trivial number, but less than 4% of the annual health and welfare benefits of $1.1 trillion. Even if the EPA's own numbers show an implausibly high ratio, more conservative valuations of likely beneficial effects still reveal benefits far higher than costs.

More generally, the Office of Management and Budget ("OMB") has, for the last several years, engaged in a full accounting of the costs and benefits of all regulation. The report shows that regulatory benefits, in the aggregate, exceed regulatory costs. While the government's own numbers should be discounted — agency accounts may well be self-serving — at least they provide a good place to start. In its 2000 report, OMB finds total regulatory benefits ranging from $254 billion to $1.8 trillion, with total costs ranging from $146 billion to $229 billion, for net benefits ranging from $25 billion to $1.65 trillion. A more disaggregated picture is also encouraging. In the transportation sector, the benefits range from $84 billion to $110 billion, with the costs from $15 billion to $18 billion, for net benefits of $66 billion to $95 billion. In the net, benefits range from $9 billion to $12 billion. Much of the uncertainty stems from uncertainty about environmental benefits and costs, producing a possible range from $73 billion in net costs to over $1.5 trillion in net benefits.

For most government action, however, the benefits do seem to exceed the costs. As especially good examples, consider the following regulations, all from recent years:

Table 10.1 Regulations Yielding Net Benefits

Regulation	2000 (net benefits in millions of dollars)	2005	2010	2015
Head impact protection	310-370	1,210-1,510	1,210-1,510	1,210-1,510
Conservation reserve program	1100	1100	1100	1100
Restriction on sale and distribution of tobacco	9,020-9820	9,020-9820	9,020-10,220	9,020-9820
Acid rain controls	260-1900	260-1900	260-1900	260-1900
Energy conservation standards for refrigerators	330	330-360	510-580	440-500
New surface water treatment	50-1,200	50-1,200	50-1,200	50-1,200
Emission standards for new highway heavy-duty engines	0	110-1200	110-1200	110-1200
Disposal of PCBs	136-736	136-736	136-736	136-736
Particulates standard	0	0	12,000-113,000	-20,000-86,000

But even though the overall picture shows no cause for alarm, a closer look at federal regulatory policy shows a wide range of problems. Perhaps foremost is exceptionally poor priority setting, with substantial resources sometimes going to small problems, and with little attention to some serious problems. There are also unnecessarily high costs, with no less than $400 billion being attributable to compliance costs each year, including $130 billion on environmental protection alone. OMB's own report shows some disturbing numbers. For the next fifteen years, OSHA's methylene chloride regulation will have annual costs of $100 million and annual benefits of $40 million; a regulation calling for roadway worker protection has benefits of $30 million, but equivalent costs; the cost-benefit ratio for airbag technology innovations seems bad, though there is uncertainty in the data; EPA's regulation for financial assurance for municipal solid waste landfills has monetized benefits of $0, but costs of $100 million, and this is expected for the next fifteen years. By way of general illustration, consider the following table, all drawn from recent regulations:

Table 10.2   Regulations Failing to Yield Net Benefits

Regulation	2000 (net benefits in millions of dollars)	2005	2010	2015
Exposure to methylene chloride	-60	-60	-60	-60
Roadway worker protection	0	0	0	0
Financial assurance for municipal solid waste landfills	-100	-100	-100	-100
Pulp and paper effluent guidelines	-150 to 0	-150 to 0	-150 to 0	-240 to 0
Ozone standards	0	-235 to 240	-840 to 1190	-9,200 to -1000
Child restraint system	-40 to 40	-40 to 40	-40 to 40	-40 to 40
Vessel response plans	-220	-220	-220	-220
Nitrogen oxide emission from new fossil fuel fired steam generating units	-57 to 29	-57 to 29	-57 to 29	-57 to 29

These figures, based on the anticipated costs and benefits of each regulation adopted in a single year, show a less than coherent overall pattern, especially when Table 10.1 is put together with Table 10.2. According to one study, better allocations of health expenditures could save, each year, 60,000 more lives at no additional cost — and such allocations could maintain the current level of lives saved with $31 billion in annual savings. The point has been dramatized by repeated demonstrations that some regulations create significant substitute risks — and that with cheaper, more effective tools, regulation could achieve its basic goals while saving billions of dollars.

In these circumstances, the most attractive parts of the movement for cost-benefit analysis have been rooted not in especially controversial judgments about what government ought to be doing, but instead in a more mundane search for pragmatic instruments designed to reduce three central problems: poor priority setting, excessively costly tools, and inattention to the unfortunate side-effects of regulation. By drawing attention to costs and benefits, it should be possible to spur the most obviously desirable regulations, to deter the most obviously undesirable ones, to encourage a broader view of consequences, and to promote a search for least-cost methods of achieving regulatory goals. Notice that, so defended, cost-benefit analysis functions not only as an obstacle to unjustified regulation but also as a spur to government as well, showing that it should attend to neglected problems. If cost-benefit balancing is supported on these highly pragmatic grounds, it might well attract support from many different people with diverse theoretical commitments.

In fact, the record of cost-benefit analysis, at least within the EPA, is generally encouraging. Assessments of costs and benefits have, for example, helped produce more stringent and rapid regulation of lead in gasoline, promoted more stringent regulation of lead in drinking water, led to stronger controls on air pollution at the Grand Canyon and the Navaho Generating Station, and produced a reformulated gasoline rule that promotes stronger controls on air pollutants. In these areas, cost-benefit analysis, far from being only a check on regulation, has indeed spurred governmental attention to serious problems.

Cost-benefit analysis has also led to regulations that accomplish statutory goals at lower cost, or that do not devote limited private and public resources to areas where they are unlikely to do much good. With respect to asbestos, for example, an analysis of benefits and costs led the EPA to tie the phase-down schedules to the costs of substitutes, and also to exempt certain products from a flat ban. With respect to lead in gasoline and control of CFCs (destructive of the ozone layer), cost-benefit analysis helped promote the use of economic incentives rather than command-and-control regulation; economic incentives are much cheaper and can make more stringent regulation possible in the first place. For regulation of sludge, protection of farm workers, water pollution regulation for the Great Lakes, and controls on organic chemicals, cost-benefit analysis helped regulators produce modifications that significantly reduced costs. For modern government, one of the most serious problems appears to be not agency use of cost-benefit analysis, but frequent noncompliance with executive branch requirements that agencies engage in such analysis.

Of course cost-benefit analysis is hardly uncontroversial. Insofar as both costs and benefits are being measured by the economic criterion of "private willingness to pay," there are many problems. Poor people often have little ability, and hence little willingness, to pay, and some people will be inadequately informed and therefore show unwillingness to pay for benefits that would improve their lives. In some circumstances, regulatory agencies should seek not private willingness to pay, but reflective public judgments as expressed in public arenas. Society is not best taken as some maximizing machine, in which aggregate output is all that matters. Sometimes a regulation producing $5 million in benefits but $6 million in costs will be worthwhile, if those who bear the costs (perhaps representing dollar losses alone?) can do so easily, and if those who receive the benefits (perhaps representing lives and illnesses averted?) are especially needy. Sometimes public deliberation, with its own norms and constraints, will reveal that government should proceed even if the costs exceed the benefits, measured in terms of private willingness to pay.

In view of these problems, the strongest arguments for cost-benefit balancing are based not only on neoclassical economics, but also on an understanding of human cognition, on democratic considerations, and on an assessment of the real-world record of such balancing. Begin with cognition. People have a hard time understanding the systemic consequences of one-shot interventions. Unless they are asked to seek a full accounting, they are likely to focus on small parts of problems, producing inadequate or even counterproductive solutions. Cost-benefit analysis is a way of producing that full accounting. Ordinary people also have difficulty in calculating probabilities, and they tend to rely on rules of thumb, or heuristics, that can lead them to make systematic errors. Cost-benefit analysis is a natural corrective here. Because of intense emotional reactions to particular incidents, people often make mistakes in thinking about the seriousness of certain risks. Cost-benefit balancing should help government resist demands for regulation that are rooted in misperceptions of facts. The idea here is not that the numbers are all that matter, but that the numbers can inform public debate simply by providing relevant information.

With respect to democracy, the case for cost-benefit analysis is strengthened by the fact that interest groups are often able to use these cognitive problems strategically, thus fending off regulation that is desirable or pressing for regulation when the argument on its behalf is fragile. Here cost-benefit analysis, taken as an input into decisions, can protect democratic processes by exposing an account of consequences to public view. Of course, public deliberation might reveal that private willingness to pay greatly understates the actual benefits of the project at issue. Values will inevitably play a role in the characterization and assessment of costs and especially benefits, but a review of the record suggests that cost-benefit balancing leads to improvements, not on any controversial view of how to value the goods at stake, but simply because such balancing leads to more stringent regulation of serious problems, less costly ways of achieving regulatory goals, and a reduction in expenditures for problems that are, by any account, relatively minor.

None of these points suggests that cost-benefit analysis is a panacea for the problems that I have identified. Everything depends on questions of implementation, and there are also hard questions about appropriate valuation, questions to which I shall return. It is possible that cost benefit balancing could provide a form of "paralysis by analysis," and thus prevent desirable regulations from going forward. I have emphasized that the numbers should not be decisive. Sometimes respect for rights, or concerns about irreversibility, justify a rejection of cost-benefit balancing. Interest groups will undoubtedly portray both costs and benefits in a self-serving manner. The central point is that cost-benefit analysis can be seen, not as opposition to some abstraction called "regulation," and not as an endorsement of the economic approach to valuation, but as a real-world instrument designed to ensure that the consequences of regulation are placed before relevant officials and the public as a whole, and intended to spur attention to neglected problems while at the same time ensuring that limited resources will be devoted to areas where they will do the most good. Thus understood, cost-benefit analysis promises to attract support from a wide range of people with diverse perspectives on contested issues — a promise realized in the apparently growing bipartisan consensus on some form of cost-benefit balancing in many domains of regulatory policy.

Frank Ackerman & Lisa Heinzerling, Pricing the Priceless: Cost-Benefit Analysis of Environmental Protection

150 U. Pa. L. Rev. 1553, 1554-81 (2002)

1. The Limits of Quantification

Cost-benefit studies of regulations focus on quantified benefits of the proposed action and generally ignore other, nonquantified, health and environmental benefits. This raises a serious problem because many benefits of environmental programs — including the prevention of many nonfatal diseases and harms to the ecosystem — either have not been quantified or are not capable of being quantified at this time. Indeed, for many environmental regulations, the only benefit that can be quantified is the prevention of cancer deaths. On the other hand, one can virtually always come up with some number for the costs of environmental regulations. Thus, in practice, cost-benefit analysis tends to skew decision making against protecting public health and the environment.

For example, regulation of workers' exposure to formaldehyde is often presented as the extreme of inefficiency, supposedly costing $72 billion per life saved. This figure is based on the finding that the regulation prevents cancers that occur only in small numbers, but which have been thoroughly evaluated in numerical terms. But the formaldehyde regulation also prevents many painful but nonfatal illnesses excluded from the $72 billion figure. If described solely as a means of reducing cancer, the regulation indeed would be very expensive. But if described as a means of reducing cancer and other diseases, the regulation would make a good deal of sense. Workplace regulation of formaldehyde is not a bad answer, but it does happen to be an answer to a different question.

The formaldehyde case is by no means unique. Often, the only regulatory benefit that can be quantified is the prevention of cancer, yet cancer has a latency period of between five and forty years. When discounted at five percent, a cancer death forty years from now has a "present value" of only one-seventh of a death today. Thus, one of the benefits that most often can be quantified — allowing it to be folded into cost-benefit analysis — is also one that is heavily discounted, making the benefits of preventive regulation seem trivial.

A. Ignoring What Cannot Be Counted

A related practical problem is that even when the existence of unquantified or unquantifiable benefits is recognized, their importance is frequently ignored. Many advocates of cost-benefit analysis concede that the decision-making process must make some room for non-quantitative considerations. Some environmental benefits never have been subjected to rigorous economic evaluation. Other important considerations in environmental protection (such as the fairness of the distribution of environmental risks) cannot be quantified and priced.

In practice, however, this kind of judgment is often forgotten, or even denigrated, once all the numbers have been crunched. No matter how many times the EPA, for example, says that one of its rules will produce many benefits — like the prevention of illness or the protection of ecosystems — that cannot be quantified, the non-quantitative aspects of its analyses are almost invariably ignored in public discussions of its policies.

When the Clinton administration's EPA proposed, for example, strengthening the standard for arsenic in drinking water, it cited many human illnesses that would be prevented by the new standard but that could not be expressed in numerical terms. Subsequent public discussion of the EPA's cost-benefit analysis of this standard, however, inevitably referred only to the EPA's numerical analysis and forgot about the cases of avoided illness that could not be quantified.

B. Overstated Costs

There is also a tendency, as a matter of practice, to overestimate the costs of regulations in advance of their implementation. This happens in part because regulations often encourage new technologies and more efficient ways of doing business; these innovations reduce the cost of compliance. It is also important to keep in mind, when reviewing cost estimates, that they are usually provided by the regulated industry itself, which has an obvious incentive to offer high estimates of costs as a way of warding off new regulatory requirements.

One study found that costs estimated in advance of regulation were more than twice the actual costs in eleven out of twelve cases. Another study found that advance total cost estimates were more than 25% higher than actual costs for fourteen out of twenty-eight regulations; advance estimates were more than 25% too low in only three of the twenty-eight cases. Before the 1990 Clean Air Act Amendments took effect, industry anticipated that the cost of sulfur reduction under the amendments would be $1500 per ton: In 2000, the actual cost was under $150 per ton: Of course, not all cost-benefit analyses overstate the actual costs of regulation, but given the technology-forcing character of environmental regulations, it is not surprising to find a marked propensity to overestimate the costs of such rules.

In a related vein, many companies have begun to discover that environmental protection actually can be good for business in some respects. Increased energy efficiency, profitable products made from waste, and decreased use of raw materials are just a few of the cost-saving or even profit-making results of turning more corporate attention to environmentally protective business practices. Cost-benefit analyses typically do not take such money-saving possibilities into account in evaluating the costs of regulation.

NOTES AND QUESTIONS

1. What are the advantages of CBA? What are the disadvantages? Is it possible to be more specific in our assessment? For example, are there certain types of regulatory problems which are more amenable to CBA or make less controversial applications of CBA? Are their certain problems which are less amendable? Consider the views of John Graham, OIRA Administrator during the George W. Bush Administration:

> Public health, safety, and environmental regulation, launched with optimism during the Progressive Era, the New Deal, and the Great Society, survived the deregulatory impulses of the early Reagan years and the Gingrich era. Sometimes called "lifesaving" regulation for short, these rules differ from curative medicine because they do not seek to improve the health of identifiable individuals. Unlike an effort to save a trapped coal miner or a patient dying from kidney disease, administrative law saves lives by reducing small probabilities of premature death, injury, or illness among large numbers of anonymous workers, consumers, travelers, and residents. The names of those whose lives will be saved are unknown when the rule is adopted and may never be known. They are sometimes called "statistical lives."
>
> Thanks to advances in probability research and statistics, we now know that federal lifesaving regulations do save lives, and there is no basis for believing that these lives are any less real than the lives saved by physicians and nurses in emergency rooms. Although the evaluation literature is not as comprehensive and robust as one would prefer, there is a variety of studies showing that specific federal rules (or combinations of rules) have saved lives, and, in fact, such rules now account for a majority of the major rules issued each year by the U.S. federal government. . . .
>
> Who are the lifesaving regulators? Measured by recent rulemaking activity, they include the Department of Agriculture (USDA), the Food and Drug Administration (FDA), the Environmental Protection Agency (EPA), the Occupational Safety and Health Administration (OSHA), and the Department of Transportation (DOT). Independent agencies such as the Nuclear Regulatory Commission (NRC) and the Consumer Product Safety Commission (CPSC) play an important role outside the purview of White House oversight. Since September 11, 2001, the Department of Homeland Security (DHS) also has been charged with lifesaving responsibilities.

John D. Graham, *Saving Lives Through Administrative Law and Economics*, 157 U. Pa. L. Rev. 395, 397-99 (2008). Which issues or agencies are not on the list?

2. Given the stakes of CBA for regulations, and how much variance there is on monetizing benefits and costs, what sorts of internal checks should an agency have to help improve the quality of its analysis?

3. How does the involvement of OIRA and OMB affect the analysis? Does Circular A-4 help address any of the issues that Professors Ackerman and Heinzerling raise? Might OIRA review hurt in other respects? What if OIRA career economists or political officials injected their own biases, perhaps focusing more heavily on costs than benefits, thereby tilting in a deregulatory direction? *See* Nicholas Bagley & Richard Revesz, *Centralized Oversight of the Regulatory State*, 106 COLUM. L. REV. 1260, 1267-70 (2006), Lisa Schultz Bressman & Michael P. Vandenbergh, *Inside the Administrative State: A Critical Look at the Practice of Presidential Control*, 105 MICH. L. REV. 47, 72-74 (2006); RICHARD L. REVESZ & MICHAEL A. LIVERMORE, RETAKING RATIONALITY: HOW COST-BENEFIT ANALYSIS CAN BETTER PROTECT THE ENVIRONMENT AND OUR HEALTH 24-45 (2008). We discuss these issues further in Chapter 9.

4. Perhaps the most insistent response by proponents of economic analysis is that the critics have offered very little by way of an alternative to CBA. An intriguing proposal was recently offered by Professors Sidney Shapiro and Christopher Schroeder, which they refer to as a pragmatic regulatory impact analysis or pragmatic RIA. *See* Sidney A. Shapiro & Christopher H. Schroeder, *Beyond Cost-Benefit Analysis: A Pragmatic Reoreintation*, 32 HARV. ENVTL. L. REV. 433, 476-81 (2008). Their approach focuses on two steps: determining the "risk trigger" and then the level of regulation set by the statutory standard. The risk trigger requires the agency to make a prediction of a particular risk. If the risk were above a particular threshold, the agency would then regulate to the level of a statutory standard, which is rarely an explicitly CBA standard. This approach aims to focus the level of regulation on the statutory standard, not the monetizing of benefits and costs, which can distort decisionmaking.

---

4. Control of Appropriations

The President also has tools to control agency funding. The President participates in the appropriations process, proposing a budget and working with Congress on annual appropriations legislation. We describe the appropriations process below at pp. 608. The President can recommend budget cuts for agencies that fail to follow administration preferences (and budget increases for those that comply). The President also has discretion to withhold funds once appropriated, unless Congress prohibits such "impoundment." *See* Train v. City of New York, 420 U.S. 35 (1975); Cincinnati Soap Co. v. United States, 301 U.S. 308, 321-22 (1937). These actions can also attract political and public scrutiny. Can you think of a way that the President can effectively achieve the same result with less potential cost?

Although the President can control agency funding, the President cannot be vested with the power to reject individual budget items in an appropriations bill. In the Line Item Veto Act of 1996, 2 U.S.C. §692(a)(1), Congress attempted to give the President authority to cancel specific items of discretionary budget authority, new direct spending, and limited tax benefits in appropriations legislation for the following year. The resulting savings would be used to reduce the budget deficit. In Clinton v. City of New York, 524 U.S. 417 (1998), the Supreme Court invalidated the Line Item Veto Act on constitutional grounds. It said that the President alone cannot amend a duly-enacted appropriations statute by repealing portions of it. See 524 U.S. at 438-39. Such action requires bicameralism and presentment. The Court had used similar logic some years earlier in INS v. Chadha, reprinted below at pp. 626. As you will see, the Court said in Chadha that one house of Congress alone cannot use a so-called "legislative veto." See 462 U.S. 919, 956-58 (1983). The legislative veto allowed one house of Congress to reverse a legally-binding agency decision, but the Court held that such action requires the support of two houses plus presidential signature. Id. We explore the Court's reasoning when we get to Chadha. Think now about the wisdom of the line-item veto. On the one hand, the line-item veto seems sensible. What if Congress inserted pork-barrel spending items into appropriations legislation because it simply could not help itself; why not let the President cancel those items and allow the savings to reduce the budget deficit? Furthermore, what is the difference between declining to spend any item that Congress authorized, which is permitted, and cancelling an item, which is not? On the other hand, the line-item veto seems problematic. If an interest group wants to preserve a specific spending item (or see one go), who must it convince? Is that how the legislative process ought to ordinarily work?

a. The Debate About Regulatory Planning and Review

Few doubt that the OIRA process is an effective tool for asserting control of agency action. But many question whether this is a good thing. Because the process is so central to presidential control, we take some time to explore the debate.

Let's start with those who endorse the OIRA process. Supporters believe that it improves the legitimacy of agency action because it increases the accountability of decisions that would otherwise be made by unelected bureaucrats. Some argue, moreover, that presidential involvement is the best way to achieve accountability; elected by a national constituency, the President arguably embodies the popular will more fully than any other elected official, including the members of Congress. For arguments along these lines, see JERRY L. MASHAW, GREED, CHAOS, AND GOVERNANCE; Elena Kagan, Presidential Administration, 114 HARV. L. REV. 2245 (2001). Some also argue that, because of its coordination function and cost-benefit focus, the OIRA process improves the efficacy and efficiency of agency rulemaking. OIRA is uniquely situated to provide coordination across federal agencies. By considering all planned regulations, it can ensure that there is no conflict or redundancy among them. OIRA can spur sluggish agencies into action, providing energy that is often missing otherwise. By providing an "outsider's" view of cost-benefit analysis, OIRA is also positioned to produce more rational or efficient regulation. Agencies, if left to their own devices, may suffer from a certain mission orientation or "tunnel vision" that causes them to overestimate benefits or underestimate costs. For arguments along these lines, see Christopher C. Demuth & Douglas H. Ginsburg, *White House Review of Agency Rulemaking*, 99 HARV. L. REV. 1075 (1986).

Yet scholars have criticized the OIRA process, and in particular, its cost-benefit component. In Chapter 10, we highlighted some general objections to cost-benefit analysis — for example, some risks are difficult to monetize, such as those to the environment or future generations. *See* pp. 581. Scholars have also criticized how OIRA performs cost-benefit analysis. They argue that OIRA focuses more on costs than benefits and thus systematically undervalues regulations. *See* Nicholas Bagley & Richard L. Revesz, *Centralized Oversight of the Regulatory State*, 106 COLUM. L. REV. 1260 (2006). On this account, OIRA generally weakens rules that impose high costs as opposed to strengthening rules that promise large benefits. Part of the cause is that OIRA employs career staffers who have been around since the Reagan era and are committed to deregulation. In short, critics contend that OIRA interposes a cost-based veto that merely inhibits or delays necessary and beneficial agency regulations.

Critics also point to broader flaws in the OIRA process. Some argue that OIRA has neither the staff nor the time to perform review in an adequate manner. *See, e.g.,* Robert V. Percival, *Presidential Management of the Administrative State: The Not-So-Unitary Executive*, 51 DUKE L.J. 963, 1006-08 (2001); Mark Seidenfeld, *A Big Picture Approach to Presidential Influence on Agency Policy-Making*, 80 IOWA L. REV. 1, 14 (1994); *but see* Steven Croley, *White House Review of Agency Rulemaking: An Empirical Investigation*, 70 U. CHI. L. REV. 821 (2003). Others contend that OIRA intervenes too late in the rulemaking process to offer meaningful input. *See, e.g.,* Alan B. Morrison, *OMB Interference with Agency Rulemaking: The Wrong Way to Write a Regulation*, 99 HARV. L. REV. 1059, 1064 (1986). In addition, some argue that the OIRA process is not an open process but a secret conduit by which regulated entities can exercise undue influence over the regulatory process. *See, e.g.,* Oliver A. Houck, *President X and the New (Approved) Decisionmaking*, 36 AM. U. L. REV. 535, 551 n.94 (1987); Morrison, *OMB Interference with Agency Rulemaking*, 99 HARV. L. REV. at 1067; Erik D. Olson, *The Quiet Shift of Power: Office of Management & Budget Supervision of Environmental Protection Agency Rulemaking under Executive Order 12,291*, 4 VA. J. NAT. RESOURCES L. 1, 28-40 (1984).

Here's a chance for you to evaluate the OIRA process for yourself. Consider the return letter reprinted below concerning a draft final rule entitled "Tire Pressure Monitoring Systems." Section 13 of the Transportation Recall Enhancement, Accountability, and Documentation Act ("TREAD Act"), 49 U.S.C. §30123 (2003), requires NHTSA to issue regulations for monitoring tire pressure to ensure proper inflation. NHTSA had proposed two different systems: direct and indirect. The direct system requires a sensor in each wheel to measure tire pressure. The indirect system infers tire pressure from information provided by a vehicle's anti-lock brake system ("ABS"). During the phase-in period of the new regulation, manufacturers could choose to install either system. But thereafter, manufacturers would have to install the direct system. OIRA found that NHTSA did not select the best approach:

February 12, 2002

Mr. Kirk K. Van Tine
General Counsel
U.S. Department of Transportation
400 Seventh Street, S.W., Room 10428
Washington, DC 20590

Dear Mr. Van Tine:

The Office of Management and Budget (OMB) has been conducting an expedited review under Executive Order No. 12866 of the draft final rule prepared by the National Highway Traffic Safety Administration (NHTSA) entitled "Tire Pressure Monitoring Systems." In accordance with recent legislation passed by Congress, the draft final rule addresses an important public safety issue: the traffic crashes, injuries and fatalities that result from operating a vehicle with underinflated tires.

OMB supports NHTSA's establishment of a safety standard in this area. However, the analysis NHTSA has performed to date does not adequately demonstrate that NHTSA has selected the best available method of achieving the regulatory objective: enhanced highway safety. Therefore, we are returning this rule to NHTSA for reconsideration of two analytic concerns related to safety. First, we have identified a regulatory alternative — one that NHTSA has not explicitly analyzed — that may provide more safety to the consumer than the draft version of the final rule. In order to analyze this alternative with care, NHTSA needs to consider the impact of regulatory alternatives on the availability of anti-lock brake systems (ABS). Second, the technical foundation for NHTSA's estimates of safety benefits needs to be better explained and subjected to sensitivity analysis. My staff is available and eager to work with NHTSA to complete this analysis and the rulemaking as expeditiously as possible.

Many vehicles on the road do not have any tire pressure monitoring system. For these vehicles, the owner or driver must take the initiative to periodically check the pressure of the vehicle's tires to ensure that each of the tires is inflated to the proper pressure level. The available evidence suggests that many people do not regularly check their tires, or at least do not take the steps to achieve optimal tire inflation. As envisioned by Congress, the draft final rule would establish a Federal Motor Vehicle Safety Standard under which tire pressure monitoring systems would have to be installed in all new passenger cars, light trucks, multi-purpose vehicles and buses weighing up to 10,000 pounds.

There are two types of tire pressure monitoring systems, both now used in some vehicles, that NHTSA believes are possible compliance choices for vehicle manufacturers. "Direct" systems monitor pressure by means of instruments installed in each wheel. Indirect systems infer tire pressure from information already available in vehicles that are equipped with anti-lock brake systems. In particular, the indirect system detects pressure differences between wheels by sensing differences in their rotational speeds. Underinflated tires have smaller diameters and thus rotate faster.

The draft final rule would establish, over a four-year phase-in period, a standard under which all new vehicles would be required to have some tire pressure monitoring system. During the phase-in period, compliance could be achieved with either indirect or direct systems. However, after the phase-in, the performance standard would be altered in a way that effectively prohibits compliance with a purely indirect system. The vehicle manufacturer would instead be compelled to comply with a direct system. NHTSA believes a so-called "hybrid" system, which would combine elements of direct and indirect tire pressure monitoring, could also meet the rule's performance standard. However, no such hybrid systems have yet been installed in vehicles and the public record provides little information about their likely performance or cost.

OMB believes that a rule permitting indirect systems may provide more overall safety than a rule that permits only direct or hybrid systems. This additional safety may be available at a lower total cost to the public. Although direct systems are capable of detecting low pressure under a greater variety of circumstances than indirect systems, the indirect system captures a substantial portion of the benefit provided by direct systems. Moreover, allowing indirect systems will reduce the incremental cost of equipping vehicles with anti-lock brakes, thereby accelerating the rate of adoption of ABS technology. About one-third of new vehicle sales currently lack anti-lock brakes necessary for an indirect system. Both experimental evidence and recent real-world data have indicated a modest net safety benefit from anti-lock brakes. Before NHTSA finalizes a rule that disallows indirect systems, OMB believes that the potential safety benefits from more vehicles with anti-lock brakes need to be considered. In a preliminary analysis attached to this memorandum, OIRA staff show that a rule permitting indirect systems may provide more overall public safety at less cost to the consumer than NHTSA's preferred alternative.

OMB is also concerned that NHTSA's estimates of the number of crashes, injuries and fatalities prevented by direct systems are based on limited data and/or assumptions that have not been fully explained or analyzed. For example, NHTSA assumes that 95% of consumers would respond promptly and effectively to a warning light indicating that the vehicle has a tire inflation problem. No data, such as estimates of driver response rates to existing safety-related warning lights, are provided to support this figure. While the safety benefit estimates stemming from reduced skidding and better control are based on a well-done study, that study unfortunately was published in 1977, before the widespread existence of front-wheel drive, radial tires and SUVs and minivans. It also appears that NHTSA's use of experimental data on shorter stopping distances from proper tire inflation was based on insufficient consideration of all of the available data. In light of the limited data and insufficiently supported assumptions, OMB suggests that NHTSA's regulatory analysis should include more sensitivity analysis of the type that is found in many previous regulatory analyses prepared by NHTSA.

NHTSA should also provide additional explanation of the data choices and uncertainties underlying its analysis.

In conclusion, OMB believes that, before issuing a final rule, NHTSA needs to provide a stronger analysis of the safety issues and benefits, including a formal analysis of a regulatory alternative that would permit indirect systems after the phase-in period. Moreover, NHTSA could analyze an option that would defer a decision about the ultimate fate of indirect systems for several more years, until the potential impact on installation of anti-lock brake systems is better understood. In addition to representing sound public policy, the consideration of the suggested regulatory alternative is required under Sections 202 and 205 of the Unfunded Mandates Act (2 U.S.C. 1532 and 1535) and under Section 1(b)(5), (8), and (11) of E.O. 12866.

Accordingly, I am returning the draft final rule for reconsideration. My staff and I are available to work with the agency in the reconsideration of this matter and in the prompt promulgation of an important safety rule.

Sincerely,

/s/

John D. Graham, Ph.D.
Administrator
Office of Information and Regulatory Affairs

Enclosure
cc: Dr. Jeffrey W. Runge

OIRA Enclosure (2/12/2002)

This enclosure describes in detail our concerns with the draft Final Economic Assessment (FEA). It presents — for illustrative purposes — an analysis of an option that has the potential to achieve substantially greater safety at lower cost than the draft final rule. The enclosure also includes a discussion of some of the major uncertainties and potential biases associated with key assumptions in the FEA and suggests possible ways to address them.

Background

After a four-year phase-in, the draft final rule would require that tire pressure monitoring systems (TPMS) be able to detect when up to four tires are 25 percent or more underinflated. The FEA includes analysis of direct and "hybrid" TPMS. Direct systems monitor tire pressure directly by means of sensors installed in each wheel. Hybrid systems would monitor tire pressure by combining elements from a direct system with elements from an indirect system. Indirect systems infer tire pressure from information already available in vehicles equipped with anti-lock brake systems (ABS). They detect pressure differences between tires by sensing differences in wheel rotational speeds. Underinflated tires have smaller diameters and thus rotate faster. No indirect systems currently available can meet a four-tire standard. The rulemaking record is also unclear on whether hybrid systems could do so.[3] Nevertheless, we assume for the sake of argument that NHTSA is correct in its belief that hybrid systems could meet a four-tire requirement.

The FEA presents quantified estimates of two components of cost: "vehicle" (e.g., hardware) and maintenance costs for each system. The benefit estimates include the value of fuel savings and reduced tire tread wear that would result from each system. The FEA presents the difference between costs and the fuel and tire wear savings as "net costs." The FEA also includes three categories of quantified safety benefits: reduced skidding and better control, shorter stopping distances, and fewer flat tires and blowouts. For direct systems, the FEA estimates a net cost (i.e., total cost minus the value of fuel economy and tire tread wear benefits) of $1,240 million per year and safety benefits of 10,271 injuries and 141 fatalities averted per year when applied to the entire on-road fleet. For hybrid systems, the FEA estimates a net cost of $862 million per year with safety benefits of 8,722 injuries and 124 fatalities averted per year.

1. Evaluation of Alternatives

The FEA does not meaningfully compare viable alternatives. Specifically, NHTSA did not analyze the benefits and costs associated with an alternative requirement that would allow indirect systems to continue to be used indefinitely (i.e., a 30 percent underinflation, 1-tire standard). There are in excess of 2 million TPMS-equipped vehicles on the road today, the vast majority of which are indirect systems.

Based on information in the Preliminary Economic Assessment (PEA) and the FEA, a requirement that allowed indirect systems indefinitely could achieve comparable and, quite possibly, substantially greater safety benefits at lower cost than those associated with the final rule. An option that allows indirect systems will provide an inducement to install anti-lock brakes (ABS) on more vehicles. We present the following analysis for illustrative purposes only. We believe that

---

[3] We were unable to locate anything in the rulemaking record indicating that hybrid systems would be able to detect four simultaneously low tires. The rulemaking record on the performance and cost of hybrid systems appears to be limited to two paragraphs in one comment. That comment stated, "The current releases of indirect TPMS will require the equivalent of the addition of two direct tire pressure sensors and a radio-frequency receiver to meet the requirement to detect two simultaneously low tires under alternative 2 [emphasis added]." Under the proposed rule, "alternative 2" would have required the detection of up to three, not four, simultaneously low tires. That comment also asserted, ". . . the maximum cost to implement these changes to be about 60% of the cost of a full direct TPMS for vehicles already equipped with an ABS." The commenter provided no further information on the performance or cost of such a system. To date, no such system has ever been produced or installed on a vehicle.

the example shows that indirect systems warrant a complete and careful analysis. At the same time, we do not consider our example to be definitive. Further refinements by NHTSA may be necessary.

A. Costs and Benefits of an Indirect System

Based on information contained in the PEA, and consistent with assumptions in the FEA, we estimate that an indirect system would cost an average of about $30 per vehicle in "vehicle" (e.g., hardware) costs and an additional $13 in maintenance costs, or a total of about $720 million per year. Indirect systems would result in about $200 million in fuel and tread wear savings combined for a net cost of about $520 million per year. We estimate this option could achieve safety benefits of about 5,000 injuries and 70 fatalities averted per year when applied to the entire on-road fleet.

B. The Anti-lock Brake Effect — Induced ABS

Indirect versus direct systems — Allowing indirect systems likely would induce vehicle manufacturers to equip a greater percentage of the new vehicle fleet with ABS.[4] This is because vehicles not equipped with ABS will need a more-expensive, direct system to comply with the rule. For direct systems, the FEA estimates vehicle cost of $66.50 per vehicle. For vehicles already equipped with ABS, the vehicle cost of an indirect system would be $13.29 per vehicle.[5]

Thus, a manufacturer who decided to install ABS in a vehicle that would not have ABS otherwise can reduce the (vehicle) cost of compliance by about $53 per vehicle. In other words, a rule that would allow indirect systems would reduce the incremental cost of adding ABS by $53, since the manufacturer could avoid the cost of a direct system.[6]

According to NHTSA, the average cost of ABS is about $240. Therefore, a manufacturer could save about 22 percent ($53/$240) of the cost of equipping a vehicle with ABS by avoiding the cost of a direct TPMS. Assuming a price elasticity of demand for ABS of 1[7] (i.e., each 1 percent decline in the price of ABS

---

[4] For model year 2000 about 68 percent of new cars and light trucks were equipped with ABS. Although the percentage of new vehicles equipped with ABS generally has increased in recent years, it appears to be leveling off. In 1999, 68.3 percent of the fleet was equipped with ABS.

[5] The average cost of $30 mentioned above is higher because it is a weighted average of both direct and indirect systems, since vehicles without ABS would require direct systems.

[6] The remainder of this analysis assumes that the consumer does not correctly perceive the difference in maintenance cost. If he or she did, the effective "discount" on ABS would be substantially greater — an additional $40 or so when comparing direct with indirect systems.

[7] We do not have an empirically-based estimate of the price elasticity of demand for anti-lock brakes. However, NHTSA reported in the draft preamble to the final rule that one vehicle manufacturer said it would add ABS to an additional 400,000 vehicles if indirect systems are permitted. This alone accounts for more than 1/3 of the additional ABS our illustrative example assumes. In public comments, all vehicle manufacturers supported a 30%, 1-tire standard. Thus it does not appear that this manufacturer made this statement in the context of a standard that today's indirect systems cannot meet.

induces a 1 percent increase in quantity demanded), a 22 percent reduction in the cost of ABS would result in a 22 percent increase in the number of new vehicles equipped with ABS. Thus, we could reasonably expect about 7.4 percent of the new vehicle fleet (22 percent of the 33 percent of the new vehicle fleet without ABS), or about 1.1 million vehicles, to be equipped with ABS as a direct result of this option.

A recent study in a peer-reviewed journal[8] estimated that light-duty vehicles equipped with ABS are between 4 and 9 percent less likely to be involved in fatal crashes of all types. (These estimates are not statistically significant. However, they appear to represent the best estimates available at this time.) Overall, there are about 40,000 fatalities per year involving these vehicles. Thus 7.4 percent of the fleet accounts for about 2,960 fatalities per year. Reducing these by 4 to 9 percent would mean 118 to 266 fatalities[9] averted per year as a result of additional ABS induced by the rule. Adding these to the 70 fatalities averted from indirect systems without the additional ABS yields a total of 188-336 fatalities averted or between 47 and 195 more than with direct systems.

We calculated the nationwide aggregate cost of the additional ABS systems as follows: About 1.1 million (7.4% × 15 million new vehicles/yr.) more vehicles would be equipped with ABS. Since the FEA already accounted for these vehicles having to install direct systems, the increment to the FEA aggregate cost estimate is about $206 million per year (1.1 million vehicles × $187 ($240 − $53)). This brings the net cost of the indirect system approach (including the cost of additional ABS systems) to about $726 ($520 + $206) million per year, or about $514 million per year less than the net cost of direct systems.

Indirect versus hybrid systems — The FEA estimated the vehicle cost of a hybrid system to be $39.90 per vehicle. This is about $26.50 less than the vehicle cost of a direct system, or about half of the savings per vehicle associated with indirect systems. Following the approach we used for indirect systems, manufacturers who choose a hybrid option over a direct system can also effectively capture the savings as a cost reduction for providing ABS. Under the same assumptions we used above, this would result in an additional 3.7% of the new vehicle fleet (about 550,000 vehicles) being equipped with ABS. This, in turn translates into an additional 59-133 more fatalities averted and about $117 million additional net cost compared with hybrid systems with no ABS effect. The total benefits for hybrid systems would then be 183-257 (124 + 59 and 124 + 133) fatalities averted per year and the net cost would be about $979 million per year. Including the ABS effect, allowing indirect systems would avert between 5 (188-183) and 79

---

[8] Farmer, Charles M., "New evidence concerning fatal crashes of passenger vehicles before and after adding antilock braking systems," ACCIDENT ANALYSIS AND PREVENTION, 33 (2001), 361-69.

[9] The study we relied upon did not estimate ABS effectiveness rates for injuries. We estimated injury reduction benefits attributable to ABS by assuming that injury reduction benefits would occur in the same proportion to fatalities (i.e., between 70 and 75 injuries per fatality) as NHTSA estimated in the FEA.

(336-257) more fatalities and about $250 million in cost per year than would hybrid systems.

The table below summarizes these estimates.

System	National Estimates (without ABS Effect)[10]				National Estimates (with ABS Effect)		
	Cost per vehicle	Annual Net Cost ($millions)	Annual Injuries Averted	Annual Fatalities Averted	Annual Net Cost ($millions)	Annual Injuries Averted	Annual Fatalities Averted
Direct	$66.50	$1,240	10,271	141	$1,240	10,271	141
Hybrid	$39.30	$ 862	8,733	124	$ 979	12,888-18,099	183-257
Indirect	$13.29	$ 520	5,000	70	$ 726	13,429-24,000	188-336

Because of this possibility, NHTSA should carefully evaluate the benefits and costs of an option that would allow indefinite use of today's indirect systems. We hope that the illustrative example we provide here will serve as a useful starting point for such an analysis. As a longer-term project, NHTSA should also evaluate the on-road performance of current direct and indirect systems.

2. Safety Benefit Estimates

The quantified safety benefits in the FEA are divided among 3 categories: reduced skidding and better control, shorter stopping distances, and fewer flat tires and blowouts. The magnitude of each is directly related to vehicle owners' responses to low pressure warning lights. This section describes some assumptions about several uncertain or unknown key parameters that affect the magnitude of the safety benefit estimates. Each assumption warrants some empirical grounding and/or sensitivity analysis.

A. Vehicle Owner Response to Warning Light

The safety benefits from a TPMS system depend critically on how vehicle owners respond when the low pressure warning light comes on. There can be no benefit if owners ignore the warning light. The FEA assumes that 95 percent of all vehicle owners will respond to the warning light promptly and appropriately. In the Preliminary Economic Assessment, NHTSA assumed 60 percent of vehicle owners would respond to a light that did not specify which tire(s) was low by inflating their tires to the correct pressure and 80 percent in cases where the

---

[10] The estimates for the direct and hybrid systems are take from the draft FEA. The estimates for an indirect system are OMB estimates based on information in the PEA and, to the maximum extent possible, consistent with assumptions NHTSA made in its draft FEA.

dashboard light indicated which tire was low. Neither the PEA nor the FEA provides an empirical basis for any of these response rates. At the same time, it is also likely that some vehicle owners will come to rely exclusively on the warning light to inform them of tire pressure and will reduce the frequency with which they normally check their tires. To the extent that this occurs, the benefits of the rule may decline, and may do so at different rates depending on the technology.

To provide a stronger foundation for its analysis, NHTSA should provide some empirical basis for this critical component of the analysis. NHTSA could, for example, perform an analysis of responses to other dashboard warnings. In any event, NHTSA should perform sensitivity analyses using alternative response rates. We believe that a carefully conducted survey and analysis of driver behavior and corresponding tire pressures in TPMS-equipped vehicles currently on the road would go a long way toward refining the estimates based on this parameter.

B. Reduced Skidding and Better Control

In the PEA, NHTSA stated it was not able to quantify this category of benefits. No commenters disagreed or suggested ways that NHTSA might do so. In the FEA, NHTSA estimated the benefits from reduced skidding and better control using a 1977 study, "Tri-Level Study of the Causes of Traffic Accidents, Final Report (Report)." This Report provides great detail on the circumstances associated with 420 crashes. It was well-done and for a long time served as a useful data source for understanding the causes of crashes. Unfortunately, because of changes in the nature of vehicles on the road, the report's value has diminished with the passage of time. The skidding and control component of the benefit estimates for this rule appears to stem from analysis of about six of the 420 crashes analyzed in the report. The small sample size alone is enough to warrant a sensitivity analysis. Perhaps more importantly, though, the relevance of the vehicles and tires involved to the fleet of vehicles that this rule will affect is not clear. For example, none of the six vehicles in the Report had front-wheel drive, none were sport utility vehicles (SUVs) or minivans, and, in all likelihood, none were equipped with radial tires. The newest of the vehicles involved in these crashes was a 1972 Pontiac. One of the six involved a 1960 Ford Falcon — a vehicle produced more than 45 years before the final rule will be fully effective. NHTSA should also provide more support for the assumption that these crashes are directly relevant to this rule.

C. Shorter Stopping Distances

Stopping distances vary greatly among vehicles and road and tire conditions. They also vary from test to test under the same vehicle, road, and tire conditions. All of the improved stopping distance benefits were based on tests of two vehicles: a Dodge Caravan minivan and a Ford Ranger pickup truck. The FEA appears to rely exclusively on the Caravan test results to estimate benefits for the passenger car fleet (but not for the minivan or SUV fleet). The FEA also appears to rely exclusively on the Ford Ranger test results to estimate benefits for the light truck fleet (including minivans and SUVs).

NHTSA chose not to continue to use results from a passenger car tested on a NHTSA test track. These results had formed part of the basis for benefit estimates in the PEA. They showed little, if any, effect of reduced pressure on stopping distances. This result is not surprising, for the same reason that the rule is expected to yield fuel economy and tread wear benefits — reduced pressure increases rolling resistance, and could be expected to improve stopping distances under at least some conditions. Although NHTSA received no comments suggesting these results were unrepresentative, it did not use them because of a belief that the test road surface was not sufficiently worn to be representative.

NHTSA does not explain why it believes the minivan test results better represent passenger car performance than NHTSA's own passenger car results. NHTSA also does not explain why it believes the pickup truck test results better represent minivan and SUV performance than the minivan test results.

Given the small sample size and variability of stopping distances, it is unclear whether any of the test results available to NHTSA are representative of much more than those particular vehicles. NHTSA should estimate benefits using its passenger car test results to represent passenger cars, the minivan test results to represent minivans and SUVs, and the pickup truck test results to represent pickup trucks. NHTSA should also perform some sensitivity calculations around the corresponding benefit estimates.

D. Flat Tires and Blowouts

In the PEA, NHTSA stated it did not have sufficient data to reliably estimate the magnitude of this category of benefits. Commenters agreed that there will be some benefits in this area.

However, no commenters disagreed with NHTSA's initial assessment that they could not be quantified. As was the case with skidding and control, none suggested ways NHTSA might estimate them. In the FEA, NHTSA produced an estimate of these benefits by assuming that 20 percent of blowouts are caused by low tire pressure. This new assumption warrants further justification and a sensitivity analysis, at the least.

NOTES AND QUESTIONS

1. In this return letter, OIRA recommended that NHTSA allow automakers to install indirect systems in new cars rather than direct systems, at their discretion. Why? OIRA claimed that allowing automakers to install indirect systems

would increase the installation of ABS and therefore improve "overall safety." How does OIRA know whether manufacturers would install more ABS? If it cannot be sure, why would OIRA prefer this option?

2. OIRA also claimed that the draft rule relied on unreliable data about the safety benefits of direct systems. Who is in a better position to evaluate such data: OIRA or NHTSA? Consider who works for OIRA: scientists or economists?

3. In its final rule, NHTSA rejected OIRA's suggestions. *See* Final Rule, Federal Motor Vehicle Safety Standards, Tire Pressure Monitoring Systems, Control and Display, 67 Fed. Reg. 38704 (2002). NHTSA argued that (1) the TREAD Act requires NHTSA to improve tire safety not overall auto safety, *id.* at 38718; (2) there was "no reliable basis" for concluding that permitting the installation of indirect systems would increase the installation of ABS, *id.* at 38719; and (3) there was "no statistically reliable basis for concluding that ABS reduces fatalities," which meant there was no reason to encourage the installation of ABS, *id.* Why was the agency free to reject OIRA's suggestions?

4. Although NHTSA did not allow automakers generally to choose indirect systems in place of direct systems, it did allow them to install indirect systems during a phase-in period. *See* Federal Motor Vehicle Safety Standard No. 138, 49 C.F.R. §571.138 pt. S4.2 (2002). The Court of Appeals for the Second Circuit reversed and remanded the rule to the agency because the rule allowed automakers to install indirect systems even for a limited time. *See* Public Citizen, Inc. v. Minetta, 340 F.3d 39 (2d Cir. 2003). Specifically, the court found that the rule in this respect was (a) contrary to the statute and (b) arbitrary and capricious. Can you make the textual argument that the rule is contrary to the statute? Section 13 of the TREAD Act provides: "The Secretary of Transportation shall complete a rulemaking for a regulation to require a warning system in new motor vehicles to indicate to the operator when *a* tire is significantly under-inflated" (emphasis added). Do both indirect and direct systems satisfy this language? Or does the language preclude one? Assuming that the statutory language permits both systems, why might NHTSA's rule be arbitrary and capricious based on the information that the agency had about how well indirect systems work for their asserted purpose?

Now consider the following prompt letter to NHTSA. Ask yourself whether the letter reveals a different limitation of OIRA — not based on the quality of its analysis but on the selectivity of its intervention. Why did OIRA choose this problem from among all those that NHTSA confronts? Does the letter offer an explanation? What if OIRA fails to issue a prompt letter in response to equally or more pressing problems — for example, NHTSA's lax investigation and regulation of faulty acceleration systems that led to a massive recall of Toyotas in 2009 and

2010, only after significant public harm? *See* Auto Safety Regulator Under Scrutiny After the Toyota Fiasco, available at *http://www.ombwatch.org/node/10851*.

December 7, 2001

The Honorable Michael P. Jackson
Deputy Secretary
Department of Transportation
400 Seventh Street, SW
Washington, DC 20590

Dear Mr. Jackson:

The purpose of this letter is to request that the Department of Transportation and the National Highway Traffic Safety Administration (NHTSA) consider giving greater priority to modifying its frontal occupant protection standard by establishing a high-speed, frontal offset crash test. Such a test would seek to improve protection for the lower extremities of automobile and light truck occupants. A frontal offset crash test — which is currently conducted in the European New Car Assessment Program and by the Insurance Institute for Highway Safety — involves crashing a portion of the test vehicle's front end (instead of the entire front end) to evaluate the structural integrity of the vehicle, including the "toe pan," which helps protect the feet and legs of occupants.

Historically, one of NHTSA's principal safety goals has been to enhance the protection of vehicle occupants involved in crashes that result in life-threatening injuries to the head, neck, and chest. Safety standards requiring the installation of seat belts and air bags have reduced the frequency and severity of such injuries. As a result, more people are surviving previously fatal crashes. However, I believe there is room for improvement in the area of lower extremity injuries. I believe that paying more attention to the protection of lower extremities could build upon NHTSA's impressive record of success in addressing upper-body injury risks. I was therefore encouraged to see an offset test rulemaking in NHTSA's recent Regulatory Agenda and urge the agency to provide this initiative significant priority.

Substantial safety improvements may be possible. Despite the existing occupant protection systems in cars and light trucks, about 3,300 people are killed and 400,000 are injured annually in frontal offset crashes. Although lower-body injuries are rarely fatal, they are often serious enough to require lengthy hospitalization and rehabilitation, and they sometimes result in years of chronic pain and impairment.

Although I realize that more thorough benefit assessment needs to be done, I suspect that the benefits of such action could substantially exceed its costs. As NHTSA noted in November 2000, a report prepared for the Australian government estimates that a new offset test may result in a 15 percent reduction in the "cost of trauma" (the product of the frequency of injuries and the cost to the public). Most of these benefits would result from a reduction in lower body and leg injuries. NHTSA's preliminary estimates then were that, for vehicles that would not currently pass this test, structural modifications would cost $14 per vehicle. Assuming that 25 percent of the fleet would need to be modified, the total annual cost to consumers would be $60 million.

If you determine that this matter should be given greater priority, a number of questions would still need to be investigated. Most importantly, NHTSA would have to refine its estimates of the specific safety benefits that a new offset test would generate. Such estimates would need to take into account potential losses in existing safety benefits due to possible changes in vehicle structure and design. For example, NHTSA would need to examine whether implementing a new offset test might create disbenefits in other crash modes such as side impacts. NHTSA would also need to estimate the number of existing vehicles that would have to be modified to pass the revised safety standard. In exploring these issues, NHTSA should assess the incremental benefits and costs of setting the new crash test at different speeds. NHTSA should also evaluate the relative merits of using different types of barriers as a potential test device. I would also encourage NHTSA to consider the possible benefits of subjecting the supporting technical and economic analyses to external peer review. I believe that taking these steps would help NHTSA ascertain the cost effectiveness of instituting the contemplated test and develop an appropriate phase-in schedule.

In requesting that NHTSA give greater priority to considering the expansion of its frontal occupant protection standard, I recognize that NHTSA faces resource constraints and other legislative mandates, such as the TREAD Act. Accordingly, I simply request that NHTSA consider whether this matter should be given greater priority in the foreseeable future. I would appreciate an initial response to this inquiry within 60 days. Please do not hesitate to contact me or Jeff Hill if you would like to discuss this matter further.

Sincerely,

/s/

John D. Graham
Administrator
Office of Information and Regulatory Affairs

cc: The Honorable Jeffrey W. Runge

5. *Presidential Directives*

The President can assert control of agency action by issuing pre-regulatory directives in the form of official memoranda to executive-branch agency heads. Such directives, particularly notable during the Clinton administration, instruct an agency to take a particular action under its existing regulatory authority — such as telling the FDA to regulate cigarettes and other tobacco products under the Food, Drug and Cosmetics Act. They are different from prompt letters because they are signed by the President not another White House official, like the OIRA Administrator. There can be no doubt that presidential directive reflects presidential preferences.

Elena Kagan, who brought to academic attention the use of presidential directives, argued that the practice had good normative implications for agency action. *See* Elena Kagan, *Presidential Administration*, 114 Harv. L. Rev. 2245 (2001). Because presidential directives come from the President, they enhance the accountability of the resulting agency action more so than other measures, whether from other White House officials or members of Congress. Because they are open to public view, they also enhance the accountability of agency action. Voters cannot evaluate what they cannot see; nor can they hold any official responsible for such action. Thus, presidential directives do not suffer from the black-box quality of much White House involvement in agency rulemaking (though return and prompt letters are also publicly available). Presidential directives have another normative value. To the extent that presidential directives spur a sluggish agency into action, they can improve regulatory efficacy.

Despite these arguments, presidential directives raise difficult legal questions. Where does the President derive authority to order an agency to take a particular action? It is one thing to review such actions to ensure that the agency is "faithfully executing" the laws or even to recommend certain actions as part of this duty. But most regulatory statutes delegate final say to agencies, not the President. Do those statutes grant implied authority to the President? *See* Kevin M. Stack, *The President's Statutory Powers to Administer the Laws*, 106 Colum. L. Rev. 263 (2006). What is the difference between making policy, by issuing a presidential directive, and influencing policy, by issuing a prompt letter or return letter or threatening to remove the agency head?

Even if legally authorized, what are the dangers of presidential directives? Perhaps presidential directives allow the President to alter agency decisions too effectively and too easily, without incurring the costs of legislation. Thus, if widely used, they would be an effective end-run around the rigors of the legislative process. Or perhaps they make it impossible for agencies to honestly evaluate other considerations, such as statutory arguments against cigarette regulation. Thus, they have a kind of a skewing effect on the administrative process in favor of presidential preferences. Do you agree? We revisit this question after reading a case called Food & Drug Administration v. Brown & Williamson Tobacco Corp., 529 U.S. 120 (2000), excerpted at pp. 690-704.

Although the use of presidential directives has attracted a lot of attention, that use appears to be quite limited. *See* David J. Barron, *From Takeover to Merger: Reforming Administrative Law in the Age of Agency Politicization*, 76 Geo. Wash. L. Rev. 1095, 1117-21 (2008) (suggesting that President Clinton issued at most half a dozen a year). The President only has so much time and personally intervenes in an official capacity (or any capacity, for that matter) on a highly selective basis. Much more prevalent is OIRA involvement, which we discussed above, and other White House and agency involvement, which we discuss below.

6. Other White House and Agency Involvement

Beyond the President and OIRA, many others also attempt to influence various agencies to change their regulations. In the White House, they sit in offices or hold positions that include: Chief of Staff, Legislative Affairs, Public Liaison, Intergovernmental Liaison, Press Secretary, White House Counsel, Domestic Policy Counsel, National Economic Council, Political Affairs, Office of the Vice President (including the Council on Competitiveness in the Bush I administration), Office of Policy Development, Office of Management and Budget (other than OIRA), Council of Economic Advisors, Council on Environmental Quality, Office of the United States Trade Representative, Office of Science and Technology Policy, and the National Security Council.

White House offices often contact an agency in informal and invisible ways, through phone calls or meetings. Sometimes they contact OIRA to advocate on their behalf in the regulatory review process. Moreover, they can hold views that conflict with one another, raising difficult questions of which office represents the President's views. If these offices impart their own views rather than the President's views, do they render agency regulations more "accountable"? Note that, of the offices mentioned above, none are run by officials who are elected or even subject to Senate confirmation. Of the White House agencies that we have discussed here, only OIRA and its parent, OMB, are run by Senate-confirmed officials.

Other federal agencies are also involved in the rulemaking activities of their siblings. The Department of Energy might contact the Department of Transportation or EPA concerning their respective regulations. The Secretary of the Treasury might contact the Chair of the Federal Reserve Board or the SEC. Such contacts, even if informal and largely invisible to outside participants, might promote inter-agency coordination. When agencies work together, they are less likely to produce overlapping or conflicting regulations. Other agencies also might transmit presidential preferences or executive-branch interests, particularly if the "target" agency is independent. Thus, other federal agencies may be an indirect source of political accountability. At the same time, these agencies might make things worse not better. They might contribute to a sense of turf warfare rather than collaboration, or they might convey narrow interests rather than broader governmental ones.

7. Congressional Control of Agency Action

Like the President, Congress seeks to assert control of agency action. Perhaps this surprises you: after all, Congress agreed to give the power away to the agency in the first place. But the impulse to delegate does not negate the impulse to control; indeed, the two go hand in hand. Once Congress decides to delegate, it has an immediate and ongoing interest in ensuring that subsequent agency action roughly tracks legislative preferences. What does this interest reflect? Why does Congress seek to assert control? Similar to the President, Congress may assert control for strategic reasons — to ensure that agency action reflects the preferences of the constituents who can help its members get reelected. Or Congress may assert control for more public-regarding reasons — to ensure that agency action comports with statutory mandates and popular preferences. What are the normative implications of congressional control? It may enhance (or decrease) political accountability, agency expertise, and other important values.

This section examines the main tools of congressional control. As with the tools of presidential control, we do not focus here on informal contacts per se, such as telephone calls or office meetings between members of Congress and agency officials. Rather, we concentrate on more formal and public means used to ensure compliance with the preferences of members of Congress, such as enacting restrictive legislation or conducting oversight hearings. We also discuss tools that Congress has sought to use but the Supreme Court has declared unconstitutional. In some sense, these tools occupy a middle ground between the informal contacts and the formal statutes that Congress can use to assert control of agency action. We will ask why the Court has rejected them.

As you explore these tools, consider how each works for Congress. As with the tools of presidential control, consider the varying degrees of formality, transparency, and effectiveness. Also consider their normative implications. Can Congress confer on agency action the same level of accountability, efficacy, or efficiency as the President? Why or why not? What dangers does congressional control of agency action impose?

Before we continue, note an additional complication: Congress must obtain information about agency action to know whether legislative intervention is necessary. We have already noted that the President also confronts this problem. How can members of Congress know when agency action departs from their preferences if they lack information about such action? Some actions are the sort that members of Congress have a personal interest in watching or are too high profile to ignore. For example, members of Congress may have a personal interest in auto safety, health care, or financial reform, and they may constantly monitor the agencies in charge. Issues like the terrorist attacks of 9-11 or Hurricane Katrina are known to all, and members of Congress join the rest of the country in watching the agencies that handle them. But most issues do not fall into either category, and members of Congress face considerable costs in monitoring them. Consider that every minute spent monitoring agency action is a minute less spent on other important (or electorally significant) activities. We have noted that Executive Order No. 12,866 is quite helpful to the White House for reducing the costs of monitoring agency action because it produces relevant information about planned and proposed regulations. On the basis of this information, the White House can decide whether intervention is necessary. Thus, the OIRA process is an informational tool as well as a control tool.

Congress also possesses informational tools that require agencies to report their activities, but those tools have not been nearly as effective for legislative monitoring. For example, Congress sometimes writes specific reporting requirements into organic statutes. NHTSA was subject to a reporting requirement in the 1966 Motor Vehicle Safety Act:

SEC. 120. (a) The Secretary shall prepare and submit to the President for transmittal to the Congress on March 1 of each year a comprehensive report on the administration of this Act for the preceding calendar year. Such report shall include but not
be restricted to (1) a thorough statistical compilation of the accidents and injuries
occurring in such year; (2) a list of Federal motor vehicle safety standards prescribed
or in effect in such year; (3) the degree of observance of applicable Federal motor
vehicle standards; (4) a summary of all current research grants and contracts
together with a description of the problems to be considered by such grants and contracts; (5) an analysis and evaluation, including relevant policy recommendations,
of research activities completed and technological progress achieved during such
year; and (6) the extent to which technical information was disseminated to the scientific community and consumer-oriented information was made available to the
motoring public.

NHTSA

This reporting requirement has limitations as a monitoring mechanism; it
pertains to implementation activities in the *preceding* calendar year. It does not
furnish information about agency action while still under consideration, earlier in
the process when political intervention is particularly effective.

In 1996, Congress enacted a generally applicable provision that goes further.
It is called the Congressional Review Act ("CRA"), 5 U.S.C. §§801-803. The
CRA requires both independent and executive-branch agencies to submit "major"
rules, as well as other information including any cost-benefit analysis of the rule,
to Congress and the General Accounting Office before the rule may take effect.
See 5 U.S.C. §801(a)(1)(B). Major rules do not become effective for at least 60
days, allowing time for congressional review. *See* 5 U.S.C. §801(a)(2)(B)(3). The
Act provides expedited procedures by which a member of Congress may propose
a joint resolution of disapproval of the rule. *See* 5 U.S.C. §802. A joint resolution
can overturn a rule either with the President's approval or with a super-majority
vote over the President's veto. *See* 5 U.S.C. §801(a). Despite the potential of the
CRA, Congress has rarely enacted a joint resolution. Perhaps Congress is confronted with too much information, which can be just as problematic as too little
information. Facing a mountain of agency documents, congressional staff members (who have lots of other work to do) have no idea even where to begin. Perhaps
Congress simply lacks the capacity to act with the requisite dispatch. How quickly
can Congress muster the support to enact a joint resolution, even with expedited
procedures? Or perhaps the information comes too late in the rulemaking process
to make less-draconian adjustments than complete disapproval of a generally
desirable rule.

How else may Congress obtain information about agency action? That is a
question that pervades our discussion of congressional control. As you read below,
watch for tools that serve an informational function in addition to or in support of
a control function.

8. *New Legislation*

To assert control of agency action, Congress can enact new legislation. Legislation might abolish an agency or restrict its authority. Less drastically, it might

preclude a particular agency regulation or compel a different regulation. The amendment to the 1966 Motor Vehicle Safety Act prohibiting ignition interlock devices, which appears later in this chapter, pp. 793-94, is a good example. Congress enacted this amendment because of widespread public resistance to the ignition interlock option that NHTSA had permitted automakers to adopt. Some might say that such legislation is absolute vindication of popular will by a politically accountable Congress. Some might regard Congress as having more self-interested motives: the electoral benefits from the legislation outweighed the costs.

Often, Congress can assert control of agency action by simply threatening to restrict an agency's authority or reverse an agency's rule. From a political standpoint, you can see that such threats have an advantage and disadvantage, which are actually flip sides of the same coin. The advantage is that threats are far easier to make than new legislation is to enact. Threats can come from any member of Congress or any congressional committee, in private settings, such as a phone call or meeting, or in public contexts, such as a press statement or oversight hearing. New legislation comes only one way. It is subject to the requirements of bicameralism and presentment. These requirements were designed as onerous to slow the production of hasty and improvident law and have been made even more so by the complexities of the modern legislative process. The disadvantage of threats is that agencies can ignore them. Agencies are free to evaluate whether Congress has the requisite political support to follow through. This is a fairly high-stakes game of chicken. Nevertheless, only new legislation is certain to produce change. When Congress amends a statute, the agency has no choice but to implement it. Pause to consider whether threats have the same normative implications as actually enacting new legislation. What if the threat only comes from one member or one committee or even one house of Congress? If the threat works to control agency action, does it enhance accountability to the same degree as a statutory amendment would?

9. *Appropriations Legislation*

Congress can also use appropriations legislation to restrict funding for a particular agency or regulatory program. When Congress creates an agency or regulatory program, it ordinarily funds them on an annual basis through separate appropriations legislation. Here is a concise description of appropriations legislation, focusing on "regular" appropriations measures:

> Congress annually considers several appropriations measures, which provide funding for numerous activities, such as national defense, education, and homeland security, as well as general government operations. These measures are considered by Congress under certain rules and practices, referred to as the *congressional appropriations process.* . . .
>
> When considering appropriations measures, Congress is exercising the power granted to it under the Constitution, which states, "No money shall be drawn from the Treasury, but in Consequence of Appropriations made by Law." The power to

appropriate is a legislative power. Congress has enforced its prerogatives through certain laws. The so-called Antideficiency Act, for example, strengthened the application of this section by, in part, explicitly prohibiting federal government employees and officers from making contracts or other obligations in advance of or in excess of an appropriation, unless authorized by law; and providing administrative and criminal sanctions for those who violate the act. Under law, public funds, furthermore, may only be used for purpose(s) for which Congress appropriated the funds. . . .

The House and Senate Committees on Appropriations have jurisdiction over the annual appropriations measures. Each committee has 12 subcommittees and each subcommittee has jurisdiction over one annual, regular appropriations bill that provides funding for departments and agencies under the subcommittee's jurisdiction. . . .

The House and Senate annually consider several regular appropriations measures. Each House and Senate appropriations subcommittee has jurisdiction over one regular bill. Due to the 2007 House and Senate appropriations committees' reorganization, each chamber considers 12 regular bills. Regular appropriations bills contain a series of unnumbered paragraphs with headings; generally reflecting a unique budget account. The basic unit of regular and supplemental appropriations bills is the account. Under these measures, funding for each department and large independent agency is distributed among several accounts. Each account, generally, includes similar programs, projects, or items, such as a "research and development" account or "salaries and expenses" account. For small agencies, a single account may fund all of the agency's activities. These acts typically provide a lump-sum amount for each of these accounts. A few accounts include a single program, project, or item, which the appropriations act funds individually. In report language, the House and Senate Committees on Appropriations provide more detailed directions to the departments and agencies on the distribution of funding among various activities funded within an account. Funding for most local projects [is] specified in report language, as opposed to the text of the appropriations bill. Congressional earmarks (referred to as congressionally directed spending items in Senate Rule XLIV) are frequently included in report language and have also been provided in a bill, amendment, or conference report. . . .

Congress has traditionally considered and approved each regular appropriations bill separately, but Congress has on occasion combined several bills together. For 19 of the past 32 years (FY1977-FY2008), Congress has packaged two or more regular appropriations bills together in one measure. These packages are referred to as omnibus appropriation measures. In these cases, Congress typically began consideration of each regular bill separately, but generally has combined some of the bills together at the conference stage. During conference on a single regular appropriations bill, the conferees typically have included in the conference report the final agreements on other outstanding regular appropriations bills, thereby creating an omnibus appropriations measure. . . .

Packaging regular appropriations bills can be an efficient means for resolving outstanding differences within Congress or between Congress and the President. The negotiators can make more convenient trade-offs between issues among several bills and complete consideration of appropriations using fewer measures.

Cong. Research Serv., The Congressional Appropriations Process: An Introduction 1, 9-11 (Dec. 2, 2008), available at *http://www.senate.gov/CRSReports/ crs-publish.cfm?pid=%26*2%404Q%2C%3B%3F%0A-*.

The appropriations process enables Congress to assert continuous control of agency action. A funding reduction can put a halt to an agency program. But agencies are likely to adjust their policies to legislative preferences in response to a threat of a budget cut. Agencies need funding to run their programs, so money is a powerful motivator. If a threat is enough, then this tool is less costly than mustering the political support to actually cut funding. Will a threat always be enough? As with any threat, agencies are free to determine whether those making them have the political support to back them up. In other words, agencies are free to determine whether the threat is credible. There is a coordination problem that complicates the analysis. The committee responsible for appropriations is different from the committee responsible for the substantive mandate, like auto safety. If the substantive committee is the one displeased with agency action, it must communicate that dissatisfaction to the appropriations committee, and the appropriations committee must agree to follow through. Still, funding threats are seen as quite powerful. Perhaps the reason is the unique nature of appropriations legislation. Funding for any particular agency program is just one item in a larger bill that reflects many diverse legislative interests and that Congress intends to pass. Funding is therefore relatively easier to alter than provisions in other bills (including bills to reduce an agency's authority or reverse an agency's rule).

10. Oversight Hearings

Congress can use oversight hearings in a variety of ways to control agency action. It can use hearings to uncover facts in aid of further legislative activity, such as statutory amendments or funding reductions. In this respect, oversight hearings can function as an informational tool. Congress can use hearings to pressure agencies to conform their policy to legislative preferences without further legislative action. This use enables Congress to assert control in a sense that we have emphasized. Congress can also use hearings to hold officials "accountable" for their actions in the traditional sense of the word — a public airing or blaming. Even if such hearings cannot change past conduct, they can enable voters to better judge those responsible for it. In addition, they can serve as a warning for the future.

The advantage of oversight hearings as a tool for controlling agency action is their relative informality. Congress need not enact legislation to move agency action in a direction consistent with its preferences. At the same time, the visibility of oversight hearings may improve their effectiveness as compared to less formal control tools, such as closed-door meetings or other contacts. Agency officials may find it more difficult to resist when doing so occurs in public view. The President may even take a public stand in reigning in the agency, so as to deflect negative attention from the administration.

To the extent that oversight hearings ensure that agency action tracks the preferences of elected officials rather than unelected bureaucrats, they can enhance the accountability of such action. Consider, however, that oversight hearings are conducted by committees of Congress. Do those committees reflect legislative preferences or idiosyncratic preferences? Do they enhance accountability as surely as more formal congressional tools? How about as compared to presidential tools? Do all presidential tools reliably reflect presidential preferences?

Depending on your standpoint, the frequency of oversight hearings is a downside. When agency officials' time, energy, and attention are consumed by oversight hearings, they cannot attend to the jobs for which they were appointed and confirmed. Even well-intentioned oversight hearings divert agency resources from their intended purposes. The claim of interference is weaker for former agency officials.

Of course, not all oversight hearings are well intentioned. They may serve political purposes but no obviously public-regarding ones. For example, oversight hearings can be used to harass or scapegoat agency officials or administrations. They can be used to improve the profile of members of Congress or their association with politically salient issues. In this regard, consider that oversight hearings are more likely in response to high-profile events and in times of divided government. (Recall the arguments from Chapter 2 concerning delegation. Congress has less reason to monitor agency action during times of unified government because it has less reason to worry that such action will depart from its preferences.)

How do oversight hearings work and what are the obstacles to their success? When a congressional committee convenes an oversight hearing, it sends a letter requesting that an agency official appear and sometimes produce documents. What happens if an agency official refuses to voluntarily appear or produce documents? In many cases, the committee will work out a compromise with the official, perhaps to provide more limited testimony or produce documents without appearing. But Congress can also use its subpoena power to compel compliance, holding officials who defy those subpoenas in contempt of Congress. A contempt citation can originate in either the House or the Senate. It is debated like any other resolution, subject to the same filibuster and procedural rules, and requires a majority vote for approval. Once approved, the House speaker or the Senate president pro tem refers it to the U.S. Attorney for the District of Columbia for prosecution. *See* 2 U.S.C. §§1992-94. Contempt of Congress is a federal misdemeanor, punishable by a maximum $100,000 fine and a maximum one-year sentence in federal prison. *See* Josh Chafetz, *Executive Branch Contempt of Congress*, 76 U. Chi. L. Rev. 1083 (2009).

In some instances, the President may assert a claim of executive privilege on behalf of agency officials. Executive privilege enables the President to protect the confidentiality of executive communications from legislative or judicial investigations. The Supreme Court has held that executive privilege, though not mentioned in the Constitution, is implicit in the notion of separation of powers. *See* United States v. Nixon, 418 U.S. 683 (1974). But the Court has left the privilege ill-defined: To what extent may the interests of the other branches overcome it? What sorts of information does it protect? Disputes between the executive and legislative branches can lead to lawsuits, although courts are reluctant to intervene and may ask the parties to work it out. The "resolution" can be quite messy for both sides.

Consider the following case study, prepared by EPA, of a famous example involving former EPA Administrator Anne Gorsuch. The Subcommittee on Oversight and Investigation of the Committee on Energy and Commerce in the House sought to examine EPA's use of federal money from the so-called "Superfund" to clean up hazardous waste sites under the Comprehensive Environmental Response, Compensation, and Liability Act of 1980 ("CERCLA") and to examine EPA's enforcement program against alleged polluters under that statute. *See* *http://www.epa.gov/safewater/dwa_old/electronic/presentations/genint/govt/i-2gorsuch.pdf.* We follow the case study with some of the actual congressional documents in the matter, which can be found in a report that the Judiciary Committee in the House filed. *See* INVESTIGATION OF THE ROLE THE DEPARTMENT OF JUSTICE IN THE WITHHOLDING OF ENVIRONMENTAL PROTECTION AGENCY DOCUMENTS FROM CONGRESS IN 1982-1983, H.R. REP. No. 99-435, at 894-97, 982, 993.

Case Study: How Congressional Checks on Executive Branch Authority Derailed an EPA Administrator

In 1981, President Ronald Reagan appointed, and the Senate confirmed, Anne Gorsuch as Administrator of EPA. Gorsuch was a lawyer who had served in the Colorado legislature, but who had no experience in managing environmental programs or large organizations. As a legislator, she was a member of a group that called itself the "crazies," whose agenda mainly consisted of State's rights and opposition to Federal energy and environmental policies. She believed in voluntarism: that left to their own devices, States would achieve better environmental protection than they would under the heavy hand of Washington. She was also known for her fierce advocacy of the doctrine of strict statutory construction, i.e., of not prescribing in regulation that which was not explicitly called for in statute.

Reagan's agenda for EPA was no secret, consisting of budget cuts and reductions in force, regulatory relief, and greater delegation of responsibility to the States. Shortly after the inauguration Reagan established a task force on regulatory relief, under the direction of James Miller, a political appointee to OMB and a deregulation enthusiast. An executive order provided OMB with veto authority over all agency regulations; the task force quickly targeted for possible deferral or cancellation several key rules relating to hazardous waste disposal and auto emissions.

While awaiting her Senate nomination hearing, Gorsuch maintained her office in the Department of the Interior, rather than at EPA. She met only infrequently with EPA's career staff and surrounded herself instead with a small group of special assistants, most of whom had connections to James Watt (the Secretary of the Interior), Coors (the owner of the brewing company and a Reagan supporter), or the Reagan campaign effort. Gorsuch's view of the Agency and its staff at the time was fairly skeptical.

Gorsuch quickly alienated career EPA staff with her aloof manner; the reported steady stream of meetings with industry representatives while at Interior;

allegations of a "hit list" of career employees to be fired or transferred; and her staff which had political experience or experience in regulated industries, but limited environmental experience. Within a few months she abolished EPA's enforcement office, farming its responsibilities out to the program offices.

Many members of Congress, including Republicans, did not display much enthusiasm either for Gorsuch's agenda or her manner in carrying it out. Gorsuch was increasingly dogged by charges, based on leaked internal documents, that she was planning to level massive FY 1983 reductions in force and budget cuts that would put operating expenditures at 40 percent below their FY 1981 level. Quickly following the furor over the proposed budget cuts, in February 1982, Gorsuch suspended a regulatory ban on the disposal of containerized hazardous waste liquids in landfills. One member of Congress (a Democrat) called the decision "a glaring and outrageous example" of EPA's "inactivity" in the hazardous waste area and another (a Republican), said that "even as we sit here . . . the trucks are rolling into 900 landfills all over America carrying a deadly legacy that our children and grandchildren will have no choice but to accept." The chemical industry offered no public support for the action, while the story received prominent play in both the national and local news media. After just 18 days Gorsuch issued a new rule restricting the disposal of liquids.

In the summer of 1982, John Dingell (D-Mich.) began an inquiry on the Agency's use of Superfund money and the slow progress of a program for which money was readily available (through the trust fund). His staff, according to one account, received a "steady stream of leaks from within the agency . . . [showing] a pattern of political manipulation interwoven with absurd incompetence." Particularly suspicious was the conduct of Rita Lavelle, Assistant Administrator for Solid Waste and Emergency Response and a former California corporate public relations specialist. In September, Dingell requested a number of documents relating to specific Superfund enforcement cases.[11] The Justice Department intervened, however, asking for all copies of the documents and instructing EPA to withhold them from Congress. Dingell issued a subpoena requiring Gorsuch to appear before the panel with the records; a month later another Congressional panel with Superfund jurisdiction issued a second subpoena to Gorsuch.

On November 30, the President, acting on the advice of his White House counsel (Ted Olsen) and the Attorney General, asserted executive privilege and instructed Gorsuch not to comply with the subpoena, explaining that "sensitive documents found in open law enforcement files should not be made available to the Congress or to the public except in extraordinary circumstances." Leaders of both parties in Congress bridled at the administration's action and the House, by a wide margin, voted Gorsuch in contempt of Congress on December 16. The Justice Department immediately filed suit to halt the contempt proceedings.

At Christmas time, freak floods led to a hazardous waste spillage and the evacuation of homes in Times Beach, Missouri. In short order after that, the

---

[11] The charge was that the administration delayed action to begin cleaning up the Stringfellow Acid Pits in California because it did not want Governor Jerry Brown (a Democrat), who was then running for the Senate, to get the credit. Rita Lavelle later testified that "there was a constant desire to tie the announcement of [Superfund] sites into election campaigns."

administration's suit was dismissed in court; Rita Lavelle was fired by Reagan (after she turned down a Gorsuch request to resign);[12] new conflict of interest allegations arose over Gorsuch staff; old controversies, such as the hit list resurfaced; more top EPA employees resigned; and the White House brought in a "management team" of experienced officials in a last-ditch attempt to abate the crisis. In early March, to her apparent disbelief, the Justice Department told Gorsuch that its responsibility to investigate the conflict of interest allegations and other charges of impropriety precluded its continued representation of her in the contempt and executive privilege proceedings. On March 9, 1983, President Reagan accepted her resignation and Gorsuch announced that Congress would have full access to the documents in question. On March 21, Reagan nominated William Ruckelshaus, EPA's first Administrator, to take Gorsuch's place as EPA Administrator. . . .

It is instructive to note that within a few years following the resignation of Anne Gorsuch, Congress enacted some of the most prescriptive environmental legislation ever passed: the Hazardous and Solid Waste Amendments of 1984, Safe Drinking Water Act Amendments of 1986, Superfund Amendments and Reauthorization Act of 1986, and the Water Quality Act of 1987. All of these statutes spelled out precisely the content of future EPA regulations and the timeframe in which EPA was to act.

---

[12] The only person indicted and found guilty of a crime was Rita Lavelle, who was convicted of perjuring herself in Congressional testimony.

LETTER FROM JOHN DINGELL TO HON. ANNE GORSUCH, SEPTEMBER 17, 1982, WITH ATTACHMENT

JOHN D. DINGELL, MICH., CHAIRMAN,

ANNE GUYDRA, MIV.	MARC L. MARKS, PA.
BHAJ BALAFFE, PA.	NORMAN F. LENT, N.Y.
ALBERT GOTL, JR., TENN.	BOB WHITTAKER, KANS.
PHILLIP N. SHARP, OHIO	DON RITTER, PA.
THOMAS A. LUKEN, OHIO	HAROLD ROGERS, KY.
RICHARD L. SHELBY, ALA.	DAVID R. OBATE, IND.
MIKE SYNAR, OKLA.	JAMES T. BROYHILL, N.C.
W. J. "BILLY" TAUZIN, LA.	
RON WYDEN, OREG.	

CONGRESS OF THE UNITED STATES
HOUSE OF REPRESENTATIVES
SUBCOMMITTEE ON OVERSIGHT AND INVESTIGATIONS
OF THE
COMMITTEE ON ENERGY AND COMMERCE
WASHINGTON, D.C. 20515

PHONE (202) 225-4441

MICHAEL F. BARRETT, JR.
CHIEF COUNSEL/STAFF DIRECTOR

September 17, 1982

The Honorable Anne M. Gorsuch
Administrator
U. S. Environmental Protection Agency
Washington, D. C. 20460

Dear Ms. Gorsuch:

On November 16 and 18, 1981, and most recently on April 2, 1982, the Subcommittee on Oversight and Investigations held hearings relating to the Environmental Protection Agency's enforcement program and the administration of the Comprehensive Environmental Response, Compensation, and Liability Act of 1980 (CERCLA). In fulfillment of our oversight responsibilities under Rule X of the Rules of the House of Representatives, the Subcommittee is continuing its review of the administration and implementation of Superfund with particular emphasis on enforcement activities related thereto. The Subcommittee is also concerned about the apparent delay by the Department of Justice (DOJ) in filing civil litigation cases which have been referred by EPA. To assist the Subcommittee in fulfilling its oversight responsibilities and specifically pursuant to Section 104(e)(2)(D) of CERCLA, the Subcommittee requests the following information:

    1)   A list of the names of the civil cases referred to the Department of Justice (DOJ) from the Environmental Protection Agency in calendar years 1980, 1981, and 1982 (to date), the date of each referral, the statutory basis for each referral, the date each case was filed by the Department of Justice, and any other disposition of each case. Information of this nature has previously been provided to the Subcommittee in various formats and the Subcommittee is now interested in establishing a comprehensive tracking system as part of its overall evaluation of EPA's enforcement program. A copy of a format which is acceptable to the Subcommittee is attached. If any of the requested information is considered to be confidential, please identify the portions of the submitted material which the agency considers to be confidential in nature.

2)   In a separate chart, please list the name and date of all
      case referrals submitted by EPA to the Department of Justice
      which seek relief in part or in whole pursuant to Section
      106 of CERCLA and Section 107 of CERCLA. In addition, for
      each case referral, whether a new referral or amendment to a
      case already in litigation, please identify the date the
      case was filed by DOJ or the complaint amended and provide a
      copy of the pleading.

3)   A copy of a July 9, 1982 memorandum from Dr. John P. Horton,
      Asssitant Administrator for Administration, to Mr. Robert
      Perry and Mrs. Rita Lavelle on the general subject of cost
      recovery for remedial and removal actions and a copy of all
      answers and materials responsive to Dr. Horton's memorandum.

4)   For each of the 160 hazardous sites on the Interim
      Priorities List, please provide a copy of (a) the action
      memorandum and any comments of the Office of Enforcement or
      the Office of General Counsel which pertain thereto, (b)
      transmittal documents from EPA headquarters to the region
      which contain comments or instructions, and (c) the record
      of decision document.

5)   EPA has entered into a cooperative agreement (CR809392010)
      with the Environmental Law Institute to do a case study cost
      analysis of remedial actions at approximately 29 hazardous
      waste sites. We understand that the Environmental Law
      Institute has completed its case study analyses on six sites
      (B&M, Gallup, Goose Farm, Fairchild Republic, Romulus,
      Strasberg) to date and expects to submit its case study
      analyses on two sites (Chemical Control and CMI) in the very
      near future. Please provide copies of the case study
      analyses for each of the above eight sites.

6)   We understand that the Office of Solid Waste and Emergency
      Response has contracted with a private law firm to prepare
      standard form administrative orders for use pursuant to
      section 106 of CERCLA and section 3008 of RCRA. Please
      provide a copy of the contract, including the contract
      justification, all work products submitted by the law firm
      in performance of the contract, any comments of the Office
      of Legal Enforcement or the Office of General Counsel
      relating to the law firm's submission, and the cost of the
      contract.

7)   Please provide a copy of all administrative orders issued
      under section 106 of CERCLA to date.

LETTER FROM JOHN DINGELL TO HON. ANNE GORSUCH, OCTOBER 14, 1982

JOHN D. DINGELL, MICH., CHAIRMAN

JIM SANTINI, NEV.
TOM WALGREN, PA.
ALBERT GORE, JR., TENN.
RONALD M. MOTTL, OHIO
THOMAS A. LUKEN, OHIO
RICHARD C. SHELBY, ALA.
MIKE SYNAR, OKLA.
W. J. "BILLY" TAUZIN, LA.
RON WYDEN, OREG.

MARC L. MARKS   PA.
NORMAN F. LENT   N.Y.
BOB WHITTAKER, KANS.
TOM RITTER, PA.
HAROLD ROGERS, KY.
DANIEL R. COATS, IND.
JAMES T. BROYHILL, N.C.

CONGRESS OF THE UNITED STATES
HOUSE OF REPRESENTATIVES
SUBCOMMITTEE ON OVERSIGHT AND INVESTIGATIONS
OF THE
COMMITTEE ON ENERGY AND COMMERCE
WASHINGTON, D.C.   20515

RAYBURN HOUSE OFFICE BUILDING
PHONE (202) 225-4441

MICHAEL F. BARRETT, JR.
CHIEF COUNSEL/STAFF DIRECTOR

October 14, 1982

HAND-DELIVERED

Honorable Anne M. Gorsuch
Administrator
Environmental Protection Agency
401 M Street, S.W.
Washington, D. C.   20460

Dear Ms. Gorsuch:

By letter dated September 17, 1982, I requested on behalf of the
Subcommittee certain documentary materials from your agency to be
delivered by October 1, 1982 to the offices of the Subcommittee on
Oversight and Investigations.

Since that time, the Department of Justice has become involved in
the matter of the availability of those materials. On Friday, October
8, 1982, copies of materials referenced in my letter were provided to
the Department of Justice. The Department has provided us with
portions of these documents, but not all of them.

There is no legal basis for withholding any of these materials.
Indeed, the Subcommittee has a clear Constitutional and statutory
right to all documents which have been requested from the
Environmental Protection Agency. In the interest of comity, the
Subcommittee has agreed to permit its staff to review those documents
which have been withheld and to make an initial determination which
documents, if any, will be needed by the Subcommittee. Such
arrangement does not, of course, waive any of the rights of the
Subcommittee with respect to obtaining documents at a future time.

Sincerely,

John D. Dingell
Chairman
Subcommittee on
Oversight and Investigations

Mr. Robert M. Perry

SUBPOENA DIRECTED TO HON. ANNE GORSUCH FROM SUBCOMMITTEE ON OVERSIGHT AND INVESTIGATIONS, HOUSE COMMITTEE ON ENERGY AND COMMERCE, SERVED OCTOBER 21, 1982

97-2-2

ORIGINAL

BY AUTHORITY OF THE HOUSE OF REPRESENTATIVES OF THE CONGRESS OF THE UNITED STATES OF AMERICA

To __Richard Frandsen, Mark Raabe, and/or__ Debra Jacobson

You are hereby commanded to summon __The Honorable Anne M. Gorsuch,__ __Administrator, Environmental Protection Agency, 401 M Street, N. W.__ __Washington, D. C. 20460__

to be and appear before the __Subcommittee on Oversight and Investigations (under__ __the authority of Rules X and XI of the Rules of__ the House of Representatives (97th Congress) of the Energy and Commerce Committee of the House of Representatives of the United States, of which the Hon. _____mittee)

__John D. Dingell__ _____ is chairman, and to bring with her

the documents described in the attachment to this subpoena (personal

appearance is not required if the described documents are received in

the Subcommittee offices (Room 2323 Rayburn HOB) at or before 4:00 p.m.,

on Friday, October 22, 1982

in their chamber in the city of Washington, on __Tuesday, October 26, 1982__

__2323 Rayburn House Office Bldg._____, at the hour of __11:30 a.m._____

then and there to testify touching matters of inquiry committed to said Committee; and he is

not to depart without leave of said Committee.

Herein fail not, and make return of this summons.

Witness my hand and the seal of the House of Representatives

of the United States, at the city of Washington, this

__14th__ day of __October_____, 19 82

Chairman

Attest:

EDMUND L. HENSHAW, JR., Clerk

NOTES AND QUESTIONS

1. The EPA case study brings together several themes from earlier chapters. For example, Administrator Gorsuch created friction with career staff from the start. We discussed the relationship between political appointees and career staffers in Chapter 8. While still located at Interior, Administrator Gorsuch was meeting with industry representatives, and those interactions may have influenced her decisions at EPA. We introduced "capture" theory in Chapter 10. In light of these facts, could you have predicted less than smooth sailing for Administrative Gorsuch?

2. Congress was frustrated in its attempt to get information and therefore to assert control of EPA Superfund and CERCLA activity. That is the point about executive privilege; it can be an obstacle to legislative oversight hearings. But this process still basically worked for Congress, didn't it? The people responsible for the supposed problems at EPA ended up gone, and officials with preferences closer to Congress's own replaced them. How did Congress further ensure changes at EPA even after Administrator Gorsuch (and Rita Lavelle) left the agency?

3. What was Administrator Gorsuch's side of the story as to executive privilege? In her 1986 book, *Are You Tough Enough?*, she wrote: "I was saying give them [Rep. Dingell's committee] anything they want and give it to them in triplicate if that'll make them happy. My attitude was based on my experience as a legislator: I believe in the legislative process, and it has to be an informed process. . . . So there came a day when the Justice Department lawyers came to me to press the idea of the confrontation over executive privilege. . . . [Receiving assurance from these lawyers that the President himself wanted her to assert what was a novel claim of executive privilege for 'enforcement-sensitive documents,' she asserted it.] [Later,] [w]hen congressional criticism about the EPA began to touch the Presidency, Mr. Reagan solved *his* problem by jettisoning me and my people, people whose only 'crime' was loyal service, following his orders. I was not the first to receive his special brand of benevolent neglect, a form of conveniently looking the other way, while his staff continues to do some very dirty work." ANNE BURFORD & JOHN GREENYA, ARE YOU TOUGH ENOUGH? 151-52, 282-83 (1986).

Because executive privilege can be an obstacle to legislative oversight hearings, it is worth discussing a bit further. Questions can arise concerning what information it protects — for example, "enforcement-sensitive" documents. In addition, questions can arise concerning to whom it applies. President George W. Bush invoked executive privilege for White House aides rather than himself or agency policymaking officials. Consider the result:

Paul Kane, West Wing Aides Cited for Contempt; Refusal to Testify Prompts House Action

Wash. Post, Feb. 15, 2008

The House yesterday escalated a constitutional showdown with President Bush, approving the first-ever contempt of Congress citations against West Wing aides and reigniting last year's battle over the scope of executive privilege.

On a 223 to 32 vote, the House approved contempt citations against White House Chief of Staff Joshua B. Bolten and former White House counsel Harriet E. Miers over their refusal to cooperate with an investigation into the mass firings of U.S. attorneys and allegations that administration officials sought to politicize the Justice Department.

The vote came after a morning of tense partisan bickering over parliamentary rules, including a GOP call for a vote on a motion to close the chamber that briefly forced lawmakers to leave a memorial service for Rep. Tom Lantos (D-Calif.), who died this week. The conflict was capped later in the day when most House Republicans walked off the floor and refused to cast a final vote. They accused Democrats of forcing a partisan vote on the contempt citations instead of approving a surveillance bill supported by Bush.

Democrats said they were left with no choice but to engage in a legal show-down with Bush because he has refused for nearly a year to allow any current or former West Wing staff member to testify in the inquiry. Citing executive privilege, the president has offered their testimony on the condition that it is taken without transcripts and not under oath.

"This is beyond arrogance. This is hubris taken to the ultimate degree," Speaker Nancy Pelosi (D-Calif.) said in the closing moments of the debate.

The administration immediately condemned the House action, noting that no White House official has ever been cited for contempt. "This action is unprecedented, and it is outrageous. It is also an incredible waste of time — time the House should spend doing the American people's legislative business," White House press secretary Dana Perino said in a statement.

Until now, the most recent Cabinet-level officials cited for contempt were two administrators of the Environmental Protection Agency, in 1982 and 1983, over their refusal to cooperate in House oversight investigations.

The contempt resolution against Bolten cites his refusal to turn over subpoenaed documents and e-mails sought by the House Judiciary Committee in its now year-long investigation into the dismissals of nine U.S. attorneys in 2006. Miers is cited for refusing to testify after she was subpoenaed to appear before the panel last summer.

The Senate Judiciary Committee has approved contempt citations for Bolten and former White House deputy chief of staff Karl Rove, who also refused to appear before that panel. The full Senate has not acted on the matter.

The furor over the fired prosecutors began in January 2007 when congressional Democrats learned that seven U.S. attorneys had been fired on the same day, Dec. 7, 2006. Most senior staff members of the Justice Department resigned as the congressional investigations unfolded, and former attorney general Alberto

R. Gonzales, who resigned in late August, is the subject of an internal investigation into whether he tampered with a likely witness.

Democrats said their votes were meant to compel more information from a White House that has blocked their efforts to complete their investigation. "Absent this resolution, the Congress has yielded to the executive the principle of whether they participate in oversight," said Rep. Artur Davis (D-Ala.).

By law, the contempt citations go to the U.S. attorney for the District of Columbia, Jeffrey A. Taylor, but the White House and the Justice Department have said that no executive branch employee will face a grand jury inquiry.

Attorney General Michael B. Mukasey has told Congress that current and former White House officials who have refused to testify in a congressional inquiry probably did so based on the Justice Department's ruling that Bush's assertion of executive privilege was proper. That means that the Justice Department cannot now criminally charge someone for defying Congress based on its own previous legal advice, he said.

Yesterday, an aide to Mukasey, who is traveling overseas, said the attorney general will review the situation but is likely to stand by that position.

House Democrats had looked ahead. They included in yesterday's resolution a second provision that allows the House general counsel to file a civil lawsuit in federal courts to compel Bolten's and Miers's testimony.

Democrats hope that this strategy will let them push the matter into federal courts, where they think they have a chance of at least establishing a legal precedent on executive privilege.

"I think we still have to establish what the law is," said Rep. Brad Miller (D-N.C.), who has helped lobby rural and moderate Democrats for five months to support the contempt motions.

Republicans said the House Judiciary Committee should accept the White House's offer of limited testimony to learn as much as they can before Bush leaves office next year. "I don't think throwing the president's chief of staff in jail is going to do the trick," said Rep. F. James Sensenbrenner Jr. (Wis.).

Many Republicans accused the Democrats of avoiding the more important business on an expiring surveillance law. "It's security for America versus partisan politics," said Rep. Eric Cantor (Va.).

Ultimately, most Republicans stormed off the floor and refused to vote on the contempt citations. Only three Republicans — Reps. Walter B. Jones (N.C.), Wayne T. Gilchrest (Md.) and Ron Paul (Tex.) — supported the contempt citations.

What happened next? After the Department of Justice directed the U.S. Attorney not to prosecute Miers and Bolton for contempt of Congress, the House Committee on the Judiciary filed a lawsuit against the Bush administration seeking civil enforcement of its subpoena authority. In October 2008, the Court of Appeals for the D.C. Circuit refused to grant their request, noting that the issue involved a serious dispute between two co-equal branches that could not be judicially resolved before the subpoenas expired in January 2009, when the 110th Congress ended. *See* Committee on the Judiciary of the United States House of Representatives v. Miers, 542 F.3d 909 (D.C. Cir. 2008). In June 2009, Miers did finally testify before members of the House Committee on the Judiciary but in a limited, closed-door session. *See* Carrie Johnson, *Miers Told House Panel of "Agitated Rove,"* WASH. POST (Aug. 12, 2009), available at *http://www.washingtonpost.com/wp-dyn/content/article/2009/08/11/AR2009081102104.html.*

———

Some agency officials resist oversight hearings without a claim of executive privilege, particularly when they view such hearings as a form of congressional harassment. But the line between harassment and "accountability" is thin. Consider the following:

Zachary Coile, EPA Chief Sits and Takes His Punishment

S.F. Chron., Jan. 25, 2008.

Environmental Protection Agency chief Stephen Johnson faced a blistering critique from lawmakers and governors Thursday for rejecting California's attempt to set the nation's most stringent greenhouse gas regulations for cars and trucks.

At his first appearance before Congress since denying California's request for a waiver to enforce its new rules, Johnson was hit from all sides. Maryland Gov. Martin O'Malley, a Democrat, called the EPA chief's decision "shameful, outrageous and irresponsible." Vermont Gov. Jim Douglas, a Republican, said the ruling infringes on states' rights and undercuts state efforts to fight climate change.

California Sen. Barbara Boxer, who chaired the hearing, accused Johnson of trying to hide documents from Congress showing that he had overruled his staff in denying the waiver last month. EPA first refused to release the documents, then turned over papers that were mostly whited out. Finally he allowed Boxer's staff this week to hand copy them under the eye of EPA lawyers.

"I have never seen such disregard and disrespect by an agency head for Congress and for the committees with the responsibility for oversight of his agency," Boxer said.

Johnson, an EPA career veteran, attempted a rope-a-dope strategy: He sat placidly while taking the pounding from lawmakers, then insisted again and again that he'd made the right call.

"While many urged me to approve or deny the California waiver request, I am bound by the criteria in the Clean Air Act, not people's opinions," he said. "My job is to make the right decision, not the easy decision."

The hearing highlighted the high stakes in the clash between California and the Bush administration over the proposed rules. Fourteen other states have now adopted California's standards and four more plan to adopt them — meaning more than half the nation's population has embraced the state's tougher regulations for vehicles.

In his testimony, Johnson tried to explain the rationale for his decision: He said the state did not show the compelling and extraordinary conditions required under the Clean Air Act to grant a waiver because global warming is an international problem and requires global, not a regional, solutions.

"Unlike pollutants covered by other waivers, greenhouse gas emissions harm the environment in California and elsewhere, regardless of where the emissions occur," he said. "Therefore, this challenge is not exclusive or unique to California."

But lawmakers were skeptical of his explanation. Many said the administration was simply seeking to block the states from taking more aggressive action to combat climate change.

"Your agency's decision to deny California a waiver just defies logic to me," said Sen. Amy Klobuchar, D-Minn. "And it's clearly a decision, I believe, that's based on politics and not on fact."

Democrats on the committee also seized on documents showing that EPA's lawyers told Johnson that California could prove that it had compelling and extraordinary conditions because of the impacts of warming on the state, from an increase in wildfires to water shortages to flooding of coastal areas.

"This is what your staff told you, and then you come out and say, 'It doesn't meet . . . the test for compelling interests,'" Boxer said. "You're walking the American taxpayers into a lawsuit that you are going to lose."

Johnson argued that it was better for the country to pursue a single national standard — such as the new fuel economy standards, passed by Congress and signed by President Bush last month — instead of what he has called a patchwork approach of regulation by the states.

But several lawmakers took strong issue with his characterization. Under the Clean Air Act, if California is granted a waiver other states are allowed to adopt the state's standards.

"The California standards do not threaten us with a regulatory patchwork," said Sen. Joe Lieberman, independent-Conn., a chief sponsor of climate change legislation in the Senate. "Two standards — one applying to the half of the country that chooses to adopt California standards and one applying to the other half — simply do not make a patchwork."

While the new federal rules would require cars and trucks to get 35 miles per gallon by 2020, California's rules would require vehicles to get significantly better mileage: 44 miles per gallon by 2020. State officials estimate the California rules would cut greenhouse gases 74 percent more than federal law.

Johnson had only one major ally Thursday: Oklahoma Sen. James Inhofe, the panel's ranking member and Congress' leading climate change skeptic. He was the only Republican lawmaker to show up at the hearing, which he denounced as political theater.

"The effect that California's politicians are trying to achieve through this waiver provision is something they cannot achieve through federal legislation — even tighter fuel economy standards than what the Congress passed in the energy bill just last month," Inhofe said.

Boxer, who has long clashed with Johnson, said she plans to continue an investigation of how he made his decision. She is requesting e-mails between the White House and EPA, which Johnson said he expects to deliver by Feb. 15.

Johnson admitted he had spoken with the president and other White House officials, but said the decision was his own.

"I was not directed by anyone," he said.

Boxer told Johnson his ruling undermines the central role of his agency in protecting public health and the environment. "You are going against your own agency's mission and you are fulfilling the mission of some special interests," she said.

Boxer, Sen. Dianne Feinstein, D-Calif., and 14 other senators introduced a bill late Thursday that would override the EPA and grant the waiver request to California and the other states.

11. Fire Alarms

In the previous section, we mentioned that oversight hearings can function not only as a tool for asserting control of agency action but also as a tool for obtaining information about agency action. In this section, we explore other tools for obtaining information about agency action. This issue is critical because without information, Congress does not know when to intervene in agency action. We have already noted that Congress has enacted statutes requiring agencies to submit information directly to it. *See* pp. 606. These mechanisms, like oversight hearings, are costly from a legislative perspective. To obtain information, Congress must devote time to calling witnesses or reading documents.

Political scientists have argued that Congress has means that enable it to monitor agency action more efficiently by shifting the responsibility and cost to others. In this regard, political scientists have distinguished between *police patrols*, which are tools that require Congress itself to monitor agency action, and *fire alarms*, which are tools that position constituents to monitor agency action and alert Congress (i.e., sound a "fire alarm") when legislative intervention is necessary. Mathew McCubbins & Thomas Schwartz, *Congressional Oversight Overlooked: Police Patrols versus Fire Alarms*, 28 AM. J. POL. SCI. 165 (1984). If oversight hearings and reporting requirements are examples of police patrols, what are examples of fire alarms?

Administrative procedures can serve as fire alarms. The prime example is notice-and-comment rulemaking, which allows any interested party to participate in the development of agency policy, acquiring information about such policy along the way and triggering legislative intervention when it departs from their preferences. *See* Mathew D. McCubbins, Roger G. Noll & Barry R. Weingast, *Administrative Procedures as Instruments of Political Control*, 3 J.L. ECON. & ORG. 243 (1987). Congress has enacted other statutes that require agencies to furnish certain sorts of information while formulating policy that may be relevant to particular groups in seeking legislative intervention. *See* 42 U.S.C. §§4321-47 (2000) (National Environmental Policy Act); 5 U.S.C. §§601-12 (Regulatory Flexibility Act); Pub. L. No. 1040121, 110 Stat. 857 (1996) (codified in scattered sections of 5, 15, and 28 U.S.C.) (Small Business Regulatory Enforcement Fairness Act). Note that some political scientists question whether administrative procedures can function as information-control mechanisms. Some contend that the connection between administrative procedures and legislative monitoring is too general and cannot be tested as an empirical matter. *See* JOHN D. HUBER & CHARLES R. SHIPAN, DELIBERATE DISCRETION? THE INSTITUTIONAL FOUNDATIONS OF BUREAUCRATIC AUTONOMY 26, 36 (2002). Others argue that providing information is insufficient to make administrative procedures useful to Congress; Congress still needs the will and the means to assert control of agency action. *See* Jerry L. Mashaw, *Explaining Administrative Process: Normative, Positive, and Critical Stories of Legal Development*, 6 J.L. ECON. & ORG. (Special Issue) 267 (1990). Note also that legal scholars tend to view administrative procedures as legal, not political, tools. They see administrative procedures, such as notice-and-comment rulemaking, as promoting notice, fairness, deliberation, and the like. But most have not really considered the simultaneous political function that administrative procedures may serve. *See* Lisa Schultz Bressman, *Procedures as Politics in Administrative Law*, 107 COLUM. L. REV. 1749 (2007).

In addition to obtaining information by placing citizens in the administrative process, Congress can obtain information by placing citizens in the judicial process. Thus, Congress has enacted so called "citizen-suit" provisions, which authorize "any person" to seek judicial review of agency action. *See, e.g.,* 16 U.S.C. §1540(g) (citizen-suit provision in Endangered Species Act). The right to seek judicial review gives citizens a greater incentive to watch agency action and report to Congress when such action departs from their preferences, in addition to or in lieu of later filing a lawsuit. It may also give agencies a greater incentive to share information with citizens; "[a]gencies are more inclined to involve and accommodate those who have the power to challenge their decisions later." Bressman, *Procedures as Politics in Administrative Law*, 107 Colum. L. Rev. at 1796. In these ways, citizen-suit provisions shift monitoring costs to citizens. They also shift monitoring costs to courts. A judicial decision can serve as a signal to Congress that legislative intervention may be necessary. As we discuss in the judicial control section, the Constitution limits the extent to which Congress can rely on citizen-suit provisions as monitoring mechanisms. *See* p. 750. As a result, citizen-suit provisions do not allow Congress to shift the costs of monitoring as broadly as it might prefer.

Finally, Congress has enacted other statutes that furnish citizens information outside the context of an administrative or judicial proceeding. For example, the Freedom of Information Act directs agencies to provide records to "any person" upon a request that "reasonably describes such records." *See* 5 U.S.C. §552 (2000); *see also* 5 U.S.C. §552b (Government in the Sunshine Act, which requires independent agencies to give reasonable notice of their meetings and make every portion of their meetings open to public observation). Although these statutes provide a number of exemptions that shield certain agency information from public view, they are important mechanisms for citizens to obtain information, on the basis of which they may invoke legislative intervention.

12. *Legislative Vetoes*

Now we turn to tools that Congress has created to assert control of agency action, but that the Supreme Court has subsequently invalidated on constitutional grounds. Thus, these are tools that Congress may not use today. Because Congress is not likely to stop searching for innovative mechanisms, it is important to understand the political advantage of these tools, as well as the constitutional objections and normative implications. We start with the legislative veto.

A legislative veto is a statutory provision that enables Congress to reverse an agency decision without enacting a new statute. There are several forms of the legislative veto: one-house, two-house, or committee. You can understand almost immediately the political appeal of such a tool. Above all else, a legislative veto enables Congress to reverse an agency decision without obtaining a presidential signature or two-thirds majority to override a presidential veto. In addition, a one-house veto dispenses with the need for bicameral consensus. Most extreme, and most tempting, is the committee veto, which places control in the small group of senators or representatives who deal with the agency on a regular basis and conduct the oversight of that agency. Yet a legislative veto, regardless of its form, has the same legal effect. It is binding on the agency, reversing its decision as if through new legislation. Therefore, even the mere threat of a veto is powerful. If you think an agency official is generally in a tough spot when called to testify at an oversight hearing, think how much more pressure the official faces if the committee can, on its own, reverse the agency's regulations.

Not surprisingly, the legislative veto has been a popular tool. As a leading legislation casebook reports, "[a] library of Congress study for period 1932 to 1975 found 295 congressional review provisions in 196 federal statutes; for the year 1975 alone, there were 58 provisions in 21 statutes." WILLIAM N. ESKRIDGE, JR. ET AL., LEGISLATION: STATUTES AND THE CREATION OF PUBLIC POLICY 1149 (4th ed.). The authors found that the trend accelerated in the late 1970s, and offer the following table:

Form of Legislative Veto	1932-78	1979-82
One-House	71	24
Two-House	65	23
Committee	0	26
Other	0	5
Totals	205	78

This list includes congressional review provisions other than "negative" legislative vetoes, which have the effect of reversing an agency decision. For example, Congress can require an agency to obtain legislative approval before a decision becomes effective, which is known as a "positive" legislative veto. Congress can also require an agency to report a decision to a specified committee and wait for a period to allow legislative review, which is known as "laying over." We discuss laying over provisions in the notes that follow the case below. (Have you seen one already?)

In 1983, the Court held that the negative form of the legislative veto is unconstitutional. With that decision, the Court invalidated more federal legislation in one day than it had invalidated in the 194 years of the republic that preceded it. Here is the decision:

Immigration & Naturalization Service v. Chadha

462 U.S. 919 (1983)

Chief Justice Burger delivered the opinion of the Court.

[This case] presents a challenge to the constitutionality of the provision in §244(c)(2) of the Immigration and Nationality Act, 8 U.S.C. §1254(c)(2), authorizing one House of Congress, by resolution, to invalidate the decision of the Executive Branch, pursuant to authority delegated by Congress to the Attorney General of the United States, to allow a particular deportable alien to remain in the United States.

[handwritten margin note: ISSUE]

Chadha is an East Indian who was born in Kenya and holds a British passport. He was lawfully admitted to the United States in 1966 on a nonimmigrant student visa. His visa expired on June 30, 1972. On October 11, 1973, the District Director of the Immigration and Naturalization Service ordered Chadha to show cause why he should not be deported for having "remained in the United States for a longer time than permitted." Pursuant to §242(b) of the Immigration and Nationality Act (Act), 8 U.S.C. §1252(b), a deportation hearing was held before an immigration judge on January 11, 1974. On the basis of evidence adduced at the hearing, affidavits submitted with the application, and the results of a character investigation conducted by the INS, the immigration judge, on June 25, 1974, ordered that Chadha's deportation be suspended. The immigration judge found that Chadha met the requirements of §244(a)(1): he had resided continuously in the United States for over seven years, was of good moral character, and would suffer "extreme hardship" if deported.

[handwritten margin note: Immig. Court]

Pursuant to §244(c)(1) of the Act, 8 U.S.C. §1254(c)(1), the immigration judge suspended Chadha's deportation and a report of the suspension was transmitted to Congress. Section 244(c)(1) provides:

[handwritten margin note: report submitted to Congress]

"Upon application by any alien who is found by the Attorney General to meet the requirements of subsection (a) of this section the Attorney General may in his discretion suspend deportation of such alien. If the deportation of any alien is suspended under the provisions of this subsection, a complete and detailed statement of the facts and pertinent provisions of law in the case shall be reported to the Congress with the reasons for such suspension. Such reports shall be submitted on the first day of each calendar month in which Congress is in session."

Once the Attorney General's recommendation for suspension of Chadha's deportation was conveyed to Congress, Congress had the power under §244(c)(2) of the Act, 8 U.S.C. §1254(c)(2), to veto the Attorney General's determination that Chadha should not be deported. Section 244(c)(2) provides:

> "(2) In the case of an alien specified in paragraph (1) of subsection (a) of this subsection —
>   if during the session of the Congress at which a case is reported, or prior to the close of the session of the Congress next following the session at which a case is reported, either the Senate or the House of Representatives passes a resolution stating in substance that it does not favor the suspension of such deportation, the Attorney General shall thereupon deport such alien or authorize the alien's voluntary departure at his own expense under the order of deportation in the manner provided by law. If, within the time above specified, neither the Senate nor the House of Representatives shall pass such a resolution, the Attorney General shall cancel deportation proceedings."

On December 12, 1975, [one week before the time to exercise the legislative veto was set to expire] Representative Eilberg, Chairman of the Judiciary Subcommittee on Immigration, Citizenship, and International Law, introduced a resolution opposing "the granting of permanent residence in the United States to [six] aliens", including Chadha. The resolution was referred to the House Committee on the Judiciary. On December 16, 1975, the resolution was discharged from further consideration by the House Committee on the Judiciary and submitted to the House of Representatives for a vote. The resolution had not been printed and was not made available to other Members of the House prior to or at the time it was voted on. So far as the record before us shows, the House consideration of the resolution was based on Representative Eilberg's statement from the floor that

> "[i]t was the feeling of the committee, after reviewing 340 cases, that the aliens contained in the resolution [Chadha and five others] did not meet these statutory requirements, particularly as it relates to hardship; and it is the opinion of the committee that their deportation should not be suspended."

The resolution was passed without debate or recorded vote. Since the House action was pursuant to §244(c)(2), the resolution was not treated as an Article I legislative act; it was not submitted to the Senate or presented to the President for his action.

[The Court first addressed questions concerning the availability of judicial review, including its jurisdiction and standing. It concluded that it had authority to review Chadha's claims.]

III

Constit. Issue

We turn now to the question whether action of one House of Congress under §244(c)(2) violates strictures of the Constitution. We begin, of course, with the presumption that the challenged statute is valid. Its wisdom is not the concern of the courts; if a challenged action does not violate the Constitution, it must be sustained. By the same token, the fact that a given law or procedure is efficient, convenient, and useful in facilitating functions of government, standing alone, will not save it if it is contrary to the Constitution. Convenience and efficiency are not the primary objectives — or the hallmarks — of democratic government and our inquiry is sharpened rather than blunted by the fact that Congressional veto provisions are appearing with increasing frequency in statutes which delegate authority to executive and independent agencies.

Explicit and unambiguous provisions of the Constitution prescribe and define the respective functions of the Congress and of the Executive in the legislative process. Since the precise terms of those familiar provisions are critical to the resolution of this case, we set them out verbatim. Art. I provides:

> "All legislative Powers herein granted shall be vested in a Congress of the United States, which shall consist of a Senate and a House of Representatives." Art. I, §1. (Emphasis added).
>
> "Every Bill which shall have passed the House of Representatives and the Senate, shall, before it becomes a Law, be presented to the President of the United States; . . ." Art. I, §7, cl. 2. (Emphasis added).
>
> "Every Order, Resolution, or Vote to which the Concurrence of the Senate and House of Representatives may be necessary (except on a question of Adjournment) shall be presented to the President of the United States; and before the Same shall take Effect, shall be approved by him, or being disapproved by him, shall be repassed by two thirds of the Senate and House of Representatives, according to the Rules and Limitations prescribed in the Case of a Bill." Art. I, §7, cl. 3. (Emphasis added).

These provisions of Art. I are integral parts of the constitutional design for the separation of powers. We have recently noted that "[t]he principle of separation of powers was not simply an abstract generalization in the minds of the Framers: it was woven into the documents that they drafted in Philadelphia in the summer of 1787." *Buckley v. Valeo*, 424 U.S., at 124. Just as we relied on the textual provision of Art. II, §2, cl. 2, to vindicate the principle of separation of powers in *Buckley*, we find that the purposes underlying the Presentment Clauses, Art. I, §7, cls. 2, 3, and the bicameral requirement of Art. I, §1 and §7, cl. 2, guide our resolution of the important question presented in this case. The very structure of the articles delegating and separating powers under Arts. I, II, and III exemplify the concept of separation of powers and we now turn to Art. I.

B

The Presentment Clauses

The records of the Constitutional Convention reveal that the requirement that all legislation be presented to the President before becoming law was uniformly accepted by the Framers. Presentment to the President and the Presidential veto were considered so imperative that the draftsmen took special pains to assure that these requirements could not be circumvented. During the final debate on Art. I, §7, cl. 2, James Madison expressed concern that it might easily be evaded by the simple expedient of calling a proposed law a "resolution" or "vote" rather than a "bill." 2 M. Farrand, The Records of the Federal Convention OF 1787 301-302. As a consequence, Art. I, §7, cl. 3, was added. *Id.*, at 304-305.

The decision to provide the President with a limited and qualified power to nullify proposed legislation by veto was based on the profound conviction of the Framers that the powers conferred on Congress were the powers to be most carefully circumscribed. It is beyond doubt that lawmaking was a power to be shared by both Houses and the President. In *The Federalist* No. 73 (H. Lodge ed. 1888), Hamilton focused on the President's role in making laws:

> "If even no propensity had ever discovered itself in the legislative body to invade the rights of the Executive, the rules of just reasoning and theoretic propriety would of themselves teach us that the one ought not to be left to the mercy of the other, but ought to possess a constitutional and effectual power of self-defense." *Id.*, at 457-458.

The President's role in the lawmaking process also reflects the Framers' careful efforts to check whatever propensity a particular Congress might have to enact oppressive, improvident, or ill-considered measures. The President's veto role in the legislative process was described later during public debate on ratification:

> "It establishes a salutary check upon the legislative body, calculated to guard the community against the effects of faction, precipitancy, or of any impulse unfriendly to the public good which may happen to influence a majority of that body. . . . The primary inducement to conferring the power in question upon the Executive is to enable him to defend himself; the secondary one is to increase the chances in favor of the community against the passing of bad laws through haste, inadvertence, or design." THE FEDERALIST No. 73, *supra*, at 458 (A. Hamilton).

The Court also has observed that the Presentment Clauses serve the important purpose of assuring that a "national" perspective is grafted on the legislative process:

> "The President is a representative of the people just as the members of the Senate and of the House are, and it may be, at some times, on some subjects, that the President elected by all the people is rather more representative of them all than are the members of either body of the Legislature whose constituencies are local and not countrywide . . . ." *Myers v. United States*, 272 U.S., at 123.

C

Bicameralism

The bicameral requirement of Art. I, §§1, 7 was of scarcely less concern to the Framers than was the Presidential veto and indeed the two concepts are interdependent. By providing that no law could take effect without the concurrence of the prescribed majority of the Members of both Houses, the Framers reemphasized their belief, already remarked upon in connection with the Presentment

Clauses, that legislation should not be enacted unless it has been carefully and fully considered by the Nation's elected officials. In the Constitutional Convention debates on the need for a bicameral legislature, James Wilson, later to become a Justice of this Court, commented:

> "Despotism comes on mankind in different shapes. Sometimes in an Executive, sometimes in a military, one. Is there danger of a Legislative despotism? Theory & practice both proclaim it. If the Legislative authority be not restrained, there can be neither liberty nor stability; and it can only be restrained by dividing it within itself, into distinct and independent branches. In a single house there is no check, but the inadequate one, of the virtue & good sense of those who compose it." 1 M. Farrand, supra, at 254.

Hamilton argued that a Congress comprised of a single House was antithetical to the very purposes of the Constitution. Were the Nation to adopt a Constitution providing for only one legislative organ, he warned:

> "we shall finally accumulate, in a single body, all the most important prerogatives of sovereignty, and thus entail upon our posterity one of the most execrable forms of government that human infatuation ever contrived. Thus we should create in reality that very tyranny which the adversaries of the new Constitution either are, or affect to be, solicitous to avert." THE FEDERALIST No. 22, supra, at 135.

These observations are consistent with what many of the Framers expressed, none more cogently than Hamilton in pointing up the need to divide and disperse power in order to protect liberty:

> "In republican government, the legislative authority necessarily predominates. The remedy for this inconveniency is to divide the legislature into different branches; and to render them, by different modes of election and different principles of action, as little connected with each other as the nature of their common functions and their common dependence on the society will admit." THE FEDERALIST No. 51 at 324.

See also THE FEDERALIST No. 62.

However familiar, it is useful to recall that apart from their fear that special interests could be favored at the expense of public needs, the Framers were also concerned, although not of one mind, over the apprehensions of the smaller states. Those states feared a commonality of interest among the larger states would work to their disadvantage; representatives of the larger states, on the other hand, were skeptical of a legislature that could pass laws favoring a minority of the people. *See* 1 M. Farrand, supra, 176-177, 484-491. It need hardly be repeated here that the Great Compromise, under which one House was viewed as representing the people and the other the states, allayed the fears of both the large and small states.

We see therefore that the Framers were acutely conscious that the bicameral requirement and the Presentment Clauses would serve essential constitutional functions. The President's participation in the legislative process was to protect the Executive Branch from Congress and to protect the whole people from improvident laws. The division of the Congress into two distinctive bodies assures that the legislative power would be exercised only after opportunity for full study and debate in separate settings. The President's unilateral veto power, in turn, was limited by the power of two thirds of both Houses of Congress to overrule a veto thereby precluding final arbitrary action of one person. *See* 1 M. Farrand, *supra*, at 99-104. It emerges clearly that the prescription for legislative action in Art. I, §§1, 7 represents the Framers' decision that the legislative power of the Federal government be exercised in accord with a single, finely wrought and exhaustively considered, procedure.

IV

The Constitution sought to divide the delegated powers of the new federal government into three defined categories, legislative, executive and judicial, to assure, as nearly as possible, that each Branch of government would confine itself to its assigned responsibility. The hydraulic pressure inherent within each of the separate Branches to exceed the outer limits of its power, even to accomplish desirable objectives, must be resisted.

Although not "hermetically" sealed from one another, *Buckley v. Valeo*, 424 U.S., at 121, the powers delegated to the three Branches are functionally identifiable. When any Branch acts, it is presumptively exercising the power the Constitution has delegated to it. *See Hampton & Co. v. United States*, 276 U.S. 394, 406. When the Executive acts, it presumptively acts in an executive or administrative capacity as defined in Art. II. And when, as here, one House of Congress purports to act, it is presumptively acting within its assigned sphere.

Beginning with this presumption, we must nevertheless establish that the challenged action under §244(c)(2) is of the kind to which the procedural requirements of Art. I, §7 apply. Not every action taken by either House is subject to the bicameralism and presentment requirements of Art. I. . . . Whether actions taken by either House are, in law and fact, an exercise of legislative power depends not on their form but upon "whether they contain matter which is properly to be regarded as legislative in its character and effect."

Examination of the action taken here by one House pursuant to §244(c)(2) reveals that it was essentially legislative in purpose and effect. In purporting to exercise power defined in Art. I, §8, cl. 4 to "establish an uniform Rule of Naturalization," the House took action that had the purpose and effect of altering the legal rights, duties and relations of persons, including the Attorney General, Executive Branch officials and Chadha, all outside the legislative branch. Section 244(c)(2) purports to authorize one House of Congress to require the Attorney General to deport an individual alien whose deportation otherwise would be cancelled under §244. The one-House veto operated in this case to overrule the Attorney General and mandate Chadha's deportation; absent the House action, Chadha would remain in the United States. Congress has acted and its action has altered Chadha's status.

The legislative character of the one-House veto in this case is confirmed by the character of the Congressional action it supplants. Neither the House of Representatives nor the Senate contends that, absent the veto provision in §244(c)(2), either of them, or both of them acting together, could effectively require the Attorney General to deport an alien once the Attorney General, in the exercise of legislatively delegated authority,[13] had determined the alien should remain in the United States. Without the challenged provision in §244(c)(2), this could have been achieved, if at all, only by legislation requiring deportation. Similarly, a veto by one House of Congress under §244(c)(2) cannot be justified as an attempt at amending the standards set out in §244(a)(1), or as a repeal of §244 as applied to Chadha. Amendment and repeal of statutes, no less than enactment, must conform with Art. I.

The nature of the decision implemented by the one-House veto in this case further manifests its legislative character. After long experience with the clumsy, time consuming private bill procedure, Congress made a deliberate choice to delegate to the Executive Branch, and specifically to the Attorney General, the authority to allow deportable aliens to remain in this country in certain specified circumstances. It is not disputed that this choice to delegate authority is precisely the kind of decision that can be implemented only in accordance with the procedures set out in Art. I. Disagreement with the Attorney General's decision on

---

[13] Congress protests that affirming the Court of Appeals in this case will sanction "lawmaking by the Attorney General. . . . Why is the Attorney General exempt from submitting his proposed changes in the law to the full bicameral process?" Brief of the United States House of Representatives 40. To be sure, some administrative agency action-rule making, for example-may resemble "lawmaking." See 5 U.S.C. §551(4), which defines an agency's "rule" as "the whole or part of an agency statement of general or particular applicability and future effect designed to implement, interpret, or prescribe law or policy . . . ." This Court has referred to agency activity as being "quasi-legislative" in character. Humphrey's Executor v. United States, 295 U.S. 602, 628 (1935). Clearly, however, "[i]n the framework of our Constitution, the President's power to see that the laws are faithfully executed refutes the idea that he is to be a lawmaker." Youngstown Sheet & Tube Co. v. Sawyer, 343 U.S. 579, 587 (1952). See Buckley v. Valeo, 424 U.S. 1, 123 (1976). When the Attorney General performs his duties pursuant to §244, he does not exercise "legislative" power. See Ernst & Ernst v. Hochfelder, 425 U.S. 185, 213-214 (1976). The bicameral process is not necessary as a check on the Executive's administration of the laws because his administrative activity cannot reach beyond the limits of the statute that created it-a statute duly enacted pursuant to Art. I, §§1, 7. The constitutionality of the Attorney General's execution of the authority delegated to him by §244 involves only a question of delegation doctrine. The courts, when a case or controversy arises, can always "ascertain whether the will of Congress has been obeyed," Yakus v. United States, 321 U.S. 414, 425, 64 S. Ct. 660, 668, 88 L. Ed. 834 (1944), and can enforce adherence to statutory standards. See Youngstown Sheet & Tube Co. v. Sawyer, 343 U.S. 579, 585 (1952); Ethyl Corp. v. EPA, 541 F.2d 1, 68 (CADC) (en banc) (separate statement of Leventhal, J.), cert. denied, 426 U.S. 941 (1976); L. Jaffe, Judicial Control of Administrative Action 320 (1965). It is clear, therefore, that the Attorney General acts in his presumptively Art. II capacity when he administers the Immigration and Nationality Act. Executive action under legislatively delegated authority that might resemble "legislative" action in some respects is not subject to the approval of both Houses of Congress and the President for the reason that the Constitution does not so require. That kind of Executive action is always subject to check by the terms of the legislation that authorized it; and if that authority is exceeded it is open to judicial review as well as the power of Congress to modify or revoke the authority entirely. A one-House veto is clearly legislative in both character and effect and is not so checked; the need for the check provided by Art. I, §§1, 7 is therefore clear. Congress' authority to delegate portions of its power to administrative agencies provides no support for the argument that Congress can constitutionally control administration of the laws by way of a Congressional veto.

Chadha's deportation — that is, Congress' decision to deport Chadha — no less than Congress' original choice to delegate to the Attorney General the authority to make that decision, involves determinations of policy that Congress can implement in only one way; bicameral passage followed by presentment to the President. Congress must abide by its delegation of authority until that delegation is legislatively altered or revoked.

This does not mean that Congress is required to capitulate to "the accretion of policy control by forces outside its chambers." Javits and Klein, *Congressional Oversight and the Legislative Veto: A Constitutional Analysis*, 52 N.Y.U. L. Rev. 455, 462 (1977). The Constitution provides Congress with abundant means to oversee and control its administrative creatures. Beyond the obvious fact that Congress ultimately controls administrative agencies in the legislation that creates them, other means of control, such as durational limits on authorizations and formal reporting requirements, lie well within Congress' constitutional power.

Finally, we see that when the Framers intended to authorize either House of Congress to act alone and outside of its prescribed bicameral legislative role, they narrowly and precisely defined the procedure for such action. There are but four provisions in the Constitution, explicit and unambiguous, by which one House may act alone with the unreviewable force of law, not subject to the President's veto:

a. The House of Representatives alone was given the power to initiate impeachments. Art. I, §2, cl. 6;
b. The Senate alone was given the power to conduct trials following impeachment on charges initiated by the House and to convict following trial. Art. I, §3, cl. 5;
c. The Senate alone was given final unreviewable power to approve or to disapprove presidential appointments. Art. II, §2, cl. 2;
d. The Senate alone was given unreviewable power to ratify treaties negotiated by the President. Art. II, §2, cl. 2.

Clearly, when the Draftsmen sought to confer special powers on one House, independent of the other House, or of the President, they did so in explicit, unambiguous terms. These carefully defined exceptions from presentment and bicameralism underscore the difference between the legislative functions of Congress and other unilateral but important and binding one-House acts provided for in the Constitution. . . .

Since it is clear that the action by the House under §244(c)(2) was not within any of the express constitutional exceptions authorizing one House to act alone, and equally clear that it was an exercise of legislative power, that action was subject to the standards prescribed in Article I. The bicameral requirement, the Presentment Clauses, the President's veto, and Congress' power to override a veto were intended to erect enduring checks on each Branch and to protect the people from the improvident exercise of power by mandating certain prescribed steps. To preserve those checks, and maintain the separation of powers, the carefully defined limits on the power of each Branch must not be eroded. To accomplish what has been attempted by one House of Congress in this case requires action in conformity with the express procedures of the Constitution's prescription for legislative action: passage by a majority of both Houses and presentment to the President.

The veto authorized by §244(c)(2) doubtless has been in many respects a convenient shortcut; the "sharing" with the Executive by Congress of its authority over aliens in this manner is, on its face, an appealing compromise. In purely practical terms, it is obviously easier for action to be taken by one House without submission to the President; but it is crystal clear from the records of the Convention, contemporaneous writings and debates, that the Framers ranked other values higher than efficiency. The records of the Convention and debates in the States preceding ratification underscore the common desire to define and limit the exercise of the newly created federal powers affecting the states and the people. There is unmistakable expression of a determination that legislation by the national Congress be a step-by-step, deliberate and deliberative process.

The choices we discern as having been made in the Constitutional Convention impose burdens on governmental processes that often seem clumsy, inefficient, even unworkable, but those hard choices were consciously made by men who had lived under a form of government that permitted arbitrary governmental acts to go unchecked. There is no support in the Constitution or decisions of this Court for the proposition that the cumbersomeness and delays often encountered in complying with explicit Constitutional standards may be avoided, either by the Congress or by the President. *See Youngstown Sheet & Tube Co. v. Sawyer*, 343 U.S. 579 (1952). With all the obvious flaws of delay, untidiness, and potential for abuse, we have not yet found a better way to preserve freedom than by making the exercise of power subject to the carefully crafted restraints spelled out in the Constitution. . . .

We hold that the congressional veto provision in §244(c)(2) . . . is constitutional. Accordingly, the judgment of the Court of Appeals is
   Affirmed.

Justice POWELL, concurring in the judgment.

The Court's decision, based on the Presentment Clauses, Art. I, §7, cls. 2 and 3, apparently will invalidate every use of the legislative veto. The breadth of this holding gives one pause. Congress has included the veto in literally hundreds of statutes, dating back to the 1930s. Congress clearly views this procedure as essential to controlling the delegation of power to administrative agencies. One reasonably may disagree with Congress' assessment of the veto's utility, but the respect due its judgment as a coordinate branch of Government cautions that our holding should be no more extensive than necessary to decide this case. In my view, the case may be decided on a narrower ground. When Congress finds that a particular person does not satisfy the statutory criteria for permanent residence in this country it has assumed a judicial function in violation of the principle of separation of powers. Accordingly, I concur only in the judgment.

... The Court thus has been mindful that the boundaries between each branch should be fixed "according to common sense and the inherent necessities of the governmental co-ordination." *J.W. Hampton, Jr. & Co. v. United States,* 276 U.S. 394, 406 (1928). But where one branch has impaired or sought to assume a power central to another branch, the Court has not hesitated to enforce the doctrine. *See Buckley v. Valeo,* 424 U.S., at 123.

Functionally, the doctrine may be violated in two ways. One branch may interfere impermissibly with the other's performance of its constitutionally assigned function. *See Nixon v. Administrator of General Services,* 433 U.S. 425, 433 (1977); *United States v. Nixon,* 418 U.S. 683 (1974). Alternatively, the doctrine may be violated when one branch assumes a function that more properly is entrusted to another. *See Youngstown Sheet & Tube Co. v. Sawyer,* supra, 343 U.S., at 587 (1952) ... This case presents the latter situation.

On its face, the House's action appears clearly adjudicatory. The House did not enact a general rule; rather it made its own determination that six specific persons did not comply with certain statutory criteria. It thus undertook the type of decision that traditionally has been left to other branches. Even if the House did not make a de novo determination, but simply reviewed the Immigration and Naturalization Service's findings, it still assumed a function ordinarily entrusted to the federal courts. *See* 5 U.S.C. §704 (providing generally for judicial review of final agency action) . . . .Where, as here, Congress has exercised a power "that cannot possibly be regarded as merely in aid of the legislative function of Congress," *Buckley v. Valeo,* 424 U.S., at 138, the decisions of this Court have held that Congress impermissibly assumed a function that the Constitution entrusted to another branch, *see id.* at 138-41.

The impropriety of the House's assumption of this function is confirmed by the fact that its action raises the very danger the Framers sought to avoid — the exercise of unchecked power. In deciding whether Chadha deserves to be deported, Congress is not subject to any internal constraints that prevent it from arbitrarily depriving him of the right to remain in this country. Unlike the judiciary or an administrative agency, Congress is not bound by established substantive rules. Nor is it subject to the procedural safeguards, such as the right to counsel and a hearing before an impartial tribunal, that are present when a court or an agency adjudicates individual rights. The only effective constraint on Congress' power is political, but Congress is most accountable politically when it prescribes rules of general applicability. When it decides rights of specific persons, those rights are subject to "the tyranny of a shifting majority."

Chief Justice Marshall observed: "It is the peculiar province of the legislature to prescribe general rules for the government of society; the application of those rules would seem to be the duty of other departments." *Fletcher v. Peck,* 6 Cranch 87, 136 (1810). In my view, when Congress undertook to apply its rules to Chadha, it exceeded the scope of its constitutionally prescribed authority. I would not reach the broader question whether legislative vetoes are invalid under the Presentment Clauses.

Justice WHITE, dissenting.

Today the Court not only invalidates §244(c)(2) of the Immigration and Nationality Act, but also sounds the death knell for nearly 200 other statutory provisions in which Congress has reserved a "legislative veto." For this reason, the Court's decision is of surpassing importance. And it is for this reason that the Court would have been well-advised to decide the case, if possible, on the narrower grounds of separation of powers, leaving for full consideration the constitutionality of other congressional review statutes operating on such varied matters as war powers and agency rulemaking, some of which concern the independent regulatory agencies.

[T]he legislative veto is more than "efficient, convenient, and useful." . . . It is an important if not indispensable political invention that allows the President and Congress to resolve major constitutional and policy differences, assures the accountability of independent regulatory agencies, and preserves Congress' control over lawmaking. Perhaps there are other means of accommodation and accountability, but the increasing reliance of Congress upon the legislative veto suggests that the alternatives to which Congress must now turn are not entirely satisfactory.

The history of the legislative veto also makes clear that it has not been a sword with which Congress has struck out to aggrandize itself at the expense of the other branches — the concerns of Madison and Hamilton. Rather, the veto has been a means of defense, a reservation of ultimate authority necessary if Congress is to fulfill its designated role under Article I as the nation's lawmaker. While the President has often objected to particular legislative vetoes, generally those left in the hands of congressional committees, the Executive has more often agreed to legislative review as the price for a broad delegation of authority. To be sure, the President may have preferred unrestricted power, but that could be precisely why Congress thought it essential to retain a check on the exercise of delegated authority.

For all these reasons, the apparent sweep of the Court's decision today is regrettable. The Court's Article I analysis appears to invalidate all legislative vetoes irrespective of form or subject. Because the legislative veto is commonly found as a check upon rulemaking by administrative agencies and upon broad-based policy decisions of the Executive Branch, it is particularly unfortunate that the Court reaches its decision in a case involving the exercise of a veto over deportation decisions regarding particular individuals. Courts should always be wary of striking statutes as unconstitutional; to strike an entire class of statutes based on consideration of a somewhat atypical and more-readily indictable exemplar of the class is irresponsible.

The reality of the situation is that the constitutional question posed today is one of immense difficulty over which the executive and legislative branches — as well as scholars and judges — have understandably disagreed. In my view, neither Article I of the Constitution nor the doctrine of separation of powers is violated by this mechanism by which our elected representatives preserve their voice in the governance of the nation. The power to exercise a legislative veto is not the power to write new law without bicameral approval or presidential consideration. The veto must be authorized by statute and may only negative what an Executive department or independent agency has proposed. On its face, the legislative veto no more allows one House of Congress to make law than does the presidential veto confer such power upon the President. Accordingly, the Court properly recognizes that it "must establish that the challenged action under §244(c)(2) is of the kind to which the procedural requirements of Art. I, §7 apply" and admits that "not every action taken by either House is subject to the bicameralism and presentation requirements of Art. I." Ante, at 2784.

The Court's holding today that all legislative-type action must be enacted through the lawmaking process ignores that legislative authority is routinely delegated to the Executive branch, to the independent regulatory agencies, and to private individuals and groups.

"The rise of administrative bodies probably has been the most significant legal trend of the last century.... They have become a veritable fourth branch of the Government, which has deranged our three-branch legal theories...." *Federal Trade Commission v. Ruberoid Co.*, 343 U.S. 470, 487 (1952) (Jackson, J. dissenting).

If Congress may delegate lawmaking power to independent and executive agencies, it is most difficult to understand Article I as forbidding Congress from also reserving a check on legislative power for itself. Absent the veto, the agencies receiving delegations of legislative or quasi-legislative power may issue regulations having the force of law without bicameral approval and without the President's signature. It is thus not apparent why the reservation of a veto over the exercise of that legislative power must be subject to a more exacting test. In both cases, it is enough that the initial statutory authorizations comply with the Article I requirements.

The Court also takes no account of perhaps the most relevant consideration: However resolutions of disapproval under §244(c)(2) are formally characterized, in reality, a departure from the status quo occurs only upon the concurrence of opinion among the House, Senate, and President. Reservations of legislative authority to be exercised by Congress should be upheld if the exercise of such reserved authority is consistent with the distribution of and limits upon legislative power that Article I provides.

The central concern of the presentation and bicameralism requirements of Article I is that when a departure from the legal status quo is undertaken, it is done with the approval of the President and both Houses of Congress — or, in the event of a presidential veto, a two-thirds majority in both Houses. This interest is fully satisfied by the operation of §244(c)(2). The President's approval is found in the Attorney General's action in recommending to Congress that the deportation order for a given alien be suspended. The House and the Senate indicate their approval of the Executive's action by not passing a resolution of disapproval within the statutory period. Thus, a change in the legal status quo — the deportability of the alien — is consummated only with the approval of each of the three relevant actors. The disagreement of any one of the three maintains the alien's pre-existing status: the Executive may choose not to recommend suspension; the

House and Senate may each veto the recommendation. The effect on the rights and obligations of the affected individuals and upon the legislative system is precisely the same as if a private bill were introduced but failed to receive the necessary approval. "The President and the two Houses enjoy exactly the same say in what the law is to be as would have been true for each without the presence of the one-House veto, and nothing in the law is changed absent the concurrence of the President and a majority in each House." *Atkins v. United States*, 556 F.2d 1028, 1064 (Ct. Claims, 1977).

[T]he history of the separation of powers doctrine is also a history of accommodation and practicality. Apprehensions of an overly powerful branch have not led to undue prophylactic measures that handicap the effective working of the national government as a whole. The Constitution does not contemplate total separation of the three branches of Government. *Buckley v. Valeo*, 424 U.S. 1, 121 (1976). "[A] hermetic sealing off of the three branches of Government from one another would preclude the establishment of a Nation capable of governing itself effectively." *Ibid.*

"[I]n determining whether the Act disrupts the proper balance between the coordinate branches, the proper inquiry focuses on the extent to which it prevents the Executive Branch from accomplishing its constitutionally assigned functions. *United States v. Nixon*, 418 U.S. [683] at 711-712. Only where the potential for disruption is present must we then determine whether that impact is justified by an overriding need to promote objectives within the constitutional authority of Congress." 433 U.S., at 443.

Section 244(c)(2) survives this test. The legislative veto provision does not "prevent the Executive Branch from accomplishing its constitutionally assigned functions." First, it is clear that the Executive Branch has no "constitutionally assigned" function of suspending the deportation of aliens. "'Over no conceivable subject is the legislative power of Congress more complete than it is over' the admission of aliens." *Kleindienst v. Mandel*, 408 U.S. 753, 766 (1972), quoting *Oceanic Steam Navigation Co. v. Stranahan*, 214 U.S. 320, 339 (1909). Nor can it be said that the inherent function of the Executive Branch in executing the law is involved. Here, §244 grants the executive only a qualified suspension authority and it is only that authority which the President is constitutionally authorized to execute.

Moreover, the Court believes that the legislative veto we consider today is best characterized as an exercise of legislative or quasi-legislative authority. Under this characterization, the practice does not, even on the surface, constitute an infringement of executive or judicial prerogative. The Attorney General's suspension of deportation is equivalent to a proposal for legislation. The nature of the Attorney General's role as recommendatory is not altered because §244 provides for congressional action through disapproval rather than by ratification. In comparison to private bills, which must be initiated in the Congress and which allow a Presidential veto to be overridden by a two-thirds majority in both Houses of Congress, §244 augments rather than reduces the executive branch's authority. So understood, congressional review does not undermine, as the Court of Appeals thought, the "weight and dignity" that attends the decisions of the Executive Branch.

Nor does §244 infringe on the judicial power, as Justice Powell would hold. Section 244 makes clear that Congress has reserved its own judgment as part of the statutory process. Congressional action does not substitute for judicial review of the Attorney General's decisions. The Act provides for judicial review of the refusal of the Attorney General to suspend a deportation and to transmit a recommendation to Congress. *INS v. Wang*, 450 U.S. 139 (1981) (per curiam). But the courts have not been given the authority to review whether an alien should be given permanent status; review is limited to whether the Attorney General has properly applied the statutory standards for essentially denying the alien a recommendation that his deportable status be changed by the Congress. Moreover, there is no constitutional obligation to provide any judicial review whatever for a failure to suspend deportation. "The power of Congress, therefore, to expel, like the power to exclude aliens, or any specified class of aliens, from the country, may be exercised entirely through executive officers; or Congress may call in the aid of the judiciary to ascertain any contested facts on which an alien's right to be in the country has been made by Congress to depend." *Fong Yue Ting v. United States*, 149 U.S. 698, 713-714 (1893).

I do not suggest that all legislative vetoes are necessarily consistent with separation of powers principles. A legislative check on an inherently executive function, for example that of initiating prosecutions, poses an entirely different question. But the legislative veto device here — and in many other settings — is far from an instance of legislative tyranny over the Executive. It is a necessary check on the unavoidably expanding power of the agencies, both executive and independent, as they engage in exercising authority delegated by Congress.

NOTES AND QUESTIONS

1. The majority invalidated all negative legislative vetoes as a violation of the constitutional lawmaking requirements of bicameralism and presentment. Justice Powell would have invalidated the legislative veto at issue in the case because it involved the exercise of judicial power. Why did the majority and Justice Powell have different understandings?

2. How do we think about the majority's focus on the legislative process? On the one hand, that focus seems overly formalistic, given the reality of the regulatory state. On the other hand, the INS and the Attorney General accorded Chadha the full rigors of the administrative process only to have that process overturned by Congress, without the full rigors of the legislative process. Perhaps the great danger of the legislative veto in Chadha's case *was* the process (or lack thereof). In the individual rights context, a version of Justice Powell's argument is that legislators should not assume the role of adjudicators because they lack an individualized, trial-type process. Does that argument prove too much? Could Congress pass a statute deporting Chadha? In any event, the larger question posed by both the majority and the concurrence: is the administrative process a better option than the legislative veto?

3. Note that most legislative vetoes reverse an agency regulation of general application rather than an adjudicatory order involving a specific person's legal status. Consider a legislative veto provision in an energy statute, which authorizes either House to disapprove by resolution certain NHTSA "energy actions" involving fuel economy and pricing. *See* Energy Policy and Conservation Act, 42 U.S.C. §6421(c) (authorizing either House to disapprove certain presidentially proposed "energy actions" involving fuel economy and pricing). Opponents of a certain energy action would only need to persuade one House of Congress to veto the action. The legislative veto makes it cheaper for private groups to skew legislation in their preferred direction. Isn't this the sort of arbitrary action that the formal legislative process is designed to inhibit (i.e., hasty and improvident law)?

4. Now consider whether the legislative veto might encourage Congress to enact especially vague statutes. Can you see why it might have this effect? Is this a *constitutional* reason to reject the legislative veto? What kind of bicameralism are we getting if Congress has a tool that allows it to retain a measure of control even when it enacts vague statutes?

5. The legislative veto also might elevate the preferences of the current Congress above those of the enacting Congress in the implementation of a statute. Suppose the enacting Congress intended the "extreme hardship" provision to be liberally applied, but a subsequent committee or coalition took a different view, which it implemented through the veto. Is this what happened in the case? If so, whose view should count?

6. Justice White argued in dissent that nothing in the Constitution prohibits the legislative veto and that the legislative veto operates as a safety valve against ever-expanding agency authority. In effect, the legislative veto restores to Congress the level of control it lost when the complexity of modern industrial society compelled it to grant broad authority to agencies. Once we acknowledge that broad delegation is necessary, shouldn't we be prepared to accept a congressional check? Does that suggest that Justice White's view is correct?

7. Think about the issue from a slightly different angle. The President possesses means short of legislation to assert control of agency action (although the President cannot possess a "line item" veto, *see* pp. 589). Doesn't Congress deserve a comparable tool? Why is it restricted to the seemingly all-or-nothing choice between statutory amendments and oversight hearings?

8. Following the *Chadha* decision, Congress continued to enact statutes that contained legislative veto provisions. *See* Louis Fisher, *The Legislative Veto: Invalidated, It Survives*, 56 LAW & CONTEMP. PROBS. 273, 275-84 (1993). Although the legislative veto provisions are not constitutional if acted upon, Congress appears to believe that agencies will take them as a warning. In 1996, Congress came up with an alternative mechanism to provide review of agency regulations as part of the Contract with America Advancement Act of 1996. It is the granddaddy of all "laying over" provisions, the Congressional Review Act ("CRA"), 5 U.S.C. §§801-803. We describe the CRA above, see p. 607. It requires agencies to submit their regulations to Congress and then wait for a certain period of time before those regulations become effective, during

which time Congress can override them by joint resolution. Why is the CRA constitutional after *Chadha*? We also noted that Congress has only repealed a single rule under the CRA, as of 2008. What does this suggest about the CRA? Is it too formal to work?

---

13. *Congressional Control of Agency Officials*

Another tool that Congress has created and the Court has rejected concerns control of agency officials. As you know, Congress has many (valid) means to assert control of agency officials. Congress has a constitutional role in the appointment of agency officials. The Constitution provides that presidential appointment of "Officers of the United States" must be made with the "Advice and Consent" of the Senate. U.S. CONST. Art. II, §2. Moreover, Congress has the ability to bring pressure to bear on particular officials once appointed, for example, by calling them to appear for an oversight hearing. The question, however, is whether Congress can seek more formal or direct means to assert control of agency officials. What if Congress created a scheme that granted itself a role in removing an agency head? Congress could then use that removal power to compel compliance with its preferences, much as the President is able to do. The Court held that such a strategy is unconstitutional.

Bowsher v. Synar

478 U.S. 714 (1986)

CHIEF JUSTICE BURGER delivered the opinion of the Court.

The question presented by these appeals is whether the assignment by Congress to the Comptroller General of the United States of certain functions under the Balanced Budget and Emergency Deficit Control Act of 1985 [Gramm-Rudman-Hollings] violates the doctrine of separation of powers.

I

. . . The purpose of the [Gramm-Rudman-Hollings] Act is to eliminate the federal budget deficit. To that end, the Act sets a "maximum deficit amount" for federal spending for each of fiscal years 1986 through 1991. The size of that maximum deficit amount progressively reduces to zero in fiscal year 1991. If in any fiscal year the federal budget deficit exceeds the maximum deficit amount by more than a specified sum, the Act requires across-the-board cuts in federal spending to reach the targeted deficit level, with half of the cuts made to defense programs and the other half made to nondefense programs.

These "automatic" reductions are accomplished through a rather compli-cated procedure, spelled out in §251, the so-called "reporting provisions" of the Act. Each year, the Directors of the Office of Management and Budget (OMB) and the Congressional Budget Office (CBO) independently estimate the amount of the federal budget deficit for the upcoming fiscal year. If that deficit exceeds the maximum targeted deficit amount for that fiscal year by more than a specified amount, the Directors of OMB and CBO independently calculate, on a program-by-program basis, the budget reductions necessary to ensure that the deficit does not exceed the maximum deficit amount. The Act then requires the Directors to report jointly their deficit estimates and budget reduction calculations to the Comptroller General.

The Comptroller General, after reviewing the Directors' reports, then reports his conclusions to the President. §251(b). The President in turn must issue a "sequestration" order mandating the spending reductions specified by the Comp-troller General. §252. There follows a period during which Congress may by legis-lation reduce spending to obviate, in whole or in part, the need for the sequestration order. If such reductions are not enacted, the sequestration order becomes effective and the spending reductions included in that order are made. . . .

Within hours of the President's signing of the Act, Congressman Synar, who had voted against the Act, filed a complaint seeking declaratory relief that the Act was unconstitutional. Eleven other Members later joined Congressman Synar's suit. A virtually identical lawsuit was also filed by the National Treasury Employ-ees Union. The Union alleged that its members had been injured as a result of the Act's automatic spending reduction provisions, which have suspended certain cost-of-living benefit increases to the Union's members.

II

[The Court first addressed the issuing of standing and found that one of the appel-lants, a member of the Union, had an injury in fact.]

III

We noted recently that "[t]he Constitution sought to divide the delegated powers of the new Federal Government into three defined categories, Legislative, Execu-tive, and Judicial." *INS v. Chadha*, 462 U.S. 919, 951 (1983). The declared pur-pose of separating and dividing the powers of government, of course, was to "diffus[e] power the better to secure liberty." *Youngstown Sheet & Tube Co. v. Sawyer*, 343 U.S. 579, 635 (1952) (Jackson, J., concurring). . . .

Other, more subtle, examples of separated powers are evident as well. Unlike parliamentary systems such as that of Great Britain, no person who is an officer of the United States may serve as a Member of the Congress. Art. I, §6. Moreover, unlike parliamentary systems, the President, under Article II, is responsible not to the Congress but to the people, subject only to impeachment proceedings which are exercised by the two Houses as representatives of the people. Art. II, §4. And even in the impeachment of a President the presiding officer of the ultimate tribunal is not a member of the Legislative Branch, but the Chief Justice of the United States. Art. I, §3.

That this system of division and separation of powers produces conflicts, confusion, and discordance at times is inherent, but it was deliberately so structured to assure full, vigorous, and open debate on the great issues affecting the people and to provide avenues for the operation of checks on the exercise of governmental power.

The Constitution does not contemplate an active role for Congress in the supervision of officers charged with the execution of the laws it enacts. The President appoints "Officers of the United States" with the "Advice and Consent of the Senate . . . ." Art. II, §2. Once the appointment has been made and confirmed, however, the Constitution explicitly provides for removal of Officers of the United States by Congress only upon impeachment by the House of Representatives and conviction by the Senate. An impeachment by the House and trial by the Senate can rest only on "Treason, Bribery or other high Crimes and Misdemeanors." Article II, §4. A direct congressional role in the removal of officers charged with the execution of the laws beyond this limited one is inconsistent with separation of powers.

This Court first directly addressed this issue in *Myers v. United States*, 272 U.S. 52 (1925). At issue in *Myers* was a statute providing that certain postmasters could be removed only "by and with the advice and consent of the Senate." The President removed one such Postmaster without Senate approval, and a lawsuit ensued. Chief Justice Taft, writing for the Court, declared the statute unconstitutional on the ground that for Congress to "draw to itself, or to either branch of it, the power to remove or the right to participate in the exercise of that power . . . would be . . . to infringe the constitutional principle of the separation of governmental powers." *Id.*, at 161.

A decade later, in *Humphrey's Executor v. United States*, 295 U.S. 602 (1935), relied upon heavily by appellants, a Federal Trade Commissioner who had been removed by the President sought backpay. *Humphrey's Executor* involved an issue not presented either in the *Myers* case or in this case — i.e., the power of Congress to limit the President's powers of removal of a Federal Trade Commissioner. 295 U.S., at 630.[14] The relevant statute permitted removal "by the President," but only "for inefficiency, neglect of duty, or malfeasance in office." Justice Sutherland, speaking for the Court, upheld the statute, holding that "illimitable power of removal is not possessed by the President [with respect to Federal Trade

---

[14] Appellants therefore are wide of the mark in arguing that an affirmance in this case requires casting doubt on the status of "independent" agencies because no issues involving such agencies are presented here. The statutes establishing independent agencies typically specify either that the agency members are removable by the President for specified causes, see, e.g., 15 U.S.C. §41 (members of the Federal Trade Commission may be removed by the President "for inefficiency, neglect of duty, or malfeasance in office"), or else do not specify a removal procedure, see, e.g., 2 U.S.C. §437c (Federal Election Commission). This case involves nothing like these statutes, but rather a statute that provides for direct congressional involvement over the decision to remove the Comptroller General. Appellants have referred us to no independent agency whose members are removable by the Congress for certain causes short of impeachable offenses, as is the Comptroller General. . . .

Commissioners]." *Id.*, at 628-629. The Court distinguished *Myers*, reaffirming its holding that congressional participation in the removal of executive officers is unconstitutional. Justice Sutherland's opinion for the Court also underscored the crucial role of separated powers in our system:

> "The fundamental necessity of maintaining each of the three general departments of government entirely free from the control or coercive influence, direct or indirect, of either of the others, has often been stressed and is hardly open to serious question. So much is implied in the very fact of the separation of the powers of these departments by the Constitution; and in the rule which recognizes their essential co-equality." 295 U.S., at 629-630.

The Court reached a similar result in *Wiener v. United States*, 357 U.S. 349 (1958), concluding that, under *Humphrey's Executor*, the President did not have unrestrained removal authority over a member of the War Claims Commission.

In light of these precedents, we conclude that Congress cannot reserve for itself the power of removal of an officer charged with the execution of the laws except by impeachment. To permit the execution of the laws to be vested in an officer answerable only to Congress would, in practical terms, reserve in Congress control over the execution of the laws. As the District Court observed: "Once an officer is appointed, it is only the authority that can remove him, and not the authority that appointed him, that he must fear and, in the performance of his functions, obey." 626 F. Supp., at 1401. The structure of the Constitution does not permit Congress to execute the laws; it follows that Congress cannot grant to an officer under its control what it does not possess.

Our decision in *INS v. Chadha*, 462 U.S. 919 (1983), supports this conclusion. To permit an officer controlled by Congress to execute the laws would be, in essence, to permit a congressional veto. Congress could simply remove, or threaten to remove, an officer for executing the laws in any fashion found to be unsatisfactory to Congress. This kind of congressional control over the execution of the laws, *Chadha* makes clear, is constitutionally impermissible.

. . . With these principles in mind, we turn to consideration of whether the Comptroller General is controlled by Congress.

IV

Appellants urge that the Comptroller General performs his duties independently and is not subservient to Congress. We agree with the District Court that this contention does not bear close scrutiny.

The critical factor lies in the provisions of the statute defining the Comptroller General's office relating to removability. Although the Comptroller General is nominated by the President from a list of three individuals recommended by the Speaker of the House of Representatives and the President pro tempore of the Senate, *see* 31 U.S.C. §703(a)(2), and confirmed by the Senate, he is removable only at the initiative of Congress. He may be removed not only by impeachment but also by joint resolution of Congress "at any time" resting on any one of the following bases:

> "(i) permanent disability;
> "(ii) inefficiency;
> "(iii) neglect of duty;
> "(iv) malfeasance; or
> "(v) a felony or conduct involving moral turpitude."

31 U.S.C. §703(e)(1)B.[15]

This provision was included, as one Congressman explained in urging passage of the Act, because Congress "felt that [the Comptroller General] should be brought under the sole control of Congress, so that Congress at any moment when it found he was inefficient and was not carrying on the duties of his office as he should and as the Congress expected, could remove him without the long, tedious process of a trial by impeachment." 61 Cong. Rec. 1081 (1921).

The removal provision was an important part of the legislative scheme, as a number of Congressmen recognized. Representative Hawley commented: "[H]e is our officer, in a measure, getting information for us. . . . If he does not do his work properly, we, as practically his employers, ought to be able to discharge him from his office." 58 Cong. Rec. 7136 (1919). Representative Sisson observed that the removal provisions would give "[t]he Congress of the United States . . . absolute control of the man's destiny in office." 61 Cong. Rec. 987 (1921). The ultimate design was to "give the legislative branch of the Government control of the audit, not through the power of appointment, but through the power of removal." 58 Cong. Rec. 7211 (1919) (Rep. Temple).

The statute permits removal for "inefficiency," "neglect of duty," or "malfeasance." These terms are very broad and, as interpreted by Congress, could sustain removal of a Comptroller General for any number of actual or perceived transgressions of the legislative will. The Constitutional Convention chose to permit impeachment of executive officers only for "Treason, Bribery, or other high Crimes and Misdemeanors." It rejected language that would have permitted impeachment for "maladministration," with Madison arguing that "[s]o vague a term will be equivalent to a tenure during pleasure of the Senate." 2 M. Farrand, Records of the Federal Convention of 1787, p. 550 (1911).

We need not decide whether "inefficiency" or "malfeasance" are terms as broad as "maladministration" in order to reject the dissent's position that removing the Comptroller General requires "a feat of bipartisanship more difficult than that required to impeach and convict." *Post*, at 3213 (White, J., dissenting). Surely no one would seriously suggest that judicial independence would be strengthened by allowing removal of federal judges only by a joint resolution finding "inefficiency," "neglect of duty," or "malfeasance." . . .

---

[15] Although the President could veto such a joint resolution, the veto could be overridden by a two-thirds vote of both Houses of Congress. Thus, the Comptroller General could be removed in the face of Presidential opposition. Like the District Court, 626 F. Supp., at 1393, n.21, we therefore read the removal provision as authorizing removal by Congress alone.

It is clear that Congress has consistently viewed the Comptroller General as an officer of the Legislative Branch. The Reorganization Acts of 1945 and 1949, for example, both stated that the Comptroller General and the GAO are "a part of the legislative branch of the Government." 59 Stat. 616. Similarly, in the Accounting and Auditing Act of 1950, Congress required the Comptroller General to conduct audits "as an agent of the Congress." 64 Stat. 835. . . .

Against this background, we see no escape from the conclusion that, because Congress has retained removal authority over the Comptroller General, he may not be entrusted with executive powers. The remaining question is whether the Comptroller General has been assigned such powers in the Balanced Budget and Emergency Deficit Control Act of 1985. . . .

Appellants suggest that the duties assigned to the Comptroller General in the Act are essentially ministerial and mechanical so that their performance does not constitute "execution of the law" in a meaningful sense. On the contrary, we view these functions as plainly entailing execution of the law in constitutional terms. Interpreting a law enacted by Congress to implement the legislative mandate is the very essence of "execution" of the law. Under §251, the Comptroller General must exercise judgment concerning facts that affect the application of the Act. He must also interpret the provisions of the Act to determine precisely what budgetary calculations are required. Decisions of that kind are typically made by officers charged with executing a statute.

The executive nature of the Comptroller General's functions under the Act is revealed in §252(a)(3) which gives the Comptroller General the ultimate authority to determine the budget cuts to be made. Indeed, the Comptroller General commands the President himself to carry out, without the slightest variation (with exceptions not relevant to the constitutional issues presented), the directive of the Comptroller General as to the budget reductions:

> "The [Presidential] order must provide for reductions in the manner specified in section 251(a)(3), must incorporate the provisions of the [Comptroller General's] report submitted under section 251(b), and must be consistent with such report in all respects. The President may not modify or recalculate any of the estimates, determinations, specifications, bases, amounts, or percentages set forth in the report submitted under section 251(b) in determining the reductions to be specified in the order with respect to programs, projects, and activities, or with respect to budget activities, within an account . . . ." §252(a)(3) (emphasis added).

See also §251(d)(3)(A).

Congress of course initially determined the content of the Balanced Budget and Emergency Deficit Control Act; and undoubtedly the content of the Act determines the nature of the executive duty. However, as *Chadha* makes clear, once Congress makes its choice in enacting legislation, its participation ends. Congress can thereafter control the execution of its enactment only indirectly — by passing new legislation. *Chadha*, 462 U.S., at 958. By placing the responsibility for execution of the Balanced Budget and Emergency Deficit Control Act in the hands of an officer who is subject to removal only by itself, Congress in effect has retained control over the execution of the Act and has intruded into the executive function. The Constitution does not permit such intrusion.

Justice STEVENS, with whom Justice MARSHALL joins, concurring in the judgment.

When this Court is asked to invalidate a statutory provision that has been approved by both Houses of the Congress and signed by the President, particularly an Act of Congress that confronts a deeply vexing national problem, it should only do so for the most compelling constitutional reasons. I agree with the Court that the "Gramm-Rudman-Hollings" Act contains a constitutional infirmity so severe that the flawed provision may not stand. I disagree with the Court, however, on the reasons why the Constitution prohibits the Comptroller General from exercising the powers assigned to him by §251(b) and §251(c)(2) of the Act. It is not the dormant, carefully circumscribed congressional removal power that represents the primary constitutional evil. Nor do I agree with the conclusion of both the majority and the dissent that the analysis depends on a labeling of the functions assigned to the Comptroller General as "executive powers." . . . Rather, I am convinced that the Comptroller General must be characterized as an agent of Congress because of his longstanding statutory responsibilities; that the powers assigned to him under the Gramm-Rudman-Hollings Act require him to make policy that will bind the Nation; and that, when Congress, or a component or an agent of Congress, seeks to make policy that will bind the Nation, it must follow the procedures mandated by Article I of the Constitution — through passage by both Houses and presentment to the President. In short, Congress may not exercise its fundamental power to formulate national policy by delegating that power to one of its two Houses, to a legislative committee, or to an individual agent of the Congress such as the Speaker of the House of Representatives, the Sergeant at Arms of the Senate, or the Director of the Congressional Budget Office. *INS v. Chadha*, 462 U.S. 919 (1983). That principle, I believe, is applicable to the Comptroller General.

Justice WHITE, dissenting.

The Court, acting in the name of separation of powers, takes upon itself to strike down the Gramm-Rudman-Hollings Act, one of the most novel and far-reaching legislative responses to a national crisis since the New Deal. The basis of the Court's action is a solitary provision of another statute that was passed over 60 years ago and has lain dormant since that time. I cannot concur in the Court's action. Like the Court, I will not purport to speak to the wisdom of the policies incorporated in the legislation the Court invalidates; that is a matter for the Congress and the Executive, both of which expressed their assent to the statute barely half a year ago. I will, however, address the wisdom of the Court's willingness to interpose its distressingly formalistic view of separation of powers as a bar to the attainment of governmental objectives through the means chosen by the Congress and the President in the legislative process established by the Constitution. Twice in the past four years I have expressed my view that the Court's recent efforts to

police the separation of powers have rested on untenable constitutional propositions leading to regrettable results. *See Northern Pipeline Construction Co. v. Mar-
athon Pipe Line Co.*, 458 U.S. 50, 92-118 (1982) (White, J., dissenting); *INS v.
Chadha*, 462 U.S. 919, 967-1003 (1983) (White, J., dissenting). Today's result is
even more misguided. As I will explain, the Court's decision rests on a feature of
the legislative scheme that is of minimal practical significance and that presents
no substantial threat to the basic scheme of separation of powers. In attaching dispositive significance to what should be regarded as a triviality, the Court neglects
what has in the past been recognized as a fundamental principle governing consideration of disputes over separation of powers:

> "The actual art of governing under our Constitution does not and cannot conform
> to judicial definitions of the power of any of its branches based on isolated clauses
> or even single Articles torn from context. While the Constitution diffuses power the
> better to secure liberty, it also contemplates that practice will integrate the dispersed
> powers into a workable government." *Youngstown Sheet & Tube Co. v. Sawyer*, 343
> U.S. 579, 635 (1952) (Jackson, J., concurring).

I have no quarrel with the proposition that the powers exercised by the Comptroller under the Act may be characterized as "executive" in that they involve the
interpretation and carrying out of the Act's mandate. I can also accept the general
proposition that although Congress has considerable authority in designating the
officers who are to execute legislation, . . . the constitutional scheme of separated
powers does prevent Congress from reserving an executive role for itself or for its
"agents." . . . I cannot accept, however, that the exercise of authority by an officer
removable for cause by a joint resolution of Congress is analogous to the impermissible execution of the law by Congress itself, nor would I hold that the congressional role in the removal process renders the Comptroller an "agent" of the
Congress, incapable of receiving "executive" power.

As the majority points out, the Court's decision in *INS v. Chadha*, 462 U.S.
919 (1983), recognizes limits on the ability of Congress to participate in or influence the execution of the laws. As interpreted in *Chadha*, the Constitution prevents Congress from interfering with the actions of officers of the United States
through means short of legislation satisfying the demands of bicameral passage
and presentment to the President for approval or disapproval. *Id.*, at 954-955.
Today's majority concludes that the same concerns that underlay *Chadha* indicate the invalidity of a statutory provision allowing the removal by joint resolution
for specified cause of any officer performing executive functions. Such removal
power, the Court contends, constitutes a "congressional veto" analogous to that
struck down in *Chadha*, for it permits Congress to "remove, or threaten to
remove, an officer for executing the laws in any fashion found to be unsatisfactory." The Court concludes that it is "[t]his kind of congressional control over the
execution of the laws" that *Chadha* condemns.

The deficiencies in the Court's reasoning are apparent. First, the Court baldly
mischaracterizes the removal provision when it suggests that it allows Congress to
remove the Comptroller for "executing the laws in any fashion found to be

unsatisfactory"; in fact, Congress may remove the Comptroller only for one or more of five specified reasons, which "although not so narrow as to deny Congress any leeway, circumscribe Congress' power to some extent by providing a basis for judicial review of congressional removal." Second, and more to the point, the Court overlooks or deliberately ignores the decisive difference between the congressional removal provision and the legislative veto struck down in *Chadha*: under the Budget and Accounting Act, Congress may remove the Comptroller only through a joint resolution, which by definition must be passed by both Houses and signed by the President. *See United States v. California*, 332 U.S. 19, 28 (1947). In other words, a removal of the Comptroller under the statute satisfies the requirements of bicameralism and presentment laid down in *Chadha*. The majority's citation of *Chadha* for the proposition that Congress may only control the acts of officers of the United States "by passing new legislation," ante, at 3192, in no sense casts doubt on the legitimacy of the removal provision, for that provision allows Congress to effect removal only through action that constitutes legislation as defined in *Chadha*.

To the extent that it has any bearing on the problem now before us, *Chadha* would seem to suggest the legitimacy of the statutory provision making the Comptroller removable through joint resolution, for the Court's opinion in *Chadha* reflects the view that the bicameralism and presentment requirements of Art. I represent the principal assurances that Congress will remain within its legislative role in the constitutionally prescribed scheme of separated powers. Action taken in accordance with the "single, finely wrought, and exhaustively considered, procedure" established by Art. I, *Chadha*, supra, at 951, should be presumptively viewed as a legitimate exercise of legislative power. That such action may represent a more or less successful attempt by Congress to "control" the actions of an officer of the United States surely does not in itself indicate that it is unconstitutional, for no one would dispute that Congress has the power to "control" administration through legislation imposing duties or substantive restraints on executive officers, through legislation increasing or decreasing the funds made available to such officers, or through legislation actually abolishing a particular office. . . .

That a joint resolution removing the Comptroller General would satisfy the requirements for legitimate legislative action laid down in *Chadha* does not fully answer the separation of powers argument, for it is apparent that even the results of the constitutional legislative process may be unconstitutional if those results are in fact destructive of the scheme of separation-of-powers. *Nixon v. Administrator of General Services*, 433 U.S. 425 (1977). The question to be answered is whether the threat of removal of the Comptroller General for cause through joint resolution as authorized by the Budget and Accounting Act renders the Comptroller sufficiently subservient to Congress that investing him with "executive" power can be realistically equated with the unlawful retention of such power by Congress itself; more generally, the question is whether there is a genuine threat of "encroachment or aggrandizement of one branch at the expense of the other," *Buckley v. Valeo*, 424 U.S., at 122. Common sense indicates that the existence of the removal provision poses no such threat to the principle of separation of powers.

The statute does not permit anyone to remove the Comptroller at will; removal is permitted only for specified cause, with the existence of cause to be determined by Congress following a hearing. Any removal under the statute would presumably be subject to post-termination judicial review to ensure that a hearing had in fact been held and that the finding of cause for removal was not arbitrary. These procedural and substantive limitations on the removal power militate strongly against the characterization of the Comptroller as a mere agent of Congress by virtue of the removal authority. Indeed, similarly qualified grants of removal power are generally deemed to protect the officers to whom they apply and to establish their independence from the domination of the possessor of the removal power. *See Humphrey's Executor v. United States*, 295 U.S., at 625-626, 629-630, 55 S. Ct., at 874-875. Removal authority limited in such a manner is more properly viewed as motivating adherence to a substantive standard established by law than as inducing subservience to the particular institution that enforces that standard. . . .

More importantly, the substantial role played by the President in the process of removal through joint resolution reduces to utter insignificance the possibility that the threat of removal will induce subservience to the Congress. As I have pointed out above, a joint resolution must be presented to the President and is ineffective if it is vetoed by him, unless the veto is overridden by the constitutionally prescribed two-thirds majority of both Houses of Congress. The requirement of Presidential approval obviates the possibility that the Comptroller will perceive himself as so completely at the mercy of Congress that he will function as its tool. If the Comptroller's conduct in office is not so unsatisfactory to the President as to convince the latter that removal is required under the statutory standard, Congress will have no independent power to coerce the Comptroller unless it can muster a two-thirds majority in both Houses — a feat of bipartisanship more difficult than that required to impeach and convict. The incremental in terrorem effect of the possibility of congressional removal in the face of a Presidential veto is therefore exceedingly unlikely to have any discernible impact on the extent of congressional influence over the Comptroller.

The practical result of the removal provision is not to render the Comptroller unduly dependent upon or subservient to Congress, but to render him one of the most independent officers in the entire federal establishment. Those who have studied the office agree that the procedural and substantive limits on the power of Congress and the President to remove the Comptroller make dislodging him against his will practically impossible.

Realistic consideration of the nature of the Comptroller General's relation to Congress thus reveals that the threat to separation of powers conjured up by the majority is wholly chimerical. The power over removal retained by the Congress is not a power that is exercised outside the legislative process as established by the Constitution, nor does it appear likely that it is a power that adds significantly to the influence Congress may exert over executive officers through other, undoubtedly constitutional exercises of legislative power and through the constitutionally guaranteed impeachment power. Indeed, the removal power is so constrained by its own substantive limits and by the requirement of Presidential approval "that, as a practical matter, Congress has not exercised, and probably will never exercise, such control over the Comptroller General that his non-legislative powers will threaten the goal of dispersion of power, and hence the goal of individual liberty, that separation of powers serves." *Ameron, Inc. v. United States Army Corps of Engineers*, 787 F.2d, at 895 (Becker, J., concurring in part).

The wisdom of vesting "executive" powers in an officer removable by joint resolution may indeed be debatable — as may be the wisdom of the entire scheme of permitting an unelected official to revise the budget enacted by Congress — but such matters are for the most part to be worked out between the Congress and the President through the legislative process, which affords each branch ample opportunity to defend its interests. The Act vesting budget-cutting authority in the Comptroller General represents Congress' judgment that the delegation of such authority to counteract ever-mounting deficits is "necessary and proper" to the exercise of the powers granted the Federal Government by the Constitution; and the President's approval of the statute signifies his unwillingness to reject the choice made by Congress. *Cf. Nixon v. Administrator of General Services*, 433 U.S., at 441. Under such circumstances, the role of this Court should be limited to determining whether the Act so alters the balance of authority among the branches of government as to pose a genuine threat to the basic division between the lawmaking power and the power to execute the law. Because I see no such threat, I cannot join the Court in striking down the Act.

NOTES AND QUESTIONS

1. The Court held that Congress cannot possess the authority to remove the Comptroller General, relying on formal categories: the power to balance the budget is "executive" and therefore cannot be vested in an agency subject to congressional control. Are you confident that you can distinguish "executive" power from "legislative" power in this case? Is there a way to reach the same conclusion even if the power is legislative? Does Justice Stevens help?
2. Does the holding in this case imperil the validity of independent agencies, those subject to a presidential "for cause" removal limitation?
3. Consider that Congress can terminate the Comptroller General only upon joint resolution, which requires the agreement of both Houses and a presidential signature. Congress could use the equivalent process (i.e., the legislative process) to cut the agency's authority or budget. Why not allow it to fire the agency's head? Will this tool be more effective as a means of controlling agency action? Is that why Congress wants it?
4. As in *Chadha*, Justice White dissents. He views the removal provision as part of a useful scheme for controlling runaway budgets. If Congress cannot be trusted to cut the budget because of the realities of the legislative process, why not allow it to use an agency for this purpose? In addition, he notes that Congress does not possess complete control over the Comptroller General any more than the President possesses complete control over independent agency

officials. Congress can remove the Comptroller General only for "good cause." Isn't this a better way to view the case? Congress does not gain much control of agency action through this scheme but overcomes its own limitations by placing authority to cut the budget in agency hands.

14. Judicial Guidance

As the previous example demonstrates, agencies can apply the tools of statutory interpretation in a manner similar to courts. Why might they fall roughly in line with judicial practice? The reason is not necessarily because that is the only way or even the best way to interpret statutes. In fact, agencies might place greater emphasis on particular tools or draw different inferences from them because of their deep familiarity with the statutory scheme and their overall responsibility for implementing the scheme. Nevertheless, agencies have incentives to interpret their statutes in ways that are likely to survive judicial review. *See* William N. Eskridge, Jr. & John Ferejohn, *The Article I, Section 7 Game*, 80 Geo. L.J. 523, (1992). The leading decision on judicial review of agency statutory interpretations is Chevron U.S.A Inc. v. Natural Resources Defense Council, Inc. 467 U.S. 837 (1984). There is much to be said about *Chevron*, particularly as it relates to how judges review agency interpretations, as we discuss in Chapter 9. Read the decision now as it relates to how agencies render those interpretations. What would agency lawyers find significant for their work in the decision?

Chevron U.S.A. Inc. v. Natural Resources Defense Council, Inc.

467 U.S. 837 (1984)

Justice MARSHALL and Justice REHNQUIST took no part in the consideration or decision of these cases.

Justice O'CONNOR took no part in the decision of these cases.

Justice STEVENS delivered the opinion of the Court.

In the Clean Air Act Amendments of 1977, Pub. L. 95-95, 91 Stat. 685, Congress enacted certain requirements applicable to States that had not achieved the national air quality standards established by the Environmental Protection Agency (EPA) pursuant to earlier legislation. The amended Clean Air Act required these "nonattainment" States to establish a permit program regulating "new or modified major stationary sources" of air pollution. Generally, a permit may not be issued for a new or modified major stationary source unless several stringent conditions are met. The EPA regulation promulgated to implement this permit requirement allows a State to adopt a plantwide definition of the term "stationary source." Under this definition, an existing plant that contains several pollution-emitting devices may install or modify one piece of equipment without meeting the permit conditions if the alteration will not increase the total emissions from the plant. The question presented by these cases is whether EPA's decision to allow States to treat all of the pollution-emitting devices within the same industrial grouping as though they were encased within a single "bubble" is based on a reasonable construction of the statutory term "stationary source."

I

The EPA regulations containing the plantwide definition of the term stationary source were promulgated on October 14, 1981. 46 Fed. Reg. 50766. Respondents filed a timely petition for review in the United States Court of Appeals for the District of Columbia Circuit pursuant to 42 U.S.C. §7607(b)(1). The Court of Appeals set aside the regulations. *Natural Resources Defense Council, Inc. v. Gorsuch*, 685 F.2d 718 (1982).

The court observed that the relevant part of the amended Clean Air Act "does not explicitly define what Congress envisioned as a 'stationary source, to which the permit program . . . should apply,'" and further stated that the precise issue was not "squarely addressed in the legislative history." *Id.* at 723. In light of its conclusion that the legislative history bearing on the question was "at best contradictory," it reasoned that "the purposes of the nonattainment program should guide our decision here." *Id.* at 726, n.39. Based on two of its precedents concerning the applicability of the bubble concept to certain Clean Air Act programs, the court stated that the bubble concept was "mandatory" in programs designed merely to maintain existing air quality, but held that it was "inappropriate" in programs enacted to improve air quality. *Id.* at 726. Since the purpose of the permit program its "raison d'etre," in the court's view — was to improve air quality, the court held that the bubble concept was inapplicable in these cases under its prior precedents. *Ibid.* It therefore set aside the regulations embodying the bubble concept as contrary to law. We granted certiorari to review that judgment, 461 U.S. 956 (1983), and we now reverse.

The basic legal error of the Court of Appeals was to adopt a static judicial definition of the term "stationary source" when it had decided that Congress itself had not commanded that definition. Respondents do not defend the legal reasoning of the Court of Appeals. Nevertheless, since this Court reviews judgments, not opinions, we must determine whether the Court of Appeals' legal error resulted in an erroneous judgment on the validity of the regulations.

II

When a court reviews an agency's construction of the statute which it administers, it is confronted with two questions. First, always, is the question whether Congress has directly spoken to the precise question at issue. If the intent of Congress is clear, that is the end of the matter; for the court, as well as the agency, must give effect to the unambiguously expressed intent of Congress. If, however, the court determines Congress has not directly addressed the precise question at issue, the court does not simply impose its own construction on the statute, as would be necessary in the absence of an administrative interpretation. Rather, if the statute is silent or ambiguous with respect to the specific issue, the question for the court is whether the agency's answer is based on a permissible construction of the statute.

The power of an administrative agency to administer a congressionally created . . . program necessarily requires the formulation of policy and the making of rules to fill any gap left, implicitly or explicitly, by Congress. *Morton v. Ruiz*, 415 U.S. 199, 231 (1974). If Congress has explicitly left a gap for the agency to fill, there is an express delegation of authority to the agency to elucidate a specific provision of the statute by regulation. Such legislative regulations are given controlling weight unless they are arbitrary, capricious, or manifestly contrary to the statute. Sometimes the legislative delegation to an agency on a particular question is implicit, rather than explicit. In such a case, a court may not substitute its own construction of a statutory provision for a reasonable interpretation made by the administrator of an agency.

We have long recognized that considerable weight should be accorded to an executive department's construction of a statutory scheme it is entrusted to administer, and the principle of deference to administrative interpretations has been consistently followed by this Court whenever decision as to the meaning or reach of a statute has involved reconciling conflicting policies, and a full understanding of the force of the statutory policy in the given situation has depended upon more than ordinary knowledge respecting the matters subjected to agency regulations. *See, e.g., National Broadcasting Co. v. United States*, 319 U.S. 190; *Labor Board v. Hearst Publications, Inc.*, 322 U.S. 111; *Republic Aviation Corp. v. Labor Board*, 324 U.S. 793; *Securities & Exchange Comm'n v. Chenery Corp.*, 332 U.S. 194; *Labor Board v. Seven-Up Bottling Co.*, 344 U.S. 344.

. . . If this choice represents a reasonable accommodation of conflicting policies that were committed to the agency's care by the statute, we should not disturb it unless it appears from the statute or its legislative history that the accommodation is not one that Congress would have sanctioned. *United States v. Shimer*, 367 U.S. 374, 382, 383 (1961). *Accord, Capital Cities Cable, Inc. v. Crisp*, ante at 699-700.

In light of these well-settled principles, it is clear that the Court of Appeals misconceived the nature of its role in reviewing the regulations at issue. Once it determined, after its own examination of the legislation, that Congress did not actually have an intent regarding the applicability of the bubble concept to the permit program, the question before it was not whether, in its view, the concept is "inappropriate" in the general context of a program designed to improve air quality, but whether the Administrator's view that it is appropriate in the context of this particular program is a reasonable one. Based on the examination of the legislation and its history which follows, we agree with the Court of Appeals that Congress did not have a specific intention on the applicability of the bubble concept in these cases, and conclude that the EPA's use of that concept here is a reasonable policy choice for the agency to make.

III

In the 1950's and the 1960's, Congress enacted a series of statutes designed to encourage and to assist the States in curtailing air pollution. See generally *Train v. Natural Resources Defense Council, Inc.*, 421 U.S. 60, 63-64 (1975). The Clean Air Amendments of 1970, Pub. L. 91-604, 84 Stat. 1676, "sharply increased federal authority and responsibility in the continuing effort to combat air pollution," 421 U.S. at 64, but continued to assign "primary responsibility for assuring air quality" to the several States, 84 Stat. 1678. Section 109 of the 1970 Amendments directed the EPA to promulgate National Ambient Air Quality Standards (NAAQS's) and §110 directed the States to develop plans (SIP's) to implement the standards within specified deadlines. In addition, §111 provided that major new sources of pollution would be required to conform to technology-based performance standards; the EPA was directed to publish a list of categories of sources of pollution and to establish new source performance standards (NSPS) for each. Section 111(e) prohibited the operation of any new source in violation of a performance standard.

Section 111(a) defined the terms that are to be used in setting and enforcing standards of performance for new stationary sources. It provided:

For purposes of this section:
＊ ＊ ＊

(3) The term "stationary source" means any building, structure, facility, or installation which emits or may emit any air pollutant.

84 Stat. 1683. In the 1970 Amendments, that definition was not only applicable to the NSPS program required by §111, but also was made applicable to a requirement of §110 that each state implementation plan contain a procedure for reviewing the location of any proposed new source and preventing its construction if it would preclude the attainment or maintenance of national air quality standards.

In due course, the EPA promulgated NAAQS's, approved SIP's, and adopted detailed regulations governing NSPS's for various categories of equipment. In one of its programs, the EPA used a plantwide definition of the term "stationary source." In 1974, it issued NSPS's for the nonferrous smelting industry that provided that the standards would not apply to the modification of major smelting units if their increased emissions were offset by reductions in other portions of the same plant.

Nonattainment

The 1970 legislation provided for the attainment of primary NAAQS's by 1975. In many areas of the country, particularly the most industrialized States, the statutory goals were not attained. In 1976, the 94th Congress was confronted with this fundamental problem, as well as many others respecting pollution control. As always in this area, the legislative struggle was basically between interests seeking strict schemes to reduce pollution rapidly to eliminate its social costs and interests advancing the economic concern that strict schemes would retard industrial development with attendant social costs. The 94th Congress, confronting these competing interests, was unable to agree on what response was in the public interest: legislative proposals to deal with nonattainment failed to command the necessary consensus.

In light of this situation, the EPA published an Emissions Offset Interpretative Ruling in December, 1976, see 41 Fed. Reg. 55524, to "fill the gap," as respondents put it, until Congress acted. The Ruling stated that it was intended to address the issue of whether and to what extent national air quality standards established under the Clean Air Act may restrict or prohibit growth of major new or expanded stationary air pollution sources. *Id.* at 55524-55525. In general, the Ruling provided that a major new source may locate in an area with air quality worse than a national standard only if stringent conditions can be met. *Id.* at 55525. The Ruling gave primary emphasis to the rapid attainment of the statute's environmental goals. Consistent with that emphasis, the construction of every new source in nonattainment areas had to meet the "lowest achievable emission rate" under the current state of the art for that type of facility. *See ibid.* The 1976 Ruling did not, however, explicitly adopt or reject the "bubble concept."

IV

The Clean Air Act Amendments of 1977 are a lengthy, detailed, technical, complex, and comprehensive response to a major social issue. A small portion of the statute — 91 Stat. 745-751 (Part D of Title I of the amended Act, 42 U.S.C. §§7501-7508) — expressly deals with nonattainment areas. The focal point of this controversy is one phrase in that portion of the Amendments.

Basically, the statute required each State in a nonattainment area to prepare and obtain approval of a new SIP by July 1, 1979. In the interim, those States were required to comply with the EPA's interpretative Ruling of December 21, 1976. 91 Stat. 745. The deadline for attainment of the primary NAAQS's was extended until December 31, 1982, and in some cases until December 31, 1987, but the SIP's were required to contain a number of provisions designed to achieve the goals as expeditiously as possible.

Most significantly for our purposes, the statute provided that each plan shall

(6) require permits for the construction and operation of new or modified major stationary sources in accordance with section 173. . . .

Id. at 747. Before issuing a permit, §173 requires (1) the state agency to determine that there will be sufficient emissions reductions in the region to offset the emissions from the new source and also to allow for reasonable further progress toward attainment, or that the increased emissions will not exceed an allowance for growth established pursuant to §172(b)(5), (2) the applicant to certify that his other sources in the State are in compliance with the SIP, (3) the agency to determine that the applicable SIP is otherwise being implemented, and (4) the proposed source to comply with the lowest achievable emission rate (LAER).

The 1977 Amendments contain no specific reference to the "bubble concept." Nor do they contain a specific definition of the term "stationary source," though they did not disturb the definition of "stationary source" contained in §111(a)(3), applicable by the terms of the Act to the NSPS program. Section 302(j), however, defines the term "major stationary source" as follows:

(j) Except as otherwise expressly provided, the terms "major stationary source" and "major emitting facility" mean any stationary facility or source of air pollutants which directly emits, or has the potential to emit, one hundred tons per year or more of any air pollutant (including any major emitting facility or source of fugitive emissions of any such pollutant, as determined by rule by the Administrator). 91 Stat. 770.

V

The legislative history of the portion of the 1977 Amendments dealing with nonattainment areas does not contain any specific comment on the "bubble concept" or the question whether a plantwide definition of a stationary source is permissible under the permit program. It does, however, plainly disclose that in the permit program Congress sought to accommodate the conflict between the economic interest in permitting capital improvements to continue and the environmental interest in improving air quality. Indeed, the House Committee Report identified the economic interest as one of the "two main purposes" of this section of the bill. It stated:

Section 117 of the bill, adopted during full committee markup establishes a new section 127 of the Clean Air Act. The section has two main purposes: (1) to allow reasonable economic growth to continue in an area while making reasonable further progress to assure attainment of the standards by a fixed date; and (2) to allow States greater flexibility for the former purpose than EPA's present interpretative regulations afford.

The new provision allows States with nonattainment areas to pursue one of two options. First, the State may proceed under EPA's present "tradeoff" or "offset" ruling. The Administrator is authorized, moreover, to modify or amend that ruling in accordance with the intent and purposes of this section.

The State's second option would be to revise its implementation plan in accordance with this new provision.

H.R. Rep. No. 95-294, p. 211 (1977).

The portion of the Senate Committee Report dealing with nonattainment areas states generally that it was intended to "supersede the EPA administrative approach," and that expansion should be permitted if a State could demonstrate that these facilities can be accommodated within its overall plan to provide for attainment of air quality standards. S. Rep. No. 95-127, p. 10 (1977). The Senate Report notes the value of case-by-case review of each new or modified major source of pollution that seeks to locate in a region exceeding an ambient standard, explaining that such a review requires matching reductions from existing sources against emissions expected from the new source in order to assure that introduction of the new source will not prevent attainment of the applicable standard by the statutory deadline. *Ibid.* This description of a case-by-case approach to plant additions, which emphasizes the net consequences of the construction or modification of a new source as well as its impact on the overall achievement of the national standards, was not, however, addressed to the precise issue raised by these cases.

Senator Muskie made the following remarks:

> I should note that the test for determining whether a new or modified source is subject to the EPA interpretative regulation [the Offset Ruling] — and to the permit requirements of the revised implementation plans under the conference bill — is whether the source will emit a pollutant into an area which is exceeding a national ambient air quality standard for that pollutant — or precursor. Thus, a new source is still subject to such requirements as "lowest achievable emission rate" even if it is constructed as a replacement for an older facility resulting in a net reduction from previous emission levels.
>
> A source — including an existing facility ordered to convert to coal — is subject to all the nonattainment requirements as a modified source if it makes any physical change which increases the amount of any air pollutant for which the standards in the area are exceeded.

123 Cong. Rec. 26847 (1977).

VI

As previously noted, prior to the 1977 Amendments, the EPA had adhered to a plantwide definition of the term "source" under a NSPS program. After adoption of the 1977 Amendments, proposals for a plantwide definition were considered in at least three formal proceedings.

In January, 1979, the EPA considered the question whether the same restriction on new construction in nonattainment areas that had been included in its December, 1976, Ruling should be required in the revised SIP's that were scheduled to go into effect in July, 1979. After noting that the 1976 Ruling was ambiguous on the question "whether a plant with a number of different processes and emission points would be considered a single source," 44 Fed. Reg. 3276 (1979), the EPA, in effect, provided a bifurcated answer to that question. In those areas that did not have a revised SIP in effect by July, 1979, the EPA rejected the plantwide definition; on the other hand, it expressly concluded that the plantwide approach would be permissible in certain circumstances if authorized by an approved SIP. It stated:

> Where a state implementation plan is revised and implemented to satisfy the requirements of Part D, including the reasonable further progress requirement, the plan requirements for major modifications may exempt modifications of existing facilities that are accompanied by intrasource offsets, so that there is no net increase in emissions. The agency endorses such exemptions, which would provide greater flexibility to sources to effectively manage their air emissions at least cost.

Ibid.

In April, and again in September, 1979, the EPA published additional comments in which it indicated that revised SIP's could adopt the plantwide definition of source in nonattainment areas in certain circumstances. *See id.* at 20372, 20379, 51924, 51951, 51958. On the latter occasion, the EPA made a formal rulemaking proposal that would have permitted the use of the "bubble concept" for new installations within a plant as well as for modifications of existing units. It explained:

> "Bubble" Exemption: The use of offsets inside the same source is called the "bubble." EPA proposes use of the definition of "source" (see above) to limit the use of the bubble under nonattainment requirements in the following respects:
> i. Part D SIPs that include all requirements needed to assure reasonable further progress and attainment by the deadline under section 172 and that are being carried out need not restrict the use of a plantwide bubble, the same as under the PSD proposal.
> ii. Part D SIPs that do not meet the requirements specified must limit use of the bubble by including a definition of "installation" as an identifiable piece of process equipment.

Significantly, the EPA expressly noted that the word "source" might be given a plantwide definition for some purposes and a narrower definition for other purposes. It wrote:

> Source means any building structure, facility, or installation which emits or may emit any regulated pollutant. "Building, structure, facility or installation" means plant in PSD areas and in nonattainment areas except where the growth prohibitions would apply or where no adequate SIP exists or is being carried out.

Id. at 51925. The EPA's summary of its proposed Ruling discloses a flexible, rather than rigid, definition of the term "source" to implement various policies and programs:

> In summary, EPA is proposing two different ways to define source for different kinds of NSR programs:
> (1) For PSD and complete Part D SIPs, review would apply only to plants, with an unrestricted plantwide bubble.
> (2) For the offset ruling, restrictions on construction, and incomplete Part D SIPs, review would apply to both plants and individual pieces of process equipment, causing the plant-wide bubble not to apply for new and modified major pieces of equipment.

In addition, for the restrictions on construction, EPA is proposing to define "major modification" so as to prohibit the bubble entirely. Finally, an alternative discussed but not favored is to have only pieces of process equipment reviewed, resulting in no plant-wide bubble and allowing minor pieces of equipment to escape NSR regardless of whether they are within a major plant. *Id.* at 51934.

In August, 1980, however, the EPA adopted a regulation that, in essence, applied the basic reasoning of the Court of Appeals in these cases. The EPA took particular note of the two then-recent Court of Appeals decisions, which had created the bright-line rule that the "bubble concept" should be employed in a program designed to maintain air quality, but not in one designed to enhance air quality. Relying heavily on those cases, EPA adopted a dual definition of "source" for nonattainment areas that required a permit whenever a change in either the entire plant, or one of its components, would result in a significant increase in emissions even if the increase was completely offset by reductions elsewhere in the plant. The EPA expressed the opinion that this interpretation was "more consistent with congressional intent" than the plantwide definition because it "would bring in more sources or modifications for review," 45 Fed. Reg. 52697 (1980), but its primary legal analysis was predicated on the two Court of Appeals decisions.

In 1981, a new administration took office and initiated a "Government-wide reexamination of regulatory burdens and complexities." 46 Fed. Reg. 16281. In the context of that review, the EPA reevaluated the various arguments that had been advanced in connection with the proper definition of the term "source" and concluded that the term should be given the same definition in both nonattainment areas and PSD areas.

In explaining its conclusion, the EPA first noted that the definitional issue was not squarely addressed in either the statute or its legislative history, and therefore that the issue involved an agency "judgment as how to best carry out the Act." *Ibid.* It then set forth several reasons for concluding that the plantwide definition was more appropriate. It pointed out that the dual definition "can act as a disincentive to new investment and modernization by discouraging modifications to existing facilities" and can actually retard progress in air pollution control by discouraging replacement of older, dirtier processes or pieces of equipment with new, cleaner ones. Moreover, the new definition would simplify EPA's rules by using the same definition of "source" for PSD, nonattainment new source review, and the construction moratorium. This reduces confusion and inconsistency. Finally, the agency explained that additional requirements that remained in place would accomplish the fundamental purposes of achieving attainment with NAAQS's as expeditiously as possible. These conclusions were expressed in a proposed rulemaking in August, 1981, that was formally promulgated in October. *See id.* at 50766.

VII

In this Court, respondents expressly reject the basic rationale of the Court of Appeals' decision. That court viewed the statutory definition of the term "source" as sufficiently flexible to cover either a plantwide definition, a narrower definition covering each unit within a plant, or a dual definition that could apply to both the entire "bubble" and its components. It interpreted the policies of the statute, however, to mandate the plantwide definition in programs designed to maintain clean air and to forbid it in programs designed to improve air quality. Respondents place a fundamentally different construction on the statute. They contend that the text of the Act requires the EPA to use a dual definition — if either a component of a plant, or the plant as a whole, emits over 100 tons of pollutant, it is a major station-ary source. They thus contend that the EPA rules adopted in 1980, insofar as they apply to the maintenance of the quality of clean air, as well as the 1981 rules which apply to nonattainment areas, violate the statute.

Statutory Language

The definition of the term "stationary source" in §111(a)(3) refers to "any build-ing, structure, facility, or installation" which emits air pollution. See supra at 846. This definition is applicable only to the NSPS program by the express terms of the statute; the text of the statute does not make this definition applicable to the per-mit program. Petitioners therefore maintain that there is no statutory language even relevant to ascertaining the meaning of stationary source in the permit pro-gram aside from §302(j), which defines the term "major stationary source." *See supra* at 851. We disagree with petitioners on this point.

The definition in §302(j) tells us what the word "major" means — a source must emit at least 100 tons of pollution to qualify — but it sheds virtually no light on the meaning of the term "stationary source." It does equate a source with a facility — a "major emitting facility" and a "major stationary source" are synony-mous under §302(j). The ordinary meaning of the term "facility" is some collec-tion of integrated elements which has been designed and constructed to achieve some purpose. Moreover, it is certainly no affront to common English usage to take a reference to a major facility or a major source to connote an entire plant, as opposed to its constituent parts. Basically, however, the language of §302(j) simply does not compel any given interpretation of the term "source."

Respondents recognize that, and hence point to §111(a)(3). Although the definition in that section is not literally applicable to the permit program, it sheds as much light on the meaning of the word "source" as anything in the stat-ute. As respondents point out, use of the words "building, structure, facility, or installation," as the definition of source, could be read to impose the permit con-ditions on an individual building that is a part of a plant. A "word may have a character of its own not to be submerged by its association." *Russell Motor Car Co. v. United States*, 261 U.S. 514, 519 (1923). On the other hand, the meaning of a word must be ascertained in the context of achieving particular objectives, and the words associated with it may indicate that the true meaning of the series is to convey a common idea. The language may reasonably be interpreted to impose the requirement on any discrete, but integrated, operation which pol-lutes. This gives meaning to all of the terms — a single building, not part of a larger operation, would be covered if it emits more than 100 tons of pollution, as would any facility, structure, or installation. Indeed, the language itself implies a "bubble concept" of sorts: each enumerated item would seem to be treated as if it were encased in a bubble. While respondents insist that each of these terms must be given a discrete meaning, they also argue that §111(a)(3) defines "source" as that term is used in §302(j). The latter section, however, equates a source with a facility, whereas the former defines "source" as a facility, among other items.

We are not persuaded that parsing of general terms in the text of the statute will reveal an actual intent of Congress. We know full well that this language is not dispositive; the terms are overlapping, and the language is not precisely directed to the question of the applicability of a given term in the context of a larger operation. To the extent any congressional "intent" can be discerned from this language, it would appear that the listing of overlapping, illustrative terms was intended to enlarge, rather than to confine, the scope of the agency's power to regulate particular sources in order to effectuate the policies of the Act.

Legislative History

In addition, respondents argue that the legislative history and policies of the Act foreclose the plantwide definition, and that the EPA's interpretation is not entitled to deference, because it represents a sharp break with prior interpretations of the Act.

Based on our examination of the legislative history, we agree with the Court of Appeals that it is unilluminating. The general remarks pointed to by respondents "were obviously not made with this narrow issue in mind, and they cannot be said to demonstrate a Congressional desire . . . ." *Jewell Ridge Coal Corp. v. Mine Workers*, 325 U.S. 161, 168-169 (1945). Respondents' argument based on the legislative history relies heavily on Senator Muskie's observation that a new source is subject to the LAER requirement. But the full statement is ambiguous, and, like the text of §173 itself, this comment does not tell us what a new source is, much less that it is to have an inflexible definition. We find that the legislative history as a whole is silent on the precise issue before us. It is, however, consistent with the view that the EPA should have broad discretion in implementing the policies of the 1977 Amendments.

More importantly, that history plainly identifies the policy concerns that motivated the enactment; the plantwide definition is fully consistent with one of those concerns — the allowance of reasonable economic growth — and, whether or not we believe it most effectively implements the other, we must recognize that the EPA has advanced a reasonable explanation for its conclusion that the regulations serve the environmental objectives as well. *See supra* at 857-859, and n.29; *see also supra* at 855, n.27. Indeed, its reasoning is supported by the public record developed in the rulemaking process, as well as by certain private studies.

Our review of the EPA's varying interpretations of the word "source" — both before and after the 1977 Amendments — convinces us that the agency primarily responsible for administering this important legislation has consistently interpreted it flexibly — not in a sterile textual vacuum, but in the context of implementing policy decisions in a technical and complex arena. The fact that the agency has from time to time changed its interpretation of the term "source" does not, as respondents argue, lead us to conclude that no deference should be accorded the agency's interpretation of the statute. An initial agency interpretation is not instantly carved in stone. On the contrary, the agency, to engage in informed rulemaking, must consider varying interpretations and the wisdom of its policy on a continuing basis. Moreover, the fact that the agency has adopted different definitions in different contexts adds force to the argument that the definition itself is flexible, particularly since Congress has never indicated any disapproval of a flexible reading of the statute.

Significantly, it was not the agency in 1980, but rather the Court of Appeals that read the statute inflexibly to command a plantwide definition for programs designed to maintain clean air and to forbid such a definition for programs designed to improve air quality. The distinction the court drew may well be a sensible one, but our labored review of the problem has surely disclosed that it is not a distinction that Congress ever articulated itself, or one that the EPA found in the statute before the courts began to review the legislative work product. We conclude that it was the Court of Appeals, rather than Congress or any of the decisionmakers who are authorized by Congress to administer this legislation, that was primarily responsible for the 1980 position taken by the agency.

Policy

The arguments over policy that are advanced in the parties' briefs create the impression that respondents are now waging in a judicial forum a specific policy battle which they ultimately lost in the agency and in the 32 jurisdictions opting for the "bubble concept," but one which was never waged in the Congress. Such policy arguments are more properly addressed to legislators or administrators, not to judges.

In these cases, the Administrator's interpretation represents a reasonable accommodation of manifestly competing interests, and is entitled to deference: the regulatory scheme is technical and complex, the agency considered the matter in a detailed and reasoned fashion, and the decision involves reconciling conflicting policies. Congress intended to accommodate both interests, but did not do so itself on the level of specificity presented by these cases. Perhaps that body consciously desired the Administrator to strike the balance at this level, thinking that those with great expertise and charged with responsibility for administering the provision would be in a better position to do so; perhaps it simply did not consider the question at this level; and perhaps Congress was unable to forge a coalition on either side of the question, and those on each side decided to take their chances with the scheme devised by the agency. For judicial purposes, it matters not which of these things occurred.

Judges are not experts in the field, and are not part of either political branch of the Government. Courts must, in some cases, reconcile competing political interests, but not on the basis of the judges' personal policy preferences. In contrast, an agency to which Congress has delegated policymaking responsibilities may, within the limits of that delegation, properly rely upon the incumbent administration's views of wise policy to inform its judgments. While agencies are not directly accountable to the people, the Chief Executive is, and it is entirely appropriate for this political branch of the Government to make such policy choices — resolving the competing interests which Congress itself either inadvertently did not resolve, or intentionally left to be resolved by the agency charged with the administration of the statute in light of everyday realities.

When a challenge to an agency construction of a statutory provision, fairly conceptualized, really centers on the wisdom of the agency's policy, rather than whether it is a reasonable choice within a gap left open by Congress, the challenge must fail. In such a case, federal judges — who have no constituency — have a duty to respect legitimate policy choices made by those who do. The responsibilities for assessing the wisdom of such policy choices and resolving the struggle between competing views of the public interest are not judicial ones: "Our Constitution vests such responsibilities in the political branches." *TVA v. Hill*, 437 U.S. 153, 195 (1978).

We hold that the EPA's definition of the term "source" is a permissible construction of the statute which seeks to accommodate progress in reducing air pollution with economic growth.

The Regulations which the Administrator has adopted provide what the agency could allowably view as . . . [an] effective reconciliation of these twofold ends. . . . *United States v. Shimer*, 367 U.S. at 383.

The judgment of the Court of Appeals is reversed.

It is so ordered.

15. *Judicial Control of Agency Statutory Interpretation*

The Court has developed separate doctrine for reviewing agency statutory interpretations. You have already encountered the leading case: Chevron U.S.A. Inc. v. Natural Resources Defense Council, Inc., 467 U.S. 837 (1984). It is difficult to over-emphasize the importance of this decision. First, it defines important features of the relationship between agencies and statutes — agencies must implement legislative enactments and their range of discretion in doing so is determined primarily by the language of those statutes. That is why we reprinted the case in the chapter on agency statutory implementation. Second, it defines important features of the relationship between agencies and courts. That is why we are revisiting it here. Note that the decision addresses this second issue in terms of the first one. It says that the stringency of judicial review should be governed by the extent to which Congress delegated basic policy decisions to the agency. If Congress wanted to constrain agency discretion by drafting precise language, then the courts should make sure that the agency abides by that language. But if Congress wanted to increase agency discretion by drafting a vaguely worded or ambiguous statute, then the courts should respect that choice and defer to the agency unless the agency chose an unreasonable interpretation. Thus, the judiciary's role is first, to enforce the boundaries of the statute and second, to assess the reasonableness of the agency interpretation.

In recent years, *Chevron* has been complicated by later decisions — so much so that scholars and judges have now begun to question whether it still contains the actual framework for judicial review of agency statutory interpretation. *See, e.g.*, William N. Eskridge, Jr. & Lauren E. Baer, *The Continuum of Deference: Supreme Court Treatment of Agency Statutory Interpretations from* Chevron *to*

Hamdan, 96 Geo. L.J. 1083, 1097-1120 (2008) (noting that *Chevron* supplies only one among many different frameworks for judicial review of agency statutory interpretations, and identifying others). In addition, scholars too numerous to mention have argued for its rearrangement or overthrow. For a sampling, see Jack M. Beerman, *End the Failed* Chevron *Experiment Now: How* Chevron *Failed and Why It Can and Should Be Overruled*, 42 Conn. L. Rev. 779 (2010) (arguing that *Chevron* has outlived its usefulness); Lisa Schultz Bressman, Chevron's *Mistake*, 58 Duke L.J. 549 (2009) (arguing that *Chevron* allows courts to find statutory meaning where none exists and should be reworked); Elizabeth V. Foote, *Statutory Interpretation or Public Administration: How* Chevron *Misconceives the Function of Agencies and Why It Matters*, 59 Admin. L. Rev. 673 (2007) (arguing that *Chevron* ignores the reality of agency statutory implementation); Matthew C. Stephenson & Adrian Vermeule, Chevron *Has Only One Step*, 95 Va. L. Rev. 597 (2009) (arguing that *Chevron* does not really have two distinct steps and should be reinterpreted). We note some of the complexities that have arisen but leave in depth coverage for a later administrative law course. Our aim is to provide a basic grounding so that you can begin to see the parameters of judicial control in this context.

Chevron U.S.A. Inc. v. Natural Resources Defense Council, Inc.

467 U.S. 837 (1984)

See pp. 571.

NOTES AND QUESTIONS

1. Step One of *Chevron* directs reviewing courts to ask whether "Congress has directly spoken to the precise issue in question," or, put differently, whether "the intent of Congress is clear." If a court finds that Congress has specified a meaning, that is the end of the matter. The court declares the meaning, which holds until and unless Congress alters it by enacting a new or amended statute. Under Step One, how clear is "clear"? The Court indicates that Congress need not resolve all doubt about the meaning of a provision in the text of the statute. Rather, courts are called upon to interpret statutory provisions applying the "traditional tools of statutory construction." That phrase should be familiar: we identified the tools of statutory interpretation in Chapter 11. Are all the tools of statutory interpretation fair game under Step One? You can see the Court applying text-based tools, including textual canons, and intent or purpose-based tools, including legislative history. What about substantive canons? Is there any reason to believe that these are off limits? How about evidence of changed circumstances? May a court consult subsequent legislative, executive, or judicial activity? Does the Court offer any clues as to the status of these tools? We will have more to say on this subject below.

2. Step Two applies when Congress has not specified a statutory meaning. It directs courts to defer to the agency interpretation as long as that interpretation is "reasonable." What reasons did the Court give for such judicial deference? Do you find each equally persuasive? Can you determine from the opinion what "reasonable" means? We will have more to say about this, too.
3. One important aspect of *Chevron* is that it permits agencies to change their interpretations of ambiguous provisions in response to changing technological, social, or political circumstances. In this case, the Reagan administration preferred the "bubble" interpretation to the prior individual smokestack interpretation. The Court deferred to the change. How can thisresult be reconciled with *State Farm*, in which the very same administration preferred to change the passive restraints rule but the Court effectively said no?
4. What exactly does "judicial deference" mean? When a court defers to an agency interpretation, it gives that interpretation the force of law. The interpretation binds the parties in the case, as well as future parties and government officials, including the agency and the courts. The only way to depart from an agency interpretation is for the agency to change it by issuing another rule or for Congress to repeal it by enacting another statute. So you can see why *Chevron* deference is a big deal for agencies and those affected by their choices. The Court agrees and has complicated *Chevron* on this force-of-law point, as we discuss below.

16. Judicial Control of Agency Action

We now turn to judicial control of agency action. Judicial control comes later than many forms of political control. As we have seen, presidential control routinely occurs in the midst of agency decisionmaking, and congressional control often does as well. Courts exercise control of agency action only by reviewing challenges to such action; generally, that process occurs only after agency action is complete or "final." For the same reason, courts exercise more limited control of agency action than political officials. Judges cannot pick up the telephone and call an agency to express their views. They cannot haul an agency in for hearings on their own initiative. They must wait until someone files a lawsuit challenging agency action. It is fair to say, however, that agencies anticipate judicial review of their actions and incorporate that prospect into their decisionmaking. They certainly know that significant regulations are likely to end up in front of a judge.

Most significant agency action is subject to judicial review. You have already encountered the Administrative Procedure Act, 5 U.S.C. §§551 *et seq. See* Appendix B. The APA not only prescribes default procedures for agency action, it contains default provisions for judicial review of agency action. Section §702 is entitled "Right of review" and provides that "[a] person suffering legal wrong because of agency action, or adversely affected or aggrieved by agency action within the meaning of a relevant statute, is entitled to judicial review thereof." Section §704 states that "[a]gency action made reviewable by statute and final agency action for which there is no other adequate remedy in a court are subject to judicial review."

The APA also specifies the "scope of review," which tells a reviewing court which standard to apply in assessing agency action. The standard that generally applies to notice-and-comment rulemaking, as well as other informal action, directs the court to hold unlawful and set aside agency action that is "arbitrary, capricious, an abuse of discretion, or otherwise not in accordance with law." 5 U.S.C. §706(2)(A). This standard is known as the "arbitrary and capricious" test. An organic statute can always specify a different standard of review (just as it can always specify different procedures than the APA). For example, an organic statute can authorize a court to set aside a notice-and-comment rule that is "unsupported by substantial evidence." The Occupational Health and Safety Act (OSHA) is one such statute. 29 U.S.C. §655(f). Under the APA, the "substantial evidence" standard is the one that generally applies to formal procedures, such as formal adjudication. See 5 U.S.C. §706(2)(E). That standard is regarded as more demanding than the arbitrary and capricious standard. By applying this heightened standard to OSHA rules, Congress subjected those rules to a more demanding level of judicial review.

How intensely should courts scrutinize agency rules under these standards? The Supreme Court, in its administrative law decisions, has elaborated and specified these standards providing guidance as to how demanding (or deferential) they should be. This section will introduce you to some of the seminal decisions on judicial review of agency action. As you read them, consider the extent to which they promote the legitimacy of agency decisionmaking. For example, to what extent do they promote rule of law values, by ensuring that agencies follow their statutes and otherwise engage in rational decisionmaking? To what extent do they promote agency expertise by ensuring that agencies rely on sound data, draw logical conclusions from the evidence, consider all relevant alternatives, and examine all important aspects of the problem? To what extent do they promote political accountability by allowing agencies to adapt to changes in presidential administrations? We will also consider whether the Court's decisions give courts too much space to approve or reject agency rules based on judicial preferences, assuming that they have this inclination. Most believe that judicial preferences should not dominate judicial review of agency decisions (or any decisions). Although the Court's administrative law decisions are consistent with this view in theory, the question is how well they work to constrain reviewing courts in practice.

17. *Judicial Control of Agency Policymaking*

We begin by examining a decision that elaborates the "arbitrary and capricious" standard of APA §706(2)(A). That decision determines how much control courts possess in reviewing the way that an agency implements its statute, setting aside for the moment what the Court regards as a discrete issue of how the agency interprets its statute. The decision is not only one of the most important in administrative law but the natural culmination of this course because it involves the passive restraints rescission that you read in Chapter 10. You have already seen the dissent of then-Justice Rehnquist. *See* p. 510. As you will recall, Justice Rehnquist argued that a change of administration was a sufficient basis to justify NHTSA's rescission: "A change in administration brought about by the people casting their votes is a perfectly reasonable basis for an executive agency's reappraisal of the costs and benefits of its programs and regulations." Motor Vehicle Manufacturers Ass'n v. State Farm Insurance Co., 463 U.S. 29, 59 (1983) (Rehnquist, J., dissenting in part). He was in the dissent; now you see the law:

Motor Vehicle Manufacturers Ass'n of the United States, Inc. v. State Farm Mutual Automobile Insurance Co.

463 U.S. 29 (1983)

Justice WHITE delivered the opinion of the Court.

The development of the automobile gave Americans unprecedented freedom to travel, but exacted a high price for enhanced mobility. Since 1929, motor vehicles have been the leading cause of accidental deaths and injuries in the United States. In 1982, 46,300 Americans died in motor vehicle accidents and hundreds of thousands more were maimed and injured. While a consensus exists that the current loss of life on our highways is unacceptably high, improving safety does not admit to easy solution. In 1966, Congress decided that at least part of the answer lies in improving the design and safety features of the vehicle itself. But much of the technology for building safer cars was undeveloped or untested. Before changes in automobile design could be mandated, the effectiveness of these changes had to be studied, their costs examined, and public acceptance considered. This task called for considerable expertise and Congress responded by enacting the National Traffic and Motor Vehicle Safety Act of 1966, (Act), 15 U.S.C. §§1381 et seq. (1976 and Supp. IV 1980). The Act, created for the purpose of "reduc[ing] traffic accidents and deaths and injuries to persons resulting from traffic accidents," 15 U.S.C. §1381, directs the Secretary of Transportation or his delegate to issue motor vehicle safety standards that "shall be practicable, shall meet the need for motor vehicle safety, and shall be stated in objective terms." 15 U.S.C. §1392(a). In issuing these standards, the Secretary is directed to consider "relevant available motor vehicle safety data," whether the proposed standard "is reasonable, practicable and appropriate" for the particular type of motor vehicle, and the "extent to which such standards will contribute to carrying out the purposes" of the Act. 15 U.S.C. §1392(f)(1), (3), (4).

The Act also authorizes judicial review under the provisions of the Administrative Procedure Act (APA), 5 U.S.C. §706 (1976), of all "orders establishing, amending, or revoking a Federal motor vehicle safety standard," 15 U.S.C.

§1392(b). Under this authority, we review today whether NHTSA [the National Highway Transportation Safety Administration, to which the Secretary has delegated authority under the Act] acted arbitrarily and capriciously in revoking the requirement in Motor Vehicle Safety Standard 208 that new motor vehicles produced after September 1982 be equipped with passive restraints to protect the safety of the occupants of the vehicle in the event of a collision. Briefly summarized, we hold that the agency failed to present an adequate basis and explanation for rescinding the passive restraint requirement and that the agency must either consider the matter further or adhere to or amend Standard 208 along lines which its analysis supports.

I

The regulation whose rescission is at issue bears a complex and convoluted history. Over the course of approximately 60 rulemaking notices, the requirement has been imposed, amended, rescinded, reimposed, and now rescinded again. . . .

II

In a statement explaining the rescission, NHTSA maintained that it was no longer able to find, as it had in 1977, that the automatic restraint requirement would produce significant safety benefits. Notice 25, 46 Fed. Reg. 53,419 (Oct. 29, 1981). This judgment reflected not a change of opinion on the effectiveness of the technology, but a change in plans by the automobile industry. In 1977, the agency had assumed that airbags would be installed in 60% of all new cars and automatic seatbelts in 40%. By 1981 it became apparent that automobile manufacturers planned to install the automatic seatbelts in approximately 99% of the new cars. For this reason, the life-saving potential of airbags would not be realized. Moreover, it now appeared that the overwhelming majority of passive belts planned to be installed by manufacturers could be detached easily and left that way permanently. Passive belts, once detached, then required "the same type of affirmative action that is the stumbling block to obtaining high usage levels of manual belts." 46 Fed. Reg., at 53421. For this reason, the agency concluded that there was no longer a basis for reliably predicting that the standard would lead to any significant increased usage of restraints at all.

In view of the possibly minimal safety benefits, the automatic restraint requirement no longer was reasonable or practicable in the agency's view. The requirement would require approximately $1 billion to implement and the agency did not believe it would be reasonable to impose such substantial costs on manufacturers and consumers without more adequate assurance that sufficient safety benefits would accrue. In addition, NHTSA concluded that automatic restraints might have an adverse effect on the public's attitude toward safety. Given the high expense and limited benefits of detachable belts, NHTSA feared that many consumers would regard the standard as an instance of ineffective regulation, adversely affecting the public's view of safety regulation and, in particular, "poisoning popular sentiment toward efforts to improve occupant restraint systems in the future." 46 Fed. Reg., at 53424. . . .

III

[The Court first determined that the "arbitrary and capricious" standard of review applies to rule rescissions, rather than a higher or lower standard. An agency is not prohibited from taking a "deregulatory" action or making any other change. And, "[w]hile the removal of a regulation may not entail the monetary expenditures and other costs of enacting a new standard, and accordingly, it may be easier for an agency to justify a deregulatory action, the direction in which an agency chooses to move does not alter the standard of judicial review established by law."]

The Department of Transportation accepts the applicability of the "arbitrary and capricious" standard. It argues that under this standard, a reviewing court may not set aside an agency rule that is rational, based on consideration of the relevant factors and within the scope of the authority delegated to the agency by the statute. We do not disagree with this formulation. The scope of review under the "arbitrary and capricious" standard is narrow and a court is not to substitute its judgment for that of the agency. Nevertheless, the agency must examine the relevant data and articulate a satisfactory explanation for its action including a "rational connection between the facts found and the choice made." *Burlington Truck Lines v. United States*, 371 U.S. 156, 168 (1962). In reviewing that explanation, we must "consider whether the decision was based on a consideration of the relevant factors and whether there has been a clear error of judgment." *Bowman Transp. Inc. v. Arkansas-Best Freight System*, 419 U.S., at 285; *Citizens to Preserve Overton Park v. Volpe*, 401 U.S., at 416. Normally, an agency rule would be arbitrary and capricious if the agency has relied on factors which Congress has not intended it to consider, entirely failed to consider an important aspect of the problem, offered an explanation for its decision that runs counter to the evidence before the agency, or is so implausible that it could not be ascribed to a difference in view or the product of agency expertise. The reviewing court should not attempt itself to make up for such deficiencies: "We may not supply a reasoned basis for the agency's action that the agency itself has not given." *SEC v. Chenery Corp.*, 332 U.S. 194, 196 (1947). We will, however, "uphold a decision of less than ideal clarity if the agency's path may reasonably be discerned." *Bowman Transp. Inc. v. Arkansas-Best Freight System*, supra, 419 U.S., at 286. *See also Camp v. Pitts*, 411 U.S. 138, 142-143 (1973) (per curiam). For purposes of this case, it is also relevant that Congress required a record of the rulemaking proceedings to be compiled and submitted to a reviewing court, 15 U.S.C. §1394, and intended that agency findings under the Motor Vehicle Safety Act would be supported by "substantial evidence on the record considered as a whole." S. REP. No. 1301, 89th Cong., 2d Sess. p. 8 (1966); H.R. REP. No. 1776, 89th Cong., 2d Sess. p. 21 (1966), U.S. Code Cong. & Admin. News 1966, p. 2716.

IV

[The Court reviewed and rejecting the reasoning of the Court of Appeals, though not the Court of Appeals' ultimate conclusion that the rule rescission was arbitrary and capricious.]

V

The ultimate question before us is whether NHTSA's rescission of the passive restraint requirement of Standard 208 was arbitrary and capricious. We conclude, as did the Court of Appeals, that it was. We also conclude, but for somewhat different reasons, that further consideration of the issue by the agency is therefore required. We deal separately with the rescission as it applies to airbags and as it applies to seatbelts.

A

The first and most obvious reason for finding the rescission arbitrary and capricious is that NHTSA apparently gave no consideration whatever to modifying the Standard to require that airbag technology be utilized. Standard 208 sought to achieve automatic crash protection by requiring automobile manufacturers to install either of two passive restraint devices: airbags or automatic seatbelts. There was no suggestion in the long rulemaking process that led to Standard 208 that if only one of these options were feasible, no passive restraint standard should be promulgated. Indeed, the agency's original proposed standard contemplated the installation of inflatable restraints in all cars.[16] Automatic belts were added as a means of complying with the standard because they were believed to be as effective as airbags in achieving the goal of occupant crash protection. 36 Fed. Reg. 12,858, 12,859 (July 8, 1971). At that time, the passive belt approved by the agency could not be detached.[17] Only later, at a manufacturer's behest, did the agency approve of the detachability feature — and only after assurances that the feature would not compromise the safety benefits of the restraint.[18] Although it was then foreseen that 60% of the new cars would contain airbags and 40% would

---

[16] While NHTSA's 1970 passive restraint requirement permitted compliance by means other than the airbag, 35 Fed. Reg. 16,927 (1970), "[t]his rule was [a] de facto air bag mandate since no other technologies were available to comply with the standard." J. Graham & P. Gorham, NHTSA. Restraints: A Case of Arbitrary and Capricious Deregulation, 35 ADMIN. L. REV. 193, 197 (1983) . . . .

[17] Although the agency suggested that passive restraint systems contain an emerg. release mechanism to allow easy extrication of passengers in the event of an accident, the agency cautioned that "[i]n the case of passive safety belts, it would be required that the release not cause belt separation, and that the system be self-restoring after operation of the release." 36 Fed. Reg. 12,866 (July 8, 1971).

[18] In April 1974, NHTSA adopted the suggestion of an automobile manufacturer that emergency release of passive belts be accomplished by a conventional latch-provided the restraint system was guarded by an ignition interlock and warning buzzer to encourage reattachment of the passive belt. 39 Fed. Reg. 14,593 (April 25, 1974). When the 1974 Amendments prohibited these devices, the agency simply eliminated the interlock and buzzer requirements, but continued to allow compliance by a detachable passive belt.

have automatic seatbelts, the ratio between the two was not significant as long as the passive belt would also assure greater passenger safety.

The agency has now determined that the detachable automatic belts will not attain anticipated safety benefits because so many individuals will detach the mechanism. Even if this conclusion were acceptable in its entirety, *see* infra, at 2871-2872, standing alone it would not justify any more than an amendment of Standard 208 to disallow compliance by means of the one technology which will not provide effective passenger protection. It does not cast doubt on the need for a passive restraint standard or upon the efficacy of airbag technology. In its most recent rule-making, the agency again acknowledged the life-saving potential of the airbag:

> "The agency has no basis at this time for changing its earlier conclusions in 1976 and 1977 that basic airbag technology is sound and has been sufficiently demonstrated to be effective in those vehicles in current use . . . ." NHTSA Final Regulatory Impact Analysis (RIA) at XI-4 (App. 264).

Given the effectiveness ascribed to airbag technology by the agency, the mandate of the Safety Act to achieve traffic safety would suggest that the logical response to the faults of detachable seatbelts would be to require the installation of airbags. At the very least this alternative way of achieving the objectives of the Act should have been addressed and adequate reasons given for its abandonment. But the agency not only did not require compliance through airbags, it did not even consider the possibility in its 1981 rulemaking. Not one sentence of its rulemaking statement discusses the airbags-only option. Because, as the Court of Appeals stated, "NHTSA's . . . analysis of airbags was nonexistent," 680 F.2d, at 236, what we said in *Burlington Truck Lines v. United States*, 371 U.S., at 167, is apropos here:

> "There are no findings and no analysis here to justify the choice made, no indication of the basis on which the [agency] exercised its expert discretion. We are not prepared to and the Administrative Procedure Act will not permit us to accept such . . . practice. . . . Expert discretion is the lifeblood of the administrative process, but 'unless we make the requirements for administrative action strict and demanding, expertise, the strength of modern government, can become a monster which rules with no practical limits on its discretion.' *New York v. United States*, 342 U.S. 882, 884 (dissenting opinion)." (footnote omitted).

We have frequently reiterated that an agency must cogently explain why it has exercised its discretion in a given manner, *Atchison, T & S.F.R. Co. v. Wichita Bd. of Trade*, 412 U.S. 800, 806 (1973). . . . ; and we reaffirm this principle again today.

The automobile industry has opted for the passive belt over the airbag, but surely it is not enough that the regulated industry has eschewed a given safety device. For nearly a decade, the automobile industry waged the regulatory equivalent of war against the airbag and lost — the inflatable restraint was proven sufficiently effective. Now the automobile industry has decided to employ a seatbelt system which will not meet the safety objectives of Standard 208. This hardly constitutes cause to revoke the standard itself. Indeed, the Motor Vehicle Safety Act was necessary because the industry was not sufficiently responsive to safety concerns. The Act intended that safety standards not depend on current technology and could be "technology-forcing" in the sense of inducing the development of superior safety design. *See Chrysler Corp. v. Dept. of Transp.*, 472 F.2d, at 672-673. If, under the statute, the agency should not defer to the industry's failure to develop safer cars, which it surely should not do, a fortiori it may not revoke a safety standard which can be satisfied by current technology simply because the industry has opted for an ineffective seatbelt design. . . .

B

Although the issue is closer, we also find that the agency was too quick to dismiss the safety benefits of automatic seatbelts. NHTSA's critical finding was that, in light of the industry's plans to install readily detachable passive belts, it could not reliably predict "even a 5 percentage point increase as the minimum level of expected usage increase." 46 Fed. Reg., at 53,423. The Court of Appeals rejected this finding because there is "not one iota" of evidence that Modified Standard 208 will fail to increase nationwide seatbelt use by at least 13 percentage points, the level of increased usage necessary for the standard to justify its cost. Given the lack of probative evidence, the court held that "only a well-justified refusal to seek more evidence could render rescission non-arbitrary." 680 F.2d, at 232.

Petitioners object to this conclusion. In their view, "substantial uncertainty" that a regulation will accomplish its intended purpose is sufficient reason, without more, to rescind a regulation. We agree with petitioners that just as an agency reasonably may decline to issue a safety standard if it is uncertain about its efficacy, an agency may also revoke a standard on the basis of serious uncertainties if supported by the record and reasonably explained. Rescission of the passive restraint requirement would not be arbitrary and capricious simply because there was no evidence in direct support of the agency's conclusion. It is not infrequent that the available data does not settle a regulatory issue and the agency must then exercise its judgment in moving from the facts and probabilities on the record to a policy conclusion. Recognizing that policymaking in a complex society must account for uncertainty, however, does not imply that it is sufficient for an agency to merely recite the terms "substantial uncertainty" as a justification for its actions. The agency must explain the evidence which is available, and must offer a "rational connection between the facts found and the choice made." *Burlington Truck Lines, Inc. v. United States*, 371 U.S., at 168. Generally, one aspect of that explanation would be a justification for rescinding the regulation before engaging in a search for further evidence.

In this case, the agency's explanation for rescission of the passive restraint requirement is not sufficient to enable us to conclude that the rescission was the product of reasoned decisionmaking. To reach this conclusion, we do not upset the agency's view of the facts, but we do appreciate the limitations of this record in supporting the agency's decision. We start with the accepted ground that if used, seatbelts unquestionably would save many thousands of lives and would prevent tens of thousands of crippling injuries. Unlike recent regulatory decisions we have reviewed . . . , the safety benefits of wearing seatbelts are not in doubt and it is not challenged that were those benefits to accrue, the monetary costs of implementing the standard would be easily justified. We move next to the fact that there is no direct evidence in support of the agency's finding that detachable automatic belts cannot be predicted to yield a substantial increase in usage. The empirical evidence on the record, consisting of surveys of drivers of automobiles equipped with passive belts, reveals more than a doubling of the usage rate experienced with manual belts.[19] Much of the agency's rulemaking statement — and much of the controversy in this case — centers on the conclusions that should be drawn from these studies. The agency maintained that the doubling of seatbelt usage in these studies could not be extrapolated to an across-the-board mandatory standard because the passive seatbelts were guarded by ignition interlocks and purchasers of the tested cars are somewhat atypical.[20] Respondents insist these studies demonstrate that Modified Standard 208 will substantially increase seatbelt usage. We believe that it is within the agency's discretion to pass upon the generalizability of these field studies. This is precisely the type of issue which rests within the expertise of NHTSA, and upon which a reviewing court must be most hesitant to intrude.

But accepting the agency's view of the field tests on passive restraints indicates only that there is no reliable real-world experience that usage rates will substantially increase. To be sure, NHTSA opines that "it cannot reliably predict even a 5 percentage point increase as the minimum level of increased usage." Notice 25, 46 Fed. Reg., at 53,423. But this and other statements that passive belts will not yield substantial increases in seatbelt usage apparently take no account of the critical difference between detachable automatic belts and current manual belts. A detached passive belt does require an affirmative act to reconnect it, but — unlike a manual seat belt — the passive belt, once reattached, will continue to function automatically unless again disconnected. Thus, inertia — a factor which the agency's own studies have found significant in explaining the current low usage rates for seatbelts[21] — works in favor of, not against, use of the protective device.

---

[19] Between 1975 and 1980, Volkswagen sold approximately 350,000 Rabbits equipped with detachable passive seatbelts that were guarded by an ignition interlock. General Motors sold 8,000 1978 and 1979 Chevettes with a similar system, but eliminated the ignition interlock on the 13,000 Chevettes sold in 1980. NHTSA found that belt usage in the Rabbits averaged 34% for manual belts and 84% for passive belts. Regulatory Impact Analysis (RIA) at IV-52, App. 108. For the 1978-1979 Chevettes, NHTSA calculated 34% usage for manual belts and 71% for passive belts. On 1980 Chevettes, the agency found these figures to be 31% for manual belts and 70% for passive belts. Ibid.

[20] "NHTSA believes that the usage of automatic belts in Rabbits and Chevettes would have been substantially lower if the automatic belts in those cars were not equipped with a use-inducing device inhibiting detachment." Notice 25, 46 Fed. Reg., at 53,422.

[21] NHTSA commissioned a number of surveys of public attitudes in an effort to better understand why people were not using manual belts and to determine how they would react to passive restraints. The surveys reveal that while 20% to 40% of the public is opposed to wearing manual belts, the larger proportion of the population does not wear belts because they forgot or found manual belts inconvenient or bothersome. RIA at IV-25; App. 81. In another survey, 38% of the surveyed group responded that they would welcome automatic belts, and 25% would "tolerate" them. See RIA at IV-37. App. 93. NHTSA did not comment upon these attitude surveys in its explanation accompanying the rescission of the passive restraint requirement.

Since 20 to 50% of motorists currently wear seatbelts on some occasions,[22] there would seem to be grounds to believe that seatbelt use by occasional users will be substantially increased by the detachable passive belts. Whether this is in fact the case is a matter for the agency to decide, but it must bring its expertise to bear on the question.

The agency is correct to look at the costs as well as the benefits of Standard 208. The agency's conclusion that the incremental costs of the requirements were no longer reasonable was predicated on its prediction that the safety benefits of the regulation might be minimal. Specifically, the agency's fears that the public may resent paying more for the automatic belt systems is expressly dependent on the assumption that detachable automatic belts will not produce more than "negligible safety benefits." 46 Fed. Reg., at 53,424. When the agency reexamines its findings as to the likely increase in seatbelt usage, it must also reconsider its judgment of the reasonableness of the monetary and other costs associated with the Standard. In reaching its judgment, NHTSA should bear in mind that Congress intended safety to be the preeminent factor under the Motor Vehicle Safety Act:

> "The Committee intends that safety shall be the overriding consideration in the issuance of standards under this bill. The Committee recognizes . . . that the Secretary will necessarily consider reasonableness of cost, feasibility and adequate lead-time." S. Rep. No. 1301, at 6, U.S. Code Cong. & Admin. News 1966, p. 2714.
>
> "In establishing standards the Secretary must conform to the requirement that the standard be practicable. This would require consideration of all relevant factors, including technological ability to achieve the goal of a particular standard as well as consideration of economic factors. Motor vehicle safety is the paramount purpose of this bill and each standard must be related thereto." H. Rep. No. 1776, at 16.

The agency also failed to articulate a basis for not requiring nondetachable belts under Standard 208. It is argued that the concern of the agency with the easy detachability of the currently favored design would be readily solved by a continuous passive belt, which allows the occupant to "spool out" the belt and create the necessary slack for easy extrication from the vehicle. The agency did not separately consider the continuous belt option, but treated it together with the ignition interlock device in a category it titled "option of use-compelling features." 46 Fed. Reg., at 53,424. The agency was concerned that use-compelling devices would "complicate extrication of [a]n occupant from his or her car." *Ibid.* "To require that passive belts contain use-compelling features," the agency observed, "could be counterproductive [given] . . . widespread, latent and irrational fear in many members of the public that they could be trapped by the seat belt after a crash." *Ibid.* In addition, based on the experience with the ignition interlock, the agency feared that use-compelling features might trigger adverse public reaction.

----

[22] Four surveys of manual belt usage were conducted for NHTSA between 1978 and 1980, leading the agency to report that 40% to 50% of the people use their belts at least some of the time. RIA, at IV-25 (App. 81).

By failing to analyze the continuous seatbelts in its own right, the agency has failed to offer the rational connection between facts and judgment required to pass muster under the arbitrary and capricious standard. We agree with the Court of Appeals that NHTSA did not suggest that the emergency release mechanisms used in nondetachable belts are any less effective for emergency egress than the buckle release system used in detachable belts. In 1978, when General Motors obtained the agency's approval to install a continuous passive belt, it assured the agency that nondetachable belts with spool releases were as safe as detachable belts with buckle releases. 43 Fed. Reg. 21,912, 21,913-14 (1978). NHTSA was satisfied that this belt design assured easy extricability: "the agency does not believe that the use of [such] release mechanisms will cause serious occupant egress problems . . . ." 43 Fed. Reg. 52,493, 52,494 (1978). While the agency is entitled to change its view on the acceptability of continuous passive belts, it is obligated to explain its reasons for doing so.

The agency also failed to offer any explanation why a continuous passive belt would engender the same adverse public reaction as the ignition interlock, and, as the Court of Appeals concluded, "every indication in the record points the other way." 680 F.2d, at 234. We see no basis for equating the two devices: the continuous belt, unlike the ignition interlock, does not interfere with the operation of the vehicle. More importantly, it is the agency's responsibility, not this Court's, to explain its decision.

VI

"An agency's view of what is in the public interest may change, either with or without a change in circumstances. But an agency changing its course must supply a reasoned analysis . . . ." *Greater Boston Television Corp. v. FCC*, 444 F.2d 841, 852 (CADC 1971). We do not accept all of the reasoning of the Court of Appeals but we do conclude that the agency has failed to supply the requisite "reasoned analysis" in this case. Accordingly, we vacate the judgment of the Court of Appeals and remand the case to that court with directions to remand the matter to the NHTSA for further consideration consistent with this opinion.

So ordered.

Justice REHNQUIST, with whom THE CHIEF JUSTICE, Justice POWELL, and Justice O'CONNOR join, concurring in part and dissenting in part.

I join parts I, II, III, IV, and V-A of the Court's opinion. In particular, I agree that, since the airbag and continuous spool automatic seatbelt were explicitly approved in the standard the agency was rescinding, the agency should explain why it declined to leave those requirements intact. In this case, the agency gave no explanation at all. Of course, if the agency can provide a rational explanation, it may adhere to its decision to rescind the entire standard.

I do not believe, however, that NHTSA's view of detachable automatic seat-belts was arbitrary and capricious. The agency adequately explained its decision to rescind the standard insofar as it was satisfied by detachable belts.

The statute that requires the Secretary of Transportation to issue motor vehicle safety standards also requires that "[e]ach such . . . standard shall be practicable [and] shall meet the need for motor vehicle safety." 15 U.S.C. §1392(a). The Court rejects the agency's explanation for its conclusion that there is substantial uncertainty whether requiring installation of detachable automatic belts would substantially increase seatbelt usage. The agency chose not to rely on a study showing a substantial increase in seatbelt usage in cars equipped with automatic seatbelts and an ignition interlock to prevent the car from being operated when the belts were not in place and which were voluntarily purchased with this equipment by consumers. *See* ante, at 2870, n.15. It is reasonable for the agency to decide that this study does not support any conclusion concerning the effect of automatic seatbelts that are installed in all cars whether the consumer wants them or not and are not linked to an ignition interlock system.

The Court rejects this explanation because "there would seem to be grounds to believe that seatbelt use by occasional users will be substantially increased by the detachable passive belts," ante, at 2872, and the agency did not adequately explain its rejection of these grounds. It seems to me that the agency's explanation, while by no means a model, is adequate. The agency acknowledged that there would probably be some increase in belt usage, but concluded that the increase would be small and not worth the cost of mandatory detachable automatic belts. 46 F.R. 53421-54323 (1981). The agency's obligation is to articulate a "rational connection between the facts found and the choice made." Ante, at 2866-2867, 2871, quoting *Burlington Truck Lines v. United States*, 371 U.S. 156, 168 (1962). I believe it has met this standard.

The agency explicitly stated that it will increase its educational efforts in an attempt to promote public understanding, acceptance, and use of passenger restraint systems. 46 F.R. 53425 (1981). It also stated that it will "initiate efforts with automobile manufacturers to ensure that the public will have [automatic crash protection] technology available. If this does not succeed, the agency will consider regulatory action to assure that the last decade's enormous advances in crash protection technology will not be lost." *Id.*, at 53426.

The agency's changed view of the standard seems to be related to the election of a new President of a different political party. It is readily apparent that the responsible members of one administration may consider public resistance and uncertainties to be more important than do their counterparts in a previous administration. A change in administration brought about by the people casting their votes is a perfectly reasonable basis for an executive agency's reappraisal of the costs and benefits of its programs and regulations. As long as the agency remains within the bounds established by Congress, it is entitled to assess administrative records and evaluate priorities in light of the philosophy of the administration.

NOTES AND QUESTIONS

1. *State Farm* tells reviewing courts that they can hold a regulation "arbitrary and capricious" and remand it to the agency for further explanation or consideration based on a host of factors short of outright policy disagreement. These factors mainly pertain to how the agency reached its decision, not what the agency decided. In this sense, *State Farm* authorizes courts to police the agency's decisionmaking process but not the substantive outcome. It imposes what many have called a "reasoned decisionmaking" requirement, encouraging agencies to issue rules that are logically sound, factually supported, and thoroughly considered. It is also known as containing the "hard look" doctrine, which enables courts to take a hard look at whether agencies have taken a hard look at their rules.

2. The Court could have interpreted the arbitrary and capricious test to authorize less intensive judicial review. The language in the APA actually comes from an old formulation of the Due Process Clause, which required courts to uphold statutes unless patently unreasonable. The Court could have directed reviewing courts to uphold an agency rule unless no reasonable agency could have adopted it. Why did it go further? Put differently, what is gained by the reasoned decisionmaking requirement? Judicial control, certainly. But for what reason? Promoting fairness and deliberation? Participation? Expertise? Accountability?

3. Should the Court have interpreted the arbitrary and capricious test to authorize more searching review? What good is reviewing the agency's process if the agency's policy choice is unsound? Should courts also review the wisdom of the policy choice?

4. How successful was the Court in holding *itself* to the line that it established between the administrative process and the outcome? What did the Court hold on the facts of the case? The Court identified two problems with the rescission. Can you identify both? Where did it arguably overstep its bounds?

5. One year after the Court decided *State Farm*, NHTSA re-imposed mandatory passive restraints in the rule, excerpted at pp. 798-99. As you will see, the rule required passive restraints unless by 1989 state laws required seat belts and met other conditions for two thirds of the U.S. population. Although most states required seat belts by that date, they failed to comply with the other conditions. Thus, automakers had no choice and began to comply with the passive restraints rule, opting mostly to install airbags. In 1991, Congress enacted a statute that required auto manufacturers to install airbags. *See* Pub. L. No. 102-240, §2508, 105 Stat. 1914, 2085 (1991). Does this suggest that the Court got it right?

6. Even if the Court got passive restraints right, *State Farm* may have unintended consequences for agency action more generally. Professors Mashaw and Harfst have argued that in response to the decision, NHTSA adopted a wait-and-see posture of issuing recalls upon discovery that motor vehicles are unsafe rather than issuing rules to make them safe. *See* JERRY L. MASHAW & DAVID L. HARFST, THE STRUGGLE FOR AUTO SAFETY 224-54 (1990). Many argue

that the hard look doctrine has the effect of "ossifying" agency action. The prospect of judicial review causes agencies to refrain from issuing rules until they have built an unassailable case, often delaying so long that the rule fails to keep pace with scientific advances or effectively address statutory goals. *See* Stephen Breyer, Breaking the Vicious Circle 49 (1993). Agencies also may choose to forego issuing rules altogether. Empirical studies suggest that the concern for ossification may be overstated. Despite hard look review, agencies continue to make plenty of rules at a reasonable speed. *See* Cary Coglianese, *Empirical Analysis and Administrative Law*, 2002 U. Ill. L. Rev. 1111, 1125-31; William S. Jordan, III, *Ossification Revisited: Does Arbitrary and Capricious Review Significantly Interfere with Agency Ability to Achieve Regulatory Goals Through Informal Rulemaking?*, 94 Nw. U. L. Rev. 393, 403-07 (2000).

E. Standing

1. Introduction

Standing is the determination of whether a specific person is the proper party to bring a matter to the court for adjudication. The Supreme Court has declared that "[i]n essence the question of standing is whether the litigant is entitled to have the court decide the merits of the dispute or of particular issues."[23]

Standing frequently has been identified by both Justices and commentators as one of the most confused areas of the law. Professor Vining wrote that it is impossible to read the standing decisions "without coming away with a sense of intellectual crisis. Judicial behavior is erratic, even bizarre. The opinions and justifications do not illuminate."[24] Thus, it is hardly surprising that standing has been the topic of extensive academic scholarship and that the doctrines are frequently attacked. Many factors account for the seeming incoherence of the law of standing. The requirements for standing have changed greatly in the past 40 years as the Court has formulated new standing requirements and reformulated old ones. The Court has not consistently articulated a test for standing; different opinions have announced varying formulations for the requirements for standing in federal court.[25] Moreover, many commentators believe that the Court has manipulated standing rules based on its views of the merits of particular cases.[26]

---

[23] Warth v. Seldin, 422 U.S. 490, 498 (1975).

[24] Joseph Vining, Legal Identity 1 (1978).

[25] The Court itself observed: "We need not mince words when we say that the concept of Art. III standing has not been defined with complete consistency in all of the various cases decided by this Court." Valley Forge Christian College v. Americans United for Separation of Church and State, 454 U.S. 464, 475 (1982).

[26] *See, e.g.,* Gene Nichol, Jr., Abusing Standing: A Comment on *Allen v. Wright*, 133 U. Pa. L. Rev. 635, 650 (1985); Mark Tushnet, The New Law of Standing: A Plea for Abandonment, 62 Cornell L. Rev. 663 (1977).

Most of all, though, the extensive attention to the standing doctrine reflects its importance in defining the role of the federal courts in American society. Basic policy considerations, about which there are strong arguments on both sides, are at the core of the law of standing. The Court has identified several values which are served by limiting who can sue in federal court.

Values Served by Limiting Standing

First, the standing doctrine promotes separation of powers by restricting the availability of judicial review.[27] The Supreme Court explained that standing "is founded in concern about the proper — and properly limited role — of the courts in a democratic society."[28] In *Allen v. Wright,* the Supreme Court declared that standing is "built on a single basic idea — the idea of separation of powers."[29] The notion is that by restricting who may sue in federal court, standing limits what matters the judiciary will address and minimizes judicial review of the actions of the other branches of government. Indeed, the Court had said that the "standing inquiry is especially rigorous [because of separation of powers concerns] when reaching the merits of a dispute would force [it] to decide whether an action taken by one of the other two branches of the federal government was unconstitutional."[30]

However, concern for separation of powers also must include preserving the federal judiciary's role in the system of government.[31] Separation of powers can be undermined either by overexpansion of the role of the federal courts or by undue restriction. Standing thus focuses attention directly on the question of what is the proper place of the judiciary in the American system of government.

Second, standing is said to serve judicial efficiency by preventing a flood of lawsuits by those who have only an ideological stake in the outcome.[32] But in light of the high costs of litigation, one must wonder how large the burden really would be without the current standing restrictions. Standing also is justified in terms of conserving the Court's political capital. The Court once stated: "Should the courts seek to expand their power so as to bring under their jurisdiction ill-defined controversies over constitutional issues, they would become the organs of political theories. Such abuse of judicial power would properly meet rebuke and restriction from other branches."[33] But the question, of course, is what constitutes judicial abuse and what is appropriate court behavior.

---

[27] *See* Antonin Scalia, The Doctrine of Standing as an Essential Element of the Separation of Powers, 17 Suffolk L. Rev. 881 (1983) (describing standing as a function of separation of powers). For a criticism of this view, *see* Nichol, Abusing Standing, *supra* note 26.

[28] Warth v. Seldin, 422 U.S. at 498.

[29] 468 U.S. 737, 752 (1984); *see also* Lewis v. Casey, 518 U.S. 343, 353 n.3 (1996) (standing "has a separation of powers component, which keeps courts within certain traditional bounds vis-à-vis the other branches, concrete adverseness or not. That is where the 'actual injury' requirement comes from.")

[30] Raines v. Byrd, 521 U.S. 811, 819 (1997).

[31] *See* Susan Bandes, The Idea of a Case, 42 Stan. L. Rev. 227 (1990).

[32] *See, e.g.,* United States v. Richardson, 418 U.S. 166, 192 (1974) (Powell, J., concurring).

[33] United Pub. Workers v. Mitchell, 330 U.S. 75, 90-91 (1947).

Third, standing is said to improve judicial decision making by ensuring that there is a specific controversy before the court and that there is an advocate with a sufficient personal concern to effectively litigate the matter. The Supreme Court has frequently quoted its words from *Baker v. Carr*, that standing requires that a plaintiff allege "such a personal stake in the outcome of the controversy as to assure that concrete adverseness which sharpens the presentation of issues upon which the court so largely depends for illumination of difficult constitutional questions."[34]

Yet the need for specificity is likely to vary; some cases present pure questions of law in which the factual context is largely irrelevant. For example, if a city government tomorrow banned all abortions within its borders, the surrounding facts in the legal challenge almost surely would be immaterial. Also, the insistence on a personal stake in the outcome of the litigation is a very uncertain guarantee of high quality advocacy. The best litigator in the country who cared deeply about an issue could not raise it without a plaintiff with standing; but a pro se litigant, with no legal training, could pursue the matter on his or her own behalf.

Fourth, standing requirements are said to serve the value of fairness by ensuring that people will raise only their own rights and concerns and that people cannot be intermeddlers trying to protect others who do not want the protection offered. The Court explained, "the courts should not adjudicate such rights unnecessarily, and it may be that in fact the holders of those rights either do not wish to assert them, or will be able to enjoy them regardless of whether the in-court litigant is successful or not."[35] But standing requirements might be quite unfair if they prevent people with serious injuries from securing judicial redress.[36]

Thus, although important values are served by the doctrine of standing, these same values also can often be furthered by expanding who has standing. Ultimately, the law of standing turns on basic normative questions about which there is no consensus.[37]

Requirements for Standing

The Supreme Court has announced several requirements for standing, all of which must be met in order for a federal court to adjudicate a case. The Court has said that some of these requirements are constitutional; that is, they are derived from the Court's interpretation of Article III and as constitutional

---

[34] 369 U.S. 186, 204 (1962).

[35] Singleton v. Wulff, 428 U.S. 106, 113-114 (1976). For an excellent explanation of this fairness argument, *see* Lea Brilmayer, The Jurisprudence of Article III: Perspectives on the "Case or Controversy" Requirement, 93 Harv. L. Rev. 297, 306-310 (1979).

[36] *See* Richard Fallon, Of Justiciability, Remedies, and Public Law Litigation: Notes on the Jurisprudence of Lyons, 59 N.Y.U. L. Rev. 1 (1984).

[37] Indeed, some prominent commentators argue that the standing doctrine is unnecessary and that standing should simply be a question on the merits of the plaintiff's claim. *See* William Fletcher, The Structure of Standing, 98 Yale L.J. 221, 223 (1988) ("The essence of a true standing question is . . . [does] the plaintiff have a legal right to judicial enforcement of an asserted legal duty? This question should be seen as a question of substantive law, answerable by reference to the statutory or constitutional provision whose protection is invoked." *Id.* at 229).

restrictions they cannot be overridden by statute. Specifically the Supreme Court has identified three constitutional standing requirements.[38] First, the plaintiff must allege that he or she has suffered or imminently will suffer an injury. Second, the plaintiff must allege that the injury is fairly traceable to the defendant's conduct. Third, the plaintiff must allege that a favorable federal court decision is likely to redress the injury. The requirement for injury is discussed in Section 10.E.2. The latter two requirements — termed causation and redressability — often have been treated by the Court as if they were a single test: Did the defendant cause the harm such that it can be concluded that limiting the defendant will remedy the injury?[39] Accordingly, these two requirements are considered together in §2.5.3 [Erwin Chemerinsky, Constitutional Law: Principles and Policies, 4th ed., (2011)].

In addition to these constitutional requirements, the Court also has identified three prudential standing principles. The Court has said that these are based not on the Constitution, but instead on prudent judicial administration. Unlike constitutional barriers, Congress may override prudential limits by statute. First, a party generally may assert only his or her own rights and cannot raise the claims of third parties not before the court. Second, a plaintiff may not sue as a taxpayer who shares a grievance in common with all other taxpayers. However, in its most recent decision, the Supreme Court indicated that the bar on citizen suits, obviously quite similar to the limit on taxpayer suits, is constitutional and not prudential.[40] Third, a party must raise a claim within the zone of interests protected by the statute in question. These three standing requirements are discussed in Sections 10.E.3, 2.5.5, and 2.5.6 [Erwin Chemerinsky, Constitutional Law: Principles and Policies, 4th ed., (2011)], respectively.[41]

Although the requirements for standing must be met in every lawsuit filed in federal court, the issue frequently arises in cases presenting important constitutional and public law statutory questions. As such, standing is crucial in defining the scope of judicial protection of constitutional rights. Because standing is jurisdictional, federal courts can raise it on their own and it may be challenged at any point in the federal court proceedings.

2. Injury

The Supreme Court has said that the core of Article III's requirement for cases and controversies is found in the rule that standing is limited to those who allege that they personally have suffered or imminently will suffer an injury. The Court explained, "[t]he plaintiff must show that he has sustained or is

---

[38] For the Court's articulation of these three constitutional standing requirements, *see, e.g.,* Northeastern Florida Contractors v. Jacksonville, 508 U.S. 656, 663-664 (1993).

[39] It should be noted that the Supreme Court indicated that causation and redressability are separate and independent standing barriers. Allen v. Wright, 468 U.S. at 758-759.

[40] Lujan v. Defenders of Wildlife, 504 U.S. 555 (1992), discussed below.

[41] Specialized standing problems, such as standing for legislators and standing for government entities, are not covered. For a discussion of these topics, *see* Erwin Chemerinsky, Federal Jurisdiction (5th ed. 2007).

immediately in danger of sustaining some direct injury as the result of the challenged official conduct and the injury or threat of injury must be both real and immediate, not conjectural or hypothetical."[42]

The injury requirement is viewed as advancing the values underlying the standing and justiciability doctrines. Requiring an injury is a key to ensuring that there is an actual dispute between adverse litigants and that the court is not being asked for an advisory opinion. The judicial role in the system of separation of powers is to prevent or redress particular injuries. Judicial resources are thought to be best saved for halting or remedying concrete injuries. An injury is said to give the plaintiff an incentive to vigorously litigate and present the matter to the court in the manner best suited for judicial resolution. An injury ensures that the plaintiff is not an intermeddler, but rather someone who truly has a personal stake in the outcome of the controversy.

Requirement for a Personally Suffered Injury

Two questions arise in implementing the injury requirement: What does it mean to say that a plaintiff must personally suffer an injury; and what types of injuries are sufficient for standing? Each issue warrants separate consideration.

The Supreme Court has declared that the "irreducible minimum" of Article III's limit on judicial power is a requirement that a party "show he personally has suffered some actual or threatened injury."[43] Two environmental cases from the early 1970s illustrate this requirement. In *Sierra Club v. Morton*, the Sierra Club sought to prevent the construction of a ski resort in Mineral King Valley in California.[44] The issue was whether the plaintiff was "adversely affected or aggrieved" so as to be entitled to seek judicial review under the Administrative Procedures Act of the Interior Department's decision. The Sierra Club, a national membership organization dedicated to protecting the environment, asserted "a special interest in the conservation and the sound maintenance of the national parks, game refuges, and forests of the country."

The Supreme Court found this insufficient for standing purposes because there was no allegation that any of the Sierra Club's members ever had used Mineral King Valley. The Court stated: "The Sierra Club failed to allege that it or its members would be affected in any of their activities or pastimes by the . . . development. Nowhere in the pleadings or affidavits did the Club state that its members use Mineral King for any purpose, much less that they use it in any way that would be significantly affected by the proposed actions of respondents."[45] The Court concluded that "a mere interest in a problem, no matter how long

---

[42] *See, e.g.,* City of Los Angeles v. Lyons, 461 U.S. 95, 101-102 (1983) (citations omitted); *see also* Lujan v. Defenders of Wildlife, 504 U.S. 555, 560 (1992) ("[By injury in fact we mean] an invasion of a legally protected interest which is (a) concrete and particularized, . . . and (b) actual or imminent, not 'conjectural' or 'hypothetical.'").

[43] Valley Forge Christian College v. Americans United for Separation of Church and State, 454 U.S. 464, 472 (1982).

[44] 405 U.S. 727 (1972).

[45] *Id.* at 735.

standing the interest and no matter how qualified the organization is in evaluating the problem, is not sufficient."[46] Justice White is quoted in *The Brethren* as saying, "Why didn't the Sierra Club have one goddamn member walk through the park and then there would have been standing to sue?"[47] In fact, on remand, the Sierra Club amended its complaint to allege that its members had used the park for activities that would be disrupted by the ski resort, and it was then accorded standing.

Sierra Club can be contrasted with another decision handed down a year later involving a group seeking to protect the environment. In *United States v. Students Challenging Regulatory Agency Procedures (SCRAP)*, the Supreme Court upheld the standing of a group of students to seek review under the Administrative Procedures Act of an Interstate Commerce Commission decision to increase freight rates.[48] A group of law students at George Washington University Law Center contended that the hike in railroad freight rates would discourage the use of recycled goods because of the extra cost of shipping them. The lawsuit claimed that a decrease in recycling would lead to more use of natural resources and thus more mining and pollution. The students maintained that their enjoyment of the forests, streams, and mountains in the Washington, D.C., area would be lessened as a result. The Supreme Court upheld the group's standing, concluding that aesthetic and environmental injuries are sufficient for standing so long as the plaintiff claims to suffer the harm personally.

A comparison of *Sierra Club* and *SCRAP* is revealing. The plaintiffs complaint must specifically allege that he or she has personally suffered an injury. Although what constitutes a sufficient injury is discussed in detail below, it is worth noting that these cases establish that an ideological interest in a matter is not enough for standing. Yet these cases also raise important policy questions. Why assume in *Sierra Club* that the only ones injured by the destruction of the park are those who already have used it? As Professor David Currie explained, why cannot a person upset by the destruction of the last grizzly bear be allowed to sue, even if he or she never has seen a grizzly?[49]

The Supreme Court has continued to apply *Sierra Club*.[50] In *Lujan v. National Wildlife Federation*, the plaintiffs challenged the federal government policy lessening the environmental protection of certain federal lands.[51] Two members of the National Wildlife Federation submitted affidavits that they used land "in the vicinity" of that which was reclassified and that the increased mining activity would destroy the area's natural beauty. The Supreme Court, however, said that this allegation was too general to establish a particular injury, and thus

---

[46] *Id.* at 739.

[47] Bob Woodward & Scott Armstrong, The Brethren 164 n.* (1979).

[48] 412 U.S. 669 (1973).

[49] David Currie, Federal Courts: Cases and Materials 42 (4th ed. 1990).

[50] *See also* Director, Office of Workers' Compensation Programs, Department of Labor v. Newport News Shipbuilding and Dry Dock Co., 514 U.S. 122 (1995) (holding that the Director of the Office of Workers' Compensation Programs is not an aggrieved person under the Longshore and Harbor Workers' Compensation Act and thus did not have standing to seek review of decisions by the Benefits Review Board that deny individuals benefits).

[51] 497 U.S. 871, 883 (1990).

the defendant was entitled to prevail on summary judgment because of the plaintiffs' lack of standing. The Court quoted the district court's finding that thousands of acres were opened to development and "[a]t a minimum, [the] . . . affidavit is ambiguous regarding whether the adversely affected lands are the ones she uses."[52] In other words, the plaintiffs were not entitled to standing unless they could demonstrate that they used specific federal land that was being mined under the new federal regulations.

The Supreme Court subsequently applied this principle in *United States v. Hays* to hold that only a person residing within an election district may argue that the lines for the district were unconstitutionally drawn in violation of equal protection.[53] The Supreme Court has held that the government may use race in drawing election district lines only if it meets strict scrutiny, even if the purpose is to increase the likelihood of electing minority-race representatives.[54] In *Hays*, the Court held that only individuals residing within a district suffer an injury from how the lines for that district are drawn. The Court said that a "plaintiff [who] resides in a racially gerrymandered district . . . has standing to challenge the legislature's action," but a plaintiff who resides outside the district fails to suffer "the injury our standing doctrine requires."[55]

It is understandable that the Court would want to limit who has standing to challenge election district lines, but it seems hard to justify restricting standing to those who actually reside within the districts. Why shouldn't a voter residing in a contiguous district, who claims to have been excluded because of the race-based districting, also have standing?[56] Drawing lines for one election district inevitably affects the lines for neighboring districts. It therefore seems arbitrary to say that those within the district suffer an injury under the equal protection clause and all others do not.

Application of Requirement for Personally Suffered Injury: *City of Los Angeles v. Lyons*

Perhaps the most important application of the requirement for a personally suffered injury is the requirement that a plaintiff seeking injunctive or declaratory relief must show a likelihood of future harm. This was the holding in *City of Los*

---

[52] *Id.* at 888 (citation omitted).
[53] 515 U.S. 737 (1995). The Court reaffirmed and applied this limitation on standing to challenge election districts in Shaw v. Hunt, 517 U.S. 899, 904-905 (1996), and Bush v. Vera, 517 U.S. 952 (1996) (plurality opinion).
[54] *See e.g.,* Miller v. Johnson, 515 U.S. 900 (1995); Shaw v. Reno, 509 U.S. 630 (1993), discussed in §9.3.5.3 and §10.8.5 [Erwin Chemerinsky, Constitutional Law: Principles and Policies, 4th ed., (2011)].
[55] 515 U.S at 745. Although the Court expressly said that the injury requirement was not met, the Court also said that the case presented a "generalized grievance." *Id.* at 745. This raises the question of whether the Court continues to believe that the generalized grievance requirement is a separate standing rule or simply another way of saying that there is not an injury sufficient for standing purposes.
[56] *But see* Pamela S. Karlan, All Over the Map: The Supreme Court's Voting Rights Trilogy, 1993 Sup. Ct. Rev. 245 (arguing that even voters who live in majority-minority districts should not have standing).

Angeles v. Lyons.[57] *Lyons* involved a suit to enjoin as unconstitutional the use of chokeholds by the Los Angeles Police Department in instances where the police were not threatened with death or serious bodily injury. Adolph Lyons, a 24-year-old black man, was stopped by the police for having a burnt-out taillight on his car. Justice Marshall describes the uncontested facts:

> After one of the officers completed a patdown search, Lyons dropped his hands, but was ordered to place them back above his head, and one of the officers grabbed Lyons' hands and slammed them into his head. Lyons complained about the pain caused by the ring of keys he was holding in his hand. Within 5 to 10 seconds, the officer began to choke Lyons by applying a forearm against his throat. As Lyons struggled for air, the officer handcuffed him, but continued to apply the chokehold until he blacked out. When Lyons regained consciousness, he was lying facedown on the ground, choking, gasping for air, and spitting up blood and dirt. He had urinated and defecated. He was issued a traffic citation and released.[58]

At the time of the suit, 16 people in Los Angeles had died from the chokehold — 12 of them black men.[59] Lyons's complaint alleged that it was the official policy of the Los Angeles Police Department to use the chokeholds in situations where officers were not faced with a threat of bodily injury or death.

The Supreme Court, in a 5-to-4 decision, ruled that Lyons did not have standing to seek injunctive relief. Although Lyons could bring a suit seeking damages for his injuries, he did not have standing to enjoin the police because he could not demonstrate a substantial likelihood that he, personally, would be choked again in the future. Justice White, writing for the Court, explained: "Lyons' standing to seek the injunction requested depended on whether he was likely to suffer future injury from the use of the chokeholds by police officers."[60] The Court concluded that "absent a sufficient likelihood that he will again be wronged in a similar way, Lyons is no more entitled to an injunction than any other citizen of Los Angeles; and a federal court may not entertain a claim by any or all citizens who no more than assert that certain practices of law enforcement officers are unconstitutional."[61] *Lyons* thus establishes that in order for a person to have standing to seek an injunction, the individual must allege a substantial likelihood that he or she will be subjected in the future to the allegedly illegal policy.

Not surprisingly, the *Lyons* decision has been strongly criticized. First, some commentators have argued that the Court incorrectly assumed that Lyons would suffer an injury in the future only if he would be choked again. The Court's critics argue that Lyons would continue to suffer a psychological injury — fear of being subjected to a similar chokehold — so long as the police policy remained unchanged.[62]

---

[57] 461 U.S. 95 (1983).
[58] *Id.* 115 (Marshall, J. dissenting).
[59] *Id.* at 115-116 (Marshall, J., dissenting).
[60] *Id.* at 105.
[61] *Id.* at 111.
[62] Gene Nichol, Jr., Rethinking Standing, 72 Cal. L. Rev. 68, 100-101 (1982).

Second, *Lyons* is criticized as representing a substantial departure from prior practice both with regard to standing and in terms of civil procedure. Never before had the Court determined standing on the basis of the remedy sought. In fact, under the Federal Rules of Civil Procedure a plaintiff is not even required to request injunctive relief in the complaint in order to receive it as a remedy.[63]

Third, critics argue that the *Lyons* rationale, if strictly followed, would have a devastating effect on a substantial amount of public law litigation. Under the *Lyons* holding, plaintiffs would have standing to seek injunctions only of ongoing practices that were likely to directly harm them in the future. For example, a student would have standing to challenge an ongoing public school practice of holding prayer sessions every morning. But in many instances, plaintiffs seek injunctions — as Adolph Lyons did — of policies sure to affect someone in the future, but where a particular victim cannot be identified in advance.

Indeed, many lower courts have applied *Lyons* to prevent judicial review of allegedly unconstitutional government policies. For example, lower federal courts have dismissed the following for lack of standing: requests for injunctions to regulate the use of the chemical mace by police; challenges to a state practice of paying police officers a bonus if their arrest led to a conviction; and attempts to halt strip searches conducted at county jails of those arrested for minor crimes.[64] Additionally, lower courts consistently have applied *Lyons* to prevent standing in suits seeking declaratory judgments where standing for injunctive relief would be unavailable.[65]

Yet defenders of the *Lyons* decision argue that Lyons was not completely denied the ability to secure review of the police department's use of chokeholds. The Court did not deny his standing to pursue a damages claim, and the constitutionality of the chokehold could be adjudicated there. The Court's rationale is that a person does not have standing to seek an injunction unless there is a reason to believe that he or she would directly benefit from the equitable relief. But critics of *Lyons* respond that unconstitutional government policies will remain in effect, especially in instances where damage suits cannot be brought or the government is willing to pay the damages in order to maintain its policy.

Since *Lyons*, the Supreme Court has reaffirmed that a plaintiff seeking injunctive or declaratory relief must show a likelihood of future injury. For example, in *County of Riverside v. McLaughlin*, the Court allowed plaintiffs standing

---

[63] For an excellent development of this and other criticisms, *see* Fallon, *supra* note 36.

[64] Curtis v. City of New Haven, 726 F.2d 65 (2d Cir. 1984) (no standing to challenge police use of mace); Brown v. Edwards, 721 F.2d 1442 (5th Cir. 1984) (no standing to challenge state policy awarding money to constables for each arrest they made that led to a conviction); Jones v. Bowman, 664 F. Supp. 433 (N.D. Ind. 1987) (no standing to challenge strip searches of women performed by county jail); John Does 1-100 v. Boyd, 613 F. Supp. 1514 (D. Minn. 1985) (no standing to challenge strip searches of people brought to the city jail for minor offenses).

[65] *See, e.g.*, Fair Employment Council of Greater Washington, Inc. v. BMC Marketing Corp., 23 F.3d 1268 (D.C. Cir. 1994) (suit for injunctive and declaratory relief to halt discriminatory placement practices dismissed based on *Lyons*); Knox v. McGinnis, 998 F.2d 1405 (7th Cir. 1993) (prisoner's suit to stop prison officials from using "black box" restraining device dismissed based on *Lyons*); Alabama Free Thought Association v. Moore, 893 F. Supp. 1522 (N.D. Ala. 1995) (dismissed based on *Lyons* request for injunctive and declaratory relief to halt judge from causing prayers to be uttered in the jury room and the placement of the Ten Commandments in the courtroom).

to challenge a county arraignment policy that allowed long delays before arraignments over weekends and holidays.[66] The Court rejected a motion to dismiss based on *Lyons* and emphasized that plaintiffs were under arrest and in custody at the time that they filed their lawsuits. The plaintiffs' complaint alleged that they were suffering a current injury and that they "would continue to suffer that injury until they received the probable cause determination to which they were entitled."[67]

In contrast, in *Lujan v. Defenders of Wildlife*, the Supreme Court considered a challenge to a revision of a federal regulation that provided that the Endangered Species Act does not apply to United States government activities outside the United States or the high seas.[68] The plaintiffs claimed that the failure to comply with the Act "with respect to certain funded activities abroad increases the rate of extinction of endangered and threatened species."[69]

The Court expressly applied *Lyons* and held that the plaintiffs lacked standing because they could not show a sufficient likelihood that they would be injured in the future by a destruction of the endangered species abroad. Two of the plaintiffs had submitted detailed affidavits describing their trips abroad and their viewing of endangered animals such as the Nile crocodile, the elephant, and the leopard. The Court said that the fact that the women had visited the areas in the past "proves nothing," and their desire to return in the future — "some day" — is insufficient for standing "without any description of concrete plans or indeed any specification of when the some day will be."[70]

Justice Blackmun wrote a vehement dissent and lamented that the requirement that a plaintiff have specific plans to return to a foreign country created only a silly formality that a plaintiff must purchase a plane ticket in order to sue.[71] Moreover, the dissent challenged the majority's assumption that a person is harmed by the destruction of the environment only if the individual has concrete plans to visit the harmed place. Justice Blackmun stated: "It cannot be seriously contended that a litigant's failure to use the precise or exact site where animals are slaughtered or where toxic waste is dumped into a river means that he or she cannot show injury."[72]

---

[66] 500 U.S. 44 (1991).

[67] *Id.* at 51.

[68] 504 U.S. 555 (1992).

[69] *Id.* at 562 (citations omitted).

[70] *Id.* at 564. *See also* Steel Co. v. Citizens for a Better Environment, 523 U.S. 83 (1998) (relying on *Lujan* to deny standing to plaintiffs who sought relief for past violations of a federal law, but did not seek compensation for themselves, and did not allege that the company was likely to violate the statute in the future).

[71] *Id.* at 592 (Blackmun, J., dissenting). For a thorough criticism of *Lujan*, *see* Cass Sunstein, What's Standing After *Lujan*: Of Citizen Suits, "Injuries," and Article III, 91 Mich. L. Rev. 163 (1992).

[72] *Id.* at 594 (Blackmun, J., dissenting).

What Injuries Are Sufficient?

The second major question concerning injury as a standing requirement is what injuries are sufficient for standing? No formula exists for determining what types of injuries are adequate to allow a plaintiff standing to sue in federal court. The law is clear that injuries to common law, constitutional, and statutory rights are sufficient for standing. More than 40 years ago, Justice Frankfurter wrote that "[a] litigant ordinarily has standing to challenge governmental action of a sort that, if taken by a private person, would create a right of action cognizable by he courts. Or standing may be based on an interest created by the Constitution or a statute."[73] Past these categories, however, it is difficult to do more than identify the types of interests that the Court has regarded as adequate bases for standing and those that have been deemed insufficient.

Injuries to Common Law Rights

Injury to rights recognized at common law — property, contracts, and torts — are sufficient for standing purposes. In fact, for a time, the Court appeared to suggest that only such injuries would be enough for standing; that standing would be granted only if there would be a cause of action at common law for similar harms caused by a private actor. In *Tennessee Electric Power Co. v. Tennessee Valley Authority*, power companies attempted to enjoin the Tennessee Valley Authority from producing and selling electricity.[74] In denying the power companies standing to restrain their potential competitor, the Court explained that standing is unavailable "unless the right invaded is a legal right — one of property, one arising out of a contract, one protected against tortious invasion, or one founded on a statute which confers a privilege.[75] Although such injuries are obviously no longer exhaustive of those required for standing, violations of common law rights remain sufficient for standing purposes.[76]

Injuries to Constitutional Rights

Injuries to constitutional rights are also adequate to accord standing. Two qualifications are important. First, it is necessary to decide which constitutional provisions bestow rights. The Supreme Court has held that suits to halt the violation of certain constitutional provisions are nonjusticiable for lack of standing

---

[73] Joint Anti-Fascist Refugee Comm. v. McGrath, 341 U.S. 123, 152-153 (1951). Justice Frankfurter also expressed the view that only these categories could be a basis for standing; this certainly no longer is true, as discussed below.

[74] 306 U.S. 118 (1939).

[75] *Id.* at 137-138.

[76] Recently, the Supreme Court ruled that "an assignee of a legal claim for money owed has standing, even when the assignee has promised to remit the proceeds of the litigation to the assignor." Sprint Communications Co. v. APCC Services, Inc., 554 U.S. 269 (2008). All of the justices assumed that the claim for money was sufficient for standing, though split 5-4 as to whether the requirement for redressability is met when the plaintiff would not actually receive the funds. This is discussed below in the consideration of redressability.

because they present "generalized grievances." For example, the Court refused to find standing for plaintiffs seeking to enjoin violations of constitutional clauses requiring a statement and account of all government expenditures and preventing members of Congress from serving in the executive branch.[77] These cases and the generalized grievance standing bar are discussed in detail in §2.5.5 [Erwin Chemerinsky, Constitutional Law: Principles and Policies, 4th ed., (2011)]. In general, a person who claims discrimination or a violation of an individual liberty, such as freedom of speech or due process of law, will be accorded standing. But someone who seeks to prevent a violation of a constitutional provision dealing with the structure of government is unlikely to be accorded standing unless the person has suffered a particular harm distinct from the rest of the population.

Second, while an injury to a constitutional right is clearly a basis for standing, here remains the question of what facts are sufficient to establish such an injury. The Supreme Court's decision in *Laird v. Tatum* is illustrative.[78] In *Laird*, the plaintiffs contended that their First Amendment rights were violated because their expression was chilled by the army's surveillance of domestic groups. The Court said that "negations of a subjective 'chill' are not an adequate substitute for a claim of specific present objective harm or a threat of specific future harm."[79] However, it should be noted that in other instances the Court has found a chilling effect on speech to be a sufficient basis for standing. For example, in 1987, the Supreme Court accorded an exhibitor of foreign films standing to challenge the Department of Justice's labeling the films as "political propaganda" under the Foreign Agents Registration Act.[80] The Court accepted as a sufficient injury the allegation that the showing of films was chilled. The underlying point is that deciding whether there is an injury to a constitutional right often requires an inquiry into the merits of the case to determine whether a constitutional right was violated.

Injuries to Statutory Rights

Violations of rights created by statute also are sufficient for standing purposes. The Supreme Court has explained that "Congress may create a statutory right or entitlement, the alleged deprivation of which can confer standing to sue even where the plaintiff would have suffered no judicially cognizable injury in the absence of statute."[81] *Trafficante v. Metropolitan Life Insurance Co.* illustrates this type of injury.[82] In *Trafficante*, two white residents of an apartment complex were accorded standing to challenge the owner's discrimination against black appli-

---

[77] *See* Schlesinger v. Reservists Comm. to Stop the War, 418 U.S. 208 (1974); United States v. Richardson, 418 U.S. 166 (1974), discussed in §2.5.5 [Erwin Chemerinsky, Constitutional Law: Principles and Policies, 4th ed., (2011)], below.
[78] 408 U.S. 1 (1972).
[79] *Id.* at 13-14.
[80] Meese v. Keene, 481 U.S. 465 (1987), discussed in greater detail in §11.2.4.5 [Erwin Chemerinsky, Constitutional Law: Principles and Policies, 4th ed., (2011)].
[81] Warth v. Seldin, 422 U.S. 490, 514 (1975).
[82] 409 U.S. 205 (1972).

cants in violation of the Civil Rights Act of 1968.[83] The Supreme Court con-cluded that the statute created a right to be free from the adverse consequences of racial discrimination and accepted the plaintiffs' claim that they were injured in being deprived of the right to live in an integrated community.[84]

The interesting question concerning injuries to statutory rights is how far Congress can expand standing pursuant to this authority. For instance, the Clean Air Act empowers "any person" to bring suit to enforce certain pollution control regulations.[85] In light of *Trafficante*, can Congress, by statute, create a right to clean air, the violation of which is a sufficient injury for standing purposes? The Court's recent decision in *Lujan v. Defenders of Wildlife* indicates that such broad authorizations for standing will not be allowed.[86]

In *Lujan*, the Court considered a challenge brought under the Endangered Species Act which provides, in part, that "any person may commence a civil suit" to enjoin a violation of the Act.[87] The Court held that Congress could not create standing in this manner. Justice Scalia, writing for the Court, stated: "To permit Congress to convert the undifferentiated public interest in executive officers' com-pliance with the law into an 'individual' right vindicable in the courts is to permit Congress to transfer from the president to the courts the Chief Executive's most important constitutional duty, to take Care that the laws be faithfully executed."[88]

The relationship between *Lujan* and *Trafficante* is unclear. Perhaps the Court will draw a distinction between statutes that create a specific statutory right, such as a right to interracial housing, and those that are essentially procedural in creating a right for any person to sue. This distinction is troubling, however, because if Congress can create a right for all citizens, such as a right to have endangered animals protected, then Congress should be able to authorize enforcement of the right.

Alternatively, the Court may interpret statutes authorizing any citizen to sue to expand standing to the maximum allowed by Article III. In other words, Con-gress in expressly permitting such citizen suits, is seen as abrogating prudential requirements and allowing standing so long as it is constitutionally permissible. Support for this view is found in the Court's decision in *Bennett v. Spear.*[89] Ranch operators and irrigation districts filed an action under the citizen suit provision of the Endangered Species Act. The plaintiffs contended that the Act was violated in the proposed use of reservoir water to protect certain species of fish. The Supreme Court upheld the plaintiffs' standing and cited *Trafficante* as an instance where "standing was expanded to the full extent permitted under Article III."[90] Although the Court did not discuss *Lujan*, its reasoning implies that in *Trafficante*, and in

---

[83] 42 U.S.C. §3604.
[84] *See, e.g., Havens Realty Corp. v. Coleman*, 455 U.S. 363 (1982); *Gladstone, Realtors v. Vil-lage of Bellwood*, 441 U.S. 91 (1979).
[85] 42 U.S.C. §7604(a).
[86] 504 U.S. 555 (1992).
[87] 16 U.S.C. §1540(g).
[88] 504 U.S. 555, 562-563 (1992).
[89] 520 U.S. 154 (1997). *Bennett's* discussion of the zone of interest test is explained below in §2.5.6 [Erwin Chemerinsky, Constitutional Law: Principles and Policies, 4th ed., (2011)].
[90] *Id.* at 165.

Bennett itself, the citizen suit provision was a basis for standing because Article III's requirements also were met; in *Lujan*, the Article III standing requirements were not satisfied.

A subsequent standing case seems to confirm that Congress retains broad authority to create injuries that are the basis for standing. In *Federal Election Commission v. Akins*, the Court held that Congress, by statute, could create a right to information and that the denial of such information was an injury sufficient to satisfy Article III.[91] A group of voters brought suit challenging a decision by the Federal Election Commission that the American Israel Public Affairs Committee was not a "political committee" subject to regulation and reporting requirements under the Federal Election Campaign Act of 1971. A federal statute authorizes suit by any person "aggrieved" by a Federal Election Commission decision.

The Court granted standing and concluded that Congress had created a right to information about political committees and that the plaintiffs were denied the information by virtue of the Federal Election Commission's decision. Justice Breyer, writing for the Court, explained: "The 'injury in fact' that respondents have suffered consists of their inability to obtain information — lists of AIPAC donors . . . and campaign-related contributions and expenditures — that on respondents' view of the law, the statute requires that AIPAC make public."[92] In other words, the statute created a right to information, albeit a right that would not exist without the statute, and the alleged infringement of that statutory right was deemed sufficient to meet Article III and to allow standing under the broad citizen suit provision for any aggrieved person.

Together *Bennett v. Spear* and *Federal Election Commission v. Akins* indicate that *Lujan* should not be read as a broad limit on Congress's ability to authorize suits. So long as the plaintiff meets Article III's injury requirement, and infringement of a statutory right is sufficient in this regard, standing is permitted under a federal statute permitting citizen suits.

Other Injuries Sufficient for Standing

Injuries to common law, constitutional, and statutory rights are sufficient for standing. But these are not the only types of injuries that permit federal court review. The Supreme Court has considered many other interests, finding some to be a sufficient basis for a claim of injury, but concluding that others were inadequate. No ascertainable principle exists to rationalize these rulings. For example, the Court has ruled that a claim of an aesthetic or environmental harm is sufficient to constitute an injury.[93] In *Lujan*, for example, the Court conceded that the "desire to use or observe an animal species, even for purely aesthetic purposes,

---

[91] 524 U.S. 11 (1998).

[92] *Id.* at 21.

[93] *See* United States v. Students Challenging Regulatory Agency Procedures, 412 U.S. 669, 686 (1973). For a creative approach to the problem of standing in environmental cases, *see* Christopher Stone, Should Trees Have Standing? — Toward Legal Rights for Natural Objects, 45 S. Cal. L. Rev. 450 (1972).

694   Chapter 10. Statutory Implementation by Agencies

is undeniably a cognizable interest for purposes of standing."[94] Also, the Court held that possible diminution of water allocations as a result of application of the Endangered Species Act was a sufficient injury for standing.[95] Most recently, in *Massachusetts v. E.P.A.*, the Court ruled that the harms from global warming are sufficient to permit a state to sue the federal Environmental Protection Agency for failure to promulgate regulations to deal with greenhouse gas emissions.[96]

Additionally, the Court has allowed standing for those suffering economic harms[97] or facing possible criminal prosecutions for their actions.[98] The Court has held that the loss of the right to sue in the forum of one's choice is an injury sufficient to convey standing.[99]

In *Clinton v. New York City*, an important decision which declared the line-item veto unconstitutional, the Court found that a change in market conditions was a sufficient injury to meet the standing requirement.[100] President Clinton used the line-item veto to cancel a tax provision that would have benefited sellers in a transaction, but not a cooperative that was purchasing their company. Nonetheless, the Court concluded that the cooperative had suffered an injury because of the change in market conditions.

But other types of interests have been deemed insufficient for standing. For instance, in *Allen v. Wright*, the Supreme Court refused to allow standing to challenge the Internal Revenue Service's policy of providing tax exemptions to private schools that discriminated on the basis of race.[101] The Court said that the plaintiffs' claim that they were stigmatized by the government's policy was insufficient to constitute an injury for standing purposes. The Court explained: "[Stigmatic injury] accords a basis for standing only to those persons who are personally denied equal treatment. . . . If the abstract stigmatic injury were cognizable, standing would extend nationwide to all members of the particular racial groups against which the Government was alleged to be discriminating by its grant of a tax exemption to a racially discriminatory school."[102]

---

[94] 504 U.S. at 562-563.

[95] Bennett v. Spear, 520 U.S. 154, 168 (1997).

[96] 549 U.S. 547 (2007).

[97] Barlow v. Collins, 397 U.S. 159 (1970); Hardin v. Kentucky Utils. Co., 390 U.S. 1 (1968); FCC v. Sanders Bros. Radio Station, 309 U.S. 470 (1940).

[98] *See* Laurence Tribe, American Constitutional Law 115 (3d ed. 2000) ("A person subject to criminal prosecution, or faced with its imminent prospect, has clearly established the requisite 'injury in fact' to oppose such prosecution by asserting any relevant constitutional or federal rights.").

[99] *See* International Primate Protection League v. Administrators of Tulane Educ. Fund, 500 U.S. 72 (1991) (allowing plaintiffs standing to challenge removal of a case from state to federal court, even though plaintiffs lacked standing to challenge the government's action, which was the basis for the lawsuit). *See also* Asarco v. Kadish, 490 U.S. 605 (1989) (a state court decision can create an injury, and therefore be the basis for standing, even if plaintiffs initially would have lacked standing to sue in federal court).

[100] 524 U.S. 417 (1998).

[101] 468 U.S. 737 (1984).

[102] *Id.* at 755-756. *Allen* also denied standing based on failure to meet the causation requirement; this is discussed below in §2.5.3 [Erwin Chemerinsky, Constitutional Law: Principles and Policies, 4th ed., (2011)].

Another example where the Court deemed a harm as insufficient to meet the injury requirement was in one of the companion cases to *Roe v. Wade*.[103] Although the Court found the claim of another plaintiff to be justiciable, the Court refused to hear the challenge brought by a married couple to a law prohibiting abortion. The couple claimed that their "marital happiness" was adversely affected because they were "forced to the choice of refraining from normal sexual relations or of endangering Mary Doe's health through a possible pregnancy."[104] The Court deemed this injury insufficient to confer standing.

It is difficult to identify a principle that explains why aesthetic or economic injuries are sufficient for standing, but stigma or marital happiness is not. The only conclusion is that in addition to injuries to common law, constitutional, and statutory rights, a plaintiff has standing if he or she asserts an injury that the Court deems sufficient for standing purposes.

3. The Limitation on Third-Party Standing

While the requirements for injury, causation, and redressability are deemed to be constitutional limits on standing, the Court also has articulated prudential standing barriers. One such nonconstitutional prudential limitation is the prohibition against third-party standing. The Court has explained that "even when the plaintiff has alleged injury sufficient to meet the 'case or controversy' requirement, the Court has held that the plaintiff generally must assert his own legal rights and interests, and cannot rest his claim to relief on the legal rights or interests of third parties."[105] In other words, a plaintiff can assert only injuries that he or she has suffered; a plaintiff cannot present the claims of third parties who are not part of the lawsuit.

The prohibition against third-party standing — sometimes termed the rule against *jus tertii* standing — serves many of the underlying objectives of the standing doctrine.[106] The Court has emphasized that the people actually affected may be satisfied and thus the ban on third-party standing avoids "the adjudication of rights which those before the Court may not wish to assert."[107] Also, the Court has stated that requiring people to assert only their own injuries improves the quality of litigation and judicial decision making. In part, this is because the Court believes that the "third parties themselves usually will be the best proponents of their own rights."[108] Furthermore, it is thought that decisions might be improved in a concrete factual situation involving an injury to a party to the lawsuit.

But the Supreme Court has recognized four major exceptions to the prohibition against third-party standing. In these situations the Court has ruled that a

---

[103] 410 U.S. 113 (1973).

[104] *Id.* at 128 (citations omitted).

[105] *Warth v. Seldin*, 422 U.S. at 499. *See also* United Food and Commercial Workers v. Brown Group, 517 U.S. 544, 557 (1996) (discussing the bar against third-party standing as prudential).

[106] *See* Henry Monaghan, Third Party Standing, 84 Colum. L. Rev. 277, 278 n.6 (1984) (defining *jus tertii* standing).

[107] *See* Duke Power Co. v. Carolina Envtl. Study Group, Inc., 438 U.S. 59, 80 (1978); *see also* Singleton v. Wulff, 428 U.S. 106, 113-114 (1976).

[108] Singleton v. Wulff, 428 U.S. at 114.

person who has suffered an injury has standing to raise the interests of third parties not before the court. It must be stressed that the person seeking to advocate the rights of third parties must meet the constitutional standing requirements of injury, causation, and redressability in addition to fitting within one of the four exceptions described below.

Exception: Where the Third Party Is Unlikely to Be Able to Sue

First, a person may assert the rights of a third party not before the court if there are substantial obstacles to the third party asserting his or her own rights and if there is reason to believe that the advocate will effectively represent the interests of the third party.[109] For example, in *Barrows v. Jackson*, the Court allowed third-party standing and permitted an individual sued for breaching a racially restrictive covenant to assert the rights of blacks in the community.[110] Barrows, a white person who had signed a racially restrictive covenant, was sued for breach of contract for allowing nonwhites to occupy the property. The defense was based on the rights of blacks, who were not parties to the lawsuit for breach of contract. The Court allowed third-party standing, permitting the white defendant to raise the interests of blacks to rent and own property in the community. The Court stated that "it would be difficult if not impossible for the persons whose rights are asserted to present their grievance before any court."[111] Because blacks were not parties to the covenant, they had no legal basis for participating in the breach of contract suit.

Another example of this exception permitting third-party standing where the third party is unlikely to assert his or her own rights is *Eisenstadt v. Baird*.[112] A Massachusetts law made it a felony to distribute contraceptives, except by physicians or pharmacists, and then only to married individuals. Baird was prosecuted for distributing contraceptive foam to unmarried individuals in violation of this statute. His defense centered on the rights of individuals to have access to and use contraceptives. In other words, he attempted to raise the rights of third parties not before the Court. The Supreme Court allowed Baird standing to present this argument, concluding that "unmarried persons denied access to contraceptives in Massachusetts . . . are not themselves subject to prosecution and, to that extent, are denied a forum in which to assert their own rights."[113]

The Supreme Court also has held that parties in a litigation may raise the claims of prospective jurors to be free from discrimination in the use of peremptory challenges. In *Powers v. Ohio*, the Supreme Court held that in addition to the constitutional interests of the parties in having a jury selected without discrimination, prospective jurors are denied equal protection if they are excluded because

---

[109] Secretary of State v. J.H. Munson Co., 467 U.S. 947, 956 (1984).
[110] 346 U.S. 249 (1953).
[111] *Id.* at 257.
[112] 405 U.S. 438 (1972).
[113] *Id.* at 446.

of their race.[114] In *Powers*, the Court ruled that a criminal defendant could represent the interests of the prospective jurors, and in subsequent cases the Court extended this to civil litigants[115] and even to prosecutors.[116] Recently, the Court applied *Powers* to find that a white defendant has standing to challenge the exclusion of African Americans from the grand jury that indicted him.[117]

This use of third-party standing fits within the well-recognized exception where individuals can represent the interests of parties who are unlikely to be able to represent their own interests. Prospective jurors who are struck on the basis of race will not know of the discriminatory pattern; nor are they likely to have an incentive to bring a challenge on their own.[118]

Exception: Close Relationship Between Plaintiff and Third Party

A second exception to the ban against third-party standing permits an individual to assert the rights of third parties where there is a close relationship between the advocate and the third party. Usually, third-party standing is permitted in such circumstances where the individual seeking standing is part of the third party's constitutionally protected activity. For example, in *Pierce v. Society of Sisters*, a parochial school was accorded standing to challenge an Oregon law requiring all children to attend public school.[119] The parochial school argued that the law requiring public school attendance violated the rights of parents to control the upbringing of their children. The parochial school was allowed third-party standing because of the close relationship between the school and the parents and because the school was part of the regulated activity of providing parochial education.

Third-party standing based on this exception has been frequently allowed. For example, doctors often have been accorded standing to raise the rights of their patients in challenging laws limiting the patients' access to contraceptives and abortions.[120] In *Singleton v. Wulff*, two physicians were accorded standing to challenge a state statute that prohibited the use of state Medicaid benefits to pay for nontherapeutic abortions (abortions that were not necessary to protect the health or life of the mother).[121] The Court observed that the doctors were injured by the statute because it denied them payments for particular medical services.

---

[114] 499 U.S. 400 (1991). The issue of discriminatory use of peremptory challenges is discussed more fully in §9.3.3.2 [Erwin Chemerinsky, Constitutional Law: Principles and Policies, 4th ed., (2011)].

[115] Edmonson v. Leesville Concrete Co., 500 U.S. 614 (1991).

[116] Georgia v. McCollum, 505 U.S. 42 (1992).

[117] Campbell v. Louisiana, 523 U.S. 392 (1998).

[118] The Court in *Powers* also said that allowing third-party standing to represent the interests of prospective jurors is justified under the second exception, discussed below: where there is a close relationship between the litigant and the injured third party. 499 U.S. at 413 (citations omitted). This rationale seems more questionable because unlike other cases where this exception has been applied, there is no personal relationship between a litigant and prospective jurors.

[119] 268 U.S. 510 (1925).

[120] *But see* Tileston v. Ullman, 318 U.S. 44 (1943) (denying standing to doctor to raise challenges to law prohibiting use of contraceptives on behalf of patients).

[121] 428 U.S. 106 (1976).

Moreover, the Court emphasized the closeness of the doctors' relationship to the patient and that "the constitutionally protected abortion decision is one in which the physician is intimately involved."[122] The Court concluded that "it generally is appropriate to allow a physician to assert the rights of women patients as against governmental interference with the abortion decision."[123]

The Court also has allowed vendors to assert the rights of their customers based on this exception to the rule against third-party standing. The most famous example of this is *Craig v. Boren*.[124] Oklahoma adopted a law permitting women to buy 3.2 percent beer at age 18, but denying men that privilege until age 21.[125] A bartender sought to challenge the law on behalf of male customers between the ages of 18 and 21. The bartender suffered economic loss from the law, thus fulfilling the injury requirement. Furthermore, the Court observed that generally "vendors and those in like positions have been uniformly permitted to resist efforts at restricting their operations by acting as advocates for the rights of third parties who seek access to their market or function."[126]

A much publicized case in which the Court refused to allow third-party standing based on this exception was *Gilmore v. Utah*.[127] Gary Gilmore was sentenced to death in the state of Utah, but chose not to pursue collateral challenges in federal court. His mother sought a stay of execution on his behalf. In a 5-to-4 decision, the Court refused to hear his mother's claim. The Court's per curiam opinion said that the defendant had waived his rights by not pursuing them. Four Justices, in a concurring opinion, said that the mother should be denied standing because there was no reason why her son could not protect and assert his own rights. The *Gilmore* case might be read as supporting the proposition that a close relationship is not enough for third-party standing; the advocate also must be part of the third party's exercise of the protected right. On the other hand, *Gilmore* might be thought of as a narrow decision in a unique factual context.

Gilmore was followed in *Whitmore v. Arkansas*, where the Supreme Court held that a death row inmate did not have standing to challenge the validity of a death sentence imposed on another inmate who elected to forgo his right of appeal to the state supreme court.[128] After Ronald Simmons chose not to appeal his death sentence, another inmate, James Whitmore, sought to intervene and appeal on Simmons's behalf. Additionally, Whitmore argued that under the Arkansas system of comparative review of death sentences, he could personally benefit from a change in Simmons's punishment. The Court rejected the assertion of third-party standing and held that "Whitmore provides no factual basis for us to conclude that the sentence imposed on a mass murderer like Simmons

---

[122] *Id.* at 117.

[123] *Id.* at 118.

[124] 429 U.S. 190 (1976).

[125] The equal protection aspect of the case is discussed in §9.4.2 [Erwin Chemerinsky, Constitutional Law: Principles and Policies, 4th ed., (2011)].

[126] *Id.* at 195. *See also* Carey v. Population Servs. Intl., 431 U.S. 678 (1977) (permitting vendor of contraceptives to challenge law on behalf of its customers).

[127] 429 U.S. 1012 (1976).

[128] 495 U.S. 149 (1990). For a discussion of *Gilmore* and *Whitmore, see* Ann Althouse, Standing, in Fluffy Slippers, 77 Va. L. Rev. 1177 (1991).

would even be relevant to a future comparative review of Whitmore's sentence."[129]

Most recently, the Court refused to allow third-party standing to a father who was suing on behalf of his daughter to challenge the use of the words "under God" in the Pledge of Allegiance in public schools.[130] In *Elk Grove Unified School District v. Newdow*, in a 5-to-3 decision (Justice Scalia recused himself in response to a motion made by Newdow based on Justice Scalia having given a speech in which he expressed his views on the case), the Court dismissed the case for lack of standing. The Court ruled that Michael Newdow lacked third-party standing to sue on behalf of his daughter. The Court stressed that the girl's mother, and not Newdow, had legal custody and the Court also emphasized a traditional unwillingness of federal courts to get involved in domestic relations matters. Justice Stevens's majority opinion declared: "In our view, it is improper for the federal courts to entertain a claim by a plaintiff whose standing to sue is founded on family law rights that are in dispute when prosecution of the lawsuit may have an adverse effect on the person who is the source of the claimed standing. When hard questions of domestic relations are sure to affect the outcome, the prudent course is for the federal court to stay its hand rather than reach out to resolve a weighty question of federal constitutional law."[131]

It is difficult to fit the Court's decision in *Newdow* in the framework of traditional standing analysis. For example, apart from third-party standing, Michael Newdow had standing based on his own interests as a parent in the religious upbringing and education of his daughter. Also, it is long-standing practice that the Supreme Court defers to appellate courts' interpretations of state law and the Ninth Circuit carefully considered California family law in concluding that the award of legal custody did not preclude a noncustodial parent from suing on behalf of a child. Perhaps the Court dismissed *Newdow* on standing grounds to avoid a highly controversial political issue. But the question then becomes whether that is an appropriate use of the justiciability doctrines.

F. The Political Question Doctrine

1. What Is the Political Question Doctrine?

Definition

The Supreme Court has held that certain allegations of unconstitutional government conduct should not be ruled on by the federal courts even though all of the jurisdictional and other justiciability requirements are met. The Court has said that constitutional interpretation in these areas should be left to the politically accountable branches of government, the president and Congress. In other words, the "political question doctrine" refers to subject matter that the Court deems to

---

[129] 495 U.S. at 157.
[130] 542 U.S. 1 (2004).
[131] *Id.* at 17.

be inappropriate for judicial review. Although there is an allegation that the Constitution has been violated, the federal courts refuse to rule and instead dismiss the case, leaving the constitutional question to be resolved in the political process.

Why Is the Political Question Doctrine Confusing?

In many ways, the political question doctrine is the most confusing of the justiciability doctrines. As Professor Martin Redish noted, "[t]he doctrine has always proven to be an enigma to commentators. Not only have they disagreed about its wisdom and validity . . . , but they also have differed significantly over the doctrine's scope and rationale."[132] First, the confusion stems from the fact that the "political question doctrine" is a misnomer; the federal courts deal with political issues all of the time. For example, in *United States v. Nixon*, the Court decided that President Nixon had to comply with a subpoena to produce tapes of presidential conversations that were needed as evidence in a criminal trial — a decision with the ultimate political effect of causing a president to resign.[133] The Supreme Court's direct involvement in the political process long has included ending racial discrimination in political primaries and elections.[134]

Second, the political question doctrine is particularly confusing because the Court has defined it very differently over the course of American history. The Court first spoke of political questions in *Marbury v. Madison*.[135] Chief Justice John Marshall wrote: "By the Constitution of the United States, the President is invested with certain important political powers, in the exercise of which he is to use his own discretion, and is accountable only to his country in his political character and to his own conscience. The subjects are political. [B]eing entrusted to the executive, the decision of the executive is conclusive. Questions, in their nature political, or which are by the constitution and laws, submitted to the executive can never be made in this court."[136] Chief Justice Marshall contrasted political questions with instances where individual rights were at stake; the latter, according to the Court, never could be political questions.[137]

The Court's definition of political questions in *Marbury v. Madison* was quite narrow. Included only were matters where the president had unlimited discretion, and there was thus no allegation of a constitutional violation. For example, presidents have the choice about whether to sign or veto a bill or who to appoint for a vacancy on the federal judiciary. Because the Constitution vests the president with plenary authority in these areas, there is no basis for a claim of a

---

[132] Martin Redish, Judicial Review and the Political Question, 79 Nw. U. L. Rev. 1031 (1985).

[133] 418 U.S. 683 (1974), discussed in §4.3 [Erwin Chemerinsky, Constitutional Law: Principles and Policies, 4th ed., (2011)].

[134] *See, e.g.*, Nixon v. Herndon, 273 U.S. 536 (1927) (declaring unconstitutional racial discrimination in the Democratic political primary in Texas). The Court said that a claim that the matter was a political question because it involved the political process was "little more than a play upon words." *Id.* at 540.

[135] 5 U.S. (1 Cranch) 137 (1803), discussed above in §2.2 [Erwin Chemerinsky, Constitutional Law: Principles and Policies, 4th ed., (2011)].

[136] *Id.* at 165-170.

[137] *Id.* at 170.

constitutional violation regardless of how the president acts. But if there is a claim of an infringement of an individual right, in other words, if the plaintiff has standing, there is not a political question under the formulation presented in *Marbury v. Madison*.[138]

In sharp contrast, the political question doctrine now includes instances where individuals allege that specific constitutional provisions have been violated and that they have suffered a concrete injury.[139] The political question doctrine definitely is not limited to instances in which the president is exercising discretion and there is no claim of unconstitutional conduct. But the Court never has explained the differing content given to the term political question; in fact, the Court even invokes *Marbury* in its modern, very different cases.

The *Baker* Criteria and Their Limited Usefulness

Finally, and perhaps most important, the political question doctrine is confusing because of the Court's failure to articulate useful criteria for deciding what subject matter presents a nonjusticiable political question. The classic, oft-quoted statement of the political question doctrine was provided in *Baker v. Carr*.[140] The Court stated:

> Prominent on the surface of any case held to involve a political question is found a textually demonstrable commitment of the issue to a coordinate political department; or a lack of judicially discoverable and manageable standards for resolving it; or the impossibility of deciding without an initial policy determination of a kind clearly for nonjudicial discretion; or the impossibility of a court's undertaking independent resolution without expressing lack of the respect due coordinate branches of government; or an unusual need for unquestioning adherence to a political decision already made; or the potentiality of embarrassment from multifarious pronouncements by various departments on one question.[141]

Virtually every case considering the political question doctrine quotes this language. But these criteria seem useless in identifying what constitutes a political question. For example, there is no place in the Constitution where the text states that the legislature or executive should decide whether a particular action constitutes a constitutional violation. The Constitution does not mention judicial review, much less limit it by creating "textually demonstrable commitments" to other branches of government. Similarly, most important constitutional provisions are written in broad, open-textured language and certainly do not include "judicially discoverable and manageable standards." The Court also speaks of

---

[138] Howard Fink & Mark Tushnet, Federal Jurisdiction: Policy and Practice 231 (2d ed. 1987) ("But notice the effect of *Marbury*'s classification: Standing is just the obverse of political questions. If a litigant claims that an individual right has been invaded, the lawsuit by definition does not involve a political question.").

[139] *See, e.g.,* Luther v. Borden, 48 U.S. (7 How.) 1 (1949) (declaring nonjusticiable a suit brought under the republican form of government clause even though the effect was to leave people in jail who contested the constitutionality of their conviction), discussed below in Section 10.F.3.

[140] 369 U.S. 186 (1962).

[141] *Id.* at 217.

determinations of a kind "clearly for a nonjudicial determination," but that hardly is a criterion that can be used to separate political questions from justiciable cases.

In other words, it is impossible for a court or a commentator to apply the *Baker v. Carr* criteria to identify what cases are political questions. As such, it hardly is surprising that the doctrine is described as confusing and unsatisfactory.

The political question doctrine can be understood only by examining the specific areas where the Supreme Court has invoked it. Specifically, the Court has considered the political question doctrine in the following areas: the republican form of government clause and the electoral process, foreign affairs, Congress's ability to regulate its internal processes, the process for ratifying constitutional amendments, instances where the federal court cannot shape effective equitable relief, and the impeachment process. Section 10.F.2 considers the basic normative question of whether there should be a political question doctrine. Sections 10.F.3 to 10.F.8 consider, in turn, each of the areas mentioned above.

2. *Should There Be a Political Question Doctrine?*

Justifications for the Political Question Doctrine

The underlying normative issue is whether the political question doctrine should exist at all. Defenders of the doctrine make several arguments. First, and most commonly, it is argued that the political question doctrine accords the federal judiciary the ability to avoid controversial constitutional questions and limits the courts' role in a democratic society. Professor Alexander Bickel was the foremost advocate of this position.[142] Professor Bickel wrote:

> Such is the foundation, in both intellect and instinct, of the political question doctrine: the Court's sense of lack of capacity, compounded in unequal part of
>
> a. the strangeness of the issue and its intractability to principled resolution;
> b. the sheer momentousness of it, which tends to unbalance judicial judgment;
> c. the anxiety, not so much that the judicial judgment will be ignored, as that perhaps it should but will not be;
> d. finally ("in a mature democracy"), the inner vulnerability, the self-doubt of an institution which is electorally irresponsible and has no earth to draw strength from.[143]

Professor Bickel contended that it was simply better for the federal courts to avoid deciding certain cases, especially so as to preserve what he perceived as the

---

[142] *See, e.g.,* Alexander Bickel, The Supreme Court, 1960 Term: Foreword: The Passive Virtues, 75 Harv. L. Rev. 40, 46 (1961); Alexander Bickel, The Least Dangerous Branch 184 (1962).

[143] Bickel, *id.,* The Least Dangerous Branch at 184. It is interesting to consider the application of the Bickel justifications for the political question doctrine to *Bush v. Gore,* 531 U.S. 98 (2000). I address this in Erwin Chemerinsky, *Bush v. Gore* Was Not Justiciable, 76 Notre Dame L. Rev. 1093 (2001). *Bush v. Gore* is discussed in detail in Chapter 10 [Erwin Chemerinsky, Constitutional Law: Principles and Policies, 4th ed., (2011)].

judiciary's fragile political legitimacy.[144] Justice Felix Frankfurter argued, on this basis, that the Court should not have decided whether malapportionment violates the Constitution,[145] and many commentators have suggested that the federal courts should not review impeachment proceedings conducted by Congress because any ruling would jeopardize the Court's credibility and prestige.[146]

A second argument for the political question doctrine is that it allocates decisions to the branches of government that have superior expertise in particular areas. For example, some argue that the Court rightly has treated many constitutional issues concerning foreign policy to be political questions because of the greater information and expertise of the other branches of government.[147]

Third, the political question doctrine is defended on the ground that the federal courts' self-interest disqualifies them from ruling on certain matters. Specifically, it is argued that the courts should not become involved in reviewing the process for ratifying constitutional amendments because amendments are the only way to overturn the Supreme Court's constitutional interpretations.[148] Justice Powell, for example, spoke of the dangers of having the Court "oversee the very constitutional process used to reverse [its] decisions."[149]

Finally, the political question doctrine is justified on separation of powers grounds as minimizing judicial intrusion into the operations of the other branches of government. The argument is that in certain cases an effective remedy would require judicial oversight of day-to-day executive or legislative conduct. For example, a lawsuit contending that there were constitutional deficiencies in training the Ohio National Guard was deemed to be a political question because a remedy would involve judicial control and supervision over the Guard's activities.[150]

Criticisms of the Political Question Doctrine

On the other hand, critics, such as Professor Martin Redish, argue that "the political question doctrine should play no role whatsoever in the exercise of the judicial review power."[151] Such critics contend, first, that the judicial role is to enforce the Constitution — that it is inappropriate to leave constitutional questions to the political branches of government.[152] The argument is that matters are

---

[144] For a more recent argument employing and expanding on Professor Bickel's views, see Jesse Choper, Judicial Review and the National Political Process (1980) (arguing that separation of powers and federalism should be deemed political questions and left to the political process so that the federal courts can reserve their institutional legitimacy for individual rights cases).

[145] Baker v. Carr, 369 U.S. at 267 (Frankfurter, J., dissenting), discussed below.

[146] See, e.g., Charles Black, Impeachment: A Handbook (1974) (discussing impeachment as a political question).

[147] See, e.g., Fritz Scharpf, Judicial Review and the Political Question: A Functional Analysis, 75 Yale L.J. 517, 567 (1966).

[148] See, e.g., Laurence Tribe, Constitutional Choices 22-23 (1985) (arguing that challenges to the constitutional amendment process should be treated as a political question).

[149] Quoted in Tribe, id. at 23.

[150] Gilligan v. Morgan, 413 U.S. 1 (1973), discussed below.

[151] Redish, supra note 132, at 1033; Erwin Chemerinsky, Interpreting the Constitution 99-105 (1987).

[152] Redish, supra note 132, at 1045-1046; Chemerinsky, supra note 151, at 99-100.

placed in a Constitution to insulate them from majoritarian control; judicial review serves to effectuate and uphold the Constitution. Thus, it is inappropriate to relegate constitutional issues to the political branches of government. Politically accountable bodies should not be entrusted to enforce any part of a document that is meant to restrain them.

Second, critics of the political question doctrine question the premise of scholars such as Professor Bickel and Justices such as Felix Frankfurter, who speak of the judiciary's fragile legitimacy. To the contrary, critics contend that the federal courts' credibility is quite robust, that there is no evidence that particular rulings have any effect on the judiciary's legitimacy, and that in any event, the courts' mission should be to uphold the Constitution and not worry about political capital.[153] The argument is that a judiciary that ducks controversial issues to preserve its credibility is likely to avoid judicial review where it is needed most, to restrain highly popular, unconstitutional government actions.

Third, critics of the political question doctrine argue that it confuses deference with abdication. The claim is that in areas where the federal courts lack expertise, they should be more deferential to the other branches of government. Likewise, the courts should be particularly deferential in reviewing the process of ratifying constitutional amendments that seek to overturn the Supreme Court's judgments. But deference need not mean abdication. Many foreign policy questions do not involve matters of expertise, but instead pose interpretive questions like those constantly resolved by the courts.[154] Also, a blatant disregard of the Constitution's requirements — for example, an amendment deemed by Congress to have been ratified even though not approved by the requisite number of states — should not be tolerated by the federal courts.[155] In other words, critics of the political question doctrine argue that the doctrine's defenders demonstrate only that on the merits, the Court should hesitate in some areas before ruling against the other branches of government; it is wrong to deem those areas to be nonjusticiable.

Is It Constitutional or Prudential?

Perhaps as a reflection of this debate, important questions remain unsettled concerning the political question doctrine. For example, it is uncertain whether the political question doctrine is constitutional, prudential, or both. Could Congress direct the federal courts to adjudicate a matter that the Supreme Court deemed to be a political question? Unlike the other justiciability doctrines, the political question doctrine is not derived from Article III's limitation of judicial power to "cases" and "controversies."

---

[153] Chemerinsky, *supra* note 151, at 133-138; *see also* Laurence Tribe, American Constitutional Law viii (3d ed. 2000) ("The highest mission of the Supreme Court . . . is not to conserve judicial credibility, but in the Constitution's own phrase, 'to form a more perfect Union.'")

[154] *See* Louis Henkin, Is There a Political Question Doctrine?, 85 Yale L.J. 597 (1976) (arguing against courts finding issues concerning foreign policy to be a political question).

[155] *See* Walter Dellinger, The Legitimacy of Constitutional Change: Rethinking the Amendment Process, 97 Harv. L. Rev. 386 (1983).

The political question doctrine might be treated as constitutional if it is thought to be based on separation of powers or textual commitments to other branches of government. On the other hand, the doctrine is prudential if it reflects the Court's concerns about preserving judicial credibility and limiting the role of an unelected judiciary in a democratic society.

3. The "Republican Form of Government" Clause and Judicial Review of the Electoral Process

Article IV, §4, of the Constitution states that "The United States shall guarantee to every State in this Union a Republican form of government." The Supreme Court consistently has held that cases alleging a violation of this clause present nonjusticiable political questions. Several scholars have urged the Court to reconsider this rule and to find cases under the republican form of government clause to be justiciable.[156] Thus far, the Court has not done so, although Justice O'Connor remarked that "the Court has suggested that perhaps not all claims under the Guarantee Clause present nonjusticiable political questions" and acknowledged that "[c]ontemporary commentators have . . . suggested that courts should address the merits of such claims, at least in some circumstances."[157]

Luther v. Borden

Luther v. Borden is the seminal case.[158] In the 1840s, Rhode Island was the only state without a state constitution. The state governed pursuant to a state charter that had been granted to it by King Charles II in 1663. As a result, in 1840, the Rhode Island legislature was badly malapportioned and controlled by a rural minority. Jamestown, for example, had one representative in the state legislature for every 180 citizens, but Providence had one representative for every 6,000 citizens.

In 1841, a convention met to draft a state constitution. A constitution was proposed and ratified. The existing government, which was sure to lose power under the new document, enacted a law prohibiting the constitution from going into effect. Nonetheless, elections were held — even though the existing government had declared voting in them to be a crime. Relatively few people participated, but a new government was chosen, headed by Thomas Dorr, who was elected governor. Dorr's government met for two days in an abandoned foundry and then disbanded.

In April 1842, a sheriff, Luther Borden, broke into the house of one of the election commissioners, Martin Luther, to search for evidence of illegal

---

[156] *See, e.g.,* Erwin Chemerinsky, Cases Under the Guarantee Clause Should be Justiciable, 65 U. Colo. L. Rev. 849 (1994); Deborah Merritt, The Guarantee Clause and State Autonomy: Federalism for a Third Century, 88 Colum. L. Rev. 1 (1988) (arguing that the guarantee clause should be seen as a basis for protecting federalism and states' rights from congressional interference); *but see* Ann Althouse, Time for Federal Courts to Enforce the Guarantee Clause? — A Response to Professor Chemerinsky, 65 U. Colo. L. Rev. 881 (1994); Louise Weinberg, Political Questions and the Guarantee Clause, 65 U. Colo. L. Rev. 887 (1994).

[157] New York v. United States, 505 U.S. 144 (1992).

[158] 48 U.S. (7 How.) 1 (1849).

participation in the prohibited election. Luther sued Borden for trespassing. Borden claimed that the search was a lawful exercise of government power. Luther, however, contended that Borden acted pursuant to an unconstitutional government's orders; he maintained that the Rhode Island government violated the republican form of government clause.

The Supreme Court held that the case posed a political question that could not be decided by a federal court. The Court stated: "Under this article of the constitution it rests with Congress to decide what government is the established one in a State. For as the United States guarantee to each state a republican government, Congress must necessarily decide what government is established in the State before it can determine whether it is republican or not."[159] The Court also explained that the case posed a political question because if the state's government was declared unconstitutional, then all of its actions would be invalidated, creating chaos in Rhode Island.[160] Additionally, the Court, in siding with Rhode Island, spoke of a lack of criteria for deciding what constitutes a republican form of government.

Luther v. Borden has been followed consistently. There is not a single instance in which the Supreme Court has deemed a state government or state action to violate the republican form of government clause.[161] In *Taylor & Marshall v. Beckham*, the Court refused to decide a claim that a state's resolution of a disputed gubernatorial race violated the republican form of government clause.[162]

Similarly, in *Pacific States Telephone & Telegraph Co. v. Oregon*, the Court again held that cases under this clause are not justiciable.[163] *Pacific States* involved a challenge to a state law, passed through a voter initiative, that taxed certain corporations. The defendant was a corporation sued by the state of Oregon for failure to pay taxes due under this law. The corporation argued that the statute was unconstitutional because the initiative process violated the republican form of government clause. The claim was that a republican form of government is one in which people elect representatives who then govern; direct democracy was said to be antithetical to a republican government. The Supreme Court held that the matter was not justiciable. The Court said that the issue was "political and governmental, and embraced within the scope of powers conferred upon Congress, and not therefore within the reach of judicial power."[164]

Reapportionment

Following these precedents, the Court declared nonjusticiable the first challenges to malapportioned state legislatures. By the middle of this century, many

---

[159] 48 U.S. at 10.

[160] *Id.* at 13-14.

[161] There are instances in which the Supreme Court decided cases on the merits under the republican form of government clause, upholding the challenged government action. *See, e.g.,* Forsyth v. Hammond, 166 U.S. 506 (1897); Foster v. Kansas ex rel. Johnson, 112 U.S. 201 (1884); Kennard v. Louisiana ex rel. Morgan, 92 U.S. 480 (1875).

[162] 178 U.S. 548 (1900).

[163] 223 U.S. 118 (1912).

[164] *Id.* at 151.

state legislatures were badly malapportioned. Legislatures had not been reapportioned after substantial growth in urban areas, with the effect that rural residents were overrepresented and urban dwellers were substantially underrepresented in state legislatures. Legislators who benefited from this system were not about to voluntarily redraw districts at the expense of their seats. Also, the rurally dominated state legislatures drew district lines for electing members of the United States House of Representatives that obviously favored their areas.

In *Colegrove v. Green*, in 1946, the Supreme Court declared nonjusticiable a challenge to the congressional districting in Illinois.[165] In an opinion by Justice Frankfurter, the Court stated: "[T]he appellants ask of this Court what is beyond its competence to grant. [E]ffective working of our government revealed this issue to be of a peculiarly political nature and therefore not fit for judicial determination. Authority for dealing with such problems resides elsewhere."[166] The Court concluded that "[c]ourts ought not to enter this political thicket."[167] Similarly, in *South v. Peters*, in 1950, the Court held that "[f]ederal courts consistently refuse to exercise their equity powers in cases posing political issues arising from a state's geographical distribution of electoral strength among its political subdivisions."[168] Only in cases alleging racial discrimination in the drawing of election districts or in holding elections did the Supreme Court approve federal court involvement.[169]

But in 1962, in the landmark decision of *Baker v. Carr*, the Supreme Court deemed justiciable claims that malapportionment violates the equal protection clause.[170] Interestingly, the Court did not overrule *Luther v. Borden*, but instead distinguished cases brought under the equal protection clause from those pursued under the republican form of government clause. Justice Brennan explained that whereas "the Guaranty Clause is not a repository of judicially manageable standards ... [j]udicial standards under the Equal Protection Clause are well-developed and familiar."[171] This seems to be a fatuous distinction because both clauses are equally vague and the principle of one-person one-vote could have been articulated and enforced under either constitutional provision.[172] Nonetheless, the Court's holding that challenges to malapportionment are justiciable was one of the most important rulings in American history.[173] The political process

---

[165] 328 U.S. 549 (1946).

[166] *Id.* at 552-554.

[167] *Id.* at 556.

[168] 339 U.S. 276, 277 (1950).

[169] *See, e.g.,* Gomillion v. Lightfoot, 364 U.S. 339 (1960) (redrawing of Tuskegee, Alabama, districts to disenfranchise blacks); Terry v. Adams, 345 U.S. 461 (1953); Smith v. Allwright, 321 U.S. 649 (1944) (discrimination against blacks in political parties).

[170] 369 U.S. 186 (1962).

[171] *Id.* at 223-226.

[172] *See* Reynolds v. Sims, 377 U.S. 533 (1964) (articulating the one-person one-vote standard), discussed in §10.8.3 [Erwin Chemerinsky, Constitutional Law: Principles and Policies, 4th ed., (2011)].

[173] Chief Justice Earl Warren remarked that the most important decisions during his tenure on the Court were those ordering reapportionment. The Warren Court: An Editorial Preface, 67 Mich. L. Rev. 219, 220 (1968).

was not likely to correct the constitutional violation, and judicial review provided democratic rule.[174]

The Supreme Court and lower courts frequently have reaffirmed that challenges to election districts are justiciable. For example, in *United States Department of Commerce v. Montana*, the Court found justiciable a challenge by Montana voters to the method of apportioning members to the United States House of Representatives.[175] The Court unanimously found the challenge to be justiciable, though it concluded that there was no constitutional violation. The Court explained that objections to apportionment by Congress should be treated no differently than challenges to state government districting decisions.

Likewise, the Supreme Court has not hesitated to decide the constitutionality of using race in drawing election districts to increase the likelihood of electing African-American and Latino representatives.[176] Although the Supreme Court acknowledged that "[f]ederal court review of districting legislation represents a serious intrusion on the most vital of local functions," the Court has made it clear that strict scrutiny must be met in order for race to be used as a predominant factor in districting.[177]

Gerrymandering

In *Vieth v. Jubelirer*,[178] the Court dismissed a challenge to partisan gerrymandering and a plurality said that such suits are inherently nonjusticiable political questions. The issue was whether partisan gerrymandering violates equal protection. Republicans controlled the Pennsylvania legislature and they drew election districts to maximize Republican seats. This, of course, is not unique to Republicans or to Pennsylvania. Except in the places where there are independent district commissions, election districts for all levels of government are drawn to maximize seats for the political party drawing the districts.

Earlier, in *Davis v. Bandemer*, the Court held that challenges to gerrymandering are justiciable.[179] But in *Vieth*, the plurality concluded that *Davis* had proved impossible to implement and the plurality opinion, written by Justice Scalia, argued that challenges to partisan gerrymandering are nonjusticiable political questions. Justice Scalia, joined by Chief Justice Rehnquist and Justices O'Connor and Thomas, said that there are no judicially discoverable or manageable standards and no basis for courts to decide when partisan gerrymandering offends the Constitution.

Justice Kennedy, concurring in the judgment, provided the fifth vote for the majority. He agreed to dismiss the case because of the lack of judicially

---

[174] *See, e.g.*, Louis Pollak, Judicial Power and the Politics of the People, 72 Yale L.J. 81, 88 (1962).

[175] 503 U.S. 442 (1992).

[176] *See, e.g.*, Shaw v. Hunt, 517 U.S. 899 (1996); Bush v. Vera, 517 U.S. 952 (1996); Miller v. Johnson, 515 U.S. 900 (1995); Shaw v. Reno, 509 U.S. 630 (1993), discussed in §9.3.5.3 and §10.8.4 [Erwin Chemerinsky, Constitutional Law: Principles and Policies, 4th ed., (2011)].

[177] Miller v. Johnson, 515 U.S. at 915.

[178] 541 U.S. 267 (2004).

[179] 478 U.S. 109 (1986).

discoverable or manageable standards, but he said that he did not believe that such standards could not be developed in the future. Thus, he disagreed with the majority opinion that challenges to partisan gerrymandering are always political questions; he said that when standards are developed, such cases can be heard. Justices Stevens, Souter, and Breyer wrote dissenting opinions, which Justice Ginsburg joined, arguing that there are standards which courts can implement.

The puzzle is how lower courts should handle challenges to partisan gerrymandering after *Vieth*. The temptation may be to always dismiss such cases as nonjusticiable political questions. But five Justices expressly rejected that position. A majority of the Justices said that such challenges can be heard if there is a manageable legal standard. But who is to decide this? Is it for each district judge to evaluate in every case whether the parties have offered such a standard? Or must they wait until the Supreme Court pronounces a standard to exist? The Court just didn't say.

The Court offered no more clarity in a subsequent decision, *League of United Latin American Citizens v. Perry*,[180] where it again dismissed a challenge to partisan gerrymandering. After Republicans gained control of the Texas legislature in 2002, they redrew districts for Congress so as to maximize likely seats for Republicans. This replaced a plan that had been drawn up by a federal district court in 2001. The redistricting was very successful. The Texas congressional delegation went from 17 Democrats and 15 Republicans in the 2002 election to 11 Democrats and 21 Republicans in the 2004 election.

Many lawsuits were brought, and again the Court considered whether partisan gerrymandering is a nonjusticiable political question and, if it is justiciable, whether it violates equal protection. Once more, there was no majority opinion for the Court. Justice Kennedy announced the judgment of the Court and stated: "We do not revisit the justiciability holding but do proceed to examine whether appellants' claims offer the Court a manageable, reliable measure of fairness for determining whether a partisan gerrymander violates the Constitution."[181] He then went on to reject the challengers' argument that mid-decade redistricting for openly partisan reasons provided a "reliable standard" for the Court to use to invalidate the Texas plan.

Justices Scalia and Thomas reiterated their view, expressed in *Vieth*, that challenges to partisan gerrymandering are always nonjusticiable political questions. Chief Justice Roberts and Justice Alito agreed with the dismissal of the suit, but without saying whether they were finding it nonjusticiable or that partisan gerrymandering did not violate equal protection. Chief Justice Roberts wrote:

> I agree with the determination that appellants have not provided "a reliable standard for identifying unconstitutional political gerrymanders." The question whether any such standard exists — that is, whether a challenge to a political gerrymander presents a justiciable case or controversy — has not been argued in these cases. I therefore take no position on that question, which has divided the Court, and I join

---

[180] 548 U.S. 399 (2006).
[181] *Id.* at 414.

the Court's disposition in Part II without specifying whether appellants have failed to state a claim on which relief can be granted, or have failed to present a justiciable controversy.[182]

Justices Stevens, Souter, Ginsburg, and Breyer again dissented from the aspect of the decision dismissing the challenge to partisan gerrymandering as being nonjusticiable. They would have reached the merits of the equal protection claim.

Although there still has not been a majority opinion holding that challenges to partisan gerrymandering are always political questions, after *Vieth* and *Perry* it is hard to imagine such a case succeeding. Five Justices — Chief Justice Roberts and Justices Scalia, Kennedy, Thomas, and Alito — likely would rule against any such challenge. The underlying normative issue is whether the federal judiciary should stay out of partisan gerrymandering because of the inherent lack of standards for determining when there is a constitutional violation, or whether the federal judiciary should review such claims to correct a serious problem in the political process that otherwise will go unremedied.

Review of Political Parties

A final area where the Court has considered the application of the political question doctrine to the electoral process involves judicial review of the activities of political parties. The Court repeatedly has held that the federal judiciary will prevent racial discrimination by political parties.[183] But other challenges to political parties, especially suits concerning the seating of delegates at national conventions, have been dismissed by the courts. In *O'Brien v. Brown*, the federal courts were asked to decide what group of delegates should be seated at the 1972 Democratic National Convention.[184] The case reached the Supreme Court three days before the convention began. Illinois delegates, led by Mayor Richard Daley, were excluded on the ground that they were not sufficiently representative of racial minorities. The Daley delegates argued that they were discriminated against and denied equal protection. Also, a group of California delegates pledged to Hubert Humphrey argued that the state's winner-take-all primary was unconstitutional. The court of appeals ruled that the case was not a political question and on the merits held for the California plaintiffs and against the Illinois plaintiffs.

The Supreme Court stayed the court of appeals decision. The Court cited *Luther v. Borden* and stated: "In light of the availability of the convention as a forum to review the recommendations of the Credentials Committee, in which process the complaining parties might obtain the relief they have sought from the federal courts, the lack of precedent to support the extraordinary relief granted by

---

[182] *Id.* at 493 (Roberts, C.J., concurring in part, concurring in the judgment in part, and dissenting in part).
[183] *See, e.g.,* Terry v. Adams, 345 U.S. 461 (1953); Smith v. Allwright, 321 U.S. 649 (1944) (discrimination against blacks in political parties), discussed in §6.4.4.2 [Erwin Chemerinsky, Constitutional Law: Principles and Policies, 4th ed., (2011)].
[184] 409 U.S. 1 (1972).

the Court of Appeals, and the large public interest in allowing the political process to function free from judicial supervision, we conclude the judgment of the Court of Appeals must be stayed."[185]

Subsequently, in *Cousins v. Wigoda*, the Court held that a state court should not interfere with the selection of delegates to a national political convention.[186] The Court did not expressly base its decision on the political question doctrine, but instead on the right of political association infringed by state oversight of the delegate selection process.

Summary

In sum, alleged violations of the republican form of government clause pose political questions, but claims that districting violates the equal protection clause are justiciable. The key normative question is whether it is desirable for the republican form of government clause to be immune from judicial application. By deeming cases under this provision always to be a political question, the Court in essence has read it out of the Constitution. Yet it seems no more lacking in content than any other open-textured constitutional provision.

4. Foreign Policy

The Supreme Court frequently has held that cases presenting issues related to the conduct of foreign affairs pose political questions.[187] In *Oetjen v. Central Leather Co.*, in 1918, the Court declared: "The conduct of the foreign relations of our Government is committed by the Constitution to the Executive and Legislature 'the political' Departments of the Government, and the propriety of what may be done in the exercise of this political power is not subject to judicial inquiry or decision."[188]

Yet the Court also has emphasized that "it is error to suppose that every case or controversy which touches foreign relations lies beyond judicial cognizance."[189] For example, the Court has upheld, on the merits, the constitutionality of the president's use of executive agreements instead of treaties to implement major foreign policy agreements.[190] Also, the Court has ruled in favor of the constitutionality of the use of the treaty power for specific subject matters.[191]

---

[185] *Id.* at 5.

[186] 419 U.S. 477 (1975).

[187] For a defense of this use of the political question doctrine, *see* Theodore Blumoff, Judicial Review, Foreign Affairs, and Legislative Standing, 25 Ga. L. Rev. 227 (1991).

[188] 246 U.S. 297, 302 (1918). *See also* Chicago & S. Air Lines v. Waterman S.S. Corp., 333 U.S. 103, 111 (1948).

[189] Baker v. Carr, 369 U.S. at 211.

[190] *See, e.g.*, Dames & Moore v. Regan, 453 U.S. 654 (1981); United States v. Pink, 315 U.S. 203, 229 (1942); United States v. Belmont, 301 U.S. 324, 330 (1937); these cases are discussed in §4.6.2 [Erwin Chemerinsky, Constitutional Law: Principles and Policies, 4th ed., (2011)].

[191] *See, e.g.*, Missouri v. Holland, 252 U.S. 416, 433 (1920) (approving the constitutionality of a treaty with Great Britain concerning migratory birds).

Thus, it is difficult to identify any principle that determines which foreign policy issues are justiciable and which present political questions. The most that can be done is to describe the areas where the political question doctrine has been applied in the realm of foreign affairs.

Areas of Foreign Policy That Pose a Political Question

First, the Supreme Court has held that the determination of when war begins or when a war ends is left to the political branches of government. In *Commercial Trust Co. v. Miller,* the question presented was whether a congressional declaration that World War I had ended prevented application of the Trading with the Enemy Act.[192] In 1921, Congress, with the approval of the president, passed a joint resolution ending the war with Germany and proclaiming peace. The issue arose over whether the congressional proclamation suspended the application of the Act. The Court stated that the power to decide when a war ends is vested exclusively in Congress.[193] Quite similarly, the Court has held that the political branches decide when hostilities begin, and hence when it is appropriate to call up the militia.[194]

Second, the Supreme Court has held that the recognition of foreign governments is a political question,[195] as are related questions concerning disputes about the diplomatic status of individuals claiming immunity.[196] In other words, issues concerning who represents a foreign state, and in what capacity, are not justiciable.

Third, the Supreme Court has held that many issues concerning the ratification and interpretation of treaties pose political questions. For example, in *Terlinden v. Ames,* the Court held that it is a political question whether a treaty survives when one country becomes part of another.[197] Subsequently, a plurality of the Court held that a challenge to President Carter's rescission of the United States treaty with Taiwan posed a nonjusticiable political question. In *Goldwater v. Carter,* Senator Barry Goldwater argued that rescission of a treaty required approval of two-thirds of the Senate.[198] Senator Goldwater contended that just as the president cannot unilaterally repeal a law, neither is it constitutional for the president to rescind a treaty without the Senate's consent. Justice Rehnquist, writing for a plurality of four Justices, said that the case posed a political question. The plurality said that there were no standards in the Constitution

---

[192] 262 U.S. 51 (1923).

[193] *Id.* at 57.

[194] *See, e.g.,* Martin v. Mott, 25 U.S. (12 Wheat.) 19, 30 (1827).

[195] *See, e.g.,* United States v. Belmont, 301 U.S. 324, 330 (1937) (Court confirmed president's power to recognize and assume diplomatic relations with the Soviet Union); Oetjen v. Central Leather Co., 246 U.S. 297 (1918). The Court also has held that the recognition of Indian tribes is left to the political process. *See, e.g.,* United States v. Sandoval, 231 U.S. 28, 45-46 (1913).

[196] *See, e.g.,* In re Baiz, 135 U.S. 403 (1890).

[197] 184 U.S. 270 (1902).

[198] 444 U.S. 996 (1979).

governing rescission of treaties and that the matter was a "dispute between coequal branches of our Government, each of which has resources available to protect and assert its interests."[199]

Fourth, federal courts frequently have declared challenges to the president's use of the war powers to constitute a political question. During the Vietnam War, several dozen cases were filed in the federal courts arguing that the war was unconstitutional because there was no congressional declaration of war. Although the Supreme Court did not rule in any of these cases, either as to justiciability or on the merits, most of the lower courts deemed the challenges to the war to constitute a political question.[200] In the same way, challenges to the constitutionality of the president's military activities in El Salvador were dismissed by the lower federal courts as posing a political question.[201] Most recently, lower courts dismissed challenges to the constitutionality of the war in Iraq as posing a nonjusticiable political question.[202]

Should Foreign Policy Issues Be a Political Question?

The application of the political question doctrine to foreign policy is extremely controversial.[203] Some contend that it is appropriate for the judiciary to stay out of foreign policy because of the greater knowledge and expertise of the president and Congress in this area. The Supreme Court once stated: "[T]he very nature of executive decisions as to foreign policy is political, not judicial. Such decisions . . . are delicate, complex, and involve large elements of prophecy. . . . They are decisions of a kind for which the Judiciary has neither aptitude, facilities nor responsibility."[204] Furthermore, it is argued that the federal courts are particularly poorly suited to evaluating the constitutionality of a war and enforcing an order halting hostilities.

---

[199] *Id.* at 1004. Justice Powell concurred in the result, arguing that the matter was not yet ripe because Congress had not taken a position on the issue. *Id.* at 997 (Powell, J., concurring in the judgment).

[200] *See, e.g.,* Holtzman v. Schlesinger, 484 F.2d 1307, 1309 (3d Cir.), *cert. denied,* 416 U.S. 936 (1973); Da Casta v. Laird, 471 F.2d 1146, 1147 (2d Cir. 1973); Sarnoff v. Connally, 457 F.2d 809, 810 (9th Cir. 1972), *cert. denied,* 409 U.S. 929 (1972); Orlando v. Laird, 443 F.2d 1039, 1043 (2d Cir.), *cert. denied,* 404 U.S. 869 (1971); Simmons v. United States, 406 F.2d 456, 460 (5th Cir.), *cert. denied,* 395 U.S. 982 (1969); *see also* Anthony D'Amato & Robert O'Neil, The Judiciary and Vietnam 51-58 (1972) (description of cases concerning the Vietnam War as a political question); Louis Henkin, Vietnam in the Courts of the United States: Political Questions, 63 Am. J. Intl. L. 284 (1969).

[201] *See, e.g.,* Crockett v. Reagan, 720 F.2d 1355 (D.C. Cir. 1983), *cert. denied,* 467 U.S. 1251 (1984); Sanchez-Espinoza v. Reagan, 770 F.2d 202 (D.C. Cir. 1985); Lowry v. Reagan, 676 F. Supp. 333 (D.D.C. 1987); *but cf.* Ramirez de Arellano v. Weinberger, 745 F.2d 1500 (D.C. Cir. 1984) (holding justiciable a claim by a United States citizen that the federal government had taken his property in Honduras for the purpose of using it as a military training site; no challenge to the legality of the military activities was present).

[202] *See,* Doe v. Bush, 322 F.3d 109 (1st Cir. 2003).

[203] *See, e.g.,* Anne-Marie Slaughter Burley, Are Foreign Affairs Different?, 106 Harv. L. Rev. 1980 (1993).

[204] Chicago & S. Air Lines v. Waterman S.S. Corp., 333 U.S. 103, 111 (1948).

Yet critics of the political question doctrine argue that constitutional questions concerning foreign affairs should be adjudicated.[205] They contend that in many cases the constitutional questions do not depend on expert information. For example, deciding what constitutes a declaration of war is an interpretive question similar to others confronted by the Supreme Court. In instances that involve expertise, the Court can hear the case and defer to the other branches of government on the merits; there is no need to deem such matters to be nonjusticiable.

Critics of the political question doctrine argue that the constitutional provisions governing foreign policy are rendered essentially meaningless without judicial enforcement. Although in some instances the other branches of government might try to uphold the Constitution even in the absence of judicial review, at times this is likely impossible. For example, in *Goldwater v. Carter*, the plaintiffs contended that rescission of a treaty required approval of two-thirds of the Senate; that is, one-third of the senators should be able to block rescission.[206] Yet there is no way that one-third of the senators can have a voice or can enforce their position — even if it is impeccably correct constitutional law — without judicial review.

Because precedents concerning judicial review of constitutional issues pertaining to foreign affairs are conflicting and very controversial, it is inevitable that in the future the Court will need to decide again whether and when challenges to the conduct of foreign policy pose a political question.

5. Congressional Self-Governance

On several occasions, the Court has considered whether the political question doctrine prevents federal court review of congressional decisions concerning its processes and members. Often, though certainly not always, the Court has held that congressional judgments pertaining to its internal governance should not be reviewed by the federal judiciary.

For example, in *Field v. Clark*, the Court dismissed a claim that a section of a bill passed by Congress was omitted from the final version of the law authenticated by the Speaker of the House and the vice president and signed by the president.[207] The Court emphasized that judicial review was unnecessary because Congress could protect its own interests by adopting additional legislation.

A key case rejecting the application of the political question doctrine to judicial review of internal congressional decisions is *Powell v. McCormack*.[208] In 1967, the House of Representatives refused to seat representative Adam Clayton Powell, even though he had been elected by his constituents. A House subcommittee found that Powell deceived Congress by presenting false travel vouchers for reimbursements and had made illegal payments to his wife with government funds. Powell and 13 of his constituents sued, arguing that the refusal to seat him

---

[205] *See, e.g.,* Redish, *supra note* 132, at 1052; Michael Tigar, Judicial Power, the Political Question Doctrine, and Foreign Relations, 17 UCLA L. Rev. 1135, 1141-1151 (1970).

[206] 444 U.S. 996 (1979).

[207] 143 U.S. 649 (1892).

[208] 395 U.S. 486 (1969).

was unconstitutional because he was properly elected and met all of the requirements stated in the Constitution for service as a representative. Although he was not seated at all during that term of Congress, he was reelected in 1968 and he was seated in 1969. Nonetheless, the Supreme Court held that his suit was not moot because his claim for back pay for the time in which he was not seated remained a live controversy.

The Constitution specifically provides, in Article I, §5, that each house of Congress may, by a vote of two-thirds of its members, expel a member. However, the Court noted that the issue in *Powell v. McCormack* was not expulsion; he was excluded, not expelled.[209]

The defendants argued that the case posed a political question because the text of the Constitution in Article I, §5, provides that each house of Congress shall "be the Judge of the Qualifications of its Members." But the Court held that the House of Representatives had discretion only to determine if a member met the qualifications stated in Article I, §2 — requirements of age, citizenship, and residence.[210] In declaring that the case was justiciable and did not pose a political question, the Court stressed the importance of allowing people to select their legislators. The Court "concluded that Art. I. §5, is at most a 'textually demonstrable commitment' to Congress to judge only the qualifications expressly set forth in the Constitution."[211]

The defendants urged the Court to dismiss the case rather than interfere with or risk conflict with another branch of government. The Court rejected that such considerations should influence its ruling. The Court stated: "Our system of government requires that federal courts on occasion interpret the Constitution in a manner at variance with the construction given the document by another branch. The alleged conflict that such an adjudication may cause cannot justify the courts' avoiding their constitutional responsibility."[212]

In *Roudebush v. Hartke*, the Court held that Article I's provision making the Senate the "judge of the elections . . . of its members" did not preclude the state from ordering a recount in a senatorial election.[213] But the Court did state that the determination of which "candidate is entitled to be seated in the Senate [poses] a non-justiciable political question."[214]

Most recently, in *United States v. Munoz-Flores*, the Court refused to apply the political question doctrine to bar a challenge to a federal assessment as violating the origination clause of the Constitution, which provides that "[a]ll bills for

---

[209] *Id.* at 506-512.

[210] The Court relied on *Powell* to declare unconstitutional a state law that limited access to the ballot for candidates for the United States House of Representatives or the United States Senate after they had served a specified number of terms. United States Term Limits v. Thornton, 514 U.S. 779 (1995). The Court again emphasized that Article I sets the only permissible qualifications for a member of Congress.

[211] 395 U.S. at 548.

[212] *Id.* at 549.

[213] 405 U.S. 15, 19 n.6 (1972) (citations omitted).

[214] *Id.* at 19.

raising revenue shall originate in the House of Representatives."[215] A federal statute required that courts collect a monetary assessment on any person convicted of a federal misdemeanor. The challenger argued that this was unconstitutional because the bill for the assessments arose in the Senate and not the House. The Court brushed aside concerns about the need for deference to Congress and the ability of the House of Representatives to protect its own interests. Justice Thurgood Marshall, writing for the Court, explained: "To be sure, the courts must develop standards for making the revenue and origination determinations, but the Government suggests no reason that developing such standards will be more difficult in this context than any other."[216]

The underlying normative question again is whether these decisions invoking the political question doctrine are proper deference to a coordinate branch of government or whether they are unjustified judicial abdication. From one view, the federal courts appropriately have refused to become involved in internal legislative matters. But from a different perspective, the courts have unjustifiably failed to enforce constitutional provisions and have eliminated an important check on Congress.

6. The Process for Ratifying Constitutional Amendments

Article V of the Constitution prescribes the manner for amending the United States Constitution. When, if at all, should federal courts hear suits contending that the process was improperly followed? Some scholars, such as Professor Laurence Tribe, argue that the courts generally should not become involved in the only mechanism that exists to directly overturn the judiciary's interpretation of the United States Constitution.[217] But others, such as Professor Walter Dellinger, contend that the federal courts must ensure that the proper procedures are followed in amending the Constitution.[218] The argument is that the very safeguards that protect the Constitution from easy alteration are rendered impotent if the political process is allowed to disregard Article V.

Nor is it fanciful to imagine that Congress might violate the procedures for ratifying amendments, as the history of the adoption of the Fourteenth Amendment demonstrates.[219] After the Civil War, Congress adopted the Fourteenth Amendment, but it was quickly rejected by enough Southern and border states to prevent its passage. Congress, furious at what it perceived as an attempt to undo the outcome of the Civil War, enacted the Reconstruction Act, which provided, in part, for military rule of the rebel states and denied those states readmission into the Union until they had ratified the Fourteenth Amendment. After the Southern states ratified the amendment, two other states that had previously approved it

---

[215] 495 U.S. 385 (1990).

[216] Id. at 395-396.

[217] See, e.g., Laurence Tribe, Constitutional Choices 22-23 (1985).

[218] Walter Dellinger, The Legitimacy of Constitutional Change: Rethinking the Amendment Process, 97 Harv. L. Rev. 386 (1983).

[219] The history of the ratification of the Fourteenth Amendment is described in *Coleman v. Miller*, 307 U.S. 433 (1939), and reviewed in Section 4.C.

rescinded their ratification. Nonetheless, the Fourteenth Amendment was deemed adopted by counting all of the Southern states that were coerced into ratifying it and including the two states that rescinded their earlier approval.

Inconsistency Among the Cases

The Supreme Court has not been consistent in deciding whether the process of ratifying amendments is a nonjusticiable political question. In some instances, the Court has allowed judicial review. In 1798, in *Hollingsworth v. Virginia*, the Court held that the president may not veto amendments passed by Congress.[220] The Court concluded that the veto power contained in Article I, §7, was confined to statutes and did not include amendments. In a case involving the ratification of the Nineteenth Amendment, *Leser v. Garnett*, the Court held that a state's certification that it had ratified an amendment was sufficient to allow it to be counted as having approved the proposed constitutional change.[221] In *Dillon v. Gloss*, the Court upheld the constitutionality of Congress's creating time limits for the ratification of amendments.[222]

Yet on other occasions, the Court has indicated that the process of ratifying amendments poses a nonjusticiable political question. In *Coleman v. Miller*, a plurality of the Court declared that Congress has "sole and complete control over the amending process, subject to no judicial review."[223] The issue in *Coleman* was whether the time period for ratifying an amendment had expired. In 1924, Congress passed a proposed amendment to prohibit the use of child labor. In 1925, the Kansas legislature rejected the proposal, but in 1937, it was approved by that state's legislature. Kansas legislators who opposed the amendment sued, arguing that the time period for ratification had lapsed and that the earlier rejection was controlling.

The Supreme Court denied review. A plurality opinion written by Justice Black stated that the process of amending the Constitution is a "political question . . . Article V . . . grants power over the amending of the Constitution to Congress alone. . . . The process itself is political in its entirety, from submission until an amendment becomes part of the Constitution, and is not subject to judicial guidance, control or interference at any point."[224]

An issue similar to that raised in *Coleman* was presented to the federal courts in *State of Idaho v. Freeman*.[225] Idaho ratified the proposed Equal Rights Amendment, but then rescinded its ratification. The plaintiffs filed suit arguing that the rescission was effective. Also, the plaintiffs contended that Congress had unconstitutionally extended the time period for ratification. The Amendment, as proposed, contained a seven-year time limit for ratification. At the expiration of this time period, Congress extended the limit by three years. The plaintiffs in *Idaho v.*

---

[220] 3 U.S. (3 Dal.) 378, 382 (1798).
[221] 258 U.S. 130 (1922).
[222] 256 U.S. 368 (1921).
[223] 307 U.S. 433, 459 (Black, J., concurring).
[224] *Id.* at 457-459.
[225] 529 F. Supp. 1107 (D. Idaho 1981), vacated 459 U.S. 809 (1982).

Freeman argued that it was impermissible for Congress to approve the extension by majority vote; they argued that the Constitution requires a two-thirds vote of both houses of Congress to propose amendments.

The federal district court found that the case was justiciable and did not pose a political question. The court said that "the courts, as a neutral third party, and having the responsibility of guardian of the Constitution" should decide the issues presented.[226] On the merits the court ruled that the extension of time for the ratification of the amendment was unconstitutional. Before appellate review of the district court's decision was completed, the three-year extension for the ratification of the Equal Rights Amendment expired without ratification by three-fourths of the states. Accordingly, the Supreme Court vacated the district court's decision and ordered the case dismissed on mootness grounds.[227]

7. *Excessive Interference with Coordinate Branches of Government*

Limiting Judicial Oversight and Intrusion

In many areas, the political question doctrine is intended to limit judicial oversight and control of the other branches of the federal government. For example, the Supreme Court's treatment of many aspects of foreign policy as political questions reflects a desire to avoid judicial intrusion into the domain of the other branches.

In *Gilligan v. Morgan*, the Supreme Court deemed not justiciable a lawsuit claiming that the government was negligent in failing to adequately train the Ohio National Guard.[228] The suit was initiated by students at Kent State University after the shooting of four students during an anti–Vietnam War protest on May 4, 1970. The plaintiffs contended that grossly inadequate training of the Guard was responsible for the unjustified use of lethal force and sought injunctive and declaratory relief.

The Supreme Court, in an opinion by Chief Justice Burger, dismissed the case as posing a political question. The Court said that allowing review "would plainly and explicitly require a judicial evaluation of a wide range of possibly dissimilar procedures and policies approved by different law enforcement agencies or other authorities. It would be inappropriate for a district judge to undertake this responsibility, in the unlikely event that he possessed the requisite technical competence to do so."[229] The Court emphasized that relief would require ongoing supervision and control of the activities of the Ohio National Guard.

Lower courts have continued to find that there is a political question when there is a challenge to the exercise of executive discretion. For instance, in *United States v. Mandel*, the Ninth Circuit concluded that the decision of the secretary of interior to place an item on the commodity control list is not judicially

---

[226] 529 F. Supp. at 1135 (citations omitted).
[227] 459 U.S. 809 (1982).
[228] 413 U.S. 1 (1973).
[229] *Id.* at 8.

reviewable.[230] The court of appeals explained that "[t]hese are quintessentially matters of policy entrusted by the Constitution to the Congress and the President, for which there are not meaningful standards of judicial review."[231] But there also are a number of lower court cases that have refused to apply the political question doctrine on this basis. For example, in *Nation Magazine v. United States Department of Defense*, a federal district court found that the political question doctrine did not bar review of the method for issuing credentials to the press during the Persian Gulf War.[232]

The Supreme Court's use of the political question doctrine to deny review has been criticized.[233] For example, it is unclear why reviewing training of the Guard and requiring standards for improved training would be more intrusive than has been judicial review of school board or prison actions. Also, it is argued that the use of the political question doctrine was unnecessary; that courts always have the power to deny equitable relief when supervision and enforcement of the equitable decree would be too difficult.[234]

8. *Impeachment and Removal from Office*: Nixon v. United States

In 1993, the Court extended the use of the political question doctrine and resolved a previously undecided issue by holding that challenges to the impeachment process are nonjusticiable. *Nixon v. United States* involved federal district court judge Walter Nixon, who had been convicted of making false statements to a grand jury.[235] Judge Nixon refused to resign from the bench and continued to collect his judicial salary while in prison. The House of Representatives adopted Articles of Impeachment. The Senate, in accord with its rules, created a committee to hold a hearing and make a recommendation to the full Senate. The committee recommended removal from office, and the entire Senate voted accordingly.

Nixon argued, however, that the Senate's procedure violated Article I, §3, of the Constitution, which provides that the "Senate shall have the sole Power to try all Impeachments." Nixon maintained that this meant that the entire Senate had to sit and hear the evidence; he contended that the use of a committee to hear testimony and make a recommendation was unconstitutional.

Chief Justice Rehnquist, writing for the Court, held that the language and structure of Article I, §3, demonstrate a textual commitment of impeachment to the Senate. The Court explained that the framers intended that there would be two proceedings against officeholders charged with wrongdoing: a judicial trial and legislative impeachment proceedings. Chief Justice Rehnquist noted that "[t]he Framers deliberately separated the two forums to avoid raising the specter of bias and to ensure independent judgments. . . . Certainly, judicial review of the

---

[230] 914 F.2d 1215 (9th Cir. 1990).
[231] *Id.* at 1223.
[232] 762 F. Supp. 1558 (S.D.N.Y. 1991).
[233] Redish, *supra* note 132, at 1055.
[234] *Id.* at 1055-1056.
[235] 506 U.S. 224 (1993).

Senate's trial would introduce the same risk of bias as would participation in the trial itself."[236]

Moreover, the Court stated that judicial review of impeachment would be inconsistent with the framers' views of impeachment in the scheme of checks and balances. The framers saw impeachment as the only legislative check on the judiciary; judicial involvement would undercut this independent check on judges.[237]

Nixon holds that the judiciary will not review the Senate's use of a committee to hold a hearing and make a recommendation on an impeachment. *Nixon* leaves open the question of whether all challenges to impeachment are nonjusticiable political questions. For example, what if the president were impeached and convicted for an act that was completely lawful and within his constitutional powers? Or what if the Senate declared the president to be convicted on the basis of a committee's determination or a vote of less than two-thirds of the senators? Although these events are certainly improbable, it also is unlikely that the Court would declare an impeachment unconstitutional in the absence of compelling circumstances.

Justice Souter, in an opinion concurring in the judgment, recognized the potential need for judicial review. He wrote: "If the Senate were to act in a manner seriously threatening the integrity of its results, convicting, say, upon a coin-toss, or upon a summary determination that an officer of the United States was simply a bad guy, judicial interference might well be appropriate."[238]

G. Ripeness

1. Introduction

Ripeness Defined

Ripeness, like mootness (discussed in the next section), is a justiciability doctrine determining when review is appropriate. While standing is concerned with who is a proper party to litigate a particular matter, ripeness and mootness determine when that litigation may occur. Specifically, the ripeness doctrine seeks to separate matters that are premature for review, because the injury is speculative and never may occur, from those cases that are appropriate for federal court action.[239]

Although the phrasing makes the questions of who may sue and when they may sue seem distinct, in practice there is an obvious overlap between the doctrines of standing and ripeness. If no injury has occurred, the plaintiff might be denied standing or the case might be dismissed as not ripe. For example, in *O'Shea v. Littleton*, the Supreme Court declared nonjusticiable a suit contending that the defendants, a magistrate and a judge, discriminated against blacks in

---

[236] *Id.* at 234.
[237] *Id.* at 233-237.
[238] *Id.* at 253 (Souter, J., concurring).
[239] Abbott Labs. v. Gardner, 387 U.S. 136, 148 (1967).

setting bail and imposing sentences.[240] The Court observed that none of the plaintiffs currently faced proceedings in the defendants' courtrooms and hence "the threat of injury from the alleged course of conduct they attack is too remote to satisfy the case-or-controversy requirement."[241] This decision could be placed under the label of either standing — no injury was alleged; or ripeness — the type of injury was adequate but had not yet occurred.

Perhaps the distinction between standing and ripeness is that standing focuses on whether the type of injury alleged is qualitatively sufficient to fulfill the requirements of Article III and whether the plaintiff has personally suffered that harm, whereas ripeness centers on whether that injury has occurred yet. Again, while the distinction will work in some instances, in others it is problematic because the question of whether the plaintiff has suffered a harm is integral to both standing and ripeness concerns. For example, in *Sierra Club v. Morton*, the Supreme Court dismissed, on standing grounds, a challenge by an environmental group to the construction of a ski resort in a national park.[242] The Court emphasized the failure of the plaintiff to allege that it or its members ever had used the park. This standing decision could be viewed as a ripeness ruling as well, if ripeness is understood as focusing on whether an injury that is sufficient to meet Article III has been suffered yet.

To the extent that the substantive requirements overlap and the result will be the same regardless of whether the issue is characterized as ripeness or standing, little turns on the choice of the label. However, for the sake of clarity, especially in those cases where the law of standing and ripeness is not identical, ripeness can be given a narrower definition that distinguishes it from standing and explains the existing case law. Ripeness properly should be understood as involving the question of *when may a party seek preenforcement review of a statute or regulation.* Customarily, a person can challenge the legality of a statute or regulation only when he or she is prosecuted for violating it. At that time, a defense can be that the law is invalid, for example, as being unconstitutional.

There is an unfairness, however, to requiring a person to violate a law in order to challenge it. A person might unnecessarily obey an unconstitutional law, refraining from the prohibited conduct, rather than risk criminal punishments. Alternatively, a person might violate a statute or regulation, confident that it will be invalidated, only to be punished when the law is upheld. A primary purpose of the Declaratory Judgment Act was to permit people to avoid this choice and obtain preenforcement review of statutes and regulations.

The Declaratory Judgment Act does not allow preenforcement review in all instances. Rather, it permits federal court decisions only "[i]n a case of actual controversy."[243] In upholding the constitutionality of the Declaratory Judgment Act, the Supreme Court emphasized that the statute did not permit advisory opinions

---

[240] 414 U.S. 488 (1974).
[241] *Id.* at 489.
[242] 405 U.S. 727 (1972), discussed in more detail in Section 10.E.2.
[243] 28 U.S.C. §2201.

because it limited federal court action to justiciable cases.[244] Ripeness, then, is best understood as the determination of whether a federal court can grant preenforcement review; for example, when may a court hear a request for a declaratory judgment, or when must it decline review?

The Supreme Court has stated that in deciding whether a case is ripe it looks primarily to two considerations: "the hardship to the parties of withholding court consideration" and "the fitness of the issues for judicial decision."[245] Ripeness is said to reflect both constitutional and prudential considerations. The focus on whether there is a sufficient injury without preenforcement review seems inextricably linked with the constitutional requirement for cases and controversies, whereas the focus on the quality of the record seems prudential.[246]

The ripeness doctrine, limiting preenforcement review, serves many of the purposes underlying the other justiciability doctrines. Ripeness advances separation of powers by avoiding judicial review in situations where it is unnecessary for the federal courts to become involved because there is not a substantial hardship to postponing review. In the leading case of *Abbott Laboratories v. Gardner*, the Court explained that the "basic rationale" of the ripeness requirement is "to prevent the courts, through avoidance of premature adjudication, from entangling themselves in abstract disagreements."[247]

Additionally, the ripeness requirement, like all justiciability doctrines, enhances judicial economy by limiting the occasion for federal court jurisdiction and the expenditure of judicial time and revenues. Perhaps most of all, ripeness is said to enhance the quality of judicial decision making by ensuring that there is an adequate record to permit effective review.[248]

As is reflected in the cases described below, the federal courts have a great deal of discretion in determining whether a case is ripe. The questions of whether there is sufficient hardship to permit preenforcement review and whether the record is adequately focused cannot be reduced to a formula. The result is that it is often difficult to distinguish why in some instances ripeness was found, but in other seemingly similar circumstances it was denied.

2. *Criteria for Determining Ripeness: The Hardship to Denying Review*

The first part of the ripeness inquiry is determining how significant is the harm to denying judicial review. The more a plaintiff can demonstrate substantial

---

[244] Aetna Life Ins. Co. v. Haworth, 300 U.S. 227, 241 (1937); for a discussion of the constitutionality of the Declaratory Judgment Act and why it is not an authorization for unconstitutional advisory opinions, *see* §2.4 [Erwin Chemerinsky, Constitutional Law: Principles and Policies, 4th ed., (2011)].

[245] Abbott Labs. v. Gardner, 387 U.S. at 149.

[246] At times, the Court describes ripeness as constitutional; *see, e.g.*, Public Serv. Commn. of Utah v. Wycoff Co., 344 U.S. 237, 242-245 (1952); but at other times, the Court describes the ripeness test as prudential; *see, e.g.*, Buckley v. Valeo, 424 U.S. 1, 114-118 (1976). In large part, this difference might reflect the aspects of ripeness at issue in particular cases.

[247] 387 U.S. at 148.

[248] *Id.*

hardship to a denial of preenforcement review, the more likely a federal court is to find ripeness. Conversely, the more speculative and uncertain the harm, the less likely it is that review will be granted.[249]

Hardship from Choice Between Possibly Unnecessary Compliance and Possible Conviction

An examination of Supreme Court ripeness decisions reveals three situations in which the Court has found there to be enough hardship to justify preenforcement review. First, when an individual is faced with a choice between forgoing allegedly lawful behavior and risking likely prosecution with substantial consequences, the federal courts will deem the case ripe rather than insist that an individual violate the law and risk the consequences. *Abbott Laboratories v. Gardner* is illustrative.[250] The Food and Drug Administration (FDA) promulgated a regulation requiring the inclusion of generic names for prescription drugs on all labels and other printed materials. Violations of the regulation were punishable by civil and criminal sanctions. Thirty-seven drug companies, accounting for 90 percent of the supply of prescription drugs in the country, challenged the regulation as exceeding the scope of the FDA's authority under the pertinent statutes. The government argued that the case was not ripe until a drug company was prosecuted for violating the regulation.

The Supreme Court disagreed and permitted preenforcement review. The Court emphasized the substantial hardship to denying preenforcement review. The Court stated: "If petitioners wish to comply they must change all their labels, advertisements and promotional materials; they must destroy stocks of printed matter; and they must invest heavily in new printing type and new supplies. The alternative to compliance . . . would risk serious criminal and civil penalties for the unlawful distribution of 'misbranded' drugs."[251]

The ripeness requirement can be understood by contrasting *Abbott Laboratories* with another case decided the same day, *Toilet Goods Association v. Gardner.*[252] An FDA regulation permitted the FDA free access to all manufacturing processes involved in the production of color additives and authorized the suspension of certifications for sales if access is denied. A cosmetic manufacturing company sought a declaratory judgment invalidating the regulation. But unlike *Abbott Laboratories,* the Court said that the matter was not ripe because there was minimal hardship to denying review. The Court explained that "a refusal to admit an inspector here would at most lead only to a suspension of certification services

---

[249] For example, in Texas v. United States, 523 U.S. 296 (1998), the Supreme Court refused to rule as to whether the preclearance provision of the Voting Rights Act of 1965 applied to the possible appointment of a magistrate to oversee school districts that failed to meet performance standards. The Court noted that no magistrate had yet been appointed and that the appointment of a magistrate was a last resort to be used only if all other means failed. The Court concluded that the case was not ripe because it was too speculative whether a magistrate ever would be appointed.

[250] 387 U.S. 136 (1967).

[251] *Id.* at 152-153.

[252] 387 U.S. 158 (1967).

to the particular party, a determination that can then be promptly challenged through an administrative procedure, which in turn is reviewable by a court."[253]

In numerous other cases as well, the Supreme Court found substantial hardship in denying judicial review because of the choice that a person faced between refraining from allegedly protected conduct or risking sanctions. For instance, in *Steffel v. Thompson*, the plaintiff sought a declaratory judgment upholding his right to distribute handbills in a shopping center.[254] On two occasions, the plaintiff attempted to distribute anti–Vietnam War literature at a shopping center; both times the owners of the property called the police. Although the plaintiff left to avoid arrest, his companions stayed and were arrested. The Supreme Court found the matter ripe because denying review would impose substantial hardship, forcing the plaintiff to choose between unnecessarily giving up possibly protected speech or risking arrest and criminal punishment. Justice Brennan, writing for the Court, spoke of the injury inflicted in placing "the hapless plaintiff between the Scylla of intentionally flouting state law and the Charybdis of forgoing what he believes to be constitutionally protected activity in order to avoid becoming enmeshed in a criminal proceeding."[255]

Similarly, in the earlier case of *Adler v. Board of Education of the City of New York*, the Court implicitly found ripe a challenge to a state law designed to eliminate "subversive persons" from the public school system.[256] The state statute contained a list of subversive organizations, and membership in any of these groups was deemed a basis for disqualification from being employed in any school. Although Justice Frankfurter dissented, arguing that the case was not ripe, the Supreme Court upheld the statute on the merits. The Court's choice to decide the case apparently reflected a conclusion that there was substantial hardship to denying review in that teachers had to either refrain from joining these organizations or risk loss of their jobs.

Thus, it is well established that a case is ripe because of the substantial hardship to denying preenforcement review when a person is forced to choose between forgoing possibly lawful activity and risking substantial sanctions. People should not be forced to exercise their rights at peril of criminal sanctions or loss of employment.

However, some Supreme Court cases deviate from this principle. For example, in *International Longshoremen's and Warehousemen's Union Local 37 v. Boyd*, the Court dismissed as not ripe a case in which resident aliens were forced to choose between giving up a job or risking permanent exclusion from the country.[257] For many years, some resident aliens in the United States went to work in Alaska during the summer. Because the case arose before Alaska became a state, the aliens sued to enjoin immigration officers from preventing their return to the United States. The Supreme Court, in an opinion by Justice Frankfurter, held that their suit was not ripe. The Court found that the situation was "hypothetical"

---

[253] *Id.* at 165.
[254] 415 U.S. 452 (1974).
[255] *Id.* at 462.
[256] 342 U.S. 485, 488 n.4 (1952).
[257] 347 U.S. 222 (1954).

and concluded that "[d]etermination of the scope and constitutionality of legislation in advance of its immediate adverse effect in the context of a concrete case involves too remote and abstract an inquiry for the proper exercise of the judicial function."[258] But this ignores the enormous hardship in forcing a person to choose between unnecessarily giving up a job or risking permanent exclusion from the country.

Like *Boyd*, the Supreme Court's decision in *United Public Workers v. Mitchell* is difficult to reconcile with the many cases holding that a case is ripe when a person is forced to choose between forgoing possibly constitutionally protected conduct or facing significant sanctions.[259] The issue in *Mitchell* was the ripeness of a challenge to the constitutionality of the Hatch Act of 1940, which prevented federal employees from taking "any active part in political management or political campaigns." The plaintiffs sought a declaratory judgment that the law violated their First Amendment rights and provided detailed affidavits listing the activities they wished to engage in. The Court found their claims to be not ripe. The Court said that the plaintiffs "seem clearly to seek advisory opinions upon broad claims. . . . A hypothetical threat is not enough. We can only speculate as to the kinds of political activity the appellants desire to engage in or as to the contents of their proposed public statements or the circumstances of their publication."[260] The Court found ripe the claims of one of the plaintiffs who was being fired for violating the Act and upheld the statute as applied to him.

The *Mitchell* Court's holding that employees had to violate the Hatch Act in order to challenge its constitutionality is unjust and inconsistent with the decisions described above. The plaintiffs in *Mitchell* suffered substantial hardship because of the Court's denial of review: They had to choose between refraining from political speech or risking loss of their jobs. In fact, 26 years later, the Court was presented with another constitutional challenge to the Hatch Act and found ripeness based on almost the same facts that were insufficient in *Mitchell*. In *United States Civil Service Commission v. National Association of Letter Carriers, AFL-CIO*, the Court found the case ripe because the plaintiffs alleged that they desired to engage in specific political activity.[261]

With reasoning quite similar to that in *Mitchell*, in *Renne v. Geary*, the Court dismissed on ripeness grounds a challenge to a provision in the California constitution that prohibits political parties and political party central committees from endorsing, supporting, or opposing candidates for nonpartisan offices.[262] The Court concluded that there was insufficient evidence that the plaintiffs were prevented from engaging in specific constitutionally protected conduct because of the law. The Court noted that "[t]he affidavit provides no indication whom the Democratic committee wished to endorse, for which office, or in what election.

---

[258] *Id.* at 224.
[259] 330 U.S. 75 (1947).
[260] *Id.* at 89-90.
[261] 413 U.S. 548 (1973). The First Amendment aspects of such restrictions on government employees are discussed in §11.3.8.2 [Erwin Chemerinsky, Constitutional Law: Principles and Policies, 4th ed., (2011)].
[262] 501 U.S. 312 (1991).

Absent a contention that [the provision] prevented a particular endorsement, and that the controversy had not become moot prior to the litigation, this allegation will not support an action in federal court."[263]

But the question arises as to why the identity of particular candidates matters for a facial challenge to the law. The record documented past enforcement of the statute, and the law undoubtedly would prevent endorsements in the future. As Justice Marshall argued in dissent: "Nothing in our analysis turn[s] on the identity of the candidates to be endorsed, the nature or precise language of the endorsements, or the mode of publicizing endorsements."[264]

Hardship Where Enforcement Is Certain

Thus, generally although not always, the Court has found substantial hardship on the basis of forcing a person to choose between refraining from possibly protected conduct and risking significant sanctions. A second situation in which the Court has found substantial hardship is where the enforcement of a statute or regulation is certain and the only impediment to ripeness is simply a delay before the proceedings commence. Where the application of a law is inevitable and consequences attach to it, the Court will find the matter ripe before the actual proceedings occur.

For example, in the *Regional Rail Reorganization Act Cases*, the Court deemed ripe a lawsuit brought by eight major railroads challenging the conveyance of their property to Conrail.[265] The district court found the case not justiciable on ripeness grounds because the reorganization plan had not yet been formulated and a special court had not yet ordered the reconveyances. But the Supreme Court held that the case was ripe, concluding: "Where the inevitability of the operation of a statute against certain individuals is patent, it is irrelevant to the existence of a justiciable controversy that there will be a time delay before the disputed provisions will come into effect."[266]

Similarly, in *Lake Carriers Association v. MacMullan*, the Court found ripe a challenge to a statute forbidding discharge of sewage from boats, even though prosecutions were definitely not imminent.[267] State officials had announced that they would not enforce the law until land-based pumpout facilities would be available, a construction process that would take a substantial amount of time. Reversing a district court decision dismissing the case as not ripe, the Supreme Court unanimously concluded that the matter was justiciable. The Court reasoned that it was inevitable that the law would be enforced and that as a result the boat owners had to begin installing new facilities on their boats in anticipation of the time when the law was implemented. This was sufficient to make the case ripe.

---

[263] *Id.* at 320.
[264] *Id.* at 342 (Marshall, J., dissenting).
[265] 419 U.S. 102 (1974).
[266] *Id.* at 143.
[267] 406 U.S. 498, 507-508 (1972).

In *Buckley v. Valeo*, the plaintiffs were allowed to challenge the method of appointing members to the Federal Election Commission in anticipation of "impending future rulings and determinations by the Commission."[268] There was no doubt that the rulings would be forthcoming; thus, the Court concluded that the plaintiffs' "claims as they bear upon the method of appointment of the Commission's members may be presently adjudicated."[269]

Hardship Because of Collateral Injuries

A third way in which the Court has found substantial hardship is based on collateral injuries that are not the primary focus of the lawsuit. *Duke Power Co. v. Carolina Environmental Study Group, Inc.* is illustrative.[270] The plaintiffs challenged the constitutionality of the Price-Anderson Act, which limited the liability of private nuclear power plants to $560 million in the event of a nuclear accident.[271] The plaintiffs contended that the statute violated the due process clause because it allowed injuries to occur without ensuring adequate compensation to the victims. There were obvious ripeness problems with this claim because it was uncertain whether an accident ever would occur, if it occurred whether the losses would exceed the limit on liability, and if it occurred and did exceed the limit whether Congress would pay the difference. Nonetheless, the Court found the matter ripe on the basis of other injuries imposed by the Price-Anderson Act. The Court explained that *but for* the Price-Anderson Act, nuclear power plants for electricity generation would not be constructed. Thus, because of the Price-Anderson Act, a reactor was about to be constructed in the plaintiffs' area and would subject them to harms such as the exposure to radiation, thermal pollution, and fear of a nuclear accident. In other words, while the primary injury that was the focus of the lawsuit was not ripe — uncompensated losses from a nuclear accident — other injuries existed to make the case justiciable.[272]

Hardship Is a Prerequisite for Ripeness

If hardship is demonstrated in any of these three ways, the case is likely to be found ripe. However, if there appears minimal harm to denying review, the case will be dismissed as not ripe. *Poe v. Ullman* is a classic example of a case dismissed for lack of ripeness.[273] Married women for whom pregnancy was medically unadvisable and their doctors filed a lawsuit challenging a Connecticut law preventing the distribution or use of contraceptives. The Court deemed the case

---

[268] 424 U.S. 1, 117 (1976).
[269] 424 U.S. 1, 117 (1976). Similarly, in *Palazzolo v. Rhode Island*, 533 U.S. 606 (2001), the Court found a takings claim to be ripe for review even though a plan had not been submitted to state court because similar requests for development had been denied.
[270] 438 U.S. 59 (1978). For an excellent analysis and criticism of this decision, *see* Jonathan Varat, Variable Justiciability and the Duke Power Case, 58 Tex. L. Rev. 273 (1980).
[271] 42 U.S.C. §2210.
[272] For a discussion of the standing aspects of *Duke Power*, *see* §2.5.3 [Erwin Chemerinsky, Constitutional Law: Principles and Policies, 4th ed., (2011)].
[273] 367 U.S. 497 (1961).

nonjusticiable because there had been only one prosecution under the law in more than 80 years. The Court noted that "contraceptives are commonly and notoriously sold in Connecticut drug stores. . . . The undeviating policy of nullification by Connecticut of its anti-contraceptive laws throughout all the long years that they have been on the statute books bespeaks more than prosecutorial paralysis. . . . The fact that Connecticut has not chosen to press the enforcement of this statute deprives these controversies of the immediacy which is an indispensable condition of constitutional adjudication."[274] The Connecticut law was subsequently declared unconstitutional in *Griswold v. Connecticut* after the state prosecuted a planned parenthood clinic.[275]

Yet the Court's decision in *Poe* was subjected to substantial criticism. The effect of the Connecticut law was to limit the availability of contraceptives, especially by preventing the opening of planned parenthood clinics. Moreover, Justice Douglas, in dissent, argued that there was sufficient hardship to justify judicial review of the Connecticut statute: "What are these people — doctors and patients — to do? Flout the law and go to prison? Violate the law surreptitiously and hope they will not get caught? By today's decision we leave them no other alternatives. It is not the choice that they need have under the regime of the declaratory judgment and our constitutional system."[276]

More recently, in *Reno v. Catholic Social Services*, the Supreme Court held that a challenge to Immigration and Naturalization Service (INS) regulations had to be dismissed on ripeness grounds because it was too speculative that anyone would be injured by the rules.[277] The Immigration Reform and Control Act of 1986 provided that before illegal aliens residing in the United States could apply for legalization, they had to apply for temporary resident status. Temporary resident status required a showing that a person continually resided in the United States since January 1, 1982, and maintained a continuous physical presence since November 6, 1986. The INS adopted many regulations to implement this law.

A class of plaintiffs, Catholic Social Services, challenged some of the INS regulations. The Supreme Court, in an opinion by Justice Souter, applied *Abbott Laboratories v. Gardner* and held that the case was not ripe for review. The Court said that it was entirely speculative whether any members of the class would be denied legalization because of the regulations. The Court said that the case might be ripe for review if the immigrants took the additional step of applying for legalization.

In other words, *Poe v. Ullman* and *Reno v. Catholic Social Services, Inc.* emphasize that a case will be dismissed on ripeness grounds if a federal court perceives the likelihood of harm as too speculative. Obviously, courts have a great deal of discretion in deciding what is a sufficient likelihood of hardship to meet the ripeness requirement.

---

[274] *Id.* at 502, 508.
[275] 381 U.S. 479 (1965), discussed in §10.3.2 [Erwin Chemerinsky, Constitutional Law: Principles and Policies, 4th ed., (2011)].
[276] 367 U.S. at 513 (Douglas, J., dissenting).
[277] 509 U.S. 43 (1993).

H. Mootness

1. Description of the Mootness Doctrine

An actual controversy must exist at all stages of federal court proceedings, at both the trial and appellate levels. If events subsequent to the filing of the case resolve the dispute, the case should be dismissed as moot. The Supreme Court, quoting Professor Henry Monaghan, explained that "mootness [is] the doctrine of standing in a time frame. The requisite personal interest that must exist at the commencement of the litigation (standing) must continue throughout its existence (mootness)."[278]

Circumstances That Might Cause a Case to Be Moot

Many different types of events might render a case moot. For example, a case is moot if a criminal defendant dies during the appeals process or if a civil plaintiff dies where the cause of action does not survive death.[279] Also, if the parties settle the matter, a live controversy obviously no longer exists.[280] If a challenged law is repealed or expires, the case is moot.[281] Essentially, any change in the facts that ends the controversy renders the case moot. Thus, a defendant's challenge to a state law denying him pretrial bail was deemed moot after his conviction,[282] and a suit by students to enjoin a school's censorship of a student newspaper was dismissed as moot after the students graduated.[283]

Why Have a Mootness Doctrine?

The Supreme Court frequently has explained that the mootness doctrine is derived from Article III's prohibition against federal courts issuing advisory opinions.[284] By definition, if a case is moot, there no longer is an actual controversy

---

[278] United States Parole Commn. v. Geraghty, 445 U.S. 388, 397 (1980), quoting Henry Monaghan, Constitutional Adjudication: The Who and When, 82 Yale L.J. 1363, 1384 (1973).

[279] Dove v. United States, 423 U.S. 325 (1976).

[280] See, e.g., United Airlines, Inc. v. McDonald, 432 U.S. 385, 400 (1977) (Powell, J., dissenting) ("The settlement of an individual claim typically moots any issues associated with it."); Stewart v. Southern Ry., 315 U.S. 283 (1942). Settlement must be distinguished from a situation in which the defendant voluntarily agrees to refrain from a practice, but is free to resume it at any time. As discussed below, the latter does not moot the case.

[281] See, e.g., Burke v. Barnes, 479 U.S. 361, 365 (1987) (bill expired during pendency of appeal, rendering moot the question of whether the president's pocket veto prevented bill from becoming law); United States Dept. of Treasury v. Galioto, 477 U.S. 556 (1986) (amendment to federal statute rendered the case moot); Kremens v. Bartley, 431 U.S. 119, 128 (1977) (statutes providing for commitment of minors to institutions were repealed, rendering the case moot); but see City of Mesquite v. Aladdin's Castle, Inc., 455 U.S. 283 (1982) (repeal of a city ordinance was not moot where the city was likely to reenact it after completion of legal proceedings), discussed below.

[282] See, e.g., Murphy v. Hunt, 455 U.S. 478, 481-482 (1982) (challenge to a state law denying bail to those accused of violent sex crimes dismissed as moot after the defendant's conviction).

[283] Board of School Commrs. v. Jacobs, 420 U.S. 128, 130 (1975).

[284] See, e.g., SEC v. Medical Comm. for Human Rights, 404 U.S. 403, 406 (1972); Hall v. Beals, 396 U.S. 45, 48 (1969). But see Honig v. Doe, 484 U.S. 305, 330 (1988) (Rehnquist, C.J., concurring) (arguing that mootness doctrine is primarily prudential and not constitutionally based).

between adverse litigants. Also, if events subsequent to the initiation of the lawsuit have resolved the matter, then a federal court decision is not likely to have any effect. Hence, neither of the prerequisites for federal court adjudication is fulfilled.[285]

Additionally, many of the values underlying the justiciability doctrines also explain the mootness rules. Mootness avoids unnecessary federal court decisions, limiting the role of the judiciary and saving the courts' institutional capital for cases truly requiring decisions.[286] On the other hand, mootness might not save judicial resources; nor is it necessary to ensure a concrete factual setting in which to decide an issue. When a case is dismissed on appeal, there is a fully developed record and an opportunity for a definitive resolution of an issue. Dismissing such a case as moot might cause the same question to be litigated in many other courts until it is finally resolved by the Supreme Court.[287]

Perhaps it is because of these competing policy considerations that the Supreme Court has spoken of "the flexible character of the Article III mootness doctrine."[288] This flexibility is manifested in four exceptions to the mootness doctrine. Cases are not dismissed as moot if there are secondary or "collateral" injuries; if the issue is deemed a wrong capable of repetition yet evading review; if the defendant voluntarily ceases an allegedly illegal practice but is free to resume it at any time; and if it is a properly certified class action suit. These exceptions are discussed below.

Procedural Issues

Procedurally, mootness can be raised by a federal court on its own at any stage of the proceedings.[289] If a case is deemed moot by the United States Supreme Court, the Court will vacate the lower court's decision and remand the case for dismissal.[290] By vacating the lower court's decision, the Supreme Court leaves the legal issue unresolved for future cases to decide.

---

[285] See Church of Scientology of California v. United States, 506 U.S. 9, 11 (1992).

[286] See, e.g., Firefighter's Local 1784 v. Stotts, 467 U.S. 561, 596 (1984) (Blackmun, J., dissenting) (a central purpose of mootness doctrine is to avoid an unnecessary ruling on the merits).

[287] Chief Justice Rehnquist urged a new exception to the mootness doctrine for cases that become moot while pending before the Supreme Court. See Honig v. Doe, 484 U.S. 305, 330 (1988). See also Gene Nichol, Moot Cases, Chief Justice Rehnquist and the Supreme Court, 22 Conn. L. Rev. 703 (1990) (arguing that mootness should be regarded as prudential and that the Supreme Court should have discretion to avoid dismissing cases that become moot while pending before the Court).

[288] United States Parole Commn. v. Geraghty, 445 U.S. at 400. For an excellent argument that mootness should be regarded as prudential and not constitutional, see Evan Lee, Deconstitutionalizing Justiciability: The Example of Mootness, 105 Harv. L. Rev. 605 (1992). Others argue that it is partially a prudential doctrine. See, e.g., Matthew I. Hall, The Partially Prudential Doctrine of Mootness, 77 Geo. Wash. L. Rev. 562 (2009).

[289] See, e.g., North Carolina v. Rice, 404 U.S. 244, 246 (1971).

[290] United States v. Munsingwear, Inc., 340 U.S. 36, 39 (1950) ("The established practice of the Court in dealing with a civil case from a court in the federal system which has become moot while on its way here or pending our decision on the merits is to reverse or vacate the judgment below and remand with a direction to dismiss.")

In *U.S. Bancorp Mortgage Co. v. Banner Mall Partnership*, the Court held that vacatur of a lower court opinion is not appropriate when a voluntary settlement of an underlying dispute makes a case moot.[291] The Court recognized that allowing such vacating of lower court opinions might facilitate settlements as losing parties may choose to settle in order to vacate an unfavorable opinion that could harm their position in future litigation. Also, vacating the lower court opinion could prevent an erroneous decision from remaining on the books. Nonetheless, the Court unanimously held that voluntary settlement does not justify vacatur of a lower court opinion. Nothing about the settlement undermines the reasoning of the lower court and warrants the vacating of its decision.[292]

Overview of the Exceptions to the Mootness Doctrine

Most of the cases dealing with the mootness issue have focused on the exceptions to the mootness doctrine. These are situations where a federal court should not dismiss a case as moot even though the plaintiff's injuries have been resolved. The common issue concerning each of these exceptions is whether the policy considerations served by them justify allowing review in a case where there is not an actual dispute between adverse litigants and where a favorable court decision will not effect a change. On the one hand, critics of these exceptions might argue that expediency does not justify a departure from Article III and that the Court wrongly has been much more flexible in carving exceptions to mootness than it has been in dealing with parallel doctrines such as standing. But others might argue that important policy objectives are served by the exceptions and that the exceptions effectuate the underlying purpose of Article III in ensuring judicial review of allegedly illegal practices.

2. Exceptions to the Mootness Doctrine: Collateral Consequences

The first exception occurs when a secondary or "collateral" injury survives after the plaintiff's primary injury has been resolved. Although this is referred to as an exception to the mootness doctrine,[293] actually the case is not moot because some injury remains that could be redressed by a favorable federal court decision.

Criminal Cases

For example, a challenge to a criminal conviction is not moot, even after the defendant has completed the sentence and is released from custody, when the defendant continues to face adverse consequences of the criminal conviction. Criminal convictions, especially for felonies, cause the permanent loss of voting privileges in many states, prevent individuals from obtaining certain occupational

---

[291] 513 U.S. 18 (1994).

[292] *See* Jill E. Fisch, Rewriting History: The Propriety of Eradicating Prior Decisional Law Through Settlement and Vacatur, 76 Cornell L. Rev. 589 (1991).

[293] Sibron v. New York, 392 U.S. 40, 53 (1968) (describing collateral consequences as an exception to the mootness doctrine).

licenses, and increase the severity of sentences if there is a future offense. Thus, the Court has concluded that even if the primary injury, incarceration, no longer exists, the secondary or collateral harms are sufficient to prevent the case from being dismissed on mootness grounds.

In *Sibron v. New York*, two defendants challenged the legality of evidence seized from them during a stop-and-frisk.[294] Although the defendants had completed their six-month sentences, the Court held that their challenge to the constitutionality of their convictions was not moot. The Court explained that "the obvious fact of life [is] that most criminal convictions do in fact entail adverse collateral legal consequences. The mere possibility that this will be the case is enough to preserve a criminal case from ending ignominiously in the limbo of mootness."[295]

Similarly, in *Carafas v. LaVallee*, a defendant convicted of burglary in state court was allowed to present a petition for habeas corpus in federal court challenging the constitutionality of his conviction despite the fact that he had been unconditionally released from custody.[296] The Court stated that "[i]n consequence of his conviction, he cannot engage in certain businesses; he cannot serve as an official of a labor union for a specified time; he cannot vote in any election held in New York State; he cannot serve as a juror. On account of these 'collateral consequences,' the case is not moot."[297]

The Court has explained that a challenge to a criminal conviction should be dismissed as moot "only if it is shown that there is no possibility that any collateral legal consequences will be imposed on the basis of the challenged conviction."[298] Therefore, a defendant convicted of two crimes, but sentenced to concurrent sentences, may challenge one of the convictions even though its reversal would not hasten his or her release from custody.[299] The Court has reasoned that the additional conviction might have future collateral consequences, such as by increasing the severity of a subsequent sentence if there is a new offense.

In fact, because the government has an interest in ensuring the conviction of criminals, the Supreme Court allows the state to continue to appeal matters even if the defendant has completed his or her sentence. In *Pennsylvania v. Mimms*, the Supreme Court granted the state's certiorari petition despite the fact that the defendant had completed the maximum three-year sentence.[300] The Court said that preventing the state from imposing the collateral consequences of a criminal conviction is of sufficient interest to the state to keep the case from being dismissed as moot.

Generally a challenge to a particular sentence, as opposed to a challenge to the conviction, is moot after the sentence has been served because there are no collateral consequences to the sentence itself. For example, in *North Carolina v.*

---

[294] 392 U.S. 40 (1968).
[295] *Id.* at 55 (citations omitted).
[296] 391 U.S. 234 (1968).
[297] *Id.* at 237-238.
[298] Sibron v. New York, 392 U.S. at 57.
[299] *See, e.g.,* Benton v. Maryland, 395 U.S. 784, 791 (1969).
[300] 434 U.S. 106,108 (1977); *see also* United States v. Villamonte-Marquez, 462 U.S. 579, 581 (1983).

Rice, a defendant contended that the state courts acted unconstitutionally in increasing his sentence on appeal.[301] The Supreme Court dismissed the case as moot because the additional sentence had been served by the time the case came before the Court.

Civil Cases

In civil litigation, a case is not moot, even if the plaintiff's primary injury is resolved, so long as the plaintiff continues to suffer some harm that a favorable court decision would remedy. For instance, a plaintiff seeking both reinstatement and back pay for alleged discrimination can continue to pursue the case even if reinstatement is granted or no longer sought.[302] The claim for back pay is adequate to keep the case from being moot. In fact, even if the amount of money damages sought is quite small, it is still sufficient to present a live controversy to the federal court. The Supreme Court explained: "Undoubtedly, not much money and seniority are involved, but the amount of money and seniority at stake does not determine mootness. As long as the parties have a concrete interest in the outcome of the litigation, the case is not moot."[303]

Likewise, a plaintiff seeking both injunctive relief and money damages can continue to pursue the case, even after the request for an equitable remedy is rendered moot.[304] For example, the Supreme Court ruled that the release of plaintiffs on parole did not moot their suit, when in addition to a release from custody, they also sought money damages for the alleged violation of their constitutional rights.[305]

More generally, so long as the federal court's decision is likely to have some effect in the future, the case should not be dismissed even though the plaintiff's primary injury has passed. The Supreme Court's decision in *Super Tire Engineering Co. v. McCorkle* is particularly instructive.[306] During a labor strike, the employers whose plants were struck filed a lawsuit challenging a state law that permitted strikers to receive public assistance through state welfare programs. Although the strike ended before the completion of the federal court litigation, the Court held that the case was not moot because a federal court decision could substantially affect future labor-management negotiations.[307] Thus, while a plaintiff's emotional concern about the outcome of the case is not enough to keep it from being moot, any continuing injury means that there is a live controversy.

---

[301] 404 U.S. 244, 246 (1977).

[302] *See, e.g.,* Firefighter's Local 1784 v. Stotts, 467 U.S. 561, 568 (1984).

[303] *Id.* at 571.

[304] Havens Realty Corp. v. Coleman, 455 U.S. 363, 370-371 (1982) (case not moot because plaintiffs would be entitled to $400 liquidated damages if defendants found liable); University of Texas v. Camenisch, 451 U.S. 390, 393 (1981) (case not moot when dispute for overpayment of money remained).

[305] Board of Pardons v. Allen, 482 U.S. 369, 371 n.1 (1987).

[306] 416 U.S. 115 (1974).

[307] The Court also reasoned that the case presented a wrong capable of repetition yet evading review, which is discussed below.

3. *Exceptions to the Mootness Doctrine: Wrongs Capable of Repetition Yet Evading Review*

Definition

Perhaps the most important exception to the mootness doctrine is for "wrongs capable of repetition yet evading review." As the title of this exception implies, some injuries occur and are over so quickly that they always will be moot before the federal court litigation process is completed. When such injuries are likely to recur, the federal court may continue to exercise jurisdiction over the plaintiff's claim notwithstanding the fact that it has become moot.[308]

Roe v. Wade presented a paradigm example of a wrong capable of repetition yet evading review.[309] The plaintiff was pregnant when she filed her complaint challenging the constitutionality of a state law prohibiting abortion. However, obviously, by the time the case reached the Supreme Court, her pregnancy was completed and she no longer sought an abortion. Hence, her case was moot; intervening circumstances meant that there no longer was a live controversy between the plaintiff and the state. But the Supreme Court refused a request to dismiss the case on mootness grounds. The Court explained that the duration of pregnancy was inherently likely to be shorter than the time required for federal court litigation. The Court concluded that the challenge to the state laws prohibiting abortions "truly could be 'capable of repetition yet evading review.'"[310]

Requirements for the Exception

Two criteria must be met in order for a matter to fit within the wrong capable of repetition yet evading review exception to the mootness doctrine. In a recent case, the Supreme Court explained: That "exception applies where '(1) the challenged action is in its duration too short to be fully litigated prior to cessation or expiration; and (2) there is a reasonable expectation that the same complaining party will be subject to the same action again.'"[311]

First, the injury must be of a type likely to happen to the plaintiff again. In other words, an injury is not deemed capable of repetition merely because someone, at some time, might suffer the same harm; there must be a reasonable chance that it will happen again to the plaintiff. The Court explained that there must be a "reasonable expectation that the same complaining party would be subjected to the same action again."[312] For instance, in *Murphy v. Hunt*, a defendant's challenge to a state law denying pretrial bail to those accused of violent sex crimes was

---

[308] A seminal case articulating this exception to the mootness doctrine was Southern Pac. Terminal Co. v. ICC, 219 U.S. 498, 514-515 (1911) (allowing a challenge to an Interstate Commerce Commission order that had expired because the Court concluded that consideration of such orders should not be defeated, "as they might be, . . . by short term orders, capable of repetition, yet evading review").

[309] 410 U.S. 113 (1973).

[310] *Id.* at 125 (citations omitted).

[311] Davis v. Federal Election Commn., 554 U.S. 724 (2008).

[312] Weinstein v. Bradford, 423 U.S. 147, 149 (1975).

dismissed as moot after the defendant's conviction.[313] The Court said that the case did not fit into the exception for wrongs capable of repetition yet evading review because there was no likelihood that the defendant would be arrested for a similar offense and denied bail in the future. The Court noted that "there must be a reasonable expectation or a demonstrated probability that the same controversy will recur involving the same complaining party. We detect no such level of probability in this case."[314] But it must be noted that in other cases — such as in *Roe* and in the election cases described below — the Court did not specifically inquire whether the plaintiff in particular was likely to suffer the same harm in the future.

Second, it must be a type of injury of inherently limited duration so that it is likely to always become moot before federal court litigation is completed. For example, a ten-day restraining order on a protest demonstration was deemed to be capable of repetition but always likely to evade review because litigation never would be completed before the ten days expired.[315]

One area where the Court consistently has found cases to fit within the exception for wrongs capable of repetition yet evading review concerns court orders imposing prior restraints on speech. For example, in *Nebraska Press Association v. Stuart*, a trial judge imposed a limit on newspaper and broadcast reports concerning a pending murder trial.[316] Although the judge's order expired when the jury was empaneled, the Supreme Court held that it was a wrong capable of repetition yet evading review because similar orders might be imposed on the media again in the future, and they would escape judicial scrutiny because the restraints would be lifted long before the appellate process was completed.[317] Likewise, challenges to a court's order excluding the press from a pretrial hearing and to a court's order excluding the press from trial in a case involving a victim under age 18 were deemed fit within this exception to the mootness doctrine.[318] In each instance, the Court reasoned that the media might be subjected to similar orders in the future and that the orders transpired so quickly as to prevent judicial review before they expired.

Another area where the Court often has applied this exception to the mootness doctrine is for challenges to election laws. Frequently, the election is over before the litigation is completed. For example, in *Moore v. Ogilvie*, a suit was brought challenging a state law requiring the obtaining of a certain number of signatures in order for an independent candidate to get on the ballot to run for president or vice president.[319] Although the election was held before the case was heard by the Supreme Court, the Court held that the case was not moot because

---

[313] 455 U.S. 478 (1982).

[314] *Id.* at 482 (citations omitted).

[315] Carroll v. President & Commrs. of Princess Anne, 393 U.S. 175 (1968), discussed in §11.2.3.3 [Erwin Chemerinsky, Constitutional Law: Principles and Policies, 4th ed., (2011)].

[316] 427 U.S. 539 (1976), discussed in §11.2.3.3 [Erwin Chemerinsky, Constitutional Law: Principles and Policies, 4th ed., (2011)].

[317] *Id.* at 546.

[318] Globe Newspaper Co. v. Superior Court, 457 U.S. 596, 602 (1982) (exclusion from trial of victim of sex crime who was under age 18); Gannett Co. v. DePasquale, 443 U.S. 368, 377 (1979) (exclusion from pretrial hearing).

[319] 394 U.S. 814 (1969).

it presented a "wrong capable of repetition, yet evading review."[320] The Court explained that the plaintiffs might again seek access to the ballot for independent candidates and that the matter would always escape review because litigation could never be completed before the election.

Similarly, in *First National Bank of Boston v. Bellotti*, the plaintiffs were allowed to pursue their challenge to a law prohibiting corporations from spending money to influence voters with regard to pending ballot initiatives.[321] The Court reasoned that the issue would likely arise in the future and there would never be enough time for the matter to be fully litigated, appealed, and decided before the completion of the election.

In *Dunn v. Blumstein*, a voter was allowed to continue to challenge a state law imposing a one-year residency requirement in the state in order to vote in state elections.[322] Although the plaintiff could vote by the time the case got to the Supreme Court, the Court held that the matter was a wrong capable of repetition yet evading review and thus should not be dismissed on mootness grounds.

In *Norman v. Reed*, the Court applied this exception to the mootness doctrine to allow a challenge to a law that created obstacles for new parties getting on the ballot.[323] Although the challenge concerned the ability to get on the ballot for an election held in 1990, the Court concluded that "[t]here would be every reason to expect the same parties to generate a similar, future controversy subject to identical time constraints if we should fail to resolve the constitutional issues that arose in 1990."[324] Thus, it was justiciable as a wrong capable of repetition yet evading review.

Most recently, in *Davis v. Federal Election Commission*, the Court allowed a challenge to a provision of the Federal Election Act to continue after the election was over.[325] Jack Davis twice ran for Congress, in 2004 and 2006, and spent enough of his own money for his campaign as to trigger the so-called "millionaire's provision" of the McCain-Feingold Bipartisan Campaign Finance Reform Act of 2001. Under this provision, the opponent of a candidate who spends more than $350,000 of his or her own money receives the benefit of higher contribution and expenditure limits. Davis filed his lawsuit challenging this provision while running for office, but the Supreme Court did not hear the case until after the election was over. Nonetheless, the Court unanimously rejected the government's argument that the case was moot (though it divided 5-4 in striking down the provision as violating the First Amendment). The Court found that this case was like others in which it held that challenges to laws regulating elections could continue after the elections were over.

But not all election cases fit within this exception to the mootness doctrine. For example, in *Illinois State Board of Elections v. Socialist Workers Party*, the plaintiffs challenged actions by the State Board of Elections that interfered with

---

[320] *Id.* at 816 (citation omitted).
[321] 435 U.S. 765, 774 (1978).
[322] 405 U.S. 330 (1972).
[323] 502 U.S. 279 (1992).
[324] *Id.* at 288.
[325] 554 U.S. 724 (2008).

their getting on the ballot.[326] The Court held that the case was moot after the election was completed because there was "no evidence creating a reasonable expectation that the ... Board will repeat its purportedly unauthorized actions in subsequent elections."[327]

Golden v. Zwickler is even more difficult to reconcile with the other election cases.[328] In *Golden*, the plaintiff filed a lawsuit in 1966 challenging a New York statute prohibiting the distribution of handbills that did not state the identity of the author. The plaintiff wanted to distribute such anonymous leaflets in connection with the 1966 congressional election. The election was completed before the matter was fully resolved in the courts, but the plaintiff maintained that there was still a live controversy because he wanted to distribute anonymous handbills again in 1968. The Supreme Court deemed the case moot. The Court said that it was speculative whether the congressman whom the plaintiff sought to campaign for would run again.[329]

The question is whether it was more speculative that the plaintiff in *Golden* would want to distribute anonymous leaflets in the future than it was in *Moore v. Ogilvie* that the plaintiffs there would want to qualify independent candidates for the ballot in the future. Was it more speculative in *Socialist Workers Party* that the plaintiffs would be frustrated in gaining access to the ballot than it was in *Bellotti* that the corporation would want to spend money in the future to oppose ballot initiatives?

In other words, the election cases reflect that the "wrong capable of repetition yet evading review exception" requires a court to determine that there is a sufficient likelihood that the harm will recur. But the courts have a great deal of discretion in deciding what is sufficient.

Perhaps the case best illustrating this discretion is *DeFunis v. Odegaard*.[330] The plaintiff, a white male, applied for admission to the University of Washington Law School and was denied acceptance. He sued the school, contending that he was discriminated against because of the school's preferential treatment of minority candidates. The trial court issued a preliminary injunction admitting the plaintiff to law school while the case was pending. By the time the case reached the United States Supreme Court, the plaintiff was in his final year of school and the school stipulated that the plaintiff would be allowed to complete his studies regardless of the outcome of the litigation. The Supreme Court held that the case was moot because "the controversy between the parties has thus clearly ceased to be definite and concrete and no longer touches the legal relations of parties having adverse legal interests."[331]

Some criticize the Court for not finding the case to constitute a wrong capable of repetition yet evading review. Professor David Currie quotes one critic as remarking that *DeFunis* "announced a new principle: 'Difficult cases are

---

[326] 440 U.S. 173 (1979).
[327] *Id.* at 187.
[328] 394 U.S. 103 (1969).
[329] *Id.* at 109-110.
[330] 416 U.S. 312 (1974).
[331] *Id.* at 316-317.

moot.'"[332] On the other hand, the Court explained that there was no chance that DeFunis again would be subjected to the law school admissions process. Moreover, there was no reason to believe that the issue would evade review because not every challenger would obtain a preliminary injunction securing law school attendance while the case was pending.[333]

In sum, a case is not dismissed, although the plaintiff's claim is moot, if the injury is one likely to recur and if the injury is of an inherently short duration that would make complete federal court review impossible. Courts have substantial discretion in deciding what is a sufficient likelihood of future injury or a sufficiently short time span for the injury to justify invoking this exception.

4. Exceptions to the Mootness Doctrine: Voluntary Cessation

Exception Defined

A case is not to be dismissed as moot if the defendant voluntarily ceases the allegedly improper behavior but is free to return to it at any time. Only if there is no reasonable chance that the defendant could resume the offending behavior is a case deemed moot on the basis of voluntary cessation.[334]

The Court explained these principles in *United States v. W. T. Grant* Co.[335] The United States sued to enjoin a practice of several corporations having similar boards of directors; the government claimed that the interlocking directorates violated federal antitrust laws. In response to the suit, the defendants said that they had eliminated the interlocking directorships and would not resume the practice. The Supreme Court said that this was not sufficient to justify dismissal of the case because the "defendant is free to return to his old ways."[336] The Court stated that "voluntary cessation of allegedly illegal conduct does not deprive the tribunal of power to hear and determine the case, i.e., does not make the case moot."[337] The Court said that "[t]he case may nevertheless be moot if the defendant can demonstrate that there is no reasonable expectation that the wrong will be repeated. The burden is a heavy one."[338] The Court said the defendants' promise to not resume the offending practice is not enough to meet this burden and render the case moot.

---

[332] David Currie, Federal Courts: Cases and Materials 77 n.3 (4th ed. 1990).

[333] 416 U.S. at 316.

[334] *See* Friends of the Earth v. Laidlaw, 528 U.S. 167, 174 (2000).

[335] 345 U.S. 629 (1953). *See also* United States v. Concentrated Phosphate Export Assn., 393 U.S. 199, 203 (1968) (citations omitted) (case not moot where defendant is "free to return to his old ways").

[336] *Id.* at 632.

[337] *Id.*

[338] *Id.* at 633 (citations omitted). See Iron Arrow Honor Socy. v. Heckler, 464 U.S. 67 (1983) (an exclusively male honorary society on campus sought to enjoin the Department of Health and Human Services from requiring the university to exclude it; while the case was pending the university announced its decision to ban the club, regardless of the government's decision, rendering the case moot); Preiser v. Newkirk, 422 U.S. 395, 401-402 (1975) (case challenging transfer of prisoner to a medium or maximum security prison dismissed as moot because he had been moved back to a minimum security unit and there was no likelihood that the wrong would be repeated).

The Court recently reaffirmed the narrowness of this exception in *Friends of the Earth, Inc. v. Laidlaw.*[339] Environmental groups brought a lawsuit pursuant to a citizen suit provision of the Clean Water Act (CWA) against the holder of a National Pollutant Discharge Elimination System (NPDES) permit, alleging that it was violating mercury discharge limits. The plaintiffs sought declaratory and injunctive relief, civil penalties, costs, and attorney fees. The defendant sought to have the case dismissed as moot on the ground that it had changed its conduct and complied with the permit requirements and had closed one of the facilities.

The Court reiterated that voluntary changes in behavior by a defendant are not sufficient to make a case moot because the defendant would be free to resume the behavior once the case was dismissed. Justice Ginsburg, writing for the Court, stated: "[T]he standard we have announced for determining whether a case has been mooted by the defendant's voluntary conduct is stringent: 'A case might become moot if subsequent events made it absolutely clear that the allegedly wrongful behavior could not reasonably be expected to recur.' The 'heavy burden of persua[ding]' the court that the challenged conduct cannot reasonably be expected to start up again lies with the party asserting mootness."[340] Indeed, Justice Ginsburg's statement of the test makes it clear that this is a very heavy burden: "[A] defendant claiming that its voluntary compliance moots a case bears the formidable burden of showing that it is absolutely clear the allegedly wrongful behavior could not reasonably be expected to recur."[341] This is quite different from standing where the burden is on the plaintiff to show that the constitutional and prudential requirements are met.[342] The Court, in *Laidlaw,* found that the defendant failed to meet its heavy burden and refused to dismiss the case based on its voluntary changes in behavior.

A recent interesting application of this exception involved a party that had prevailed in the lower court making the case moot while it was pending in the Supreme Court. In *City of Erie v. Pap's A.M.,*[343] the defendant, the owner of a nude dancing establishment, successfully challenged a city ordinance prohibiting public nudity that was adopted to close that business. While the case was pending in the Supreme Court, the business closed and the defendant moved for the Court to dismiss the matter on mootness grounds. The Court refused and said that the case was not moot because the company still had the license for the business and could reopen it at any time and also because the city continued to be injured by the injunction of the ordinance entered by the state court.[344] The defendant also said that he was 72 years old and retired. The Court said that this was not sufficient: "Several members of this Court can attest, however, that the 'advanced age' of Pap's owner, 72, does not make it 'absolutely clear' that a life of quiet retirement is his only reasonable expectation."[345]

---

[339] 528 U.S. 167 (2000).
[340] *Id.* at 189 (citation omitted).
[341] *Id.* at 190.
[342] *Id.*
[343] 529 U.S. 277 (2000).
[344] *Id.* at 287.
[345] *Id.* at 288.

Statutory Change

Usually, a statutory change is enough to render a case moot, even though the legislature possesses the power to reinstate the allegedly invalid law after the lawsuit is dismissed. For example, in *Kremens v. Bartley*, the state repealed statutes challenged as unconstitutional in that they permitted involuntary commitment of juveniles.[346] The Supreme Court said that the legislative action made the case moot. Likewise, in *Massachusetts v. Oakes*, the Court dismissed a challenge to an overbreadth challenge to a Massachusetts law prohibiting nude photography of minors.[347] The law was amended while the case was pending, and the Court ruled that "overbreadth analysis is inappropriate if the statute being challenged has been amended or repealed."[348]

However, the Court also has held that a repeal of a challenged law does not render a case moot if there is a reasonable possibility that the government would reenact the law if the proceedings were dismissed. In *City of Mesquite v. Aladdin's Castle, Inc.*, a city law limited licensing of video arcades and amusement centers.[349] The plaintiff challenged the ordinance as being unconstitutionally vague in prohibiting licensing of operations that have "connections with criminal elements." The city repealed this language from the ordinance while the case was pending. Nonetheless, the Court held that the case was not moot. Justice Stevens, writing for the majority, explained: "It is well settled that a defendant's voluntary cessation of a challenged practice does not deprive a federal court of its power to determine the legality of the practice. . . . In this case the City's repeal of the objectionable language would not preclude it from reenacting precisely the same provision if the District Court's judgment were vacated."[350]

Similarly, in *Northeastern Florida Contractors v. Jacksonville*, the Court refused to dismiss as moot a challenge to a city ordinance that provided preference in contracting for minority-owned businesses.[351] The Court explained that "[t]here is no mere risk that Jacksonville will repeat its allegedly wrongful conduct; it already has done so. Nor does it matter that the new ordinance differs in certain respects from the old one. . . . [I]f that were the rule, a defendant could moot a case by repealing the challenged statute and replacing it with one that differs only in some insignificant respect."[352] The Court said that the new statute posed the same basic constitutional question, and thus the repeal of the earlier law did not moot the case.

The difficulty is determining why in some situations a legislative repeal is deemed to make a case moot, yet in other cases it does not. In all instances, the legislature is free to reenact the law. In *Aladdin's Castle*, the Court said that "[t]he

---

[346] 431 U.S. 119, 132 (1977).
[347] 491 U.S. 576 (1989).
[348] *Id.* at 582. *See also* Lewis v. Continental Bank Corp., 494 U.S. 472 (1990) (change in the law rendered the case moot).
[349] 455 U.S. 283 (1982).
[350] *Id.* at 289.
[351] 508 U.S. 656 (1993). The standing aspects of the case are discussed in §2.5.3 [Erwin Chemerinsky, Constitutional Law: Principles and Policies, 4th ed., (2011)].
[352] *Id.* at 662.

test for mootness in cases such as this is a stringent one. Mere voluntary cessation of allegedly illegal conduct does not moot a case. . . . A case might become moot if subsequent events made it absolutely clear that the allegedly wrongful behavior could not reasonably be expected to recur."[353] Yet in other cases described above, the Court concluded that legislative repeal was enough to make a case moot, although the law could have been readopted after the conclusion of the legal proceedings. The key appears to be that cases will not be dismissed as moot if the Court believes that there is a likelihood of reenactment of a substantially similar law if the lawsuit is dismissed.

Compliance with a Court Order

Compliance with a court order renders a case moot only if there is no possibility that the allegedly offending behavior will resume once the order expires or is lifted. For example, a case was not moot when a court order caused a union to end its boycott because the union could resume the boycott as soon as the order was removed.[354] Similarly, the voluntary cessation exception was applied to prevent dismissal of a case when a union stopped its picketing in response to a court injunction, but contested the constitutionality of that injunction and wished to challenge allegedly illegal harassment of its members.[355]

Vitek v. Jones illustrates the inability of court orders to render a case moot where the offending practices can resume if the orders are lifted.[356] In *Vitek*, the plaintiffs challenged the ability of state prisons to transfer prisoners to mental hospitals without providing adequate notice and an opportunity for a hearing. A court permanently enjoined these transfers imposed without due process protections. Although the transfers halted, the Court held that the case was not moot because "it is not absolutely clear absent the injunction that the allegedly wrongful behavior could not reasonably be expected to recur."[357]

But a case can be dismissed as moot if a court order produces a change in behavior and it is deemed unlikely that the offending conduct will resume. *County of Los Angeles v. Davis* is instructive.[358] The plaintiffs, representing present and future black and Mexican-American applicants to the Los Angeles County Fire Department, brought a class action suit challenging alleged discriminatory hiring practices. The district court found a violation of federal civil rights statutes and permanently enjoined the discriminatory practices. The fire department complied with the injunction, discarding its preemployment screening test and hiring many new minority applicants.

The Supreme Court held that the case was moot. The Court explained that a case may become moot if "it can be said with assurance that there is no reasonable

[353] 455 U.S. 283, 289.
[354] Bakery Drivers v. Wagshal, 333 U.S. 437 (1948).
[355] Alice v. Medrano, 416 U.S. 802, 810 (1974).
[356] 445 U.S. 480 (1980). The procedural due process issues raised in *Vitek* are discussed in §7.4.2 [Erwin Chemerinsky, Constitutional Law: Principles and Policies, 4th ed., (2011)].
[357] *Id.* at 487 (citations omitted).
[358] 440 U.S. 625 (1979).

expectation that the alleged violation will recur, [and] interim relief or events have completely and irrevocably eradicated the effects of the alleged violation."[359] The Court said that the defendant had eliminated the use of the invalidated civil service examination and showed no propensity for reinstituting it and that the defendant had changed its hiring so that more than 50 percent of new recruits were racial minorities. As such, the Court deemed the case moot.

In short, under the voluntary cessation exception to the mootness doctrine the central question is whether the defendant has the ability to resort to the allegedly improper behavior that was voluntarily stopped. Only if the defendant can show that there is no reasonable chance that the conduct can resume should a federal court dismiss a case as moot when a defendant voluntarily halts a challenged practice.

5. *Exceptions to the Mootness Doctrine: Class Actions*

The Supreme Court has taken a particularly flexible approach to the mootness doctrine in class action suits. In a series of cases, the Supreme Court has held that a properly certified class action suit may continue even if the named plaintiff's claims are rendered moot. The Court has reasoned that the "class of unnamed persons described in the certification acquired a legal status separate from the interest asserted by the [plaintiff]," and thus so long as the members of the class have a live controversy, the case can continue.[360] Furthermore, the Court has concluded that a plaintiff may continue to appeal the denial of class certification even after his or her particular claim is mooted.

Properly Certified Class Action Not Moot

Sosna v. Iowa was the first major departure from traditional mootness rules for class action suits.[361] The plaintiff, Mrs. Sosna, initiated a class action suit challenging an Iowa law requiring residence in the state for one year in order to obtain a divorce from an Iowa court. The class action was properly certified, and the district court ruled against the plaintiffs on the merits. While the appeals were pending, Mrs. Sosna satisfied the durational residency requirement, thus resolving her claim. The Supreme Court, in an opinion by Justice Rehnquist, held that the suit was not moot. The Court emphasized that the controversy "remains very much alive for the class of persons she has been certified to represent."[362] The Court explained that a class action suit should not be dismissed on mootness grounds so long as the named plaintiff had a live controversy when the suit was filed, there was a properly certified class action, and there are members of the class whose claims are not moot.

---

[359] *Id.* at 631.
[360] Sosna v. Iowa, 419 U.S. 393, 399 (1975).
[361] *Id.*
[362] *Id.* at 401. The Court also explained that the case could fit into the exception for wrongs capable of repetition yet evading review because of the fact that residency requirement was shorter than the usual course of litigation. *Id.* at 401 n.9.

The Supreme Court applied *Sosna* in other cases involving class action suits. For example, in *Gerstein v. Pugh*, a properly certified class action suit challenged the constitutionality of a Florida practice of holding individuals without a judicial hearing determining probable cause.[363] Although the named plaintiff's claim was resolved because the pretrial detention ended, the case was not moot because there was a properly certified class action and the members of the class continued to present a live controversy.

In several cases, decided the same year as *Sosna*, the Supreme Court concluded that the mootness doctrine required the dismissal of class action suits that were not properly certified when the named plaintiff's claim became moot.[364] The underlying rationale seems to be that when there is a properly certified class action, the entire class is the actual plaintiff, and as long as a live controversy exists for some of the plaintiffs, the case should not be deemed moot.

The Court expanded the exception for class action suits in *Franks v. Bowman Transportation Co.*[365] In *Franks*, the plaintiff brought a class action suit challenging alleged employment discrimination. By the time the case came to the Supreme Court, it was clear that the named plaintiff did not have a possible claim of discrimination even though other class members did. The Court said that even if the named plaintiff never had a legitimate claim for relief, a class action is not moot when it was properly certified and when some members continue to have live claims.

Appeals of Denial of Class Certification Not Moot

Sosna, Gerstein, and *Franks* all involved properly certified class actions. The Court first considered noncertified class actions in *United Airlines, Inc. v. McDonald*.[366] There the Court held that a member of the proposed class may intervene to challenge and appeal the denial of class certification after the named plaintiff's claims are mooted.

Subsequently, the Court held that a person seeking to initiate a class action suit may continue to appeal the denial of certification even after his or her own claims are rendered moot. In *United States Parole Commission v. Geraghty*, a prisoner who was denied parole on the basis of the Parole Commission's guidelines sought to bring a class action suit challenging the guidelines.[367] The district court refused to certify a class action, and the plaintiff appealed. While the appeal was pending, the plaintiff was released from prison.

Even though a class action never was certified, the Court held that the case was not moot. The Court explained that the members of the proposed class still had a live controversy, justifying continued federal judicial consideration of

---

[363] 420 U.S. 103 (1975).
[364] *See, e.g.*, Indianapolis School Commrs. v. Jacobs, 420 U.S. 128 (1975); Weinstein v. Bradford, 423 U.S. 147 (1975); *see also* Pasadena City Bd. of Educ. v. Spangler, 427 U.S 424 (1976); Franks v. Bowman Transportation Co., 424 U.S. 747 (1976).
[365] 424 U.S. 747 (1976).
[366] 432 U.S. 385, 393 (1973).
[367] 445 U.S. 388 (1980).

whether the class should be certified. The Court stated "that an action brought on behalf of a class does not become moot upon expiration of the named plaintiff's substantive claim, even though class certification has been denied. The proposed representative retains a 'personal stake' in obtaining class certification sufficient to assure that Art. III values are not undermined. If the appeal results in a reversal of the class certification denial, and a class subsequently is properly certified, the merits of the class claim then may be adjudicated pursuant to the holding in *Sosna*."[368] Similarly, in *Deposit Guaranty National Bank v. Roper,* decided the same day as *Geraghty,* the Court held that the named plaintiffs in a proposed class action suit could continue to appeal the denial of class certification even after the plaintiffs settled their personal claims.[369] In *Roper,* the plaintiffs sought to bring a class action suit to challenge the interest charged by Bank Americard. The plaintiffs agreed to a settlement that paid them the full sum they claimed as damages. The Court said that the plaintiffs could continue to appeal the denial of class certification. The Court explained that the plaintiffs maintained a "personal stake in the appeal" because they had "a continuing individual interest in the resolution of the class certification question in their desire to shift part of the costs of litigation to those who will share in its benefits if the class is certified and ultimately prevails."[370] The Court explained that other class members had a live controversy, and allowing the settlement to end the litigation would give defendants an incentive to "buy off" named plaintiffs in class action litigation.[371]

The exception for class action suits makes sense in that it focuses on the interests of the class, rather than simply looking to the named plaintiff's claims. As long as the class presents a live controversy, the status of any particular member's claim is irrelevant. Thus, the Court has properly concluded that a properly certified class action is not moot simply because the named plaintiff's controversy is resolved. Nor should the mootness of the plaintiff's claim prevent an appeal of the denial of class certification. This mootness exception furthers the underlying purposes of the federal rules concerning class actions and is consistent with Article III, because there is an actual dispute between adverse litigants and a favorable federal court decision will make a difference for the class members.

---

[368] *Id.* at 404.
[369] 445 U.S. 326 (1980).
[370] *Id.* at 336.
[371] *Id.* at 339.

CHAPTER 11

STATUTORY INTERPRETATION BY COURTS

Courts are often called upon to interpret statutes. This chapter examines how they do so. With the emergence of the regulatory state, courts are not the only (or even the primary) institutions that interpret statutes; agencies and others are also involved, as we discuss in Chapters 10 and 9. But even when an agency is the primary interpreter of a statute, courts are still charged with reviewing the agency's interpretation. Understanding how courts interpret statutes, regardless of whether an agency is involved, is essential for understanding the regulatory state.

To discuss how courts interpret statutes, we make a distinction between the tools and theories of statutory interpretation. A *tool of statutory interpretation* is an instrument for ascertaining the meaning of a statute. For example, a dictionary is a tool of statutory interpretation because it can assist a court in understanding the ordinary meaning of a contested word. Legislative history, like a Senate Committee Report, is also a tool of statutory interpretation because it can assist a court in determining the intent of the legislature or the purpose of the statute. When you read a judicial opinion, you will see courts using these and other tools to interpret statutes. As a lawyer, you will use these tools and others when making statutory arguments to courts.

A *theory of statutory interpretation* is a normative view of how courts should interpret statutes. There are many different theories of statutory interpretation, and legal academics and judges have engaged in a longstanding debate about which is best. As you will see, a particular theory of statutory interpretation may lead a court to exclude or deemphasize particular tools. For example, *textualism* permits courts to rely on dictionaries as a source of statutory meaning but prohibits them from relying on indications of legislative intent in legislative history. By contrast, *intentionalism* instructs courts to implement legislative intent, even when that intent is not clear from the plain meaning of the statutory text and discernible only through other sources. These theories are helpful to lawyers because they provide insight into how particular judges will interpret statutes — for example, Justice Scalia is a textualist, while now-retired Justice Stevens is an intentionalist. In addition, theories of statutory interpretation are useful for evaluating the tools of statutory interpretation. Textualism offers a biting critique of legislative history, intentionalism of plain meaning, and so on. But, as you will see, judges rarely expressly or consistently rely on any particular theory when interpreting a statute; they do, however, rely on the tools of statutory interpretation.

In this chapter, we first present the tools of statutory interpretation and then the theories of statutory interpretation. We follow with some positive descriptions of judicial behavior. Do courts really interpret statutes by applying whichever tools or theories of statutory interpretation they believe are best? Do they favor an approach that is more pragmatic or political or intuitive? These questions should interest lawyers who want to understand actual judicial behavior.

A. A Classic of Statutory Interpretation

Before we turn to the tools and theories of statutory interpretation, we present a concrete example of statutory interpretation for you to keep in mind as you read this chapter. We could have chosen an auto safety example, to pick up on the theme that runs through most of this book. Instead, we begin with a famous decision: *Church of the Holy Trinity v. United States*. Over time, this decision has attracted more criticism than praise. Whatever your view, it is a classic illustration of the major tools and theories of statutory interpretation. As you read this opinion, see if you can identify the different interpretive "moves" that the Supreme Court makes.

Church of the Holy Trinity v. United States

143 U.S. 457 (1892)

Justice BREWER delivered the opinion of the court.

Plaintiff in error is a corporation duly organized and incorporated as a religious society under the laws of the state of New York. E. Walpole Warren was, prior to September, 1887, an alien residing in England. In that month the plaintiff in error made a contract with him, by which he was to remove to the city of New York, and enter into its service as rector and pastor; and, in pursuance of such contract, Warren did so remove and enter upon such service. It is claimed by the United States that this contract on the part of the plaintiff in error was forbidden by [an act of February 26, 1885, chapter 164]. . . . ; and an action was commenced to recover the penalty prescribed by that act. The circuit court held that the contract was within the prohibition of the statute, and rendered judgment accordingly, and the single question presented for our determination is whether it erred in that conclusion.

The first section describes the act forbidden, and is in these words:

> "*Be it enacted by the senate and house of representatives of the United States of America, in congress assembled,* that from and after the passage of this act it shall be unlawful for any person, company, partnership, or corporation, in any manner

whatsoever, to prepay the transportation, or in any way assist or encourage the importation or migration, of any alien or aliens, any foreigner or foreigners, into the United States, its territories, or the District of Columbia, under contract or agreement, parol or special, express or implied, made previous to the importation or migration of such alien or aliens, foreigner or foreigners, to perform labor or service of any kind in the United States, its territories, or the District of Columbia."

It must be conceded that the act of the corporation is within the letter of this section, for the relation of rector to his church is one of service, and implies labor on the one side with compensation on the other. Not only are the general words "labor" and "service" both used, but also, as it were to guard against any narrow interpretation and emphasize a breadth of meaning, to them is added "of any kind"; and, further, as noticed by the circuit judge in his opinion, the fifth section, which makes specific exceptions, among them professional actors, artists, lecturers, singers, and domestic servants, strengthens the idea that every other kind of labor and service was intended to be reached by the first section.[*] While there is great force to this reasoning, we cannot think Congress intended to denounce with penalties a transaction like that in the present case. It is a familiar rule that a thing may be within the letter of the statute and yet not within the statute, because not within its spirit nor within the intention of its makers. This has been often asserted, and the Reports are full of cases illustrating its application. This is not the substitution of the will of the judge for that of the legislator; for frequently words of general meaning are used in a statute, words broad enough to include an act in question, and yet a consideration of the whole legislation, or of the circumstances surrounding its enactment, or of the absurd results which follow from giving such broad meaning to the words, makes it unreasonable to believe that the legislator intended to include the particular act.. . . .

[As the Court noted in U. S. v. Kirby, 7 Wall. 482, 486:] "All laws should receive a sensible construction. General terms should be so limited in their application as not to lead to injustice, oppression, or an absurd consequence. It will always, therefore, be presumed that the legislature intended exceptions to its language which would avoid results of this character. The reason of the law in such cases should prevail over its letter. The common sense of man approves the judgment mentioned by Puffendorf, that the Bolognian law which enacted 'that whoever drew blood in the streets should be punished with the utmost severity,' did not extend to the surgeon who opened the vein of a person that fell down in the street in a fit. The same common sense accepts the ruling, cited by Plowden, that the statute of 1 Edw. II., which enacts that a prisoner who breaks prison shall be guilty of felony, does not extend to a prisoner who breaks out when the prison is on fire, 'for he is not to be hanged because he would not stay to be burnt.' And we

---

[*] [Section 5 provides in relevant part:

[N]or shall the provisions of this act apply to professional actors, artists, lecturers or singers, nor to persons employed strictly as personal or domestic servants: Provided, That nothing in this act shall be construed as prohibiting any individual from assisting any member of his family or any relative or personal friend, to migrate from any foreign country to the United States, for purposes of settlement here. — EDS.]

think that a like common sense will sanction the ruling we make, that the act of congress which punishes the obstruction or retarding of the passage of the mail, or of its carrier, does not apply to a case of temporary detention of the mail caused by the arrest of the carrier upon an indictment for murder."

Among other things which may be considered in determining the intent of the legislature is the title of the act. We do not mean that it may be used to add to or take from the body of the statute, but it may help to interpret its meaning. The title of this act is, "An act for the punishment of certain crimes against the United States." It would seem that offenses against the United States, not offenses against the human race, were the crimes which the legislature intended by this law to punish.

It will be seen that words as general as those used in the first section of this act were by that decision limited, and the intent of congress with respect to the act was gathered partially, at least, from its title. Now, the title of this act is, "An act to prohibit the importation and migration of foreigners and aliens under contract or agreement to perform labor in the United States, its territories, and the District of Columbia." Obviously the thought expressed in this reaches only to the work of the manual laborer, as distinguished from that of the professional man. No one reading such a title would suppose that congress had in its mind any purpose of staying the coming into this country of ministers of the gospel, or, indeed, of any class whose toil is that of the brain. The common understanding of the terms "labor" and "laborers" does not include preaching and preachers, and it is to be assumed that words and phrases are used in their ordinary meaning. So whatever of light is thrown upon the statute by the language of the title indicates an exclusion from its penal provisions of all contracts for the employment of ministers, rectors, and pastors.

Again, another guide to the meaning of a statute is found in the evil which it is designed to remedy; and for this the court properly looks at contemporaneous events, the situation as it existed, and as it was pressed upon the attention of the legislative body. The situation which called for this statute was briefly but fully stated by Mr. Justice Brown when, as district judge, he decided the case of *U.S. v. Craig*, 28 Fed. Rep. 795, 798: "The motives and history of the act are matters of common knowledge. It had become the practice for large capitalists in this country to contract with their agents abroad for the shipment of great numbers of an ignorant and servile class of foreign laborers, under contracts by which the employer agreed, upon the one hand, to prepay their passage, while, upon the other hand, the laborers agreed to work after their arrival for a certain time at a low rate of wages. The effect of this was to break down the labor market, and to reduce other laborers engaged in like occupations to the level of the assisted immigrant. The evil finally became so flagrant that an appeal was made to congress for relief by the passage of the act in question, the design of which was to raise the standard of foreign immigrants, and to discountenance the migration of those who had not sufficient means in their own hands, or those of their friends, to pay their passage."

It appears, also, from the petitions, and in the testimony presented before the committees of congress, that it was this cheap, unskilled labor which was making the trouble, and the influx of which congress sought to prevent. It was never suggested that we had in this country a surplus of brain toilers, and, least of all, that the market for the services of Christian ministers was depressed by foreign competition. Those were matters to which the attention of congress, or of the people, was not directed. So far, then, as the evil which was sought to be remedied interprets the statute, it also guides to an exclusion of this contract from the penalties of the act.

A singular circumstance, throwing light upon the intent of congress, is found in this extract from the report of the senate committee on education and labor, recommending the passage of the bill: "The general facts and considerations which induce the committee to recommend the passage of this bill are set forth in the report of the committee of the house. The committee report the bill back without amendment, although there are certain features thereof which might well be changed or modified, in the hope that the bill may not fail of passage during the present session. Especially would the committee have otherwise recommended amendments, substituting for the expression, 'labor and service,' whenever it occurs in the body of the bill, the words 'manual labor' or 'manual service,' as sufficiently broad to accomplish the purposes of the bill, and that such amendments would remove objections which a sharp and perhaps unfriendly criticism may urge to the proposed legislation. The committee, however, believing that the bill in its present form will be construed as including only those whose labor or service is manual in character, and being very desirous that the bill become a law before the adjournment, have reported the bill without change." Page 6059, Congressional Record, 48th Cong. And, referring back to the report of the committee of the house, there appears this language: "It seeks to restrain and prohibit the immigration or importation of laborers who would have never seen our shores but for the inducements and allurements of men whose only object is to obtain labor at the lowest possible rate, regardless of the social and material well-being of our own citizens, and regardless of the evil consequences which result to American laborers from such immigration. This class of immigrants care nothing about our institutions, and in many instances never even heard of them. They are men whose passage is paid by the importers. They come here under contract to labor for a certain number of years. They are ignorant of our social condition, and, that they may remain so, they are isolated and prevented from coming into contact with Americans. They are generally from the lowest social stratum, and live upon the coarsest food, and in hovels of a character before unknown to American workmen. They, as a rule, do not become citizens, and are certainly not a desirable acquisition to the body politic. The inevitable tendency of their presence among us is to degrade American labor, and to reduce it to the level of the imported pauper labor." Page 5359, Congressional Record, 48th Cong.

We find, therefore, that the title of the act, the evil which was intended to be remedied, the circumstances surrounding the appeal to congress, the reports of the committee of each house, all concur in affirming that the intent of congress was simply to stay the influx of this cheap, unskilled labor.

But, beyond all these matters, no purpose of action against religion can be imputed to any legislation, state or national, because this is a religious people.

This is historically true. From the discovery of this continent to the present hour, there is a single voice making this affirmation. The commission to Christopher Columbus, prior to his sail westward, is from "Ferdinand and Isabella, by the grace of God, king and queen of Castile," etc., and recites that "it is hoped that by God's assistance some of the continents and islands in the ocean will be discovered," etc. The first colonial grant, that made to Sir Walter Raleigh in 1584, was from "Elizabeth, by the grace of God, of England, France and Ireland, queen, defender of the faith," etc.; and the grant authorizing him to enact statutes of the government of the proposed colony provided that "they be not against the true Christian faith nowe professed in the Church of England.". . . .

The first charter of Virginia, granted by King James I in 1606, after reciting the application of certain parties for a charter, commenced the grant in these words: "'We, greatly commending, and graciously accepting of, their Desires for the Furtherance of so noble a Work, which may, by the Providence of Almighty God, hereafter tend to the Glory of his Divine Majesty, in propagating of Christian Religion to such People.". . . .

If we examine the constitutions of the various states, we find in them a constant recognition of religious obligations. Every constitution of every one of the 44 states contains language which, either directly or by clear implication, recognizes a profound reverence for religion, and an assumption that its influence in all human affairs is essential to the well-being of the community. This recognition may be in the preamble, such as is found in the constitution of Illinois, 1870: "We, the people of the state of Illinois, grateful to Almighty God for the civil, political, and religious liberty which He hath so long permitted us to enjoy, and looking to Him for a blessing upon our endeavors to secure and transmit the same unimpaired to succeeding generations," etc.

It may be only in the familiar requisition that all officers shall take an oath closing with the declaration, "so help me God." It may be in clauses like that of the constitution of Indiana, 1816, art. 11, §4: "The manner of administering an oath or affirmation shall be such as is most consistent with the conscience of the deponent, and shall be esteemed the most solemn appeal to God. . . . ."

Even the constitution of the United States, which is supposed to have little touch upon the private life of the individual, contains in the first amendment a declaration common to the constitutions of all the states, as follows: "Congress shall make no law respecting an establishment of religion, or prohibiting the free exercise thereof," etc., and also provides in article 1, §7, (a provision common to many constitutions,) that the executive shall have 10 days (Sundays excepted) within which to determine whether he will approve or veto a bill.. . . .

If we pass beyond these matters to a view of American life, as expressed by its laws, its business, its customs, and its society, we find every where a clear recognition of the same truth. Among other matters note the following: The form of oath universally prevailing, concluding with an appeal to the Almighty; the custom of opening sessions of all deliberative bodies and most conventions with prayer; the prefatory words of all wills, "In the name of God, amen"; the laws respecting the observance of the Sabbath, with the general cessation of all secular business, and the closing of courts, legislatures, and other similar public assemblies on that day;

the churches and church organizations which abound in every city, town, and hamlet; the multitude of charitable organizations existing everywhere under Christian auspices; the gigantic missionary associations, with general support, and aiming to establish Christian missions in every quarter of the globe. These, and many other matters which might be noticed, add a volume of unofficial declarations to the mass of organic utterances that this is a Christian nation. In the face of all these, shall it be believed that a congress of the United States intended to make it a misdemeanor for a church of this country to contract for the services of a Christian minister residing in another nation?. . . .

The judgment will be reversed, and the case remanded for further proceedings in accordance with this opinion.

NOTES AND QUESTIONS

1. *A Preview of Interpretive Tools. Holy Trinity* illustrates many of the tools of statutory interpretation that we will study in this chapter.

   a. *Text.* The Court begins with the concession that the Church's act is "within the letter of this section" prohibiting the payment for aliens to enter the country. In what sense is the importation of the pastor within the letter of the provision at issue? That provision reads in relevant part:

   > [I]t shall be unlawful for any person, company, partnership, or corporation, in any manner whatsoever, to prepay the transportation, or in any way assist or encourage the importation or migration, of any alien or aliens, any foreigner or foreigners, into the United States, its territories, or the District of Columbia, under contract or agreement, parol or special, express or implied, made previous to the importation or migration of such alien or aliens, foreigner or foreigners, to perform labor or service of any kind in the United States, its territories, or the District of Columbia.

   Holy Trinity, 143 U.S. at 457 (citing statute). Make the argument that the pastor falls within the letter of this provision. Can you make the opposite argument?

   b. *Title.* In making the argument that the statute did not apply to the Church's action, the Court relies on the title of the statute. The title was "An act to prohibit the importation and migration of foreigners and aliens under contract or agreement to perform labor in the United States, its territories, and the District of Columbia." What conclusions does the Court draw from this language? Should the title play such an important role in interpreting provisions of a statute? It is part of the law that Congress enacted and the President signed. What arguments are there that the title (or section headings) should control or function as a strong guide for interpreting provisions of a statute? What are the arguments that the title should *not* have controlled here?

c. *Statutory Purpose and Statutory Context.* The Court does not stop at the text of the statute to determine its meaning. Rather, it invokes the purpose of the Act to guide its interpretation. In particular, the Court states that the purpose of the Act was to prevent the influx of "cheap, unskilled labor," which was viewed as harming the labor market in the United States. Because the problem of unskilled labor was the "evil" that Congress sought to address, the statute had no application to "brain toilers," such as the pastor in the case. Why did the Court cite the purpose of the Act rather than simply relying on the text? How did the Court determine that the purpose of the Act was to prevent the influx of cheap labor? Was this purpose in the actual minds of the legislators who wrote the Act or did the Court glean it from the circumstances surrounding the statute — which is to say, the statutory context?

d. *Legislative Intent and Legislative History.* To interpret the statute, the Court also relies upon the proceedings and reports surrounding the passage of the Act. These proceedings and reports are part of the legislative history of the statute. The Court quotes extensively from Senate and House Committee Reports recommending passage of the bill. The Senate Report specifically noted that the Senate Committee would have preferred substituting "manual labor" or "manual service" for the phrase "labor and service" to remove objections. The Senate Committee, however, did not recommend making that change. Preferring passage of the bill prior to Congress's adjournment, the committee nonetheless suggested "labor and service" provisions "will be construed as including only those whose labor or service is manual in character." What inferences does the Court in *Holy Trinity* draw from this report? Do those inferences appear to be strong or weak ones?

What happens when the legislative history conflicts with the statutory text? Which should control? Many read *Holy Trinity* as permitting the legislative history to trump the statutory text and thus have condemned the decision for this result. Justice Scalia reflects this view in his dissenting opinion in Zuni Public School Dist. No. 89 v. Department of Education, 550 U.S. 81, 108 (2007) (Scalia, J., dissenting): "[T]oday," Justice Scalia writes, "*Church of the Holy Trinity* arises, Phoenix-like, from the ashes. The Court's contrary assertions aside, today's decision is nothing other than the elevation of judge-supposed legislative intent over clear statutory text." What does Justice Scalia mean by "judge-supposed legislative intent"?

In this regard, consider Professor Adrian Vermeule's evaluation of the legislative history of the statute in *Holy Trinity*. Vermeule has shown that the legislative history as a whole (rather than the select parts on which the Court relied) supports the view that Congress sought the Act to apply to "any employee, manual or professional, except those specifically exempted." Adrian Vermeule, *Legislative History and the Limits of Judicial Competence: The Untold Story of* Holy Trinity Church, 50 STAN. L. REV. 1833, 1845 (1998). Vermeule focuses on the exceptions for "professional actors, singers and lecturers," suggesting that, absent these exceptions, the Act would apply to these "brain toilers." *Id.* at 1846. According to Vermeule, members of the House viewed the bill as including "brain toilers" and accordingly argued for broader exceptions to protect these categories. Meanwhile, activities in the Senate demonstrated an understanding that the bill applied only to manual laborers, despite the claim to the contrary in the Senate Report. In particular, in response to a question in the floor debate as to whether the bill applied to lawyers, artists, painters, engravers, great authors, bookkeepers, and so on, Senator Blair — a committee member and floor manager of the bill — conceded that "the bill applies to them. Perhaps the bill ought to be further amended." *Id.* at 1850. Does Vermeule's version of the legislative history affect your view of the Court's decision? Does it carry a more general warning for courts about placing great weight on legislative history? We will examine the arguments for and against the use of legislative history in detail.

2. *A Preview of Interpretive Theories.* When courts interpret statutes, they often reveal an underlying theory of statutory interpretation — that is, a general sense for how statutes should be interpreted as a normative matter. Courts rarely refer to theories of interpretation by name in written opinions. Indeed, when *Holy Trinity* was decided, neither courts nor academics devoted much time to describing or debating interpretive theories. That phenomenon began in the twentieth century. Nevertheless, the Court in *Holy Trinity* has something to offer on this score. For example, it stated that its ultimate aim in interpreting the statute was to determine the way in which "Congress intended" the statute to be applied.

In this respect, *Holy Trinity* reflects a widely shared assumption that the primary role for courts is to serve as "faithful agents" of Congress in interpreting statutes, that is, to "identify and enforce the legal directives that an appropriately informed interpreter would conclude the enacting legislature meant to establish." Caleb Nelson, *What Is Textualism?*, 91 Va. L. Rev. 347, 353-54 (2005). Most theories of statutory interpretation rest on this assumption (or some version of it). It reflects the view that law should be made by Congress not courts, which has roots in notions of legislative supremacy and judicial restraint. But some depart from it, viewing courts more as partners with Congress rather than as faithful agents of Congress at the time the statute was enacted.

The following subsections provide a brief chronological description of the basic theories of statutory interpretation, using *Holy Trinity* as the jumping off point for each. The description is intended to be detailed enough for you to begin to develop a working vocabulary of the theories, which are discussed at greater length in section E [Lisa Schultz Bressman et al., The Regulatory State, 1st ed., (2010)] of this chapter.

a. *Intentionalism.* Under one of the earliest approaches to statutory interpretation, courts looked to find the actual or specific meaning that Congress meant for a particular word or phrase to carry. Intentionalists interpret statutory provisions by relying on sources that most directly bear on actual legislative intent, including the text of the statute, its legislative history, and the conditions at the time of enactment. Where do you see intentionalism at work in *Holy Trinity*? What did Congress intend when it wrote the word "labor"?

b. *Purposivism.* In the 1930s, the realist movement cast doubt on the quest for an actual, discernible legislative intent. At best, legal realists asserted, legislative intent is difficult to reconstruct given the complexities of the legislative process. How can a court know with confidence what Congress actually intended a particular word or phrase to mean? At worst, legislative intent is incoherent. No group as large and diverse as Congress can share a unified intent. Collective legislative intent simply does not exist. In response, courts began to shift their focus away from the actual intent of Congress to the broad purposes of the statute. They still examined the same sort of sources: text, legislative history, and circumstances at the time of enactment. But the inquiry concerning what Congress intended to accomplish was no longer at the level of the specific meaning of words but rather at the overall aims of the statute. Even in earlier cases such as *Holy Trinity*, you can see purposivism at work. What was the purpose of the statute, and how does that purpose affect the meaning of the words of the statute, including "labor"?

c. *Legal Process Purposivism.* In the 1950s, a group of scholars refined purposivism to make it a more objective theory. The Legal Process thinkers doubted the possibility of discerning actual statutory purpose, just as the realists before them doubted the possibility of discerning actual legislative intent. Nevertheless, they recognized that every statute has a purpose simply because it is an affirmative act meant to accomplish something. They suggested that courts inquire into that purpose by asking what a reasonable legislature would have sought to accomplish under the circumstances. Thus, courts should interpret statutes assuming that the legislature was "made up of reasonable persons pursuing reasonable purposes reasonably." HENRY M. HART, JR. & ALBERT SACKS, THE LEGAL PROCESS: BASIC PROBLEMS IN THE MAKING AND APPLICATION OF LAW 1378 (William N. Eskridge, Jr. & Philip P. Frickey eds., 1994). The Legal Process approach asked courts to construct the reasonable purpose or purposes of statutes based on the available evidence, including the text, legislative history, and contextual evidence. It continued through the next significant wave of regulatory statutes in the 1960s and 1970s.

    Can you see any foreshadowing of Legal Process purposivism in *Holy Trinity*? What do you make of the religious discussion? There the Court stated that a purpose against religion would not be attributed to the legislature. Was the Court saying it would not have been reasonable for Congress, if acting reasonably, to have applied the statute to religious workers given that the United States at that time was a "Christian nation"? (This is not to say that Legal Process scholars would endorse the religious discussion in the opinion.)

d. *Imaginative Reconstruction.* A modern variant of intentionalism applies when Congress has not foreseen or considered a particular problem.

Judge Posner is the leading proponent of this theory, which is called imaginative reconstruction. It does not purport to uncover the actual intent of Congress; indeed, it applies when Congress failed to appreciate an issue and therefore cannot be understood as having an intention as to that issue. Imaginative reconstruction asks the court to stand in the shoes of Congress, asking how the enacting legislature would have resolved the issue if it had envisioned it.

Do you see any seeds of this theory in *Holy Trinity?* Is this a better understanding of the religious discussion? (Again, that is not to say that proponents of imaginative reconstruction would endorse this religious discussion in the Court's opinion.) Was the Court conceding that Congress probably had not thought about whether the statute applies to pastors, reasoning instead that Congress would not have applied the statute to pastors if it had thought about the issue?

e.   *Textualism and New Textualism.* In the late 1980s and 1990s, textualism began to ascend as a prominent theory of statutory interpretation, and it remains so today. Judges always have looked to the text of statutes to see if it reveals a meaning. But textualists set themselves apart by refusing to consult sources like legislative history in search of legislative intent or statutory purpose. Textualists are committed to the view that the text should be the sole tool of interpretation, though they believe that the text should be interpreted in its statutory context rather than in isolation. This view has both constitutional and pragmatic underpinnings. Textualists argue that intent- and purpose-based analyses do not comport with constitutional or rule-of-law values because only the text is enacted into law. Furthermore, textualists join ranks with realists in believing that the legislature has no intent or purpose other than to forge compromises in the chaotic and messy environment of the legislative process. The text manifests those compromises. Textualists also find support in the law-and-economics movement, which views legislators as writing statutes to deliver benefits to powerful interest groups. By sticking to the text, courts can confine such groups to the deals that they extracted rather than allowing them to find more generous interpretations in the legislative history.

The members of the majority in *Holy Trinity* were not textualists, which you know because they looked well beyond the text in support of their interpretation. You see the Court employing textual tools when it construes the words of the provision first on their own and then in the context of the broader statute, including the title. But there is a great difference between textual analysis and textualist theory.

f.   *Dynamic Interpretation.* There is another theory that is not really reflected in *Holy Trinity*: dynamic interpretation. Dynamic interpretation sees courts more as partners with Congress than as faithful agents of the enacting Congress in developing the meaning of statutes. Partly, this theory is based on the reality of the judicial process. When courts interpret statutes, they generally act as if they are not imposing their own background understandings and core values but are simply recovering the intent of the legislature, the purpose of the statute, or the meaning of the text. In truth, dynamic theorists claim, courts are applying their own understandings and values in order to interpret statutes. Because such an approach is inevitable, particularly as statutes age, courts ought to be honest about their method of interpretation. There is something to this, right? Just from reading *Holy Trinity*, you have a sense that text-, intent-, and purpose-based approaches do not always point in the same direction or yield a single, objective result. Perhaps the results vary more with judicial understandings and core values than courts are willing to acknowledge.

Dynamic theorists also argue that their partnership or pragmatic approach is normatively desirable. Some suggest that the courts should approach statutes as they approach the common law, construing them in light of legal and social developments that have occurred over time. Others argue that courts should take particular note of current legislative preferences because these preferences determine whether a statute or an interpretation could be enacted today, and therefore are more objective than picking and choosing among original meanings. Overall, these theorists view courts as (a) producing the best interpretations of statutes, and (b) best serving Congress when taking account of social and legal developments.

3. Following *Holy Trinity*, how would you advise Grace Church, also located in Manhattan, if it sought to enter a contract to pay a group of bricklayers from Italy to come and build an extension to its chapel, including the carving of several new gargoyles? Following *Holy Trinity*, how would you advise a mosque if it sought to enter into a contract with an Egyptian muezzin, by which the mosque would pay for the muezzin's transportation to New York City and the muezzin, in return, would begin service for the mosque?

4. Recall that the 1966 Motor Vehicle Safety Act authorizes NHTSA to set minimum performance standards for new motor vehicles and provides that all standards "shall be practicable, shall meet the need for motor vehicle safety, and shall be stated in objective terms." §103. Assume NHTSA issued a standard that forced manufacturers to develop new technology in order to meet its safety requirements (say a tire-pressure detection method that has not yet been developed). Several auto manufacturers challenge the standard, arguing that it was not "practicable" because it depended on technology not currently in use. Consider the potential sources for determining the meaning of "practicable":

The provision itself.

Webster's Third New International Dictionary defines "practicable" as "possible or practical to perform," "capable of being put into practice, done or accomplished," and "feasible."

Other provisions of the same statute.

The express purpose of the Act is "to reduce traffic accidents and deaths and injuries to persons resulting from traffic accidents." 15 U.S.C. §1381.

The Act establishes a research and development section within the agency itself. *See* 15 U.S.C. §1395.

The Act permits the Secretary to extend the effective date beyond the usual statutory maximum of one year from the date of issuance. 15 U.S.C. §1392(c).

The legislative history of the statute.

The Senate Committee Report, in a section entitled "Purpose and Need," states: "[T]his legislation reflects the faith that the restrained and responsible exercise of Federal authority can channel the creative energies and vast technology of the automobile industry into a vigorous and competitive effort to improve the safety of vehicles." S. Rep. 1301, 89th Cong., 2d. Sess. 2 U.S.C.C.A.N. 2709 (1966).

The same report adds: "While the bill reported by the committee authorizes the Secretary to make grants or award contracts for research in certain cases, a principal aim is to encourage the auto industry itself to engage in greater auto safety and safety-related research." *Id.* at 2718.

The report, explaining the effective date provision, states: "The power to specify a later effective date is needed because it may be a practical economic and engineering impossibility, as well as a source of great hardship and unnecessary additional cost, to require that all vehicle changes required by any new safety standard, whatever its scope or subject matter, be accomplished by all manufacturers on all their vehicles within 1 year." *Id.* at 2714.

The House Committee Report states: "In establishing standards the Secretary must conform to the requirement that the standard is practicable. This would include consideration of all relevant factors, including technological ability to achieve the goal of a particular standard as well as consideration of economic factors." H.R. Rep. 1776, p. 16.

The Automobile Manufacturers Association transmitted to the House Committee several amendments to HR 13228 (the House Bill) proposing a requirement that: ".... the Secretary, in proposing and issuing orders establishing, amending, or withdrawing Federal motor vehicle safety standards under this section, shall be guided so far as practicable by the following criteria, and the Secretary shall include in each such order findings of fact with respect thereto:.... (2) The standard shall be consistent with the continuation or adoption by motor vehicle manufacturers of efficient designing, engineering, and manufacturing practices, and with innovation, progressiveness, and customary model changes in the automotive industry. (3) The standard, the means of complying with the standard, and the methods of testing for compliance should embody feasible devices and techniques that are available or can be made available in a reasonable time and at costs commensurate with the benefit to be achieved..... (5) The standard should be made effective so as to allow adequate time for compliance, taking into account the time required for designing, engineering, tooling and production....." Hearings Before the Committee on Interstate and Foreign

Commerce, U.S. House of Representatives, 89th Cong., 2d Sess., on H.R. 13228, "Part 2, Traffic Safety," p. 1203.

If you were a lawyer for NHTSA, which sources would you emphasize and which arguments would you make in your brief defending the agency's technology-forcing standard as "practicable" under the 1966 Act? Alternatively, if you were a lawyer for the automakers, which sources would you stress and which arguments would you make? How might either the lawyer for NHTSA or the automaker use *Holy Trinity*? Finally, if you were a judge, how would you rule and why? Suppose that one of your judicial colleagues refused to consult the legislative history. How would that refusal influence the interpretation of the word "practicable"?

B. How Should the Constitution Be Interpreted?

The Inevitable Need for Interpretation

A constant theme throughout this book and throughout all of constitutional law concerns how should the document be interpreted. In applying any law — be it a statute, regulation, or Constitution — judges must decide what it means. Three factors make constitutional interpretation uniquely complicated and produce a great many of the interpretive questions before the Supreme Court.

First, countless problems arise that the Constitution does not expressly consider. When may the president remove executive officers? When, if at all, do federal laws impermissibly infringe upon state sovereignty? May states adopt laws that place a substantial burden on interstate commerce? These problems are less a matter of deciding the meaning of a particular phrase in the Constitution and more a reflection of the reality that countless issues of governance are not dealt with in any of the language of the Constitution. Long ago, Chief Justice John Marshall expressed this when he explained that the Constitution was not meant to have the "prolixity of a legal code," but instead, "[i]ts nature . . . requires, that only its great outlines should be marked, its important objects designated. . . . [W]e must never forget that it is a constitution we are expounding. . . . [A]constitution, intended to endure for ages to come, and consequently, to be adapted to the various crises of human affairs."[1] Because the Constitution is just an outline, a blueprint for government, it does not address myriad questions that courts must face.

Second, even where there are constitutional provisions, much of the Constitution is written in open-textured language using phrases such as "commerce among the states," "necessary and proper," "freedom of speech," "due process of law," "liberty," "taking," "equal protection," and "cruel and unusual punishment." How should the Court decide the content and meaning of these and other similar clauses that are found throughout the Constitution?

---

[1] McCulloch v. Maryland, 17 U.S. (4 Wheat.) 316, 407, 415 (1819). *McCulloch* is discussed in detail in §3.2 [Erwin Chemerinsky, Constitutional Law: Principles and Policies, 4th ed., (2011)].

There is no doubt that this open-textured language is what has allowed the Constitution to survive for over 200 years and to govern a world radically different from the one that existed when it was drafted. But it is this very nature of the Constitution that requires that courts interpret it and decide its meaning.

Third, inevitably in constitutional law, courts must face the question of what, if any, government justifications are sufficient to permit the government to interfere with a fundamental right or to discriminate. Even though the First Amendment says that Congress shall make "no law" abridging freedom of speech, that provision never has been regarded as an absolute. Once it is recognized that there can be laws preventing perjury or, to use a classic example, forbidding falsely shouting "fire" in a crowded theater, the issue becomes how to draw a line as to when the government can regulate speech.[2]

Although the Fourteenth Amendment says that states shall not deny any person equal protection of the laws, inevitably states must draw distinctions among people. For instance, every state requires that people be 16 in order to get a driver's license, and that they have a low income in order to receive welfare benefits. These, and an infinite variety of other laws, can be challenged as treating people unequally, and courts must decide when differences in treatment are justified and when they deny equal protection. The point is that in interpreting and applying the Constitution, courts must decide what, if any, justifications permit deviating from the text, or interfering with a right, or discriminating.

Although these issues of interpretation arise in every area of constitutional law, there has been an especially heated scholarly and public debate over the question of whether it is appropriate for the Court to interpret the Constitution to protect rights that are not expressly stated in the text.[3] The paradigm issue concerning this debate has been whether the Court should have recognized a constitutional right of women to terminate their pregnancies in the absence of an explicit textual provision or framers' intent supporting such a right.[4]

The Debate Between Originalism and Nonoriginalism

Over the last few decades, the debate frequently has been characterized as one between originalism, sometimes synonymously called interpretivism, and nonoriginalism, sometimes termed noninterpretivism. Originalism is the view that "judges deciding constitutional issues should confine themselves to enforcing norms that are stated or clearly implicit in the written Constitution."[5] In contrast, nonoriginalism is the "contrary view that courts should go beyond that set of

---

[2] The example of falsely shouting "fire" in a crowded theater comes from Justice Oliver Wendell Holmes's opinion in Schenck v. United States, 249 U.S. 47, 52 (1919), discussed in §11.3.2.2 [Erwin Chemerinsky, Constitutional Law: Principles and Policies, 4th ed., (2011)].

[3] See, e.g., Robert H. Bork, The Tempting of America (1990); Mark Tushnet, Red, White, and Blue: A Critical Analysis of Constitutional Law (1988); John Hart Ely, Democracy and Distrust (1980); Michael J. Perry, The Constitution, the Courts, and Human Rights (1982).

[4] See Roe v. Wade, 410 U.S. 113 (1973).

[5] Ely, supra note 3, at 1. See Steven G. Calabresi, ed., Originalism: A Quarter Century of Debate (2007) (a collection of essays advocating originalism and discussing arguments for and against it.)

references and enforce norms that cannot be discovered within the four corners of the document."[6]

Originalists believe that the Court should find a right to exist in the Constitution only if it is expressly stated in the text or was clearly intended by its framers. If the Constitution is silent, originalists say it is for the legislature, unconstrained by the courts, to decide the law. Nonoriginalists think that it is permissible for the Court to interpret the Constitution to protect rights that are not expressly stated or clearly intended. Originalists believe that the meaning of a constitutional provision was set when it was adopted and that it can be changed solely by amendment; nonoriginalists believe that the Constitution's meaning can evolve by amendment and by interpretation. For example, originalists argue that it was wrong for the Court to strike down state laws prohibiting the use of contraceptives and forbidding abortion.[7] Because the Constitution is silent about reproductive freedom and there is no evidence that the framers intended to protect such a right, originalists argue that the matter is left entirely to the legislatures to govern as they deem appropriate. Nonoriginalists, by contrast, believe that it was appropriate for the Court to decide that the word "liberty" includes a right of privacy and that reproductive freedom is an essential aspect of privacy.

The disagreement between originalists and nonoriginalists is not only about whether the Court should recognize unenumerated rights. Originalists and nonoriginalists also disagree over how the Court should decide the meaning of particular constitutional provisions. For example, an issue arose before the Supreme Court as to whether the Fourth Amendment requires that police officers "knock and announce" before searching a residence.[8] Justice Thomas, following his originalist philosophy, decided the issue by considering the law as of 1791 when the Fourth Amendment was adopted and concluded that knock and announce is generally required because it was part of the law at that time. For a nonoriginalist, such historical practice might be of interest, but is not necessarily decisive because the meaning of the Constitution is not limited to what the framers experienced or intended.

Simply stated, the disagreement between originalists and nonoriginalists is basically over how the Constitution should evolve. Originalists explicitly state that amendment is the only legitimate means for constitutional evolution.[9] If there is to be a right to use contraceptives or a right to abortion, originalists would say that the Constitution must be amended.

In contrast, nonoriginalists believe that the Constitution's meaning is not limited to what the framers intended; rather, the meaning and application of constitu-

---

[6] Id.

[7] See Griswold v. Connecticut, 381 U.S. 479 (1965) (declaring unconstitutional Connecticut law prohibiting the use of contraceptives); Roe v. Wade, 410 U.S. 113 (1973) (declaring unconstitutional Texas law prohibiting abortion).

[8] Wilson v. Arkansas, 514 U.S. 927 (1995).

[9] See, e.g., Raoul Berger, G. Edward White's Apology for Judicial Activism, 63 Tex. L. Rev. 367, 372 (1984); William Van Alstyne, Interpreting this Constitution: The Unhelpful Contributions of Special Theories of Judicial Review, 35 U. Fla. L. Rev. 209, 234-235 n.66 (1983).

tional provisions should evolve by interpretation.[10] The fact that the framers of the Fourteenth Amendment did not intend to prohibit gender discrimination or to apply the Bill of Rights to the states is not decisive for the nonoriginalist in deciding what the Constitution means. In recent years, this discussion has been expressed as a debate over whether the document is a "living Constitution."

It is important to recognize that the Supreme Court, at various times, has professed adherence to each of these competing philosophies. In *South Carolina v. United States*, in 1905, the Court stated: "The Constitution is a written instrument. As such its meaning does not alter. That which it meant when adopted, it means now."[11] But there are equally strong statements from the Court rejecting an originalist approach. In *Home Building and Loan Assn. v. Blaisdell*, in 1934, the Court declared:

> It is no answer to say that this public need was not apprehended a century ago, or to insist that what the provision of the Constitution meant to the vision of that day it must mean to the vision of our time. If by the statement that what the Constitution meant at the time of its adoption it means today, it is intended to say that the great clauses of the Constitution must be confined to the interpretation which the framers, with the conditions and outlook of their time, would have placed upon them, the statement carries its own refutation. It was to guard against such a narrow conception that Chief Justice John Marshall uttered the memorable warning — " We must never forget that it is a constitution we are expounding."[12]

Countless other quotations from the Court can be found endorsing and rejecting both originalism and nonoriginalism.

The Range of Alternatives Within Originalism and Nonoriginalism

There are not only two approaches to interpreting the Constitution, but a wide range of alternative views exist within both originalism and nonoriginalism. Originalism and nonoriginalism are general categories more than unitary philosophies. Within originalism, there are those who might be termed strict originalists, who believe that the Court must follow the literal text and the specific intent of its drafters.[13] A strict originalist, for example, is likely to believe that the Court was wrong in ordering desegregation of public schools because the Congress that ratified the Fourteenth Amendment also approved the segregation of the District of Columbia public schools. But there also are more moderate originalists who are "more concerned with the adopters' general purposes than with their intentions

---

[10] *See, e.g.*, Gregg v. Georgia, 428 U.S. 153, 227 (1975) (Brennan, J., dissenting) (arguing that the cruel and unusual punishment clause should be interpreted according to contemporary norms); *see also* Peter Irons, Brennan v. Rehnquist: The Battle for the Constitution (1994); Bernard Schwartz, Brennan v. Rehnquist — Mirror Images in Constitutional Construction, 19 Okla. City U. L. Rev. 213 (1994).

[11] 199 U.S. 437, 448 (1905).

[12] 290 U.S. 398, 442-443 (1934).

[13] *See, e.g.*, Raoul Berger, Government by Judiciary (1977).

in a very precise sense."[14] A moderate originalist likely would argue that the Court was correct in ordering school desegregation because it advances the general purpose of the equal protection clause even if it does not follow the framers' specific views.

Because the framers' intent can be stated at many different levels of abstraction, the distinction between strict and moderate originalism is not always clear. Yet there is a difference between believing that the specific conceptions of the framers are binding and believing that the framers' general concepts are controlling, but that their particular conceptions need not be followed.[15]

In recent years, Justice Antonin Scalia has propounded a different version of originalism, one that focuses on finding the "original meaning" of constitutional provisions.[16] Justice Scalia says that original meaning is to be found in the historical practices and understandings of the time, not the views of the document's drafters.[17] As with other forms of originalism, Justice Scalia believes that the Constitution's meaning is fixed and unchanging until it is amended.

There are a great many varieties of nonoriginalism. This is inevitable because nonoriginalism describes what *doesn't* control interpretation; it does not specify what should be looked to in deciding the meaning of the Constitution. Some, including often the Supreme Court, say that tradition should be a, or even *the*, guide in interpreting the Constitution.[18] The tension between specific and abstract originalism replicates itself in the use of tradition as a method of interpretation. Justice Scalia, for example, has said that when the Court looks to tradition in deciding the meaning of due process, it should consider only traditions stated at the most specific level of abstraction.[19] Justice Brennan rejected this view and would allow the Court to follow traditions stated more generally.[20]

Another strand of nonoriginalism emphasizes the Court's role in implementing the processes of government. Some believe that the Court may decide cases based on contemporary values, but only when it is dealing with issues concerning the process of government, such as in ensuring fair representation and adjudication.[21] Professor John Hart Ely, for example, argued that the Court is justified in

[14] Paul Brest, The Misconceived Quest for the Original Understanding. 60 B.U. L. Rev. 204, 205 (1980).
[15] The distinction between concepts and conceptions is from Ronald Dworkin, Taking Rights Seriously 134-136 (1978).
[16] See, e.g., Antonin Scalia, A Matter of Interpretation: Federal Courts and the Law (1997).
[17] I have described and analyzed this approach to constitutional interpretation in more detail in Erwin Chemerinsky, The Jurisprudence of Justice Scalia: A Critical Appraisal, 22 U. Haw. L. Rev. 385 (2000).
[18] See, e.g., Poe v. Ullman, 367 U.S. 497, 522-555 (Harlan, J., dissenting); Adamson v. California, 332 U.S. 46, 59-68 (1947) (Frankfurter J., concurring) (describing tradition as the basis for interpreting due process). Another view of tradition is advanced in Barry Friedman & Scott B. Smith, The Sedimentary Constitution, 147 U. Pa. L. Rev. 1 (1998) (constitutional interpretation should account for all that has occurred with regard to a constitutional provision throughout American history).
[19] See, e.g., Michael H. v. Gerald D., 491 U.S. 110, 127 n.6 (1989) (plurality opinion).
[20] Id. at 137-141 (Brennan, J., dissenting). See also Laurence Tribe & Michael Dorf, On Reading the Constitution (1991) (discussing the debate over the use of tradition and its level of abstraction).
[21] See Ely, supra note 3, at 73-75.

being nonoriginalist when it follows a "participation-oriented, representation rein-forcing approach."[22] Ely argues that nonoriginalism is appropriate when the Court is providing "procedural fairness in the resolution of individual disputes" or by "ensuring broad participation in the processes and distributions of govern-ment."[23] Ely maintains that the Court has special expertise in the area of proce-dure and also that judicial review in this realm is consistent with majority rule because it is perfecting democracy, whereas other judicial review must be limited because it is inconsistent with democratic principles.

Other nonoriginalists believe that the Court should discern and implement the "natural law" in interpreting the Constitution.[24] Still others say that the Court should identify and follow the deeply embedded moral consensus that exists in society.[25] Often nonoriginalists reject limiting the Constitution to the enumera-tions in the text or the framers' intent but don't articulate a specific philosophy for how meaning should be given to the Constitution.

The Basic Arguments for Originalism

The issue of how the Constitution should be interpreted confronts all branches and levels of government; all officeholders take an oath to uphold the Constitution and are therefore required to interpret the document. Yet the debate between originalism and nonoriginalism has focused on which approach the judi-ciary should follow in interpreting the Constitution.

Originalists make two primary arguments for their approach. First, some origi-nalists argue that the very nature of interpreting a document requires that its meaning be limited to its specific text and its framers' intentions. Professor Walter Benn Michaels, for example, stated that "any interpretation of the Constitution that really is an interpretation . . . of the Constitution . . . is always and only an interpretation of what the Constitution originally meant."[26] Professor Edward Melvin wrote that "when a judge takes his oath to uphold the Constitution he promises to carry out the intention of its framers."[27]

Second, and more commonly, originalists argue that their approach is desir-able to constrain the power of unelected judges in a democratic society.[28] The argument is that the basic premise of American democracy is majority rule; "the political principle that governmental policymaking — . . . decisions as to which values among competing values shall prevail, and as to how those values shall be

---

[22] *Id.* at 87.

[23] *Id.*

[24] *See, e.g.,* Harry V. Jaffa, Original Intent and the Framers of the Constitution: A Disputed Question (1994).

[25] *See, e.g.,* Larry G. Simon, The Authority of the Framers of the Constitution: Can Originalist Interpretation Be Justified?, 73 Cal. L. Rev. 1482, 1505-1510 (1985) (describing constitutional inter-pretation based on "deeply layered consensus"); Harry H. Wellington, Common Law Rules and Constitutional Double Standards: Some Notes on Adjudication, 83 Yale L.J. 221, 284 (1973).

[26] Walter Benn Michaels, Response to Perry and Simon, 58 S. Cal. L. Rev. 673, 673 (1985).

[27] Edward J. Melvin, Judicial Activism: The Violation of the Oath, 27 Cath. Law. 283, 284 (1982).

[28] *See, e.g.,* Robert Bork, Neutral Principles and Some First Amendment Problems, 47 Ind. L.J. 1 (1971).

implemented — ought to be subject to control by persons accountable to the electorate."[29] The claim is that judicial review is a "deviant institution in American democracy" because it permits unelected judges to overturn the decisions of popularly accountable officials.[30] Alexander Bickel termed this the "counter-majoritarian difficulty," and it has been at the core of the debate over the proper method of judicial review.[31]

Originalists argue, therefore, that the Court is justified in invalidating government decisions only when it is following values clearly stated in the text or intended by the framers. Raoul Berger, for example, contends that "activist judicial review is inconsistent with democratic theory because it substitutes the policy choices of unelected, unaccountable judges for those of the people's representatives."[32] Robert Bork similarly remarked that a "Court that makes rather than implements value choices cannot be squared with the presuppositions of a democratic society."[33]

As to the former argument, that interpretation requires originalism, the nonoriginalist reply is that it is a tautology; it defines interpretation as requiring originalism and then concludes that only originalism is a legitimate method of interpretation. Nonoriginalists argue that both theories claim to be interpreting the Constitution and that neither is inherently the proper approach.

The second argument, based on democracy, has produced a variety of answers. Some nonoriginalists dispute the definition of democracy as majority rule that originalists rely on. They argue that neither descriptively nor normatively should American democracy be defined as majority rule.[34] The framers openly and explicitly distrusted majority rule, and therefore virtually every government institution that they created had strong anti-majoritarian features. As described above in Section 4.B, the Constitution exists primarily to shield some matters from easy change by political majorities.[35] Judicial review implementing a counter-majoritarian document is inherently anti-majoritarian. Some critics of originalism argue that a preferable definition of American democracy includes both

---

[29] Perry, *supra* note 3, at 9; *see also* Ely, *supra* note 3, at 5, 7.

[30] Alexander Bickel, The Least Dangerous Branch 18 (1962).

[31] *Id.* at 16-17. Professor Barry Friedman has written an excellent series of articles tracing the history of the counter-majoritarian difficulty. *See, e.g.,* Barry Friedman, The History of the Counter-Majoritarian Difficulty, Part Four: Law's Politics, 148 U. Pa. L. Rev. 971 (2000); Barry Friedman, The History of the Counter-Majoritarian Difficulty, Part One: The Road to Judicial Supremacy, 73 N.Y.U. L. Rev. 333 (1998).

[32] Raoul Berger, Ely's Theory of Judicial Review, 42 Ohio St. L.J. 87, 87 (1981).

[33] Bork, *supra* note 28, at 6.

[34] *See, e.g.,* Erwin Chemerinsky, Foreword: The Vanishing Constitution, 103 Harv. L. Rev. 43, 74-76 (1989).

[35] Justice Jackson eloquently expressed this view of the Bill of Rights:

The very purpose of a Bill of Rights was to withdraw certain subjects from the vicissitudes of political controversy, to place them beyond the reach of majorities and officials and to establish them as legal principles to be applied by the courts. One's right to life, liberty, and property, to free speech, a free press, freedom of worship and assembly, and other fundamental rights may not be submitted to vote: they depend on the outcome of no elections.

West Va. Bd. of Educ. v. Barnette, 319 U.S. 624, 638 (1943).

substantive values and procedural norms such as majority rule.[36] Nonoriginalist judicial review advancing these substantive values is therefore consistent with this broader definition of democracy.

However, some critics of originalism accept the originalists' definition of democracy as majority rule, but purport to offer a theory that reconciles judicial review with majority rule. John Ely, for example, argues that his process-based theory is consistent with democracy because judicial review reinforces majority rule when it ensures fair representation and procedures.[37] Michael Perry contends that judicial review is consistent with majority rule so long as Congress retains the power to restrict the jurisdiction of the Supreme Court.[38]

Also, some critics of originalism argue that originalist judicial review is itself inconsistent with majority rule and therefore cannot claim any advantage over nonoriginalism.[39] The claim is that all judicial review, including originalist review, involves unelected judges overturning policies enacted by electorally accountable officials.

Originalists often answer this by claiming that originalist judicial review is democratic because the people consented to the adoption of the Constitution.[40] But nonoriginalists reply that it is wrong to say that the people consented to the Constitution because less than 5 percent of the population participated in the ratification process.[41] More important, it is erroneous to say that originalist review is democratic because the people ratified the Constitution because not a person alive today — and not even most of our ancestors — voted in its favor.[42] Democracy is defined by originalists to require decisions by current majorities; majority rule does not exist if society is governed by decisions of past majorities that cannot be overruled by a majority of the current population.

The Basic Arguments for Nonoriginalism

Three major arguments are often advanced to support nonoriginalism. First, nonoriginalists maintain that it is desirable to have the Constitution evolve by interpretation and not only by amendment. The cumbersome amendment process, requiring approval by two-thirds of both Houses of Congress and three-fourths of the states, makes it likely that few amendments will be added to the Constitution. Only 17 amendments have been added in more than two centuries. The claim is that nonoriginalist review is necessary if the Constitution is to meet the needs of a changing society.

---

[36] See, e.g., Mark Tushnet, Red, White and Blue: A Critical Analysis of Constitutional Law 71 (1988).

[37] Ely, supra note 3, at 101-104.

[38] Perry, supra note 3, at 126; the authority of Congress to restrict federal court jurisdiction is discussed at §2.9 [Erwin Chemerinsky, Constitutional Law: Principles and Policies, 4th ed., (2011)].

[39] See, e.g., Erwin Chemerinsky, Interpreting the Constitution 17-20 (1987).

[40] Bork, supra note 28, at 3.

[41] Max Lerner, Constitution and Court as Symbols, 46 Yale L.J. 1290, 1296 (1937).

[42] Brest, supra note 14, at 225.

Nonoriginalists argue, for example, that equal protection in the last half of the twentieth century must mean that government-mandated racial segregation is unacceptable, yet there is strong evidence that the framers of the Fourteenth Amendment approved this practice.[43] The drafters of the equal protection clause did not intend to protect women from discrimination,[44] but it is widely accepted that the clause should apply to gender discrimination. Indeed, the argument is made that under originalism it would be unconstitutional to elect a woman as president or vice president because the Constitution refers to these officeholders with the word "he," and the framers clearly intended that they be male.[45]

Moderate originalists respond to this by contending that all of these problems could be avoided under their approach because eliminating segregation, stopping gender discrimination, and allowing women to be elected president or vice president are consistent with the framers' general intentions. But nonoriginalists counter that moderate originalism fails in its goal of constraining judges and is actually indistinguishable from nonoriginalism. The intent behind a constitutional provision can be stated at many different levels of abstraction. Is the intent behind the equal protection clause protecting former slaves, protecting blacks, protecting racial minorities, protecting all "discrete and insular" minorities, or protecting everyone in society from unjust discrimination? Deciding the level of abstraction necessarily requires a value choice by the justices.[46] Moreover, at the highest level of abstraction, the framers desired liberty and equality; almost any imaginable court decision can be justified as consistent with these values.

A second major argument for nonoriginalism is that there is not an unambiguous, knowable framers' intent that can be found to resolve constitutional questions. Instead, the process of determining the framers' intent invariably is a process of interpretation that is affected by contemporary values; in other words, it is indistinguishable from nonoriginalism. In part, the argument is that there is not a single framer or group of framers. The framers include the drafters of a provision, the members of the House and Senate that voted for it, and the members of the state conventions and legislatures that ratified it.[47] Moreover, even if a particular group is chosen as authoritative for purposes of constitutional decision making, there is not a single intent but, rather, many and perhaps conflicting reasons for

---

[43] The same Congress that ratified the Fourteenth Amendment also approved the segregation of the District of Columbia public schools. *See* Ronald Dworkin, Law's Empire 360 (1986). This legislation was later declared unconstitutional in *Boiling v. Sharpe*, 347 U.S. 497 (1954), discussed in §9.3.3.1 [Erwin Chemerinsky, Constitutional Law: Principles and Policies, 4th ed., (2011)]. *But see* Michael McConnell, Originalism and the Desegregation Decisions, 81 Va. L. Rev. 947 (1995) (arguing that the framers of the Fourteenth Amendment did intend to desegregate public schools).

[44] *See, e.g.,* The Slaughter-House Cases, 83 U.S. (16 Wall.) 36, 81 (1872) (stating that the equal protection clause was meant only to protect racial minorities and never would be extended beyond this).

[45] Richard B. Saphire, Judicial Review in the Name of the Constitution, 8 U. Dayton L. Rev. 745, 796-797 (1983).

[46] Paul Brest, The Fundamental Rights Controversy: The Essential Contradictions of Normative Constitutional Scholarship, 90 Yale L.J. 1063, 1091-1092 (1981) ("The fact is that all adjudication requires making choices among the levels of generality on which to articulate principles, and all such choices are inherently non-neutral.").

[47] *See* John G. Wofford, The Blinding Light: The Use of History in Constitutional Interpretation, 31 U. Chi. L. Rev. 502, 508-509 (1964).

adopting a particular constitutional provision.[48] Ronald Dworkin remarked that "there are no, or very few, relevant collective intentions, or perhaps only collective intentions that are indeterminate rather than decisive one way or another."[49]

Nonoriginalists argue further that even if the group is determined and even if somehow a way of arriving at collective intent could be found, the historical materials are too incomplete to support authoritative conclusions. Jeffrey Shaman explains that the "Journal of the Constitutional Convention, which is the primary record of the Framers' intent, is neither complete nor necessarily accurate."[50] As Justice Jackson eloquently remarked: "Just what our forefathers did envision, or would have envisioned had they foreseen modern conditions, must be divined from materials almost as enigmatic as the dreams Joseph was called upon to interpret for Pharaoh."[51]

Third, some nonoriginalists argue that nonoriginalism is the preferable method of interpretation because it is the approach intended by the framers. In other words, the claim is that following originalism requires that originalism be abandoned because the framers did not intend this method of interpretation. Professor Jeff Powell stated: "It is commonly assumed that the 'interpretive intention' of the Constitution's framers was that the Constitution would be construed in accordance with what future interpreters could gather of the framers' own purposes, expectations, and intentions. Inquiry shows that assumption to be incorrect. Of the numerous hermeneutical options that were available in the framers' day . . . none corresponds to the modern notion of intentionalism."[52] In other words, the framers probably did not intend that their intent would govern later interpretations of the Constitution.

Originalists disagree with each of these arguments. As to the first, that nonoriginalism leads to better results, originalists argue that the appropriate method of changing the Constitution is through amendment, not interpretation. Originalists argue that nonoriginalism improperly empowers unelected judges to displace the decisions of popularly elected officials and that, historically, nonoriginalism has produced undesirable decisions, such as those invalidating economic regulations in the first third of this century.[53]

As to the second argument, on the difficulty of determining the framers' intent, originalists maintain that if the intent on a particular issue cannot be determined, then it is a matter that should be left to the political process. Robert Bork wrote: "It follows that the choice of 'fundamental values' by the Court cannot be justified. Where constitutional materials do not clearly specify the value to be preferred, there is no principled way to prefer any claimed human value to any other."[54]

---

[48] Ely, *supra* note 3, at 18.

[49] Ronald Dworkin, The Forum of Principle, 56 N.Y.U. L. Rev. 469, 477 (1981).

[50] Jeffrey Shaman, The Constitution, the Supreme Court, and Creativity, 9 Hastings Const. L.Q. 257, 267 (1982).

[51] Youngstown Sheet & Tube Co. v. Sawyer, 343 U.S. 579, 592 (1952) (Jackson, J., concurring).

[52] H. Jefferson Powell, The Original Understanding of Original Intent, 98 Harv. L. Rev. 885, 948 (1985).

[53] *See* Bork, *supra* note 3, at 4449.

[54] Bork, *supra* note 28, at 8.

Finally, originalists argue that the framers did intend that their approach be followed in constitutional interpretation. Robert Bork declared that "not even a scintilla of evidence supports the argument that the framers and the ratifiers of the various amendments intended the judiciary to develop new individual rights, which correspondingly create new disabilities for democratic government.... If the framers really intended to delegate to judges the function of creating new rights by the method of moral philosophy, one would expect they would say so."[55]

Conclusion

This discussion of constitutional interpretation, of course, is not a comprehensive presentation of the arguments on either side of the debate but rather a summary of some of the most frequently advanced points. The debate over how the Constitution should be interpreted will continue as long as there is a Constitution. Yet the issue of how the Constitution should be interpreted is crucial and manifests itself expressly or implicitly in all areas of constitutional law and all of the topics discussed in this book.

District of Columbia v. Heller

128 S. Ct. 2783 (2008)

Justice SCALIA delivered the opinion of the Court.

We consider whether a District of Columbia prohibition on the possession of usable handguns in the home violates the Second Amendment to the Constitution.

I

The District of Columbia generally prohibits the possession of handguns. It is a crime to carry an unregistered firearm, and the registration of handguns is prohibited. See D.C.Code §§7-2501.01(12), 7-2502.01(a), 7-2502.02(a)(4) (2001). Wholly apart from that prohibition, no person may carry a handgun without a license, but the chief of police may issue licenses for 1-year periods. See §§22-4504(a), 22-4506. District of Columbia law also requires residents to keep their lawfully owned firearms, such as registered long guns, "unloaded and dissembled or bound by a trigger lock or similar device" unless they are located in a place of business or are being used for lawful recreational activities. See §7-2507.02.[56]

Respondent Dick Heller is a D.C. special police officer authorized to carry a handgun while on duty at the Federal Judicial Center. He applied for a registration certificate for a handgun that he wished to keep at home, but the District refused. He thereafter filed a lawsuit in the Federal District Court for the District

---

[55] Robert H. Bork, The Impossibility of Finding Welfare Rights in the Constitution, 1979 Wash. U. L.Q. 695, 697.

[56] There are minor exceptions to all of these prohibitions, none of which is relevant here. [Footnote by the Court.]

of Columbia seeking, on Second Amendment grounds, to enjoin the city from enforcing the bar on the registration of handguns, the licensing requirement insofar as it prohibits the carrying of a firearm in the home without a license, and the trigger-lock requirement insofar as it prohibits the use of "functional firearms within the home."

II

We turn first to the meaning of the Second Amendment.

A

The Second Amendment provides: "A well regulated Militia, being necessary to the security of a free State, the right of the people to keep and bear Arms, shall not be infringed." In interpreting this text, we are guided by the principle that "[t]he Constitution was written to be understood by the voters; its words and phrases were used in their normal and ordinary as distinguished from technical meaning."

The two sides in this case have set out very different interpretations of the Amendment. Petitioners and today's dissenting Justices believe that it protects only the right to possess and carry a firearm in connection with militia service. Respondent argues that it protects an individual right to possess a firearm unconnected with service in a militia, and to use that arm for traditionally lawful purposes, such as self-defense within the home.

The Second Amendment is naturally divided into two parts: its prefatory clause and its operative clause. The former does not limit the latter grammatically, but rather announces a purpose. The Amendment could be rephrased, "Because a well regulated Militia is necessary to the security of a free State, the right of the people to keep and bear Arms shall not be infringed." Although this structure of the Second Amendment is unique in our Constitution, other legal documents of the founding era, particularly individual-rights provisions of state constitutions, commonly included a prefatory statement of purpose.

Logic demands that there be a link between the stated purpose and the command. The Second Amendment would be nonsensical if it read, "A well regulated Militia, being necessary to the security of a free State, the right of the people to petition for redress of grievances shall not be infringed." But apart from that clarifying function, a prefatory clause does not limit or expand the scope of the operative clause.

1. Operative Clause

a. "Right of the People." The first salient feature of the operative clause is that it codifies a "right of the people." The unamended Constitution and the Bill of Rights use the phrase "right of the people" two other times, in the First Amendment's Assembly-and-Petition Clause and in the Fourth Amendment's Search-and-Seizure Clause. The Ninth Amendment uses very similar terminology. All three of these instances unambiguously refer to individual rights, not "collective" rights, or rights that may be exercised only through participation in some corporate body.

What is more, in all six other provisions of the Constitution that mention "the people," the term unambiguously refers to all members of the political community, not an unspecified subset. This contrasts markedly with the phrase "the militia" in the prefatory clause. As we will describe below, the "militia" in colonial America consisted of a subset of "the people" — those who were male, able bodied, and within a certain age range. Reading the Second Amendment as protecting only the right to "keep and bear Arms" in an organized militia therefore fits poorly with the operative clause's description of the holder of that right as "the people."

We start therefore with a strong presumption that the Second Amendment right is exercised individually and belongs to all Americans.

b. "Keep and bear Arms." We move now from the holder of the right — "the people" — to the substance of the right: "to keep and bear Arms."

Before addressing the verbs "keep" and "bear," we interpret their object: "Arms." The 18th-century meaning is no different from the meaning today. The 1773 edition of Samuel Johnson's dictionary defined "arms" as "weapons of offence, or armour of defence." 1 Dictionary of the English Language 107 (4th ed.) (hereinafter Johnson). Timothy Cunningham's important 1771 legal dictionary defined "arms" as "any thing that a man wears for his defence, or takes into his hands, or useth in wrath to cast at or strike another." 1 A New and Complete Law Dictionary (1771). The term was applied, then as now, to weapons that were not specifically designed for military use and were not employed in a military capacity.

Some have made the argument, bordering on the frivolous, that only those arms in existence in the 18th century are protected by the Second Amendment. We do not interpret constitutional rights that way. Just as the First Amendment protects modern forms of communications, and the Fourth Amendment applies to modern forms of search, the Second Amendment extends, prima facie, to all instruments that constitute bearable arms, even those that were not in existence at the time of the founding.

We turn to the phrases "keep arms" and "bear arms." Johnson defined "keep" as, most relevantly, "[t]o retain; not to lose," and "[t]o have in custody." Webster defined it as "[t]o hold; to retain in one's power or possession." No party has apprised us of an idiomatic meaning of "keep Arms." Thus, the most natural reading of "keep Arms" in the Second Amendment is to "have weapons."

The phrase "keep arms" was not prevalent in the written documents of the founding period that we have found, but there are a few examples, all of which favor viewing the right to "keep Arms" as an individual right unconnected with militia service.

From our review of founding-era sources, we conclude that this natural meaning was also the meaning that "bear arms" had in the 18th century. In numerous instances, "bear arms" was unambiguously used to refer to the carrying of weapons outside of an organized militia. The most prominent examples are those most relevant to the Second Amendment: Nine state constitutional provisions written in the 18th century or the first two decades of the 19th, which enshrined a right of citizens to "bear arms in defense of themselves and the state" or "bear arms in defense of himself and the state." It is clear from those formulations that "bear arms" did not refer only to carrying a weapon in an organized military unit.

Justice Stevens places great weight on James Madison's inclusion of a conscientious-objector clause in his original draft of the Second Amendment: "but no person religiously scrupulous of bearing arms, shall be compelled to render military service in person." He argues that this clause establishes that the drafters of the Second Amendment intended "bear Arms" to refer only to military service. It is always perilous to derive the meaning of an adopted provision from another provision deleted in the drafting process. In any case, what Justice Stevens would conclude from the deleted provision does not follow. It was not meant to exempt from military service those who objected to going to war but had no scruples about personal gunfights. Quakers opposed the use of arms not just for militia service, but for any violent purpose whatsoever — so much so that Quaker frontiersmen were forbidden to use arms to defend their families, even though "[i]n such circumstances the temptation to seize a hunting rifle or knife in self-defense . . . must sometimes have been almost overwhelming." Thus, the most natural interpretation of Madison's deleted text is that those opposed to carrying weapons for potential violent confrontation would not be "compelled to render military service," in which such carrying would be required.

Finally, Justice Stevens suggests that "keep and bear Arms" was some sort of term of art, presumably akin to "hue and cry" or "cease and desist." This suggestion usefully evades the problem that there is no evidence whatsoever to support a military reading of "keep arms." And even if "keep and bear Arms" were a unitary phrase, we find no evidence that it bore a military meaning. Although the phrase was not at all common (which would be unusual for a term of art), we have found instances of its use with a clearly nonmilitary connotation.

c. Meaning of the Operative Clause. Putting all of these textual elements together, we find that they guarantee the individual right to possess and carry weapons in case of confrontation. This meaning is strongly confirmed by the historical background of the Second Amendment. We look to this because it has always been widely understood that the Second Amendment, like the First and Fourth Amendments, codified a pre-existing right. The very text of the Second Amendment implicitly recognizes the pre-existence of the right and declares only that it "shall not be infringed."

There seems to us no doubt, on the basis of both text and history, that the Second Amendment conferred an individual right to keep and bear arms. Of course the right was not unlimited, just as the First Amendment's right of free speech was not. Thus, we do not read the Second Amendment to protect the right of citizens to carry arms for any sort of confrontation, just as we do not read the First Amendment to protect the right of citizens to speak for any purpose. Before turning to limitations upon the individual right, however, we must determine whether the prefatory clause of the Second Amendment comports with our interpretation of the operative clause.

2.   Prefatory Clause

The prefatory clause reads: "A well regulated Militia, being necessary to the security of a free State. . . ."

a. "Well-Regulated Militia." In United States v. Miller (1939), we explained that "the Militia comprised all males physically capable of acting in concert for the common defense." That definition comports with founding-era sources.

Petitioners take a seemingly narrower view of the militia, stating that "[m]ilitias are the state- and congressionally-regulated military forces described in the Militia Clauses (art. I, §8, cls. 15-16)." Although we agree with petitioners' interpretive assumption that "militia" means the same thing in Article I and the Second Amendment, we believe that petitioners identify the wrong thing, namely, the organized militia. Unlike armies and navies, which Congress is given the power to create ("to raise . . . Armies"; "to provide . . . a Navy," Art. I, §8, cls. 12-13), the militia is assumed by Article I already to be in existence. Congress is given the power to "provide for calling forth the militia," §8, cl. 15; and the power not to create, but to "organiz[e]" it — and not to organize "a" militia, which is what one would expect if the militia were to be a federal creation, but to organize "the" militia, connoting a body already in existence, ibid., cl. 16. This is fully consistent with the ordinary definition of the militia as all able-bodied men.

Finally, the adjective "well-regulated" implies nothing more than the imposition of proper discipline and training.

b. "Security of a Free State." The phrase "security of a free state" meant "security of a free polity," not security of each of the several States as the dissent below argued. There are many reasons why the militia was thought to be "necessary to the security of a free state." First, of course, it is useful in repelling invasions and suppressing insurrections. Second, it renders large standing armies unnecessary — an argument that Alexander Hamilton made in favor of federal control over the militia. Third, when the able-bodied men of a nation are trained in arms and organized, they are better able to resist tyranny.

3.   Relationship between Prefatory Clause and Operative Clause

We reach the question, then: Does the preface fit with an operative clause that creates an individual right to keep and bear arms? It fits perfectly, once one knows the history that the founding generation knew and that we have described above. That history showed that the way tyrants had eliminated a militia consisting of all the able-bodied men was not by banning the militia but simply by taking away the people's arms, enabling a select militia or standing army to suppress political opponents. This is what had occurred in England that prompted codification of the right to have arms in the English Bill of Rights.

It is therefore entirely sensible that the Second Amendment's prefatory clause announces the purpose for which the right was codified: to prevent elimination of the militia. The prefatory clause does not suggest that preserving the militia was the only reason Americans valued the ancient right; most undoubtedly thought it even more important for self-defense and hunting. But the threat that the new Federal Government would destroy the citizens' militia by taking away their arms was the reason that right — unlike some other English rights — was codified in a written Constitution. Justice Breyer's assertion that individual self-defense is merely a "subsidiary interest" of the right to keep and bear arms is profoundly mistaken. He bases that assertion solely upon the prologue — but that can only show that self-defense had little to do with the right's codification; it was the central component of the right itself.

B

Our interpretation is confirmed by analogous arms-bearing rights in state constitutions that preceded and immediately followed adoption of the Second Amendment. Four States adopted analogues to the Federal Second Amendment in the period between independence and the ratification of the Bill of Rights. Two of them — Pennsylvania and Vermont — clearly adopted individual rights unconnected to militia service.

North Carolina also codified a right to bear arms in 1776. Many colonial statutes required individual arms-bearing for public-safety reasons — such as the 1770 Georgia law that "for the security and defence of this province from internal dangers and insurrections" required those men who qualified for militia duty individually "to carry fire arms" "to places of public worship."

The 1780 Massachusetts Constitution presented another variation on the theme: "The people have a right to keep and to bear arms for the common defence. . . ." Once again, if one gives narrow meaning to the phrase "common defence" this can be thought to limit the right to the bearing of arms in a state-organized military force. But once again the State's highest court thought otherwise. Writing for the court in an 1825 libel case, Chief Justice Parker wrote: "The liberty of the press was to be unrestrained, but he who used it was to be responsible in cases of its abuse; like the right to keep fire arms, which does not protect him who uses them for annoyance or destruction."

We therefore believe that the most likely reading of all four of these pre- Second Amendment state constitutional provisions is that they secured an individual right to bear arms for defensive purposes.

Between 1789 and 1820, nine States adopted Second Amendment analogues. The historical narrative that petitioners must endorse would thus treat the Federal Second Amendment as an odd outlier, protecting a right unknown in state constitutions or at English common law, based on little more than an overreading of the prefatory clause.

C

Justice Stevens relies on the drafting history of the Second Amendment — the various proposals in the state conventions and the debates in Congress. It is dubious to rely on such history to interpret a text that was widely understood to codify a pre-existing right, rather than to fashion a new one. But even assuming that this legislative history is relevant, Justice Stevens flatly misreads the historical record.

It is true, as Justice Stevens says, that there was concern that the Federal Government would abolish the institution of the state militia. That concern found expression, however, not in the various Second Amendment precursors proposed in the State conventions, but in separate structural provisions that would have given the States concurrent and seemingly nonpre-emptible authority to organize, discipline, and arm the militia when the Federal Government failed to do so.

D

We now address how the Second Amendment was interpreted from immediately after its ratification through the end of the 19th century. Three important founding-era legal scholars interpreted the Second Amendment in published writings. All three understood it to protect an individual right unconnected with militia service. We have found only one early 19th-century commentator who clearly conditioned the right to keep and bear arms upon service in the militia — and he recognized that the prevailing view was to the contrary.

The 19th-century cases that interpreted the Second Amendment universally support an individual right unconnected to militia service. Many early 19th- century state cases indicated that the Second Amendment right to bear arms was an individual right unconnected to militia service, though subject to certain restrictions.

In the aftermath of the Civil War, there was an outpouring of discussion of the Second Amendment in Congress and in public discourse, as people debated whether and how to secure constitutional rights for newly free slaves. Since those discussions took place 75 years after the ratification of the Second Amendment, they do not provide as much insight into its original meaning as earlier sources. Yet those born and educated in the early 19th century faced a widespread effort to limit arms ownership by a large number of citizens; their understanding of the origins and continuing significance of the Amendment is instructive.

Blacks were routinely disarmed by Southern States after the Civil War. Those who opposed these injustices frequently stated that they infringed blacks' constitutional right to keep and bear arms. Needless to say, the claim was not that blacks were being prohibited from carrying arms in an organized state militia. It was plainly the understanding in the post-Civil War Congress that the Second Amendment protected an individual right to use arms for self-defense. Every late-19th-century legal scholar that we have read interpreted the Second Amendment to secure an individual right unconnected with militia service.

E

We now ask whether any of our precedents forecloses the conclusions we have reached about the meaning of the Second Amendment. Justice Stevens places overwhelming reliance upon this Court's decision in United States v. Miller (1939). *Miller* did not hold that and cannot possibly be read to have held that. The judgment in the case upheld against a Second Amendment challenge two men's federal convictions for transporting an unregistered short-barreled shotgun in interstate commerce, in violation of the National Firearms Act. It is entirely clear that the Court's basis for saying that the Second Amendment did not apply was not that the defendants were "bear[ing] arms" not "for . . . military purposes" but for "nonmilitary use." Rather, it was that the type of weapon at issue was not eligible for Second Amendment protection. Beyond that, the opinion provided no explanation of the content of the right.

This holding is not only consistent with, but positively suggests, that the Second Amendment confers an individual right to keep and bear arms (though only arms that "have some reasonable relationship to the preservation or efficiency of a well regulated militia"). Had the Court believed that the Second Amendment protects only those serving in the militia, it would have been odd to examine the character of the weapon rather than simply note that the two crooks were not militiamen. *Miller* stands only for the proposition that the Second Amendment right, whatever its nature, extends only to certain types of weapons.

It is particularly wrongheaded to read *Miller* for more than what it said, because the case did not even purport to be a thorough examination of the Second Amendment. The respondent made no appearance in the case, neither filing a brief nor appearing at oral argument; the Court heard from no one but the Government.

We conclude that nothing in our precedents forecloses our adoption of the original understanding of the Second Amendment.

III

Like most rights, the right secured by the Second Amendment is not unlimited. From Blackstone through the 19th-century cases, commentators and courts routinely explained that the right was not a right to keep and carry any weapon whatsoever in any manner whatsoever and for whatever purpose. For example, the majority of the 19th-century courts to consider the question held that prohibitions on carrying concealed weapons were lawful under the Second Amendment or state analogues. Although we do not undertake an exhaustive historical analysis today of the full scope of the Second Amendment, nothing in our opinion should be taken to cast doubt on longstanding prohibitions on the possession of firearms by felons and the mentally ill, or laws forbidding the carrying of firearms in sensitive places such as schools and government buildings, or laws imposing conditions and qualifications on the commercial sale of arms.

We also recognize another important limitation on the right to keep and carry arms. *Miller* said, as we have explained, that the sorts of weapons protected were those "in common use at the time." We think that limitation is fairly supported by the historical tradition of prohibiting the carrying of "dangerous and unusual weapons."

It may be objected that if weapons that are most useful in military service — M-16 rifles and the like — may be banned, then the Second Amendment right is completely detached from the prefatory clause. But as we have said, the conception of the militia at the time of the Second Amendment's ratification was the body of all citizens capable of military service, who would bring the sorts of lawful weapons that they possessed at home to militia duty. It may well be true today that a militia, to be as effective as militias in the 18th century, would require sophisticated arms that are highly unusual in society at large. Indeed, it may be true that no amount of small arms could be useful against modern-day bombers and tanks. But the fact that modern developments have limited the degree of fit between the prefatory clause and the protected right cannot change our interpretation of the right.

IV

We turn finally to the law at issue here. As we have said, the law totally bans handgun possession in the home. It also requires that any lawful firearm in the home be disassembled or bound by a trigger lock at all times, rendering it inoperable.

As the quotations earlier in this opinion demonstrate, the inherent right of self-defense has been central to the Second Amendment right. The handgun ban amounts to a prohibition of an entire class of "arms" that is overwhelmingly chosen by American society for that lawful purpose. The prohibition extends, moreover, to the home, where the need for defense of self, family, and property is most acute. Under any of the standards of scrutiny that we have applied to enumerated constitutional rights, banning from the home "the most preferred firearm in the nation to 'keep' and use for protection of one's home and family," would fail constitutional muster.

We must also address the District's requirement (as applied to respondent's handgun) that firearms in the home be rendered and kept inoperable at all times. This makes it impossible for citizens to use them for the core lawful purpose of self-defense and is hence unconstitutional. The District argues that we should interpret this element of the statute to contain an exception for self-defense. But we think that is precluded by the unequivocal text, and by the presence of certain other enumerated exceptions: "Except for law enforcement personnel . . . , each registrant shall keep any firearm in his possession unloaded and disassembled or bound by a trigger lock or similar device unless such firearm is kept at his place of business, or while being used for lawful recreational purposes within the District of Columbia." D.C.Code §7-2507.02. The nonexistence of a self-defense exception is also suggested by the D.C. Court of Appeals' statement that the statute forbids residents to use firearms to stop intruders.

Justice Breyer moves on to make a broad jurisprudential point: He criticizes us for declining to establish a level of scrutiny for evaluating Second Amendment restrictions. He proposes, explicitly at least, none of the traditionally expressed levels (strict scrutiny, intermediate scrutiny, rational basis), but rather a judge-empowering "interest-balancing inquiry" that "asks whether the statute burdens a protected interest in a way or to an extent that is out of proportion to the statute's salutary effects upon other important governmental interests."

We know of no other enumerated constitutional right whose core protection has been subjected to a freestanding "interest-balancing" approach. The very enumeration of the right takes out of the hands of government — even the Third Branch of Government — the power to decide on a case-by-case basis whether the right is really worth insisting upon. A constitutional guarantee subject to future judges' assessments of its usefulness is no constitutional guarantee at all.

Constitutional rights are enshrined with the scope they were understood to have when the people adopted them, whether or not future legislatures or (yes) even future judges think that scope too broad. We would not apply an "interest-balancing" approach to the prohibition of a peaceful neo-Nazi march through Skokie. The First Amendment contains the freedom-of-speech guarantee that the people ratified, which included exceptions for obscenity, libel, and disclosure of state secrets, but not for the expression of extremely unpopular and wrong-headed views. The Second Amendment is no different. Like the First, it is the very product of an interest-balancing by the people — which Justice Breyer would now conduct for them anew. And whatever else it leaves to future evaluation, it surely elevates above all other interests the right of law-abiding, responsible citizens to use arms in defense of hearth and home.

Justice Breyer chides us for leaving so many applications of the right to keep and bear arms in doubt, and for not providing extensive historical justification for those regulations of the right that we describe as permissible. But since this case represents this Court's first in-depth examination of the Second Amendment, one should not expect it to clarify the entire field. And there will be time enough to expound upon the historical justifications for the exceptions we have mentioned if and when those exceptions come before us.

In sum, we hold that the District's ban on handgun possession in the home violates the Second Amendment, as does its prohibition against rendering any lawful firearm in the home operable for the purpose of immediate self-defense. Assuming that Heller is not disqualified from the exercise of Second Amendment rights, the District must permit him to register his handgun and must issue him a license to carry it in the home.

* * *

We are aware of the problem of handgun violence in this country, and we take seriously the concerns raised by the many amici who believe that prohibition of handgun ownership is a solution. The Constitution leaves the District of Columbia a variety of tools for combating that problem, including some measures regulating handguns. But the enshrinement of constitutional rights necessarily takes certain policy choices off the table. These include the absolute prohibition of handguns held and used for self-defense in the home. Undoubtedly some think that the Second Amendment is outmoded in a society where our standing army is the pride of our Nation, where well-trained police forces provide personal security, and where gun violence is a serious problem. That is perhaps debatable, but what is not debatable is that it is not the role of this Court to pronounce the Second Amendment extinct.

Justice STEVENS, with whom Justice SOUTER, Justice GINSBURG, and Justice BREYER join, dissenting.

The question presented by this case is not whether the Second Amendment protects a "collective right" or an "individual right." Surely it protects a right that can be enforced by individuals. But a conclusion that the Second Amendment protects an individual right does not tell us anything about the scope of that right.

Guns are used to hunt, for self-defense, to commit crimes, for sporting activities, and to perform military duties. The Second Amendment plainly does not protect the right to use a gun to rob a bank; it is equally clear that it does encompass the right to use weapons for certain military purposes. Whether it also protects the right to possess and use guns for nonmilitary purposes like hunting and personal self-defense is the question presented by this case. The text of the Amendment, its history, and our decision in United States v. Miller (1939), provide a clear answer to that question.

The Second Amendment was adopted to protect the right of the people of each of the several States to maintain a well-regulated militia. It was a response to concerns raised during the ratification of the Constitution that the power of Congress to disarm the state militias and create a national standing army posed an intolerable threat to the sovereignty of the several States. Neither the text of the Amendment nor the arguments advanced by its proponents evidenced the slightest interest in limiting any legislature's authority to regulate private civilian uses of firearms. Specifically, there is no indication that the Framers of the Amendment intended to enshrine the common-law right of self-defense in the Constitution.

In 1934, Congress enacted the National Firearms Act, the first major federal firearms law. Upholding a conviction under that Act, this Court held that, "[i]n the absence of any evidence tending to show that possession or use of a 'shotgun having a barrel of less than eighteen inches in length' at this time has some reasonable relationship to the preservation or efficiency of a well regulated militia, we cannot say that the Second Amendment guarantees the right to keep and bear such an instrument." United States v. Miller. The view of the Amendment we took in *Miller* — that it protects the right to keep and bear arms for certain military purposes, but that it does not curtail the Legislature's power to regulate the nonmilitary use and ownership of weapons — is both the most natural reading of the Amendment's text and the interpretation most faithful to the history of its adoption.

Since our decision in *Miller*, hundreds of judges have relied on the view of the Amendment we endorsed there; we ourselves affirmed it in 1980. See Lewis v. United States (1980). No new evidence has surfaced since 1980 supporting the view that the Amendment was intended to curtail the power of Congress to regulate civilian use or misuse of weapons. Indeed, a review of the drafting history of the Amendment demonstrates that its Framers rejected proposals that would have broadened its coverage to include such uses.

Even if the textual and historical arguments on both sides of the issue were evenly balanced, respect for the well-settled views of all of our predecessors on this Court, and for the rule of law itself, would prevent most jurists from endorsing such a dramatic upheaval in the law.

In this dissent I shall first explain why our decision in *Miller* was faithful to the text of the Second Amendment and the purposes revealed in its drafting history. I shall then comment on the postratification history of the Amendment, which makes abundantly clear that the Amendment should not be interpreted as limiting the authority of Congress to regulate the use or possession of firearms for purely civilian purposes.

I

The text of the Second Amendment is brief. It provides: "A well regulated Militia, being necessary to the security of a free State, the right of the people to keep and bear Arms, shall not be infringed."

Three portions of that text merit special focus: the introductory language defining the Amendment's purpose, the class of persons encompassed within its reach, and the unitary nature of the right that it protects.

"A well regulated Militia, being necessary to the security of a free State"

The preamble to the Second Amendment makes three important points. It identifies the preservation of the militia as the Amendment's purpose; it explains that the militia is necessary to the security of a free State; and it recognizes that the militia must be "well regulated." In all three respects it is comparable to provisions in several State Declarations of Rights that were adopted roughly contemporaneously with the Declaration of Independence. Those state provisions highlight the importance members of the founding generation attached to the maintenance of state militias; they also underscore the profound fear shared by many in that era of the dangers posed by standing armies.

The preamble thus both sets forth the object of the Amendment and informs the meaning of the remainder of its text. Such text should not be treated as mere surplusage, for "[i]t cannot be presumed that any clause in the constitution is intended to be without effect." Marbury v. Madison (1803).

The Court today tries to denigrate the importance of this clause of the Amendment by beginning its analysis with the Amendment's operative provision and returning to the preamble merely "to ensure that our reading of the operative clause is consistent with the announced purpose." That is not how this Court ordinarily reads such texts, and it is not how the preamble would have been viewed at the time the Amendment was adopted.

"The right of the people"

The centerpiece of the Court's textual argument is its insistence that the words "the people" as used in the Second Amendment must have the same meaning, and protect the same class of individuals, as when they are used in the First and Fourth Amendments. According to the Court, in all three provisions — as well as the Constitution's preamble, "the term unambiguously refers to all members of the political community, not an unspecified subset." But the Court itself reads the Second Amendment to protect a "subset" significantly narrower than the class of persons protected by the First and Fourth Amendments; when it finally drills down on the substantive meaning of the Second Amendment, the Court limits the protected class to "law-abiding, responsible citizens." But the class of persons protected by the First and Fourth Amendments is not so limited; for even felons (and presumably irresponsible citizens as well) may invoke the protections of those constitutional provisions. The Court offers no way to harmonize its conflicting pronouncements.

"To keep and bear Arms"

Although the Court's discussion of these words treats them as two "phrases" — as if they read "to keep" and "to bear" — they describe a unitary right: to possess arms if needed for military purposes and to use them in conjunction with military activities.

As a threshold matter, it is worth pausing to note an oddity in the Court's interpretation of "to keep and bear arms." Unlike the Court of Appeals, the Court does not read that phrase to create a right to possess arms for "lawful, private purposes." Instead, the Court limits the Amendment's protection to the right "to possess and carry weapons in case of confrontation." No party or amicus urged this interpretation; the Court appears to have fashioned it out of whole cloth. But although this novel limitation lacks support in the text of the Amendment, the Amendment's text does justify a different limitation: the "right to keep and bear arms" protects only a right to possess and use firearms in connection with service in a state-organized militia.

The term "bear arms" is a familiar idiom; when used unadorned by any additional words, its meaning is "to serve as a soldier, do military service, fight." 1 Oxford English Dictionary 634 (2d ed. 1989). It is derived from the Latin arma ferre, which, translated literally, means "to bear [ferre] war equipment [arma]."

The Amendment's use of the term "keep" in no way contradicts the military meaning conveyed by the phrase "bear arms" and the Amendment's preamble. To the contrary, a number of state militia laws in effect at the time of the Second Amendment's drafting used the term "keep" to describe the requirement that militia members store their arms at their homes, ready to be used for service when necessary. The Virginia military law, for example, ordered that "every one of the said officers, non-commissioned officers, and privates, shall constantly keep the aforesaid arms, accoutrements, and ammunition, ready to be produced whenever called for by his commanding officer." "[K]eep and bear arms" thus perfectly describes the responsibilities of a framing-era militia member.

* * *

When each word in the text is given full effect, the Amendment is most naturally read to secure to the people a right to use and possess arms in conjunction with service in a well-regulated militia. So far as appears, no more than that was contemplated by its drafters or is encompassed within its terms. Even if the meaning of the text were genuinely susceptible to more than one interpretation, the burden would remain on those advocating a departure from the purpose identified in the preamble and from settled law to come forward with persuasive new arguments or evidence. The textual analysis offered by respondent and embraced by the Court falls far short of sustaining that heavy burden.

Indeed, not a word in the constitutional text even arguably supports the Court's overwrought and novel description of the Second Amendment as "elevat

[ing] above all other interests" "the right of law-abiding, responsible citizens to use arms in defense of hearth and home."

II

The proper allocation of military power in the new Nation was an issue of central concern for the Framers. The compromises they ultimately reached, reflected in Article I's Militia Clauses and the Second Amendment, represent quintessential examples of the Framers' "splitting the atom of sovereignty."

It is strikingly significant that Madison's first draft omitted any mention of nonmilitary use or possession of weapons. Rather, his original draft repeated the essence of the two proposed amendments sent by Virginia, combining the substance of the two provisions succinctly into one, which read: "The right of the people to keep and bear arms shall not be infringed; a well armed, and well regulated militia being the best security of a free country; but no person religiously scrupulous of bearing arms, shall be compelled to render military service in person."

Madison's decision to model the Second Amendment on the distinctly military Virginia proposal is therefore revealing, since it is clear that he considered and rejected formulations that would have unambiguously protected civilian uses of firearms. When Madison prepared his first draft, and when that draft was debated and modified, it is reasonable to assume that all participants in the drafting process were fully aware of the other formulations that would have protected civilian use and possession of weapons and that their choice to craft the Amendment as they did represented a rejection of those alternative formulations.

Madison's initial inclusion of an exemption for conscientious objectors sheds revelatory light on the purpose of the Amendment. It confirms an intent to describe a duty as well as a right, and it unequivocally identifies the military character of both. The objections voiced to the conscientious-objector clause only confirm the central meaning of the text.

The history of the adoption of the Amendment thus describes an overriding concern about the potential threat to state sovereignty that a federal standing army would pose, and a desire to protect the States' militias as the means by which to guard against that danger. But state militias could not effectively check the prospect of a federal standing army so long as Congress retained the power to disarm them, and so a guarantee against such disarmament was needed. As we explained in *Miller*: "With obvious purpose to assure the continuation and render possible the effectiveness of such forces the declaration and guarantee of the Second Amendment were made. It must be interpreted and applied with that end in view." The evidence plainly refutes the claim that the Amendment was motivated by the Framers' fears that Congress might act to regulate any civilian uses of weapons. And even if the historical record were genuinely ambiguous, the burden would remain on the parties advocating a change in the law to introduce facts or arguments "'newly ascertained[]'"; the Court is unable to identify any such facts or arguments.

[IV]

The Court concludes its opinion by declaring that it is not the proper role of this Court to change the meaning of rights "enshrine[d]" in the Constitution. But the right the Court announces was not "enshrined" in the Second Amendment by the Framers; it is the product of today's law-changing decision. The majority's exegesis has utterly failed to establish that as a matter of text or history, "the right of law-abiding, responsible citizens to use arms in defense of hearth and home" is "elevate[d] above all other interests" by the Second Amendment.

Until today, it has been understood that legislatures may regulate the civilian use and misuse of firearms so long as they do not interfere with the preservation of a well-regulated militia. The Court's announcement of a new constitutional right to own and use firearms for private purposes upsets that settled understanding, but leaves for future cases the formidable task of defining the scope of permissible regulations. Today judicial craftsmen have confidently asserted that a policy choice that denies a "law-abiding, responsible citize[n]" the right to keep and use weapons in the home for self-defense is "off the table." Given the presumption that most citizens are law abiding, and the reality that the need to defend oneself may suddenly arise in a host of locations outside the home, I fear that the District's policy choice may well be just the first of an unknown number of dominoes to be knocked off the table.

I do not know whether today's decision will increase the labor of federal judges to the "breaking point" envisioned by Justice Cardozo, but it will surely give rise to a far more active judicial role in making vitally important national policy decisions than was envisioned at any time in the 18th, 19th, or 20th centuries.

The Court properly disclaims any interest in evaluating the wisdom of the specific policy choice challenged in this case, but it fails to pay heed to a far more important policy choice — the choice made by the Framers themselves. The Court would have us believe that over 200 years ago, the Framers made a choice to limit the tools available to elected officials wishing to regulate civilian uses of weapons, and to authorize this Court to use the common-law process of case-by-case judicial lawmaking to define the contours of acceptable gun control policy. Absent compelling evidence that is nowhere to be found in the Court's opinion, I could not possibly conclude that the Framers made such a choice.

Justice BREYER, with whom Justice STEVENS, Justice SOUTER, and Justice GINSBURG join, dissenting.

We must decide whether a District of Columbia law that prohibits the possession of handguns in the home violates the Second Amendment. The majority, relying upon its view that the Second Amendment seeks to protect a right of personal self-defense, holds that this law violates that Amendment. In my view, it does not.

I

The majority's conclusion is wrong for two independent reasons. The first reason is that set forth by Justice Stevens — namely, that the Second Amendment protects militia-related, not self-defense-related, interests. These two interests are sometimes intertwined. To assure 18th-century citizens that they could keep arms for militia purposes would necessarily have allowed them to keep arms that they could have used for self-defense as well. But self-defense alone, detached from any militia-related objective, is not the Amendment's concern.

The second independent reason is that the protection the Amendment provides is not absolute. The Amendment permits government to regulate the interests that it serves. Thus, irrespective of what those interests are — whether they do or do not include an independent interest in self-defense — the majority's view cannot be correct unless it can show that the District's regulation is unreasonable or inappropriate in Second Amendment terms. This the majority cannot do.

In respect to the first independent reason, I agree with Justice Stevens, and I join his opinion. In this opinion I shall focus upon the second reason. I shall show that the District's law is consistent with the Second Amendment even if that Amendment is interpreted as protecting a wholly separate interest in individual self-defense. That is so because the District's regulation, which focuses upon the presence of handguns in high-crime urban areas, represents a permissible legislative response to a serious, indeed life-threatening, problem.

Thus I here assume that one objective (but, as the majority concedes, not the primary objective) of those who wrote the Second Amendment was to help assure citizens that they would have arms available for purposes of self-defense. Even so, a legislature could reasonably conclude that the law will advance goals of great public importance, namely, saving lives, preventing injury, and reducing crime. The law is tailored to the urban crime problem in that it is local in scope and thus affects only a geographic area both limited in size and entirely urban; the law concerns handguns, which are specially linked to urban gun deaths and injuries, and which are the overwhelmingly favorite weapon of armed criminals; and at the same time, the law imposes a burden upon gun owners that seems proportionately no greater than restrictions in existence at the time the Second Amendment was adopted. In these circumstances, the District's law falls within the zone that the Second Amendment leaves open to regulation by legislatures.

[II]

I therefore begin by asking a process-based question: How is a court to determine whether a particular firearm regulation (here, the District's restriction on handguns) is consistent with the Second Amendment? What kind of constitutional standard should the court use? How high a protective hurdle does the Amendment erect?

The question matters. The majority is wrong when it says that the District's law is unconstitutional "[u]nder any of the standards of scrutiny that we have applied to enumerated constitutional rights." How could that be? It certainly would not be unconstitutional under, for example, a "rational basis" standard, which requires a court to uphold regulation so long as it bears a "rational relationship" to a "legitimate governmental purpose." The law at issue here, which in part seeks to prevent gun-related accidents, at least bears a "rational relationship" to that "legitimate" life-saving objective.

Respondent proposes that the Court adopt a "strict scrutiny" test, which would require reviewing with care each gun law to determine whether it is "narrowly tailored to achieve a compelling governmental interest." But the majority implicitly, and appropriately, rejects that suggestion by broadly approving a set of laws — prohibitions on concealed weapons, forfeiture by criminals of the Second Amendment right, prohibitions on firearms in certain locales, and governmental regulation of commercial firearm sales — whose constitutionality under a strict scrutiny standard would be far from clear.

Indeed, adoption of a true strict-scrutiny standard for evaluating gun regulations would be impossible. That is because almost every gun-control regulation will seek to advance (as the one here does) a "primary concern of every government — a concern for the safety and indeed the lives of its citizens." The Court has deemed that interest, as well as "the Government's general interest in preventing crime," to be "compelling," and the Court has in a wide variety of constitutional contexts found such public-safety concerns sufficiently forceful to justify restrictions on individual liberties. Thus, any attempt in theory to apply strict scrutiny to gun regulations will in practice turn into an interest-balancing inquiry, with the interests protected by the Second Amendment on one side and the governmental public-safety concerns on the other, the only question being whether the regulation at issue impermissibly burdens the former in the course of advancing the latter.

I would simply adopt such an interest-balancing inquiry explicitly. The fact that important interests lie on both sides of the constitutional equation suggests that review of gun-control regulation is not a context in which a court should effectively presume either constitutionality (as in rational-basis review) or unconstitutionality (as in strict scrutiny). Rather, "where a law significantly implicates competing constitutionally protected interests in complex ways," the Court generally asks whether the statute burdens a protected interest in a way or to an extent that is out of proportion to the statute's salutary effects upon other important governmental interests. Any answer would take account both of the statute's effects upon the competing interests and the existence of any clearly superior less restrictive alternative. Contrary to the majority's unsupported suggestion that this sort of "proportionality" approach is unprecedented, the Court has applied it in various constitutional contexts, including election-law cases, speech cases, and due process cases.

In applying this kind of standard the Court normally defers to a legislature's empirical judgment in matters where a legislature is likely to have greater expertise and greater institutional factfinding capacity. Nonetheless, a court, not a legislature, must make the ultimate constitutional conclusion, exercising its "independent judicial judgment" in light of the whole record to determine whether a law exceeds constitutional boundaries.

[III]

A

No one doubts the constitutional importance of the statute's basic objective, saving lives. But there is considerable debate about whether the District's statute helps to achieve that objective.

First, consider the facts as the legislature saw them when it adopted the District statute. As stated by the local council committee that recommended its adoption, the major substantive goal of the District's handgun restriction is "to reduce the potentiality for gun-related crimes and gun-related deaths from occurring within the District of Columbia." The committee concluded, on the basis of "extensive public hearings" and "lengthy research," that "[t]he easy availability of firearms in the United States has been a major factor contributing to the drastic increase in gun-related violence and crime over the past 40 years." It reported to the Council "startling statistics," regarding gun-related crime, accidents, and deaths, focusing particularly on the relation between handguns and crime and the proliferation of handguns within the District.

The committee informed the Council that guns were "responsible for 69 deaths in this country each day," for a total of "[a]pproximately 25,000 gun-deaths . . . each year," along with an additional 200,000 gun-related injuries. Three thousand of these deaths, the report stated, were accidental. A quarter of the victims in those accidental deaths were children under the age of 14. And according to the committee, "[f]or every intruder stopped by a homeowner with a firearm, there are 4 gun-related accidents within the home."

In respect to local crime, the committee observed that there were 285 murders in the District during 1974 — a record number. The committee report furthermore presented statistics strongly correlating handguns with crime. Of the 285 murders in the District in 1974, 155 were committed with handguns. Ibid. This did not appear to be an aberration, as the report revealed that "handguns [had been] used in roughly 54% of all murders" (and 87% of murders of law enforcement officers) nationwide over the preceding several years. Nor were handguns only linked to murders, as statistics showed that they were used in roughly 60% of robberies and 26% of assaults. "A crime committed with a pistol," the committee reported, "is 7 times more likely to be lethal than a crime committed with any other weapon." The committee furthermore presented statistics regarding the availability of handguns in the United States, and noted that they had "become easy for juveniles to obtain," even despite then-current District laws prohibiting juveniles from possessing them.

Next, consider the facts as a court must consider them looking at the matter as of today. Petitioners, and their amici, have presented us with more recent statistics that tell much the same story that the committee report told 30 years ago. At the least, they present nothing that would permit us to second-guess the Council in respect to the numbers of gun crimes, injuries, and deaths, or the role of handguns.

From 1993 to 1997, there were 180,533 firearm-related deaths in the United States, an average of over 36,000 per year. Over that same period there were an additional 411,800 nonfatal firearm-related injuries treated in U.S. hospitals, an average of over 82,000 per year. Of these, 62% resulted from assaults, 17% were unintentional, 6% were suicide attempts, 1% were legal interventions, and 13% were of unknown causes.

The statistics are particularly striking in respect to children and adolescents. In over one in every eight firearm-related deaths in 1997, the victim was someone under the age of 20. Firearm-related deaths account for 22.5% of all injury deaths between the ages of 1 and 19. More male teenagers die from firearms than from all natural causes combined. Persons under 25 accounted for 47% of hospital-treated firearm injuries between June 1, 1992, and May 31, 1993.

Handguns are involved in a majority of firearm deaths and injuries in the United States. From 1993 to 1997, 81% of firearm-homicide victims were killed by handgun. In the same period, for the 41% of firearm injuries for which the weapon type is known, 82% of them were from handguns. Firearm Injury and Death From Crime 4. And among children under the age of 20, handguns account for approximately 70% of all unintentional firearm-related injuries and deaths. In particular, 70% of all firearm-related teenage suicides in 1996 involved a handgun.

Handguns also appear to be a very popular weapon among criminals. In a 1997 survey of inmates who were armed during the crime for which they were incarcerated, 83.2% of state inmates and 86.7% of federal inmates said that they were armed with a handgun. Statistics further suggest that urban areas, such as the District, have different experiences with gun-related death, injury, and crime, than do less densely populated rural areas. A disproportionate amount of violent and property crimes occur in urban areas, and urban criminals are more likely than other offenders to use a firearm during the commission of a violent crime.

Finally, the linkage of handguns to firearms deaths and injuries appears to be much stronger in urban than in rural areas. "[S]tudies to date generally support the hypothesis that the greater number of rural gun deaths are from rifles or shotguns, whereas the greater number of urban gun deaths are from handguns."

Finally, consider the claim of respondent's amici that handgun bans cannot work; there are simply too many illegal guns already in existence for a ban on legal guns to make a difference. In a word, they claim that, given the urban sea of pre-existing legal guns, criminals can readily find arms regardless. Nonetheless, a legislature might respond, we want to make an effort to try to dry up that urban sea, drop by drop. And none of the studies can show that effort is not worthwhile.

In a word, the studies to which respondent's amici point raise policy-related questions. They succeed in proving that the District's predictive judgments are controversial. But they do not by themselves show that those judgments are incorrect; nor do they demonstrate a consensus, academic or otherwise, supporting that conclusion.

Thus, it is not surprising that the District and its amici support the District's handgun restriction with studies of their own. One in particular suggests that, statistically speaking, the District's law has indeed had positive life-saving effects. See Loftin, McDowall, Weirsema, & Cottey, Effects of Restrictive Licensing of Handguns on Homicide and Suicide in the District of Columbia, 325 New England J.

Med. 1615 (1991). Others suggest that firearm restrictions as a general matter reduce homicides, suicides, and accidents in the home. Still others suggest that the defensive uses of handguns are not as great in number as respondent's amici claim.

Respondent and his amici reply to these responses; and in doing so, they seek to discredit as methodologically flawed the studies and evidence relied upon by the District. The upshot is a set of studies and counterstudies that, at most, could leave a judge uncertain about the proper policy conclusion. But from respondent's perspective any such uncertainty is not good enough. That is because legislators, not judges, have primary responsibility for drawing policy conclusions from empirical fact. And, given that constitutional allocation of decisionmaking responsibility, the empirical evidence presented here is sufficient to allow a judge to reach a firm legal conclusion.

In particular this Court, in First Amendment cases applying intermediate scrutiny, has said that our "sole obligation" in reviewing a legislature's "predictive judgments" is "to assure that, in formulating its judgments," the legislature "has drawn reasonable inferences based on substantial evidence." And judges, looking at the evidence before us, should agree that the District legislature's predictive judgments satisfy that legal standard. That is to say, the District's judgment, while open to question, is nevertheless supported by "substantial evidence."

There is no cause here to depart from [that] standard for the District's decision represents the kind of empirically based judgment that legislatures, not courts, are best suited to make. In fact, deference to legislative judgment seems particularly appropriate here, where the judgment has been made by a local legislature, with particular knowledge of local problems and insight into appropriate local solutions.

For these reasons, I conclude that the District's statute properly seeks to further the sort of life-preserving and public-safety interests that the Court has called "compelling."

B

I next assess the extent to which the District's law burdens the interests that the Second Amendment seeks to protect. Respondent and his amici, as well as the majority, suggest that those interests include: (1) the preservation of a "well regulated Militia"; (2) safeguarding the use of firearms for sporting purposes, e.g., hunting and marksmanship; and (3) assuring the use of firearms for self-defense. For argument's sake, I shall consider all three of those interests here.

1

The District's statute burdens the Amendment's first and primary objective hardly at all. As previously noted, there is general agreement among the Members of the Court that the principal (if not the only) purpose of the Second Amendment is found in the Amendment's text: the preservation of a "well regulated Militia." What scant Court precedent there is on the Second Amendment teaches that the Amendment was adopted "[w]ith obvious purpose to assure the continuation and render possible the effectiveness of [militia] forces" and "must be interpreted and applied with that end in view."

2

The majority briefly suggests that the "right to keep and bear Arms" might encompass an interest in hunting. But in enacting the present provisions, the District sought "to take nothing away from sportsmen." And any inability of District residents to hunt near where they live has much to do with the jurisdiction's exclusively urban character and little to do with the District's firearm laws. For reasons similar to those I discussed in the preceding subsection — that the District's law does not prohibit possession of rifles or shotguns, and the presence of opportunities for sporting activities in nearby States — I reach a similar conclusion, namely, that the District's law burdens any sports-related or hunting-related objectives that the Amendment may protect little, or not at all.

3

The District's law does prevent a resident from keeping a loaded handgun in his home. And it consequently makes it more difficult for the householder to use the handgun for self-defense in the home against intruders, such as burglars. As the Court of Appeals noted, statistics suggest that handguns are the most popular weapon for self defense. To that extent the law burdens to some degree an interest in self-defense that for present purposes I have assumed the Amendment seeks to further.

C

In weighing needs and burdens, we must take account of the possibility that there are reasonable, but less restrictive alternatives. Are there other potential measures that might similarly promote the same goals while imposing lesser restrictions? Here I see none.

The reason there is no clearly superior, less restrictive alternative to the District's handgun ban is that the ban's very objective is to reduce significantly the number of handguns in the District, say, for example, by allowing a law enforcement officer immediately to assume that any handgun he sees is an illegal handgun. And there is no plausible way to achieve that objective other than to ban the guns.

D

The upshot is that the District's objectives are compelling; its predictive judgments as to its law's tendency to achieve those objectives are adequately supported; the law does impose a burden upon any self-defense interest that the Amendment seeks to secure; and there is no clear less restrictive alternative. I turn now to the final portion of the "permissible regulation" question: Does the District's law disproportionately burden Amendment-protected interests? Several considerations, taken together, convince me that it does not.

First, the District law is tailored to the life-threatening problems it attempts to address. The law concerns one class of weapons, handguns, leaving residents free to possess shotguns and rifles, along with ammunition. The area that falls within its scope is totally urban. That urban area suffers from a serious handgun-fatality problem. The District's law directly aims at that compelling problem. And there is no less restrictive way to achieve the problem-related benefits that it seeks.

Second, the self-defense interest in maintaining loaded handguns in the home to shoot intruders is not the primary interest, but at most a subsidiary interest, that the Second Amendment seeks to serve. The Second Amendment's language, while speaking of a "Militia," says nothing of "self-defense."

Further, any self-defense interest at the time of the Framing could not have focused exclusively upon urban-crime related dangers. Two hundred years ago, most Americans, many living on the frontier, would likely have thought of self-defense primarily in terms of outbreaks of fighting with Indian tribes, rebellions such as Shays' Rebellion, marauders, and crime-related dangers to travelers on the roads, on footpaths, or along waterways. Insofar as the Framers focused at all on the tiny fraction of the population living in large cities, they would have been aware that these city dwellers were subject to firearm restrictions that their rural counterparts were not. They are unlikely then to have thought of a right to keep loaded handguns in homes to confront intruders in urban settings as central. And the subsequent development of modern urban police departments, by diminishing the need to keep loaded guns nearby in case of intruders, would have moved any such right even further away from the heart of the amendment's more basic protective ends.

Nor, for that matter, am I aware of any evidence that handguns in particular were central to the Framers' conception of the Second Amendment. The lists of militia-related weapons in the late 18th-century state statutes appear primarily to refer to other sorts of weapons, muskets in particular.

Third, irrespective of what the Framers could have thought, we know what they did think. Samuel Adams, who lived in Boston, advocated a constitutional amendment that would have precluded the Constitution from ever being "construed" to "prevent the people of the United States, who are peaceable citizens, from keeping their own arms." And he doubtless knew that Massachusetts law prohibited Bostonians from keeping loaded guns in the house. So how could Samuel Adams have advocated such protection unless he thought that the protection was consistent with local regulation that seriously impeded urban residents from using their arms against intruders? It seems unlikely that he meant to deprive the Federal Government of power (to enact Boston-type weapons regulation) that he kn[e]w Boston had and (as far as we know) he would have thought constitutional under the Massachusetts Constitution.

Fourth, a contrary view, as embodied in today's decision, will have unfortunate consequences. The decision will encourage legal challenges to gun regulation throughout the Nation. Because it says little about the standards used to evaluate regulatory decisions, it will leave the Nation without clear standards for resolving those challenges. And litigation over the course of many years, or the mere specter of such litigation, threatens to leave cities without effective protection against gun violence and accidents during that time. As important, the majority's decision threatens severely to limit the ability of more knowledgeable, democratically elected officials to deal with gun-related problems. But I cannot understand how one can take from the elected branches of government the right to decide whether to insist upon a handgun-free urban populace in a city now facing a serious crime problem and which, in the future, could well face environmental or other emergencies that threaten the breakdown of law and order.

For these reasons, I conclude that the District's measure is a proportionate, not a disproportionate, response to the compelling concerns that led the District to adopt it.

INDEX